Pro VB 2010 and the .NET 4 Platform

Andrew Troelsen
and Vidya Vrat Agarwal

Pro VB 2010 and the .NET 4 Platform

ISBN-13 (pbk): 978-1-4302-2985-8

ISBN-13 (electronic): 978-1-4302-2986-5

Printed and bound in the United States of America 9 8 7 6 5 4 3 2 1

Trademarked names may appear in this book. Rather than use a trademark symbol with every occurrence of a trademarked name, we use the names only in an editorial fashion and to the benefit of the trademark owner, with no intention of infringement of the trademark.

Distributed to the book trade worldwide by Springer-Verlag New York, Inc., 233 Spring Street, 6th Floor, New York, NY 10013. Phone 1-800-SPRINGER, fax 201-348-4505, e-mail orders-ny@springer-sbm.com, or visit www.springeronline.com.

For information on translations, please e-mail rights@apress.com, or visit www.apress.com.

Apress and friends of ED books may be purchased in bulk for academic, corporate, or promotional use. eBook versions and licenses are also available for most titles. For more information, reference our Special Bulk Sales–eBook Licensing web page at www.apress.com/info/bulksales.

The information in this book is distributed on an "as is" basis, without warranty. Although every precaution has been taken in the preparation of this work, neither the author(s) nor Apress shall have any liability to any person or entity with respect to any loss or damage caused or alleged to be caused directly or indirectly by the information contained in this work.

The source code for this book is available to readers at www.apress.com.

To the memory of my wonderful grandmother, Maxine. I love you, Gerta.
Rest peacefully.

—Andrew Troelsen

To my lovely wife, sweet daughters, and my parents. I love you all.

—Vidya Vrat Agarwal

Contents at a Glance

Contents

About the Authors

■**Andrew Troelsen** fondly recalls his very first computer, an Atari 400 complete with a tape deck storage device and a black and white TV serving as a monitor (which his parents permitted him to have in his bedroom - thanks guys!). He also is grateful to the legacy *Compute!* magazine, a B.A. degree in mathematical linguistics, and three years of formal Sanskrit. All of these artifacts have greatly influenced his current career.

Andrew is currently employed with Intertech (`www.intertech.com`), a .NET and Java training and consulting center.

He has authored a number of books, including *Developer's Workshop to COM and ATL 3.0* (Wordware Publishing, 2000), *COM and .NET Interoperability* (Apress, 2002) and *Visual Basic 2008 and the .NET 3.5 Platform: An Advanced Guide* (Apress, 2008).

■**Vidya Vrat Agarwal** is a Microsoft .NET purist. He started working on Microsoft .NET with its 1st beta release. He has been involved in software development, evangelism, consultation, corporate training, and T3 programs on Microsoft .NET for various employers and corporate clients. Vidya is a published author for Apress titles *Beginning C# 2008 Databases: From Novice to Professional*, *Beginning VB 2008 Databases: From Novice to Professional*, and *Pro ASP.NET 3.5 in VB 2008: Includes Silverlight 2Pro*. He is also a technical reviewer of many books published by Apress.

Vidya works with Lionbridge Technologies (Nasdaq:LIOX) as a Technical Architect. He lives with his wife, Rupali, and daughter, Pearly. Vidya runs a Bellevue .NET User Group, `www.BellevueDotNet.com`, and blogs at `http://dotnetpassion.blogspot.com`.

About the Technical Reviewer

Andy Olsen is a freelance consultant and trainer based in the UK. Andy has been working with .NET since the days of the first beta and is actively involved with the latest features in the .NET 4 platform. Andy lives by the sea in Swansea with his wife, Jayne, and children. Andy enjoys running along the sea front (with regular coffee stops along the way), skiing, and following the swans and ospreys. Andy can be reached at andyo@olsensoft.com.

Acknowledgments

I would like to thank my wife, Rupali, for being so understanding, patient, and helpful and supporting me to live with my passion. It's not only hard but seems impossible for a wife to live with a person who works on four books in approximately three years in addition to nine technical review assignments and many other things. At the end all looks great, but all this work is based on the sacrifices my wife and daughter made every day. Rupali, I am so fortunate to have you in my life, you always allowed me to live with my second companion: my laptop. Pearly, you are the best kid a father can imagine to have; I know what I have missed while working on these assignments. Thanks for helping me to remain focused. Many, many thanks to both of you. I love you the most.

I would like to thank my Technical Reviewer, Andy Olsen. I do admire his technical skills, he is very detailed, and his contribution in getting this done is worth appreciation. Thanks, Andy.

I also would like to thank Debra Kelly, the Managing Coordinating Editor at Apress, who didn't only coordinate all the deliverables with me but who also fixed the minor technical revisions for me so I could work on the major revisions in that chapter. Thanks a ton Debra.

I am also grateful to the copyediting team, Mary Behr, Patrick Meader, Katie Stence, and Sharon Terdeman, for fixing the text and punctuations and making it perfect for the readers. No book can hit the market without you guys. Thanks a lot.

—Vidya Vrat Agarwal

Introduction

This book has been fully updated to provide coverage on the new features of the VB 2010 programming language, as well as the new features of the .NET 4 Platform. Here you will find information on the new Dynamic Language Runtime (DLR), the Task Parallel Library (TPL), Parallel LINQ (PLINQ), the ADO.NET Entity Framework (EF), and several "minor" (but very useful) updates, such as named arguments, optional parameters, the Lazy(Of T) class type, and so on.

In addition to covering all the new bits, this book continues to provide you with a rock-solid foundation of the VB language as a whole, the pillars of object oriented programming (OOP), assembly configuration, database access (through ADO.NET), as well as the process of building desktop GUI applications, web applications, and distributed systems (among other topics).

As with the earlier editions, this edition presents the VB programming language and .NET base class libraries using a friendly and approachable tone (or so I have been told!). As well, this new edition remains focused on providing you with the information you need to build software solutions today, rather than spending too much time examining esoteric details that few individuals will ever actually care about.

We're a Team, You and I

Technology authors write for a demanding group of people (I should know—I'm one of them). You know that building software solutions using any platform (e.g., .NET, Java, and COM) is extremely complicated and is highly specific to your department, company, client base, and subject matter. Perhaps you work in the electronic publishing industry, develop systems for the state or local government, or work at NASA or a branch of the military. Speaking for myself, I have developed children's educational software (Oregon Trail / Amazon Trail anyone?), various n-tier systems, and projects within the medical and financial industries. The chances are almost 100 percent that the code you write at your place of employment has little to do with the code I write at mine (unless we happened to work together previously!).

Therefore, in this book, I have deliberately chosen to avoid creating examples that tie the example code to a specific industry or vein of programming. Given this, I explain VB, OOP, the CLR, and the .NET 4 base class libraries using industry-agnostic examples. Rather than having every blessed example fill a grid with data, calculate payroll, or whatnot, I'll stick to subject matter everyone can relate to: automobiles (with some geometric structures and employee payroll systems thrown in for good measure). And that's where you come in.

My job is to explain the VB programming language and the core aspects of the .NET platform as well as I possibly can. I will also do everything I can to equip you with the tools and strategies you need to continue your studies at this book's conclusion.

Your job is to take this information and apply it to your specific programming assignments. I obviously appreciate that your projects most likely don't revolve around automobiles with friendly pet names (e.g., Zippy the BMW and a Yugo named Clunker), but that's what applied knowledge is all about!

You should also understand that no single book, regardless of its size, can possibly cover every single detail you might wish to hear. In my 15 years as a corporate educator, I can *easily say with confidence* that when engineers say terms such as *real world* or *practical*, what they are actually saying is something close to: "I want to hear information that will help me on my immediate programming assignment." While I completely understand this request, the written word can only go so far, especially since I most likely have not made your acquaintance. Rest assured, once you understand the topics and concepts presented within this text, you will be in a perfect position to build .NET solutions that map to your own unique programming environment.

An Overview of This Book

Chapter 1: Introducing VB 2010

This lays out the conceptual framework necessary for the remainder of this book. I examine a number of limitations and complexities found within the technologies prior to .NET, and follow that with an overview of how .NET and VB attempt to simplify the current state of affairs.

Chapter 2: Building Visual Basic 2010 Applications

The goal of this chapter is to provide you with a tour of the major programming tools a VB 2010 programmer may leverage during the development process. You begin by learning how to generate .NET assemblies using nothing other than the free VB 2010 compiler and Notepad. Next, you are introduced to the TextPad and Notepad++ applications and walked through the process of using these tools to edit and compile *.vb code files. You will also examine two feature-rich IDEs, starting with Microsoft's Visual VB 2010 Express and Visual Studio 2010 Professional.

Chapter 3: Core VB 2010 Programming Constructs, Part I

This chapter begins your formal investigation of the VB 2010 programming language. Here you will learn about the role of the Main() method and numerous details regarding the intrinsic data types of the .NET platform. You will also examine iteration and decision constructs, and narrowing and widening operations.

Chapter 4: Core VB Programming Constructs, Part II

This chapter completes your examination of the core aspects of VB 2010. You'll see how pass parameters by value, by reference, and as output parameters. This chapter will examine the role of optional or named parameters and how to define and invoke methods taking parameter arrays.

Chapter 5: Defining Encapsulated Class Types

This chapter begins your examination of object-oriented programming (OOP) using the VB programming language. Focusing mainly on encapsulation, you'll learn about the access modifiers of VB 2010 and the role of type properties, object initialization syntax, and partial classes. It also illustrates several class design techniques and related keywords, such as Me, Shared, and Const.

Chapter 6: Understanding Inheritance and Polymorphism

Here, you will examine the remaining pillars of OOP (inheritance and polymorphism), which allow you to build families of related class types. As you do this, you will examine the role of Overridable methods, MustInherit methods, and the nature of the *polymorphic interface.* Last but not least, this chapter will explain the role of the supreme base class of the .NET platform, System.Object.

Chapter 7: Understanding Structured Exception Handling

The point of this chapter is to discuss how to handle runtime anomalies in your code base through the use of structured exception handling. Not only will you learn about the VB keywords that allow you to handle such problems (Try, Catch, Throw, and Finally), but you will also come to understand the distinction between application-level and system-level exceptions. In addition, this chapter will examine various tools within Visual Studio 2010 that allow you to debug the exceptions that escape your notice.

Chapter 8: Understanding Object Lifetime

The final chapter of this part examines how the CLR manages memory using the .NET garbage collector. Here you will come to understand the role of application roots, object generations, and the System.GC type. Once you understand the basics, you will examine the topics of *disposable objects* (using the IDisposable Interface) and the finalization process (using the System.Object.Finalize() method). This chapter will also investigate a new .NET 4 class, Lazy(Of T), which allows you to define data that will not be allocated until requested by a caller. As you will see, this feature can be very helpful when you wish to ensure you do not clutter the heap with objects that are not actually required by your programs.

Chapter 9: Working with Interfaces

The material in this chapter builds upon your understanding of object-based development by covering the topic of interface-based programming. Here, you will learn how to define classes and structures that support multiple behaviors, how to discover these behaviors at runtime, and how to selectively hide particular behaviors using *explicit interface implementation.* In addition to creating a number of custom interfaces, you will also learn how to implement standard interfaces found within the .NET platform. You will use these to build objects that can be sorted, copied, enumerated and compared.

Chapter 10: Understanding Generics

This chapter explores the topic of *generics*. As you will see, generic programming gives you a way to create types and type members, which contain various *placeholders* that can be specified by the caller. In a nutshell, generics greatly enhance application performance and type safety. Not only will you explore various generic types within the System.Collections.Generic namespace, but you will also learn how to build your own generic methods and types (with and without constraints).

Chapter 11: Delegates, Events, and Lambdas

The purpose of this chapter is to demystify the *delegate* type. Simply put, a .NET delegate is an object that *points* to other methods in your application. Using this type, you can build systems that allow multiple objects to engage in a two-way conversation. After you have examined the use of .NET delegates, you will then be introduced to the VB Event keyword, which you can use to simplify the manipulation of raw delegate programming. You will wrap up this chapter by investigating the role of the VB lambda statements Function and Sub and exploring the connection between delegates, anonymous methods, and lambda expressions.

Chapter 12: Advanced VB 2010 Language Features

This chapter deepens your understanding of the VB 2010 programming language by introducing you to a number of advanced programming techniques. Here, you will learn how to overload operators and create custom conversion routines (both implicit and explicit) for your types. You will also learn how to work with *extension methods*, *anonymous types*, and *partial methods*.

Chapter 13: LINQ to Objects

This chapter will begin your examination of Language Integrated Query (LINQ). LINQ allows you to build strongly typed *query expressions* that can be applied to a number of LINQ targets to manipulate *data* in the broadest sense of the word. Here, you will learn about LINQ to Objects, which allows you to apply LINQ expressions to containers of data (e.g., arrays, collections, and custom types). This information will serve you well as you encounter a number of additional LINQ APIs throughout the remainder of this book (e.g., LINQ to XML, LINQ to DataSet, PLINQ, and LINQ to Entities).

Chapter 14: Configuring .NET Assemblies

At a very high level, *assembly* is the term used to describe a *.dll or *.exe binary file created with a .NET compiler. However, the true story of .NET assemblies is far richer than that. Here you will learn the distinction between single-file and multi-file assemblies, as well as how to build and deploy each entity. You'll also examine how you can configure private and shared assemblies using XML-based *.config files and publisher policy assemblies. Along the way, you will investigate the internal structure of the global assembly cache (GAC), including some changes to the GAC as of .NET 4.

Chapter 15: Type Reflection, Late Binding, and Attribute-Based Programming

Chapter 15 continues your examination of .NET assemblies by checking out the process of runtime type discovery using the System.Reflection namespace. Using the types of this namespace, you can build applications that can read an assembly's metadata on the fly. You will also learn how to load and create types at runtime dynamically using *late binding*. The final topic of this chapter will explore the role of .NET attributes (both standard and custom). To illustrate the usefulness of each of these topics, the chapter shows you how to construct an extendable Windows Forms application.

Chapter 16: Processes, AppDomains, and Object Contexts

Now that you have a solid understanding of assemblies, this chapter dives deeper into the composition of a loaded .NET executable. The goal of this chapter is to illustrate the relationship between processes, application domains, and contextual boundaries. These topics provide the proper foundation for Chapter 19, where you will examine the construction of multithreaded applications.

Chapter 17: Understanding CIL and the Role of Dynamic Assemblies

The goal of this chapter is twofold. In the first half (more or less), you will examine the syntax and semantics of CIL in much greater detail than in previous chapters. The remainder of this chapter will cover the role of the System.Reflection.Emit namespace. You can use these types to build software that can generate .NET assemblies in memory at runtime. Formally speaking, assemblies defined and executed in memory are termed *dynamic assemblies*. You should not confuse this term with a *dynamic type*, which is the subject of Chapter 18.

Chapter 18: Dynamic Types and the Dynamic Language Runtime

.NET 4 introduces a new aspect of the .NET runtime environment called the *dynamic language runtime*. Using the DLR and the VB 2010 dynamic typing, you can define data that is not truly resolved until runtime. Using these features simplifies some very complex .NET programming tasks dramatically. In this chapter, you will learn some practical uses of dynamic data, including how to leverage the .NET reflection APIs in a streamlined manner, as well as how to communicate with legacy COM libraries a minimum of fuss and bother.

Chapter 19: Multithreaded and Parallel Programming

This chapter examines how to build multithreaded applications and illustrates a number of techniques you can use to author thread-safe code. The chapter opens by revisiting the .NET delegate type to ensure, explaining a delegate's intrinsic support for asynchronous method invocations. Next, you will investigate the types within the System.Threading namespace. The remainder of this chapter covers a brand new .NET 4 API called the *Task Parallel Library* (TPL). Using the TPL, .NET developers can build applications that distribute their workload across all available CPUs in a wickedly simple manner. At this point, you will also learn about the role of Parallel LINQ (PINQ), which provides a way to create LINQ queries that scale across multiple machine cores.

Chapter 20: File I/O and Object Serialization

The System.IO namespace allows you to interact with a machine's file and directory structure. Over the course of this chapter, you will learn how to create (and destroy) a directory system programmatically. You will also learn how to move data into and out of various streams (e.g., file based, string based, and memory based). The latter part of this chapter will examine the object serialization services of the .NET platform. Simply put, *serialization* allows you to persist the state of an object (or a set of related objects) into a stream for later use. *Deserialization* (as you might expect) is the process of plucking an object from the stream into memory for consumption by your application. Once you understand the basics, you will learn how to customize the serialization process using the ISerializable interface and a set of .NET attributes.

Chapter 21: ADO.NET Part I: The Connected Layer

In this first of three database-centric chapters, you will take your first look at the database access API of the .NET platform, ADO.NET. Specifically, this chapter will introduce you to the role of .NET data providers and how to communicate with a relational database using the *connected layer* of ADO.NET, which is represented by connection objects, command objects, transaction objects, and data reader objects. Be aware that this chapter will also walk you through the creation of a custom database and the first iteration of a custom data access library (AutoLotDAL.dll); you will use this library throughout the remainder of this book.

Chapter 22: ADO.NET Part II: The Disconnected Layer

This chapter continues your study of database manipulation by examining the *disconnected layer* of ADO.NET. Here, you will learn the role of the DataSet type, data adapter objects. You will also learn about the many tools of Visual Studio 2010 that can greatly simplify the creation of data-driven applications. Along the way, you will learn how to bind DataTable objects to user interface elements, as well as how to apply LINQ queries to in-memory DataSet objects using LINQ to DataSet.

Chapter 23: ADO.NET Part III: The Entity Framework

This chapter wraps up your investigation of ADO.NET by examining the role of the Entity Framework (EF). Essentially, EF is a way for you to author data access code using strongly typed classes that directly map to your business model. Here, you will come to understand the role of EF Object Services, the Entity Client and Object Context, and the composition of an *.edmx file. While doing so, you will learn to interact with relational databases using LINQ to Entities. You will also build the final version of your custom data access library (AutoLotDAL.dll), which you will use in several of the remaining chapters of the book.

Chapter 24: Introducing LINQ to XML

Chapter 14 introduced you to the core LINQ programming model—specifically LINQ to Objects. Here, you will deepen your understanding of Language Integrated Query by examining how to apply LINQ queries to XML documents. You will begin by learning about the "warts" that were present in .NET's initial foray into XML manipulation as you use the types of the System.Xml.dll assembly. With this brief history lesson behind you, you will explore how to create XML documents in memory, how to persist them to the hard drive, and how to navigate their contents using the LINQ programming model (LINQ to XML).

Chapter 25: Introducing Windows Communication Foundation

Until this point in the book, all of the sample applications have executed on a single computer. In this chapter, you will learn about the Windows Communication Foundation (WCF) API that allows you to build distributed applications in a symmetrical manner, regardless of their underlying plumbing. This chapter will expose you to the construction of WCF services, hosts, and clients. As you will see, WCF services are extremely flexible because they allow clients and hosts to leverage XML-based configuration files to specify addresses, bindings, and contracts declaratively. This chapter will also showcase a number of helpful shortcuts that introduced in .NET 4.

Chapter 26: Introducing Windows Workflow Foundation

Of all the .NET APIs, Windows Workflow Foundation (WF) can provide the biggest source of confusion for new developers. In fact, with the release of .NET 4, the initial incarnation of the WF API (introduced in .NET 3.0) has been given a complete, and total, reboot. In this chapter, you will begin by learning about the role of a workflow-enabled application, and you will come to understand the various ways to model business processes using the .NET 4 WF API. Next, you will examine the scope of the WF 4 activity library, as well as learn how to build custom activities that will use the custom database access library you created earlier in the book.

Chapter 27: Introducing Windows Presentation Foundation and XAML

Essentially, WPF allows you to build extremely interactive and media-rich front ends for desktop applications (and indirectly, web applications). Unlike Windows Forms, this supercharged UI framework integrates a number of key services (e.g., 2D and 3D graphics, animations, and rich documents) into a single, unified object model. In this chapter, you will begin your examination of WPF and the Extendable Application Markup Language (XAML). Here, you will learn how to build WPF programs without XAML, using nothing but XAML, and by using a combination of both approaches. You will wrap up the chapter by building a custom XAML editor that you will use for the remainder of the WPF-centric chapters.

Chapter 28: Programming with WPF Controls

This chapter will expose you to the process of using intrinsic WPF controls and layout managers. For example, you will learn to build menu systems, splitter windows, toolbars, and status bars. This chapter will also introduce you to a number of WPF APIs (and their related controls), including the WPF Documents API, the WPF Ink API, and the data-binding model. Just as importantly, this chapter will begin your investigation of Expression Blend IDE, which simplifies the task of creating rich UIs for a WPF application.

Chapter 29: WPF Graphical Rendering Services

WPF is a graphically intensive API; given this fact, WPF provides three ways to render graphics: *shapes*, *drawings and geometries*, and *visuals*. In this chapter, you will evaluate each option and learn about a number of important graphics primitives (e.g., brushes, pens, and transformations) along the way. This chapter will also examine a number of ways in which Expression Blend can help you simplify the process of creating WPF graphics, as well as how to perform hit-testing operations against graphical data.

Chapter 30: WPF Resources, Animations, and Styles

This chapter will introduce you to three important (and interrelated) topics that will deepen your understanding of the Windows Presentation Foundation API. The first order of business is to learn the role of *logical resources*. As you will see, the logical resource (also termed an *object resource*) system provides a way for you to name and refer to commonly used objects within a WPF application. Next, you will learn how to define, execute, and control an animation sequence. Despite what you might be thinking, however, WPF animations are not limited to the confines of video game or multimedia applications. You will wrap up the chapter by learning about the role of WPF styles. Similar to a web page that uses CSS or the ASP.NET theme engine, a WPF application can define a common look-and-feel for a set of controls.

Chapter 31: WPF Control Templates and UserControls

This chapter concludes your investigation of the WPF programming model by introducing you to the process of building customized controls. This chapter begins by examining two topics that are important when creating a custom control: *dependency properties* and *routed events*. Once you understand these topics, you will learn about the role of a *default template*, as well as how to view them programmatically at runtime. Once this foundation has been laid, the remainder of this chapter will examine how to build custom UserControl classes using Visual Studio 2010 and Expression Blend, including the .NET 4 Visual State Manager (VSM).

Chapter 32: Building ASP.NET Web Pages

This chapter begins your study of web application development using ASP.NET. As you will see, server-side scripting code has now been replaced with real object-oriented languages. This chapter will examine the construction of an ASP.NET web page, the underlying programming model, and other key aspects of ASP.NET, such as your choice of web server and the use of Web.config files.

Chapter 33: ASP.NET Web Controls, Master Pages, and Themes

Whereas the previous chapter showed you how to construct ASP.NET Page objects, this chapter will examine the controls that populate the internal control tree. Here, you will examine the core ASP.NET web controls, including validation controls, the intrinsic site navigation controls, and various data-binding operations. This chapter will also illustrate the role of *master pages* and the ASP.NET theme engine, which is a server-side alternative to traditional style sheets.

Chapter 34: ASP.NET State Management Techniques

This chapter extends your understanding of ASP.NET by examining various ways to handle state management under .NET. Like classic ASP, ASP.NET allows you to create cookies and application-level and session-level variables quite easily. However, ASP.NET also introduces a new state management technique: the application cache. Once you look at the numerous ways to handle state with ASP.NET, you will examine the role of the HttpApplication base class and learn how to alter the runtime behavior of your web application dynamically using the Web.config file.

Appendix A: Programming with Windows Forms

The original desktop GUI toolkit that shipped with the .NET platform is called *Windows Forms*. This appendix will walk you through the role of this UI framework and illustrate how to build main windows, dialog boxes, and menu systems. You will also learn about the role of form inheritance and see how to render 2D graphical data using the System.Drawing namespace. You will wrap things up by building a (semi-capable) painting application that illustrates the various topics discussed throughout this appendix.

Appendix B: Platform-Independent .NET Development with Mono

Last but not least, Appendix B covers how to use an open source implementation of the .NET platform named *Mono*. You can use Mono to build feature-rich .NET applications that can be created, deployed, and executed upon a variety of operating systems, including Mac OS X, Solaris, AIX, and numerous other Linux distributions. Given that Mono is largely comparable with Microsoft's .NET platform, you already know most of what Mono has to offer. Therefore, this appendix will focus on the Mono installation process, Mono development tools, and Mono runtime engine.

Obtaining This Book's Source Code

You can find all of the code examples contained in this book available as a free download from the Source Code/Download area of the Apress website. Simply navigate to www.apress.com, select the Source Code/Download link, and look up this title by name. Once you are on the home page for *Pro VB 2010 and the .NET 4 Platform*, you can download a self-extracting *.zip file. After you unzip the contents, you will find that the code has been partitioned on a chapter-by-chapter basis.

On a related note, be aware that you will find Source Code notes such as the following in many of the book's chapters. These notes serves as your visual cue that you can load the example under discussion into Visual Studio 2010 for further examination and modification:

■ **Source Code** This is a source code note that refers you to a specific directory in the ZIP archive!

To open a solution into Visual Studio 2010, use the File ➤ Open ➤ Project/Solution menu option, and then navigate to the correct *.sln file within the correct subdirectory of the unzipped archive.

Obtaining Updates for This Book

As you read through this text, you might find an occasional grammatical or code error (although I sure hope not). If this is the case, please accept my apologies. Being human, I am sure that a glitch or two might be present, despite my best efforts. If this is the case, you can obtain the current errata list from the Apress website (again, this is located on the home page for this book.

Take care,
Andrew Troelsen (the guy on the Gunflint Trail)

■■■

## CHAPTER 1

Introducing VB 2010

Every few years or so, the modern-day programmer must be willing to perform a self-inflicted knowledge transplant to stay current with the new technologies of the day. The languages (C++, Visual Basic 6.0, Java), frameworks (MFC, ATL, STL), architectures (COM, CORBA, EJB) and APIs that were touted as the silver bullets of software development eventually become overshadowed by something better, or at the very least something new.

Regardless of the frustration you can feel when upgrading your internal knowledge base, it is frankly unavoidable. To this end, the goal of this book is to examine the details of Microsoft's current offering within the landscape of software engineering: the .NET 4.0 platform and the VB 2010 programming language.

The point of this chapter is to lay the conceptual groundwork for the remainder of the book. Here you will find a high-level discussion of a number of .NET-related topics such as assemblies, the Common Intermediate Language (CIL), and just-in-time (JIT) compilation. In addition to previewing some keywords of the VB 2010 programming language, you will also come to understand the relationship between various aspects of the .NET Framework, such as the Common Language Runtime (CLR), the Common Type System (CTS), and the Common Language Specification (CLS).

This chapter also provides you with a survey of the functionality supplied by the .NET 4.0 base class libraries, sometimes abbreviated as BCLs or alternatively as FCLs (Framework class libraries). Here, you will also overview the language-agnostic and platform-independent nature of the .NET platform (yes, it's true; .NET is not confined to the Windows operating system). As you would hope, many of these topics are explored in further detail throughout the remainder of this text.

Understanding the Previous State of Affairs

Before examining the specifics of the .NET universe, it's helpful to consider some of the issues that motivated the genesis of Microsoft's current platform. To get in the proper mind-set, let's begin this chapter with a brief and painless history lesson to remember our roots and understand the limitations of the previous state of affairs (after all, admitting you have a problem is the first step toward finding a solution). After completing this quick tour of life as we knew it, we turn our attention to the numerous benefits provided by VB 2010 and the .NET 4.0 platform.

Life As a C/Windows API Programmer

Traditionally speaking, developing software for the Windows family of operating systems involved using the C programming language in conjunction with the Windows application programming interface

(API). While it is true that numerous applications have been successfully created using this time-honored approach, few of us would disagree that building applications using the raw API is a complex undertaking.

The first obvious problem is that C is a very terse language. C developers are forced to contend with manual memory management, ugly pointer arithmetic, and ugly syntactical constructs. Furthermore, given that C is a structured language, it lacks the benefits provided by the object-oriented approach (can anyone say *spaghetti code*?). When you combine the thousands of global functions and data types defined by the Windows API to an already formidable language, it is little wonder that there are so many buggy applications floating around today.

Life As a C++/MFC Programmer

One vast improvement over raw C/API development is the use of the C++ programming language. In many ways, C++ can be thought of as an object-oriented *layer* on top of C. Thus, even though C++ programmers benefit from the famed Pillars of OOP (encapsulation, inheritance, and polymorphism), they are still at the mercy of the painful aspects of the C language (e.g., manual memory management, ugly pointer arithmetic, and ugly syntactical constructs).

Despite its complexity, many C++ frameworks exist today. For example, the Microsoft Foundation Classes (MFC) provides the developer with a set of C++ classes that facilitate the construction of Windows applications. The main role of MFC is to wrap a *sane subset* of the underlying Windows API behind a number of classes, magic macros, and numerous code-generation tools (aka *wizards*). Regardless of the helpful assistance offered by the MFC framework (as well as many other C++-based windowing toolkits), the fact of the matter is that C++ programming remains a difficult and error-prone experience, given its historical roots in C.

Life As a Visual Basic 6.0 Programmer

Due to a heartfelt desire to enjoy a simpler lifestyle, many programmers shifted away from the world of C(++)-based frameworks to kinder, gentler languages such as Visual Basic 6.0 (VB6). VB6 became popular due to its ability to build complex user interfaces, code libraries (e.g., COM servers), and database access logic with minimal fuss and bother. Much more than MFC, VB6 hid the complexities of the raw Windows API from view using a number of integrated code wizards, intrinsic VB data types, classes, and VB-specific functions.

The major downfall of VB6 (which has been rectified given the advent of the .NET platform) is that it is *not* a fully object-oriented language; rather, it is *object based*. For example, VB6 does not allow the programmer to establish *is-a* relationships between classes (i.e., no classical inheritance) and has no intrinsic support for parameterized object construction. Moreover, VB6 doesn't provide the ability to build multithreaded applications unless you are willing to drop down to low-level API calls (which is complex at best and dangerous at worst).

■ **Note** The Visual Basic language used within the .NET platform (which is often referred to as VB.NET), has very little relationship to VB6. For example, modern day VB supports operator overloading, classical inheritance, type constructors and generics.

Life As a Java Programmer

Enter Java. Java is an object-oriented programming (OOP) language with its syntactic roots in C++. As many of you are aware, Java's strengths are far greater than its support for platform independence. As a language, Java cleans up many unsavory syntactical aspects of C++. As a platform, Java provides programmers with a large number of predefined packages that contain various type definitions. Using these types, Java programmers are able to build "100% Pure Java" applications complete with database connectivity, messaging support, web-enabled front ends, and a rich desktop user interface (among other services).

Although Java is a very elegant language, one potential problem is that using Java typically means that you must use Java front to back during the development cycle. In effect, Java offers little hope of language integration, as this goes against the grain of Java's primary goal—a single programming language for every need. In reality, however, there are millions of lines of existing code out there in the world that would ideally like to commingle with newer Java code. Sadly, Java makes this task problematic. While Java does provide a limited ability to access non-Java APIs, there is little support for true cross-language integration.

Life As a COM Programmer

The Component Object Model (COM) was Microsoft's previous application development framework, which first appeared on the programming landscape circa 1991 (or 1993, if you regard COM's introduction with the birth of OLE 1.0). COM is an architecture that says, in effect, "If you build your types in accordance with the rules of COM, you end up with a block of *reusable binary code.*" These binary blobs of COM code are often called "COM servers".

One benefit of a binary COM server is that it can be accessed in a language-independent manner. Thus, C++ programmers can build COM classes that can be used by VB6; Delphi programmers can use COM classes built using C, and so forth. However, as you may be aware, COM's language independence is somewhat limited. For example, there is no way to derive a new COM class using an existing COM class (as COM has no support for classical inheritance). Rather, are limited to reuse via the *has-a* relationship.

Another benefit of COM is its location-transparent nature. Using constructs such as the system registry, application identifiers (AppIDs), stubs, proxies, and the COM runtime environment, programmers can avoid the need to work with raw sockets, RPC calls, and other low-level details when building a distributed application. For example, consider the following VB6 COM client code:

```
' The MyCOMClass class could have be written in
' any COM-aware language, and may be located anywhere
' on the network (including your local machine).
Dim obj as MyCOMClass
Set obj = New MyCOMClass   ' Location resolved using AppID.
obj.DoSomeWork
```

Although COM can be considered a very successful object model, it is extremely complex under the hood (at least until you have spent many months exploring its plumbing—especially if you happen to be a C++ programmer). To help simplify the development of COM binaries, programmers can make use of numerous COM-aware frameworks. For example, the Active Template Library (ATL) provides a set of C++ classes, templates, and macros to ease the creation of COM servers.

Many other languages also hide a good part of the COM infrastructure from view. However, language support alone is not enough to hide the complexity of COM. Even when you choose a relatively simple COM-aware language such as VB6, you are still forced to contend with fragile registration entries and numerous deployment-related issues (collectively, and somewhat comically, termed *DLL hell*).

The Complexity of COM Data Type Representation

Although COM certainly facilitates the construction of software applications using a variety of different programming languages, the language-independent nature of COM was not as straightforward as one would hope.

Some of the complexity is due to the simple fact that applications that are woven together using diverse languages are completely unrelated from a syntactic point of view. For example, JScript has a syntax much like C, while VBScript is a subset of VB6. The COM servers that are created to run under the COM+ runtime (a Windows OS feature which provides common services to custom code libraries [transactions, object lifetime, security, etc]) have an entirely different look and feel from the web-centric ASP pages that invoke them. The result was a rather confused mishmash of technologies.

Furthermore, and perhaps more important, each language and/or technology has its own *type system* (that may look nothing like another's type system). Beyond the fact that each API ships with its own collection of prefabricated code, even basic data types cannot always be treated identically. A `CComBSTR` in ATL is not quite the same as a `String` in VB6, both of which have nothing to do with a `char*` in C.

Given that each language has its own unique type system, COM programmers typically needed to be very careful with building public methods on public COM classes. For example, if a C++ developer needed to create a method that returned an array of integers to a VB6 application, they would be up to their eyeballs in complex COM API calls to construct a `SAFEARRAY` structure, which could easily require dozens of line of code. In the COM world, the `SAFEARRAY` data type is the only way to build an array that all COM frameworks understand. If the C++ developer simply returned a native C++ array, VB6 would have no clue what to do with it.

Similar complexities could be found when building methods that manipulate simple string data, references to other COM objects, or even a trivial BOOLEAN value! To put it politely, COM programming is a very *asymmetrical* discipline.

The .NET Solution

So much for the brief history lesson. The bottom line is that life as a Windows programmer has historically been tough. The .NET Framework is a rather radical and brute-force approach to making our lives easier. As you will see during the remainder of this book, the .NET Framework is a software platform for building systems on the Windows family of operating systems, as well as on numerous non-Microsoft operating systems such as Mac OS X and various Unix/Linux distributions. To set the stage, here is a quick rundown of some core features provided courtesy of .NET.

- *Interoperability with existing code*: This is (of course) a good thing. Existing COM binaries can commingle (i.e., interop) with newer .NET binaries and vice versa. As of .NET 4.0, interoperability has been further simplified with the addition of the `dynamic` keyword (covered in Chapter 18).

- *Support for numerous programming languages*: .NET applications can be created using any number of programming languages (C#, Visual Basic, F#, S#, and so on).

- *A common runtime engine shared by all .NET-aware languages*: One aspect of this engine is a well-defined set of types that each .NET-aware language understands.

- *Complete and total language integration*: .NET supports cross-language inheritance, cross-language exception handling, and cross-language debugging of code.

- *A comprehensive base class library*: This library provides shelter from the complexities of raw API calls and offers a consistent object model used by all .NET-aware languages.

- *No more COM plumbing*: `IClassFactory`, `IUnknown`, `IDispatch`, IDL code, and the variant-compliant data types (e.g., `BSTR`, `SAFEARRAY`) have no place in a .NET binary.

- *A simplified deployment model*: Under .NET, there is no need to register a binary unit into the system registry. Furthermore, .NET allows multiple versions of the same `*.dll` to exist in harmony on a single machine.

As you can most likely gather from the previous bullet points, the .NET platform has nothing to do with COM (beyond the fact that both frameworks originated from Microsoft). In fact, the only way .NET and COM types can interact with each other is using the interoperability layer.

Introducing the Building Blocks of the .NET Platform (the CLR, CTS, and CLS)

Now that you know some of the benefits provided by .NET, let's preview three key (and interrelated) entities that make it all possible: the CLR, CTS, and CLS. From a programmer's point of view, .NET can be understood as a runtime environment and a comprehensive base class library. The runtime layer is properly referred to as the *Common Language Runtime*, or *CLR*. The primary role of the CLR is to locate, load, and manage .NET types on your behalf. The CLR also takes care of a number of low-level details such as memory management, application hosting, handling threads, and performing various security checks.

Another building block of the .NET platform is the *Common Type System*, or *CTS*. The CTS specification fully describes all possible data types and programming constructs supported by the runtime, specifies how these entities can interact with each other, and details how they are represented in the .NET metadata format (more information on metadata later in this chapter; see Chapter 15 for complete details).

Understand that a given .NET-aware language might not support each and every feature defined by the CTS. The *Common Language Specification, or CLS,* is a related specification that defines a subset of common types and programming constructs that all .NET programming languages can agree on. Thus, if you build .NET types that only expose CLS-compliant features, you can rest assured that all .NET-aware languages can consume them. Conversely, if you make use of a data type or programming construct that is outside of the bounds of the CLS, you cannot guarantee that every .NET programming language can interact with your .NET code library. Thankfully, as you will see later in this chapter, it is very simple to tell your VB compiler to check all of your code for CLS compliance.

The Role of the Base Class Libraries

In addition to the CLR and CTS/CLS specifications, the .NET platform provides a base class library that is available to all .NET programming languages. Not only does this base class library encapsulate various primitives such as threads, file input/output (I/O), graphical rendering systems, and interaction with various external hardware devices, but it also provides support for a number of services required by most real-world applications.

For example, the base class libraries define types that facilitate database access, manipulation of XML documents, programmatic security, and the construction of web-enabled as well as traditional desktop and console-based front ends. From a high level, you can visualize the relationship between the CLR, CTS, CLS, and the base class library, as shown in Figure 1-1.

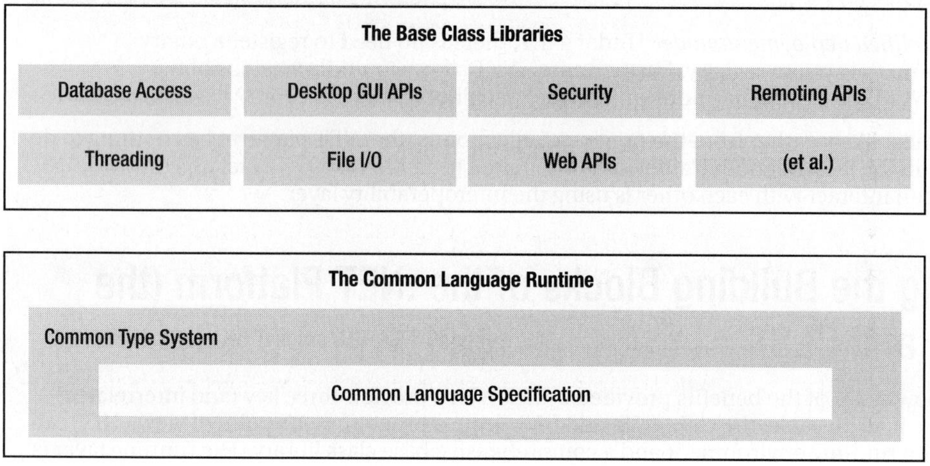

The Base Class Libraries			
Database Access	Desktop GUI APIs	Security	Remoting APIs
Threading	File I/O	Web APIs	(et al.)

The Common Language Runtime
Common Type System
Common Language Specification

Figure 1-1. The CLR, CTS, CLS, and base class library relationship

What Visual Basic 2010 Brings to the Table

Given that .NET is such a radical departure from previous technologies, Microsoft crafted a new programming language, VB, specifically for this platform.

- VB 1.0 through VB 6.0 were the original (pre-.NET) languages.

- Then Microsoft introduced .NET, and came out with a .NET version of VB (named VB.NET).

- Then over the last few years, Microsoft has dropped the ".NET" suffix so that it's just named VB now. The latest version is named VB 2010, as ships with Visual Studio 2010.

From now on in this book, we will say VB 2010. If we want to say something about a non .NET version of VB, we'll explicitly say VB6 or VB in general.

VB 2010 is a programming language with a core syntax that looks somewhat similar to the syntax of VB 6.0. The truth of the matter is that many VB 2010 syntactic constructs are modeled after various aspects of Visual Basic 6.0 and C++. For example, like VB6, VB 2010 supports the notion of formal type properties (as opposed to traditional getter and setter methods) and the ability to declare methods taking a varying number of arguments (via parameter arrays). Like C++, VB 2010 allows you to overload operators, as well as create structures, enumerations, and callback functions (via delegates).

Moreover, as you work through this text, you will quickly see that VB 2010 supports a number of features traditionally found in various functional languages (e.g., LISP or Haskell) such as lambda expressions and anonymous types. Furthermore, with the advent of LINQ (*Language Integrated Query*), VB 2010 supports a number of constructs that make it quite unique in the programming landscape.

Due to the fact that VB 2010 is a hybrid of numerous languages, the result is a product that is as syntactically clean—if not cleaner—as Java, is about as simple as VB6, and provides just about as much power and flexibility as C++ (without the associated ugly bits). Here is a partial list of core VB features that are found in all versions of the language.

- VB does not support pointers

- Full support for classical inheritance and classical polymorphism

- Strongly typed keywords to define classes, structures, enumerations, delegates, and interfaces. Given these new keywords, VB 2010 code is always contained within a `*.vb` file (in contrast to the VB6-centric `*.cls`, `*.bas`, and `*.frm` files)

- Full support for interface-based programming techniques. Automatic memory management through garbage collection

- Formal syntactic constructs for classes, interfaces, structures, enumerations, and delegates

- VB 2010 does support Operator Oveloading. For example, if we have a Money class, we can define how operators such as + and – work for Money objects

- Support for attribute-based programming. This brand of development allows you to annotate types and their members to further qualify their behavior

With the release of .NET 2.0 (circa 2005), the VB .NET programming language was updated to support numerous new bells and whistles, most notability the following:

- The ability to build generic types and generic members. Using generics, you are able to build very efficient and type-safe code that defines numerous *placeholders* specified at the time you interact with the generic item.

- Support for anonymous methods, which allow you to supply an inline function anywhere a delegate type is required. For example, you can provide an anonymous method to handle a button click event in a GUI application.

- Numerous simplifications to the delegate/event model, including covariance, contravariance, and method group conversion. (If some of these terms are unfamiliar, fear not. You'll learn about such details over the course of the book.)

- The ability to define a single type across multiple code files (or if necessary, as an in-memory representation) using the `Partial` keyword.

.NET 3.5 (released circa 2008) added even more functionality to the VB .NET programming language, including the following features:

- Support for strongly typed queries (e.g., LINQ) used to interact with various forms of data.

- Support for anonymous types that allow you to model the *shape* of a type rather than its behavior. For example, it lets you create objects without writing a class definition for the data type.

- The ability to extend the functionality of an existing type (without sub-classing) using extension methods.

- Inclusion of a lambda operator (=>), which even further simplifies working with .NET delegate types.

- A new object initialization syntax, which allows you to set property values at the time of object creation.

The current release of the.NET platform version 4.0 updates VB .NET yet again with a handful of features. While the following list of new constructs may seem rather limited, you see just how useful they can be as you work through this text.

- Support for optional method parameters, as well as named method parameters.

- Support for dynamic lookup of members at runtime via the `dynamic` keyword. As you will see in Chapter 18 this provides a unified approach to invoking members on the fly, regardless of which framework the member implemented (COM, IronPython, HTML DOM, or via .NET reflection services).

- Related to the previous point, .NET 4.0 greatly simplifies how VB applications can interact with legacy COM servers by removing the dependency on interop assemblies and support for optional `ref` arguments.

- Working with generic types is much more intuitive, given that you can easily map generic data to and from general `System.Object` collections via covariance and contravariance.

Perhaps the most important point to understand about the VB 2010 language is that it can only produce code that can execute within the .NET runtime (you could never use VB 2010 to build a native COM server or an unmanaged C/C++ API application). Officially speaking, the term used to describe the code targeting the .NET runtime is *managed code*. The binary unit that contains the managed code is termed an *assembly* (more details on assemblies in just a bit). Conversely, code that cannot be directly hosted by the .NET runtime is termed *unmanaged code*.

Additional .NET-Aware Programming Languages

Understand that VB is not the only language that can be used to build .NET applications. When you install the freely downloadable Microsoft .NET 4.0 Framework Software Development Kit (SDK), as well as when you install Visual Studio 2010, you will be given five managed languages out of the box: C#, Visual Basic, C++/CLI, JScript .NET, and F#.

■ **Note** F# is a new .NET language based on the ML family of functional languages, especially OCaml. While F# can be used as a purely functional language, it also has support for OOP constructs and the .NET base class libraries. If you are interested in learning more about this managed language, navigate online to the official F# homepage, `http://msdn.microsoft.com/fsharp`.

In addition to the managed languages provided by Microsoft, there are .NET compilers for Smalltalk, COBOL, and Pascal (to name a few). Although this book focuses almost exclusively on VB, you may be interested in the following web site:

`http://www.dotnetlanguages.net`

If you click the Resources link at the top of the homepage, you will find a list of .NET programming languages and related links where you are able to download various compilers (see Figure 1-2).

Figure 1-2. DotNetLanguages.net is one of many sites documenting known .NET programming languages.

While I assume you are primarily interested in building .NET programs using the syntax of VB, I encourage you to visit this site, as you are sure to find many .NET languages worth investigating at your leisure (LISP .NET, anyone?).

Life in a Multi-Language World

As developers first come to understand the language-agnostic nature of .NET, numerous questions arise. The most prevalent of these questions would have to be, "If all .NET languages compile down to managed code, why do we need more than one compiler?" There are a number of ways to answer this question. First, we programmers are a *very* particular lot when it comes to our choice of programming language. Some of us prefer languages that offer human-readable syntactic token (such as the Visual Basic family of language).Others enjoy a language full of semicolons and curly brackets with as few language keywords as possible (such as C++ and Java). Still others may want to leverage their mainframe skills while moving to the .NET platform (via COBOL .NET).

Now, be honest. If Microsoft were to build a single "official" .NET language derived from the C/C++/Java family of languages, can you really say all programmers would be happy with this choice? Or, if the only "official" .NET language were based on Fortran syntax, imagine all the folks out there who would ignore .NET altogether. Because the .NET runtime couldn't care less which language was used to build a block of managed code, .NET programmers can stay true to their syntactic preferences and share the compiled code among teammates, departments, and external organizations (regardless of which .NET language others choose to use).

Another excellent byproduct of integrating various .NET languages into a single unified software solution is the simple fact that all programming languages have their own sets of strengths and weaknesses. For example, some programming languages offer excellent intrinsic support for advanced mathematical processing. Others offer superior support for financial calculations, logical calculations, interaction with mainframe computers, and so forth. When you take the strengths of a particular programming language and then incorporate the benefits provided by the .NET platform, everybody wins.

Of course, in reality the chances are quite good that you will spend much of your time building software using your .NET language of choice. However, once you master the syntax of one .NET language, it is very easy to learn another. This is also quite beneficial, especially to the software consultants of the world. If your language of choice happens to be VB .NET but you are placed at a client site that has committed to C#, you are still able to leverage the functionality of the .NET Framework, and you should be able to understand the overall structure of the code base with minimal fuss and bother. Enough said.

An Overview of .NET Assemblies

Regardless of which .NET language you choose to program with, understand that despite the fact that .NET binaries take the same file extension as COM servers and unmanaged Windows binaries (`*.dll` or `*.exe`), they have absolutely no internal similarities. For example, `*.dll` .NET binaries do not export methods to facilitate communications with the COM runtime (given that .NET is *not* COM). Furthermore, .NET binaries are not described using COM type libraries and are not registered into the system registry. Perhaps most important, .NET binaries do not contain platform-specific instructions, but rather platform-agnostic *Intermediate Language* (*IL*) and type metadata. Figure 1-3 shows the big picture of the story thus far.

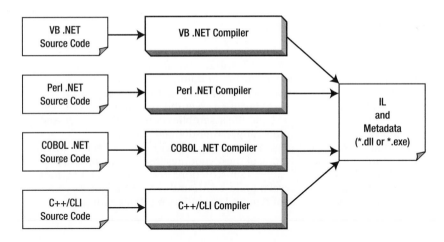

Figure 1-3. All .NET-aware compilers emit IL instructions and metadata.

▪ **Note** There is one point to be made regarding the abbreviation "IL." During the development of .NET, the official term for IL was Microsoft Intermediate Language (MSIL). However, with the final release of .NET, the term was changed to Common Intermediate Language (CIL). Thus, as you read the .NET literature, understand that IL, MSIL, and CIL are all describing the same entity. In keeping with the current terminology, I will use the abbreviation CIL throughout this text.

When a *.dll or *.exe has been created using a .NET-aware compiler, the binary blob is termed an *assembly*. You will examine numerous details of .NET assemblies in Chapter 14. However, to facilitate the discussion of the .NET runtime environment, you do need to understand some basic properties of this new file format.

As mentioned, an assembly contains CIL code, which is conceptually similar to Java bytecode in that it is not compiled to platform-specific instructions until absolutely necessary. Typically, "absolutely necessary" is the point at which a block of CIL instructions (such as a method implementation) is referenced for use by the .NET runtime.

In addition to CIL instructions, assemblies also contain *metadata* that describes in vivid detail the characteristics of every "type" living within the binary. For example, if you have a class named SportsCar, the type metadata describes details such as SportsCar's base class, which interfaces are implemented by SportsCar (if any), as well as a full description of each member supported by the SportsCar type. .NET metadata is always present within an assembly, and is automatically generated by a .NET-aware language compiler.

Finally, in addition to CIL and type metadata, assemblies themselves are also described using metadata, which is officially termed a *manifest*. The manifest contains information about the current version of the assembly, culture information (used for localizing string and image resources), and a list of all externally referenced assemblies that are required for proper execution. You'll examine various tools that can be used to examine an assembly's types, metadata, and manifest information over the course of the next few chapters.

Single-File and Multi-File Assemblies

In a great number of cases, there is a simple one-to-one correspondence between a .NET assembly and the binary file (*.dll or *.exe). Thus, if you are building a .NET *.dll, it is safe to consider that the binary and the assembly are one and the same. Likewise, if you are building an executable desktop application, the *.exe can simply be referred to as the assembly itself. As you'll see in Chapter 14, however, this is not completely accurate. Technically speaking, if an assembly is composed of a single *.dll or *.exe module, you have a *single-file assembly*. Single-file assemblies contain all the necessary CIL, metadata, and associated manifest in an autonomous, single, well-defined package.

Multi-file assemblies, on the other hand, are composed of numerous .NET binaries, each of which is termed a *module*. When building a multi-file assembly, one of these modules (termed the *primary module*) must contain the assembly manifest (and possibly CIL instructions and metadata for various types). The other related modules contain a module-level manifest, CIL, and type metadata. As you might suspect, the primary module documents the set of required secondary modules within the assembly manifest.

■ **Note** Chapter 14 will examine the distinction between single-file and multi-file assemblies in detail. Be aware, however, that Visual Studio 2010 can only be used to build single file assemblies. In the rare case that you need to build a multi-file assembly, you must make use of command-line tools.

The Role of the Common Intermediate Language

Let's examine CIL code, type metadata, and the assembly manifest in a bit more detail. CIL is a language that sits above any particular platform-specific instruction set. For example, the following VB code models a trivial calculator. Don't concern yourself with the exact syntax for now, but do notice the format of the **Add()** method in the **Calc** class.

```
'Calc.vb
Namespace CalculatorExample

    Module Program

        Sub Main()
            Dim c As New Calc()
            Dim ans As Integer = c.Add(10, 84)
            Console.WriteLine("10 + 84 is {0}.", ans)

            ' Wait for user to press the Enter key before shutting down.
            Console.ReadLine()
        End Sub

    End Module
```

```
Public Class Calc
    Public Function Add(ByVal x As Integer, ByVal y As Integer) As Integer
        Return x + y
    End Function
End Class
```

```
End Namespace
```

Now go to Program ➤ Microsoft Visual Studio 2010 ➤ Visual Studio Tools, and open Visual Studio Command Prompt(2010). In the opened VS 2010 cmd window, type **vbc.exe <your_project_path>\ Calc.vb** and press enter. Once you compile this code file using the VB .NET compiler (**vbc.exe**), you end up with a single-file ***.exe** assembly (e.g., named **Calc.exe**) that contains a manifest, CIL instructions, and metadata describing each aspect of the **Calc** and **Program** classes.

■ **Note** Chapter 2 examines the details of compiling code using the VB .NET compiler, as well as the use of graphical IDEs such as Microsoft Visual Studio 2010, Microsoft Visual Basic 2010 Express.

For example, if you were to open this assembly using **ildasm.exe** (examined a little later in this chapter), you would find that the **Add()** method is represented using CIL such as the following:

```
.method public instance int32  Add(int32 x,
int32 y) cil managed
{
  // Code size        9 (0x9)
  .maxstack  2
  .locals init (int32 V_0)
  IL_0000:  ldarg.1
  IL_0001:  ldarg.2
  IL_0002:  add.ovf
  IL_0003:  stloc.0
  IL_0004:  br.s        IL_0007
  IL_0006:  ldloc.0
  IL_0007:  ret
} // end of method Calc::Add
```

Don't worry if you are unable to make heads or tails of the resulting CIL for this method—Chapter 17 will describe the basics of the CIL programming language. The point to concentrate on is that the VB 2010 compiler emits CIL, not platform-specific instructions.

Now, recall that this is true of all .NET-aware compilers. To illustrate, assume you created this same application using C#, rather than Visual Basic 2010.

```
// Calc.cs
using System;

namespace CalculatorExample
{

    // static members.
    class Program
    {
        public static void Main()
        {
            Calc c = new Calc();
            int ans = c.Add(10, 84);
            Console.WriteLine("10 + 84 is {0}.", ans);
            Console.ReadLine();
        }
    }

    class Calc
    {
        public int Add(int x, int y)
        {
            return x + y;
        }
    }

}
```

If you examine the CIL for the **Add()** method, you find similar instructions (slightly tweaked by the C# compiler, csc.exe).

```
..method public hidebysig instance int32  Add(int32 x,
int32 y) cil managed
{
  // Code size        9 (0x9)
  .maxstack  2
  .locals init (int32 V_0)
  IL_0000:  nop
  IL_0001:  ldarg.1
  IL_0002:  ldarg.2
  IL_0003:  add
  IL_0004:  stloc.0
  IL_0005:  br.s        IL_0007
  IL_0007:  ldloc.0
  IL_0008:  ret
} // end of method Calc::Add
```

■ **Source Code** The Calc.cs and Calc.vb code files are included under the Chapter 1 subdirectory.

Benefits of CIL

At this point, you might be wondering exactly what is gained by compiling source code into CIL rather than directly to a specific instruction set. One benefit is language integration. As you have already seen, each .NET-aware compiler produces nearly identical CIL instructions. Therefore, all languages are able to interact within a well-defined binary arena.

Furthermore, given that CIL is platform-agnostic, the .NET Framework itself is platform-agnostic, providing the same benefits Java developers have grown accustomed to (e.g., a single code base running on numerous operating systems). In fact, there is an international standard for the VB language, and a large subset of the .NET platform and implementations already exist for many non-Windows operating systems (more details at the conclusion of this chapter). In contrast to Java, however, .NET allows you to build applications using your language of choice.

Compiling CIL to Platform-Specific Instructions

Due to the fact that assemblies contain CIL instructions rather than platform-specific instructions, CIL code must be compiled on the fly before use. The entity that compiles CIL code into meaningful CPU instructions is a Just-In-Time (JIT) compiler, which sometimes goes by the friendly name of *Jitter*. The .NET runtime environment leverages a JIT compiler for each CPU targeting the runtime, each optimized for the underlying platform.

For example, if you are building a .NET application to be deployed to a handheld device (such as a Windows mobile device), the corresponding Jitter is well equipped to run within a low-memory environment. On the other hand, if you are deploying your assembly to a back-end server (where memory is seldom an issue), the Jitter will be optimized to function in a high-memory environment. In this way, developers can write a single body of code that can be efficiently JIT compiled and executed on machines with different architectures.

Furthermore, as a given Jitter compiles CIL instructions into corresponding machine code, it will cache the results in memory in a manner suited to the target operating system. In this way, if a call is made to a method named `PrintDocument()`, the CIL instructions are compiled into platform-specific instructions on the first invocation and retained in memory for later use. Therefore, the next time `PrintDocument()` is called, there is no need to recompile the CIL.

■ **Note** It is also possible to perform a "pre-JIT" of an assembly when installing your application using the `ngen.exe` command-line tool that ships with the .NET 4.0 Framework SDK. Doing so may improve startup time for graphically intensive applications.

The Role of .NET Type Metadata

In addition to CIL instructions, a .NET assembly contains full, complete, and accurate metadata, which describes each and every type (e.g., class, structure, enumeration) defined in the binary, as well as the members of each type (e.g., properties, methods, events). Thankfully, it is always the job of the compiler (not the programmer) to emit the latest and greatest type metadata. Because .NET metadata is so wickedly meticulous, assemblies are completely self-describing entities.

To illustrate the format of .NET type metadata, let's take a look at the metadata that has been generated for the `Add()` method of the VB 2010 `Calc` class you examined previously (the metadata generated for the C# version of the `Add()` method is similar).

```
TypeDef #7 (02000008)
-------------------------------------------------------
        TypDefName: CalculatorExample.Calc   (02000008)
        Flags     : [Public] [AutoLayout] [Class] [AnsiClass]   (00000001)
        Extends   : 01000003 [TypeRef] System.Object
        Method #1 (06000012)
        ---------------------------------------------------------
        MethodName: .ctor (06000012)
        Flags      : [Public] [ReuseSlot] [SpecialName] [RTSpecialName] [.ctor]   (00001806)
                RVA       : 0x00002218
                ImplFlags : [IL] [Managed]   (00000000)
                CallCnvntn: [DEFAULT]
                hasThis
                ReturnType: Void
                No arguments.

        Method #2 (06000013)
        ---------------------------------------------------------
        MethodName: Add (06000013)
        Flags     : [Public] [ReuseSlot]   (00000006)
        RVA       : 0x00002220
        ImplFlags : [IL] [Managed]   (00000000)
        CallCnvntn: [DEFAULT]
        hasThis
        ReturnType: I4
        2 Arguments
          Argument #1:  I4
          Argument #2:  I4
        2 Parameters
         (1) ParamToken : (08000004) Name : x flags: [none] (00000000)
         (2) ParamToken : (08000005) Name : y flags: [none] (00000000)
```

Metadata is used by numerous aspects of the .NET runtime environment, as well as by various development tools. For example, the IntelliSense feature provided by tools such as Visual Studio 2010 is made possible by reading an assembly's metadata at design time. Metadata is also used by various object-browsing utilities, debugging tools, and the VB compiler itself. To be sure, metadata is the backbone of numerous .NET technologies including Windows Communication Foundation (WCF), reflection, late binding, and object serialization. Chapter 15 will formalize the role of .NET metadata.

The Role of the Assembly Manifest

Last but not least, remember that a .NET assembly also contains metadata that describes the assembly itself (technically termed a *manifest*). Among other details, the manifest documents all external assemblies required by the current assembly to function correctly, the assembly's version number, copyright information, and so forth. Like type metadata, it is always the job of the compiler to generate the assembly's manifest. Here are some relevant details of the manifest generated when compiling the `Calc.vb` code file shown earlier in this chapter (assume the assembly is named `Calc.exe`).

```
// Metadata version: v4.0.21006
.assembly extern mscorlib
{
  .publickeytoken = (B7 7A 5C 56 19 34 E0 89 )                       //
.z\V.4..
  .ver 4:0:0:0
}
.assembly extern Microsoft.VisualBasic
{
  .publickeytoken = (B0 3F 5F 7F 11 D5 0A 3A )                       //
.?_....:
  .ver 10:0:0:0
}
.assembly extern System
{
  .publickeytoken = (B7 7A 5C 56 19 34 E0 89 )                       //
.z\V.4..
  .ver 4:0:0:0
}
.assembly CalculatorExample
{
  .custom instance void
[mscorlib]System.Runtime.CompilerServices.RuntimeCompatibilityAttribute::.ctor()

= ( 01 00 01 00 54 02 16 57 72 61 70 4E 6F 6E 45 78   // ....T..WrapNonEx


63 65 70 74 69 6F 6E 54 68 72 6F 77 73 01 )          // ceptionThrows.
  .custom instance void
[mscorlib]System.Runtime.CompilerServices.CompilationRelaxationsAttribute::.ctor(int32) = (
01 00 08 00 00 00 00 00 )
  .hash algorithm 0x00008004
  .ver 0:0:0:0
}
.module CalculatorExample.exe
// MVID: {B92DE364-319E-4C35-9BCD-90479054BD0E}
.imagebase 0x00400000
.file alignment 0x00000200
.stackreserve 0x00100000
.subsystem 0x0003        // WINDOWS_CUI
.corflags 0x00000001     // ILONLY
// Image base: 0x00650000
```

In a nutshell, this manifest documents the set of external assemblies required by `Calc.exe` (via the `.assembly extern` directive) as well as various characteristics of the assembly itself (e.g., version number, module name). Chapter 14 will examine the usefulness of manifest data in much more detail.

Understanding the Common Type System

A given assembly may contain any number of distinct types. In the world of .NET, *type* is simply a general term used to refer to a member from the set {class, interface, structure, enumeration, delegate}. When you build solutions using a .NET-aware language, you will most likely interact with many of these types. For example, your assembly may define a single class that implements some number of interfaces. Perhaps one of the interface methods takes an enumeration type as an input parameter and returns a structure to the caller.

Recall that the CTS is a formal specification that documents how types must be defined in order to be hosted by the CLR. Typically, the only individuals who are deeply concerned with the inner workings of the CTS are those building tools and/or compilers that target the .NET platform. It is important, however, for all .NET programmers to learn about how to work with the five types defined by the CTS in their language of choice. Here is a brief overview.

CTS Class Types

Every .NET-aware language supports, at the very least, the notion of a *class type*, which is the cornerstone of OOP. A class may be composed of any number of members (such as constructors, properties, methods, and events) and data points (fields). In VB, classes are declared using the `Class` keyword.

```
' A VB class type with 1 method.
Class Calc
    Public Function Add(x As Integer, y As Integer) As Integer
            Return x + y
    End Function
End Class
```

Chapter 5 will begin your examination of building CTS class types with VB; however, Table 1-1 documents a number of characteristics pertaining to class types.

Table 1-1. CTS Class Characteristics

Class Characteristic	Meaning in Life
Is the class NotInheritable or not?	NotInheritable classes cannot function as a base class to other classes.
Does the class implement any interfaces?	An interface is a collection of abstract members that provide a contract between the object and object user. The CTS allows a class to implement any number of interfaces.
Is the class MustInherit or concrete?	MustInherit classes cannot be directly instantiated, but are intended to define common behaviors for derived types. Concrete classes can be instantiated directly.
What is the visibility of this class?	Each class can be configured with a visibility keyword such as `public` or `Friend`. Basically, this controls if the class may be used by external assemblies or only from within the defining assembly.

CTS Interface Types

Interfaces are nothing more than a named collection of abstract member definitions, which may be supported (i.e., implemented) by a given class or structure. In VB, interface types are defined using the `Interface` keyword. By convention, all .NET interfaces begin with a capital letter I, as in the following example:

```
' A VB interface type is usually
' declared as public, to allow types in other
' assemblies to implement their behavior.

Public Interface IDraw
    Sub Draw()
End Interface
```

On their own, interfaces are of little use. However, when a class or structure implements a given interface in its unique way, you are able to request access to the supplied functionality using an interface reference in a polymorphic manner. Interface-based programming will be fully explored in Chapter 9.

CTS Structure Types

The concept of a structure is also formalized under the CTS. Simply put, a *structure* can be thought of as a lightweight class type having value-based semantics. For more details on the subtleties of structures, see Chapter 4. Typically, structures are best suited for modeling geometric and mathematical data and are created in VB using the `Structure` keyword.

```
' A VB structure type.
Structure Point
        ' Structures can contain fields.
        Public xPos As Integer, yPos As Integer

        ' Structures can contain parameterized constructors.
        Public Sub New(x As Integer, y As Integer)
                xPos = x
                yPos = y
        End Sub

        ' Structures may define methods.
        Public Sub PrintPosition()
                Console.WriteLine("({0}, {1})", xPos, yPos)
        End Sub
End Structure
```

CTS Enumeration Types

Enumerations are a handy programming construct that allow you to group name/value pairs. For example, assume you are creating a video game application that allows the player to select one of three character categories (Wizard, Fighter, or Thief). Rather than keeping track of simple numerical values to represent each possibility, you could build a custom enumeration using the Enum keyword.

```
' A VB enumeration type.
Enum CharacterType
        Wizard = 100
        Fighter = 200
        Thief = 300
End Enum
```

By default, the storage used to hold each item is a 32-bit integer; however, it is possible to alter this storage slot if need be (e.g., when programming for a low-memory device such as a Windows mobile device). Also, the CTS demands that enumerated types derive from a common base class, System.Enum. As you will see in Chapter 4, this base class defines a number of interesting members that allow you to extract, manipulate, and transform the underlying name/value pairs programmatically.

CTS Delegate Types

A .NET delegate is a *class* that derives from System.MulticastDelegate, rather than a simple pointer to a raw memory address. In VB, delegates are declared using the Delegate keyword.

```
' This VB delegate type can "point to" any method
' returning an Integer and taking two Integers as input.
Delegate Function BinaryOp(x As Integer, y As Integer) As Integer
```

Delegates are useful when you wish to provide a way for one entity to forward a call to another entity and provide the foundation for the .NET event architecture. As you will see in Chapters 11 and 19, delegates have intrinsic support for multicasting (i.e., forwarding a request to multiple recipients) and asynchronous method invocations (i.e., invoking the method on a secondary thread).

CTS Type Members

Now that you have previewed each of the types formalized by the CTS, realize that most types take any number of *members*. Formally speaking, a type member is constrained by the set {constructor, finalizer, static constructor, nested type, operator, method, property, indexer, field, read-only field, constant, event}.

The CTS defines various *adornments* that may be associated with a given member. For example, each member has a given visibility trait (e.g., Public, Private, Protected). Some members may be declared as MustOverride (to enforce a polymorphic behavior on derived types) as well as Overridable (to define a canned, but overridable, implementation). Also, most members may be configured as Shared (bound at the class level) or instance (bound at the object level). The creation of type members is examined over the course of the next several chapters.

■ **Note** As described in Chapter 10, the VB language also supports the creation of generic types and generic members.

Intrinsic CTS Data Types

The final aspect of the CTS to be aware of for the time being is that it establishes a well-defined set of fundamental data types. Although a given language typically has a unique keyword used to declare an intrinsic CTS data type, all language keywords ultimately resolve to the same type defined in an assembly named `mscorlib.dll`. Consider Table 1-2, which documents how key CTS data types are expressed in various .NET languages.

Table 1-2. The Intrinsic CTS Data Types

CTS Data Type	VB Keyword	C# Keyword	C++/CLI Keyword
System.Byte	Byte	Byte	unsigned char
System.SByte	SByte	Sbyte	signed char
System.Int16	Short	Short	Short
System.Int32	Integer	Int	int or long
System.Int64	Long	Long	__int64

Continued

CTS Data Type	VB Keyword	C# Keyword	C++/CLI Keyword
System.UInt16	UShort	Ushort	unsigned short
System.UInt32	UInteger	Uint	unsigned int or unsigned long
System.UInt64	ULong	Ulong	unsigned __int64
System.Single	Single	Float	Float
System.Double	Double	Double	double
System.Object	Object	Object	object^
System.Char	Char	Char	wchar_t
System.String	String	String	String^
System.Decimal	Decimal	Decimal	Decimal
System.Boolean	Boolean	Bool	Bool

Given the fact that the unique keywords of a managed language are simply shorthand notations for a real type in the System namespace, we no longer have to worry about overflow/underflow conditions for numerical data, or how strings and Booleans are internally represented across different languages. Consider the following code snippets, which define 32-bit numerical variables in C# and VB using language keywords as well as the formal CTS data type:

```
' Define some "Integers" in VB.
Dim i As Integer = 0
Dim j As System.Int32 = 0
```

```
// Define some "ints" in C#.
int i = 0;
System.Int32 j = 0;
```

Understanding the Common Language Specification

As you are aware, different languages express the same programming constructs in unique, language-specific terms. For example, in VB .NET you typically make use of the ampersand (&), while in C# you denote string concatenation using the plus operator (+). Even when two distinct languages express the same programmatic idiom (e.g., a function with no return value), the chances are very good that the syntax will appear quite different on the surface.

```
' VB method returning nothing.
Public Sub MyMethod()
  ' Some interesting code...
End Sub
```

```
// C# method returning nothing.
public void MyMethod()
{
  // Some interesting code...
}
```

As you have already seen, these minor syntactic variations are inconsequential in the eyes of the .NET runtime, given that the respective compilers (`vbc.exe` or `csc.exe`, in this case) emit a similar set of CIL instructions. However, languages can also differ with regard to their overall level of functionality. For example, a .NET language may or may not have a keyword to represent unsigned data, and may or may not support pointer types. Given these possible variations, it would be ideal to have a baseline to which all .NET-aware languages are expected to conform.

The CLS is a set of rules that describe in vivid detail the minimal and complete set of features a given .NET-aware compiler must support to produce code that can be hosted by the CLR, while at the same time be accessed in a uniform manner by all languages that target the .NET platform. In many ways, the CLS can be viewed as a *subset* of the full functionality defined by the CTS.

The CLS is ultimately a set of rules that compiler builders must conform to if they intend their products to function seamlessly within the .NET universe. Each rule is assigned a simple name (e.g., CLS Rule 6) and describes how this rule affects those who build the compilers as well as those who (in some way) interact with them. The crème de la crème of the CLS is the mighty Rule 1.

- *Rule 1*: CLS rules apply only to those parts of a type that are exposed outside the defining assembly.

Given this rule, you can (correctly) infer that the remaining rules of the CLS do not apply to the logic used to build the inner workings of a .NET type. The only aspects of a type that must conform to the CLS are the member definitions themselves (i.e., naming conventions, parameters, and return types). The implementation logic for a member may use any number of non-CLS techniques, as the outside world won't know the difference.

To illustrate, the following VB 2010 `Add()` method is not CLS compliant, as the parameters and return values make use of unsigned data (which is not a requirement of the CLS):

```
Class Calc
        ' Exposed unsigned data is not CLS compliant!
        Public Function Add(x As ULong, y As ULong) As ULong
                Return x + y
        End Function
End Class
```

However, if you were to only make use of unsigned data internally in a method as follows

```
Class Calc
        Public Function Add(x As Integer, y As Integer) As Integer
            ' As this ULong variable is only used internally,
            ' we are still CLS compliant.
            Dim temp As ULong = 0
```

```
            Return x + y
        End Function
End Class
```

you have still conformed to the rules of the CLS and can rest assured that all .NET languages are able to invoke the `Add()` method.

Of course, in addition to Rule 1, the CLS defines numerous other rules. For example, the CLS describes how a given language must represent text strings, how enumerations should be represented internally (the base type used for storage), how to define Shared members, and so forth. Luckily, you don't have to commit these rules to memory to be a proficient .NET developer. Again, by and large, an intimate understanding of the CTS and CLS specifications is only of interest to tool/compiler builders.

Ensuring CLS Compliance

As you will see over the course of this book, VB does define a number of programming constructs that are not CLS compliant. The good news, however, is that you can instruct the VB compiler to check your code for CLS compliance using a single .NET attribute.

```
' Tell the VB  compiler to check for CLS compliance.
<Assembly: System.CLSCompliant(True)>
```

Chapter 15 dives into the details of attribute-based programming. Until then, simply understand that the `<CLSCompliant>` attribute will instruct the VB compiler to check each and every line of code against the rules of the CLS. If any CLS violations are discovered, you receive a compiler error and a description of the offending code.

Understanding the Common Language Runtime

In addition to the CTS and CLS specifications, the final TLA (three-letter abbreviation) to contend with at the moment is the CLR. Programmatically speaking, the term *runtime* can be understood as a collection of services that are required to execute a given compiled unit of code. For example, when developers make use of the MFC to create a new application, they are aware that their program requires the MFC runtime library (i.e., `mfc42.dll`). Other popular languages also have a corresponding runtime: VB6 programmers are tied to a runtime module or two (e.g., `msvbvm60.dll`), and Java developers are tied to the Java Virtual Machine (JVM), for example.

The .NET platform offers yet another runtime system. The key difference between the .NET runtime and the various other runtimes I just mentioned is the fact that the .NET runtime provides a single well-defined runtime layer that is shared by *all* languages and platforms that are .NET-aware.

The crux of the CLR is physically represented by a library named `mscoree.dll` (aka the Common Object Runtime Execution Engine). When an assembly is referenced for use, `mscoree.dll` is loaded automatically, which in turn loads the required assembly into memory. The runtime engine is responsible for a number of tasks. First and foremost, it is the entity in charge of resolving the location of an assembly and finding the requested type within the binary by reading the contained metadata. The CLR then lays out the type in memory, compiles the associated CIL into platform-specific instructions, performs any necessary security checks, and then executes the code in question.

In addition to loading your custom assemblies and creating your custom types, the CLR will also interact with the types contained within the .NET base class libraries when required. Although the entire base class library has been broken into a number of discrete assemblies, the key assembly is mscorlib.dll, which contains a large number of core types that encapsulate a wide variety of common programming tasks as well as the core data types used by all .NET languages. When you build .NET solutions, you automatically have access to this particular assembly.

Figure 1-4 illustrates the workflow that takes place between your source code (which is making use of base class library types), a given .NET compiler, and the .NET execution engine.

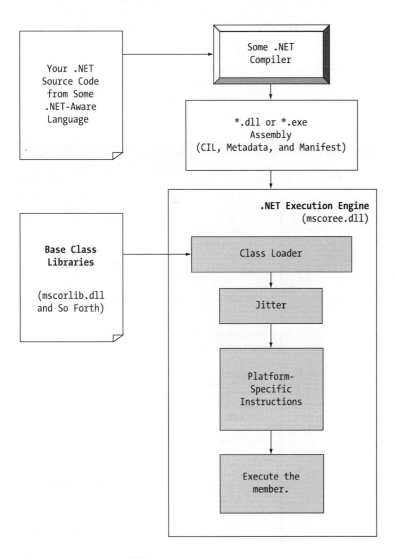

Figure 1-4. mscoree.dll in action

The Assembly/Namespace/Type Distinction

Each of us understands the importance of code libraries. The point of libraries such as MFC, Java Enterprise Edition, and ATL is to give developers a well-defined set of existing code to leverage in their applications. However, the VB language does not come with a language-specific code library. Rather, VB developers leverage the language-neutral .NET libraries. To keep all the types within the base class libraries well organized, the .NET platform makes extensive use of the *namespace* concept.

A namespace is a grouping of semantically related types contained in an assembly. For example, the System.IO namespace contains file I/O-related types, the System.Data namespace defines basic database types, and so on. It is very important to point out that a single assembly (such as mscorlib.dll) can contain any number of namespaces, each of which can contain any number of types.

To clarify, Figure 1-5 shows a screenshot of the Visual Studio 2010 Object Browser utility. This tool allows you to examine the assemblies referenced by your current project, the namespaces within a particular assembly, the types within a given namespace, and the members of a specific type. Note that the mscorlib.dll assembly contains many different namespaces (such as System.IO), each with its own semantically related types (e.g., BinaryReader).

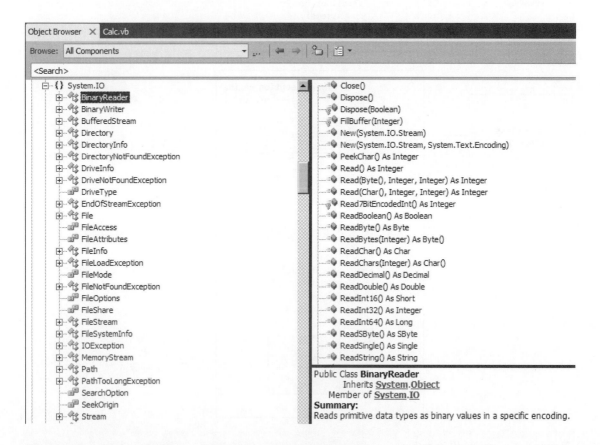

Figure 1-5. A single assembly can have any number of namespaces.

The key difference between this approach and a language-specific library such as MFC is that any language targeting the .NET runtime makes use of the *same* namespaces and *same* types. For example, the following three programs all illustrate the ubiquitous "Hello World" application, written in VB, C# and C++/CLI:

```
' Hello world in VB

Imports System

Public Module MyApp
  Sub Main()
    Console.WriteLine("Hi from VB")
  End Sub
End Module
```

```
// Hello world in C#
using System;

public class MyApp
{
  static void Main()
  {
    Console.WriteLine("Hi from C#");
  }
}
```

```
// Hello world in C++/CLI
#include "stdafx.h"
using namespace System;

int main(array<System::String ^> ^args)
{
  Console::WriteLine(L"Hi from C++/CLI");
  return 0;
}
```

Notice that each language is making use of the `Console` class defined in the `System` namespace. Beyond minor syntactic variations, these three applications look and feel very much alike, both physically and logically.

Clearly, your primary goal as a .NET developer is to get to know the wealth of types defined in the (numerous) .NET namespaces. The most fundamental namespace to get your hands around initially is named `System`. This namespace provides a core body of types that you will need to leverage time and again as a .NET developer. In fact, you cannot build any sort of functional VB .NET application without at least making a reference to the `System` namespace, as the core data types (e.g., `System.Int32`, `System.String`) are defined here. Table 1-3 offers a rundown of some (but certainly not all) of the .NET namespaces grouped by related functionality.

Table 1-3. A Sampling of .NET Namespaces

.NET Namespace	Meaning in Life
System	Within System, you find numerous useful types dealing with intrinsic data, mathematical computations, random number generation, environment variables, and garbage collection, as well as a number of commonly used exceptions and attributes.
System.Collections System.Collections.Generic	These namespaces define a number of stock container types, as well as base types and interfaces that allow you to build customized collections.
System.Data System.Data.Common System.Data.EntityClient System.Data.SqlClient	These namespaces are used for interacting with relational databases using ADO.NET.
System.IO System.IO.Compression System.IO.Ports	These namespaces define numerous types used to work with file I/O, compression of data, and port manipulation.
System.Reflection System.Reflection.Emit	These namespaces define types that support runtime type discovery as well as dynamic creation of types.
System.Runtime.InteropServices	This namespace provides facilities to allow .NET types to interact with unmanaged code (e.g., C-based DLLs and COM servers) and vice versa.
System.Drawing System.Windows.Forms	These namespaces define types used to build desktop applications using .NET's original UI toolkit (Windows Forms).
System.Windows System.Windows.Controls System.Windows.Shapes	The System.Windows namespace is the root for several namespaces that represent the Windows Presentation Foundation (WPF) UI toolkit.
System.Linq System.Xml.Linq System.Data.DataSetExtensions	These namespaces define types used when programming against the LINQ API.
System.Web	This is one of many namespaces that allow you to build ASP.NET web applications.
System.ServiceModel	This is one of many namespaces used to build distributed applications using the Windows Communication Foundation API.

.NET Namespace	Meaning in Life
System.Workflow.Runtime System.Workflow.Activities	These are two of many namespaces that define types used to build "workflow-enabled" applications using the Windows Workflow Foundation API.
System.Threading System.Threading.Tasks	This namespace defines numerous types to build multithreaded applications that can distribute workloads across multiple CPUs.
System.Security	Security is an integrated aspect of the .NET universe. In the security-centric namespaces, you find numerous types dealing with permissions, cryptography, and so on.
System.Xml	The XML-centric namespaces contain numerous types used to interact with XML data.

The Role of the Microsoft Root Namespace

I'm sure you noticed while reading over the listings in Table 1-3, that System is the root namespace for a good number of nested namespaces (e.g., System.IO, System.Data). As it turns out, however, the .NET base class library defines a number of topmost root namespaces beyond System, the most useful of which is named Microsoft.

Any namespace nested within Microsoft (e.g., Microsoft.VisualBasic, Microsoft.ManagementConsole, Microsoft.Win32) contains types that are used to interact with services unique to the Windows operating system. Given this point, you should not assume that these types could be used successfully on other .NET-enabled operating systems such as Mac OS X. For the most part, this text will not dig into the details of the Microsoft rooted namespaces, so be sure to consult the .NET Framework 4.0 SDK documentation if you are so interested.

■ **Note** Chapter 2 will illustrate the use of the .NET Framework 4.0 SDK documentation, which provides details regarding every namespace, type, and member found within the base class libraries.

Accessing a Namespace Programmatically

It is worth reiterating that a namespace is nothing more than a convenient way for us mere humans to logically understand and organize related types. Consider again the System namespace. From your perspective, you can assume that System.Console represents a class named Console that is contained within a namespace called System. However, in the eyes of the .NET runtime, this is not so. The runtime engine only sees a single entity named System.Console.

In VB .NET, the `Imports` keyword simplifies the process of referencing types defined in a particular namespace. Here is how it works. Let's say you are interested in building a graphical desktop application using the Windows Forms API. The main window renders a bar chart based on some information obtained from a back-end database and displays your company logo. While learning the types each namespace contains takes study and experimentation, here are some possible candidates to reference in your program.

```
'Here are all the namespaces used to build this application.
Imports System                    ' General base class library types.
Imports System.Drawing            ' Graphical rendering types.
Imports System.Windows.Forms      ' Windows Forms GUI widget types.
Imports System.Data               ' General data-centric types.
Imports System.Data.SqlClient     ' MS SQL Server data access types.
```

Once you have specified some number of namespaces (and set a reference to the assemblies that define them), you are free to create instances of the types they contain. For example, if you are interested in creating an instance of the `Bitmap` class (defined in the `System.Drawing` namespace), you can write

```
' Explicitly list the namespaces used by this file.
    Imports System
    Imports System.Drawing

    Class Program
        Public Sub DisplayLogo()
                ' Create a 20 * 20 pixel bitmap.
                Dim companyLogo As New Bitmap(20, 20)
                ....
        End Sub
End Class
```

Because your code file is importing `System.Drawing`, the compiler is able to resolve the `Bitmap` class as a member of this namespace. If you did not specify the `System.Drawing` namespace, you would be issued a compiler error. However, you are free to declare variables using a *fully qualified name* as well.

```
' Not listing System.Drawing namespace!
    Imports System

    Class Program
        Public Sub DisplayLogo()
                ' Using fully qualified name.
                Dim companyLogo As New System.Drawing.Bitmap(20, 20)
                ....
        End Sub
End Class
```

While defining a type using the fully qualified name provides greater readability, I think you'd agree that the `VB Imports` keyword reduces keystrokes. In this text, I will avoid the use of fully qualified names (unless there is a definite ambiguity to be resolved) and opt for the simplified approach of the `VB Imports` keyword.

However, always remember that the `Imports` keyword is simply a shorthand notation for specifying a type's fully qualified name, and either approach results in the *exact* same underlying CIL (given the fact that CIL code always makes use of fully qualified names) and has no effect on performance or the size of the assembly.

Referencing External Assemblies

In addition to specifying a namespace via the VB .NET `Imports` keyword, you also need to tell the VB .NET compiler the name of the assembly containing the actual CIL definition for the referenced type. As mentioned, many core .NET namespaces are defined within `mscorlib.dll`. However, the `System.Drawing.Bitmap` class is contained within a separate assembly named `System.Drawing.dll`. A vast majority of the .NET Framework assemblies are located under a specific directory termed the *global assembly cache* (GAC). On a Windows machine, this can be located by default under C:\Windows\Assembly, as shown in Figure 1-6.

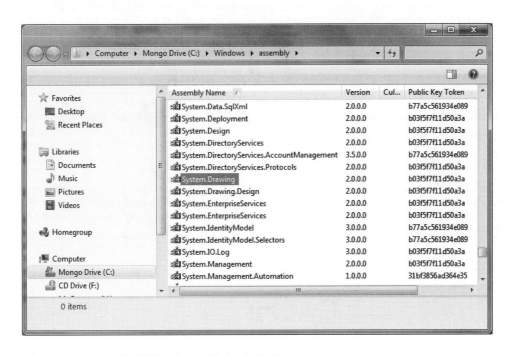

Figure 1-6. Many .NET libraries reside in the GAC.

Depending on the development tool you are using to build your .NET applications, you will have various ways to inform the compiler which assemblies you wish to include during the compilation cycle. You'll examine how to do so in the next chapter, so I'll hold off on the details for now.

■ **Note** With the release of .NET 4.0, Microsoft has opted to isolate .NET 4.0 assemblies in a unique location, which is independent from C:\Windows\Assembly. Chapter 14 will address this point in detail.

Exploring an Assembly Using ildasm.exe

If you are beginning to feel a tad overwhelmed at the thought of gaining mastery over every namespace in the .NET platform, just remember that what makes a namespace unique is that it contains types that are somehow *semantically related*. Therefore, if you have no need for a user interface beyond a simple Console Application, you can forget all about the `System.Windows.Forms`, `System.Windows`, and `System.Web` namespaces (among others). If you are building a painting application, the database namespaces are most likely of little concern. Like any new set of prefabricated code, you learn as you go.

The Intermediate Language Disassembler utility (`ildasm.exe`, which ships with the .NET Framework 4.0 SDK), allows you to load up any .NET assembly and investigate its contents, including the associated manifest, CIL code, and type metadata. By default, `ildasm.exe` should be installed under C:\Program Files\Microsoft SDKs\Windows\v7.0A\bin (if you cannot find `ildasm.exe` in this location, simply search your machine for a file named `ildasm.exe`).

■ **Note** You can easily run `ildasm.exe` by opening a Visual Studio 2010 Command Prompt, and type "ildasm" (without the quotes) followed by the Enter key.

Once you run this tool, proceed to the File | Open menu command and navigate to an assembly you wish to explore. By way of illustration, here is the `Calc.exe` assembly generated based on the `Calc.vb` file shown earlier in this chapter (see Figure 1-7). `ildasm.exe` presents the structure of an assembly using a familiar tree-view format.

D:\vidya\My Task File\Chapter_01\Code_VB_01\Calc\...
File View Help
D:\vidya\My Task File\Chapter_01\Code_VB_01\Calc\Calc\bin\Debug\Ca
MANIFEST
Calc
Calc.My
Calc.CalculatorExample
.class private abstract auto ansi sealed
.custom instance void [Microsoft.VisualBasic]Microsoft.Visual
Calc
.class nested public auto ansi
.ctor : void()
Add : int32(int32,int32)
Main : void()
.assembly Calc
{

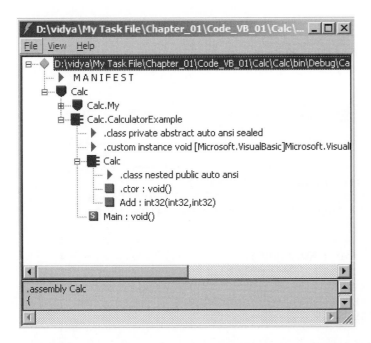

Figure 1-7. ildasm.exe allows you to see the CIL code, manifest, and metadata within a .NET assembly.

Viewing CIL Code

In addition to showing the namespaces, types, and members contained in a given assembly, `ildasm.exe` also allows you to view the CIL instructions for a given member. For example, if you were to double-click the `Main()` method of the `Program` class, a separate window would display the underlying CIL (see Figure 1-8).

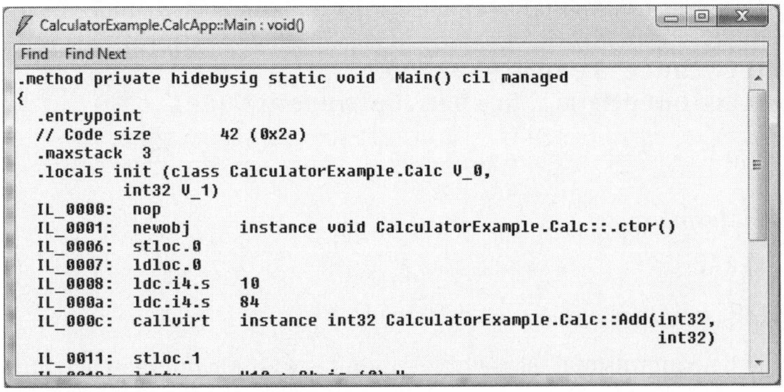

CalculatorExample.CalcApp::Main : void()
Find Find Next
.method private hidebysig static void Main() cil managed
{
.entrypoint
// Code size 42 (0x2a)
.maxstack 3
.locals init (class CalculatorExample.Calc V_0,
int32 V_1)
IL_0000: nop
IL_0001: newobj instance void CalculatorExample.Calc::.ctor()
IL_0006: stloc.0
IL_0007: ldloc.0
IL_0008: ldc.i4.s 10
IL_000a: ldc.i4.s 84
IL_000c: callvirt instance int32 CalculatorExample.Calc::Add(int32,
int32)
IL_0011: stloc.1

Figure 1-8. Viewing the underlying CIL

Viewing Type Metadata

If you wish to view the type metadata for the currently loaded assembly, press Ctrl+M. Figure 1-9 shows the metadata for the Calc.Add() method.

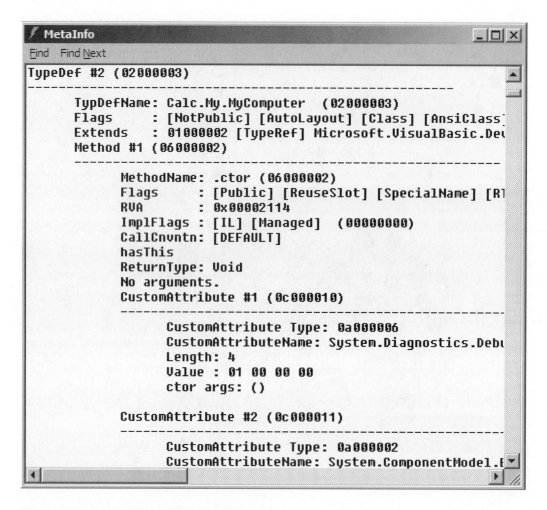

Figure 1-9. Viewing type metadata via ildasm.exe

Viewing Assembly Metadata (aka the Manifest)

Finally, if you are interested in viewing the contents of the assembly's manifest, simply double-click the MANIFEST icon (see Figure 1-10).

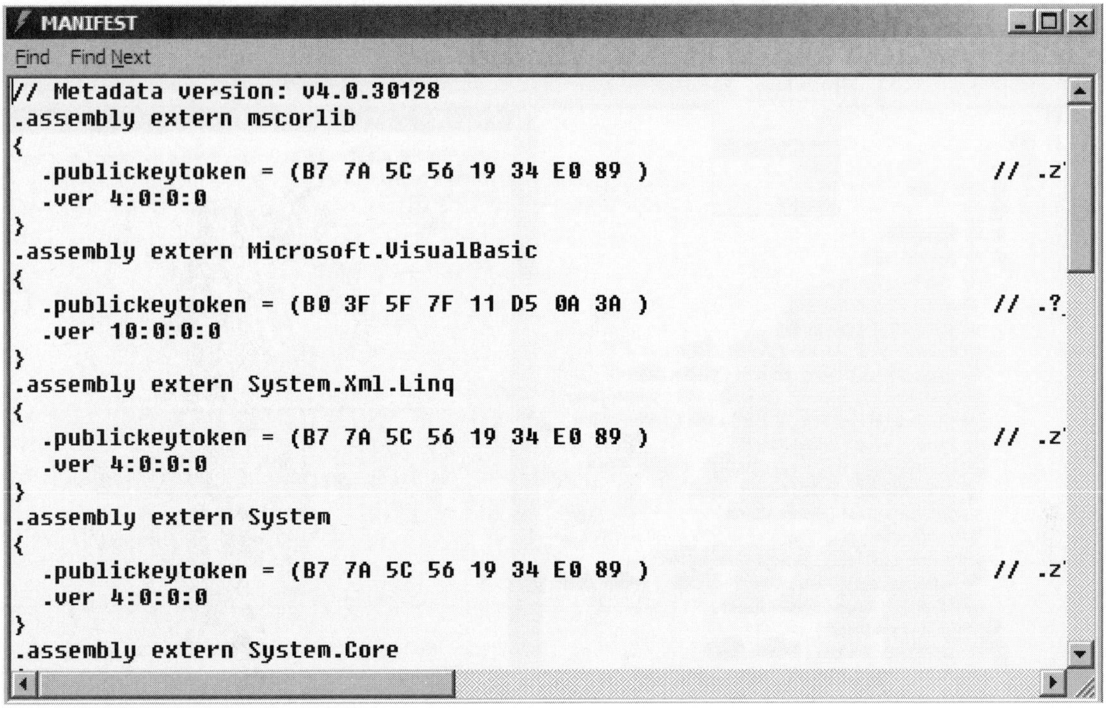

```
// Metadata version: v4.0.30128
.assembly extern mscorlib
{
  .publickeytoken = (B7 7A 5C 56 19 34 E0 89 )              // .z
  .ver 4:0:0:0
}
.assembly extern Microsoft.VisualBasic
{
  .publickeytoken = (B0 3F 5F 7F 11 D5 0A 3A )              // .?
  .ver 10:0:0:0
}
.assembly extern System.Xml.Linq
{
  .publickeytoken = (B7 7A 5C 56 19 34 E0 89 )              // .z
  .ver 4:0:0:0
}
.assembly extern System
{
  .publickeytoken = (B7 7A 5C 56 19 34 E0 89 )              // .z
  .ver 4:0:0:0
}
.assembly extern System.Core
```

Figure 1-10. Viewing manifest data via ildasm.exe

To be sure, `ildasm.exe` has more options than shown here, and I will illustrate additional features of the tool where appropriate in the text.

Exploring an Assembly Using Reflector

While using `ildasm.exe` is a very common task when you wish to dig into the guts of a .NET assembly, the one gotcha is that you are only able to view the underlying CIL code, rather than looking at an assembly's implementation using your managed language of choice. Thankfully, many .NET object browsers and decompilers are available for download, including the very popular Reflector.

This free tool can be downloaded from `http://www.red-gate.com/products/reflector`. Once you have unzipped the archive, you are able to run the tool. When you open this tool for the first time, it will show you a "Start Default Assembly List" dialog from which you can choose the version of assembly. In this tool you can plug in any assembly you wish using the File | Open menu option. Figure 1-11 shows our `Calc.exe` application once again.

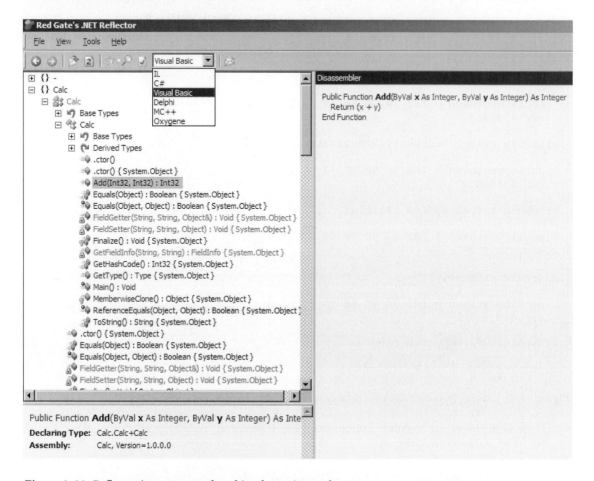

Figure 1-11. Reflector is a very popular object browsing tool.

Notice that `reflector.exe` supports a Disassembler window (opened by pressing the space bar) as well as a drop-down list box that allows you to view the underlying code base in your language of choice (including, of course, CIL code). I'll leave it up to you to check out the number of intriguing features found within this tool.

■ **Note** Be aware that over the course of the remainder of the book, I'll make use of both `ildasm.exe` as well as `reflector.exe` to illustrate various concepts. So take a moment to download Reflector if you have not already done so.

Deploying the .NET Runtime

It should come as no surprise that .NET assemblies can be executed only on a machine that has the .NET Framework installed. For an individual who builds .NET software, this should never be an issue, as your development machine will be properly configured at the time you install the freely available .NET Framework 4.0 SDK (as well as commercial .NET development environments such as Visual Studio 2010).

However, if you deploy your application to a computer that does not have .NET installed, it will fail to run. For this reason, Microsoft provides a setup package named **dotNetFx40_Full_x86.exe** that can be freely shipped and installed along with your custom software. This installation program can be downloaded from Microsoft's general download area (**http://www.microsoft.com/downloads**).

Once **dotNetFx40_Full_x86.exe** is installed, the target machine will now contain the .NET base class libraries, .NET runtime (**mscoree.dll**), and additional .NET infrastructure (such as the GAC).

■ **Note** The Vista and Windows 7 operating systems are preconfigured with the necessary .NET runtime infrastructure. However, if you are deploying your application to a different Microsoft OS, such as Windows XP, you will want to ensure the target machine has the .NET runtime environment installed and configured.

The .NET Client Profile Runtime

The **dotNetFx40_Full_x86.exe** setup program weighs in at approximately 35 MB in size. If you were deploying your application to the end user via a CD, this would not be an issue, as your setup program could simply run the executable if the machine were not configured correctly.

However, if the end user were required to download **dotNetFx40_Full_x86.exe** using a low-speed Internet connection, this could be a bit of a burden. To address this situation, Microsoft introduced an alternative setup program termed the *client profile* (**dotNetFx40_Client_x86.exe**), which can also be downloaded for free from the Microsoft download site.

As the name implies, this setup program installs a subset of the .NET base class libraries, in addition to the necessary runtime infrastructure. While the client profile is more lightweight than its big brother (approximately 28 MB in size), the target machine will not have the same libraries as a "Full" .NET installation. The omitted assemblies of the client profile can be optionally installed on the target machine when the end user performs a Windows Update.

■ **Note** Both the full and client runtime profiles do have 64-bit counterparts, dotNetFx40_Full_x86_x64.exe and dotNetFx40_Client_x86_x64.exe respectively.

The Platform-Independent Nature of .NET

To close this chapter, allow me to briefly comment on the platform-independent nature of the .NET platform. To the surprise of most developers, .NET assemblies can be developed and executed on non-

Microsoft operating systems—Mac OS X, various Linux distributions, Solaris, as well as the Apple iPhone device (via the MonoTouch API). To understand how this is possible, you need to come to terms with yet another abbreviation in the .NET universe: CLI (Common Language Infrastructure).

When Microsoft released the .NET compliant programming language and the .NET platform, they also crafted a set of formal documents that described the syntax and semantics of the CIL language, the .NET assembly format, core .NET namespaces, and the mechanics of a hypothetical .NET runtime engine (known as the Virtual Execution System, or VES).

Better yet, these documents have been submitted to (and ratified by) Ecma International as official international standards (`http://www.ecma-international.org`). The specification of interest is:

- *ECMA-335*: The Common Language Infrastructure (CLI)

The importance of these documents becomes clear when you understand that they enable third parties to build distributions of the .NET platform for any number of operating systems and/or processors. ECMA-335 is the more "meaty" of the two specifications, so much so that is has been broken into six partitions, as shown in Table 1-4.

Table 1-4. *Partitions of the CLI*

Partitions of ECMA-335	Meaning in Life
Partition I: Concepts and Architecture	Describes the overall architecture of the CLI, including the rules of the CTS and CLS, and the mechanics of the .NET runtime engine.
Partition II: Metadata Definition and Semantics	Describes the details of .NET metadata and the assembly format.
Partition III: CIL Instruction Set	Describes the syntax and semantics of CIL code.
Partition IV: Profiles and Libraries	Gives a high-level overview of the minimal and complete class libraries that must be supported by a .NET distribution.
Partition V	Debug Interchange Format
Partition VI: Annexes	Provides a collection of odds-and-ends details such as class library design guidelines and the implementation details of a CIL compiler.

Be aware that Partition IV (Profiles and Libraries) defines only a *minimal* set of namespaces that represent the core services expected by a CLI distribution (e.g., collections, console I/O, file I/O, threading, reflection, network access, core security needs, XML data manipulation). The CLI does *not* define namespaces that facilitate web development (ASP.NET), database access (ADO.NET), or desktop graphical user interface (GUI) application development (Windows Forms/Windows Presentation Foundation).

The good news, however, is that the mainstream .NET distributions extend the CLI libraries with Microsoft-compatible equivalents of ASP.NET, ADO.NET, and Windows Forms in order to provide full-featured, production-level development platforms. To date, there are two major implementations of the CLI (beyond Microsoft's Windows-specific offering). Although this text focuses on the creation of .NET applications using Microsoft's .NET distribution, Table 1-5 provides information regarding the Mono and Portable .NET projects.

Table 1-5. Open Source .NET Distributions

Distribution	Meaning in Life
`http://www.mono-project.com`	The Mono project is an open source distribution of the CLI that targets various Linux distributions (e.g., openSUSE, Fedora) as well as Windows and Mac OS X / iPhone devices.
`http://www.gnu.org/software/dotgnu/`	Portable.NET is another open source distribution of the CLI that runs on numerous operating systems. Portable.NET aims to target as many operating systems as possible (e.g., Windows, AIX, BeOS, Mac OS X, Solaris, all major Linux distributions).

Both Mono and Portable.NET provide an ECMA-compliant VB .NET compiler, .NET runtime engine, code samples, documentation, as well as numerous development tools that are functionally equivalent to the tools that ship with Microsoft's .NET Framework 4.0 SDK. Furthermore, Mono and Portable.NET collectively ship with a C#, Java, and C complier.

▓ **Note** Coverage of creating cross-platform .NET applications using Mono can be found in Appendix B.

Summary

The point of this chapter was to lay out the conceptual framework necessary for the remainder of this book. I began by examining a number of limitations and complexities found within the technologies prior to .NET, and followed up with an overview of how .NET and VB attempt to simplify the current state of affairs.

.NET basically boils down to a runtime execution engine (`mscoree.dll`) and base class library (`mscorlib.dll` and associates). The Common Language Runtime (CLR) is able to host any .NET binary (aka assembly) that abides by the rules of managed code. As you have seen, assemblies contain CIL instructions (in addition to type metadata and the assembly manifest) that are compiled to platform-specific instructions using a just-in-time (JIT) compiler. In addition, you explored the role of the Common Language Specification (CLS) and Common Type System (CTS).

This was followed by an examination of the `ildasm.exe` and `reflector.exe` object browsing utilities, as well as coverage of how to configure a machine to host .NET applications using the full and client profiles. I wrapped up by briefly addressing the platform-independent nature of VB and the .NET platform, a topic further examined in Appendix B.

■ ■ ■

Building Visual Basic 2010 Applications

As a VB 2010 programmer, you may choose among numerous tools to build .NET applications. The point of this chapter is to provide a tour of various .NET development options, including, of course, Visual Studio 2010. The chapter opens, however, with an examination of working with the VB 2010 command-line compiler, **vbc.exe**, and the simplest of all text editors, the Notepad application that ships with the Microsoft Windows OS as well as the freely downloadable Notepad++.

While you could work through this entire text using nothing other than **vbc.exe** and a basic text editor, I'd bet you are also interested in working with feature-rich integrated development environments (IDEs). As you will see, this IDE rivals the functionality of many commercial .NET development environments. After briefly examining the Visual Basic 2010 Express IDE (which is also free), you will be given a guided tour of the key features of Visual Studio 2010.

■ **Note** Over the course of this chapter, you will encounter some VB 2010 syntax we have not formally examined. If you are unfamiliar with the syntax, don't fret. Chapter 3 will formally begin your examination of the VB 2010 language.

The Role of the .NET Framework 4.0 SDK

One common misconception regarding .NET development is the belief that programmers must purchase a copy of Visual Studio in order to build their VB 2010 applications. The truth of the matter is that you are able to build any sort of .NET program using the freely downloadable .NET Framework 4.0 Software Development Kit (SDK). This SDK provides you with numerous managed compilers, command-line utilities, sample code, the .NET class libraries, and a complete documentation system.

■ **Note** The .NET Framework 4.0 SDK setup program (`dotnetfx40_full_setup.exe`) can be obtained from the .NET download web site (`http://msdn.microsoft.com/netframework`).

Now, be aware that if you are going to be using Visual Studio 2010 or Visual Basic 2010 Express, you have no need to manually install the .NET Framework 4.0 SDK. When you install either of these products, the SDK is installed automatically, thereby giving you everything you need out of the box.

However, if you are *not* going to be using a Microsoft IDE as you work through this text, be sure to install the SDK before proceeding.

The Visual Studio 2010 Command Prompt

When you install the .NET Framework 4.0 SDK, Visual Studio 2010, or Visual Basic 2010 Express, you will end up with a number of new directories on your local hard drive, each of which contains various .NET development tools. Many of these tools are driven from the command prompt, so if you wish to use these utilities from any Windows command window, you will need to register these paths with the operating system.

While you could update your PATH variable manually to do so, you can save yourself some time by simply making use of the Visual Studio 2010 Command Prompt that is accessible from the Start ➤ All Programs ➤ Microsoft Visual Studio 2010 ➤ Visual Studio Tools folder (see Figure 2-1).

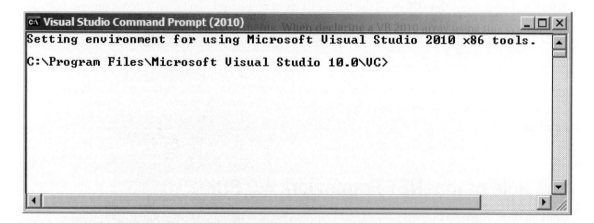

Figure 2-1. The Visual Studio 2010 command prompt

The benefit of using this particular command prompt is that it has been preconfigured to provide access to each of the .NET development tools. Assuming you have a .NET development environment installed, type the following command and press the Enter key:

```
vbc -?
```

If all is well, you should see a list of command-line arguments of the VB 2010 command-line compiler (where **vbc** stands for the *visual basic compiler*).

Building VB 2010 Applications Using vbc.exe

While it is true that you may never decide to build a large-scale application using nothing but the VB 2010 command-line compiler, it is important to understand the basics of how to compile your code files by hand. I can think of a few reasons you should get a grip on the process.

- The most obvious reason is the simple fact that you might not have a copy of Visual Studio 2010 or another graphical IDE.

- You may be in a university setting where you are prohibited from using code generation tools/IDEs in the classroom.

- You plan to make use of automated build tools, such as MSBuild, which require you to know the command-line options of the tools you are utilizing.

- You want to deepen your understanding of VB 2010. When you use graphical IDEs to build applications, you are ultimately instructing **vbc.exe** how to manipulate your VB 2010 input files. In this light, it's edifying to see what takes place behind the scenes.

Another nice by-product of working with **vbc.exe** in the raw is that you become that much more comfortable manipulating other command-line tools included with the .NET Framework 4.0 SDK. As you will see throughout this book, a number of important utilities are accessible only from the command line.

To illustrate how to build a .NET application IDE-free, we will build a simple executable assembly named **TestApp.exe** using the VB 2010 command-line compiler and Notepad. First, you need some source code. Open Notepad (using the Start ➤ All Programs ➤ Accessories menu option) and enter the following trivial VB 2010 class definition:

```
'A Simple VB Application
Module Program
      Sub Main()
         Console.WriteLine("Testing! 1, 2, 3")
      End Sub
End Module
```

Once you have finished, save the file in a convenient location (e.g., C:\VbcExample) as **TestApp.vb**. Now let's get to know the core options of the VB compiler.

■ **Note** As a convention, all VB 2010 code files take a *.vb file extension. The name of the file does not need to have any mapping to the name of the type (or types) it is defining.

Specifying Input and Output Targets

The first point of interest is to understand how to specify the name and type of assembly to create (e.g., a console application named MyShell.exe, a code library named MathLib.dll, a Windows Presentation Foundation application named Halo8.exe). Each possibility is represented by a specific flag passed into vbc.exe as a command-line parameter (see Table 2-1).

Table 2-1. Output Options of the VB 2010 Compiler

Option	Meaning in Life
/out	This option is used to specify the name of the assembly to be created. By default, the assembly name is the same as the name of the initial input *.vb file.
/target:exe	This option builds an executable console application. This is the default assembly output type, and thus may be omitted when building this type of application.
/target:library	This option builds a single-file *.dll assembly.
/target:module	This option builds a *module*. Modules are elements of multi-file assemblies (fully described in Chapter 15).
/target:winexe	Although you are free to build graphical user interface–based applications using the /target:exe option, /target:winexe prevents a console window from appearing in the background.

■ **Note** The options sent to the command-line compiler (as well as most other command-line tools) can be prefixed with either a dash (-) or a slash (/).

To compile TestApp.vb into a console application named TestApp.exe, change to the directory containing your source code file

```
cd C:\VbcExample
```

and enter the following command set (note that command-line flags must come before the name of the input files, not after):

```
vbc /target:exe TestApp.vb
```

Here I did not explicitly specify an /out flag; therefore, the executable will be named TestApp.exe given that TestApp is the name of the input file. Also be aware that most of the VB 2010 compiler flags support an abbreviated version, such as /t rather than /target (you can view all abbreviations by entering vbc -? at the command prompt).

```
vbc /t:exe TestApp.vb
```

Furthermore, given that the /t:exe flag is the default output used by the VB compiler, you could also compile TestApp.vb simply by typing

```
vbc TestApp.vb
```

TestApp.exe can now be run from the command line by typing the name of the executable, as shown in Figure 2-2.

Figure 2-2. TestApp.exe in action

Referencing External Assemblies

Next, let's examine how to compile an application that makes use of types defined in a separate .NET assembly. And just in case you are wondering how the VB 2010 compiler understood your reference to the System.Console type, recall from Chapter 1 that mscorlib.dll is *automatically referenced* during the compilation process (if for some strange reason you wish to disable this feature, you may specify the /nostdlib option of vbc.exe).

Let's update the TestApp application to display a Windows Forms message box. Open your TestApp.vb file and modify it as follows:

```vb
' Add this!
Imports System.Windows.Forms

Module TestApp
    Sub Main()
        Console.WriteLine("Testing! 1, 2, 3")

        ' Add this!
        MessageBox.Show("Hello...")
    End Sub
End Module
```

Notice you are importing the `System.Windows.Forms` namespace via the VB 2010 **Imports** keyword (introduced in Chapter 1). Recall that when you explicitly list the namespaces used within a given ***.vb** file, you avoid the need to make use of fully qualified names of a type (which can lead to hand cramps).

At the command line, you must inform **vbc.exe** which assembly contains the namespaces you are using. Given that you have made use of the `System.Windows.Forms.MessageBox` class, you must specify the `System.Windows.Forms.dll` assembly using the **/reference** flag (which can be abbreviated to **/r**).

```
vbc /r:System.Windows.Forms.dll TestApp.vb
```

If you now rerun your application, you should see a message box appear (see Figure 2-3) in addition to the console output.

Figure 2-3. *Your first Windows Forms application*

Referencing Multiple External Assemblies

On a related note, what if you need to reference numerous external assemblies using **vbc.exe**? Simply list each assembly using a comma-delimited list. You don't need to specify multiple external assemblies for the current example, but some sample usage follows:

```
vbc /r:System.Windows.Forms.dll,System.Drawing.dll *.vb
```

■ **Note** As explained a bit later in this chapter, the VB 2010 compiler will automatically reference a set of core .NET assemblies (such as `System.Windows.Forms.dll`) even if they are not specified using the /r flag.

Compiling Multiple Source Files

The current incarnation of the **TestApp.exe** application was created using a single ***.vb** source code file. While it is perfectly permissible to have all of your .NET types defined in a single ***.vb** file, most projects are composed of multiple ***.vb** files to keep your code base a bit more flexible. Assume you have authored a new class contained in a new file named **HelloMsg.vb**.

```
'The HelloMessage Class

Imports System.Windows.Forms
Public Class HelloMessage
  Public Sub Speak()
  MessageBox.Show("Hello...")
  End Sub
End Class
```

Now, update your initial **TestApp** class to make use of this new class type and comment out the previous Windows Forms logic.

```
' Don't need this anymore.
' Imports System.Windows.Forms

Module TestApp
  Sub Main()
        Console.WriteLine("Testing! 1, 2, 3")
        ' Don't need this anymore either.
        ' MessageBox.Show("Hello...")
        ' Use the HelloMessage class!
        Dim h As New HelloMsg()
        h.Speak()
  End Sub
End Module
```

You can compile your VB 2010 files by listing each input file explicitly.

```
vbc /r:System.Windows.Forms.dll TestApp.vb HelloMsg.vb
```

As an alternative, the VB 2010 compiler allows you to make use of the wildcard character (*) to inform **vbc.exe** to include all ***.vb** files contained in the project directory as part of the current build.

```
vbc /r:System.Windows.Forms.dll *.vb
```

When you run the program again, the output is identical to the previous compiled code. The only difference between the two applications is the fact that the current logic has been split among multiple files.

Working with VB 2010 Response Files

As you might guess, if you were to build a complex VB 2010 application at the command prompt, you would have to specify a tedious number of input options to inform the compiler how to process your source code. To help lessen your typing burden, the VB 2010 compiler honors the use of *response files*.

VB 2010 response files contain all the instructions to be used during the compilation of your current build. By convention, these files end in a ***.rsp** (response) extension. Assume that you have created a response file named **TestApp.rsp** that contains the following options (as you can see, comments are denoted with the # character):

```
# This is the response file
# for the TestApp.exe example
# of Chapter 2.

# External assembly references.
/r:System.Windows.Forms.dll

# output and files to compile (using wildcard syntax).
/target:exe /out:TestApp.exe *.vb
```

Now, assuming this file is saved in the same directory as the VB source code files to be compiled, you are able to build your entire application as follows (note the use of the @ symbol):

```
vbc @TestApp.rsp
```

If the need should arise, you can also specify multiple *.rsp files as input (e.g., vbc @FirstFile.rsp @SecondFile.rsp @ThirdFile.rsp). If you take this approach, be aware that the compiler processes the command options as they are encountered. Therefore, command-line arguments in a later *.rsp file can override options in a previous response file.

Also note that flags listed explicitly on the command line before a response file will be overridden by the specified *.rsp file. Thus, if you were to enter the following:

```
vbc /out:MyCoolApp.exe @TestApp.rsp
```

the name of the assembly would still be TestApp.exe (rather than MyCoolApp.exe), given the /out:TestApp.exe flag listed in the TestApp.rsp response file. However, if you list flags after a response file, the flag will override settings in the response file.

■ **Note** The effect of the /reference flag is cumulative. Regardless of where you specify external assemblies (before, after, or within a response file), the end result is a summation of each reference assembly.

The Default Response File (vbc.rsp)

The final point to be made regarding response files is that the VB compiler has an associated default response file (vbc.rsp), which is located in the same directory as vbc.exe itself (which is by default installed under C:\Windows\Microsoft.NET\Framework\<version>, where <version> is a given version of the platform). If you were to open this file using Notepad, you will find that numerous .NET assemblies have already been specified using the /r: flag, including various libraries for web development, LINQ programming, data access, and other core libraries (beyond mscorlib.dll).

When you are building your VB 2010 programs using vbc.exe, this response file will be automatically referenced, even when you supply a custom *.rsp file. Given the presence of the default response file, the current TestApp.exe application could be successfully compiled using the following command set (as System.Windows.Forms.dll is referenced within vbc.rsp):

```
vbc /out:TestApp.exe *.vb
```

CHAPTER 2 ■ BUILDING VISUAL BASIC 2010 APPLICATIONS

In the event that you wish to disable the automatic reading of **vbc.rsp**, you can specify the **/noconfig** option.

```
vbc @TestApp.rsp /noconfig
```

■ **Note** If you reference assemblies (via the **/r** option) that you do not actually make use of, they are ignored by the compiler. Therefore, you have no need to worry about "code bloat."

Obviously, the VB 2010 command-line compiler has many other options that can be used to control how the resulting .NET assembly is to be generated. You'll see other important features where necessary over the course of this text, however full details of these options can be found within the .NET Framework 4.0 SDK documentation.

■ **Source Code** The VbcExample application can be found under the Chapter 2 subdirectory.

Building .NET Applications Using Notepad++

Another text editor I'd like to quickly point out is the open source (and freely downloadable) Notepad++ application. This tool can be obtained from **http://notepad-plus.sourceforge.net**. Unlike the simple Windows Notepad application, Notepad++ allows you to author code in a variety of languages and supports various plug-in utilities. In addition, Notepad++ provides a few other niceties, including the following:

- Out-of-the-box support for VB 2010 keywords (including keyword Color coding)

- Support for *syntax folding*, which allows you to collapse and expand groups of code statements within the editor (similar to Visual Studio 2010/VB 2010 Express)

- The ability to zoom in/zoom out text via Ctrl-mouse wheel

- Configurable autocompletion for a variety of VB 2010 keywords and .NET namespaces

Regarding this last point, the Ctrl+space keyboard combination will activate VB 2010 autocompletion support (see Figure 2-4).

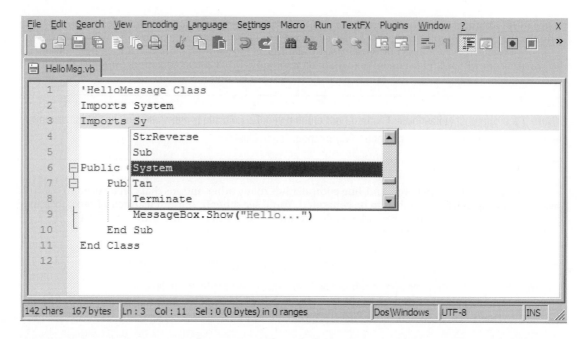

Figure 2-4. Autocompletion using Notepad++

■ **Note** The options displayed by the autocomplete window can be modified and extended. Simply open up the C:\Program Files\Notepad++\plugins\APIs\vbxml file for editing and add any additional entries.

I won't go into too many details of Notepad++ beyond what we have examined here. If you require more assistance, select the ? ➤ Help content menu option.

Building .NET Applications Using Visual Basic 2010 Express

During the summer of 2004, Microsoft introduced a new line of IDEs that fall under the designation of *Express* products (http://msdn.microsoft.com/express). To date, there are various members of the Express family (all of which are *completely free* and supported and maintained by Microsoft Corporation), including the following:

- *Visual Web Developer 2010 Express*: A lightweight tool for building dynamic ASP.NET web sites and WCF services

- *Visual Basic 2010 Express*: A streamlined programming tool ideal for novice programmers who want to learn how to build applications using the user-friendly syntax of Visual Basic

- *Visual Basic 2010 Express and Visual C++ 2010 Express*: Targeted IDEs for students and enthusiasts who wish to learn the fundamentals of computer science in their syntax of choice

- *SQL Server Express*: An entry-level, database management system geared toward hobbyists, enthusiasts, and student developers

Some Unique Features of Visual Basic 2010 Express

By and large, the Express products are slimmed-down versions of their Visual Studio 2010 counterparts and are primarily targeted at .NET hobbyists and students. Visual Basic 2010 Express provides various object browsing tools, a Windows Forms designer, the Add References dialog box, IntelliSense capabilities, and code expansion templates.

However, Visual Basic 2010 Express offers a few (important) features currently not available in other IDEs, including the following:

- Rich support for Windows Presentation Foundation (WPF) XAML applications

- IntelliSense for new Visual Basic 2010 syntactical constructs including named and optional parameters

- The ability to download additional free templates that support Xbox 360 development, WPF applications with Twitter integration, and much more

Consider Figure 2-5, which illustrates using Visual Basic 2010 Express to author the XAML markup for a WPF project.

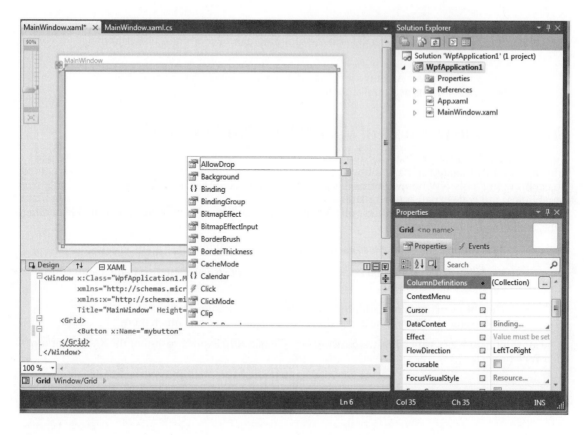

Figure 2-5. Visual Basic 2010 Express has integrated support for .NET 4.0 APIs.

Because the look and feel of Visual Basic 2010 Express is so similar to that of Visual Studio 2010, I do not provide a walk-through of this particular IDE here. You are free to use this IDE as you work through the book, but do be aware that Visual Basic 2010 Express does not support project templates form building ASP.NET web sites. If you wish to also build web applications, be sure to download Visual Web Developer 2010, also available from `http://msdn.microsoft.com/express`.

Building .NET Applications Using Visual Studio 2010

If you are a professional .NET software engineer, the chances are extremely good that your employer has purchased Microsoft's premier IDE, Visual Studio 2010, for your development endeavors (`http://msdn.microsoft.com/vstudio`). This tool is far and away the most feature-rich, enterprise-ready IDE examined in this chapter. Of course, this power comes at a price, which will vary based on the version of Visual Studio 2010 you purchase. As you might suspect, each version supplies a unique set of features.

■ **Note** There is a staggering number of members within the Visual Studio 2010 family. My assumption during the remainder of this text is that you have chosen to make use of Visual Studio 2010 Professional as your IDE of choice.

Although I will assume you have a copy of Visual Studio 2010 Professional, understand that owning a copy of this IDE is *not required* to use this edition of the text. In the worst case, I may examine an option that is not provided by your IDE. However, rest assured that all of this book's sample code will compile just fine when processed by your tool of choice.

■ **Note** Once you download the source code for this book from the Source Code/Downloads area of the Apress web site (http://www.apress.com), you may load the current example into Visual Studio 2010 (or VB 2010 Express) by double-clicking the example's *.sln file. If you are not using Visual Studio 2010/Basic 2010 Express, you will need to manually insert the provided *.vb files into your IDE's project work space.

Some Unique Features of Visual Studio 2010

Visual Studio 2010 ships with the expected GUI designers, code snippet support, database manipulation tools, object and project browsing utilities, and an integrated help system. Unlike many of the IDEs we have already examined, Visual Studio 2010 provides numerous additions. Here is a partial list.

- Visual XML editors/designers
- Support for Windows mobile device development
- Support for Microsoft Office development
- Designer support for Windows Workflow Foundation projects
- Integrated support for code refactoring
- Visual class designer tools

To be completely honest, Visual Studio 2010 provides so many features that it would take an entire book (a rather large book at that) to fully describe every aspect of the IDE. *This is not that book*. However, I do want to point out some of the major features in the pages that follow. As you progress through the text, you'll learn more about the Visual Studio 2010 IDE where appropriate.

Targeting the .NET Framework Using the New Project Dialog Box

If you are following along, create a new VB Console Application (named Vs2010Example) using the File ➤ New ➤ Project menu item. As you can see in Figure 2-6, Visual Studio 2010 supports the ability to select which version of the .NET Framework you wish to build against (2.0, 3.x, or 4.0) using the drop-down list box on the top-center of the New Project dialog box. For each project in this text, you can simply leave the default selection of .NET Framework 4.0.

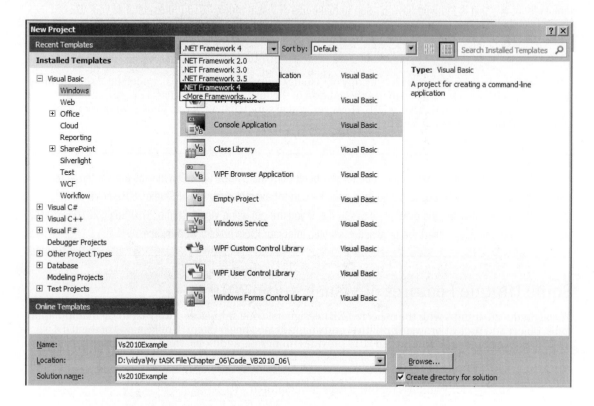

Figure 2-6. Visual Studio 2010 allows you to target a particular version of the .NET Framework.

Using the Solution Explorer Utility

The Solution Explorer utility (accessible from the View menu) allows you to view the set of all content files and referenced assemblies that comprise the current project (see Figure 2-7).

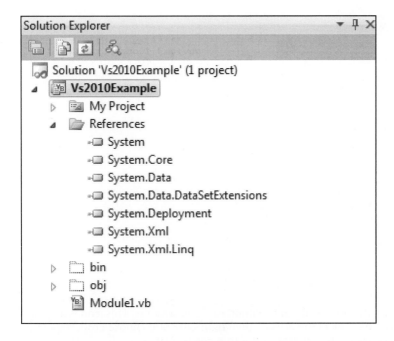

Figure 2-7. The Solution Explorer utility

Before you get to see the referenced assemblies, you need to click on the "Show All Files" icon located in the toolbar in the Solution Explorer pane, as shown highlighted in Figure 2-7 (the second icon from left). After clicking on this you will notice that the References folder of Solution Explorer displays a list of each assembly you have currently referenced, which will differ based on the type of project you select and the version of the Framework you are compiling against.

Referencing External Assemblies

When you need to reference additional assemblies, right-click the References folder and select Add Reference. At this point, you can select your assembly from the resulting dialog box (this is essentially the way Visual Studio allows you to specify the **/reference** option of the command-line compiler). The .NET tab (see Figure 2-8) displays a number of commonly used .NET assemblies; however, the Browse tab allows you to navigate to any .NET assembly on your hard drive. Also, the very useful Recent tab keeps a running tally of frequently referenced assemblies you have used in other projects.

Figure 2-8. *The Add Reference dialog box*

Viewing Project Properties

Finally, notice the first icon on the toolbar located in the Solution Explorer window. This icon is named Properties. When you click on this icon or select the project, then right-click and choose Properties, you are presented with a sophisticated project configuration editor (see Figure 2-9).

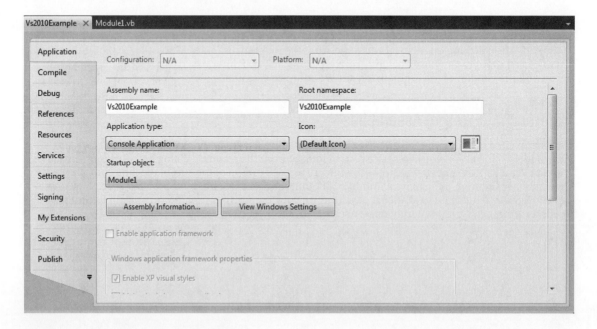

Figure 2-9. *The Project Properties window*

You will see various aspects of the Project Properties window as you progress through this book. However, if you take some time to poke around, you will see that you can establish various security settings, strongly name your assembly, deploy your application, insert application resources, and configure pre- and post-build events.

The Class View Utility

The next tool to examine is the Class View utility, which you can load from the View menu. The purpose of this utility is to show all of the types in your current project from an object-oriented perspective (rather than a file-based view of Solution Explorer). The top pane displays the set of namespaces and their types, while the bottom pane displays the currently selected type's members (see Figure 2-10).

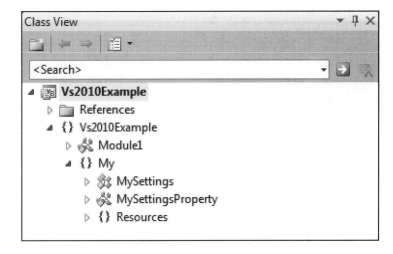

Figure 2-10. The Class View utility

When you double click on a type or type member using the Class View tool, Visual Studio will automatically open the correct VB 2010 code file, and place your mouse cursor at the correct location. Another nice feature of the Visual Studio 2010 Class View tool is that you are able to open up any referenced assembly and drill into the contained namespaces, types, and members (Figure 2-11).

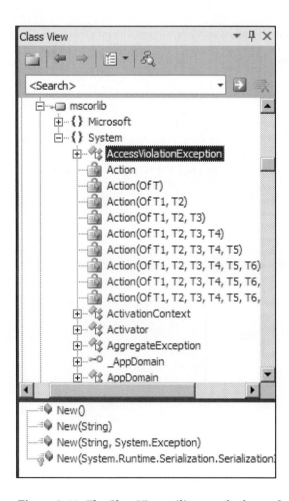

Figure 2-11. The Class View utility can also be used to view referenced assemblies.

The Object Browser Utility

Visual Studio 2010 also provides a second utility to investigate the set of referenced assemblies within your current project. Activate the Object Browser using the View menu, and then select the assembly you wish to investigate (see Figure 2-12).

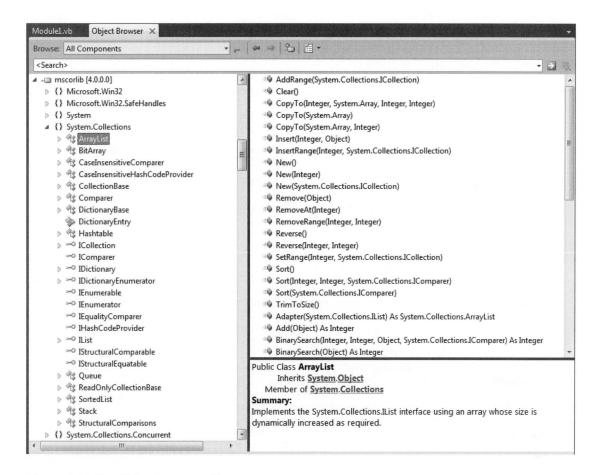

Figure 2-12. *The Object Browser utility*

Integrated Support for Code Refactoring

One major feature that ships with Visual Studio 2010 is support to *refactor* existing code. Simply put, refactoring is a formal and mechanical process whereby you improve an existing code base. In the bad old days, refactoring typically involved a ton of manual labor. Luckily, Visual Studio 2010 does a great deal to automate the refactoring process.

Using the Refactor menu (which will only be available when a code file is active), related keyboard shortcuts, smart tags, and/or context-sensitive mouse clicks, you can dramatically reshape your code with minimal fuss and bother. Table 2-2 defines some common refactorings recognized by Visual Studio 2010.

Table 2-2. Visual Studio 2010 Refactorings

Refactoring Technique	Meaning in Life
Extract Method	Allows you to define a new method based on a selection of code statements
Encapsulate Field	Turns a public field into a private field encapsulated by a VB 2010 property
Extract Interface	Defines a new interface type based on a set of existing type members
Reorder Parameters	Provide a way to reorder member arguments
Remove Parameters	Remove a given argument from the current list of parameters (as you would expect)
Rename	Allows you to rename a code token (method name, field, local variable, and so on) throughout a project

To illustrate refactoring in action, update your `Main()` method with the following simple code:

```
Module Module1
    Sub Main()
        ' Set up Console UI (CUI)
        Console.Title = "My Rocking App"
        Console.ForegroundColor = ConsoleColor.Yellow
        Console.BackgroundColor = ConsoleColor.Blue
        Console.WriteLine("**********************************")
        Console.WriteLine("***** Welcome to My Rocking App *****")
        Console.WriteLine("**********************************")
        Console.BackgroundColor = ConsoleColor.Black

        ' Wait for Enter key to be pressed.
        Console.ReadLine()
    End Sub
End Module
static void Main(string[] args)
{
  // Set up Console UI (CUI)
  Console.Title = "My Rocking App";
  Console.ForegroundColor = ConsoleColor.Yellow;
  Console.BackgroundColor = ConsoleColor.Blue;
  Console.WriteLine("**********************************");
  Console.WriteLine("***** Welcome to My Rocking App *****");
  Console.WriteLine("**********************************");
  Console.BackgroundColor = ConsoleColor.Black;
```

```
// Wait for Enter key to be pressed.
  Console.ReadLine();
}
```

While there is nothing wrong with the preceding code as it now stands, imagine that you want to display this welcome message at various places throughout your program. Rather than retyping the same exact console user interface logic, it would be ideal to have a helper function that could be called to do so.

First, create a new Sub and name it ConfigureCUI. Select each code statement within `Main()` (except the final call to `Console.ReadLine()`) using the editor. Then cut these lines and paste them into the new ConfigureCUI sub.

When you have finished, you will find that your `Main()` method calls the newly created `ConfigureCUI()` method, which now contains the previously selected code.

```
Module Module1
      Sub Main()
            ConfigureCUI()
            ' Wait for key press to close.
            Console.ReadLine()
      End Sub
      Sub ConfigureCUI()
            ' Set up Console UI (CUI)
            Console.Title = "My Rocking App"
            Console.ForegroundColor = ConsoleColor.Yellow
            Console.BackgroundColor = ConsoleColor.Blue
            Console.WriteLine("**********************************")
            Console.WriteLine("***** Welcome to My Rocking App *****")
            Console.WriteLine("**********************************")
            Console.BackgroundColor = ConsoleColor.Black
      End Sub
End Module
```

This is a simple example of using the built-in refactorings of Visual Studio 2010, and you'll see additional examples here and there over the course of this text.

Code Expansions Techniques

Visual Studio 2010 (as well as Visual Basic 2010 Express) is capable of inserting prefabricated blocks of VB 2010 code using menu selections, context-sensitive mouse clicks, and/or keyboard shortcuts. The number of available code expansions is impressive and can be grouped together as snippets.

- *Snippets*: These templates insert common code blocks at the location of the mouse cursor.

To see this functionality firsthand, assume that you wish to iterate over the incoming parameters of the `Main()` method using a `For Each` construct. Rather than typing the code in by hand, you can activate the `For Each` code snippet. When you have done so, the IDE will dump out a `For Each` code template at the current location of the mouse cursor.

To illustrate, place the mouse cursor in the next line of `Main()`. One way to activate a code snippet is to right-click the mouse and click on the Insert Snippet menu option. Here, you will find a list of all code snippets of this category (press the Esc key to dismiss the pop-up menu). To access the `For Each` code snippet, you need to double-click and choose "Code Patterns – Conditional and Loops." Choose `For Each` from the provided list of options, as shown in Figure 2-13. Notice how the icon for a code snippet looks a bit like a torn piece of paper.

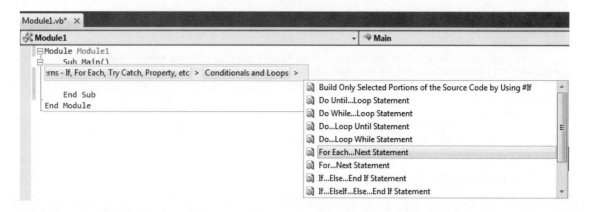

Figure 2-13. Activating a code snippet

Once you find the snippet you want to activate, press the Tab key twice. This will autocomplete the entire snippet and leave a set of placeholders that you can fill in to complete the snippet.

▪ **Note** All code expansion templates are XML-based descriptions of the code to generate within the IDE. Using Visual Studio 2010 (as well as Visual Basic 2010 Express), you can create your own custom code templates. Details of how to do so can be found in my article "Investigating Code Snippet Technology" at `http://msdn.microsoft.com`.

The Visual Class Designer

Visual Studio 2010 gives us the ability to design classes visually (this capability is not included in Visual Basic 2010 Express). The Class Designer utility allows you to view and modify the relationships of the types (classes, interfaces, structures, enumerations, and delegates) in your project. Using this tool, you are able to visually add (or remove) members to (or from) a type and have your modifications reflected in the corresponding VB 2010 file. Also, as you modify a given VB 2010 file, changes are reflected in the class diagram.

To work with this aspect of Visual Studio 2010, the first step is to insert a new class diagram file. There are many ways to do so, one of which is to click the View Class Diagram button located on Solution Explorer's right side (see Figure 2-14; be sure your project—not the solution—is the selected item in the window).

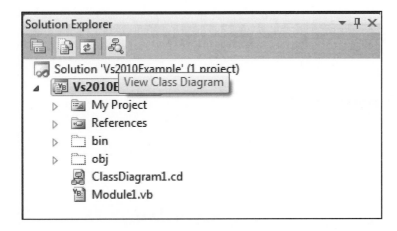

Figure 2-14. Inserting a class diagram file

Once you do, you will find class icons that represent the classes in your current project. If you click the arrow icon for a given type, you can show or hide the type's members (see Figure 2-15).

■ **Note** Using the Class Designer toolbar, you can fine-tune the display options of the designer surface.

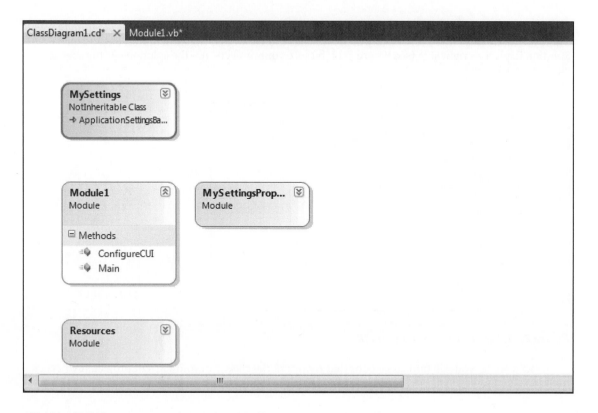

Figure 2-15. The Class Diagram viewer

This utility works in conjunction with two other aspects of Visual Studio 2010: the Class Details window (activated using the View ➤ Other Windows menu) and the Class Designer Toolbox (activated using the View ➤ Toolbox menu item). The Class Details window not only shows you the details of the currently selected item in the diagram, but also allows you to modify existing members and insert new members on the fly (see Figure 2-16).

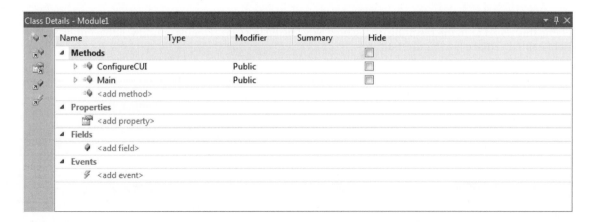

Figure 2-16. The Class Details window

The Class Designer Toolbox, which can be activated using the View menu, allows you to insert new types into your project (and create relationships between these types) visually (see Figure 2-17). (Be aware you must have a class diagram as the active window to view this toolbox.) As you do so, the IDE automatically creates new VB 2010 type definitions in the background.

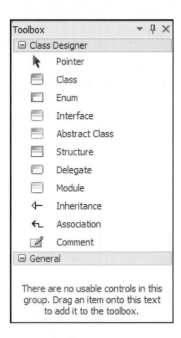

Figure 2-17. The Class Designer Toolbox

By way of example, drag a new Class from the Class Designer Toolbox onto your Class Designer. Name this class Car in the resulting dialog box. Now, using the Class Details window, add a Public String field named petName (see Figure 2-18).

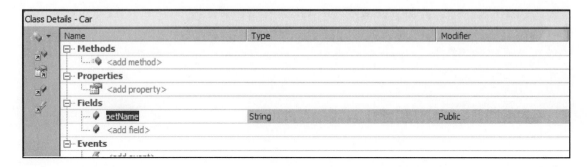

Figure 2-18. Adding a field with the Class Details window

If you now look at the VB 2010 definition of the Car class, you will see it has been updated accordingly (minus the additional code comments).

```
Public Class Car
        ' Public data is typically a bad idea; however,
        ' it keeps this example simple.
        Public petName As String
End Class
```

Now, activate the designer file once again and drag another new Class onto the designer named SportsCar. Now, select the Inheritance icon from the Class Designer Toolbox and click the top of the SportsCar icon. Next, click the mouse on top of the Car class icon. If you performed these steps correctly, you have just derived the SportsCar class from Car (see Figure 2-19).

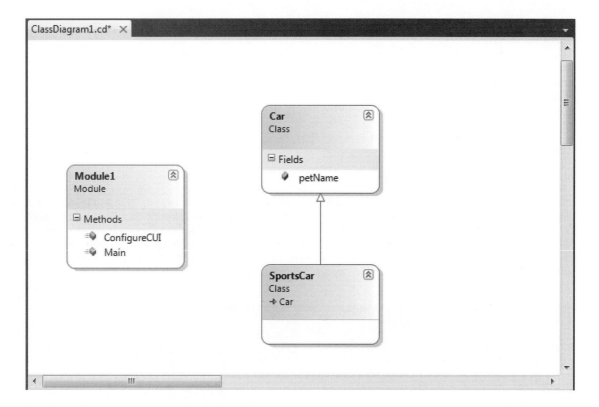

Figure 2-19. Visually deriving from an existing class

To complete this example, update the generated **SportsCar** class with a public method named **GetPetName()** authored as follows:

```
Public Class SportsCar
        Inherits Car
        Public Function GetPetName() As String
                petName = "Fred"
                Return petName
        End Function
End Class
```

You will make use of these (and other) visual tools of Visual Studio 2010 over the course of this book. However, you should now feel a bit more comfortable regarding the basics of the IDE.

■ **Note** The concept of Inheritance will be fully examined in Chapter 6.

The Integrated .NET Framework 4.0 SDK Documentation System

The final aspect of Visual Studio 2010 you *must* be comfortable with from the outset is the fully integrated help system. The .NET Framework 4.0 SDK documentation is extremely good, very readable, and full of useful information. Given the huge number of predefined .NET types (which number well into the thousands), you must be willing to roll up your sleeves and dig into the provided documentation. If you resist, you are doomed to a long, frustrating, and painful existence as a .NET developer.

If you have an internet connection, you can view the .NET Framework 4.0 SDK documentation online at the following web address:

```
http://msdn.microsoft.com/library
```

Of course, if you do not have a live internet connection, this is not very useful. Thankfully, you can install the same help system locally to your computer. Assuming you have already installed Visual Studio 2010, navigate to the All Programs | Microsoft Visual Studio 2010 | Visual Studio Tools folder using your Windows Start button, and select the Manage Help Settings tool. Once you have done so, you can then elect to add the help documentation you are interested in, as seen in Figure 2-20 (if hard drive space allows, I'd recommend adding all possible documentation).

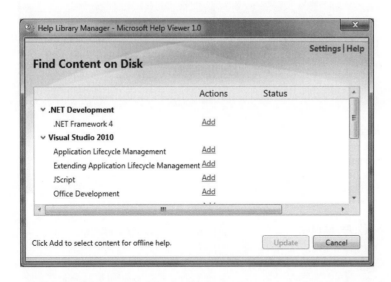

Figure 2-20. *The Help Library Manager allows you to download a local copy of the .NET Framework 4.0 SDK Documentation.*

■ **Note** Beginning with .NET 4.0, the help system is viewed via your current web browser, even if you do a local installation of the .NET Framework 4.0 SDK documentation.

Once the local help system is installed, the simplest way to interact with the documentation is to select a VB 2010 keyword, type name or member name within the Visual Studio 2010 code window, and press the F1 key. This will automatically open a documentation window for the selected item. For example, select the `String` keyword within your `Car` class definition. Once you press F1, you will see the Help page appear.

Another useful aspect of the documentation is the Search edit box located on the upper left area of the display. Here you can enter in the name of any namespace, type, or member and navigate to the correct location. If you were to try to search for the `System.Reflection` namespace, you would be able to learn about the details of this namespace, examine the contained types, view code examples, and so forth (Figure 2-21)

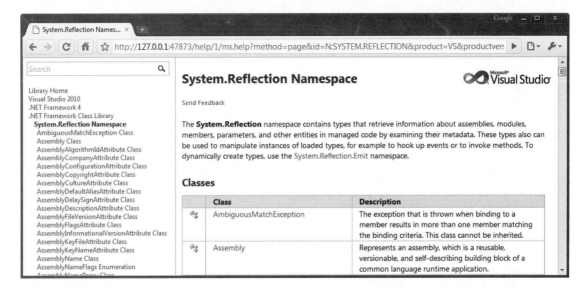

Figure 2-21. The Search edit box allows you to look up items of interest.

Each node in the tree defines the set of types in a given namespace, the members of a given type, and the parameters of a given member. Furthermore, when you view the help page for a given type, you will be told the name of the assembly and namespace that contains the type in question (located at the top of said page). As you read through the remainder of this book, I assume that you will dive into this very, very critical node to read up on additional details of the entity under examination.

■ **Note** At the risk of sounding like a broken record, I really can't emphasize enough how important it is that you learn to use the .NET Framework 4.0 SDK documentation. No book, no matter how lengthy, can cover every aspect of the .NET platform. Make sure you take some time to get comfortable using the help system—you'll thank yourself later.

Summary

So as you can see, you have many new toys at your disposal! The point of this chapter was to provide you with a tour of the major programming tools a VB 2010 programmer may leverage during the development process. You began the journey by learning how to generate .NET assemblies using nothing other than the free VB 2010 compiler and Notepad. Next, you were introduced to the TextPad and Notepad++ applications and walked through the process of using these tools to edit and compile *.vb code files.

You also examined two feature-rich IDEs, starting with Microsoft's VB 2010 Express and Visual Studio 2010 Professional. While this chapter only scratched the surface of each tool's functionality, you should be in a good position to explore your chosen IDE at your leisure (and remember that you'll see additional features of Visual Studio 2010 as you progress through the book).

CHAPTER 3

■ ■ ■

Core VB 2010 Programming Constructs, Part I

This chapter begins your formal investigation of the VB 2010 programming language by presenting a number of bite-sized, stand-alone topics you must be comfortable with as you explore the .NET Framework. The first order of business is to understand the role of the Module keyword and the composition of an executable program's entry point: the Main() method. Next, you will investigate the fundamental VB 2010 data types (and their equivalent types in the System namespace) including an examination of the System.String and System.Text.StringBuilder class types.

Once you know the details of the fundamental .NET data types, you will then examine a number of data type conversion techniques, including narrowing operations and widening operations.

This chapter will also examine the ability to *implicitly* define a local variable. As you will see later in this book, implicit typing is extremely helpful, if not occasionally mandatory, when working with the LINQ technology set. We wrap up this chapter by quickly examining the core operators, iteration constructs, and decision constructs used to build valid VB 2010 code statements.

The Role of the Module Type

Visual Basic 2010 supports a specific programming construct termed a *module*, which is declared with the Module keyword. For example, when you create a Console Application project using Visual Studio 2010, you automatically receive a *.vb file that contains the following code:

```
Module Module1
    Sub Main()
    End Sub
End Module
```

Under the hood, the Module keyword defines a class type, with a few notable exceptions. First and foremost, any public function, subroutine, property, or member variable defined within the scope of a module is exposed as a "shared member" that is directly accessible throughout an application. Simply put, shared members allow you to simulate a global scope within your application that is roughly analogous to the functionality provided by a VB6 *.bas file (full details on shared members can be found in Chapter 5).

Given that members in a module are directly accessible, you are not required to prefix the module's name when accessing its contents. To illustrate working with modules, create a new Console Application project (named FunWithModules), and update your initial code file as follows:

```
Module Module1
  Sub Main()
    ' Show banner.
    DisplayBanner()

    ' Get user's name and say howdy.
    GreetUser()
  End Sub

  Sub DisplayBanner()
    ' Get the current color of the console text.
    Dim currColor As ConsoleColor = Console.ForegroundColor

    ' Set text color to yellow.
    Console.ForegroundColor = ConsoleColor.Yellow
    Console.WriteLine("******* Welcome to FunWithModules *******")
    Console.WriteLine("This simple program illustrates the role")
    Console.WriteLine("of the Module type.")
    Console.WriteLine("*****************************************")

    ' Reset to previous color of your console text.
    Console.ForegroundColor = currColor
    Console.WriteLine()
  End Sub

  Sub GreetUser()
    Dim userName As String
    Console.Write("Please enter your name: ")
    userName = Console.ReadLine()
    Console.WriteLine("Hello there {0}. Nice to meet ya.", userName)
  End Sub
End Module
```

Figure 3-1 shows one possible output.

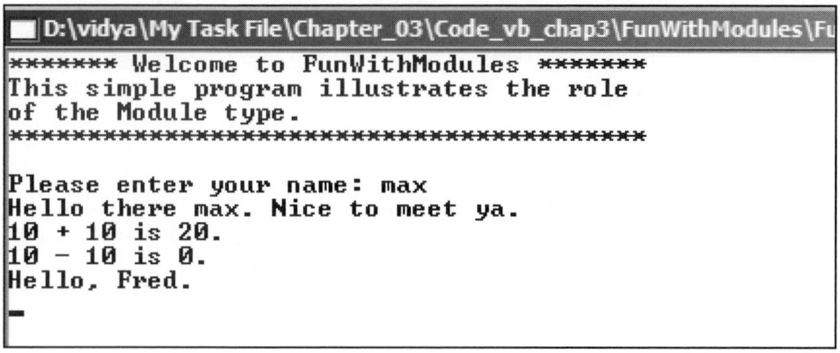

Figure 3-1. Modules at work

Projects with Multiple Modules

In our current example, notice that the Main() method is able to directly call the DisplayBanner() and GreetUser() methods. Because these methods are defined within the same module as Main(), we are not required to prefix the name of our module (Module1) to the member name. However, if you wish to do so, you could retrofit Main() as follows:

```
Sub Main()
  ' Show banner.
  Module1.DisplayBanner()

  ' Get user's name and say howdy.
  Module1.GreetUser()
End Sub
```

In the current example, this is a completely optional bit of syntax (there is no difference in terms of performance or the size of the compiled assembly). However, assume you were to define a new module (MyModule) in your project (within the same *.vb file, for example), which defines an identically formed GreetUser() method:

```
Module MyModule
    Public Sub GreetUser()
        Console.WriteLine("Hello user...")
    End Sub
End Module
```

If you wish to call MyModule.GreetUser() from within the Main() method, you would now need to *explicitly* prefix the module's name. If you do not specify the name of the module, the Main() method automatically calls the Module1.GreetUser() method, as it is in the same module scope as Main():

```
Sub Main()
    ' Show banner.
    DisplayBanner()
    ' Call the GreetUser() method in MyModule.
    MyModule.GreetUser()
End Sub
```

Again, understand that when a single project defines multiple modules, you are not required to prefix the module name unless the methods are ambiguous. Thus, if your current project were to define yet another module named MyMathModule

```
Module MyMathModule
    Function Add(ByVal x As Integer, ByVal y As Integer) As Integer
        Return x + y
    End Function

    Function Subtract(ByVal x As Integer, ByVal y As Integer) As Integer
        Return x - y
    End Function
End Module
```

you could directly invoke the Add() and Subtract() functions anywhere within your application (or optionally prefix the module's name):

```
Sub Main()
    ...
    ' Add some numbers.
    Console.WriteLine("10 + 10 is {0}.", Add(10, 10))

    ' Subtract some numbers
    ' (module prefix optional).
    Console.WriteLine("10 - 10 is {0}.", MyMathModule.Subtract(10, 10))
End Sub
```

■ **Note** If you are new to the syntax of BASIC languages, rest assured that Chapter 4 will cover the details of building functions and subroutines.

Modules Are Not Creatable

Another trait of the module type is that it cannot be directly created using the VB 2010 New keyword (any attempt to do so will result in a compiler error). Therefore, the following code is illegal:

```
' Nope! Error, can't allocate modules!
Dim m as New Module1()
```

Rather, a module simply exposes shared members.

■ **Note** If you already have a background in object-oriented programming, be aware that module types cannot be used to build class hierarchies, as they are implicitly "not inheritable". Furthermore, unlike "normal" classes, modules cannot implement interfaces.

Renaming Your Initial Module

By default, Visual Studio 2010 names the initial module type of a Console Application using the rather nondescript `Module1`. If you were to change the name of the module defining your `Main()` method to a more fitting name (`Program`, for example), the compiler will generate an error such as the following:

```
'Sub Main' was not found in 'FunWithModules.Module1'.
```

In order to inform Visual Studio 2010 of the new module name, you are required to reset the "startup object" using the Application tab of the My Project dialog box, as you see in Figure 3-2. To view this dialog box, double-click "My Project" in Solution Explorer. Once you do so, you will be able to compile your application without error.

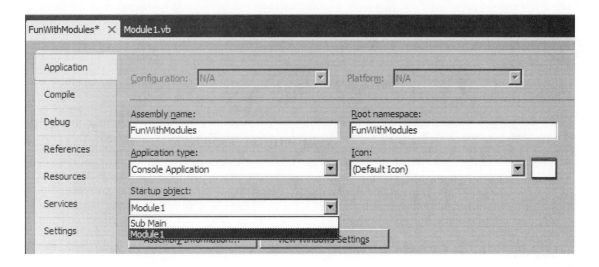

Figure 3-2. Resetting the module name

Members of Modules

To wrap up our investigation of module types, do know that modules can have additional members beyond subroutines and functions. If you wish to define field data (as well as other members, such as properties or events), you are free to do so. For example, assume you wish to update `MyModule` to contain a single piece of public string data. Note that the `GreetUser()` method will now print out this value when invoked:

```
Module MyModule
    Public UserName As String
    Sub GreetUser()
        Console.WriteLine("Hello, {0}.", UserName)
    End Sub
End Module
```

Like any module member, the `UserName` field can be directly accessed by any part of your application. For example:

```
Sub Main()
    ...
    ' Set user's name and call second form of GreetUser().
    UserName = "Fred"
    MyModule.GreetUser()
    ...
End Sub
```

■ **Source Code** The FunWithModules project is located under the Chapter 3 subdirectory.

The Anatomy of a Simple VB 2010 Program

VB 2010 demands that all program logic be contained within a type definition (recall from Chapter 1 that type is a general term referring to a member of the set {class, interface, structure, enumeration, delegate}). Unlike many other languages, in VB 2010 it is not possible to create global functions or global points of data, (although, as we've just seen, you can achieve the same effect as globals by defining members within a Module). In VB 2010, all data members and methods must be contained within a type definition. To get the ball rolling, create a new Console Application project named SimpleVBApp. You might agree that the code within the initial `Module1.vb` file is rather uneventful.

```
Module Module1
    Sub Main()
    End Sub
End Module
```

Given this, update the `Main()` method of your Module1 with the following code statements:

```
Module Module1
    Sub Main()
        ' Display a simple message to the user.
        Console.WriteLine("***** My First VB App *****")
        Console.WriteLine("Hello World!")
        Console.WriteLine()

        ' Wait for Enter key to be pressed before shutting down.
        Console.ReadLine()
    End Sub
End Class
```

Here we have a definition for a Module that supports a single method named `Main()`. By default, Visual Studio 2010 names the module type defining `Main()` *Module1*; however, you are free to change this if you so choose (as we discussed earlier). Every executable VB 2010 application (console program, Windows desktop program, or Windows service) must contain a class defining a `Main()` method, which is used to signify the entry point of the application.

`Main()` method is implicitly "shared," as indeed are all members in a module. We'll examine the details of "shared" members in Chapter 5. For the time being, simply understand that Shared members are scoped to the module/class level (rather than the object level) and can thus be invoked without the need to first create a new module/class instance.

■ **Note** VB 2010 is case insensitive. Therefore, *Main* is the same as *main*, and *Readline* is the same as *readLine*. When you type in keywords (e.g., `Public`, `Private`, `Class`, `MustInherit`), Visual Studio will always capitalize the first letter (plus the first letter of any embedded words). It's also conventional to use the same capitalization strategy for namespaces, types, and member names (e.g., `Console.WriteLine`, `System.Windows.Forms.MessageBox`, `System.Data.SqlClient`). As a rule of thumb, whenever you receive a compiler error regarding "undefined symbols", be sure to check your spelling!

At the moment, the `Main()` method has no parameters. It's also possible to declare `Main()` to take an array of strings as a parameter, which can contain any number of incoming command-line arguments (you'll see how to access them momentarily). Also notice that `Main()` has been defined as a `Sub`, meaning we do not explicitly define a return value using the `Return` keyword before exiting the method scope.

The logic of `Module1` is within `Main()` itself. Here, you make use of the `Console` class, which is defined within the `System` namespace. Among its set of members is the Shared `WriteLine()` which, as you might assume, sends a text string and carriage return to the standard output. You also make a call to `Console.ReadLine()` to ensure the command prompt launched by the Visual Studio 2010 IDE remains visible during a debugging session until you press the Enter key.

Variations on the Main() Method

By default, Visual Studio 2010 will generate `Main()` as a `Sub` (i.e., no return type) and no parameters. This is not the only possible form of `Main()`, however. It is permissible to construct your application's entry point using any of the following signatures (assuming it is contained within a VB 2010 class or structure definition):

```
' Integer return type, array of Strings as the parameter.
Function Main(ByVal args() As String) As Integer
    ' Must return a value before exiting!
    Return 0
End Function

' No return type, no parameters.
Sub Main()
End Sub

' Integer return type, no parameters.
Function Main() As Integer
    ' Must return a value before exiting!
    Return 0
End Function
```

Obviously, your choice of how to construct `Main()` will be based on two questions. First, do you want to return a value to the system when `Main()` has completed and your program terminates? If so, you have to declare `Main()` as a Function with an Integer return type, rather than as a **Sub**. Second, do you need to process any user-supplied, command-line parameters? If so, they will be stored in the array of **Strings**. Let's examine all of our options in more detail.

Specifying an Application Error Code

While a vast majority of your `Main()` methods will be defined as **Subs**, you can also define `Main()` as a **Function** with an **Integer** return type. By convention, returning the value 0 indicates the program has terminated successfully, while another value (such as **-1**) represents an error condition (be aware that the value 0 is automatically returned, even if you define `Main()` as a **Sub** (with no explicit return value).

On the Windows operating system, an application's return value is stored within a system environment variable named **%ERRORLEVEL%**. If you were to create an application that programmatically launches another executable (a topic examined in Chapter 16), you can obtain the value of **%ERRORLEVEL%** using the Shared **System.Diagnostics.Process.ExitCode** property.

Given that an application's return value is passed to the system at the time the application terminates, it is obviously not possible for an application to obtain and display its final error code while running. However, to illustrate how to view this error level upon program termination, begin by updating the `Main()` method as follows:

```
' Note we are now returning an Integer, rather than Sub.
Function Main() As Integer
    ' Display a message and wait for Enter key to be pressed.
    Console.WriteLine("***** My First VB App *****")
    Console.WriteLine("Hello World!")
    Console.WriteLine()
    Console.ReadLine()
    ' Return an arbitrary error code.
    Return -1
End Function
```

Now let's capture the return value of `Main()` with the help of a batch file. Using Windows Explorer, navigate to the folder containing your compiled application (for example, C:\SimpleVBApp\bin\Debug). Add a new text file (named **SimpleVBApp.bat**) to the Debug folder that contains the following instructions (if you have not authored ***.bat** files before, don't concern yourself with the details; this is a test . . . this is only a test):

```
@echo off

rem A batch file for SimpleVBApp.exe
rem which captures the app's return value.

SimpleVBApp
@if "%ERRORLEVEL%" == "0" goto success

:fail
  echo This application has failed!
  echo return value = %ERRORLEVEL%
  goto end
:success
  echo This application has succeeded!
  echo return value = %ERRORLEVEL%
  goto end
:end
  echo All Done.
```

At this point, open a command prompt and navigate to the folder containing your executable and new ***.bat** file. Execute the batch logic by typing its name and pressing the Enter key. You should find the output shown in Figure 3-3, given that your `Main()` method is returning **-1**. Had the `Main()` method returned **0**, you would see the message "This application has succeeded!" print to the console.

Figure 3-3. Capturing an application's return value via a batch file

Again, a vast majority (if not all) of your VB 2010 applications will define `Main()` as a `Sub`, which, as you recall, implicitly returns the error code of zero. To this end, the `Main()` methods used in this text (beyond the current example) will indeed be defined as `Subs` (and the remaining projects will certainly not need to make use of batch files to capture return codes).

Processing Command-Line Arguments

Now that you better understand the return value of the `Main()` method, let's examine the incoming array of `String` data. Assume that you now wish to update your application to process any possible command-line parameters. One way to do so is using a VB 2010 `For` loop. (Note that VB 2010 iteration constructs will be examined in some detail near the end of this chapter.)

```
Function Main(ByVal args As String()) As Integer
   Console.WriteLine("***** Fun with Main() *****")

   ...
   ' Get command-line args.
   For i = 0 To args.Length - 1
       Console.WriteLine("Arg: {0}", args(i))
   Next
   Console.ReadLine()
   Return -1
End Function
```

Here you are checking to see whether the array of `String`s contains some number of items using the `Length` property of `System.Array`. As you'll see in Chapter 4, all VB 2010 arrays actually alias the `System.Array` class and therefore share a common set of members. As you loop over each item in the array, its value is printed to the console window. Supplying the arguments at the command line is equally simple, as shown in Figure 3-4.

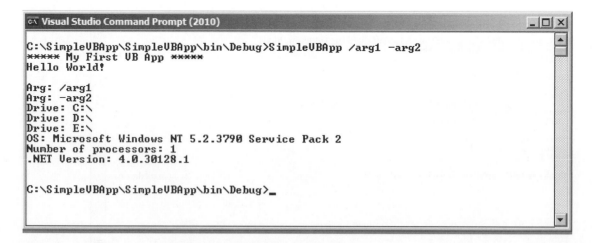

Figure 3-4. Supplying arguments at the command line

As an alternative to the standard **For** loop, you may iterate over an incoming **String** array using the VB 2010 **For Each** construct. Here is some sample usage.

```
' Notice you have no need to check the size of the array when using "For 'Each".
Function Main(ByVal args As String()) As Integer
    ....
        ' Process any incoming args using For Each.
        For Each arg In args
            Console.WriteLine("Arg: {0}", arg)
        Next
        Console.ReadLine()
        Return -1
End Function
```

Finally, you are also able to access command-line arguments using the Shared **GetCommandLineArgs()** method of the **System.Environment** type. The return value of this method is an array of **Strings**. The first index identifies the name of the application itself, while the remaining elements in the array contain the individual command-line arguments. Note that when using this approach, it is no longer necessary to define **Main()** as taking a **String** array as the input parameter, although there is no harm in doing so.

```
Function Main(ByVal args As String()) As Integer
    ...
        ' Get arguments using System.Environment.
        Dim theArgs As String() = Environment.GetCommandLineArgs()
        For Each arg In theArgs
            Console.WriteLine("Arg: {0}", arg)
        Next
        Console.ReadLine()
        Return -1
End Function
```

Of course, it is up to you to determine which command-line arguments your program will respond to (if any) and how they must be formatted (such as with a - or / prefix). Here we simply passed in a series of options that were printed directly to the command prompt. Assume, however, you were creating a new video game and programmed your application to process an option named -godmode. If the user starts your application with the flag, you know he is, in fact, *a cheater* and you can take an appropriate course of action.

Specifying Command-Line Arguments with Visual Studio 2010

In the real world, an end user has the option of supplying command-line arguments when starting a program. However, during the development cycle, you may wish to specify possible command-line flags for testing purposes. To do so with Visual Studio 2010, double-click the My Project icon from Solution Explorer and select the Debug tab on the left side. From there, specify values using the command-line arguments text box (see Figure 3-5).

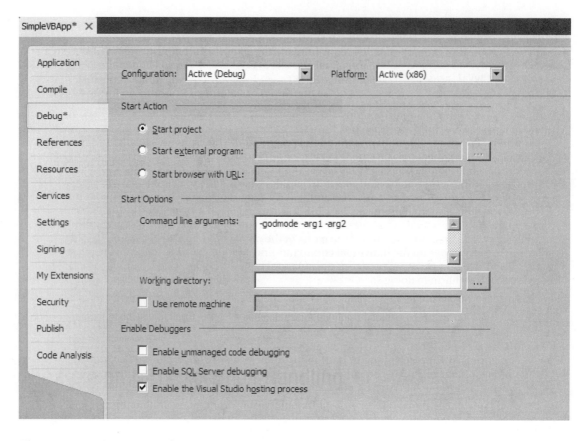

Figure 3-5. Setting command arguments via Visual Studio 2010

Once you have established such command-line arguments, they will automatically be passed to the Main() method when debugging or running your application within the Visual Studio IDE.

An Interesting Aside: Some Additional Members of the System.Environment Class

The Environment class exposes a number of extremely helpful methods beyond GetCommandLineArgs(). Specifically, this class allows you to obtain a number of details regarding the operating system currently hosting your .NET application using various Shared members. To illustrate the usefulness of System.Environment, update your Main() method to call a helper method named ShowEnvironmentDetails():

```
Function Main(ByVal args As String()) As Integer
  ...
  'Helper method within the Module1.
  ShowEnvironmentDetails()
  Console.ReadLine()
  Return -1
End Function
```

Implement this method within your **Program** class to call various members of the **Environment** type.

```
Sub ShowEnvironmentDetails()
    ' Print out the drives on this machine,
    ' and other interesting details.
    For Each drive In Environment.GetLogicalDrives()
        Console.WriteLine("Drive: {0}", drive)
    Next
    Console.WriteLine("OS: {0}", Environment.OSVersion)
    Console.WriteLine("Number of processors: {0}",
                    Environment.ProcessorCount)
    Console.WriteLine(".NET Version: {0}", Environment.Version)
End Sub
```

Figure 3-6 shows a possible test run of invoking this method. If you did not specify command-line arguments via the Visual Studio 2010 Debug tab, you will not find them printed to the console.

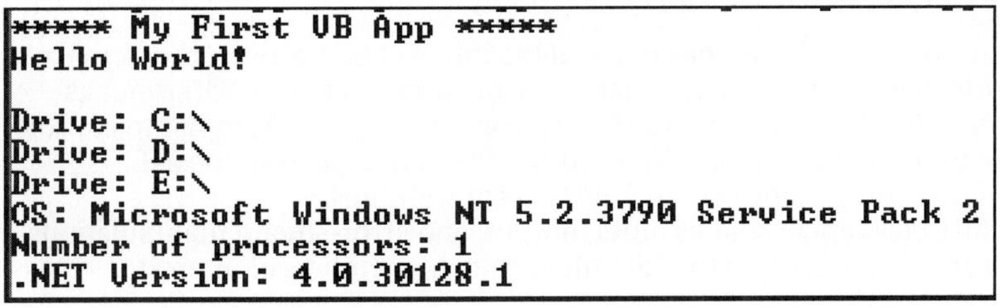

Figure 3-6. *Displaying system environment variables*

The **Environment** type defines members other than those shown in the previous example. Table 3-1 documents some additional properties of interest; however, be sure to check out the .NET Framework 4.0 SDK documentation for full details.

Table 3-1. Select Properties of System.Environment

Property	Meaning in Life
ExitCode	Gets or sets the exit code for the application.
MachineName	Gets the name of the current machine.
NewLine	Gets the newline symbol for the current environment.
StackTrace	Gets the current stack trace information for the application.
SystemDirectory	Returns the full path to the system directory.
UserName	Returns the name of the user that started this application.

■ **Source Code** The SimpleVBApp project is located under the Chapter 3 subdirectory.

The System.Console Class

Almost all of the example applications created over the course of the initial chapters of this book make extensive use of the **System.Console** class. While it is true that a console user interface (CUI) is not as enticing as a graphical user interface (GUI) or web-application, restricting the early examples to console programs will allow us to keep focused on the syntax of VB 2010 and the core aspects of the .NET platform, rather than dealing with the complexities of building GUIs or web sites.

As its name implies, the **Console** class encapsulates input, output, and error-stream manipulations for console-based applications. Table 3-2 lists some (but definitely not all) members of interest.

Table 3-2. Select Members of System.Console

Member	Meaning in Life
Beep()	This method forces the console to emit a beep of a specified frequency and duration.
BackgroundColor ForegroundColor	These properties set the background/foreground colors for the current output. They may be assigned any member of the ConsoleColor enumeration.
BufferHeight BufferWidth	These properties control the height/width of the console's buffer area.

Member	Meaning in Life
`Title`	This property sets the title of the current console.

`WindowHeight`
`WindowWidth`
`WindowTop`
`WindowLeft`
	These properties control the dimensions of the console in relation to the established buffer.

`Clear()`	This method clears the established buffer and console display area.

Basic Input and Output with the Console Class

In addition to the members in Table 3-2, the `Console` type defines a set of methods to capture input and output, all of which are Shared and are therefore called by prefixing the name of the class (`Console`) to the method name. As you have seen, `WriteLine()` pumps a text string (including a carriage return) to the output stream. The `Write()` method pumps text to the output stream without a carriage return. `ReadLine()` allows you to receive information from the input stream up until the Enter key is pressed, while `Read()` is used to capture a single character from the input stream.

To illustrate basic I/O using the `Console` class, create a new Console Application project named BasicConsoleIO and update your `Main()` method to call a helper method named `GetUserData()`:

```
Module Module1
    Sub Main()
        Console.WriteLine("***** Basic Console I/O *****")
        GetUserData()
        Console.ReadLine()
    End Sub
End Module
```

Implement this method within the `Module1` with logic that prompts the user for some bits of information and echoes each item to the standard output stream. For example, we could ask the user for his or her name and age (which we will treat as a text value for simplicity, rather than the expected numerical value) as follows:

```
Sub GetUserData()

    ' Get name and age.
    Console.Write("Please enter your name: ")
    Dim userName As String = Console.ReadLine()
    Console.Write("Please enter your age: ")
    Dim userAge As String = Console.ReadLine()
```

```
    ' Change echo color, just for fun.
    Dim prevColor As ConsoleColor = Console.ForegroundColor
    Console.ForegroundColor = ConsoleColor.Yellow

    ' Echo to the console.
    Console.WriteLine("Hello {0}!  You are {1} years old.",
                        userName, userAge)
    ' Restore previous color.
    Console.ForegroundColor = prevColor
End Sub
```

Not surprisingly, when you run this application, the input data is printed to the console (using a custom color to boot!).

Formatting Console Output

During these first few chapters, you may have noticed numerous occurrences of tokens such as {0} and {1} embedded within various string literals. Simply put, when you are defining a string literal that contains segments of data whose value is not known until runtime, you are able to specify a placeholder within the literal using this curly-bracket syntax. At runtime, the value(s) passed into `Console.WriteLine()` are substituted for each placeholder.

The first parameter to `WriteLine()` represents a string literal that contains optional place-holders designated by {0}, {1}, {2}, and so forth. Be very aware that the first ordinal number of a curly-bracket placeholder always begins with 0. The remaining parameters to `WriteLine()` are simply the values to be inserted into the respective placeholders.

■ **Note** If you have more uniquely numbered curly-bracket placeholders than fill arguments, you will receive a format exception at runtime.

It is also permissible for a given placeholder to repeat within a given string. For example, if you are a Beatles fan and want to build the string "9, Number 9, Number 9", you would write:

```
' John says...
Console.WriteLine("{0}, Number {0}, Number {0}", 9)
```

Also know that it is possible to position each placeholder in any location within a string literal, and it need not follow an increasing sequence. For example, consider the following code snippet:

```
' Prints: 20, 10, 30
Console.WriteLine("{1}, {0}, {2}", 10, 20, 30)
```

Formatting Numerical Data

If you require more elaborate formatting for numerical data, each placeholder can optionally contain various format characters. Table 3-3 shows the most common formatting options.

Table 3-3. .NET Numerical Format Characters

String Format Character	Meaning in Life
C or c	Used to format currency. By default, the flag will prefix the local cultural symbol (a dollar sign [$] for U.S. English).
D or d	Used to format decimal numbers. This flag may also specify the minimum number of digits used to pad the value.
E or e	Used for exponential notation. Casing controls whether the exponential constant is uppercase (E) or lowercase (e).
F or f	Used for fixed-point formatting. This flag may also specify the minimum number of digits used to pad the value.
G or g	Stands for *general.* This character can be used to format a number to fixed or exponential format.
N or n	Used for basic numerical formatting (with commas).
X or x	Used for hexadecimal formatting. If you use an uppercase X, your hex format will also contain uppercase characters.

These format characters are suffixed to a given placeholder value using the colon token (e.g., {0:C}, {1:d}, {2:X}). To illustrate, update the Main() method to call a new helper function named FormatNumericalData(). Implement this method in your Module1 Module to format a fixed numerical value in a variety of ways.

```
' Now make use of some format tags.
Sub FormatNumericalData()
        Console.WriteLine("The value 99999 in various formats:")
        Console.WriteLine("c format: {0:c}", 99999)
        Console.WriteLine("d9 format: {0:d9}", 99999)
        Console.WriteLine("f3 format: {0:f3}", 99999)
        Console.WriteLine("n format: {0:n}", 99999)
        ' Notice that upper- or lowercasing for hex
        ' determines if letters are upper- or lowercase.
        Console.WriteLine("E format: {0:E}", 99999)
        Console.WriteLine("e format: {0:e}", 99999)
        Console.WriteLine("X format: {0:X}", 99999)
        Console.WriteLine("x format: {0:x}", 99999)
End Sub
```

Figure 3-7 shows the output for our current application.

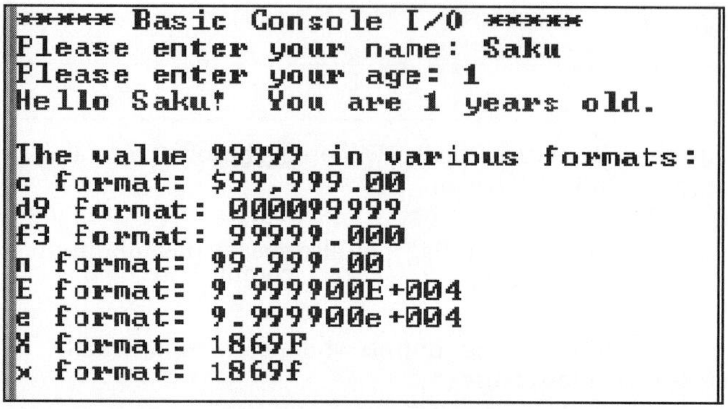

```
***** Basic Console I/O *****
Please enter your name: Saku
Please enter your age: 1
Hello Saku! You are 1 years old.

The value 99999 in various formats:
c format: $99,999.00
d9 format: 000099999
f3 format: 99999.000
n format: 99,999.00
E format: 9.999900E+004
e format: 9.999900e+004
X format: 1869F
x format: 1869f
```

Figure 3-7. Basic console I/O (with .NET string formatting)

Beyond controlling how numerical data is formatted, the .NET platform provides additional tokens that may appear in a string literal that controls spacing and positioning of content. Furthermore, the tokens applied to numerical data can be applied to other data types (such as enumerations or the DateTime type) to control data formatting. Also, be aware that it is possible to build a custom class (or structure) that defines a custom formatting scheme through the implementation of the ICustomFormatter interface.

You'll see additional formatting examples where required throughout this text; however, if you are interested in digging into .NET string formatting further, look up *formatting types* within the .NET Framework 4.0 SDK documentation.

■ **Source Code** The BasicConsoleIO project is located under the Chapter 3 subdirectory.

Formatting Numerical Data Beyond Console Applications

On a final note, be aware that the use of the .NET string formatting characters is not limited to console programs. This same formatting syntax can be used when calling the Shared String.Format() method. This can be helpful when you need to compose textual data at runtime for use in any application type (e.g., desktop GUI app, ASP.NET web app, XML web services).

For example, assume you are building a graphical Windows Forms desktop application and need to format a string for display in a message box.

```
Sub DisplayMessage()
    ' Using string.Format() to format a String literal.
    Dim userMessage As String = String.Format
        ("100000 in hex is {0:x}", 100000)
    ' You would need to reference System.Windows.Forms.dll
    ' in order to compile this line of code!
    System.Windows.Forms.MessageBox.Show(userMessage)
End Sub
```

Notice how `String.Format()` returns a new `String` object, which is formatted according to the provided flags. After this point, you are free to use the textual data as you see fit.

System Data Types and VB 2010 Shorthand Notation

Like any programming language, VB 2010 defines an intrinsic set of fundamental data types, which are used to represent local variables, member variables, return values, and parameters. Unlike other programming languages, however, these keywords are much more than simple compiler-recognized tokens. Rather, the VB 2010 data type keywords are actually shorthand notations for full-blown types in the `System` namespace. Table 3-4 lists each system data type, its range, the corresponding VB 2010 keyword, and the type's compliance with the common language specification (CLS).

■ **Note** Recall from Chapter 1 that CLS-compliant .NET code can be used by any managed programming language. If you expose non–CLS-compliant data from your programs, other languages may not be able to make use of it.

Table 3-4. *The Intrinsic Data Types of VB 2010*

VB 2010 Shorthand	CLS Compliant?	System Type	Range	Meaning in Life
Boolean	Yes	System.Boolean	True or False	Represents truth or falsity
Sbyte	No	System.SByte	−128 to 127	Signed 8-bit number
Byte	Yes	System.Byte	0 to 255	Unsigned 8-bit number
Short	Yes	System.Int16	−32,768 to 32,767	Signed 16-bit number
UShort	No	System.UInt16	0 to 65,535	Unsigned 16-bit number
Integer	Yes	System.Int32	−2,147,483,648 to 2,147,483,647	Signed 32-bit number
UInteger	No	System.UInt32	0 to 4,294,967,295	Unsigned 32-bit number

Continued

VB 2010 Shorthand	CLS Compliant?	System Type	Range	Meaning in Life
Long	Yes	System.Int64	−9,223,372,036,854,775,808 to 9,223,372,036,854,775,807	Signed 64-bit number
ULong	No	System.UInt64	0 to 18,446,744,073,709,551,615	Unsigned 64-bit number
Char	Yes	System.Char	U+0000 to U+ffff	Single 16-bit Unicode character
Single	Yes	System.Single	$\pm 1.5 \times 10^{-45}$ to $\pm 3.4 \times 10^{38}$	32-bit floating-point number
Double	Yes	System.Double	$\pm 5.0 \times 10^{-324}$ to $\pm 1.7 \times 10^{308}$	64-bit floating-point number
Decimal	Yes	System.Decimal	$\pm 1.0 \times 10^{-28}$ to $\pm 7.9 \times 10^{28}$	96-bit signed number
String	Yes	System.String	Limited by system memory	Represents a set of Unicode characters
Object	Yes	System.Object	Can store any data type in an object variable	The base class of all types in the .NET universe

■ **Note** By default, a floating point number is treated as a Double. To declare a Single variable, you can use the suffix f or F to the raw numerical value (for example, 5.3F). As well, raw whole numbers default to an Integer data type. To set the underlying data type to a Long, suffix l or L (4L).

Each of the numerical types, such as Short or Integer, map to a corresponding *structure* in the System namespace. Simply put, structures are *value types* allocated on the stack. On the other hand, String and Object are *reference types,* meaning the data stored in the variable is allocated on the managed heap. You will examine full details of value and reference types in Chapter 4. For the time being, however, simply understand that value types can be allocated into memory very quickly and have a fixed and predictable lifetime.

Variable Declaration and Initialization

When you are declaring a local variable (e.g., a variable within a member scope), you use the `Dim varName As dataType` syntax. To begin, create a new Console Application project named BasicDataTypes. Update the `Module1` Module with the following helper method that is called from within `Main()`:

```
Sub LocalVarDeclarations()
    Console.WriteLine("=> Data Declarations:")
    ' Local variables are declared as so:
    ' Dim varName As dataType
    Dim myInt As Integer
    Dim myString As String

    Console.WriteLine()
End Sub
```

It's good practice to assign an initial value to your local data points at the time of declaration. You may do so on a single line, or by separating the declaration and assignment into two code statements.

```
Sub LocalVarDeclarations()
    Console.WriteLine("=> Data Declarations:")
    ' Local variables are declared and initialized as follows:
    ' Dim varName As dataType = initialValue
    Dim myInt As Integer = 0
    ' You can also declare and assign on two lines.
    Dim myString As String
    myString = "This is my character data"
    Console.WriteLine()
End Sub
```

It is also permissible to declare multiple variables of the same underlying type on a single line of code, as in the following three Boolean variables:

```
Sub LocalVarDeclarations()
    Console.WriteLine("=> Data Declarations:")
    Dim myInt As Integer = 0
    Dim myString As String
    myString = "This is my character data"
    ' Declare 3 Booleans on a single line.
    Dim b1 As Boolean = True, b2 As Boolean = False, b3 As Boolean = b1
    Console.WriteLine()
End Sub
```

Since the VB 2010 `Boolean` keyword is simply a shorthand notation for the `System.Boolean` structure, it is also possible to allocate any data type using its full name (of course, the same point holds true for any VB 2010 data type keyword). Here is the final implementation of `LocalVarDeclarations()`:

```
Sub LocalVarDeclarations()
    Console.WriteLine("=> Data Declarations:")

    ' Local variables are declared and initialized as follows:
    ' Dim varName As dataType = initialValue
    Dim myInt As Integer = 0
    Dim myString As String
    myString = "This is my character data"

    ' Declare 3 Booleans on a single line.
    Dim b1 As Boolean = True, b2 As Boolean = False, b3 As Boolean = b1

    ' Use System data type to declare a Boolean.
    Dim b4 As System.Boolean = False
    Console.WriteLine("Your data: {0}, {1}, {2}, {3}, {4}, {5}",
                    myInt, myString, b1, b2, b3, b4)
    Console.WriteLine()
End Sub
```

Intrinsic Data Types and the New Operator

All intrinsic data types support what is known as a *default constructor* (see Chapter 5). This feature allows you to create a variable using the New keyword, which automatically sets the variable to its default value.

- Boolean variables are set to False.

- Numeric data is set to 0 (or 0.0 in the case of floating-point data types).

- Char variables are set to a single empty character.

- BigInteger variables are set to 0.

- DateTime variables are set to 1/1/0001 12:00:00 AM.

- Object references (including Strings) are set to Nothing.

■ **Note** The BigInteger data type seen in the previous list is a new .NET 4.0 programming feature, which will be explained in just a bit.

Although it is more cumbersome to use the New keyword when creating a basic data type variable, the following is syntactically well-formed VB code:

```
Sub NewingDataTypes()
    Console.WriteLine("=> Using New to create variables:")

    Dim b As New Boolean()    ' Set to False.
    Dim i As New Integer()    ' Set to 0.
    Dim d As New Double()     ' Set to 0.
    Dim dt As New DateTime()  ' Set to 1/1/0001 12:00:00 AM

    Console.WriteLine("{0}, {1}, {2}, {3}", b, i, d, dt)
    Console.WriteLine()
End Sub
```

The Data Type Class Hierarchy

It is very interesting to note that even the primitive .NET data types are arranged in a *class hierarchy*. If you are new to the world of inheritance, you will discover the full details in Chapter 6. Until then, just understand that types at the top of a class hierarchy provide some default behaviors that are granted to the derived types. The relationship between these core system types can be understood as shown in Figure 3-8.

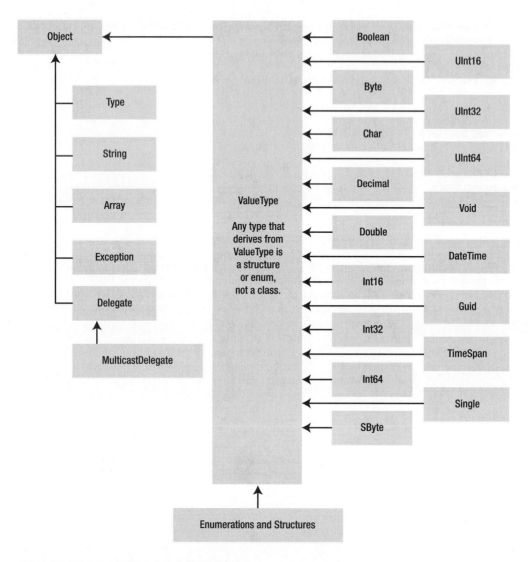

Figure 3-8. *The class hierarchy of system types*

Notice that each of these types ultimately derive from `System.Object`, which defines a set of methods (e.g., `ToString()`, `Equals()`, `GetHashCode()`) common to all types in the .NET base class libraries (these methods are fully detailed in Chapter 6).

Also note that many numerical data types derive from a class named `System.ValueType`. Descendents of `ValueType` are automatically allocated on the stack and therefore have a very predictable lifetime and are quite efficient. On the other hand, types that do not have `System.ValueType` in their inheritance chain (such as `System.Type`, `System.String`, `System.Array`, `System.Exception`, and `System.Delegate`) are not allocated on the stack, but on the garbage-collected heap.

Without getting too hung up on the details of System.Object and System.ValueType , just understand that because a VB 2010 keyword (such as Integer) is simply shorthand notation for the corresponding system type (in this case, System.Int32), the following is perfectly legal syntax, given that System.Int32 (the VB 2010 Integer) eventually derives from System.Object and therefore can invoke any of its Public members, as illustrated by this additional helper method:

```
Sub ObjectFunctionality()
    Console.WriteLine("=> System.Object Functionality:")
    ' A VB Integer is really a shorthand for System.Int32.
    ' which inherits the following members from System.Object.
    Console.WriteLine("12.GetHashCode() = {0}", 12.GetHashCode())
    Console.WriteLine("12.Equals(23) = {0}", 12.Equals(23))
    Console.WriteLine("12.ToString() = {0}", 12.ToString())
    Console.WriteLine("12.GetType() = {0}", 12.GetType())
    Console.WriteLine()
End Sub
```

If you were to call this method from within Main(), you would find the output shown in Figure 3-9.

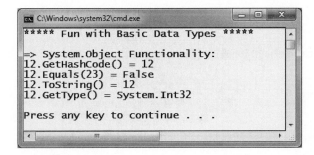

Figure 3-9. *All types (even numerical data) extend System.Object*

Members of Numerical Data Types

To continue experimenting with the intrinsic VB 2010 data types, understand that the numerical types of .NET support MaxValue and MinValue properties that provide information regarding the range a given type can store. In addition to the MinValue/MaxValue properties, a given numerical system type may define further useful members. For example, the System.Double type allows you to obtain the values for epsilon and infinity (which may be of interest to those of you with a mathematical flare). To illustrate, consider the following helper function:

```
Sub DataTypeFunctionality()
    Console.WriteLine("=> Data type Functionality:")
    Console.WriteLine("Max of Integer: {0}", Integer.MaxValue)
    Console.WriteLine("Min of Integer: {0}", Integer.MinValue)
```

```
        Console.WriteLine("Max of Double: {0}", Double.MaxValue)
        Console.WriteLine("Min of Double: {0}", Double.MinValue)

        Console.WriteLine("Double.Epsilon: {0}", Double.Epsilon)
        Console.WriteLine("Double.PositiveInfinity: {0}",
                        Double.PositiveInfinity)
        Console.WriteLine("Double.NegativeInfinity: {0}",
                        Double.NegativeInfinity)
        Console.WriteLine()
End Sub
```

Members of System.Boolean

Next, consider the System.Boolean data type. The only valid assignment a VB 2010 Boolean can take is from the set {True | False}. Given this point, it should be clear that System.Boolean does not support a MinValue/MaxValue property set, but rather TrueString/FalseString (which yields the string "True" or "False", respectively). Add the following code statements to the DataTypeFunctionality() helper method:

```
Console.WriteLine("Boolean.FalseString: {0}", Boolean.FalseString)
Console.WriteLine("Boolean.TrueString: {0}", Boolean.TrueString)
```

Figure 3-10 shows the output of invoking DataTypeFunctionality() from within Main().

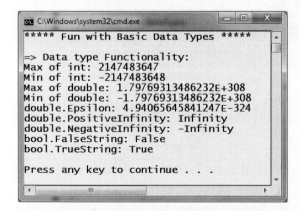

Figure 3-10. Select functionality of various data types

Members of System.Char

VB 2010 textual data is represented by the String and Char keywords, which are simple shorthand notations for System.String and System.Char, both of which are Unicode under the hood. As you may already know, a String represents a contiguous set of characters (e.g., "Hello"), while the Char can represent a single slot in a String (e.g., "H"c).

The System.Char type provides you with a great deal of functionality beyond the ability to hold a single point of character data. Using the Shared methods of System.Char, you are able to determine whether a given character is numerical, alphabetical, a point of punctuation, or whatnot. Consider the following method:

```
Sub CharFunctionality()

    Console.WriteLine("=> char type Functionality:")
    Dim myChar As Char = "a"c
    Console.WriteLine("char.IsDigit('a'): {0}", Char.IsDigit(myChar))
    Console.WriteLine("char.IsLetter('a'): {0}",
                    Char.IsLetter(myChar))
    Console.WriteLine("char.IsWhiteSpace('Hello There', 5): {0}",
                    Char.IsWhiteSpace("Hello There", 5))
    Console.WriteLine("char.IsWhiteSpace('Hello There', 6): {0}",
                    Char.IsWhiteSpace("Hello There", 6))
    Console.WriteLine("char.IsPunctuation('?'): {0}",
                    Char.IsPunctuation("?"c))
    Console.WriteLine()
End Sub
```

As illustrated in the previous code snippet, many members of System.Char have two calling conventions: a single character or a string with a numerical index that specifies the position of the character to test.

Parsing Values from String Data

The .NET data types provide the ability to generate a variable of their underlying type given a textual equivalent (e.g., parsing). This technique can be extremely helpful when you wish to convert a bit of user input data (such as a selection from a GUI-based, drop-down list box) into a numerical value. Consider the following parsing logic within a method named ParseFromStrings():

```
Sub ParseFromStrings()
    Console.WriteLine("=> Data type parsing:")

    Dim b As Boolean = Boolean.Parse("True")
    Console.WriteLine("Value of b: {0}", b)

    Dim d As Double = Double.Parse("99.884")
    Console.WriteLine("Value of d: {0}", d)

    Dim i As Integer = Integer.Parse("8")
    Console.WriteLine("Value of i: {0}", i)

    Dim c As Char = Char.Parse("w")
    Console.WriteLine("Value of c: {0}", c)

    Console.WriteLine()
End Sub
```

System.DateTime and System.TimeSpan

The System namespace defines a few useful data types for which there is no VB 2010 keyword, such as the DateTime and TimeSpan structures (I'll leave the investigation of System.Guid and System.Void, as shown in Figure 3-8, to interested readers).

The DateTime type contains data that represents a specific date (month, day, year) and time value, both of which may be formatted in a variety of ways using the supplied members. The TimeSpan structure allows you to easily define and transform units of time using various members.

```
Sub UseDatesAndTimes()
    Console.WriteLine("=> Dates and Times:")

    ' This constructor takes (year, month, day)
    Dim dt As New DateTime(2010, 10, 17)

    ' What day of the month is this?
    Console.WriteLine("The day of {0} is {1}", dt.Date, dt.DayOfWeek)

    ' Month is now December.
    dt = dt.AddMonths(2)
    Console.WriteLine("Daylight savings: {0}",
                    dt.IsDaylightSavingTime())

    ' This constructor takes (hours, minutes, seconds)
    Dim ts As New TimeSpan(4, 30, 0)
    Console.WriteLine(ts)
    ' Subtract 15 minutes from the current TimeSpan and
    ' print the result.
    Console.WriteLine(ts.Subtract(New TimeSpan(0, 15, 0)))
End Sub
```

The .NET 4.0 System.Numerics Namespace

.NET 4.0 introduces a new namespace named System.Numerics, which defines a structure named BigInteger. As its name implies, the BigInteger data type can be used when you need to represent humongous numerical values (sadly, such as the national debt of the United States), which are not constrained by a fixed upper or lower limit.

■ **Note** The System.Numerics namespace defines a second structure named Complex, which allows you to model mathematically complex numerical data (e.g., imaginary data, real data, hyperbolic tangents). Consult the .NET Framework 4.0 SDK documentation if you are interested.

While many of your .NET applications may never need to make use of the `BigInteger` structure, if you do find the need to define a massive numerical value, your first step is to import the `System.Numerics.dll` assembly into your project. If you wish to follow along with the current example, perform the following tasks:

1. Select the Project ➤ Add Reference… menu option of Visual Studio.

2. Select the .NET tab from the resulting dialog box.

3. Locate and select the `System.Numerics` assembly within the list of presented libraries.

4. Press the OK button.

Once you have done so, add the following Imports statement to the file, which will be using the `BigInteger` data type:

```
' BigInteger lives here!
Imports System.Numerics
```

At this point, you can create a `BigInteger` variable using the `New` operator. Within the constructor you can specify a numerical value, including floating point data. However, recall that when you define a literal whole number (such as 500), the runtime will default the data type to an `Integer`. Likewise, literal floating point data (such as 55.333) will default to a `Double`. How, then, can you set `BigInteger` to a massive value while not overflowing the default data types used for raw numerical values?

The simplest approach is to establish the massive numerical value as a string literal, which can be converted into a `BigInteger` variable via the Shared `Parse()` method. If required, you can also pass in a byte array directly to the constructor of the `BigInteger` class.

■ **Note** Once you assign a value to a `BigInteger` variable, you cannot change it, as the data is immutable. However, the `BigInteger` class defines a number of members that will return new `BigInteger` objects based on your data modifications (such as the Shared `Multiply()` method used in the proceeding code sample).

In any case, once you have defined a `BigInteger` variable, you will find this class defines very similar members as other intrinsic VB 2010 data types (e.g., `Single`, `Integer`). In addition, the `BigInteger` class defines several Shared members that allow you to apply basic mathematical expressions (such as adding and multiplying) to `BigInteger` variables. Here is an example of working with the `BigInteger` class:

```
Sub UseBigInteger()
    Console.WriteLine("=> Use BigInteger:")
    Dim biggy As BigInteger =
    BigInteger.Parse("9999999999999999999999999999999999999999")

    Console.WriteLine("Value of biggy is {0}", biggy)
    Console.WriteLine("Is biggy an even value?: {0}", biggy.IsEven)
    Console.WriteLine("Is biggy a power of two?: {0}",
                    biggy.IsPowerOfTwo)
```

```
    Dim reallyBig As BigInteger = BigInteger.Multiply(biggy,
    BigInteger.Parse("888888888888888888888888888888888888888"))

    Console.WriteLine("Value of reallyBig is {0}", reallyBig)
End Sub
```

It is also important to note that the `BigInteger` data type responds to VB's 2010 intrinsic mathematical operators, such as +, -, and *. Therefore, rather than calling `BigInteger.Multiply()` to multiply two huge numbers, you could author the following code:

```
    Dim reallyBig2 As BigInteger = biggy * reallyBig
```

At this point, I hope you understand that the VB 2010 keywords representing basic data types have a corresponding type in the .NET base class libraries, each of which exposes a fixed functionality. While I have not detailed each member of these data types, you are in a great position to dig into the details as you see fit. Be sure to consult the .NET Framework 4.0 SDK documentation for full details regarding the various .NET data types.

■ **Source Code** The BasicDataTypes project is located under the Chapter 3 subdirectory.

Working with String Data

`System.String` provides a number of methods you would expect from such a utility class, including methods that return the length of the character data, find substrings within the current string, and convert to and from uppercase/lowercase. Table 3-5 lists some (but by no means all) of the interesting members.

Table 3-5. *Select Members of System.String*

String Member	Meaning in Life
Length	This property returns the length of the current string.
Compare()	This Shared method compares two strings.
Contains()	This method determines whether a string contains a specific substring.
Equals()	This method tests whether two String objects contain identical character data.
Format()	This Shared method formats a string using other primitives (e.g., numerical data, other strings) and the {0} notation examined earlier in this chapter.
Insert()	This method inserts a string within a given string.

String Member	Meaning in Life
PadLeft() PadRight()	These methods are used to pad a string with some characters.
Remove() Replace()	Use these methods to receive a copy of a string with modifications (characters removed or replaced).
Split()	This method returns a **String** array containing the substrings in this instance that are delimited by elements of a specified **Char** array or **String** array.
Trim()	This method removes all occurrences of a set of specified characters from the beginning and end of the current string.
ToUpper() ToLower()	These methods create a copy of the current string in uppercase or lowercase format, respectively.

Basic String Manipulation

Working with the members of **System.String** is as you would expect. Simply declare a **String** variable and make use of the provided functionality via the dot operator. Be aware that a few of the members of **System.String** are Shared members and are, therefore, called at the class (rather than the object) level. Assume you have created a new Console Application project named FunWithStrings. Author the following method, which should be called from within **Main()**:

```
Sub BasicStringFunctionality()

        Console.WriteLine("=> Basic String functionality:")
        Dim firstName As String = "Freddy"
        Console.WriteLine("Value of firstName: {0}", firstName)
        Console.WriteLine("firstName has {0} characters.",
                        firstName.Length)
        Console.WriteLine("firstName in uppercase: {0}",
                        firstName.ToUpper())
        Console.WriteLine("firstName in lowercase: {0}",
                        firstName.ToLower())
        Console.WriteLine("firstName contains the letter y?: {0}",
                        firstName.Contains("y"))
        Console.WriteLine("firstName after replace: {0}",
                        firstName.Replace("dy", ""))
        Console.WriteLine()
End Sub
```

Not too much to say here, as this method simply invokes various members, such as ToUpper() and Contains(), on a local **String** variable to yield various formats and transformations. Figure 3-11 shows the initial output.

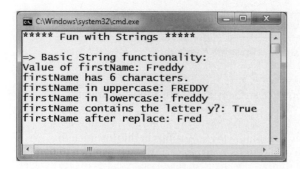

Figure 3-11. Basic string manipulation

While this output may not seem too surprising, the output seen via calling the `Replace()` method is a tad bit misleading. In reality, the `firstName` variable has not changed at all; rather, we receive back a new `String` in a modified format. We will revisit the immutable nature of strings in just a few moments.

String Concatenation

`String` variables can be connected together to build larger `String`s via the VB 2010 **&** or + operators (**&** is preferred, because it allows you to concatenate a String to a non-String such as a number). As you may know, this technique is formally termed *string concatenation*. Consider the following new helper method:

```
Sub StringConcatenation()
    Console.WriteLine("=> String concatenation:")
    Dim s1 As String = "Programming the "
    Dim s2 As String = "PsychoDrill(PTP)"
    Dim s3 As String = s1 & s2
    Console.WriteLine(s3)
    Console.WriteLine()
End Sub
```

You may be interested to know that the VB 2010 **&** symbol is processed by the compiler to emit a call to the Shared `String.Concat()` method. In fact, if you were to compile the previous code and open the assembly within **ildasm.exe** (see Chapter 1), you would find the common intermediate language (CIL) code shown in Figure 3-12.

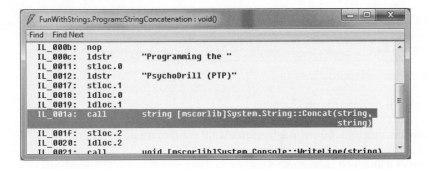

Figure 3-12. The VB 2010 & operator results in a call to String.Concat().

Given this, it is possible to perform string concatenation by calling `String.Concat()` directly (although you really have not gained anything by doing so—in fact, you have incurred additional keystrokes!).

```
Sub StringConcatenation()
        Console.WriteLine("=> String concatenation:")
        Dim s1 As String = "Programming the "
        Dim s2 As String = "PsychoDrill (PTP)"
        Dim s3 As String = String.Concat(s1, s2)
        Console.WriteLine(s3)
        Console.WriteLine()
End Sub
```

Special Character Constants

If you have developed any application in a C-based language, then you might have used various *escape characters*, which qualify how the character data should be printed to the output stream. In C-based language we call them an escape character; an escape character begins with a backslash, followed by a specific token.

In Visual Basic 2010 we can achieve a similar effect with the help of some character constants. These constants belong to the `ControlChars` class, which is member of the `Microsoft.VisualBasic` namespace, which is the default added to each Visual Basic 2010 application.

In case you are a bit rusty on the meanings behind these constant characters, Table 3-6 lists the more common options.

Table 3-6. Special Character Constants

Character	Meaning in Life
Back (VbBack)	Represents a backspace character.
Cr(VbCr)	Represents a carriage return character.
CrLf(VbCrLf)	Represents a carriage return/line feed character combination.
Lf(VbLf)	Represents a line feed character.
NewLine(VbNewLine)	Represents a new line character.
Tab(vbTab)	Represents a tab character.

For example, to print a string that contains a tab between each word and then enters a new line before the last character, you can make use of the **vbTab** and **VbCrLfconstant** characters. Consider the following:

```
Sub ConstantChars()
  Console.WriteLine("=> Constant characters: ")

  Console.WriteLine("Model" + VbTab + "Color"+ VbTab + "Speed" + VbCrLf + "Pet Name")
```

End SubStrings and Equality

As fully explained in Chapter 4, a *reference type* is an object allocated on the garbage-collected managed heap. By default, when you perform a test for equality on reference types (via the VB 2010 = and <> operators), you will be returned **True** if the references are pointing to the same object in memory. However, even though the **String** data type is indeed a reference type, the equality operators have been redefined to compare the *values* of **String** objects, not the object in memory to which they refer.

```
Sub StringEquality()
    Console.WriteLine("=> String equality:")
    Dim s1 As String = "Hello!"
    Dim s2 As String = "Yo!"
    Console.WriteLine("s1 is {0}", s1)
    Console.WriteLine("s2 is {0}", s2)
    Console.WriteLine()

    'Test these strings for equality
    Console.WriteLine("s1 = s2: {0}", s1 = s2)
    Console.WriteLine("s1 = Hello!: {0}", s1 = "Hello!")
    Console.WriteLine("s1 = HELLO!: {0}", s1 = "HELLO!")
    Console.WriteLine("s1 = hello!: {0}", s1 = "hello!")
    Console.WriteLine("s1.Equals(s2): {0}", s1.Equals(s2))
```

```
    Console.WriteLine("Yo!.Equals(s2): {0}", "Yo!".Equals(s2))
    Console.WriteLine()
End Sub
```

The VB 2010 equality operators perform a case-sensitive, character-by-character equality test on `String` objects. Therefore, `"Hello!"` is not equal to `"HELLO!"`, which is different from `"hello!"`. Also, keeping the connection between `String` and `System.String` in mind, notice that we are able to test for equality using the `Equals()` method of `String` as well as the baked-in equality operators. Finally, given that every string literal (such as `"Yo!"`) is a valid `System.String` instance, we are able to access string-centric functionality from a fixed sequence of characters.

Strings Are Immutable

One of the interesting aspects of `System.String` is that once you assign a `String` object with its initial value, the character data *cannot be changed*. At first glance, this might seem like a flat-out lie, given that we are always reassigning strings to new values and because the `System.String` type defines a number of methods that appear to modify the character data in one way or another (such as uppercasing and lowercasing). However, if you look more closely at what is happening behind the scenes, you will notice the methods of the `String` type are, in fact, returning you a brand-new `String` object in a modified format.

```
Sub StringsAreImmutable()
    ' Set initial String value
    Dim s1 As String = "This is my string."
    Console.WriteLine("s1 = {0}", s1)

    ' Uppercase s1?
    Dim upperString As String = s1.ToUpper()
    Console.WriteLine("upperString = {0}", upperString)

    ' Nope! s1 is in the same format!
    Console.WriteLine("s1 = {0}", s1)
End Sub
```

If you examine the relevant output in Figure 3-13, you can verify that the original `String` object (`s1`) is not uppercased when calling `ToUpper()`, rather you are returned a *copy* of the `String` in a modified format.

Figure 3-13. Strings are immutable.

The same law of immutability holds true when you use the VB 2010 assignment operator. To illustrate, comment out (or delete) any existing code within **StringsAreImmutable()** (to decrease the amount of generated CIL code) and add the following code statements:

```
Sub StringsAreImmutable()
    Dim s2 As String = "My other string"
    s2 = "New string value"
    Console.WriteLine(s2)
End Sub
```

Now, compile your application and load the assembly into **ildasm.exe** (again, see Chapter 1). Figure 3-14 shows what you would find if you were to generate CIL code for the **StringsAreImmutable()** method.

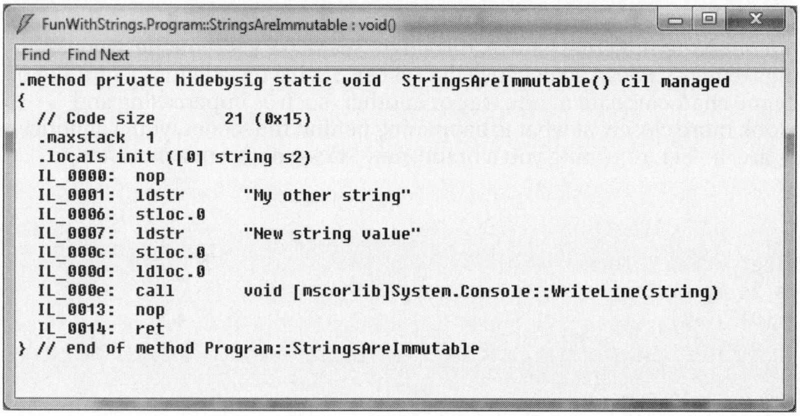

```
FunWithStrings.Program::StringsAreImmutable : void()
Find   Find Next
.method private hidebysig static void  StringsAreImmutable() cil managed
{
  // Code size       21 (0x15)
  .maxstack  1
  .locals init ([0] string s2)
  IL_0000:  nop
  IL_0001:  ldstr      "My other string"
  IL_0006:  stloc.0
  IL_0007:  ldstr      "New string value"
  IL_000c:  stloc.0
  IL_000d:  ldloc.0
  IL_000e:  call       void [mscorlib]System.Console::WriteLine(string)
  IL_0013:  nop
  IL_0014:  ret
} // end of method Program::StringsAreImmutable
```

Figure 3-14. Assigning a value to a String object results in a new String object.

Although we have yet to examine the low-level details of the CIL, note the numerous calls to the **ldstr** (load string) opcode. Simply put, the **ldstr** opcode of the CIL loads a new **String** object on the managed heap. The previous **String** object that contained the value **"My other string."** will eventually be garbage collected.

So, what exactly are we to gather from this insight? In a nutshell, the **String** class can be inefficient and result in bloated code if misused, especially when performing string concatenation. If you need to represent basic character data such as a U.S. Social Security number, first or last names, or simple bits of text used within your application, the **String** class is the perfect choice.

However, if you are building an application that makes heavy use of textual data (such as a word processing program), it would be a very bad idea to represent the word processing data using **String** objects, as you will most certainly (and often indirectly) end up making unnecessary copies of string data. So what is a programmer to do? Glad you asked.

The System.Text.StringBuilder Type

Given that the **String** type can be inefficient when used with reckless abandon, the .NET base class libraries provide the **System.Text** namespace. Within this (relatively small) namespace lives a class named `StringBuilder`. Like the `System.String` class, the `StringBuilder` defines methods that allow you to replace or format segments, for example. When you wish to use this type in your VB 2010 code files, your first step is to make sure the following namespace is imported into your code file:

```
' StringBuilder lives here!
Imports System.Text
```

What is unique about the `StringBuilder` is that when you call members of this type, you are directly modifying the object's internal character data (making it more efficient), not obtaining a copy of the data in a modified format. When you create an instance of the `StringBuilder`, you can supply the object's initial startup values via one of many *constructors*. If you are new to the topic of constructors, simply understand that constructors allow you to create an object with an initial state when you apply the `New` keyword. Consider the following usage of `StringBuilder`:

```
Sub FunWithStringBuilder()
    Console.WriteLine("=> Using the StringBuilder:")

    Dim sb As New StringBuilder("**** Fantastic Games ****")
    sb.Append(vbLf)
    sb.AppendLine("Half Life")
    sb.AppendLine("Beyond Good and Evil")
    sb.AppendLine("Deus Ex 2")
    sb.AppendLine("System Shock")
    Console.WriteLine(sb.ToString())

    sb.Replace("2", "Invisible War")
    Console.WriteLine(sb.ToString())
    Console.WriteLine("sb has {0} chars.", sb.Length)
    Console.WriteLine()
End Sub
```

Here we have constructed a `StringBuilder` set to the initial value `"**** Fantastic Games ****"`. As you can see, we are appending to the internal buffer and are able to replace or remove characters at will. By default, a `StringBuilder` is only able to initially hold a string of 16 characters or fewer (but will expand automatically if necessary); however, this default starting value can be changed via an additional constructor argument.

```
' Make a StringBuilder with an initial size of 256.
Dim sb As New StringBuilder("**** Fantastic Games ****",256)
```

If you append more characters than the specified limit, the `StringBuilder` object will copy its data into a new instance and grow the buffer by the specified limit. Figure 3-15 shows the output of the current helper method.

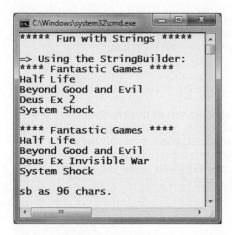

Figure 3-15. *The StringBuilder is more efficient than string.*

■ **Source Code** The FunWithStrings project is located under the Chapter 3 subdirectory.

Narrowing and Widening Data Type Conversions

Now that you understand how to interact with intrinsic VB 2010 data types, let's examine the related topic of *data type conversion*. Assume you have a new Console Application project named TypeConversions that defines the following module:

```
Module Module1

    Sub Main()
        Console.WriteLine("***** Fun with type conversions *****")

        ' Add two Shorts and print the result
        Dim numb1 As Short = 9, numb2 As Short = 10
        Console.WriteLine("{0} + {1} = {2}", numb1, numb2,
                        Add(numb1,numb2))
        Console.ReadLine()
    End Sub

    Function Add(ByVal x As Integer, ByVal y As Integer) As Integer
        Return x + y
    End Function

End Module
```

Notice that the Add() method expects to be sent two Integer parameters. However, the Main() method is, in fact, sending in two Short variables. While this might seem like a complete and total mismatch of data types, the program compiles and executes without error, returning the expected result of 19.

The reason the compiler treats this code as syntactically sound is due to the fact that there is no possibility for loss of data. Given that the maximum value of a Short (32,767) is well within the range of an Integer (2,147,483,647), the compiler implicitly *widens* each Short to an Integer. Formally speaking, *widening* is the term used to define an implicit *upward cast* that does not result in a loss of data.

■ **Note** Look up *Type Conversion Tables* in the .NET Framework 4.0 SDK documentation if you wish to see permissible widening (and narrowing, see below) conversions for each VB 2010 data type.

Although this implicit widening worked in our favor for the previous example, other times this "feature" can be the source of compile-time errors (to see these errors, you must add an Option Strict On statement right at the top of your code file). By means of an example, assume that you have set values to numb1 and numb2 that (when added together) overflow the maximum value of a Short. Also, assume you are storing the return value of the Add() method within a new local Short variable, rather than directly printing the result to the console.

```
Sub Main()
    Console.WriteLine("***** Fun with type conversions *****")

    ' Compiler error below!
    Dim numb1 As Short = 30000, numb2 As Short = 30000
    Dim answer As Short = Add(numb1, numb2)

    Console.WriteLine("{0} + {1} = {2}", numb1, numb2, answer)
    Console.ReadLine()
End Sub
```

In this case, the compiler reports the following error (assuming you have set Option Strict On, as mentioned previously):

```
Option Strict On disallows implicit conversions from 'Integer' to 'Short'.
```

The problem is that although the Add() method is capable of returning an Integer with the value 60,000 (as this fits within the range of a System.Int32), the value cannot be stored in a Short, as it overflows the bounds of this data type. Formally speaking, the CLR was unable to apply a *narrowing operation*. As you can guess, narrowing is the logical opposite of widening, in that a larger value is stored within a smaller data type variable.

It is important to point out that all narrowing conversions result in a compiler error (providing you have set Option Strict On, of course), even when you can reason that the narrowing conversion should indeed succeed. For example, the following code also results in a compiler error:

```
' Another compiler error!
Sub NarrowingAttempt()
    Dim myByte As Byte = 0
    Dim myInt As Integer = 200
    myByte = myInt

    Console.WriteLine("Value of myByte: {0}", myByte)
End Sub
```

Here, the value contained within the Integer variable (myInt) is safely within the range of a byte; therefore, you would expect the narrowing operation to not result in a runtime error. However, given that VB 2010 is a language built with type safety in mind, we do indeed receive a compiler error.

When you wish to inform the compiler that you are willing to receive a possible overflow exception due to a narrowing operation, you must apply an *explicit cast* using the VB 2010 CType keyword. Consider the following update to Module1 and the resulting output in Figure 3-16.

```
Option Strict On

Module Module1
    Sub Main()
        Console.WriteLine("***** Fun with type conversions *****")
        Dim numb1 As Short = 30000, numb2 As Short = 30000

        ' Explicitly cast the Integer into a Short (and allow possible overflow exception).
        Dim answer As Short = CType(Add(numb1, numb2), Short)
        Console.WriteLine("{0} + {1} = {2}", numb1, numb2, answer)
        NarrowingAttempt()
        Console.ReadLine()
    End Sub

    Function Add(ByVal x As Integer, ByVal y As Integer) As Integer
        Return x + y
    End Function

    Sub NarrowingAttempt()
        Dim myByte As Byte = 0
        Dim myInt As Integer = 200

        ' Explicitly cast the Integer into a Byte (no loss of data).
        myByte = CType(myInt, Byte)
        Console.WriteLine("Value of myByte: {0}", myByte)
    End Sub
End Module
```

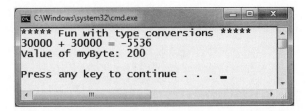

Figure 3-16. OOPS! We lost some data when adding our numbers!

■ **Note** CType is the general casting keyword in VB 2010. You can use it to cast an expression to any type (such as Short or Byte in the previous examples). VB 2010 also provides a simpler syntax for casting to common types, using keywords such as CShort and CByte. For example, you can rewrite CType(myInt, Byte) as simply CByte(myInt).

Trapping Narrowing Data Conversions

As you have just witnessed, an explicit cast allows you to force the compiler to apply a narrowing conversion, even when doing so may result in a loss of data. In the case of the NarrowingAttempt() method, this was not a problem, as the value 200 can fit snuggly within the range of a Byte. However, in the case of adding the two Shorts within Main(), the end result is completely unacceptable. (30,000 + 30,000 overflows the range of a Short and causes an overflow exception). If you suspect overflow exceptions might occur, you should handle OverflowExceptions manually to prevent your program from crashing.

To illustrate the use of these keywords, assume you have a new method that attempts to add two Bytes, each of which has been assigned a value that is safely below the maximum (255). If you were to add the values of these types (casting the returned Integer to a Byte), you would assume that the result would be the exact sum of each member.

```
Sub ProcessBytes()
    Dim b1 As Byte = 100
    Dim b2 As Byte = 250
    Dim sum As Byte = CByte(Add(b1, b2))

    ' sum should hold the value 350. However, we find the value 94!
    Console.WriteLine("sum = {0}", sum)
End Sub
```

When you run this application, you get an overflow exception. Chapter 7 will examine all the details of structured exception handling and the use of the **Try** and **Catch** keywords. Without getting too hung up on the specifics at this point, the following code shows how to handle this exception:

```vb
Sub ProcessBytes()
    Dim b1 As Byte = 100
    Dim b2 As Byte = 250

    'Handle overflow exceptions
    Try
        Dim sum As Byte = CByte(Add(b1, b2))
        Console.WriteLine("sum = {0}", sum)
    Catch ex As OverflowException
        Console.WriteLine(ex.Message)
    End Try
End Sub
```

Understanding Option Strict

Option Strict ensures compile-time (rather than runtime) notification of any narrowing conversion so it can be corrected in a timely fashion. If we are able to identify these narrowing conversions upfront, we can take a corrective course of action and decrease the possibility of nasty runtime errors.

A Visual Basic 2010 project, as well as specific *.vb files within a given project, can elect to enable or disable implicit narrowing via the Option Strict directive. When turning this option On, you are informing the compiler to check for such possibilities during the compilation process. Thus, if you were to add the following to the very top of your current file

```vb
' Option directives must be the very first code statements in a *.vb file!
Option Strict On
```

you would now find a compile-time error for each implicit narrowing conversion, as shown in Figure 3-17.

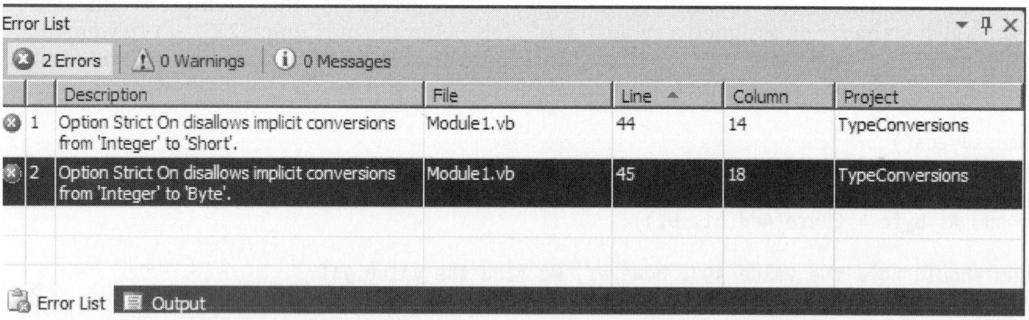

		Description	File	Line ▲	Column	Project
⊗	1	Option Strict On disallows implicit conversions from 'Integer' to 'Short'.	Module1.vb	44	14	TypeConversions
⊗	2	Option Strict On disallows implicit conversions from 'Integer' to 'Byte'.	Module1.vb	45	18	TypeConversions

Error List — ⊗ 2 Errors | ⚠ 0 Warnings | ⓘ 0 Messages

Error List   Output

Figure 3-17. Option Strict disables automatic narrowing of data.

Here, we have enabled Option Strict on a single file within our project. This approach can be useful when you wish to selectively allow narrowing conversions within specific *.vb files. However, if you wish to enable Option Strict for each and every file in your project, you can do so using the Compile tab of the My Project dialog box, as shown in Figure 3-18.

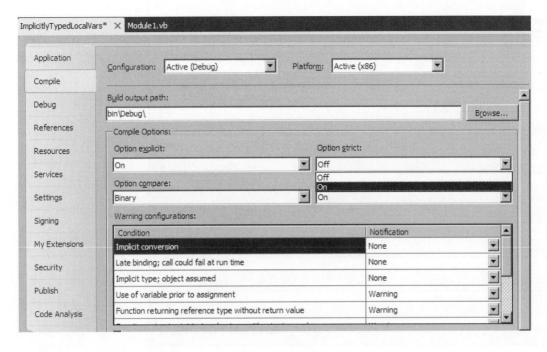

Figure 3-18. Enabling Option Strict *on the project level*

■ **Note** Under Visual Studio 2010, Option Strict is disabled for new Visual Basic 2010 projects. I would recommend, however, that you always enable this setting for each application you are creating, given that it is far better to resolve problems at compile time than runtime!

Setting Project-wide Overflow Checking

If you are creating an application that should never allow silent overflow to occur, you may find yourself in the annoying position of wrapping numerous lines of code. As an alternative, the VB 2010 compiler supports the overflow check flag as "Remove integer overflow checks". When not checked, all of your arithmetic will be evaluated for overflow. If overflow has been discovered, you will still receive a runtime exception.

To enable this flag using Visual Studio 2010, open your project's property page and click the Advanced Compile Options button on the Compile tab. From the resulting dialog box, select Check for Remove integer overflow checks (see Figure 3-19).

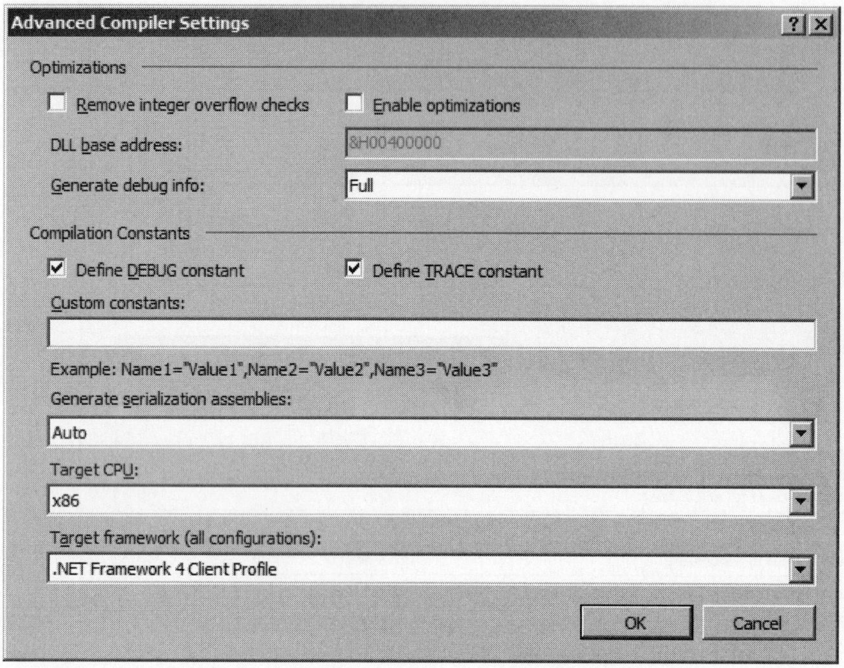

Figure 3-19. Enabling project-wide overflow/underflow data checking

Enabling this setting can be very helpful when you're creating a debug build. Once all of the overflow exceptions have been squashed out of the code base, you're free to disable the /checked flag for subsequent builds (which will increase the runtime performance of your application).

The Role of System.Convert

To wrap up the topic of data type conversions, I'd like to point out the fact that the System namespace defines a class named Convert that can also be used to widen or narrow data.

```
Sub NarrowWithConvert()
    Dim myByte As Byte = 0
    Dim myInt As Integer = 200
    myByte = Convert.ToByte(myInt)
    Console.WriteLine("Value of myByte: {0}", myByte)
End Sub
```

One benefit of using System.Convert is that it provides a language-neutral manner to convert between data types (for example, the VB 2010 language syntax for casting is completely different from the VB 2010 language syntax). However, given that VB 2010 provides explicit conversion keywords, using the Convert type to do your data type conversions is usually nothing more than a matter of personal preference.

Understanding Implicitly Typed Local Variables

Up until this point in the chapter, when we have been defining local variables, we've *explicitly* specified the underlying data type of said variable.

```
Sub DeclareExplicitVars()
    ' Explicitly typed local variables
    ' are declared as follows:
    ' Dim variableName As dataType = initialValue
    Dim myInt As Integer = 0
    Dim myBool As Boolean = True
    Dim myString As String = "Time, marches on..."
End Sub
```

While it is always good practice to explicitly specify the data type of each variable, the VB 2010 language does provide for *implicitly typing* of local variables, whereby you omit the `As dataType` part of the variable declaration syntax. When you do so, the compiler will automatically infer the underlying data type based on the initial value used to initialize the local data point.

To illustrate the role of implicit typing, create a new Console Application project named ImplicitlyTypedLocalVars. Notice how the local variables within the previous method can now be declared as follows:

```
Sub DeclareImplicitVars()
    ' Implicitly typed local variables
    ' are declared as follows:
    ' Dim variableName = initialValue
    Dim myInt = 0
    Dim myBool = True
    Dim myString = "Time, marches on..."
End Sub
```

In this case, the compiler is able to infer, given the initially assigned value, that `myInt` is, in fact, a `System.Int32`, `myBool` is a `System.Boolean`, and `myString` is indeed of type `System.String`. You can verify this by printing out the type name via *reflection*. As you will see in much more detail in Chapter 15, reflection is the act of determining the composition of a type at runtime. For example, using reflection, you can determine the data type of an implicitly typed local variable. Update your method with the following code statements:

```
Sub DeclareImplicitVars()

    ' Implicitly typed local variables.
    Dim myInt = 0
    Dim myBool = True
    Dim myString = "Time, marches on..."
```

```
    ' Print out the underlying type.
    Console.WriteLine("myInt is a: {0}", myInt.GetType().Name)
    Console.WriteLine("myBool is a: {0}", myBool.GetType().Name)
    Console.WriteLine("myString is a: {0}", myString.GetType().Name)
End Sub
```

■ **Note** Be aware that you can use this implicit typing for any type including arrays, generic types (see Chapter 10), and your own custom types. You'll see other examples of implicit typing over the course of this book.

If you were to call the `DeclareImplicitVars()` method from within `Main()`, you'd find the output shown in Figure 3-20.

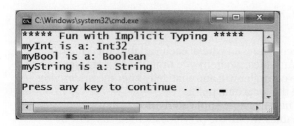

Figure 3-20. *Reflecting over implicitly defined local variables*

Restrictions on Implicitly Typed Variables

There are, of course, various restrictions regarding the use of implicitly typed variables. First and foremost, implicit typing applies *only* to local variables in a method or property scope. It is illegal to use implicitly typed to define return values, parameters, or field data of a custom type. For example, the following class definition will result in various compile-time errors (assuming you have set Option Strict On):

```
Public Class ThisWillNeverCompile
  ' Error! Cannot use implicit types for field data
  Private Dim myInt = 10

  ' Error! Cannot use implicit types for parameters or return values
  Public Function MyMethod(ByVal x, ByVal y)
  End Function
End Class
```

Also, local implicitly typed variables *must* be assigned an initial value at the exact time of declaration.

```
' Error! Must assign a value!
Dim myData

' Error! Must assign value at exact time of declaration!
Dim myInt
myInt = 0
```

Furthermore, it is permissible to assign the value of an implicitly typed local variable to the value of other variables, implicitly typed or not.

```
' This is OK!
Dim myInt = 0
Dim anotherInt = myInt

Dim myString As String = "Wake up!"
Dim myData = myString
```

Also, it is permissible to return an implicitly typed local variable to the caller, provided the method return type is the same underlying type as the implicitly typed data point.

```
Function GetAnInt() As Integer
    Dim retVal = 9
    Return retVal
End Function
```

Implicit Typed Data Is Strongly Typed Data

Be very aware that implicit typing of local variables results in *strongly typed data*. Therefore, use of implicitly typed variables is *not* the same technique used with scripting languages (such as JavaScript or Perl) or the COM **Variant** data type, where a variable can hold values of different types over its lifetime in a program (often termed *dynamic typing*).

Rather, type inference keeps the strongly typed aspect of the VB 2010 language and affects only the declaration of variables at compile time. After that, the data point is treated as if it were declared with that type; assigning a value of a different type into that variable will result in a compile-time error (if you have set Option Strict On).

```
Sub ImplicitTypingIsStrongTyping()
    ' The compiler knows "s" is a System.String.
    Dim s = "This variable can only hold String data!"
    s = "This is fine..."

    ' Can invoke any member of the underlying type.
    Dim upper As String = s.ToUpper()
    Console.WriteLine(s)

    ' Error! Can't assign numerical data to a string!
    s = 44
End Sub
```

Usefulness of Implicitly Typed Local Variables

Now that you have seen the syntax used to declare implicitly typed local variables, I am sure you are wondering when to make use of this construct? First and foremost, using implicitly typed variables simply for the sake of doing so really brings little to the table. Doing so can be confusing to others reading your code, as it becomes harder to quickly determine the underlying data type and therefore more difficult to understand the overall functionality of the variable. So if you know you need an Integer, declare an Integer!

However, as you will see beginning in Chapter 13, the LINQ technology set makes use of *query expressions* that can yield dynamically created result sets based on the format of the query itself. In these cases, implicit typing is extremely helpful, as we do not need to explicitly define the type that a query may return, which in some cases would be literally impossible to do. Without getting hung up on the following LINQ example code, see if you can figure out the underlying data type of subset:

```
Sub QueryOverInts()
  Dim numbers As Integer() = {10, 20, 30, 40, 1, 2,3, 8}

  ' LINQ query!
  Dim subset = From i In numbers Where i < 10 Select i
  Console.Write("Values in subset: ")

  For Each x In subset
      Console.Write("{0} ", x)
  Next

  ' Hmm...what type is subset?
  Console.WriteLine()
  Console.WriteLine("subset is a: {0}", subset.GetType().Name)
  Console.WriteLine("subset is defined in: {0}",
                    subset.GetType().Namespace)
End Sub
```

I'll let the interested reader verify the underlying data type of subset by executing the preceding code (and it is not an array of integers!). In any case, it should be clear that implicit typing does have its place within the LINQ technology set. In fact, it could be argued that the *only time* one would make use of implicitly typed variables is when defining data returned from a LINQ query. Remember, if you know you need an Integer, just declare an Integer! Overuse of implicit typing (via the Dim keyword) is considered bad style in production code.

■ **Source Code** The ImplicitlyTypedLocalVars project can be found under the Chapter 3 subdirectory.

VB 2010 Iteration Constructs

All programming languages provide ways to repeat blocks of code until a terminating condition has been met. Regardless of which language you have used in the past, the VB 2010 iteration statements should not raise too many eyebrows and should require little explanation. VB 2010 provides the following four iteration constructs:

- `For` loop

- `For Each/In` loop

- `While` loop

- `Do/While` loop

Let's quickly examine each looping construct in turn, using a new Console Application project named IterationsAndDecisions.

The For Loop

When you need to iterate over a block of code a fixed number of times, the `For` statement provides a good deal of flexibility. In essence, you are able to specify how many times a block of code repeats itself, as well as the terminating condition. Without belaboring the point, here is a sample of the syntax, which outputs the numbet 0, 1, 2, 3, (note that the upper limit in a `For` loop is inclusive):

```
' A basic for loop.
Sub ForAndForEachLoop()
    ' Note! "i" is only visible within the scope of the for loop.
    For i As Integer=0 To 3
        Console.WriteLine("Number is: {0} ", i)
    Next
    ' "i" is not visible here.
End Sub
```

When building a VB 2010 `For` statement, you can make use of the `GoTo`, `Continue`, and `Exit For` keywords. I'll assume that you will bend this iteration construct as you see fit. Consult the .NET Framework 4.0 SDK documentation if you require further details on the VB 2010 `For` keyword.

The For Each Loop

The VB 2010 `For Each` keyword allows you to iterate over all items within an array (or a collection object; see Chapter 10) without the need to test for an upper limit. Here are two examples using `For Each`—one to traverse an array of strings and the other to traverse an array of integers.

```
' Iterate array items using foreach.
Sub ForAndForEachLoop()
    ...
    Dim carTypes As String() = {"Ford", "BMW", "Yugo", "Honda"}
    For Each c As String In carTypes
        Console.WriteLine(c)
    Next
```

```
    Dim myInts As Integer() = {10, 20, 30, 40}
    For Each i As Integer In myInts
        Console.WriteLine(i)
    Next
End Sub
```

In addition to iterating over simple arrays, For Each is also able to iterate over system-supplied or user-defined collections. I'll hold off on the details until Chapter 9, as this aspect of the For Each keyword entails an understanding of interface-based programming and the role of the IEnumerator and IEnumerable interfaces.

Use of Implicitly Typed Variables Within For Each Constructs

It is also possible to make use of implicit typing within a For Each looping construct. As you would expect, the compiler will correctly infer the correct "type of type." Consider the following method, which iterates over a local array of integers:

```
Sub ImplicitTypingInForEachLoop()
  Dim myInts As Integer() = {10, 20, 30, 40}

  'Use of implicit typing in For Each loop
  For Each item In myInts
      Console.WriteLine("Item value: {0}", item)
  Next
End Sub
```

Understand that in this example there is no compelling reason to use implicit typing in our For Each loop, as we can clearly see that we are indeed iterating over an array of integers. But once again, when using the LINQ programming model it can be very useful, and in some cases absolutely mandatory.

The While and Do/While Looping Constructs

The While looping construct is useful should you wish to execute a block of statements until some terminating condition has been reached. Within the scope of a While loop, you will need to ensure this terminating event is indeed established; otherwise, you will be stuck in an endless loop. In the following example, the message "In While loop" will be continuously printed until the user terminates the loop by entering *yes* at the command prompt:

```
Sub ExecuteWhileLoop()
    Dim userIsDone As String = ""

  ' Test on a lower-class copy of the string.
  While userIsDone.ToLower() <> "yes"
      Console.Write("Are you done? [yes] [no]: ")
      userIsDone = Console.ReadLine()
      Console.WriteLine("In While loop")
  End While
End Sub
```

Closely related to the While loop is the Do/While statement. Like a simple While loop, Do/While is used when you need to perform some action an undetermined number of times. The difference is that Do/While loops are guaranteed to execute the corresponding block of code at least once. In contrast, it is possible that a simple While loop may never execute if the terminating condition is false from the onset.

```
Sub ExecuteDoWhileLoop()
    Dim userIsDone As String = ""
    Do
        Console.WriteLine("In do/while loop")
        Console.Write("Are you done? [yes] [no]: ")
        userIsDone = Console.ReadLine()
    Loop While userIsDone.ToLower() <> "yes"
End Sub
```

Decision Constructs and the Relational/Equality Operators

Now that you can iterate over a block of statements, the next related concept is how to control the flow of program execution. VB 2010 defines two simple constructs to alter the flow of your program, based on various contingencies:

- The If/Then/Else statement
- The Select/Case statement

The If/Then/Else Statement

First up is our good friend the If/Then/Else statement. The If/Then/Else statement in VB 2010 operates only on Boolean expressions, not ad hoc values such as –1 or 0. Given this, If/Then/Else statements typically involve the use of the VB 2010 operators shown in Table 3-7 in order to obtain a literal Boolean value.

Table 3-7. VB 2010 Relational and Equality Operators

VB 2010 Equality/Relational Operator	Example Usage	Meaning in Life
=	if(age = 30)	Returns True only if each expression is the same.
<>	if("Foo" <> myStr)	Returns True only if each expression is different.

<
>
<=
>=
	if(bonus < 2000)
	if(bonus > 2000)
	if(bonus <= 2000)
	if(bonus >= 2000)
		Returns True if expression A (bonus) is less than, greater than, less than or equal to, or greater than or equal to expression B (2000).

If you've ever written any code in C or C++, you need to be aware that the old tricks of testing a condition for a value not equal to zero will not work in VB2010 Let's say you want to see whether the `String` you are working with is longer than zero characters. You may be tempted to write the following:

```
Sub ExecuteIfElse()
    ' This will give you a compiler error if you have set Option Strict On, given that Length
returns an Integer, not a Boolean.
    Dim stringData As String = "My textual data"
        If stringData.Length Then
            Console.WriteLine("string is greater than 0 characters")
        End If
End Sub
```

If you wish to make use of the `String.Length` property to determine truth or falsity, you need to modify your conditional expression to resolve to a Boolean.

```
'  Always legal, as this resolves to either True or False.
If stringData.Length  > 0 Then
    Console.WriteLine("string is greater than 0 characters")
End If
```

An `If` statement may be composed of complex expressions as well and can contain `Else` statements to perform more complex testing. To build complex expressions, VB 2010 offers an expected set of logical operators, as shown in Table 3-8.

Table 3-8. VB Logical Operators

Logical Operator	Example	Meaning in Life
And	if(age = 30 And name = "Fred")	AND operator. Returns `True` if all expressions are `True`. Note that both expressions will always be evaluated, even if the first expression is `False`.
Or	if(age = 30 Or name = "Fred")	Or operator. Returns `True` if at least one expression is `True`. Note that both expressions will always be evaluated, even if the first expression is `True`.
Not	if(Not myBool)	NOT operator. Returns `True` if `False`, or `False` if `True`.
AndAlso	If age = 30 AndAlso name = "Fred" Then	Conditional AND operator that supports *short-circuiting*, meaning if the first expression is `False`, the second expression is not evaluated
OrElse	If age = 30 OrElse name = "Fred" Then	Conditional Or operator that supports *short-circuiting*, meaning if the first expression is `True`, the second expression is not evaluated.

The Select/Case Statement

The other simple selection construct offered by VB 2010 is the **Select/Case** statement. The **Select/Case** statement allows you to handle program flow based on a predefined set of choices. For example, the following logic prints a specific string message based on one of two possible selections (the **Case Else** case handles an invalid selection):

```vb
' Switch on a numerical value.
Sub ExecuteSwitch()
    Console.WriteLine("1 [C#], 2 [VB]")
    Console.Write("Please pick your language preference: ")
    Dim langChoice As String = Console.ReadLine()

    Dim n As Integer = Integer.Parse(langChoice)
    Select Case n
        Case 1
            Console.WriteLine("Good choice, C# is a fine language.")
        Case 2
            Console.WriteLine("VB: OOP, multithreading, and more!")
        Case Else
            Console.WriteLine("Well...good luck with that!")
    End Select
End Sub
```

One nice feature of the VB 2010 **Select/Case** statement is that you can evaluate string data in addition to numeric data. Here is an updated **Select/Case** statement that does this very thing (notice we have no need to parse the user data into a numeric value with this approach):

```vb
Sub ExecuteSwitchOnString()
    Console.WriteLine("C# or VB")
    Console.Write("Please pick your language preference: ")
    Dim langChoice As String = Console.ReadLine()

    Select Case langChoice
        Case "VB"
            Console.WriteLine("VB: OOP, multithreading and more!")
        Case "C#"
            Console.WriteLine("Good choice, C# is a fine language.")
        Case Else
      Console.WriteLine("Well...good luck with that!")
    End Select
End Sub
```

■ **Source Code** The IterationsAndDecisions project is located under the Chapter 3 subdirectory.

That wraps up your look at the looping and decision keywords of VB 2010, and the common operators that are used to build complex statements. I've tried to keep this part of the chapter short and to the point, as I am assuming you have experience using similar keywords (`If`, `For`, `Select/Case`, etc.) in your current programming language. If you require more information, look up the topic of interest within the .NET Framework 4.0 SDK Documentation.

Summary

The goal of this chapter was to expose you to numerous core aspects of the VB 2010 programming language. Here, we examined the commonplace constructs in any application you may be interested in building. After examining the role of an application object, you learned that every VB 2010 executable program must have a type defining a `Main()` method, which serves as the program's entry point. Within the scope of `Main()`, you typically create any number of objects that work together to breathe life into your application.

Next, we dove into the details of the built-in data types of VB 2010 and came to understand that each data type keyword (e.g., `Integer`) is really a shorthand notation for a full-blown type in the `System` namespace (`System.Int32` in this case). Given this, each VB 2010 data type has a number of built-in members. Along the same vein, you also learned about the role of *widening* and *narrowing*.

We wrapped up by checking out the role of implicit typing. As we discussed, the most useful place for implicit typing is when working with the LINQ programming model. Finally, we quickly examined the various iteration and decision constructs supported by VB 2010. Now that you have an understanding of some of the basic nuts and bolts, the next chapter completes our examination of core language features. After that you will be well prepared to examine the object-oriented features of VB 2010.

CHAPTER 4

■ ■ ■

Core VB 2010 Programming Constructs, Part II

This chapter picks up where the previous chapter left off, and completes your investigation of the core aspects of the VB 2010 programming language. We begin by examining various details regarding the construction of VB 2010 methods, exploring the `ByRef` and `ParamArray` keywords. Along the way, you will also examine useful language features such as optional and named parameters.

After you examine the topic of *method overloading*, the next task is to investigate the details behind manipulating arrays using the syntax of VB 2010 and get to know the functionality contained within the related `System.Array` class type.

In addition, this chapter provides a discussion regarding the construction of enumeration and structure types, including a fairly detailed examination of the distinction between a *value type* and a *reference type*. We wrap this up by examining the role of nullable data types. Once you have completed this chapter, you will be in a perfect position to learn the object oriented capabilities of VB 2010, beginning in Chapter 5.

Methods and Parameter Modifiers

To begin this chapter, let's examine the details of defining methods. Just like the `Main()` method (see Chapter 3), your custom methods may or may not take parameters and may or may not return values to the caller. As you will see over the next several chapters, methods can be implemented within the scope of classes or structures (as well as prototyped within interface types) and may be decorated with various keywords (e.g., `Friend`, `Overridable`, `Public`, `Shadows`) to qualify their behavior. At this point in the text, it's useful to discuss the general format of methods in VB 2010. Let's say you have a module named Module1. You can define methods as follows (remember, all methods in a Module are implicitly Shared, which means they can be called directly without creating a Module instance):

```
Module Module1

    ' General syntax for Subs (which don't return a value):
    ' Public Sub MethodName(params)

    ' General syntax for functions (which do return a value):
    ' Public Function MethodName(params) As returnType
```

```
' Example function, takes some parameters and returns an Integer:
Public Function Add(ByVal x As Integer,
        ByVal y As Integer) As Integer
    Return x + y
End Function

End Module
```

While the definition of a method in VB 2010 is quite straightforward, there are a handful of keywords that you can use to control how arguments are passed to the method in question. These are listed in Table 4-1.

Table 4-1. VB 2010 Parameter Modifiers

Parameter Modifier	Meaning in Life
ByVal	If a parameter is not marked with a parameter modifier, it is assumed to be passed by value, meaning the called method receives a copy of the original data.
<Out()>	Output parameters declared using the <Out()> attribute, which is part of the System.Runtime.Interop.Services namespace, must be assigned by the method being called, and therefore are passed by reference. If the called method fails to assign output parameters, you are issued a compiler error.
ByRef	The value is initially assigned by the caller and may be optionally reassigned by the called method (as the data is also passed by reference). No compiler error is generated if the called method fails to assign a ByRef parameter.
ParamArray	This parameter modifier allows you to send in a variable number of arguments as a single logical parameter. A method can have only a single ParamArray modifier, and it must be the final parameter of the method. In reality, you may not need to use the ParamArray modifier all too often, however be aware that numerous methods within the base class libraries do make use of this VB 2010 language feature.
Optional	This marks an argument that does not need to be specified by the caller.

To illustrate the use of these keywords, create a new Console Application project named FunWithMethods. Now, let's walk through the role of each keyword.

The ByVal Parameter Modifier

The default manner in which a parameter is sent into a method is *by value*. Simply put, if you do not mark an argument with a parameter modifier, a copy of the data is passed into the method. As explained at the end of this chapter, exactly *what* is copied will depend on whether the parameter is a value type or a reference type. For the time being, assume the following method within your module that operates on two numerical data types passed by value:

```
' The ByVal keyword indicates that arguments are passed by value.
Function Add(ByVal x As Integer, ByVal y As Integer) As Integer

        Dim ans As Integer = x + y
        ' Caller will not see these changes
        ' as you are modifying a copy of the
        ' original data.
        x = 10000
        y = 88888
    Return ans
End Function
```

Numerical data falls under the category of *value types*. Therefore, if you change the values of the parameters within the scope of the member, the caller is blissfully unaware, given that you are changing the values on a *copy* of the caller's original data:

```
Sub Main()
        Console.WriteLine("***** Fun with Methods *****" & vbLf)

        ' Pass two variables in by value.
        Dim x As Integer = 9, y As Integer = 10
        Console.WriteLine("Before call: X: {0}, Y: {1}", x, y)
        Console.WriteLine("Answer is: {0}", Add(x, y))
        Console.WriteLine("After call: X: {0}, Y: {1}", x, y)
        Console.ReadLine()
End Sub
```

As you would hope, the values of x and y remain identical before and after the call to Add(), as shown in the following:

```
***** Fun with Methods *****



Before call: X: 9, Y: 10

Answer is: 19

After call: X: 9, Y: 10
```

The ByRef Modifier

Some "methods need to be created in such a way that the caller should be able to realize any reassignments that have taken place within the method scope. For example, you might have a method that needs to change incoming character data, assign an incoming parameter to a new object in memory, or simply modify the value of a numerical argument. For this very reason, VB 2010 supplies the ByRef keyword.

Let's check out the use of the ByRef keyword by way of a method that swaps two String variables:

```
' Reference parameters.
Public Sub SwapStrings(ByRef s1 As String, ByRef s2 As String)
    Dim tempStr As String = s1
    s1 = s2
    s2 = tempStr
End Sub
```

This method can be called as follows:

```
Sub Main()
    Console.WriteLine("***** Fun with Methods *****")
    ...
    Dim s1 As String = "Flip"
    Dim s2 As String = "Flop"
    Console.WriteLine("Before: {0}, {1} ", s1, s2)

    SwapStrings(s1, s2)
    Console.WriteLine("After: {0}, {1} ", s1, s2)
    Console.ReadLine()
End Sub
```

Here, the caller has assigned an initial value to local string data (s1 and s2). Once the call to SwapStrings() returns, s1 now contains the value "Flop", while s2 reports the value "Flip":

```
Before: Flip, Flop

After: Flop, Flip
```

■ **Note** The VB 2010 ByRef keyword will be revisited later in this chapter in the section "Understanding Value Types and Reference Types." As you will see, the behavior of this keyword changes just a bit depending on whether the argument is a value type (structure) or reference type (class).

The <Out()> Attribute

Next, you have the use of *output parameters*. Methods that have been defined to take output parameters (via the <Out()> attribute, which comes under the `System.Runtime.InteropServices namespace`) are under obligation to assign them to an appropriate value before exiting the method scope (if you fail to do so, you will receive compiler errors).

To illustrate, here is an alternative version of the `Add()` method that returns the sum of two integers using the VB 2010 `<Out()>` attribute (note the physical return value of this method is now `Sub` (doesn't return a value):

```
' Output parameters must be assigned by the called method.
Shared Sub Add(ByVal x As Integer, ByVal y As Integer, < Out()>
             ByRef ans As Integer)
  ans = x + y
End Sub
```

Calling a method with output parameters doesn't require the use of the `<Out()>` attribute. However, the local variables, which are passed as output variables, are not required to be assigned before passing them in as output arguments (if you do so, the original value is lost after the call). The reason the compiler allows you to send in seemingly unassigned data is due to the fact that the method being called *must* make an assignment. The following code is an example:

```
Sub Main()
        Console.WriteLine("***** Fun with Methods *****")
        ' No need to assign initial value to local variables
        ' used as output parameters, provided the first time
        ' you use them is as output arguments.
        Dim ans As Integer
        Add(90, 90, ans)
        Console.WriteLine("90 + 90 = {0}", ans)
        Console.ReadLine()
End Sub
```

The previous example is intended to be illustrative in nature; you really have no reason to return the value of your summation using an output parameter. However, the VB 2010 `<Out()>` attribute does serve a very useful purpose: it allows the caller to obtain multiple return values from a single method invocation.

```
' Returning multiple output parameters.
Sub FillTheseValues(<Out()> ByRef a As Integer, <Out()> ByRef b As
  String, <Out()> ByRef c As Boolean)
    a = 9
    b = "Enjoy your string."
    c = True
End Sub
```

The caller would be able to invoke the `FillTheseValues()` method. Do notice that you don't need to use the `<Out()>` attribute when you invoke the method, as well as when you implement the method:

```
Sub Main()
    Console.WriteLine("***** Fun with Methods *****")
    Dim i As Integer
    Dim str As String
    Dim b As Boolean
    FillTheseValues(i, str, b)

    Console.WriteLine("Int is: {0}", i)
    Console.WriteLine("String is: {0}", str)
    Console.WriteLine("Boolean is: {0}", b)
    Console.ReadLine()
End Sub
```

Finally, always remember that a method that defines output parameters *must* assign the parameter to a valid value before exiting the method scope. Therefore, the following code will result in a compiler error, as the output parameter has not been assigned within the method scope:

```
Sub ThisWontCompile(<Out()> ByRef a As Integer)
    Console.WriteLine("Error! Forgot to assign output arg!")
End Sub
```

The ParamArray Modifier

VB 2010 supports the use of *parameter arrays* using the `ParamArray` keyword. To understand this language feature you must (as the name implies) understand how to manipulate VB 2010 arrays. If this is not the case, you may wish to return to this section once you read the section "Array Manipulation in VB 2010" found a bit later in this chapter.

The `ParamArray` keyword allows you to pass into a method a variable number of identically typed parameters as a *single logical parameter*. As well, arguments marked with the `ParamArray` keyword can be processed if the caller sends in a strongly typed array or a comma-delimited list of items. Yes, this can be confusing! To clear things up, assume you wish to create a function that allows the caller to pass in any number of arguments and return the calculated average.

If you were to prototype this method to take an array of `Doubles`, this would force the caller to first define the array, then fill the array, and finally pass it into the method. However, if you define `CalculateAverage()` to take a `ParamArray` of Double data types, the caller can simply pass a comma-delimited list of `Doubles`. The .NET runtime will automatically package the set of `Doubles` into an array of type `Double` behind the scenes:

```
' Return average of "some number" of Doubles.
Function CalculateAverage(ParamArray ByVal values() As Double)
                        As Double
    Console.WriteLine("You sent me {0} Doubles.", values.Length)

    Dim sum As Double = 0
    If values.Length = 0 Then
        Return sum
    End If
```

```
        For i = 0 To values.Length - 1
            sum += values(i)
        Next
        Return (sum / values.Length)
End Function
```

This method has been defined to take a parameter array of doubles. What this method is in fact saying is, "Send me any number of **Doubles** (including zero) and I'll compute the average." Given this, you can call **CalculateAverage()** in any of the following ways:

```
Sub Main()
    Console.WriteLine("***** Fun with Methods *****")
    ...

    ' Pass in a comma-delimited list of Doubles...
    Dim average As Double
    average = CalculateAverage(4, 3.2, 5.7, 64.22, 87.2)
    Console.WriteLine("Average of data is: {0}", average)

    ' ...or pass an array of Doubles.
    Dim data As Double() = {4, 3.2, 5.7}
    average = CalculateAverage(data)
    Console.WriteLine("Average of data is: {0}", average)

    ' Average of 0 is 0!
    Console.WriteLine("Average of data is: {0}", CalculateAverage())
    Console.ReadLine()
End Sub
```

If you did not make use of the **ParamArray** modifier in the definition of **CalculateAverage()**, the first invocation of this method would result in a compiler error, as the compiler would be looking for a version of **CalculateAverage()** which took five **Double** arguments.

■ **Note** To avoid any ambiguity, VB 2010 demands a method only support a single **ParamArray** argument, which must be the final argument in the parameter list.

As you might guess, this technique is nothing more than a convenience for the caller, given that the array is created by the CLR as necessary. By the time the array is within the scope of the method being called, you are able to treat it as a full-blown .NET array that contains all the functionality of the **System.Array** base class library type. Consider the following output:

```
You sent me 5 Doubles.

Average of data is: 32.864

You sent me 3 Doubles.

Average of data is: 4.3


You sent me 0 Doubles.

Average of data is: 0
```

Defining Optional Parameters

VB 2010 also allows you to create methods which can take *optional arguments*. This technique allows the caller to invoke a single method while omitting arguments deemed unnecessary, provided the caller is happy with the specified defaults.

■ **Note** As you will see in Chapter 18, one of the key uses of optional arguments is to simplify interaction with COM objects.. Several Microsoft object models (e.g., Microsoft Office) expose their functionality via COM objects, many of which were written long ago to make use of optional parameters.

To illustrate working with optional arguments, assume you have a method named EnterLogData(), which defines a single optional parameter:

```
Sub EnterLogData(ByVal message As String,
                 Optional ByVal owner As String =  "Programmer")
    Console.Beep()
    Console.WriteLine("Error: {0}", message)
    Console.WriteLine("Owner of Error: {0}", owner)
End Sub
```

Here, the final **String** argument has been assigned the default value of **"Programmer"**, via an assignment within the parameter definition. Given this, we can call EnterLogData() from within Main() in two manners:

```
Sub Main()
        Console.WriteLine("***** Fun with Methods *****")
        ...
        EnterLogData("Oh no! Grid can't find data")
        EnterLogData("Oh no! I can't find the payroll data", "CFO")
        Console.ReadLine()
End Sub
```

Because the first invocation of `EnterLogData()` did not specify a second `String` argument, we would find that the programmer is the one responsible for losing data for the grid, while the CFO misplaced the payroll data (as specified by the second argument in the second method call).

One very important thing to be aware of, is that the value assigned to an optional parameter must be known at compile time, and cannot be resolved at runtime (if you attempt to do so, you'll receive compile time errors!). To illustrate, assume you wish to update `EnterLogData()` with the following extra optional parameter:

```
'Error! The default value for an optional arg must be known
'at compile time!
Sub EnterLogData(ByVal message As String,
                Optional ByVal owner As String = "Programmer",
                Optional ByVal timeStamp As DateTime = DateTime.Now)
    Console.Beep()
    Console.WriteLine("Error: {0}", message)
    Console.WriteLine("Owner of Error: {0}", owner)
    Console.WriteLine("Time of Error: {0}", timeStamp)
End Sub
```

This will not compile, as the value of the `Now` property of the `DateTime` class is resolved at runtime, not compile time.

■ **Note** To avoid ambiguity, optional parameters must always be packed onto the *end* of a method signature. It is a compiler error to have optional parameters listed before non-optional parameters.

Invoking Methods using Named Parameters

Another interesting language feature in VB 2010 is its support for *named arguments*. To be honest, at first glance, this language construct may appear to do little more than result in confusing code. And to continue being completely honest, this could be the case! Much like optional arguments, named parameters simplify the process of working with the COM interoperability layer (again, see Chapter 18).

Named arguments allow you to invoke a method by specifying parameter values in any order you choose. Thus, rather than passing parameters solely by position (as you will do in most cases), you can choose to specify each argument by name using a := operator. To illustrate the use of named arguments, assume we have added the following method to our module:

```vb
Sub DisplayFancyMessage(ByVal textColor As ConsoleColor,
                        ByVal backgroundColor As ConsoleColor,
                        ByVal message As String)

    ' Store old colors to restore once message is printed.
    Dim oldTextColor As ConsoleColor = Console.ForegroundColor
    Dim oldbackgroundColor As ConsoleColor = Console.BackgroundColor

    ' Set new colors and print message.
    Console.ForegroundColor = textColor
    Console.BackgroundColor = backgroundColor
    Console.WriteLine(message)

    ' Restore previous colors.
    Console.ForegroundColor = oldTextColor
    Console.BackgroundColor = oldbackgroundColor
End Sub
```

Now, the way `DisplayFancyMessage()` was written, you would expect the caller to invoke this method by passing two `ConsoleColor` variables followed by a `String` type. However, using named arguments, the following calls are completely fine:

```vb
Sub Main()
    Console.WriteLine("***** Fun with Methods *****")
    …
    DisplayFancyMessage(message:="Wow!  Very Fancy indeed!",
                textColor:=ConsoleColor.DarkRed,
                backgroundColor:=ConsoleColor.White)

    DisplayFancyMessage(backgroundColor:=ConsoleColor.Green,
                message:="Testing...",
                textColor:=ConsoleColor.DarkBlue)

    Console.ReadLine()
End Sub
```

One minor gotcha regarding named arguments is that if you begin to invoke a method using positional parameters, they must be listed before any named parameters. In other words, named arguments must always be packed onto the end of a method call. The following code is an example:

```vb
' This is OK, as positional args are listed before named args.
DisplayFancyMessage(ConsoleColor.Blue, message:= "Testing...",
backgroundColor:=ConsoleColor.White)

' This is an ERROR, as positional args are listed after named args.
DisplayFancyMessage(message:= "Testing...",
backgroundColor:= ConsoleColor.White, ConsoleColor.Blue)
```

This restriction aside, you might still be wondering when you would ever want to use this language feature. After all, if you need to specify three arguments to a method, why bother flipping around their position?

Well, as it turns out, if you have a method that defines optional arguments, this feature can actually be really helpful. Assume `DisplayFancyMessage()` has been rewritten to now support optional arguments, as you have assigned fitting defaults:

```
Sub DisplayFancyMessage(
        Optional ByVal textColor As ConsoleColor = ConsoleColor.Blue,
        Optional ByVal backgroundColor As ConsoleColor = ConsoleColor.White,
        Optional ByVal message As String = "Test Message")
 ...
End Sub
```

Given that each argument has a default value, named arguments allows the caller to only specify the parameter(s) for which they do not wish to receive the defaults. Therefore, if the caller wants the value "Hello!" to appear in blue text surrounded by a white background, they can simply say:

```
DisplayFancyMessage(message:="Hello!")
```

Or, if the caller wants to see "Test Message" print out with a green background containing blue text, they can invoke DisplayFancyMessage():

```
DisplayFancyMessage(backgroundColor!= ConsoleColor.Green)
```

As you can see, optional arguments and named parameters do tend to work hand in hand. To wrap up our examination of building VB 2010 methods, I need to address the topic of *method overloading*.

■ **Source Code** The FunWithMethods application is located under the Chapter 4 subdirectory.

Understanding Method Overloading

Like other modern object-oriented languages, VB 2010 allows a method to be *overloaded*. Simply put, when you define a set of identically named method that differ by the number (or type) of parameters, the method in question is said to be overloaded.

To understand why overloading is so useful, consider life as a Visual Basic 6.0 developer. Assume you are using VB6 to build a set of methods that return the sum of various incoming data types (`Integers`, `Doubles`, and so on). Given that VB6 does not support method overloading, you would be required to define a unique set of methods that essentially do the same thing (return the sum of the arguments):

```
' VB6 code examples.
Public Function AddInts(ByVal x As Integer, ByVal y As Integer) As Integer
  AddInts = x + y
End Function

Public Function AddDoubles(ByVal x As Double, ByVal y As Double) As Double
  AddDoubles = x + y
End Function
```

```
Public Function AddLongs(ByVal x As Long, ByVal y As Long) As Long
   AddLongs = x + y
End Function
```

Not only can code such as this become tough to maintain, but the caller must now be painfully aware of the name of each method. Using overloading, you are able to allow the caller to call a single method named Add(). Again, the key is to ensure that each version of the method has a distinct set of arguments (methods differing only by return type are not unique enough).

■ **Note** As explained in Chapter 10, it is possible to build generic methods that take the concept of overloading to the next level. Using generics, you can define "placeholders" for a method implementation that are specified at the time you invoke the member.

To check this out firsthand, create a new Console Application project named MethodOverloading. Now, consider the following code:

```
' VB 2010 code.

Module Module1
    Sub Main()
    End Sub

    ' Overloaded Add() method.
    Function Add(ByVal x As Integer, ByVal y As Integer) As Integer
        Return x + y
    End Function

    Function Add(ByVal x As Double, ByVal y As Double) As Double
        Return x + y
    End Function

    Function Add(ByVal x As Long, ByVal y As Long) As Long
        Return x + y
    End Function
End Module
```

The caller can now simply invoke Add() with the required arguments and the compiler is happy to comply, given the fact that the compiler is able to resolve the correct implementation to invoke given the provided arguments:

```
Sub Main()
        Console.WriteLine("***** Fun with Method Overloading *****" & vbLf)
        ' Calls Integer version of Add()
        Console.WriteLine(Add(10, 10))
```

```
        ' Calls Long version of Add()
        Console.WriteLine(Add(900000000000, 900000000000))

        ' Calls Double version of Add()
        Console.WriteLine(Add(4.3, 4.4))
        Console.ReadLine()
End Sub
```

The Visual Studio 2010 IDE provides assistance when calling overloaded methods to boot. When you type in the name of an overloaded method (such as our good friend `Console.WriteLine()`), IntelliSense will list each version of the method in question. Note that you are able to cycle through each version of an overloaded method using the up and down arrow keys shown in Figure 4-1.

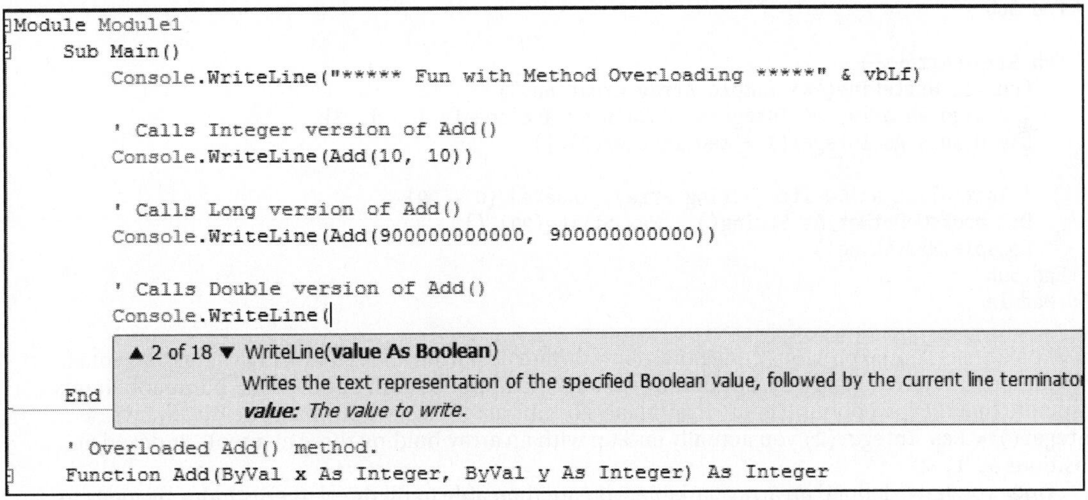

```
Module Module1
    Sub Main()
        Console.WriteLine("***** Fun with Method Overloading *****" & vbLf)

        ' Calls Integer version of Add()
        Console.WriteLine(Add(10, 10))

        ' Calls Long version of Add()
        Console.WriteLine(Add(900000000000, 900000000000))

        ' Calls Double version of Add()
        Console.WriteLine(

        ┌─────────────────────────────────────────────────────────────────────────────┐
        │ ▲ 2 of 18 ▼  WriteLine(value As Boolean)                                       │
        │              Writes the text representation of the specified Boolean value, followed by the current line terminato│
    End │              value: The value to write.                                        │
        └─────────────────────────────────────────────────────────────────────────────┘
    ' Overloaded Add() method.
    Function Add(ByVal x As Integer, ByVal y As Integer) As Integer
```

Figure 4-1. Visual Studio IntelliSense for overloaded methods

---

■ **Source Code** The MethodOverloading application is located under the Chapter 4 subdirectory.

That wraps up our initial examination of building methods using the syntax of VB 2010. Next, let's check out how to build and manipulate arrays, enumerations, and structures. After this point, we will wrap up the chapter with an examination of 'nullable data types' and the `Nullable(Of T)` and If(x,y) in VB 2010.

Understanding VB 2010 Arrays

As I would guess you are already aware, an *array* is a set of data items, accessed using a numerical index. More specifically, an array is a set of contiguous data points of the same type (an array of Integers, an array of strings, an array of SportsCars, and so on). Declaring an array with VB 2010 is quite straightforward. To illustrate, create a new Console Application project (named FunWithArrays) that contains a helper method named SimpleArrays(), invoked from within Main():

```
Module Module1
    Sub Main()
        Console.WriteLine("***** Fun with Arrays *****")
        SimpleArrays()
        Console.ReadLine()
    End Sub

    Sub SimpleArrays()
        Console.WriteLine("=> Simple Array Creation.")
        ' Assign an array of Integers containing 3 elements {0, 1, 2}
        Dim myInts As Integer() = New Integer(2) {}

        ' Initialize a 100 item String array, indexed {0 - 99}
        Dim booksOnDotNet As String() = New String(99) {}
        Console.WriteLine()
    End Sub
End Module
```

Look closely at the previous code comments. When declaring a VB 2010 array using this syntax, the number used in the array declaration represents the upper bound, not the total number of items. Also note that the lower bound of an array always begins at 0. Thus, when you write Dim myInts As Integer() = New Integer(2) you actually end up with an array holding three elements, indexed at positions 0, 1, 2.

Once you have defined an array variable, you are then able to fill the elements index by index as shown in the updated SimpleArrays() method:

```
Sub SimpleArrays()
        Console.WriteLine("=> Simple Array Creation.")

        ' Create and fill an array of 3 Integers
        Dim myInts As Integer() = New Integer(2) {}
        myInts(0) = 100
        myInts(1) = 200
        myInts(2) = 300

        ' Now print each value.
        For Each I As Integer In myInts
          Console.WriteLine(i)
        Next
        Console.WriteLine()
End Sub
```

■ **Note** Do be aware that if you declare an array, but do not explicitly fill each index, each item will be set to the default value of the data type (e.g., an array of Booleans will be set to False or an array of Integers will be set to 0).

VB 2010 Array Initialization Syntax

In addition to filling an array element by element, you are also able to fill the items of an array using VB 2010 *array initialization syntax*. To do so, specify each array item within the scope of curly brackets ({}). This syntax can be helpful when you are creating an array of a known size and wish to quickly specify the initial values. For example, consider the following alternative array declarations:

```
Sub ArrayInitialization()
        Console.WriteLine("=> Array Initialization.")

        ' Array initialization syntax using the New keyword.
        Dim stringArray As String() = New String() {"one", "two", "three"}
        Console.WriteLine("stringArray has {0} elements", stringArray.Length)

        ' Array initialization syntax without using the New keyword.
        Dim boolArray As Boolean() = {False, False, True}
        Console.WriteLine("boolArray has {0} elements", boolArray.Length)

        ' Array initialization with New keyword and size.
        Dim intArray As Integer() = New Integer(3) {20, 22, 23, 0}
        Console.WriteLine("intArray has {0} elements", intArray.Length)
        Console.WriteLine()
End Sub
```

Notice that when you make use of this "curly bracket" syntax, you do not need to specify the size of the array (seen when constructing the **stringArray** variable), given that this will be inferred by the number of items within the scope of the curly brackets. Also notice that use of the New keyword is optional (shown when constructing the **boolArray** type).

In the case of the **intArray** declaration, again recall the numeric value specified represents the value of the upper bound, not the number of elements in the array. If there is a mismatch between the declared size and the number of initializers, you are issued a compile-time error. The following is an example:

```
' OOPS! Mismatch of size and elements!
Dim intArray As Integer() = New Integer(2) {20, 22, 23, 0}
```

Implicitly Typed Local Arrays

In the previous chapter, you learned about the topic of implicitly typed local variables. Recall that when you declare a local variable using Dim, you can omit the type name in the declaration. The compiler will infer the type based on the value you assign to the variable. You can use the same approach to define *implicitly typed local arrays.* Using this technique, you can allocate a new array variable without specifying the type contained within the array itself:

```
Sub DeclareImplicitArrays()
    Console.WriteLine("=> Implicit Array Initialization.")
    ' a is really Integer().
    Dim a = {1, 10, 100, 1000}
    Console.WriteLine("a is a: {0}", a.ToString())

    ' b is really Double().
    Dim b = {1, 1.5, 2, 2.5}
    Console.WriteLine("b is a: {0}", b.ToString())

    ' c is really String().
    Dim c = {"hello", Nothing, "world"}
    Console.WriteLine("c is a: {0}", c.ToString())
    Console.ReadLine()
End Sub
```

If you call this method from Main(), you'll see the following output:

```
=> Implicit Array Initialization.

a is a: System.Int32[]

b is a: System.Double[]

c is a: System.String[]
```

This is because the array ToString() method displays an array using [ ] notation (this is reminiscent of C# syntax, because C# uses [ ] rather than ( ) to denote arrays).

Of course, just as when you allocate an array using explicit VB 2010 syntax, the items in the array's initialization list must be of the same underlying type (e.g., all Integers, all Strings, or all SportsCars). Unlike what you might be expecting, an implicitly typed local array does not default to System.Object; thus the following generates a compile-time error (note, you must add Option Strict On at the top of your code to see this error message):

```
' Error! Mixed types!
Dim d = { 1, "one", 2, "two", False }
```

Defining an Array of Objects

In most cases, when you define an array, you do so by specifying the explicitly type of item that can be within the array variable. While this seems quite straightforward, there is one notable twist. As you will come to understand in Chapter 6, System.Object is the ultimate base class to each and every type (including fundamental data types) in the .NET type system. Given this fact, if you were to define an array of Objects, the subitems could be anything at all. Consider the following ArrayOfObjects() method (which again can be invoked from Main() for testing):

```
Sub ArrayOfObjects()
        Console.WriteLine("=> Array of Objects.")

        ' An array of objects can be anything at all.
        Dim myObjects As Object() = New Object(3) {}
        myObjects(0) = 10
        myObjects(1) = False
        myObjects(2) = New DateTime(1969, 3, 24)
        myObjects(3) = "Form & Void"

        For Each obj As Object In myObjects
                ' Print the type and value for each item in array.
                Console.WriteLine("Type: {0}, Value: {1}", obj.GetType(), obj)
        Next
        Console.WriteLine()
End Sub
```

Here, as you are iterating over the contents of myObjects, you print out the underlying type of each item using the GetType() method of System.Object as well as the value of the current item. Without going into too much detail regarding System.Object.GetType() at this point in the text, simply understand that this method can be used to obtain the fully qualified name of the item (Chapter 15 examines the topic of type information and reflection services in detail). The following output shows the result of calling ArrayOfObjects().

```
=> Array of Objects.

Type: System.Int32, Value: 10

Type: System.Boolean, Value: False

Type: System.DateTime, Value: 3/24/1969 12:00:00 AM

Type: System.String, Value: Form & Void
```

Working with Multidimensional Arrays

In addition to the single-dimension arrays you have seen thus far, VB 2010 also supports two varieties of multidimensional arrays. The first of these is termed a *rectangular array*, which is simply an array of multiple dimensions, where each row is of the same length. To declare and fill a multidimensional rectangular array, proceed as follows:

```
Sub RectMultidimensionalArray()
        Console.WriteLine("=> Rectangular multidimensional array.")
        ' A rectangular MD array.
        Dim myMatrix As Integer(,)
        myMatrix = New Integer(5, 5) {}
```

```vb
        ' Populate rows 0 - 5, and columns 0 - 5.
        For i=0 To 5
                        For j=0 To 5
                        myMatrix(i, j) = i * j
                Next
        Next

        ' Print rows 0 - 5, and columns 0 - 5.
                        For i=0 To 5
                        For j=0 To 5
        Console.Write(myMatrix(i, j) & vbTab)
                Next
        Console.WriteLine()
                Next
        Console.WriteLine()
End Sub
```

The second type of multidimensional array is termed a *jagged array*. As the name implies, jagged arrays contain some number of inner arrays, each of which may have a unique upper limit, for example:

```vb
Sub JaggedMultidimensionalArray()

        Console.WriteLine("=> Jagged multidimensional array.")

        ' A jagged MD array (i.e., an array of arrays).
        ' Here we have an array of 5 different arrays.
        Dim myJagArray As Integer()() = New Integer(4)() {}

        ' Create the jagged array.
        For i=0 To myJagArray.Length - 1
                myJagArray(i) = New Integer(i + 6) {}
        Next

        ' Print each row (remember, each element is defaulted to zero!)
        For i=0 To 4
                For j=0 To myJagArray(i).Length - 1
                        Console.Write(myJagArray(i)(j) & " ")
                Next
                Console.WriteLine()
        Next
        Console.WriteLine()
End Sub
```

Figure 4-2 shows the output of calling each of the RectMultidimensionalArray() and JaggedMultidimensionalArray() methods within Main().

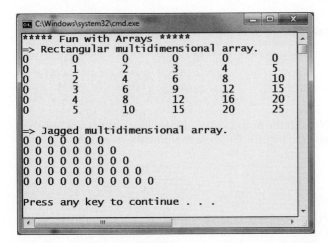

Figure 4-2. Rectangular and jagged multidimensional arrays

Arrays As Arguments or Return Values

Once you have created an array, you are free to pass it as an argument or receive it as a member return value. For example, the following PrintArray() method takes an incoming array of integers and prints each member to the console, while the GetStringArray() method populates an array of strings and returns it to the caller:

```vb
Sub PrintArray(ByVal myInts As Integer())
      For i=0 To myInts.Length - 1
          Console.WriteLine("Item {0} is {1}", i, myInts(i))
      Next
End Sub

Function GetStringArray() As String()
      Dim theStrings As String() = {"Hello", "from", "GetStringArray"}
    Return theStrings
End Function
```

These methods may be invoked as you would expect:

```vb
Sub PassAndReceiveArrays()

      Console.WriteLine("=> Arrays as params and return values.")
      ' Pass array as parameter.
      Dim ages As Integer() = {20, 22, 23, 0}
      PrintArray(ages)
```

```
        ' Get array as return value.
        Dim strs As String() = GetStringArray()
        For Each s In strs
        Console.WriteLine(s)
        Next
        Console.WriteLine()
End Sub
```

At this point, hopefully you feel comfortable with the process of defining, filling, and examining the contents of a VB 2010 array variable. To complete the picture, let's now examine the role of the `System.Array` class.

The System.Array Base Class

Every array you create gathers much of its functionality from the `System.Array` class. Using these common members, you are able to operate on an array using a consistent object model. Table 4-2 gives a rundown of some of the more interesting members (be sure to check the .NET Framework 4.0 SDK documentation for full details).

Table 4-2. Select Members of System.Array

Member of Array Class	Meaning in Life
Clear()	This Shared method sets a range of elements in the array to empty values (0 for numbers, Nothing for object references, False for Booleans).
CopyTo()	This method is used to copy elements from the source array into the destination array.
Length	This property returns the number of items within the array.
Rank	This property returns the number of dimensions of the current array.
Reverse()	This Shared method reverses the contents of an one-dimensional array.
Sort()	This Shared method sorts a one-dimensional array of intrinsic types. If the elements in the array implement the `IComparer` interface, you can also sort your custom types (see Chapter 9).

Let's see some of these members in action. The following helper method makes use of the Shared `Reverse()` and `Clear()` methods to pump out information about an array of string types to the console:

```
Sub SystemArrayFunctionality()
        Console.WriteLine("=> Working with System.Array.")
        ' Initialize items at startup.
        Dim gothicBands As String() = {"Tones on Tail", "Bauhaus",
                              "Sisters of Mercy"}
        ' Print out names in declared order.
```

```
        Console.WriteLine("-> Here is the array:")
        For i=0 To gothicBands.Length - 1
                ' Print a name
                Console.Write(gothicBands(i) & ", ")
        Next
                Console.WriteLine(vbLf)

        ' Reverse them...
        Array.Reverse(gothicBands)
        Console.WriteLine("-> The reversed array")

        ' ... and print them.
        For i=0 To gothicBands.Length - 1
                ' Print a name
                Console.Write(gothicBands(i) & ", ")
        Next
                Console.WriteLine(vbLf)

        ' Clear out all but the final member.
        Console.WriteLine("-> Cleared out all but one...")
        Array.Clear(gothicBands, 1, 2)
        For i=0 To gothicBands.Length - 1
                ' Print a name
                Console.Write(gothicBands(i) & ", ")
        Next
        Console.WriteLine()
End Sub
```

If you invoke this method from within Main(), you will get the output shown here.

```
=> Working with System.Array.

-> Here is the array:

Tones on Tail, Bauhaus, Sisters of Mercy,


-> The reversed array

Sisters of Mercy, Bauhaus, Tones on Tail,


-> Cleared out all but one...

Sisters of Mercy, , ,
```

Notice that many members of System.Array are defined as Shared members and are therefore called at the class level (for example, the Array.Sort() or Array.Reverse() methods). Methods such as these are passed in the array you wish to process. Other methods of System.Array (such as the Length property) are bound at the object level, thus you are able to invoke the member directly on the array.

■ **Source Code** The FunWithArrays application is located under the Chapter 4 subdirectory.

Understanding the Enum Type

Recall from Chapter 1 that the .NET type system is composed of classes, structures, enumerations, interfaces, and delegates. To begin exploration of these types, let's check out the role of the *enumeration* (or simply, *Enum*) using a new Console Application project named FunWithEnums.

When building a system, it is often convenient to create a set of symbolic names that map to known numerical values. For example, if you are creating a payroll system, you may want to refer to the type of employees using constants such as vice president, manager, contractor, and grunt. VB 2010 supports the notion of custom enumerations for this very reason. For example, here is an enumeration named EmpType:

```
' A custom enumeration.
Enum EmpType
    Manager        ' = 0
    Grunt          ' = 1
    Contractor     ' = 2
    VicePresident  ' = 3
End Enum
```

The EmpType enumeration defines four named constants, corresponding to discrete numerical values. By default, the first element is set to the value zero (0), followed by an *n+1* progression. You are free to change the initial value as you see fit. For example, if it made sense to number the members of EmpType as 102 through 105, you could do so as follows:

```
' Begin with 102.
Enum EmpType
    Manager = 102  ' = 102
    Grunt          ' = 103
    Contractor     ' = 104
    VicePresident  ' = 105
End Enum
```

Enumerations do not necessarily need to follow a sequential ordering, and need not have unique values. If (for some reason or another) it makes sense to establish your EmpType as shown here, the compiler continues to be happy:

```
' Elements of an enumeration need not be sequential!
Enum EmpType
        Manager = 10
        Grunt = 1
        Contractor = 100
        VicePresident = 9
End Enum
```

Controlling the Underlying Storage for an Enum

By default, the storage type used to hold the values of an enumeration is a `System.Int32` (the VB 2010 `Integer`); however, you are free to change this to your liking. VB 2010 enumerations can be defined in a similar manner for any of the core system types (`Byte`, `Short`, `Integer`, or `Long`). For example, if you want to set the underlying storage value of `EmpType` to be a `Byte` rather than an `Integer`, you can write the following:

```
' This time, EmpType maps to an underlying Byte.
Enum EmpType As Byte
        Manager = 10
        Grunt = 1
        Contractor = 100
        VicePresident = 9
End Enum
```

Changing the underlying type of an enumeration can be helpful if you are building a .NET application that will be deployed to a low-memory device (such as a .NET-enabled cell phone or PDA) and need to conserve memory wherever possible. Of course, if you do establish your enumeration to use a `Byte` as storage, each value must be within its range! For example, the following version of `EmpType` will result in a compiler error, as the value 999 cannot fit within the range of a byte:

```
' Compile time error!  999 is too big for a Byte!
Enum EmpType As Byte
        Manager = 10
        Grunt = 1
        Contractor = 100
        VicePresident = 999
End Enum
```

Declaring Enum Variables

Once you have established the range and storage type of your enumeration, you can use it in place of so-called "magic numbers." Because enumerations are nothing more than a user-defined data type, you are able to use them as function return values, method parameters, local variables, and so forth. Assume you have a method named `AskForBonus()`, taking an `EmpType` variable as the sole parameter. Based on the value of the incoming parameter, you will print out a fitting response to the pay bonus request:

```
Module Module1
    Sub Main()
        Console.WriteLine("**** Fun with Enums *****")
        ' Make a contractor type.
        Dim emp As EmpType = EmpType.Contractor
        AskForBonus(emp)
        Console.ReadLine()
    End Sub

    ' Enums as parameters.
    Sub AskForBonus(ByVal e As EmpType)
        Select Case e
            Case EmpType.Manager
        Console.WriteLine("How about stock options instead?")
            Case EmpType.Grunt
        Console.WriteLine("You have got to be kidding...")
            Case EmpType.Contractor
        Console.WriteLine("You already get enough cash...")
                                        Case EmpType.VicePresident
        Console.WriteLine("VERY GOOD, Sir!")
            End Select
    End Sub
End Module
```

Notice that when you are assigning a value to an Enum variable, you must scope the Enum name (`EmpType`) to the value (`Grunt`). Because enumerations are a fixed set of name/value pairs, it is illegal to set an Enum variable to a value that is not defined directly by the enumerated type:

```
Sub ThisMethodWillNotCompile()

    ' Error! SalesManager is not in the EmpType enum!
    Dim emp As EmpType = EmpType.SalesManager

    ' Error! Forgot to scope Grunt value to EmpType enum!
    emp = Grunt
End Sub
```

The System.Enum Type

The interesting thing about .NET enumerations is that they gain functionality from the `System.Enum` class type. This class defines a number of methods that allow you to interrogate and transform a given enumeration. One helpful method is the Shared `Enum.GetUnderlyingType()`, which as the name implies returns the data type used to store the values of the enumerated type (`System.Byte` in the case of the current `EmpType` declaration). We must enclose the Enum class name in square brackets like this: [Enum]. This tells the compiler that we're talking about the Enum *class name* rather than the Enum *keyword*.

```
Sub Main()
        Console.WriteLine("**** Fun with Enums *****")
        ' Make a contractor type.
        Dim emp As EmpType = EmpType.Contractor
        AskForBonus(emp)

        ' Print storage for the enum.
        Console.WriteLine("EmpType uses a {0} for storage",
                [Enum].GetUnderlyingType(emp.GetType()))
        Console.ReadLine()
End Sub
```

If you were to consult the Visual Studio 2010 object browser, you would be able to verify that the Enum.GetUnderlyingType() method requires you to pass in a **System.Type** as the first parameter. As fully examined in Chapter 16, **Type** represents the metadata description of a given .NET entity.

One possible way to obtain metadata (as shown previously) is to use the **GetType()** method, which is common to all types in the .NET base class libraries. Another approach is to make use of the VB 2010 **GetType** operator. One benefit of doing so is that you do not need to have a variable of the entity you wish to obtain a metadata description of:

```
' This time use GetType to extract a Type.
Console.WriteLine("EmpType uses a {0} for storage",
                [Enum].GetUnderlyingType(GetType(EmpType)))
```

Dynamically Discovering an Enum's Name/Value Pairs

Beyond the Enum.GetUnderlyingType() method, all VB 2010 enumerations support a method named ToString(), which returns the string name of the current enumeration's value. The following code is an example:

```
Sub Main()
        Console.WriteLine("**** Fun with Enums *****")
        Dim emp As EmpType = EmpType.Contractor

        ' Prints out "emp is a Contractor".
        Console.WriteLine("emp is a {0}.", emp.ToString())
        Console.ReadLine()
End Sub
```

If you are interested in discovering the value of a given enumeration variable, rather than its name, you can simply cast the Enum variable against the underlying storage type. The following is an example:

```
Sub Main()
        Console.WriteLine("**** Fun with Enums *****")
        Dim emp As EmpType = EmpType.Contractor

        ' Prints out "Contractor = 100".
        Console.WriteLine("{0} = {1}", emp.ToString(), CByte(emp))
        Console.ReadLine()
End Sub
```

■ **Note** The Shared `Enum.Format()` method provides a finer level of formatting options by specifying a desired format flag. Consult the .NET Framework 4.0 SDK documentation for full details of the `System.Enum.Format()` method.

`System.Enum` also defines another Shared method named `GetValues()`. This method returns an instance of `System.Array`. Each item in the array corresponds to a member of the specified enumeration. Consider the following method, which will print out each name/value pair within any enumeration you pass in as a parameter:

```
' This method will print out the details of any Enum.
Sub EvaluateEnum(ByVal e As System.Enum)

    Console.WriteLine("=> Information about {0}", e.GetType().Name)
    Console.WriteLine("Underlying storage type: {0}",
                        [Enum].GetUnderlyingType(e.GetType()))

    ' Get all name/value pairs for incoming parameter.
    Dim enumData As Array = [Enum].GetValues(e.GetType())
    Console.WriteLine("This enum has {0} members.", enumData.Length)

    ' Now show the string name and associated value.
    For i=0 To enumData.Length - 1
        Console.WriteLine("Name: {0}, Value: {0:D}", enumData.GetValue(i))
    Next
    Console.WriteLine()
End Sub
```

To test this new method, update your `Main()` method to create variables of several enumeration types declared in the `System` namespace (as well as an `EmpType` enumeration for good measure). The following code is an example:

```
Sub Main()
        Console.WriteLine("**** Fun with Enums *****")
        Dim e2 As EmpType = EmpType.Contractor

        ' These types are Enums in the System namespace.
        Dim day As DayOfWeek = DayOfWeek.Monday
        Dim cc As ConsoleColor = ConsoleColor.Gray
        EvaluateEnum(e2)
        EvaluateEnum(day)
        EvaluateEnum(cc)
        Console.ReadLine()
End Sub
```

The output is shown in Figure 4-3.

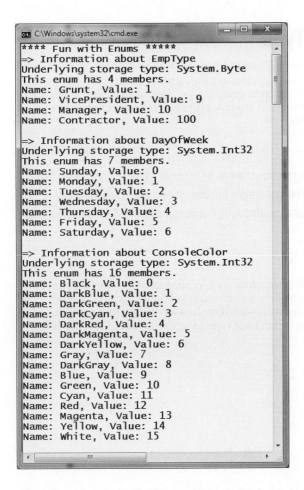

Figure 4-3. Dynamically discovering name/value pairs of enumeration types.

As you will see over the course of this text, enumerations are used extensively throughout the .NET base class libraries. For example, ADO.NET makes use of numerous enumerations to represent the state of a database connection (e.g., opened or closed), the state of a row in a DataTable (e.g., changed, new, or detached). Therefore, when you make use of any enumeration, always remember that you are able to interact with the name/value pairs using the members of System.Enum.

■ **Source Code** The FunWithEnums project is located under the Chapter 4 subdirectory.

Understanding the Structure Type

Now that you understand the role of enumeration types, let's examine the use of .NET *structures*. Structure types are well suited for modeling mathematical, geometrical, and other "atomic" entities in your application. A structure (like an enumeration) is a user-defined type; however, structures are not simply a collection of name/value pairs. Rather, structures are types that can contain any number of data fields and members that operate on these fields.

■ **Note** If you have a background in OOP, you can think of a structure as a "lightweight class type," given that structures provide a way to define a type that supports encapsulation, but cannot be used to build a family of related types. When you need to build a family of related types through inheritance, you will need to make use of class types.

On the surface, the process of defining and using structures is very simple, but as they say, the devil is in the details. To begin understanding the basics of structure types, create a new project named FunWithStructures. In VB 2010 structures are created using the **Structure** keyword. Define a new structure named **Point**, which defines two member variables of type **Integer** and a set of methods to interact with said data:

```
Structure Point
    ' Fields of the structure.
    Public X As Integer
    Public Y As Integer

    ' Add 1 to the (X, Y) position.
    Public Sub Increment()
        X += 1
        Y += 1
    End Sub

    ' Subtract 1 from the (X, Y) position.
    Public Sub Decrement()
        X -= 1
        Y -= 1
    End Sub

    ' Display the current position.
    Public Sub Display()
        Console.WriteLine("X = {0}, Y = {1}", X, Y)
    End Sub
End Structure
```

Here, you have defined your two integer fields (X and Y) using the **Public** keyword, which is an access control modifier (Chapter 5 furthers this discussion). Declaring data with the **Public** keyword ensures the caller has direct access to the data from a given **Point** variable (via the dot operator).

■ **Note** It is typically considered bad style to define Public data within a class or structure. Rather, you will want to define *Private* data, which can be accessed and changed using *Public* properties. These details will be examined in Chapter 5.

Here is a `Main()` method that takes our `Point` type out for a test drive:

```
Sub Main()
    Console.WriteLine("***** A First Look at Structures *****" & vbLf)

    ' Create an initial Point.
    Dim myPoint As Point
    myPoint.X = 349
    myPoint.Y = 76
    myPoint.Display()

    ' Adjust the X and Y values.
    myPoint.Increment()
    myPoint.Display()
    Console.ReadLine()
End Sub
```

The output is as you would expect:

```
***** A First Look at Structures *****


X = 349, Y = 76

X = 350, Y = 77
```

Creating Structure Variables

When you wish to create a structure variable, you have a variety of options. Here, you simply create a `Point` variable and assign each piece of Public field data before invoking its members.

```
Dim p1 As Point
p1.X = 10
p1.Display()

Dim p2 As Point
p2.X = 10
p2.Y = 10
p2.Display()
```

As an alternative, we can create structure variables using the VB 2010 **New** keyword, which will invoke the structure's *default constructor*. By definition, a default constructor does not take any arguments. The benefit of invoking the default constructor of a structure is that each piece of field data is automatically set to its default value:

```
' Set all fields to default values
' using the default constructor.
Dim p1 As New Point()

' Prints X=0,Y=0
p1.Display()
```

It is also possible to design a structure with a *custom constructor*. This allows you to specify the values of field data upon variable creation, rather than having to set each data member field by field. Chapter 5 will provide a detailed examination of constructors; however, to illustrate, update the **Point** structure with the following code:

```
Structure Point

    ' Fields of the structure.
    Public X As Integer
    Public Y As Integer

    ' A custom constructor.
    Public Sub New(XPos As Integer, YPos As Integer)
            X = XPos
            Y = YPos
    End Sub
    ...
End Structure
```

With this, we could now create **Point** variables as follows:
```
' Call custom constructor.
Dim p2 As New Point(50, 60)

' Prints X=50,Y=60
p2.Display()
```

As mentioned, working with structures on the surface is quite simple. However, to deepen your understanding of this type, you need to explore the distinction between a .NET value type and a .NET reference type.

■ **Source Code** The FunWithStructures project is located under the Chapter 4 subdirectory.

Understanding Value Types and Reference Types

■ **Note** The following discussion of value types and reference types assumes that you have a background in object-oriented programming. If this is not the case, you may wish to skip to the final section in this chapter (Understanding VB 2010 Nullable Types) and return to this section once you have read Chapters 5 and 6.

Unlike arrays, strings, or enumerations, VB 2010 structures do not have an identically named representation in the .NET library (that is, there is no `System.Structure` class), but are implicitly derived from `System.ValueType.` Simply put, the role of `System.ValueType` is to ensure that the derived type (e.g., any structure) is allocated on the *stack* rather than the garbage collected *heap*. Simply put, data allocated on the stack can be created and destroyed very quickly, as its lifetime is determined by the defining scope. Heap allocated data, on the other hand, is monitored by the .NET garbage collector, and has a lifetime that is determined by a large number of factors, which will be examined in Chapter 8.

Functionally, the only purpose of `System.ValueType` is to override the Overridable methods defined by `System.Object` to use value-based, versus reference-based, semantics. As you may know, overriding is the process of changing the implementation of a virtual (or possibly abstract) method defined within a base class. The base class of `ValueType` is `System.Object`. In fact, the instance methods defined by `System.ValueType` are identical to those of `System.Object`:

```
' Structures and enumerations implicitly extend System.ValueType.
Public MustInherit Class ValueType
        Inherits Object

        Public Overridable Function Equals(obj As Object) As Boolean
        Public Overridable Function GetHashCode() As Integer
        Public Function GetType() As Type
        Public Overridable Function ToString() As String

End Class
```

Given the fact that value types are using value-based semantics, the lifetime of a structure (which includes all numerical data types [`Integer`, `Single`], as well as any enum or custom structure) is very predictable. When a structure variable falls out of the defining scope, it is removed from memory immediately:

```
' Local structures are popped off
' the stack when a method returns.
Sub LocalValueTypes()
        ' Recall! "Integer" is really a System.Int32 structure.
        Dim i As Integer = 0
        ' Recall! Point is a structure type.
        Dim p As New Point()
End Sub    ' "i" and "p" popped off the stack here!
```

Value Types, References Types, and the Assignment Operator

When you assign one value type to another, a member-by-member copy of the field data is achieved. In the case of a simple data type such as System.Int32, the only member to copy is the numerical value. However, in the case of your Point, the X and Y values are copied into the new structure variable. To illustrate, create a new Console Application project named ValueAndReferenceTypes, then copy your previous Point definition into your new namespace. Next, add the following method to your module:

```
' Assigning two intrinsic value types results in
' two independent variables on the stack.
Sub ValueTypeAssignment()

        Console.WriteLine("Assigning value types" & vbLf)
        Dim p1 As New Point(10, 10)
        Dim p2 As Point = p1

        ' Print both points.
        p1.Display()
        p2.Display()

        ' Change p1.X and print again. p2.X is not changed.
        p1.X = 100
        Console.WriteLine(vbLf & "=> Changed p1.X" & vbLf)
        p1.Display()
        p2.Display()
End Sub
```

Here you have created a variable of type Point (named p1) that is then assigned to another Point (p2). Because Point is a value type, you have two copies of the Point type on the stack, each of which can be independently manipulated. Therefore, when you change the value of p1.X, the value of p2.X is unaffected:

```
Assigning value types


X = 10, Y = 10

X = 10, Y = 10


=> Changed p1.X


X = 100, Y = 10

X = 10, Y = 10
```

In stark contrast to value types, when you apply the assignment operator to reference types (meaning all class instances), you are redirecting what the reference variable points to in memory. To illustrate, create a new class type named PointRef that has the exact same members as the Point structures:

```
Class PointRef
    ' Same members as Point structure.
    ...
End Class
```

Now, make use of your PointRef type within the following new method. Note that beyond using the PointRef class, rather than the Point structure, the code is identical to the ValueTypeAssignment() method.

```
Sub ReferenceTypeAssignment()

        Console.WriteLine("Assigning reference types" & vbLf)
        Dim p1 As New PointRef(10, 10)
        Dim p2 As PointRef = p1

        ' Print both point refs.
        p1.Display()
        p2.Display()
```

```
        ' Change p1.X and print again.
        p1.X = 100
        Console.WriteLine(vbLf & "=> Changed p1.X" & vbLf)
        p1.Display()
        p2.Display()
End Sub
```

In this case, you have two references pointing to the same object on the managed heap. Therefore, when you change the value of X using the **p2** reference, **p1.X** reports the same value. Assuming you have called this new method within Main(), your output should look like the following:

```
Assigning reference types



X = 10, Y = 10

X = 10, Y = 10



=> Changed p1.X



X = 100, Y = 10

X = 100, Y = 10
```

Value Types Containing Reference Types

Now that you have a better feeling for the basic differences between value types and reference types, let's examine a more complex example. Assume you have the following reference (class) type that maintains an informational String that can be set using a custom constructor:

```
Public Class ShapeInfo
        Public infoString As String
        Public Sub New(ByVal info As String)
            infoString = info
        End Sub
End Class
```

Now assume that you want to contain a variable of this class type within a value type named **Rectangle**. To allow the caller to set the value of the inner **ShapeInfo** member variable, you also provide a custom constructor. Here is the complete definition of the **Rectangle** type:

```
Structure Rectangle
```

CHAPTER 4 ■ CORE VB 2010 PROGRAMMING CONSTRUCTS, PART II

```
' The Rectangle structure contains a reference type member.
Public rectInfo As ShapeInfo

Public rectTop As Integer, rectLeft As Integer, rectBottom As Integer,
 rectRight As Integer

Public Sub New(ByVal info As String,ByVal top As Integer,
          ByVal left As Integer,ByVal bottom As Integer,
          ByVal right As Integer)

    rectInfo = New ShapeInfo(info)
    rectTop = top
    rectBottom = bottom
    rectLeft = left
    rectRight = right
End Sub

Public Sub Display()
    Console.WriteLine("String = {0},"&
          "Top = {1}, Bottom = {2}, Left = {3}, Right = {4}",
              rectInfo.infoString, rectTop, rectBottom, rectLeft, rectRight)
End Sub
End Structure
```

At this point, you have contained a reference type within a value type. The million dollar question now becomes, what happens if you assign one **Rectangle** variable to another? Given what you already know about value types, you would be correct in assuming that the integer data (which is indeed a structure) should be an independent entity for each **Rectangle** variable. But what about the internal reference type? Will the object's state be fully copied, or will the reference to that object be copied? To answer this question, define the following method and invoke it from **Main()**.

```
Sub ValueTypeContainingRefType()

        ' Create the first Rectangle.
        Console.WriteLine("-> Creating r1")
        Dim r1 As New Rectangle("First Rect", 10, 10, 50, 50)

        ' Now assign a new Rectangle to r1.
        Console.WriteLine("-> Assigning r2 to r1")
        Dim r2 As Rectangle = r1

        ' Change some values of r2.
        Console.WriteLine("-> Changing values of r2")
        r2.rectInfo.infoString = "This is new info!"
        r2.rectBottom = 4444
```

159

```
        ' Print values of both rectangles.
        r1.Display()
        r2.Display()
End Sub
```

The output can be seen in the following:

```
-> Creating r1

-> Assigning r2 to r1

-> Changing values of r2

String = This is new info!, Top = 10, Bottom = 50, Left = 10, Right = 50

String = This is new info!, Top = 10, Bottom = 4444, Left = 10, Right = 50
```

As you can see, when you change the value of the informational string using the r2 reference, the r1 reference displays the same value. By default, when a value type contains other reference types, assignment results in a copy of the references. In this way, you have two independent structures, each of which contains a reference pointing to the same object in memory (i.e., a shallow copy). When you want to perform a deep copy, where the state of internal references is fully copied into a new object, one approach is to implement the ICloneable interface (as you will do in Chapter 9).

■ **Source Code** The ValueAndReferenceTypes project is located under the Chapter 4 subdirectory.

Passing Reference Types by Value

Reference types or value types can obviously be passed as parameters to methods. However, passing a reference type (e.g., a class) by reference is quite different from passing it by value. To understand the distinction, assume you have a simple Person class defined in a new Console Application project named RefTypeValTypeParams, defined as follows:

```
Public Class Person
        Public personName As String
        Public personAge As Integer

        ' Constructors.
        Public Sub New(ByVal name As String,ByVal age As Integer)
                personName = name
                personAge = age
        End Sub
```

```
        Public Sub New()
        End Sub

        Public Sub Display()
                Console.WriteLine("Name: {0}, Age: {1}", personName, personAge)
        End Sub
End Class
```

Now, what if you create a method that allows the caller to send in the **Person** object by value (note the use of the **ByVal** keyword):

```
Sub SendAPersonByValue(ByVal p As Person)
        ' Change the age of "p"?
        p.personAge = 99

        ' Will the caller see this reassignment?
        p = New Person("Nikki", 99)
End Sub
```

Notice how the **SendAPersonByValue()** method attempts to reassign the incoming **Person** reference to a new **Person** object as well as change some state data. Now let's test this method using the following **Main()** method:

```
Sub Main()
        ' Passing ref-types by value.
        Console.WriteLine("***** Passing Person object by value *****")
        Dim fred As New Person("Fred", 12)
        Console.WriteLine(vbLf & "Before by value call, Person is:")

        fred.Display()
        SendAPersonByValue(fred)
        Console.WriteLine(vbLf & "After by value call, Person is:")
        fred.Display()
        Console.ReadLine()
End Sub
```

The following is the output of this call.

```
***** Passing Person object by value *****


Before by value call, Person is:

Name: Fred, Age: 12


After by value call, Person is:

Name: Fred, Age: 99
```

As you can see, the value of `personAge` has been modified. This behavior seems to fly in the face of what it means to pass a parameter "by value." Given that you were able to change the state of the incoming `Person`, what was copied? The answer: a copy of the reference to the caller's object. Therefore, as the `SendAPersonByValue()` method is pointing to the same object as the caller, it is possible to alter the object's state data. What is not possible is to reassign what the reference *is pointing to*.

Passing Reference Types by Reference

Now assume you have a `SendAPersonByReference()` method, which passes a reference type by reference (note the `ByRef` parameter modifier):

```
Sub SendAPersonByReference(ByRef p As Person)
        ' Change some data of "p".
        p.personAge = 555

        ' "p" is now pointing to a new object on the heap!
        p = New Person("Nikki", 999)
End Sub
```

As you might expect, this allows complete flexibility of how the callee is able to manipulate the incoming parameter. Not only can the callee change the state of the object, but if it so chooses, it may also reassign the reference to a new `Person` type. Now ponder the following updated `Main()` method:

```
Sub Main()
        ' Passing ref-types by ref.
        Console.WriteLine("***** Passing Person object by reference *****")
        Dim mel As New Person("Mel", 23)
        Console.WriteLine("Before by ref call, Person is:")

        mel.Display()
        SendAPersonByReference(mel)
        Console.WriteLine("After by ref call, Person is:")
        mel.Display()
        Console.ReadLine()
End Sub
```

Notice the following output:

```
***** Passing Person object by reference *****

Before by ref call, Person is:

Name: Mel, Age: 23

After by ref call, Person is:

Name: Nikki, Age: 999
```

As you can see, an object named Mel returns after the call as an object named Nikki, as the method was able to change what the incoming reference pointed to in memory. The golden rule to keep in mind when passing reference types is the following:

- If a reference type is passed by reference, the callee may change the values of the object's state data as well as the object it is referencing.

- If a reference type is passed by value, the callee may change the values of the object's state data but not the object it is referencing.

■ **Source Code** The RefTypeValTypeParams project is located under the Chapter 4 subdirectory.

Final Details Regarding Value Types and Reference Types

To wrap up this topic, consider the information in Table 4-3, which summarizes the core distinctions between value types and reference types.

Table 4-3. Value Types and Reference Types Side by Side

Intriguing Question	Value Type	Reference Type
Where is this type allocated?	Allocated on the stack.	Allocated on the managed heap.
How is a variable represented?	Value type variables are local copies.	Reference type variables are pointing to the memory occupied by the allocated instance.
What is the base type?	Must derive from `System.ValueType`.	Can derive from any other type (except `System. ValueType`), as long as that type is not "NotInheritable" (more details on this in Chapter 6).
Can this type function as a base to other types?	No. Value types are always sealed and cannot be inherited from.	Yes. If the type is not NotInheritable, it may function as a base to other types.
What is the default parameter passing behavior?	Variables are passed by value (i.e., a copy of the variable is passed into the called function).	For value types, the object is copied-by-value. For reference types, the reference is copied-by-value.
Can this type override `System.Object.Finalize()`?	No. Value types are never placed onto the heap and therefore do not need to be finalized.	Yes, indirectly (more details on this in Chapter 8).
Can I define constructors for this type?	Yes, but the default constructor is reserved (i.e., your custom constructors must all have arguments).	But of course!
When do variables of this type die?	When they fall out of the defining scope	When the object is garbage collected.

Despite their differences, value types and reference types both have the ability to implement interfaces and may support any number of fields, methods, overloaded operators, constants, properties, and events.

Understanding VB 2010 Nullable Types

To wrap up this chapter, let's examine the role of *nullable data type* using a final Console Application named NullableTypes. As you know, CLR data types have a fixed range and are represented as a type in the `System` namespace. For example, the `System.Boolean` data type can be assigned a value from the set

{True, False}. Now, recall that all of the numerical data types (as well as the Boolean data type) are *value types*. VB 2010 actually allows you to assign Nothing to value types, as in the following example:

```
Sub Main()
        ' VB lets you assign Nothing to value types
        ' but it actually means "assign the default value" to the variable
        ' (i.e. it doesn't actually set the variables to Nothing!)
                Dim myBool As Boolean = Nothing
                Dim myInt As Integer = Nothing

        ' Reference types work the way you might expect
        ' i.e. it actually sets the variables to Nothing.
                Dim myString As String = Nothing
End Sub
```

Since the release of .NET 2.0, it has been possible to create truly nullable data types. Simply put, a nullable type can represent all the values of its underlying type, plus the value Nothing. Thus, if we declare a nullable Boolean, it could be assigned a value from the set {True, False, Nothing} (and we really do mean Nothing here; i.e., a null reference). This can be extremely helpful when working with relational databases, given that it is quite common to encounter undefined columns in database tables. Without the concept of a nullable data type, there is no convenient manner in VB 2010 to represent a numerical data point with no value.

To define a nullable variable type, a variable is declared of the Nullable(Of T) type. Do note that this syntax is only legal when applied to value types. If you attempt to create a nullable reference type (including Strings), you are issued a compile-time error. Like a nonnullable variable, local nullable variables must be assigned an initial value before you can use them:

```
Sub LocalNullableVariables()

        ' Define some local nullable types.
        Dim nullableInt As Nullable(Of Integer) = 10
        Dim nullableDouble As Nullable(Of Double) = 3.14
        Dim nullableBool As Nullable(Of Boolean) = Nothing
        Dim nullableChar As Nullable(Of Char) = "a"C
        Dim arrayOfNullableInts As Nullable(Of Integer)() =
                    New Nullable(Of Integer)(10) {}
End Sub
```

Nullable(Of T) is a generic structure, where T represents any value type you care to pass in (such as Integer and Point). Although we will not examine generics until Chapter 10, it is important to understand that the System. Nullable(Of T) type provides a set of members that all nullable types can make use of.

For example, you are able to programmatically discover whether the nullable variable indeed has been assigned a Nothing value using the HasValue property or the IsNot operator. The assigned value of a nullable type may be obtained directly or via the Value property.

Working with Nullable Types

As stated, nullable data types can be particularly useful when you are interacting with databases, given that columns in a data table may be intentionally empty (e.g., undefined). To illustrate, assume the following class, which simulates the process of accessing a database that has a table containing two columns that may be null. Note that the GetIntFromDatabase() method is not assigning a value to the nullable Integer member variable, while GetBoolFromDatabase() is assigning a valid value to the Nullable(Of Boolean) member:

```
Public Class DatabaseReader
' Nullable data field.
Public numericValue As Nullable(Of Integer) = Nothing
Public boolValue As Nullable(Of Boolean) = True

' Note the nullable return type.
Public Function GetIntFromDatabase() As Nullable(Of Integer)
Return numericValue
End Function

' Note the nullable return type.
Public Function GetBoolFromDatabase() As Nullable(Of Boolean)
Return boolValue
End Function
End Class
```

Now, assume the following Main() method, which invokes each member of the DatabaseReader class, and discovers the assigned values using the HasValue and Value members as well as using the VB equality operator (not equal, to be exact):

```
Sub Main()
        Console.WriteLine("***** Fun with Nullable Data *****" & vbLf)
        Dim dr As New DatabaseReader()
        ' Get Integer from "database".
        Dim i As Nullable(Of Integer) = dr.GetIntFromDatabase()
        If i.HasValue Then
                Console.WriteLine("Value of 'i' is: {0}", i.Value)
        Else
                Console.WriteLine("Value of 'i' is undefined.")
        End If

        ' Get Boolean from "database".
        Dim b As Nullable(Of Boolean) = dr.GetBoolFromDatabase()
        If b IsNot Nothing Then
                Console.WriteLine("Value of 'b' is: {0}", b.Value)
        Else
                Console.WriteLine("Value of 'b' is undefined.")
        End If
        Console.ReadLine()
End Sub
```

The Nullable If Operator

The final aspect of nullable types to be aware of is that they can make use of the VB 2010 nullable If operator. This operator allows you to assign a value to a nullable type if the retrieved value is in fact

Nothing. For this example, assume you wish to assign a local nullable integer to 100 if the value returned from GetIntFromDatabase() is Nothing (of course, this method is programmed to *always* return Nothing, but I am sure you get the general idea):

```
Sub Main()
        Console.WriteLine("***** Fun with Nullable Data *****" & vbLf)
        Dim dr As New DatabaseReader()
        ...

        ' If the value from GetIntFromDatabase() is Nothing,
        ' assign local variable to 100.
        Dim myData As Integer = If(dr.GetIntFromDatabase(), 100)
        Console.WriteLine("Value of myData: {0}", myData)
        Console.ReadLine()
End Sub
```

The benefit of using the nullable If operator is that it provides a more compact version of a traditional If/Else condition. However, if you wish, you could have authored the following, functionally equivalent code to ensure that if a value comes back as Nothing, it will indeed be set to the value 100:

```
Dim moreData As Nullable(Of Integer) = dr.GetIntFromDatabase()
If Not moreData.HasValue Then
        moreData = 100
End If
Console.WriteLine("Value of moreData: {0}", moreData)
```

■ **Source Code** The NullableTypes application is located under the Chapter 4 subdirectory.

Summary

This chapter began with an examination of several VB 2010 keywords that allow you to build custom methods. You saw how to pass parameters by value, by reference, and as output parameters. You also learned about the role of optional or named parameters and how to define and invoke methods taking parameter arrays.

Once we investigated the topic of method overloading, the bulk of this chapter examined several details regarding how arrays, enumerations, and structures are defined in VB 2010 and represented within the .NET base class libraries. Along the way, you examined several details regarding value types and reference types, including how they respond when passing them as parameters to methods, and how to interact with nullable data types.

With this, our initial investigation of the VB 2010 programming language is complete! In the next chapter, you will begin to dig into the details of object-oriented development.

CHAPTER 5

■ ■ ■

Defining Encapsulated Class Types

In the previous two chapters, you investigated a number of core syntactical constructs that are commonplace to any .NET application you may be developing. Here, you will begin your examination of the object-oriented capabilities of VB 2010. The first order of business is to examine the process of building well-defined class types that support any number of *constructors*. Once you understand the basics of defining classes and allocating objects, the remainder of this chapter will examine the role of *encapsulation*. Along the way you will understand how to define class properties as well as the role of Shared members, object initialization syntax, read-only fields, constant data, and partial classes.

Introducing the VB 2010 Class Type

As far as the .NET platform is concerned, the most fundamental programming construct is the *class type*. Formally, a class is a user-defined type that is composed of field data (often called *member variables*) and members that operate on this data (such as constructors, properties, methods, events, and so forth). Collectively, the set of field data represents the "state" of a class instance (otherwise known as an *object*). The power of object-based languages such as VB 2010 is that by grouping data and related functionality in a unified class definition, you are able to model your software after entities in the real world.

To get the ball rolling, create a new VB 2010 Console Application named SimpleClassExample. Next, insert a new class file (named **Car.vb**) into your project using the Project ➤ Add Class... menu selection, choose the Class icon from the resulting dialog box as shown in Figure 5-1, and click the Add button.

A class is defined in VB 2010 using the **Class** keyword. Here is the simplest possible declaration:

```
Public Class Car
End Class
```

Once you have defined a class type, you will need to consider the set of member variables that will be used to represent its state. For example, you may decide that cars maintain an **Integer** data type to represent the current speed and a **String** data type to represent the car's friendly pet name. Given these initial design notes, update your **Car** class as follows:

```
Public Class Car
      'The state of the car
        Public petName As String
        Public currSpeed As Integer
End Class
```

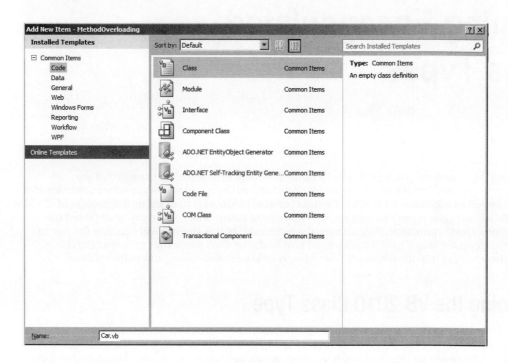

Figure 5-1. *Inserting a new VB 2010 class type*

Notice that these member variables are declared using the `Public` access modifier. Public members of a class are directly accessible once an object of this type has been created. Recall the term "object" is used to represent an instance of a given class type created using the `New` keyword.

■ **Note** Field data of a class should seldom (if ever) be defined as Public. To preserve the integrity of your state data, it is a far better design to define data as Private (or possibly Protected) and allow controlled access to the data via type properties (as shown later in this chapter). However, to keep this first example as simple as possible, Public data fits the bill.

After you have defined the set of member variables that represent the state of the class, the next design step is to establish the members that model its behavior. For this example, the Car class will define one method named SpeedUp() and another named PrintState(). Update your class as so:

```
Public Class Car

        'The 'state' of the Car.
        Public petName As String
        Public currSpeed As Integer

        'The functionality of the Car.
        Public Sub PrintState()
Console.WriteLine("{0} is going {1} MPH.", petName, currSpeed)
        End Sub

        Public Sub SpeedUp(delta As Integer)
                currSpeed += delta
        End Sub
End Class
```

PrintState() is more or less a diagnostic function that will simply dump the current state of a given Car object to the command window. SpeedUp() will increase the speed of the Car by the amount specified by the incoming Integer parameter. Now, update your Main() method in the Module1 Module with the following code:

```
Module Module1
    Sub Main()
     Console.WriteLine("***** Fun with Class Types *****" & vbLf)

        'Allocate and configure a Car object.
        Dim myCar As New Car()
        myCar.petName = "Henry"
        myCar.currSpeed = 10

        'Speed up the car a few times and print out the
      'new state.
        For i=0 to 10
                myCar.SpeedUp(5)
                myCar.PrintState()
        Next
        Console.ReadLine()
    End Sub
End Module
```

Once you run your program, you will see that the **Car** variable (**myCar**) maintains its current state throughout the life of the application, as shown in the following code:

```
***** Fun with Class Types *****


Henry is going 15 MPH.

Henry is going 20 MPH.

Henry is going 25 MPH.

Henry is going 30 MPH.

Henry is going 35 MPH.

Henry is going 40 MPH.

Henry is going 45 MPH.

Henry is going 50 MPH.

Henry is going 55 MPH.

Henry is going 60 MPH.

Henry is going 65 MPH.
```

Allocating Objects with the New Keyword

As shown in the previous code example, objects must be allocated into memory using the **New** keyword. If you do not make use of the **New** keyword and attempt to make use of your class variable in a subsequent code statement, you will receive a compiler error. For example, the following **Main()** method will not compile:

```
Sub Main()
        Console.WriteLine("***** Fun with Class Types *****" & vbLf)

        ' Error! Forgot to use 'New' to create object!
        Dim myCar As Car
        myCar.petName = "nFred"
End Sub
```

To correctly create an object using the **New** keyword, you may define and allocate a **Car** object on a single line of code:

```
Sub Main()
        Console.WriteLine("***** Fun with Class Types *****" & vbLf)
        Dim myCar As New Car()
        myCar.petName = "Fred"
End Sub
```

As an alternative, if you wish to declare a variable and allocate a class instance on separate lines of code, you may do so as follows:

```
Sub Main()
        Console.WriteLine("***** Fun with Class Types *****" & vbLf)

        Dim myCar As Car
        myCar = New Car()
        myCar.petName = "Fred"
End Sub
```

Here, the first code statement simply declares a reference to a yet-to-be-determined Car object. It is not until you assign a reference to an object that this reference points to a valid object in memory.

In any case, at this point we have a trivial class that defines a few points of data and some basic methods. To enhance the functionality of the current Car class, we need to understand the role of *constructors*.

Understanding Constructors

Given that objects have state (represented by the values of an object's member variables), a programmer will typically want to assign relevant values to the object's field data before use. Currently, the Car class demands that the petName and currSpeed fields be assigned on a field-by-field basis. For the current example, this is not too problematic, given that we have only two public data points. However, it is not uncommon for a class to have dozens of fields to contend with. Clearly, it would be undesirable to author 20 initialization statements to set 20 points of data!

Thankfully, VB 2010 supports the use of *constructors*, which allow the state of an object to be established at the time of creation. A constructor is a special method of a class that is called indirectly when creating an object using the New keyword. However, unlike a "normal" method, constructors never have a return value (not even Sub) and are always implemented as a subroutine named New().

The Role of the Default Constructor

Every VB 2010 class is provided with a freebee *default constructor* that you may redefine if need be. By definition, a default constructor never takes arguments. After allocating the new object into memory, the default constructor ensures that all field data of the class is set to an appropriate default value (see Chapter 3 for information regarding the default values of VB 2010 data types).

If you are not satisfied with these default assignments, you may redefine the default constructor to suit your needs. To illustrate, update your VB 2010 **Car** class as follows:

```
Public Class Car
    ' The 'state' of the Car.
        Public petName As String
        Public currSpeed As Integer

        'A custom default constructor.
        Public Sub New()
                petName = "Chuck"
                currSpeed = 10
        End Sub
        ...
End Class
```

In this case, we are forcing all **Car** objects to begin life named **Chuck** at a rate of 10 mph. With this, you are able to create a **Car** object set to these default values as follows:

```
Module Module1
    Sub Main()
        Console.WriteLine("***** Fun with Class Types *****" & vbLf)

        'Invoking the default constructor.
        Dim chuck As New Car()

        ' Prints "Chuck is going 10 MPH."
        chuck.PrintState()
        ...
    End Sub
End Module
```

Defining Custom Constructors

Typically, classes define additional constructors beyond the default. In doing so, you provide the object user with a simple and consistent way to initialize the state of an object directly at the time of creation. Ponder the following update to the **Car** class, which now supports a total of three constructors:

```
Public Class Car
    'The 'state' of the Car.
        Public petName As String
        Public currSpeed As Integer

        Public Sub New()
                petName = "Chuck"
                currSpeed = 10
        End Sub
```

```vb
        'Here, currSpeed will receive the
       'default value of an Integer (zero).
        Public Sub New(ByVal pn As String)
                petName = pn
        End Sub

        'Let caller set the full state of the Car.
        Public Sub New(ByVal pn As String, ByVal cs As Integer)
                petName = pn
                currSpeed = cs
        End Sub
        ...
End Class
```

Keep in mind that what makes one constructor different from another (in the eyes of the VB 2010 compiler) is the number of and type of constructor arguments. Recall from Chapter 4, when you define a method of the same name that differs by the number or type of arguments, you have overloaded the method. Thus, the Car class has overloaded the constructor to provide a number of ways to create an object at the time of declaration. In any case, you are now able to create Car objects using any of the public constructors. For example:

```vb
Sub Main()
        Console.WriteLine("***** Fun with Class Types *****" & vbLf)

        'Make a Car called Chuck going 10 MPH.
        Dim chuck As New Car()
        chuck.PrintState()

        'Make a Car called Mary going 0 MPH.
        Dim mary As New Car("Mary")
        mary.PrintState()

        'Make a Car called Daisy going 75 MPH.
        Dim daisy As New Car("Daisy", 75)
        daisy.PrintState()
   ...
End Sub
```

The Default Constructor Revisited

As you have just learned, all classes are provided with a free default constructor. Thus, if you insert a new class into your current project named Motorcycle, defined like so:

```vb
Public Class Motorcycle

        Public Sub PopAWheely()
                Console.WriteLine("Yeeeeeee Haaaaaeewww!")
        End Sub
End Class
```

you are able to create an instance of the `Motorcycle` type via the default constructor out of the box:

```
Sub Main()
        Console.WriteLine("***** Fun with Class Types *****" & vbLf)
        Dim mc As New Motorcycle()
        mc.PopAWheely()
        ...
End Sub
```

However, as soon as you define a custom constructor, the default constructor is silently removed from the class and is no longer available! Think of it this way: if you do not define a custom constructor, the VB 2010 compiler grants you a default in order to allow the object user to allocate an instance of your type with field data set to the correct default values. However, when you define a unique constructor, the compiler assumes you have taken matters into your own hands.

Therefore, if you wish to allow the object user to create an instance of your type with the default constructor, as well as your custom constructor, you must *explicitly* redefine the default. To this end, understand that in a vast majority of cases, the implementation of the default constructor of a class is intentionally empty, as all you require is the ability to create an object with default values. Consider the following update to the `Motorcycle` class:

```
Public Class Motorcycle
        Public driverIntensity As Integer

        Public Sub PopAWheely()
                For i=0 to driverIntensity
                        Console.WriteLine("Yeeeeeee Haaaaaeewww!")
                Next
        End Sub

        'Put back the default constructor, which will
          'set all data members to default vaules.
        Public Sub New()
        End Sub

        Public Sub New(ByVal intensity As Integer)
                driverIntensity = intensity
        End Sub
End Class
```

The Role of the Me Keyword

VB 2010 supplies a `Me` keyword that provides access to the current class instance. One possible use of the `Me` keyword is to resolve scope ambiguity, which can arise when an incoming parameter is named identically to a data field of the type. Of course, ideally you would simply adopt a naming convention that does not result in such ambiguity; however, to illustrate this use of the `Me` keyword, update your `Motorcycle` class with a new `String` field (named `name`) to represent the driver's name. Next, add a method named `SetDriverName()` implemented as follows:

```
Public Class Motorcycle

        Public driverIntensity As Integer

        'New members to represent the name of the driver.
        Public name As String
        Public Sub SetDriverName(ByVal name As String)
                name = name
        End Sub
        ...
End Class
```

This code will compile just fine. To illustrate, update `Main()` to call `SetDriverName()` and then print out the value of the `name` field, you may be surprised to find that the value of the `name` field is an empty string!

```
'Make a Motorcycle with a rider named Tiny?
Dim c As New Motorcycle(5)
c.SetDriverName("Tiny")
c.PopAWheely()

'Prints an empty name value!
Console.WriteLine("Rider name is {0}", c.name)
```

The problem is that the implementation of `SetDriverName()` is assigning the incoming parameter *back to itself* given that the compiler assumes `name` is referring to the variable currently in the method scope rather than the `name` field at the class scope. To inform the compiler that you wish to set the current object's `name` data field to the incoming `name` parameter, simply use `Me` to resolve the ambiguity:

```
Public Sub SetDriverName(ByVal name As String)
        Me.name = name
End Sub
```

Do understand that if there is no ambiguity, you are not required to make use of the `Me` keyword when a class wishes to access its own data fields or members, as `Me` is implied. For example, if we rename the `String` data member from `name` to `driverName` (which will also require you to update your `Main()` method) the use of `Me` is optional as there is no longer a scope ambiguity:

```
Public Class Motorcycle
    Public driverIntensity As Integer
    Public driverName As String

    Public Sub SetDriverName(ByVal name As String)
        'These two statements are functionally the same.
        driverName = name
        Me.driverName = name
    End Sub
    ...
End Class
```

Even though there is little to be gained when using Me in unambiguous situations, you may still find Me keyword useful when implementing class members, as IDEs such as Visual Studio 2010 will enable IntelliSense when Me is specified. This can be very helpful when you have forgotten the name of a class member and want to quickly recall the definition. Consider Figure 5-2.

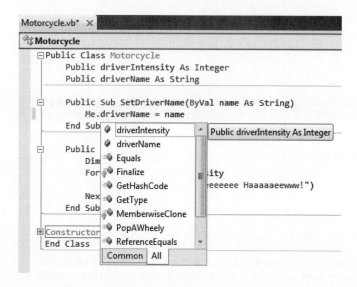

Figure 5-2. The IntelliSense of Me

■ **Note** It is a compiler error to use the Me keyword within the implementation of a Shared member. As you will see, Shared members operate on the class (not object) level, and therefore at the class level, there is no current object (thus no Me)!

Chaining Constructor Calls Using Me

Another use of the Me keyword is to design a class using a technique termed *constructor chaining*. This language feature is helpful when you have a class that defines multiple constructors. Given the fact that constructors often validate the incoming arguments to enforce various business rules, it can be quite common to find redundant validation logic within a class's constructor set. Consider the following updated Motorcycle:

```
Public Class Motorcycle

        Public driverIntensity As Integer
        Public driverName As String

        'Redundent constructor logic!
        Public Sub New()
        End Sub

        Public Sub New(ByVal intensity As Integer)
                If intensity > 10 Then
                        intensity = 10
                End If
                driverIntensity = intensity
        End Sub

        Public Sub New(ByVal intensity As Integer,ByVal name As String)
                If intensity > 10 Then
                        intensity = 10
                End If
                driverIntensity = intensity
                driverName = name
        End Sub
        ...
End Class
```

Here, perhaps in an attempt to ensure the safety of the rider, each constructor is ensuring that the intensity level is never greater than 10. While this is all well and good, you do have redundant code statements in two constructors. This is less than ideal, as you are now required to update code in multiple locations if your rules change (for example, if the intensity should not be greater than 5).

One way to improve the current situation is to define a method in the Motorcycle class that will validate the incoming argument(s). If you were to do so, each constructor could make a call to this method before making the field assignment(s). While this approach does allow you to isolate the code you need to update when the business rules change, you are now dealing with the following redundancy:

```
Public Class Motorcycle

        Public driverIntensity As Integer
        Public driverName As String

        'Constructors.
        Public Sub New()
        End Sub

        Public Sub New(ByVal intensity As Integer)
                SetIntensity(intensity)
        End Sub
```

```
        Public Sub New(ByVal intensity As Integer,ByVal name As String)
                SetIntensity(intensity)
                driverName = name
        End Sub

        Public Sub SetIntensity(ByVal intensity As Integer)
                If intensity > 10 Then
                        intensity = 10
                End If
                driverIntensity = intensity
        End Sub
        ...
End Class
```

A cleaner approach is to designate the constructor that takes the *greatest number of arguments* as the "master constructor" and have its implementation perform the required validation logic. The remaining constructors can make use of `Me.New()` to forward the incoming arguments to the master constructor and provide any additional parameters as necessary. In this way, you only need to worry about maintaining a single constructor for the entire class, while the remaining constructors are basically empty.

Here is the final iteration of the `Motorcycle` class (with one additional constructor for the sake of illustration). Note that when you use `Me.New()` to call another constructor, this must be the first statement in your constructor.

```
Public Class Motorcycle

        Public driverIntensity As Integer
        Public driverName As String

        'Constructor chaining.
        Public Sub New()
        End Sub

        Public Sub New(ByVal intensity As Integer)
                Me.New(intensity, "")
        End Sub

        Public Sub New(ByVal name As String)
                Me.New(0, name)
        End Sub

        'This is the 'master' constructor that does all the real work.
        Public Sub New(ByVal intensity As Integer,ByVal name As String)
                If intensity > 10 Then
                        intensity = 10
                End If
```

```
                driverIntensity = intensity
                driverName = name
        End Sub
        ...
End Class
```

Understand that using the Me keyword to chain constructor calls is never mandatory. However, when you make use of this technique, you do tend to end up with a more maintainable and concise class definition. Again, using this technique you can simplify your programming tasks, as the real work is delegated to a single constructor (typically the constructor that has the most parameters), while the other constructors simply "pass the buck."

Observing Constructor Flow

On a final note, do know that once a constructor passes arguments to the designated master constructor (and that constructor has processed the data), the constructor invoked originally by the caller will finish executing any remaining code statements. To clarify, update each of the constructors of the Motorcycle class with a fitting call to Console.WriteLine():

```
Public Class Motorcycle

        Public driverIntensity As Integer
        Public driverName As String

        'Constructor chaining.
        Public Sub New()
                Console.WriteLine("In default ctor")
        End Sub

        Public Sub New(ByVal intensity As Integer)
                Me.New(intensity, "")
                Console.WriteLine("In ctor taking an Integer")
        End Sub

        Public Sub New(ByVal name As String)
                Me.New(0, name)
                Console.WriteLine("In ctor taking a String")
        End Sub

        'This is the 'master' constructor that does all the real work.
        Public Sub New(ByVal intensity As Integer,ByVal name As String)
                Console.WriteLine("In master ctor ")
                If intensity > 10 Then
                        intensity = 10
                End If
                driverIntensity = intensity
                driverName = name
        End Sub
        ...
End Class
```

Now, ensure your `Main()` method exercises a `Motorcycle` object as follows:

```
Sub Main()
        Console.WriteLine("***** Fun with class Types *****" & vbLf)

        ' Make a Motorcycle.
        Dim c As New Motorcycle(5)
        c.SetDriverName("Tiny")
        c.PopAWheely()
        Console.WriteLine("Rider name is {0}", c.driverName)
        Console.ReadLine()
End Sub
```

With this, ponder the output from the previous `Main()` method:

```
***** Fun with class Types *****


In master ctor

In ctor taking an Integer

Yeeeeeee Haaaaaeewww!

Yeeeeeee Haaaaaeewww!

Yeeeeeee Haaaaaeewww!

Yeeeeeee Haaaaaeewww!

Yeeeeeee Haaaaaeewww!

Yeeeeeee Haaaaaeewww!

Rider name is Tiny
```

As you can see, the flow of constructor logic is as follows:

- You create your object by invoking the constructor requiring a single `Integer`.

- This constructor forwards the supplied data to the master constructor and provides any additional startup arguments not specified by the caller.

- The master constructor assigns the incoming data to the object's field data.

- Control is returned to the constructor originally called, and executes any remaining code statements.

The nice thing about using constructor chaining is that this programming pattern will work with .NET platform and any version of the VB.NET language but not for an un-managed version like VB6 or earlier. However, if you are targeting .NET 4.0 and higher, you can further simplify your programming tasks by making use of optional arguments as an alternative to traditional constructor chaining.

Revisiting Optional Arguments

In Chapter 4, you learned about optional and named arguments. Recall that optional arguments allow you to define supplied default values to incoming arguments. If the caller is happy with these defaults, they are not required to specify a unique value, however they may do so to provide the object with custom data. Consider the following version of Motorcycle which now provides a number of ways to construct objects using a *single* constructor definition:

```
Public Class Motorcycle

    'Single constructor using optional args.
Public Sub New(Optional ByVal intensity As Integer=0,Optional ByVal name As String="")
            If intensity > 10 Then
                    intensity = 10
            End If
            driverIntensity = intensity
            driverName = name
        End Sub
    ...
End Class
```

With this one constructor, you are now able to create a new Motorcycle object using zero, one, or two arguments. Recall that named argument syntax allows you to essentially skip over acceptable default settings (see Chapter 3).

```
Sub MakeSomeBikes()
        ' driverName = "" , driverIntensity = 0
          Dim m1 As New Motorcycle()
Console.WriteLine("Intensity= {0}, Name= {1} ", m1. driverIntensity, m1.driverName)

        ' driverName = "Tiny", driverIntensity = 0
        Dim m2 As New Motorcycle(name:"Tiny")
Console.WriteLine("Intensity= {0}, Name= {1} ", m2. driverIntensity, m2.driverName)

        ' driverName = "", driverIntensity = 7
        Dim m3 As New Motorcycle(7)
Console.WriteLine("Intensity= {0}, Name= {1}", m3. driverIntensity, m3.driverName)
End Sub
```

While the use of optional/named arguments is a very slick way to streamline how you define the set of constructors used by a given class, do always remember that this syntax will lock you into compiling your software under VB 2010 and running your code under .NET 4.0. If you need to build classes which can run under any version of the .NET platform, it is best to stick to classical constructor chaining techniques.

In any case, at this point you are able to define a class with field data (aka member variables) and various members such as methods and constructors. Next up, let's formalize the role of the **Shared** keyword.

■ **Source Code** The SimpleClassExample project is included under the Chapter 5 subdirectory.

Understanding the Shared Keyword

A VB 2010 class may define any number of *Shared members* using the **Shared** keyword. When you do so, the member in question must be invoked directly from the class level, rather than from an object reference. To illustrate the distinction, consider your good friend **System.Console**. As you have seen, you do not invoke the **WriteLine()** method from the object level:

```
'Error!  WriteLine() is not an object level method!
Dim c As New Console()
c.WriteLine("I can't be printed...")
```

but instead simply prefix the class name to the Shared **WriteLine()** member:

```
'Correct!  WriteLine() is a Shared method.
Console.WriteLine("Thanks...")
```

Simply put, Shared members are items that are deemed (by the class designer) to be so commonplace that there is no need to create an instance of the type when invoking the member. While any class can define Shared members, they are most commonly found within "utility classes." For example, if you were to use the Visual Studio 2010 object browser (via the View ➤ Object Browser menu item) to view the **System** namespace of **mscorlib.dll**, you will see that all of the members of the **Console**, **Math**, **Environment**, and **GC** classes (among others) expose all of their functionality via Shared members.

Defining Shared Methods

Assume you have a new Console Application project named SharedMethods and have inserted a class named **Teenager** that defines a Shared method named **Complain()**. This method returns a random **string**, obtained in part by calling a Shared helper function named **GetRandomNumber()**:

```
Public Class Teenager

        Public Shared r As New Random()

        Public Function GetRandomNumber(ByVal upperLimit As Short) As    Integer
                Return r.Next(upperLimit)
        End Function

        Public Shared Function Complain() As String
        Dim messages As String() = {"Do I have to?", "He started it!", "I'm too tired...",
        "I hate school!", "You are sooooooo wrong!"}
                Return messages(GetRandomNumber(5))
        End Function
End Class
```

Notice that the **System.Random** member variable and the **GetRandomNumber()** helper function method have also been declared as Shared members of the **Teenager** class, given the rule that Shared members such as the **Complain()** method can operate only on other Shared members.

■ **Note** Allow me to repeat myself: Shared members can operate only on Shared data and call Shared methods of the defining class. If you attempt to make use of nonShared class data or call a nonShared method of the class within a Shared member's implementation, you'll receive compile-time errors.

Like any Shared member, to call **Complain()**, prefix the name of the defining class:

```
Sub Main()
        Console.WriteLine("***** Fun with Shared Methods *****" & vbLf)

For i=0 To 5
                Console.WriteLine(Teenager.Complain())
        Next
        Console.ReadLine()
End Sub
```

■ **Source Code** The SharedMethods application is located under the Chapter 5 subdirectory.

Defining Shared Field Data

In addition to Shared methods, a class may also define Shared field data such as the **Random** member variable seen in the previous **Teenager** class. Understand that when a class defines nonShared data (properly referred to as *instance data*), each object of this type maintains an independent copy of the field. For example, assume a class that models a savings account is defined in a new Console Application project named SharedData:

```
'A simple savings account class.
Public Class SavingsAccount
        Public currBalance As Double

        Public Sub New(ByVal balance As Double)
            currBalance = balance
        End Sub
End Class
```

When you create SavingsAccount objects, memory for the currBalance field is allocated for each object. Shared data, on the other hand, is allocated once and Shared among all objects of the same class category. To illustrate the usefulness of Shared data, add a Shared point of data named currInterestRate to the SavingsAccount class, which is set to a default value of 0.04:

```
'A simple savings account class.
Public Class SavingsAccount
        Public currBalance As Double
        Public Shared currInterestRate As Double = 0.04

        Public Sub New(ByVal balance As Double)
            currBalance = balance
        End Sub
End Class
```

If you were to create three instances of SavingsAccount in Main()as follows:

```
Sub Main()
        Console.WriteLine("***** Fun with Shared Data *****" & vbLf)
        Dim s1 As New SavingsAccount(50)
Dim s2 As New SavingsAccount(100)
        Dim s3 As New SavingsAccount(10000.75)
        Console.ReadLine()
End Sub
```

the in-memory data allocation would look something like Figure 5-3.

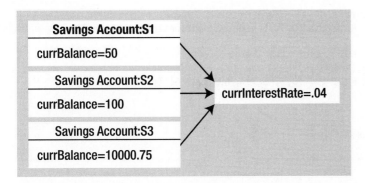

Figure 5-3. Shared data is allocated once and Shared among all instances of the class.

Let's update the `SavingsAccount` class to define two Shared methods to get and set the interest rate value:

```
'A simple savings account class.
Public Class SavingsAccount

        Public currBalance As Double

        'A Shared point of data.
        Public Shared currInterestRate As Double = 0.04

        Public Sub New(ByVal balance As Double)
                currBalance = balance
        End Sub

        'Shared members to get/set interest rate.
Public Shared Function GetInterestRate() As Double
                Return currInterestRate
        End Function

        Public Shared Sub SetInterestRate(ByVal newRate As Double)
                currInterestRate = newRate
        End Sub

End Class
```

Now, observe the following usage:

```
Sub Main()
        Console.WriteLine("***** Fun with Shared Data *****" & vbLf)

        Dim s1 As New SavingsAccount(50)
        Dim s2 As New SavingsAccount(100)
```

```
        'Print the current interest rate.
        Console.WriteLine("Interest Rate is: {0}", SavingsAccount.GetInterestRate())

        'Make new object, this does NOT 'reset' the interest rate
        Dim s3 As New SavingsAccount(10000.75)
        Console.WriteLine("Interest Rate is: {0}", SavingsAccount.GetInterestRate())
        Console.ReadLine()
End Sub
```

The output of the previous Main() is seen here:

```
***** Fun with Shared Data *****



Interest Rate is: 0.04

Interest Rate is: 0.04
```

As you can see, when you create new instances of the SavingsAccount class, the value of the Shared data is not reset, as the CLR will allocate the data into memory exactly one time. After that point, all objects of type SavingsAccount operate on the same value.

When designing any VB 2010 class, one of your design challenges is to determine which pieces of data should be defined as Shared members, and which should not. While there are no hard and fast rules, remember that a Shared data field is Shared by all objects of that type. Therefore, if you are defining a point of data that *all* objects should share between them, Shared is the way to go.

Consider what would happen if the interest rate variable were *not* defined using the Shared keyword. This would mean every SavingsAccount object would have its own copy of the currInterestRate field. Now, assume you created 100 SavingsAccount objects, and need to change the interest rate. That would require you to call the SetInterestRate() method 100 times! Clearly, this would not be a very useful way to model shared data. Again, shared data is perfect when you have a value that should be common to all objects of that category.

Defining Shared Constructors

Recall that constructors are used to set the value of an object's data at the time of creation. Thus, if you were to assign a value to a Shared data member within an instance-level constructor, you won't be surprised to find that the value is reset each time you create a new object! For example, assume you have updated the SavingsAccount class as follows:

```
Public Class SavingsAccount

    Public currBalance As Double
        Public Shared currInterestRate As Double
```

```
        'Notice that our constructor is setting
        'the Shared currInterestRate value.

        Public Sub New(ByVal balance As Double)
              Console.WriteLine("Setting currInterestRate to 0.04")
                    currInterestRate = 0.04
                    currBalance = balance
          End Sub
          ...
End Class
```

If you execute the previous `Main()` method, you would see that the `currInterestRate` variable is reset each time you create a new `SavingsAccount` object, and it is always set to `0.04`. Clearly, setting the values of Shared data in a normal instance level constructor sort of defeats the whole purpose. Every time you make a new object, the class level data is reset! One approach to setting a Shared field is to use member initialization syntax, as you did originally:

```
Public Class SavingsAccount
        Public currBalance As Double

        'A Shared point of data.
        Public Shared currInterestRate As Double = 0.04
        ...
End Class
```

This approach will ensure the Shared field is assigned only once, regardless of how many objects you create. However, what if the value for your Shared data needed to be obtained at runtime? For example, in a typical banking application, the value of an interest rate variable would be read from a database or external file. To perform such tasks requires a method scope such as a constructor to execute the code statements.

For this very reason, VB 2010 allows you to define a Shared constructor, which allows you to safely set the values of your Shared data. Consider the following update:

```
Public Class SavingsAccount
        Public currBalance As Double
        Public Shared currInterestRate As Double

        Public Sub New(ByVal balance As Double)
                currBalance = balance
        End Sub

        ' A Shared constructor!
        Shared Sub New()
                Console.WriteLine("In Shared ctor!")
                currInterestRate = 0.04
        End Sub
        ...
End Class
```

Simply put, a Shared constructor is a special constructor that is an ideal place to initialize the values of Shared data when the value is not known at compile time (e.g., you need to read in the value from an external file or generate a random number). Here are a few points of interest regarding Shared constructors:

- A given class may define only a single Shared constructor. In other words, the Shared constructor cannot be overloaded.

- A Shared constructor should not be declared as Public and cannot take any parameters.

- A Shared constructor executes exactly one time, regardless of how many objects of the type are created.

- The runtime invokes the Shared constructor when it creates an instance of the class or before accessing the first Shared member invoked by the caller.

- The Shared constructor executes before any instance-level constructors.

Given this modification, when you create new `SavingsAccount` objects, the value of the Shared data is preserved, as the Shared member is set only one time within the Shared constructor, regardless of the number of objects created.

Defining Modules in VB 2010

Visual Basic 2010 supports a specific programming construct termed a *module*, which is declared with the `Module` keyword. For example, when you create a Console Application project using Visual Studio 2010, you automatically receive a `*.vb` file that contains the following code:

```
Module Module1
  Sub Main()
  End Sub
End Module
```

Under the hood, the `Module` keyword defines a class type, with a few notable exceptions. First and foremost, any Public function, subroutine, property, or member variable defined within the scope of a module is exposed as a "shared member" that is directly accessible throughout an application. Simply put, *Shared members* allow you to simulate a global scope within your application.

You can add a Module to your VB 2010 Project by selecting the project by right-clicking and then choose Module from the provided templates, as shown in Figure 5-4.

Figure 5-4. Add a Module to your VB 2010 Project

■ **Note** If you need to implement shared functionality (for example, to provide general utility functionality) it's a good practice to define a Module.

At first glance, this might seem like a fairly useless feature, given that a class that cannot be created does not appear all that helpful. However, if you create a class that contains nothing but Shared members and/or constant data, the class has no need to be instantiated in the first place. Consider the following new Shared class type:

```
' Modules can only contain Shared members.
' You can't actually use the Shared keyword explicitly
' members are Shared implicitly
Module TimeUtilModule
    Public Sub PrintTime()
        Console.WriteLine(DateTime.Now.ToShortTimeString())
    End Sub

    Public Sub PrintDate()
        Console.WriteLine(DateTime.Today.ToShortDateString())
    End Sub
End Module
```

Given that all the members in Module are implicitly Shared, you cannot create an instance of TimeUtilModule using the New keyword. Rather, all functionality is exposed via module name itself:

```
Sub Main()
        Console.WriteLine("***** Fun with Shared Data *****" & vbLf)

        'This is just fine.
        TimeUtilModule PrintDate()
        TimeUtilModule PrintTime()

        'Compiler error! Can't create and instance of a Module!
        Dim u As New TimeUtilModule()
    ...
End Sub
```

There are a few other ways to achieve the effect of a non-instantiable type. The only way to prevent the creation of a Module class that only exposed Shared functionality was to either redefine the default constructor using the Private keyword or mark the class as an abstract type using the VB 2010 MustInherit keyword (full details regarding abstract types are in Chapter 6). Consider the following approaches:

```
Public Class TimeUtilClass2
    'Redefine the default ctor as Private
    'to prevent creation.
    Private Sub New()
    End Sub

    Public Shared Sub PrintTime()
            Console.WriteLine(DateTime.Now.ToShortTimeString())
    End Sub

    Public Shared Sub PrintDate()
            Console.WriteLine(DateTime.Today.ToShortDateString())
    End Sub

End Class

' Define type as MustInherit to prevent creation.
Public MustInherit Class TimeUtilClass3
        Public Shared Sub PrintTime()
                Console.WriteLine(DateTime.Now.ToShortTimeString())
        End Sub

        Public Shared Sub PrintDate()
                Console.WriteLine(DateTime.Today.ToShortDateString())
        End Sub
End Class
```

While these constructs are still permissible, the use of modules is a cleaner solution and more type-safe, given that the previous two techniques allowed nonshared members to appear within the class definition without error. This would be a big problem! If you had a class that was no longer creatable, you would have a chunk of functionality (e.g., all the non-shared items) which could not be used!

At this point in the chapter you hopefully feel comfortable defining simple class types containing constructors, fields, and various Shared (and nonshared) members. Now that you have the basics under your belt, you can formally investigate the three pillars of object-oriented programming.

■ **Source Code** The SharedData project is located under the Chapter 5 subdirectory.

Defining the Pillars of OOP

All object-based languages (VB 2010, C#, Java, C++, Smalltalk etc.) must contend with three core principals, often called the pillars of object-oriented programming (OOP):

- *Encapsulation*: How does this language hide an object's internal implementation details and preserve data integrity?

- *Inheritance*: How does this language promote code reuse

- *Polymorphism*: How does this language let you treat related objects in a similar way?

Before digging into the syntactic details of each pillar, it is important that you understand the basic role of each. Here is an overview of each pillar, which will be examined in full detail over the remainder of this chapter and the next.

The Role of Encapsulation

The first pillar of OOP is called *encapsulation*. This trait boils down to the language's ability to hide unnecessary implementation details from the object user. For example, assume you are using a class named DatabaseReader, which has two primary methods named Open() and Close():

```
'Assume this class encapsulates the details of opening and closing a database.
Dim dbReader As New DatabaseReader()
dbReader.Open("C:\AutoLot.mdf")

'Do something with data file and close the file.
dbReader.Close()
```

The fictitious DatabaseReader class encapsulates the inner details of locating, loading, manipulating, and closing the data file. Programmers love encapsulation, as this pillar of OOP keeps coding tasks simpler. There is no need to worry about the numerous lines of code that are working behind the scenes to carry out the work of the DatabaseReader class. All you do is create an instance and send the appropriate messages (e.g., "Open the file named AutoLot.mdf located on my C drive").

Closely related to the notion of encapsulating programming logic is the idea of data protection. Ideally, an object's state data should be specified using the Private (or possibly Protected) keyword. In this way, the outside world must ask politely in order to change or obtain the underlying value. This is a good thing, as publicly declared data points can easily become corrupted (hopefully by accident rather than intent!). You will formally examine this aspect of encapsulation in just a bit.

The Role of Inheritance

The next pillar of OOP, *inheritance*, boils down to the language's ability to allow you to build new class definitions based on existing class definitions. In essence, inheritance allows you to extend the behavior of a base (or *parent*) class by inheriting core functionality into the derived subclass (also called a *child class*). Figure 5-5 shows a simple example.

You can read the diagram in Figure 5-5 as "A Hexagon is-a Shape that is-an Object." When you have classes related by this form of inheritance, you establish *"is-a" relationships* between types. The "is-a" relationship is termed *inheritance*.

Here, you can assume that Shape defines some number of members that are common to all descendents (maybe a value to represent the color to draw the shape, and other values to represent the height and width). Given that the Hexagon class extends Shape, it inherits the core functionality defined by Shape and Object, as well as defining additional hexagon-related details of its own (whatever those may be).

■ **Note** Under the .NET platform, System.Object is always the topmost parent in any class hierarchy, which defines some general functionality for all types, fully described in Chapter 6.

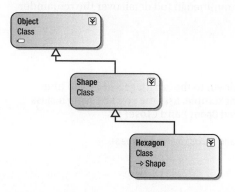

Figure 5-5. The "is-a" relationship

There is another form of code reuse in the world of OOP: the containment/delegation model also known as the "has-a" relationship or aggregation. This form of reuse is not used to establish parent/child relationships. Rather, the "has-a" relationship allows one class to define a member variable of another class and expose its functionality (if required) to the object user indirectly.

For example, assume you are again modeling an automobile. You might want to express the idea that a car "has-a" radio. It would be illogical to attempt to derive the `Car` class from a `Radio`, or vice versa (a `Car` "is-a" `Radio`? I think not!). Rather, you have two independent classes working together, where the `Car` class creates and exposes the `Radio`'s functionality:

```
Public Class Radio
        Public Sub Power(ByVal turnOn As Boolean)
                Console.WriteLine("Radio on: {0}", turnOn)
        End Sub
End Class

Public Class Car
        'Car 'has-a' Radio
        Private myRadio As New Radio()

        Public Sub TurnOnRadio(ByVal onOff As Boolean)
        'Delegate call to inner object.
                myRadio.Power(onOff)
        End Sub
End Class
```

Notice that the object user has no clue that the `Car` class is making use of an inner `Radio` object.

```
Sub Main()
      'Call is forwarded to Radio internally.
        Dim viper As New Car()
        viper.TurnOnRadio(False)
End Sub
```

The Role of Polymorphism

The final pillar of OOP is *polymorphism*. This trait captures a language's ability to treat related objects in a similar manner. Specifically, this tenant of an object-oriented language allows a base class to define a set of members (formally termed the *polymorphic interface*) that are available to all descendents. A class's polymorphic interface is constructed using any number of *Overridable* or *MustOverride* members (see Chapter 6 for full details).

In a nutshell, an *Overridable member* is a member in a base class that defines a default implementation that may be changed (or more formally speaking, *overridden*) by a derived class. In contrast, a *MustOverride method* is a member in a base class that does not provide a default implementation, but does provide a signature. When a class derives from a base class defining a *MustOverride* method, it *must* be overridden by a derived type. In either case, when derived types override the members defined by a base class, they are essentially redefining how they respond to the same request.

To preview polymorphism, let's provide some details behind the shapes hierarchy shown in Figure 5-6. Assume that the Shape class has defined an Overridable method named `Draw()` that takes no parameters. Given the fact that every shape needs to render itself in a unique manner, subclasses such as Hexagon and Circle are free to override this method to their own liking (see Figure 5-6).

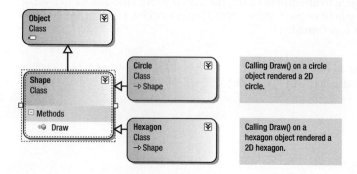

Figure 5-6. Classical polymorphism

Once a polymorphic interface has been designed, you can begin to make various assumptions in your code. For example, given that Hexagon and Circle derive from a common parent (Shape), an array of Shape objects could contain anything deriving from this base class. Furthermore, given that Shape defines a polymorphic interface to all derived types (the `Draw()` method in this example), you can assume each member in the array has this functionality.

Consider the following `Main()` method, which instructs an array of Shape-derived objects to render themselves using the `Draw()` method:

```vb
Module Module1
    Sub Main()
        Dim myShapes As Shape() = New Shape(2) {}

        myShapes(0) = New Hexagon()
        myShapes(1) = New Circle()
        myShapes(2) = New Hexagon()

        For Each s As Shape In myShapes
            'Use the polymorphic interface!
            s.Draw()
        Next
        Console.ReadLine()
    End Sub
End Module
```

This wraps up our brisk overview of the pillars of OOP. Now that you have the theory in your mind, the remainder of this chapter explores further details of how encapsulation is handled under VB 2010. Chapter 6 will tackle the details of inheritance and polymorphism.

VB 2010 Access Modifiers

When working with encapsulation, you must always take into account which aspects of a type are visible to various parts of your application. Specifically, types (classes, interfaces, structures, enumerations, and delegates) as well as their members (properties, methods, constructors, and fields) are defined using a specific keyword to control how "visible" the item is to other parts of your application. Although VB 2010 defines numerous keywords to control access, they differ on where they can be successfully applied (type or member). Table 5-1 documents the role of each access modifier and where it may be applied.

Table 5-1. *VB 2010 Access Modifiers*

VB 2010 Access Modifier	May Be Applied To	Meaning in Life
Public	Types or type members	Public items have no access restrictions. A Public member can be accessed from within the class itself as well as any derived class. A Public type can be accessed from other external assemblies.
Private	Type members or nested types	Private items can only be accessed by the class (or structure) that defines the item.
Protected	Type members or nested types	Protected items can be accessed by the class which defines it, and any child class. However, Protected items cannot be accessed from the outside world using the VB 2010 dot operator.
Friend	Types or type members	Friend items are accessible only within the current assembly. Therefore, if you define a set of Friend types within a .NET class library, other assemblies are not able to make use of them.
Protected Friend	Type members or nested types	When the Protected and Friend keywords are combined on an item, the item is accessible within the defining assembly, the defining class, and by derived classes.

In this chapter, you are only concerned with the Public and Private keywords. Later chapters will examine the role of the Friend and Protected Friend modifiers (useful when you build .NET code libraries) and the Protected modifier (useful when you are creating class hierarchies).

The Default Access Modifiers

By default, a type's set of properties, subroutines, and functions are implicitly Public, while a type's set of fields are *implicitly* Private. Thus, the following class definition is automatically set to Public, while the type's default constructor is automatically set to Public:

```
'A Public class with a default constructor.
Public Class Radio
        Sub New()
        End Sub
End Class
```

Access Modifiers and Nested Types

As mentioned in Table 5-1, the `Private`, `Protected`, and `Protected Friend` access modifiers can be applied to a *nested type*. Chapter 6 will examine nesting in detail. What you need to know at this point, however, is that a nested type is a type declared directly within the scope of a class or structure. By way of example, here is a private enumeration (named `Color`) nested within a public class (named `SportsCar`):

```
Public Class SportsCar
        'OK! Nested types can be marked Private.
        Private Enum CarColor
                Red
                Green
                Blue
        End Enum
End Class
```

Here, it is permissible to apply the `Private` access modifier on the nested type. However, nonnested types (such as the `SportsCar`) can only be defined with the `Public` or `Friend` modifiers. Therefore, the following class definition is illegal:

```
'Error! Nonnested types cannot be marked Private!
Private Class SportsCar
End Class
```

Now that you have seen the access modifiers at work, you are ready to formally investigate the first pillar of OOP.

The First Pillar: VB 2010 Encapsulation Services

The concept of encapsulation revolves around the notion that an object's internal data should not be directly accessible from an object instance. Rather, if the caller wants to alter the state of an object, the user does so indirectly using accessor (i.e., "getter") and mutator (i.e., "setter") methods. In VB 2010, encapsulation is enforced at the syntactic level using the `Public`, `Private`,`Friend`, and `Protected Friend` keywords. To illustrate the need for encapsulation services, assume you have created the following class definition:

```
'A class with a single public field.
Public Class Book
        Public numberOfPages As Integer
End Class
```

The problem with public data is that the data itself has no ability to "understand" whether the current value to which they are assigned is valid with regard to the current business rules of the system.

As you know, the upper range of a VB 2010 Integer is quite large (2,147,483,647). Therefore, the compiler allows the following assignment:

```
' Humm. That is one heck of a mini-novel!
Sub Main()
        Dim miniNovel As New Book()
        miniNovel.numberOfPages = 30000000
End Sub
```

Although you have not overflowed the boundaries of the **Integer** data type, it should be clear that a mini-novel with a page count of 30,000,000 pages is a bit unreasonable. As you can see, public fields do not provide a way to trap logical upper (or lower) limits. If your current system has a business rule that states a book must be between 1 and 1,000 pages, you are at a loss to enforce this programmatically. Because of this, Public fields typically have no place in a production-level class definition.

■ **Note** To be more specific, members of a class that represent an object's state should not be marked as Public. As you will see later in this chapter, Public constants and Public read-only fields are a-okay.

Encapsulation provides a way to preserve the integrity of an object's state data. Rather than defining Public fields (which can easily foster data corruption), you should get in the habit of defining *Private data*, which is indirectly manipulated using one of two main techniques:

- Define a pair of accessor (Get) and mutator (Set) methods.

- Define a .NET property.

Whichever technique you choose, the point is that a well-encapsulated class should protect its data and hide the details of how it operates from the prying eyes of the outside world. This is often termed *black box programming*. The beauty of this approach is that an object is free to change how a given method is implemented under the hood. It does this without breaking any existing code making use of it, provided that the parameters and return values of the method remain constant.

Encapsulation Using Traditional Accessors and Mutators

Over the remaining pages in this chapter, you will be building a fairly complete class that models a general employee. To get the ball rolling, create a new Console Application named EmployeeApp and insert a new class file (named **Employee.vb**) using the Project ➤ Add class menu item. Update the **Employee** class with the following fields, methods, and constructors:

```vbnet
Public Class Employee

    'Field data.
    Private empName As String
    Private empID As Integer
    Private currPay As Single

    'Constructors.
      Public Sub New()
      End Sub

      Public Sub New(Optional ByVal name As String = "", Optional ByVal   id As Integer =
      0, Optional ByVal pay As Single = 0.0)
              empName = name
              empID = id
              currPay = pay
      End Sub

    'Methods.
    Public Sub GiveBonus(ByVal amount As Single)
            currPay += amount
    End Sub

    Public Sub DisplayStats()
            Console.WriteLine("Name: {0}", empName)
            Console.WriteLine("ID: {0}", empID)
            Console.WriteLine("Pay: {0}", currPay)
End Sub

End Class
```

Notice that the fields of the Employee class are currently defined using the **Private** keyword. Given this, the empName, empID, and currPay fields are not directly accessible from an object variable:

```vbnet
Sub Main()

    'Error! Cannot directly access Private members
    'from an object!
    Dim emp As New Employee()
    emp.empName = "Marv"

End Sub
```

If you want the outside world to interact with a worker's full name, tradition dictates defining an accessor (get method) and a mutator (set method). The role of a 'get' method is to return to the caller the current value of the underlying state data. A 'set' method allows the caller to change the current value of the underlying state data, so long as the defined business rules are met.

To illustrate, let's encapsulate the empName field. To do so, add the following Public methods to the Employee class. Notice that the SetName() method performs a test on the incoming data, to ensure the String is 15 characters or less. If it is not, an error prints to the console and returns without making a change to the empName field:

■ **Note** If this were a production level class, you would also make to check the character length for an employee's name within your constructor logic. Ignore this detail for the time being, you will clean up this code in just a bit when you examine .NET property syntax.

```
Public Class Employee

    'Field data.
    Private empName As String
    ...
    'Accessor (get method)
    Public Function GetName() As String
        Return empName
    End Function

    'Mutator (set method)
    Public Sub SetName(ByVal name As String)
        'Do a check on incoming value
    'before making assignment.
        If name.Length > 15 Then
            Console.WriteLine("Error!  Name must be less than 16 characters!")
        Else
            empName = name
        End If
    End Sub

End Class
```

This technique requires two uniquely named methods to operate on a single data point. To test your new methods, update your Main() method as follows:

```
Sub Main()
    Console.WriteLine("***** Fun with Encapsulation *****" & vbLf)

    Dim emp As New Employee("Marvin", 456, 30000)
    emp.GiveBonus(1000)
    emp.DisplayStats()
```

```
        'Use the Get/Set methods to interact with the object's name.
        emp.SetName("Marv")
        Console.WriteLine("Employee is named: {0}", emp.GetName())
        Console.ReadLine()
End Sub
```

Because of the code in your **SetName()** method, if you attempted to specify more than 15 characters (see below), you would find the hard-coded error message print to the console:

```
Sub Main()
        Console.WriteLine("***** Fun with Encapsulation *****" & vbLf)
        ...
        'Longer than 15 characters! Error will print to console.
        Dim emp2 As New Employee()
        emp2.SetName("Xena the warrior princess")
        Console.ReadLine()
End Sub
```

So far so good. You have encapsulated the private **empName** field using two methods named **GetName()** and **SetName()**. If you were to further encapsulate the data in the **Employee** class, you would need to add various additional methods (**GetID()**, **SetID()**, **GetCurrentPay()**, **SetCurrentPay()** for example). Each of the mutator methods could have within it various lines of code to check for additional business rules. While this could certainly be done, the VB 2010 language has a useful alternative notation to encapsulate class data.

Encapsulation Using .NET Properties

Although you can encapsulate a piece of field data using traditional get and set methods, .NET languages prefer to enforce data encapsulation state data using *properties*. First of all, understand that properties are just a simplification for "real" accessor and mutator methods. Therefore, as a class designer, you are still able to perform any internal logic necessary before making the value assignment (e.g., uppercase the value, scrub the value for illegal characters, check the bounds of a numerical value, and so on).

Here is the updated **Employee** class, now enforcing encapsulation of each field using property syntax rather than traditional get and set methods:

```
Public Class Employee

        Private empName As String
        Private empID As Integer
        Private currPay As Single

        'Properties!
        Public Property Name() As String
        Get
        Return empName
        End Get
                Set(ByVal value As String)
                        If value.Length > 15 Then
                                Console.WriteLine("Error!  Name must be less
                                        than 16 characters!")
```

```
            Else
                        empName = value
                End If
        End Set
     End Property

     ' We could add additional business rules to the sets of these  properties,
     'however there is no need to do so for this example.
     Public Property ID() As Integer
            Get
        Return empID
            End Get
            Set(ByVal value As Integer)
                    empID = value
            End Set
     End Property

     Public Property Pay() As Single
            Get
                    Return currPay
            End Get
            Set(ByVal value As Single)
                    currPay = value
            End Set
     End Property
     ...
End Class
```

A VB 2010 property is composed of a **Property** keyword, a **Get/End Get** scope (accessor) and **Set/End Set** scope (mutator), and a value parameter that is directly within the property itself. A **Get** accessor is meant for reading the value from a property, and **Set** is used to assign a value to the property, which is achieved by the value parameter. Notice that the property specifies the type of data it is encapsulating by what appears to be a return value. Also take note that, like a method, properties make use of the **Property** keyword and parentheses when being defined. Consider the commentary on your current **ID** property:

```
        ' The 'Integer' represents the type of data this property encapsulates.
        ' The data type must be identical to the related field (empID).
        Public Property ID() As Integer
                Get
                                Return empID
                End Get
                Set(ByVal value As Integer)
                                empID = value
                End Set
        End Property
```

Within a 'Set' scope of a property, you use a token named **value**, which is used to represent the incoming value used to assign the property by the caller. This token is *not* a true VB 2010 keyword, but it is what is known as a *contextual keyword*. This contextual keyword (value) always represents the value being assigned by the caller, and it will always be the same underlying data type as the property itself. Thus, notice how the **Name** property can still test the range of the **String** as so:

```
Public Property Name() As String
  Get
        Return empName
  End Get
  Set(ByVal value As String)
         If value.Length > 15 Then
Console.WriteLine("Error!  Name must be less than 16 characters!")
       Else
                  empName = value
          End If
   End Set
End Property
```

Once you have these properties in place, it appears to the caller that it is getting and setting a *public point* of data; however, the correct **Get** and **Set** block is called behind the scenes to preserve encapsulation:

```
Sub Main()
        Console.WriteLine("***** Fun with Encapsulation *****" & vbLf)

        Dim emp As New Employee("Marvin", 456, 30000)
        emp.GiveBonus(1000)
        emp.DisplayStats()

        'Set and get the Name property.
        emp.Name = "Marv"
        Console.WriteLine("Employee is named: {0}", emp.Name)
        Console.ReadLine()
End Sub
```

Properties (as opposed to accessors and mutators) also make your types easier to manipulate, in that properties are able to respond to the intrinsic operators of VB 2010. To illustrate, assume that the **Employee** class type has an internal Private member variable representing the age of the employee. Here is the relevant update (notice the use of constructor chaining):

```
Public Class Employee
...
        'New field and property.
        Private empAge As Integer
```

```
    Public Property Age() As Integer
    Get
                        Return empAge
    End Get
    Set(ByVal value As Integer)
                        empAge = value
    End Set
    End Property

    'Updated constructors
    Public Sub New()
    End Sub

    Public Sub New(ByVal n As String,ByVal i As Integer,
    ByVal p As Single)
            Me.New(n, 0, i, p)
    End Sub

    Public Sub New(ByVal n As String,ByVal a As Integer,
    ByVal i As Integer,ByVal p  As Single)
            empName = n
            empAge = a
    empID = i
            currPay = p
    End Sub

    'Updated DisplayStats() method now accounts for age.
    Public Sub DisplayStats()
            Console.WriteLine("Name: {0}", empName)
            Console.WriteLine("ID: {0}", empID)
            Console.WriteLine("Age: {0}", empAge)
            Console.WriteLine("Pay: {0}", currPay)
    End Sub

End Class
```

Now assume you have created an **Employee** object named **joe**. On his birthday, you wish to increment the age by one. Using traditional accessor and mutator methods, you would need to write code such as the following:

```
Dim joe As New Employee()
joe.SetAge(joe.GetAge() + 1)
```

However, if you encapsulate **empAge** using a property named **Age**, you are able to simply write

```
Dim joe As New Employee()
joe.Age += 1
```

Using Properties within a Class Definition

Properties, specifically the 'Set' portion of a property, are common places to package up the business rules of your class. Currently, the Employee class has a Name property which ensures the name is no more than 15 characters. The remaining properties (ID, Pay and Age) could also be updated with any relevant logic.

While this is well and good, also consider what a class constructor typically does internally. It will take the incoming parameters, check for valid data, and then make assignments to the internal Private fields. Currently your master constructor does *not* test the incoming string data for a valid range, so you could update this member as so:

```
Public Sub New(ByVal n As String,ByVal a As Integer,ByVal iAs Integer,ByVal p As Single)

    'Humm, this seems like a problem...
    If name.Length > 15 Then
                Console.WriteLine("Error!  Name must be less than 16    characters!")
    Else
                empName = n
      empAge = a
                empID = i
      currPay = p
    End If
End Sub
```

I am sure you can see the problem with this approach. The Name property and your master constructor are performing the same error checking! If you were also making checks on the other data points, you would have a good deal of duplicate code. To streamline your code, and isolate all of your error checking to a central location, you will do well if you *always* use properties within your class whenever you need to get or set the values. Consider the following updated constructor:

```
Public Sub New(ByVal n As String,ByVal a As Integer,ByVal i As Integer,ByVal p As Single)
    'Better!  Use properties when setting class data.
    ' This reduces the amount of duplicate error checks.
    Name = n
    Age = a
    ID = i
    Pay = p
End Sub
```

Beyond updating constructors to use properties when assigning values, it is good practice to use properties throughout a class implementation, to ensure your business rules are always enforced. In many cases, the only time when you directly make reference to the underlying Private piece of data is within the property itself. With this in mind, here is your updated Employee class:

```vb
Public Class Employee

        'Field data.
        Private empName As String
        Private empID As Integer
        Private currPay As Single
        Private empAge As Integer

        'Constructors.
        Public Sub New()
        End Sub

        Public Sub New(ByVal n As String,ByVal i As Integer,ByVal    ByVal p As Single)
                Me.New(n, 0, i, p)
        End Sub

Public Sub New(ByVal n As String,ByVal a As Integer,ByVal i As Integer,ByVal p As Single)
                Name = n
                Age = a
                ID = i
                Pay = p
        End Sub

        ' Methods.
        Public Sub GiveBonus(ByVal amount As Single)
                Pay += amount
        End Sub

        Public Sub DisplayStats()
                Console.WriteLine("Name: {0}", Name)
                Console.WriteLine("ID: {0}", ID)
                Console.WriteLine("Age: {0}", Age)
                Console.WriteLine("Pay: {0}", Pay)
        End Sub

        'Properties as before...
        ...
End Class
```

Internal Representation of Properties

Many programmers who use traditional accessor and mutator methods, often name these methods using get_ and set_ prefixes (e.g., get_Name() and set_Name()). This naming convention itself is not problematic as far as VB 2010 is concerned. However, it is important to understand that under the hood, a property is represented in CIL code using this same naming convention.

For example, if you open up the EmployeeApp.exe assembly using ildasm.exe, you see that each property is mapped to hidden get_XXX()/set_XXX() methods called internally by the CLR (see Figure 5-7).

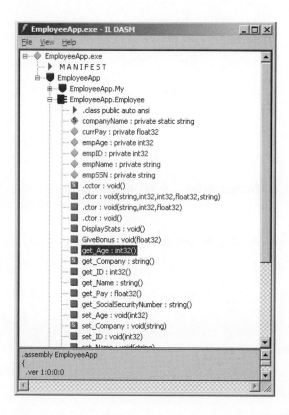

Figure 5-7. *A property is represented by get/set methods internally.*

Assume the Employee type now has a Private String member variable named empSSN to represent an individual's Social Security number, which is manipulated by a property named SocialSecurityNumber (and also assume you have updated your type's custom constructors and DisplayStats() method to account for this new piece of field data).

```
'Add support for a new field representing the employee's SSN.
Public Class Employee
    ...
    Private empSSN As String
    Public Property SocialSecurityNumber() As String
        Get
            Return empSSN
        End Get
        Set(ByVal value As String)
            empSSN = value
        End Set
    End Property

    'Constructors
    Public Sub New()
```

```
            End Sub

Public Sub New(ByVal n As String,ByVal i As Integer,ByVal p As Single)
            Me.New(n, 0, i, p, "")
        End Sub

Public Sub New(ByVal n As String,ByVal a As Integer,ByVal i As Integer,ByVal↵
 p As Single,ByVal s As String)
            Name = n
            Age = a
            ID = i
            Pay = p
            SocialSecurityNumber = s
        End Sub

        Public Sub DisplayStats()
            Console.WriteLine("Name: {0}", Name)
            Console.WriteLine("ID: {0}", ID)
            Console.WriteLine("Age: {0}", Age)
            Console.WriteLine("Pay: {0}", Pay)
            Console.WriteLine("SSN: {0}", SocialSecurityNumber)
        End Sub
        ...
End Class
```

When the compiler sees a property named SocialSecurityNumber(), it generates methods named get_ SocialSecurityNumber() and set_ SocialSecurityNumber(). If you tend to define these two methods in the same class, you would be issued compile-time errors:

```
'Remember, a property really maps to a Get_/Set_ pair!
Public Class Employee

    ...
    Public Function get_SocialSecurityNumber() As String
            Return empSSN
    End Function

    Public Sub set_SocialSecurityNumber(ByVal ssn As String)
            empSSN = ssn
    End Sub

End Class
```

■ **Note** The .NET base class libraries always favor type properties over traditional accessor and mutator methods when encapsulating field data. Therefore, if you wish to build custom classes that integrate well with the .NET platform, avoid defining traditional get and set methods.

Controlling Visibility Levels of Property Get/Set Statements

Unless you say otherwise, the visibility of get and set logic is solely controlled by the access modifier of the property declaration:

```
' The Get and Set logic is both Public,
' given the declaration of the property.Public Property SocialSecurityNumber() As String
        Get
                Return empSSN
        End Get
        Set(ByVal value As String)
                empSSN = value
        End Set
End Property
```

In some cases, it would be useful to specify unique accessibility levels for get and set logic. To do so, simply prefix an accessibility keyword to the appropriate Get or Set keyword (the unqualified scope takes the visibility of the property's declaration):

```
' Object users can only get the value, however
' the Employee class and derived types can set the value.
Public Property SocialSecurityNumber() As String
        Get
                Return empSSN
        End Get
        Protected Set(ByVal value As String)
                empSSN = value
        End Set
End Property
```

In this case, the set logic of SocialSecurityNumber can only be called by the current class and derived classes and therefore cannot be called from an object instance. Again, the Protected keyword will be formally detailed in the next chapter when we examine inheritance and polymorphism.

Read-Only and Write-Only Properties

When encapsulating data, you may wish to configure a *read-only property*. To do so, use the ReadOnly keyword and omit the Set block. Likewise, if you wish to have a *write-only Property*, use the WriteOnly keyword and omit the Get block. While there is no need to do so for the current example, here is how the SocialSecurityNumber property could be retrofitted as read-only:

```
Public ReadOnly Property SocialSecurityNumber() As String
        Get
                Return empSSN
        End Get
End Property
Public WriteOnly Property PhoneNumber () As String
        Set(ByVal value As String)
            pNumber = value
        End Set
```

```
End Property
```

Given this adjustment, the only manner in which an employee's Social Security number can be set is through a constructor argument.

```
Public Sub New(ByVal n As String,ByVal a As Integer,ByVal i As  Integer,ByVal p As
Single,ByVal s As String)
        Name = n
        Age = a
        ID = i
        Pay = p

        'OOPS!  This is no longer possible if the property is read only.
        SocialSecurityNumber = s
End Sub
```

If you did make this property read only, your only choice would be to use the underlying ssn member variable within your constructor logic or in any other place where you want to set the Social Security numbers.

Shared Properties

VB 2010 also supports Shared properties. Recall from earlier in this chapter that Shared members are accessed at the class level, not from an instance (object) of that class. For example, assume that the Employee type defines a Shared point of data to represent the name of the organization employing these workers. You may encapsulate the field with a Shared property as follows:

```
'Shared properties must operate on Shared data!
Public Class Employee

    ...
        Private Shared companyName As String
        Public Shared Property Company() As String
                Get
                        Return companyName
                End Get
```

```
            Set(ByVal value As String)
                    companyName = value
            End Set
      End Property
      ...
End Class
```

Shared properties are manipulated in the same manner as Shared methods, as shown here:

```
'Interact with the Shared property.
Sub Main()

    Console.WriteLine("***** Fun with Encapsulation *****" & vbLf)

    'Set company.
    Employee.Company = "Intertech Training"
    Console.WriteLine("These folks work at {0}.", Employee.Company)
    Dim emp As New Employee("Marvin", 24, 456, 30000, "111-11-1111")
    emp.GiveBonus(1000)
    emp.DisplayStats()
    Console.ReadLine()

End Sub
```

Finally, recall that classes can support Shared constructors. Thus, if you wanted to ensure that the name of the Shared companyName field was always assigned to "Intertech Training," you would write the following:

```
'Shared constructors are used to initialize Shared data.
Public Class Employee
        Private Shared comapanyName As String

        Shared Sub New()
                companyName = "Intertech Training"
        End Sub
End Class
```

Using this approach, there is no need to explicitly call the Company property to set the initial value:

```
'Automatically set to "Intertech Training" via Shared constructor.
Sub Main()
        Console.WriteLine("These folks work at {0}", Employee.Company)
End Sub
```

To wrap up the story thus far, recall that VB 2010 prefers properties to encapsulate data. These syntactic entities are used for the same purpose as traditional accessor (get)/mutator (set) methods. The benefit of properties is that the users of your objects are able to manipulate the internal data point using a single named item.

■ **Source Code** The EmployeeApp project can be found under the Chapter 5 subdirectory.

Understanding Automatic Properties

When .NET 3.5 was released, the VB 2010 language offered yet another way to define simple encapsulation services with minimal code, using automatic property syntax. To illustrate, create a new VB 2010 Console Application project named AutoProps. Now, insert a new VB 2010 class file (**Car.vb**) that defines the following class, which encapsulates a single point of data using classic property syntax.

```
'A Car type using standard property
'syntax.
Public Class Car

        Private carName As String = ""
        Public Property PetName() As String
                Get
                        Return carName
                End Get
                Set(ByVal value As String)
                        carName = value
                End Set
        End Property

End Class
```

While it is very true that most VB 2010 properties contain business rules within their set scope, it is not too uncommon that some properties literally have nothing more to do than simply assign and return the value straightaway as you see here. In these cases, it can become rather verbose to define Private backing fields and simple property definitions multiple times. By way of an example, if you are modeling a class that requires 15 Private points of field data, you end up authoring 15 related properties that are little more than thin wrappers for encapsulation services.

To streamline the process of providing simple encapsulation of field data, you may use *automatic property syntax*. As the name implies, this feature will offload the work of defining a Private backing field and the related VB 2010 property member to the compiler using a new bit of syntax. Consider the reworking of the Car class, which uses this syntax to quickly create three properties:

```
Public Class Car
      'Automatic properties!
      Public Property PetName() As StringPublic Property Speed() As Integer
      Public Property Color() As String
End Class
```

When defining automatic properties, you simply specify the access modifier, underlying data type, and property name. At compile time, your type will be provided with an autogenerated Private backing field and a fitting implementation of the Get/Set logic.

■ **Note** The name of the autogenerated Private backing field is not visible within your VB 2010 code base. The names of these auto-generated fields would be _petName, _speed and _color. The only way to see it is to make use of a tool such as ildasm.exe.

Unlike traditional VB 2010 properties, however, it is *not* possible to build read-only or write-only automatic properties. While you might think you can just omit the Get or Set within your property declaration as follows:

```
'Read-only property? Error!
Public ReadOnly Property MyReadOnlyProp() As Integer

'Write only property? Error!
Public WriteOnly Property MyWriteOnlyProp() As Integer
```

this will result in a compiler error. When you are defining an automatic property, it must support both read and write functionality.

Interacting with Automatic Properties

Because the compiler will define the Private backing field at compile time, the class defining automatic properties will always need to use property syntax to Get and Set the underlying value. This is important to note because many programmers make direct use of the Private fields *within* a class definition, which is not possible in this case. For example, if the Car class were to provide a DisplayStats() method, it would need to implement this method using the property name:

```
Public Class Car
'Automatic properties!
        Public Property PetName() As String
        Public Property Speed() As Integer
        Public Property Color() As String

        Public Sub DisplayStats()
                Console.WriteLine("Car Name: {0}", PetName)
                Console.WriteLine("Speed: {0}", Speed)
                Console.WriteLine("Color: {0}", Color)
        End Sub
End Class
```

When you are using an object defined with automatic properties, you will be able to assign and obtain the values using the expected property syntax:

```
Sub Main()
        Console.WriteLine("** Fun with Automatic Properties **" & vbLf)

        Dim c As New Car()

        c.PetName = "Frank"
        c.Speed = 55
        c.Color = "Red"

        Console.WriteLine("Your car is named {0}?  That's odd...",  c.PetName)
        c.DisplayStats()
        Console.ReadLine()
End Sub
```

Regarding Automatic Properties and Default Values

When you use automatic properties to encapsulate numerical or Boolean data, you are able to use the autogenerated type properties straightaway within your code base, as the hidden backing fields will be assigned a safe default value that can be used directly(e.g., Integer fields will be set to 0, Boolean fields will be set to False, and so on). However, be very aware that if you use automatic property syntax with reference types (e.g., String), the hidden private reference type will be set to a default value of Nothing.

Consider the following new Class named Garage, which makes use of two automatic properties:

```
Public Class Garage
'The hidden Integer backing field is set to zero!
        Public Property NumberOfCars() As Integer

        'The hidden Car backing field is set to Nothing!
        Public Property MyAuto() As Car
End Class
```

Given VB's 2010 default values for field data, you would be able to print out the value of NumberOfCars as is (as it is automatically assigned the value of zero), but if you directly invoke MyAuto, you will receive a "null reference exception" at runtime, as the Car member variable used in the background has not been assigned to a new object:

```
Sub Main()
        ...
        Dim g As New Garage()
        'OK, prints default value of zero.
        Console.WriteLine("Number of Cars: {0}", g.NumberOfCars)

        'Runtime error! Backing field is currently Nothing
        Console.WriteLine(g.MyAuto.PetName)
        Console.ReadLine()
End Sub
```

Given that the Private backing fields are created at compile time, you will be unable to make use of VB 2010 field initialization syntax to allocate the reference type directly with the New keyword. Therefore, this work will need to be done with class constructors to ensure the object comes to life in a safe manner. For example:

```
Public Class Garage
        'The hidden backing field is set to zero!
        Public Property NumberOfCars() As Integer

        'The hidden backing field is set to Nothing
        Public Property MyAuto() As Car

        'Must use constructors to override default
        'values assigned to hidden backing fields.
        Public Sub New()
                MyAuto = New Car()
                NumberOfCars = 1
        End Sub

        Public Sub New(ByVal car As Car,ByVal number As Integer)
                MyAuto = car
                NumberOfCars = number
        End Sub
End Class
```

With this update, you could now place a Car object into the Garage object as so:

```
Sub Main()
        Console.WriteLine("**Fun with Automatic Properties***" & vbLf)

        'Make a car.
        Dim c As New Car()

        c.PetName = "Frank"
        c.Speed = 55
        c.Color = "Red"
        c.DisplayStats()

        'Put car in the garage.
        Dim g As New Garage()

        g.MyAuto = c
Console.WriteLine("Number of Cars in garage: {0}", g.NumberOfCars)
        Console.WriteLine("Your car is named: {0}", g.MyAuto.PetName)
        Console.ReadLine()
End Sub
```

As you most likely agree, this is a very nice feature of the VB 2010 programming language, as you can define a number of properties for a class using a streamlined syntax. Be aware of course that if you are building a property that requires additional code beyond getting and setting the underlying Private field (such as data validation logic, writing to an event log, communicating with a database, etc.), you will be required to define a "normal" .NET property type by hand. VB 2010 automatic properties never do more than provide simple encapsulation for an underlying piece of (compiler generated) Private data.

■ **Source Note** The AutoProps project can be found under the Chapter 5 subdirectory.

Understanding Object Initializer Syntax

As seen throughout this chapter, a constructor allows you to specify start up values when creating a new object. On a related note, properties allow you to get and set underlying data in a safe manner. When you are working with other people's classes, including the classes found within the .NET base class library, it is not too uncommon to discover that there is not a single constructor which allows you to set every piece of underlying state data. Given this point, a programmer is typically forced to pick the best constructor possible, after which he or she makes assignments using a handful of provided properties.

To help streamline the process of getting an object up and running, VB 2010 offers *object initializer syntax*. Using this technique, it is possible to create a new object and assign a slew of properties and/or Public fields in a few lines of code. Syntactically, an object initializer consists of a With Keyword, followed by a set of {}. Within the {},use a dot, followed by the name of Public field or property you want to set, and then assign it the value you want to give it. To see this syntax in action, create a new Console Application named ObjectInitializers. Now, consider a simple class named **Point**, created using automatic properties (which is not mandatory for this example, but helps us write some very concise code):

```
Public Class Point
        Public Property X() As Integer
        Public Property Y() As Integer

        Public Sub New(ByVal xVal As Integer,ByVal yVal As Integer)
                X = xVal
                Y = yVal
        End Sub

        Public Sub New()
        End Sub

        Public Sub DisplayStats()
                Console.WriteLine("[{0}, {1}]", X, Y)
        End Sub
End Class
```

217

Now consider how we can make **Point** objects using any of the following approaches:

```
Sub Main()
    Console.WriteLine("***** Fun with Object Init Syntax *****" & vbLf)

    'Make a Point by setting each property manually.
    Dim firstPoint As New Point()

    firstPoint.X = 10
    firstPoint.Y = 10
    firstPoint.DisplayStats()

    'Or make a Point via a custom constructor.
    Dim anotherPoint As New Point(20, 20)
    anotherPoint.DisplayStats()

    'Or make a Point using object init syntax.
    Dim finalPoint As New Point With {.X = 30, .Y = 30}
    finalPoint.DisplayStats()
    Console.ReadLine()

End Sub
```

The final **Point** variable is not making use of a custom constructor (as one might do traditionally), but is rather setting values to the public **X** and **Y** properties. Behind the scenes, the type's default constructor is invoked, followed by setting the values to the specified properties. To this end, object initialization syntax is just shorthand notations for the syntax used to create an object using a default constructor, and setting the state data property by property.

Calling Custom Constructors with Initialization Syntax

The previous examples initialized **Point** objects by implicitly calling the default constructor on the type:

```
' Here, the default constructor is called implicitly.
Dim finalPoint As New Point With {.X = 30, .Y = 30}
```

If you wish to be very clear about this, it is permissible to explicitly call the default constructor as follows:

```
' Here, the default constructor is called explicitly.
Dim finalPoint As New Point() With {.X = 30, .Y = 30}
```

Do be aware that when you are constructing a type using the new initialization syntax, you are able to invoke *any* constructor defined by the class. Our **Point** type currently defines a two-argument constructor to set the (*x, y*) position. Therefore, the following **Point** declaration results in an **X** value of **100** and a **Y** value of **100**, regardless of the fact that our constructor arguments specified the values **10** and **16**:

```
'Calling a custom constructor.
Dim finalPoint As New Point(10,16) With {.X =100, .Y =100}
```

Given the current definition of your **Point** type, calling the custom constructor while using initialization syntax is not terribly useful (and more than a bit verbose). However, if your **Point** type provides a new constructor that allows the caller to establish a color (via a custom Enum named PointColor), the combination of custom constructors and object initialization syntax becomes clear. Assume you have updated **Point** as follows:

```vb
Public Enum PointColor
        LightBlue
        BloodRed
        Gold
End Enum

Public Class Point
        Public Property X() As Integer
        Public Property Y() As Integer
        Public Property Color() As PointColor

Public Sub New(ByVal xVal As Integer,ByVal yVal As Integer)
                X = xVal
                Y = yVal
                Color = PointColor.Gold
        End Sub

        Public Sub New(ByVal ptColor As PointColor)
                Color = ptColor
        End Sub

        Public Sub New()
                Color = PointColor.BloodRed
        End Sub

        Public Sub DisplayStats()
                Console.WriteLine("[{0}, {1}]", X, Y)
                Console.WriteLine("Point is {0}", Color)
        End Sub

End Class
```

With this new constructor, you can now create a golden point (positioned at 90, 20) as follows:

```vb
'Calling a more interesting custom constructor with init syntax.
Sub Main()
   Dim goldPoint As New Point(PointColor.Gold) with {.X=90,.Y=20}
   goldPoint.DisplayStats()
End Sub
```

Nested Objects

As briefly mentioned earlier in this chapter (and fully examined in Chapter 6), the "has-a" relationship allows us to compose new classes by defining member variables of existing classes. For example, assume you now have a `Rectangle` class, which makes use of the `Point` type to represent its upper-left/bottom-right coordinates. Since automatic properties set reference-type variables to `Nothing`, you will implement this new Class using 'traditional' property syntax:

```
Public Class Rectangle

        Dim objTL As New Point()
        Dim objBR As New Point()

        Public Property TopLeft() As Point
            Get
                Return objTL
            End Get
            Set(ByVal value As Point)
                objTL = value
            End Set
        End Property

         Public Property BottomRight() As Point
             Get
                 Return objBR
             End Get
             Set(ByVal value As Point)
                 objBR = value
             End Set
         End Property

        Public Sub DisplayStats()
            Console.WriteLine("[TopLeft: {0}, {1}, {2} BottomRight: {3}, {4}, {5}]",
objTL.X, objTL.Y, objTL.Color, objBR.X, objBR.Y, objBR.Color)
        End Sub
End Class
```

Using object initialization syntax, you could create a new `Rectangle` object and set the inner `Point`s as follows:

```
'Create and initialize a Rectangle.
Dim myRect As New Rectangle With {
        .TopLeft = New Point With {.X = 10, .Y = 10}, _
        .BottomRight = New Point With {.X = 200, .Y = 200}}
```

Again, the benefit of object initialization syntax is that it basically decreases the number of keystrokes (assuming there is not a suitable constructor). Here is the traditional approach to establishing a similar `Rectangle`:

```
'Old-school approach.
Dim r As New Rectangle()
```

```
Dim p1 As New Point()
p1.X = 10
p1.Y = 10
r.TopLeft = p1
Dim p2 As New Point()
p2.X = 200
p2.Y = 200
r.BottomRight = p2
```

While you might feel object initialization syntax can take a bit of getting used to, once you get comfortable with the code, you'll be quite pleased at how quickly you can establish the state of a new object with minimal fuss and bother.

To wrap up this chapter, allow me to close with three bite-sized topics which will round out your understanding of building well encapsulated classes, specifically constant data, read only fields, and partial class definitions.

Working with Constant Field Data

VB 2010 offers the `Const` keyword to define constant data, which can never change after the initial assignment. As you might guess, this can be helpful when you are defining a set of known values for use in your applications that are logically connected to a given class.

Assume you are building a utility class named `MyMathClass` that needs to define a value for the value PI (which you will assume to be 3.14). Begin by creating a new Console Application project named ConstData. Given that you would not want to allow other developers to change this value in code, PI could be modeled with the following constant:

```
Public Class MyMathClass
        Public Const PI As Double = 3.14
End Class

Module Module1
    Sub Main()

        Console.WriteLine("***** Fun with Const *****" & vbLf)
        Console.WriteLine("The value of PI is: {0}", MyMathClass.PI)
        'Error! Can't change a constant!
      MyMathClass.PI = 3.1444
        Console.ReadLine()

    End Sub
End Module
```

Notice that you are referencing the constant data defined by `MyMathClass` using a class name prefix (i.e., `MyMathClass.PI`). This is due to the fact that constant fields of a class are implicitly *Shared*. However, it is permissible to define and access a local constant variable within a method or property. By way of example:

```
Sub LocalConstStringVariable()
    ' A local constant data point can be directly accessed.
    Const  fixedStr As String = "Fixed string Data"
    Console.WriteLine(fixedStr)

    ' Error!
    fixedStr = "This will not work!"
End Sub
```

Regardless of where you define a constant piece of data, the one point to always remember is that the initial value assigned to the constant must be specified at the time you define the constant. Thus, if you were to modify your MyMathClass in such a way that the value of PI is assigned in a class constructor as follows:

```
Public Class MyMathClass
    'Try to set PI in ctor?
    'Public Const PI As Double
    Public Sub New()
        'Error!
        PI = 3.14
    End Sub
End Class
```

you would receive a compile-time error. The reason for this restriction has to do with the fact the value of constant data must be known at compile time. Constructors, as you know, are invoked at runtime.

Understanding Read-Only Fields

Closely related to constant data is the notion of *read-only field data* (which should not be confused with a read-only property). Like a constant, a read-only field cannot be changed after the initial assignment. However, unlike a constant, the value assigned to a read-only field can be determined at runtime, and therefore can legally be assigned within the scope of a constructor, but nowhere else.

This can be very helpful when you don't know the value of a field until runtime, perhaps because you need to read an external file to obtain the value, but wish to ensure that the value will not change after that point. For the sake of illustration, assume the following update to MyMathClass:

```
Public Class MyMathClass

    ' Read-only fields can be assigned in ctors,
    ' (or in the declaration itself)but nowhere else.
        Public ReadOnly PI As Double
        Public Sub New()
                PI = 3.14
        End Sub
End Class
```

Again, any attempt to make assignments to a field marked ReadOnly outside the scope of a constructor results in a compiler error:

```
Public Class MyMathClass

        Public ReadOnly PI As Double
        Public Sub New()
           PI = 3.14
        End Sub

        ' Error!
        Public Sub ChangePI()
            ' PI = 3.14444
        End Sub
End Class
```

Shared Read-Only Fields

Unlike a constant field, read-only fields are *not* implicitly Shared. Thus, if you wish to expose PI from the class level, you must explicitly make use of the **Shared** keyword. If you know the value of a Shared read-only field at compile time, the initial assignment looks very similar to that of a constant:

```
Public Class MyMathClass
        Public Shared ReadOnly PI As Double = 3.14
End Class

Module Module1
        Sub Main()
            Console.WriteLine("***** Fun with ReadOnly *****")
            Console.WriteLine("The value of PI is: {0}", MyMathClass.PI)
            Console.ReadLine()
        End Sub
End Module
```

However, if the value of a Shared read-only field is not known until runtime, you must make use of a Shared Function as described earlier in this chapter:

```
Public Class MyMathClass
      Public Shared ReadOnly PI As Double = ComputeValueForPI()
      Private Shared Function ComputeValueForPI() As Double
            Return 3.14
      End Function

End Class
```

■ **Source Code** The ConstData project is included under the Chapter 5 subdirectory.

Understanding Partial Types

Last but not least, it is important to understand the role of the VB 2010 `Partial` keyword. A production level class could very easily consist of hundreds and hundreds of lines of code. As well, given that a typical class is defined within a single `*.vb` file, you could end up with a very long file indeed. When you are creating your classes, it is often the case that much of the code can be basically ignored once accounted for. For example, field data, properties, and constructors tend to remain as-is during production, while methods tend to be modified quite often.

If you wish, you can partition a single class across multiple VB 2010 files, to isolate the boilerplate code from more readily useful members. To illustrate, open up the `EmployeeApp` project you created previously in this chapter into Visual Studio. Once you have done so, open the `Employee.vb` file for editing. Currently, this single file contains code from all aspects of the class:

```
Public Class Employee
     ' Field Data
     ' Constructors
     ' Methods
     ' Properties
End Class
```

Using partial classes, you could choose to move the constructors and properties into a brand new file named `Employee.Internal.vb` (please note, the name of the file is irrelevant; here I just tacked on the word Internal to represent the guts of the class). The first step is to add the `Partial` keyword to the current class definition and cut the code to be placed into the new file:

```
'Employee.vb
Partial Public Class Employee

'Methods

'Properties
End Class
```

Next, assuming you have inserted a new class file into your project, you can move the data fields and constructors to the new file using a simple cut/paste operation. In addition, you need not to add the

Partial keyword to this aspect of the class definition because when one part is Partial then whole thing is Partial. For example:

```
'Employee.Internal.vb
    Public class Employee

'Field data

'Constructors
End Class
```

■ **Note** A partial class can be defined over any number of VB 2010 code files, and only one aspect of the partial class needs to be marked with the Partial keyword. As long as each aspect of the partial class is defined in the same namespace, the compiler will assume they are related.

Once you compile the modified project, you should see no difference whatsoever. The whole idea of a partial class is only realized during design time. Once the application has been compiled, there is just a single, unified class within the assembly. The only requirement when defining partial types is that the type's name (Employee in this case) is identical and defined within the same .NET namespace.

To be honest, you will most likely not need to make use of partial class definitions too often. However, Visual Studio uses them in the background all the time. Later in this book when you start to look into GUI application development in Windows Forms, Windows Presentation Foundation, or ASP.NET, you'll see that Visual Studio isolates designer generated code into a partial class, leaving you to focus on your application specific programming logic.

■ **Source Code** The EmployeeAppWithPartial project can be found under the Chapter 5 subdirectory.

Summary

The point of this chapter was to introduce you to the role of the VB 2010 class type. As you have seen, classes can take any number of *constructors* that enable the object user to establish the state of the object upon creation. This chapter also illustrated several class design techniques (and related keywords). Recall that the Me keyword can be used to obtain access to the current object, the Shared keyword allows you to define fields and members that are bound at the class (not object) level, and the Const keyword (and ReadOnly modifier) allows you to define a point of data that can never change after the initial assignment.

The bulk of this chapter dug into the details of the first pillar of OOP: encapsulation. Here you learned about the access modifiers of VB 2010 and the role of type properties, object initialization syntax, and partial classes. With this behind you, you are now able to turn to the next chapter where you will learn to build a family of related classes using inheritance and polymorphism.

CHAPTER 6

■ ■ ■

Understanding Inheritance and Polymorphism

The previous chapter examined the first pillar of OOP: encapsulation. At that time, you learned how to build a single well-defined class type with constructors and various members (fields, properties, constants, and read-only fields). This chapter will focus on the remaining two pillars of OOP: inheritance and polymorphism.

First, you will learn how to build families of related classes using *inheritance*. As you will see, this form of code reuse allows you to define common functionality in a parent class that can be leveraged, and possibly altered, by child classes. Along the way, you will learn how to establish a *polymorphic interface* into the class hierarchies using Overridable and MustOverride members. I wrap up by examining the role of the ultimate parent class in the .NET base class libraries: System.Object.

The Basic Mechanics of Inheritance

Recall from the previous chapter that inheritance is the aspect of OOP that facilitates code reuse. Specifically speaking, code reuse comes in two flavors: inheritance (the "is-a" relationship) and the containment/delegation model (the "has-a" relationship). Let's begin this chapter by examining the classical "is-a" inheritance model.

When you establish "is-a" relationships between classes, you are building a dependency between two or more class types. The basic idea behind classical inheritance is that new classes can be created using existing classes as a starting point. To begin with a very simple example, create a new Console Application project named BasicInheritance. Now assume you have designed a class named Car that models some basic details of an automobile:

```
' A simple base class.
Public Class Car

        Public ReadOnly maxSpeed As Integer
        Private currSpeed As Integer

        Public Sub New(ByVal max As Integer)
                maxSpeed = max
        End Sub
End Sub
```

```
        Public Sub New()
                maxSpeed = 55
        End Sub

        Public Property Speed() As Integer
                Get
                        Return currSpeed
                End Get
                Set(ByVal value As Integer)
                        currSpeed = value
                        If currSpeed > maxSpeed Then
                                currSpeed = maxSpeed
                        End If
                End Set
        End Property
End Class
```

Notice that the Car class is making use of encapsulation services to control access to the Private currSpeed field using a Public property named Speed. At this point, you can exercise your Car type as follows:

```
Module Module1
        Sub Main()

                Console.WriteLine("***** Basic Inheritance *****" & vbLf)
                Dim myCar As New Car(80)
                myCar.Speed = 50
                Console.WriteLine("My car is going {0} MPH", myCar.Speed)
                Console.ReadLine()

        End Sub
End Module
```

Specifying the Parent Class of an Existing Class

Now assume you wish to build a new class named MiniVan. Like a basic Car, you wish to define the MiniVan class to support a maximum speed, current speed, and a property named Speed to allow the object user to modify the object's state. Clearly, the Car and MiniVan classes are related; in fact, it can be said that a MiniVan "is-a" Car. The "is-a" relationship (formally termed *classical inheritance*) allows you to build new class definitions that extend the functionality of an existing class.

The existing class that will serve as the basis for the new class is termed a base or parent class. The role of a base class is to define all the common data and members for the classes that extend it. The extending classes are formally termed derived or child classes. In VB you make use of the Inherits keyword on the next line of the class definition to establish an "is-a" relationship between classes:

```
'MiniVan 'is-a' Car.
Public Class MiniVan
        Inherits Car
End Class
```

What have you gained by extending your `MiniVan` from the `Car` base class? Simply put, `MiniVan` objects now have access to each Public member defined within the parent class.

■ **Note** Although constructors are typically defined as public, a derived class never inherits the constructors of a parent class.

Given the relation between these two class types, you could now make use of the `MiniVan` class like so:

```
Sub Main()
        Console.WriteLine("***** Basic Inheritance *****" & vbLf)
        ...
        'Now make a MiniVan object.
        Dim myVan As New MiniVan()
        myVan.Speed = 10
        Console.WriteLine("My van is going {0} MPH", myVan.Speed)
        Console.ReadLine()
End Sub
```

Notice that although you have not added any members to the `MiniVan` class, you have direct access to the Public `Speed` property of your parent class, and have thus reused code. This is a far better approach than creating a `MiniVan` class that has the exact same members as `Car` such as a `Speed` property. If you did duplicate code between these two classes, you would need to now maintain two bodies of code, which is certainly a poor use of your time.

Always remember, that inheritance preserves encapsulation; therefore, the following code results in a compiler error, as Private members can never be accessed from an object reference.

```
Sub Main()
        Console.WriteLine("***** Basic Inheritance *****" & vbLf)
        ...
        'Make a MiniVan object.
        Dim myVan As New MiniVan()
        myVan.Speed = 10
        Console.WriteLine("My van is going {0} MPH", myVan.Speed)

        'Error! Can't access private members!
        myVan.currSpeed = 55
        Console.ReadLine()
End Sub
```

On a related note, if the `MiniVan` defined its own set of members, it would not be able to access any Private member of the `Car` base class. Again, Private members can *only* be accessed by the class that defines it.

```
'MiniVan derives from Car.
Public Class MiniVan
        Inherits Car

        Public Sub TestMethod()
            'OK! Can access Public members
          'of a parent within a derived type.
            Speed = 10

            'Error! Cannot access Private
          'members of parent within a derived type.
            currSpeed = 10
        End Sub
End Class
```

Regarding Multiple Base Classes

Speaking of base classes, it is important to keep in mind that VB 2010 demands that a given class have exactly *one* direct base class. It is not possible to create a class type that directly derives from two or more base classes (this technique [which is supported in unmanaged C++] is known as *multiple inheritance*, or simply *MI*). If you attempted to create a class that specifies two direct parent classes as shown in the following code, you will receive compiler errors.

```
'Illegal! The .NET platform does not allow
'multiple inheritance for classes!
Public Class WontWork
        Inherits BaseClassOne
        Inherits BaseClassTwo
End Class
```

As examined in Chapter 9, the .NET platform does allow a given class to implement any number of discrete interfaces. In this way, a VB 2010 type can exhibit a number of behaviors while avoiding the complexities associated with MI. On a related note, while a class can have only one direct base class, it is permissible for an interface to directly derive from multiple interfaces. Using this technique, you can build sophisticated interface hierarchies that model complex behaviors (again, see Chapter 9).

The NotInheritable Keyword

VB 2010 supplies another keyword, NotInheritable, that prevents inheritance from occurring. When you mark a class as NotInheritable, the compiler will not allow you to derive from this type. For example, assume you have decided that it makes no sense to further extend the MiniVan class:

```
'The MiniVan class cannot be extended!
Public NotInheritable Class MiniVan
        Inherits Car
End Class
```

If you (or a teammate) were to attempt to derive from this class, you would receive a compile-time error:

```
'Error! Cannot extend
'a class marked with the NotInheritable keyword!
Public Class DeluxeMiniVan
        Inherits MiniVan

End Class
```

Most often, making a class NotInheritable makes the best sense when you are designing a utility class. For example, the System namespace defines numerous NotInheritable classes. You can verify this for yourself by opening up the Visual Studio 2010 Object Browser (via the View menu) and selecting the String class within the System namespace of the mscorlib.dll assembly. Notice in Figure 6-1 the use of the NotInheritable keyword seen within the Summary window.

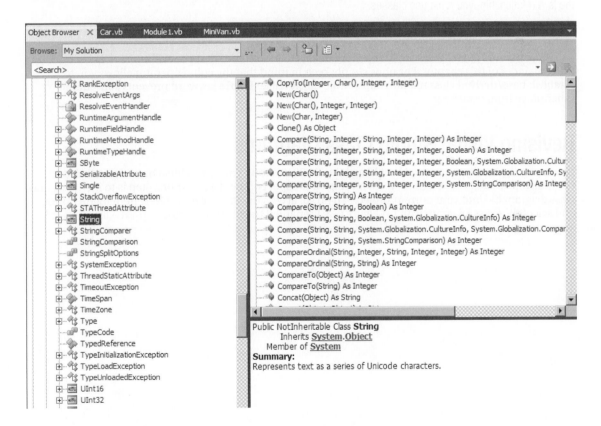

Figure 6-1. The base class libraries define numerous `NotInheritable` *types*

Thus, just like the `MiniVan`, if you attempted to build a new class that extends `System.String`, you will receive a compile-time error:

```
'Another error! Cannot extend
' a class marked as NotInheritable!
Public Class MyString
        Inherits String
End Class
```

■ **Note** In Chapter 4 you learned that VB 2010 structures are always implicitly `NotInheritable` (see Table 4-3). Therefore, you can never derive one structure from another structure, a class from a structure or a structure from a class. Structures can only be used to model standalone, atomic, user defined-data types. If you wish to leverage the Is-A relationship, you must use classes.

As you would guess, there are many more details to inheritance that you will come to know during the remainder of this chapter. For now, simply keep in mind that the colon operator allows you to establish base/derived class relationships, while the `NotInheritable` keyword prevents subsequent inheritance from occurring.

Revising Visual Studio Class Diagrams

In Chapter 2, I briefly mentioned that Visual Studio 2010 allows you to establish base/derived class relationships visually at design time. To leverage this aspect of the IDE, your first step is to include a new class diagram file into your current project. To do so, access the Project ➤ Add New Item menu option and select the Class Diagram icon (in Figure 6-2, I renamed the file from `ClassDiagram1.cd` to `Cars.cd`).

Figure 6-2. Inserting a new class diagram

Once you click the Add button, you will be presented with a blank designer surface. To add types to a class designer, simply drag each file from the Solution Explorer window onto the surface. Also recall that if you delete an item from the visual designer (simply by selecting it and pressing the Delete key), this will not destroy the associated source code, but simply removes the item off the designer surface. The current class hierarchy is shown in Figure 6-3.

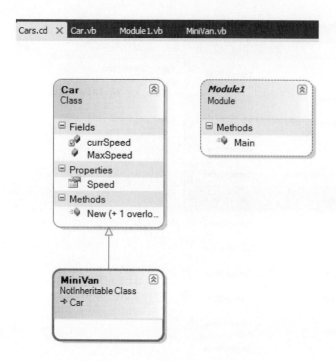

Figure 6-3. *The visual designer of Visual Studio*

■ **Note** As a shortcut, if you wish to automatically add all of your project's current types to a designer surface, select the Project node within the Solution Explorer and then click the View Class Diagram button in the upper right of the Solution Explorer window.

Beyond simply displaying the relationships of the types within your current application, recall from Chapter 2 that you can also create brand new types and populate their members using the Class Designer toolbox and Class Details window.

If you wish to make use of these visual tools during the remainder of the book, feel free. However, always make sure you analyze the generated code so you have a solid understanding of what these tools have done on your behalf.

■ **Source Code** The BasicInheritance project is located under the Chapter 6 subdirectory.

The Second Pillar of OOP: The Details of Inheritance

Now that you have seen the basic syntax of inheritance, let's create a more complex example and get to know the numerous details of building class hierarchies. To do so, you will be reusing the Employee class you designed in Chapter 5. To begin, create a brand new VB 2010 Console Application named Employees.

Next, activate the Project Add Existing Item menu option and navigate to the location of your Employee.vb and Employee.Internals.vb files you created in the EmployeeApp example of previous chapter. Select each of them (via a Ctrl-click) and click the Add button. Visual Studio 2010 responds by copying each file into the current project.

■ **Note** As a sanity check, compile and run your new project by pressing Ctrl+F5. The program will not do anything at this point; however, this will ensure you do not have any compiler errors.

Your goal is to create a family of classes that model various types of employees in a company. Assume that you wish to leverage the functionality of the Employee class to create two new classes (SalesPerson and Manager). The class hierarchy you will be building initially over the next several pages looks something like what you see in Figure 6-4 (be aware that you will not see individual fields in your diagram if you make use of VB 2010 automatic property syntax).

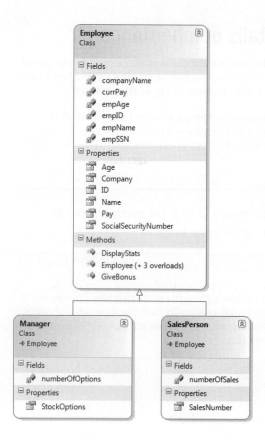

Figure 6-4. *The initial Employees hierarchy*

As illustrated in Figure 6-4, you can see that a `SalesPerson` "is-a" `Employee` (as is a `Manager`). Remember that under the classical inheritance model, base classes (such as `Employee`) are used to define general characteristics that are common to all descendents. Subclasses (such as `SalesPerson` and `Manager`) extend this general functionality while adding more specific functionality.

For your example, you will assume that the `Manager` class extends `Employee` by recording the number of stock options, while the `SalesPerson` class maintains the number of sales made. Insert a new class file (`Manager.vb`) that defines the `Manager` class with the following property:

```
'Managers need to know their number of stock options.
Public Class Manager
        Inherits Employee

        Public Property Stockoptions As Integer
End Class
```

Next, add another new class file (`SalesPerson.vb`) that defines the `SalesPerson` class with a fitting automatic property:

```
'Salespeople need to know their number of sales.
Public Class SalesPerson
        Inherits Employee

        Public Property SalesNumber As Integer
End Class
```

Now that you have established an "is-a" relationship, `SalesPerson` and `Manager` have automatically inherited all public members of the `Employee` base class. To illustrate, update your `Main()` method as follows:

```
'Create a subclass object and access base class functionality.
Module Module1
    Sub Main()

            Console.WriteLine("**The Employee Class Hierarchy**" & vbLf)
            Dim danny As New SalesPerson()
            danny.Age = 31
            danny.Name = "Danny"
            danny.SalesNumber = 50
                Console.ReadLine()
    End Sub
End Module
```

Controlling Base Class Creation with the MyBase Keyword

Currently, `SalesPerson` and `Manager` can only be created using the freebee default constructor (see Chapter 5). With this in mind, assume you have added a new six-argument constructor to the `Manager` type, which is invoked as follows:

```
Sub Main()
        ...
        ' Assume Manager has a constructor matching this signature:
        '(ByVal fullName As String, ByVal age As Integer,
        'ByVal empID As Integer, ByVal currPay As Single,
        'ByVal ssn As String, ByVal numbOfOpts As Integer)
        Dim chucky As New Manager("Chucky", 50, 92, 100000, "333-23-2322", 9000)
        Console.ReadLine()
End Sub
```

If you look at the parameter list, you can clearly see that most of these arguments should be stored in the member variables defined by the `Employee` base class. To do so, you might implement this custom constructor on the `Manager` class as follows:

```
'Manager class constructor
Public Sub New(ByVal fullName As String, ByVal age As Integer,
              ByVal empID As Integer, ByVal currPay As Single,
              ByVal ssn As String,  ByVal numbOfOpts As Integer)

        'This property is defined by the Manager class.
        Me.StockOptions = numbOfOpts

        'Assign incoming parameters using the
        'Inherited properties of the Parent class.
        Me.ID = empID
        Me.Age = age
        Me.Name = fullName
        Me.Pay = currPay

        'OOPS! This would be a compiler error,
        'if the SSN property were read-only!
        Me.SocialSecurityNumber = ssn
End Sub
```

The first issue with this approach is that if you defined any property as read-only (for example, the `SocialSecurityNumber` property), you are unable to assign the incoming **string** parameter to this field, as seen in the final code statement of this custom constructor.

The second issue is that you have indirectly created a rather inefficient constructor, given the fact that under VB, 2010 unless you say otherwise, the default constructor of a base class is called automatically before the logic of the derived constructor is executed. After this point, the current implementation accesses numerous Public properties of the `Employee` base class to establish its state. Thus, you have really made seven hits (five inherited properties and two constructor calls) during the creation of a `Manager` object!

To help optimize the creation of a derived class, you will do well to implement your subclass constructors to explicitly call an appropriate custom base class constructor, rather than the default. In this way, you are able to reduce the number of calls to inherited initialization members (which saves processing time). Let's retrofit the custom constructor of the `Manager` type to do this very thing using the `MyBase` keyword:

```
'Manager class constructor
Public Sub New(ByVal fullName As String, ByVal age As Integer,
              ByVal empID As Integer, ByVal currPay As Single,
              ByVal ssn As String, ByVal numbOfOpts As Integer)

        MyBase.New(fullName, age, empID, currPay, ssn)
        ' This field is defined by the Manager class.
        Me.StockOptions = numbOfOpts
End Sub
```

Here, the first statement within your custom constructor is making use of the `MyBase` keyword. In this situation, you are explicitly calling the five-argument constructor defined by `Employee` and saving yourself unnecessary calls during the creation of the child class. The custom `SalesPerson` constructor looks almost identical:

```
'As a general rule, all subclasses should explicitly call an 'appropriate.
' base class constructor.
Public Class SalesPerson

    Public Sub New(ByVal fullName As String,
                   ByVal empAge As Integer,
                   ByVal empID As Integer,
                   ByVal currPay As Single, _
                   ByVal ssn As String,
                   ByVal numbOfSales As Integer)

                   'Pass these arguments to the parent's constructor.
                   MyBase.New(fullName, empAge, empID, currPay, ssn)

                   'This belongs with us!
                   Me.SalesNumber= numbOfSales
    End Sub
End Class
```

Also be aware that you may use the `MyBase` keyword anytime a subclass wishes to access a public or protected member defined by a parent class. Use of this keyword is not limited to constructor logic. You will see examples using `MyBase` in this manner during our examination of polymorphism later in this chapter.

Finally, recall that once you add a custom constructor to a class definition, the default constructor is silently removed. Therefore, be sure to redefine the default constructor for the `SalesPerson` and `Manager` types, for example:

```
Public Sub New()
End Sub
```

Keeping Family Secrets: The Protected Keyword

As you already know, Public items are directly accessible from anywhere, while Private items can only be accessed by the class that has defined it. Recall from Chapter 5 that VB 2010 takes the lead of many other modern object languages and provides an additional keyword to define member accessibility: `Protected`.

When a base class defines Protected data or Protected members, it establishes a set of items that can be accessed directly by any descendent. If you wish to allow the `SalesPerson` and `Manager` child classes to directly access the data sector defined by `Employee`, you can update the original `Employee` class definition as follows:

```
'Protected state data.
Partial Public Class Employee

        'Derived classes can now directly access this information.
        Protected empName As String
        Protected empID As Integer
        Protected currPay As Single
```

```
    Protected empAge As Integer
    Protected empSSN As String
    Protected Shared companyName As String
    ...
End Class
```

The benefit of defining Protected members (rather than Private members) in a base class is that derived types no longer have to access the data indirectly using Public methods or properties. The possible downfall, of course, is that when a derived type has direct access to its parent's internal data, it is very possible to accidentally bypass existing business rules found within Public properties. When you define Protected members, you are creating a level of trust between the parent and child class, as the compiler will not catch any violation of your type's business rules.

Finally, understand that as far as the object user is concerned, Protected data is regarded as Private (as the user is "outside" of the family). Therefore, the following is illegal:

```
Sub Main()

    'Error! Can't access Protected data from object instance.
    Dim emp As New Employee()
        emp.empName = "Fred"
End Sub
```

■ **Note** Although `Protected` field data can break encapsulation, it is quite safe (and useful) to define `Protected` methods. When building class hierarchies, it is very common to define a set of methods that are only for use by derived types.

Adding a NotInheritable Class

Recall that a `NotInheritable` class cannot be extended by other classes. As mentioned, this technique is most often used when you are designing a utility class. However, when building class hierarchies, you might find that a certain branch in the inheritance chain should be "capped off," as it makes no sense to further extend the linage. For example, assume you have added yet another class to your program (`PTSalesPerson`) that extends the existing `SalesPerson` type. Figure 6-5 shows the current update.

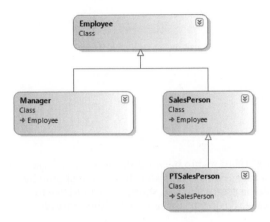

Figure 6-5. The PTSalesPerson *class*

PTSalesPerson is a class representing, of course, a part-time salesperson. For the sake of argument, let's say that you wish to ensure that no other developer is able to subclass from PTSalesPerson. (After all, how much more part-time can you get than "part-time"?) Again, to prevent others from extending a class, make use of the NotInheritable keyword:

```
NotInheritable Class PTSalesPerson
                Inherits SalesPerson

    Public Sub New(ByVal fullName As String,
                ByVal age As Integer,
                ByVal empID As Integer,
                ByVal currPay As Single,
                ByVal ssn As String,
                ByVal numbOfSales As Integer)

        MyBase.New(fullName, age, empID, currPay, ssn, numbOfSales)
    End Sub
            ' Assume other members here...
End Class
```

Given that NotInheritable classes cannot be extended, you may wonder if it is possible to reuse the functionality found within a class marked NotInheritable? Glad you asked! If you wish to build a new class that leverages the functionality of a NotInheritable class, your one option is to make use of the containment/delegation model (aka the "has-a" relationship).

Programming for Containment/Delegation

Recall that code reuse comes in two flavors. You have just explored the classical "is-a" relationship. Before you examine the third pillar of OOP (polymorphism), let's examine the "has-a" relationship (also known as the *containment/delegation model* or *aggregation*). Assume you have created a new class that models an employee benefits package:

```
'This new type will function as a contained class.
Public Class BenefitPackage

        'Assume we have other members that represent
        'dental/health benefits, and so on.

        Public Function ComputePayDeduction() As Double
                    Return 125
        End Function
End Class
```

Obviously, it would be rather odd to establish an "is-a" relationship between the BenefitPackage class and the employee types. (Employee "is-a" BenefitPackage? I don't think so.) However, it should be clear that some sort of relationship between the two could be established. In short, you would like to express the idea that each employee "has-a" BenefitPackage. To do so, you can update the Employee class definition as follows:

```
'Employees now have benefits.
Partial Public Class Employee

        'Contain a BenefitPackage object.
        Protected empBenefits As New BenefitPackage()
        ...
End Class
```

At this point, you have successfully contained another object. However, to expose the functionality of the contained object to the outside world requires delegation. *Delegation* is simply the act of adding Public members to the containing class that make use of the contained object's functionality.

For example, you could update the Employee class to expose the contained empBenefits object using a custom property as well as make use of its functionality internally using a new method named GetBenefitCost():

```
Partial Public Class Employee

        'Contain a BenefitPackage object.
        Protected empBenefits As New BenefitPackage()

        'Expose certain benefit behaviors of object.
        Public Function GetBenefitCost() As Double
                Return empBenefits.ComputePayDeduction()
        End Function

        'Expose object through a custom property.
        Public Property Benefits() As BenefitPackage
                Get
                        Return empBenefits
                End Get
```

```
                Set(ByVal value As BenefitPackage)

                        empBenefits = value
                End Set
        End Property
        ...
End Class
```

In the following updated `Main()` method, notice how you can interact with the internal `BenefitsPackage` type defined by the `Employee` type:

```
Sub Main()

        Console.WriteLine("***The Employee Class Hierarchy ***" & vbLf)
        Dim chucky As New Manager("Chucky", 50, 92, 100000, "333-23
                                  -2322", 9000)

        Dim cost As Double = chucky.GetBenefitCost()
        Console.ReadLine()
End Sub
```

Understanding Nested Type Definitions

The previous chapter briefly mentioned the concept of nested types, which is a spin on the "has-a" relationship you have just examined. In VB 2010 (as well as other .NET languages), it is possible to define a type (enum, class, interface, struct, or delegate) directly within the scope of a class or structure. When you have done so, the nested (or "inner") type is considered a member of the nesting (or "outer") class, and in the eyes of the runtime can be manipulated like any other member (fields, properties, methods, and events). The syntax used to nest a type is quite straightforward:

```
Public Class OuterClass

        'A Public nested type can be used by anybody.
        Public Class PublicInnerClass
        End Class

        ' A Private nested type can only be used by members
        'of the containing class.
        Private Class PrivateInnerClass
        End Class

End Class
```

Although the syntax is clean, understanding why you might want to do this may not readily apparent. To understand this technique, ponder the following traits of nesting a type:

- Nested types allow you to gain complete control over the access level of the inner type, as they may be declared privately (recall that non-nested classes cannot be declared using the `Private` keyword).

- Because a nested type is a member of the containing class, it can access Private members of the containing class.

- Oftentimes, a nested type is only useful as a helper for the outer class, and is not intended for use by the outside world.

When a type nests another class type, it can create member variables of the type, just as it would for any point of data. However, if you wish to make use of a nested type from outside of the containing type, you must qualify it by the scope of the nesting type. Consider the following code:

```
Sub Main()

        'Create and use the Public inner class. OK!
        Dim inner As OuterClass.PublicInnerClass
        inner = New OuterClass.PublicInnerClass()

        'Compiler Error! Cannot access the Private class.
        Dim inner2 As OuterClass.PrivateInnerClass
        inner2 = New OuterClass.PrivateInnerClass()
End Sub
```

To make use of this concept within the employees example, assume you have now nested the `BenefitPackage` directly within the `Employee` class type:

```
Partial Public Class Employee

        Public Class BenefitPackage

                'Assume we have other members that represent
               'dental/health benefits, and so on.
                Public Function ComputePayDeduction() As Double
                        Return 125
                End Function
        End Class
        ...
End Class
```

The nesting process can be as "deep" as you require. For example, assume you wish to create an enumeration named `BenefitPackageLevel`, which documents the various benefit levels an employee may choose. To programmatically enforce the tight connection between `Employee`, `BenefitPackage`, and `BenefitPackageLevel`, you could nest the enumeration as follows:

```
'Employee nests BenefitPackage.
Partial Public Class Employee

        'BenefitPackage nests BenefitPackageLevel.
        Public Class BenefitPackage
                Public Enum BenefitPackageLevel
                    Standard
                    Gold
                    Platinum
                End Enum
                Public Function ComputePayDeduction() As Double
                    Return 125
                End Function
        End Class
        ...
End Class
```

Because of the nesting relationships, note how you are required to make use of this enumeration:

```
Sub Main()
    ...
        'Define my benefit level.
        Dim myBenefitLevel As Employee.BenefitPackage.BenefitPackageLevel =
        Employee.BenefitPackage.BenefitPackageLevel.Platinum
        Console.ReadLine()
End Sub
```

Excellent! At this point you have been exposed to a number of keywords (and concepts) that allow you to build hierarchies of related types via classical inheritance, containment, and nested types. If the details aren't crystal clear right now, don't sweat it. You will be building a number of additional hierarchies over the remainder of this text. Next up, let's examine the final pillar of OOP: polymorphism.

The Third Pillar of OOP: VB's Polymorphic Support

Recall that the Employee base class defined a method named GiveBonus(), which was originally implemented as follows:

```
Partial Public Class Employee
    ..
        Public Sub GiveBonus(ByVal amount As Single)
            Pay += amount
        End Sub
    ...
End Class
```

Because this method has been defined with the Public keyword, you can now give bonuses to salespeople and managers (as well as part-time salespeople):

```
Sub Main()

        Console.WriteLine("** The Employee Class Hierarchy***" & vbLf)
        'Give each employee a bonus?
        Dim chucky As New Manager("Chucky", 50, 92, 100000, "333-23-2322", 9000)

        chucky.GiveBonus(300)
        chucky.DisplayStats()
        Console.WriteLine()

        Dim fran As New SalesPerson("Fran", 43, 93, 3000, "932-32-3232", 31)
        fran.GiveBonus(200)
        fran.DisplayStats()
        Console.ReadLine()
End Sub
```

The problem with the current design is that the publicly inherited `GiveBonus()` method operates identically for all subclasses. Ideally, the bonus of a salesperson or part-time salesperson should take into account the number of sales. Perhaps managers should gain additional stock options in conjunction with a monetary bump in salary. Given this, you are suddenly faced with an interesting question: "How can related types respond differently to the same request?" Again, glad you asked!

The Overridable and Overrides Keywords

Polymorphism provides a way for a subclass to define its own version of a method defined by its base class, using the process termed *method overriding*. To retrofit your current design, you need to understand the meaning of the `Overridable` and `Overrides` keywords. If a base class wishes to define a method that *may be* (but does not have to be) overridden by a subclass, it must mark the method with the `Overridable` keyword:

```
Partial Public Class Employee

        'This method can now be 'overridden' by a derived class.
        Public Overridable Sub GiveBonus(ByVal amount As Single)
            Pay += amount
            End Sub
    ...
End Class
```

When a subclass wishes to change the implementation details of an `Overridable` method, it does so using the `Overrides` keyword. For example, the `SalesPerson` and `Manager` could override `GiveBonus()` as follows (assume that `PTSalesPerson` will not override `GiveBonus()` and therefore simply inherits the version defined by `SalesPerson`):

```
Public Class SalesPerson
        Inherits Employee
        ...
        'A salesperson's bonus is influenced by the number of sales.
        Public Overrides Sub GiveBonus(ByVal amount As Single)

          Dim salesBonus As Integer = 0
          If SalesNumber >= 0 AndAlso SalesNumber <= 100 Then
              salesBonus = 10
          Else
              If SalesNumber >= 101 AndAlso SalesNumber <= 200 Then
                  salesBonus = 15
              Else
                  salesBonus = 20
              End If
          End If
          MyBase.GiveBonus(amount * salesBonus)
        End Sub
End Class

Public Class Manager
        Inherits Employee
        ...
        Public Overrides Sub GiveBonus(ByVal amount As Single)

          MyBase.GiveBonus(amount)
          Dim r As New Random()
          StockOptions += r.Next(500)
        End Sub

End Class
```

Notice how each overridden method is free to leverage the default behavior using the `MyBase` keyword. In this way, you have no need to completely reimplement the logic behind `GiveBonus()`, but can reuse (and possibly extend) the default behavior of the parent class.

Also assume that the current `DisplayStats()` method of the `Employee` class has been declared as Overridable. By doing so, each subclass can override this method to account for displaying the number of sales (for salespeople) and current stock options (for managers). For example, consider the `Manager`'s version of the `DisplayStats()` method (the `SalesPerson` class would implement `DisplayStats()` in a similar manner to show the number of sales):

```
Public Overrides Sub DisplayStats()
        MyBase.DisplayStats()
        Console.WriteLine("Number of Stock Options: {0}", StockOptions)
End Sub
```

Now that each subclass can interpret what these `Overridable` methods means to itself, each object instance behaves as a more independent entity:

```
Sub Main()

        Console.WriteLine("*** The Employee Class Hierarchy ***" & vbLf)
        'A better bonus system!
        Dim chucky As New Manager("Chucky", 50, 92, 100000, "333-23-2322",  9000)

        chucky.GiveBonus(300)
        chucky.DisplayStats()
        Console.WriteLine()
        Dim fran As New SalesPerson("Fran", 43, 93, 3000, "932-32-3232", 31)
        fran.GiveBonus(200)
        fran.DisplayStats()
        Console.ReadLine()
End Sub
```

The following output shows a possible test run of your application thusfar:

```
***** The Employee Class Hierarchy *****


Name: Chucky

ID: 92

Age: 50

Pay: 100300

SSN: 333-23-2322

Number of Stock Options: 9337


Name: Fran

ID: 93

Age: 43

Pay: 5000

SSN: 932-32-3232

Number of Sales: 31
```

Overriding Overridable Members Using Visual Studio 2010

As you may have already noticed, when you are overriding a member, you must recall the type of each and every parameter—not to mention the method name and parameter passing conventions (**ByVal**, **ByRef**, and **ParamArray**). Visual Studio 2010 has a very helpful feature that you can make use of when overriding an Overridable member. If you type the word "Overrides" within the scope of a class type (then hit the spacebar), IntelliSense will automatically display a list of all the Overridable members defined in your parent classes, as you see in Figure 6-6.

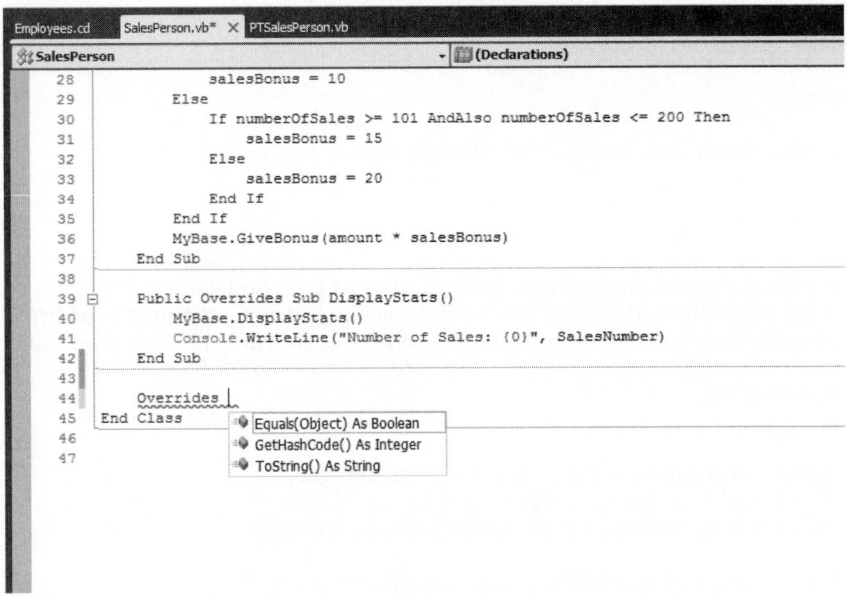

Figure 6-6. *Quickly viewing Overridable methods à la Visual Studio 2010*

When you select a member and hit the Enter key, the IDE responds by automatically filling in the method stub on your behalf. Note that you also receive a code statement that calls your parent's version of the Overridable member (you are free to delete this line if it is not required). For example, if you used this technique when overriding the **DisplayStats()** method, you might find the following autogenerated code:

```
Public Overrides Sub DisplayStats()
      MyBase.DisplayStats()
End Sub
```

NotOverridable Members

Recall that the NotOverridable keyword can be applied to a class type to prevent other types from extending its behavior via inheritance. As you may remember, you sealed PTSalesPerson as you assumed it made no sense for other developers to extend this line of inheritance any further.

On a related note, sometimes you may not wish to mark an entire class as NotInheritable, but simply want to prevent derived types from overriding particular Overridable methods. For example, assume you do not want part-time salespeople to obtain customized bonuses. To prevent the PTSalesPerson class from overriding the Overridable GiveBonus() method, you could apply the NotOverridable keyword to this method in the SalesPerson class as follows:

```
'SalesPerson has sealed the GiveBonus() method!
Public Class SalesPerson
      Inherits Employee
      ...
      Public NotOverridable Overrides Sub GiveBonus(ByVal amount As Single)
      ....
      End Sub
End Class
```

Here, SalesPerson has indeed overridden the Overridable GiveBonus() method defined in the Employee class; however, it has explicitly marked it as NotOverridable. Thus, if you attempted to override this method in the PTSalesPerson class you receive compile-time errors, as shown in the following code:

```
NotInheritable Class PTSalesPerson
    Inherits SalesPerson

      Public Sub New(ByVal fullName As String, ByVal age As Integer,
                    ByVal empID As Integer, ByVal currPay As Single,
                    ByVal ssn As String, ByVal numbOfSales As Integer)

      MyBase.New(fullName, age, empID, currPay, ssn, numbOfSales)
      End Sub

      'Compiler error!  Can't override this method
      'in the PTSalesPerson class, as it was NotInheritable.
      Public  Overrides Sub GiveBonus(ByVal amount As Single)
      End Sub
End Class
```

Understanding Abstract Classes and the MustInherit Keyword

Currently, the Employee base class has been designed to supply various data members for its descendents, as well as supply two Overridable methods (GiveBonus() and DisplayStats()) that may be overridden by a given descendent. While this is all well and good, there is a rather odd byproduct of the current design; you can directly create instances of the Employee base class:

```
'What exactly does this mean?
Dim X As New Employee()
```

In this example, the only real purpose of the `Employee` base class is to define common members for all subclasses. In all likelihood, you did not intend anyone to create a direct instance of this class, reason being that the `Employee` type itself is too general of a concept. For example, if I were to walk up to you and say, "I'm an employee!" I would bet your very first question to me would be, "What *kind* of employee are you?" Are you a consultant, trainer, admin assistant, copyeditor, or White House aide?

Given that many base classes tend to be rather nebulous entities, a far better design for this example is to prevent the ability to directly create a new `Employee` object in code. In VB 2010, you can enforce this programmatically by using the `MustInherit` keyword in the class definition, thus creating an *abstract base class*:

```
'Update the Employee class as MustInherit
'to prevent direct instantiation.
Partial Public MustInherit Class Employee
  ...
End Class
```

With this, if you now attempt to create an instance of the `Employee` class, you are issued a compile-time error:

```
'Error! Cannot create an instance of a MustInherit class!
Dim X As New Employee()
```

At first glance it might seem very strange to define a class that you cannot directly create. Recall however that base classes (`MustInherit` or not) are very useful, in that they contain all of the common data and functionality of derived types. Using this form of abstraction, we are able to model that the "idea" of an employee is completely valid; it is just not a concrete entity. Also understand that although we cannot *directly* create a `MustInherit` class, it is still assembled in memory when derived classes are created. Thus, it is perfectly fine (and common) for `MustInherit` classes to define any number of constructors that are called *indirectly* when derived classes are allocated.

At this point, you have constructed a fairly interesting employee hierarchy. You will add a bit more functionality to this application later in this chapter when examining VB 2010 casting rules. Until then, Figure 6-7 illustrates the core design of your current types.

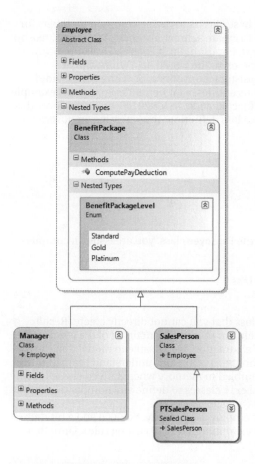

Figure 6-7. The Employee hierarchy

■ **Source Code** The Employees project is included under the Chapter 6 subdirectory.

Understanding the Polymorphic Interface

When a class has been defined as an `abstract` base class (via the `MustInherit` keyword), it may define any number of *abstract members. To define an abstract member, you qualify it with the* `MustOverride` *keyword.*) Abstract members can be used whenever you wish to define a member that does *not* supply a default implementation, but *must* be accounted for by each derived class. By doing so, you enforce a *polymorphic interface* on each descendent, leaving them to contend with the task of providing the details behind your `MustOverride` methods.

Simply put, a `MustInherit` base class's polymorphic interface simply refers to its set of `Overridable` and `MustOverride` methods. This is much more interesting than first meets the eye, as this trait of OOP allows you to build easily extendable and flexible software applications. To illustrate, you will be implementing (and slightly modifying) the hierarchy of shapes briefly examined in Chapter 5 during the overview of the pillars of OOP. To begin, create a new VB 2010 Console Application project named Shapes.

In Figure 6-8, notice that the `Hexagon` and `Circle` types each extend the `Shape` base class. Like any base class, `Shape` defines a number of members (a `PetName` property and `Draw()` method in this case) that are common to all descendents.

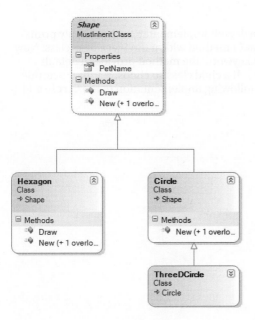

Figure 6-8. *The shapes hierarchy*

Much like the employee hierarchy, you should be able to tell that you don't want to allow the object user to create an instance of `Shape` directly, as it is too abstract of a concept. Again, to prevent the direct creation of the `Shape` type, you could define it as a `MustInherit` class. As well, given that you wish the derived types to respond uniquely to the `Draw()` method, let's mark it as `Overridable` and define a default implementation:

```
'The MustInherit base class of the hierarchy
Public MustInherit Class Shape

    Public Sub New()
        PetName = "NoName"
    End Sub
```

```
    Public Sub New(ByVal name As String)
        PetName = name
    End Sub

    Public Property PetName As String

    'A single Overridable method.
    Public Overridable Sub Draw()
        Console.WriteLine("Inside Shape.Draw()")
    End Sub
End Class
```

Notice that the `Overridable Draw()` method provides a default implementation that simply prints out a message that informs you that you are calling the `Draw()` method within the `Shape` base class. Now recall that when a method is marked with the `Overridable` keyword, the method provides a default implementation that all derived types automatically inherit. If a child class so chooses, it *may* override the method but does not *have* to. Given this, consider the following implementation of the `Circle` and `Hexagon` types:

```
'Circle DOES NOT override Draw().
Public Class Circle
    Inherits Shape

    Public Sub New()
    End Sub

    Public Sub New(ByVal name As String)
        MyBase.New(name)
    End Sub

End Class

'Hexagon DOES override Draw().
Public Class Hexagon
    Inherits Shape

    Public Sub New()
    End Sub

    Public Sub New(ByVal name As String)
        MyBase.New(name)
    End Sub

    Public Overrides Sub Draw()
        Console.WriteLine("Drawing {0} the Hexagon", PetName)
    End Sub
End Class
```

The usefulness of `MustOverride` methods becomes crystal clear when you once again remember that subclasses are *never required* to override `Overridable` methods (as in the case of `Circle`). Therefore, if you create an instance of the `Hexagon` and `Circle` types, you'd find that the `Hexagon` understands how to "draw" itself correctly or at least print out an appropriate message to the console. The `Circle`, however, is more than a bit confused:

```
Sub Main()

        Console.WriteLine("** Fun with Polymorphism **" & vbLf)
        Dim hex As New Hexagon("Beth")
        hex.Draw()
        Dim cir As New Circle("Cindy")
        'Calls base class implementation!
        cir.Draw()
        Console.ReadLine()
End Sub
```

Now consider the following output of the previous `Main()` method:

```
***** Fun with Polymorphism *****


Drawing Beth the Hexagon

Inside Shape.Draw()
```

Clearly, this is not a very intelligent design for the current hierarchy. To force each child class to override the `Draw()` method, you can define `Draw()` as a `MustOverride` method of the `Shape` class, which by definition means you provide no default implementation whatsoever:

```
Public MustInherit Class Shape
    …
    ' A single MustOverride method.
    Public MustOverride Sub Draw()
    ...
End Class
```

■ **Note** `MustOverride` methods can only be defined in `MustInherit` classes. If you attempt to do otherwise, you will be issued a compiler error.

Methods marked with `MustOverride` are pure protocol. They simply define the name, return type (if any), and parameter set (if required). Here, the `MustInherit Shape` class informs the derived types "I have a method named `Draw()` that takes no arguments and returns nothing. If you derive from me, you figure out the details."

Given this, you are now obligated to override the `Draw()` method in the `Circle` class. If you do not, `Circle` is also assumed to be a noncreatable `MustInherit` type that must be adorned with the `MustInherit` keyword (which is obviously not very useful in this example). Here is the code update:

```
'If we did not implement the MustOverride Draw() method,Circle would also     'be considered
MustInherit!
Public Class Circle
    Inherits Shape

    Public Sub New()
    End Sub

    Public Sub New(ByVal name As String)
        MyBase.New(name)
    End Sub

    Public Overrides Sub Draw()
        Console.WriteLine("Drawing {0} the Circle", PetName)
    End Sub
End Class
```

The short answer is that you can now make the assumption that anything deriving from **Shape** does indeed have a unique version of the `Draw()` method. To illustrate the full story of polymorphism, consider the following code:

```
Module Module1
    Sub Main()

        Console.WriteLine("***** Fun with Polymorphism *****" & vbLf)

        'Make an array of Shape-compatible objects.
        Dim myShapes As Shape() = {New Hexagon(), New Circle(), New Hexagon("Mick"), New
        Circle("Beth"), New Hexagon("Linda")}

        'Loop over each item and interact with the
        'polymorphic interface.
```

```
        For Each s As Shape In myShapes
                s.Draw()
        Next

        Console.ReadLine()
    End Sub
End Module
```

Here is the output from the modified `Main()` method:

```
***** Fun with Polymorphism *****


Drawing NoName the Hexagon

Drawing NoName the Circle

Drawing Mick the Hexagon

Drawing Beth the Circle

Drawing Linda the Hexagon
```

This `Main()` method illustrates polymorphism at its finest. Although it is not possible to *directly* create an instance of a `MustInherit` base class (the `Shape`), you are able to freely store references to any subclass with a `MustInherit` base variable. Therefore, when you are creating a `Shape` array, the array can hold any object deriving from the `Shape` base class (if you attempt to place `Shape`-incompatible objects into the array, you receive a compiler error).

Given that all items in the `myShapes` array do indeed derive from `Shape`, you know they all support the same "polymorphic interface" (or said more plainly, they all have a `Draw()` method). As you iterate over the array of `Shape` references, it is at runtime that the underlying type is determined. At this point, the correct version of the `Draw()` method is invoked in memory.

This technique also makes it very simple to safely extend the current hierarchy. For example, assume you derived more classes from the `MustInherit Shape` base class (`Triangle`, `Square`, etc.). Due to the polymorphic interface, the code within your `For Each` loop would not have to change in the slightest as the compiler enforces that only `Shape`-compatible types are placed within the `myShapes` array.

Understanding Member Shadowing

VB 2010 provides a facility that is the logical opposite of method overriding termed *shadowing*. Formally speaking, if a derived class defines a member that is identical to a member defined in a base class, the derived class has *shadowed* the parent's version. In the real world, the possibility of this occurring is the greatest when you are subclassing from a class you (or your team) did not create yourselves (for example, if you purchase a third-party .NET software package).

For the sake of illustration, assume you receive a class named `ThreeDCircle` from a coworker (or classmate) that defines a subroutine named `Draw()` taking no arguments:

```
Public Class ThreeDCircle
        Public Sub Draw()
                Console.WriteLine("Drawing a 3D Circle")
        End Sub
End Class
```

You figure that a `ThreeDCircle` "is-a" `Circle`, so you derive from your existing `Circle` type:

```
Public Class ThreeDCircle
        Inherits Circle

        Public Sub Draw()
                Console.WriteLine("Drawing a 3D Circle")
        End Sub
End Class
```

Once you recompile, you find a warning in the Visual Studio 2010 error window (see Figure 6-9).

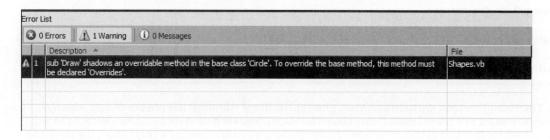

Figure 6-9. Oops! You just shadowed a member in your parent class

The problem is that you have a derived class (`ThreeDCircle`) which contains a method that is identical to an inherited method.

To address this issue, you have two options. You could simply update the parent's version of `Draw()` using the `Overrides` keyword (as suggested by the compiler). With this approach, the `ThreeDCircle` type is able to extend the parent's default behavior as required. However, if you don't have access to the code defining the base class (again, as would be the case in many third-party libraries), you would be unable to modify the `Draw()` method as an Overridable member, as you don't have access to the code file!

As an alternative, you can include the `Shadows` keyword to the offending `Draw()` member of the derived type (`ThreeDCircle` in this example). Doing so explicitly states that the derived type's implementation is intentionally designed to effectively ignore the parent's version (again, in the real world, this can be helpful if external .NET software somehow conflicts with your current software).

```
'This class extends Circle and hides the inherited Draw() method.
Public Class ThreeDCircle
        Inherits Circle

        'Hide any Draw() implementation above me.
        Public Shadows Sub Draw()
                Console.WriteLine("Drawing a 3D Circle")
        End Sub
End Class
```

You can also apply the `Shadows` keyword to any member type inherited from a base class (field, constant, Shared member, or property). As a further example, assume that `ThreeDCircle` wishes to hide the inherited `PetName` property:

```
Public Class ThreeDCircle
    Inherits Circle

    'Hide the PetName property above me.
    Public Shadows Property PetName As String

    'Hide any Draw() implementation above me.
    Public Shadows Sub Draw()
        Console.WriteLine("Drawing a 3D Circle")
    End Sub

End Class
```

Finally, be aware that it is still possible to trigger the base class implementation of a shadowed member using an explicit cast, as described in the next section. For example:

```
Sub Main()
        ...
        'This calls the Draw() method of the ThreeDCircle.
        Dim o As New ThreeDCircle()
        o.Draw()

        'This calls the Draw() method of the parent!
        DirectCast(o, Circle).Draw()
        Console.ReadLine()
End Sub
```

■ **Source Code** The Shapes project can be found under the Chapter 6 subdirectory.

Understanding Base Class/Derived Class Casting Rules

Now that you can build a family of related class types, you need to learn the rules of class *casting operations*. To do so, let's return to the Employees hierarchy created earlier in this chapter. Under the

.NET platform, the ultimate base class in the system is **System.Object**. Therefore, everything "is-a" **Object** and can be treated as such. Given this fact, it is legal to store an instance of any type within an object variable:

```
Sub CastingExamples()

    'A Manager "is-a" System.Object, so we can
    'store a Manager reference in an object variable just fine.
    Dim frank As Object = New Manager("Frank Zappa", 9, 3000, 40000,
                                      "111-11-1111", 5)
End Sub
```

In the **Employees** example, **Managers**, **SalesPerson**, and **PTSalesPerson** types all extend **Employee**, so you can store any of these objects in a valid base class reference. Therefore, the following statements are also legal:

```
Sub CastingExamples()
    ' A Manager "is-a" System.Object, so we can
    ' store a Manager reference in an Object variable just fine.
    Dim frank As Object = New Manager("Frank Zappa", 9, 3000, 40000, "111-11-1111", 5)

    ' A Manager "is-an" Employee too.
    Dim moonUnit As Employee = New Manager("MoonUnit Zappa", 2, 3001, 20000,
                                           "101-11-1321", 1)

    ' A PTSalesPerson "is-a" SalesPerson.
    Dim jill As SalesPerson = New PTSalesPerson("Jill", 834, 3002, 100000,
                                                "111-12-1119", 90)

End Sub
```

The first law of casting between class types is that when two classes are related by an "is-a" relationship, it is always safe to store a derived object within a base class reference. Formally, this is called an *implicit cast*, as "it just works" given the laws of inheritance. This leads to some powerful programming constructs. For example, assume you have defined a new method within your current **Program** class:

```
Sub GivePromotion(ByVal emp As Employee)

    'Increase pay...
    ' Give new parking space in company garage...
    Console.WriteLine("{0} was promoted!", emp.Name)
End Sub
```

Because this method takes a single parameter of type **Employee**, you can effectively pass any descendent from the **Employee** class into this method directly, given the "is-a" relationship:

```
Sub CastingExamples()

        ' A Manager "is-a" System.Object, so we can
        ' store a Manager reference in an Object variable just fine.
        Dim frank As Object = New Manager("Frank Zappa", 9, 3000, 40000, "111-11-1111", 5)
        GivePromotion(DirectCast(frank, Manager))

        ' A Manager "is-an" Employee too.
        Dim moonUnit As Employee = New Manager("MoonUnit Zappa", 2, 3001, 20000,
                                                "101-11-1321", 1)
        GivePromotion(moonUnit)

        ' A PTSalesPerson "is-a" SalesPerson.
        Dim jill As SalesPerson = New PTSalesPerson("Jill", 834, 3002, 100000,
                                                "111-12-1119", 90)
        GivePromotion(jill)
End Sub
```

The previous code compiles given the implicit cast from the base class type (Employee) to the derived type. However, what if you also wanted to fire Frank Zappa (currently stored in a general System.Object reference)? If you pass the frank object directly into this method, you will find a compiler error as follows

```
'Error!Dim frank As Object = New Manager("Frank Zappa", 9, 3000, 40000, "111-11-1111", 5)
GivePromotion(frank)
```

You only get the error if Option Strict is On, which provides strong typing and prevents unintended type conversions with data loss. The problem is that you are attempting to pass in a variable which Is-NOT-A Employee, but a more general System.Object. Given the fact that object is higher up the inheritance chain than Employee, the compiler will not allow for an implicit cast, in an effort to keep your code as type safe as possible.

Even though you can figure out that the object reference is pointing to an Employee compatible class in memory, the compiler cannot, as that will not be known until runtime. You can satisfy the compiler by performing an *explicit cast*. This is the second law of casting: you can in such cases explicitly downcast using the VB 2010 casting operator. The basic template to follow when performing an explicit cast looks something like the following:

```
DirectCast(referenceIHave, ClassIWantToCastTo )
```

Thus, to pass the Object variable into the GivePromotion() method, you must author the following code:

```
' OK!
GivePromotion(DirectCast(frank, Manager))
```

The VB TryCast Keyword

Be very aware that explicit casting is evaluated at *runtime*, not compile time. Therefore, if you were to author the following VB 2010 code:

```
' Ack! You can't cast frank to a Hexagon, but this compiles fine!
Dim hex As Hexagon = DirectCast(frank, Hexagon)
```

you would compile without error, but would receive a runtime error, or more formally a *runtime exception*. Chapter 7 will examine the full details of structured exception handling; however, it is worth pointing out for the time being when you are performing an explicit cast, you can trap the possibility of an invalid cast using the **Try** and **Catch** keywords (again, see Chapter 7 for full details):

```
' Catch a possible invalid cast.
Try
        Dim hex As Hexagon = DirectCast(frank, Hexagon)
Catch ex As InvalidCastException
        Console.WriteLine(ex.Message)
End Try
```

While this is a fine example of defensive programming, VB 2010 provides the **TryCast** keyword to quickly determine at runtime whether a given type is compatible with another. When you use the **TryCast** keyword, you are able to determine compatibility by checking against a **Nothing** return value. Consider the following:

```
'Use 'TryCast' to test compatability.
        Dim hex2 As Hexagon = TryCast(frank, Hexagon)

If hex2 Is Nothing Then
        Console.WriteLine("Sorry, frank is not a Hexagon...")
End If
```

The VB Is Keyword

Given that the **GivePromotion()** method has been designed to take any possible type derived from **Employee**, one question on your mind may be how this method can determine which derived type was sent into the method. On a related note, given that the incoming parameter is of type **Employee**, how can you gain access to the specialized members of the **SalesPerson** and **Manager** types?

In addition to the **TryCast** keyword, the VB 2010 language provides the **Is** keyword to determine whether two items are compatible. Unlike the **TryCast** keyword, however, the **Is** keyword returns **False**, rather than a **Nothing** reference, if the types are incompatible. Consider the following implementation of the **GivePromotion()** method:

```
Sub GivePromotion(ByVal emp As Employee)

        Console.WriteLine("{0} was promoted!", emp.Name)

        If TypeOf emp Is SalesPerson Then
                Console.WriteLine("{0} made {1} sale(s)!", emp.Name, (DirectCast(emp,
                SalesPerson)).SalesNumber)
                Console.WriteLine()
        End If

        If TypeOf emp Is Manager Then
                Console.WriteLine("{0} had {1} stock options...", emp.Name,
                (DirectCast(emp, Manager)).StockOptions)
                Console.WriteLine()
        End If
End Sub
```

Here you are performing a runtime check to determine what the incoming base class reference is actually pointing to in memory. Once you determine whether you received a SalesPerson or Manager type, you are able to perform an explicit cast to gain access to the specialized members of the class. Also notice that you are not required to wrap your casting operations within a Try/Catch construct, as you know that the cast is safe if you enter either If scope, given your conditional check.

The Master Parent Class: System.Object

To wrap up this chapter, I'd like to examine the details of the master parent class in the .NET platform: Object. As you were reading the previous section, you may have noticed that the base classes in your hierarchies (Car, Shape, Employee) never explicitly specify their parent classes:

```
'Who is the parent of Car?
Public Class Car
...
End Class
```

In the .NET universe, every type ultimately derives from a base class named System.Object (which can be represented by the VB 2010 Object keyword [uppercase 'O']). The Object class defines a set of common members for every type in the framework. In fact, when you do build a class that does not explicitly define its parent, the compiler automatically derives your type from Object. If you want to be very clear in your intentions, you are free to define classes that derive from Object as follows:

```
'Here we are explicitly deriving from System.Object.
Public Class Car
        Inherits Object
        ...
End Class
```

Like any class, `System.Object` defines a set of members. In the following formal VB 2010 definition, note that some of these items are declared `Overridable`, which specifies that a given member may be overridden by a subclass, while others are marked with `Shared` (and are therefore called at the class level):

```
Public Class Object

        'Overridable members.
        Public Overridable Function Equals(ByVal obj As Object) As Boolean

        Protected Overridable Sub Finalize()
        Public Overridable Function GetHashCode() As Integer
        Public Overridable Function ToString() As String

        'Instance level, non-Overridable members.
        Public Function GetType() As Type
        Protected Function MemberwiseClone() As Object

        'Shared members.
        Public Function Equals(ByVal objA As Object,ByVal  objB As Object) As Boolean

        Public Function ReferenceEquals(ByVal objA As Object,ByVal objB As Object)
        As Boolean
End Class
```

Table 6-1 offers a rundown of the functionality provided by some of the methods you're most likely to make use of.

Table 6-1. Core Members of System.Object

Instance Method of Object Class	Meaning in Life
Equals()	By default, this method returns **True** only if the items being compared refer to the exact same item in memory. Thus, **Equals()** is used to compare object references, not the state of the object. Typically, this method is overridden to return **True** only if the objects being compared have the same internal state values (that is, value-based semantics). Be aware that if you override **Equals()**, you should also override **GetHashCode()**, as these methods are used internally by **Hashtable** types to retrieve subobjects from the container. Also recall from Chapter 4, that the **ValueType** class overrides this method for all structures, so they work with value-based comparisons.
Finalize()	For the time being, you can understand this method (when overridden) is called to free any allocated resources before the object is destroyed. I talk more about the CLR garbage collection services in Chapter 8.
GetHashCode()	This method returns an **Integer** that identifies a specific object instance.
ToString()	This method returns a string representation of this object, using the **<namespace>.<type name>** format (termed the *fully qualified name*). This method will often be overridden by a subclass to return a tokenized string of name/value pairs that represent the object's internal state, rather than its fully qualified name.
GetType()	This method returns a **Type** object that fully describes the object you are currently referencing. In short, this is a Runtime Type Identification (RTTI) method available to all objects (discussed in greater detail in Chapter 15).
MemberwiseClone()	This method exists to return a member-by-member copy of the current object, which is often used when cloning an object (see Chapter 9).

To illustrate some of the default behavior provided by the **Object** base class, create a new VB 2010 Console Application named ObjectOverrides. Insert a new VB 2010 class type that contains the following empty class definition for a type named **Person**:

```
'Remember! Person extends Object.
Public Class Person
End Class
```

Now, update your **Main()** method to interact with the inherited members of **System.Object** as follows:

```
Module Module1
    Sub Main()

        Console.WriteLine("***** Fun with System.Object *****" & vbLf)
        Dim p1 As New Person()

        'Use inherited members of System.Object.
        Console.WriteLine("ToString: {0}", p1.ToString())
        Console.WriteLine("Hash code: {0}", p1.GetHashCode())
        Console.WriteLine("Type: {0}", p1.[GetType]())

        'Make some other references to p1.
        Dim p2 As Person = p1
        Dim o As Object = p2

        'Are the references pointing to the same object in memory?
        If o.Equals(p1) AndAlso p2.Equals(o) Then
                Console.WriteLine("Same instance!")
        End If
        Console.ReadLine()

    End Sub
End Module
```

Here is the output of the current `Main()` method.

```
***** Fun with System.Object *****



ToString: ObjectOverrides.Person

Hash code: 46104728

Type: ObjectOverrides.Person

Same instance!
```

First, notice how the default implementation of `ToString()` returns the fully qualified name of the current type (`ObjectOverrides.Person`). As you will see later during the examination of building custom namespaces in Chapter 14, every VB 2010 project defines a "root namespace," which has the same name of the project itself. Here, you created a project named ObjectOverrides; thus the `Person` type (as well as the `Program` class) have both been placed within the `ObjectOverrides` namespace.

The default behavior of Equals() is to test whether two variables are pointing to the same object in memory. Here, you Declare a new **Person** variable named **p1**. At this point, a new **Person** object is placed on the managed heap. **p2** is also of type **Person**. However, you are not creating a *new* instance, but rather assigning this variable to reference **p1**. Therefore, **p1** and **p2** are both pointing to the same object in memory, as is the variable **o** (of type **Object**, which was thrown in for good measure). Given that **p1**, **p2**, and **o** all point to the same memory location, the equality test succeeds.

Although the canned behavior of **System.Object** can fit the bill in a number of cases, it is quite common for your custom types to override some of these inherited methods. To illustrate, update the **Person** class to support some properties representing an individual's first name, last name, and age, each of which can be set by a custom constructor:

```vb
'Remember! Person extends Object.
Public Class Person

        Public Property FirstName As String
        Public Property LastName As String
        Public Property Age As Integer

        Public Sub New(ByVal firstName As String, ByVal lastName As String, _
        ByVal age As Byte)
                Me.FirstName = firstName
                Me.LastName = lastName
                Me.Age = age
        End Sub

        Public Sub New()
        End Sub

End Class
```

Overriding System.Object.ToString()

Many classes that you create can benefit from overriding ToString() in order to return a string textual representation of the type's current state. This can be quite helpful for purposes of debugging (among other reasons). How you choose to construct this string is a matter of personal choice; however, a recommended approach is to separate each name/value pair with semicolons and wrap the entire string within square brackets (many types in the .NET base class libraries follow this approach). Consider the following overridden ToString() for your **Person** class:

```vb
Public Overrides Function ToString() As String

    Dim myState As String
    myState = String.Format("[First Name: {0}; Last Name: {1};
    Age: {2}]", FirstName, LastName, Age)

    Return myState
End Function
```

This implementation of `ToString()` is quite straightforward, given that the **Person** class only has three pieces of state data. However, always remember that a proper `ToString()` override should also account for any data defined *up the chain of inheritance*.

When you override `ToString()` for a class extending a custom base class, the first order of business is to obtain the `ToString()` value from your parent using the **MyBase** keyword. Once you have obtained your parent's string data, you can append the derived class's custom information.

Overriding System.Object.Equals()

Let's also override the behavior of `Object.Equals()` to work with value-based semantics. Recall that by default, `Equals()` returns **True** only if the two objects being compared reference the same object instance in memory. For the **Person** class, it may be helpful to implement `Equals()` to return **true** if the two variables being compared contain the same state values (e.g., FirstName, LastName, and Age).

First of all, notice that the incoming argument of the `Equals()` method is a general **System.Object**. Given this, your first order of business is to ensure the caller has indeed passed in a **Person** object, and as an extra safeguard, to make sure the incoming parameter is not **Nothing**.

Once you have established the caller has passed you an allocated **Person**, one approach to implement `Equals()` is to perform a field-by-field comparison against the data of the incoming object to the data of the current object:

```
Public Overrides Function Equals(ByVal obj As Object) As Boolean

    If TypeOf obj Is Person AndAlso obj <> Nothing Then

        Dim temp As Person
        temp = DirectCast(obj, Person)

        If temp.FirstName = Me.FirstName AndAlso temp.LastName =
        Me.LastName AndAlso temp.Age = Me.Age Then
                Return True
        Else
                Return False
        End If
    End If

    Return False
End Function
```

Here, you are examining the values of the incoming object against the values of your internal values (note the use of the Me keyword). If the name and age of each are identical, you have two objects with the exact same state data and therefore return **True**. Any other possibility results in returning **False**.

While this approach does indeed work, you can certainly imagine how labor intensive it would be to implement a custom `Equals()` method for nontrivial types that may contain dozens of data fields. One common shortcut is to leverage your own implementation of `ToString()`. If a class has a prim-and-proper implementation of `ToString()` that accounts for all field data up the chain of inheritance, you can simply perform a comparison of the object's string data:

```
'No need to cast 'obj' to a Person anymore,
'as everything has a ToString() method.
Public  Overrides Function Equals(ByVal obj As Object) As Boolean
                Return obj.ToString() = Me.ToString()
End Function
```

Notice in this case that we no longer need to check if the incoming argument is of the correct type (a Person in our example), as everything in .NET supports a ToString() method. Even better, we no longer need to perform a property-by-property equality check, as we are not simply testing the value returned from ToString().

Overriding System.Object.GetHashCode()

When a class overrides the Equals() method, you should also override the default implementation of GetHashCode(). Simply put, a *hash code* is a numerical value that represents an object as a particular state. For example, if you create two String variables that hold the value Hello, you would obtain the same hash code. However, if one of the String objects were in all lowercase (hello), you would obtain different hash codes.

By default, System.Object.GetHashCode() uses your object's current location in memory to yield the hash value. However, if you are building a custom type that you intend to store in a Hashtable type (within the System.Collections namespace), you should always override this member, as the Hashtable will be internally invoking Equals() and GetHashCode() to retrieve the correct object.

> ■ **Note** To be more specific, the System.Collections.Hashtable class calls GetHashCode() internally to gain an general idea where the object is located, but a subsequent (internal) call to Equals() determines the exact match.

Although you are not going to place your Person into a System.Collections.Hashtable, for completion, let's override GetHashCode(). There are many algorithms that can be used to create a hash code, some fancy, others not so fancy. Most of the time, you are able to generate a hash code value by leveraging the System.String's GetHashCode() implementation.

Given that the String class already has a solid hash code algorithm that is using the character data of the String to compute a hash value, if you can identify a piece of field data on your class that should be unique for all instances (such as a Social Security number), simply call GetHashCode() on that point of field data. Thus, if the Person class defined a SSN property, we could author the following code:

```
'Return a hash code based on a point of unique string data.
Public Overrides Function GetHashCode() As Integer
        Return SSN.GetHashCode()
End Function
```

If you cannot find a single point of unique **string** data, but you have overridden **ToString()**, call **GetHashCode()** on your own string representation:

```
'Return a hash code based on the person's ToString() value.
Public Overrides Function GetHashCode() As Integer
      Return Me.ToString().GetHashCode()
End Function
```

Testing Your Modified Person Class

Now that you have overridden the Overridable members of **Object**, update **Main()** to test your updates.

```
Sub Main()

        Console.WriteLine("***** Fun with System.Object *****" & vbLf)
        Dim p1 As New Person("Homer", "Simpson", 50)

        ' NOTE:  We want these to be identical to test
        ' the Equals() and GetHashCode() methods.
        Dim p1 As New Person("Homer", "Simpson", 50)
        Dim p2 As New Person("Homer", "Simpson", 50)

        'Get stringified version of objects.
        Dim p2 As New Person("Homer", "Simpson", 50)
        Console.WriteLine("p1.ToString() = {0}", p1.ToString())
        Console.WriteLine("p2.ToString() = {0}", p2.ToString())

        'Test Overridden Equals()
        Console.WriteLine("p1 = p2?: {0}", p1.Equals(p2))

        'Test hash codes.
        Console.WriteLine("Same hash codes?: {0}", p1.GetHashCode() = p2.GetHashCode())
        Console.WriteLine()

        'Change age of p2 and test again.
        p2.Age = 45
        Console.WriteLine("p1.ToString() = {0}", p1.ToString())
        Console.WriteLine("p2.ToString() = {0}", p2.ToString())
        Console.WriteLine("p1 = p2?: {0}", p1.Equals(p2))
        Console.WriteLine("Same hash codes?: {0}", p1.GetHashCode() = p2.GetHashCode())
        Console.ReadLine()
End Sub
```

The output can be seen here:

```
***** Fun with System.Object *****


p1.ToString() = [First Name: Homer; Last Name: Simpson; Age: 50]

p2.ToString() = [First Name: Homer; Last Name: Simpson; Age: 50]

p1 = p2?: True

Same hash codes?: True


p1.ToString() = [First Name: Homer; Last Name: Simpson; Age: 50]

p2.ToString() = [First Name: Homer; Last Name: Simpson; Age: 45]

p1 = p2?: False

Same hash codes?: False
```

The Shared Members of System.Object

In addition to the instance-level members you have just examined, System.Object does define two (very helpful) Shared members that also test for value-based or reference-based equality. Consider the following code:

```
Sub SharedMembersOfObject()

        'Shared members of System.Object.
        Dim p3 As New Person("Sally", "Jones", 4)
        Dim p4 As New Person("Sally", "Jones", 4)

        Console.WriteLine("P3 and P4 have same state: {0}",
                Object.Equals(p3, p4))
        Console.WriteLine("P3 and P4 are pointing to same object: {0}",
                Object.ReferenceEquals(p3, p4))
End Sub
```

Here, you are able to simply send in two objects (of any type) and allow the `System.Object` class to determine the details automatically. These methods can be very helpful when you have redefined equality for a custom type, yet still need to quickly determine whether two reference variables point to the same location in memory (via the Shared `ReferenceEquals()` method).

■ **Source Code** The ObjectOverrides project is located under the Chapter 6 subdirectory.

Summary

This chapter explored the role and details of inheritance and polymorphism. Over these pages you were introduced to numerous new keywords and tokens to support each of these techniques. Parent types are able to define any number of Overridable and/or MustOverride members to establish a polymorphic interface. Derived types override such members using the `Overrides` keyword.

In addition to building numerous class hierarchies, this chapter also examined how to explicitly cast between base and derived types, and wrapped up by diving into the details of the cosmic parent class in the .NET base class libraries: `System.Object`.

CHAPTER 7

■■■

Understanding Structured Exception Handling

In this chapter you will learn how to handle runtime anomalies in your VB 2010 code through the use of *structured exception handling* (often cryptically abbreviated as SEH). Not only will you examine the VB 2010 keywords that allow you to handle such matters (`Try`, `Catch`, `Throw`, `Finally`), you will also come to understand the distinction between application-level and system-level exceptions, as well as the role of the `System.Exception` base class. This discussion will lead into the topic of building custom exceptions, and, finally, to a quick look at the exception-centric debugging tools of Visual Studio 2010.

Ode to Errors, Bugs, and Exceptions

Despite what our (sometimes inflated) egos may tell us, no programmer is perfect. Writing software is a complex undertaking, and given this complexity, it is quite common for even the best software to ship with various...problems. Sometimes the problem is caused by "bad code" (such as overflowing the bounds of an array). Other times, a problem is caused by bogus user input that has not been accounted for in the application's code base (e.g., a phone number input field assigned to the value "Chucky"). Now, regardless of the cause of the problem, the end result is that the application does not work as expected. To help frame the upcoming discussion of structured exception handling, allow me to provide definitions for three commonly used anomaly-centric terms:

- *Bugs*: These are, simply put, errors made by the programmer. For example, suppose you are programming with unmanaged C++. If you fail to delete dynamically allocated memory, resulting in a memory leak, you have a bug.

- *User errors*: User errors, on the other hand, are typically caused by the individual running your application, rather than by those who created it. For example, an end user who enters a malformed string into a text box could very well generate an error *if* you fail to handle this faulty input in your code base.

- *Exceptions*: Exceptions are typically regarded as runtime anomalies that are difficult, if not impossible, to account for while programming your application. Possible exceptions include attempting to connect to a database that no longer exists, opening a corrupted XML file, or trying to contact a machine that is currently offline. In each of these cases, the programmer (or end user) has little control over these "exceptional" circumstances.

Given these definitions, it should be clear that .NET structured *exception* handling is a technique for dealing with runtime *exceptions*. However, even for the bugs and user errors that have escaped your view, the CLR will often generate a corresponding exception that identifies the problem at hand. The .NET base class libraries define numerous exceptions, such as `FormatException`, `IndexOutOfRangeException`, `FileNotFoundException`, `ArgumentOutOfRangeException`, and so forth.

Within the .NET nomenclature, an "exception" accounts for bugs, bogus user input, and runtime errors, even though we programmers may view each of these as a distinct issue. However, before we get too far ahead of ourselves, let's formalize the role of structured exception handling and check out how it differs from traditional error-handling techniques.

■ **Note** To make the code examples used in this book as clean as possible, I will not catch every possible exception that may be thrown by a given method in the base class libraries. In your production level projects, you should, of course, make liberal use of the techniques presented in this chapter.

The Role of .NET Exception Handling

Prior to .NET, error handling under the Windows operating system was a confused mishmash of techniques. Many programmers rolled their own error-handling logic within the context of a given application. For example, a development team could define a set of numerical constants that represented known error conditions, and make use of them as method return values. By way of an example, consider the following partial C code:

```
/* A very C-style error trapping mechanism. */
#define E_FILENOTFOUND 1000

int SomeFunction()
{
  // Assume something happens in this function
  // that causes the following return value.
  return E_FILENOTFOUND;
}

void main()
{
  int retVal = SomeFunction();
  if(retVal == E_FILENOTFOUND)
    printf("Cannot find file...");
}
```

This approach is less than ideal, given the fact that the constant `E_FILENOTFOUND` is little more than a numerical value, and is far from being a helpful agent regarding how to deal with the problem. Ideally, you would like to wrap the error's name, a descriptive message, and other helpful information about this error condition into a single, well-defined package (which is exactly what happens under structured exception handling).

In addition to a developer's ad hoc techniques, the Windows API defines hundreds of error codes that come by way of `#defines`, `HRESULTs`, and far too many variations on the simple Boolean (`bool`, `BOOL`, `VARIANT_BOOL`, and so on). Furthermore, many C++ COM developers (and indirectly, many VB6 COM developers) made use of a small set of standard COM interfaces (e.g., `ISupportErrorInfo`, `IErrorInfo`, `ICreateErrorInfo`) to return meaningful error information to a COM client.

The obvious problem with these older techniques is the tremendous lack of symmetry. Each approach is more or less tailored to a given technology, a given language, and perhaps even a given project. To put an end to this madness, the .NET platform provides a standard technique to send and trap runtime errors: structured exception handling (SEH).

The beauty of this approach is that developers now have a unified approach to error handling, which is common to all languages targeting the .NET platform. Therefore, the way in which a VB 2010 programmer handles errors is syntactically similar to that of a C# programmer, or a C++ programmer using C++/CLI.

As an added bonus, the syntax used to throw and catch exceptions across assemblies and machine boundaries is identical. For example, if you use VB 2010 to build a Windows Communication Foundation (WCF) service, you can throw a SOAP fault to a remote caller, using the same keywords that allow you to throw an exception between methods in the same application.

Another bonus of .NET exceptions is that rather than receiving a cryptic numerical value that simply identifies the problem at hand, exceptions are objects that contain a human-readable description of the problem, as well as a detailed snapshot of the call stack that triggered the exception in the first place. Furthermore, you are able to give the end user help-link information that points the user to a URL that provides details about the error, as well as custom programmer-defined data.

The Atoms of .NET Exception Handling

Programming with structured exception handling involves the use of four interrelated entities:

- A class type that represents the details of the exception

- A member that *throws* an instance of the exception class to the caller under exceptional circumstances

- A block of code on the caller's side that invokes the exception-prone member

- A block of code on the caller's side that will process (or *catch*) the exception should it occur

The VB 2010 programming language offers four keywords (`Try`, `Catch`, `Throw`, and `Finally`) that allow you to throw and handle exceptions. The object that represents the problem at hand is a class extending `System.Exception` (or a descendent thereof). Given this fact, let's check out the role of this exception-centric base class.

The System.Exception Base Class

All user- and system-defined exceptions ultimately derive from the `System.Exception` base class, which in turn derives from `System.Object`. Here is the crux of this class (note that some of these members are Overridable and may thus be overridden by derived classes):

```
Public Class Exception
        Implements ISerializable, _Exception

        ' Public constructors
        Public Sub New(ByVal  message As String, ByVal innerException As Exception)
        Public Sub New(ByVal message As String)

        Public Sub New()


        ...
        ' Methods
        Public Overridable Function GetBaseException() As Exception

Public Overridable Sub GetObjectData(iByVal info As SerializationInfo, ByVal context↵
 As StreamingContext)

        ' Properties
        Public Overridable ReadOnly Property Data() As IDictionary
        Public Overridable Property HelpLink() As String

        Public ReadOnly Property InnerException() As Exception
        Public Overridable ReadOnly Property Message() As String
        Public Overridable Property Source() As String
        Public Overridable ReadOnly Property StackTrace() As String

        Public ReadOnly Property TargetSite() As MethodBase

        ...
End Class
```

As you can see, many of the properties defined by `System.Exception` are read-only in nature. This is due to the fact that derived types will typically supply default values for each property. For example, the default message of the `IndexOutOfRangeException` type is "Index was outside the bounds of the array."

■ **Note** The `Exception` class implements two .NET interfaces. Although we have yet to examine interfaces (see Chapter 9), just understand that the `_Exception` interface allows a .NET exception to be processed by an unmanaged code base (such as a COM application), while the `ISerializable` interface allows an exception object to be persisted across boundaries (such as a machine boundary).

Table 7-1 describes the most important members of `System.Exception`.

Table 7-1. *Core Members of the System.Exception Type*

System.Exception Property	Meaning in Life
Data	This read-only property retrieves a collection of key/value pairs (represented by an object implementing `IDictionary`) that provide additional, programmer-defined information about the exception. By default, this collection is empty.
HelpLink	This property gets or sets a URL to a help file or web site describing the error in full detail.
InnerException	This read-only property can be used to obtain information about the previous exception(s) that caused the current exception to occur. The previous exception(s) are recorded by passing them into the constructor of the most current exception.
Message	This read-only property returns the textual description of a given error. The error message itself is set as a constructor parameter.
Source	This property gets or sets the name of the assembly, or the object, that threw the current exception.
StackTrace	This read-only property contains a string that identifies the sequence of calls that triggered the exception. As you might guess, this property is very useful during debugging or if you wish to dump the error to an external error log.
TargetSite	This read-only property returns a `MethodBase` object, which describes numerous details about the method that threw the exception (invoking `ToString()` will identify the method by name).

The Simplest Possible Example

To illustrate the usefulness of structured exception handling, we need to create a class that will throw an exception under the correct (or one might say *exceptional)* circumstances. Assume we have created a new VB 2010 Console Application project (named SimpleException) that defines two class types (`Car` and `Radio`) associated by the "has-a" relationship. The `Radio` type defines a single method that turns the radio's power on or off:

```
Public Class Radio
        Public Sub TurnOn(Byval IsOn As Boolean)
                If IsOn Then
                        Console.WriteLine("Jamming...")
                Else
                        Console.WriteLine("Quiet time...")
                End If
        End Sub
End Class
```

In addition to leveraging the Radio class via containment/delegation, the Car class (shown below) is defined in such a way that if the user accelerates a Car object beyond a predefined maximum speed (specified using a constant member variable named MaxSpeed), its engine explodes, rendering the Car unusable (captured by a private Boolean member variable named carIsDead).

Beyond these points, the Car type has a few properties to represent the current speed and a user supplied "pet name," as well as various constructors to set the state of a new Car object. Here is the complete definition (with code annotations):

```
Public Class Car
    ' Constant for maximum speed.
    Public Const MaxSpeed As Integer = 100

    ' Car properties.
    Public Property CurrentSpeed() As Integer
    Public Property PetName() As String

    ' Is the car still operational?
    Private carIsDead As Boolean

    ' A car has-a radio.
    Private theMusicBox As New Radio()

    ' Constructors.
    Public Sub New()
    End Sub
    Public Sub New(ByVal name As String, ByVal speed As Integer)
        CurrentSpeed = speed
        PetName = name
    End Sub

    Public Sub CrankTunes(ByVal state As Boolean)
        ' Delegate request to inner object.
        theMusicBox.TurnOn(state)
    End Sub

    ' See if Car has overheated.
    Public Sub Accelerate(ByVal delta As Integer)
        If carIsDead Then
            Console.WriteLine("{0} is out of order...", PetName)
        Else
            CurrentSpeed += delta
```

```
            If CurrentSpeed > MaxSpeed Then
                Console.WriteLine("{0} has overheated!", PetName)
                CurrentSpeed = 0
                carIsDead = True
            Else
                Console.WriteLine("=> CurrentSpeed = {0}", CurrentSpeed)
            End If
        End If
    End Sub
End Class
```

Now, if we implement a `Main()` method that forces a `Car` object to exceed the predefined maximum speed (set to 100, in the Car class) as shown here:

```
Module Module1
    Sub Main()
        Console.WriteLine("***** Simple Exception Example *****")
        Console.WriteLine("=> Creating a car and stepping on it!")
        Dim myCar As New Car("Zippy", 20)
        myCar.CrankTunes(True)

        For i As Integer = 0 To 9
            myCar.Accelerate(10)
        Next
        Console.ReadLine()
    End Sub
End Module
```

we would see the following output:

```
***** Simple Exception Example *****

=> Creating a car and stepping on it!

Jamming...

=> CurrentSpeed = 30

=> CurrentSpeed = 40

=> CurrentSpeed = 50

=> CurrentSpeed = 60

=> CurrentSpeed = 70

=> CurrentSpeed = 80
```

```
=> CurrentSpeed = 90

=> CurrentSpeed = 100

Zippy has overheated!

Zippy is out of order...
```

Throwing a General Exception

Now that we have a functional `Car` class, I'll demonstrate the simplest way to throw an exception. The current implementation of `Accelerate()` simply displays an error message if the caller attempts to speed up the `Car` beyond its upper limit.

To retrofit this method to throw an exception if the user attempts to speed up the automobile after it has met its maker, you want to create and configure a new instance of the `System.Exception` class, setting the value of the read-only `Message` property via the class constructor. When you wish to send the exception object back to the caller, use the VB 2010 `Throw` keyword. Here is the relevant code update to the `Accelerate()` method:

```
' This time, throw an exception if the user speeds up beyond MaxSpeed.
Public Sub Accelerate(ByVal delta As Integer)
        If carIsDead Then
                Console.WriteLine("{0} is out of order...", PetName)
        Else
                CurrentSpeed += delta
                If CurrentSpeed > MaxSpeed Then
                        carIsDead = True
                        CurrentSpeed = 0

                        ' Use the "Throw" keyword to raise an exception.
                        Throw New Exception(String.Format("{0} has overheated!", PetName))
                Else
                        Console.WriteLine("=> CurrentSpeed = {0}", CurrentSpeed)
                End If
        End If
End Sub
```

Before examining how a caller would catch this exception, a few points of interest. First of all, when you are throwing an exception, it is always up to you to decide exactly what constitutes the error in question, and when an exception should be thrown. Here, you are making the assumption that if the program attempts to increase the speed of a `Car` object that has expired, a `System.Exception` object should be thrown to indicate the `Accelerate()` method cannot continue (which may or may not be a valid assumption; this will be a judgment call on your part based on the application you are creating).

Alternatively, you could implement `Accelerate()` to recover automatically without needing to throw an exception in the first place. By and large, exceptions should be thrown only when a more terminal condition has been met (for example, not finding a necessary file, failing to connect to a database, and the like). Deciding exactly what justifies throwing an exception is a design issue you must always contend with. For our current purposes, assume that asking a doomed automobile to increase its speed is cause to throw an exception.

Catching Exceptions

Because the `Accelerate()` method now throws an exception, the caller needs to be ready to handle the exception should it occur. When you are invoking a method that may throw an exception, you make use of a `Try/Catch` block. Once you have caught the exception object, you are able to invoke the members of the exception object to extract the details of the problem.

What you do with this data is largely up to you. You may wish to log this information to a report file, write the data to the Windows event log, e-mail a system administrator, or display the problem to the end user. Here, you will simply dump the contents to the console window:

```
Module Module1
    'Handle the thrown exception.
    Sub Main()
            Console.WriteLine("***** Simple Exception Example *****")
            Console.WriteLine("=> Creating a car and stepping on it!")
            Dim myCar As New Car("Zippy", 20)
            myCar.CrankTunes(True)

            ' Speed up past the car's max speed to
            ' trigger the exception.
            Try
              For i As Integer = 0 To 9
                  myCar.Accelerate(10)
              Next
            Catch e As Exception
              Console.WriteLine(vbLf & "*** Error! ***")
              Console.WriteLine("Method: {0}", e.TargetSite)
              Console.WriteLine("Message: {0}", e.Message)
              Console.WriteLine("Source: {0}", e.Source)
            End Try

            ' The error has been handled, processing continues with the
              next statement.
            Console.WriteLine(vbLf & "***** Out of exception logic *****")
            Console.ReadLine()
        End Sub
End Module
```

In essence, a `Try` block is a section of statements that may throw an exception during execution. If an exception is detected, the flow of program execution is sent to the appropriate `Catch` block. On the other hand, if the code within a `Try` block does not trigger an exception, the `Catch` block is skipped entirely, and all is right with the world. The following output shows a test run of this program.

```
***** Simple Exception Example *****

=> Creating a car and stepping on it!

Jamming...

=> CurrentSpeed = 30

=> CurrentSpeed = 40

=> CurrentSpeed = 50

=> CurrentSpeed = 60

=> CurrentSpeed = 70

=> CurrentSpeed = 80

=> CurrentSpeed = 90


*** Error! ***

Method: Void Accelerate(Int32)

Message: Zippy has overheated!

Source: SimpleException


***** Out of exception logic *****
```

As you can see, once an exception has been handled, the application is free to continue on from the point after the Catch block. In some circumstances, a given exception may be critical enough to warrant the termination of the application. However, in a good number of cases, the logic within the exception handler will ensure the application can continue on its merry way (although it may be slightly less functional, such as not being able to connect to a remote data source).

Configuring the State of an Exception

Currently, the `System.Exception` object configured within the `Accelerate()` method simply establishes a value exposed to the `Message` property (via a constructor parameter). As shown previously in Table 7-1, however, the `Exception` class also supplies a number of additional members (`TargetSite`, `StackTrace`, `HelpLink`, and `Data`) that can be useful in further qualifying the nature of the problem. To spruce up our current example, let's examine further details of these members on a case-by-case basis.

The TargetSite Property

The `System.Exception.TargetSite` property allows you to determine various details about the method that threw a given exception. As shown in the previous `Main()` method, printing the value of `TargetSite` will display the return type, name, and parameter types of the method that threw the exception. However, `TargetSite` does not return just a vanilla-flavored string, but rather a strongly typed `System.Reflection.MethodBase` object. This type can be used to gather numerous details regarding the offending method, as well as the class that defines the offending method. To illustrate, assume the previous `Catch` logic has been updated as follows:

```
Module Module1
    Sub Main()
        ...
        ' TargetSite actually returns a MethodBase object.
        Catch e As Exception
            Console.WriteLine(vbLf & "*** Error! ***")
            Console.WriteLine("Member name: {0}", e.TargetSite)
            Console.WriteLine("Class defining member: {0}", e.TargetSite.DeclaringType)
            Console.WriteLine("Member type: {0}", e.TargetSite.MemberType)
            Console.WriteLine("Message: {0}", e.Message)
            Console.WriteLine("Source: {0}", e.Source)
        End Try
        Console.WriteLine(vbLf & "***** Out of exception logic *****")
        Console.ReadLine()
        End Sub
End Module
```

This time, you make use of the `MethodBase.DeclaringType` property to determine the fully qualified name of the class that threw the error (`SimpleException.Car` in this case) as well as the `MemberType` property of the `MethodBase` object to identify the type of member (such as a property vs. a method) where this exception originated. In this case, the `Catch` logic would display the following:

```
*** Error! ***

Member name: Void Accelerate(Int32)

Class defining member: SimpleException.Car

Member type: Method

Message: Zippy has overheated!

Source: SimpleException
```

The StackTrace Property

The System.Exception.StackTrace property allows you to identify the series of calls that resulted in the exception. Be aware that you never set the value of StackTrace as it is established automatically at the time the exception is created. To illustrate, assume you have once again updated your Catch logic:

```
Catch e As Exception
    ...
        Console.WriteLine("Stack: {0}", e.StackTrace)
End Try
```

If you were to run the program, you would find the following stack trace is printed to the console (your line numbers and file paths may differ, of course):

```
Stack: at SimpleException.Car.Accelerate(Int32 delta)

in c:\MyApps\SimpleException\car.vb:line 65 at SimpleException.Program.Main()

in c:\MyApps\SimpleException\Program.vb:line 21
```

The string returned from StackTrace documents the sequence of calls that resulted in the throwing of this exception. Notice how the bottommost line number of this string identifies the first call in the sequence, while the topmost line number identifies the exact location of the offending member. Clearly, this information can be quite helpful during the debugging or logging of a given application, as you are able to "follow the flow" of the error's origin.

The HelpLink Property

While the TargetSite and StackTrace properties allow programmers to gain an understanding of a given exception, this information is of little use to the end user. As you have already seen, the System.Exception.Message property can be used to obtain human-readable information that can be displayed to the current user. In addition, the HelpLink property can be set to point the user to a specific URL or standard Windows help file that contains more detailed information.

By default, the value managed by the HelpLink property is an empty string. If you wish to fill this property with a more interesting value, you need to do so before throwing the System.Exception object. Here are the relevant updates to the Car.Accelerate() method:

```
Public Sub Accelerate(ByVal delta As Integer)
        If carIsDead Then
                Console.WriteLine("{0} is out of order...", PetName)
        Else
                CurrentSpeed += delta
                If CurrentSpeed > MaxSpeed Then
                        carIsDead = True
                        CurrentSpeed = 0

                        ' We need to call the HelpLink property, thus we need to
                        ' create a local variable before throwing the Exception object.
                        Dim ex As New Exception(String.Format("{0} has overheated!",
                                                PetName))
                        ex.HelpLink = "http://www.CarsRUs.com"
                        Throw ex
                Else
                        Console.WriteLine("=> CurrentSpeed = {0}", CurrentSpeed)
                End If
        End If
End Sub
```

The Catch logic could now be updated to print out this help link information as follows:

```
Catch e As Exception
        ...
        Console.WriteLine("Help Link: {0}", e.HelpLink)
End Try
```

The Data Property

The Data property of System.Exception allows you to fill an exception object with relevant auxiliary information (such as a time stamp). The Data property returns an object implementing an interface named IDictionary, defined in the System.Collections namespace. Chapter 9 examines the role of interface-based programming as well as the System.Collections namespace. For the time being, just understand that dictionary collections allow you to create a set of values that are retrieved using a specific key. Observe the next update to the Car.Accelerate() method:

```
Public Sub Accelerate(ByVal delta As Integer)
        If carIsDead Then
                Console.WriteLine("{0} is out of order...", PetName)
        Else
                CurrentSpeed += delta
                If CurrentSpeed > MaxSpeed Then
                        carIsDead = True
                        CurrentSpeed = 0
```

```
                        ' We need to call the HelpLink property, thus we need
                        ' to create a local variable before throwing the Exception object.
                        Dim ex As New Exception(String.Format("{0} has overheated!",↩
                                          PetName))
                        ex.HelpLink = "http://www.CarsRUs.com"

                        ' Stuff in custom data regarding the error.
                        ex.Data.Add("TimeStamp", String.Format("The car exploded at {0}",↩
                                          DateTime.Now))
                        ex.Data.Add("Cause", "You have a lead foot.")
                        Throw ex
                Else
                        Console.WriteLine("=> CurrentSpeed = {0}", CurrentSpeed)
                End If
        End If
End Sub
```

To successfully enumerate over the key/value pairs, you must first make sure to specify an `Imports` directive for the `System.Collections` namespace, since you will use a `DictionaryEntry` type in the file containing the class implementing your `Main()` method:

```
Imports System.Collections
```

Next, you need to update the `Catch` logic to test that the value returned from the `Data` property is not `Nothing` (the default value). After that, you make use of the `Key` and `Value` properties of the `DictionaryEntry` type to print the custom data to the console:

```
Catch e As Exception
        ...
        ' By default, the data field is empty, so check for null.
        Console.WriteLine(vbLf & "-> Custom Data:")
        If e.Data IsNot Nothing Then
                For Each de As DictionaryEntry In e.Data
                        Console.WriteLine("-> {0}: {1}", de.Key, de.Value)
                Next
        End If
End Try
```

With this, here's the final output you'd see:

```
***** Simple Exception Example *****

=> Creating a car and stepping on it!

Jamming...

=> CurrentSpeed = 30

=> CurrentSpeed = 40
```

```
=> CurrentSpeed = 50

=> CurrentSpeed = 60

=> CurrentSpeed = 70

=> CurrentSpeed = 80

=> CurrentSpeed = 90


*** Error! ***

Member name: Void Accelerate(Int32)

Class defining member: SimpleException.Car

Member type: Method

Message: Zippy has overheated!

Source: SimpleException

Stack: at SimpleException.Car.Accelerate(Int32 delta)

        at SimpleException.Program.Main(String[] args)

Help Link: http://www.CarsRUs.com


-> Custom Data:

-> TimeStamp: The car exploded at 1/12/2010 8:02:12 PM

-> Cause: You have a lead foot.


***** Out of exception logic *****
```

The **Data** property is very useful in that it allows us to pack in custom information regarding the error at hand, without requiring the building of a brand-new class type to extend the **Exception** base class (which, prior to .NET 2.0, was our only option!). As helpful as the **Data** property may be, however, it is still common for .NET developers to build strongly typed exception classes, which handle custom data using strongly typed properties.

This approach allows the caller to catch a specific **exception**-derived type, rather than having to dig into a data collection to obtain additional details. To understand how to do this, we need to examine the distinction between system-level and application-level exceptions.

■ **Source Code** The SimpleException project is included under the Chapter 7 subdirectory.

System-Level Exceptions (System.SystemException)

The .NET base class libraries define many classes that ultimately derive from **System.Exception**. For example, the **System** namespace defines core exception classes such as **ArgumentOutOfRangeException**, **IndexOutOfRangeException**, **StackOverflowException**, and so forth. Other namespaces define exceptions that reflect the behavior of that namespace. For example, **System.Drawing.Printing** defines printing exceptions, **System.IO** defines input/output-based exceptions, **System.Data** defines database-centric exceptions, and so forth.

Exceptions that are thrown by the .NET platform are (appropriately) called *system exceptions*. These exceptions are regarded as non-recoverable, fatal errors. System exceptions derive directly from a base class named **System.SystemException**, which in turn derives from **System.Exception** (which derives from **System.Object**):

```
Public Class SystemException
        Inherits Exception
        ' Various constructors.
End Class
```

Given that the **System.SystemException** type does not add any additional functionality beyond a set of custom constructors, you might wonder why **SystemException** exists in the first place. Simply put, when an exception type derives from **System.SystemException**, you are able to determine that the .NET runtime is the entity that has thrown the exception, rather than the code base of the executing application. You can verify this quite simply using the VB 2010 **TypeOf** construct:

```
' True! NullReferenceException is-a SystemException.
Dim nullRefEx As New NullReferenceException()

Console.WriteLine("NullReferenceException is-a SystemException? : {0}", TypeOf nullRefEx↩
  Is SystemException)
```

Application-Level Exceptions (System.ApplicationException)

Given that all .NET exceptions are class types, you are free to create your own application-specific exceptions. However, due to the fact that the **System.SystemException** base class represents exceptions thrown from the CLR, you may naturally assume that you should derive your custom exceptions from the `System.Exception` type. You could do this, but you could instead derive from the `System.ApplicationException` class:

```
Public Class ApplicationException
       Inherits Exception
       '  Various constructors.
End Class
```

Like `SystemException`, `ApplicationException` does not define any additional members beyond a set of constructors. Functionally, the only purpose of `System.ApplicationException` is to identify the source of the error. When you handle an exception deriving from `System.ApplicationException`, you can assume the exception was raised by the code base of the executing application, rather than by the .NET base class libraries or .NET runtime engine.

Building Custom Exceptions, Take One

While you can always throw instances of `System.Exception` to signal a runtime error (as shown in the first example), it is sometimes advantageous to build a *strongly typed exception* that represents the unique details of your current problem. For example, assume you wish to build a custom exception (named `CarIsDeadException`) to represent the error of speeding up a doomed automobile. The first step is to derive a new class from `System.Exception`/`System.ApplicationException` (by convention, all exception classes end with the "Exception" suffix; in fact, this is a .NET best practice).

■ **Note** As a rule, all custom exception classes should be defined as Public classes (recall, the default access modifier of a non-nested type is Friend). The reason is that exceptions are often passed outside of assembly boundaries, and should therefore be accessible to the calling code base.

Create a new Console Application project named CustomException, and copy the previous `Car.vb` and `Radio.vb` files into your new project using the Project ➤ Add Existing Item menu option. Next, add the following class definition:

```
' This custom exception describes the details of the car-is-dead condition.
Public Class CarIsDeadException
       Inherits ApplicationException
End Class
```

As with any class, you are free to include any number of custom members that can be called within the `Catch` block of the calling logic. You are also free to override any Overridable members defined by your parent classes. For example, we could implement the `CarIsDeadException` by overriding the Overridable `Message` property.

As well, rather than populating a data dictionary (via the `Data` property) when throwing our exception, our constructor allows the sender to pass in a time stamp and reason for the error. Finally, the time stamp data and cause of the error can be obtained using strongly typed properties:

```
Public Class CarIsDeadException
        Inherits ApplicationException

        Private messageDetails As String = String.Empty
        Public Property ErrorTimeStamp() As DateTime

        Public Property CauseOfError() As String

        Public Sub New()
        End Sub
        Public Sub New(ByVal message As String, ByVal cause As String, ByVal time↵
                                        As DateTime)
                messageDetails = message
                CauseOfError = cause
                ErrorTimeStamp = time
        End Sub

        ' Override the Exception.Message property.
        Public Overrides ReadOnly Property Message() As String
                Get
                        Return String.Format("Car Error Message: {0}", messageDetails)
                End Get
        End Property
End Class
```

Here, the CarIsDeadException class maintains a Private field (messageDetails) that represents data regarding the current exception, which can be set using a custom constructor. Throwing this exception from the Accelerate() method is straightforward. Simply allocate, configure, and throw a CarIsDeadException type rather than a System.Exception (notice that in this case, we no longer need to fill the data collection manually):

```
' Throw the custom CarIsDeadException.
Public Sub Accelerate(ByVal delta As Integer)
        ...
        Dim ex As New CarIsDeadException(String.Format("{0} has overheated!", PetName),↵
  "You have a lead foot", DateTime.Now)
        ex.HelpLink = "http://www.CarsRUs.com"
        Throw ex
        ...
End Sub
```

To catch this incoming exception, your Catch scope can now be updated to catch a specific CarIsDeadException type (however, given that CarIsDeadException "is-a" System.Exception, it is still permissible to catch a System.Exception as well):

```
Module Module1
        Sub Main()
                Console.WriteLine("***** Fun with Custom Exceptions *****" & vbLf)
                Dim myCar As New Car("Rusty", 90)
```

```
            Try
            ' Trip exception.
            myCar.Accelerate(50)
            Catch e As CarIsDeadException
            Console.WriteLine(e.Message)
            Console.WriteLine(e.ErrorTimeStamp)
            Console.WriteLine(e.CauseOfError)
             End Try
            Console.ReadLine()
        End Sub
End Module
```

So, now that you understand the basic process of building a custom exception, you may wonder when you are required to do so. Typically, you only need to create custom exceptions when the error is tightly bound to the class issuing the error (for example, a custom file-centric class that throws a number of file-related errors, a `Car` class that throws a number of car-related errors, a data access object that throws errors regarding a particular database table, and so forth). In doing so, you provide the caller with the ability to handle numerous exceptions on a descriptive error-by-error basis.

Building Custom Exceptions, Take Two

The current `CarIsDeadException` type has overridden the virtual `System.Exception.Message` property in order to configure a custom error message, and has supplied two custom properties to account for additional bits of data. In reality, however, you are not required to override the Overridable `Message` property, as you could simply pass the incoming message to the parent's constructor as follows:

```
Public Class CarIsDeadException
        Inherits ApplicationException

        Public Property ErrorTimeStamp() As DateTime

        Public Property CauseOfError() As String

        Public Sub New()
        End Sub

        ' Feed message to parent constructor.
        Public Sub New(ByVal message As String,ByVal  cause As String,ByVal  time↵
                    As DateTime)
            MyBase.New(message)
            CauseOfError = cause
            ErrorTimeStamp = time
        End Sub
End Class
```

Notice that this time you have *not* defined a String variable to represent the message, and have *not* overridden the `Message` property. Rather, you are simply passing the parameter to your base class constructor. With this design, a custom exception class is little more than a uniquely named class deriving from `System.ApplicationException`, (with additional properties if appropriate), devoid of any base class overrides.

Don't be surprised if most (if not all) of your custom exception classes follow this simple pattern. Many times, the role of a custom exception is not necessarily to provide additional functionality beyond what is inherited from the base classes, but to supply a *strongly named type* that clearly identifies the nature of the error, so the client can provide different handler-logic for different types of exceptions.

Building Custom Exceptions, Take Three

If you wish to build a truly prim-and-proper custom exception class, you would want to make sure your type adheres to .NET best practices. Specifically, this requires that your custom exception

- Derives from `ApplicationException`

- Is marked with the `<System.Serializable>` attribute

- Defines a default constructor

- Defines a constructor that sets the inherited `Message` property

- Defines a constructor to handle "inner exceptions"

- Defines a constructor to handle the serialization of your type

Now, based on your current background with .NET, you may have no idea regarding the role of attributes or object serialization, which is just fine. I'll address these topics later in the text (see Chapter 15 for information on attributes and Chapter 20 for details on serialization services). However, to complete our examination of building custom exceptions, here is the final iteration of `CarIsDeadException`, which accounts for each of these special constructors:

```
<Serializable()> _
Public Class CarIsDeadException
        Inherits ApplicationException

        Public Sub New()
        End Sub
        Public Sub New(ByVal message As String)
                MyBase.New(message)
        End Sub
        Public Sub New(ByVal message As String,ByVal  inner As System.Exception)
                MyBase.New(message, inner)
        End Sub
        Protected Sub New(ByVal info As System.Runtime.Serialization.SerializationInfo,↵
                        ByVal context As System.Runtime.Serialization.StreamingContext)
                MyBase.New(info, context)
        End Sub

        ' Any additional custom properties, constructors and data members...
End Class
```

Given that building custom exceptions that adhere to .NET best practices really differ by only their name, you will be happy to know that Visual Studio 2010 provides a code snippet template named "Exception" (see Figure 7-1) that will autogenerate a new exception class that adheres to .NET best practices. (Recall from Chapter 2, a code snippet can be activated by right-clicking in the code editor and choosing the Insert Snippet option. Thereafter you need to choose the option that includes the Exception handling related code snippet, as shown in Figure 7-1.)

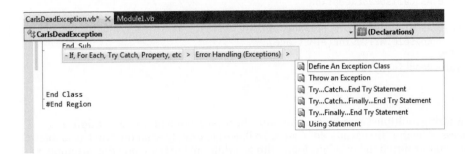

Figure 7-1. The Exception code snippet template

■ **Source Code** The CustomException project is included under the Chapter 7 subdirectory.

Processing Multiple Exceptions

In its simplest form, a `Try` block has a single `Catch` block. In reality, though, you often run into situations where the statements within a `Try` block could trigger *numerous* possible exceptions. Create a new VB 2010 Console Application project named `ProcessMultipleExceptions`, add the `Car.vb`, `Radio.vb`, and `CarIsDeadException.vb` files from the previous CustomException example into the new project (via Project ► Add Existing Item).

Now, update the `Car`'s `Accelerate()` method to also throw a predefined base class library `ArgumentOutOfRangeException` if you pass an invalid parameter (which we will assume is any value less than zero). Note the constructor of this exception class takes the name of the offending argument as the first `string`, followed by a message describing the error.

```
' Test for invalid argument before proceeding.
Public Sub Accelerate(ByVal delta As Integer)
        If delta < 0 Then
Throw New ArgumentOutOfRangeException("delta", "Speed must be greater than zero!")
        End If
        ...
End Sub
```

The `Catch` logic could now specifically respond to each type of exception:

```
Module Module1
        Sub Main()
                Console.WriteLine("***** Handling Multiple Exceptions *****" & vbLf)
                Dim myCar As New Car("Rusty", 90)
```

```
        Try
                ' Trip Arg out of range exception.
                myCar.Accelerate(-10)
        Catch e As CarIsDeadException
                Console.WriteLine(e.Message)
        Catch e As ArgumentOutOfRangeException
                Console.WriteLine(e.Message)
        End Try
        Console.ReadLine()
End Sub
End Module
```

When you are authoring multiple Catch blocks, you must be aware that when an exception is thrown, it will be processed by the "first available" Catch. To illustrate exactly what the "first available" Catch means, assume you retrofitted the previous logic with an additional Catch scope that attempts to handle all exceptions beyond CarIsDeadException and ArgumentOutOfRangeException by catching a general System.Exception as follows:

```
' This code will not compile!
Module Module1
Sub Main()
        Console.WriteLine("***** Handling Multiple Exceptions *****" & vbLf)
        Dim myCar As New Car("Rusty", 90)

        Try
                ' Trigger an argument out of range exception.
                myCar.Accelerate(-10)
        Catch e As Exception
                ' Process all other exceptions?
                Console.WriteLine(e.Message)
        Catch e As CarIsDeadException
                Console.WriteLine(e.Message)
        Catch e As ArgumentOutOfRangeException
                Console.WriteLine(e.Message)
        End Try
        Console.ReadLine()
End Sub
End Module
```

This exception-handling logic generates compile-time errors. The problem is due to the fact that the first Catch block can handle *anything* derived from System.Exception (given the "is-a" relationship), including the CarIsDeadException and ArgumentOutOfRangeException types. Therefore, the final two Catch blocks are unreachable!

The rule of thumb to keep in mind is to make sure your Catch blocks are structured such that the very first Catch is the most specific exception (i.e., the most derived type in an exception-type inheritance chain), leaving the final Catch for the most general (i.e., the base class of a given exception inheritance chain, in this case System.Exception).

Thus, if you wish to define a Catch block that will handle any errors beyond CarIsDeadException and ArgumentOutOfRangeException, you could write the following:

```
' This code compiles just fine.
Module Module1
     Sub Main()
               Console.WriteLine("***** Handling Multiple Exceptions *****" & vbLf)
               Dim myCar As New Car("Rusty", 90)
               Try
                     ' Trigger an argument out of range exception.
                     myCar.Accelerate(-10)
               Catch e As CarIsDeadException
                     Console.WriteLine(e.Message)
               Catch e As ArgumentOutOfRangeException
                     Console.WriteLine(e.Message)
               ' This will catch any other exception
               ' beyond CarIsDeadException or
               ' ArgumentOutOfRangeException.
               Catch e As Exception
                     Console.WriteLine(e.Message)
               End Try
               Console.ReadLine()
     End Sub
End Module
```

■ **Note** Where at all possible, always favor catching specific exception classes, rather than a general System.Exception. Though it might appear to make life simple in the short term (you may think, "Ah! This catches all the other things I don't care about."), in the long term you could end up with strange runtime crashes, as a more serious error was not directly dealt with in your code. Remember, a final Catch block that deals with System.Exception tends to be very general indeed.

General Catch Statements

VB 2010 also supports a "general" Catch scope that does not explicitly receive the exception object thrown by a given member:

```
' A generic catch.
Module Module1
     Sub Main()
               Console.WriteLine("***** Handling Multiple Exceptions *****" & vbLf)
               Dim myCar As New Car("Rusty", 90)
               Try
                     myCar.Accelerate(90)
               Catch
                     Console.WriteLine("Something bad happened...")
               End Try
               Console.ReadLine()
     End Sub
End Module
```

Obviously, this is not the most informative way to handle exceptions, since you have no way to obtain meaningful data about the error that occurred (such as the method name, call stack, or custom message). Nevertheless, VB 2010 does allow for such a construct, which can be helpful when you want to handle all errors in a very, very general fashion.

Rethrowing Exceptions

When you catch an exception, it is permissible for the logic in a Catch block to *rethrow* the exception up the call stack to the previous caller. To do so, simply use the Throw keyword within a Catch block. This passes the exception up the chain of calling logic, which can be helpful if your Catch block is only able to partially handle the error at hand:

```
' Passing the buck.
Module Module1
      Sub Main()
      ...
                  ' Speed up car logic...
                  Try
                  Catch e As CarIsDeadException
                          ' Do any partial processing of this error and pass the buck.
                          Throw
                  End Try

      ...
      End Sub
End Module
```

Be aware that in this example code, the ultimate receiver of CarIsDeadException is the CLR, since it is the Main() method rethrowing the exception. Because of this, your end user is presented with a system-supplied error dialog box. Typically, you would only rethrow a partial handled exception to a caller that has the ability to handle the incoming exception more gracefully.

Notice as well that we are not explicitly rethrowing the CarIsDeadException object, but rather making use of the Throw keyword with no argument. We're not creating a new exception object; we're just rethrowing the original exception object (with all its original information). Doing so preserves the context of the original target.

Inner Exceptions

As you may suspect, it is entirely possible to trigger an exception at the time you are handling another exception. For example, assume you are handling a CarIsDeadException within a particular Catch scope, and during the process you attempt to record the stack trace to a file on your C: drive named carErrors.txt (you must import the System.IO namespace to gain access to these I/O-centric types):

```
      Catch e As CarIsDeadException
       ' Attempt to open a file named carErrors.txt on the C drive.
       Dim fs As FileStream = File.Open("C:\carErrors.txt", FileMode.Open)
       ...
End Try
```

Now, if the specified file is not located on your C: drive, the call to `File.Open()` results in a `FileNotFoundException`! Later in this text, you will learn all about the `System.IO` namespace where you'll discover how to programmatically determine whether a file exists on the hard drive before attempting to open the file in the first place (thereby avoiding the exception altogether). However, to stay focused on the topic of exceptions, assume the exception has been raised.

When you encounter an exception while processing another exception, best practice states that you should record the new exception object as an "inner exception" within a new object of the same type as the initial exception. (That was a mouthful!) The reason you need to allocate a new object of the exception being handled is that the only way to document an inner exception is via a constructor parameter. Consider the following code:

```
Catch e As CarIsDeadException
        Try
        ....
                Dim fs As FileStream = File.Open("C:\carErrors.txt", FileMode.Open)
        Catch e2 As Exception
                ' Throw an exception that records the new exception,
                ' as well as the message of the first exception.
                Throw New CarIsDeadException(e.Message, e2)
        End Try
End Try
```

Notice in this case, we have passed in the `FileNotFoundException` object as the second parameter to the `CarIsDeadException` constructor. Once we have configured this new object, we throw it up the call stack to the next caller Much like the act of rethrowing an exception, recording inner exceptions is usually only useful when the caller has the ability to gracefully catch the exception in the first place. If this is the case, the caller's `Catch` logic can make use of the `InnerException` property to extract the details of the inner exception object.

The Finally Block

A `Try`/`Catch` scope may also define an optional `Finally` block. The purpose of a `Finally` block is to ensure that a set of code statements will *always* execute, exception (of any type) or not. To illustrate, assume you wish to always power down the car's radio before exiting `Main()`, regardless of any handled exception:

```
Module Module1
        Sub Main()
                Console.WriteLine("***** Handling Multiple Exceptions *****" & vbLf)
                Dim myCar As New Car("Rusty", 90)
                myCar.CrankTunes(True)

                Try
                        ' Speed up car logic.

                Catch e As CarIsDeadException
                                ' Process CarIsDeadException.
```

```
                Catch e As ArgumentOutOfRangeException
                        ' Process ArgumentOutOfRangeException.

                Catch e As Exception
                        ' Process any other Exception.

                Finally
                        ' This will always occur. Exception or not.
                        myCar.CrankTunes(False)

                End Try
                Console.ReadLine()
        End Sub
End Module
```

If you did not include a **Finally** block, the radio would not be turned off if an exception is encountered (which may or may not be problematic). In a more real-world scenario, when you need to dispose of objects, close a file, detach from a database (or whatever), a **Finally** block ensures a location for proper cleanup.

Who Is Throwing What?

Given that a method in the .NET Framework could throw any number of exceptions under various circumstances, a logical question is, "How do I know which exceptions may be thrown by a given base class library method?" The ultimate answer is simple: consult the .NET Framework 4.0 SDK documentation. Each method in the help system documents the exceptions a given member may throw.

For those coming to .NET from a Java background, understand that type members are not prototyped with the set of exceptions they may throw (in other words, .NET does not support checked exceptions). For better or for worse, you are not required to handle each and every exception thrown from a given member.

The Result of Unhandled Exceptions

At this point, you might be wondering what would happen if you do not handle an exception thrown in your direction? Assume that the logic in **Main()** increases the speed of the **Car** object beyond the maximum speed, without the benefit of **Try/Catch** logic:

```
Module Module1
        Sub Main()
                Console.WriteLine("***** Handling Multiple Exceptions *****" & vbLf)
                Dim myCar As New Car("Rusty", 90)
                myCar.Accelerate(500)
                Console.ReadLine()
        End Sub
End Module
```

The result of ignoring an exception would be rather obstructive to the end user of your application, as an "unhandled exception" dialog box is displayed (see Figure 7-2).

Figure 7-2. The result of not dealing with exceptions

Debugging Unhandled Exceptions Using Visual Studio

Do be aware that Visual Studio 2010 supplies a number of tools that help you debug unhandled custom exceptions. Again, assume you have increased the speed of a Car object beyond the maximum. If you start a debugging session within Visual Studio 2010 (using the Debug ➤ Start Debugging menu selection), Visual Studio automatically breaks at the time the uncaught exception is thrown. Better yet, you are presented with a window (see Figure 7-3) displaying the value of the Message property.

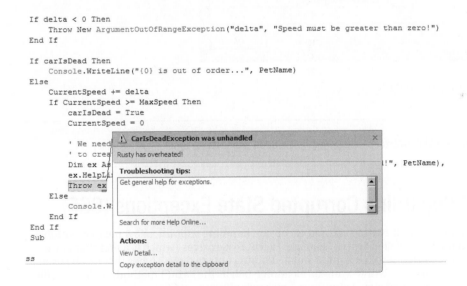

Figure 7-3. Debugging unhandled custom exceptions with Visual Studio 2010

■ **Note** If you fail to handle an exception thrown by a method in the .NET base class libraries, the Visual Studio 2010 debugger breaks at the statement that called the offending method.

If you click the View Detail link, you will find the details regarding the state of the object (see Figure 7-4).

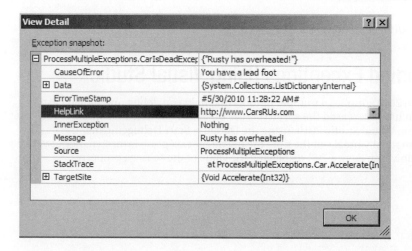

Figure 7-4. Viewing exception details

■ **Source Code** The ProcessMultipleExceptions project is included under the Chapter 7 subdirectory.

A Brief Word Regarding Corrupted State Exceptions (CSE)

To wrap up our examination of VB 2010 structured exception handling support, allow me to mention a brand-new .NET 4.0 namespace called `System.Runtime.ExceptionServices` (which is a member of the `mscorlib.dll` assembly). This namespace is quite small, defining only two class types that can be used if you wish to equip various methods within your application (such as the `Main()` method) with the ability to intercept and process "corrupted state exceptions," otherwise known as *CSEs*.

As you learned back in Chapter 1, the .NET platform sits on top of the hosting operating system (such as Microsoft Windows). Now, based on your background in Windows programming, you may recall that the low-level Windows API has a very unique set of rules regarding the treatment of runtime errors, which look little like .NET's structured exception handling techniques.

Within the Windows API, it is possible to trap extremely low-level errors that represent "corrupted state" errors. Simply put, if the Windows OS sends out a corrupted state error, your program is in very bad shape. So much so, that there is no hope of recovery and the only corrective course of action is to terminate the program.

■ **Note** As a .NET programmer, the only times you may accidentally trigger a CSE error is if your VB 2010 code is using platform invocation services (to talk directly to the Windows API).

Before the release of .NET 4.0, the CLR would allow these very low-level, OS-specific errors to be trapped using a general `System.Exception Catch` block. The problem, however, was that if a CSE exception was somehow encountered and trapped within such a `Catch` block, the .NET platform did not (and still does not) provide much by way of elegant recovery code.

Now, with the release of .NET 4.0, the CLR will *not* allow CSEs to be automatically caught within your .NET applications. Most of the time, this is exactly what you would want. However, if you did still wish to receive notifications of these OS-level errors (which would typically be only if you had some legacy code that required such notifications), you can make use of the `<Handle ProcessCorruptedStateExceptions>` attribute.

While we have not yet examined the role of .NET attributes (see Chapter 15), for now just understand that this attribute can be applied on any method of your application, and when you do this, the method in question will have a chance to deal with these low-level OS errors. By way of a simple example, assuming you have imported the `System.Runtime.ExceptionServices` namespace into your VB 2010 code file, you could build the following `Main()` method:

```vb
<HandledProcessCorruptedStateExceptions()> _
Function Main() As Integer
        Try
                ' Assume Main() is invoking a method which
                ' runs the entire program.
                RunMyApplication()
        Catch ex As Exception
                ' If we get here, we know something really bad happended.
                ' Just print out the message and exit the program...we are
                ' doomed!
                Console.WriteLine("Ack!  Huge problem: {0}", ex.Message)
                Return -1
        End Try
        Return 0
End Function
```

Here we have a `Main()` method that does little more than call a second method that deals with the entire running of the application. For this example, we will assume that `RunMyApplication()` makes liberal use of `Try/Catch` logic to deal with any expected error. However, since `Main()` has been marked with the `<HandledProcessCorruptedStateExceptions>` attribute, if a CSE error is encountered, the catching of the `System.Exception` is our last chance to do *something* before the program is terminated.

Here, the `Main()` method returns an `Integer`, (rather than `Sub`, which has no return value). As explained in Chapter 3, by convention, returning zero to the OS indicates the application exits without error, while any other value (typically a negative number) signifies an error.

This text will not deal with the processing of these low-level Windows OS errors, and therefore, I won't comment on the role of `System.Runtime.ExceptionServices` beyond this point. If you are in need of further details, consult the .NET 4.0 Framework SDK documentation.

Summary

In this chapter, you examined the role of structured exception handling. When a method needs to send an error object to the caller, it will allocate, configure, and throw a specific `System.Exception` derived type via the VB 2010 `Throw` keyword. The caller is able to handle any possible incoming exceptions using the VB 2010 `Catch` keyword and an optional `Finally` scope.

When you are creating your own custom exceptions, you ultimately create a class type deriving from `System.ApplicationException`, which denotes an exception thrown from the currently executing application. In contrast, error objects deriving from `System.SystemException` represent critical (and fatal) errors thrown by the CLR. Last but not least, this chapter illustrated various tools within Visual Studio 2010 that can be used to create custom exceptions (according to .NET best practices) as well as debug exceptions.

CHAPTER 8

■ ■ ■

Understanding Object Lifetime

At this point in the text, you have learned a great deal about how to build custom class types using VB 2010. Now you will see how the CLR manages allocated class instances (aka, objects) via *garbage collection*. VB 2010 programmers never directly deallocate a managed object from memory (recall there is no `Delete` keyword in the VB 2010 language). Rather, .NET objects are allocated to a region of memory termed the *managed heap*, where they will be automatically destroyed by the garbage collector "sometime in the future."

Once you have looked at the core details of the collection process, you'll learn how to programmatically interact with the garbage collector using the `System.GC` class type. Next, you'll examine how the `Overridable System.Object.Finalize()` method and `IDisposable` interface can be used to build classes that release internal *unmanaged resources* in a timely manner.

You will also delve into some new functionality of the garbage collector introduced with .NET 4.0, including background garbage collections and lazy instantiation using the generic `System.Lazy(Of T)` class. By the time you have completed this chapter, you will have a solid understanding of how .NET objects are managed by the CLR.

Classes, Objects, and References

To frame the topics covered in this chapter, it is important to further clarify the distinction between classes, objects, and references. Recall that a class is nothing more than a blueprint that describes how an instance of this type will look and feel in memory. Classes, of course, are defined within a code file (which in VB 2010 takes a `*.vb` extension by convention). Consider a simple `Car` class defined within a new VB 2010 Console Application project named SimpleGC:

```vb
' Car.vb
Public Class Car
        Public Property CurrentSpeed() As Integer

        Public Property PetName() As String

        Public Sub New()
        End Sub
```

```vb
        Public Sub New(ByVal name As String, ByVal speed As Integer)
                PetName = name
                CurrentSpeed = speed
        End Sub

        Public Overrides Function ToString() As String
                Return String.Format("{0} is going {1} MPH", PetName, CurrentSpeed)
        End Function
End Class
```

Once a class is defined, you can allocate any number of objects using the VB 2010 `New` keyword. Understand, however, that the `New` keyword returns a *reference* to the object on the heap, not the actual object itself. If you declare the reference variable as a local variable in a method scope, it is stored on the stack for further use in your application. When you wish to invoke members on the object, apply the VB 2010 dot operator to the stored reference:

```vb
Module Module1
        Sub Main()
                Console.WriteLine("***** GC Basics *****")

                ' Create a new Car object on
                ' the managed heap. We are
                ' returned a reference to this
                ' object ("refToMyCar").
                Dim refToMyCar As New Car("Zippy", 50)

                ' The VB 2010 dot operator (.) is used
                ' to invoke members on the object
                ' using our reference variable.
                Console.WriteLine(refToMyCar.ToString())
                Console.ReadLine()
        End Sub
End Module
```

Figure 8-1 illustrates the class, object, and reference relationship.

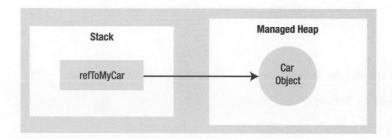

Figure 8-1. References to objects on the managed heap

■ **Note** Recall from Chapter 4 that structures are *value types* that are always allocated directly on the stack and are never placed on the .NET managed heap. Heap allocation only occurs when you are creating instances of classes.

The Basics of Object Lifetime

When you are building your VB 2010 applications, you are correct to assume that the .NET runtime environment will take care of the managed heap without your direct intervention. In fact, the golden rule of .NET memory management is simple:

■ **Rule** Allocate a class instance onto the managed heap using the New keyword and forget about it.

Once instantiated, the garbage collector will destroy an object when it is no longer needed. The next obvious question, of course, is, "How does the garbage collector determine when an object is no longer needed?" The short (i.e., incomplete) answer is that the garbage collector removes an object from the heap when it is *unreachable* by any part of your code base. Assume you have a method in your Module Module1 that allocates a local Car object:

```
Sub MakeACar()
    ' If myCar is the only reference to the Car object,
    ' it *may* be destroyed when this method returns.
    Dim myCar As New Car()
End Sub
```

Notice that this Car reference (myCar) has been created directly within the MakeACar() method and has not been passed outside of the defining scope (via a Return value or ByRef parameters). Thus, once this method call completes, the myCar reference is no longer reachable, and the associated Car object is now a candidate for garbage collection. Understand, however, that you can't guarantee that this object will be reclaimed from memory immediately after MakeACar() has completed. All you can assume at this point is that when the CLR performs the next garbage collection, the myCar object could be safely destroyed.

As you will most certainly discover, programming in a garbage-collected environment greatly simplifies your application development. In stark contrast, C++ programmers are painfully aware that if they fail to manually delete heap-allocated objects, memory leaks are never far behind. In fact, tracking down memory leaks is one of the most time-consuming (and tedious) aspects of programming in unmanaged environments. By allowing the garbage collector to take charge of destroying objects, the burden of memory management has been lifted from your shoulders and placed onto those of the CLR.

■ **Note** If you happen to have a background in COM development, note that .NET objects do not maintain an internal reference counter, and therefore managed objects do not expose methods such as AddRef() or Release().

The CIL of new

When the VB 2010 compiler encounters the New keyword, it emits a CIL newobj instruction into the method implementation. If you compile the current example code and investigate the resulting assembly using ildasm.exe, you'd find the following CIL statements within the MakeACar() method:

```
.method public static void  MakeACar() cil managed
{ // Code size       9 (0x9)
  .maxstack  1
  .locals init ([0] class SimpleGC.Car  myCar)
  IL_0000:  nop
  IL_0001:  newobj      instance void SimpleGC.Car::.ctor()
  IL_0006:  stloc.0
  IL_0007:  nop
  IL_0008:  ret
} //end of methodModule1:MakeACar
```

Before we examine the exact rules that determine when an object is removed from the managed heap, let's check out the role of the CIL newobj instruction in a bit more detail. First, understand that the managed heap is more than just a random chunk of memory accessed by the CLR. The .NET garbage collector is quite a tidy housekeeper of the heap, given that it will compact empty blocks of memory (when necessary) for purposes of optimization. To aid in this endeavor, the managed heap maintains a pointer (commonly referred to as the *next object pointer* or *new object pointer*) that identifies exactly where the next object will be located.

That said, the newobj instruction tells the CLR to perform the following core operations:

- Calculate the total amount of memory required for the object to be allocated (including the memory required by the data members and the base classes).

- Examine the managed heap to ensure that there is indeed enough room to host the object to be allocated. If there is, the specified constructor is called and the caller is ultimately returned a reference to the new object in memory, whose address just happens to be identical to the last position of the next object pointer.

- Finally, before returning the reference to the caller, advance the next object pointer to point to the next available slot on the managed heap.

The basic process is illustrated in Figure 8-2.

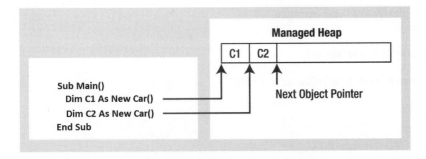

Figure 8-2. The details of allocating objects onto the managed heap

As your application is busy allocating objects, the space on the managed heap may eventually become full. When processing the newobj instruction, if the CLR determines that the managed heap does not have sufficient memory to allocate the requested type, it will perform a garbage collection in an attempt to free up memory. Thus, the next rule of garbage collection is also quite simple:

■ **Rule** If the managed heap does not have sufficient memory to allocate a requested object, a garbage collection will occur.

Exactly *how* this garbage collection occurs, however, depends on which version of the .NET platform your application is running under. You'll look at the differences a bit later in this chapter.

Setting Object References to Nothing

Those of you who created COM objects using Visual Basic 6.0 know that it was always preferable to set their references to Nothing when you were finished using them. Under the covers, the reference count of the COM object was decremented by one, and the object could be removed from memory if its reference count equaled 0. In a similar fashion, C/C++ programmers often set pointer variables to null to ensure they are no longer referencing unmanaged memory.

Given these facts, you might wonder what the end result is of assigning object references to Nothing under VB 2010. For example, assume the MakeACar() subroutine has now been updated as follows:

```
Sub MakeACar()
      Dim myCar As New Car()
      myCar = Nothing
End Sub
```

When you assign object references to Nothing, the compiler generates CIL code that ensures the reference (myCar in this example) no longer points to any object. If you once again made use of ildasm.exe to view the CIL code of the modified MakeACar(), you would find the ldnull opcode (which pushes a Nothing value on the virtual execution stack) followed by a **stloc.0** opcode (which sets the Nothing reference on the variable):

```
.method public static void  MakeACar() cil managed
{ // Code size        11 (0xb)
  .maxstack  1
  .locals init ([0] class SimpleGC.Car myCar)
  IL_0000:  nop
  IL_0001:  newobj       instance void SimpleGC.Car::.ctor()
  IL_0006:  stloc.0
  IL_0007:  ldnull
  IL_0008:  stloc.0
  IL_0009:  nop
  IL_000a:  ret
} //end of method Program::MakeACar
```

What you must understand, however, is that assigning a reference to Nothing does not in any way force the garbage collector to fire up at that exact moment and remove the object from the heap. The only thing you have accomplished is explicitly clipping the connection between the reference and the object it previously pointed to. Given this point, setting references to Nothing under VB 2010 is far less consequential than doing so in VB 6.0 or C-based languages; however, doing so will certainly not cause any harm.

The Role of Application Roots

Now, back to the topic of how the garbage collector determines when an object is no longer needed. To understand the details, you need to be aware of the notion of *application roots*. Simply put, a *root* is a storage location containing a reference to an object on the managed heap. Strictly speaking, a root can fall into any of the following categories:

- References to global objects (though these are not allowed in VB2010 CIL code does permit allocation of global objects)

- References to any Shared objects/Shared fields

- References to local objects within an application's code base

- References to object parameters passed into a method

- References to objects waiting to be *finalized* (described later in this chapter)

- Any CPU register that references an object

During a garbage collection process, the runtime will investigate objects on the managed heap to determine whether they are still reachable (i.e., rooted) by the application. To do so, the CLR will build an *object graph*, which represents each reachable object on the heap. Object graphs are explained in some detail during the discussion of object serialization in Chapter 20. For now, just understand that object graphs are used to document all reachable objects. As well, be aware that the garbage collector will never graph the same object twice, thus avoiding the nasty circular reference count found in COM programming.

Assume the managed heap contains a set of objects named A, B, C, D, E, F, and G. During a garbage collection, these objects (as well as any internal object references they may contain) are examined for active roots. Once the graph has been constructed, unreachable objects (which we will assume are objects C and F) are marked as garbage. Figure 8-3 diagrams a possible object graph for the scenario just described (you can read the directional arrows using the phrase *depends on* or *requires,* for example, E depends on G and B, A depends on nothing, and so on).

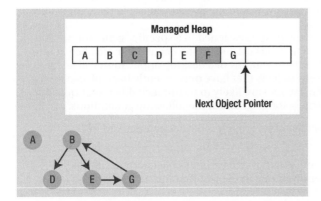

Figure 8-3. Object graphs are constructed to determine which objects are reachable by application roots

Once an object has been marked for termination (C and F in this case—as they are not accounted for in the object graph), they are swept from memory. At this point, the remaining space on the heap is compacted, which in turn causes the CLR to modify the set of active application roots (and the underlying pointers) to refer to the correct memory location (this is done automatically and transparently). Last but not least, the next object pointer is readjusted to point to the next available slot. Figure 8-4 illustrates the resulting readjustment.

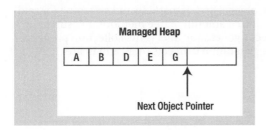

Figure 8-4. A clean and compacted heap

■ **Note** Strictly speaking, the garbage collector makes use of two distinct heaps, one of which is specifically used to store very large objects. This heap is less frequently consulted during the collection cycle, given possible performance penalties involved with relocating large objects. Regardless, it is safe to consider the managed heap as a single region of memory.

Understanding Object Generations

When the CLR is attempting to locate unreachable objects, is does not literally examine each and every object placed on the managed heap. Doing so, obviously, would involve considerable time, especially in larger (i.e., real-world) applications.

To help optimize the process, each object on the heap is assigned to a specific "generation." The idea behind generations is simple: the longer an object has existed on the heap, the more likely it is to stay there. For example, the class that defined the main window of a desktop application will be in memory until the program terminates. Conversely, objects that have only recently been placed on the heap (such as an object allocated within a method scope) are likely to be unreachable rather quickly. Given these assumptions, each object on the heap belongs to one of the following generations:

- *Generation 0*: Identifies a newly allocated object that has never been marked for collection.

- *Generation 1*: Identifies an object that has survived a garbage collection (i.e., it was marked for collection but was not removed due to the fact that the sufficient heap space was acquired).

- *Generation 2*: Identifies an object that has survived more than one sweep of the garbage collector.

■ **Note** Generations 0 and 1 are termed ephemeral generations. As explained in the next section, you will see that the garbage collection process does treat ephemeral generations differently.

The garbage collector will investigate all generation 0 objects first. If marking and sweeping (or said more plainly, getting rid of) these objects results in the required amount of free memory, any surviving objects are promoted to generation 1. To see how an object's generation affects the collection process, ponder Figure 8-5, which diagrams how a set of surviving generation 0 objects (A, B, and E) are promoted once the required memory has been reclaimed.

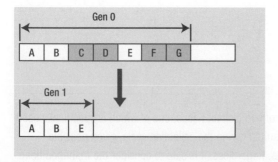

Figure 8-5. Generation 0 objects that survive a garbage collection are promoted to generation 1

If all generation 0 objects have been evaluated, but additional memory is still required, generation 1 objects are then investigated for reachability and collected accordingly. Surviving generation 1 objects are then promoted to generation 2. If the garbage collector *still* requires additional memory, generation 2 objects are evaluated. At this point, if a generation 2 object survives a garbage collection, it remains a generation 2 object given the predefined upper limit of object generations.

The bottom line is that by assigning a generational value to objects on the heap, newer objects (such as local variables) will be removed quickly, while older objects (such as a program's application object) are not "bothered" as often.

Concurrent Garbage Collection under .NET 1.0 - 3.5

Prior to .NET 4.0, the runtime would clean up unused objects using a technique termed *concurrent garbage collection.* Under this model, when a collection takes place for any generation 0 or generation 1 objects (recall these are *ephemeral generations*), the garbage collector temporarily suspends all active *threads* within the current process to ensure that the application does not access the managed heap during the collection process.

We will examine the topic of threads in Chapter 19; however, for the time being, simply regard a thread as a path of execution within a running executable. Once the garbage collection cycle has completed, the suspended threads are permitted to carry on their work. Thankfully, the .NET 3.5 (and earlier) garbage collector was highly optimized; you seldom (if ever) noticed this brief interruption in your application.

As an optimization, concurrent garbage collection allowed objects that were not located in one of the ephemeral generations to be cleaned up on a dedicated thread. This decreased (but didn't eliminate) the need for the .NET runtime to suspect active threads. Moreover, concurrent garbage collection allowed your program to continue allocating objects on the heap during the collection of non-ephemeral generations.

Background Garbage Collection under .NET 4.0

.NET 4.0 changes the way the garbage collector deals with thread suspension when it cleans up objects on the managed heap, using *background garbage collection.* Despite its name, this does not mean that all garbage collection now takes place on additional background threads of execution. Rather, if a background garbage collection is taking place for objects living in a non-ephemeral generation, the .NET runtime is now able to collect objects on the ephemeral generations using a dedicated background thread.

On a related note, the .NET 4.0 garbage collection has been improved to further reduce the amount of time a given thread involved with garbage collection details must be suspended. The end result of these changes is that the process of cleaning up unused objects living in generation 0 or generation 1 has been optimized and can result in better runtime performance of your programs (which is really important for real-time systems that require small (and predictable) GC stop time).

Do understand, however, that the introduction of this new garbage collection model has no effect on how you build your .NET applications. For all practical purposes, you can simply allow the .NET garbage collector to perform its work without your direct intervention (and be happy that the folks at Microsoft are improving the collection process in a transparent manner).

The System.GC Type

The base class libraries provide a class type named System.GC that allows you to programmatically interact with the garbage collector using a set of Shared members. Now, do be very aware that you will seldom (if ever) need to make use of this class directly in your code. Typically, the only time you will use the members of System.GC is when you are creating classes that make internal use of *unmanaged resources*. This could be the case if you are building a class that makes calls into the Windows C-based API using the .NET platform invocation protocol, or perhaps due to some very low level and complicated COM interop logic. Table 8-1 provides a rundown of some of the more interesting members (consult the .NET Framework 4.0 SDK documentation for complete details).

Table 8-1. Select Members of the System.GC Type

System.GC Member	Description
AddMemoryPressure() RemoveMemoryPressure()	Allows you to specify a numerical value that represents the calling object's "urgency level" regarding the garbage collection process. Be aware that these methods should alter pressure *in tandem* and thus never remove more pressure than the total amount you have added.
Collect()	Forces the GC to perform a garbage collection. This method has been overloaded to specify a generation to collect, as well as the mode of collection (via the GCCollectionMode enumeration).
CollectionCount()	Returns a numerical value representing how many times a given generation has been swept.
GetGeneration()	Returns the generation to which an object currently belongs.
GetTotalMemory()	Returns the estimated amount of memory (in bytes) currently allocated on the managed heap. A Boolean parameter specifies whether the call should wait for garbage collection to occur before returning.
MaxGeneration	Returns the maximum number of generations supported on the target system. Under Microsoft's .NET 4.0, there are three possible generations: 0, 1, and 2.
SuppressFinalize()	Sets a flag indicating that the specified object should not have its Finalize() method called.
WaitForPendingFinalizers()	Suspends the current thread until all finalizable objects have been finalized. This method is typically called directly after invoking GC.Collect().

■ **Note**.NET 3.5 Service Pack 1 added the ability to receive notifications when a garbage collection is about to occur using a handful of new members. While this can be helpful in some limited scenarios, most applications will not need such functionality, and therefore I have chosen not to cover the details in this edition. If you are interested, look up "Garbage Collection Notifications" in the .NET Framework 4.0 SDK documentation.

To illustrate how the `System.GC` type can be used to obtain various garbage collection–centric details, consider the following `Main()` method, which makes use of several members of `GC`:

```
Module Module1
    Sub Main()
        Console.WriteLine("***** Fun with System.GC *****")
        ' Print out estimated number of bytes on heap.
        Console.WriteLine("Estimated bytes on heap: {0}", GC.GetTotalMemory(False))
        ' MaxGeneration is zero based, so add 1 for display purposes.
        Console.WriteLine("This OS has {0} object generations." & vbLf, (GC.MaxGeneration +
1))

        Dim refToMyCar As New Car("Zippy", 100)
        Console.WriteLine(refToMyCar.ToString())
        ' Print out generation of refToMyCar object.
        Console.WriteLine("Generation of refToMyCar is: {0}", GC.GetGeneration(refToMyCar))
        Console.ReadLine()
        End Sub
    End Module
```

Forcing a Garbage Collection

Again, the whole purpose of the .NET garbage collector is to manage memory on our behalf. However, in some very rare circumstances, it may be beneficial to programmatically force a garbage collection using `GC.Collect()`. Specifically:

- Your application is about to enter into a block of code that you don't want interrupted by a possible garbage collection.

- Your application has just finished allocating an extremely large number of objects and you wish to remove as much of the acquired memory as soon as possible.

If you determine it may be beneficial to have the garbage collector check for unreachable objects, you could explicitly trigger a garbage collection, as follows:

```
Module Module1
  Sub Main()
        ...
    ' Force a garbage collection and wait for
    ' each object to be finalized.
    GC.Collect()
```

```
        GC.WaitForPendingFinalizers()
        ...
    End Sub
End Module
```

When you manually force a garbage collection, you should always make a call to
GC.WaitForPendingFinalizers(). With this approach, you can rest assured that all *finalizable objects*
(described in the next section) have had a chance to perform any necessary cleanup before your
program continues. Under the hood, GC.WaitForPendingFinalizers() will suspend the calling "thread"
during the collection process. This is a good thing, as it ensures your code does not invoke methods on
an object currently being destroyed!

The GC.Collect() method can also be supplied a numerical value that identifies the oldest
generation on which a garbage collection will be performed. For example, to instruct the CLR to
investigate only generation 0 objects, you would write the following:

```
Module Module1
Sub Main()
        ...
' Only investigate generation 0 objects.
    GC.Collect(0)
    GC.WaitForPendingFinalizers()
        ...
    End Sub
End Module
```

As well, the Collect() method can also be passed in a value of the GCCollectionMode enumeration as
a second parameter, to fine-tune exactly how the runtime should force the garbage collection. This enum
defines the following values:

```
Public Enum GCCollectionMode
            [Default]          ' Forced is the current default.
            Forced             ' Tells the runtime to collect immediately!
            Optimized          ' Allows the runtime to determine
                               ' whether the current time is optimal to reclaim objects.
End Enum
```

As with any garbage collection, calling GC.Collect() promotes surviving generations. To illustrate,
assume that our Main() method has been updated as follows:

```
Module Module1
    Sub Main()
    Console.WriteLine("***** Fun with System.GC *****")
    ' Print out estimated number of bytes on heap.
        Console.WriteLine("Estimated bytes on heap: {0}", GC.GetTotalMemory(False))
    ' MaxGeneration is zero based.
        Console.WriteLine("This OS has {0} object generations." & vbLf, (GC.MaxGeneration +
1))
```

```vb
    Dim refToMyCar As New Car("Zippy", 100)
        Console.WriteLine(refToMyCar.ToString())
    ' Print out generation of refToMyCar.
        Console.WriteLine(vbLf & "Generation of refToMyCar is: {0}",
GC.GetGeneration(refToMyCar))
    ' Make a ton of objects for testing purposes.
        Dim tonsOfObjects As Object() = New Object(49999) {}
    For i As Integer = 0 To 49999
                tonsOfObjects(i) = New Object()
        Next
    ' Collect only gen 0 objects.
        GC.Collect(0, GCCollectionMode.Forced)
        GC.WaitForPendingFinalizers()
    ' Print out generation of refToMyCar.
        Console.WriteLine("Generation of refToMyCar is: {0}", GC.GetGeneration(refToMyCar))
    ' See if tonsOfObjects[9000] is still alive.
        If tonsOfObjects(9000) IsNot Nothing Then
Console.WriteLine("Generation of tonsOfObjects[9000] is: {0}",
GC.GetGeneration(tonsOfObjects(9000)))
    Else
            Console.WriteLine("tonsOfObjects[9000] is no longer alive.")
    End If
    ' Print out how many times a generation has been swept.
    Console.WriteLine(vbLf & "Gen 0 has been swept {0} times", GC.CollectionCount(0))
        Console.WriteLine("Gen 1 has been swept {0} times", GC.CollectionCount(1))
        Console.WriteLine("Gen 2 has been swept {0} times", GC.CollectionCount(2))
    Console.ReadLine()
    End Sub
End Module
```

Here, we have purposely created a very large array of **object** types (50,000to be exact) for testing purposes. As you can see from the output that follows, even though this `Main()` method only made one explicit request for a garbage collection (via the `GC.Collect()` method), the CLR performed a number of them in the background.

```
***** Fun with System.GC *****

Estimated bytes on heap: 162260

This OS has 3 object generations.



Zippy is going 100 MPH
```

```
Generation of refToMyCar is: 0

Generation of refToMyCar is: 1

Generation of tonsOfObjects[9000] is: 1



Gen 0 has been swept 1 times

Gen 1 has been swept 0 times

Gen 2 has been swept 0 times
```

At this point, I hope you feel more comfortable regarding the details of object lifetime. In the next section, we'll examine the garbage collection process a bit further by addressing how you can build *finalizable objects* as well as *disposable objects*. Be very aware that the following techniques are useful only if you are building managed classes that maintain internal unmanaged resources.

■ **Source Code** The SimpleGC project is included under the Chapter 8 subdirectory.

Building Finalizable Objects

In Chapter 6, you learned that the supreme base class of .NET, System.Object, defines an Overridable method named Finalize(). The default implementation of this method does nothing whatsoever:

```
' System.Object
Public Class [Object]
        ...
        Protected Overridable Sub Finalize()
        End Sub
End Class
```

When you override Finalize() for your custom classes, you establish a specific location to perform any necessary cleanup logic for your type. Given that this member is defined as Protected, it is not possible to directly call an object's Finalize() method from a class instance via the dot operator. Rather, the *garbage collector* will call an object's Finalize() method (if supported) before removing the object from memory.

■ **Note** It is illegal to override `Finalize()` on structure types. This makes perfect sense given that structures are value types, which are never allocated on the heap to begin with and therefore are not garbage collected! However, if you create a structure that contains unmanaged resources that need to be cleaned up, you can implement the `IDisposable` interface (described shortly).

Of course, a call to `Finalize()` will (eventually) occur during a "natural" garbage collection or when you programmatically force a collection via `GC.Collect()`. In addition, a type's finalizer method will automatically be called when the application domain hosting your application is unloaded from memory. Depending on your background in .NET, you may know that application domains (or simply AppDomains) are used to host an executable assembly and any necessary external code libraries. If you are not familiar with this .NET concept, you will be by the time you've finished Chapter 16. For now, note that when your AppDomain is unloaded from memory, the CLR automatically invokes finalizers for every finalizable object created during its lifetime.

Now, despite what your developer instincts may tell you, the vast majority of your VB 2010 classes will not require any explicit cleanup logic or a custom finalizer. The reason is simple: if your classes are just making use of other managed objects, everything will eventually be garbage-collected. The only time you would need to design a class that can clean up after itself is when you are using *unmanaged* resources (such as raw OS file handles, raw unmanaged database connections, chunks of unmanaged memory, or other unmanaged resources). Under the .NET platform, unmanaged resources are obtained by directly calling into the API of the operating system using Platform Invocation Services (PInvoke) or as a result of some very elaborate COM interoperability scenarios. Given this, consider the next rule of garbage collection:

■ **Rule** The only reason to override `Finalize()` is if your VB 2010 class is making use of unmanaged resources via PInvoke or complex COM interoperability tasks (typically via various members defined by the `System.Runtime.InteropServices.Marshal` type).

Overriding System.Object.Finalize()

In the rare case that you do build a VB 2010 class that uses unmanaged resources, you will obviously want to ensure that the underlying memory is released in a predictable manner. Suppose you have created a new VB 2010 Console Application named `SimpleFinalize` and inserted a class named `MyResourceWrapper` that uses an unmanaged resource (whatever that may be) and you want to override `Finalize()`. The odd thing about doing so in VB 2010 is that you can't do it using the expected `Overrides` keyword:

```
Public Class MyResourceWrapper

        Protected Overrides Sub Finalize()
        End Sub
End Class
```

Here is a custom Finalizer for MyResourceWrapper that will issue a system beep when invoked. Obviously, this example is only for instructional purposes. A real-world Finalizer would do nothing more than free any unmanaged resources and would *not* interact with other managed objects, even those referenced by the current object, as you can't assume they are still alive at the point the garbage collector invokes your Finalize() method:

```vb
Public Class MyResourceWrapper
        ' Override System.Object.Finalize()
        Protected Overrides Sub Finalize()
                ' Clean up any unmanaged resources here!
                ' Beep when destroyed (testing purposes only!)
                Console.Beep()
        End Sub
End Class
```

While the previous implementation of Finalize() is syntactically correct, best practices state that a proper finalization routine should explicitly call the Finalize() method of its base class after your custom finalization logic. This ensures that any unmanaged resources up the chain of inheritance are cleaned up as well. Furthermore, to make a Finalize() method as robust as possible, you should wrap your code statements within a Try/Finally construct, as this will ensure that the finalization occurs even in the event of a runtime exception (see previous chapter). Given these notes, here is a prim-and-proper Finalize() method:

```vb
' Override System.Object.Finalize()
Public Class MyResourceWrapper
    Protected Overrides Sub Finalize()
            Try
                    ' Clean up unmanaged resources here.
                    ' Beep when destroyed (testing purposes only!)
                    Console.Beep()
            Finally
                    MyBase.Finalize()
            End Try
    End Sub
End Class
```

If you were to examine this VB 2010 Finalize method using ildasm.exe, you would see that the compiler inserts some necessary error-checking code. First, the code statements within the scope of your Finalize() method are placed within a Try block (see Chapter 7). The related Finally block ensures that your base classes' Finalize() method will always execute, regardless of any exceptions encountered within the try scope:

```
.method family strict virtual instance void
  Finalize() cil managed
{
  // Code size       22 (0x16)
  .maxstack  1
  IL_0000:    nop
  IL_0001:    nop
  .try
```

```
{
  IL_0002:  call                    void[mscorlib]System.Console::Beep()
  IL_0007:  nop
  IL_0008:  leave.s                 IL_0013
} // end .try
finally
{
  IL_000a:  nop
  IL_000b:  idarg.0
  IL_000c:  call                    instance void [mscorlib]System.Object::Finalize()
  IL_0011:  nop
  IL_0012:  endfinally
} // end handler
IL_0013:  nop
IL_0014:  nop
IL_0015:  ret
} // end of method MyResourceWrapper::Finalize
```

If you then tested the MyResourceWrapper type, you would find that a system beep occurs when the application terminates, given that the CLR will automatically invoke finalizers upon AppDomain shutdown:

```
Sub Main()
        Console.WriteLine("***** Fun with Finalizers *****" & vbLf)
        Console.WriteLine("Hit the return key to shut down this app")
        Console.WriteLine("and force the GC to invoke Finalize()")
        Console.WriteLine("for finalizable objects created in this AppDomain.")
        Console.ReadLine()
        Dim rw As New MyResourceWrapper()
End Sub
```

■ **Source Code** The SimpleFinalize project is included under the Chapter 8 subdirectory.

Detailing the Finalization Process

Not to beat a dead horse, but always remember that the role of the Finalize() method is to ensure that a .NET object can clean up unmanaged resources when it is garbage-collected. Thus, if you are building a class that does not make use of unmanaged entities (by far the most common case), finalization is of little use. In fact, if at all possible, you should design your types to avoid supporting a Finalize() method for the very simple reason that finalization takes time.

When you allocate an object onto the managed heap, the runtime automatically determines whether your object supports a custom Finalize() method. If so, the object is marked as *finalizable*, and a pointer to this object is stored on an internal queue named the *finalization queue*. The finalization queue is a table maintained by the garbage collector that points to each and every object that must be finalized before it is removed from the heap.

When the garbage collector determines it is time to free an object from memory, it examines each entry on the finalization queue and copies the object off the heap to yet another managed structure termed the *finalization reachable* table (often abbreviated as freachable, and pronounced "eff-reachable"). At this point, a separate thread is spawned to invoke the `Finalize()` method for each object on the freachable table *at the next garbage collection.* Given this, it will take at the very least two garbage collections to truly finalize an object.

The bottom line is that while finalization of an object does ensure an object can clean up unmanaged resources, it is still nondeterministic in nature, and due to the extra behind-the-curtains processing, considerably slower.

Building Disposable Objects

As you have seen, Finalizers can be used to release unmanaged resources when the garbage collector kicks in. However, given that many unmanaged objects are "precious items" (such as raw database or file handles), it may be valuable to release them as soon as possible instead of relying on a garbage collection to occur. As an alternative to overriding `Finalize()`, your class could implement the `IDisposable` Interface, which defines a single method named `Dispose()`:

```
Public Interface IDisposable
        Sub Dispose()
End Interface
```

If you are new to interface-based programming, Chapter 9 will take you through the details. In a nutshell, an interface is a collection of abstract members a class or structure may support. When you do support the `IDisposable` interface, the assumption is that when the *object user* is finished using the object, the object user manually calls `Dispose()` before allowing the object reference to drop out of scope. In this way, an object can perform any necessary cleanup of unmanaged resources without incurring the hit of being placed on the finalization queue and without waiting for the garbage collector to trigger the class's finalization logic.

■ **Note** Structures and class types can both implement `IDisposable` (unlike overriding `Finalize()`, which is reserved for class types), as the object user (not the garbage collector) invokes the `Dispose()` method.

To illustrate the use of this interface, create a new VB 2010 Console Application named SimpleDispose. Here is an updated `MyResourceWrapper` class that now implements `IDisposable`, rather than overriding `System.Object.Finalize()`:

```
' Implementing IDisposable.
Public Class MyResourceWrapper
    Implements IDisposable
    ' The object user should call this method
    ' when they finish with the object.
```

```
        Public Sub Dispose() Implements IDisposable. Dispose
                ' Clean up unmanaged resources...
                ' Dispose other contained disposable objects...
                ' Just for a test.
                Console.WriteLine("***** In Dispose! *****")
        End Sub
End Class
```

Notice that a `Dispose()` method is not only responsible for releasing the type's unmanaged resources, but should also call `Dispose()` on any other contained disposable methods. Unlike with `Finalize()`, it is perfectly safe to communicate with other managed objects within a `Dispose()` method. The reason is simple: the garbage collector has no clue about the `IDisposable` interface and will never call `Dispose()`. Therefore, when the object user calls this method, the object is still living a productive life on the managed heap and has access to all other heap-allocated objects. The calling logic is straightforward:

```
Module Module1
    Sub Main()
            Console.WriteLine("***** Fun with Dispose *****" & vbLf)
            ' Create a disposable object and call Dispose()
            ' to free any internal resources.
            Dim rw As New MyResourceWrapper()
            rw.Dispose()
            Console.ReadLine()
    End Sub
End Module
```

Of course, before you attempt to call `Dispose()` on an object, you will want to ensure the type supports the `IDisposable` interface. While you will typically know which base class library types implement `IDisposable` by consulting the .NET Framework 4.0 SDK documentation, a programmatic check can be accomplished using the **is** or **as** keywords discussed in Chapter 6:

```
Module Module1
    Sub Main()
            Console.WriteLine("***** Fun with Dispose *****" & vbLf)
            Dim rw As New MyResourceWrapper()
            If TypeOf rw Is IDisposable Then
                    rw.Dispose()
            End If
            Console.ReadLine()
    End Sub
End Module
```

This example exposes yet another rule of working with garbage-collected types:

■ **Rule** Always call `Dispose()` on any object you directly create if the object supports `IDisposable`. The assumption you should make is that if the class designer chose to support the `Dispose()` method, the type has some cleanup to perform.

There is one caveat to the previous rule. A number of types in the base class libraries that do implement the `IDisposable` interface provide a (somewhat confusing) alias to the `Dispose()` method, in an attempt to make the disposal-centric method sound more natural for the defining type. By way of an example, while the `System.IO.FileStream` class implements `IDisposable` (and therefore supports a `Dispose()` method), it also defines a `Close()` method that is used for the same purpose:

```
' Assume you have imported
' the System.IO Namespace...
Sub DisposeFileStream()
    Dim fs As New FileStream("myFile.txt", FileMode.OpenOrCreate)

    ' Confusing, to say the least!
    ' These method calls do the same thing!
    fs.Close()
    fs.Dispose()
End Sub
```

While it does feel more natural to "close" a file rather than "dispose" of one, this doubling up of disposal-centric methods can be confusing. For the few types that do provide an alias, just remember that if a type implements `IDisposable`, calling `Dispose()` is always a correct course of action.

Using Keyword with VB 2010

When you are handling a managed object that implements `IDisposable`, it is quite common to make use of structured exception-handling to ensure the type's `Dispose()` method is called in the event of a runtime exception:

```
Module Module1
    Sub Main()
        Console.WriteLine("***** Fun with Dispose *****" & vbLf)
        Dim rw As New MyResourceWrapper()

        Try

                ' Use the members of rw.

        Finally
                ' Always call Dispose(), error or not.
                rw.Dispose()
        End Try
    End Sub
End Module
```

While this is a fine example of defensive programming, the truth of the matter is that few developers are thrilled by the prospects of wrapping each and every disposable type within a Try/Finally block just to ensure the Dispose() method is called. To achieve the same result in a much less obtrusive manner, VB 2010 supports a special bit of syntax that looks like this:

```
Module Module1
    Sub Main()
        Console.WriteLine("***** Fun with Dispose *****" & vbLf)
        ' Dispose() is called automatically when the
        'Using scope exits.Using rw As New MyResourceWrapper()
                ' Use rw object.
        End Using
    End Sub
End Module
```

If you looked at the CIL code of the Main() method using ildasm.exe, you would find the using syntax does indeed expand to Try/Final logic, with the expected call to Dispose():

```
.method public static void Main() cil managed
{
...
  .try
  {
    ...
  }  // end .try
  finally
  {
...
  IL_002a:  callvirt instance void [mscorlib]
    System.IDisposable::Dispose()
  }  // end handler
...
} // end of method Program::Main
```

■ **Note** If you attempt to "use" an object that does not implement IDisposable, you will receive a compiler error.

While this syntax does remove the need to manually wrap disposable objects within Try/Finally logic, the VB 2010 Using keyword invokes a Dispose() method. When you are working with .NET types that support the IDisposable Interface, this syntactical construct will ensure that the object "being used" will automatically have its Dispose() method called once the Using block has exited.

Also, be aware that it is possible to declare multiple objects *of the same type* within a Using scope. As you would expect, the compiler will inject code to call Dispose() on each declared object:

```
Module Program
    Sub Main()
        Console.WriteLine("***** Fun with Dispose *****" & vbLf)

        ' Use a comma-delimited list to declare multiple objects to dispose.
        Using rw As New MyResourceWrapper(), rw2 As New MyResourceWrapper()
        ' Use rw and rw2 objects.
        End Using
    End Sub
End Module
```

■ **Source Code** The `SimpleDispose` project is included under the Chapter 8 subdirectory.

Building Finalizable and Disposable Types

At this point, we have seen two different approaches to constructing a class that cleans up internal unmanaged resources. On the one hand, you can override `System.Object.Finalize()`. Using this technique, you have the peace of mind that comes with knowing the object cleans itself up when garbage-collected (whenever that may be) without the need for user interaction. On the other hand, you can implement `IDisposable` to provide a way for the object user to clean up the object as soon as it is finished. However, if the caller forgets to call `Dispose()`, the unmanaged resources may be held in memory indefinitely.

As you might suspect, it is possible to blend both techniques into a single class definition. By doing so, you gain the best of both models. If the object user does remember to call `Dispose()`, you can inform the garbage collector to bypass the finalization process by calling `GC.SuppressFinalize()`. If the object user forgets to call `Dispose()`, the object will eventually be finalized and have a chance to free up the internal resources. The good news is that the object's internal unmanaged resources will be freed one way or another.

Here is the next iteration of `MyResourceWrapper`, which is now finalizable and disposable, defined in a VB 2010 Console Application named FinalizableDisposableClass:

```
'A sophisticated resource wrapper.
Public Class MyResourceWrapper
        Implements IDisposable

    'The garbage collector will call this method if the
    ' object user forgets to call Dispose().
    Protected Overrides Sub Finalize()
        'Clean up any internal unmanaged resources.
        'Do **not** call Dispose() on any managed objects.
        Try
        Finally
            MyBase.Finalize()
        End Try
    End Sub
```

```
    'The object user will call this method to clean up
    'resources ASAP.
    Public Sub Dispose()
        Implements IDisposable.Dispose
        'Clean up unmanaged resources here.
        'Call Dispose() on other contained disposable objects.
        'No need to finalize if user called Dispose(),
        'so suppress finalization.
        GC.SuppressFinalize(Me)
    End Sub
End Class
```

Notice that this `Dispose()` method has been updated to call `GC.SuppressFinalize()`, which informs the CLR that it is no longer necessary to call the destructor when this object is garbage-collected, given that the unmanaged resources have already been freed via the `Dispose()` logic.

A Formalized Disposal Pattern

The current implementation of `MyResourceWrapper` does work fairly well; however, we are left with a few minor drawbacks. First, the `Finalize()` and `Dispose()` methods each have to clean up the same unmanaged resources. This could result in duplicate code, which can easily become a nightmare to maintain. Ideally, you would define a private helper function that is called by either method.

Next, you'd like to make sure that the `Finalize()` method does not attempt to dispose of any managed objects, while the `Dispose()` method should do so. Finally, you'd also like to be certain the object user can safely call `Dispose()` multiple times without error. Currently, our `Dispose()` method has no such safeguards.

To address these design issues, Microsoft defined a formal, prim-and-proper disposal pattern that strikes a balance between robustness, maintainability, and performance. Here is the final (and annotated) version of `MyResourceWrapper`, which makes use of this official pattern:

```
Public Class MyResourceWrapper
        Implements IDisposable

        'Used to determine if Dispose()
            'has already been called.
        Private disposed As Boolean = False

        Public Sub Dispose()
                Implements IDisposable. Dispose
            'Call our helper method.
                'Specifying "True" signifies that
                    'the object user triggered the cleanup.
                CleanUp(True)
                'Now suppress finalization.
                GC.SuppressFinalize(Me)
        End Sub
```

```vb
        Private Sub CleanUp(ByVal disposing As Boolean)
            'Be sure we have not already been disposed!
                If Not Me.disposed Then
                    ' If disposing equals true, dispose all
                                  ' managed resources.
                        If disposing Then
                                'Dispose managed resources.
                        End If
                        'Clean up unmanaged resources here.
                End If
                disposed = True
        End Sub

        Protected Overrides Sub Finalize()
                    Try
                    'Call our helper method.
                    'Specifying "False" signifies that
                    'the GC triggered the cleanup.
                        CleanUp(False)
                Finally
                        MyBase.Finalize()
                End Try
        End Sub
End Class
```

Notice that `MyResourceWrapper` now defines a Private helper method named `CleanUp()`. By specifying `True` as an argument, we indicate that the object user has initiated the cleanup, so we should clean up all managed *and* unmanaged resources. However, when the garbage collector initiates the cleanup, we specify `False` when calling `CleanUp()` to ensure that internal disposable objects are *not* disposed (as we can't assume they are still in memory!). Last but not least, our `Boolean` member variable (`disposed`) is set to `True` before exiting `CleanUp()` to ensure that `Dispose()` can be called numerous times without error.

■ **Note** After an object has been "disposed", it's still possible for the client to invoke members on it as it is still in memory. Therefore, a robust resource wrapper class would also need to update each member of the class with additional coding logic that says, in effect, "if I am disposed, do nothing and return from the member."

To test our final iteration of `MyResourceWrapper`, add a call to `Console.Beep()` within the scope of your finalizer:

```vb
Protected Overrides Sub Finalize()
        Try
        Console.Beep()

        ' Call our helper method.
            ' Specifying "False" signifies that
            ' the GC triggered the cleanup.
```

```
                CleanUp(False)
        Finally
            MyBase.Finalize()
        End Try
End Sub
```

Next, update `Main()` as follows:

```
Module Module1
    Sub Main()
        Console.WriteLine("***** Dispose()  Platter *****")

        'Call Dispose() manually, this will not call the finalizer.
        Dim rw As New MyResourceWrapper()
        rw.Dispose()

        'Don't call Dispose(), this will trigger the finalizer
            'and cause a beep.
        Dim rw2 As New MyResourceWrapper()
    End Sub
End Module
```

Notice that we are explicitly calling `Dispose()` on the `rw` object. However, we have "forgotten" to call `Dispose()` on the `rw2` object, and therefore, when the application terminates, we hear a single beep. If you were to comment out the call to `Dispose()` on the `rw` object, you would hear two beeps.

■ **Source Code** The FinalizableDisposableClass project is included under the Chapter 8 subdirectory.

That concludes our investigation of how the CLR manages your objects via garbage collection. While there are additional (somewhat esoteric) details regarding the collection process I haven't covered here (such as weak references and object resurrection), you are now in a perfect position for further exploration on your own. To wrap this chapter up, we will examine a brand new .NET 4.0 programming feature called "Lazy Instantiation" of objects.

Understanding Lazy Object Instantiation

■ **Note** This section assumes you are comfortable with the topics of .NET generics and .NET delegates. If that's not the case, you may want to return to this section once you have completed Chapters 10 and 11.

When you are creating classes, you may occasionally need to account for a particular member variable in code, which may never actually be needed, in that the object user may not call the method (or property) that makes use of it. Fair enough. However, this can be very problematic if the member variable in question requires a large amount of memory to be instantiated.

For example, assume you are writing a class that encapsulates the operations of a digital music player. In addition to the expected methods, such as Play(), Pause(), and Stop(), you also want to provide the ability to return a collection of Song objects (via a class named AllTracks), which represents every single digital music file on the device.

If you'd like to follow along, create a new Console Application named LazyObjectInstantiation, and define the following class types:

```vb
'Represents a single song.
Public Class Song
        Public Property Artist() As String
        Public Property TrackName() As String
        Public Property TrackLength() As Double
End Class

'Represents all songs on a player.
Public Class AllTracks
    'Our media player can have a maximum
    ' of 10,000 songs.
        Private allSongs As Song() = New Song(9999) {}
        Public Sub New()
                        'Assume we fill up the array
                         'of Song objects here.
                Console.WriteLine("Filling up the songs!")
        End Sub
End Class

'The MediaPlayer has-a AllTracks object.
Public Class MediaPlayer
                'Assume these methods do something useful.
        Public Sub Play()
                'Play a song
        End Sub

        Public Sub Pause()
                'Pause the song
        End Sub

        Public Sub [Stop]()
                'Stop playback
        End Sub

        Private allSongs As New AllTracks()

        Public Function GetAllTracks() As AllTracks
        'Return all of the songs.
                Return allSongs
        End Function
End Class
```

The current implementation of MediaPlayer makes the assumption that the object user will want to obtain a list of songs via the GetAllTracks() method. Well, what if the object user does *not* need to obtain this list? No matter, the AllTracks member variable will create 10,000 Song objects in memory:

```
Module Module1
    ..
    Sub Main()
     'This caller does not care about getting all songs,
           'but indirectly created 10,001 objects!
     Dim myPlayer As New MediaPlayer()
     myPlayer.Play()
     Console.ReadLine()
    End Sub
End Module
```

Clearly, you would rather not create 10,000 objects that nobody will use, as that will add a good deal of stress to the .NET garbage collector. While you could manually add some code to ensure the all Songs object is only created if used (perhaps using the factory method design pattern), there is an easier way.

With the release of .NET 4.0, the base class libraries provide a very interesting generic class named Lazy(Of T), defined in the System namespace of mscorlib.dll. This class allows you to define data that will *not* be created unless your code base actually makes use of it. As this is a generic class, you must specify the type of item to be created on first use, which can be any type with the .NET base class libraries or a custom type you have authored yourself. To enable lazy instantiation of the AllTracks member variable, you can simply replace this:

```
'The MediaPlayer has-a AllTracks object.
Public Class MediaPlayer
    ...
        Private allSongs As New AllTracks()
        Public Function GetAllTracks() As AllTracks
                'Return all of the songs.
                Return allSongs
        End Function
End Class
```

with this:

```
'The MediaPlayer has-a generic Lazy<Of AllTracks> object.
Public Class MediaPlayer
    ...
        Private allSongs As New Lazy(Of AllTracks)()
        Public Function GetAllTracks() As AllTracks
              'Return all of the songs.
                Return allSongs.Value
        End Function
End Class
```

Beyond the fact that we are now representing the `AllTracks` member variable as a `Lazy(Of AllTracks)` type, notice that the implementation of the previous `GetAllTracks()` method has also been updated. Specifically, we must make use of the read-only `Value` property of the `Lazy(Of AllTracks)` class to obtain the actual stored data (in this case, the `AllTracks` object that is maintaining the 10,000 `Song` objects).

With this simple update, notice how the following updated `Main()` method will indirectly allocate the `Song` objects only if `GetAllTracks()`is indeed called:

```
Module Module1
    Sub Main()
        Console.WriteLine("***** Fun with Lazy Instantiation *****" & vbLf)
        'No allocation of AllTracks object here!
        Dim myPlayer As New MediaPlayer()
        myPlayer.Play()

        'Allocation of AllTracks happens when you call GetAllTracks().
        Dim yourPlayer As New MediaPlayer()
        Dim yourMusic As AllTracks = yourPlayer.GetAllTracks()
        Console.ReadLine()
    End Sub
End Module
```

Customizing the Creation of the Lazy Data

When you declare a `Lazy(Of T)` variable, the actual internal data type is created using the Default constructor:

```
'default constructor of AllTracks is called when the Lazy(Of AllTracks)
'variable is used.
Private allSongs As New Lazy(Of AllTracks)()
```

While this might be fine in some cases, what if the `AllTracks` class had some additional constructors, and you want to ensure the correct one is called? Furthermore, what if you have some extra work do to (beyond simply creating the `AllTracks` object) when the `Lazy(Of AllTracks)` variable is made? As luck would have it, the `Lazy(Of AllTracks)` class allows you to specify a generic delegate as an optional parameter, which will specify a method to call during the creation of the wrapped type.

The generic delegate in question is of type `System.Func(Of T)`, which can point to a method that returns the same data type being created by the related `Lazy(Of AllTracks)` variable and can take up to 16 arguments (which are typed using generic type parameters). In most cases, you will not need to specify any parameters to pass to the method pointed to by `Func(Of T)`. Furthermore, to greatly simplify the use of the required `Func(OF T)`, I'd recommend using a lambda expression (see Chapter 11 for details regarding the delegate/lambda relationship).

With this in mind, here is a final version of `MediaPlayer` that adds a bit of custom code when the wrapped `AllTracks` object is created. Remember, this method must return a new instance of the type wrapped by `Lazy(Of AllTracks)` before exiting, and you can use any constructor you choose (here, we are still invoking the default constructor of `AllTracks`):

```
Public Class MediaPlayer
        .
        'Use a Lambda expression to add additional code
        'when the AllTracks Object is made.
        Private allSongs As New Lazy(Of AllTracks)(
                Function()
                Console.WriteLine("Creating AllTracks object!")
                        Return New AllTracks()
                        End Function)
        Public Function GetAllTracks() As AllTracks
            'Return all of the songs.
            Return allSongs.Value
        End Function
End Class
```

Sweet! Hopefully you can see the usefulness of the **Lazy(Of AllTracks)** class. Essentially, this new generic class allows you to ensure expensive objects are only allocated when the object user requires them. If you find this topic useful for your projects, you may also want to look up the **System.Lazy(Of T)** class in the .NET Framework 4.0 SDK documentation for further examples of how to program for "lazy instantiation".

■ **Source Code** The LazyObjectInstantiation project is included under the Chapter 8 subdirectory.

Summary

The point of this chapter was to demystify the garbage collection process. As you have seen, the garbage collector will only run when it is unable to acquire the necessary memory from the managed heap (or when a given AppDomain unloads from memory). When a collection does occur, you can rest assured that Microsoft's collection algorithm has been optimized by the use of object generations, secondary threads for the purpose of object finalization, and a managed heap dedicated to hosting large objects.

This chapter also illustrated how to programmatically interact with the garbage collector using the **System.GC** class type. As mentioned, the only time you will really need to do so is when you are building finalizable or disposable class types that operate on unmanaged resources.

Recall that finalizable types are classes that have overridden the Overridable **System.Object.Finalize()** method to clean up unmanaged resources at the time of garbage collection. Disposable objects, on the other hand, are classes that implement the **IDisposable** interface, which should be called by the object user when it is finished using said object. Finally, you learned about an official "disposal" pattern that blends both approaches.

We wrapped up this chapter with a look at a new .NET 4.0 generic class named **Lazy(Of T)**. As you have seen, you can use this class to delay the creation of an expensive (in terms of memory consumption) object until the caller actually requires it. By doing so, you can help reduce the number of objects stored on the managed heap, and therefore ease the stress on the runtime garbage collector.

CHAPTER 9

■ ■ ■

Working with Interfaces

This chapter builds on your current understanding of object-oriented development by examining the topic of interface-based programming. Here you'll learn how to define and implement interfaces, and come to understand the benefits of building types that support multiple behaviors. Along the way, I'll also discuss a number of related topics, such as obtaining interface references, explicit interface implementation, and the construction of interface hierarchies.

We'll also examine a number of standard interfaces defined within the .NET base class libraries. As you will see, your custom classes and structures are free to implement these predefined interfaces to support a number of advanced behaviors such as object cloning, object enumeration, and object sorting.

Understanding Interface Types

To begin this chapter, allow me to provide a formal definition of the interface type. An *interface* is nothing more than a named set of *abstract members*. Recall from Chapter 6 that abstract methods are pure protocol in that they do not provide a default implementation. The specific members defined by an interface depend on the exact behavior it is modeling. Yes, it's true. An interface expresses a *behavior* that a given class or structure may choose to support. Furthermore, as you will see in this chapter, a class (or structure) can support as many interfaces as necessary, thereby supporting (in essence) multiple behaviors.

As you might guess, the .NET base class libraries ship with hundreds of predefined interface types that are implemented by various classes and structures. For example, as you will see in Chapter 21, ADO.NET ships with multiple data providers that allow you to communicate with a particular database management system. Thus, under ADO.NET we have numerous connection objects to choose among (SqlConnection, OracleConnection, OdbcConnection, etc.).

Regardless of the fact that each connection object has a unique name, is defined within a different namespace, and (in some cases) is bundled within a different assembly, all connection objects implement a common interface named IDbConnection:

```
'The IDbConnection Interface defines a common
'set of members supported by all connection objects.
Public Interface IDbConnection
    Inherits IDisposable
```

```
    'Methods
    Function BeginTransaction() As IDbTransaction
Function BeginTransaction(ByVal il As IsolationLevel) As  IDbTransaction

    Sub ChangeDatabase(ByVal databaseName As String)
    Sub Close()

    Function CreateCommand() As IDbCommand
    Sub Open()

    'Properties
    Property ConnectionString As String
    ReadOnly Property ConnectionTimeout As Integer
    ReadOnly Property Database As String
    ReadOnly Property State As ConnectionState
End Interface
```

■ **Note** By convention, .NET interfaces are prefixed with a capital letter "I." When you are creating your own custom interfaces, it is considered a best practice to do the same.

Don't concern yourself with the details of what these members actually do at this point. Simply understand that the IDbConnection interface defines a set of members that are common to all ADO.NET connection objects. Given this, you are guaranteed that every connection object supports members such as Open(), Close(), CreateCommand(), and so forth. Furthermore, given that interface members are always implicitly MustOverride, each connection object is free to implement these methods in its own unique manner.

Another example: the System.Windows.Forms namespace defines a class named Control, which is a base class to a number of Windows Forms GUI widgets (DataGridView, Label, StatusBar, TreeView, etc.). The Control class implements an interface named IDropTarget, which defines basic drag-and-drop functionality:

```
Public Interface IDropTarget
    'Methods
    Sub OnDragDrop(ByVal e As DragEventArgs)
    Sub OnDragEnter(ByVal e As DragEventArgs)
    Sub OnDragLeave(ByVal e As EventArgs)
    Sub OnDragOver(ByVal e As DragEventArgs)
End Interface
```

Based on this interface, you can correctly assume that any class that extends System.Windows.Forms.Control supports four methods named OnDragDrop(), OnDragEnter(), OnDragLeave(), and OnDragOver().

As you work through the remainder of this book, you'll be exposed to dozens of interfaces that ship with the .NET base class libraries. As you will see, these interfaces can be implemented on your own custom classes and structures to define types that integrate tightly within the framework.

Interface Types vs. Abstract Base Classes

Given your work in Chapter 6, the interface type may seem very similar to a MustInherit base class. Recall that when a class is marked as MustInherit, it *may* define any number of MustOverride members to provide a polymorphic interface to all derived types. However, even when a class does define a set of MustOverride members, it is also free to define any number of constructors, field data, concrete members (with implementation), and so on. Interfaces, on the other hand, *only* contain MustOverride member definitions.

The polymorphic interface established by a MustInherit parent class suffers from one major limitation in that *only derived types* support the members defined by the parent. However, in larger software systems, it is very common to develop multiple class hierarchies that have no common parent beyond System.Object. Given that MustOverride members in a MustInherit base class apply only to derived types, we have no way to configure types in different hierarchies to support the same polymorphic interface. By way of example, assume you have defined the following MustInherit class:

```
Public MustInherit Class CloneableType
    'Only derived types can support this
    '"polymorphic interface." Classes in other
    'hierarchies have no access to this MustOverride
    'member.
    Public MustOverride Function Clone() As Object
End Class
```

Given this definition, only members that extend CloneableType are able to support the Clone() method. If you create a new set of classes that do not extend this base class, you can't gain this polymorphic interface. Also you may recall, that VB 2010 does not support multiple inheritance for classes. Therefore, if you wanted to create a MiniVan that is-a Car and is-a CloneableType, you are unable to do so:

```
' Nope! Multiple Inheritance is not possible in VB 2010
' for classes.
Public Class MiniVan
    Inherits Car
    Inherits CloneableType
End Class
```

As you would guess, interface types come to the rescue. Once an interface has been defined, it can be implemented by any class or structure, in any hierarchy, within any namespace or any assembly (written in any .NET programming language). As you can see, interfaces are *highly* polymorphic. Consider the standard .NET interface named ICloneable defined in the System namespace. This interface defines a single method named Clone():

```
Public Interface ICloneable
        Function Clone() As Object
End Interface
```

If you examine the .NET Framework 4.0 SDK documentation, you'll find that a large number of seemingly unrelated types (System.Array, System.Data.SqlClient.SqlConnection, System.OperatingSystem, System.String, etc.) all implement this interface. Although these types have no common parent (other than System.Object), we can treat them polymorphically via the ICloneable interface type.

For example, if you had a method named `CloneMe()` that took an `ICloneable` interface parameter, you could pass this method any object that implements said interface. Consider the following simple `Program` class defined within a Console Application named ICloneableExample:

```
Module Module1
    Sub Main()
        Console.WriteLine("***** A First Look at Interfaces *****" & vbLf)

        'All of these classes support the ICloneable interface.
        Dim myStr As String = "Hello"
        Dim unixOS As New OperatingSystem(PlatformID.Unix, New Version())
        Dim sqlCnn As New System.Data.SqlClient.SqlConnection()

        'Therefore, they can all be passed into a method taking ICloneable.
        CloneMe(myStr)
        CloneMe(unixOS)
        CloneMe(sqlCnn)
        Console.ReadLine()
    End Sub

    Private Sub CloneMe(ByVal c As ICloneable)
        'Clone whatever we get and print out the name.
        Dim theClone As Object = c.Clone()
        Console.WriteLine("Your clone is a: {0}", theClone.GetType().Name)
    End Sub
End Module
```

When you run this application, the class name of each class prints out to the console, via the `GetType()` method you inherit from `System.Object` (Chapter 15 provides full coverage of this method and .NET reflection services).

___

■ **Source Code** The ICloneableExample project is located under the Chapter 9 subdirectory.

___

Another limitation of traditional abstract base classes is that *each derived type* must contend with the set of `MustInherit` members and provide an implementation. To see this problem, recall the shapes hierarchy we defined in Chapter 6. Assume we defined a new `MustInherit` method in the `Shape` base class named `GetNumberOfPoints()`, which allows derived types to return the number of points required to render the shape:

```
MustInherit Class Shape
    ...
    'Every derived class must now support this method!
    Public MustOverride Function GetNumberOfPoints() As Byte
End Class
```

Clearly, the only type that has any points in the first place is **Hexagon**. However, with this update, *every* derived class (**Circle**, **Hexagon**, and **ThreeDCircle**) must now provide a concrete implementation of this function even if it makes no sense to do so.

Again, the interface type provides a solution. If you define an interface that represents the behavior of "having points," you can simply plug it into the **Hexagon** type, leaving **Circle** and **ThreeDCircle** untouched.

Defining Custom Interfaces

Now that you better understand the overall role of interface types, let's see an example of defining and implementing custom interfaces. To begin, create a brand-new Console Application named CustomInterface. Using the Project ➤ Add Existing Item menu option, insert the file(s) containing your shape type definitions (**Shapes.vb** in the book's solution code) created back in Chapter 6 during the **Shapes** example.

Now, insert a new interface into your project named **IPointy** using the Project ➤ Add New Item menu option, as shown in Figure 9-1.

Figure 9-1. Interfaces, like classes, can be defined in any *.vb file

337

At a syntactic level, an interface is defined using the VB 2010 `Interface` keyword. Unlike a class, interfaces never specify a base class (not even `System.Object`; however, as you will see later in this chapter, an interface can specify base interfaces). Moreover, the members of an interface never specify an access modifier (as all interface members are implicitly Public and MustOverride). To get the ball rolling, here is a custom interface defined in VB 2010:

```vb
' This Interface defines the behavior of "having points."
Public Interface IPointy
    ' Implicitly Public and MustOverride.
    ReadOnly Property Points() As Byte
End Interface
```

Remember that when you define interface members, you do not define an implementation scope for the member in question. Interfaces are pure protocol, and therefore never define an implementation (that is up to the supporting class or structure). Therefore, the following version of `IPointy` would result in various compiler errors:

```vb
' Ack! Errors abound!
Public Interface IPointy
        ' Error! Interfaces cannot have fields!
        Public numbOfPoints As Integer

        ' Error! Interfaces do not have constructors!
        Public Sub New()
          numbOfPoints = 0
        End Sub

        ' Error! Interfaces don't provide an implementation of members!
        Function GetNumberOfPoints() As Byte
         Return numbOfPoints
        End Function
End Interface
```

In any case, this initial `IPointy` interface defines a single method. However, .NET interface types are also able to define any number of property prototypes. For example, you could create the `IPointy` interface to use a read-only property rather than a traditional accessor method:

```vb
'The pointy behavior as a read-only property.
Public Interface IPointy
    ReadOnly Property Points() As Byte
End Interface
```

■ **Note** Interface types can also contain event (see Chapter 11) and indexer (see Chapter 12) definitions.

Interface types are quite useless on their own, as they are nothing more than a named collection of MustOverride members. For example, you can't allocate interface types as you would a class or structure:

```
'Ack! Illegal to allocate Interface Types.
Sub Main()
        Dim p As New IPointy() 'Compiler error!
End Sub
```

Interfaces do not bring much to the table until they are implemented by a class or structure. Here, **IPointy** is an interface that expresses the behavior of "having points." The idea is simple: some classes in the shapes hierarchy have points (such as the **Hexagon**), while others (such as the **Circle**) do not.

Implementing an Interface

When a class (or structure) chooses to extend its functionality by supporting interfaces types, it does so using the **Implements** keyword. When your class type derives directly from **System.Object**, you are free to simply list the interface(s) supported by the class, as the VB 2010 compiler will extend your types from **System.Object** if you do not say otherwise. On a related note, given that structures always derive from **System.ValueType** (see Chapter 4 for full details), simply list each interface via **Implements** keyword directly after the structure definition. Ponder the following examples:

```
' This class derives from System.Object and
' implements a single Interface.
Public Class Pencil
        Implements IPointy
...
End Class

' This class also derives from System.Object
' and implements a single Interface.
Public Class SwitchBlade
        Inherits Object
        Implements IPointy
...
End Class

' This class derives from a custom base class
' and implements a single Interface.
Public Class Fork
        Inherits Utensil
        Implements IPointy
...
End Class
```

```
' This structure implicitly derives from System.ValueType and
'implements two Interfaces.
Public Structure Arrow
        Implements ICloneable
        Implements IPointy
...
End Structure
```

You will notice that the **Implements** keyword is used *twice* later in the examples. First, the class definition is updated to list each interface supported by the type. Second, the **Implements** keyword is used to "attach" the interface member to a member on the class itself. At first glance, this can appear to be quite redundant; however, as you will see later in this chapter, this approach can be quite helpful when you need to resolve name clashes that can occur when a type implements multiple interfaces.

Understand that implementing an interface is an all-or-nothing proposition. The supporting type is not able to selectively choose which members it will implement. Given that the **IPointy** interface defines a single read-only property, this is not too much of a burden. However, if you are implementing an interface that defines ten members (such as the **IDbConnection** interface shown earlier), the type is now responsible for fleshing out the details of all ten abstract entities.

For this example, insert a new class type named **Triangle** that is-a **Shape** and supports **IPointy**. Note that the implementation of the read-only **Points** property simply returns the correct number of points (3).

```
'New Shape derived class named Triangle.
Public Class Triangle
    Inherits Shape
    Implements IPointy

    Public Sub New()
    End Sub

    Public Sub New(ByVal name As String)
        MyBase.New(name)
    End Sub

    Public Overrides Sub Draw()
        Console.WriteLine("Drawing {0} the Triangle", PetName)
    End Sub

    'IPointy Implementation.
    Public ReadOnly Property Points() As Byte Implements IPointy.Points
        Get
            Return 3
        End Get
    End Property
End Class
```

Now, update your existing **Hexagon** type to also support the **IPointy** interface type:

```
' Hexagon now implements IPointy.
Public Class Hexagon
    Inherits Shape
    Implements IPointy

    Public Sub New()
    End Sub

    Public Sub New(ByVal name As String)
        MyBase.New(name)
    End Sub
    Public Overrides Sub Draw()
        Console.WriteLine("Drawing {0} the Hexagon", PetName)
    End Sub

    ' IPointy Implementation.
    Public ReadOnly Property Points() As Byte Implements IPointy.Points
        Get
            Return 6
        End Get
    End Property
End Class
```

To sum up the story so far, the Visual Studio 2010 class diagram shown in Figure 9-2 illustrates **IPointy**-compatible classes using the popular "lollipop" notation. Notice again that **Circle** and **ThreeDCircle** do not implement **IPointy**, as this behavior makes no sense for these particular classes.

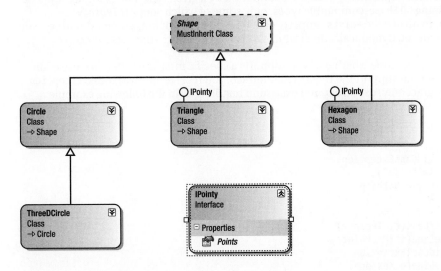

Figure 9-2. The shapes hierarchy, now with interfaces

■ **Note** To display or hide interface names on the class designer, right-click on the interface icon and select the Collapse or Expand option.

Invoking Interface Members at the Object Level

Now that you have some classes that support the `IPointy` interface, the next question is how you interact with the new functionality. The most straightforward way to interact with functionality supplied by a given interface is to invoke the members directly from the object level (provided the interface members are not implemented explicitly; more details later in the section "Resolving Name Clashes via Explicit Interface Implementation"). For example, consider the following `Main()` method:

```
Module Module1
   Sub Main()
        Console.WriteLine("***** Fun with Interfaces *****" & vbLf)

        ' Call Points property defined by IPointy.
        Dim hex As New Hexagon()
        Console.WriteLine("Points: {0}", hex.Points)
        Console.ReadLine()
   End Sub
End Module
```

This approach works fine in this particular case, given that you are well aware that the `Hexagon` type has implemented the interface in question and therefore has a `Points` property. Other times, however, you may not be able to determine which interfaces are supported by a given type. For example, suppose you have an array containing 50 `Shape`-compatible types, only some of which support `IPointy`. Obviously, if you attempt to invoke the `Points` property on a type that has not implemented `IPointy`, you receive an error. So how can you dynamically determine if a class or structure supports the correct interface?

One way to determine at runtime whether a type supports a specific interface is to make use of an explicit cast. If the type does not support the requested interface, you receive an `InvalidCastException`. To handle this possibility gracefully, use structured exception handling as in the following example:

```
Module Module1
   Sub Main()
        ...
' Catch a possible InvalidCastException.
      Dim c As New Circle("Lisa")
      Dim itfPt As IPointy = Nothing

      Try
          itfPt = DirectCast(c, IPointy)
          Console.WriteLine(itfPt.Points)
      Catch e As InvalidCastException
          Console.WriteLine(e.Message)
      End Try
```

```
        Console.ReadLine()
    End Sub
End Module
```

While you could use **Try/Catch** logic and hope for the best, it would be ideal to determine which interfaces are supported before invoking the interface members in the first place. Let's see two ways of doing so.

Obtaining Interface References: The TryCast Keyword

You can determine whether a given type supports an interface by using the **TryCast** keyword, introduced in Chapter 6. If the object can be treated as the specified interface, you are returned a reference to the interface in question. If not, you receive a **Nothing** reference. Therefore, be sure to check against a **Nothing** value before proceeding:

```
Module Module1
    Sub Main()
        ...
        ' Can we treat hex2 as IPointy?
        Dim hex2 As New Hexagon("Peter")
        Dim itfPt2 As IPointy = TryCast(hex2, IPointy)

        If itfPt2 IsNot Nothing Then
            Console.WriteLine("Points: {0}", itfPt2.Points)
        Else
            Console.WriteLine("OOPS! Not pointy...")
        End If
        Console.ReadLine()
    End Sub
End Module
```

Notice that when you use the **TryCast** keyword, you have no need to use **Try/Catch** logic, given that if the reference is not **Nothing**, you know you are calling on a valid interface reference.

Obtaining Interface References: The Is Keyword

You may also check for an implemented interface using the **Is** keyword (also first discussed in Chapter 6). If the object in question is not compatible with the specified interface, you are returned the value **False**. On the other hand, if the type is compatible with the interface in question, you can safely call the members without needing to use **Try/Catch** logic.

To illustrate, assume we have an array of **Shape** types containing some members that implement **IPointy**. Notice how we are able to determine which item in the array supports this interface using the **Is** keyword, as shown in this retrofitted **Main()** method:

```
Module Program

  Sub Main()
      Console.WriteLine("***** Fun with Interfaces *****" & vbLf)
      'Make an array of Shapes.
        Dim myShapes As Shape() = {New Hexagon(), New Circle(), New Triangle("Joe"),↵
New Circle("JoJo")}

      For i = 0 To myShapes.Length - 1
          'Recall the Shape base class defines an MustOverride Draw()
          'member, so all shapes know how to draw themselves.
          myShapes(i).Draw()

          ' Who's pointy?
          If TypeOf myShapes(i) Is IPointy Then
              Console.WriteLine("-> Points: {0}", (DirectCast(myShapes(i),↵
IPointy)).Points)
          Else
              Console.WriteLine("-> {0}'s not pointy!", myShapes(i).PetName)
          End If

          Console.WriteLine()

      Next
      Console.ReadLine()
    End Sub
End Module
```

The output is as follows:

```
***** Fun with Interfaces *****



Drawing NoName the Hexagon

-> Points: 6



Drawing NoName the Circle

-> NoName's not pointy!
```

```
Drawing Joe the Triangle

-> Points: 3



Drawing JoJo the Circle

-> JoJo's not pointy!
```

Interfaces As Parameters

Given that interfaces are valid .NET types, you may construct methods that take interfaces as parameters, as illustrated by the CloneMe() method earlier in this chapter. For the current example, assume you have defined another interface named IDraw3D:

```vb
' Models the ability to render a type in stunning 3D.
Public Interface IDraw3D
    Sub Draw3D()
End Interface
```

Next, assume that two of your three shapes (ThreeDCircle and Hexagon) have been configured to support this new behavior:

```vb
' Circle supports IDraw3D Interface.
Public Class ThreeDCircle
    Inherits Circle
    Implements IDraw3D
    ...
    Public Sub Draw3D() Implements IDraw3D.Draw3D
        Console.WriteLine("Drawing a 3D Circle")
    End Sub
End Class

' Hexagon now implements IPointy and IDraw3D.
Public Class Hexagon
    Inherits Shape
    Implements IPointy
    Implements IDraw3D
    ...
    Public Sub Draw3D() Implements IDraw3D.Draw3D
        Console.WriteLine("Drawing a 3D Hexagon")
    End Sub
End Class
```

Figure 9-3 presents the updated Visual Studio 2010 class diagram.

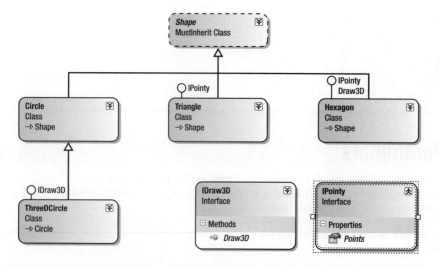

Figure 9-3. *The updated shapes hierarchy*

If you now define a method taking an **IDraw3D** interface as a parameter, you can effectively send in any object implementing **IDraw3D.** (If you attempt to pass in a type not supporting the necessary interface, you receive a compile-time error.) Consider the following method defined within your Module1 Module:

```
'I'll draw anyone supporting IDraw3D.
Sub DrawIn3D(ByVal itf3d As IDraw3D)
        Console.WriteLine("-> Drawing IDraw3D compatible type")
        itf3d.Draw3D()
End Sub
```

We could now test whether an item in the **Shape** array supports this new interface, and if so, pass it into the **DrawIn3D()** method for processing:

```
Sub Main()

        Console.WriteLine("***** Fun with Interfaces *****" & vbLf)

        'Make an array of Shapes.
        Dim myShapes As Shape() = {New Hexagon(), New Circle(), New   Triangle("Joe"), New
Circle("JoJo")}
```

```
        For i = 0 To myShapes.Length - 1
          ...
            ' Can I draw you in 3D?
            If TypeOf myShapes(i) Is IDraw3D Then
                DrawIn3D(DirectCast(myShapes(i), IDraw3D))
            End If
        Next
End Sub
```

Here is the output of the updated application. Notice that only the **Hexagon** object prints out in 3D, as the other members of the **Shape** array do not implement the **IDraw3D** interface.

```
***** Fun with Interfaces *****


Drawing NoName the Hexagon

-> Points: 6

-> Drawing IDraw3D compatible type

Drawing Hexagon in 3D!



Drawing NoName the Circle

-> NoName's not pointy!



Drawing Joe the Triangle

-> Points: 3



Drawing JoJo the Circle

-> JoJo's not pointy!
```

Interfaces As Return Values

Interfaces can also be used as method return values. For example, you could write a method that takes an array of Shape objects and returns a reference to the first item that supports IPointy:

```
'This method returns the first object in the
'array that implements IPointy.
Function FindFirstPointyShape(ByVal shapes As Shape()) As IPointy

    For Each s As Shape In shapes
        If TypeOf s Is IPointy Then
            Return TryCast(s, IPointy)
        End If
    Next

    Return Nothing
End Function
```

You could interact with this method as follows:

```
Sub Main()
    Console.WriteLine("***** Fun with Interfaces *****" & vbLf)

    'Make an array of Shapes.
    Dim myShapes As Shape() = {New Hexagon(), New Circle(), New    Triangle("Joe"), New
Circle("JoJo")}

    'Get first pointy item.
    Dim firstPointyItem As IPointy = FindFirstPointyShape(myShapes)
    Console.WriteLine("The item has {0} points", firstPointyItem.Points)
...
End Sub
```

Arrays of Interface Types

Recall that the same interface can be implemented by numerous types, even if they are not within the same class hierarchy and do not have a common parent class beyond System.Object. This can yield some very powerful programming constructs. For example, assume you have developed three new class types within your current project that model kitchen utensils (via Knife and Fork classes) and another modeling gardening equipment (à la PitchFork). Consider Figure 9-4.

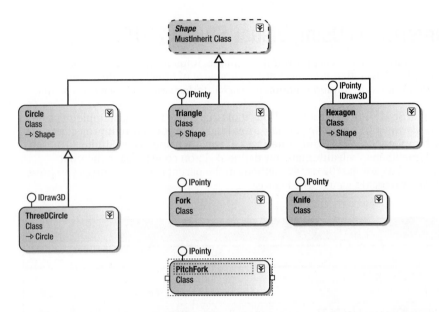

Figure 9-4. Recall that interfaces can be "plugged into" any type in any part of a class hierarchy

If you defined the PitchFork, Fork, and Knife types, you could now define an array of IPointy-compatible objects. Given that these members all support the same interface, you can iterate through the array and treat each item as an IPointy-compatible object, regardless of the overall diversity of the class hierarchies:

```
Sub Main()
        'This array can only contain types that
      'implement the IPointy Interface.
        Dim myPointyObjects As IPointy() = {New Hexagon(), New Knife(),
        New Triangle(), New Fork(), New PitchFork()}

        For Each i As IPointy In myPointyObjects
            Console.WriteLine("Object has {0} points.", i.Points)
        Next
        Console.ReadLine()
End Sub
```

■ **Source Code** The CustomInterface project is located under the Chapter 9 subdirectory.

Implementing Interfaces Using Visual Studio 2010

Although interface-based programming is a very powerful technique, implementing interfaces may entail a healthy amount of typing. Given that interfaces are a named set of MustOverride members, you are required to type in the definition and implementation for *each* interface method on *each* type that supports the behavior.

As you would hope, Visual Studio 2010 supports various tools that make the task of implementing interfaces less burdensome. By way of a simple test, insert a final class into your current project named PointyTestClass. This class implements the IPointy interfaces. If you are using Visual Studio 2010, you will find that the integrated IntelliSense will automatically define skeleton code for each member defined by the interfaces (as well as any MustOverride methods in the parent class) as soon as you press the Enter key at the end of an Implements clause (see Figure 9-5).

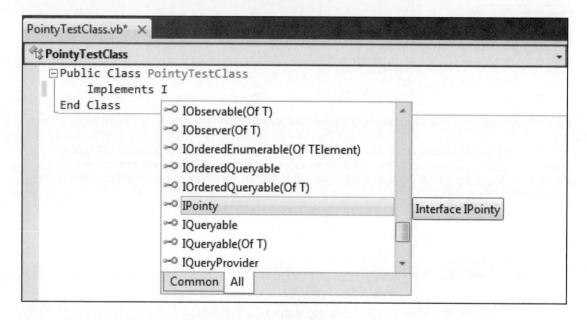

Figure 9-5. Implementing interfaces using Visual Studio 2010

```
Public Class PointTestClass
                Implements IPointy

  Public Overrides Sub Draw()
  End Sub

  Public ReadOnly Property Points() As Byte Implements IPointy.Points
        Get
        End Get
  End Property
End Class
```

Notice that the Implements keyword is used *twice*. First, the class definition is updated to list each interface supported by the type. Second, the Implements keyword is used to "attach" the interface member to a member on the class itself. At first glance, this can appear to be quite redundant; however, as you will see later in this chapter, this approach can be quite helpful when you need to resolve name clashes that can occur when a type implements multiple interfaces.

Resolving Name Clashes via Explicit Interface Implementation

As shown earlier in this chapter, a single class or structure can implement any number of interfaces. Given this, there is always the possibility you may implement interfaces that contain identical members, and therefore have a name clash to contend with. To illustrate various manners in which you can resolve this issue, create a new Console Application named InterfaceNameClash. Now design three interfaces that represent various locations to which an implementing type could render its output:

```
' Draw image to a Form.
Public Interface IDrawToForm
    Sub Draw()
End Interface

' Draw to buffer in memory.
Public Interface IDrawToMemory
    Sub Draw()
End Interface

' Render to the printer.
Public Interface IDrawToPrinter
    Sub Draw()
End Interface
```

Notice that each interface defines a method named Draw(), with the identical signature (which happen to be no arguments). If you now wish to support each of these interfaces on a single class type named Octagon, the IDE will automatically generate three different Public members on the class, following the rather nondescript naming convention of suffixing a numerical value after the interface member name:

```
' To resolve name clashes,
' the IDE will autogenerate unique names where necessary.
Public Class Octagon
  Implements IDrawToForm, IDrawToMemory, IDrawToPrinter

  Public Sub Draw() Implements IDrawToForm.Draw
  End Sub

  Public Sub Draw1() Implements IDrawToMemory.Draw
  End Sub
```

```
    Public Sub Draw2() Implements IDrawToPrinter.Draw
    End Sub
End Class
```

Although the generated method names (Draw1(), Draw2(), etc.) leave something to be desired, it should be clear that the coding logic used to render image data to a window, a region of memory, or a piece of paper is quite different.

Clearly, the sort of code required to render the image to a window is quite different from the code needed to render the image to a networked printer or a region of memory. When you implement several interfaces that have identical members, you can resolve this sort of name clash using *explicit interface implementation* syntax. Consider the following update to the Octagon type:

```
Public Class Octagon
    Implements IDrawToForm, IDrawToMemory, IDrawToPrinter
    ' Explicitly bind Draw() implementations
    ' to a given interface.
    Public Sub Draw() Implements IDrawToForm.Draw
        Console.WriteLine("Drawing to form..")
    End Sub

    Public Sub RenderToMemory() Implements IDrawToMemory.Draw
        Console.WriteLine("Drawing to memory...")
    End Sub

    Public Sub Print() Implements IDrawToPrinter.Draw
        Console.WriteLine("Printing to a printer...")
    End Sub
End Class
```

As you can see, when explicitly implementing an interface member, the general pattern breaks down to

```
returnType InterfaceName.MethodName(params)
```

Note that when using this syntax, you do not supply an access modifier; explicitly implemented members are automatically Private. For example, the following is illegal syntax:

```
' Error! No access modifer!
Public Sub Draw() Implements IDrawToForm.Draw
    Console.WriteLine("Drawing to form...")
End Sub
```

Because explicitly implemented members are always implicitly Private, these members are no longer available from the object level. In fact, if you were to apply the dot operator to an Octagon type, you would find that IntelliSense does not show you any of the Draw() members (see Figure 9-6).

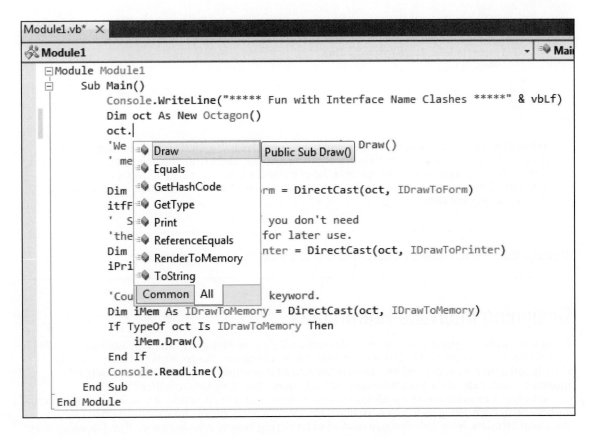

```
Module1.vb* ×

Module1                                                                    ▾  Mai

  Module Module1
    Sub Main()
        Console.WriteLine("***** Fun with Interface Name Clashes *****" & vbLf)
        Dim oct As New Octagon()
        oct.|
        'We  ▣  Draw              Public Sub Draw()   Draw()
        '  me ▣  Equals
        Dim    ▣  GetHashCode       rm = DirectCast(oct, IDrawToForm)
        itfF   ▣  GetType
        '   S  ▣  Print              you don't need
        'the   ▣  ReferenceEquals    for later use.
        Dim    ▣  RenderToMemory     nter = DirectCast(oct, IDrawToPrinter)
        iPri   ▣  ToString

        'Cou   Common   All          keyword.
        Dim iMem As IDrawToMemory = DirectCast(oct, IDrawToMemory)
        If TypeOf oct Is IDrawToMemory Then
            iMem.Draw()
        End If
        Console.ReadLine()
    End Sub
End Module
```

Figure 9-6. Explicitly implemented interface members are not exposed from the object level

As expected, you must make use of explicit casting to access the required functionality. For example:

```
Module Moodule1
    Sub Main()
        Console.WriteLine("** Fun with Interface Name Clashes **" & vbLf)
        Dim oct As New Octagon()

        ' We now must use casting to access the Draw()
        ' members.
        Dim itfForm As IDrawToForm = DirectCast(oct, IDrawToForm)
        itfForm.Draw()

        ' Shorthand notation if you don't need
        ' the interface variable for later use.
        Dim iPrint As IDrawToPrinter = DirectCast(oct, IDrawToPrinter)
        iPrint.Draw()
```

```
            ' Could also use the "Is" keyword.
            Dim iMem As IDrawToMemory = DirectCast(oct, IDrawToMemory)
            If TypeOf oct Is IDrawToMemory Then
                iMem.Draw()
            End If
            Console.ReadLine()
        End Sub
End Module
```

While this syntax is quite helpful when you need to resolve name clashes, you can use explicit interface implementation simply to hide more "advanced" members from the object level. In this way, when the object user applies the dot operator, he or she will see only a subset of the type's overall functionality. However, those who require the more advanced behaviors can extract out the desired interface via an explicit cast.

■ **Source Code** The InterfaceNameClash project is located under the Chapter 9 subdirectory.

Designing Interface Hierarchies

Interfaces can be arranged in an interface hierarchy. Like a class hierarchy, when an interface extends an existing interface, it inherits the MustOverride members defined by the parent(s). Of course, unlike class-based inheritance, derived interfaces never inherit true implementation. Rather, a derived interface simply extends its own definition with additional MustOverride members.

Interface hierarchies can be useful when you wish to extend the functionality of an existing interface without breaking existing code bases. To illustrate, create a new Console Application named InterfaceHierarchy. Now, let's design a new set of rendering-centric interfaces such that IDrawable is the root of the family tree:

```
Public Interface IDrawable
    Sub Draw()
End Interface
```

Given that IDrawable defines a basic drawing behavior, we could now create a derived interface that extends this interface with the ability to render in modified formats, for example:

```
Public Interface IAdvancedDraw
    Inherits IDrawable
        Sub DrawInBoundingBox(ByVal top As Integer, ByVal left As Integer,
        ByVal bottom As Integer, ByVal right As Integer)
        Sub DrawUpsideDown()
End Interface
```

Given this design, if a class were to implement **IAdvancedDraw**, it would now be required to implement each and every member defined up the chain of inheritance (specifically, the **Draw()**, **DrawInBoundingBox()**, and **DrawUpsideDown()** methods):

```
Public Class BitmapImage
    Implements IAdvancedDraw

    Public Sub Draw() Implements IDrawable.Draw
        Console.WriteLine("Drawing...")
    End Sub

        Public Sub DrawInBoundingBox(ByVal top As Integer, ByVal left As Integer, _
        ByVal bottom As Integer, ByVal right As Integer) _
                Implements IAdvancedDraw.DrawInBoundingBox
        Console.WriteLine("Drawing in a box...")
    End Sub

    Public Sub DrawUpsideDown() Implements IAdvancedDraw.DrawUpsideDown
        Console.WriteLine("Drawing upside down!")
    End Sub
End Class
```

Now, when we make use of the **BitmapImage**, we are able to invoke each method at the object level (as they are all **Public**), as well as extract out a reference to each supported interface explicitly via casting:

```
Module Module1
    Sub Main()

        Console.WriteLine("***** Simple Interface Hierarchy *****")

        ' Call from object level.
        Dim myBitmap As New BitmapImage()
        myBitmap.Draw()
        myBitmap.DrawInBoundingBox(10, 10, 100, 150)
        myBitmap.DrawUpsideDown()

        ' Get IAdvancedDraw explicitly.
        Dim iAdvDraw As IAdvancedDraw
        iAdvDraw = DirectCast(myBitmap, IAdvancedDraw)
        iAdvDraw.DrawUpsideDown()
        Console.ReadLine()
    End Sub
End Module
```

■ **Source Code** The InterfaceHierarchy project is located under the Chapter 9 subdirectory.

Multiple Inheritance with Interface Types

Unlike class types, a single interface can extend multiple base interfaces, allowing us to design some very powerful and flexible abstractions. Create a new Console Application project named MIInterfaceHierarchy. Here is another collection of interfaces that model various rendering and shape abstractions. Notice that the IShape interface is extending both IDrawable and IPrintable:

```
' Multiple inheritance for interface types is a-okay.
Public Interface IDrawable
    Sub Draw()
End Interface

Interface IPrintable
    Sub Print()
    Sub Draw() ' <-- Note possible name clash here!
End Interface

' Multiple interface inheritance. OK!
Interface IShape
    Inherits IDrawable
    Inherits IPrintable
    Function GetNumberOfSides() As Integer
End Interface
```

Figure 9-7 illustrates the current interface hierarchy.

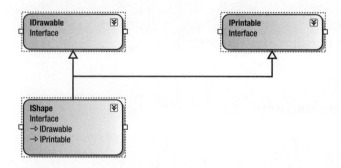

Figure 9-7. *Unlike classes, interfaces can extend multiple interface types*

Now, the million dollar question is, if you have a class supporting IShape, how many methods will it be required to implement? The answer: it depends. If you want to provide a simple implementation of the Draw() method, you need only provide three members, as shown in the following Rectangle type:

```
Public Class Rectangle
    Implements IShape

    Public Function GetNumberOfSides() As Integer _
        Implements IShape.GetNumberOfSides
        Return 4
    End Function

    Public Sub Dra_Draw()  Implements IDrawable.Draw
        Console.WriteLine("Drawing...")
    End Sub
    Public Sub Print() Implements IPrintable.Print
        Console.WriteLine("Printing...")
    End Sub
End Class
```

If you'd rather have specific implementations for each **Draw()** method (which in this case would make the most sense), you can resolve the name clash using the interface **IPrintable.Draw** implementation for the **Draw()** method explicitly, as shown in the following **Square** type:

```
Public Class Square
    Implements IShape

    Sub Print_Draw() Implements IPrintable.Draw
        'Draw to Printer ...
    End Sub

    Sub Dra_Draw() Implements IDrawable.Draw
        'Draw to Screen ...
    End Sub

    Public Sub Print() Implements IPrintable.Print
        'Print ...
    End Sub

    Public Function GetNumberOfSides() As Integer _
        Implements IShape.GetNumberOfSides
        Return 4
    End Function
End Class
```

Hopefully, at this point you feel more comfortable with the process of defining and implementing custom interfaces using the VB 2010 syntax. To be honest, interface-based programming can take awhile to get comfortable with, so if you are in fact still scratching your head just a bit, this is a perfectly normal reaction.

Do be aware, however, that interfaces are a fundamental aspect of the .NET Framework. Regardless of the type of application you are developing (web-based, desktop GUIs, data-access libraries, etc.), working with interfaces will be part of the process. To summarize the story thus far, remember that interfaces can be extremely useful when

- You have a single hierarchy where only a subset of the derived types supports a common behavior.

- You need to model a common behavior that is found across multiple hierarchies with no common parent class beyond `System.Object`.

Now that you have drilled into the specifics of building and implementing custom interfaces, the remainder of the chapter examines a number of predefined interfaces contained within the .NET base class libraries.

■ **Source Code** The MlInterfaceHierarchy project is located under the Chapter 9 subdirectory.

Building Enumerable Types (IEnumerable and IEnumerator)

To begin examining the process of implementing existing .NET interfaces, let's first look at the role of `IEnumerable` and `IEnumerator`. Recall that VB 2010 supports keywords named `For Each` that allow you to iterate over the contents of any array type:

```
' Iterate over an array of items.
Dim myArrayOfInts As Integer() = New Integer() {10, 20, 30, 40}

For Each i As Integer In myArrayOfInts
    Console.WriteLine(i)
Next
```

While it may seem that only array types can make use of this construct, the truth of the matter is any type supporting a method named `GetEnumerator()` can be evaluated by the `For Each` construct. To illustrate, begin by creating a new Console Application project named CustomEnumerator. Next, add the `Car.vb` and `Radio.vb` files defined in the SimpleException example of Chapter 7 (via the Project ➤ Add Existing Item menu option).

Now, insert a new class named `Garage` that stores a set of `Car` objects within a `System.Array`:

```
' Garage contains a set of Car objects.
Public Class Garage

    'Fill with some Car objects upon startup.
    Private carArray As Car() = New Car(3) {}

    Public Sub New()
        carArray(0) = New Car("Rusty", 30)
        carArray(1) = New Car("Clunker", 55)
        carArray(2) = New Car("Zippy", 30)
        carArray(3) = New Car("Fred", 30)
    End Sub
End Class
```

Ideally, it would be convenient to iterate over the **Garage** object's subitems using the **For Each** construct, just like an array of data values:

```
Module Module1
    Sub Main()

        Console.WriteLine("**Fun with IEnumerable / IEnumerator**" & vbLf)
        Dim carLot As New Garage()
        'Hand over each car in the collection?
        For Each c As Car In carLot
                Console.WriteLine("{0} is going {1} MPH", c.PetName, c.CurrentSpeed)
                Next
        Console.WriteLine()
    End Sub

End Module
```

Sadly, the compiler informs you that the **Garage** class does not implement a method named **GetEnumerator()**. This method is formalized by the **IEnumerable** interface, which is found lurking within the **System.Collections** namespace.

■ **Note** In the next chapter you will learn about the role of generics and the **System.Collections.Generic** namespace. As you will see, this namespace contain generic versions of IEnumerable/IEnumerator that provide a more type-safe way to iterate over subobjects.

Classes or structures that support this behavior advertise that they are able to expose contained subitems to the caller (in this example, the **For Each** construct itself):

```
' This interface informs the caller' that the object's subitems can be enumerated.
Public Interface IEnumerable
  Function GetEnumerator() As IEnumerator
End Interface
```

As you can see, the **GetEnumerator()** method returns a reference to yet another interface named **System.Collections.IEnumerator**. This interface provides the infrastructure to allow the caller to traverse the internal objects contained by the **IEnumerable**-compatible container:

```
' This interface allows the caller to
' obtain a container's subitems.
Public Interface IEnumerator

    ' Advance the internal position of the cursor.
    Function MoveNext() As Boolean
```

```
' Get the current item (read-only property).
ReadOnly Property Current As Object

' Reset the cursor before the first member.
Sub Reset()

End Interface
```

If you wish to update the **Garage** type to support these interfaces, you could take the long road and implement each method manually. While you are certainly free to provide customized versions of GetEnumerator(), MoveNext(), Current, and Reset(), there is a simpler way. As the **System.Array** type (as well as many other collection classes) already implements IEnumerable and IEnumerator, you can simply delegate the request to the **System.Array** as follows:

```
Imports system.Collections
Public Class Garage
  Implements IEnumerable

  Private carArray () As Car = New Car(3) {}

  Public Sub New()
   carArray(0) = New Car("Rusty", 30)
   carArray(1) = New Car("Clunker", 55)
   carArray(2) = New Car("Zippy", 30)
   carArray(3) = New Car("Fred", 30)
  End Sub

  Public Function GetEnumerator() As IEnumerator _
    Implements IEnumerable.GetEnumerator
    Return carArray.GetEnumerator()
  End Function
End Class
```

Once you have updated your **Garage** type, you can now safely use the type within the VB 2010 **For Each** construct. Furthermore, given that the GetEnumerator() method has been defined publicly, the object user could also interact with the IEnumerator type:

```
'Manually work with IEnumerator.
Dim i As IEnumerator = carLot.GetEnumerator()
i.MoveNext()
Dim myCar As Car = DirectCast(i.Current, Car)
Console.WriteLine("{0} is going {1} MPH", myCar.PetName, myCar.CurrentSpeed)
```

```
you may wish to define GetEnumerator() as Private, to hide this member from the object
level:
Public Function GetEnumerator() As System.Collections.IEnumerator _
  Implements IEnumerable.GetEnumerator

    ' Return the array object's IEnumerator.
    Return carArray.GetEnumerator()
End Function
```

Building Cloneable Objects (ICloneable)

As you recall from Chapter 6, `System.Object` defines a member named `MemberwiseClone()`. This method is used to obtain a shallow copy of the current object. Object users do not call this method directly as it is protected. However, a given object may call this method itself during the cloning process. To illustrate, create a new Console Application named CloneablePoint that defines a class named **Point**:

```
'A class named Point.
Public Class Point

    Public Property X() As Integer
    Public Property Y() As Integer

    Public Sub New(ByVal xPos As Integer, ByVal yPos As Integer)
        X = xPos
        Y = yPos
    End Sub

    Public Sub New()
    End Sub

    ' Override Object.ToString().
    Public Overrides Function ToString() As String
Return String.Format("X = {0}; Y = {1}", X, Y)
    End Function
End Class
```

Given what you already know about reference types and value types (Chapter 4), you are aware that if you assign one reference variable to another, you have two references pointing to the same object in memory. Thus, the following assignment operation results in two references to the same **Point** object on the heap; modifications using either reference affect the same object on the heap:

```
Module Module1
    Sub Main())

        Console.WriteLine("*** Fun with Object Cloning ***" & vbLf)
        Dim p1 As New Point(50, 50)
        Dim p2 As Point = p1
        p2.X = 0
        Console.WriteLine(p1)
        Console.WriteLine(p2)
        Console.ReadLine()
    End Sub
End Module
```

When you want to give your custom type the ability to return an identical copy of itself to the caller, you may implement the standard ICloneable interface. As shown at the start of this chapter, this type defines a single method named Clone():

```
Public Interface ICloneable
        Function Clone() As Object
End Interface
```

■ **Note** The usefulness of the ICloneable interface is a topic of debate within the .NET community. The problem has to do with the fact that the official specification does not explicitly say that objects implementing this interface must return a *deep copy* of the object (i.e., internal reference types of an object result in brand-new objects with identical state). Thus, it is technically possible that objects implementing ICloneable actually return a *shallow copy* of the interface (i.e., internal references point to the same object on the heap), which clearly generates a good deal of confusion. In our example, I am assuming we are implementing Clone() to return a full, deep copy of the object.

Obviously, the implementation of the Clone() method varies among types. However, the basic functionality tends to be the same: copy the values of your member variables into a new object instance of the same type, and return it to the user. To illustrate, ponder the following update to the Point class:

```
' The Point now supports "clone-ability."
Public Class Point
    Implements ICloneable

    Public Property X() As Integer
    Public Property Y() As Integer

    Public Sub New(ByVal xPos As Integer, ByVal yPos As Integer)
        X = xPos
        Y = yPos
    End Sub

    Public Sub New()
    End Sub

    ' Override Object.ToString().
    Public Overrides Function ToString() As String
        Return String.Format("X = {0}; Y = {1}", X, Y)
    End Function

    ' Return a copy of the current object.
    Public Function Clone() As Object Implements ICloneable.Clone
        Return New Point(Me.X, Me.Y)
    End Function
End Class
```

In this way, you can create exact stand-alone copies of the `Point` type, as illustrated by the following code:

```
Module Module1
    Sub Main()

        Console.WriteLine("***** Fun with Object Cloning *****" & vbLf)

        ' Notice Clone() returns a plain object type.
        ' You must perform an explicit cast to obtain the derived type.
        Dim p3 As New Point(100, 100)
        Dim p4 As Point = DirectCast(p3.Clone(), Point)

        ' Change p4.X (which will not change p3.X).
        p4.X = 0

        ' Print each object.
        Console.WriteLine(p3)
        Console.WriteLine(p4)
        Console.ReadLine()
    End Sub
End Module
```

While the current implementation of `Point` fits the bill, you can streamline things just a bit. Because the `Point` type does not contain any internal reference type variables, you could simplify the implementation of the `Clone()` method as follows:

```
Public Function Clone() As Object Implements ICloneable.Clone
    ' Copy each field of the Point member by member.
    Return Me.MemberwiseClone()
End Function
```

Be aware, however, that if the `Point` did contain any reference type member variables, `MemberwiseClone()` will copy the references to those objects (i.e., a *shallow copy*). If you wish to support a true deep copy, you will need to create a new instance of any reference type variables during the cloning process. Let's see an example.

A More Elaborate Cloning Example

Now assume the `Point` class contains a reference type member variable of type `PointDescription`. This class maintains a point's friendly name as well as an identification number expressed as a `System.Guid` (if you don't come from a COM background, know that a globally unique identifier [GUID] is a statistically unique 128-bit number). Here is the implementation:

```
' This class describes a point.
Public Class PointDescription

    Public Property PetName() As String
    Public Property PointID() As Guid

    Public Sub New()
        PetName = "No-name"
        PointID = Guid.NewGuid()
    End Sub
End Class
```

The initial updates to the **Point** class itself included modifying **ToString()** to account for these new bits of state data, as well as defining and creating the **PointDescription** reference type. To allow the outside world to establish a pet name for the **Point**, you also update the arguments passed into the overloaded constructor:

```
'A class named Point.
Public Class Point
    Implements ICloneable

    Public Property X() As Integer
    Public Property Y() As Integer
    Public desc As New PointDescription()

Public Sub New(ByVal xPos As Integer, ByVal yPos As Integer, ByVal petName As String)
        X = xPos
        Y = yPos
        desc.PetName = petName
    End Sub

    Public Sub New(ByVal xPos As Integer, ByVal yPos As Integer)
        X = xPos
        Y = yPos
    End Sub

    Public Sub New()
    End Sub

    ' Override Object.ToString().
    Public Overrides Function ToString() As String
        Return String.Format("X = {0}; Y = {1}; Name = {2};" _
                    & vbLf & "ID = {3}" & vbLf, X, Y, desc.PetName, desc.PointID)
    End Function

    ' Return a copy of the current object.
    Public Function Clone() As Object Implements ICloneable.Clone
            Return Me.MemberwiseClone()
    End Function
End Class
```

Notice that you did not yet update your `Clone()` method. Therefore, when the object user asks for a clone using the current implementation, a shallow (member-by-member) copy is achieved. To illustrate, assume you have updated `Main()` as follows:

```
Module Module1
    Sub Main()
        Console.WriteLine("***** Fun with Object Cloning *****" & vbLf)
        Console.WriteLine("Cloned p3 and stored new Point in p4")

        Dim p3 As New Point(100, 100, "Jane")
        Dim p4 As Point = DirectCast(p3.Clone(), Point)
        Console.WriteLine("Before modification:")
        Console.WriteLine("p3: {0}", p3)
        Console.WriteLine("p4: {0}", p4)

        p4.desc.PetName = "My new Point"
        p4.X = 9
        Console.WriteLine(vbLf & "Changed p4.desc.petName and p4.X")
        Console.WriteLine("After modification:")
        Console.WriteLine("p3: {0}", p3)
        Console.WriteLine("p4: {0}", p4)

        Console.ReadLine()
    End Sub
End Module
```

Notice in the following output that while the value types have indeed been changed, the internal reference types maintain the same values, as they are "pointing" to the same objects in memory (Specifically, note that the pet name for both objects is now "My new Point").

```
***** Fun with Object Cloning *****


Cloned p3 and stored new Point in p4

Before modification:

p3: X = 100; Y = 100; Name = Jane;

ID = 133d66a7-0837-4bd7-95c6-b22ab0434509


p4: X = 100; Y = 100; Name = Jane;

ID = 133d66a7-0837-4bd7-95c6-b22ab0434509
```

Changed p4.desc.petName and p4.X

After modification:

p3: X = 100; Y = 100; Name = My new Point;

ID = 133d66a7-0837-4bd7-95c6-b22ab0434509

p4: X = 9; Y = 100; Name = My new Point;

ID = 133d66a7-0837-4bd7-95c6-b22ab0434509

To have your `Clone()` method make a complete deep copy of the internal reference types, you need to configure the object returned by `MemberwiseClone()` to account for the current point's name (the `System.Guid` type is in fact a structure, so the numerical data is indeed copied). Here is one possible implementation:

```
' Now we need to adjust for the PointDescription memb
Public Function Clone() As Object Implements ICloneable.Clone
            ' First get a shallow copy.
      Dim newPoint As Point = DirectCast(Me.MemberwiseClone(), Point)

        ' Then fill in the gaps.
  Dim currentDesc As New PointDescription()
        currentDesc.PetName = Me.desc.PetName
        newPoint.desc = currentDesc
        Return newPoint
End Function
```

If you rerun the application once again and view the output (see below), you see that the `Point` returned from `Clone()` does copy its internal reference type member variables (note the pet name is now unique for both p3 and p4).

***** Fun with Object Cloning *****

Cloned p3 and stored new Point in p4

Before modification:

```
p3: X = 100; Y = 100; Name = Jane;

ID = 51f64f25-4b0e-47ac-ba35-37d263496406


p4: X = 100; Y = 100; Name = Jane;

ID = 0d3776b3-b159-490d-b022-7f3f60788e8a



Changed p4.desc.petName and p4.X

After modification:

p3: X = 100; Y = 100; Name = Jane;

ID = 51f64f25-4b0e-47ac-ba35-37d263496406


p4: X = 9; Y = 100; Name = My new Point;

ID = 0d3776b3-b159-490d-b022-7f3f60788e8a
```

To summarize the cloning process, if you have a class or structure that contains nothing but value types, implement your `Clone()` method using `MemberwiseClone()`. However, if you have a custom type that maintains other reference types, you need to create a new object that takes into account each reference type member variable.

■ **Source Code** The CloneablePoint project is located under the Chapter 9 subdirectory.

Building Comparable Objects (IComparable)

The `System.IComparable` interface specifies a behavior that allows an object to be sorted based on some specified key. Here is the formal definition:

```vb
' This interface allows an object to specify its
' relationship between other like objects.
Public Interface IComparable
        Function CompareTo(ByVal o As Object) As Integer
End Interface
```

■ **Note** The generic version of this interface (IComparable(Of T)) provides a more type-safe manner to handle comparisons between objects. You'll examine generics in Chapter 10.

Let's assume you have a new Console Application named ComparableCar that defines the following updated **Car** class (notice that we have basically just added a new property to represent a unique ID for each car and a modified constructor):

```vb
Public Class Car
    ...
    Public Property CurrentSpeed() As Integer
    Public Property PetName() As String
    Public Property CarID() As Integer

    'Constructors.
    Public Sub New()
    End Sub

        Public Sub New(ByVal name As String, ByVal currSp As Integer, ByVal id As Integer)
        CurrentSpeed = currSp
        PetName = name
        CarID = id
    End Sub
    ...
End Class
```

Now assume you have an array of **Car** objects as follows:

```vb
Module Module1
    Sub Main()
        Console.WriteLine("***** Fun with Object Sorting *****" & vbLf)

        'Make an array of Car types.
        Dim myAutos As Car() = New Car(4) {}
        myAutos(0) = New Car("Rusty", 80, 1)
        myAutos(1) = New Car("Mary", 40, 234)
        myAutos(2) = New Car("Viper", 40, 34)
        myAutos(3) = New Car("Mel", 40, 4)
        myAutos(4) = New Car("Chucky", 40, 5)
    End Sub
End Module
```

The `System.Array` class defines a Shared method named `Sort()`. When you invoke this method on an array of intrinsic types (`Integer`, `Short`, `String`, etc.), you are able to sort the items in the array in numeric/alphabetic order as these intrinsic data types implement `IComparable`. However, what if you were to send an array of `Car` types into the `Sort()` method as follows?

```
'Sort my cars?
Array.Sort(myAutos)
```

If you run this test, you would get a runtime exception, as the `Car` class does not support the necessary interface. When you build custom types, you can implement `IComparable` to allow arrays of your types to be sorted. When you flesh out the details of `CompareTo()`, it will be up to you to decide what the baseline of the ordering operation will be. For the `Car` type, the internal `CarID` seems to be the logical candidate:

```
' The iteration of the Car can be ordered
' based on the CarID.
Public Class Car
    Implements IComparable
    ...
     'IComparable implementation.
     Function CompareTo(ByVal obj As Object) As Integer Implements
     IComparable.CompareTo

        Dim temp As Car = TryCast(obj, Car)
        If temp IsNot Nothing Then
            If Me.CarID > temp.CarID Then
                Return 1
            End If
            If Me.CarID < temp.CarID Then
                Return -1
            Else
                Return 0
            End If
        Else
            Throw New ArgumentException("Parameter is not a Car!")
        End If
    End Function

    ...
End Class
```

As you can see, the logic behind `CompareTo()` is to test the incoming object against the current instance based on a specific point of data. The return value of `CompareTo()` is used to discover whether this type is less than, greater than, or equal to the object it is being compared with (see Table 9-1).

Table 9-1. CompareTo() Return Values

CompareTo() **Return Value**	**Description**
Any number less than zero	This instance comes before the specified object in the sort order.
Zero	This instance is equal to the specified object.
Any number greater than zero	This instance comes after the specified object in the sort order.

We can streamline the previous implementation of CompareTo() given the fact that the VB 2010 Integer data type (which is just a shorthand notation for the CLR System.Int32) implements IComparable. You could implement the Car's CompareTo() as follows:

```
Function CompareTo(ByVal obj As Object) As Integer Implements IComparable.CompareTo
        Dim temp As Car = TryCast(obj, Car)
        If temp IsNot Nothing Then
            Return Me.CarID.CompareTo(temp.CarID)
        Else
            Throw New ArgumentException("Parameter is not a Car!")
        End If
    End Function
```

In either case, so that your **Car** type understands how to compare itself to like objects, you can write the following user code:

```
Module Module1
    Sub Main()
        Console.WriteLine("**** Fun with Object Sorting ****" & vbLf)

        'Make an array of Car objects.
        ...
        Console.WriteLine("Here is the unordered set of cars:")

        For Each c As Car In myAutos
            Console.WriteLine("{0} {1}", c.CarID, c.PetName)
        Next
        Console.WriteLine()

        ' Now, sort them using IComparable!
        Array.Sort(myAutos)

        ' Display sorted array.
        Console.WriteLine("Here is the ordered set of cars:")
        For Each c As Car In myAutos
            Console.WriteLine("{0} {1}", c.CarID, c.PetName)
        Next
        Console.ReadLine()
    End Sub
End Module
```

Here is the output from the previous `Main()` method:

```
***** Fun with Object Sorting *****


Here is the unordered set of cars:

1 Rusty

234 Mary

34 Viper

4 Mel

5 Chucky


Here is the ordered set of cars:

1 Rusty

4 Mel

5 Chucky

34 Viper

234 Mary
```

Specifying Multiple Sort Orders (IComparer)

In this version of the `Car` type, you used the car's ID as the base of the sort order. Another design might have used the pet name of the car as the basis of the sorting algorithm (to list cars alphabetically). Now, what if you wanted to build a `Car` that could be sorted by ID as well as by pet name? If this is the type of behavior you are interested in, you need to make friends with another standard interface named `IComparer`, defined within the `System.Collections` namespace as follows:

```
' A general way to compare two objects.
Interface IComparer
        Function Compare(ByVal o1 As Object,ByVal o2 As Object) As Integer
End Interface
```

371

■ **Note** The generic version of this interface (IComparer(Of T)) provides a more type-safe manner to handle comparisons between objects. You'll examine generics in Chapter 10.

Unlike the `IComparable` interface, `IComparer` is typically *not* implemented on the type you are trying to sort (i.e., the `Car`). Rather, you implement this interface on any number of helper classes, one for each sort order (pet name, car ID, etc.). Currently, the `Car` type already knows how to compare itself against other cars based on the internal car ID. Therefore, allowing the object user to sort an array of `Car` object by pet name will require an additional helper class that implements `IComparer`. Here's the code (be sure to import the `System.Collections` namespace in the code file):

```
' This helper class is used to sort an array of Cars by pet name.
Public Class PetNameComparer
    Implements IComparer

        'Test the pet name of each object.
        Function Compare(ByVal o1 As Object, ByVal o2 As Object) As Integer Implements
        IComparer.Compare
            Dim t1 As Car = TryCast(o1, Car)
            Dim t2 As Car = TryCast(o2, Car)
        If t1 IsNot Nothing AndAlso t2 IsNot Nothing Then
            Return String.Compare(t1.PetName, t2.PetName)
        Else
            Throw New ArgumentException("Parameter is not a Car!")
        End If
    End Function
End Class
```

The object user code is able to make use of this helper class. `System.Array` has a number of overloaded `Sort()` methods, one that just happens to take an object implementing `IComparer`.

```
Module Module1
    Sub Main()
        ...
        ' Dump sorted array.
        Array.Sort(myAutos, New PetNameComparer())
        Console.WriteLine("Ordering by pet name:")
        For Each c As Car In myAutos
            Console.WriteLine("{0} {1}", c.CarID, c.PetName)
        Next
        Console.ReadLine()
        ...
    End Sub
End Module
```

Custom Properties, Custom Sort Types

It is worth pointing out that you can make use of a custom Shared property in order to help the object user along when sorting your Car types by a specific data point. Assume the Car class has added a Shared read-only property named SortByPetName that returns an instance of an object implementing the IComparer interface (PetNameComparer, in this case):

```
' We now support a custom property to return
' the correct IComparer interface.
Public Class Car
    Implements IComparable
    ...
    'Property to return the SortByPetName comparer.
    Public Shared ReadOnly Property SortByPetName() As IComparer
        Get
            Return DirectCast(New PetNameComparer(), IComparer)
        End Get
    End Property
End Class
```

The object user code can now sort by pet name using a strongly associated property, rather than just "having to know" to use the stand-alone PetNameComparer class type:

```
' Sorting by pet name made a bit cleaner.
Array.Sort(myAutos, Car.SortByPetName)
Array.Sort(myAutos, Car.SortByPetName);
```

■ **Source Code** The ComparableCar project is located under the Chapter 9 subdirectory.

Hopefully, at this point you not only understand how to define and implement your own interfaces, but also understand their usefulness. To be sure, interfaces are found within every major .NET namespace, and you will continue working with various standard interfaces over the remainder of this text.

Summary

An interface can be defined as a named collection of *MustOverride members*. Because an interface does not provide any implementation details, it is common to regard an interface as a behavior that may be supported by a given type. When two or more classes implement the same interface, you can treat each type the same way (interface-based polymorphism) even if the types are defined within unique class hierarchies.

VB 2010 provides the `Interface` keyword to allow you to define a new interface. As you have seen, a type can support as many interfaces as necessary. Furthermore, it is permissible to build interfaces that derive from multiple base interfaces.

In `addition` to building your custom interfaces, the .NET libraries define a number of standard (i.e., framework-supplied) interfaces. As you have seen, you are free to build custom types that implement these predefined interfaces to gain a number of desirable traits such as cloning, sorting, and enumerating.

CHAPTER 10

■■■

Understanding Generics

The most primitive container for application data within the .NET platform is the **System.Array** class. As you saw in Chapter 4, VB 2010 arrays allow you to define a set of identically typed items (including an array of **System.Objects**, which essentially represents an array of any type of data) of a fixed upper limit. While basic arrays can be useful to manage small amounts of known data, there are many other times where you require a more flexible data structure, such as a dynamically growing and shrinking container, or a container that can only hold objects that meet a specific criteria (e.g., only objects deriving from a specific base class or only objects implementing a particular interface).

When the .NET platform was first released, programmers frequently used the **System.Collections** namespace to account for more flexible ways to manage bits of data in an application. However, in .NET 2.0 the VB programming language was enhanced to support a feature termed *generics*; and with this change, a brand new collection-centric namespace was introduced in the base class libraries: **System.Collections.Generic**.

As you will learn in this chapter, generic containers are far superior in many ways to their non-generic counterparts because they provide greater type safety and performance benefits. Once you've seen the motivation for generics, you will learn about the commonly used classes and interfaces within **System.Collections.Generic**. The remainder of this chapter examines how to build your own generic types. As you do this, you will learn about the role of *constraints*, which allow you to build extremely type safe containers.

■ **Note** It is also possible to create generic delegate types, which you will learn about in the next chapter.

The Issues with Non-Generic Collections

When the .NET platform was first released, programmers frequently used the **System.Collections** namespace of **mscorlib.dll**. Here, developers were provided with a set of classes that allowed them to manage and organize large amounts of data. Table 10-1 documents some of the more commonly used collection classes, and the core interfaces they implement.

Table 10-1. Commonly Used Classes of `System.Collections`

System.Collections Class	Meaning in Life	Key Implemented Interfaces
ArrayList	Represents a dynamically sized collection of objects listed in sequential order.	IList, ICollection, IEnumerable, and ICloneable
Hashtable	Represents a collection of key/value pairs that are organized based on the hash code of the key.	IDictionary, ICollection, IEnumerable, and ICloneable
Queue	Represents a standard first-in, first-out (FIFO) queue.	ICollection, IEnumerable, and ICloneable
SortedList	Represents a collection of key/value pairs that are sorted by the keys and are accessible by key and by index.	IDictionary, ICollection, IEnumerable, and ICloneable
Stack	A last-in, first-out (LIFO) stack providing push and pop (and peek) functionality.	ICollection, IEnumerable, and ICloneable

The interfaces implemented by these classic collection classes provide huge insights into their overall functionality. Table 10-2 documents the overall nature of these key interfaces, some of which you worked with first-hand in Chapter 9.

Table 10-2. Key Interfaces Supported by Classes of `System.Collections`

System.Collections Interface	Meaning in Life
ICollection	Defines general characteristics (e.g., size, enumeration, and thread safety) for all non-generic collection types.
ICloneable	Allows the implementing object to return a copy of itself to the caller.
IDictionary	Allows a non-generic collection object to represent its contents using key/value pairs.
IEnumerable	Returns an object implementing the IEnumerator interface (see next table entry).
IEnumerator	Enables **foreach** style iteration of collection items.
IList	Provides behavior to add, remove, and index items in a sequential list of objects.

In addition to these core classes (and interfaces), the `System.Collections.Specialized` namespace of `System.dll` added a few (pardon the redundancy) specialized collection types such as `BitVector32`, `ListDictionary`, `StringDictionary`, and `StringCollection`. This namespace also contains many additional interfaces and abstract base classes that you can use as a starting point for creating custom collection classes.

While it is true that many successful .NET applications have been built over the years using these "classic" collection classes (and interfaces), history has shown that use of these types can result in a number of issues.

The first issue is that using the `System.Collections` and `System.Collections.Specialized` classes can result in some poorly performing code, especially when you are manipulating data structures (e.g., value types). As you'll see momentarily, the CLR must perform a number of memory transfer operations when you store structures in a classic collection class, which can hurt runtime execution speed.

The second issue is that these classic collection classes are not type safe because they were (by-and-large) developed to operate on `System.Objects`, and they could therefore contain anything at all. If a .NET developer needed to create a highly type safe collection (e.g., a container that can only hold objects implementing a certain interface), the only real choice was to create a brand new collection class by hand. Doing so was not too labor intensive, but it was a tad bit on the tedious side.

Given these (and other) issues, .NET 2.0 introduced a brand new set of collection classes, which are packaged up in the `System.Collections.Generic` namespace. Any new project created with .NET 2.0 and higher should ignore the legacy, non-generic classes in favor of the corresponding generic classes.

■ **Note** This is worth repeating: Any .NET application built with .NET 2.0 or higher should ignore the classes in `System.Collections` in favor of the classes in `System.Collections.Generic`.

Before you look at how to use generics in your programs, you'll find it helpful to examine the issues of non-generic collection classes a bit closer; this will help you understand better the problems generics intend to solve in the first place. If you wish to follow along, create a new Console Application named IssuesWithNon-genericCollections. Next, import the `System.Collections` namespace to the top of your VB 2010 code file:

```
Imports System.Collections
```

The Issue of Performance

As you might recall from Chapter 4, the .NET platform supports two broad categories of data: value types and reference types. Given that .NET defines two major categories of types, you might occasionally need to represent a variable of one category as a variable of the other category. To do so, VB 2010 provides a simple mechanism, termed boxing, to store the data in a value type within a reference variable. Assume that you have created a local variable of type `Integer` in a method called `SimpleBoxUnboxOperation()`:

```
Sub SimpleBoxUnboxOperation()
    ' Make an Integer value type
    Dim myInt As Integer = 25
End Sub
```

If, during the course of your application, you were to represent this value type as a reference type, you would *box* the value, as follows:

```
Sub SimpleBoxUnboxOperation()
    ' Make an Integer value type
    Dim myInt As Integer = 25

    ' Box the Integer into an object reference.
    Dim boxedInt As Object = myInt
End Sub
```

Boxing can be formally defined as the process of explicitly assigning a value type to a `System.Object` variable. When you box a value, the CLR allocates a new object on the heap and copies the value type's value (25, in this case) into that instance. What is returned to you is a reference to the newly allocated heap-based object. If you use this technique, you don't need to use of a set of wrapper classes to treat stack data temporarily as heap-allocated objects.

The opposite operation is also permitted through unboxing. Unboxing is the process of converting the value held in the object reference back into a corresponding value type on the stack. Syntactically speaking, an unboxing operation looks like a normal casting operation. However, the semantics are quite different. The CLR begins by verifying that the receiving data type is equivalent to the boxed type; and if so, it copies the value back into a local stack-based variable. For example, the following unboxing operations work successfully, given that the underlying type of the `boxedInt` is indeed an `Integer`:

```
Sub SimpleBoxUnboxOperation()

    ' Make an Integer value type.
    Dim myInt As Integer = 25

    ' Box the Integer into an object reference.
    Dim boxedInt As Object = myInt

    ' Unbox in the wrong data type to trigger
    'runtime exception.

    Dim unboxedInt As Long = DirectCast(boxedInt, Long)
End Sub
```

When the VB 2010 compiler encounters boxing/unboxing syntax, it emits CIL code that contains the box/unbox op codes. If you were to examine your compiled assembly using `ildasm.exe`, you would find the following:

```
.method public static void SimpleBoxUnboxOperation() cil managed
{
  // Code size 25 (0x19)
  .maxstack  1
  .locals init ([0] object boxInt, [1] int32 myInt, [2] int64 unboxedInt)
  IL_0000:  nop
  IL_0001:  ldc.i4.s 25
  IL_0003:  stloc.1
  IL_0004:  ldloc.1
  IL_0005:  box      [mscorlib]System.Int32
```

```
    IL_000a:  stloc.0
    IL_000b:  ldloc.0
    IL_000c:  unbox  [mscorlib]System.Int64
    IL_0011:  ldobj  [mscorlib]System.Int64
    IL_0016:  stloc.2
    IL_0017:  nop
    IL_0018:  ret
} // end of method Program::SimpleBoxUnboxOperation
```

Remember that unlike when performing a typical cast, you *must* unbox into an appropriate data type. If you attempt to unbox a piece of data into the incorrect variable, an `InvalidCastException` exception will be thrown. To be perfectly safe, you should wrap each unboxing operation in Try/Catch logic; however, this would be quite labor intensive to do for every unboxing operation. Consider the following code update, which will throw an error because you're attempting to unbox the boxed `Integer` into a `Long`:

```
Sub SimpleBoxUnboxOperation()

        ' Make an Integer value type.
        Dim myInt As Integer = 25

        ' Box the Integer into an object reference.
        Dim boxedInt As Object = myInt

        ' Unbox in the wrong data type to trigger
        'runtime exception.
        Try
            Dim unboxedInt As Long = DirectCast(boxedInt, Long)
        Catch ex As InvalidCastException
            Console.WriteLine(ex.Message)
        End Try
End Sub
```

At first glance, boxing/unboxing might seem like a rather uneventful language feature that is more academic than practical. After all, You will seldom store a local value type in a local `object` variable, as seen here. However, it turns out that the boxing/unboxing process is quite helpful because it allows you to assume everything can be treated as a `System.Object`, while the CLR takes care of the memory-related details on your behalf.

Let's look at a practical use of these techniques. Assume you have created a non-generic `System.Collections.ArrayList` to hold onto a batch of numeric (stack-allocated) data. If you were to examine the members of `ArrayList`, you would find they are prototyped to operate on `System.Object` data. Now consider the `Add()`, `Insert()`, `Remove()` methods, as well as the class indexer:

```
Public Class ArrayList
    Inherits Object
    Implements IList
    Implements ICollection
    Implements IEnumerable
    Implements ICloneable
```

```
...
        Public Overridable Function Add(ByVal value As Object) As Integer

Public Overridable Sub Insert(ByVal index As Integer, ByVal value As Object)
        Public Overridable Sub Remove(ByVal obj As Object)

Public Overridable Property Item(ByVal index As Integer) As Object

End Class
```

ArrayList has been built to operate on objects, which represent data allocated on the heap, so it might seem strange that the following code compiles and executes without throwing an error:

```
Sub WorkWithArrayList()

        ' Value types are automatically boxed when
        ' passed to a member requesting an object.
        Dim myInts As New ArrayList()
        myInts.Add(10)
        myInts.Add(20)
        myInts.Add(35)
        Console.ReadLine()
End Sub
```

Although you pass in numerical data directly into methods requiring an object, the runtime automatically boxes the stack-based data on your behalf.

Later, if you wish to retrieve an item from the ArrayList using the type indexer, you must unbox the heap-allocated object into a stack-allocated integer using a casting operation. Remember that the indexer of the ArrayList is returning System.Objects, not System.Int32s:

```
Sub WorkWithArrayList()

        'Value types are automatically boxed when
        ' passed to a member requesting an object.
        Dim myInts As New ArrayList()
        myInts.Add(10)
        myInts.Add(20)
        myInts.Add(35)

        'Unboxing occurs when an object is converted back to
        'stack based data.
        Dim i As Integer = DirectCast(myInts(0), Integer)

        ' Now it is reboxed, as WriteLine() requires object types!
        Console.WriteLine("Value of your Integer: {0}", i)
        Console.ReadLine()
End Sub
```

Again, note that the stack-allocated `System.Int32` is boxed prior to the call to `ArrayList.Add()` so it can be passed in the required `System.Object`. Also note that the `System.Object` is unboxed back into a `System.Int32` once it is retrieved from the `ArrayList` using the type indexer, only to be boxed *again* when it is passed to the `Console.WriteLine()` method, as this method is operating on `System.Object` variables.

Boxing and unboxing are convenient from a programmer's point of view, but this simplified approach to stack/heap memory transfer comes with the baggage of performance issues (in both speed of execution and code size) and a lack of type safety. To understand the performance issues, ponder the steps that must occur to box and unbox a simple integer:

1. A new object must be allocated on the managed heap.

2. The value of the stack-based data must be transferred into that memory location.

3. When unboxed, the value stored on the heap-based object must be transferred back to the stack.

4. The now unused object on the heap will (eventually) be garbage collected.

Although this particular `WorkWithArrayList()` method won't cause a major bottleneck in terms of performance, you could certainly feel the impact if an `ArrayList` contained thousands of integers that your program manipulates on a somewhat regular basis. In an ideal world, you could manipulate stack-based data in a container without any performance issues. Ideally, it would be nice if you did not have to have to bother plucking data from this container using Try/Catch scopes (this is exactly what generics let you achieve).

The Issue of Type Safety

You touched on the issue of type safety when you looked at unboxing operations. Recall that you must unbox your data into the same data type it was declared as before boxing. However, there is another aspect of type safety you must keep in mind in a generic-free world: the fact that a majority of the classes of `System.Collections` can typically hold anything whatsoever because their members are prototyped to operate on `System.Objects`. For example, this method builds an `ArrayList` of random bits of unrelated data:

```
Sub ArrayListOfRandomObjects()

    ' The ArrayList can hold anything at all.
    Dim allMyObjects As New ArrayList()
    allMyObjects.Add(True)

    Dim osVer As New OperatingSystem(PlatformID.MacOSX, New Version(10, 0))
    allMyObjects.Add(osVer)
    allMyObjects.Add(66)
    allMyObjects.Add(3.14)
End Sub
```

In some cases, you will require an extremely flexible container that can hold literally anything (as seen here). However, most of the time you desire a *type-safe* container that can only operate on a particular type of data point. For example, you might need a container that can only hold database connections, bitmaps, or `IPointy`-compatible objects.

Prior to generics, the only way you could address this issue of type safety was to create a custom (strongly typed) collection class manually. Assume you wish to create a custom collection that can only contain objects of type `Person`:

```vb
Public Class Person
        Public Property Age() As Integer
        Public Property FirstName() As String
        Public Property LastName() As String

        Public Sub New()
        End Sub

        Public Sub New(ByVal firstName As String, ByVal lastName As String, ByVal age As Integer)
                Me.Age = age
                Me.FirstName = firstName
                Me.LastName = lastName
        End Sub

        Public Overrides Function ToString() As String
                Return String.Format("Name: {0} {1}, Age: {2}", ↩
                FirstName, LastName, Age)
        End Function
End Class
```

To build a *person only collection,* you could define a `System.Collections.ArrayList` member variable within a class named `PersonCollection` and configure all members to operate on strongly typed `Person` objects, rather than on `System.Object` types. Here is a simple example (a production-level custom collection could support many additional members and might extend an abstract base class from the `System.Collections` namespace):

```vb
Public Class PersonCollection
    Implements IEnumerable

    Private arPeople As New ArrayList()

    ' Cast for caller.
    Public Function GetPerson(ByVal pos As Integer) As Person
        Return DirectCast(arPeople(pos), Person)
    End Function

    ' Only insert Person objects.
    Public Sub AddPerson(ByVal p As Person)
        arPeople.Add(p)
    End Sub

    Public Sub ClearPeople()
        arPeople.Clear()
    End Sub
```

```
    Public ReadOnly Property Count() As Integer
        Get
            Return arPeople.Count
        End Get
    End Property

    ' Foreach enumeration support.
Function GetEnumerator() As IEnumerator Implements        IEnumerable.GetEnumerator
        Return arPeople.GetEnumerator()
    End Function
End Class
```

Notice that the PersonCollection class implements the IEnumerable interface, which allows a For Each-like iteration over each contained item. Also notice that your GetPerson() and AddPerson() methods have been prototyped to operate only on Person objects, not bitmaps, strings, database connections, or other items. With these types defined, you are now assured of type safety, given that the VB 2010 compiler will be able to determine any attempt to insert an incompatible data type:

```
Sub UsePersonCollection()

        Console.WriteLine("***** Custom Person Collection *****" & vbLf)

        Dim myPeople As New PersonCollection()
        myPeople.AddPerson(New Person("Homer", "Simpson", 40))
        myPeople.AddPerson(New Person("Marge", "Simpson", 38))
        myPeople.AddPerson(New Person("Lisa", "Simpson", 9))
        myPeople.AddPerson(New Person("Bart", "Simpson", 7))
        myPeople.AddPerson(New Person("Maggie", "Simpson", 2))

        ' This would be a compile-time error!
    ' myPeople.AddPerson(New Car())
        For Each p As Person In myPeople
            Console.WriteLine(p)
        Next
End Sub
```

While custom collections do ensure type safety, this approach leaves you in a position where you must create an (almost identical) custom collection for each unique data type you wish to contain. Thus, if you need a custom collection that can operate only on classes deriving from the Car base class, you need to build a highly similar collection class:

```
Public Class CarCollection
    Implements IEnumerable

    Private arCars As New ArrayList()

    'Cast for caller.
    Public Function GetCar(ByVal pos As Integer) As Car
        Return DirectCast(arCars(pos), Car)
    End Function
```

```vb
    'Only insert Car objects.
    Public Sub AddCar(ByVal c As Car)
        arCars.Add(c)
    End Sub
    Public Sub ClearCars()
        arCars.Clear()
    End Sub
    Public ReadOnly Property Count() As Integer
        Get
            Return arCars.Count
        End Get
    End Property

    'For Each enumeration support.
    Function GetEnumerator() As IEnumerator Implements
            IEnumerable.GetEnumerator

        Return arCars.GetEnumerator()
    End Function
End Class
```

However, a custom collection class does nothing to solve the issue of boxing/unboxing penalties. Even if you were to create a custom collection named IntCollection that you designed to operate only on System.Int32 items, you would have to allocate some type of object to hold the data (e.g., System.Array and ArrayList):

```vb
Public Class IntCollection
    Implements IEnumerable

    Private arInts As New ArrayList()

    ' Unbox for caller.
    Public Function GetInt(ByVal pos As Integer) As Integer
        Return DirectCast(arInts(pos), Integer)
    End Function

    ' Boxing operation!
    Public Sub AddInt(ByVal i As Integer)
        arInts.Add(i)
    End Sub

    Public Sub ClearInts()
        arInts.Clear()
    End Sub

    Public ReadOnly Property Count() As Integer
        Get
            Return arInts.Count
        End Get
    End Property
```

```
    Function GetEnumerator() As IEnumerator Implements
        IEnumerable.GetEnumerator

        Return arInts.GetEnumerator()
    End Function
End Class
```

Regardless of which type you might choose to hold the integers, you cannot escape the boxing dilemma using non-generic containers.

When you use generic collection classes, you rectify all of the previous issues, including boxing/unboxing penalties and a lack of type safety. Also, the need to build a custom (generic) collection class manually becomes quite rare. Rather than having to build unique classes that can contain people, cars, and integers, you can use a generic collection class and specify the type of type. Consider the following method, which uses a generic List(Of T) class (in the System.Collections.Generic namespace) to contain various types of data in a strongly typed manner (don't fret the details of generic syntax at this time):

```
Sub UseGenericList()

        Console.WriteLine("***** Fun with Generics *****" & vbLf)

        ' This List(Of T) can only hold Person objects.
        Dim morePeople As New List(Of Person)()
        morePeople.Add(New Person("Frank", "Black", 50))
        Console.WriteLine(morePeople(0))

        ' This List(Of T) can only hold integers.
        Dim moreInts As New List(Of Integer)()
        moreInts.Add(10)
        moreInts.Add(2)
        Dim sum As Integer = moreInts(0) + moreInts(1)

        ' Compile-time error! Can't add Person object
        ' to a list of Integers!
        ' moreInts.Add(new Person());
End Sub
```

The first List(Of T) object can *only* contain Person objects. Therefore, you do not need to perform a cast when plucking the items from the container, which makes this approach more type safe. The second List(Of T) can *only* contain integers, all of which are allocated on the stack; in other words, there is no hidden boxing or unboxing as you found with the non-generic ArrayList.

Here is a short list of the benefits generic containers provide over their non-generic counterparts:

- Generics provide better performance because they do not result in boxing or unboxing penalties.

- Generics are more type safe because they can only contain the type of type you specify.

- Generics greatly reduce the need to build custom collection types because the base class library provides several prefabricated containers.

■ **Source Code** You can find the IssuesWithNonGenericCollections project under the Chapter 10 directory.

The Role of Generic Type Parameters

You can find generic classes, interfaces, structures, and delegates sprinkled throughout the .NET base class libraries, and these might be part of any .NET namespace.

■ **Note** Only classes, structures, interfaces, and delegates can be written generically; enum types cannot.

When you see a generic item listed in the .NET Framework 4.0 SDK documentation or the Visual Studio 2010 object browser, you will notice a pair of parentheses with a letter or other token sandwiched within. Figure 10-1 shows a number of generic items in the System.Collections.Generic namespace, including the highlighted List(Of T) class.

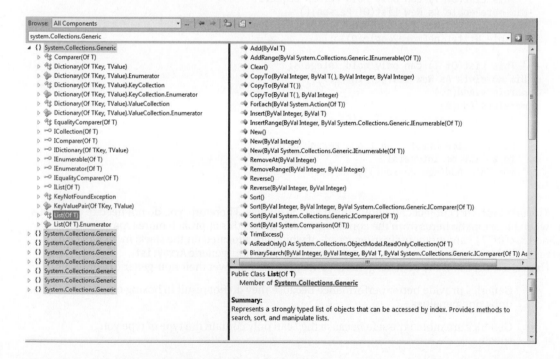

Figure 10-1. Generic Items Supporting Type Parameters

Formally speaking, you call these tokens *type parameters*; however, in more user friendly terms, you can simply call them *placeholders*.

■ **Note** The name of a type parameter (placeholder) is irrelevant, and it is up to the individual who created the generic item. However, typically *T* is used to represent types, *TKey* or *K* is used for keys, and *TValue* or *V* is used for values.

When you create a generic object, implement a generic interface, or invoke a generic member, it is up to you to supply a value to the type parameter. You'll see many examples in this chapter, and throughout the remainder of the text. However, to set the stage, let's see the basics of interacting with generic types and members.

Specifying Type Parameters for Generic Classes / Structures

When you create an instance of a generic class or structure, you specify the type parameter when you declare the variable and when you invoke the constructor. As you saw in the preceding code example, UseGenericList() defined two List(Of T) objects:

```
' This List(Of T) can only hold Person objects.
Dim morePeople As New List(Of Person)()
```

You can read the preceding snippet as *a List (Of T), where T is of type Person*. Or, more simply, you can read it as *a list of person objects*. Once you specify the type parameter of a generic item, it cannot be changed (remember: generics are all about type safety). When you specify a type parameter for a generic class or structure, all occurrences of the placeholder(s) are now replaced with your supplied value.

If you were to view the full declaration of the generic List(Of T) class using the Visual Studio 2010 object browser, you would see that the placeholder T is used throughout the definition of the List(Of T) type. Here is a partial listing:

```
Public Class List(Of T)
    Implements IList(Of T)
    Implements ICollection(Of T)
    Implements IEnumerable(Of T)
    Implements IList
    Implements ICollection
    Implements IEnumerable

    Public Sub Add(ByVal item As T)
    Public Function AsReadOnly() As ReadOnlyCollection(Of T)
    Public Function BinarySearch(ByVal item As T) As Integer
    Public Function Contains(ByVal item As T) As Boolean
```

```
        Public Sub CopyTo(ByVal array As T())
        Public Function FindIndex(ByVal match As System.Predicate(Of T))
                            As Integer

        Public Function FindLast(ByVal match As System.Predicate(Of T)) As T
        Public Function Remove(ByVal item As T) As Boolean
        Public Function RemoveAll(ByVal match As System.Predicate(Of T))
                            As Integer

        Public Function ToArray() As T()
        Public Function TrueForAll(ByVal match As System.Predicate(Of T))
                            As Boolean
        Public Property Item(ByVal index As Integer) As T
End Class
```

When you create a List(Of T) specifying Person objects, it is as if the List(Of T) type were defined as follows:

```
Public Class List(Of T)
    Implements IList(Of T)
    Implements ICollection(Of T)
    Implements IEnumerable(Of T)
    Implements IList
    Implements ICollection
    Implements IEnumerable

    Public Sub Add(ByVal item As Person)
    Public Function AsReadOnly() As ReadOnlyCollection(Of Person)
    Public Function BinarySearch(ByVal item As Person) As Integer
    Public Function Contains(ByVal item As Person) As Boolean
    Public Sub CopyTo(ByVal array As Person())

    Public Function FindIndex(ByVal match As System.Predicate
                            (Of Person)) As Integer

    Public Function FindLast(ByVal match As System.Predicate
                            (Of Person)) As Person

    Public Function Remove(ByVal item As Person) As Boolean
    Public Function RemoveAll(ByVal match As System.Predicate
                            (Of Person)) As Integer

    Public Function ToArray() As Person()
    Public Function TrueForAll(ByVal match As System.Predicate
                            (Of Person)) As Boolean

    Public Property Item(ByVal index As Integer) As Person
End Class
```

Of course, when you create a generic List(Of T) variable, the compiler does not literally create a brand new implementation of the List(Of T) class. Rather, it will address only the members of the generic type you actually invoke.

■ **Note** In the next chapter, you will learn about generic delegates, which will also require you to specify a type parameter when creating them.

Specifying Type Parameters for Generic Members

It is fine for a non-generic class or structure to support a handful of generic members (e.g., methods and properties). In these cases, you would also need to specify the placeholder value at the time you invoke the method. For example, System.Array supports several generic methods (which were added in .NET 2.0). Specifically, the Shared Sort() method now has a generic counterpart named Sort(Of T). Consider the following code snippet, where T is of type Integer:

```
Dim myInts As Integer() = {10, 4, 2, 33, 93}
'Specify the placeholder to the generic
'Sort(Of T) method.
Array.Sort(Of Integer)(myInts)
For Each i As Integer In myInts
    Console.WriteLine(i)
Next
```

Specifying Type Parameters for Generic Interfaces

It is common to implement generic interfaces when you building classes or structures that need to support various framework behaviors (e.g., cloning, sorting, and enumeration). In Chapter 9, you learned about a number of non-generic interfaces, such as IComparable, IEnumerable, IEnumerator, and IComparer. Recall that the non-generic IComparable interface was defined like this:

```
Public Interface IComparable
        Function CompareTo(ByVal obj As Object) As Integer
End Interface
```

In Chapter 9, you also implemented this interface on your Car class to enable sorting in a standard array. However, the code required a several runtime checks and casting operations because the parameter was a general System.Object:

```
Public Class Car
  Implements IComparable
```

```
    'IComparable implementation.
    Public Function CompareTo(ByVal obj As Object) As Integer
        Implements  System.IComparable.CompareTo
            Dim temp As Car = CType(obj, Car)

        If temp IsNot Nothing Then
            If Me.carID > temp.carID Then
                Return 1
            End If

            If Me.carID < temp.carID Then
                Return -1
            Else
                Return 0
            End If
        Else
            Throw New ArgumentException("Parameter is not a car")
        End If
    End Function
End Class
```

Now assume you use the generic counterpart of this interface:

```
Public Interface IComparable(Of T)
    Function CompareTo(ByVal obj As T) As Integer
End Interface
```

In this case, your implementation code will be cleaned up considerably:

```
Public Class Car
    Implements IComparable(Of Car)

    'IComparable(Of T) implementation.
    Function CompareTo(ByVal obj As Car) As Integer Implements
    IComparable(Of Car).CompareTo

        If Me.CarID > obj.CarID Then
            Return 1
        End If

        If Me.CarID < obj.CarID Then
            Return -1
        Else
            Return 0
        End If
    End Function
End Class
```

Here you do not need to check whether the incoming parameter is a **Car** because it can *only* be a **Car**! If someone were to pass in an incompatible data type, you would get a compile-time error.

Now that you have a better handle on how to interact with generic items, as well as the role of type parameters (aka placeholders), you're ready to examine the classes and interfaces of the `System.Collections.Generic` namespace.

The System.Collections.Generic Namespace

You can find the bulk of the `System.Collections.Generic` namespace in the `mscorlib.dll` and `System.dll` assemblies. At the opening of this chapter, I briefly mentioned some of the core non-generic interfaces implemented by the non-generic collection classes. Not too surprisingly, the `System.Collections.Generic` namespace defines generic replacements for many of them.

In fact, you can find a number of the generic interfaces that extend their non-generic counterparts! This might seem odd; however, by doing so, implementing classes will also support the legacy functionally found in their non-generic siblings. For example, `IEnumerable(Of T)` extends `IEnumerable`. Table 10-3 documents the core generic interfaces you'll encounter when working with the generic collection classes.

■ **Note** If you have worked with generics prior to .NET 4.0, you should be aware of the new `ISet(Of T)` and `SortedSet(Of T)` types, which you'll learn more about later in this chapter.

Table 10-3. Key Interfaces Supported by Classes of `System.Collections.Generic`

System.Collections Interface	Meaning in Life
`ICollection(Of T)`	Defines general characteristics (e.g., size, enumeration, and thread safety) for all generic collection types.
`IComparer(Of T)`	Defines a way to compare to objects.
`IDictionary(Of TKey, TValue)`	Allows a generic collection object to represent its contents using key/value pairs.
`IEnumerable(Of T)`	Returns the `IEnumerator(Of T)` interface for a given object.
`IEnumerator(Of T)`	Enables `foreach`-style iteration over a generic collection.
`IList(Of T)`	Provides behavior to add, remove, and index items in a sequential list of objects.
`ISet(Of T)`	Provides the base interface for the abstraction of sets.

The `System.Collections.Generic` namespace also defines several classes that implement many of these key interfaces. Table 10-4 describes some commonly used classes of this namespace, the interfaces they implement, and their basic functionality.

Table 10-4. Classes of `System.Collections.Generic`

Generic Class	Supported Key Interfaces	Meaning in Life
`Dictionary(Of TKey, TValue)`	`ICollection(Of T)`, `IDictionary(Of TKey, TValue)`, `IEnumerable(Of T)`	This represents a generic collection of keys and values.
`List(Of T)`	`ICollection(Of T)`, `IEnumerable(Of T)`, `IList(Of T)`	This is a dynamically resizable sequential list of items.
`LinkedList(Of T)`	`ICollection(Of T)`, `IEnumerable(Of T)`	This represents a doubly linked list.
`Queue(Of T)`	`ICollection` (not a typo! This is the non-generic collection interface), `IEnumerable(Of T)`	This is a generic implementation of a first-in, first-out (FIFO) list.
`SortedDictionary(Of TKey, TValue)`	`ICollection(Of T)`, `IDictionary(Of TKey, TValue)`, `IEnumerable(Of T)`	This is a generic implementation of a sorted set of key/value pairs.
`SortedSet(Of T)`	`ICollection(Of T)`, `IEnumerable(Of T)`, `ISet(Of T)`	This represents a collection of objects that is maintained in sorted order with no duplication.
`Stack(Of T)`	`ICollection` (not a typo! This is the non-generic collection interface), `IEnumerable(Of T)`	This is a generic implementation of a last-in, first-out (LIFO) list.

The `System.Collections.Generic` namespace also defines many auxiliary classes and structures that work in conjunction with a specific container. For example, the `LinkedListNode(Of T)` type represents a node within a generic `LinkedList(Of T)`, the `KeyNotFoundException` exception is raised when attempting to grab an item from a container using a nonexistent key, and so forth.

It is also worth pointing out that `mscorlib.dll` and `System.dll` are not the only assemblies which add new types to the `System.Collections.Generic` namespace. For example, `System.Core.dll` adds the `HashSet(Of T)` class to the mix. Be sure to consult the .NET Framework 4.0 SDK documentation for full details of the `System.Collections.Generic` namespace.

In any case, your next task is to learn how to use some of these generic collection classes. Before you do however, allow me to illustrate a VB 2010 language feature (first introduced in .NET 3.5) that simplifies the way you populate generic (and non-generic) collection containers with data.

Understanding Collection Initialization Syntax

In Chapter 4, you learned about *object initialization syntax*, which allows you to set properties on a new variable at the time of construction. Closely related to this is *collection initialization syntax*. This VB 2010 language feature makes it possible to populate many containers (such as `ArrayList` or `List(Of T)`) with items by using syntax similar to what you use to populate a basic array.

■ Note You can only apply collection initialization syntax to classes that support an `Add()` method, which is formalized by the `ICollection(Of T)/ICollection` interfaces.

Consider the following examples:

```vb
' Init a standard array.
Dim myArrayOfInts As Integer() = {0, 1, 2, 3, 4, 5, _6, 7, 8, 9}

' Init a generic List(Of T) of Integers.
Dim myGenericList As New List(Of Integer) From{1,2,3}

'Init an ArrayList with numerical data.
Dim myList As New ArrayList() From {0,1,2,3,4,5,6,7,8,9}
```

If your container is managing a collection of classes, you can blend object initialization syntax with collection initialization syntax to yield some functional code. You might recall the `Point` class from Chapter 5, which defined two properties named X and Y. If you wish to build a generic `List(Of T)` of `Point` objects, you can write the following:

```vb
Dim myListOfPoints As
  New List(Of Point)() From
  { _
        New Point() With { _
            .X = 2, _
            .Y = 2 _
        }, _
        New Point() With { _
            .X = 3, _
            .Y = 3 _
        }, _
        New Point(PointColor.BloodRed) With { _
            .X = 4, _
            .Y = 4 _
        }
  }

For Each pt As Point In myListOfPoints
    Console.WriteLine(pt)
Next
```

Again, the benefit of this syntax is that you save yourself numerous keystrokes. While the nested curly brackets can become difficult to read if you don't mind your formatting, imagine the amount of code that would be required to fill the following `List(Of T)` of `Rectangle`s if you did not have collection initialization syntax (you might recall from Chapter 4 that you created a `Rectangle` class that contained two properties encapsulating `Point` objects):

```vb
Dim myListOfRects As New List(Of Rectangle)() From
{ _
    New Rectangle() With
    { _
        .TopLeft = New Point() With
        { _
                    .X = 10, _
                    .Y = 10 _
        }, _
        .BottomRight = New Point() With
        { _
                    .X = 200, _
                    .Y = 200 _
        } _
    }, _
    New Rectangle() With
    { _
        .TopLeft = New Point() With
        { _
                    .X = 2, _
                    .Y = 2 _
        }, _
        .BottomRight = New Point() With
        { _
                    .X = 100, _
                    .Y = 100 _
        } _
    }, _
    New Rectangle() With
    { _
        .TopLeft = New Point() With
        { _
                    .X = 5, _
                    .Y = 5 _
        }, _
        .BottomRight = New Point() With
        { _
                    .X = 90, _
                    .Y = 75 _
        } _
    } _
}

For Each r In myListOfRects
    Console.WriteLine(r)
Next
```

Working with the List(Of T) Class

Create a brand new Console Application project named **FunWithGenericCollections**. This project type automatically references mscorlib.dll and System.dll, so you have access to a majority of the common generic collection classes. In VB 2010 most of the namespaces like System.Collections.Generic are added by default, but they are not listed in the code file as Imports statements. These namespaces are listed in the References tab of the Project Properties. You can access the properties option by selecting and right-clicking on the project.

The first generic class you will examine is the List(Of T), which you've already seen once or twice in this chapter. The List(Of T) class is bound to be your most frequently used type in the System.Collections.Generic namespace because it allows you to resize the contents dynamically. To illustrate the basics of this type, ponder the following method in your Program class, which leverages List(Of T) to manipulate the set of Person objects seen earlier in this chapter; you might recall that these Person objects defined three properties (Age, FirstName, and LastName) and a custom ToString() implementation:

```vb
Public Sub UseGenericList()

        ' Make a List of Person objects, filled with
        ' collection / object init syntax.
        Dim people As New List(Of Person) From
        { _
            New Person() With {.FirstName = "Homer", .LastName = "Simpson",  .Age = 47}, _
            New Person() With {.FirstName = "Marge", .LastName = "Simpson", .Age = 45}, _
            New Person() With {.FirstName = "Lisa", .LastName = "Simpson", .Age = 9}, _
            New Person() With {.FirstName = "Bart", .LastName = "Simpson", .Age = 8}
        }

        'Print out # of items in List.
        Console.WriteLine("Items in list: {0}", people.Count)

        ' Enumerate over list.
        For Each p As Person In people
            Console.WriteLine(p)
        Next

        ' Insert a new person.
        Console.WriteLine(vbLf & "->Inserting new person.")
        people.Insert(2, New Person() With
        { _
         .FirstName = "Maggie", _
         .LastName = "Simpson", _
         .Age = 2 _
        })
        Console.WriteLine("Items in list: {0}", people.Count)

        ' Copy data into a new array.
        Dim arrayOfPeople As Person() = people.ToArray()
        For i As Integer = 0 To arrayOfPeople.Length - 1
        Console.WriteLine("First Names: {0}", arrayOfPeople(i).FirstName)
        Next
End Sub
```

Here you use initialization syntax to populate your List(Of T) with objects, as a shorthand notation for calling Add() *n* number of times. Once you print out the number of items in the collection (as well as enumerate over each item), you invoke Insert(). As you can see, Insert() allows you to plug a new item into the List(Of T) at a specified index.

Finally, notice the call to the ToArray() method, which returns an array of Person objects based on the contents of the original List(Of T). From this array, you loop over the items again using the array's indexer syntax. If you call this method from within Main(), you get the following output:

```
***** Fun with Generic Collections *****


Items in list: 4

Name: Homer Simpson, Age: 47

Name: Marge Simpson, Age: 45

Name: Lisa Simpson, Age: 9

Name: Bart Simpson, Age: 8


->Inserting new person.

Items in list: 5

First Names: Homer

First Names: Marge

First Names: Maggie

First Names: Lisa

First Names: Bart
```

The List(Of T) class defines many additional members of interest, so be sure to consult the .NET Framework 4.0 SDK documentation for more information. Next, let's look at a few more generic collections, specifically Stack(Of T), Queue(Of T) and SortedSet(Of T). This should get you in a great position to understand your basic choices regarding how to hold your custom application data.

Working with the Stack(Of T) Class

The Stack(Of T) class represents a collection that maintains items using a last-in, first-out manner. As you might expect, Stack(Of T) defines members named Push() and Pop() to place items onto or remove items from the stack. The following method creates a stack of Person objects:

```
Sub UseGenericStack()
     Dim stackOfPeople As New Stack(Of Person)()
        stackOfPeople.Push(New Person With
        {
             .FirstName = "Homer",
             .LastName = "Simpson", .Age = 47
        })
        stackOfPeople.Push(New Person With
        {
             .FirstName = "Marge",
             .LastName = "Simpson", .Age = 45
        })

        stackOfPeople.Push(New Person With
        {
             .FirstName = "Lisa",
             .LastName = "Simpson", .Age = 9
        })

        ' Now look at the top item, pop it, and look again.
        Console.WriteLine("First person is: {0}", stackOfPeople.Peek())
        Console.WriteLine("Popped off {0}", stackOfPeople.Pop())

        Console.WriteLine(vbLf & "First person is: {0}",
        stackOfPeople.Peek())

        Console.WriteLine("Popped off {0}", stackOfPeople.Pop())

        Console.WriteLine(vbLf & "First person item is: {0}",
        stackOfPeople.Peek())

        Console.WriteLine("Popped off {0}", stackOfPeople.Pop())

        Try
             Console.WriteLine(vbLf & "nFirst person is: {0}"
                             ,stackOfPeople.Peek())
             Console.WriteLine("Popped off {0}", stackOfPeople.Pop())
        Catch ex As InvalidOperationException
             Console.WriteLine(vbLf & "Error! {0}", ex.Message)
        End Try
End Sub
```

Here, you build a stack that contains three people, added in the order of their first names: Homer, Marge, and Lisa. As you peek into the stack, you will always see the object at the top first; therefore, the first call to Peek() reveals the third Person object. After a series of Pop() and Peek() calls, the stack eventually empties, at which time additional Peek() and Pop() calls raise a system exception. You can see the output for this here:

```
***** Fun with Generic Collections *****


First person is: Name: Lisa Simpson, Age: 9

Popped off Name: Lisa Simpson, Age: 9


First person is: Name: Marge Simpson, Age: 45

Popped off Name: Marge Simpson, Age: 45


First person item is: Name: Homer Simpson, Age: 47

Popped off Name: Homer Simpson, Age: 47


Error! Stack empty.
```

Working with the Queue(Of T) Class

Queues are containers that ensure items are accessed in a first-in, first-out manner. Sadly, we humans are subject to queues all day long: lines at the bank, lines at the movie theater, and lines at the morning coffeehouse. When you need to model a scenario in which items are handled on a first-come, first-served basis, you will find the Queue(Of T) class fits the bill. In addition to the functionality provided by the supported interfaces, Queue defines the key members shown in Table 10-5.

Table 10-5. Members of the Queue(Of T) *Type*

Select Member of Queue(Of T)	Meaning in Life
Dequeue()	Removes and returns the object at the beginning of the Queue(Of T).
Enqueue()	Adds an object to the end of the Queue(Of T).
Peek()	Returns the object at the beginning of the Queue(Of T) without removing it.

Now let's put these methods to work. You can begin by leveraging your **Person** class again and building a Queue(Of T) object that simulates a line of people waiting to order coffee. First, assume you have the following helper method:

```
Sub GetCoffee(ByVal p As Person)
    Console.WriteLine("{0} got coffee!", p.FirstName)
End Sub
```

Now assume you have this additional helper method, which calls **GetCoffee()** internally:

```
Sub UseGenericQueue()

    ' Make a Q with three people.
    Dim peopleQ As New Queue(Of Person)()

peopleQ.Enqueue(New Person With {.FirstName = "Homer",
 .LastName = "Simpson", .Age = 47})

peopleQ.Enqueue(New Person With {.FirstName = "Marge",
 .LastName = "Simpson", .Age = 45})

peopleQ.Enqueue(New Person With {.FirstName = "Lisa",
 .LastName = "Simpson", .Age = 9})

    'Peek at first person in Q.
Console.WriteLine("{0} is first in line!", peopleQ.Peek().FirstName)
    GetCoffee(peopleQ.Dequeue())
    GetCoffee(peopleQ.Dequeue())
    GetCoffee(peopleQ.Dequeue())

    'Try to de-Q again?
    Try
        GetCoffee(peopleQ.Dequeue())
    Catch e As InvalidOperationException
        Console.WriteLine("Error! {0}", e.Message)
    End Try
End Sub
```

Here you insert three items into the `Queue(Of T)` class using its `Enqueue()` method. The call to `Peek()` allows you to view (but not remove) the first item currently in the `Queue`. Finally, the call to `Dequeue()` removes the item from the line and sends it into the `GetCoffee()` helper function for processing. Note that if you attempt to remove items from an empty queue, a runtime exception is thrown. Here is the output you receive when calling this method:

```
***** Fun with Generic Collections *****


Homer is first in line!

Homer got coffee!

Marge got coffee!

Lisa got coffee!

Error! Queue empty.
```

Working with the SortedSet(Of T) Class

The final generic collection class you will look was introduced with the release of .NET 4.0. The `SortedSet(Of T)` class is useful because it automatically ensures that the items in the set are sorted when you insert or remove items. However, you do need to inform the `SortedSet(Of T)` class exactly *how* you want it to sort the objects, by passing in as a constructor argument an object that implements the generic `IComparer(Of T)` interface.

Begin by creating a brand new class named `SortPeopleByAge`, which implements `IComparer(Of T)`, where T is of type `Person`. Recall that this interface defines a single method named `Compare()`, where you can author whatever logic you require for the comparison. Here is a simple implementation of this class:

```vb
Public Class SortPeopleByAge
    Implements IComparer(Of Person)

    Public Function Compare(ByVal firstPerson As Person,
                    ByVal secondPerson As Person) _
            As Integer Implements Generic.IComparer _
            Of FunWithGenericCollections.Person).Compare

        If firstPerson.Age > secondPerson.Age Then
            Return 1
        End If
```

```
                If firstPerson.Age < secondPerson.Age Then
                        Return -1
                Else
                        Return 0
                End If
        End Function
End Class
```

Now update your **Module1** Module with the following new method, which I assume you will call from **Main()**:

```
Sub UseSortedSet()

    ' Make some people with different ages.
    Dim setOfPeople As New SortedSet(Of Person)(New SortPeopleByAge()) From
    { New Person() With {.FirstName = "Homer", .LastName = "Simpson",
      .Age = 47}, _
      New Person() With {.FirstName = "Marge", .LastName = "Simpson",
      .Age = 45}, _
      New Person() With {.FirstName = "Lisa", .LastName = "Simpson",
      .Age = 9}, _
      New Person() With {.FirstName = "Bart", .LastName = "Simpson",
      .Age = 8} _
    }

    ' Note the items are sorted by age!
    For Each p As Person In setOfPeople
        Console.WriteLine(p)
    Next
    Console.WriteLine()

    ' Add a few new people, with various ages.
    setOfPeople.Add(New Person() With
      { _
        .FirstName = "Saku", _
        .LastName = "Jones", _
        .Age = 1 _
      })
    setOfPeople.Add(New Person() With
      { _
        .FirstName = "Mikko", _
        .LastName = "Jones", _
        .Age = 32 _
      })

    For Each p As Person In setOfPeople
        Console.WriteLine(p)
    Next
End Sub
```

When you run your application, the listing of objects is now always ordered based on the value of the Age property, regardless of the order you inserted or removed objects:

```
***** Fun with Generic Collections *****


Name: Bart Simpson, Age: 8

Name: Lisa Simpson, Age: 9

Name: Marge Simpson, Age: 45

Name: Homer Simpson, Age: 47


Name: Saku Jones, Age: 1

Name: Bart Simpson, Age: 8

Name: Lisa Simpson, Age: 9

Name: Mikko Jones, Age: 32

Name: Marge Simpson, Age: 45

Name: Homer Simpson, Age: 47
```

Awesome! At this point, you should feel more comfortable, but just about the benefits of generic programming, but also with using generic types in the .NET base class libraries. To conclude this chapter, you will learn how to build your own custom generic types and generic methods, as well as why you might want to.

■ **Source Code** You can find the FunWithGenericCollections project under the Chapter 10 directory.

Creating Custom Generic Methods

While most developers typically use the existing generic types within the base class libraries, it is also possible to build your own generic members and custom generic types. Let's look at how to incorporate custom generics into your own projects. The first step is to build a generic swap method. Begin by creating a new console application named CustomGenericMethods.

When you build custom generic methods, you achieve a supercharged version of traditional method overloading. In Chapter 2, you learned that overloading is the act of defining multiple versions of a single method, which differ by the number of, or type of, parameters.

While overloading is a useful feature in an object oriented language, one problem is that you can easily end up with a ton of methods that essentially do the same thing. For example, assume you need to build some methods that can switch two pieces of data using a simple swap routine. You might begin by authoring a new method that can operate on integers, like this:

```
' Swap two Integers.
Sub Swap(ByRef a As Integer, ByRef b As Integer)
        Dim temp As Integer
        temp = a
        a = b
        b = temp
End Sub
```

So far, so good. But now assume you also need to swap two **Person** objects; this would require authoring a new version of **Swap()**:

```
' Swap two Person objects.
Sub Swap(ByRef a As Person, ByRef b As Person)
        Dim temp As Person
        temp = a
        a = b
        b = temp
End Sub
```

No doubt, you can see where this is going. If you also needed to swap floating point numbers, bitmaps, cars, buttons and whatnot, you would have to build even more methods, which would become a maintenance nightmare. You could build a single (non-generic) method that operated on **object** parameters, but then you face all the issues you examined earlier in this chapter, including boxing, unboxing, a lack of type safety, explicit casting, and so on.

Whenever you have a group of overloaded methods that only differ by incoming arguments, this is your clue that generics could make your life easier. Consider the following generic **Swap(Of T)** method that can swap any two *T*s:

```
' This method will swap any two items.
' as specified by the type parameter (Of T).
Sub Swap(Of T)(ByRef a As T, ByRef b As T)
        Console.WriteLine("You sent the Swap() method a {0}", GetType(T))
        Dim temp As T
        temp = a
        a = b
        b = temp
End Sub
```

Notice how a generic method is defined by specifying the type parameters after the method name, but before the parameter list. Here, you state that the **Swap(Of T)()** method can operate on any two parameters of type (T). To spice things up a bit, you also print out the type name of the supplied placeholder to the console using VB 2010 **GetType()** method. Now consider the following **Main()** method, which swaps integers and strings:

```vb
Sub Main()
    Console.WriteLine("*** Fun with Custom Generic Methods ***" & vbLf)

        'Swap 2 Integers.
        Dim a As Integer = 10, b As Integer = 90
        Console.WriteLine("Before swap: {0}, {1}", a, b)
        Swap(Of Integer)(a, b)
        Console.WriteLine("After swap: {0}, {1}", a, b)
        Console.WriteLine()

        'Swap 2 strings.
        Dim s1 As String = "Hello", s2 As String = "There"
        Console.WriteLine("Before swap: {0} {1}!", s1, s2)
        Swap(Of String)(s1, s2)
        Console.WriteLine("After swap: {0} {1}!", s1, s2)
        Console.ReadLine()
End Sub
```

The output looks like this:

```
***** Fun with Custom Generic Methods *****


Before swap: 10, 90

You sent the Swap() method a System.Int32

After swap: 90, 10


Before swap: Hello There!

You sent the Swap() method a System.String

After swap: There Hello!
```

The major benefit of this approach is that you have only one version of `Swap(Of T)()` to maintain, yet it can operate on any two items of a given type in a type safe manner. Better yet, stack-based items stay on the stack, while heap-based items stay on the heap!

Inference of Type Parameters

When you invoke generic methods such as `Swap(Of T)`, you can optionally omit the type parameter if (and only if) the generic method requires arguments because the compiler can infer the type parameter based on the member parameters. For example, you could swap two `System.Boolean` values by adding the following code to `Main()`:

```
'Compiler will infer System.Boolean.
Dim b1 As Boolean = True, b2 As Boolean = False
Console.WriteLine("Before swap: {0}, {1}", b1, b2)
Swap(b1, b2)
Console.WriteLine("After swap: {0}, {1}", b1, b2)
```

Even though the compiler is able to discover the correct type parameter based on the data type used to declare `b1` and `b2`, you should get in the habit of always specifying the type parameter explicitly:

```
Swap(Of Boolean)(b1, b2)
```

This makes it clear to your fellow programmers that this method is indeed generic. Moreover, inference of type parameters only works if the generic method has at least one parameter. For example, assume you have the following generic method in your `Program` class:

```
Public Sub DisplayBaseClass(Of T)()
    Console.WriteLine("Base class of {0} is: {1}.", GetType(T),
    GetType(T).BaseType)
End Sub
```

In this case, you must supply the type parameter upon invocation:

```
Sub Main()
        ...

        ' Must supply type parameter if
        ' the method does not take params.
        DisplayBaseClass(Of Integer)()
        DisplayBaseClass(Of String)()
        ' Compiler error! No params? Must supply placeholder!
        ' DisplayBaseClass()
        Console.ReadLine()
        ...
End Sub
```

Currently, the generic `Swap(Of T)` and `DisplayBaseClass(Of T)` methods are defined within the application's `Module1` Module. Of course, as with any method, you are free to define these members in a separate module type (`MyGenericMethods`) if you would prefer to do it that way:

```
Public Module MyGenericMethods
    ' This method will swap any two items.
    ' as specified by the type parameter (Of T).
    Public Sub Swap(Of T)(ByRef a As T, ByRef b As T)
        Console.WriteLine("You sent the Swap() method a {0}", GetType(T))
```

```
        Dim temp As T
        temp = a
        a = b
        b = temp
    End Sub

    Public Sub DisplayBaseClass(Of T)()
 Console.WriteLine("Base class of {0} is: {1}.", GetType(T)
                    ,GetType(T).BaseType)
    End Sub
End Module
```

The `Swap(Of T)` and `DisplayBaseClass(Of T)` methods have been scoped within a new Module (and are therefore implicitly Shared), so you need to specify the type's name when invoking either member, as in this example:

```
MyGenericMethods.Swap(Of Integer)(a, b)
```

Of course, generic methods do not need to be Shared. If `Swap(Of T)` and `DisplayBaseClass(Of T)` were instance level (methods in a class), you would simply make an instance of `MyGenericMethods` and invoke them using the object variable:

```
Dim c As New MyGenericMethods()
c.Swap(Of Integer)(a,b)
```

■ **Source Code** You can find the CustomGenericMethods project under the Chapter 10 directory.

Creating Custom Generic Structures and Classes

Now that you understand how to define and invoke generic methods, it's time to turn your attention to the construction of a generic structure (the process of building a generic class is identical) within a new Console Application project named `GenericPoint`. Assume you have built a generic `Point` structure that supports a single type parameter that represents the underlying storage for the (`x, y`) coordinates. The caller can then create `Point(Of T)` types as follows:

```
'Point using Integers.
Dim p As New Point(Of Integer)(10, 10)

' Point using Double.
Dim p2 As New Point(Of Double)(5.4, 3.3)
```

Here is the complete definition of Point(Of T), with some analysis to follow:

```vb
'A generic Point structure.
Public Structure Point(Of T)

    Private xPos As T
    Private yPos As T

    Public Sub New(ByVal xVal As T, ByVal yVal As T)
        xPos = xVal
        yPos = yVal
    End Sub

    Public Property X() As T
        Get
            Return xPos
        End Get
        Set(ByVal value As T)
            xPos = value
        End Set
    End Property

    Public Property Y() As T
        Get
            Return yPos
        End Get
        Set(ByVal value As T)
            yPos = value
        End Set
    End Property

    Public Overrides Function ToString() As String
        Return String.Format("[{0}, {1}]", xPos, yPos)
    End Function

    Public Sub ResetPoint()
        xPos = Nothing
        yPos = Nothing
    End Sub
End Structure
```

The Nothing Keyword in Generic Code

As you can see, Point(Of T) leverages its type parameter in the definition of the field data, constructor arguments, and property definitions. Notice that, in addition to overriding ToString(), Point(Of T) defines a method named ResetPoint() that resets X and Y to Nothing:

```
'The "Nothing" keyword is overloaded in VB 2010.
'When used with generics, it represents the
'value of a type parameter.
Public Sub ResetPoint()
        X = Nothing
        Y = Nothing
End Sub
```

With the introduction of generics, the VB 2010 Nothing keyword can be can also be used to set a type parameter to its default value. This is helpful because a generic type does not know the actual placeholders up front, which means it cannot safely assume what the default value will be. The defaults for a type parameter are as follows:

- Numeric values will be equivalent to 0.

- Reference types will be equivalent to Nothing.

- Fields of a structure are set to 0 (for value types) or Nothing (for reference types).

For Point(Of T), you can set the X and Y values to 0 directly because it is safe to assume the caller will supply only numerical data. However, you can also increase the overall flexibility of the generic type by using the Nothing syntax. In any case, you can now exercise the methods of Point(Of T):

```
Module Module1
    Sub Main()

        Console.WriteLine("***** Fun with Generic Structures *****\n")

        ' Point using Integers.
        Dim p As New Point(Of Integer)(10, 10)
        Console.WriteLine("p.ToString()={0}", p.ToString())
        p.ResetPoint()
        Console.WriteLine("p.ToString()={0}", p.ToString())
        Console.WriteLine()

        ' Point using Doubles.
        Dim p2 As New Point(Of Double)(5.4, 3.3)
        Console.WriteLine("p2.ToString()={0}", p2.ToString())
        p2.ResetPoint()
        Console.WriteLine("p2.ToString()={0}", p2.ToString())

        Console.ReadLine()

    End Sub
End Module
```

Here is the output:

```
***** Fun with Generic Structures *****


p.ToString()=[10, 10]

p.ToString()=[0, 0]


p2.ToString()=[5.4, 3.3]

p2.ToString()=[0, 0]
```

■ **Source Code** You can find the GenericPoint project under the Chapter 10 subdirectory.

Generic Base Classes

Generic classes can be the base class to other classes, which means they can define any number of Overrideable or MustOverride methods. However, the derived types must abide by a few rules to ensure that the nature of the generic abstraction flows through. First, if a non-generic class extends a generic class, the derived class must specify a type parameter:

```vb
' Assume you have created a custom
' generic list class.
Public Class MyList(Of T)
        Private listOfData As New List(Of T)()
End Class

' Non-generic classes must specify the type
' parameter when deriving from a
' generic base class.
Public Class MyStringList
        Inherits MyList(Of String)
End Class
```

Second, if the generic base class defines generic Overrideable or MustOverride methods, the derived type must override the generic methods using the specified type parameter:

```
' A generic class with an Overridable method.
Public Class MyList(Of T)
    Private listOfData As New List(Of T)()
    Public Overridable Sub Insert(ByVal data As T)
    End Sub
End Class

Public Class MyStringList
    Inherits MyList(Of String)

    'Must substitute the type parameter used in the
    'parent class in derived methods.
    Public Overrides Sub Insert(ByVal data As String)
    End Sub
End Class
```

Third, if the derived type is generic as well, the child class can (optionally) reuse the type placeholder in its definition. However, be aware that any constraints (see next section) placed on the base class must be honored by the derived type, as in this example:

```
' Note that we now have a default constructor constraint (see next section).
Public Class MyList(Of T As New)

    Private listOfData As New List(Of T)()

    Public Overridable Sub Insert(ByVal data As T)
    End Sub
End Class


' Derived type must honor constraints.
Public Class MyReadOnlyList(Of T As New)
    Inherits MyList(Of T)

    Public Overrides Sub Insert(ByVal data As T)
    End Sub
End Class
```

Again, in your day-to-day programming tasks, creating custom generic class hierarchies will most likely not be a common task. Nevertheless, doing so is possible (as long as you abide by the rules).

Constraining Type Parameters

As this chapter illustrates, any generic item has at least one type parameter that you need to specify at the time you interact with the generic type or member. This alone allows you to build some type safe code; however, the .NET platform allows you to use the **As** keyword to get extremely specific about what a given type parameter must look like.

Using this keyword, you can add a set of constraints to a given type parameter, which the VB 2010 compiler will check at compile time. Specifically, you can constrain a type parameter as described in Table 10-6.

Table 10-6. Possible Constraints for Generic Type Parameters

Generic Constraint	Meaning in Life
`T As Structure`	The type parameter (`Of T`) must have `System.ValueType` in its chain of inheritance; in other words, (`Of T`) must be a structure.
`T As Class`	The type parameter (`Of T`) must not have `System.ValueType` in its chain of inheritance (e.g., (`Of T`) must be a reference type).
`T As New`	The type parameter (`Of T`) must have a default constructor. This is helpful if your generic type must create an instance of the type parameter because you cannot assume you know the format of custom constructors. Note that this constraint must be listed last on a multiconstrained type.
`T As NameOfBaseClass`	The type parameter (`Of T`) must be derived from the class specified by `NameOfBaseClass`.
`T As NameOfInterface`	The type parameter (`Of T`) must implement the interface specified by NameOfInterface. You can separate multiple interfaces as a comma-delimited list.

Unless you need to build some extremely type safe custom collections, you might never need to use the **As** keyword in your VB 2010 projects. Regardless, the following handful of (partial) code examples illustrate how to work with the **As** keyword.

Examples Using the As Keyword

Begin by assuming that you have created a custom generic class, and you want to ensure that the type parameter has a default constructor. This could be useful when the custom generic class needs to create instances of the T because the default constructor is the only constructor that is potentially common to all types. Also, constraining T in this way lets you get compile-time checking; if T is a reference type, then programmer remembered to redefine the default in the class definition (you might recall that the default constructor is removed in classes when you define your own):

```
'MyGenericClass derives from Object, while
'contained items must have a default ctor.
Public Class MyGenericClass(Of T As New)
    '...
End Class
```

Notice that the **As** clause specifies which type parameter is being constrained. If you have more than one constraint, pop the constraints into curly braces {}, as in the next example:

```
' MyGenericClass derives from Object, while
'contained items must be a class implementing IDrawable
'and must support a default ctor.
Public Class MyGenericClass(Of T As {Class, IDrawable, New})
    ' ...
End Class
```

In this case, T has three requirements. It must be a reference type (not a structure), as marked with the **class** token. Second, T must implement the **IDrawable** interface. Third, it must also have a default constructor

If you ever create a custom generic collection class that specifies multiple type parameters, you can specify a unique set of constraints for each, using separate **As** clauses:

```
'K must extend SomeBaseClass and have a default ctor,
'while T must be a structure and implement the
'generic IComparable interface.
Public Class MyGenericClass(Of K As {SomeBaseClass, New}, T As {Structure, IComparable(Of↩
   T)})
    ' ...
End Class
```

You will rarely encounter cases where you need to build a complete custom generic collection class; however, you can use the **As** keyword on generic methods, as well. For example, if you want to specify that your generic **Swap(Of T)()** method can only operate on structures, you would update the method like this:

```
'This method will swap any structure, but not classes.
Sub Swap(Of T As Structure)(ByRef a As T, ByRef b As T)
    ' ...
End Sub
```

Note that if you were to constrain the **Swap()** method in this manner, you would no longer be able to swap **string** objects (as is shown in the sample code) because **String** is a reference type.

The Lack of Operator Constraints

I want to make one more comment on generic methods and constraints as this chapter draws to a close. When you create generic methods, it might come as a surprise to you that it causes a compiler error if you apply any VB 2010 operators (+, -, *, etc.) on the type parameters. For example, imagine the usefulness of a class that can **Add()**, **Subtract()**, **Multiply()**, and **Divide()** generic types:

```
'Compiler error! Cannot apply
'operators to type parameters!
Public Class BasicMath(Of T)
    Public Function Add(ByVal arg1 As T, ByVal arg2 As T) As T
        Return arg1 + arg2
    End Function
End Class
```

```
    Public Function Subtract(ByVal arg1 As T, ByVal arg2 As T) As T
        Return arg1 - arg2
    End Function

    Public Function Multiply(ByVal arg1 As T, ByVal arg2 As T) As T
        Return arg1 * arg2
    End Function

    Public Function Divide(ByVal arg1 As T, ByVal arg2 As T) As T
        Return arg1 / arg2
    End Function
End Class
```

Unfortunately, the preceding BasicMath class will not compile. While this might seem like a major restriction, you need to remember that generics are generic. Of course, the numerical data can work just fine with the binary operators of VB 2010. However, for the sake of argument, if (Of T) were a custom class or structure type, the compiler could assume the class supports the +, -, *, and / operators. Ideally, VB 2010 would allow a generic type to be constrained by supported operators:

```
'Illustrative code only!
Public Class BasicMath(Of T As Operator +,Operator -,Operator *,Operator /)

    Public Function Add(ByVal arg1 As T, ByVal arg2 As T) As T
        Return arg1 + arg2
    End Function
    Public Function Subtract(ByVal arg1 As T, ByVal arg2 As T) As T
        Return arg1 - arg2
    End Function
    Public Function Multiply(ByVal arg1 As T, ByVal arg2 As T) As T
        Return arg1 * arg2
    End Function
    Public Function Divide(ByVal arg1 As T, ByVal arg2 As T) As T
        Return arg1 / arg2
    End Function
End Class
```

Alas, operator constraints are not supported under the current version of VB 2010. However, it is possible (albeit it requires a bit more work) to achieve the desired effect by defining an interface that supports these operators (VB 2010 interfaces can define operators!) and then specify an interface constraint of the generic class. In any case, this wraps up this book's initial look at building custom generic types. In the next chapter, you will pick up the topic of generics once again in the course of examining the .NET delegate type.

Summary

This chapter began by examining the issues associated with the classic containers found within the System.Collections namespace. While these types remain supported for purposes of backward compatibility, new .NET applications will benefit from using the generic counterparts within the System.Collections.Generic namespace instead.

As you have seen, a generic item allows you to specify placeholders (type parameters) that you specify at the time of object creation (or invocation, in the case of generic methods). Essentially, generics provide a solution to the boxing and type-safety issues that plagued .NET 1.1 software development. Also, generic types largely remove the need to build custom collection types.

While you will most often simply use the generic types provided in the .NET base class libraries, you will also able to create your own generic types (and generic methods). When you do so, you have the option of specifying any number of constraints (using the **As** keyword) to increase the level of type safety and ensure that you perform operations on types of a *known quantity* that are guaranteed to exhibit certain basic capabilities.

CHAPTER 11

■ ■ ■

Delegates, Events, and Lambdas

Up to this point in the text, most of the applications you developed added various bits of code to `Main()`, which, in some way or another, sent requests *to* a given object. However, many applications require that an object be able to communicate *back to* the entity that created it using a callback mechanism. While callback mechanisms can be used in any application, they are especially critical for graphical user interfaces in that controls (such as a button) need to invoke external methods under the correct circumstances (when the button is clicked, when the mouse enters the button surface, and so forth).

Under the .NET platform, the *delegate* type is the preferred means of defining and responding to callbacks within applications. Essentially, the .NET delegate type is a type-safe object that "points to" a method or a list of methods that can be invoked at a later time. Unlike the approach taken in some programming languages (such as traditional function pointers in C and C++), however, .NET delegates are classes that have built-in support for multicasting and asynchronous method invocation.

In this chapter, you will learn how to create and manipulate delegate types, then you'll investigate the VB 2010 `Event` keyword, which streamlines the process of working with delegate types. Along the way, you will also examine several delegate- and event-centric language features of VB 2010, including anonymous methods and method group conversions.

I wrap up this chapter by examining *lambda expressions*. Using the VB 2010 lambda statement (`Function`), you can specify a block of code statements (and the parameters to pass to those code statements) wherever a strongly typed delegate is required. As you will see, a lambda expression is little more than an anonymous method in disguise, and provides a simplified approach to working with delegates.

Understanding the .NET Delegate Type

Before formally defining .NET delegates, let's gain a bit of perspective. Historically, the Windows API made frequent use of C-style function pointers to create entities termed *callback functions,* or simply *callbacks*. Using callbacks, programmers were able to configure one function to report back to (call back) another function in the application. With this approach, Windows developers were able to handle button-clicking, mouse-moving, menu-selecting, and general bidirectional communications between two entities in memory.

The problem with standard C-style callback functions is that they represent little more than a raw address in memory. Ideally, you should be able to configure callbacks to include additional type-safe information such as the number of (and types of) parameters and the return type (if any) of the method pointed to. Sadly, this is not the case in traditional callback functions and, as you may suspect, they can therefore be a frequent source of bugs, hard crashes, and other runtime disasters. Nevertheless, callbacks are useful entities.

In the .NET Framework, callbacks are still possible, and this functionality is accomplished in a much safer and more object-oriented manner using *delegates*. In essence, a delegate is a type-safe object that points to another method (or possibly a list of methods) in the application, which can be invoked at a later time. Specifically, a delegate maintains three important pieces of information:

- The *address* of the method on which it makes calls

- The *parameters* (if any) of this method

- The *return type* (if any) of this method

■ **Note** .NET delegates can point to either Shared or instance methods.

Once a delegate object has been created and given the necessary information, it may dynamically invoke the method(s) it points to at runtime. Every delegate in the .NET Framework (including your custom delegates) is automatically endowed with the ability to call its methods *synchronously* or *asynchronously*. This fact greatly simplifies programming tasks, given that you can call a method on a secondary thread of execution without manually creating and managing a Thread object.

■ **Note** We will examine the asynchronous behavior of delegate types during our investigation of the System.Threading namespace in Chapter 19.

Defining a Delegate Type in VB 2010

When you want to create a delegate type in VB 2010, you use the Delegate keyword. The name of your delegate type can be whatever you desire. However, you must define the delegate to match the signature of the method(s) it will point to. For example, assume you wish to build a delegate type named BinaryOp that can point to any method that returns an Integer and takes two Integers as input parameters:

```
'This delegate can point to any method,
'taking two Integers and returning an Integer.
Public Delegate Function BinaryOp(ByVal x As Integer, ByVal y As Integer) As Integer
```

When the VB 2010 compiler processes delegate types, it automatically generates a NotInheritable class deriving from System.MulticastDelegate. This class (in conjunction with its base class, System.Delegate) provides the necessary infrastructure for the delegate to hold onto a list of methods to be invoked at a later time. For example, if you examine the BinaryOp delegate using ildasm.exe, you would find the class shown in Figure 11-1.

As you can see, the compiler-generated BinaryOp class defines three public methods. Invoke() is perhaps the key method, as it is used to invoke each method maintained by the delegate object in a *synchronous* manner, meaning the caller must wait for the call to complete before continuing on its way. Strangely enough, the synchronous Invoke() method need not be called explicitly from your VB 2010 code. As you will see in just a bit, `Invoke()` is called behind the scenes when you make use of the appropriate VB 2010 syntax.

`BeginInvoke()` and `EndInvoke()` provide the ability to call the current method *asynchronously* on a separate thread of execution. If you have a background in multithreading, you know that one of the most common reasons developers create secondary threads of execution is to invoke methods that require time to complete. Although the .NET base class libraries supply an entire namespace devoted to multithreaded programming (`System.Threading`), delegates provide this functionality out of the box.

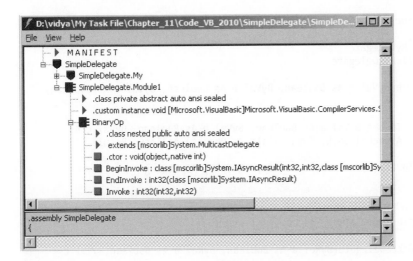

Figure 11-1. The VB 2010 Delegate keyword represents a NotInheritable class deriving from System.MulticastDelegate

Now, how exactly does the compiler know how to define the `Invoke()`, `BeginInvoke()`, and `EndInvoke()` methods? To understand the process, here is the crux of the compiler-generated `BinaryOp` class type (***bold italic*** marks the items specified by the defined delegate type):

```
Public NotInheritable Class BinaryOp
        Inherits System.MulticastDelegate

        Public Function Invoke(ByVal x As Integer,ByVal y As Integer) As Integer

        Public Function BeginInvoke(ByVal x As Integer,ByVal y As Integer,ByVal cb As
        AsyncCallback,ByVal state As Object) As IAsyncResult

        Public Function EndInvoke(ByVal result As IAsyncResult) As Integer

End Class
```

First, notice that the parameters and return type defined for the `Invoke()` method exactly match the definition of the `BinaryOp` delegate. The initial parameters to `BeginInvoke()` members (two Integers in our case) are also based on the `BinaryOp` delegate; however, `BeginInvoke()` will always provide two final parameters (of type `AsyncCallback` and `Object`) that are used to facilitate asynchronous method invocations. Finally, the return type of `EndInvoke()` is identical to the original delegate declaration and will always take as a sole parameter an object implementing the `IAsyncResult` interface.

Let's see another example. Assume you have defined a delegate type that can point to any method returning a `String` and receiving three `System.Boolean` input parameters:

```
Public Delegate Function MyDelegate(ByVal a As Boolean,ByVal b As Boolean,ByVal c As
Boolean) As String
```

This time, the compiler-generated class breaks down as follows:

```
Public NotInheritable Class MyDelegate
        Inherits System.MulticastDelegate

        Public Function Invoke(ByVal a As Boolean, ByVal b As Boolean, ByVal c As Boolean)
        As String

        Public Function BeginInvoke(ByVal a As Boolean, ByVal b As Boolean, ByVal c As
        Boolean, ByVal cb As AsyncCallback, ByVal state As Object) As IAsyncResult

        Public Function EndInvoke(ByVal result As IAsyncResult) As String
End Class
```

Delegates can also "point to" methods that contain any number of `ByRef` parameters (). For example, assume the following delegate type:

```
Public Delegate Function MyOtherDelegate(ByRef a As Boolean, ByRef b As Boolean,ByVal c↵
 As Integer) As String
```

The signatures of the `Invoke()` and `BeginInvoke()` methods look as you would expect; however, check out the `EndInvoke()` method, which now includes the set of all `ByRef` arguments defined by the delegate type:

```
Public NotInheritable Class MyOtherDelegate
        Inherits System.MulticastDelegate

        Public Function Invoke(ByRef a As Boolean, ByRef b As Boolean,ByVal c As Integer)
        As String


        Public Function BeginInvoke(ByRef a As Boolean, ByRef b As Boolean,ByVal c As
        Integer,ByVal cb As AsyncCallback,ByVal state As Object) As IAsyncResult

        Public Function EndInvoke(ByRef a As Boolean, ByRef b As Boolean,ByVal result As
        IAsyncResult) As String

End Class
```

To summarize, a VB 2010 delegate type definition results in a `NotInheritable` class with three compiler-generated methods whose parameter and return types are based on the delegate's declaration. The following pseudo-code approximates the basic pattern:

```
'This is only pseudo-code
Public NotInheritable Class DelegateName
        Inherits System.MulticastDelegate

        Public Function Invoke(ByVal allDelegateInputRefAndOutParams) As delegateReturnValue

        Public Function BeginInvoke(ByVal allDelegateInputRefAndOutParams, ByVal cb As
        AsyncCallback, ByVal state As Object) As IAsyncResult

        Public Function EndInvoke(ByVal allDelegateInputRefAndOutParams, ByVal result As
        IAsyncResult) As delegateReturnValue
End Class
```

The System.MulticastDelegate and System.Delegate Base Classes

So, when you build a type using the VB 2010 Delegate keyword, you indirectly declare a class type that derives from System.MulticastDelegate. This class provides descendents with access to a list that contains the addresses of the methods maintained by the delegate object, as well as several additional methods (and a few overloaded operators) to interact with the invocation list. Here are some select members of System.MulticastDelegate:

```
Public MustInherit Class MulticastDelegate
        Inherits [Delegate]

        'Returns the list of methods "pointed to."
        Public NotOverridable Overrides Function GetInvocationList() As [Delegate]()

        'Overloaded operators.
        Public Shared Operator =(ByVal d1 As MulticastDelegate, ByVal d2 As
        MulticastDelegate) As Boolean

        Public Shared Operator <>(ByVal d1 As MulticastDelegate, ByVal d2 As
        MulticastDelegate) As Boolean

        'Used internally to manage the list of methods
        'maintained by the delegate.
        Private_invocationCount As IntPtr
        Private  invocationList As Object
End Class
```

System.MulticastDelegate obtains additional functionality from its parent class, System.Delegate. Here is a partial snapshot of the class definition:

```
Public MustInherit Class [Delegate]
        Implements ICloneable
        Implements ISerializable
```

```
'Methods to interact with the list of functions.
Public Shared Function Combine(ByVal ParamArray delegates As [Delegate]()) As
[Delegate]

Public Shared Function Combine(ByVal a As [Delegate], ByVal b As [Delegate]) As
[Delegate]

Public Shared Function Remove(ByVal source As [Delegate], ByVal value As [Delegate])
As [Delegate]

Public Shared Function RemoveAll(ByVal source As [Delegate], ByVal value As
[Delegate]) As [Delegate]

'Overloaded operators.
Public Shared Operator =(ByVal d1 As [Delegate], ByVal d2 As [Delegate]) As Boolean

Public Shared Operator <>(ByVal d1 As [Delegate], ByVal d2 As [Delegate]) As Boolean

'Properties that expose the delegate target.
Public ReadOnly Property Method() As MethodInfo
Public ReadOnly Property Target() As Object
```

```
End Class
```

Now, understand that you can never directly derive from these base classes in your code (it is a compiler error to do so). Nevertheless, when you use the **Delegate** keyword, you have indirectly created a class that "is-a" **MulticastDelegate**. Table 11-1 documents the core members common to all delegate types.

Table 11-1. Select Members of System.MultcastDelegate/System.Delegate

Member	Meaning in Life
Method	This property returns a **System.Reflection.MethodInfo** object that represents details of a Shared method maintained by the delegate.
Target	If the method to be called is defined at the object level (rather than a Shared method), **Target** returns an object that represents the method maintained by the delegate. If the value returned from **Target** equals **Nothing**, the method to be called is a Shared member.
Combine()	This Shared method adds a method to the list maintained by the delegate.
GetInvocationList()	This method returns an array of **System.Delegate** objects, each representing a particular method that may be invoked.
Remove() RemoveAll()	These Shared methods remove a method (or all methods) from the delegate's invocation list.

The Simplest Possible Delegate Example

To be sure, delegates can cause a great deal of confusion when encountered for the first time. Thus, to get the ball rolling, let's take a look at a very simple Console Application program (named SimpleDelegate) that makes use of the BinaryOp delegate type you've seen previously. Here is the complete code, with analysis to follow:

```
'This delegate can point to any method,
'taking two Integers and returning an Integer.
Public Delegate Function BinaryOp(ByVal x As Integer,
                                  ByVal y As Integer) As Integer
'This class contains methods BinaryOp will point to.
Public Class SimpleMath

        Public Shared Function Add(ByVal x As Integer,
                                   ByVal y As Integer) As Integer

            Return x + y
        End Function

        Public Shared Function Subtract(ByVal x As Integer,
                                        ByVal y As Integer) As Integer

            Return x - y
        End Function
End Class

Module Module1

    Sub Main()
        Console.WriteLine("***** Simple Delegate Example *****" & vbLf)

        'Create a BinaryOp delegate object that
        'points to "SimpleMath.Add()".
        Dim b As New BinaryOp(AddressOf SimpleMath.Add)

        'Invoke Add() method indirectly using delegate object.
        Console.WriteLine("10 + 10 is {0}", b(10, 10))
        Console.ReadLine()
    End Sub
End Module
```

Again, notice the format of the BinaryOp delegate type declaration; it specifies that BinaryOp delegate objects can point to any method taking two Integers and returning an Integer (the actual name of the method pointed to is irrelevant). Here, we have created a class named SimpleMath, which defines two Shared methods that (surprise, surprise) match the pattern defined by the BinaryOp delegate.

When you want to insert the target method to a given delegate object, simply pass in the name of the method to the delegate's constructor:

```
' Create a BinaryOp delegate object that
' "points to" SimpleMath.Add().
Dim b As New BinaryOp(SimpleMath.Add)
```

At this point, you are able to invoke the member pointed to using a syntax that looks like a direct function invocation:

```
'Invoke() is really called here!
Console.WriteLine("10 + 10 is {0}", b(10, 10))
```

Under the hood, the runtime actually calls the compiler-generated `Invoke()` method on your `MulticastDelegate` derived class. You can verify this for yourself if you open your assembly in `ildasm.exe` and examine the CIL code within the `Main()` method:

```
.method public  static void Main() cil managed
{
...
  callvirt instance int32 SimpleDelegate .BinaryOp::Invoke(int32, int32)
}
```

Although VB 2010 does not require you to explicitly call `Invoke()` within your code base, you are free to do so. Thus, the following code statement is also permissible:

```
Console.WriteLine("10 + 10 is {0}", b.Invoke(10, 10))
```

Recall that .NET delegates are *type safe*. Therefore, if you attempt to pass a delegate a method that does not match the pattern, you receive a compile-time error. To illustrate, assume the `SimpleMath` class now defines an additional method named `SquareNumber()`, which takes a single Integer as input:

```
Public Class SimpleMath
        ...
        Public Shared Function SquareNumber(ByVal a As Integer) As Integer
            Return a * a
        End Function
End Class
```

Given that the `BinaryOp` delegate can *only* point to methods that take two Integers and return an Integer, the following code is illegal and will not compile:

```
'Compiler error! Method does not match delegate pattern!
Dim b As New BinaryOp(AddressOf SimpleMath.Add)
```

Investigating a Delegate Object

Let's spice up the current example by creating a Shared method (named `DisplayDelegateInfo()`) within the `Module1` Module. This method will print out the names of the method(s) maintained by a delegate object as well as the name of the class defining the method. To do this, we will iterate over the `System.Delegate` array returned by `GetInvocationList()`, invoking each object's `Target` and `Method` properties:

```
Sub DisplayDelegateInfo(ByVal delObj As [Delegate])
        'Print the names of each member in the
        'delegate's invocation list.
        For Each d As [Delegate] In delObj.GetInvocationList()
            Console.WriteLine("Method Name: {0}", d.Method)
            Console.WriteLine("Type Name: {0}", d.Target)
        Next
End Sub
```

Assuming you have updated your `Main()` method to actually call this new helper method, you would find the output shown below:

```
***** Simple Delegate Example *****


Method Name: Int32 Add(Int32, Int32)

Type Name:

10 + 10 is 20
```

Notice that the name of the type (`SimpleMath`) is currently *not* displayed when calling the `Target` property. The reason has to do with the fact that our `BinaryOp` delegate is pointing to a *Shared method* and therefore there is no object to reference! However, if we update the `Add()` and `Subtract()` methods to be non-Shared (simply by deleting the `Shared` keywords), we could create an instance of the `SimpleMath` class and specify the methods to invoke using the object reference:

```
Sub Main()
        Console.WriteLine("***** Simple Delegate Example *****" & vbLf)

        '.NET delegates can also point to instance methods as well.
        Dim m As New SimpleMath()
        Dim b As New BinaryOp(AddressOf m.Add)

        'Show information about this object.
        DisplayDelegateInfo(b)

        Console.WriteLine("10 + 10 is {0}", b(10, 10))
        Console.ReadLine()
End Sub
```

In this case, we would find the output shown here.

```
***** Simple Delegate Example *****


Method Name: Int32 Add(Int32, Int32)

Type Name: SimpleDelegate.SimpleMath

10 + 10 is 20
```

■ **Source Code** The SimpleDelegate project is located under the Chapter 11 subdirectory.

Sending Object State Notifications Using Delegates

Clearly, the previous SimpleDelegate example was intended to be purely illustrative in nature, given that there would be no compelling reason to define a delegate simply to add two numbers! To provide a more realistic use of delegate types, let's use delegates to define a Car class that has the ability to inform external entities about its current engine state. To do so, we will take the following steps:

- Define a new delegate type that will send notifications to the caller.

- Declare a member variable of this delegate in the Car class.

- Create a helper function on the Car that allows the caller to specify the method to call back to.

- Implement the Accelerate() method to invoke the delegate's invocation list under the correct circumstances.

To begin, create a new Console Application project named CarDelegate. Now, define a new Car class that looks initially like this:

```
Public Class Car
    ' Internal state data.
    Public Property CurrentSpeed() As Integer
    Public Property MaxSpeed() As Integer
    Public Property PetName() As String

    ' Is the car alive or dead?
    Private carIsDead As Boolean
```

```
    Public Sub New()
        MaxSpeed = 100
    End Sub

    Public Sub New(ByVal name As String, ByVal maxSp As Integer, ByVal currSp As Integer)
        CurrentSpeed = currSp
        MaxSpeed = maxSp
        PetName = name
    End Sub
End Class
```

Now, consider the following updates, which address the first three points:

```
Public Class Car

    ' 1) Define the delegate type.
    Public Delegate Sub CarEngineHandler(ByVal msgForCaller As String)

    ' 2) Define a member variable of the delegate.
    Private listOfHandlers As CarEngineHandler

    ' 3) Add registration function for the caller.
    Public Sub RegisterWithCarEngine(ByVal methodToCall As CarEngineHandler)
            listOfHandlers = methodToCall
    End Sub
End Class
```

Notice in this example that we define the delegate types directly within the scope of the **Car** class. As you explore the base class libraries, you will find it is quite common to define a delegate within the scope of the type it naturally works with. Our delegate type, **CarEngineHandler**, can point to any method taking a single **String** as input and having no return value.

Next, note that we declare a Private member variable of our delegate (named **listOfHandlers**), and a helper function (named **RegisterWithCarEngine()**) that allows the caller to assign a method to the delegate's invocation list.

■ **Note** Strictly speaking, we could have defined our delegate member variable as Public, therefore avoiding the need to create additional registration methods. However, by defining the delegate member variable as Private, we are enforcing encapsulation services and providing a more type-safe solution. You'll revisit the risk of Public delegate member variables later in this chapter when you look at the VB 2010 Event keyword.

At this point, we need to create the **Accelerate()** method. Recall, the point here is to allow a **Car** object to send engine-related messages to any subscribed listener. Here is the update:

```
Public Sub Accelerate(ByVal delta As Integer)

    'If this car is 'dead', send dead message.
```

```
            If carIsDead Then
                If listOfHandlers IsNot Nothing Then
                    listOfHandlers("Sorry, this car is dead...")
                End If
            Else
                CurrentSpeed += delta
                ' Is this car 'almost dead'?
                  If 10 = (MaxSpeed - CurrentSpeed) AndAlso listOfHandlers IsNot Nothing Then
                    listOfHandlers("Careful buddy! Gonna blow!")
                End If

                If CurrentSpeed >= MaxSpeed Then
                    carIsDead = True
                Else
                    Console.WriteLine("CurrentSpeed = {0}", CurrentSpeed)
                End If
            End If
    End Sub
```

Notice that before we invoke the methods maintained by the `listOfHandlers` member variable, we are checking it against a `Nothing` value. The reason is that it will be the job of the caller to allocate these objects by calling the `RegisterWithCarEngine()` helper method. If the caller does not call this method and we attempt to invoke the delegate's invocation list, we will trigger a `NullReferenceException` and bomb at runtime—which would obviously be a bad thing! Now that we have the delegate infrastructure in place, observe the updates to the `Module1` Module:

```
Module Module1
    Sub Main()

        Console.WriteLine("*** Delegates as event enablers ***" & vbLf)

        'First, make a Car object.
         Dim c1 As New Car("SlugBug", 100, 10)

        'Now tell the car which method to call
        ' when it wants to send us messages
        c1.RegisterWithCarEngine(New Car.CarEngineHandler(
                    AddressOf OnCarEngineEvent))

        'Speed up (this will trigger the events).
        Console.WriteLine("***** Speeding up *****")

        For i = 0 To 5
            c1.Accelerate(20)
        Next
        Console.ReadLine()
    End Sub

    'This is the target for incoming events
    Public Sub OnCarEngineEvent(ByVal msg As String)
        Console.WriteLine(vbLf & "***** Message From Car Object *****")
```

```
        Console.WriteLine("=> {0}", msg)
        Console.WriteLine("********************************" & vbLf)
    End Sub

End Module
```

The `Main()` method begins by simply making a new `Car` object. Since we are interested in hearing about the engine events, our next step is to call our custom registration function, `RegisterWithCarEngine()`. Recall that this method expects to be passed an instance of the nested `CarEngineHandler` delegate, and as with any delegate, we specify a "method to point to" as a constructor parameter.

The trick in this example is that the method in question is located back in the `Module1` Module! Again, notice that the `OnCarEngineEvent()` method is a dead-on match to the related delegate in that it takes a `string` as input and has no return value. Consider the output of the current example:

```
***** Delegates as event enablers *****


***** Speeding up *****

CurrentSpeed = 30

CurrentSpeed = 50

CurrentSpeed = 70


***** Message From Car Object *****

=> Careful buddy!  Gonna blow!

********************************


CurrentSpeed = 90


***** Message From Car Object *****

=> Sorry, this car is dead...

********************************
```

Enabling Multicasting

Recall that .NET delegates have the built-in ability to *multicast*. In other words, a delegate object can maintain a list of methods to call, rather than just a single method. When you wish to add multiple methods to a delegate object, you will need to call System.Delegate.Combine(). To enable multicasting on the Car type, we could update the RegisterWithCarEngine() method as follows:

```
Public Class Car

    'Now with multicasting support!
    'Note we are now using the System.Delegate.Combine() method not
    'the assignment operator (=).
    Public Sub RegisterWithCarEngine(ByVal methodToCall As    CarEngineHandler)
            Dim del As [Delegate] = System.Delegate.Combine
            (listOfHandlers, methodToCall)

            listOfHandlers = CType(del, CarEngineHandler)
    End Sub
    ...
End class
```

With this simple change, the caller can now register multiple targets for the same callback notification. Here, our second handler prints the incoming message in uppercase, just for display purposes:

```
Module Module1
    Sub Main()

        Console.WriteLine("***** Delegates as event enablers *****" & vbLf)

        'First, make a Car object.
        Dim c1 As New Car("SlugBug", 100, 10)

        'Register multiple targets for the notifications.
        c1.RegisterWithCarEngine(New Car.CarEngineHandler(AddressOf OnCarEngineEvent))

        Dim handler2 As New Car.CarEngineHandler(AddressOf OnCarEngineEvent2)
        c1.RegisterWithCarEngine(OnCarEngineEvent2)

        'Speed up (this will trigger the events).
        Console.WriteLine("***** Speeding up *****")
        For i = 0 To 5
                c1.Accelerate(20)
        Next
        Console.ReadLine()
    End Sub

    'We now have TWO methods that will be called by the Car
    'when sending notifications.
    Public Sub OnCarEngineEvent(ByVal msg As String)
        Console.WriteLine(vbLf & "***** Message From Car Object *****")
```

```
        Console.WriteLine("=> {0}", msg)
        Console.WriteLine("*******************************" & vbLf)
    End Sub

    Public Sub OnCarEngineEvent2(ByVal msg As String)
        Console.WriteLine("=> {0}", msg.ToUpper())
    End Sub
End Module
```

It's quite enlightening to take a look at the CIL when you're using delegates. Here's the CIL for RegisterWithCarEngine():

```
.method public instance void  RegisterWithCarEngine(class CarDelegate.Car/CarEngineHandler↵
 methodToCall) cil managed
{
  // Code size       28 (0x1c)
  .maxstack  2
  .locals init ([0] class [mscorlib]System.Delegate del)
  IL_0000:  nop
  IL_0001:  ldarg.0
  IL_0002:  ldfld       class CarDelegate.Car/CarEngineHandler↵
 CarDelegate.Car::listOfHandlers
  IL_0007:  ldarg.1
  IL_0008:  call        class [mscorlib]System.Delegate↵
 [mscorlib]System.Delegate::Combine(class [mscorlib]System.Delegate,

class [mscorlib]System.Delegate)
  IL_000d:  stloc.0
  IL_000e:  ldarg.0
  IL_000f:  ldloc.0
  IL_0010:  castclass   CarDelegate.Car/CarEngineHandler
  IL_0015:  stfld       class CarDelegate.Car/CarEngineHandler↵
 CarDelegate.Car::listOfHandlers
  IL_001a:  nop
  IL_001b:  ret
} // end of method Car::RegisterWithCarEngine
```

Removing Targets from a Delegate's Invocation List

The Delegate class also defines a Shared Remove() method that allows a caller to dynamically remove a method from a delegate object's invocation list. This makes it simple to allow the caller to "unsubscribe" from a given notification at runtime. If you want to allow the caller to detach from the event notifications, you could add the following additional helper methods to the Car type:

```
Public Class Car
...
    Public Sub UnRegisterWithCarEngine(ByVal methodToCall As CarEngineHandler)
        Dim del As [Delegate] =System.Delegate.Remove(
        listOfHandlers, methodToCall)
        listOfHandlers = CType(del, CarEngineHandler)
    End Sub
End Class
```

With the current updates to the **Car** class, we could stop receiving the engine notification on the second handler by updating **Main()** as follows:

```
Sub Main()
        Console.WriteLine("***** Delegates as event enablers *****" & vbLf)
        'First, make a Car object.
        Dim c1 As New Car("SlugBug", 100, 10)

        'Register multiple targets for the notifications.
        c1.RegisterWithCarEngine(New Car.CarEngineHandler(AddressOf OnCarEngineEvent))

        'This time, hold onto the delegate object,
        'so we can unregister later.
        Dim handler2 As New Car.CarEngineHandler(AddressOf OnCarEngineEvent2)
        c1.RegisterWithCarEngine(handler2)

        'Speed up (this will trigger the events).
        Console.WriteLine("***** Speeding up *****")
        For i = 0 To 5
            c1.Accelerate(20)
        Next

       'Unregister from the second handler.
        c1.UnRegisterWithCarEngine(handler2)

        'We won't see the 'upper case' message anymore!
        Console.WriteLine("***** Speeding up *****")
        For i = 0 To 5
            c1.Accelerate(20)
        Next
        Console.ReadLine()
End Sub
```

One difference in **Main()** is that this time we are creating a **Car.CarEngineHandler** object and storing it in a local variable so we can use this object to unregister with the notification later on. Thus, the second time we speed up the **Car** object, we no longer see the uppercase version of the incoming message data, as we have removed this target from the delegates invocation list.

■ **Source Code** The CarDelegate project is located under the Chapter 11 subdirectory.

Method Group Conversion Syntax

In the previous CarDelegate example, we explicitly created instances of the `Car.CarEngineHandler` delegate object in order to register and unregister with the engine notifications:

```
Sub Main()
    Dim c1 As New Car("SlugBug", 100, 10)

    'Register multiple targets for the notifications.
    c1.RegisterWithCarEngine(New Car.CarEngineHandler(AddressOf OnCarEngineEvent))

    Dim handler2 As New Car.CarEngineHandler(AddressOf OnCarEngineEvent2)

    c1.RegisterWithCarEngine(handler2)
        ...
End Sub
```

To be sure, if you need to call any of the inherited members of `MulticastDelegate` or `Delegate`, manually creating a delegate variable is the most straightforward way of doing so. However, in most cases, you don't really need to hang onto the delegate object. Rather, you typically only need to use the delegate object in order to pass in the method name as a constructor parameter.

As a simplification, VB 2010 provides a shortcut termed *method group conversion*. This feature allows you to supply a direct method name, rather than a delegate object, when calling methods that take delegates as arguments.

■ **Note** As you will see later in this chapter, you can also use method group conversion syntax to simplify how you register with a VB 2010 event.

To illustrate, create a new Console Application named CarDelegateMethodGroupConversion and insert the file containing the `Car` class you defined in the CarDelegate project. Now, consider the following `Module`, which uses method group conversion to register and unregister from the engine notifications:

```
Module Module1
    Sub Main()
        Console.WriteLine("***** Method Group Conversion *****" & vbLf)

        Dim c1 As New Car()

        ' Register the simple method name.
        c1.RegisterWithCarEngine(AddressOf CallMeHere)
```

```
        Console.WriteLine("***** Speeding up *****")
        For i As Integer = 0 To 5
            c1.Accelerate(20)
        Next

        ' Unregister the simple method name.
        c1.UnRegisterWithCarEngine(AddressOf CallMeHere)

        ' No more notifications!
        For i As Integer = 0 To 5
            c1.Accelerate(20)
        Next
        Console.ReadLine()
    End Sub

    Sub CallMeHere(ByVal msg As String)
        Console.WriteLine("=> Message from Car: {0}", msg)
    End Sub
End Module
```

Notice that we are not directly allocating the associated delegate object, but rather simply specifying a method that matches the delegate's expected signature (a method returning **Sub** and taking a single **String** in this case). Understand that the VB 2010 compiler is still ensuring type safety. Thus, if the **CallMeHere()** method did not take a **string** and return **void**, we would be issued a compiler error.

■ **Source Code** The CarDelegateMethodGroupConversion project is located under the Chapter 11 subdirectory.

Understanding Delegate Covariance

As you may have noticed, each of the delegates created thus far point to methods returning simple numerical data types (or to **Subs** having no return values). However, assume you have a new Console Application named DelegateCovariance that defines a delegate type that can point to methods returning a custom class type (be sure to include your **Car** class definition in this new project):

```
'Define the delegate type.
Public Delegate Function ObtainCarDelegate() As Car
```

Of course, you would be able to define a target for the delegate as expected:

```
Module Module1
    ' Define a single delegate that may return a Car
    ' or SportsCar.
    Public Delegate Function ObtainVehicalDelegate() As Car
```

```
    Sub Main()
        Console.WriteLine("***** Delegate Covariance *****" & vbLf)
        Dim targetA As New ObtainVehicalDelegate(AddressOf GetBasicCar)
        Dim c As Car = targetA()
        Console.WriteLine("Obtained a {0}", c)
        Console.ReadLine()

    End Sub

     Public Function GetBasicCar() As Car
         Return New Car("Zippy", 100, 55)
    End Function
End Module
```

Now, what if you were to derive a new class from the **Car** type named **SportsCar** and you wanted to create a delegate type that can point to methods returning this class type? Prior to .NET 2.0, you would be required to define an entirely new delegate to do so, given that delegates were so type-safe that they did not honor the basic laws of inheritance:

```
'Define a new delegate type pointing to
'methods that return a SportsCar object.
Public Delegate Function ObtainSportsCarDelegate() As SportsCar
```

As we now have two delegate types, we must create an instance of each to obtain **Car** and **SportsCar** types:

```
Module Module1
    Public Delegate Function ObtainCarDelegate() As Car
    Public Delegate Function ObtainSportsCarDelegate() As SportsCar

    Public Function GetBasicCar() As Car
        Return New Car()
    End Function

    Public Function GetSportsCar() As SportsCar
        Return New SportsCar()
    End Function

    Sub Main()
        Console.WriteLine("***** Delegate Covariance *****" & vbLf)

        Dim targetA As New ObtainCarDelegate(AddressOf GetBasicCar)
        Dim c As Car = targetA()
        Console.WriteLine("Obtained a {0}", c)

        Dim targetB As New ObtainSportsCarDelegate(AddressOf GetSportsCar)
        Dim sc As SportsCar = targetB()
        Console.WriteLine("Obtained a {0}", sc)
        Console.ReadLine()
    End Sub
End Module
```

Given the laws of classic inheritance, it would be ideal to build a single delegate type that can point to methods returning either `Car` or `SportsCar` objects (after all, a `SportsCar` "is-a" `Car`). *Covariance* (which also goes by the term *relaxed delegates*) allows for this very possibility. Simply put, covariance allows you to build a single delegate that can point to methods returning class types related by classical inheritance.

■ **Note** In a similar vein, *contravariance* allows you to create a single delegate that can point to numerous methods that receive objects related by classical inheritance. Consult the .NET Framework 4.0 SDK documentation for further details.

```
Module Module1

    'Define a single delegate type that can point to
    'methods that return a Car or SportCar.
    Public Delegate Function ObtainVehicleDelegate() As Car

    Public Function GetBasicCar() As Car
        Return New Car()
    End Function

    Public Function GetSportsCar() As SportsCar
        Return New SportsCar()
    End Function

    Sub Main()
        Console.WriteLine("***** Delegate Covariance *****" & vbLf)

        Dim targetA As New ObtainVehicleDelegate(AddressOf GetBasicCar)
        Dim c As Car = targetA()
        Console.WriteLine("Obtained a {0}", c)

        'Covariance allows this target assignment.
        Dim targetB As New ObtainVehicleDelegate(AddressOf GetSportsCar)
        Dim sc As SportsCar = DirectCast(targetB(), SportsCar)
        Console.WriteLine("Obtained a {0}", sc)
        Console.ReadLine()
    End Sub
End Module
```

Notice that the `ObtainVehicleDelegate` delegate type has been defined to point to methods returning a strongly typed `Car` type. Given covariance, however, we can point to methods returning derived types as well. To obtain access to the members of the derived type, simply perform an explicit cast.

■ **Source Code** The DelegateCovariance project is located under the Chapter 11 subdirectory.

Understanding Generic Delegates

Recall from the previous chapter that VB 2010 does allow you to define generic delegate types. For example, assume you wish to define a delegate type that can call any Sub that receives a single parameter. If the argument in question may differ, you could model this using a type parameter. To illustrate, consider the following code within a new Console Application named GenericDelegate:

```vb
'This generic delegate can call any Sub
'that takes a single type parameter.
Public Delegate Sub MyGenericDelegate(Of T)(ByVal arg As T)

Module Module1
    Sub Main()
        Console.WriteLine("***** Generic Delegates *****" & vbLf)

        'Register targets.
        Dim strTarget As New MyGenericDelegate(Of String)
                        (AddressOf StringTarget)
        strTarget("Some String data")

        Dim intTarget As New MyGenericDelegate(Of Integer)
                        (AddressOf IntegerTarget)
        intTarget(9)
        Console.ReadLine()
    End Sub

    Sub StringTarget(ByVal arg As String)
        Console.WriteLine("arg in uppercase is: {0}", arg.ToUpper())
    End Sub

    Sub IntegerTarget(ByVal arg As Integer)
        arg += 1
        Console.WriteLine("incremented arg is {0}", arg)
    End Sub
End Module
```

Notice that MyGenericDelegate(Of T) defines a single type parameter that represents the argument to pass to the delegate target. When creating an instance of this type, you are required to specify the value of the type parameter as well as the name of the method the delegate will invoke. Thus, if you specified a String type, you send a String value to the target method:

```vb
'Create an instance of MyGenericDelegate(Of T)
'with String as the type parameter.
Dim strTarget As New MyGenericDelegate(Of String)(AddressOf StringTarget)
strTarget("Some String data")
```

Given the format of the strTarget object, the StringTarget() method must now take a single String as a parameter:

```
Sub StringTarget(ByVal arg As String)
      Console.WriteLine("arg in uppercase is: {0}", arg.ToUpper())
End Sub
```

Simulating Generic Delegates Without Generics

Generic delegates offer a more flexible way to specify the method to be invoked in a type-safe manner. Before the introduction of generics in .NET 2.0, you could achieve a similar end result using a System.Object parameter:

```
Public Delegate Sub MyDelegate(ByVal arg As Object)
```

Although this allows you to send any type of data to a delegate target, you do so without type safety and with possible boxing penalties. For instance, assume you have created two instances of MyDelegate, both of which point to the same method, MyTarget. Note the boxing/unboxing penalties as well as the inherent lack of type safety:

```
Module Module1
    Sub Main()
        ...
        'Register target with "traditional" delegate syntax.
        Dim d As New MyDelegate(AddressOf MyTarget)
        d("More string data")

        ' Method group conversion syntax.
        Dim d2 As MyDelegate = AddressOf MyTarget

        ' Boxing penalty.
        d2(9)
        Console.ReadLine()
    End Sub

    ' Due to a lack of type safety, we must
    ' determine the underlying type before casting.
    Public Sub MyTarget(ByVal arg As Object)
        If TypeOf arg Is Integer Then
            ' Unboxing penalty.
            Dim i As Integer = CInt(arg)
            i += 1
            Console.WriteLine("incremented arg is: {0}",i)
        End If

        If TypeOf arg Is String Then
            Dim s As String = CStr(arg)
            Console.WriteLine("arg in uppercase is: {0}", s.ToUpper())
        End If
```

```
    End Sub
End Module
```

When you send out a value type to the target site, the value is boxed and unboxed once it is received by the target method. As well, given that the incoming parameter could be anything at all, you must dynamically check the underlying type before casting. Using generic delegates, you can still obtain the desired flexibility without the issues.

■ **Source Code** The GenericDelegate project is located under the Chapter 11 directory.

That wraps up our first look at the .NET delegate type. We will look at some additional details of working with delegates at the conclusion of this chapter and again in Chapter 19 during our examination of multithreading. Now let's move on to the related topic of the VB 2010 Event keyword.

Understanding VB 2010 Events

Delegates are fairly interesting constructs in that they enable objects in memory to engage in a two-way conversation. However, working with delegates in the raw can entail the creation of some boilerplate code (defining the delegate, declaring necessary member variables, and creating custom registration and unregistration methods to preserve encapsulation, etc.).

Moreover, when you use delegates in the raw as your application's callback mechanism, if you do not define a class's delegate member variables as Private, the caller will have direct access to the delegate objects. In this case, the caller could reassign the variable to a new delegate object (effectively deleting the current list of functions to call) and, worse yet, the caller would be able to directly invoke the delegate's invocation list. To illustrate this problem, consider the following reworking (and simplification) of the previous CarDelegate example:

```
Public Class Car
    Public Delegate Sub CarEngineHandler(ByVal msgForCaller As String)

    ' Now a public member!
    Public listOfHandlers As CarEngineHandler

    'Just fire out the Exploded notification.
    Public Sub Accelerate(ByVal delta As Integer)
        If listOfHandlers IsNot Nothing Then
            listOfHandlers("Sorry, this car is dead...")
        End If
    End Sub
End Class
```

Notice that we no longer have Private delegate member variables encapsulated with custom registration methods. Because these members are indeed Public, the caller can directly access the listOfHandlers member variable and reassign this type to new CarEngineHandler objects and invoke the delegate whenever it so chooses:

```
Module Module1
    Sub Main()
        Console.WriteLine("***** Agh!  No Encapsulation! *****" & vbLf)

        'Make a Car.
         Dim myCar As New Car()

        'We have direct access to the delegate!
        myCar.listOfHandlers = New Car.CarEngineHandler(
                        AddressOf CallWhenExploded)
        myCar.Accelerate(10)

        'We can now assign to a whole new object...
        'confusing at best.
        myCar.listOfHandlers = New Car.CarEngineHandler(AddressOf↵
                        CallHereToo)
        myCar.Accelerate(10)

         'The caller can also directly invoke the delegate!
         myCar.listOfHandlers.Invoke("hee, hee, hee...")
         Console.ReadLine()
    End Sub

    Sub CallWhenExploded(ByVal msg As String)
        Console.WriteLine(msg)
    End Sub

     Sub CallHereToo(ByVal msg As String)
        Console.WriteLine(msg)
     End Sub
End Module
```

Exposing Public delegate members breaks encapsulation, which not only can lead to code that is hard to maintain (and debug) but could also open your application to possible security risks! Here is the output of the current example:

```
***** Agh!  No Encapsulation! *****



Sorry, this car is dead...

Sorry, this car is dead...

hee, hee, hee...
```

Obviously, you would not want to give other applications the power to change what a delegate is pointing to or to invoke the members without your permission.

■ **Source Code** The PublicDelegateProblem project is located under the Chapter 11 subdirectory.

The VB 2010 Event Keyword

As a shortcut, so you don't have to build custom methods to add or remove methods to a delegate's invocation list, VB 2010 provides the **Event** keyword. When the compiler processes the **Event** keyword, you are automatically provided with registration and unregistration methods as well as any necessary member variables for your delegate types. These delegate member variables are *always* declared Private, and therefore they are not directly exposed from the object firing the event. To be sure, the **Event** keyword is little more than syntactic sugar in that it simply saves you some typing time.

Defining an event is a two-step process. First, you need to define a delegate type that will hold the list of methods to be called when the event is fired. Next, you declare an event (using the VB 2010 **Event** keyword) in terms of the related delegate type.

To illustrate the **Event** keyword, create a new Console Application named **CarEvents**. In this iteration of the **Car** class, we will define two events named **AboutToBlow** and **Exploded**. These events are associated to a single delegate type named **CarEngineHandler**. Here are the initial updates to the **Car** class:

```
Public Class Car
    ...
    'This delegate works in conjunction with the
    'Car's events.
    Public Delegate Sub CarEngineHandler(ByVal msg As String)

    'This car can send these events.
    Public Event Exploded As CarEngineHandler
    Public Event AboutToBlow As CarEngineHandler
    ...
End Class
```

Firing an event is as simple as specifying the event by name (with any specified parameters) using the **RaiseEvent** keyword, along with any required parameters as defined by the associated delegate. To ensure that the caller has indeed registered with the event, you will want to check the event against **Nothing** before invoking the delegate's method set. With these points in mind, here is the new iteration of the **Car**'s **Accelerate()** method:

```
Public Sub Accelerate(ByVal delta As Integer)

        'If the car is dead, fire Exploded event.
        If carIsDead Then
            RaiseEvent Exploded("Sorry, this car is dead...")
        Else
            CurrentSpeed += delta
            'Almost dead?
            If 10 = MaxSpeed - CurrentSpeed Then
                    RaiseEvent AboutToBlow("Careful buddy!  Gonna blow!")
            End If
```

```
                'Still OK!
                If CurrentSpeed >= MaxSpeed Then
                        carIsDead = True
                Else
                        Console.WriteLine("CurrentSpeed = {0}", CurrentSpeed)
                End If
        End If
End Sub
```

With this, you have configured the car to send two custom events without having to define custom registration functions or declare delegate member variables. You will see the usage of this new automobile in just a moment, but first, let's check the event architecture in a bit more detail.

Events under the Hood

A VB 2010 event actually encapsulates a good deal of information. Each time you declare an event with the Event keyword, the compiler generates the following information within the defining class:

- A new hidden nested delegate type is defined automatically within your class. The name of this delegate type is always EventName+EventHandler. For example, if you have an event named Exploded, the autogenerated delegate type is named ExplodedEventHandler.

- Two hidden Public functions, one having an "add_" prefix, the other having a "remove_" prefix, are automatically added to your class. These are used internally to call Delegate.Combine() and Delegate.Remove() in order to add and remove methods to and from the list maintained by the delegate.

- A new hidden member variable is added to your class that represents a new instance of the autogenerated delegate type.

Each prefix is followed by the name of the VB 2010 event. For example, the Exploded event results in two hidden methods named add_Exploded() and remove_Exploded(). If you were to check out the CIL instructions behind add_AboutToBlow(), you would find a call to Delegate.Combine() method. Consider the partial CIL code:

```
.method public specialname instance void
        add_AboutToBlow(class CarEvents.Car/CarEngineHandler obj) cil managed synchronized
  {
    .custom instance void [mscorlib]System.Diagnostics.DebuggerNonUserCodeAttribute::↩
.ctor() = ( 01 00 00 00 )
    // Code size       25 (0x19)
    .maxstack  8
    IL_0000:  ldarg.0
    IL_0001:  ldarg.0
    IL_0002:  ldfld      class CarEvents.Car/CarEngineHandler↩
CarEvents.Car::AboutToBlowEvent
    IL_0007:  ldarg.1
    IL_0008:  call       class [mscorlib]System.Delegate↩
[mscorlib]System.Delegate::Combine(class [mscorlib]System.Delegate,
```

```
class [mscorlib]System.Delegate)
    IL_000d:  castclass  CarEvents.Car/CarEngineHandler
    IL_0012:  stfld        class CarEvents.Car/CarEngineHandler↵
CarEvents.Car::AboutToBlowEvent
    IL_0017:  nop
    IL_0018:  ret
  } // end of method Car::add_AboutToBlow
```

Furthermore, remove_AboutToBlow() makes the call to Delegate.Remove() automatically, passing in the incoming AboutToBlowEventHandler delegate:

```
.method public specialname instance void
        remove_AboutToBlow(class CarEvents.Car/CarEngineHandler obj) cil managed↵
synchronized
  {
    .custom instance void [mscorlib]System.Diagnostics.DebuggerNonUserCodeAttribute::↵
.ctor() = ( 01 00 00 00 )
    // Code size       25 (0x19)
    .maxstack  8
    IL_0000:  ldarg.0
    IL_0001:  ldarg.0
    IL_0002:  ldfld        class CarEvents.Car/CarEngineHandler↵
CarEvents.Car::AboutToBlowEvent
    IL_0007:  ldarg.1
    IL_0008:  call         class [mscorlib]System.Delegate↵
[mscorlib]System.Delegate::Remove(class [mscorlib]System.Delegate,

class [mscorlib]System.Delegate)
    IL_000d:  castclass  CarEvents.Car/CarEngineHandler
    IL_0012:  stfld        class CarEvents.Car/CarEngineHandler↵
CarEvents.Car::AboutToBlowEvent
    IL_0017:  nop
    IL_0018:  ret
  } // end of method Car::remove_AboutToBlow
```

The CIL instructions for the event declaration itself (which appears in ildasm.exe as an inverted green triangle icon) makes use of the .addon and .removeon CIL tokens to connect the correct add_XXX() and remove_XXX() methods:

```
.event CarEvents.Car/CarEngineHandler AboutToBlow
  {
.   addon instance void CarEvents.Car::add_AboutToBlow(class
    CarEvents.Car/CarEngineHandler)

    .removeon instance void CarEvents.Car::remove_AboutToBlow(class
    CarEvents.Car/CarEngineHandler)
  } // end of event Car::AboutToBlow
```

Perhaps most importantly, if you were to check out the CIL behind this iteration of the `Accelerate()` method, you would find that the delegate is invoked on your behalf. Here is a partial snapshot of the CIL that invokes the invocation list maintained by the `ExplodedEventHandler` delegate:

```
.method public instance void  Accelerate(int32 delta) cil managed
{
  ...
  IL_001d:  ldloc.0
    IL_001e:  ldstr       "Sorry, this car is dead..."
    IL_0023:  callvirt    instance
                 void CarEvents.Car/CarEngineHandler::Invoke(string)
    IL_0028:  nop
    IL_0029:  br.s        IL_00a5

}
```

As you can see, the VB 2010 `Event` keyword is quite helpful, given that it builds and manipulates raw delegates on your behalf. As you saw earlier in this chapter, however, you are able to directly manipulate delegates if you so choose.

Listening to Incoming Events

VB 2010 events also simplify the act of registering the caller-side event handlers. Rather than having to specify custom helper methods, the caller simply makes use of `AddHandler` and `RemoveHandler` directly (which triggers the correct **add_XXX()** or **remove_XXX()** method in the background). When you wish to register with an event, follow the pattern shown here:

```
'AddHandler NameOfObject.NameOfEvent,AddressOf functiontocall
AddHandler c1.AboutToBlow, AddressOf CarExploded
```

When you wish to detach from a source of events, use the `RemoveHandler`, using the following pattern:
```
RemoveHandler c1.AboutToBlow, AddressOf CarExploded
```

Given these very predictable patterns, here is the refactored `Main()` method, now using the C# event registration syntax:

```
Module Module1

    Sub Main()
        Console.WriteLine("***** Fun with Events *****" & vbLf)

        Dim c1 As New Car("SlugBug", 100, 10)

        'Register event handlers.
        AddHandler c1.AboutToBlow, AddressOf CarIsAlmostDoomed
        AddHandler c1.AboutToBlow, AddressOf CarAboutToBlow
        AddHandler c1.Exploded, AddressOf CarExploded
```

```vbnet
        Console.WriteLine("***** Speeding up *****")

        For i = 0 To 5
            c1.Accelerate(20)
        Next

        RemoveHandler c1.AboutToBlow, AddressOf CarExploded

        Console.WriteLine(vbLf & "***** Speeding up *****")

        For i = 0 To 5
            c1.Accelerate(20)
        Next
        Console.ReadLine()
    End Sub

    Public Sub CarAboutToBlow(ByVal msg As String)
        Console.WriteLine(msg)
    End Sub

    Public Sub CarIsAlmostDoomed(ByVal msg As String)
        Console.WriteLine("=> Critical Message from Car: {0}", msg)
    End Sub

    Public Sub CarExploded(ByVal msg As String)
        Console.WriteLine(msg)
    End Sub
End Module
```

To even further simplify event registration, you can use method group conversion. Consider the following iteration of `Main()`:

```vbnet
Sub Main()
        Console.WriteLine("***** Fun with Events *****" & vbLf)

        Dim c1 As New Car("SlugBug", 100, 10)

        'Register event handlers.
        AddHandler c1.AboutToBlow, AddressOf CarIsAlmostDoomed
        AddHandler c1.AboutToBlow, AddressOf CarAboutToBlow
        AddHandler c1.Exploded, AddressOf CarExploded

        Console.WriteLine("***** Speeding up *****")

        For i = 0 To 5
            c1.Accelerate(20)
        Next
        RemoveHandler c1.Exploded, AddressOf CarExploded
        Console.WriteLine(vbLf & "***** Speeding up *****")
```

```
        For i = 0 To 5
            c1.Accelerate(20)
        Next
        Console.ReadLine()
End Sub
```

Simplifying Event Registration Using Visual Studio 2010

Visual Studio 2010 offers assistance with the process of registering event handlers. When you apply the **AddHandler** syntax during event registration, you will find an IntelliSense window displayed, inviting you to hit the Space key to autocomplete the associated delegate instance (see Figure 11-2).

Console.WriteLine(msg)
End Sub
#End Region
Public Sub HookIntoEvents()
Dim newCar As New Car()
AddHandler newCar.
End S
End Modul
AddHandler Object As Event, Object As Delegate
AboutToBlow
Public Event AboutToBlow(msg As String)
Accelerate
CarEngineHandler
CurrentSpeed
Exploded
MaxSpeed
PetName
Common
All

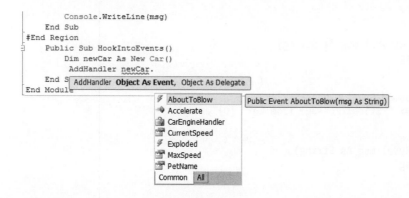

Figure 11-2. Delegate selection IntelliSense

After you hit the Space key, you are invited to enter the name of the event handler to be generated, prefixed with the **AddressOf** keyword (or simply accept the default name), as shown in Figure 11-3.

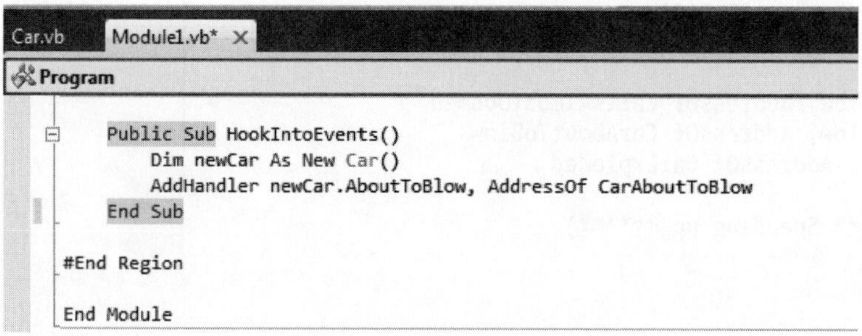

Car.vb
Module1.vb*
Program
Public Sub HookIntoEvents()
Dim newCar As New Car()
AddHandler newCar.AboutToBlow, AddressOf CarAboutToBlow
End Sub
#End Region
End Module

Figure 11-3. Delegate target format IntelliSense

IntelliSense is available to all .NET events in the base class libraries. This IDE feature is a massive time-saver, given that it saves you from having to search the .NET help system to figure out both the correct delegate to use with a particular event and the format of the delegate target method.

■ **Source Code** The CarEvents project is located under the Chapter 11 subdirectory.

Creating Custom Event Arguments

Truth be told, there is one final enhancement we could make to the current iteration of the Car class that mirrors Microsoft's recommended event pattern. As you begin to explore the events sent by a given type in the base class libraries, you will find that the first parameter of the underlying delegate is a System.Object, while the second parameter is a descendent of System.EventArgs.

The System.Object argument represents a reference to the object that sent the event (such as the Car), while the second parameter represents information regarding the event at hand. The System.EventArgs base class represents an event that is not sending any custom information:

```
Public Class EventArgs
    Public Shared ReadOnly Empty As System.EventArgs
    Public Sub New()
    End Sub
End Class
```

For simple events, you can pass an instance of EventArgs directly. However, when you wish to pass along custom data, you should build a suitable class deriving from EventArgs. For our example, assume you have a class named CarEventArgs, which maintains a string representing the message sent to the receiver:

```
Public Class CarEventArgs
    Inherits EventArgs

    Public ReadOnly msg As String
    Public Sub New(ByVal message As String)
        msg = message
    End Sub
End Class
```

With this, you would now update the CarEngineHandler delegate type definition as follows (the events would be unchanged):

```
Public Class Car
    ...
        Public Delegate Sub CarEngineHandler(ByVal sender As Object, ByVal e As
        CarEventArgs)
    ...
End Class
```

Here, when firing the events from within the **Accelerate()** method, you would now need to supply a reference to the current **Car** (via the **Me** keyword) and an instance of the **CarEventArgs** type. For example, consider the following partial update:

```
Public Sub Accelerate(ByVal delta As Integer)

    'If the car is dead, fire Exploded event.
    If carIsDead Then

        RaiseEvent Exploded(Me, New CarEventArgs
        ("Sorry, this  car is dead..."))
            ....
    End If
End Sub
```

On the caller's side, all you would need to do is update your event handlers to receive the incoming parameters and obtain the message via the read-only field. For example:

```
Public Sub CarAboutToBlow(ByVal sender As Object, ByVal e As CarEventArgs)
        Console.WriteLine("{0} says: {1}", sender, e.msg)
End Sub
```

If the receiver wishes to interact with the object that sent the event, you can explicitly cast the **System.Object**. From this reference, you can make use of any Public member of the object that sent the event notification:

```
Public Sub CarAboutToBlow(ByVal sender As Object, ByVal e As CarEventArgs)
    'Just to be safe, perform a
    'runtime check before casting.
    If TypeOf sender Is Car Then
        Dim c As Car = DirectCast(sender, Car)
        Console.WriteLine("Critical Message from {0}: {1}", c.PetName, e.msg)
    End If
End Sub
```

■ **Source Code** The PrimAndProperCarEvents project is located under the Chapter 11 subdirectory.

The Generic EventHandler(Of T) Delegate

Given that so many custom delegates take an **object** as the first parameter and an **EventArgs** descendent as the second, you could further streamline the previous example by using the generic **EventHandler(Of T)** type, where T is your custom **EventArgs** type. Consider the following update to the **Car** type (notice how we no longer need to define a custom delegate type at all):

```
Public Class Car
    Public Event Exploded As EventHandler(Of CarEventArgs)
    Public Event AboutToBlow As EventHandler(Of CarEventArgs)
    ...
End Class
```

The Main() method could then use EventHandler(Of CarEventArgs) anywhere we previously specified CarEventHandler (or, once again, use method group conversion):

```
Module Module1
    Sub Main()
        Console.WriteLine("***** Prim and Proper Events *****" & vbLf)

        'Make a car as usual
        Dim c1 As New Car("SlugBug", 100, 10)

        ' Register event handlers.
        AddHandler c1.AboutToBlow, AddressOf CarIsAlmostDoomed
        AddHandler c1.AboutToBlow, AddressOf CarAboutToBlow

        Dim d As New EventHandler(Of CarEventArgs)(AddressOf CarExploded)
        AddHandler c1.Exploded, d
        ...
    End Sub
End Module
```

Great! At this point, you have seen the core aspects of working with delegates and events in the VB 2010 language. While you could use this information for just about all of your callback needs, we will wrap up this chapter with a look at some final simplifications, specifically anonymous methods and lambda expressions.

■ **Source Code** The PrimAndProperCarEvents (Generic) project is located under the Chapter 11 subdirectory.

Understanding VB 2010 Anonymous Methods

As you have seen, when a caller wishes to listen to incoming events, it must define a custom method in a class (or structure) that matches the signature of the associated delegate, for example:

```
Module Module1
    Sub Main()
        Dim t As New SomeType()
        'Assume "SomeDelegate" can point to methods taking no
        'args and having no return value.
        AddHandler t.SomeEvent,AddressOf MyEventHandler
    End Sub
```

```
        'Typically only called by the SomeDelegate object.
        Public Sub MyEventHandler()
            'Do something when event is fired.
        End Sub
End Module
```

When you think about it, however, methods such as `MyEventHandler()` are seldom intended to be called by any part of the program other than the invoking delegate. As far as productivity is concerned, it is a bit of a bother (though in no way a showstopper) to manually define a separate method to be called by the delegate object.

To address this point, it is possible to associate an event directly to a block of code statements at the time of event registration. Formally, such code is termed an *anonymous method*. To illustrate the syntax, check out the following `Main()` method, which handles the events sent from the `Car` class using anonymous methods, rather than specifically named event handlers:

```
Module Module1
    Sub Main()

    Console.WriteLine("***** Anonymous Methods *****" & vbLf)
    Dim c1 As New Car("SlugBug", 100, 10)

    'Register event handlers as anonymous methods.
    AddHandler c1.AboutToBlow, Sub()
                                Console.WriteLine("Eek! Going too fast!")
                            End Sub

     AddHandler c1.AboutToBlow, Sub(sender As Object, e As CarEventArgs)
                        Console.WriteLine("Message from Car: {0}", e.msg)
                            End Sub

    AddHandler c1.Exploded, Sub(sender As Object, e As CarEventArgs)
                        Console.WriteLine("Fatal Message from Car: {0}", e.msg)
                            End Sub

     'This will eventually trigger the events.
      For i As Integer = 0 To 5
            c1.Accelerate(20)
      Next

      Console.ReadLine()
    End Sub
End Module
```

■ **Note** The Statement (`Sub` or `Function`) block of an anonymous method must be terminated by an `End Function` or `End Sub`. If you fail to do so, you are issued a compilation error.

Again, notice that the `Module1` type no longer defines specific Shared event handlers such as `CarAboutToBlow()` or `CarExploded()`. Rather, the unnamed (aka anonymous) methods are defined inline at the time the caller is handling the event using the `AddHandler` syntax. The basic syntax of an anonymous method matches the following pseudo-code:

```
Module Module1
    Sub Main()
      Dim t As New SomeType()
      AddHandler t.SomeEvent,Sub(optionallySpecifiedDelegateArgs)
                        '...
                        End Sub

    End Sub
End Module
```

When handling the first `AboutToBlow` event within the previous `Main()` method, notice that you are not specifying the arguments passed from the delegate:

```
AddHandler c1.AboutToBlow,
          Sub(sender As Object, e As CarEventArgs)
              Console.WriteLine("Eek! Going too fast!")
          End Sub
```

Strictly speaking, you are not required to receive the incoming arguments sent by a specific event. However, if you wish to make use of the possible incoming arguments, you will need to specify the parameters prototyped by the delegate type (as shown in the second handling of the `AboutToBlow` and `Exploded` events). For example:

```
AddHandler c1.AboutToBlow,
          Sub(sender As Object, e As CarEventArgs)
              Console.WriteLine("Critical Message from Car: {0}", e.msg)
          End Sub
```

Accessing Local Variables

Anonymous methods are interesting in that they are able to access the local variables of the method that defines them. Formally speaking, such variables are termed *outer variables* of the anonymous method. A few important points about the interaction between an anonymous method scope and the scope of the defining method should be mentioned:

- An anonymous method cannot access `ByRef` parameters of the defining method

- An anonymous method cannot have a local variable with the same name as a local variable in the outer method

- An anonymous method can access instance variables (or Shared variables, as appropriate) in the outer class scope

- An anonymous method can declare local variables with the same name as outer class member variables (the local variables have a distinct scope and hide the outer class member variables)

Assume our `Main()` method defined a local Integer named **aboutToBlowCounter**. Within the anonymous methods that handle the **AboutToBlow** event, we will increment this counter by 1 and print out the tally before `Main()` completes:

```
Sub Main()
        Console.WriteLine("***** Anonymous Methods *****" & vbLf)

        Dim aboutToBlowCounter As Integer = 0

        'Make a car as usual
        Dim c1 As New Car("SlugBug", 100, 10)

        ' Register event handlers as anonymous methods.
        AddHandler c1.AboutToBlow,Sub()
                aboutToBlowCounter  = aboutToBlowCounter + 1
                Console.WriteLine("Eek! Going too fast!")
            End sub

        AddHandler c1.AboutToBlow,Sub(sender As Object, e As        CarEventArgs)
                aboutToBlowCounter += 1
                Console.WriteLine("Message from Car: {0}", e.msg)
            End Sub

        AddHandler c1.Exploded,Sub(sender As Object, e As CarEventArgs)
            Console.WriteLine("Critical Message from Car: {0}", e.msg)
           End Sub
    ...
        Console.WriteLine("AboutToBlow event was fired {0} times.", aboutToBlowCounter)
        Console.ReadLine()
End Sub
```

Once you run this updated `Main()` method, you will find the final `Console.WriteLine()` reports the **AboutToBlow** event was fired twice.

■ **Source Code** The AnonymousMethods project is located under the Chapter 11 subdirectory.

Understanding Lambda Expressions

To conclude our look at the .NET event architecture, we will examine VB 2010 *lambda expressions*. As just explained, VB 2010 supports the ability to handle events "inline" by assigning a block of code statements directly to an event using anonymous methods, rather than building a stand-alone method to be called by the underlying delegate. Lambda expressions are nothing more than a very concise way to author anonymous methods and ultimately simplify how we work with the .NET delegate type.

To set the stage for our examination of lambda expressions, create a new Console Application named SimpleLambdaExpressions. To begin, consider the FindAll() method of the generic List(Of T) class. This method can be called when you need to extract out a subset of items from the collection, and is prototyped like so:

```
'Method of the System.Collections.Generic.List(Of T) class.
Public Function FindAll(ByVal match As Predicate(Of T)) As List(Of T)
```

As you can see, this method returns a new List(Of T) that represents the subset of data. Also notice that the sole parameter to FindAll() is a generic delegate of type System.Predicate(Of T). This delegate can point to any method returning a Boolean, and takes a single type parameter as the only input parameter:

```
'This delegate is used by FindAll() method
'to extract out the subset.
Public Delegate Function Predicate(Of T)(ByVal obj As T) As Boolean
```

When you call FindAll(), each item in the List(Of T) is passed to the method pointed to by the Predicate(Of T) object. The implementation of said method will perform some calculations to see if the incoming data matches the necessary criteria, and return True or False. If this method returns True, the item will be added to the new List(Of T) that represents the subset. (Got all that?)

Before we see how lambda expressions can simplify working with FindAll(), let's work the problem out in longhand notation, using the delegate objects directly. Add a method (named TraditionalDelegateSyntax()) within your Module1 type that interacts with the System.Predicate(Of T) type to discover the even numbers in a List(Of T) of Integers:

```
Module Module1
    Sub Main()
        Console.WriteLine("***** Fun with Lambdas *****" & vbLf)
        TraditionalDelegateSyntax()
        Console.WriteLine()
        Console.ReadLine()
    End Sub

    Sub TraditionalDelegateSyntax()
        ' Make a list of Integers.
        Dim list As New List(Of Integer)()
        list.AddRange(New Integer() {20, 1, 4, 8, 9, 44})

        ' Call FindAll() using traditional delegate syntax.
        Dim callback As New Predicate(Of Integer)(AddressOf IsEvenNumber)
        Dim evenNumbers As List(Of Integer) = list.FindAll(callback)

        Console.WriteLine("Here are your even numbers:")
        For Each evenNumber As Integer In evenNumbers
            Console.Write("{0}" & vbTab, evenNumber)
        Next
        Console.WriteLine()
    End Sub
```

```
    ' Target for the Predicate() delegate.
    Private Function IsEvenNumber(ByVal i As Integer) As Boolean
        ' Is it an even number?
        Return (i Mod 2) = 0
    End Function
End Module
```

Here, we have a method (`IsEvenNumber()`) that is in charge of testing the incoming Integer parameter to see whether it is even or odd via the VB 2010 modulo operator, `Mod`. If you execute your application, you will find the numbers 20, 4, 8, and 44 print out to the console.

While this traditional approach to working with delegates behaves as expected, the `IsEvenNumber()` method is invoked only in very limited circumstances—specifically when we call `FindAll()`, which leaves us with the baggage of a full method definition. If we were to instead use an anonymous method, our code would clean up considerably. Consider the following new method of the `Module1` Module:

```
Private Sub AnonymousMethodSyntax()

    ' Make a list of Integers.
    Dim list As New List(Of Integer)()
    list.AddRange(New Integer() {20, 1, 4, 8, 9, 44})

    'Now, use an anonymous method.
    Dim evenNumbers As List(Of Integer) = list.FindAll(Function(i As Integer)
    (i Mod 2) = 0)
    Console.WriteLine("Here are your even numbers:")

    For Each evenNumber As Integer In evenNumbers
        Console.Write("{0}" & vbTab, evenNumber)
    Next
    Console.WriteLine()
End Sub
```

In this case, rather than directly creating a `Predicate(Of T)` delegate type and then authoring a stand-alone method, we are able to inline a method anonymously. While this is a step in the right direction, we are still required to use the `Function` keyword (or a strongly typed `Predicate(Of T)`), and we must ensure that the parameter list is a dead-on match. As well, as you may agree, the syntax used to define an anonymous method can be viewed as being a bit hard on the eyes, which is even more apparent here:

```
Dim evenNumbers As List(Of Integer) = list.FindAll(
        Function(i)
            Console.WriteLine("value of i is currently: {0}", i)
            Dim isEven As Boolean = ((i Mod 2) = 0)
            Return isEven
        End Function)
```

Lambda expressions can be used to simplify the call to `FindAll()` even more. When you make use of lambda syntax, there is no trace of the underlying `Function` object whatsoever. Consider the following new method to the `Module1` Module:

```
Private Sub LambdaExpressionSyntax()
        ' Make a list of Integers.
        Dim list As New List(Of Integer)()
        list.AddRange(New Integer() {20, 1, 4, 8, 9, 44})

        ' Now ,use a VB 2010 lambda expression.
        Dim evenNumbers As List(Of Integer) = list.FindAll(
            Function(i)
                Dim isEven As Boolean = ((i Mod 2) = 0)
                Return isEven
            End Function)
        Console.WriteLine("Here are your even numbers:")
        For Each evenNumber As Integer In evenNumbers
            Console.Write("{0}" & vbTab, evenNumber)
        Next
        Console.WriteLine()
End Sub
```

In this case, notice the rather strange statement of code passed into the `FindAll()` method, which is in fact a lambda expression. In this iteration of the example there is no trace of the `Predicate(Of T)` delegate. Also note that we have not authored a separate method in our module to test for odd or even numbers. All we have specified is the lambda expression:

```
Function(i) (i Mod 2) = 0
```

Before I break this syntax down, first understand that lambda expressions can be used anywhere you would have used an anonymous method or a strongly typed delegate (typically with far fewer keystrokes). Under the hood, the VB 2010 compiler translates the expression into a standard anonymous method making use of the `Predicate(Of T)` delegate type (which can be verified using `ildasm.exe` or `reflector.exe`). Specifically, the following code statement:

```
'This lambda expression...
Dim evenNumbers As List(Of Integer)=list.FindAll(Function(i)(i Mod 2)=  0)
```

is compiled into the following approximate VB 2010 code:

```
'...becomes this anonymous method.
Dim evenNumbers As List(Of Integer) = list.FindAll(Function(i)
                                      Return (i Mod 2) = 0
                                      End Function)
```

Dissecting a Lambda Expression

A VB 2010 lambda expression is written using the `Function` statement, followed by a set of parameter names wrapped in parentheses, followed by a single code statement that will process these arguments. From a very high level, a lambda expression can be understood as follows:

```
Function or Sub(ArgumentsToProcess) StatementToProcessThem
End Function / End Sub
```

Within our `LambdaExpressionSyntax()` method, things break down like so:

```
'"i" is our parameter list.
'"(i Mod 2) = 0" is our statement set to process "i".
Dim evenNumbers As List(Of Integer) = list.FindAll(Function(i) (i Mod 2) = 0)
```

The parameters of a lambda expression can be explicitly or implicitly typed. Currently, the underlying data type representing the i parameter (an Integer) is determined implicitly. The compiler is able to figure out that i is an Integer based on the context of the overall lambda expression and the underlying delegate. However, it is also possible to explicitly define the type of each parameter in the expression, by wrapping the data type and variable name in a pair of parentheses as follows:

```
'Now, explicitly state the parameter type.
Dim evenNumbers As List(Of Integer) = list.FindAll(Function(i As Integer) (i Mod 2) = 0)
```

The parameters of a lambda expression can be explicitly or implicitly typed. Currently, the underlying data type representing the i parameter (an Integer) is determined implicitly. The compiler is able to figure out that i is an Integer based on the context of the overall lambda expression and the underlying delegate. However, it is also possible to explicitly define the type of each parameter in the expression by making use of an **As** clause:

```
Dim evenNumbers As List(Of Integer) = list.FindAll(Function(i) (i Mod 2) = 0)
```

Now that you have seen the various ways to build a lambda expression, how can we read this lambda statement in human-friendly terms? Leaving the raw mathematics behind, the following explanation fits the bill:

```
' My list of parameters (in this case a single Integer named i)
' will be processed by the expression ((i Mod 2) = 0).
Dim evenNumbers As List(Of Integer) = list.FindAll(Function(i) (i Mod 2) = 0)
```

Processing Arguments Within Multiple Statements

Our first lambda expression was a single statement that ultimately evaluated to a Boolean. However, as you know, many delegate targets must perform a number of code statements. For this reason, VB 2010 allows you to build lambda expressions using multiple statement blocks. When your expression must process the parameters using multiple lines of code, you can do so by denoting a scope for these statements using the expected **End Function** or **End Sub**. Consider the following example update to our `LambdaExpressionSyntax()` method:

```
Private Sub LambdaExpressionSyntax()

        ' Make a list of Integers.
        Dim list As New List(Of Integer)()
        list.AddRange(New Integer() {20, 1, 4, 8, 9, 44})

        ' Now process each argument within a group of
        ' code statements.
        Dim evenNumbers As List(Of Integer) = list.FindAll(
            Function(i)
```

```
                Console.WriteLine("value of i is currently: {0}", i)
                Dim isEven As Boolean = ((i Mod 2) = 0)
                Return isEven
            End Function)

        Console.WriteLine("Here are your even numbers:")
        For Each evenNumber As Integer In evenNumbers
            Console.Write("{0}" & vbTab, evenNumber)
        Next
        Console.WriteLine()
End Sub
```

In this case, our parameter list (again, a single Integer named i) is being processed by a set of code statements. Beyond the calls to `Console.WriteLine()`, our modulo statement has been broken into two code statements for increased readability. Assuming each of the methods we've looked at in this section are called from within `Main()`:

```
Sub Main()
        Console.WriteLine("***** Fun with Lambdas *****" & vbLf)

        TraditionalDelegateSyntax()
        AnonymousMethodSyntax()
        Console.WriteLine()
        LambdaExpressionSyntax()
        Console.ReadLine()
End Sub
```

we will find the following output:

```
***** Fun with Lambdas *****


Here are your even numbers:

20      4       8       44

Here are your even numbers:

20      4       8       44


value of i is currently: 20

value of i is currently: 1

value of i is currently: 4
```

CHAPTER 11 ■ DELEGATES, EVENTS, AND LAMBDAS

```
value of i is currently: 8

value of i is currently: 9

value of i is currently: 44

Here are your even numbers:

20      4       8       44
```

■ **Source Code** The SimpleLambdaExpressions project can be found under the Chapter 11 subdirectory.

Lambda Expressions with Multiple (or Zero) Parameters

The lambda expressions you have seen here processed a single parameter. This is not a requirement, however, as a lambda expression may process multiple arguments—or none. To illustrate the first scenario, create a Console Application named LambdaExpressionsMultipleParams. Next, assume the following incarnation of the SimpleMath type:

```
Public Class SimpleMath
    Public Delegate Sub MathMessage(ByVal msg As String, ByVal result As Integer)

    Private mmDelegate As MathMessage

    Public Sub SetMathHandler(ByVal target As MathMessage)
        mmDelegate = target
    End Sub

    Public Sub Add(ByVal x As Integer, ByVal y As Integer)
        If mmDelegate IsNot Nothing Then
            mmDelegate.Invoke("Adding has completed!", x + y)
        End If
    End Sub
End Class
```

Notice that the `MathMessage` delegate is expecting two parameters. To represent them as a lambda expression, our `Main()` method might be written as follows:

```
Sub Main()
        'Register w/ delegate as a lambda expression.
        Dim m As New SimpleMath()

        m.SetMathHandler(Sub(msg, result)
        Console.WriteLine("Message: {0}, Result: {1}", msg, result)
                          End Sub)

        'This will execute the lambda expression.
        m.Add(10, 10)
        Console.ReadLine()
End Sub
```

Here, we are leveraging type inference, as our two parameters have not been strongly typed for simplicity. However, we could call `SetMathHandler()` as follows:

```
m.SetMathHandler(Sub(msg as String, result as Integer)
                            Console.WriteLine("Message: {0}, Result: {1}", msg, result)
                End Sub)
```

Finally, if you are using a lambda expression to interact with a delegate taking no parameters at all, you may do so by supplying a pair of empty parentheses as the parameter. Thus, assuming you have defined the following delegate type:

```
Public Delegate Function VerySimpleDelegate() As String
```

you could handle the result of the invocation as follows:

```
'Prints "Enjoy your string!" to the console.
Dim d As New VerySimpleDelegate(Function()
        Return "Enjoy your string!"
        End Function)
Console.WriteLine(d.Invoke())
```

■ **Source Code** The LambdaExpressionsMultipleParams project can be found under the Chapter 11 subdirectory.

Retrofitting the CarEvents Example Using Lambda Expressions

Given that the whole reason for lambda expressions is to provide a clean, concise manner to define an anonymous method (and therefore indirectly a manner to simplify working with delegates), let's retrofit the PrimAndProperCarEvents project we created earlier in this chapter. Here is a simplified version of that project's `Module1` Module, which makes use of lambda expression syntax (rather than the raw delegates) to hook into each event sent from the `Car` object:

```
Module Module1
    Sub Main()
        Console.WriteLine("***** More Fun with Lambdas *****" & vbLf)
        'Make a car as usual.
        Dim c1 As New Car("SlugBug", 100, 10)

        'Hook into events with lambdas!
        AddHandler c1.AboutToBlow, Sub(sender, e)
                                       Console.WriteLine(e.msg)
                                   End Sub

        AddHandler c1.Exploded, Sub(sender, e)
                                    Console.WriteLine(e.msg)
                                End Sub
        'Speed up (this will generate the events).
        Console.WriteLine(vbLf & "***** Speeding up *****")

        For i = 0 To 5
            c1.Accelerate(20)
        Next

        Console.ReadLine()
    End Sub

End Module
```

Hopefully, at this point you can see the overall role of lambda expressions and understand how they provide a "functional manner" to work with anonymous methods and delegate types. Although the new VB 2010 lambda statements (Function and Sub) might take a while to get used to, always remember a lambda expression can be broken down to the following simple equation:

```
Function /Sub(ArgumentsToProcess) StatementToProcessThem
End Function/ End Sub
```

It is worth pointing out that the LINQ programming model also makes substantial use of lambda expressions to help simplify your coding efforts. You will examine LINQ beginning in Chapter 13.

■ **Source Code** The CarEventsWithLambdas project can be found under the Chapter 11 subdirectory.

Summary

In this chapter, you have examined a number of ways in which multiple objects can partake in a bidirectional conversation. First, you looked at the VB 2010 `Delegate` keyword, which is used to indirectly construct a class derived from `System.MulticastDelegate`. As you saw, a delegate object maintains a list of methods to call when told to do so. These invocations may be made synchronously (using the `Invoke()` method) or asynchronously (via the `BeginInvoke()` and `EndInvoke()` methods). Again, the asynchronous nature of .NET delegate types will be examined in Chapter 19.

You then examined the VB 2010 `Event` and `RaiseEvent` keywords, which, when used in conjunction with a delegate type, can simplify the process of sending your event notifications to waiting callers. As shown via the resulting CIL, the .NET event model maps to hidden calls on the `System.Delegate`/`System.MulticastDelegate` types. In this light, the VB 2010 `Event` keyword is purely optional in that it simply saves you some typing time.

This chapter also explored a VB 2010 language feature termed *anonymous methods*. Using this syntactic construct, you are able to directly associate a block of code statements to a given event. As you have seen, anonymous methods are free to ignore the parameters sent by the event and have access to the "outer variables" of the defining method. You also examined a simplified way to register events using *method group conversion*.

Finally, we wrapped things up by looking at the VB 2010 *lambda* statement (`Function and Sub`). As shown, this syntax is a great shorthand notation for authoring anonymous methods, where a stack of arguments can be passed into a group of statements for processing.

■ ■ ■

## CHAPTER 12

Advanced VB 2010 Language Features

In this chapter, you'll deepen your understanding of the VB 2010 programming language by examining a number of more advanced syntactic constructs. To begin, you'll learn how to implement and use an *indexer method*. This VB 2010 mechanism enables you to build custom types that provide access to internal subitems using an array-like syntax. Once you learn how to build an indexer method, you'll see how to overload various operators (+, -, <, >, and so forth), and how to create custom explicit and implicit conversion routines for your types (and you'll learn why you may want to do this).

Next, you'll examine three topics that are particularly useful when working with LINQ-centric APIs (though you can use them outside of the context of LINQ)—extension methods, partial methods, and anonymous types.

Understanding Indexer Methods

As a programmer, you are certainly familiar with the process of accessing individual items contained within a simple array using the index operator (()), for example:

```
Module Module1
    Sub Main(ByVal args As String())

        'Loop over incoming command line arguments
        'using index operator.
        For i=0 To args.Length - 1
            Console.WriteLine("Args: {0}", args(i))
        Next

        'Declare an array of local Integers.
        Dim myInts As Integer() = {10, 9, 100, 432, 9874}
```

```
        'Use the index operator to access each element.
        For j=0 To myInts.Length - 1
                Console.WriteLine("Index {0}  = {1} ", j, myInts(j))
        Next
        Console.ReadLine()
    End Sub
End Module
```

This code is by no means a major newsflash. However, the VB 2010 language provides the capability to design custom classes and structures that may be indexed just like a standard array, by defining an *indexer method.* This particular feature is most useful when you are creating custom collection classes (generic or nongeneric).

Before examining how to implement a custom indexer, let's begin by seeing one in action. Assume you have added support for an indexer method to the custom `PeopleCollection` type developed in Chapter 10 (specifically, the CustomNonGenericCollection project). Observe the following usage within a new Console Application named SimpleIndexer:

```
'Indexers allow you to access items in an array-like fashion.
Module Module1
    Sub Main()
        Console.WriteLine("***** Fun with Indexers *****" & vbLf)

        Dim myPeople As New PeopleCollection()

        'Add objects with indexer syntax.
        myPeople(0) = New Person("Homer", "Simpson", 40)
        myPeople(1) = New Person("Marge", "Simpson", 38)
        myPeople(2) = New Person("Lisa", "Simpson", 9)
        myPeople(3) = New Person("Bart", "Simpson", 7)
        myPeople(4) = New Person("Maggie", "Simpson", 2)

        'Now obtain and display each item using indexer.
        For i = 0 To myPeople.Count - 1
            Console.WriteLine("Person number: {0}", i)
            Console.WriteLine("Name: {0} {1}", myPeople(i).FirstName, myPeople(i).LastName)
            Console.WriteLine("Age: {0}", myPeople(i).Age)
            Console.WriteLine()
        Next
        Console.ReadLine()
    End Sub
End Module
```

As you can see, indexers behave much like a custom collection supporting the `IEnumerator` and `IEnumerable` interfaces (or their generic counterparts) in that they provide access to a container's subitems. The major difference, of course, is that rather than accessing the contents using the `For Each` construct, you are able to manipulate the internal collection of sub-objects just like a standard array.

Now for the big question: How do you configure the `PeopleCollection` class (or any custom class or structure) to support this functionality? An indexer is represented as a slightly modified VB 2010 property definition. In its simplest form, an indexer is created using the `Item` keyword. Here is the required update for the `PeopleCollection` class from Chapter 10 located under the `IssuesWithNonGenericCollections` folder:

```
Public Class PeopleCollection
    Implements IEnumerable

    Private arPeople As New ArrayList()

    'Custom indexer for this class.
    Default Public Property Item(ByVal index As Integer) As Person
        Get
            Return DirectCast(arPeople(index), Person)
        End Get
        Set(ByVal value As Person)
            arPeople.Insert(index, value)
        End Set
    End Property
    ...
End Class
```

Apart from using the Item keyword, the indexer looks just like any other VB 2010 property declaration. For example, the role of the Get scope is to return the correct object to the caller. Here, we are doing so by delegating the request to the indexer of the ArrayList object! This can be achieved by calling the Insert() method of the ArrayList inside the Set scope.

As you can see, indexers are yet another form of syntactic sugar, given that this functionality can also be achieved using "normal" Public methods such as AddPerson() or GetPerson(). Nevertheless, when you support indexer methods on your custom collection types, they integrate well into the fabric of the .NET base class libraries.

While creating indexer methods is quite commonplace when you are building custom collections, do remember that generic types give you this very functionality out of the box. Consider the following method, which makes use of a generic List(Of T) of Person objects. Note that you can simply use the indexer of List(Of T) directly, for example:

```
Sub UseGenericListOfPeople()

    Dim myPeople As New List(Of Person)()
    myPeople.Add(New Person("Lisa", "Simpson", 9))
    myPeople.Add(New Person("Bart", "Simpson", 7))

    'Change first person with indexer.
    myPeople(0) = New Person("Maggie", "Simpson", 2)

    'Now obtain and display each item using indexer.
    For i = 0 To myPeople.Count - 1
        Console.WriteLine("Person number: {0}", i)
            Console.WriteLine("Name: {0} {1}", myPeople(i).FirstName,
            myPeople(i).LastName)
            Console.WriteLine("Age: {0}", myPeople(i).Age)
            Console.WriteLine()
    Next
End Sub
```

■ **Source Code** The SimpleIndexer project is located under the Chapter 12 subdirectory.

Indexing Data Using String Values

The current PeopleCollection class defined an indexer that allowed the caller to identify subitems using a numerical value. Understand, however, that this is not a requirement of an indexer method. Suppose you'd prefer to contain the Person objects using a System.Collections.Generic.Dictionary(Of TKey, TValue) rather than an ArrayList. Given that ListDictionary types allow access to the contained types using a string token (such as a person's first name), you could define an indexer as follows:

```vb
Public Class PeopleCollection
    Implements IEnumerable

    Dim listPeople As New Dictionary(Of String, Person)()

    'This indexer returns a person based on a string index.
    Default Public Property Item(ByVal name As String) As Person
        Get
            Return DirectCast(listPeople(name), Person)
        End Get
        Set(ByVal value As Person)
            listPeople(name) = value
        End Set
    End Property

    Public Sub ClearPeople()
        listPeople.Clear()
    End Sub

    Public ReadOnly Property Count() As Integer
        Get
            Return listPeople.Count
        End Get
    End Property

    Function GetEnumerator() As IEnumerator Implements IEnumerable.GetEnumerator
        Return listPeople.GetEnumerator()
    End Function
End Class
```

The caller would now be able to interact with the contained **Person** objects as shown here:

```
Module Module1

    Sub Main()
        Console.WriteLine("***** Fun with Indexers *****" & vbLf)
        Dim myPeople As New PeopleCollection()
        myPeople("Homer") = New Person("Homer", "Simpson", 40)
        myPeople("Marge") = New Person("Marge", "Simpson", 38)

        'Get "Homer" and print data.
        Dim homer As Person = myPeople("Homer")

        Console.WriteLine(homer.ToString())
        Console.ReadLine()
    End Sub

End Module
```

Again, if you were to use the generic **Dictionary(Of TKey, TValue)** type directly, you'd gain the indexer method functionality out of the box, without building a custom, non-generic class supporting a String indexer.

■ **Source Code** The StringIndexer project is located under the Chapter 12 subdirectory.

Overloading Indexer Methods

Understand that indexer methods may be overloaded on a single class or structure. Thus, if it makes sense to allow the caller to access subitems using a numerical index or a String value, you might define multiple indexers for a single type. By way of example, if you have ever programmed with ADO.NET (.NET's native database-access API), you may recall that the **DataSet** type supports a property named **Tables**, which returns to you a strongly typed **DataTableCollection** type. As it turns out, **DataTableCollection** defines three indexers to get and set **DataTable** objects—one by ordinal position, and the others by a friendly string moniker and optional containing namespace:

```
Public NotInheritable Class DataTableCollection
    Inherits InternalDataCollectionBase

    ...
    'Overloaded indexers!
    Public ReadOnly Property Item(ByVal name As String) As DataTable

    Public ReadOnly Property Item(ByVal name As String, ByVal
    tableNamespace As String) As DataTable

    Public ReadOnly Property Item(ByVal index As Integer) As DataTable

End Class
```

465

Note that a number of types in the base class libraries support indexer methods. So be aware, even if your current project does not require you to build custom indexers for your classes and structures, that many types already support this syntax.

Indexers with Multiple Dimensions

You can also create an indexer method that takes multiple parameters. Assume you have a custom collection that stores subitems in a 2D array. If this is the case, you may define an indexer method as follows:

```
Public Class SomeContainer
    Private my2DintArray As Integer(,) = New Integer(10, 10) {}

    Public Property Item(ByVal row As
    Integer,ByVal column As Integer) As Integer
        'get or set value from 2D array
    End Function
End Class
```

Again, unless you are building a highly stylized custom collection class, you won't have much need to build a multi-dimensional indexer. Still, once again ADO.NET showcases how useful this construct can be. The ADO.NET DataTable is essentially a collection of rows and columns, much like a piece of graph paper or the general structure of a Microsoft Excel spreadsheet.

While DataTable objects are typically populated on your behalf using a related "data adapter," the following code illustrates how to manually create an in-memory DataTable containing three columns (for the first name, last name, and age of each record). Notice how once we have added a single row to the DataTable, we use a multidimensional indexer to drill into each column of the first (and only) row. (If you are following along, you'll need to import the System.Data namespace into your code file.)

```
Sub MultiIndexerWithDataTable()

        'Make a simple DataTable with 3 columns.
        Dim myTable As New DataTable()
        myTable.Columns.Add(New DataColumn("FirstName"))
        myTable.Columns.Add(New DataColumn("LastName"))
        myTable.Columns.Add(New DataColumn("Age"))

        'Now add a row to the table.
        myTable.Rows.Add("Mel", "Appleby", 60)

        'Use multi-dimension indexer to get details of first row.
        Console.WriteLine("First Name: {0}", myTable.Rows(0)(0))
        Console.WriteLine("Last Name: {0}", myTable.Rows(0)(1))
        Console.WriteLine("Age : {0}", myTable.Rows(0)(2))
End Sub
```

Do be aware that we'll take a rather deep dive into ADO.NET beginning with Chapter 21, so if some of the previous code seems unfamiliar, fear not. The main point of this example is that indexer methods can support multiple dimensions, and if used correctly, can simplify the way you interact with contained subobjects in custom collections.

Indexer Definitions on Interface Types

Indexers can be defined on a given .NET interface type to allow supporting types to provide a custom implementation. Here is a simple example of an interface that defines a protocol for obtaining String objects using a numerical indexer:

```
Public Interface IStringContainer
    'This interface defines an indexer that returns
    'Strings based on a numerical index.
    Property Item(ByVal index As Integer) As String
End Interface
```

With this interface definition, any class or structure that implements this interface must now support a read/write indexer that manipulates subitems using a numerical value.

That wraps up the first major topic of this chapter. While understanding the syntax of VB 2010 indexers is important, as explained in Chapter 10, typically the only time a programmer needs to build a custom generic collection class is to add *constraints* to the type parameters. If you happen to build such a class, adding a custom indexer will make your collection class look and feel like the standard collection classes in the .NET base class libraries.

Now let's examine a language feature that lets you build custom classes or structures that respond uniquely to the intrinsic operators of VB 2010. Allow me to introduce operator overloading.

Understanding Operator Overloading

VB 2010, like any programming language, has a canned set of tokens that are used to perform basic operations on intrinsic types. For example, you know that the + operator can be applied to two Integers in order to yield a larger Integer:

```
' The + operator applied to Integers.
Dim a As Integer = 100
Dim b As Integer = 240
Dim c As Integer = a + b  ' c is now 340
```

Once again, this is no major newsflash, but have you ever stopped and noticed how the same + operator can be applied to most intrinsic VB 2010 data types? For example, consider this code:

```
' The + operator applied to Strings.
Dim s1 As String = "Hello"
Dim s2 As String = " world!"
Dim s3 As String = s1 + s2  ' s3 is now "Hello world!"
```

In essence, the + operator functions in specific ways based on the supplied data types (Strings or Integers in this case). When the + operator is applied to numerical types, the result is the summation of the operands. However, when the + operator is applied to String types, the result is String concatenation.

The VB 2010 language gives you the capability to build custom classes and structures that also respond uniquely to the same set of basic tokens (such as the + operator). Be aware that you cannot overload every intrinsic VB 2010 operator. Table 12-1 outlines the "overloadability" of the core operators.

Table 12-1. Overloadability of VB 2010 Operators

VB 2010 Operator	Overloadability
+, -, Not, IsTrue, IsFalse	These unary operators can be overloaded.
+, -, *, /, &, \, ^, And, Or, Xor	These binary operators can be overloaded.
=, <>, <, >, <=, >=	The comparison operators of VB 2010 (which are technically also binary operators) can be overloaded. VB 2010 will demand that "like" operators (i.e., < and >, <= and >=, = and <>) are overloaded together to keep the defining type consistent.
CType	The CType operator can be overloaded to implement a custom conversion routine.

Overloading Binary Operators

To illustrate the process of overloading binary operators, assume the following simple Point class is defined in a new Console Application named OverloadedOps:

```
Public Class Point

    Public Property X() As Integer
    Public Property Y() As Integer

    Public Sub New(ByVal xPos As Integer, ByVal yPos As Integer)
        X = xPos
        Y = yPos
    End Sub

    Public Overrides Function ToString() As String
        Return String.Format("[{0}, {1}]", Me.X, Me.Y)
    End Function
End Class
```

Now, logically speaking, it makes sense to "add" Points together. For example, if you added together two Point variables, you should receive a new Point that is the summation of the X and Y values. Of course, it may also be helpful to subtract one Point from another. Ideally, you would like to be able to author the following code:

```
Module Module1
  Sub Main()
    Console.WriteLine("***** Fun with Overloaded Operators *****" & vbLf)

    ' Make two points.
    Dim ptOne As New Point(100, 100)
    Dim ptTwo As New Point(40, 40)
```

```
      Console.WriteLine("ptOne = {0}", ptOne)
      Console.WriteLine("ptTwo = {0}", ptTwo)

      'Add the points to make a bigger point?
      Console.WriteLine("ptOne + ptTwo: {0} ", ptOne + ptTwo)

      'Subtract the points to make a smaller point?
      Console.WriteLine("ptOne - ptTwo: {0} ", ptOne - ptTwo)
      Console.ReadLine()
  End Sub
End Module
```

However, as our **Point** now stands, we will receive compile-time errors, as the **Point** type does not know how to respond to the + or - operators.

To equip a custom type to respond uniquely to intrinsic operators, VB 2010 provides the **Operator** keyword, which you can use only in conjunction with Shared methods. When you overload a binary operator (such as + and -), you will most often pass in two arguments that are the same type as the defining class (a **Point** in this example), as illustrated in the following code update:

```
Public Class Point
    …
    'overloaded operator +
    Public Shared Operator +(ByVal p1 As Point, ByVal p2 As Point) As Point
        Return New Point(p1.X + p2.X, p1.Y + p2.Y)
    End Operator

    'overloaded operator -
    Public Shared Operator -(ByVal p1 As Point, ByVal p2 As Point) As Point
        Return New Point(p1.X - p2.X, p1.Y - p2.Y)
    End Operator
End Class
```

The logic behind operator + is simply to return a brand new **Point** object based on the summation of the fields of the incoming **Point** parameters. Thus, when you write **pt1 + pt2**, under the hood you can envision the following hidden call to the Shared operator + method:

```
' Pseudo-code: Dim p3 As Point=Point.Operator +(p1, p2)
Dim p3 As New Point(10,10)
p3=p1+p2
```

Likewise, **p1 – p2** maps to the following:

```
'  Pseudo-code: Dim p4 As Point= Point.Operator -(p1, p2)
Dim p4 As New Point(60,40)
p4=p1-p2
```

With this update, our program now compiles, and we find we are able to add and subtract `Point` objects:

```
ptOne = [100, 100]

ptTwo = [40, 40]

ptOne + ptTwo: [140, 140]

ptOne - ptTwo: [60, 60]
```

When you are overloading a binary operator, you are not required to pass in two parameters of the same type. If it makes sense to do so, one of the arguments can differ. For example, here is an overloaded operator + that allows the caller to obtain a new `Point` that is based on a numerical adjustment:

```
Public Class Point
    …
    Public Shared Operator + (ByVal p1 As Point,
                              ByVal change As Integer) As Point
        Return New Point(p1.X + change, p1.Y + change)
    End Operator

    Public Shared Operator + (ByVal change As Integer,
                              ByVal p1 As Point)  As Point
        Return New Point(p1.X + change, p1.Y + change)
    End Operator
End Class
```

Notice that you need both versions of the method if you want the arguments to be passed in either order (i.e., you can't just define one of the methods and expect the compiler to automatically support the other one). We are now able to use these new versions of operator + as follows:

```
'Prints [110, 110]
Dim biggerPoint As New Point(110,110)
biggerPoint = ptOne + 10
Console.WriteLine("ptOne + 10 = {0}", biggerPoint)

'Prints [120, 120]
Console.WriteLine("10 + biggerPoint = {0}", 10 + biggerPoint)
Console.WriteLine()
```

And What of the += and −= Operators?

If you overload the + and - operators in VB 2010, you get the += and -= operators for free. Thus, given that the `Point` structure has already overloaded the + and - operators, you can write the following:

```
Sub  Main()
...          ...
        ' Freebie +=
        Dim ptThree As New Point(90, 5)
        Console.WriteLine("ptThree = {0}", ptThree)
        ptThree += ptTwo
        Console.WriteLine("ptThree += ptTwo: {0}", ptThree)

        ' Freebie -=
        Dim ptFour As New Point(0, 500)
        Console.WriteLine("ptFour = {0}", ptFour)
        ptFour -= ptThree
        Console.WriteLine("ptFour -= ptThree: {0}", ptFour)

        Console.ReadLine()
End Sub
```

Overloading Unary Operators

VB 2010 also allows you to overload various unary operators, such as `IsTrue` and `IsFalse`. When you overload a unary operator, you also define a Shared method via the `Operator` keyword; however, in this case you simply pass in a single parameter that is the same type as the defining class/structure. For example, if you were to update the `Point` with the following overloaded operators:

```
Public Class Point

    '...

    Public Sub New(ByVal xVal As Integer)
        X = xVal
    End Sub

    'calculate IsTrue of Point.
    Public Shared Operator IsTrue(ByVal p1 As Point) As Boolean
        Return (p1.X <> 0 OrElse p1.Y <> 0)
    End Operator

    'calculate IsFalse of Point.
    Public Shared Operator IsFalse(ByVal p1 As Point) As Boolean
        Return (p1.X = 0 AndAlso p1.Y = 0)
    End Operator
End Class
```

you could determine if a Point is "true" like this:

```
Sub Main()

    Dim pt1 As New Point(2, 4)   ' This is a "True" Point
    If (pt1) Then
        Console.WriteLine("pt1 is True")
```

```
    Else
        Console.WriteLine("pt1 is False")
    End If

    Dim pt2 As New Point(0, 0)  ' This is a "False" Point.
    If (pt2) Then
        Console.WriteLine("pt2 is True")
    Else
        Console.WriteLine("pt2 is False")
    End If

End Sub
```

Overloading Equality Operators

As you may recall from Chapter 6, `System.Object.Equals()` can be overridden to perform value-based (rather than referenced-based) comparisons between reference types. If you choose to override `Equals()` (and the often related `System.Object.GetHashCode()` method), it is trivial to overload the equality operators (= and <>). To illustrate, here is the updated `Point` type:

```
'This incarnation of Point also overloads the = and <> operators.

Public Class Point
    ...
        Public Overrides Function Equals(ByVal o As Object) As Boolean
            Return o.ToString() = Me.ToString()
        End Function

        Public Overrides Function GetHashCode() As Integer
            Return Me.ToString().GetHashCode()
        End Function

        'Now let's overload the = and <> operators.
        Public Shared Operator =(ByVal p1 As Point, ByVal p2 As Point) As Boolean
            Return p1.Equals(p2)
        End Operator

        Public Shared Operator <>(ByVal p1 As Point, ByVal p2 As Point) As Boolean
            Return Not p1.Equals(p2)
        End Operator
    ...
End Class
```

Notice how the implementation of operator = and operator <> simply makes a call to the overridden `Equals()` method to get the bulk of the work done. Given this, you can now exercise your `Point` class as follows:

```
' Make use of the overloaded equality operators.
Sub Main()
...
    Console.WriteLine("ptOne = ptTwo : {0}", ptOne = ptTwo)
    Console.WriteLine("ptOne <>. ptTwo : {0}", ptOne <> ptTwo)
...
End Sub
```

As you can see, it is quite intuitive to compare two objects using the well-known = and <> operators rather than making a call to `Object.Equals()`. If you do overload the equality operators for a given class, keep in mind that VB 2010 demands that if you override the = operator, you must also override the <> operator (if you forget, the compiler will let you know).

Overloading Comparison Operators

In Chapter 9, you learned how to implement the `IComparable` interface in order to compare the relationship between two like objects. You can, in fact, also overload the comparison operators (<, >, <=, and >=) for the same class. As with the equality operators, VB 2010 demands that if you overload <, you must also overload >. The same holds true for the <= and >= operators. If the `Point` type overloaded these comparison operators, the object user could now compare `Point`s as follows:

```
'Using the overloaded < and > operators.
Sub Main()
    ...
        Console.WriteLine("ptOne < ptTwo : {0}", ptOne < ptTwo)
        Console.WriteLine("ptOne > ptTwo : {0}", ptOne > ptTwo)
        Console.ReadLine()
End Sub
```

Assuming you have implemented the `IComparable` interface, overloading the comparison operators is trivial. Here is the updated class definition:

```
'Point is also comparable using the comparison operators.
Public Class Point
    Implements IComparable
...
    Public Function CompareTo(ByVal obj As Object) As Integer Implements
    IComparable.CompareTo
        If TypeOf obj Is Point Then

            Dim p As Point = DirectCast(obj, Point)
            If Me.X > p.X AndAlso Me.Y > p.Y Then
                Return 1
            End If
```

```
            If Me.X < p.X AndAlso Me.Y < p.Y Then
                Return -1
            Else
                Return 0
            End If
        Else
            Throw New ArgumentException()
        End If
    End Function

    Public Shared Operator <(ByVal p1 As Point, ByVal p2 As Point) As Boolean
        Return (p1.CompareTo(p2) < 0)
    End Operator

    Public Shared Operator >(ByVal p1 As Point, ByVal p2 As Point) As Boolean
        Return (p1.CompareTo(p2) > 0)
    End Operator

    Public Shared Operator <=(ByVal p1 As Point, ByVal p2 As Point) As Boolean
        Return (p1.CompareTo(p2) <= 0)
    End Operator

    Public Shared Operator >=(ByVal p1 As Point, ByVal p2 As Point) As Boolean
        Return (p1.CompareTo(p2) >= 0)
    End Operator
..
End Class
```

The Internal Representation of Overloaded Operators

Like any VB 2010 programming element, overloaded operators are represented using specific CIL syntax. To begin examining what takes place behind the scenes, open the **OverloadedOps.exe** assembly using **ildasm.exe**. As you can see from Figure 12-1, the overloaded operators are internally expressed via hidden methods, such as **op_Addition()**, **op_Subtraction()**, **op_Equality()**, and so on.

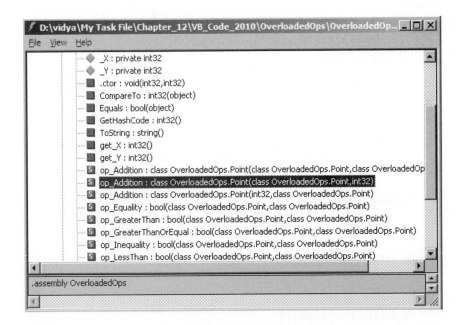

Figure 12-1. In terms of CIL, overloaded operators map to hidden methods

Now, if you were to examine the specific CIL instructions for the **op_Addition** method (the one that takes two Point parameters), you would find that the **specialname** method decoration has also been inserted by the compiler:

```
.method public  specialname static
  class OverloadedOps.Point
  op_Addition(class OverloadedsOps.Point p1,
          class OverloadedOps.Point p2) cil managed
{
  ...
}
```

The truth of the matter is that any operator that you may overload equates to a specially named method in terms of CIL. Table 12-2 documents the VB 2010 operator-to-CIL mapping for the most common VB 2010 operators.

Table 12-2. VB 2010 Operator-to-CIL Special Name Road Map

Intrinsic VB 2010 Operator	CIL Representation
+	op_Addition()
-	op_Subtraction()
*	op_Multiply()
/	op_Division()
=	op_Equality()
>	op_GreaterThan()
<	op_LessThan()
<>	op_Inequality()
>=	op_GreaterThanOrEqual()
<=	op_LessThanOrEqual()
-=	op_SubtractionAssignment()

Final Thoughts Regarding Operator Overloading

As you have seen, VB 2010 provides the capability to build types that can respond uniquely to various intrinsic, well-known operators. Now, before you go and retrofit all your classes to support such behavior, you must be sure that the operator(s) you are about to overload make some sort of logical sense in the world at large.

For example, let's say you overloaded the multiplication operator for the MiniVan class. What exactly would it mean to multiply two MiniVan objects? Not much. In fact, it would be very confusing for teammates to see the following use of MiniVan objects.

```
' Huh?! This is far from intuitive...
Dim newVan As MiniVan = myVan * yourVan
```

Overloading operators is generally useful only when you're building utility types. Strings, points, rectangles, fractions, and hexagons make good candidates for operator overloading. People, managers, cars, database connections, and web pages do not. As a rule of thumb, if an overloaded operator makes it *harder* for the user to understand a type's functionality, don't do it. Use this feature wisely.

Also, be aware that even if you do not generally overload operators for your custom classes, numerous types in the base class libraries have already done so. For example, the System.Drawing.dll assembly provides a Windows Forms-centric Point definition that overloads numerous operators. Notice the operator icon from the Visual Studio 2010 Object Browser shown in Figure 12-2.

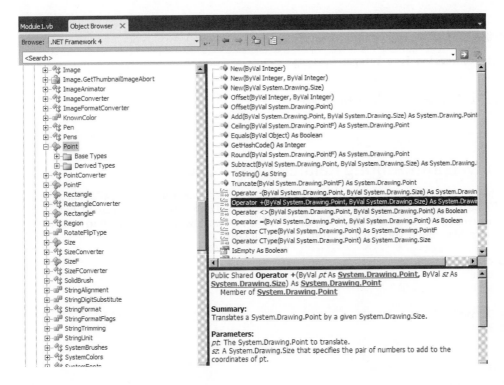

Figure 12-2. Numerous types in the base class libraries have already overloaded operators.

■ **Source Code** The OverloadedOps project is located under the Chapter 12 subdirectory.

Understanding Custom Type Conversions

Let's now examine a topic closely related to operator overloading: custom type conversions. To set the stage for the discussion, let's quickly review the notion of explicit and implicit conversions between numerical data and related class types.

Recall: Numerical Conversions

In terms of the intrinsic numerical types (**SByte**, **Integer**, **Single** etc.), an explicit conversion is required when you attempt to store a larger value in a smaller container as this may result in a loss of data. Basically, this is your way to tell the compiler, "Leave me alone, I know what I am trying to do." An explicit conversion can be achieved with the help of VB constructs such as **CInt** and **CLng**. Conversely, an implicit conversion happens automatically when you attempt to place a smaller type in a destination type that will not result in a loss of data:

```
Sub Main()
Dim a As Integer = 123

        'Implicit conversion from Integer to Long
        Dim b As Long = a

        'Explicit conversion from Long to Integer
        Dim c As Integer = CInt(b)
End Sub
```

Recall: Conversions Among Related Class Types

As shown in Chapter 6, class types may be related by classical inheritance (the "is-a" relationship). In this case, the VB 2010 conversion process allows you to cast up and down the class hierarchy. For example, a derived class can always be implicitly cast to a base type. However, if you wish to store a base class type in a derived variable, you must perform an explicit cast:

```
'Two related class types.
Public Class Base
End Class

Public Class Derived
    Inherits Base
End Class

Module Module1
    Sub Main()

        'Implicit cast between derived type to base.
        Dim myBaseType As Base
        myBaseType = New Derived()

        'Must explicitly cast to store base reference.
        Dim myDerivedType As Derived = CType(myBaseType, Derived)
    End Sub
End Module
```

This explicit cast works due to the fact that the **Base** and **Derived** classes are related by classical inheritance. However, what if you have two class types in *different hierarchies* with no common parent (other than **System.Object**) that require conversions? Given that they are not related by classical inheritance, explicit casting offers no help.

On a related note, consider value types, such as structures. Assume you have two .NET structures named **Square** and **Rectangle**. Given that structures cannot leverage classic inheritance (as they are always **NotInheritable**), you have no natural way to cast between these seemingly related types.

While you could create helper methods in the structures (such as **Rectangle.ToSquare()**), VB 2010 lets you build custom conversion routines that allow your types to respond to the **CType** operator. Therefore, if you configured the structures correctly, you would be able to use the following syntax to explicitly convert between them as follows:

```
'Convert a Rectangle to a Square!
Dim rect As Rectangle
rect.Width = 3
rect.Height = 10
Dim sq As Square = CType(rect, Square)
```

Creating Custom Conversion Routines

Begin by creating a new Console Application named CustomConversions. VB 2010 provides two keywords, Narrowing and Widening, that you can use to control how your types respond during an attempted conversion. Assume you have the following class definitions:

```
Public Class Rectangle
    Public Property Width() As Integer
    Public Property Height() As Integer

    Public Sub New(ByVal w As Integer, ByVal h As Integer)
        Width = w
        Height = h
    End Sub

    Public Sub New()
    End Sub

    Public Sub Draw()
        For i = 0 To Height - 1
            For j = 0 To Width - 1
                Console.Write("*")
            Next
            Console.WriteLine()
        Next
    End Sub

    Public Overrides Function ToString() As String
        Return String.Format("[Width = {0}; Height = {1}]", Width, Height)
    End Function
End Class

Public Class Square
    Public Property Length() As Integer

    Public Sub New(ByVal l As Integer)
        Length = l
    End Sub

    Public Sub New()
    End Sub
```

```
    Public Sub Draw()
        For i = 0 To Length - 1
            For j = 0 To Length - 1
                Console.Write("*")
            Next
            Console.WriteLine()
        Next
    End Sub

    Public Overrides Function ToString() As String
        Return String.Format("[Length = {0}]", Length)
    End Function

    'Rectangles can be explicitly converted
    'into Squares.
    Public Shared Narrowing Operator CType(ByVal r As Rectangle) As Square
        Dim s As New Square()
        s.Length = r.Height
        Return s
    End Operator
End Class
```

Notice that this iteration of the **Square** type defines an explicit conversion operator (using the **Narrowing** keyword). Like the process of overloading an operator, conversion routines make use of the VB 2010 **Operator** keyword, in conjunction with the **Narrowing** or **Widening** keyword, and must be defined as Shared. The incoming parameter is the entity you are converting *from*, while the operator type is the entity you are converting *to*.

In this case, the assumption is that a square (being a geometric pattern in which all sides are of equal length) can be obtained from the height of a rectangle. Thus, you are free to convert a **Rectangle** into a **Square** as follows:

```
Module Module1
    Sub Main()
        Console.WriteLine("***** Fun with Conversions *****" & vbLf)

        'Make a Rectangle.
  Dim r As New Rectangle(15, 4)
        Console.WriteLine(r.ToString())
        r.Draw()
        Console.WriteLine()

        'Convert r into a Square,
        'based on the height of the Rectangle.
        Dim s As Square = CType(r, Square)
        Console.WriteLine(s.ToString())
        s.Draw()
        Console.ReadLine()
    End Sub
End Module
```

The output can be seen in Figure 12-3.

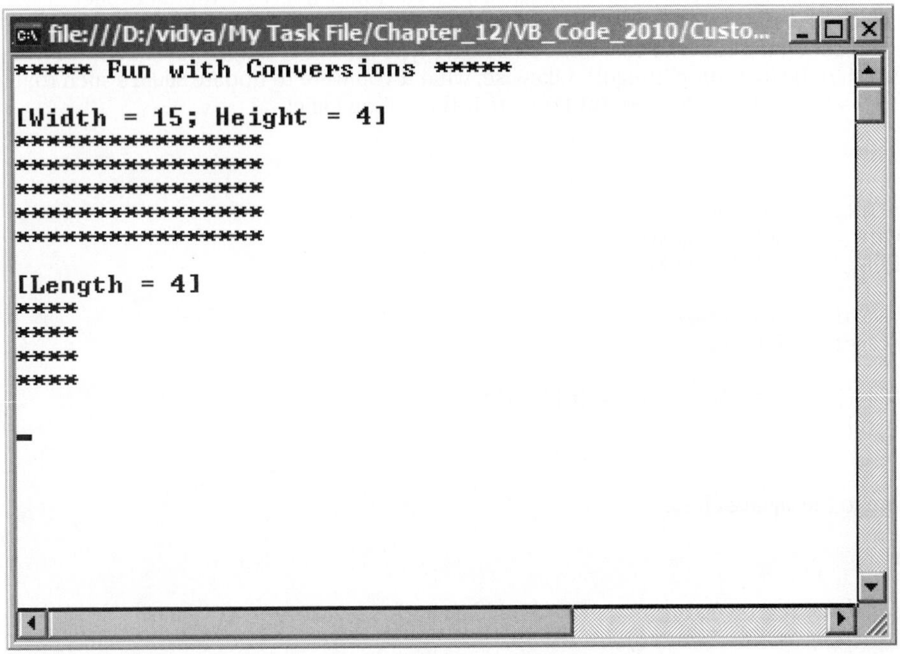

Figure 12-3. Converting a Rectangle structure to a Square structure

While it may not be all that helpful to convert a **Rectangle** into a **Square** within the same scope, assume you have a function that has been designed to take **Square** parameters.

```
'This method requires a Square type.
Sub DrawSquare(ByVal sq As Square)
    Console.WriteLine(sq.ToString())
    sq.Draw()
End Sub
```

Using your explicit conversion operation on the **Square** type, you can now pass in **Rectangle** types for processing using an explicit cast:

```
Sub Main()
  ...
  'Convert Rectangle to Square to invoke method.
  Dim rect As New Rectangle(10, 5)
  DrawSquare(CType(rect, Square))
  Console.ReadLine()
End Sub
```

Additional Explicit Conversions for the Square Type

Now that you can explicitly convert Rectangles into Squares, let's examine a few additional explicit conversions. Given that a square is symmetrical on all sides, it might be helpful to provide an explicit conversion routine that allows the caller to cast from an Integer type into a Square (which, of course, will have a side length equal to the incoming Integer). Likewise, what if you were to update Square such that the caller can cast from a Square into a System.Int32? Here is the calling logic:

```
Sub Main()
  ...
    'Converting an Integer to a Square.
    Dim sq2 As Square = CType(90, Square)
    Console.WriteLine("sq2 = {0}", sq2)

    'Converting a Square to an Integer.
    Dim side As Integer = CInt(sq2)

    Console.WriteLine("Side length of sq2 = {0}", side)
    Console.ReadLine()
End Sub
```

and here is the update to the Square class:

```
Public Class Square
...
    Public Shared Narrowing Operator CType(ByVal sideLength As Integer) As Square
            Dim newSq As New Square()
            newSq.Length = sideLength
            Return newSq
    End Operator

    Public Shared Narrowing Operator CType(ByVal s As Square) As Integer
        Return s.Length
    End Operator

End Class
```

To be honest, converting from a Square into an Integer may not be the most intuitive (or useful) operation. However, it does point out a very important fact regarding custom conversion routines: the compiler does not care what you convert to or from, as long as you have written syntactically correct code.

Thus, as with overloading operators, just because you can create an explicit cast operation for a given type does not mean you should. Typically, this technique will be most helpful when you're creating .NET structure types, given that they are unable to participate in classical inheritance (where casting comes for free).

Defining Implicit Conversion Routines

Thus far, you have created various custom explicit conversion operations. However, what about the following implicit conversion?

```vb
Sub Main()
...
    'Attempt to make an implicit cast?
    Dim s3 As New Square()
    s3.Length = 83
    Dim rect2 As Rectangle = s3
    Console.ReadLine()
End Sub
```

This code will not compile, given that you have not provided an implicit conversion routine for the Rectangle type. Now here is the catch: it is illegal to define explicit and implicit conversion functions on the same type if they do not differ by their return type or parameter set. This might seem like a limitation; however, the second catch is that when a type defines an *implicit* conversion routine, it is legal for the caller to make use of the *explicit* cast syntax!

Confused? To clear things up, let's add an implicit conversion routine to the Rectangle structure using the VB 2010 Widening keyword (note that the following code assumes the width of the resulting Rectangle is computed by multiplying the side of the Square by 2):

```vb
Public Class Rectangle

    Public Shared Widening Operator CType(ByVal s As Square) As Rectangle
        Dim r As New Rectangle()
        r.Height = s.Length
        'Assume the length of the new Rectangle with
        '(Length x 2)
        r.Width = s.Length * 2
        Return r
    End Operator
End Class
```

With this update, you are now able to convert between types as follows:

```vb
Sub Main()
        'an Implicit cast OK!
        Dim s3 As New Square()
        s3.Length = 7
        Dim rect2 As Rectangle = s3
        Console.WriteLine("rect2 = {0}", rect2)
        DrawSquare(s3)

        'Explicit cast syntax still OK!
        Dim s4 As New Square()
        s4.Length = 3
        Dim rect3 As Rectangle = CType(s4, Rectangle)
        Console.WriteLine("rect3 = {0}", rect3)
        Console.ReadLine()
End Sub
```

The Internal Representation of Custom Conversion Routines

Like overloaded operators, methods that are qualified with the Narrowing or Widening keywords have "special" names in terms of CIL: op_Implicit and op_Explicit, respectively (see Figure 12-4).

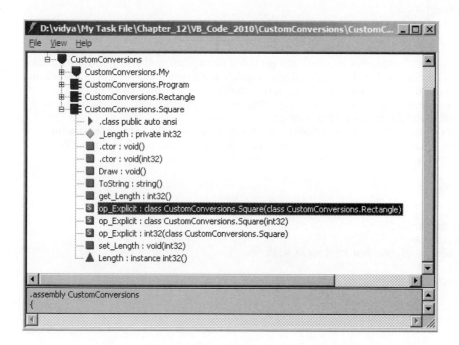

Figure 12-4. CIL representation of user-defined conversion routines

---

■ **Note** The Visual Studio 2010 Object Browser shows custom conversion operators using the "explicit operator" and "implicit operator" icons.

That wraps up our look at defining custom conversion routines. As with overloaded operators, remember that this bit of syntax is simply a shorthand notation for "normal" member functions, and in this light it is always optional. When used correctly, however, custom structures can be used more naturally, as they can be treated as true class types related by inheritance.

■ **Source Code** The CustomConversions project is located under the Chapter 12 subdirectory.

Understanding Extension Methods

.NET 3.5 introduced the concept of *extension methods*, which allow you to tack on new functionality to precompiled types on the fly. As you know, once a type is defined and compiled into a .NET assembly, its definition is, more or less, final. The only way to add new members, update members, or remove members is to recode and recompile the code base into an updated assembly (or take more drastic measures, such as importing the `System.Reflection.Emit` namespace to dynamically reshape a compiled type in memory).

In VB 2010, it is now possible to define extension methods. In a nutshell, extension methods allow existing compiled types (specifically, classes, structures, or interface implementations) as well as types currently being compiled (such as types in a project that contains extension methods) to gain new functionality without needing to directly update the type being extended.

This technique can be quite helpful when you need to inject new functionality into types for which you do not have an existing code base. It can also be handy when you need to force a type to support a set of members (in the interest of polymorphism), but cannot modify the original type declaration. Using extension methods, you can add functionality to precompiled types while providing the illusion these methods were there all along.

■ **Note** Understand that extension methods do not literally change the compiled code base! This technique only adds members to a type within the context of the current application.

When you define extension methods, the first restriction is that they must be defined within a Module. The second point is that all extension methods are defined under the `<Extension()>` attribute from the `System.Runtime.CompilerServices` namespace. The first parameter in an extension method definition specifies which data type the method extends. When the method is run, the first parameter is bound to the instance of the data type that invokes the method. The third point is that every extension method can be called either from the correct instance in memory or statically via the defining Module! Sound strange? Let's look at a full example to clarify matters.

Defining Extension Methods

Create a new Console Application named ExtensionMethods. Now, assume you are authoring a utility Module named `MyExtensions` that defines two extension methods. The first method allows any object in the .NET base class libraries to have a brand-new method named `DisplayDefiningAssembly()` that makes use of types in the `System.Reflection` namespace to display the assembly of the specified type.

■ **Note** You will formally examine the reflection API in Chapter 15. If you are new to the topic, simply understand that reflection allows you to discover the structure of assemblies, types, and type members at runtime.

The second extension method, named `ReverseDigits()`, allows any `System.Int32` to obtain a new version of itself where the value is reversed digit by digit. For example, if an Integer with the value 1234 called `ReverseDigits()`, the Integer returned is set to the value 4321. Consider the following module implementation (be sure to import the `System.Reflection` and `System.Runtime.CompilerServices` namespace if you are following along):

```
Imports System.Reflection
Imports System.Runtime.CompilerServices

Module MyExtensions

    'This method allows any object to display the assembly
    'it is defined in.
    <Extension()> _
    Public Sub DisplayDefiningAssembly(ByVal obj As Object)

Console.WriteLine("{0} lives here: => {1}" & vbLf, obj.GetType().Name, ↵
  Assembly.GetAssembly(obj.GetType()).GetName().Name)
    End Sub

    'This method allows any any Integer to reverse its digits.
    'for example, 56 would return 65.
    <Extension()> _
    Public Function ReverseDigits(ByVal i As Integer) As Integer

        'Translate Integer into a character string, and then
        'get all the characters.
        Dim digits As Char() = i.ToString().ToCharArray()

        'Now reverse items in the array.
        Array.Reverse(digits)

        'Put back into String.
        Dim newDigits As New String(digits)

        'Finally, return the modified String back as an Integer.
        Return Integer.Parse(newDigits)
    End Function
End Module
```

Given that `DisplayDefiningAssembly()` has been prototyped to extend `System.Object`, any type in any assembly now has this new member. However, `ReverseDigits()` has been prototyped to only extend Integer types, and therefore if anything other than an Integer attempts to invoke this method, you will receive a compile-time error.

Understand that a given extension method can have multiple parameters, The first parameter always indicates the type being extended. Subsequent parameters are the "real parameters" you want to pass into the method.

For example, here is an overloaded extension method defined in another utility Module named `TesterUtilModule`:

```
Imports System.Reflection
Imports System.Runtime.CompilerServices

Public Module TesterUtilClass
    'Every Int32 now has a Foo() method...
    <Extension()> _
    Public Sub Foo(ByVal i As Integer)
        Console.WriteLine("{0} called the Foo() method.", i)
    End Sub

    '...which has been overloaded to take a String!
    <Extension()> _
    Public Sub Foo(ByVal i As Integer, ByVal msg As String)
        Console.WriteLine("{0} called Foo() and told me: {1}", i, msg)
    End Sub
End Module
```

Invoking Extension Methods on an Instance Level

Now that we have these extension methods, look at how all objects (which of course means everything in the .NET base class libraries) have a new method named DisplayDefiningAssembly(), while System.Int32 types (and only Integers) have methods named ReverseDigits() and Foo():

```
Sub Main()

    Console.WriteLine("***** Fun with Extension Methods *****" & vbLf)
    'The Integer has assumed a new identity!
    Dim myInt As Integer = 12345678
    myInt.DisplayDefiningAssembly()

    'So this has the DataSet!
    Dim d As New System.Data.DataSet()
    d.DisplayDefiningAssembly()

    'And the SoundPlayer!
    Dim sp As New System.Media.SoundPlayer()
    sp.DisplayDefiningAssembly()

    'Use new Integer functionality.
    Console.WriteLine("Value of myInt: {0}", myInt)
    Console.WriteLine("Reversed digits of myInt: {0}",
        myInt.ReverseDigits())

    myInt.Foo()
    myInt.Foo("Integers that Foo?  Who would have thought it!")

    Dim b2 As Boolean = True
```

```
    'Error! Booleans don't have the Foo() method!
    'b2.Foo()

    Console.ReadLine()
End Sub
```

Here is the output.

```
***** Fun with Extension Methods *****


Int32 lives here: => mscorlib


DataSet lives here: => System.Data


SoundPlayer lives here: => System


Value of myInt: 12345678

Reversed digits of myInt: 87654321

12345678 called the Foo() method.

12345678 called Foo() and told me: Ints that Foo?  Who would have thought it!
```

Invoking Extension Methods as Shared Methods

Recall that extension methods are marked with the `<Extension ()>` attribute, followed by the type of item the method is applicable to. If you peek at what is happening behind the scenes (as verified by a tool such as `ildasm.exe`), you will find that the compiler simply calls the "normal" Shared method, passing in the variable calling the method as a parameter (e.g., it is the value of Me). Consider the following VB 2010 code, which approximates the code substitution that took place:

```
Sub Main()

    Console.WriteLine("***** Fun with Extension Methods *****" & vbLf)
    Dim myInt As Integer = 12345678
    MyExtensions.DisplayDefiningAssembly(myInt)

    Dim d As System.Data.DataSet = New DataSet()
    MyExtensions.DisplayDefiningAssembly(d)

    Dim sp As System.Media.SoundPlayer = New System.Media.SoundPlayer()
    MyExtensions.DisplayDefiningAssembly(sp)

    Console.WriteLine("Value of myInt: {0}", myInt)
    Console.WriteLine("Reversed digits of myInt: {0}",
      MyExtensions.ReverseDigits(myInt))

        TesterUtilModule. Foo(myInt)
        TesterUtilModule. Foo(myInt, "Ints that Foo?  Who would have thought it!")
End Sub
```

Given that calling an extension method from an object (thereby making it seem that the method is in fact an instance-level method) is just some smoke-and-mirrors effect provided by the compiler, you are always free to call extension methods as normal Shared methods using the expected VB 2010 syntax (as just shown)..

The Scope of an Extension Method

As just explained, extension methods are implicitly Shared methods that can be invoked from an instance of the extended type. Given this flavor of syntactic sugar, it is really important to point out that unlike a "normal" method, extension methods do not have direct access to the members of the type they are extending; said another way, extending is not inheriting. Consider the following simple Car type:

```
Public Class Car

  Public Speed As Integer

  Public Function SpeedUp() As Integer
        Speed += 1
        Return Speed
  End Function
End Class
```

If you were to build an extension method for the Car type named SlowDown(), you would not have direct access to the members of Car within the scope of the extension method as this is not classical inheritance. Therefore, the following would result in a compiler error:

```
Public Module CarExtensions
    <Extension()> _
    Public  Function SlowDown(ByVal c As Car) As Integer
        ' Error! This method is not deriving from Car!
        c.Speed -= 1
        Return c.Speed
    End Function
End Module
```

The problem here is that the Shared SlowDown() extension method is attempting to access the Speed field of the Car type. However, because SlowDown() is a Shared member of the CarExtensions class, Speed does not exist in this context! What is permissible, however, is to make use of the first parameter to access all Public members (and *only* the Public members) of the type being extending. Thus, the following code compiles as expected:

```
Imports System.Runtime.CompilerServices

Public Module CarExtensions

    <Extension()> _
    Public  Function SlowDown(ByVal c As Car) As Integer
        ' OK!
        c.Speed -= 1
        Return c.Speed
    End Function
End Module
```

At this point, you could create a Car object and invoke the SpeedUp() and SlowDown() methods as follows:

```
Sub UseCar()
    Dim c As New Car()
    Console.WriteLine("Speed: {0}", c.SpeedUp())
    Console.WriteLine("Speed: {0}", c.SlowDown())
End Sub
```

Importing Types That Define Extension Methods

When you partition a set of modules containing extension methods in a unique namespace, other namespaces in that assembly will make use of the standard VB 2010 Imports keyword to import not only the modules themselves, but also each of the supported extension methods. This is important to remember, because if you do not explicitly import the correct namespace, the extension methods are not available for that VB 2010 code file.

In effect, although it can appear on the surface that extension methods are global in nature, they are in fact limited to the namespaces that define them or the namespaces that import them. Thus, if we wrap the definitions of our modules (MyExtensions, TesterUtilModule, and CarExtensions) into a namespace named MyExtensionMethods as follows:

```
Namespace MyExtensionMethods

        Module MyExtensions
        ...
        End Module
        Module TesterUtilClass
        ...
        End Module
        Module CarExtensions
        ...
        End Module
End Namespace
```

other namespaces in the project would need to explicitly import the MyExtensionMethods namespace to gain the extension methods defined by these types. Therefore, the following is a compiler error:

```
'Here is our only Imports directive.
Imports System

Namespace MyNewApp
        Public Class JustATest
                Sub SomeMethod()

                        'Error! Need to import MyExtensionMethods
                        'namespace to extend Integer with Foo()!
                          Dim i As Integer = 0
                          i.Foo()

                End Sub
        End Class
End Namespace
```

The IntelliSense of Extension Methods

Given the fact that extension methods are not literally defined on the type being extended, it is certainly possible to become confused when examining an existing code base. For example, assume you have imported a namespace that defined some number of extension methods authored by a teammate. As you are authoring your code, you might create a variable of the extended type, apply the dot operator, and find dozens of new methods that are not members of the original class definition!

Thankfully, Visual Studio's IntelliSense mechanism marks all extension methods with a unique, blue down-arrow icon (see Figure 12-5).

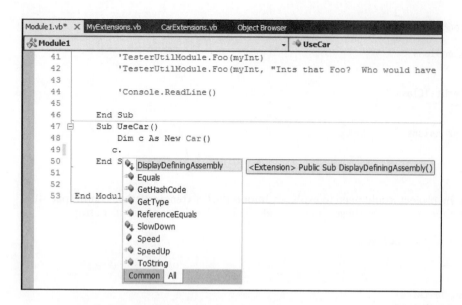

Figure 12-5. The IntelliSense of extension methods

Any method marked with this visual icon is a friendly reminder that the method is defined outside of the original class definition via an extension method.

■ **Source Code** The ExtensionMethods project can be found under the Chapter 12 subdirectory.

Building and Using Extension Libraries

The previous example extended the functionality of various types (such as the System.Int32 type) for use by the current console application. However, I am sure you can imagine the usefulness of building a.NET code library that defines extensions that can be referenced by multiple applications. As luck would have it, doing so is very straightforward.

Chapter 14 will delve into the details of creating and configuring custom libraries; however, if you wish to follow along for this example, create a new Class Library project named MyExtensionsLibrary. Next, rename your initial VB 2010 code file to MyExtensions.vb and copy the MyExtensions Module definition in your new namespace:

```
Imports System.Reflection
Imports System.Runtime.CompilerServices

'Be sure to Imports System.Reflection
Public Module MyExtensions
```

```
          'Same implementation as before.
          <Extension()> _
          Public Sub DisplayDefiningAssembly(ByVal obj As Object)
                ...
          End Sub

          'Same implementation as before.
          <Extension()> _
          Public Function ReverseDigits(ByVal i As Integer) As Integer
                ...
          End Function
End Module
```

> ■ **Note** If you wish to export extension methods from a .NET code library, the defining type must be declared with the Public keyword (recall that the default access modifier for a type is Friend).

At this point, you can compile your library and reference the `MyExtensionsLibrary.dll` assembly within new .NET projects. When you do so, the new functionality provided to `System.Object` and `System.Int32` can be used by any application that references the library.

To test this out, add a new Console Application project (named MyExtensionsLibraryClient). Next, add a reference to the `MyExtensionsLibrary.dll` assembly. Within the initial code file, specify that you are using the `MyExtensionsLibrary` namespace and author some simple code that invokes these new methods on a local Integer:

```
Imports MyExtensionsLibrary

Module Module1
     Sub Main()
             Console.WriteLine("*Using Library with Extensions*" & vbLf)

             'This time, these extension methods
             'have been defined within an external
             '.NET class library.
             Dim myInt As Integer = 987

             myInt.DisplayDefiningAssembly()
             Console.WriteLine("{0} is reversed to {1}", myInt,

             myInt.ReverseDigits())
             Console.ReadLine()
     End Sub
End Module
```

Microsoft recommends placing types that have extension methods in a dedicated assembly (within a dedicated namespace). The reason is simply to reduce cluttering of your programming environment. By way of example, if you were to author a core library for your company that every application was expected to make use of, and if the root namespace of that library defined 30 extension methods, the end result would be that all applications would see these methods pop up in IntelliSense (even if they are not required).

■ **Source Code** The MyExtensionsLibrary and MyExtensionsLibraryClient projects can be found under the Chapter 12 subdirectory.

Extending Interface Types via Extension Methods

At this point, you have seen how to extend classes (and, indirectly, structures that follow the same syntax) with new functionality via extension methods. To wrap up our investigation of VB 2010 extension methods, allow me to point out that it is possible to extend an interface type with new methods; however, the semantics of such an action are sure to be a bit different from what you might expect.

Create a new Console Application named InterfaceExtensions and define a simple interface type (IBasicMath) that contains a single method named Add(). Next, implement this interface on a class type (MyCalc) in a fitting manner, for example:

```
' Define a normal interface in VB 2010.
Interface IBasicMath
        Function Add(ByVal x As Integer, ByVal y As Integer) As Integer
End Interface

'Implementation of IBasicMath.
Public Class MyCalc
   Implements IBasicMath

   Public Function Add(ByVal x As Integer, ByVal y As Integer) As Integer
      Implements IBasicMath.Add
      Return x + y
   End Function
End Class
```

Now, assume you do not have access to the code definition of IBasicMath, but wish to add a new member (such as a subtraction method) to expand its behavior. You might attempt to author the following extension class to do so:

```
Module MathExtensions

   ' Extend IBasicMath with Substract
   <Extension()> _
   Public Function Subtract(ByVal itf As IBasicMath, ByVal x As
      Integer, ByVal y As Integer) As Integer

End Module
```

However, this will result in compile-time errors. When you extend an interface with new members, you must also supply an implementation of these members! This seems to fly in the face of the very nature of interface types, as interfaces do not provide implementations, only definitions. Nevertheless, you are required to define your extension method outside the MathExtensions class into the module as follows:

```
< Extension()> _
Public Function Subtract(ByVal itf As IBasicMath, ByVal x As Integer, ByVal y As Integer)↵
 As Integer

        Return x - y
End Function
```

At this point, you might assume you could create a variable of type IBasicMath and directly invoke Subtract(). Again, if this were possible (which it is not), it would destroy the nature of .NET interface types. In reality, what we have actually said here is "Any class in my project implementing IBasicMath now has a Subtract() method, implemented in this manner." As before, all the basic rules apply, therefore the namespace defining MyCalc must have access to the namespace defining MathExtensions. Consider the following Main() method:

```
Sub Main()
        Console.WriteLine("***** Extending an interface *****" & vbLf)

        'Call IBasicMath members from MyCalc object.
        Dim c As New MyCalc()
        Console.WriteLine("1 + 2 = {0}", c.Add(1, 2))
        Console.WriteLine("1 - 2 = {0}", c.Subtract(1, 2))

        'Can also cast into IBasicMath to invoke extension.
        Console.WriteLine("30 - 9 = {0}", (DirectCast(c, IBasicMath)).Subtract(30, 9))

        'This would NOT work!
        'Dim itfBM As New IBasicMath()
        'itfBM.Subtract(10, 10)

        Console.ReadLine()
End Sub
```

That wraps up our examination of VB 2010 extension methods. Remember that this particular language feature can be very useful whenever you wish to extend the functionality of a type, even if you do not have access to the original source code (or if the type is NotInheritable), for the purposes of polymorphism. And, much like implicitly typed local variables, extension methods are a key element of working with the LINQ API. As you will see in the next chapter, numerous existing types in the base class libraries have been extended with new functionality, via extension methods, to allow them to integrate with the LINQ programming model.

■ **Source Code** The InterfaceExtension project can be found under the Chapter 12 subdirectory.

Understanding Partial Methods

Since the release of .NET 2.0, it has been possible to build partial class definitions using the `Partial` keyword (see Chapter 5). Recall that this bit of syntax allows you to partition the full implementation of a type across multiple code files (or other locations, such as in memory). As long as each aspect of the partial type has the same fully qualified name, the end result is a single "normal" compiled class type in the assembly being constructed.

VB 2010 recycles the role of the `Partial` keyword in that it can now be applied on the method level. In a nutshell, this allows you to prototype a method in one file, yet implement it in another file. VB 2010 partial methods have a number of important restrictions:

- Partial methods can only be defined within a partial class.

- Partial methods must be `Subs`(they can't be `Functions`).

- Partial methods can have arguments (including parameters modified by `ByRef` or `ParamArray`).

- Partial methods must be explicitly specified as Private.

Even stranger is the fact that a partial method may or may not be emitted into the compiled assembly! Let's see an example to clarify matters.

A First Look at Partial Methods

To see the implications of defining a partial method, create a new Console Application project named PartialMethods. Now, define a new class named `CarLocator` within a VB 2010 file named `CarLocator.vb`:

```vb
'CarLocator.vb
Partial Public Class CarLocator

    'This member will always be part of the CarLocator class.
    Public Function CarAvailableInZipCode(ByVal zipCode As String) As Boolean

        'This call *may* be part of this method implementation.
        VerifyDuplicates(zipCode)

        'Assume some interesting database logic here...
        Return True
    End Function

    'This member *may* be part of the CarLocator class!
    Partial Private Sub VerifyDuplicates(ByVal make As String)
    End Sub
End Class
```

Notice that the `VerifyDuplicates()` method has been defined with the `Partial` modifier. Also notice that the `CarAvailableInZipCode()` method is making a call to `VerifyDuplicates()` within its implementation.

If you were to compile this application as it now stands and open the compiled assembly in a tool such as ildasm.exe or reflector.exe, you would find no trace of the VerifyDuplicates() method in the CarLocator class, and no trace of the call to VerifyDuplicates() within CarAvailableInZipCode()! With the project as it now stands, you really authored the following definition of the CarLocator class as far as the compiler is concerned:

```
Public Class CarLocator
        Public Function CarAvailableInZipCode(ByVal zipCode As String) As Boolean
                Return True
        End Function
End Class
```

The reason for this strange stripping away of code has to do with the fact that the partial VerifyDuplicates() method was never given a true implementation. If you were to now add a new file to your project (named perhaps CarLocatorImpl.vb) that defined the remainder of the partial method:

```
'CarLocatorImpl.vb
'We don't need to specify a class as Partial multiple times.
Public Class CarLocator

    'Must not declare this method as Partial
    'otherwise it will produce a compilation error.
    Private Sub VerifyDuplicates(ByVal make As String)
        'Assume some expensive data validation
        'takes place here...
    End Sub
End Class
```

you would find that the full scope of the CarLocator class is taken into account at compile time, as shown in the following approximate VB 2010 code:

```
Public Class CarLocator

        Public Function CarAvailableInZipCode(ByVal zipCode As String) As Boolean
                Me.VerifyDuplicates(zipCode)
                Return True
        End Function

        Private Sub VerifyDuplicates(ByVal make As String)
        End Sub
End Class
```

As you can see, when a method is defined with the Partial keyword, the compiler will determine if it should be emitted into the assembly based on whether the method has a method body or is simply an empty signature. If there is no method body, all traces of the method (invocations, metadata descriptions, prototypes) are stripped out during the compilation cycle.

In some ways, VB 2010 partial methods are a strongly typed version of *conditional code compilation* (via the #If, #ElseIf, #Else, and #End If preprocessor directives). The major difference, however, is that a partial method will be completely ignored during the compilation cycle (regardless of build settings) if there is not a supporting implementation.

Uses of Partial Methods

Given the restrictions that come with partial methods, most notably that they must be explicitly Private and always be Subs (rather than Functions), it is hard to see many useful applications of this new language feature. Truth be told, out of all of the language features of VB 2010, partial methods seem among those likely to be used the least.

In the current example, the VerifyDuplicates() method was marked as Partial for illustrative purposes. However, imagine that this method, if implemented, had to perform some very intensive calculations.

By marking this method with the Partial modifier, other class builders have the *option* of providing implementation details if they so choose. In this case, partial methods provide a cleaner solution than using preprocessor directives, supplying "dummy" implementations to Overridable methods, or throwing NotImplementedException objects.

The most common use of this syntax is to define what are termed lightweight events. This technique enables class designers to provide method hooks, similar to event handlers, that developers may choose to implement or not. As a naming convention, such lightweight event-handling methods take an On prefix, for example:

```
'CarLocator.vb
Public Partial Class CarLocator

    'This member will always be part of the CarLocator class.
    Public Function CarAvailableInZipCode(ByVal zipCode As String) As Boolean
    ...
        OnZipCodeLookup(zipCode)
        Return True
    End Function
    ...
    'A 'lightweight' event handler.
    Partial Private Sub OnZipCodeLookup(ByVal make As String)
    End Sub
End Class
```

If any class builders wish to be informed when the CarAvailableInZipCode() method has been called, they can provide an implementation of the OnZipCodeLookup() method. If they do not care, they simply do nothing.

■ **Source Code** The PartialMethods project can be found under the Chapter 12 subdirectory.

Understanding Anonymous Types

As an OO programmer, you know the benefits of defining classes to represent the state and functionality of a given programming entity. To be sure, whenever you need to define a class that is intended to be reused across projects and provides numerous bits of functionality through a set of methods, events, properties, and custom constructors, creating a new VB 2010 class is common practice and often mandatory.

However, there are other times when you would like to define a class simply to model a set of encapsulated (and somehow related) data points without any associated methods, events, or other custom functionality. Furthermore, what if this type is only to be used internally to your current application and it's not intended to be reused? If you need such a "temporary" type, earlier versions of VB 2010 would require you to nevertheless build a new class definition by hand:

```
Friend Class SomeClass

    ' Define a set of Private member variables...

    ' Make a property for each member variable...

    ' Override ToString() to account for each member variable...

    ' Override GetHashCode() and Equals() to work with value based equality...
End Class
```

While building such a class is not rocket science, it can be rather labor-intensive if you are attempting to encapsulate more than a handful of members (although automatic properties do help in this regard). These days, we are provided with a massive shortcut for this very situation (termed *anonymous types*) that in many ways is a natural extension of VB 2010 anonymous methods syntax (examined in Chapter 11).

When you define an anonymous type, you do so by making use of the Dim keyword without the declaration of type specifier (see Chapter 3) in conjunction with object initialization syntax (see Chapter 5). To illustrate, create a new Console Application named AnonymousTypes. Now, update Main() with the following anonymous class, which models a simple car type:

```
Sub Main()
        Console.WriteLine("***** Fun with Anonymous Types *****" & vbLf)

        ' Make an anonymous type representing a car.
        Dim myCar = New With { _
                .Color = "Bright Pink", _
                .Make = "Saab", _
                .CurrentSpeed = 55 _
        }

        ' Now show the color and make.
        Console.WriteLine("My car is a {0} {1}.", myCar.Color, myCar.Make)
        Console.ReadLine()
End Sub
```

Again note that the myCar variable must be implicitly typed, which makes good sense as we are not modeling the concept of an automobile using a strongly typed class definition. At compile time, the VB 2010 compiler will autogenerate a uniquely named class on our behalf. Given the fact that this class name is not visible from VB 2010, the use of implicit typing using the Dim keyword without type specifier is mandatory.

Also notice that we have to specify (using object initialization syntax) the set of properties that model the data we are attempting to encapsulate. Once defined, these values can then be obtained using standard VB 2010 property invocation syntax.

The Internal Representation of Anonymous Types

All anonymous types are automatically derived from System.Object, and therefore support each of the members provided by this base class. Given this, we could invoke ToString(), GetHashCode(), Equals(), or GetType() on the implicitly typed myCar object. Assume our module defines the following helper function:

```
Sub ReflectOverAnonymousType(ByVal obj As Object)

        Console.WriteLine("obj is an instance of: {0}", obj.GetType().Name)
        Console.WriteLine("Base class of {0} is {1}", obj.GetType().Name, _
        obj.GetType().BaseType)

        Console.WriteLine("obj.ToString() = {0}", obj.ToString())
        Console.WriteLine("obj.GetHashCode() = {0}", obj.GetHashCode())
        Console.WriteLine()
End Sub
```

Now assume we invoke this method from Main(), passing in the myCar object as the parameter:

```
Sub Main()
        Console.WriteLine("***** Fun with Anonymous types *****" & vbLf)

        ' Make an anonymous type representing a car.
        Dim myCar = New With { _
         .Color = "Bright Pink", _
         .Make = "Saab", _
         .CurrentSpeed = 55 _
        }

        ' Reflect over what the compiler generated.
        ReflectOverAnonymousType(myCar)
        Console.ReadLine()
End Sub
```

The output will look similar to the following:

```
***** Fun with Anonymous types *****



obj is an instance of: VB$AnonymousType_0`3

Base class of VB$AnonymousType_0`3 is System.Object

obj.ToString() = { Color = Bright Pink, Make = Saab, CurrentSpeed = 55 }

obj.GetHashCode() = 46104728
```

First of all, notice that in this example, the myCar object is of type VB$AnonymousType_0`3 (your name may differ). Remember that the assigned type name is completely determined by the compiler and is not directly accessible in your VB 2010 code base.

Perhaps most important, notice that each name/value pair defined using the object initialization syntax is mapped to an identically named read-only property and a corresponding private read-only backing field. The following VB 2010 code approximates the compiler-generated class used to represent the myCar object (which again can be verified using tools such as reflector.exe or ildasm.exe):

```
private auto ansi sealed VB$AnonymousType_0`3<T0,T1,T2>
 {
  // Read-only fields
 .field private !T0 $Color
 .field private !T1 $Make
 .field private !T2 $CurrentSpeed

  // Default constructor
method public specialname rtspecialname
         instance void  .ctor(!T0 Color,
                              !T1 Make,
                              !T2 CurrentSpeed) cil managed

  // Overridden methods
.method public strict virtual instance bool
          Equals(object o) cil managed

.method public strict virtual instance int32
          GetHashCode() cil managed
  .method public strict virtual instance string
         ToString() cil managed

  // Read-only properties
.property instance !T0 Color()
  {
    .get instance !T0 VB$AnonymousType_0`3::get_Color()
    .set instance void VB$AnonymousType_0`3::set_Color(!T0)
  } // end of property VB$AnonymousType_0`3::Color
  .property instance !T1 Make()
  {
    .get instance !T1 VB$AnonymousType_0`3::get_Make()
    .set instance void VB$AnonymousType_0`3::set_Make(!T1)
  } // end of property VB$AnonymousType_0`3::Make
  .property instance !T2 CurrentSpeed()
  {
    .get instance !T2 VB$AnonymousType_0`3::get_CurrentSpeed()
    .set instance void VB$AnonymousType_0`3::set_CurrentSpeed(!T2)
  }
}
```

The Implementation of ToString() and GetHashCode()

All anonymous types automatically derive from `System.Object` and are provided with an overridden version of `Equals()`, `GetHashCode()`, and `ToString()`. The `ToString()` implementation simply builds a string from each name/value pair, for example:

```
Public Overrides Function ToString() As String

        Dim builder As New StringBuilder()
        builder.Append("{ Color = ")
        builder.Append(Me.i__Field(Of Color))
        builder.Append(", Make = ")
        builder.Append(Me.i__Field (Of Make))
        builder.Append(", CurrentSpeed = ")
        builder.Append(Me.i__Field (Of CurrentSpeed))
        builder.Append(" }")
        Return builder.ToString()
End Function
```

The `GetHashCode()` implementation computes a hash value based on the value of each member variable of the anonymous type. Using this implementation of `GetHashCode()`, two anonymous types will yield the same hash value if (and only if) they have the same set of properties that have been assigned the same values. Given this implementation, anonymous types are well suited to be contained within a `Hashtable` container.

The Semantics of Equality for Anonymous Types

While the implementation of the overridden `ToString()` and `GetHashCode()` methods is fairly straightforward, you may be wondering how the `Equals()` method has been implemented. For example, if we were to define two "anonymous cars" variables that specify the same name/value pairs, would these two variables be considered equal or not? To see the results firsthand, update your `Program` type with the following new method:

```
Sub EqualityTest()

        ' Make 2 anonymous classes with identical name/value pairs.
        Dim firstCar = New With { _
         .Color = "Bright Pink", _
         .Make = "Saab", _
         .CurrentSpeed = 55 _
        }
        Dim secondCar = New With { _
         .Color = "Bright Pink", _
         .Make = "Saab", _
         .CurrentSpeed = 55 _
        }

        ' Are they considered equal when using Equals()?
        If firstCar.Equals(secondCar) Then
            Console.WriteLine("Same anonymous object!")
```

```
        Else
            Console.WriteLine("Not the same anonymous object!")
        End If

        ' Are they considered equal when using =?
        If (firstCar.GetType() = secondCar.GetType()) Then
            Console.WriteLine("Same anonymous object!")
        Else
            Console.WriteLine("Not the same anonymous object!")
        End If

        ' Are these objects the same underlying type?
        If firstCar.GetType().Name = secondCar.GetType().Name Then
            Console.WriteLine("We are both the same type!")
        Else
            Console.WriteLine("We are different types!")
        End If

        ' Show all the details.
        Console.WriteLine()

        ReflectOverAnonymousType(firstCar)
        ReflectOverAnonymousType(secondCar)
End Sub
```

Assuming you have called this method from within `Main()`, Figure 12-6 shows the (somewhat surprising) output.

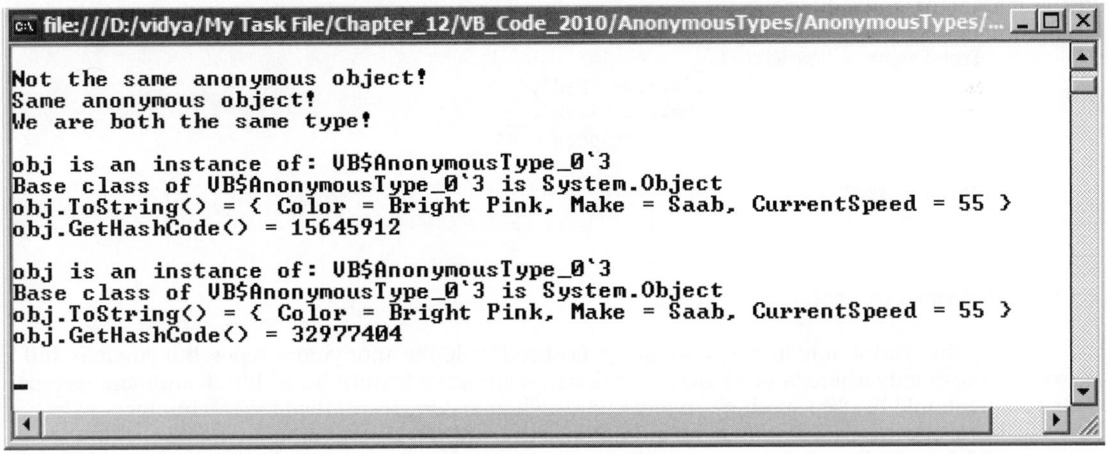

Figure 12-6. The equality of anonymous types

When you run this test code, you will see that the first conditional test where you call `Equals()` returns `true`, and therefore the message "Same anonymous object!" prints out to the screen. This is because the compiler-generated `Equals()` method makes use of value-based semantics when testing for equality (e.g., checking the value of each field of the objects being compared).

However, the second conditional test (which makes use of the VB 2010 equality operator, =) prints out "Not the same anonymous object!", which may seem at first glance to be a bit counterintuitive. This result is due to the fact that anonymous types do *not* receive overloaded versions of the VB 2010 equality operators (= and <>). Given this, when you test for equality of anonymous types using the VB 2010 equality operators (rather than the `Equals()` method), the *references*, not the values maintained by the objects, are being tested for equality.

Last but not least, in our final conditional test (where we examine the underlying type name), we find that the anonymous types are instances of the same compiler-generated class type (in this example, `VB$AnonymousType_0`3`), due to the fact that `firstCar` and `secondCar` have the same properties (`Color`, `Make`, and `CurrentSpeed`).

This illustrates an important but subtle point: the compiler will only generate a new class definition when an anonymous type contains unique names of the anonymous type. Thus, if you declare identical anonymous types (again, meaning the same names) within the same assembly, the compiler generates only a single anonymous type definition.

Anonymous Types Containing Anonymous Types

It is possible to create an anonymous type that is composed of other anonymous types. For example, assume you wish to model a purchase order that consists of a timestamp, a price point, and the automobile purchased. Here is a new (slightly more sophisticated) anonymous type representing such an entity:

```
' Make an anonymous type that is composed of another.
Dim purchaseItem = New With { _
        .TimeBought = DateTime.Now, _
        .ItemBought = New With { _
                            .Color = "Red", _
                            .Make = "Saab", _
                            .CurrentSpeed = 55 _
                                }, _
        .Price = 34.000 _
    }
```

```
ReflectOverAnonymousType(purchaseItem)
```

At this point, you should understand the syntax used to define anonymous types, but you may still be wondering exactly where (and when) to use this new language feature. To be blunt, anonymous type declarations should be used sparingly, typically only when making use of the LINQ technology set (see Chapter 14). You would never want to abandon the use of strongly typed classes/structures simply for the sake of doing so, given anonymous types' numerous limitations, which include the following:

- You don't control the name of the anonymous type.
- Anonymous types always extend `System.Object`.
- The fields and properties of an anonymous type are always read-only.

- Anonymous types cannot support events, custom methods, custom operators, or custom overrides.

- Anonymous types are always implicitly `NotInheritable`

- Anonymous types are always created using the default constructor.

However, when programming with the LINQ technology set, you will find that in many cases this syntax can be very helpful when you want to quickly model the overall *shape* of an entity rather than its functionality.

■ **Source Code** The AnonymousTypes project can be found under the Chapter 12 subdirectory.

Summary

The purpose of this chapter was to deepen your understanding of the VB 2010 programming language. First you investigated various advanced type construction techniques (indexer methods, overloaded operators, and custom conversion routines).

Next, you examined the role of extension methods, anonymous types, and partial methods. As you'll see in some detail in the next chapter, these features are very useful when working with LINQ-centric APIs (though you can use them anywhere in your code, should they be useful). Recall that anonymous methods allow you to quickly model the "shape" of a type, while extension methods allow you to tack on new functionality to types, without the need to subclass.

CHAPTER 13

■ ■ ■

LINQ to Objects

Regardless of the type of application you are creating using the .NET platform, your program will certainly need to access some form of data as it executes. To be sure, data can be found in numerous locations, including XML files, relational databases, in-memory collections, and primitive arrays. Historically speaking, based on the location of said data, programmers needed to make use of very different and unrelated APIs. The Language Integrated Query (LINQ) technology set, introduced initially in .NET 3.5, provides a concise, symmetrical, and strongly typed manner to access a wide variety of data stores. In this chapter you will begin your investigation of LINQ, by focusing on LINQ to Objects.

Before you dive into LINQ to Objects proper, the first part of this chapter quickly reviews the key VB 2010 programming constructs which enable LINQ. As you work through this chapter, you will find that implicitly typed local variables, object initialization syntax, lambda expressions, extension methods, and anonymous types will be quite useful.

Once this supporting infrastructure is reviewed, the remainder of the chapter will introduce you to the LINQ model and its role in the .NET platform. Here, you will come to learn the role of query operators and query expressions, which allow you to define statements that will interrogate a data source to yield the requested result set. Along the way, you will build numerous LINQ examples that interact with data contained within arrays as well as various collection types (both generic and nongeneric) and understand the assemblies, namespaces, and types that represent the LINQ to Objects API.

■ **Note** The information in this chapter is the foundation for future chapters of the book which examine additional LINQ technologies including LINQ to XML (Chapter 25), Parallel LINQ (Chapter 19), and LINQ to Entities (Chapter 23).

LINQ Specific Programming Constructs

From a very high level, LINQ can be understood as a strongly typed query language, embedded directly into the grammar of VB 2010 itself. Using LINQ, you can build any number of expressions which have a look-and-feel similar to that of a database SQL query. However, a LINQ query can be applied to any number of data stores, including stores that have nothing to do with a literal relational database.

■ **Note** Although LINQ queries look similar to SQL queries, the syntax is *not* identical. In fact, many LINQ queries seem to be the exact opposite format of a similar database query! If you attempt to map LINQ directly to SQL, you will surely become frustrated. To keep your sanity, I'd recommend that you try your best to regard LINQ queries as unique entities, which just "happen to look" similar to SQL.

When LINQ was first introduced to the .NET platform in version 3.5, the VB 2010 (and C#) languages were each expanded with a large number of new programming constructs used to support the LINQ technology set. Specifically, the VB 2010 language uses the following core LINQ-centric features:

- Implicitly typed local variables

- Object/collection initialization syntax

- Lambda expressions

- Extension methods

- Anonymous types

These features have already been explored in detail within various chapters of the text. However, to get the ball rolling, let's quickly review each feature in turn, just to make sure we are all in the proper mindset.

Implicit Typing of Local Variables

In Chapter 3, you learned about the `Dim` keyword without declaring the type specifier (e.g., no `As` integer) of VB 2010. This technique allows you to define a local variable without explicitly specifying the underlying data type. The variable, however, is strongly typed as the compiler will determine the correct data type based on the initial assignment. Recall the following code example from Chapter 3:

```
Sub DeclareImplicitVars()
        'Implicitly typed local variables.
        Dim myInt = 0
        Dim myBool = True
        Dim myString = "Time, marches on..."

        'Print out the underlying type.
        Console.WriteLine("myInt is a: {0}", myInt.GetType().Name)
        Console.WriteLine("myBool is a: {0}", myBool.GetType().Name)
        Console.WriteLine("myString is a: {0}", myString.GetType().Name)
End Sub
```

This language feature is very helpful, and often mandatory, when using LINQ. As you will see during this chapter, many LINQ queries will return a sequence of data types which are not known until compile time. Given that the underlying data type is not known until the application is compiled, you obviously can't declare a variable explicitly!

Object and Collection Initialization Syntax

Chapter 5 explored the role of object initialization syntax, which allows you to create a class or structure variable, and set any number of its Public properties, in one fell swoop. The end result is a very compact (yet still easy on the eyes) syntax which can be used to get your objects ready for use. Also recall from Chapter 10, the VB 2010 language allows you to use a very similar syntax to initialize collections of objects. Consider the following code snippet which uses collection initialization syntax to fill a List(Of T) of Rectangle objects, each of which maintains two Point objects to represent an (x,y) position:

```
Dim myListOfRects As New List(Of Rectangle)From { _
    New Rectangle With {.TopLeft = New Point With {.X = 10, .Y = 10}, _
        .BottomRight = New Point With {.X = 200, .Y = 200}},
    New Rectangle With {.TopLeft = New Point With {.X = 2, .Y = 2}, _
        .BottomRight = New Point With {.X = 100, .Y = 100}},
    New Rectangle With {.TopLeft = New Point With {.X = 5, .Y = 5}, _
        .BottomRight = New Point With {.X = 90, .Y = 75}}}
```

While you are never required to use collection/object initialization syntax, you do end up with a more compact code base. Furthermore, this syntax, when combined with implicit typing of local variables, allows you to declare an anonymous type, which is very useful when creating a LINQ projection. You'll learn about LINQ projections later in this chapter.

Lambda Expressions

The VB 2010 lambda expression Sub was fully explored in Chapter 11. Recall that a lambda expression can be used to invoke a method that requires a strongly typed delegate as an argument. Lambdas greatly simplify how you work with .NET delegates, in that they reduce the amount of code you have to author by hand. Recall that a lambda expression can be broken down into the following usage:

```
Sub(ArgumentsToProcess) StatementToProcessThem
End Sub
```

In Chapter 11, I walked you through how to interact with the FindAll() method of the generic List(Of T) class using three different approaches. After working with the raw Predicate(Of T) delegate and a VB 2010 anonymous method, you eventually arrived with the following (extremely concise) iteration which used the following lambda expression:

```
Sub LambdaExpressionSyntax()
        ' Make a list of Integers.
        Dim list As New List(Of Integer)()
        list.AddRange(New Integer() {20, 1, 4, 8, 9, 44})

        'VB 2010 lambda expression.
        Dim evenNumbers As List(Of Integer) = list.FindAll(
            Function(i)
                    Return (i Mod 2) = 0)
            End Function)
```

```
        Console.WriteLine("Here are your even numbers:")
        For Each evenNumber As Integer In evenNumbers
            Console.Write("{0}" & vbTab, evenNumber)
        Next
        Console.WriteLine()
    End Sub
```

Lambdas will be very useful when working with the underlying object model of LINQ. As you will soon find out, the VB 2010 LINQ query operators are simply a shorthand notation for calling true-blue methods on a class named `System.Linq.Enumerable`. These methods typically always require delegates (the `Func(Of T)` delegate in particular) as parameters, which are used to process your data to yield the correct result set. Using lambdas, you can streamline your code, and allow the compiler to infer the underlying delegate.

Extension Methods

VB 2010 extension methods allow you to tack on new functionality to existing classes without the need to subclass. As well, extension methods allow you to add new functionality to `NotInheritable` classes and structures, which could never be subclassed in the first place. Recall from Chapter 12 when you define extension methods:

- They must be defined within a Module.

- All extension methods are defined under the `<Extension()>` attribute from the `System.Runtime.CompilerServices` namespace. The first parameter in an extension method definition specifies which data type the method extends. When the method is run, the first parameter is bound to the instance of the data type that invokes the method.

- Every extension method can be called either from the correct instance in memory or statically via the defining `Shared` class.

- Finally, you can't have a `ByRef` parameter definition in the extension method, and they must be `Sub` rather than a `Function`.

For an example, see the following code:

```
Public Module ObjectExtensions
    <System.Runtime.CompilerServices.Extension()> _
    Public  Sub DisplayDefiningAssembly(obj As Object)
        Console.WriteLine("{0} lives here:" & vbLf & vbTab & "->{1}" & _
            vbLf, obj.GetType().Name, Assembly.GetAssembly(obj.GetType()))
    End Sub
End Module
```

To use this extension, an application must first set a reference to the external assembly that contains the extension method implementation using the Add Reference dialog of Visual Studio 2010. At this point, simply import the defining namespace, and code away:

```
Sub Main()
        'Since everything extends System.Object, all classes
        'can use this extension.
        Dim myInt As Integer = 12345678
        myInt.DisplayDefiningAssembly()

        Dim d As New System.Data.DataSet()
        d.DisplayDefiningAssembly()
        Console.ReadLine()
End Sub
```

When you working with LINQ, you will seldom, if ever, be required to manually build your own extension methods. However, as you create LINQ query expressions, you will in fact be making use of numerous extension methods already defined by Microsoft. In fact, each VB 2010 LINQ query operator is a shorthand notation for making a manual call on an underlying extension method, typically defined by the System.Linq.Enumerable utility class.

Anonymous Types

The final VB 2010 language feature I'd like to quickly review is that of anonymous types which was fully explored in Chapter 12. This feature can be used to quickly model the "shape" of data, by allowing the compiler to generate a new class definition at compile time, based on a supplied set of name/value pairs. Recall that this type will be composed using value based semantics, and each Overridable method of System.Object will be overridden accordingly. To define an anonymous type, declare an implicitly typed variable and specify the data's shape using object initialization syntax:

```
' Make an anonymous type that is composed of another.
  Dim purchaseItem = New With { _
          .TimeBought = DateTime.Now, _
          .ItemBought = New With { _
                                   .Color = "Red", _
                                   .Make = "Saab", _
                                   .CurrentSpeed = 55 _
                                   }, _
                                   .Price = 34.0 _
                  }
```

LINQ makes frequent use of anonymous types when you wish to project new forms of data on the fly. For example, assume you have a collection of Person objects, and wish to use LINQ to obtain information on the age and social security number of each. Using a LINQ projection, you can allow the compiler to generate a new anonymous type that contains your information.

Understanding the Role of LINQ

That wraps up our quick review of the VB 2010 language features that allow LINQ to work its magic. However, why have LINQ in the first place? Well, as software developers, it is hard to deny that the vast majority of our programming time is spent obtaining and manipulating data. When speaking of "data," it is very easy to immediately envision information contained within relational databases. However, another popular location in which data exists is within XML documents (`*.config` files, locally persisted `DataSet`s, or in-memory data returned from WCF services).

Data can be found in numerous places beyond these two common homes for information. For instance, say you have an array or generic `List(Of T)` type containing 300 Integers, and you want to obtain a subset that meets a given criterion (e.g., only the odd or even members in the container, only prime numbers, only nonrepeating numbers greater than 50). Or perhaps you are making use of the reflection APIs and need to obtain only metadata descriptions for each class deriving from a particular parent class within an array of `Type`s. Indeed, data is *everywhere*.

Prior to .NET 3.5, interacting with a particular flavor of data required programmers to make use of very diverse APIs. Consider, for example, Table 13-1, which illustrates several common APIs used to access various types of data (I'm sure you can think of many other examples).

Table 13-1. Ways to Manipulate Various Types of Data

The Data You Want	How to Obtain It
Relational data	`System.Data.dll`, `System.Data.SqlClient.dll`, etc.
XML document data	`System.Xml.dll`
Metadata tables	The `System.Reflection` namespace
Collections of objects	`System.Array` and the `System.Collections`/`System.Collections.Generic` namespaces

Of course, nothing is wrong with these approaches to data manipulation. In fact, when programming with .NET 4.0/VB 2010, you can (and will) certainly make direct use of ADO.NET, the XML namespaces, reflection services, and the various collection types. However, the basic problem is that each of these APIs is an island unto itself, which offers very little in the way of integration. True, it is possible (for example) to save an ADO.NET `DataSet` as XML, and then manipulate it via the `System.Xml` namespaces, but nonetheless, data manipulation remains rather asymmetrical.

The LINQ API is an attempt to provide a consistent, symmetrical manner in which programmers can obtain and manipulate "data" in the broad sense of the term. Using LINQ, you are able to create directly within the VB 2010 programming language constructs called query expressions. These query expressions are based on numerous query operators that have been intentionally designed to look and feel very similar (but not quite identical) to a SQL expression.

The twist, however, is that a query expression can be used to interact with numerous types of data— even data that has nothing to do with a relational database. Strictly speaking, "LINQ" is the term used to describe this overall approach to data access. However, based on where you are applying your LINQ queries, you will encounter various terms, such as the following:

- **LINQ to Objects**: This term refers to the act of applying LINQ queries to arrays and collections.

- **LINQ to XML**: This term refers to the act of using LINQ to manipulate and query XML documents.

- **LINQ to DataSet**: This term refers to the act of applying LINQ queries to ADO.NET `DataSet` objects.

- **LINQ to Entities**: This aspect of LINQ allows you to make use of LINQ queries within the ADO.NET Entity Framework (EF) API.

- **Parallel LINQ** (aka, PLINQ): Allows for parallel processing of data returned from a LINQ query.

To be sure, Microsoft seems quite dedicated to integrating LINQ support deeply within the .NET programming environment. As time goes on, it would be very safe to bet that LINQ will become an integral part of the .NET base class libraries, languages, and Visual Studio itself.

LINQ Expressions Are Strongly Typed

It is also very important to point out that a LINQ query expression (unlike a traditional SQL statement) is *strongly typed*. Therefore, the VB 2010 compiler will keep us honest and make sure that these expressions are syntactically well formed. On a related note, query expressions have metadata representation within the assembly that makes use of them, as the VB 2010 LINQ query operators always make a rich underlying object model. Tools such as Visual Studio 2010 can use this metadata for useful features such as IntelliSense, autocompletion, and so forth.

The Core LINQ Assemblies

As mentioned in Chapter 2, the New Project dialog of Visual Studio 2010 has the option of selecting which version of the .NET platform you wish to compile against. When you opt to compile against .NET 3.5 or higher, each of the project templates will automatically reference the key LINQ assemblies, which can be viewed using the Solution Explorer. Table 13-2 documents the role of the key LINQ assemblies. However, you will encounter additional LINQ libraries over the remainder of this book.

Table 13-2. Core LINQ-centric Assemblies

Assembly	Meaning in Life
System.Core.dll	Defines the types that represent the core LINQ API. This is the one assembly you must have access to if you wish to use any LINQ API, including LINQ to Objects.
System.Data.DataSetExtensions.dll	Defines a handful of types to integrate ADO.NET types into the LINQ programming paradigm (LINQ to DataSet).
System.Xml.Linq.dll	Provides functionality for using LINQ with XML document data (LINQ to XML).

In order to work with LINQ to Objects, you must make sure that every VB 2010 code file that contains LINQ queries imports the System.Linq namespace (defined within System.Core.dll). If you do not do so, you will run into a number of problems. As a very good rule of thumb, if you see a compiler error looking similar to this:

```
Error 1 Could not find an implementation of the query pattern for source type 'Integer()'.
'Where' not found. Are you missing a reference to 'System.Core.dll' or a using directive for
'System.Linq'?
```

The chances are extremely good that your VB 2010 file does not have the following using directive (and believe me, I speak from experience!):

```
Imports System.Linq
```

Applying LINQ Queries to Primitive Arrays

To begin examining LINQ to Objects, let's build an application that will apply LINQ queries to various array objects. Create a Console Application named LinqOverArray, and define a helper method within the module named QueryOverStrings(). In this method, create a String array containing six or so items of your liking (here I listed out a batch of video games I am currently attempting to finish). Make sure to have at least two entries that contain numerical values, and a few that have embedded spaces.

```
Sub QueryOverStrings()
        'Assume we have an array of Strings.
        Dim currentVideoGames As String() = {"Morrowind", "Uncharted 2",    "Fallout 3",
        "Daxter", "System Shock 2"}
End Sub
```

Now, update Main() to invoke QueryOverStrings():

```
Sub Main()
        Console.WriteLine("***** Fun with LINQ to Objects *****" & vbLf)
        QueryOverStrings()
        Console.ReadLine()
End Sub
```

When you have any array of data, it is very common to extract a subset of items based on a given requirement. Maybe you want to obtain only the subitems that contain a number (e.g., System Shock 2, Uncharted 2, and Fallout 3), have more or less than some number of characters, or don't contain embedded spaces (e.g., Morrowind or Daxter). While you could certainly perform such tasks using members of the System.Array type and a bit of elbow grease, LINQ query expressions can greatly simplify the process.

Going on the assumption that you wish to obtain from the array only items that contain an embedded blank space, and you want these items listed in alphabetical order, you could build the following LINQ query expression:

```
Sub QueryOverStrings()
        'Assume we have an array of Strings.
         Dim currentVideoGames As String() = {"Morrowind", "Uncharted 2", "Fallout 3",
        "Daxter", "System Shock 2"}
```

```
'Build a query expression to find the items in the array
'that have an embedded space.
Dim subset As IEnumerable(Of String) = From g In currentVideoGames _
Where g.Contains(" ") _
Order By g _
Select g

'Print out the results.
For Each s As String In subset
    Console.WriteLine("Item: {0}", s)
Next
End Sub
```

Notice that the query expression created here makes use of the From, In, Where, Order By, and Select LINQ query operators. You will dig into the formalities of query expression syntax later in this chapter. However, even now you should be able to read this statement roughly as "Give me the items inside of currentVideoGames that contain a space, ordered alphabetically."

Here, each item that matches the search criteria has been given the name "g" (as in "game"); however, any valid VB 2010 variable name would do:

```
Dim subset As IEnumerable(Of String) = From g In currentVideoGames _
    Where g.Contains(" ") _
    Order By g _
    Select g
```

Notice that the returned sequence is held in a variable named subset, typed as a type that implements the generic version of IEnumerable(Of T), where T is of type System.String (after all, you are querying an array of strings). Once you obtain the result set, you then simply print out each item using a standard foreach construct. If you run your application, you will find the following output:

```
***** Fun with LINQ to Objects *****

Item: Fallout 3

Item: System Shock 2

Item: Uncharted 2
```

Once Again, Without LINQ

To be sure, LINQ is never necessary. If you so choose, you could have found the same result set by forgoing LINQ altogether and making use of programming primitives such as If statements and For loops. Here is a method which yields the same result as the QueryOverStrings() method, but in a much more verbose manner:

```
Sub QueryOverStringsLongHand()
    'Assume we have an array of Strings.
        Dim currentVideoGames As String() = {"Morrowind", "Uncharted 2", "Fallout 3",
        "Daxter", "System Shock 2"}

        Dim gamesWithSpaces As String() = New String(4) {}
        For i = 0 To currentVideoGames.Length - 1
            If currentVideoGames(i).Contains(" ") Then
                gamesWithSpaces(i) = currentVideoGames(i)
            End If
        Next

        'Now sort them.
        Array.Sort(gamesWithSpaces)

        'Print out the results.
         For Each s As String In gamesWithSpaces
            If s IsNot Nothing Then
                Console.WriteLine("Item: {0}", s)
            End If
        Next
        Console.WriteLine()
End Sub
```

While I am sure you can think of ways to tweak the previous method, the fact remains that LINQ queries can be used to radically simplify the process of extracting new subsets of data from a source. Rather than building nested loops, complex If/Else logic, temporary data types, and so on, the VB 2010 compiler will perform the dirty work on your behalf, once you create a fitting LINQ query.

Reflecting Over a LINQ Result Set

Now, assume the module defines an additional helper method named ReflectOverQueryResults() that will print out various details of the LINQ result set (note the parameter is a System.Object, to account for multiple types of result sets):

```
Sub ReflectOverQueryResults(ByVal resultSet As Object)
        Console.WriteLine("***** Info about your query *****")
        Console.WriteLine("resultSet is of type: {0}",
                    resultSet.GetType().Name)

        Console.WriteLine("resultSet location: {0}",
        resultSet.GetType().Assembly.GetName().Name)
End Sub
```

Assuming you have called this method within QueryOverStrings() directly after printing out the obtained subset, if you run the application, you will see the subset is really an instance of the generic OrderedEnumerable(Of TElement, TKey) type (represented in terms of CIL code as WhereSelectEnumerableIterator`2), which is an internal abstract type residing in the System.Core.dll assembly:

```
***** Info about your query *****

resultSet is of type: WhereSelectEnumerableIterator`2

resultSet location: System.Core
```

■ **Note** Many of the types that represent a LINQ result are hidden by the Visual Studio 2010 object browser. Make use of `ildasm.exe` or `reflector.exe` to see these internal, hidden types if you are interested.

LINQ and Implicitly Typed Local Variables

While the current sample program makes it relatively easy to determine that the result set can be captured as an enumeration of **string** object (e.g., **IEnumerable(Of String)**), I would guess that it is *not* clear that **subset** is really of type **OrderedEnumerable(Of TElement, TKey)**.

Given the fact that LINQ result sets can be represented using a good number of types in various LINQ-centric namespaces, it would be tedious to define the proper type to hold a result set, because in many cases the underlying type may not be obvious or even directly accessible from your code base (and as you will see, in some cases the type is generated at compile time).

To further accentuate this point, consider the following additional helper method defined within the module (which I assume you will invoke from within the **Main()** method):

```
Sub QueryOverInts()
        Dim numbers As Integer() = {10, 20, 30, 40, 1, 2,3, 8}

        'Get numbers less than ten.
        Dim subset As IEnumerable(Of Integer) = From i In numbers
                                                Where i < 10 Select i

        For Each i As Integer In subset
            Console.WriteLine("Item: {0}", i)
        Next
        ReflectOverQueryResults(subset )
End Sub
```

In this case, the **subset** variable is a completely different underlying type. This time, the type implementing the **IEnumerable(Of Integer)** interface is a low-level class named **WhereSelectArrayIterator`2**.

```
Item: 1

Item: 2

Item: 3

Item: 8



***** Info about your query *****

resultSet is of type: WhereSelectArrayIterator`2

resultSet location: System.Core
```

Given the fact that the exact underlying type of a LINQ query is certainly not obvious, these first examples have represented the query results as an IEnumerable(Of T) variable, where T is the type of data in the returned sequence (String, Integer, etc.). However, this is still rather cumbersome. To add insult to injury, given that IEnumerable(Of T) extends the nongeneric IEnumerable interface, it would also be permissible to capture the result of a LINQ query as follows:

```
'Get numbers less than ten.
Dim subset As IEnumerable = From i In numbers Where i < 10 Select i
```

Thankfully, implicit typing cleans things up considerably when working with LINQ queries:

```
Sub QueryOverInts()
        Dim numbers As Integer() = {10, 20, 30, 40, 1, 2,3, 8}

        ' Use implicit typing here...
        Dim subset = From i In numbers Where i < 10 Select i

        '...and here!
        For Each i In subset
            Console.WriteLine("Item:{0}", i)
            ReflectOverQueryResults(subset)
        Next

End Sub
```

As a rule of thumb, you will always want to make use of implicit typing when capturing the results of a LINQ query. Just remember, however, that (in a vast majority of cases), the *real* return value is a type implementing the generic IEnumerable(Of T) interface.

Exactly what this type is under the covers (`OrderedEnumerable(Of TElement, TKey)`, `WhereSelectArrayIterator`2`, etc.) is irrelevant, and not necessary to discover. As seen in the previous code example, you can simply use the `Dim` keyword without a type specifier in a `For Each` construct to iterate over the fetched data.

LINQ and Extension Methods

Although the current example does not have you author any extension methods directly, you are in fact using them seamlessly in the background. LINQ query expressions can be used to iterate over data containers that implement the generic `IEnumerable(Of T)` interface. However, the .NET `System.Array` class type (used to represent our array of strings and array of integers) does *not* implement this contract:

```
'The System.Array type does not seem to implement the correct
'infrastructure for query expressions!
       Public MustInherit Class Array
       Implements
       ICloneable,IList,ICollection,IEnumerable,IStructuralComparable,IStructuralEquatable
       ...
End Class
```

While `System.Array` does not directly implement the `IEnumerable(Of T)` interface, it indirectly gains the required functionality of this type (as well as many other LINQ-centric members) via the Shared `System.Linq.Enumerable` class type.

This utility class defines a good number of generic extension methods (such as `Aggregate(Of T)()`, `First(Of T)()`, `Max(Of T)()`, etc.), which `System.Array` (and other types) acquire in the background. Thus, if you apply the **dot** operator on the **currentVideoGames** local variable, you will find a good number of members *not* found within the formal definition of `System.Array` (see Figure 13-1).

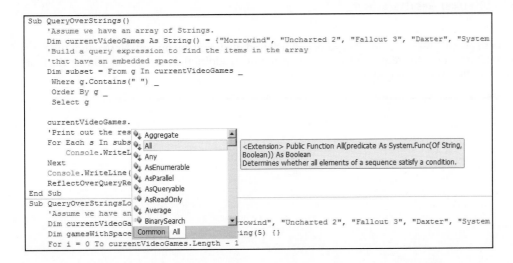

Figure 13-1. The System.Array type has been extended with members of System.Linq.Enumerable

The Role of Deferred Execution

Another important point regarding LINQ query expressions is that they are not actually evaluated until you iterate over the sequence. Formally speaking, this is termed deferred execution. The benefit of this approach is that you are able to apply the same LINQ query multiple times to the same container, and rest assured you are obtaining the latest and greatest results. Consider the following update to the QueryOverInts() method:

```
Sub QueryOverInts()
        Dim numbers As Integer() = {10, 20, 30, 40, 1, 2,3, 8}

        'Get numbers less than ten.
        Dim subset = From i In numbers Where i < 10 Select i

        'LINQ statement evaluated here!
        For Each i In subset
            Console.WriteLine("{0} < 10", i)
        Next
        Console.WriteLine()

        'Change some data in the array.
        numbers(0) = 4

        'Evaluated again!
        For Each j In subset
            Console.WriteLine("{0} < 10", j)
        Next

        Console.WriteLine()
        ReflectOverQueryResults(subset)
End Sub
```

If you were to execute the program yet again, you will find the following output. Notice that the second time you iterate over the requested sequence, you find an additional member, as you set the first item in the array to be a value less than ten:

```
1 < 10

2 < 10

3 < 10

8 < 10


4 < 10

1 < 10
```

2 < 10

3 < 10

8 < 10

One very useful aspect of Visual Studio 2010 is that if you set a breakpoint before the evaluation of a LINQ query, you are able to view the contents during a debugging session. Simply locate your mouse cursor above the LINQ result set variable (**subset** in Figure 13-2). When you do, you will be given the option of evaluating the query at that time by expanding the Results View option.

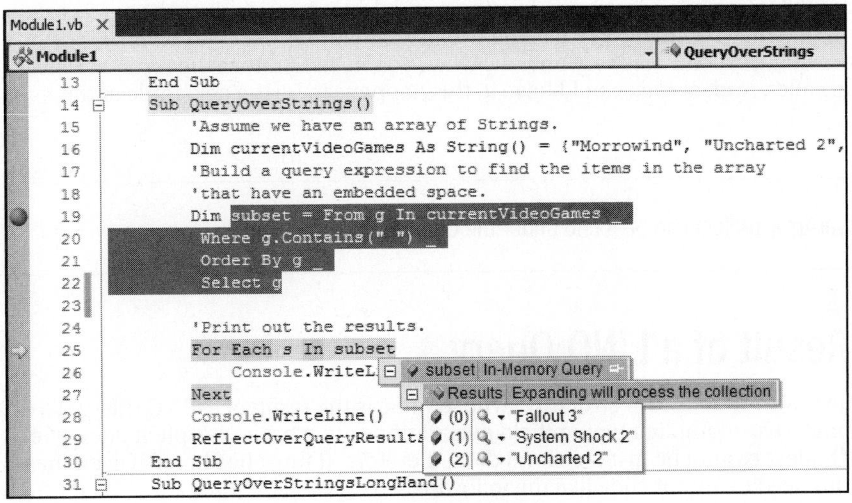

```vb
13        End Sub
14 ⊟    Sub QueryOverStrings()
15            'Assume we have an array of Strings.
16            Dim currentVideoGames As String() = {"Morrowind", "Uncharted 2",
17            'Build a query expression to find the items in the array
18            'that have an embedded space.
19            Dim subset = From g In currentVideoGames _
20                Where g.Contains(" ") _
21                Order By g _
22                Select g
23
24            'Print out the results.
25            For Each s In subset
26                Console.WriteL
27            Next
28            Console.WriteLine()
29            ReflectOverQueryResults
30        End Sub
31 ⊟    Sub QueryOverStringsLongHand()
```

✔ subset In-Memory Query
  ✔ Results Expanding will process the collection
    ● (0) 🔍 ▾ "Fallout 3"
    ● (1) 🔍 ▾ "System Shock 2"
    ● (2) 🔍 ▾ "Uncharted 2"

Figure 13-2. Debugging LINQ expressions

The Role of Immediate Execution

When you wish to evaluate a LINQ expression from outside the confines of `For Each` logic, you are able to call any number of extension methods defined by the `Enumerable` type as `ToArray(Of T)()`, `ToDictionary(Of TSource,TKey)()`, and `ToList(Of T)()`. These methods will cause a LINQ query to execute at the exact moment you call them, to obtain a snapshot of the data. Once you have done so, the snapshot of data may be independently manipulated:

```vbnet
Sub ImmediateExecution()

        Dim numbers As Integer() = {10, 20, 30, 40, 1, 2,3, 8}

        'Get data RIGHT NOW as Integer().
        Dim subsetAsIntArray As Integer() = (From i In numbers _
                                    Where i < 10 Select i).ToArray()

        'Get data RIGHT NOW as List(Of Integer).
        Dim subsetAsListOfInts As List(Of Integer) = (From i In numbers _
                                    Where i < 10 Select i).ToList() _
End Sub
```

Notice that the entire LINQ expression is wrapped within parentheses to cast it into the correct underlying type (whatever that may be) in order to call the extension methods of `Enumerable`.

The usefulness of immediate execution is very obvious when you need to return the results of a LINQ query to an external caller. And, as luck would have it, this happens to be the next topic of the chapter!

■ **Source Code** The LinqOverArray project can be found under the Chapter 13 subdirectory.

Returning the Result of a LINQ Query

It is possible to define a field within a class (or structure) whose value is the result of a LINQ query. To do so, however, you cannot make use of implicit typing (field declarations must have an explicit data type), and the target of the LINQ query cannot be instance level data; therefore, it must be Shared. Given these limitations, you will seldom need to author code like the following:

```vbnet
Public Class LINQBasedFieldsAreClunky

        Private Shared currentVideoGames As String() = {"Morrowind", "Uncharted 2",
        "Fallout 3", "Daxter", "System Shock 2"}

        'Can't use implicit typing here! Must know type of subset!
        Dim subset As IEnumerable(Of String) = From g In currentVideoGames _
                Where g.Contains(" ") _
                Order By g _
                Select g

    Public Sub PrintGames()
            For Each item In subset
                    Console.WriteLine(item)
            Next
        End Sub
End Class
```

More often than not, LINQ queries are defined within the scope of a method or property. Moreover, to simplify your programming, the variable used to hold the result set will be stored in an implicitly typed local variable using the `Dim` keyword without declaring **a** type specifier. Now, recall from Chapter 3 that implicitly typed variables cannot be used to define parameters, return values, or fields of a class or structure.

Given this point, you may wonder exactly how you could return a query result to an external caller. The answer is, it depends. If you have a result set consisting of strongly typed data such as an array of strings or a `List(Of T)` of `Cars`, you could abandon the use of **implicitly typed** variables and use a proper `IEnumerable(Of T)` or `IEnumerable` type (again, as `IEnumerable(Of T)` extends `IEnumerable`). Consider the following example for a new Console Application named LinqRetValues:

```
Module Module1

    Sub Main()
        Console.WriteLine("***** LINQ Transformations *****" & vbLf)
        Dim subset As IEnumerable(Of String) = GetStringSubset()
        For Each item As String In subset
            Console.WriteLine(item)
        Next

        Console.ReadLine()
    End Sub

    Function GetStringSubset() As IEnumerable(Of String)
        Dim colors As String() = {"Light Red", "Green", "Yellow", "Dark Red",
          "Red", "Purple"}

        'Note subset is an IEnumerable(Of String) compatible object.
        Dim theRedColors As IEnumerable(Of String) = From c In colors _
          Where c.Contains("Red") _
          Select c
        Return theRedColors
    End Function
End Module
```

The results are as expected:

```
Light Red

Dark Red

Red
```

Returning LINQ Results via Immediate Execution

This example works as expected, only because the return value of the `GetStringSubset()` and the LINQ query within this method has been strongly typed. If you define subset as an implicitly-typed variable, it would be permissible to return the value *only* if the method is still prototyped to return IEnumerable(Of String) (and if the implicitly typed local variable is in fact compatible with the specified return type).

Because it is a tad bit inconvenient to operate on IEnumerable(Of T), you could make use of immediate execution. For example, rather than returning IEnumerable(Of String), you could simply return a String(), provided that you transform the sequence to a strongly typed array. Consider this new method of the module, which does this very thing:

```
Function GetStringSubsetAsArray() As String()

        Dim colors As String() = {"Light Red", "Green", "Yellow",
        "Dark Red", "Red", "Purple"}

        Dim theRedColors = From c In colors _
                    Where c.Contains("Red") _
                    Select c

        'Map results into an array.
        Return theRedColors.ToArray()
End Function
```

With this, the caller can be blissfully unaware that their result came from a LINQ query, and simply work with the array of strings as expected. For an example, see the following code:

```
For Each item As String In GetStringSubsetAsArray()
    Console.WriteLine(item)
Next
```

Immediate execution is also critical when attempting to return to the caller the results of a LINQ projection. You'll examine this topic a bit later in the chapter. However, next up, let's look at how to apply LINQ queries to generic and nongeneric collection objects.

■ **Source Code** The LinqRetValues project can be found under the Chapter 13 subdirectory.

Applying LINQ Queries to Collection Objects

Beyond pulling results from a simple array of data, LINQ query expressions can also manipulate data within members of the System.Collections.Generic namespace, such as the List(Of T) type. Create a new Console Application project named LinqOverCollections, and define a basic Car class that maintains a current speed, color, make, and pet name as shown in the following code:

```
Class Car
        Public Property PetName() As String
        Public Property Color() As String
        Public Property Speed() As Integer
        Public Property Make() As String
End Class
```

Now, within your `Main()` method define a local `List(Of T)` variable of type `Car`, and make use of object initialization syntax to fill the list with a handful of new `Car` objects:

```
Sub Main()
        Console.WriteLine("***** LINQ over Collections *****" & vbLf)
        'Make a List(Of T) of Car objects.
        Dim myCars As New List(Of Car) From _
        {
        New Car With {.PetName = "Henry", .Color = "Silver", .Speed = 100, .Make = "BMW"},

        New Car With {.PetName = "Daisy", .Color = "Tan", .Speed = 90, .Make = "BMW"},

        New Car With {.PetName = "Mary", .Color = "Black", .Speed = 55, .Make = "VW"},

        New Car With {.PetName = "Clunker", .Color = "Rust", .Speed = 5, .Make = "Yugo"},
        New Car With {.PetName = "Melvin", .Color = "White", .Speed = 43, .Make = "Ford"}
        }
        Console.ReadLine()
End Sub
```

Accessing Contained Subobjects

Applying a LINQ query to a generic container is no different than doing so with a simple array, as LINQ to Objects can be used on any type implementing `IEnumerable(Of T)`. This time, your goal is to build a query expression to select only the `Car` objects within the `myCars` list, where the speed is greater than 55.

Once you get the subset, you will print out the name of each `Car` object by calling the `PetName` property. Assume you have the following helper method (taking a `List(Of Car)` parameter), which is called from within `Main()`:

```
Sub GetFastCars(ByVal myCars As List(Of Car))

        'Find all Car objects in the List(), where the Speed is
        'greater than 55.
        Dim fastCars = From c In myCars _
                    Where c.Speed > 55 _
                    Select c
        For Each car In fastCars
                Console.WriteLine("{0} is going too fast!", car.PetName)
        Next
End Sub
```

Notice that your query expression is only grabbing items from the `List(Of T)` where the `Speed` property is greater than 55. If you run the application, you will find that "Henry" and "Daisy" are the only two items that match the search criteria.

If you want to build a more complex query, you might wish to only find the BMWs that have a `Speed` value above 90. To do so, simply build a compound Boolean statement using the VB 2010 `AndAlso` operator:

```vb
Sub GetFastBMWs(ByVal myCars As List(Of Car))
      'Find the fast BMWs!
      Dim fastCars = From c In myCars _
       Where c.Speed > 90 AndAlso c.Make = "BMW" _
       Select c
      For Each car In fastCars
          Console.WriteLine("{0} is going too fast!", car.PetName)
      Next
End Sub
```

In this case, the only pet name printed out is "Henry".

Applying LINQ Queries to Nongeneric Collections

Recall that the query operators of LINQ are designed to work with any type implementing IEnumerable (Of T) (either directly or via extension methods). Given that System.Array has been provided with such necessary infrastructure, it may surprise you that the legacy (nongeneric) containers within System.Collections have not. Thankfully, it is still possible to iterate over data contained within nongeneric collections using the generic Enumerable.OfType(Of T)() extension method.

The OfType(Of T)() method is one of the few members of Enumerable that does not extend generic types. When calling this member off a nongeneric container implementing the IEnumerable interface (such as the ArrayList), simply specify the type of item within the container to extract a compatible IEnumerable(Of T) object. In code, you can store this data point using an implicitly typed variable.

Consider the following new method which fills an ArrayList with a set of Car objects (be sure to import the System.Collections namespace into your Module1.vb file).

```vb
Sub LINQOverArrayList()
      Console.WriteLine("***** LINQ over ArrayList *****")

      'Here is a nongeneric collection of cars.
      Dim myCars As New ArrayList() From {
      New Car With {.PetName = "Henry", .Color = "Silver", .Speed = 100, .Make = "BMW"},
      New Car With {.PetName = "Daisy", .Color = "Tan", .Speed = 90, .Make = "BMW"},
      New Car With {.PetName = "Mary", .Color = "Black", .Speed = 55, .Make = "VW"},
      New Car With {.PetName = "Clunker", .Color = "Rust", .Speed = 5, .Make = "Yugo"},
      New Car With {.PetName = "Melvin", .Color = "White", .Speed = 43, .Make = "Ford"}
      }

      'Transform ArrayList into an IEnumerable(Of T)-compatible type.
      Dim myCarsEnum = myCars.OfType(Of Car)()

      'Create a query expression.
      Dim fastCars = From c In myCarsEnum _
                     Where c.Speed > 55 _
                     Select c

      For Each car In fastCars
          Console.WriteLine("{0} is going too fast!", car.PetName)
      Next
End Sub
```

Similar to the previous examples, this method, when called from `Main()` will only display the names "Henry" and "Daisy", based on the format of our LINQ query.

Filtering Data Using OfType(Of T)()

As you know, nongeneric types are capable of containing any combination of items, as the members of these containers (again, such as the `ArrayList`) are prototyped to receive `System.Objects`. For example, assume an `ArrayList` contains a variety of items, only a subset of which are numerical. If you want to obtain a subset that contains only numerical data, you can do so using `OfType(Of T)()`, since it filters out each element whose type is different from the given type during the iterations:

```
Sub OfTypeAsFilter()

        'Extract the Integers from the ArrayList.
        Dim myStuff As New ArrayList()
        myStuff.AddRange(New Object() {10, 400, 8, False, New Car(), "String data"})
        Dim myInts = myStuff.OfType(Of Integer)()

        'Prints out 10, 400, and 8.
        For Each i As Integer In myInts
             Console.WriteLine("Int value: {0}", i)
        Next
End Sub
```

Great! At this point, you have had a chance to apply LINQ queries to arrays, generic collections, and nongeneric collections. These containers held both VB 2010 primitive types (integers, String data) as well as custom classes. The next task is to learn about many additional LINQ operators, which can be used to build more complex, and useful queries.

■ **Source Code** The LinqOverCollections project can be found under the Chapter 13 subdirectory.

Investigating the VB 2010 LINQ Query Operators

VB 2010 defines a good number of query operators out of the box. Table 13-3 documents some of the more commonly used query operators.

■ **Note** The .NET Framework 4.0 SDK documentation provides full details regarding each of the VB 2010 LINQ operators. Look up the topic "LINQ General Programming Guide" for more information.

Table 13-3. Various LINQ Query Operators

Query Operators	Meaning in Life
`From, In`	Used to define the backbone for any LINQ expression, which allows you to extract a subset of data from a fitting container.
`Where`	Used to define a restriction for which items to extract from a container.
`Select`	Used to select a sequence from the container.
`Join, On,`	Performs joins based on specified key. Remember, these "joins" do not need to have anything to do with data in a relational database.
`Order By, ascending, descending`	Allows the resulting subset to be ordered in ascending or descending order.
`Group, By`	Yields a subset with data grouped by a specified value.

In addition to the partial list of operators shown in Table 13-3, the `System.Linq.Enumerable` class provides a set of methods that do not have a direct VB 2010 query operator shorthand notation, but are instead exposed as extension methods. These generic methods can be called to transform a result set in various manners (`Reverse(Of T)`, `ToArray(Of T)`, `ToList(Of T)`, etc.). Some are used to extract singletons from a result set, others perform various set operations (`Distinct(Of T)`, `Union(Of T)`, `Intersect(Of T)`, etc.), and still others aggregate results (`Count(Of T)`, `Sum(Of T)`, `Min(Of T)`, `Max(Of T)`, etc.).

To begin digging into more intricate LINQ queries, create a new Console Application named FunWithLinqExpressions. Next, you need to define an array or collection of some sample data. For this project, you will make an array of `ProductInfo` objects, defined in the following code:

```
Public Class ProductInfo
    Public Property Name() As String
    Public Property Description() As String
    Public Property NumberInStock() As Integer

    Public Overrides Function ToString() As String
     Return String.Format("Name={0}, Description={1}, Number in Stock={2}", Name,
     Description, NumberInStock)
    End Function
End Class
```

Now populate an array with a batch of `ProductInfo` objects within your `Main()` method:

```
Sub Main()

        'This array will be the basis of our testing...
        Console.WriteLine("***** Fun with Query Expressions *****" & vbLf)
```

```
Dim itemsInStock() As ProductInfo=
{
New ProductInfo() With
{.Name = "Mac's Coffee",.Description ="Coffee with TEETH",      .NumberInStock = 24},
New ProductInfo() With
{.Name = "Milk Maid Milk", .Description = "Milk cow's love", .NumberInStock = 100},
New ProductInfo() With
{.Name = "Pure Silk Tofu", .Description = "Bland as Possible",
 .NumberInStock = 120},
New ProductInfo() With
{.Name = "Cruchy Pops", .Description = "Cheezy, peppery goodness",
.NumberInStock = 2},
New ProductInfo() With
{.Name = "RipOff Water", .Description = "From the tap to your wallet",
 .NumberInStock = 100},
New ProductInfo() With
{.Name = "Classic Valpo Pizza", .Description = "Everyone   loves pizza!",
.NumberInStock = 73}
}
    'We will call various methods here!
Console.ReadLine()
End Sub
```

Basic Selection Syntax

Because the syntactical correctness of a LINQ query expression is validated at compile time, you need to remember that the ordering of these operators is critical. In the simplest terms, every LINQ query expression is built using the From, In, and Select operators. Here is the general template to follow:

```
Dim result = From matchingItem In container Select matchingItem
```

The item after the From operator represents an item that matches the LINQ query criteria, which can be named anything you choose. The item after the In operator, represents the data container to search (an array, collection, or XML document).

Here is a very simple query, doing nothing more than selecting every item in the container (similar in behavior to a database Select * SQL statement). Consider the following:

```
Sub SelectEverything(ByVal products As ProductInfo())
      'Get everything.
      Console.WriteLine("All product details:")

      Dim allProducts = From p In products _
                    Select p

      For Each prod In allProducts
          Console.WriteLine(prod.ToString())
      Next
End Sub
```

To be honest, this query expression is not entirely useful, given that your subset is identical to that of the data in the incoming parameter. If you wish, you could use this incoming parameter to extract only the Name values of each car using the following selection syntax:

```
Sub ListProductNames(ByVal products As ProductInfo())

        'Now get only the names of the products.
        Console.WriteLine("Only product names:")

        Dim names = From p In products _
                    Select p.Name

        For Each n In names
            Console.WriteLine("Name: {0}", n)
        Next
End Sub
```

Obtaining Subsets of Data

To obtain a specific subset from a container, you can make use of the Where operator. When doing so, the general template now becomes the following code:

```
Dim result = From item In container Where BooleanExpression Select item
```

Notice that the Where operator expects an expression that resolves to a Boolean. For example, to extract from the ProductInfo() argument only the items that have more than 25 items on hand, you could author the following code:

```
Sub GetOverstock(ByVal products As ProductInfo())

        'Get only the items where we have more than
        '25 in stock.
        Console.WriteLine("The overstock items!")
        Dim overstock = From p In products _
                        Where p.NumberInStock > 25 _
                        Select p

        For Each c As ProductInfo In overstock
            Console.WriteLine(c.ToString())
        Next
End Sub
```

As seen earlier in this chapter, when you are building a Where clause, it is permissible to make use of any valid VB 2010 operators to build complex expressions. For example, recall the query that only extracts out the BMWs going at least 100 mph:

```
'Get BMWs going at least 100 mph.
Dim onlyFastBMWs = From c In myCars _
                   Where c.Speed >= 100 AndAlso c.Make = "BMW" _
                   Select c
                   For Each c In onlyFastBMWs
                           Console.WriteLine("{0} is going {1} MPH",   c.PetName, c.Speed)
                   Next
```

Projecting New Data Types

It is also possible to project new forms of data from an existing data source. Let's assume that you wish to take the incoming `ProductInfo()` parameter and obtain a result set that accounts only for the name and description of each item. To do so, you can define a `Select` statement that dynamically yields a new anonymous type:

```
Sub GetNamesAndDescriptions(ByVal products As ProductInfo())

        Console.WriteLine("Names and Descriptions:")
        Dim nameDesc = From p In products _
                        Select p.Name, p.Description

        For Each item In nameDesc
            'Could also use Name and Description properties directly.
            Console.WriteLine(item.ToString())
        Next
End Sub
```

Always remember that when you have a LINQ query that makes use of a projection, you have no way of knowing the underlying data type, as this is determined at compile time. In these cases, the use of implicit type variables is mandatory. As well, recall that you cannot create methods with implicitly typed return values. Therefore, the following method would not compile:

```
Function GetProjectedSubset()

        Dim products() As ProductInfo = {
                    New ProductInfo With {.Name = "Mac's Coffee", .Description =
                    "Coffee with TEETH", .NumberInStock = 24},

                    New ProductInfo With {.Name = "Milk Maid Milk",
                    .Description = "Milk cow's love", .NumberInStock = 100},

                    New ProductInfo With {.Name = "Pure Silk Tofu",
                    .Description = "Bland as Possible", .NumberInStock = 120},
                    New ProductInfo With {.Name = "Cruchy Pops",
                    .Description = "Cheezy, peppery goodness", .NumberInStock = 2},

                    New ProductInfo With {.Name = "RipOff Water",
                    .Description = "From the tap to your wallet", .NumberInStock = 100},
```

```
                    New ProductInfo With {.Name = "Classic Valpo Pizza",
                        .Description = "Everyone loves pizza!", .NumberInStock = 73}
                        }
        Dim nameDesc = From p In products _
                        Select p.Name, p.Description

    Return nameDesc
End Function
```

When you wish to return projected data to a caller, one approach is to transform the query result into a .NET `System.Array` object using the `ToArray()` extension method. Thus, if you were to update your query expression as follows:

```
'Return value is now an Array.
Function GetProjectedSubset()

    …
    Return nameDesc
End Function
```

you could invoke and process the data from `Main()` as follows:

```
Dim objs As Array = GetProjectedSubset()

For Each o As Object In objs
    'Calls ToString() on each anonymous object.
    Console.WriteLine(o)
Next
```

Note that you have to use a literal `System.Array` object and cannot make use of the VB 2010 array declaration syntax, given that you don't know the underlying type of type, as you are operating on a compiler generated anonymous class! Also note that you are not specifying the type parameter to the generic `ToArray(Of T)()` method, as you once again don't know the underlying data type until compile time, which is too late for your purposes.

The obvious problem is that you lose any strong typing, as each item in the `Array` object is assumed to be of type `Object`. Nevertheless, when you need to return a LINQ result set which is the result of a projection operation, transforming the data into an `Array` type (or another suitable container via other members of the `Enumerable` type) is mandatory.

Obtaining Counts Using Enumerable

When you are projecting new batches of data, you may need to discover exactly how many items have been returned into the sequence. Any time you need to determine the number of items returned from a LINQ query expression, simply make use of the `Count()` extension method of the `Enumerable` class. For example, the following method will find all `String` objects in a local array which have a length greater than six characters:

```
Sub GetCountFromQuery()

        Dim currentVideoGames As String() =
                {"Morrowind", "BioShock", "Half Life 2: Episode 1",
                "The Darkness", "Daxter", "System Shock 2"}

        'Get count from the query.
        Dim numb As Integer = (From g In currentVideoGames _
                                Where g.Length > 6 _
                                Select g).Count()

        'Print out the number of items.
        Console.WriteLine("{0} items honor the LINQ query.", numb)
End Sub
```

Reversing Result Sets

You can reverse the items within a result set quite simply using the Reverse(Of T)() extension method of the Enumerable class. For example, the following method selects all items from the incoming ProductInfo() parameter in reverse:

```
Sub ReverseEverything(ByVal products As ProductInfo())

        Console.WriteLine("Product in reverse:")
        Dim allProducts = From p In products _
                            Select p

        For Each prod In allProducts.Reverse()
            Console.WriteLine(prod.ToString())
        Next
End Sub
```

Sorting Expressions

As you have seen over this chapter's initial examples, a query expression can take an Order By operator to sort items in the subset by a specific value. By default, the order will be ascending; thus, ordering by a String would be alphabetical, ordering by numerical data would be lowest to highest, and so forth. If you wish to view the results in a descending order, simply include the Descending operator. Ponder the following method:

```
Sub AlphabetizeProductNames(ByVal products As ProductInfo())

        'Get names of products, alphabetized.
        Dim subset = From p In products _
                    Order By p.Name
                    Select p
        Console.WriteLine("Ordered by Name:")
```

```
        For Each p In subset
            Console.WriteLine(p.ToString())
        Next
End Sub
```

Although ascending order is the default, you are able to make your intentions very clear by making use of the Ascending operator:

```
Dim subset = From p In products _
             Order By p.Name Ascending _
             Select p
```

If you wish to get the items in descending order, you can do so via the Descending operator:

```
Dim subset = From p In products _
             Order By p.Name Descending _
             Select p
```

LINQ As a Better Venn Diagramming Tool

The Enumerable class supports a set of extension methods which allows you to use two (or more) LINQ queries as the basis to find unions, differences, concatenations, and intersections of data. First of all, consider the Except() extension method, which will return a LINQ result set that contains the differences between two containers, which in this case, is the value "Yugo":

```
Sub DisplayDiff()
        Dim myCars As New List(Of String)({"Yugo", "Aztec", "BMW"})
        Dim yourCars As New List(Of String)({"BMW", "Saab", "Aztec"})

        Dim carDiff = (From c In myCars _
                       Select c).Except(From c2 In yourCars _
                       Select c2)
        Console.WriteLine("Here is what you don't have, but I do:")

        For Each s As String In carDiff
            'Prints Yugo
            Console.WriteLine(s)
        Next
End Sub
```

The Intersect() method will return a result set that contains the common data items in a set of containers. For example, the following method returns the sequence, "Aztec" and "BMW".

```
Sub DisplayIntersection()
        Dim myCars As New List(Of String)({"Yugo", "Aztec", "BMW"})
        Dim yourCars As New List(Of String)({"BMW", "Saab", "Aztec"})
```

```
        'Get the common members.
        Dim carIntersect = (From c In myCars _
                            Select c).Intersect(From c2 In yourCars _
                            Select c2)
        Console.WriteLine("Here is what we have in common:")

        For Each s As String In carIntersect
            'Prints Aztec and BMW
            Console.WriteLine(s)
        Next
End Sub
```

The Union() method, as you would guess, returns a result set that includes all members of a batch of LINQ queries. Like any proper union, you will not find repeating values if a common member appears more than once. Therefore, the following method will print out the values "Yugo", "Aztec", "BMW", and "Saab":

```
Sub DisplayUnion()
        Dim myCars As New List(Of String)({"Yugo", "Aztec", "BMW"})
        Dim yourCars As New List(Of String)({"BMW", "Saab", "Aztec"})

        'Get the union of these containers.
        Dim carUnion = (From c In myCars _
                        Select c).Union(From c2 In yourCars _
                        Select c2)
        Console.WriteLine("Here is everything:")

        For Each s As String In carUnion
            'Prints all common members
            Console.WriteLine(s)
        Next
End Sub
```

Finally, the Concat() extension method returns a result set that is a direct concatenation of LINQ result sets. For example, the following method prints out the results "Yugo", "Aztec", "BMW", "BMW", "Saab", and "Aztec":

```
Sub DisplayConcat()
        Dim myCars As New List(Of String)({"Yugo", "Aztec", "BMW"})
        Dim yourCars As New List(Of String)({"BMW", "Saab", "Aztec"})

        ' Prints:
        'Yugo, Aztec, BMW, BMW, Saab, Aztec.
        Dim carConcat = (From c In myCars _
                        Select c).Concat(From c2 In yourCars _
                        Select c2)

        For Each s As String In carConcat
            Console.WriteLine(s)
        Next
End Sub
```

Removing Duplicates

When you call the Concat()extension method, you could very well end up with redundant entries in the fetched result, which could be exactly what you want in some cases. However, in other cases, you might wish to remove duplicate entries in your data. To do so, simply call the Distinct() extension method, as seen here:

```
Sub DisplayConcatNoDups()
        Dim myCars As New List(Of String)({"Yugo", "Aztec", "BMW"})
        Dim yourCars As New List(Of String)({"BMW", "Saab", "Aztec"})
        'Prints:
        'Yugo Aztec BMW Saab.
        Dim carConcat = (From c In myCars _
                         Select c).Concat(From c2 In yourCars _
                         Select c2)

        For Each s As String In carConcat.Distinct()
            Console.WriteLine(s)
        Next
End Sub
```

LINQ Aggregation Operations

LINQ queries can also be designed to perform various aggregation operations on the result set. The Count() extension method is one such aggregation example. Other possibilities include obtaining an average, max, min, or sum of values using the Max(), Min(), Average(), or Sum() members of the Enumerable class. Here is a simple example:

```
Sub AggregateOps()
        'Various aggregation examples.
        Dim winterTemps As Double() = {2, -21.3, 8, -4, 0, 8.2}

        Console.WriteLine("Max temp: {0}",
                          (From t In winterTemps _Select t).Max())
        Console.WriteLine("Min temp: {0}",
                          (From t In winterTemps _Select t).Min())
        Console.WriteLine("Avarage temp: {0}",
                          (From t In winterTemps _Select t).Average())
        Console.WriteLine("Sum of all temps: {0}",
                          (From t In winterTemps _Select t).Sum())
End Sub
```

These examples should give you enough knowledge to feel comfortable with the process of building LINQ query expressions. While there are additional operators you have not yet examined, you will see additional examples later in this text when you learn about related LINQ technologies. To wrap up your first look at LINQ, the remainder of this chapter will dive into the details between the VB 2010 LINQ query operators and the underlying object model.

■ **Source Code** The FunWithLinqExpressions project can be found under the Chapter 13 subdirectory.

The Internal Representation of LINQ Query Statements

At this point, you have been introduced to the process of building query expressions using various VB 2010 query operators (such as `From`, `In`, `Where`, `Order By`, and `Select`). Also, you discovered that some functionality of the LINQ to Objects API can only be accessed when calling extension methods of the `Enumerable` class. The truth of the matter, however, is that when compiled, the VB 2010 compiler actually translates all VB 2010 LINQ operators into calls on methods of the `Enumerable` class. In fact, if you were really a glutton for punishment, you could build all of your LINQ statements using nothing but the underlying object model.

A great many of the methods of `Enumerable` have been prototyped to take delegates as arguments. In particular, many methods require a generic delegate named `Func(Of T)` defined within the `System` namespace of `System.Core.dll`. For example, consider the `Where()` method of `Enumerable` which is called on your behalf when you use the VB 2010 `Where` LINQ query operator:

```
'Overloaded versions of the Enumerable.Where(Of T)() method.
' Note the second parameter is of type System.Func(Of T).
<Extension> _
Public Shared Function Where(Of TSource)(ByVal source As IEnumerable(Of TSource),ByVal
predicate As System.Func(Of TSource, Integer,Boolean)) As IEnumerable(Of TSource)

<Extension> _
Public Shared Function Where(Of TSource)(ByVal source As IEnumerable(Of TSource),ByVal
predicate As System.Func(Of TSource, Boolean)) As IEnumerable(Of TSource)
```

The `Func(Of T)` delegate (as the name implies) represents a pattern for a given function with a set of arguments and a return value. If you were to examine this type using the Visual Studio 2010 object browser, you'll notice that the `Func(Of T)` delegate can take between zero and four input arguments (here typed T1, T2, T3, and T4 and named **arg1**, **arg2**, **arg3**, and **arg4**), and a return type denoted by TResult:

```
'The various formats of the Func(Of T) delegate.
Public Delegate Function Func(Of T1, T2, T3, T4, TResult)(ByVal arg1 As T1, ByVal arg2↵
  As T2, ByVal arg3 As T3, ByVal arg4 As T4) As TResult
Public Delegate Function Func(Of T1, T2, T3, TResult)(ByVal arg1 As T1, ByVal arg2↵
  As T2, ByVal arg3 As T3) As TResult

Public Delegate Function Func(Of T1, T2, TResult)(ByVal arg1 As T1, ByVal arg2↵
  As T2) As TResult

Public Delegate Function Func(Of T1, TResult)(ByVal arg1 As T1) As TResult

Public Delegate Function Func(Of TResult)() As TResult
```

Given that many members of `System.Linq.Enumerable` demand a delegate as input, when invoking them, you can manually create a new delegate type and author the necessary target methods, make use of a VB 2010 anonymous method, or define a proper lambda expression. Regardless of which approach you take, the end result is identical.

While it is true that making use of VB 2010 LINQ query operators is far and away the simplest way to build a LINQ query expression, let's walk through each of these possible approaches just so you can see the connection between the VB 2010 query operators and the underlying `Enumerable` type.

Building Query Expressions with Query Operators (Revisited)

To begin, create a new Console Application named LinqUsingEnumerable. The module will define a series of helper methods (each of which is called within the `Main()` method) to illustrate the various manners in which you can build LINQ query expressions.

The first method, `QueryStringsWithOperators()`, offers the most straightforward way to build a query expression and is identical to the code seen in the LinqOverArray example found earlier in this chapter:

```
Sub QueryStringWithOperators()
    Console.WriteLine("***** Using Query Operators *****")

Dim currentVideoGames As String() = {"Morrowind", "Uncharted 2", "Fallout 3", "Daxter", ↵
 "System Shock 2"}

    Dim subset = From game In currentVideoGames _
        Where game.Contains(" ") _
        Order By game _
        Select game

    For Each s As String In subset
        Console.WriteLine("Item: {0}", s)
    Next
End Sub
```

The obvious benefit of using VB 2010 query operators to build query expressions is the fact that the `Func(Of T)` delegates and calls on the `Enumerable` type are out of sight and out of mind, as it is the job of the VB 2010 compiler to perform this translation. To be sure, building LINQ expressions using various query operators (`from`, `in`, `where`, or `orderby`) is the most common and straightforward approach.

Building Query Expressions Using the Enumerable Type and Lambda Expressions

Keep in mind that the LINQ query operators used here are simply shorthand versions for calling various extension methods defined by the `Enumerable` type. Consider the following `QueryStringsWithEnumerableAndLambdas()` method, which is processing the local String array now making direct use of the `Enumerable` extension methods:

```
Sub QueryStringsWithEnumerableAndLambdas()

        Console.WriteLine("** Using Enumerable / Lambda Expressions ***")

        Dim currentVideoGames As String() = {"Morrowind", "Uncharted 2",
        "Fallout 3", "Daxter", "System Shock 2"}

        'Build a query expression using extension methods
        'granted to the Array via the Enumerable type.
        Dim subset = currentVideoGames.Where(
                            Function(game) game.Contains("  ")).OrderBy
                            (Function(game) game).Select(Function(game) game)

    'Print out the results.
    For Each game In subset
            Console.WriteLine("Item: {0}", game)
    Next
    Console.WriteLine()

End Sub
```

Here, you begin by calling the `Where()` extension method on the `currentVideoGames` String array. Recall the `Array` class receives this via an extension method granted by `Enumerable`. The `Enumerable.Where()` method requires a `System.Func(Of T1, TResult)` delegate parameter. The first type parameter of this delegate represents the `IEnumerable(Of T)` compatible data to process (an array of strings in this case), while the second type parameter represents the method result data, which is obtained from a single statement fed into the lambda expression.

The return value of the `Where()` method is hidden from view in this code example, but under the covers you are operating on an `OrderedEnumerable` type. From this object, you call the generic `OrderBy()` method, which also requires a `Func(Of T)` delegate parameter. This time, you are simply passing each item in turn via a fitting lambda expression. The end result of calling `OrderBy()` is a new ordered sequence of the initial data.

Last but not least, you call the `Select()` method off the sequence returned from `OrderBy()`, which results in the final set of data that is stored in an implicitly typed variable named subset.

To be sure, this "long hand" LINQ query is a bit more complex to tease apart than the previous VB 2010 LINQ query operator example. Part of the complexity is no doubt due to the chaining together of calls using the dot operator. Here is the exact same query, with each step broken into discrete chunks:

```
Sub QueryStringsWithEnumerableAndLambdas2()
        Console.WriteLine("*** Using Enumerable / Lambda Expressions **")

        Dim currentVideoGames As String() = {"Morrowind", "Uncharted 2",
        "Fallout 3", "Daxter", "System Shock 2"}

        'Break it down!.
        Dim gamesWithSpaces = currentVideoGames.Where(Function(game) game.Contains(" "))

        Dim orderedGames = gamesWithSpaces.OrderBy(Function(game) game)
        Dim subset = orderedGames.Select(Function(game) game)
```

```
        'Print out the results.
        For Each game In subset
            Console.WriteLine("Item: {0}", game)
        Next
        Console.WriteLine()
End Sub
```

As you may agree, building a LINQ query expression using the methods of the Enumerable class directly is much more verbose than making use of the VB 2010 query operators. As well, given that the methods of Enumerable require delegates as parameters, you will typically need to author lambda expressions to allow the input data to be processed by the underlying delegate target.

Building Query Expressions Using the Enumerable Type and Anonymous Methods

Given that VB 2010 lambda expressions are simply shorthand notations for working with anonymous methods, consider the third query expression created within the QueryStringsWithAnonymousMethods() helper function:

```
Sub QueryStringsWithAnonymousMethods()

        Console.WriteLine("***** Using Anonymous Methods *****")
        Dim currentVideoGames As String() = {"Morrowind", "Uncharted 2",
        "Fallout 3", "Daxter", "System Shock 2"}

        'Build the necessary Func(Of T) delegates using anonymous methods.
        Dim searchFilter As Func(Of String, Boolean) = Function(game As     String)
            Return game.Contains(" ")
        End Function

        Dim itemToProcess As Func(Of String, String) = Function(s As String)
            Return s
        End Function

        'Pass the delegates into the methods of Enumerable.
        Dim subset = currentVideoGames.Where(
        searchFilter).OrderBy(itemToProcess).Select(itemToProcess)

        'Print out the results.
        For Each game In subset
            Console.WriteLine("Item: {0}", game)
        Next

        Console.WriteLine()
End Sub
```

This iteration of the query expression is even more verbose, because you are manually creating the Func(Of T) delegates used by the Where(), OrderBy(), and Select() methods of the Enumerable class. On the plus side, the anonymous method syntax does keep all the delegate processing contained within a single method definition. Nevertheless, this method is functionally equivalent to the

`QueryStringsWithEnumerableAndLambdas()` and `QueryStringsWithOperators()` methods created in the previous sections.

Building Query Expressions Using the Enumerable Type and Raw Delegates

Finally, if you want to build a query expression using the *really verbose approach,* you could avoid the use of lambdas/anonymous method syntax and directly create delegate targets for each `Func(Of T)` type. Here is the final iteration of your query expression, modeled within a new class type named `VeryComplexQueryExpression`:

```
Public Class VeryComplexQueryExpression

    Public Shared Sub QueryStringsWithRawDelegates()
                Console.WriteLine("***** Using Raw Delegates *****")

                Dim currentVideoGames As String() = {"Morrowind", "Uncharted 2",
                "Fallout 3", "Daxter", "System Shock 2"}

                'Build the necessary Func(Of T) delegates.
                Dim searchFilter As New Func(Of String, Boolean)(AddressOf Filter)
                Dim itemToProcess As New Func(Of String, String)(AddressOf ProcessItem)

                'Pass the delegates into the methods of Enumerable.
                Dim subset = currentVideoGames.Where(searchFilter).
                OrderBy(itemToProcess).Select(itemToProcess)

                'Print out the results.
                For Each game In subset
                Console.WriteLine("Item: {0}", game)
                Next
                Console.WriteLine()
    End Sub

    'Delegate targets.
    Public Shared Function Filter(ByVal game As String) As Boolean
        Return game.Contains(" ")
    End Function

    Public Shared Function ProcessItem(ByVal game As String) As String
        Return game
    End Function

End Class
```

You can test this iteration of your String processing logic by calling this method within the `Main()` method of your module as follows:

```
VeryComplexQueryExpression.QueryStringsWithRawDelegates()
```

If you were to now run the application to test each possible approach, it should not be too surprising that the output is identical regardless of the path taken. Keep the following points in mind regarding how LINQ query expressions are represented under the covers:

- Query expressions are created using various VB 2010 query operators.

- Query operators are simply shorthand notations for invoking extension methods defined by the `System.Linq.Enumerable` type.

- Many methods of `Enumerable` require delegates (`Func(Of T)` in particular) as parameters.

- Any method requiring a delegate parameter can instead be passed a lambda expression.

- Lambda expressions are simply anonymous methods in disguise (which greatly improve readability).

- Anonymous methods are shorthand notations for allocating a raw delegate and manually building a delegate target method.

Whew! That might have been a bit deeper under the hood than you wish to have gone, but I hope this discussion has helped you understand what the user-friendly VB 2010 query operators are actually doing behind the scenes.

■ **Note** The LinqUsingEnumerable project can be found under the Chapter 13 subdirectory.

Summary

LINQ is a set of related technologies that attempts to provide a single, symmetrical manner to interact with diverse forms of data. As explained over the course of this chapter, LINQ can interact with any type implementing the `IEnumerable(Of T)` interface, including simple arrays as well as generic and nongeneric collections of data.

As you have seen, working with LINQ technologies is accomplished using several VB 2010 language features. For example, given the fact that LINQ query expressions can return any number of result sets, it is common to use implicitly typed variables to represent the underlying data type. Also, lambda expressions, object initialization syntax, and anonymous types can all be used to build very functional and compact LINQ queries.

More importantly, you have seen how the VB 2010 LINQ query operators are simply shorthand notations for making calls on Shared members of the `System.Linq.Enumerable` type. As shown, most members of `Enumerable` operate on `Func(Of T)` delegate types, which can take literal method addresses, anonymous methods, or lambda expressions as input to evaluate the query.

CHAPTER 14

■ ■ ■

Configuring .NET Assemblies

Each of the applications in this book's first thirteen chapters was developed along the lines of traditional "stand-alone" applications, with all of the custom programming logic packaged within a single executable file (*.exe). However, a major aspect of the .NET platform is the notion of *binary reuse*, where applications make use of the types contained within various external assemblies (aka code libraries). In this chapter, we'll examine the core details of creating, deploying, and configuring .NET assemblies.

You'll learn the construction of .NET namespaces and the distinction between single-file and multi-file assemblies, as well as private and shared assemblies. Next, you'll explore exactly how the .NET runtime resolves the location of an assembly, and you'll come to understand the global assembly cache (GAC), application configuration files (*.config files), publisher policy assemblies, and the System.Configuration namespace.

Observing the Root Namespace

Notice that when you create a Class Library project, you receive little more than an empty class definition for a type named Class1. Your goal when building a *.dll assembly is to populate the binary with any number of classes, interfaces, enumerations, structures, and delegates for the task at hand. Given this, it is important to point out that all of the skills you have developed during the previous chapters apply directly to a Class Library project. The only noticeable difference between a *.dll and *.exe assembly is how the image is loaded from disk.

In any case, double-click the My Project icon within Solution Explorer. Notice that the Application tab contains a text area that defines the root namespace, which as mentioned is by default named identically to the project you have just created, as you see in Figure 14-1.

You are always free to rename your root namespace as you see fit. Recall that a namespace does not need to be defined within an identically named assembly. Consider again our good friend mscorlib.dll. This core .NET assembly does **not** define a namespace named mscorlib. Rather the mscorlib.dll assembly defines a good number of unique namespaces (System.IO, System, System.Threading, System.Collections, etc.). This brings up another very important point: a single assembly can contain any number of uniquely named namespaces. In fact, it is also possible to have a single namespace defined across multiple assemblies. For example, the System.IO namespace is partially defined in mscorlib.dll as well as System.dll.

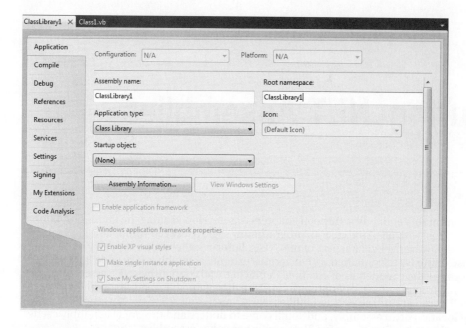

Figure 14-1. The root namespace

Defining Namespaces Beyond the Root

To illustrate the role of the VB 2010 **Namespace** keyword, update your initial ***.vb** file with the following code:

```
' This type is in the root namespace,
' which is (by default) the same name
' as the initial project.
Public Class SomeClass
End Class

' This namespace is nested within the
' root. Therefore the fully qualified
' name of this class is ClassLibrary1.MyTypes.SomeClass
Namespace MyTypes
  Public Class SomeClass
  End Class

  ' It is possible to nest namespaces within other
  ' namespaces to gain a greater level of structure.
  ' Thus, the fully qualified name of this enum is:
  ' ClassLibrary1.MyTypes.MyEnums.TestEnum
```

```
Namespace MyEnums
   Public Enum TestEnum
      TestValue
   End Enum
 End Namespace
End Namespace
```

Notice that the `Namespace` keyword allows us to create customized namespaces that are nested within the root. To see the impact of this firsthand, open the Visual Studio 2010 Object Browser (via the View menu) and expand the tree view representing your project. As you can see, your single assembly defines three custom namespaces named `ClassLibrary1`, `ClassLibrary1.MyTypes`, and `ClassLibrary1.MyTypes.MyEnums` (the additional "My" namespaces are autogenerated as a convenience for VB 2010 programmers).

■ **Note** Since the release of .NET 2.0, VB projects have access to an autogenerated namespace named My, which provides instant access to machine and project resources. Look up "My" within the .NET Framework 3.5 SDK documentation for full details.

Defining Custom Namespaces

Before diving into the details of assembly deployment and configuration, you must know how to create custom .NET namespaces. Up to this point in the text, you've been building small test programs that leverage existing namespaces in the .NET universe (`System` in particular). However, when you build your own custom applications, it can be very helpful to group your related types into custom namespaces. In VB 2010, this is accomplished using the `Namespace` keyword. Explicitly defining custom namespaces is even more important when creating .NET `*.dll` assemblies, as other developers will need to import your custom namespaces in order to use your types. Before you create your custom namespace, make sure you delete the default root namespace.

To investigate the issues firsthand, begin by creating a new Console Application named CustomNamespaces. Now, assume you are developing a collection of geometric classes named `Square`, `Circle`, and `Hexagon`. Given their similarities, you would like to group them all together into a unique namespace within the `CustomNamespaces.exe` assembly called `MyShapes`. You have two basic approaches. First, you can choose to define all classes in a single VB 2010 file (`ShapesLib.vb`) as follows:

```
'ShapesLib.vb
Namespace MyShapes

    'Circle class
    Public Class Circle
        'Interesting methods...
    End Class

    'Hexagon class
    Public Class Hexagon
        'More interesting methods...
    End Class
```

```
        'Square class
        Public Class Square
            'Even more interesting methods...
        End Class
End Namespace
```

Alternatively, you can split a single namespace into multiple VB 2010 files. To ensure each type is packaged into the same logical group, simply wrap the given class definitions in the same namespace scope:

```
'Circle.vb
Namespace MyShapes
    Public Class Circle
        'Interesting methods...
    End Class
End Namespace
```

```
'Hexagon.vb
Namespace MyShapes
    Public Class Hexagon
        'More interesting methods...
    End Class
End Namespace
```

```
'Square.vb
Namespace MyShapes
    Public Class Square
        'Even more interesting methods...
    End Class
End Namespace
```

In both cases, notice how the MyShapes namespace acts as the conceptual "container" of these classes. When another namespace (such as CustomNamespaces) needs to import types defined within a separate namespace, you make use of the Imports keyword, just as you would when using types in the .NET base class libraries:

```
' Make use of types defined the MyShapes namespace.
Imports MyShapes

Namespace CustomNamespaces
    Module Module1
        Sub Main()
            Dim h As New Hexagon()
            Dim c As New Circle()
            Dim s As New Square()
        End Sub
    End Module
End Namespace
```

For this particular example, the assumption is that the VB 2010 file(s) that define the MyShapes namespace are part of the same Console Application project that contains the file defining the CustomNamespaces namespace; in other words, all of the files are used to compile a single .NET executable assembly.

If you defined the MyShapes namespace within an external assembly, you might need to set a reference to that library before you could compile successfully. You'll learn all the details of building applications that make use of external libraries during the course of this chapter.

■ **Note** Once you have defined your own custom namespace and removed the default root namespace, then you need to define the startup object in the Application tab from the project properties.

Resolving Name Clashes with Fully Qualified Names

Technically speaking, you are not required to use the VB 2010 Imports keyword when referring to types defined in external namespaces. You could use the *fully qualified name* of the type, which, as you recall from Chapter 1, is the type's name prefixed with the defining namespace:

```
' Note we are not importing MyShapes anymore.
Namespace CustomNamespaces
    Module Module1
        Sub Main()
            Dim h As New MyShapes.Hexagon()
            Dim c As New MyShapes.Circle()
            Dim s As New MyShapes.Square()
        End Sub
    End Module
End Namespace
```

Typically there is no need to use a fully qualified name. Not only does it require a greater number of keystrokes, it also makes no difference whatsoever in terms of code size or execution speed. In fact, in CIL code, types are *always* defined with the fully qualified name. In this light, the VB 2010 Imports keyword is simply a typing time-saver.

However, fully qualified names can be very helpful (and sometimes necessary) to avoid potential name clashes when using multiple namespaces that contain identically named types. Assume you have a new namespace termed My3DShapes, which defines three classes capable of rendering a shape in stunning 3D:

```
'Another shape-centric namespace.
Namespace My3DShapes
    '3D Circle class
    Public Class Circle
    End Class
```

```
        '3D Hexagon class
        Public Class Hexagon
        End Class

        '3D Square class
        Public Class Square
        End Class
End Namespace
```

If you update the Module Module1 as seen next, you are issued a number of compile-time errors, because both namespaces define identically named classes:

```
' Ambiguities abound!
Imports MyShapes
Imports My3DShapes

Namespace CustomNamespaces
    Module Module1
        Sub Main()

            ' Which namespace do I reference?
            ' Compiler error!
            Dim h As New Hexagon()

            ' Compiler error!
            Dim c As New Circle()

            ' Compiler error!
            Dim s As New Square()
        End Sub
    End Module
End Namespace
```

The ambiguity can be resolved using the type's fully qualified name:

```
' We have now resolved the ambiguity.
Sub Main()
    Dim h As New My3DShapes.Hexagon()
    Dim c As New My3DShapes.Circle()
    Dim s As New MyShapes.Square()
End Sub
```

Resolving Name Clashes with Aliases

The VB 2010 Imports keyword also lets you create an alias for a type's fully qualified name. When you do so, you define a token that is substituted for the type's full name at compile time. Defining aliases provides a second way to resolve name-clashes, for example:

```
Imports MyShapes
Imports My3DShapes

' Resolve the ambiguity using a custom alias.
Imports The3DHexagon =My3DShapes.Hexagon

Namespace CustomNamespaces
    Module Module1
        Sub Main()
            ' This is really creating a My3DShapes.Hexagon object.
            Dim h2 As New The3DHexagon()
            '...
        End Sub
    End Module
End Namespace
```

This alternative Imports syntax also lets you create an alias for a lengthy namespace. One of the longer namespaces in the base class library is `System.Runtime.Serialization.Formatters.Binary`, which contains a member named `BinaryFormatter`. If you wish, you can create an instance of the `BinaryFormatter` as follows:

```
Imports bfHome = System.Runtime.Serialization.Formatters.Binary

Namespace MyApp
    Module ShapeTester
        Sub Main()
            Dim b As New bfHome.BinaryFormatter()
        End Sub
    End Module
End Namespace
```

as well as with a traditional Imports directive:

```
Imports System.Runtime.Serialization.Formatters.Binary

Namespace MyApp
    Module ShapeTester
        Sub Main()
            Dim b As New BinaryFormatter()
        End Sub
    End Module
End Namespace
```

At this point in the game, there is no need to concern yourself with what the `BinaryFormatter` class is used for (you'll examine this class in Chapter 20). For now, simply remember that the VB 2010 **Imports** keyword can be used to define aliases for lengthy fully qualified names or, more commonly, to resolve name-clashes that can arise when importing multiple namespaces that define identically named types.

> ■ **Note** Be aware that overuse of VB 2010 aliases can result in a confusing code base. If other programmers on your team are unaware of your custom aliases, they may assume the aliases refer to types in the .NET base class libraries and become quite confused when they can't find these tokens in the .NET 4.0 framework SDK documentation!

Creating Nested Namespaces

When organizing your types, you are free to define namespaces within other namespaces. The .NET base class libraries do so in numerous places to provide deeper levels of type organization. For example, the IO namespace is nested within System, to yield System.IO. If you want to create a root namespace containing the existing My3DShapes namespace, you can update your code as follows:

```
'Nesting a namespace.
Namespace Chapter14

    Namespace My3DShapes

        '3D Circle class
        Class Circle
        End Class

        '3D Hexagon class
        Class Hexagon
        End Class

        '3D Square class
        Class Square
        End Class

    End Namespace

End Namespace
```

In many cases, the role of a root namespace is simply to provide a further level of scope, and therefore it may not define any types directly within its scope (as in the case of the **Chapter14** namespace). If this is the case, a nested namespace can be defined using the following compact form:

```
'Nesting a namespace (take two).
Namespace Chapter14.My3DShapes
        '3D Circle class
        Class Circle
        End Class

        ' 3D Hexagon class
        Class Hexagon
        End Class
```

```
        ' 3D Square class
        Class Square
        End Class
End Namespace
```

Given that you have now nested the `My3DShapes` namespace within the `Chapter14` root namespace, you need to update any existing `Imports` directives and type aliases:

```
Imports Chapter14.My3DShapes
Imports The3DHexagon = Chapter14.My3DShapes.Hexagon
```

■ **Source Code** The CustomNamespaces project is located under the Chapter 14 subdirectory.

The Role of .NET Assemblies

.NET applications are constructed by piecing together any number of *assemblies*. Simply put, an assembly is a versioned, self-describing binary file hosted by the CLR. Now, despite the fact that .NET assemblies have exactly the same file extensions (`*.exe` or `*.dll`) as previous Windows binaries (including legacy COM servers), they have very little in common with those files under the hood. Thus, to set the stage for the information to come, let's consider some of the benefits provided by the assembly format.

Assemblies Promote Code Reuse

As you have built your Console Applications over the previous chapters, it may have seemed that *all* of the applications' functionality was contained within the executable assembly you were constructing. In reality, your applications were leveraging numerous types contained within the always accessible .NET code library, `mscorlib.dll` (recall that the VB 2010 compiler references `mscorlib.dll` automatically), and in the case of some examples, `System.Windows.Forms.dll`.

As you may know, a *code library* (also termed a *class library*) is a `*.dll` that contains types intended to be used by external applications. When you are creating executable assemblies, you will no doubt be leveraging numerous system-supplied and custom code libraries as you create your application. Do be aware, however, that a code library need not take a `*.dll` file extension. It is perfectly possible (although not very common) for an executable assembly to make use of types defined within an external executable file. In this light, a referenced `*.exe` can also be considered a code library.

Regardless of how a code library is packaged, the .NET platform allows you to reuse types in a language-independent manner. For example, you could create a code library in VB 2010 and reuse that library in any other .NET programming language. It is possible not only to allocate types across languages, but also to derive from them. A base class defined in VB 2010 could be extended by a class authored in C#. Interfaces defined in Pascal.NET can be implemented by structures defined in VB 2010, and so forth. The point is that when you begin to break apart a single monolithic executable into numerous .NET assemblies, you achieve a *language-neutral* form of code reuse.

Assemblies Establish a Type Boundary

Recall that a type's *fully qualified name* is composed by prefixing the type's namespace (e.g., `System`) to its name (e.g., `Console`). Strictly speaking, however, the assembly in which a type resides further establishes a type's identity. For example, if you have two uniquely named assemblies (say, `MyCars.dll` and `YourCars.dll`) that both define a namespace (`CarLibrary`) containing a class named `SportsCar`, they are considered unique types in the .NET universe.

Assemblies Are Versionable Units

.NET assemblies are assigned a four-part numerical version number of the form *<major>.<minor>.<build>.<revision>*. (If you do not explicitly provide a version number, the assembly is automatically assigned a version of 1.0.0.0, given the default Visual Studio project settings.) This number, in conjunction with an optional *public key value*, allows multiple versions of the same assembly to coexist in harmony on a single machine. Formally speaking, assemblies that provide public key information are termed *strongly named*. As you will see in this chapter, by using a strong name, the CLR is able to ensure that the correct version of an assembly is loaded on behalf of the calling client.

Assemblies Are Self-Describing

Assemblies are regarded as *self-describing* in part because they record every external assembly they must have access to in order to function correctly. Thus, if your assembly requires `System.Windows.Forms.dll` and `System.Drawing.dll`, this will be documented in the assembly's *manifest*. Recall from Chapter 1 that a manifest is a blob of metadata that describes the assembly itself (name, version, required external assemblies, etc.).

In addition to manifest data, an assembly contains metadata that describes the composition (member names, implemented interfaces, base classes, constructors, and so forth) of every contained type. Because an assembly is documented in such detail, the CLR does *not* consult the Windows system registry to resolve its location (quite the radical departure from Microsoft's legacy COM programming model). As you will discover during this chapter, the CLR makes use of an entirely new scheme to resolve the location of external code libraries.

Assemblies Are Configurable

Assemblies can be deployed as "private" or "shared." Private assemblies reside in the same directory (or possibly a subdirectory) as the client application that uses them. Shared assemblies, on the other hand, are libraries intended to be consumed by numerous applications on a single machine and are deployed to a specific directory termed the *global assembly cache*, or *GAC*.

Regardless of how you deploy your assemblies, you are free to author XML-based configuration files. Using these configuration files, you can instruct the CLR to "probe" for assemblies at a specific location, load a specific version of a referenced assembly for a particular client, or consult an arbitrary directory on your local machine, your network location, or a web-based URL. You'll learn a good deal more about XML configuration files throughout this chapter.

Understanding the Format of a .NET Assembly

Now that you've learned about several benefits provided by the .NET assembly, let's shift gears and get a better idea of how an assembly is composed under the hood. Structurally speaking, a .NET assembly (*.dll or *.exe) consists of the following elements:

- A Windows file header
- A CLR file header
- CIL code
- Type metadata
- An assembly manifest
- Optional embedded resources

While the first two elements (the Windows and CLR headers) are blocks of data you can typically always ignore, they do deserve some brief consideration. Here's an overview of each element.

The Windows File Header

The Windows file header establishes the fact that the assembly can be loaded and manipulated by the Windows family of operating systems. This header data also identifies the kind of application (console-based, GUI-based, or *.dll code library) to be hosted by Windows. If you open a .NET assembly using the dumpbin.exe utility (via a Visual Studio 2010 command prompt) and specify the /headers flag as so:

```
dumpbin /headers CarLibrary.dll
```

you can view an assembly's Windows header information. Here is the (partial) Windows header information for the CarLibrary.dll assembly you will build a bit later in this chapter (if you would like to run dumpbin.exe yourself right now, you can specify the name of any *.dll or *.exe you wrote during this book in place of CarLibrary.dll):

```
Dump of file CarLibrary.dll


PE signature found

File Type: DLL


FILE HEADER VALUES

            14C machine (x86)
```

```
           3 number of sections

     4C01DE81 time date stamp Sun Aug 17  01:19:51  2010

           0 file pointer to symbol table

           0 number of symbols

          E0 size of optional header

        2102 characteristics

             Executable

             32 bit word machine

             DLL


OPTIONAL HEADER VALUES

         10B magic # (PE32)

        8.00 linker version

        2E00 size of code

         E00 size of initialized data

           0 size of uninitialized data

        4DEE entry point (00402CDE)

        2000 base of code

        6000 base of data

      400000 image base (00400000 to 00407FFF)

        2000 section alignment

         200 file alignment

        4.00 operating system version

        0.00 image version
```

```
4.00 subsystem version

   0 Win32 version

C000 size of image

 400 size of headers

   0 checksum

   2 subsystem (Windows CUI)
```

...

Now, remember that the vast majority of .NET programmers will never need to concern themselves with the format of the header data embedded in a .NET assembly. Unless you happen to be building a new .NET language compiler (where you *would* care about such information), you are free to remain blissfully unaware of the grimy details of the header data. Do be aware, however, that this information is used under the covers when Windows loads the binary image into memory.

The CLR File Header

The CLR header is a block of data that all .NET assemblies must support (and do support, courtesy of the VB 2010 compiler) in order to be hosted by the CLR. In a nutshell, this header defines numerous flags that enable the runtime to understand the layout of the managed file. For example, flags exist that identify the location of the metadata and resources within the file, the version of the runtime the assembly was built against, the value of the (optional) public key, and so forth. If you supply the /clrheader flag to dumpbin.exe like so:

```
dumpbin /clrheader CarLibrary.dll
```

you are presented with the internal CLR header information for a given .NET assembly, as shown here:

```
Dump of file CarLibrary.dll

File Type: DLL


  clr Header:

        48 cb

      2.05 runtime version

      2A48 [2358] RVA [size] of MetaData Directory
```

```
          3 flags

              IL Only

              32-Bit Required

          0 entry point token

      2050 [0] RVA [size] of Resources Directory

          0 [0] RVA [size] of StrongNameSignature Directory

          0 [0] RVA [size] of CodeManagerTable Directory

          0 [0] RVA [size] of VTableFixups Directory

          0 [0] RVA [size] of ExportAddressTableJumps Directory

          0 [0] RVA [size] of ManagedNativeHeader Directory


  Summary

      2000 .reloc

      2000 .rsrc

      2000 .sdata

      4000 .text
```

Again, as a .NET developer you will not need to concern yourself with the gory details of an assembly's CLR header information. Just understand that every .NET assembly contains this data, which is used behind the scenes by the .NET runtime as the image data loads into memory. Now let's turn our attention to some information that is much more useful in our day-to-day programming tasks.

CIL Code, Type Metadata, and the Assembly Manifest

At its core, an assembly contains CIL code, which, as you recall, is a platform- and CPU-agnostic intermediate language. At runtime, the internal CIL is compiled on the fly using a just-in-time (JIT) compiler, according to platform- and CPU-specific instructions. Given this design, .NET assemblies can indeed execute on a variety of architectures, devices, and operating systems. (Although you can live a happy and productive life without understanding the details of the CIL programming language, Chapter 17 offers an introduction to the syntax and semantics of CIL.)

An assembly also contains metadata that completely describes the format of the contained types, as well as the format of external types referenced by this assembly. The .NET runtime uses this metadata to resolve the location of types (and their members) within the binary, lay out types in memory, and facilitate remote method invocations. You'll check out the details of the .NET metadata format in Chapter 16 during our examination of reflection services.

An assembly must also contain an associated *manifest* (also referred to as *assembly metadata*). The manifest documents each *module* within the assembly, establishes the version of the assembly, and also documents any *external* assemblies referenced by the current assembly (unlike legacy COM type libraries, which did not provide a way to document external dependencies). As you will see over the course of this chapter, the CLR makes extensive use of an assembly's manifest during the process of locating external assembly references.

■ **Note** As you will see a bit later in this chapter, a .NET module is a term used to define the parts in a multifile assembly.

Optional Assembly Resources

Finally, a .NET assembly may contain any number of embedded resources, such as application icons, image files, sound clips, or string tables. In fact, the .NET platform supports *satellite assemblies* that contain nothing but localized resources. This can be useful if you wish to partition your resources based on a specific culture (English, German, etc.) for the purposes of building international software. The topic of building satellite assemblies is outside the scope of this text; however, you will learn how to embed application resources into an assembly during our examination of the Windows Presentation Foundation API in Chapter 30.

Single-File and Multifile Assemblies

Technically speaking, an assembly can be composed of multiple *modules*. A module is really nothing more than a general term for a valid .NET binary file. In most situations, an assembly is in fact composed of a single module. In this case, there is a one-to-one correspondence between the (logical) assembly and the underlying (physical) binary (hence the term *single-file assembly*).

Single-file assemblies contain all of the necessary elements (header information, CIL code, type metadata, manifest, and required resources) in a single `*.exe` or `*.dll` package. Figure 14-2 illustrates the composition of a single-file assembly.

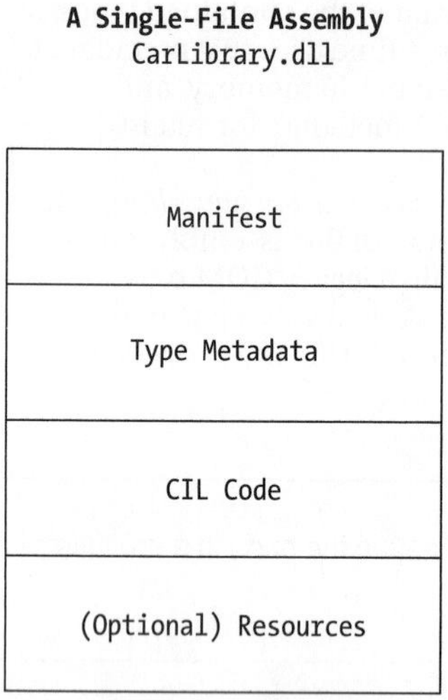

A Single-File Assembly
   CarLibrary.dll

Manifest
Type Metadata
CIL Code
(Optional) Resources

Figure 14-2. A single-file assembly

A multifile assembly, on the other hand, is a set of .NET `modules` that are deployed and versioned as a single logical unit. Formally speaking, one of these `modules` is termed the `primary module` and contains the assembly-level manifest (as well as any necessary CIL code, metadata, header information, and optional resources). The manifest of the primary module records each of the related `module` files it is dependent upon.

As a naming convention, the secondary modules in a multifile assembly take a `*.netmodule` file extension; however, this is not a requirement of the CLR. Secondary `*.netmodules` also contain CIL code and type metadata, as well as a *module-level manifest*, which simply records the externally required assemblies of that specific module.

The major benefit of constructing multifile assemblies is that they provide a very efficient way to download content. For example, assume you have a machine that is referencing a remote multifile assembly composed of three modules, where the primary module is installed on the client. If the client requires a type within a secondary remote `*.netmodule`, the CLR will download the binary to the local machine on demand to a specific location termed the *download cache*. If each `*.netmodule` is 5MB, I'm sure you can see the benefit (compared with downloading a single 15MB file).

Another benefit of multifile assemblies is that they enable modules to be authored using multiple .NET programming languages (which is very helpful in larger corporations, where individual departments tend to favor a specific .NET language). Once each of the individual modules has been compiled, the modules can be logically "connected" into a logical assembly using the VB 2010 command-line compiler.

In any case, do understand that the modules that compose a multifile assembly are not literally linked together into a single (larger) file. Rather, multifile assemblies are only logically related by information contained in the primary module's manifest. Figure 14-3 illustrates a multifile assembly composed of three modules, each authored using a unique .NET programming language.

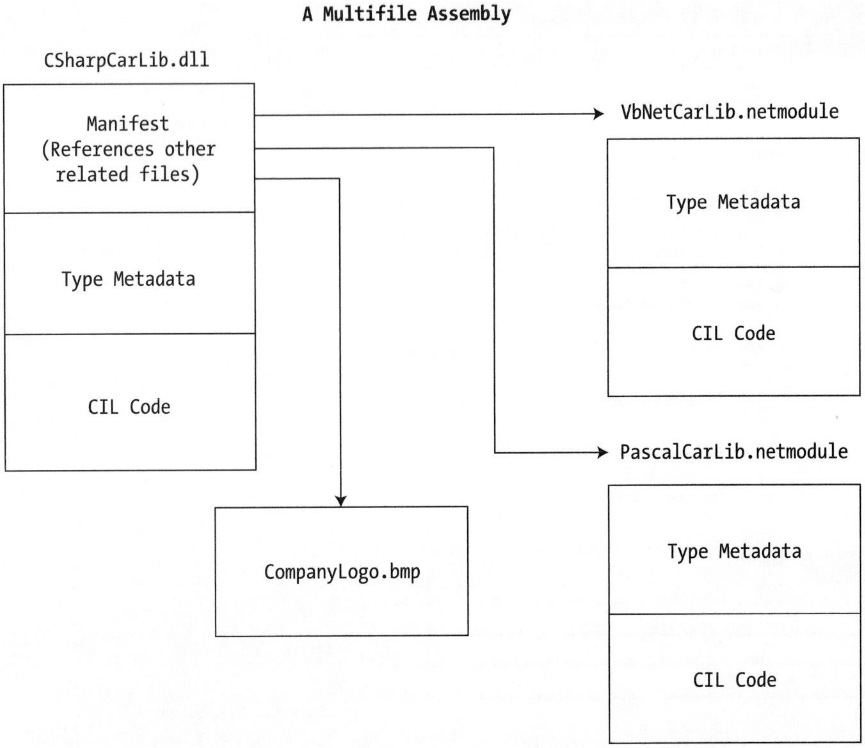

A Multifile Assembly

CSharpCarLib.dll

Manifest (References other related files)
Type Metadata
CIL Code

VbNetCarLib.netmodule

Type Metadata
CIL Code

PascalCarLib.netmodule

Type Metadata
CIL Code

CompanyLogo.bmp

Figure 14-3. The primary module records secondary modules in the assembly manifest

At this point you should have a better understanding of the internal composition of a .NET binary file. With that out of the way, we are ready to look at the building and configuring a variety of code libraries.

Building and Consuming a Single-File Assembly

To begin exploring the world of .NET assemblies, you'll first create a single-file *.dll assembly (named CarLibrary) that contains a small set of public types. To build a code library using Visual Studio 2010, select the Class Library project workspace via the File ➤ New Project… menu option (see Figure 14-4).

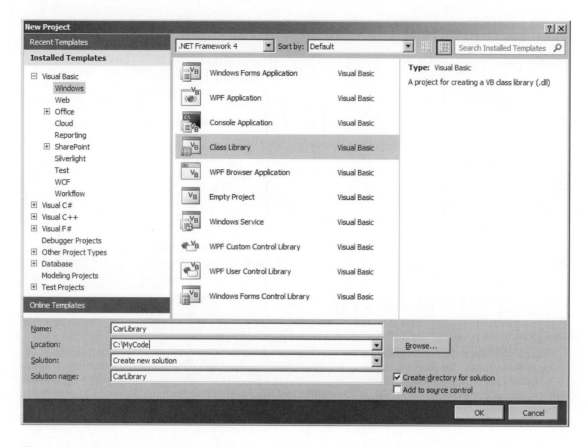

Figure 14-4. Creating a VB 2010 code library

The design of your automobile library begins with a `MustInherit` base class named `Car` that defines various state data via automatic property syntax. This class also has a single `MustOverride` method named `TurboBoost()`, which makes use of a custom enumeration (`EngineState`) representing the current condition of the car's engine:

```
'Represents the state of the engine.
Public Enum EngineState
    engineAlive
    engineDead
End Enum

'The MustInherit base class in the hierarchy.
Public MustInherit Class Car
```

```
        Public Property PetName() As String
        Public Property CurrentSpeed() As Integer
        Public Property MaxSpeed() As Integer

        Protected egnState As EngineState = EngineState.engineAlive

        Public ReadOnly Property EngineState() As EngineState
            Get
                Return egnState
            End Get
        End Property

        Public MustOverride Sub TurboBoost()

        Public Sub New()
        End Sub

        Public Sub New(ByVal name As String, ByVal maxSp As Integer,
            ByVal currSp As Integer)
                PetName = name
                MaxSpeed = maxSp
                CurrentSpeed = currSp
        End Sub
End Class
```

Now assume you have two direct descendents of the **Car** type named **MiniVan** and **SportsCar**. Each overrides the **MustOverride TurboBoost()** method by displaying an appropriate message via a Windows Forms message box. Insert a new VB 2010 class file into your project named **DerivedCars.vb**, which contains the following code:

```
Imports System.Windows.Forms

Public Class SportsCar
  Inherits Car

        Public Sub New()
        End Sub

        Public Sub New(ByVal name As String, ByVal maxSp As Integer,
            ByVal currSp As Integer)
            MyBase.New(name, maxSp, currSp)
        End Sub

        Public Overrides Sub TurboBoost()
            MessageBox.Show("Ramming speed!", "Faster is better...")
        End Sub
End Class
```

```
Public Class MiniVan
  Inherits Car

    Public Sub New()
    End Sub

    Public Sub New(ByVal name As String, ByVal maxSp As Integer,
          ByVal currSp As Integer)
          MyBase.New(name, maxSp, currSp)
    End Sub

    Public Overrides Sub TurboBoost()
        'Minivans have poor turbo capabilities!
        egnState = EngineState.engineDead
        MessageBox.Show("Eek!", "Your engine block exploded!")
    End Sub
End Class
```

Notice how each subclass implements `TurboBoost()` using the Windows Form's `MessageBox` class, which is defined in the `System.Windows.Forms.dll` assembly. For your assembly to make use of the types defined within this external assembly, the CarLibrary project must set a reference to this binary via the Add Reference dialog box (see Figure 14-5), which you can access through the Visual Studio Project ➤ Add Reference menu selection.

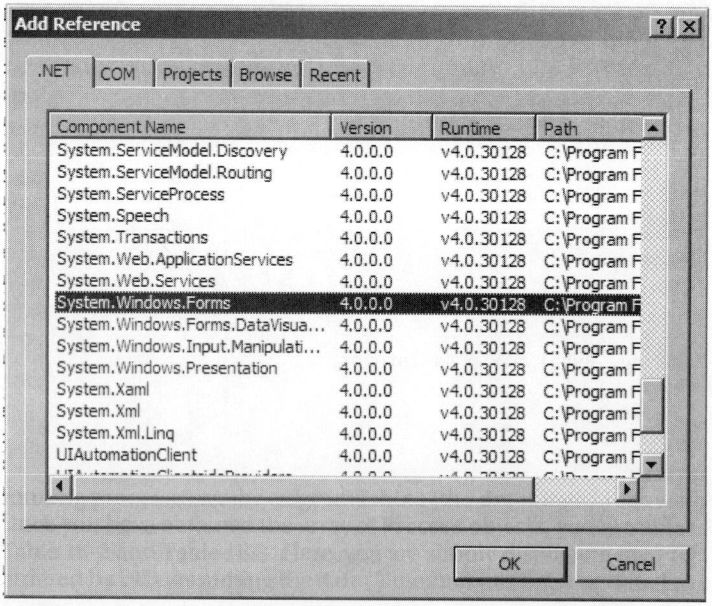

Figure 14-5. Referencing external .NET assemblies using the Add Reference dialog box

It is *really* important to understand that the assemblies displayed in the .NET tab of the Add Reference dialog box do not represent each and every assembly on your machine. The Add Reference dialog box will *not* display your custom assemblies, and it does *not* display all assemblies located in the GAC. Rather, this dialog box simply presents a list of common assemblies that Visual Studio 2010 is preprogrammed to display. When you are building applications that require the use of an assembly not listed within the Add Reference dialog box, you need to click the Browse tab to manually navigate to the *.dll or *.exe in question.

■ **Note** Be aware that the Recent tab of the Add Reference dialog box keeps a running list of previously referenced assemblies. This can be handy, as many .NET projects tend to use the same core set of external libraries.

Exploring the Manifest

Before using CarLibrary.dll from a client application, let's check out how the code library is composed under the hood. Assuming you have compiled this project, load CarLibrary.dll into ildasm.exe (see Figure 14-6).

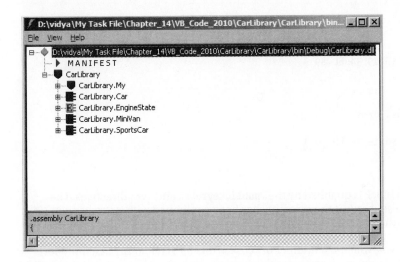

Figure 14-6. CarLibrary.dll loaded into ildasm.exe

Now, open the manifest of CarLibrary.dll by double-clicking the MANIFEST icon. The first code block in a manifest specifies all external assemblies required by the current assembly to function correctly. As you recall, CarLibrary.dll made use of types within mscorlib.dll and System.Windows.Forms.dll, both of which are listed in the manifest using the .assembly extern token:

```
// Metadata version: v4.0.30128
.assembly extern mscorlib
{
  .publickeytoken = (B7 7A 5C 56 19 34 E0 89 )
  .ver 4:0:0:0
}
.assembly extern Microsoft.VisualBasic
{
  .publickeytoken = (B0 3F 5F 7F 11 D5 0A 3A )
  .ver 4:0:0:0
}

.assembly extern System.Xml.Linq
{
  .publickeytoken = (B7 7A 5C 56 19 34 E0 89 )
  .ver 4:0:0:0
}

.assembly extern System
{
  .publickeytoken = (B7 7A 5C 56 19 34 E0 89 )
  .ver 4:0:0:0
}

.assembly extern System.Core
{
  .publickeytoken = (B7 7A 5C 56 19 34 E0 89 )
  .ver 4:0:0:0
}

.assembly extern System.Windows.Forms
{
  .publickeytoken = (B7 7A 5C 56 19 34 E0 89 )
  .ver 4:0:0:0
}
```

Here, each `.assembly extern` block is qualified by the `.publickeytoken` and `.ver` directives. The `.publickeytoken` instruction is present only if the assembly has been configured with a *strong name* (more details on strong names in the section "Understanding Strong Names" later in this chapter). The `.ver` token defines (of course) the numerical version identifier of the referenced assembly.

After the external references, you will find a number of `.custom` tokens that identify assembly-level attributes (copyright information, company name, assembly version, etc.). Here is a (very) partial listing of this chunk of MANIFEST data:

```
.assembly CarLibrary
{
  custom instance void ...AssemblyCompanyAttribute...
  custom instance void ...AssemblyCompilationAttribute...
  custom instance void ...RuntimeCompatibilityAttribute...
  custom instance void ...AssemblyProductAttribute...
  .custom instance void ...AssemblyDescriptionAttribute...
```

```
    .custom instance void ...AssemblyTitleAttribute...
     custom instance void ...TargetFrameworkAttribute...
    .custom instance void ...AssemblyTrademarkAttribute...
    . custom instance void ...AssemblyCopyrightAttribute...
    ....
    .ver 1:0:0:0
}
.module CarLibrary.dll
```

Typically these settings are established visually using the Properties editor of your current project. Now, switching back to Visual Studio 2010, if you single-click on the Properties icon within the Solution Explorer, you can click on the "Assembly Information..." button located on the (automatically selected) Application tab. This will bring up the GUI editor shown in Figure 14-7.

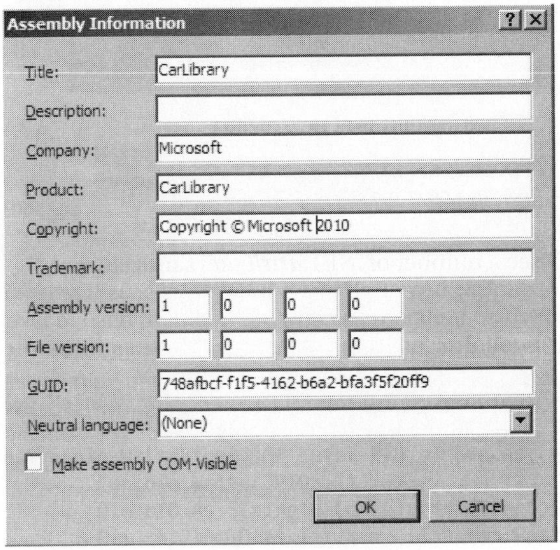

Figure 14-7. Editing assembly information using Visual Studio's Properties editor

When you save your changes, the GUI editor updates your project's `AssemblyInfo.vb` file, which is maintained by Visual Studio 2010 and can be viewed by expanding the My Project node in the Solution Explorer; see Figure 14-8).

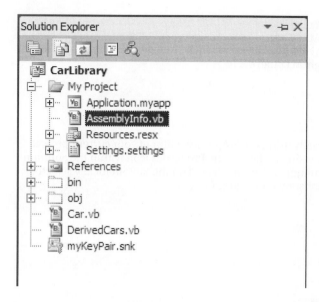

Figure 14-8. The AssemblyInfo.vb file is updated as you use the GUI Properties editor

If you view the contents of this VB 2010 file, you'll see a number of .NET *attributes* sandwiched between square brackets, for example:

```
<Assembly: AssemblyTitle("CarLibrary")>
<Assembly: AssemblyDescription("")>
<Assembly: AssemblyCompany("Microsoft")>
<Assembly: AssemblyProduct("CarLibrary")>
<Assembly: AssemblyCopyright("Copyright © Microsoft 2010")>
<Assembly: AssemblyTrademark("")>
```

Chapter 15 examines the role of attributes in depth, so don't sweat the details at this point. For now, just be aware that a majority of the attributes in `AssemblyInfo.vb` will be used to update the `.custom` token values within an assembly MANIFEST.

Exploring the CIL

Recall that an assembly does not contain platform-specific instructions; rather, it contains platform-agnostic common intermediate language (CIL) instructions. When the .NET runtime loads an assembly into memory, the underlying CIL is compiled (using the JIT compiler) into instructions that can be understood by the target platform. For example, if you double-click the `TurboBoost()` method of the `SportsCar` class, `ildasm.exe` will open a new window showing the CIL tokens that implement this method:

```
.method public strict virtual instance void
  TurboBoost() cil managed
{
  // Code size       19 (0x13)
  .maxstack  8
  IL_0000:  nop
  IL_0001:  ldstr   "Ramming speed!"
  IL_0006:  ldstr   "Faster is better..."
  IL_000b:  call    valuetype [System.Windows.Forms]System.Windows.Forms.DialogResult
    [System.Windows.Forms]System.Windows.Forms.MessageBox::Show(string, string)
  IL_0010:  pop
  IL_0011:  nop
  IL_0012:  ret
} // end of method
SportsCar::TurboBoost
```

Again, while most .NET developers don't need to be deeply concerned with the details of CIL on a daily basis, Chapter 17 provides more details on its syntax and semantics. Believe it or not, understanding the grammar of CIL can be helpful when you are building more complex applications that require advanced services, such as runtime construction of assemblies (again, see Chapter 17).

Exploring the Type Metadata

Before we build some applications that make use of our custom .NET library, if you press the Ctrl+M keystroke combination, **ildasm.exe** displays the metadata for each type within the **CarLibrary.dll** assembly (see Figure 14-9).

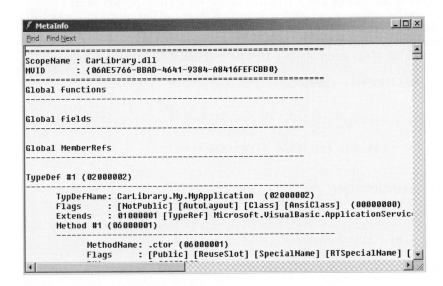

Figure 14-9. Type metadata for the types within CarLibrary.dll

As explained in the next chapter, an assembly's metadata is a very important element of the .NET platform, and serves as the backbone for numerous technologies (object serialization, late binding, extendable applications, etc.). In any case, now that you have looked inside the `CarLibrary.dll` assembly, you can build some client applications that make use of your types!

■ **Source Code** The CarLibrary project is located under the Chapter 14 subdirectory.

Building a VB 2010 Client Application

Because each of the `CarLibrary` types has been declared using the `Public` keyword, other assemblies are able to use them as well. Recall that you may also define types using the VB 2010 `Friend` keyword (in fact, this is the default VB 2010 access mode). Friend types can be used only by the assembly in which they are defined. External clients can neither see nor create types marked with the `Friend` keyword.

■ **Note** .NET does provide a way to specify "friend assemblies" that allow Friend types to be consumed by a set of specified assemblies. Look up the InternalsVisibleToAttribute class in the .NET Framework 4.0 SDK documentation for details if you are interested; however, be aware that the construction of friend assemblies is quite rare.

To use your library's functionality, create a new VB 2010 Console Application project named VisualBasicCarClient. Once you have done so, set a reference to `CarLibrary.dll` using the Browse tab of the Add Reference dialog box (if you compiled `CarLibrary.dll` using Visual Studio, your assembly is located under the \bin\Debug subdirectory of the CarLibrary project folder). At this point you can build your client application to make use of the external types. Update your initial VB 2010 file as follows:

```
' Don't forget to import the CarLibrary namespace!
Imports CarLibrary

Public Module Module1
    Sub Main()
        Console.WriteLine("***** VB 2010 CarLibrary Client App *****")

        ' Make a sports car.
        Dim viper As New SportsCar("Viper", 240, 40)
        viper.TurboBoost()

        ' Make a minivan.
        Dim mv As New MiniVan()
        mv.TurboBoost()
        Console.ReadLine()
    End Sub
End Module
```

This code looks just like the code of the other applications developed thus far in the text. The only point of interest is that the VB 2010 client application is now making use of types defined within a separate custom assembly. Go ahead and run your program. As you'd expect, the execution of this program results in the display of various message boxes.

It is important to point out that Visual Studio 2010 placed a copy of `CarLibrary.dll` into the `\bin\Debug` folder of the VisualBasicCarClient project folder. This can be verified by clicking the Show All Files button of the Solution Explorer (see Figure 14-10).

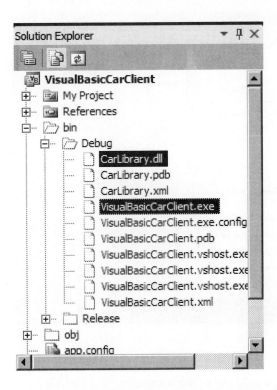

Figure 14-10. *Visual Studio 2010 copies private assemblies to the client's directory*

As explained later in this chapter, `CarLibrary.dll` has been configured as a "private" assembly (which is the automatic behavior for all Visual Studio 2010 Class Library projects). When you reference private assemblies in new applications (such as `VisualBasicCarClient.exe`), the IDE responds by placing a copy of the library in the client application's output directory.

■ **Source Code** The VisualBasicCarClient project is located under the Chapter 14 subdirectory.

Building a C# Client Application

To illustrate the language-agnostic attitude of the .NET platform, let's create another Console Application (CSharpCarClient), this time using C# (see Figure 14-11). Once you have created the project, set a reference to **CarLibrary.dll** using the Add Reference dialog box, which can be activated by the Project ➤ Add Reference menu option.

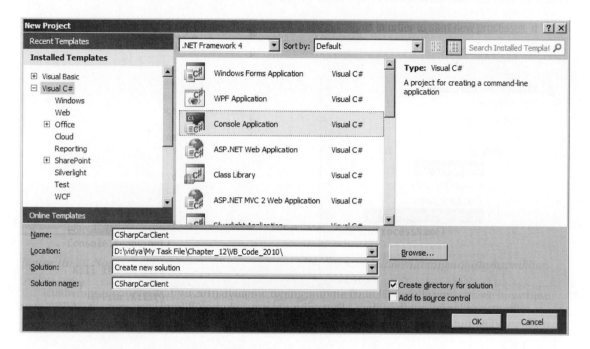

Figure 14-11. Creating a C# Console Application

Like VB 2010, C# requires you to list each namespace used within the current file. However, C# offers the **using** keyword rather than the VB 2010 **Imports** keyword, so add the following **using** statement within the **program.cs** code file:

```csharp
using CarLibrary;
public class program
{
    public static void Main(string[] args)
    {
    }
}
```

Notice that the **Main()** method is defined within a C# **program** class. In any case, to exercise the **MiniVan** and **SportsCar** types using the syntax of C#, update your **Main()** method as follows:

```
public static void Main(string[] args)
{
    Console.WriteLine("***** C# CarLibrary Client App *****");
        // Local variables are declared.
        MiniVan myMiniVan = new MiniVan();
        myMiniVan.TurboBoost();
        SportsCar mySportsCar = new SportsCar();
        mySportsCar.TurboBoost();
        Console.ReadLine();
}
```

This code looks just like the code of the other applications developed thus far in the text. The only point of interest is that the C# client application is now making use of types defined within a separate custom assembly. When you compile and run your application, you will once again find a series of message boxes displayed. Furthermore, this new client application has its own local copy of CarLibrary.dll located under the bin\Debug folder.

Cross-Language Inheritance in Action

A very enticing aspect of .NET development is the notion of *cross-language inheritance*. To illustrate, let's create a new C# class that derives from SportsCar (which was authored using VB 2010). First, add a new class file to your current C# application (by selecting the Project ➤ Add Class menu option) named PerformanceCar.cs. Update the initial class definition by deriving from SportsCar. Then, override the abstract TurboBoost() method:

```
using CarLibrary;
//This C# class is deriving from the VB 2010 SportsCar.
public class PerformanceCar : SportsCar
{
        public override void TurboBoost()
        {
                Console.WriteLine("Zero to 60 in a cool 4.8 seconds...");
        }
}
```

To test this new class type, update the program's Main() method as follows:

```
Public static void Main(string[] args)
{
        ...
        PerformanceCar dreamCar = new PerformanceCar();
        //Use Inherited property.
        dreamCar.PetName = "Hank";
        dreamCar.TurboBoost();
        Console.ReadLine();
}
```

Notice that the **dreamCar** object is able to invoke any public member (such as the **PetName** property) found up the chain of inheritance, regardless of the fact that the base class was defined in a completely different language and in a completely different assembly! The ability to extend classes across assembly boundaries in a language-independent manner is a very natural aspect of the .NET development cycle. This makes it very easy to use compiled code written by individuals who would rather not build their shared code with VB 2010.

■ **Source Code** The CSharpCarClient project is located under the Chapter 14 subdirectory.

Building and Consuming a Multifile Assembly

Now that you have constructed and consumed a single-file assembly, let's examine the process of building a multifile assembly. Recall that a multifile assembly is simply a collection of related modules that is deployed and versioned as a single logical unit. At the time of this writing, the Visual Studio IDE does not support a VB 2010 multifile assembly project template. Therefore, you will need to make use of the command-line compiler (**vbc.exe**) to build such a beast.

To describe the process, you will build a multifile assembly named **AirVehicles**. The primary module (**airvehicles.dll**) will contain a single class type named **Helicopter**. The related manifest (also contained in **airvehicles.dll**) will catalog an additional *.netmodule file named **ufo.netmodule** that contains another class type named (of course) **Ufo**. Although both class types are physically contained in separate binaries, you will group them into a single namespace named **AirVehicles**. You'll create both classes using VB 2010 (although you could certainly mix and match languages if you desire).

To begin, open a simple text editor (such as Notepad) and create the following **Ufo** class definition and save it to a file named **ufo.vb**:

```
Namespace AirVehicles
    Public Class Ufo
        Public Sub AbductHuman()
            Console.WriteLine("Resistance is futile")
        End Sub
    End Class
End Namespace
```

To compile this class into a .NET module, open a Visual Studio 2010 Command Prompt, navigate to the folder containing **ufo.vb** and issue the following command to the VB 2010 compiler (the **module** option of the **/target** flag instructs **vbc.exe** to produce a *.netmodule as opposed to a *.dll or an *.exe file):

```
vbc.exe /t:module ufo.vb
```

If you now look in the folder that contains the **ufo.vb** file, you should see a new file named **ufo.netmodule** (take a peek in your working directory). Next, create a new file named **helicopter.vb** that contains the following class definition:

```
Namespace AirVehicles
    Public Class Helicopter
        Public Sub TakeOff()
            Console.WriteLine("Helicopter taking off!")
        End Sub
    End Class
End Namespace
```

Given that `airvehicles.dll` is the intended name of the primary module of this multifile assembly, you will need to compile `helicopter.vb` using the `/t:library` and `/out:` options. To enlist the `ufo.netmodule` binary into the assembly manifest, you must also specify the `/addmodule` flag. The following command does the trick:

```
vbc /t:library /addmodule:ufo.netmodule /out:airvehicles.dll helicopter.vb
```

At this point, your directory should contain the primary `airvehicles.dll` module as well as the secondary `ufo.netmodule` binaries.

Exploring the ufo.netmodule File

Now, using `ildasm.exe`, open `ufo.netmodule`. As you can see, `*.netmodule`s contain a *module-level manifest*; however, its sole purpose is to list each external assembly referenced by the code base. Given that the `Ufo` class did little more than make a call to `Console.WriteLine()`, you find the following core information:

```
.assembly extern mscorlib
{
  .publickeytoken = (B7 7A 5C 56 19 34 E0 89 )
  .ver 4:0:0:0
}
.assembly extern Microsoft.VisualBasic
{
  .publickeytoken = (B0 3F 5F 7F 11 D5 0A 3A )
  // .?_....:
  .ver 10:0:0:0
}
.module ufo.netmodule
```

Exploring the airvehicles.dll File

Next, using `ildasm.exe`, open the primary `airvehicles.dll` module and investigate the assembly-level manifest. Notice that the `.file` token documents the associated modules in the multifile assembly (`ufo.netmodule` in this case). The `.class extern` tokens are used to document the names of the external types referenced for use from the secondary module (`Ufo`). Here is the relevant information:

```
.assembly extern mscorlib
{
  .publickeytoken = (B7 7A 5C 56 19 34 E0 89 )
  .ver 4:0:0:0
  ...
}
...
.assembly airvehicles
{
...
  .hash algorithm 0x00008004
  .ver 0:0:0:0
}
.file ufo.netmodule
...
.class extern public AirVehicles.Ufo
{
  .file ufo.netmodule
  .class 0x02000002
}
.module airvehicles.dll
```

Again, realize that the only entity that links together **airvehicles.dll** and **ufo.netmodule** is the assembly manifest. These two binary files have not been merged into a single, larger ***.dll**.

Consuming a Multifile Assembly

The consumers of a multifile assembly couldn't care less that the assembly they are referencing is composed of numerous modules. To keep things simple, let's create a new VB 2010 client application at the command line. Create a new file named **Client.vb** with the following module definition. When you are done, save it in the same location as your multifile assembly.

```
Imports AirVehicles

Module Client

    Sub Main()
        Console.WriteLine("***** Multifile Assembly Client *****")
        Dim h As New Helicopter()
        h.TakeOff()

        'This will load the *.netmodule on demand.
        Dim u As New Ufo()
        u.AbductHuman()
        Console.ReadLine()
    End Sub

End Module
```

To compile this executable assembly at the command line, use the VB 2010 command-line compiler, **vbc.exe**, with the following command set:

```
vbc /r:airvehicles.dll Client.vb
```

Notice that when you are referencing a multifile assembly, the compiler needs to be supplied only with the name of the primary module (the `*.netmodules` are loaded on demand by the CLR when used by the client's code base). In and of themselves, `*.netmodules` do not have an individual version number and can't be directly loaded by the CLR. Individual `*.netmodules` can be loaded only by the primary module (e.g., the file that contains the assembly manifest).

■ **Note** Visual Studio 2010 also allows you to reference a multifile assembly. Simply use the Add References dialog box and select the primary module. Any related *.netmodules are copied during the process.

At this point, you should feel comfortable with the process of building both single-file and multifile assemblies. To be completely honest, chances are very good that all of your assemblies will be single-file entities. Nevertheless, multifile assemblies can prove helpful when you wish to break a large physical binary into modular units (which are quite useful for remote download scenarios). Next up, let's formalize the concept of a private assembly.

■ **Source Code** The MultifileAssembly code files are included under the Chapter 14 subdirectory.

Understanding Private Assemblies

Technically speaking, the code libraries you've created thus far in this chapter have been deployed as *private assemblies*. Private assemblies must be located within the same directory as the client application that's using them (the *application directory*) or a subdirectory thereof. Recall that when you set a reference to **CarLibrary.dll** while building the **VisualBasicCarClient.exe** and **CSharpCarClient.exe** applications, Visual Studio 2010 responded by placing a copy of **CarLibrary.dll** within the client's application directory (at least, after the first compilation).

When a client program uses the types defined within this external assembly, the CLR simply loads the local copy of **CarLibrary.dll**. Because the .NET runtime does not consult the system registry when searching for referenced assemblies, you can relocate the **VisualBasicCarClient.exe** (or **CSharpCarClient.exe**) and **CarLibrary.dll** assemblies to a new location on your machine and run the application (this is often termed *Xcopy deployment*).

Uninstalling (or replicating) an application that makes exclusive use of private assemblies is a no-brainer: simply delete (or copy) the application folder. Unlike with COM applications, you do not need to worry about dozens of orphaned registry settings. More important, you do not need to worry that the removal of private assemblies will break any other applications on the machine.

The Identity of a Private Assembly

The full identity of a private assembly consists of the friendly name and numerical version, both of which are recorded in the assembly manifest. The *friendly name* is simply the name of the module that contains the assembly's manifest minus the file extension. For example, if you examine the manifest of the CarLibrary.dll assembly, you find the following:

```
.assembly CarLibrary
{
...
  .ver 1:0:0:0
}
```

Given the isolated nature of a private assembly, it should make sense that the CLR does not bother to use the version number when resolving its location. The assumption is that private assemblies do not need to have any elaborate version checking, as the client application is the only entity that "knows" of its existence. because of this, it is (very) possible for a single machine to have multiple copies of the same private assembly in various application directories.

Understanding the Probing Process

The .NET runtime resolves the location of a private assembly using a technique called *probing*, which is much less invasive than it sounds. Probing is the process of mapping an external assembly request to the location of the requested binary file. Strictly speaking, a request to load an assembly may be either *implicit* or *explicit*. An implicit load request occurs when the CLR consults the manifest in order to resolve the location of an assembly defined using the .assembly extern tokens:

```
// An implicit load request.
.assembly extern CarLibrary
{ ... }
```

An explicit load request occurs programmatically using the Load() or LoadFrom() method of the System.Reflection.Assembly class type, typically for the purposes of late binding and dynamic invocation of type members. You'll examine these topics further in Chapter 15, but for now you can see an example of an explicit load request in the following code:

```
' An explicit load request based on a friendly name.
Dim asm As Assembly = Assembly.Load("CarLibrary.CarLibrary.")
```

In either case, the CLR extracts the friendly name of the assembly and begins probing the client's application directory for a file named CarLibrary.dll. If this file cannot be located, an attempt is made to locate an executable assembly based on the same friendly name (for example, CarLibrary.exe). If neither file can be located in the application directory, the runtime gives up and throws a FileNotFoundException exception at runtime.

■ **Note** Technically speaking, if a copy of the requested assembly cannot be found within the client's application directory, the CLR will also attempt to locate a client subdirectory with the exact same name as the assembly's friendly name (e.g., C:\MyClient\CarLibrary). If the requested assembly resides within this subdirectory, the CLR will load the assembly into memory.

Configuring Private Assemblies

While it is possible to deploy a .NET application by simply copying all required assemblies to a single folder on the user's hard drive, you will most likely want to define a number of subdirectories to group related content. For example, assume you have an application directory named C:\MyApp that contains VisualBasicCarClient.exe. Under this folder might be a subfolder named MyLibraries that contains CarLibrary.dll.

Regardless of the intended relationship between these two directories, the CLR will *not* probe the MyLibraries subdirectory unless you supply a configuration file. Configuration files contain various XML elements that allow you to influence the probing process. Configuration files must have the same name as the launching application and take a *.config file extension, and they must be deployed in the client's application directory. Thus, if you wish to create a configuration file for VisualBasicCarClient.exe, it must be named VisualBasicCarClient.exe.config, and be located (for this example) under the C:\MyApp directory.

To illustrate the process, create a new directory on your C: drive named MyApp using Windows Explorer. Next, copy VisualBasicCarClient.exe and CarLibrary.dll to this new folder, and run the program by double-clicking the executable. Your program should run successfully at this point. Next, create a new subdirectory under C:\MyApp named MyLibraries (see Figure 14-12), and move CarLibrary.dll to this location.

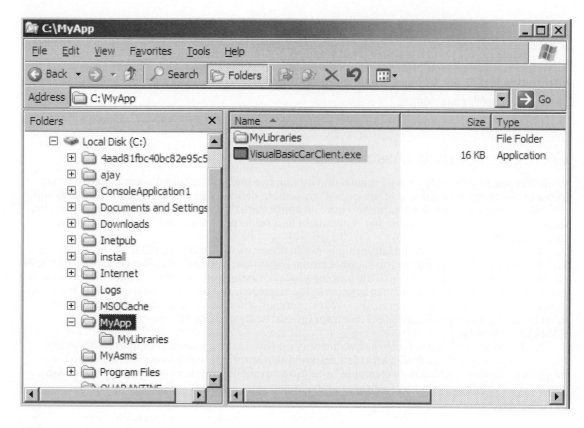

Figure 14-12. CarLibrary.dll now resides under the MyLibraries subdirectory

Try to run your client program again. Because the CLR could not locate an assembly named CarLibrary directly within the application directory, you are presented with a rather nasty unhandled `FileNotFoundException` exception.

To instruct the CLR to probe under the MyLibraries subdirectory, create a new configuration file named `VisualBasicCarClient.exe.config` using any text editor, and save the file in the folder containing the `VisualBasicCarClient.exe` application, which, in this example is `C:\MyApp`. Open this file and enter the following content exactly as shown (be aware that XML is case sensitive!):

```
<configuration>
  <runtime>
    <assemblyBinding xmlns="urn:schemas-microsoft-com:asm.v1">
      <probing privatePath="MyLibraries"/>
    </assemblyBinding>
  </runtime>
</configuration>
```

.NET `*.config` files always open with a root element named `<configuration>`. The nested `<runtime>` element may specify an `<assemblyBinding>` element, which nests a further element named `<probing>`. The `privatePath` attribute is the key point in this example, as it is used to specify the subdirectories relative to the application directory where the CLR should probe.

Once you've finished creating `VisualBasicCarClient.exe.config`, run the client by double-clicking the executable in Windows Explorer. You should find that `VisualBasicCarClient.exe` executes without a hitch (if this is not the case, double-check your `*.config` file for typos).

Do note that the `<probing>` element does not specify *which* assembly is located under a given subdirectory. In other words, you cannot say, "CarLibrary is located under the MyLibraries subdirectory, but MathLibrary is located under the OtherStuff subdirectory." The `<probing>` element simply instructs the CLR to investigate all specified subdirectories for the requested assembly until the first match is encountered.

■ **Note** Be very aware that the privatePath attribute cannot be used to specify an absolute (`C:\SomeFolder\SomeSubFolder`) or relative (`..\\SomeFolder\\AnotherFolder`) path! If you wish to specify a directory outside the client's application directory, you will need to use a completely different XML element named `<codeBase>` (more details on this element later in the chapter).

Multiple subdirectories can be assigned to the `privatePath` attribute using a semicolon-delimited list. You have no need to do so at this time, but here is an example that informs the CLR to consult the MyLibraries and MyLibraries\Tests client subdirectories:

```
<probing privatePath="MyLibraries;MyLibraries\Tests"/>
```

Next, for testing purposes, change the name of your configuration file (in one way or another) and attempt to run the program once again. The client application should now fail. Remember that `*.config` files must be prefixed with the same name as the related client application. By way of a final test, open your configuration file for editing and capitalize any of the XML elements. Once the file is saved, your client should fail to run once again (as XML is case sensitive).

■ **Note** Understand that the CLR will load the very first assembly it finds during the probing process. For example, if the C:\MyApp folder did contain a copy of `CarLibrary.dll`, it will be loaded into memory, while the copy under MyLibraries is effectively ignored.

Configuration Files and Visual Studio 2010

While you are always able to create XML configuration files by hand using your text editor of choice, Visual Studio 2010 allows you create a configuration file during the development of the client program. To illustrate, load the `VisualBasicCarClient` solution into Visual Studio 2010 and insert a new Application Configuration File item using the Project ➤ Add New Item menu selection (see Figure 14-13).

Figure 14-13. Inserting a new app.config file into a new Visual Studio 2010 project

Before you click the OK button, take note that the file is named `app.config` (don't rename it!). If you look in the Solution Explorer window, you will find `App.config` has been inserted into your current project (Figure 14-14).

Figure 14-14. Edit the app.config file to store the necessary data for client applications.

At this point, you are free to enter the necessary XML elements for the client you happen to be creating. Now, here is the cool thing. Each time you compile your project, Visual Studio 2010 will automatically copy the data in `app.config` to the `\bin\Debug` directory using the proper naming convention (such as `VisualBasicCarClient`solution`.exe.config`). However, this behavior will happen only if your configuration file is indeed named `app.config`; see Figure 14-15.

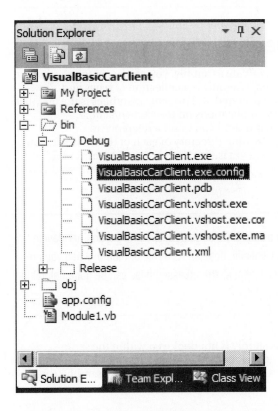

Figure 14-15. The contents of app.config will be copied to a correctly named *.config in your output directory

Using this approach, all you need to do is maintain `app.config`, and Visual Studio 2010 will ensure your application directory contains the latest and greatest configuration data (even if you happen to rename your project).

■ **Note** Using `app.config` files within Visual Studio 2010 is always recommended. If you manually add a `*config` file to your `bin\Debug` folder via Windows Explorer, Visual Studio 2010 may delete or change your file at the next compilation!

Understanding Shared Assemblies

Now that you understand how to deploy and configure a private assembly, you can begin to examine the role of a *shared assembly*. Like a private assembly, a shared assembly is a collection of types and (optional) resources. The most obvious difference between shared and private assemblies is the fact that a single copy of a shared assembly can be used by several applications on the same machine.

Consider all the applications created in this text that required you to set a reference to `System.Windows.Forms.dll`. If you were to look in the application directory of each of these clients, you would *not* find a private copy of this .NET assembly. The reason is that `System.Windows.Forms.dll` has been deployed as a shared assembly. Clearly, if you need to create a machine-wide class library, this is the way to go.

■ **Note** Deciding whether a code library should be deployed as a private or shared library is yet another design issue to contend with, and this will be based on many project-specific details. As a rule of thumb, when you are building libraries that need to be used by a wide variety of applications, shared assemblies can be quite helpful in that they can be updated to new versions very easily (as you will see).

As suggested in the previous paragraph, a shared assembly is not deployed within the same directory as the application that uses it. Rather, shared assemblies are installed into the Global Assembly Cache (GAC). The GAC is located in a subdirectory of your Windows directory named Assembly (e.g., `C:\Windows\assembly`), as shown in Figure 14-16.

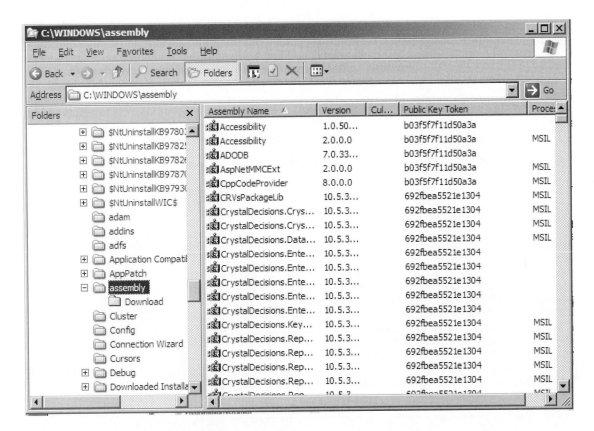

Figure 14-16. The global assembly cache

■ **Note** You cannot install executable assemblies (*.exe) into the GAC. Only assemblies that take the *.dll file extension can be deployed as a shared assembly.

Understanding Strong Names

Before you can deploy an assembly to the GAC, you must assign it a *strong name*, which is used to uniquely identify the publisher of a given .NET binary. Understand that a "publisher" can be an individual programmer, a department within a given company, or an entire company.

In some ways, a strong name is the modern-day .NET equivalent of the COM globally unique identifier (GUID) identification scheme. If you have a COM background, you may recall that AppIDs are GUIDs that identify a particular COM application. Unlike COM GUID values (which are nothing more than 128-bit numbers), strong names are based (in part) on two cryptographically related keys (*public keys* and *private keys*), which are much more unique and resistant to tampering than a simple GUID.

Formally, a strong name is composed of a set of related data, much of which is specified using assembly-level attributes:

- The friendly name of the assembly (which, you recall, is the name of the assembly minus the file extension)

- The version number of the assembly (assigned using the `<AssemblyVersion>` attribute)

- The public key value (assigned using the `<AssemblyKeyFile>` attribute)

- An optional culture identity value for localization purposes (assigned using the `<AssemblyCulture>` attribute)

- An embedded *digital signature* created using a hash of the assembly's contents and the private key value

To provide a strong name for an assembly, your first step is to generate public/private key data using the .NET Framework 4.0 SDK's `sn.exe` utility (which you'll do in a moment). The `sn.exe` utility generates a file (typically ending with the `*.snk` [Strong Name Key] file extension) that contains data for two distinct but mathematically related keys, the public key and the private key. Once the VB 2010 compiler is made aware of the location of your `*.snk` file, it will record the full public key value in the assembly manifest using the `.publickey` token at the time of compilation.

The VB 2010 compiler will also generate a hash code based on the contents of the entire assembly (CIL code, metadata, and so forth). As you recall from Chapter 6, a *hash code* is a numerical value that is statistically unique for a fixed input. Thus, if you modify any aspect of a .NET assembly (even a single character in a string literal) the compiler yields a different hash code. This hash code is combined with the private key data within the `*.snk` file to yield a digital signature embedded within the assembly's CLR header data. The process of strongly naming an assembly is illustrated in Figure 14-17.

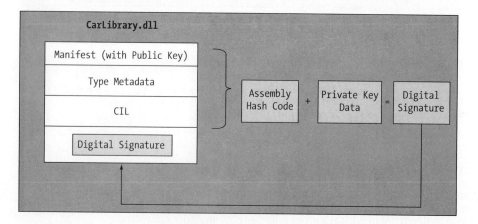

Figure 14-17. At compile time, a digital signature is generated and embedded into the assembly based in part on public and private key data

Understand that the actual `private key` data is not listed anywhere within the manifest, but is used only to digitally sign the contents of the assembly (in conjunction with the generated hash code). Again, the whole idea of using public/private key data is to ensure that no two companies, departments, or individuals have the same identity in the .NET universe. In any case, once the process of assigning a strong name is complete, the assembly may be installed into the GAC.

■ **Note** Strong names also provide a level of protection against potential evildoers tampering with your assembly's contents. Given this point, it is considered a .NET best practice to strongly name every assembly (including `*.exe` assemblies), regardless of whether it is deployed to the GAC.

Generating Strong Names at the Command Line

Let's walk through the process of assigning a strong name to the `CarLibrary` assembly created earlier in this chapter. These days, you will most likely generate the required *.snk file using Visual Studio 2010, however in the bad old days (circa 2003), the only option for strongly signing an assembly was to do so at the command line. Let's see how to do this.

The first order of business is to generate the required key data using the `sn.exe` utility. Although this tool has numerous command-line options, all you need to concern yourself with for the moment is the k flag, which instructs the tool to generate a new file containing the public/private key information. Create a new folder on your C drive named `MyTestKeyPair` and change to that directory using the Visual Studio 2010 command prompt. Next, issue the following command to generate a file named `MyTestKeyPair.snk`:

```
sn -k MyTestKeyPair.snk
```

Now that you have your key data, you need to inform the VB 2010 compiler exactly where `MyTestKeyPair.snk` is located. Recall from earlier in this chapter, when you create any new VB 2010 project workspace using Visual Studio 2010, one of the initial project files (located under the My Project node of Solution Explorer) is named `AssemblyInfo.vb`. This file contains a number of attributes that describe the assembly itself. The `<AssemblyKeyFile>` assembly-level attribute can be added to your `AssemblyInfo.vb` file to inform the compiler of the location of a valid `*.snk` file. Simply specify the path as a string parameter, for example:

```
<Assembly: AssemblyKeyFile("C:\MyTestKeyPair\MyTestKeyPair.snk")> _
```

■ **Note** When you manually specify the `<AssemblyKeyFile>` attribute, Visual Studio 2010 will generate a warning informing you to use the /keyfile option of `vbc.exe` or to establish the key file via the Visual Studio 2010 Properties window. You'll use the IDE to do so in just a moment (so feel free to ignore the generated warning).

Because the version of a shared assembly is one aspect of a strong name, selecting a version number for `CarLibrary.dll` is a necessary detail. In the `AssemblyInfo.vb` file, you will find another attribute named `<AssemblyVersion>`. Initially the value is set to `1.0.0.0`:

```
<Assembly: AssemblyVersion("1.0.0.0")> _
```

A .NET version number is composed of the four parts (*<major>.<minor>.<build>.<revision>*). While specifying a version number is entirely up to you, you can instruct Visual Studio 2010 to automatically increment the build and revision numbers as part of each compilation using the wildcard token, rather than with a specific build and revision value. We have no need to do so for this example; however, consider the following:

```
'Format: <Major number>.<Minor number>.<Build number>.<Revision number>
'Valid values for each part of the version number are between 0 and 65535.
<Assembly: AssemblyVersion("1.0.*")> _
```

At this point, the VB 2010 compiler has all the information needed to generate strong name data (as you are not specifying a unique culture value via the `<AssemblyCulture>` attribute, you "inherit" the culture of your current machine, which in my case would be US English).

Compile your CarLibrary code library, open your assembly into `ildasm.exe`, and check the manifest. You will now see that a new `.publickey` tag is used to document the full public key information, while the `.ver` token records the version specified via the `<AssemblyVersion>` attribute (see Figure 14-18).

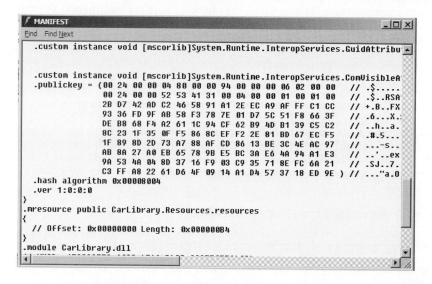

Figure 14-18. A strongly named assembly records the public key in the manifest

Great! At this point we could deploy our shared `CarLibrary.dll` assembly to the GAC. However, remember that these days, .NET developers can use Visual Studio to create strongly named assemblies using a friendly user interface rather than the cryptic `sn.exe` command line tool. Before seeing how to do so, be sure you delete (or comment out) the following line of code from your AssemblyInfo.vb file (assuming you manually added this line during this section of the text):

```
' <Assembly: AssemblyKeyFile("C:\MyTestKeyPair\MyTestKeyPair.snk")> _
```

Generating Strong Names using Visual Studio 2010

Visual Studio 2010 allows you to specify the location of an existing *.snk file using the project's Properties page, as well as generate a new *.snk file. To do so for the CarLibrary project, first double-click on the My Project icon of the Solution Explorer, and select the Signing tab. Next, select the Sign the assembly check box, and choose the New... option (see Figure 14-19).

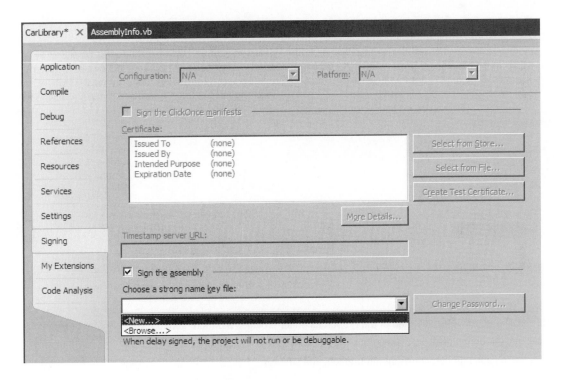

Figure 14-19. Creating a new *.snk file using Visual Studio 2010

Once you have done so, you will be asked to provide a name for your new *.snk file (such as myKeyFile.snk) and you'll have the option to password-protect your file (which is not required for this example); see Figure 14-20.

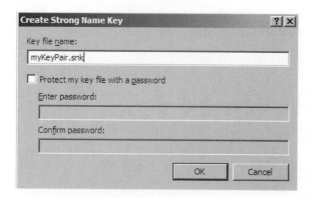

Figure 14-20. Naming the new *.snk file using Visual Studio 2010

At this point, you will see your *.snk file within the Solution Explorer (Figure 14-21). Every time you build your application, this data will be used to assign a proper strong name to the assembly.

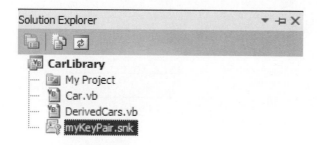

Figure 14-21. Visual Studio 2010 will now strongly sign your assembly with each compilation

---

■ **Note** Recall that the Application tab of the Properties editor provides a button named Assembly Information. When clicked, the button displays a dialog box that allows you to establish numerous assembly-level attributes, including the version number, copyright information, and so forth.

Installing Strongly Named Assemblies to the GAC

The final step is to install the (now strongly named) CarLibrary.dll into the GAC. While the preferred way to deploy assemblies to the GAC in a production setting is to create a Windows MSI installer package (or use a commercial installer program such as InstallShield), the .NET Framework 4.0 SDK ships with a command-line tool named gacutil.exe, which can be useful for quick tests.

■ **Note** You must have administrator rights to interact with the GAC on your machine, which may including adjusting the User Access Control (UAC) settings on Windows Vista or Windows 7.

Table 14-1 documents some relevant options of `gacutil.exe` (specify the `/?` flag when you run the program to see each option).

Table 14-1. Various Options of `gacutil.exe`

Option	Meaning in Life
/i	Installs a strongly named assembly into the GAC
/u	Uninstalls an assembly from the GAC
/l	Displays the assemblies (or a specific assembly) in the GAC

To install a strongly named assembly using `gacutil.exe`, first open a Visual Studio 2010 Command Prompt, change to the directory containing `CarLibrary.dll`, for example (your path may differ!):

```
cd C:\MyCode\CarLibrary\bin\Debug
```

Next, install the library using the `-i` command:

```
gacutil -i CarLibrary.dll
```

Once you have done so, you can verify that the library has been deployed by specifying the `-l` command (note that you omit the file extension when using the `/l` command):

```
gacutil -l CarLibrary
```

If all is well, you should see the following output to the Console window (you will find a unique `PublicKeyToken` value, as expected):

```
The Global Assembly Cache contains the following assemblies:

  CarLibrary, Version=1.0.0.0, Culture=neutral, PublicKeyToken=3898c264cf96df22,
processorArchitecture=MSIL
```

Viewing the .NET 4.0 GAC using Windows Explorer

If you read previous editions of this book that covered .NET 1.0-.NET 3.5, this is where I would be telling you to open your machine's Windows Explorer and view your installed CarLibrary in the GAC, simply by navigating to `C:\Windows\assembly`.

However (and this is a very big however), if you attempted to do so now, you would be stunned to find that you *cannot* see the expected CarLibrary icon under `C:\Windows\assembly`, even though `gacutil.exe` has verified the library has been installed!

With the release of .NET 4.0, the GAC has been split in two. Specifically, under `C:\Windows\assembly` you will find the location of the .NET 1.0-.NET 3.5 base class libraries (as well as various oddball assemblies, including libraries from third-party vendors). However, when you compile an assembly under .NET 4.0, and deploy it to the GAC using `gacutil.exe`, your library will be deployed to a brand-new location: `C:\Windows\Microsoft.NET\assembly\GAC_MSIL`.

Under this new folder, you will find a set of subdirectories, each of which is named identically to the friendly name of a particular code library (for example, `\System.Windows.Forms`, `\System.Core`, and so on). Beneath a given friendly name folder, you'll find yet another subdirectory that always takes the following naming convention:

`v4.0_major.minor.build.revision__publicKeyTokenValue`

The "v4.0" prefix denotes that the library compiled under .NET version 4.0. That prefix is followed by a single underbar, then the version of the library in question, which in this example is version 1.0.0.0 of CarLibrary.dll. After a pair of underbars, you'll see the publickeytoken value based on your strong name. Figure 14-22 shows the directory structure of my version of `CarLibrary.dll` on my Windows 7 operating system.

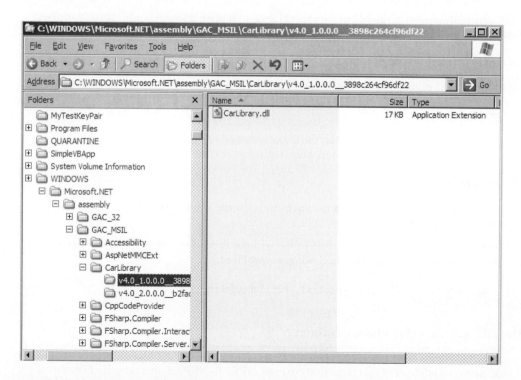

Figure 14-22. The strongly named, shared CarLibrary (version 1.0.0.0)

Consuming a Shared Assembly

When you are building applications that use a shared assembly, the only difference from consuming a private assembly is in how you reference the library using Visual Studio 2010. In reality, there is no difference as far as the tool is concerned—you still use the Add Reference dialog box. However, this dialog box will *not* allow you to reference the assembly by browsing to the `C:\Windows\assembly` folder, which is specific to .NET 3.5 and earlier.

■ **Note** Seasoned .NET developers may recall that even when you navigated to `C:\Windows\assembly`, the Visual Studio Add Reference dialog refused to let you reference shared libraries! Because of this, developers had to maintain a separate copy of the library, simply for the purpose of referencing the assembly. The story under Visual Studio 2010 is much nicer. Read on...

When you need to reference an assembly that has been deployed to the .NET 4.0 GAC, you will need to browse to the `"v4.0_major.minor.build.revision__publicKeyTokenValue"` directory for your particular library via the Browse tab (see Figure 14-23).

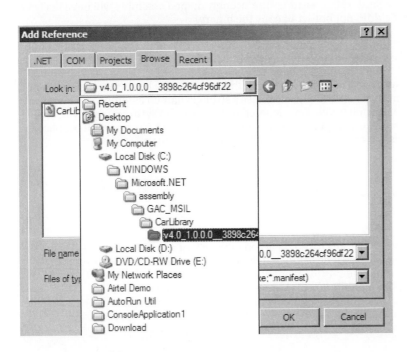

Figure 14-23. Referencing the strongly named, shared CarLibrary (version 1.0.0.0) using Visual Studio 2010

This (somewhat confusing) fact aside, create a new VB 2010 Console Application named SharedCarLibClient and reference your **CarLibrary.dll** assembly as just described. As you would hope, you can now see an icon in your Solution Explorer's Reference folder (you might have to click the Show All Files icon at the top of Solution Explorer to see the References folder). If you select the **CarLibrary.dll** icon and then view the Properties window (accessible from the Visual Studio View menu), you'll notice that the Copy Local property of the selected CarLibrary is now set to False. In any case, author the following test code in your new client application:

```
Imports CarLibrary

Module Module1
    Sub Main()
        Console.WriteLine("***** Shared Assembly Client *****")
        Dim c As New SportsCar()
        c.TurboBoost()
        Console.ReadLine()
    End Sub
End Module
```

Once you have compiled your client application, navigate to the directory that contains **SharedCarLibClient.exe** using Windows Explorer and notice that Visual Studio 2010 has *not* copied **CarLibrary.dll** to the client's application directory. When you reference an assembly whose manifest contains a **.publickey** value, Visual Studio 2010 assumes the strongly named assembly will most likely be deployed to the GAC, and therefore does not bother to copy the binary.

Exploring the Manifest of SharedCarLibClient

Recall that when you generate a strong name for an assembly, the entire public key is recorded in the assembly manifest. On a related note, when a client references a strongly named assembly, its manifest records a condensed hash value of the full public key, denoted by the **.publickeytoken** tag. If you open the manifest of **SharedCarLibClient.exe** using **ildasm.exe**, you would find the following (your public key token value will of course differ, as it is computed based on the public key value):

```
.assembly extern CarLibrary
{
  .publickeytoken = (33 A2 BC 29 43 31 E8 B9 )
  .ver 1:0:3814:8504
}
```

If you compare the value of the public key token recorded in the client manifest with the public key token value shown in the GAC, you will find a dead-on match. Recall that a public key represents one aspect of the strongly named assembly's identity. Given this, the CLR will only load version 1.0.0.0 of an assembly named **CarLibrary** that has a public key that can be hashed down to the value 33A2BC294331E8B9. If the CLR does not find an assembly meeting this description in the GAC (and did not find a private assembly named **CarLibrary** in the client's directory), a **FileNotFoundException** exception is thrown.

■ **Source Code** The SharedCarLibClient application can be found under the Chapter 14 subdirectory.

Configuring Shared Assemblies

Like private assemblies, shared assemblies can be configured using a client *.config file. Of course, because shared assemblies are deployed to a well-known location (the .NET 4.0 GAC), you don't use the <privatePath> element as you did for private assemblies (although if the client is using both shared and private assemblies, the <privatePath> element may still exist in the *.config file).

You can use application configuration files in conjunction with shared assemblies whenever you wish to instruct the CLR to bind to a *different* version of a specific assembly, effectively bypassing the value recorded in the client's manifest. This can be useful for a number of reasons. For example, imagine that you have shipped version 1.0.0.0 of an assembly and later discover a major bug. One corrective action would be to rebuild the client application to reference the correct version of the bug-free assembly (say, 1.1.0.0) and redistribute the updated client and new library to every target machine.

Another option is to ship the new code library and a *.config file that automatically instructs the runtime to bind to the new (bug-free) version. As long as the new version has been installed into the GAC, the original client runs without recompilation, redistribution, or fear of having to update your resume.

Here's another example: you have shipped the first version of a bug-free assembly (1.0.0.0), and after a month or two, you add new functionality to the assembly to yield version 2.0.0.0. Obviously, existing client applications that were compiled against version 1.0.0.0 have no clue about these new types, given that their code base makes no reference to them.

New client applications, however, wish to make reference to the new functionality in version 2.0.0.0. Under .NET, you are free to ship version 2.0.0.0 to the target machines, and have version 2.0.0.0 run alongside the older version 1.0.0.0. If necessary, existing clients can be dynamically redirected to load version 2.0.0.0 (to gain access to the implementation refinements), using an application configuration file without needing to recompile and redeploy the client application.

Freezing the Current Shared Assembly

To illustrate how to dynamically bind to a specific version of a shared assembly, open Windows Explorer and copy the current version of the compiled CarLibrary.dll assembly (1.0.0.0) into a distinct subdirectory (I called mine "CarLibrary Version 1.0.0.0") to symbolize the freezing of this version (see Figure 14-24).

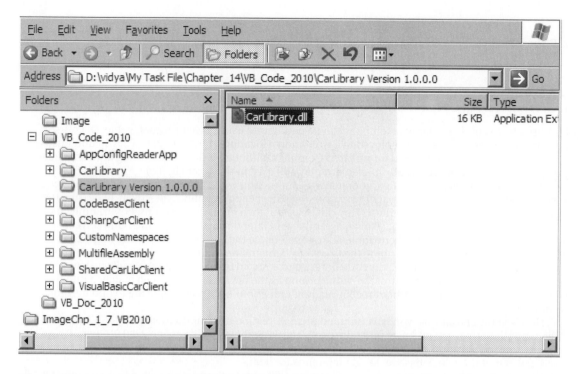

Figure 14-24. Freezing the current version of CarLibrary.dll

Building Shared Assembly Version 2.0.0.0

Now, open your existing CarLibrary project and update your code base with a new **enum** type named **MusicMedia** that defines four possible musical devices:

```
'Which type of music player does this car have?
Public Enum MusicMedia
    musicCd
    musicTape
    musicRadio
    musicMp3
End Enum
```

As well, add a new Public method to the Car type that allows the caller to turn on one of the given media players (be sure to import the System.Windows.Forms namespace within Car.vb if necessary):

```
'The MustInherit base class in the hierarchy.
Public MustInherit Class Car
...

        Public Sub TurnOnRadio(ByVal musicOn As Boolean, ByVal mm As MusicMedia)
            If musicOn Then
                    MessageBox.Show(String.Format("Jamming {0}", mm))
            Else
                    MessageBox.Show("Quiet time...")
            End If
        End Sub
End Class
```

Update the constructors of the Car class to display a MessageBox that verifies you are indeed using CarLibrary 2.0.0.0:

```
Public MustInherit Class Car
    ...
    Public Sub New()
            MessageBox.Show("CarLibrary Version 2.0!")
    End Sub

    Public Sub New(ByVal name As String, ByVal maxSp As Integer, ByVal currSp As Integer)
            MessageBox.Show("CarLibrary Version 2.0!")
            PetName = name
            MaxSpeed = maxSp
            CurrentSpeed = currSp
    End Sub

End Class
```

Last but not least, before you recompile your new library, update the version to be 2.0.0.0. Recall you can do so in a visual manner by double-clicking on the My **Properties** icon of the Solution Explorer and clicking on the Assembly Information... button on the Application tab. Once you do, simply update the Assembly Version number (Figure 14-25).

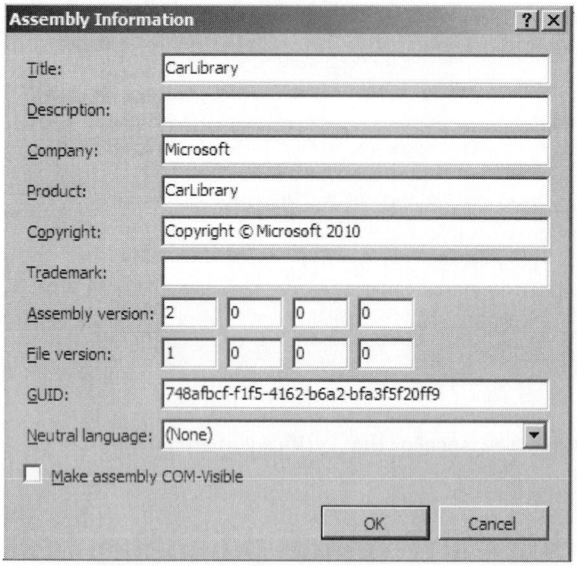

Figure 14-25. Setting the version number of CarLibrary.dll to 2.0.0.0

If you look in your project's \bin\Debug folder, you'll see that you have a new version of this assembly (2.0.0.0), while version 1.0.0.0 is safe in storage in the CarLibrary Version 1.0.0.0 directory. Install this new assembly into the 4.0 GAC using gacutil.exe as described earlier in this chapter. Notice that you now have two versions of the same assembly (see Figure 14-26).

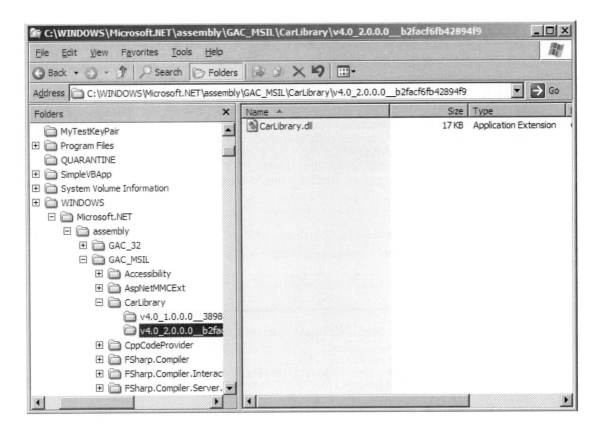

Figure 14-26. Side-by-side execution of a shared assembly

If you run the current SharedCarLibClient.exe program by double-clicking the icon in Windows Explorer, you should *not* see the "CarLibrary Version 2.0!" message box appear, as the manifest is specifically requesting version 1.0.0.0. How then can you instruct the CLR to bind to version 2.0.0.0? Glad you asked!

■ **Note** Visual Studio 2010 will automatically reset references when you compile your applications! Therefore, if you run your SharedCarLibClient.exe application within Visual Studio 2010, it will grab CarLibrary.dll version 2.0.0.0! If you accidentally ran your application in this way, simply delete the current CarLibrary.dll reference and select version 1.0.0.0 (which I suggested you place in a folder named CarLibrary Version 1.0.0.0).

Dynamically Redirecting to Specific Versions of a Shared Assembly

When you want to tell the CLR to load a version of a shared assembly other than the version listed in the manifest, you can build a *.config file that contains a <dependentAssembly> element. When doing so, you will need to create an <assemblyIdentity> subelement that specifies the friendly name of the assembly listed in the client manifest (CarLibrary, for this example) and an optional culture attribute (which can be assigned an empty string or omitted altogether if you wish to use the default culture for the machine). Moreover, the <dependentAssembly> element will define a <bindingRedirect> subelement to define the version *currently* in the manifest (via the oldVersion attribute) and the version in the GAC to load instead (via the newVersion attribute).

Create a new configuration file in the application directory of SharedCarLibClient named SharedCarLibClient.exe.config that contains the following XML data.

■ **Note** The value of your public key token will be different from what you see in the following markup, and it can be obtained either by examining the client manifest using ildasm.exe or via the GAC.

```
<configuration>
  <runtime>
    <assemblyBinding xmlns="urn:schemas-microsoft-com:asm.v1">
      <dependentAssembly>
        <assemblyIdentity name="CarLibrary"
                          publicKeyToken=" b2facf6fb42894f9"
                          culture="neutral"/>
        <bindingRedirect oldVersion= "1.0.0.0"
                         newVersion= "2.0.0.0"/>
      </dependentAssembly>
    </assemblyBinding>
  </runtime>
</configuration>
```

Now run the SharedCarLibClient.exe program by double-clicking the executable from Windows Explorer. You should see the message that version 2.0.0.0 has loaded.

Multiple <dependentAssembly> elements can appear within a client's configuration file. Although there's no need for this example, assume that the manifest of SharedCarLibClient.exe also references version 2.5.0.0 of an assembly named MathLibrary. If you wanted to redirect to version 3.0.0.0 of MathLibrary (in addition to version 2.0.0.0 of CarLibrary), the SharedCarLibClient.exe.config file would look like the following:

```
<configuration>
  <runtime>
    <assemblyBinding xmlns="urn:schemas-microsoft-com:asm.v1">
        <!-- Controls Binding to CarLibrary -->
      <dependentAssembly>
        <assemblyIdentity name="CarLibrary"
                          publicKeyToken=" b2facf6fb42894f9"
                          culture=""/>
```

```
        <bindingRedirect oldVersion= "1.0.0.0" newVersion= "2.0.0.0"/>
      </dependentAssembly>

      <!-- Controls Binding to MathLibrary -->
      <dependentAssembly>
        <assemblyIdentity name="MathLibrary"
                          publicKeyToken="33A2BC294331E8B9"
                          culture=""/>
        <bindingRedirect oldVersion= "2.5.0.0" newVersion= "3.0.0.0"/>
      </dependentAssembly>
    </assemblyBinding>
  </runtime>
</configuration>
```

■ **Note** It is possible to specify a range of old version numbers via the `oldVersion` attribute; for example, `<bindingRedirect oldVersion="1.0.0.0-1.2.0.0" newVersion="2.0.0.0"/>` informs the CLR to use version 2.0.0.0 for any older version within the range of 1.0.0.0 to 1.2.0.0.

Understanding Publisher Policy Assemblies

The next configuration issue we'll examine is the role of *publisher policy assemblies*. As you've just seen, `*.config` files can be constructed to bind to a specific version of a shared assembly, thereby bypassing the version recorded in the client manifest. While this is all well and good, imagine you're an administrator who now needs to reconfigure *all* client applications on a given machine to rebind to version 2.0.0.0 of the `CarLibrary.dll` assembly. Given the strict naming convention of a configuration file, you would need to duplicate the same XML content in numerous locations (assuming you are, in fact, aware of the locations of the executables using CarLibrary!). Clearly this would be a maintenance nightmare.

Publisher policy allows the publisher of a given assembly (you, your department, your company, or what have you) to ship a binary version of a `*.config` file that is installed into the GAC along with the newest version of the associated assembly. The benefit of this approach is that client application directories do *not* need to contain specific `*.config` files. Rather, the CLR will read the current manifest and attempt to find the requested version in the GAC. However, if the CLR finds a publisher policy assembly, it will read the embedded XML data and perform the requested redirection *at the level of the GAC.*

Publisher policy assemblies are created at the command line using a .NET utility named **al.exe** (the assembly linker). Though this tool provides many options, building a publisher policy assembly requires passing in only the following input parameters:

- The location of the `*.config` or `*.xml` file containing the redirecting instructions
- The name of the resulting publisher policy assembly
- The location of the `*.snk` file used to sign the publisher policy assembly
- The version numbers to assign the publisher policy assembly being constructed

If you wish to build a publisher policy assembly that controls `CarLibrary.dll`, the command set is as follows (which must be entered on a single line within the command window):

```
al /link: CarLibraryPolicy.xml /out:policy.1.0.CarLibrary.dll
/keyf:C:\MyKey\myKey.snk /v:1.0.0.0
```

Here, the XML content is contained within a file named `CarLibraryPolicy.xml`. The name of the output file (which must be in the format `policy.<major>.<minor>.assemblyToConfigure`) is specified using the obvious `/out` flag. In addition, note that the name of the file containing the public/private key pair will also need to be supplied via the `/keyf` option. Remember, publisher policy files are shared, and therefore must have strong names!

Once the `al.exe` tool has executed, the result is a new assembly that can be placed into the GAC to force all clients to bind to version 2.0.0.0 of `CarLibrary.dll`, without the use of a specific client application configuration file. Using this technique, you can design a machinewide redirection for all applications using a specific version (or range of versions) of an existing assembly.

Disabling Publisher Policy

Now, assume you (as a system administrator) have deployed a publisher policy assembly (and the latest version of the related assembly) to the GAC of a client machine. As luck would have it, nine of the ten affected applications rebind to version 2.0.0.0 without error. However, the remaining client application (for whatever reason) blows up when accessing `CarLibrary.dll` 2.0.0.0. (As we all know, it is next to impossible to build backward-compatible software that works 100 percent of the time.)

In such a case, it is possible to build a configuration file for a specific troubled client that instructs the CLR to *ignore* the presence of any publisher policy files installed in the GAC. The remaining client applications that are happy to consume the newest .NET assembly will simply be redirected via the installed publisher policy assembly. To disable publisher policy on a client-by-client basis, author a (properly named) `*.config` file that makes use of the `<publisherPolicy>` element and set the `apply` attribute to `no`. When you do so, the CLR will load the version of the assembly originally listed in the client's manifest.

```
<configuration>
  <runtime>
    <assemblyBinding xmlns="urn:schemas-microsoft-com:asm.v1">
      <publisherPolicy apply="no" />
    </assemblyBinding>
  </runtime>
</configuration>
```

Understanding the \<codeBase\> Element

Application configuration files can also specify *code bases*. The `<codeBase>` element can be used to instruct the CLR to probe for dependent assemblies located at arbitrary locations (such as network end points, or an arbitrary machine path outside a client's application directory).

If the value assigned to a `<codeBase>` element is located on a remote machine, the assembly will be downloaded on demand to a specific directory in the GAC termed the *download cache*. Given what you have learned about deploying assemblies to the GAC, it should make sense that assemblies loaded from a `<codeBase>` element will need to be assigned a strong name (after all, how else could the CLR install remote assemblies to the GAC?). If you are interested, you can view the content of your machine's download cache by supplying the `/ldl` option to `gacutil.exe`:

```
gacutil /ldl
```

■ **Note** Technically speaking, the `<codeBase>` element can be used to probe for assemblies that do not have a strong name. However, the assembly's location must be relative to the client's application directory (and thus is little more than an alternative to the `<privatePath>` element).

To see the `<codeBase>` element in action, create a Console Application named CodeBaseClient, set a reference to `CarLibrary.dll` version 2.0.0.0, and update the initial file as follows:

```vb
Imports CarLibrary

Module Module1
    Sub Main()
        Console.WriteLine("***** Fun with CodeBases *****")
        Dim c As New SportsCar()
        Console.WriteLine("Sports car has been allocated.")
        Console.ReadLine()
    End Sub
End Module
```

Given that `CarLibrary.dll` has been deployed to the GAC, you are able to run the program as is. However, to illustrate the use of the `<codeBase>` element, create a new folder under your C: drive (perhaps `C:\MyAsms`) and place a copy of `CarLibrary.dll` version 2.0.0.0 into this directory.

Now, add an `app.config` file to the CodeBaseClient project (as explained earlier in this chapter) and author the following XML content (remember that your `.publickeytoken` value will differ; consult your GAC as required):

```xml
<?xml version="1.0" encoding="utf-8" ?>
<configuration>
    <system.diagnostics>
        <sources>
                <!-- This section defines the logging configuration for My.Application.Log
-->
```

```
            <source name="DefaultSource" switchName="DefaultSwitch">
                <listeners>
                  <add name="FileLog"/>
                  <!-- Uncomment the below section to write to the Application Event Log -->
                    <!--<add name="EventLog"/>-->
                </listeners>
            </source>
        </sources>
        <switches>
            <add name="DefaultSwitch" value="Information" />
        </switches>
        <sharedListeners>
            <add name="FileLog"
                type="Microsoft.VisualBasic.Logging.FileLogTraceListener,
Microsoft.VisualBasic, Version=8.0.0.0, Culture=neutral, PublicKeyToken=b03f5f7f11d50a3a,
processorArchitecture=MSIL"
                initializeData="FileLogWriter"/>
            <!-- Uncomment the below section and replace APPLICATION_NAME with the name of
your application to write to the Application Event Log -->
            <!--<add name="EventLog" type="System.Diagnostics.EventLogTraceListener"
initializeData="APPLICATION_NAME"/> -->
        </sharedListeners>
    </system.diagnostics>

  <runtime>
    <assemblyBinding xmlns="urn:schemas-microsoft-com:asm.v1">
      <dependentAssembly>
    <assemblyIdentity name=" CarLibrary" publicKeyToken="b2facf6fb42894f9" />
        <codeBase version="2.0.0.0" href="file:///C:/MyAsms/CarLibrary.dll" />
      </dependentAssembly>
    </assemblyBinding>
  </runtime>
</configuration>
```

As you can see, the `<codeBase>` element is nested within the `<assemblyIdentity>` element, which makes use of the `name` and `publicKeyToken` attributes to specify the friendly name as associated `publicKeyToken` values. The `<codeBase>` element itself specifies the version and location (via the `href` property) of the assembly to load. If you were to delete version 2.0.0.0 of `CarLibrary.dll` from the GAC, this client would still run successfully, as the CLR is able to locate the external assembly under C:\MyAsms.

■ **Note** If you place assemblies at random locations on your development machine, you are in effect re-creating the system registry (and the related DLL hell), given that if you move or rename the folder containing your binaries, the current bind will fail. With that in mind, use `<codeBase>` with caution.

The `<codeBase>` element can also be helpful when referencing assemblies located on a remote networked machine. Assume you have permission to access a folder located at `http://www.MySite.com`. To download the remote `*.dll` to the GAC's download cache on your local machine, you could update the `<codeBase>` element as follows:

```
<codeBase version="2.0.0.0"
  href="http://www.MySite.com/Assemblies/CarLibrary.dll" />
```

■ **Source Code** The CodeBaseClient application can be found under the Chapter 14 subdirectory.

The System.Configuration Namespace

Currently, all of the `*.config` files shown in this chapter have made use of well-known XML elements that are read by the CLR to resolve the location of external assemblies. In addition to these recognized elements, it is perfectly permissible for a client configuration file to contain application-specific data that has nothing to do with binding heuristics. Given this, it should come as no surprise that the .NET Framework provides a namespace that allows you to programmatically read the data within a client configuration file.

The `System.Configuration` namespace provides a small set of types you can use to read custom data from a client's `*.config` file. These custom settings must be contained within the scope of an `<appSettings>` element. The `<appSettings>` element contains any number of `<add>` elements that define key/value pairs to be obtained programmatically.

For example, assume you have an `App.config` file for a Console Application named AppConfigReaderApp that defines two application specific values, listed like so:

```
<configuration>
  <appSettings>
    <add key="TextColor" value="Green" />
    <add key="RepeatCount" value="8" />
  </appSettings>
</configuration>
```

Reading these values for use by the client application is as simple as calling the instance-level `GetValue()` method of the `System.Configuration.AppSettingsReader` type. As shown in the following code, the first parameter to `GetValue()` is the name of the key in the `*.config` file, whereas the second parameter is the underlying type of the key (obtained via the VB 2010 `GetType()` operator):

```
Imports System.Configuration

Module Module1
    Sub Main()
        Console.WriteLine("***** Reading <appSettings> Data *****" & vbLf)
```

603

```
        'Get our custom data from the *.config file.
        Dim ar As New AppSettingsReader()
          Dim numbOfTimes As Integer = CInt(ar.GetValue("RepeatCount", GetType(Integer)))

          Dim textColor As String = CStr(ar.GetValue("TextColor", GetType(String)))
          Console.ForegroundColor = CInt([Enum].Parse(GetType(ConsoleColor), textColor))

        'Now print a message correctly.
        For i = 0 To numbOfTimes - 1
              Console.WriteLine("Howdy!")
        Next
        Console.ReadLine()
     End Sub
End Module
```

As you work throughout the remainder of the book, you will find many other important sections that can be found within a client (or web-based) configuration file. To be sure, the deeper you dive into .NET programming, the more critical an understanding of XML configuration files become.

■ **Source Code** The AppConfigReaderApp application can be found under the Chapter 14 subdirectory.

Summary

This chapter drilled down into the details of how the CLR resolves the location of externally referenced assemblies. You began by examining the content within an assembly: headers, metadata, manifests, and CIL. Then you constructed single-file and multifile assemblies and a handful of client applications (written in a language-agnostic manner).

As you have seen, assemblies can be private or shared. Private assemblies are copied to the client's subdirectory, whereas shared assemblies are deployed to the GAC, provided they have been assigned a strong name. Finally, private and shared assemblies can be configured using a client-side XML configuration file or, alternatively, via a publisher policy assembly.

■ ■ ■

Type Reflection, Late Binding, and Attribute-Based Programming

As shown in the previous chapter, assemblies are the basic unit of deployment in the .NET universe. Using the integrated object browsers of Visual Studio 2010 (and numerous other IDEs), you are able to examine the types within a project's referenced set of assemblies. Furthermore, external tools such as `ildasm.exe` and `reflector.exe` allow you to peek into the underlying CIL code, type metadata, and assembly manifest for a given .NET binary. In addition to this design-time investigation of .NET assemblies, you are also able to *programmatically* obtain this same information using the `System.Reflection` namespace. To this end, the first task of this chapter is to define the role of reflection and the necessity of .NET metadata.

The remainder of the chapter examines a number of closely related topics, all of which hinge upon reflection services. For example, you'll learn how a .NET client may employ dynamic loading and late binding to activate types it has no compile-time knowledge of. You'll also learn how to insert custom metadata into your .NET assemblies through the use of system-supplied and custom attributes. To put all of these (seemingly esoteric) topics into perspective, the chapter closes by demonstrating how to build several "snap-in objects" that you can plug into an extendable Windows Forms application.

The Necessity of Type Metadata

The ability to fully describe types (classes, interfaces, structures, enumerations, and delegates) using metadata is a key element of the .NET platform. Numerous .NET technologies, such as object serialization, .NET remoting, XML web services, and Windows Communication Foundation (WCF), require the ability to discover the format of types at runtime. Furthermore, cross-language interoperability, numerous compiler services, and an IDE's IntelliSense capabilities all rely on a concrete description of *type*.

Regardless of (or perhaps due to) its importance, metadata is not a new idea supplied by the .NET Framework. Java, CORBA, and COM all have similar concepts. For example, COM type libraries (which are little more than compiled IDL code) are used to describe the types contained within a COM server. Like COM, .NET code libraries also support type metadata. Of course, .NET metadata has no syntactic similarities to COM IDL.

Recall that the `ildasm.exe` utility allows you to view an assembly's type metadata using the Ctrl+M keyboard option (see Chapter 1). Thus, if you were to open any of the `*.dll` or `*.exe` assemblies created over the course of this book (such as the **CarLibrary.dll** created in the previous chapter) using **ildasm.exe** and press Ctrl+M, you would find the relevant type metadata (see Figure 15-1).

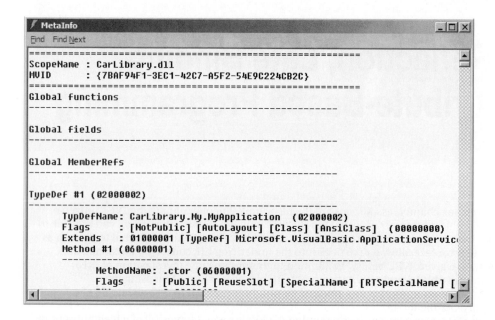

Figure 15-1. Viewing an assembly's metadata using ildasm.exe

As you can see, **ildasm.exe**'s display of .NET type metadata is very verbose (the actual binary format is much more compact). In fact, if I were to list the entire metadata description representing the **CarLibrary.dll** assembly, it would span several pages. Given that this act would be a woeful waste of paper, let's just glimpse into some key metadata descriptions of the **CarLibrary.dll** assembly.

■ **Note** Don't be too concerned with the exact syntax of each and every piece of .NET metadata in the next few sections. The bigger point to absorb is that .NET metadata is very descriptive and lists each internally defined (and externally referenced) type found within a given code base.

Viewing (Partial) Metadata for the EngineState Enumeration

Each type defined within the current assembly is documented using a **TypeDef #n** token (where **TypeDef** is short for *type definition*). If the type being described uses a type defined within a separate .NET assembly, the referenced type is documented using a **TypeRef #n** token (where **TypeRef** is short for *type reference*). A **TypeRef** token is a pointer (if you will) to the referenced type's full metadata definition in an external assembly. In a nutshell, .NET metadata is a set of tables that clearly mark all type definitions (**TypeDef**s) and referenced types (**TypeRef**s), all of which can be viewed using **ildasm.exe**'s metadata window.

As far as `CarLibrary.dll` goes, one `TypeDef` is the metadata description of the `CarLibrary.EngineState` enumeration (your number may differ; `TypeDef` numbering is based on the order in which the VB 2010 compiler processes the file):

```
TypeDef #9 (0200000a)
-------------------------------------------------------
  TypDefName: CarLibrary.EngineState  (0200000A)
  Flags     : [Public] [AutoLayout] [Class] [Sealed] [AnsiClass]  (00000101)
  Extends   : 0100000E [TypeRef] System.Enum
  Field #1 (0400000e)
-------------------------------------------------------
    Field Name: value__  (0400000E)
    Flags     : [Public] [SpecialName] [RTSpecialName]  (00000606)
    CallCnvntn: [FIELD]
    Field type:  I4

  Field #2 (0400000F)
-------------------------------------------------------
    Field Name: engineAlive (0400000F)
    Flags     : [Public] [Static] [Literal] [HasDefault]  (00008056)
    DefltValue: (I4) 0
    CallCnvntn: [FIELD]
    Field type:  ValueClass CarLibrary.EngineState
...
```

Here, the `TypDefName` token is used to establish the name of the given type, which in this case is the custom `CarLibrary.EngineState` enum. The `Extends` metadata token is used to document the base type of a given .NET type (in this case, the referenced type, `System.Enum`). Each field of an enumeration is marked using the `Field #n` token. For brevity, I have simply listed the metadata for `CarLibrary.EngineState.engineAlive`.

Viewing (Partial) Metadata for the Car Type

Here is a partial dump of the `Car` class that illustrates the following:

- How fields are defined in terms of .NET metadata

- How methods are documented via .NET metadata

- How an automatic property is represented in .NET metadata

```
TypeDef #10 (0200000b)
-------------------------------------------------------
  TypDefName: CarLibrary.Car  (0200000B)
  Flags : [Public] [AutoLayout] [Class] [Abstract]
          [AnsiClass] (00100081)
  Extends : 01000003 [TypeRef] System.Object
...
```

```
Method #1 (06000001)
---------------------------------------------------------
  MethodName: get_PetName (06000020)
  Flags     : [Public] [ReuseSlot] [SpecialName]  (00000806)
  RVA       : 0x000027c0
  ImplFlags : [IL] [Managed]  (00000000)
  CallCnvntn: [DEFAULT]
  hasThis
  ReturnType: String
  No arguments.

...

  Method #2 (06000021)
---------------------------------------------------------
  MethodName: set_PetName (06000021)
  Flags     : [Public] [ReuseSlot] [SpecialName]  (00000806)
  RVA       : 0x000027d8
  ImplFlags : [IL] [Managed]  (00000000)
  CallCnvntn: [DEFAULT]
  hasThis
  ReturnType: Void
  1 Arguments
    Argument #1:  String
  1 Parameters
    (1) ParamToken : (08000026) Name : AutoPropertyValue flags: [none] (00000000)
...

Property #1 (17000009)
---------------------------------------------------------
  Prop.Name : PetName (17000009)
  Flags     : [none] (00000000)
  CallCnvntn: [PROPERTY]
  hasThis
  ReturnType: String
  No arguments.
  DefltValue:
  Setter    : (06000021) set_PetName
  Getter    : (06000020) get_PetName
  0 Others
  ...
```

First, note that the Car class metadata marks the type's base class (System.Object) and includes various flags that describe how this type was constructed (e.g., [Public], [Abstract], and whatnot). Methods (such as our Car's constructor) are described in regard to their parameters, return value, and name.

First, note that the Car class metadata marks the type's base class and includes various flags that describe how this type was constructed (e.g., [Public] and [Abstract]). Methods (such as our Car's constructor, denoted by .ctor) are described in regard to their parameters, return value, and name. Finally, note how properties are mapped to their internal get/set methods using the .NET metadata

Setter/Getter tokens. As you would expect, the derived Car types (SportsCar and MiniVan) are described in a similar manner.

Examining a TypeRef

Recall that an assembly's metadata will describe not only the set of internal types (Car, EngineState, etc.), but also any external types the internal types reference. For example, given that CarLibrary.dll has defined two enumerations, you find a TypeRef block for the System.Enum type:

```
TypeRef #14 (0100000e)
-------------------------------------------------------
Token:              0x0100000e
ResolutionScope:    0x23000001
TypeRefName:        System.Enum
```

Documenting the Defining Assembly

The ildasm.exe metadata window also allows you to view the .NET metadata that describes the assembly itself using the Assembly token. As you can see from the following (partial) listing, information documented within the Assembly table is (surprise, surprise!) the same information that can be viewable via the MANIFEST icon. The following is a partial dump of the manifest of CarLibrary.dll (version 2.0.0.0):

```
Assembly
-------------------------------------------------------
  Token: 0x20000001
  Name : CarLibrary
  Public Key     : 00 24 00 00 04 80 00 00  // Etc...

  Hash Algorithm : 0x00008004
  Version:  2.0.0.0
  Major Version: 0x00000002
  Minor Version: 0x00000000
  Build Number: 0x00000000
  Revision Number: 0x00000000
  Locale: <null>
  Flags : [PublicKey] ...
```

Documenting Referenced Assemblies

In addition to the Assembly token and the set of TypeDef and TypeRef blocks, .NET metadata also makes use of AssemblyRef #n tokens to document each external assembly. Given that the CarLibrary.dll makes use of the System.Windows.Forms.MessageBox class, you find an AssemblyRef for the System.Windows.Forms assembly, as shown in the following code:

```
AssemblyRef #6 (23000006)
---------------------------------------------------------
  Token: 0x23000006
  Public Key or Token: b7 7a 5c 56 19 34 e0 89
  Name: System.Windows.Forms
  Version: 4.0.0.0
  Major Version: 0x00000004
  Minor Version: 0x00000000
  Build Number: 0x00000000
  Revision Number: 0x00000000
  Locale: <null>
  HashValue Blob:
  Flags: [none] (00000000)
```

Documenting String Literals

The final point of interest regarding .NET metadata is the fact that each and every string literal in your code base is documented under the User Strings token.

```
User Strings
---------------------------------------------------------
70000001 : (23) L" CarLibrary Version 2.0!"
70000031 : (11) L"Jamming {0{"
70000049 : (13) L" Quiet time..."
70000065 : (14) L"Ramming speed!"
70000083 : (19) L"Faster is better..."
700000ab : (15) L"Cranking tunes!"
700000cd : (4)   L"Eek!"
700000d5:  (27) L"your engine block exploded! "
7000010d:  (20) L"CarLibrary.Resources"
```

> ■ **Note** As illustrated in this last metadata listing, always be aware that all strings are clearly documented in the assembly metadata. This could have huge security consequences if you were to use string literals to capture passwords, credit card numbers, or other sensitive information.

The next question on your mind may be (in the best-case scenario) "How can I leverage this information in my applications?" or (in the worst-case scenario) "Why should I care about metadata?" To address both points of view, allow me to introduce .NET reflection services. Be aware that the usefulness of the topics presented over the pages that follow may be a bit of a head-scratcher until this chapter's endgame. So hang tight.

■ **Note** You will also find a number of `CustomAttribute` tokens displayed by the MetaInfo window, which documents the attributes applied within the code base. You'll learn about the role of .NET attributes later in this chapter.

Understanding Reflection

In the .NET universe, *reflection* is the process of runtime type discovery. Using reflection services, you are able to programmatically obtain the same metadata information displayed by `ildasm.exe` using a friendly object model. For example, through reflection, you can obtain a list of all types contained within a given `*.dll` or `*.exe` assembly (or even within a `*.netmodule` file, if you have a multi-file assembly), including the methods, fields, properties, and events defined by a given type. You can also dynamically discover the set of interfaces supported by a given type, the parameters of a method, and other related details (base classes, namespace information, manifest data, and so forth).

Like any namespace, `System.Reflection` (which is defined in `mscorlib.dll`) contains a number of related types. Table 15-1 lists some of the core items you should be familiar with.

Table 15-1. A Sampling of Members of the `System.Reflection` Namespace

Type	Meaning in Life
Assembly	This `MustInherit` class contains a number of Shared methods that allow you to load, investigate, and manipulate an assembly.
AssemblyName	This class allows you to discover numerous details behind an assembly's identity (version information, culture information, and so forth).
EventInfo	This `MustInherit` class holds information for a given event.
FieldInfo	This `MustInherit` class holds information for a given field.
MemberInfo	This is the `MustInherit` base class that defines common behaviors for the `EventInfo`, `FieldInfo`, `MethodInfo`, and `PropertyInfo` types.
MethodInfo	This `MustInherit` class contains information for a given method.
Module	This `MustInherit` class allows you to access a given module within a multi-file assembly. When we use the word "module" here we are talking about "net modules", not Modules as in Shared Classes in VB 2010.
ParameterInfo	This class holds information for a given parameter.
PropertyInfo	This `MustInherit` class holds information for a given property.

To understand how to leverage the `System.Reflection` namespace to programmatically read .NET metadata, you need to first come to terms with the `System.Type` class.

The System.Type Class

The System.Type class defines a number of members that can be used to examine a type's metadata, a great number of which return types from the System.Reflection namespace. For example, Type.GetMethods() returns an array of MethodInfo objects, Type.GetFields() returns an array of FieldInfo objects, and so on. The complete set of members exposed by System.Type is quite expansive; however, Table 15-2 offers a partial snapshot of the members supported by System.Type (see the .NET Framework 4.0 SDK documentation for full details).

Table 15-2. Select Members of System.Type

Type	Meaning in Life
IsAbstract IsArray IsClass	These properties (among others) allow you to discover a number of basic traits about the Type you are referring to (e.g., if it is an abstract entity, an array, a nested class, and so forth).
IsCOMObject IsEnum IsGenericTypeDefinition IsGenericParameter IsInterface IsPrimitive IsNestedPrivate IsNestedPublic IsSealed IsValueType	
GetConstructors() GetEvents() GetFields() GetInterfaces() GetMembers() GetMethods() GetNestedTypes() GetProperties()	These methods (among others) allow you to obtain an array representing the items (interface, method, property, etc.) you are interested in. Each method returns a related array (e.g., GetFields() returns a FieldInfo array, GetMethods() returns a MethodInfo array, etc.). Be aware that each of these methods has a singular form (e.g., GetMethod(), GetProperty(), etc.) that allows you to retrieve a specific item by name, rather than an array of all related items.
FindMembers()	This method returns a MemberInfo array based on search criteria.
GetType()	This Shared method returns a Type instance given a string name.
InvokeMember()	This method allows "late binding" for a given item. You'll learn about late binding later in this chapter.

Obtaining a Type Reference Using System.Object.GetType()

You can obtain an instance of the `Type` class in a variety of ways. However, the one thing you cannot do is directly create a `Type` object using the `New` keyword, as `Type` is a `MustInherit` class. Regarding your first choice, recall that `System.Object` defines a method named `GetType()`, which returns an instance of the `Type` class that represents the metadata for the current object:

```
' Obtain type information using a SportsCar instance.
Dim sc As New SportsCar()
Dim t As Type = sc.GetType()
```

Obviously, this approach will only work if you have compile-time knowledge of the type you wish to reflect over (`SportsCar` in this case) and currently have an instance of the type in memory. Given this restriction, it should make sense that tools such as `ildasm.exe` do not obtain type information by directly calling `System.Object.GetType()` for each type, given the `ildasm.exe` was not compiled against your custom assemblies!

Obtaining a Type Reference Using System.Type.GetType()

To obtain type information in a more flexible manner, you may call the Shared `GetType()` member of the `System.Type` class and specify the fully qualified string name of the type you are interested in examining. Using this approach, you do *not* need to have compile-time knowledge of the type you are extracting metadata from, given that `Type.GetType()` takes an instance of the omnipresent `System.String`.

■ **Note** When I say you do not need compile-time knowledge when calling `Type.GetType()`, I am referring to the fact that this method can take any string value whatsoever (rather than a strongly typed variable). Of course, you would still need to know the name of the type in a "stringified" format!

The `Type.GetType()` method has been overloaded to allow you to specify two Boolean parameters, one of which controls whether an exception should be thrown if the type cannot be found, and the other of which establishes the case sensitivity of the string. To illustrate, ponder the following:

```
'Obtain type information using the Shared Type.GetType() method
'(don't throw an exception if SportsCar cannot be found and ignore  case).
Dim t As Type = Type.GetType("CarLibrary.SportsCar", False, True)
```

In the previous example, notice that the string you are passing into `GetType()` makes no mention of the assembly containing the type. In this case, the assumption is that the type is defined within the currently executing assembly. However, when you wish to obtain metadata for a type within an external private assembly, the string parameter is formatted using the type's fully qualified name, followed by a comma, followed by the friendly name of the assembly containing the type:

```
'Obtain type information for a type within an external assembly.
Dim t As Type = Type.GetType("CarLibrary.SportsCar, CarLibrary")
```

As well, do know that the string passed into **Type.GetType()** may specify a plus token (+) to denote a *nested type*. Assume you wish to obtain type information for an enumeration (**SpyOptions**) nested within a class named **JamesBondCar**. To do so, you would write the following:

```
' Obtain type information for a nested enumeration
' within the current assembly.
Dim t As Type = Type.GetType("CarLibrary.JamesBondCar+SpyOptions")
```

Obtaining a Type Reference Using GetType()

The final way to obtain type information is using the VB 2010 **GetType** operator:

```
'Get the Type using GetType.
Dim t As Type = GetType(SportsCar)
```

Like **Type.GetType()**, the **GetType** operator is helpful in that you do not need to first create an object instance to extract type information. However, your code base must still have compile-time knowledge of the type you are interested in examining.

Building a Custom Metadata Viewer

To illustrate the basic process of reflection (and the usefulness of **System.Type**), let's create a Console Application named **MyTypeViewer**. This program will display details of the methods, properties, fields, and supported interfaces (in addition to some other points of interest) for any type within **mscorlib.dll** (recall all .NET applications have automatic access to this core framework class library) or a type within **MyTypeViewer** itself. Once the application has been created, be sure to import the **System.Reflection** namespace.

```
' Need to import this namespace to do any reflection!
Imports System.Reflection
```

Reflecting on Methods

The **Module1** Module will be updated to define a number of **Subs**, each of which takes a single **System.Type** parameter. First you have **ListMethods()**, which (as you might guess) prints the name of each method defined by the incoming type. Notice how **Type.GetMethods()** returns an array of **System.Reflection.MethodInfo** objects, which can be enumerated over using a standard **For Each** loop:

```
'Display method names of type.
Sub ListMethods(ByVal t As Type)
        Console.WriteLine("***** Methods *****")
        Dim mi As MethodInfo() = t.GetMethods()

        For Each m As MethodInfo In mi
        Console.WriteLine("->{0}", m.Name)
        Next
        Console.WriteLine()
End Sub
```

Here, you are simply printing the name of the method using the `MethodInfo.Name` property. As you might guess, `MethodInfo` has many additional members that allow you to determine whether the method is Shared, `Overridable`, generic, or `MustOverride`. As well, the `MethodInfo` type allows you to obtain the method's return value and parameter set. You'll spruce up the implementation of `ListMethods()` in just a bit.

If you wish, you could also build a fitting LINQ query to enumerate the names of each method. Recall from Chapter 13, LINQ to Objects allows you to build strongly typed queries which can be applied to in-memory object collections. As a good rule of thumb, whenever you find blocks of looping or decision programming logic, you could make use of a related LINQ query. For example, you could rewrite the previous method as so:

```
'Display method names of type.
Sub ListMethods(ByVal t As Type)
        Console.WriteLine("***** Methods *****")
        Dim methodNames = From n In t.GetMethods() _
          Select n

        For Each name In methodNames
            Console.WriteLine("->{0}", name)
        Next
        Console.WriteLine()
End Sub
```

Reflecting on Fields and Properties

The implementation of `ListFields()` is similar. The only notable difference is the call to `Type.GetFields()` and the resulting `FieldInfo` array. Again, to keep things simple, you are printing out only the name of each field using a LINQ query.

```
'Display field names of type.
Sub ListFields(ByVal t As Type)
        Console.WriteLine("***** Fields *****")
        Dim fieldNames = From f In t.GetFields() _
                        Select f.Name

        For Each name In fieldNames
            Console.WriteLine("->{0}", name)
        Next
        Console.WriteLine()
End Sub
```

The logic to display a type's properties is similar as well.

```
'Display property names of type.
Sub ListProps(ByVal t As Type)
        Console.WriteLine("***** Properties *****")
        Dim propNames = From p In t.GetProperties() _
                        Select p.Name
```

```
        For Each name In propNames
            Console.WriteLine("->{0}", name)
        Next
        Console.WriteLine()
End Sub
```

Reflecting on Implemented Interfaces

Next, you will author a method named `ListInterfaces()` that will print out the names of any interfaces supported on the incoming type. The only point of interest here is that the call to `GetInterfaces()` returns an array of `System.Types`! This should make sense given that interfaces are, indeed, types:

```
' Display implemented interfaces.
Sub ListInterfaces(ByVal t As Type)
        Console.WriteLine("***** Interfaces *****")
        Dim ifaces = From i In t.GetInterfaces() _
                        Select i

        For Each i As Type In ifaces
            Console.WriteLine("->{0}", i.Name)
        Next
End Sub
```

■ **Note** Be aware that a majority of the "get" methods of `System.Type` (`GetMethods()`, `GetInterfaces()`, etc) have been overloaded to allow you to specify values from the `BindingFlags` enumeration. This provides a greater level of control on exactly what should be searched for (e.g., only Shared members, only Public members, include Private members, etc). Consult the .NET Framework 4.0 SDK documentation for details.

Displaying Various Odds and Ends

Last but not least, you have one final helper method that will simply display various statistics (indicating whether the type is generic, what the base class is, whether the type is NotInheritable, and so forth) regarding the incoming type:

```
'Just for good measure.
Sub ListVariousStats(ByVal t As Type)
    Console.WriteLine("***** Various Statistics *****")
    Console.WriteLine("Base class is: {0}", t.BaseType)
    Console.WriteLine("Is type MustInherit? {0}", t.IsAbstract)
    Console.WriteLine("Is type NotInheritable? {0}", t.IsSealed)
    Console.WriteLine("Is type generic? {0}",          t.IsGenericTypeDefinition)
    Console.WriteLine("Is type a class type? {0}", t.IsClass)
    Console.WriteLine()
End Sub
```

Implementing Main()

The Main() method of the Module1 Module prompts the user for the fully qualified name of a type. Once you obtain this string data, you pass it into the Type.GetType() method and send the extracted System.Type into each of your helper methods. This process repeats until the user enters **Q** to terminate the application:

```
Sub Main()
    Console.WriteLine("***** Welcome to MyTypeViewer *****")
    Dim typeName As String = ""

    Do
        Console.WriteLine(vbLf & "Enter a type name to evaluate")
        Console.Write("or enter Q to quit: ")

        ' Get name of type.
        typeName = Console.ReadLine()

        ' Does user want to quit?
        If typeName.ToUpper() = "Q" Then
            Exit Do
        End If

        ' Try to display type.
        Try
            Dim t As Type = Type.GetType(typeName)
            Console.WriteLine("")
            ListVariousStats(t)
            ListFields(t)
            ListProps(t)
            ListMethods(t)
            ListInterfaces(t)
        Catch
            Console.WriteLine("Sorry, can't find type")
        End Try
    Loop While True
End Sub
```

At this point, MyTypeViewer.exe is ready to take out for a test drive. For example, run your application and enter the following fully qualified names (be aware that the manner in which you invoked Type.GetType() requires case-sensitive string names):

- System.Int32
- System.Collections.ArrayList
- System.Threading.Thread
- System.Void
- System.IO.BinaryWriter
- System.Math

- System.Console
- MyTypeViewer.Program

For example, here is some partial output when specifying System.Math.

```
***** Welcome to MyTypeViewer *****


Enter a type name to evaluate

or enter Q to quit: System.Math


***** Various Statistics *****

Base class is: System.Object

Is type MustInherit? True

Is type NotInheritable? True

Is type generic? False

Is type a class type? True


***** Fields *****

->PI

->E


***** Properties *****
```

```
***** Methods *****

->Acos

->Asin

->Atan

->Atan2

->Ceiling

->Ceiling

->Cos

...
```

Reflecting on Generic Types

When you call `Type.GetType()` in order to obtain metadata descriptions of generic types, you must make use of a special syntax involving a "back tick" character (`) followed by a numerical value that represents the number of type parameters the type supports. For example, if you wish to print out the metadata description of `System.Collections.Generic.List(Of T)`, you would need to pass the following string into your application:

```
System.Collections.Generic.List`1
```

Here, you are using the numerical value of `1`, given that `List(Of T)` has only one type parameter. However, if you wish to reflect over `Dictionary(Of TKey, TValue)`, you would supply the value `2`:

```
System.Collections.Generic.Dictionary`2
```

Reflecting on Method Parameters and Return Values

So far, so good! Let's make a minor enhancement to the current application. Specifically, you will update the `ListMethods()` helper method to list not only the name of a given method, but also the return type and incoming parameter types. The `MethodInfo` type provides the `ReturnType` property and `GetParameters()` method for these very tasks. In the following modified code, notice that you are building a string that contains the type and name of each parameter using a nested `For Each` loop (without the use of LINQ):

```vb
Sub ListMethods(ByVal t As Type)
    Console.WriteLine("***** Methods *****")
    Dim mi As MethodInfo() = t.GetMethods()
```

```
    For Each m As MethodInfo In mi
        Dim retVal As String = m.ReturnType.FullName()

        Dim paramInfo As String = "( "
        For Each pi As ParameterInfo In m.GetParameters()
            paramInfo &= String.Format("{0} {1} ",
                                    pi.ParameterType,    pi.Name)
        Next
        paramInfo &= " )"

        Console.WriteLine("->{0} {1} {2}", retVal, m.Name, paramInfo)
    Next
    Console.WriteLine("")
End Sub
```

If you now run this updated application, you will find that the methods of a given type are much more detailed. If you enter your good friend, System.Object as input to the program, the following methods will display:

```
***** Methods *****

->System.String ToString (  )

->System.Boolean Equals ( System.Object obj  )

->System.Boolean Equals ( System.Object objA System.Object objB  )

->System.Boolean ReferenceEquals ( System.Object objA System.Object objB  )

->System.Int32 GetHashCode (  )

->System.Type GetType (  )
```

The current implementation of ListMethods() is helpful, in that you can directly investigate each parameter and method return type using the System.Reflection object model. As an extreme shortcut, be aware that each of the XXXInfo types (MethodInfo, PropertyInfo, EventInfo, etc.) have overridden ToString() to display the signature of the item requested. Thus, you could also implement ListMethods() as follows (once again using LINQ, where you simply select all MethodInfo objects, rather than only the Name values):

```
Sub ListMethods(ByVal t As Type)
    Console.WriteLine("***** Methods *****")
    Dim methodNames = From n In t.GetMethods() _
                Select n
```

```
    For Each name In methodNames
      Console.WriteLine("->{0}", name)
    Next
    Console.WriteLine()
End Sub
```

Interesting stuff, huh? Clearly the `System.Reflection` namespace and `System.Type` class allow you to reflect over many other aspects of a type beyond what `MyTypeViewer` is currently displaying. As you would hope, you can obtain a type's events, get the list of any generic parameters for a given member, and glean dozens of other details.

Nevertheless, at this point you have created a (somewhat capable) object browser. The major limitation, of course, is that you have no way to reflect beyond the current assembly (`MyTypeViewer`) or the always accessible `mscorlib.dll`. This begs the question, "How can I build applications that can load (and reflect over) assemblies not referenced at compile time?" Glad you asked.

■ **Source Code** The MyTypeViewer project can be found under the Chapter 15 subdirectory.

Dynamically Loading Assemblies

In the previous chapter, you learned all about how the CLR consults the assembly manifest when probing for an externally referenced assembly. However, there will be many times when you need to load assemblies on the fly programmatically, even if there is no record of said assembly in the manifest. Formally speaking, the act of loading external assemblies on demand is known as a *dynamic load*.

`System.Reflection` defines a class named `Assembly`. Using this class, you are able to dynamically load an assembly as well as discover properties about the assembly itself. Using the `Assembly` type, you are able to dynamically load private or shared assemblies, as well as load an assembly located at an arbitrary location. In essence, the `Assembly` class provides methods (`Load()` and `LoadFrom()` in particular) that allow you to programmatically supply the same sort of information found in a client-side `*.config` file.

To illustrate dynamic loading, create a brand-new Console Application named ExternalAssemblyReflector. Your task is to construct a `Main()` method that prompts for the friendly name of an assembly to load dynamically. You will pass the `Assembly` reference into a helper method named `DisplayTypes()`, which will simply print the names of each class, interface, structure, enumeration, and delegate it contains. The code is refreshingly simple:

```
Imports System.Reflection
Imports System.IO  ' For FileNotFoundException definition.

Module Module1
    Sub DisplayTypesInAsm(ByVal asm As Assembly)
        Console.WriteLine(vbLf & "***** Types in Assembly *****")
        Console.WriteLine("->{0}", asm.FullName)

        Dim types As Type() = asm.GetTypes()
```

```
        For Each t As Type In types
            Console.WriteLine("Type: {0}", t)
        Next
        Console.WriteLine("")
    End Sub

    Sub Main()
        Console.WriteLine("***** External Assembly Viewer *****")

        Dim asmName As String = ""
        Dim asm As Assembly = Nothing
        Do
            Console.WriteLine(vbLf & "Enter an assembly to evaluate")
            Console.Write("or enter Q to quit: ")

            'Get name of assembly.
            asmName = Console.ReadLine()
            If asmName.ToUpper() = "Q" Then
                Exit Do
            End If

            'Try to load assembly.
            Try
                asm = Assembly.Load(asmName)
                DisplayTypesInAsm(asm)
            Catch
                Console.WriteLine("Sorry, can't find assembly.")
            End Try
        Loop While True
    End Sub
End Module
```

Notice that the Shared **Assembly.Load()** method has been passed only the friendly name of the assembly you are interested in loading into memory. Thus, if you wish to reflect over **CarLibrary.dll**, you will need to copy the **CarLibrary.dll** binary to the \bin\Debug directory of the ExternalAssemblyReflector application to run this program. Once you do, you will find output similar to the following:

```
***** External Assembly Viewer *****


Enter an assembly to evaluate

or enter Q to quit: CarLibrary
```

```
***** Types in Assembly *****

->CarLibrary, Version=2.0.0.0, Culture=neutral, PublicKeyToken= null

Type: CarLibrary.My.MyApplication

Type: CarLibrary.My.MyComputer

Type: CarLibrary.My.MyProject

Type: CarLibrary.My.MyProject+MyWebServices

Type: CarLibrary.My.MyProject+ThreadSafeObjectProvider`1[T]

Type: CarLibrary.My.InternalXmlHelper

Type: CarLibrary.My.InternalXmlHelper+RemoveNamespaceAttributesClosure

Type: CarLibrary.MusicMedia

Type: CarLibrary.EngineState

Type: CarLibrary.Car

Type: CarLibrary.SportsCar

Type: CarLibrary.MiniVan

Type: CarLibrary.My.Resources.Resources

Type: CarLibrary.My.MySettings

Type: CarLibrary.My.MySettingsProperty
```

If you wish to make ExternalAssemblyReflector more flexible, you can update your code to load the external assembly using `Assembly.LoadFrom()` rather than `Assembly.Load()`:

```
Try
    asm = Assembly.LoadFrom(asmName)
    DisplayTypesInAsm(asm)
...
```

By doing so, you can enter an absolute path to the assembly you wish to view (e.g., C:\MyApp\MyAsm.dll). Essentially, `Assembly.LoadFrom()` allows you to programmatically supply a `<codeBase>` value. With this adjustment, you can now pass in a full path to your console application. Thus, if `CarLibrary.dll` was located under `C:\MyCode`, you could enter the following:

```
***** External Assembly Viewer *****


Enter an assembly to evaluate

or enter Q to quit: C:\MyCode\CarLibrary.dll


***** Types in Assembly *****

->CarLibrary, Version=2.0.0.0, Culture=neutral, PublicKeyToken= nullType:

CarLibrary.My.MyApplication

Type: CarLibrary.My.MyComputer

Type: CarLibrary.My.MyProject

Type: CarLibrary.My.MyProject+MyWebServices

Type: CarLibrary.My.MyProject+ThreadSafeObjectProvider`1[T]

Type: CarLibrary.My.InternalXmlHelper

Type: CarLibrary.My.InternalXmlHelper+RemoveNamespaceAttributesClosure

Type: CarLibrary.EngineState

Type: CarLibrary.MusicMedia

Type: CarLibrary.Car

Type: CarLibrary.SportsCar

Type: CarLibrary.MiniVan

Type: CarLibrary.My.Resources.Resources

Type: CarLibrary.My.MySettings

Type: CarLibrary.My.MySettingsProperty
```

■ **Source Code** The ExternalAssemblyReflector project is included in the Chapter 15 subdirectory.

Reflecting on Shared Assemblies

The `Assembly.Load()` method has been overloaded a number of times. One variation allows you to specify a culture value (for localized assemblies) as well as a version number and public key token value (for shared assemblies). Collectively speaking, the set of items identifying an assembly is termed the *display name*. The format of a display name is a comma-delimited string of name/value pairs that begins with the friendly name of the assembly, followed by optional qualifiers (that may appear in any order). Here is the template to follow (optional items appear in parentheses):

```
Name (,Version = major.minor.build.revision) (,Culture = culture token)
(,PublicKeyToken= public key token)
```

When you're crafting a display name, the convention `PublicKeyToken=null` indicates that binding and matching against a non–strongly named assembly is required. Additionally, `Culture=""` indicates matching against the default culture of the target machine, for example:

```
' Load version 1.0.0.0 of CarLibrary using the default culture.
Dim a As Assembly = Assembly.Load("CarLibrary, Version=1.0.0.0, PublicKeyToken=null,
Culture="""")
```

Also be aware that the `System.Reflection` namespace supplies the `AssemblyName` type, which allows you to represent the preceding string information in a handy object variable. Typically, this class is used in conjunction with `System.Version`, which is an OO wrapper around an assembly's version number. Once you have established the display name, it can then be passed into the overloaded `Assembly.Load()` method:

```
' Make use of AssemblyName to define the display name.
Dim asmName As New AssemblyName("CarLibrary")
Dim v As New Version("1.0.0.0")
asmName.Version = v
Dim a As Assembly = Assembly.Load(asmName)
```

To load a shared assembly from the GAC, the `Assembly.Load()` parameter must specify a `PublicKeyToken` value. For example, assume you have a new Console Application named SharedAsmReflector, and wish to load version 4.0.0.0 of the `System.Windows.Forms.dll` assembly provided by the .NET base class libraries. Given that the number of types in this assembly is quite large, the following application only prints out the names of public enums, using a simple LINQ query:

```
Imports System.Reflection

Module Module1
    Sub DisplayInfo(ByVal a As Assembly)
        Console.WriteLine("***** Info about Assembly *****")
        Console.WriteLine("Loaded from GAC? {0}", a.GlobalAssemblyCache)
        Console.WriteLine("Asm Name: {0}", a.GetName().Name)
```

```
            Console.WriteLine("Asm Version: {0}", a.GetName().Version)
            Console.WriteLine("Asm Culture: {0}",a.GetName().
                                    CultureInfo.DisplayName)
            Console.WriteLine(vbLf & "Here are the public enums:")

            'Use a LINQ query to find the public enums.
            Dim types As Type() = a.GetTypes()
            Dim publicEnums = From pe In types _
                Where pe.IsEnum AndAlso pe.IsPublic _
                Select pe

            For Each pe In types
                Console.WriteLine(pe)
            Next
    End Sub

    Sub Main()
        Console.WriteLine("**** The Shared Asm Reflector App ****" & vbLf)

        'Load System.Windows.Forms.dll from GAC.
        Dim displayName As String = "System.Windows.Forms," &
            "Version=4.0.0.0," & "PublicKeyToken=b77a5c561934e089," &
            "Culture="""

        Dim asm As Assembly = Assembly.Load(displayName)
        DisplayInfo(asm)
        Console.WriteLine("Done!")
        Console.ReadLine()
    End Sub
End Module
```

■ **Source Code** The SharedAsmReflector project is included in the Chapter 15 subdirectory.

At this point, you should understand how to use some of the core members of the System.Reflection namespace to discover metadata at runtime. Of course, I realize despite the "cool factor," you likely will not need to build custom object browsers at your place of employment too often. Do recall, however, that reflection services are the foundation for a number of very common programming activities, including *late binding*.

Understanding Late Binding

Simply put, *late binding* is a technique in which you are able to create an instance of a given type and invoke its members at runtime without having hard-coded compile-time knowledge of its existence. When you are building an application that binds late to a type in an external assembly, you have no reason to set a reference to the assembly; therefore, the caller's manifest has no direct listing of the assembly.

At first glance, it is not easy to see the value of late binding. It is true that if you can "bind early" to an object (e.g., set an assembly reference and allocate the type using the VB 2010 New keyword), you should opt to do so. For one reason, early binding allows you to determine errors at compile time, rather than at runtime. Nevertheless, late binding does have a critical role in any extendable application you may be building. You will have a chance to build such an "extendable" program at the end of this chapter in the section "Building an Extendable Application"; until then, let's examine the role of the Activator class.

The System.Activator Class

The System.Activator class (defined in mscorlib.dll) is the key to the .NET late binding process. For the current example, you are only interested in the Activator.CreateInstance() method, which is used to create an instance of a type à la late binding. This method has been overloaded numerous times to provide a good deal of flexibility. The simplest variation of the CreateInstance() member takes a valid Type object that describes the entity you wish to allocate into memory on the fly.

Create a new Console Application named LateBindingApp, and import the System.IO and System.Reflection namespace via the VB 2010 Imports keyword. Now, update the Module1 Module as follows:

```
Imports System.Reflection
Imports System.IO

'This program will load an external library,
'and create an object using late binding.
Module Module1
    Sub Main()
        Console.WriteLine("***** Fun with Late Binding *****")

        'Try to load a local copy of CarLibrary.
        Dim a As Assembly = Nothing

        Try
            a = Assembly.Load("CarLibrary")
        Catch ex As FileNotFoundException
            Console.WriteLine(ex.Message)
            Return
        End Try

        If a IsNot Nothing Then
            CreateUsingLateBinding(a)
        End If
        Console.ReadLine()
    End Sub

    Sub CreateUsingLateBinding(ByVal asm As Assembly)
        Try
            'Get metadata for the MiniVan type.
            Dim miniVanType As Type = asm.GetType("CarLibrary.MiniVan")
```

```
        ' Create the MiniVan on the fly.
        Dim obj As Object = Activator.CreateInstance(miniVanType)
        Console.WriteLine("Created a {0} using late binding!", obj)

    Catch ex As Exception
        Console.WriteLine(ex.Message)
    End Try
  End Sub
End Module
```

Now, before you run this application, you will need to manually place a copy of `CarLibrary.dll` into the bin\Debug folder of this new application using Windows Explorer. The reason is that you are calling `Assembly.Load()`, therefore the CLR will only probe in the client folder (if you wish, you could enter a path to the assembly using `Assembly.LoadFrom()`, however there is no need to do so) .

■ **Note** Don't set a reference to CarLibrary.dll using Visual Studio for this example! That will record this library in the client's manifest. The whole point of late binding is that you are trying to create an object which is not known at compile time.

Notice that the `Activator.CreateInstance()` method returns a `System.Object` rather than a strongly typed `MiniVan`. Therefore, if you apply the dot operator on the `obj` variable, you will fail to see any members of the `MiniVan` class. At first glance, you may assume you can remedy this problem with an explicit cast:

```
'Cast to get access to the members of MiniVan?
'Nope!  Compiler error!
Dim obj As Object = DirectCast(Activator.CreateInstance(miniVanType), MiniVan)
```

However, because your program has not set a reference to `CarLibrary.dll`, you cannot make use of the VB 2010 `Imports` keyword to import the `CarLibrary` namespace, and therefore you can't use a `MiniVan` during the casting operation! Remember that the whole point of late binding is to create instances of objects for which there is no compile-time knowledge. Given this, how can you invoke the underlying methods of the `MiniVan` object stored in the `System.Object` reference? The answer, of course, is by using reflection.

Invoking Methods with No Parameters

Assume you wish to invoke the `TurboBoost()` method of the `MiniVan`. As you recall, this method will set the state of the engine to "dead" and display an informational message box. The first step is to obtain a `MethodInfo` object for the `TurboBoost()` method using `Type.GetMethod()`. From the resulting `MethodInfo`, you are then able to call `MiniVan.TurboBoost` using `Invoke()`. `MethodInfo.Invoke()` requires you to send in all parameters that are to be given to the method represented by `MethodInfo`. These parameters are represented by an array of `System.Object` types (as the parameters for a given method could be any number of various entities).

Given that `TurboBoost()` does not require any parameters, you can simply pass `Nothing` (meaning "this method has no parameters"). Update your `CreateUsingLateBinding()` method as follows:

```
Sub CreateUsingLateBinding(ByVal asm As Assembly)
  Try
      'Get metadata for the Minivan type.
      Dim miniVanType As Type = asm.GetType("CarLibrary.MiniVan")

      'Create the MiniVan on the fly.
      Dim obj As Object = Activator.CreateInstance(miniVanType)
      Console.WriteLine("Created a {0} using late binding!", obj)

      'Get info for TurboBoost.
      Dim mi As MethodInfo = miniVanType.GetMethod("TurboBoost")

      'Invoke method ('Nothing' for no parameters).
      mi.Invoke(obj, Nothing)
  Catch ex As Exception
      Console.WriteLine(ex.Message)
  End Try
End Sub
```

At this point, you will see the message box shown in Figure 15-2, once the `TurboBoost()` method is invoked.

Figure 15-2. *Late-bound method invocation*

Invoking Methods with Parameters

When you wish to use late binding to invoke a method requiring parameters, you will package up the arguments as a loosely typed array of `objects`. Recall that version 2.0.0.0 of `CarLibrary.dll` defined the following method in the `Car` class:

```
Public Sub TurnOnRadio(ByVal musicOn As Boolean, ByVal mm As MusicMedia)
    If musicOn Then
        MessageBox.Show(String.Format("Jamming {0}", mm))
    Else
        MessageBox.Show("Quiet time...")
    End If
End Sub
```

This method takes two parameters: a Boolean representing if the automobile's music system should be turned on or off, and an enum which represents the type of music player. Recall this enum was structured as so:

```
Public Enum MusicMedia
    musicCd    '0
    musicTape  '1
    musicRadio '2
    musicMp3   '3
End Enum
```

Here is a new method of the `Module1` Module, which invokes `TurnOnRadio()`. Notice that you are using the underlying numerical values of the `MusicMedia` enumeration, to specify a "radio" media player.

```
Sub InvokeMethodWithArgsUsingLateBinding(ByVal asm As Assembly)
    Try
        'First, get a metadata description of the sports car.
        Dim sport As Type = asm.GetType("CarLibrary.SportsCar")

        'Now, create the sports car.
        Dim obj As Object = Activator.CreateInstance(sport)

        'Invoke TurnOnRadio() with arguments.
        Dim mi As MethodInfo = sport.GetMethod("TurnOnRadio")
        mi.Invoke(obj, New Object() {True, 2})

    Catch ex As Exception
        Console.WriteLine(ex.Message)
    End Try
End Sub
```

Hopefully, at this point, you can see the relationships among reflection, dynamic loading, and late binding. To be sure, the reflection API provides many additional features beyond what has been covered here, but you should be in good shape to dig into more details if you are interested.

Again, you still may wonder exactly *when* you might make use of these techniques in your own applications. The conclusion of this chapter should shed light on this question; however, the next topic under investigation is the role of .NET attributes.

■ **Source Code** The LateBindingApp project is included in the Chapter 15 subdirectory.

Understanding the Role of .NET Attributes

As illustrated at beginning of this chapter, one role of a .NET compiler is to generate metadata descriptions for all defined and referenced types. In addition to this standard metadata contained within any assembly, the .NET platform provides a way for programmers to embed additional metadata into an assembly using *attributes*. In a nutshell, attributes are nothing more than code annotations that can be applied to a given type (class, interface, structure, etc.), member (property, method, etc.), assembly, or module.

The idea of annotating code using attributes is not new. COM IDL provided numerous predefined attributes that allowed developers to describe the types contained within a given COM server. However, COM attributes were little more than a set of keywords. If a COM developer needed to create a custom attribute, he or she could do so, but it was referenced in code by a 128-bit number (GUID), which was cumbersome at best.

.NET attributes are class types that extend the abstract `System.Attribute` base class. As you explore the .NET namespaces, you will find many predefined attributes that you are able to make use of in your applications. Furthermore, you are free to build custom attributes to further qualify the behavior of your types by creating a new type deriving from `Attribute`.

The .NET base class library provides a number of attributes in various namespaces. Table 15-3 gives a snapshot of some—but by *absolutely* no means all—predefined attributes.

Table 15-3. A Tiny Sampling of Predefined Attributes

Attribute	Meaning in Life
`<CLSCompliant()>`	Enforces the annotated item to conform to the rules of the Common Language Specification (CLS). Recall that CLS-compliant types are guaranteed to be used seamlessly across all .NET programming languages.
`<DllImport()>`	Allows .NET code to make calls to any unmanaged C- or C++-based code library, including the API of the underlying operating system. Do note that `<DllImport()>` is not used when communicating with COM-based software.
`<Obsolete()>`	Marks a deprecated type or member. If other programmers attempt to use such an item, they will receive a compiler warning describing the error of their ways.
`<Serializable()>`	Marks a class or structure as being "serializable," meaning it is able to persist its current state into a stream.
`<NonSerialized()>`	Specifies that a given field in a class or structure should not be persisted during the serialization process.
`<WebMethod()>`	Marks a method as being invokable via HTTP requests and instructs the CLR to serialize the method return value as XML.

Understand that when you apply attributes in your code, the embedded metadata is essentially useless until another piece of software explicitly reflects over the information. If this is not the case, the blurb of metadata embedded within the assembly is ignored and completely harmless.

Attribute Consumers

As you would guess, the .NET 4.0 Framework SDK ships with numerous utilities that are indeed on the lookout for various attributes. The VB 2010 compiler (`vbc.exe`) itself has been preprogrammed to discover the presence of various attributes during the compilation cycle. For example, if the VB 2010 compiler encounters the `<CLSCompliant()>` attribute, it will automatically check the attributed item to ensure it is exposing only CLS-compliant constructs. By way of another example, if the VB 2010 compiler discovers an item attributed with the `<Obsolete()>` attribute, it will display a compiler warning in the Visual Studio 2010 Error List window.

In addition to development tools, numerous methods in the .NET base class libraries are preprogrammed to reflect over specific attributes. For example, if you wish to persist the state of an object to file, all you are required to do is annotate your class or structure with the `<Serializable()>` attribute. If the `Serialize()` method of the `BinaryFormatter` class encounters this attribute, the object is automatically persisted to file in a compact binary format.

The .NET CLR is also on the prowl for the presence of certain attributes. One famous .NET attribute is `<WebMethod()>`, used to build XML web services using ASP.NET. If you wish to expose a method via HTTP requests and automatically encode the method return value as XML, simply apply `<WebMethod()>` to the method and the CLR handles the details. Beyond web service development, attributes are critical to the operation of the .NET security system, Windows Communication Foundation, and COM/.NET interoperability (and so on).

Finally, you are free to build applications that are programmed to reflect over your own custom attributes as well as any attribute in the .NET base class libraries. By doing so, you are essentially able to create a set of "keywords" that are understood by a specific set of assemblies.

Applying Attributes in VB 2010

To illustrate the process of applying attributes in VB 2010, create a new Console Application named ApplyingAttributes. Assume you wish to build a class named `Motorcycle` that can be persisted in a binary format. To do so, simply apply the `<Serializable()>` attribute to the class definition. If you have a field that should not be persisted, you may apply the `<NonSerialized()>` attribute:

```
'This class can be saved to disk.
<Serializable()> _
Public Class Motorcycle
        'However this field will not be persisted.
        <NonSerialized()> _
        Private weightOfCurrentPassengers As Single

        'These fields are still serializable.
        Private hasRadioSystem As Boolean
        Private hasHeadSet As Boolean
        Private hasSissyBar As Boolean
End Class
```

■ **Note** An attribute applies to the "very next" item. For example, the only nonserialized field of the `Motorcycle` class is `weightOfCurrentPassengers`. The remaining fields are serializable given that the entire class has been annotated with `<Serializable()>`.

At this point, don't concern yourself with the actual process of object serialization (Chapter 20 examines the details). Just notice that when you wish to apply an attribute, the name of the attribute is sandwiched between Angle brackets.

Once this class has been compiled, you can view the extra metadata using `ildasm.exe`. Notice that these attributes are recorded using the **serializable** token (see the red triangle immediately inside the `Motorcycle` class) and the **notserialized** token (on the `weightOfCurrentPassengers` field; see Figure 15-3).

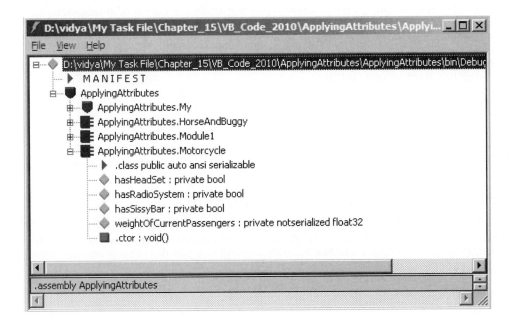

Figure 15-3. Attributes shown in `ildasm.exe`

As you might guess, a single item can be attributed with multiple attributes. Assume you have a legacy VB 2010 class type (`HorseAndBuggy`) that was marked as serializable, but is now considered obsolete for current development. Rather than deleting the class definition from your code base (and risk breaking existing software), you can mark the class with the `<Obsolete()>` attribute. To apply multiple attributes to a single item, simply use a comma-delimited list:

```
<Serializable(), Obsolete("Use another vehicle!")> _
Public Class HorseAndBuggy
    '....
End Class
```

As an alternative, you can also apply multiple attributes on a single item by stacking each attribute as follows (the end result is identical):

```
<Serializable()>
<Obsolete("Use another vehicle!")> _
Public Class HorseAndBuggy
    '....
End Class
```

VB 2010 Attribute Shorthand Notation

If you were consulting the .NET Framework 4.0 SDK documentation, you may have noticed that the actual class name of the `<Obsolete()>` attribute is `ObsoleteAttribute`, not `Obsolete`. As a naming convention, all .NET attributes (including custom attributes you may create yourself) are suffixed with the `Attribute` token. However, to simplify the process of applying attributes, the VB 2010 language does not require you to type in the `Attribute` suffix. Given this, the following iteration of the `HorseAndBuggy` type is identical to the previous (it just involves a few more keystrokes):

```
<SerializableAttribute()>
<ObsoleteAttribute("Use another vehicle!")> _
Public Class HorseAndBuggy
    ' ....
End Class
```

Be aware that this is a courtesy provided by VB 2010. Not all .NET-enabled languages support this shorthand attribute syntax.

Specifying Constructor Parameters for Attributes

Notice that the `<Obsolete()>` attribute is able to accept what appears to be a constructor parameter. If you view the formal definition of the `<Obsolete()>` attribute using the Code Definition window (which can be opened using the View menu of Visual Studio 2010), you will find that this class indeed provides a constructor receiving a `System.String`:

```
Public NotInheritable Class ObsoleteAttribute
        Inherits Attribute

        Public Sub New(ByVal message As String,ByVal err As Boolean)
        ...

        Public Sub New(ByVal message As String)
        ...

        Public Sub New()
        ...

        Public ReadOnly Property IsError() As Boolean
        Public ReadOnly Property Message() As String
End Class
```

Understand that when you supply constructor parameters to an attribute, the attribute is *not* allocated into memory until the parameters are reflected upon by another type or an external tool. The string data defined at the attribute level is simply stored within the assembly as a blurb of metadata.

The Obsolete Attribute in Action

Now that `HorseAndBuggy` has been marked as obsolete, if you were to allocate an instance of this type:

```
Sub Main()
    Dim mule As New HorseAndBuggy()
End Sub
```

you would find that the supplied string data is extracted and displayed within the Error List window of Visual Studio 2010, as well as one the offending line of code when you hover your mouse cursor above the obsolete type (see Figure 15-4).

Figure 15-4. Attributes in action

In this case, the "other piece of software" that is reflecting on the <Obsolete()> attribute is the VB 2010 compiler. Hopefully, at this point, you should understand the following key points regarding .NET attributes:

- Attributes are classes that derive from System.Attribute.

- Attributes result in embedded metadata.

- Attributes are basically useless until another agent reflects upon them.

- Attributes are applied in VB 2010 using angle brackets.

Next up, let's examine how you can build your own custom attributes and a piece of custom software that reflects over the embedded metadata.

■ **Source Code** The ApplyingAttributes project is included in the Chapter 15 subdirectory.

Building Custom Attributes

The first step in building a custom attribute is to create a new class deriving from System.Attribute. Keeping in step with the automobile theme used throughout this book, assume you have created a brand new VB 2010 Class Library project named AttributedCarLibrary. This assembly will define a handful of vehicles, each of which is described using a custom attribute named VehicleDescriptionAttribute:

```
'A custom attribute.
Public NotInheritable Class VehicleDescriptionAttribute
        Inherits System.Attribute

        Public Property Description() As String

        Public Sub New(ByVal vehicalDescription As String)
            Description = vehicalDescription
        End Sub

        Public Sub New()
        End Sub
End Class
```

As you can see, VehicleDescriptionAttribute maintains a piece of string data manipulated using an automatic property (Description). Beyond the fact that this class derived from System.Attribute, there is nothing unique to this class definition.

■ **Note** For security reasons, it is considered a .NET best practice to design all custom attributes as NotInheritable.

Applying Custom Attributes

Given that VehicleDescriptionAttribute is derived from System.Attribute, you are now able to annotate your vehicles as you see fit. For testing purposes, add the following class definitions to your new class library:

```
'Assign description using a "named property."<Serializable()> _
<VehicleDescription(Description:="My rocking Harley")> _
Public Class Motorcycle
End Class

<SerializableAttribute()> _
<ObsoleteAttribute("Use another vehicle!")> _
<VehicleDescription("The old gray mare, she ain't what she used to  be...")> _
Public Class HorseAndBuggy
End Class

<VehicleDescription("A very long, slow, but feature-rich auto")> _
Public Class Winnebago
End Class
```

Named Property Syntax

Notice that the description of the Motorcycle is assigned a description using a new bit of attribute-centric syntax termed a *named property*. In the constructor of the first <VehicleDescription()> attribute, you set the underlying string data by using the Description property. If this attribute is reflected upon by an external agent, the value is fed into the Description property (named property syntax is legal only if the attribute supplies a writable .NET property).

In contrast, the HorseAndBuggy and Winnebago types are not making use of named property syntax and are simply passing the string data via the custom constructor. In any case, once you compile the AttributedCarLibrary assembly, you can make use of ildasm.exe to view the injected metadata descriptions for your type. For example, Figure 15-5 shows an embedded description of the Winnebago class.

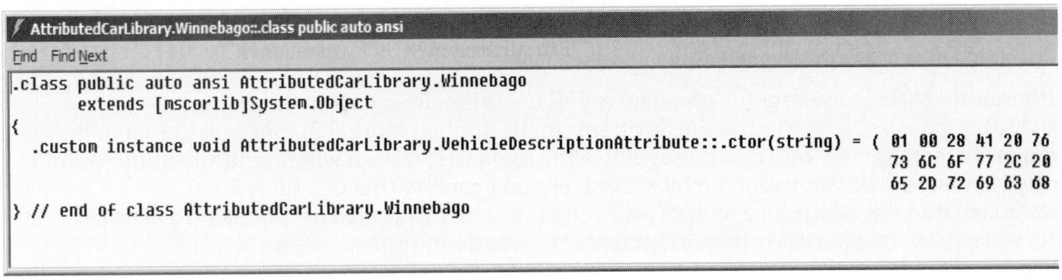

```
 AttributedCarLibrary.Winnebago::.class public auto ansi

Find  Find Next

.class public auto ansi AttributedCarLibrary.Winnebago
        extends [mscorlib]System.Object
{
   .custom instance void AttributedCarLibrary.VehicleDescriptionAttribute::.ctor(string) = ( 01 00 28 41 20 76
                                                                                             73 6C 6F 77 2C 20
                                                                                             65 2D 72 69 63 68
} // end of class AttributedCarLibrary.Winnebago
```

Figure 15-5. Embedded vehicle description data

Restricting Attribute Usage

By default, custom attributes can be applied to just about any aspect of your code (methods, classes, properties, and so on). Thus, if it made sense to do so, you could use VehicleDescription to qualify methods, properties, or fields (among other things):

```
<VehicleDescription("A very long, slow, but feature-rich auto")> _
Public Class Winnebago
        <VehicleDescription("My rocking CD player")> _
        Sub PlayMusic(ByVal IsOn As Boolean)
                '...
        End Sub
End Class
```

In some cases, this is exactly the behavior you require. Other times, however, you may want to build a custom attribute that can be applied only to select code elements. If you wish to constrain the scope of a custom attribute, you will need to apply the <AttributeUsage()>attribute on the definition of your custom attribute. The <AttributeUsage()> attribute allows you to supply any combination of values (via an OR operation) from the AttributeTargets enumeration:

```
'This enumeration defines the possible targets of an attribute.
Public Enum AttributeTargets
        All
        Assembly
        [Class]
        Constructor
        [Delegate]
        [Enum]
```

```
    [Event]
    Field
    GenericParameter
    [Interface]
    Method
    [Module]
    Parameter
    [Property]
    ReturnValue
    Struct
End Enum
```

Furthermore, `<AttributeUsage()>` also allows you to optionally set a named property (`AllowMultiple`) that specifies whether the attribute can be applied more than once on the same item (the default is `False`). As well, `<AttributeUsage()>` allows you to establish whether the attribute should be inherited by derived classes using the `Inherited` named property (the default is `True`).

To establish that the `<VehicleDescription()>` attribute can be applied only once on a class or structure, you can update the `VehicleDescriptionAttribute` definition as follows:

```
'This time, we are using the AttributeUsage attribute
'to annotate our custom attribute.
<AttributeUsage(AttributeTargets.Class Or _
 AttributeTargets.Struct ,Inherited:=False)> _
Public NotInheritable Class VehicleDescriptionAttribute
        Inherits System.Attribute
    ...
End Class
```

With this, if a developer attempted to apply the `<VehicleDescription()>` attribute on anything other than a class or structure, he or she is issued a compile-time error.

Assembly-Level (and Module-Level) Attributes

It is also possible to apply attributes on all types within a given module (for a multi-file assembly; see Chapter 14) or all modules within a given assembly using the `<Module:>` and `<Assembly:>` tags, respectively. For example, assume you wish to ensure that every public member of every public type defined within your assembly is CLS compliant.

■ **Note** Chapter 1 mentioned the role of CLS compliant assemblies. Recall that a CLS compliant assembly can be used by all .NET programming languages out-of-the-box. If you create Public members of Public types which expose non-CLS compliant programming constructs (such as unsigned data or pointer parameters), other .NET languages may not be able to use your functionality. Therefore, if you are building VB 2010 code libraries which need to be used by a wide variety of .NET languages, checking for CLS compliance is a must.

To do so, simply add the following assembly level attribute at the very top of any VB 2010 source code file. Be very aware that all assembly or module-level attributes must be listed outside the scope of any namespace scope! If you add assembly (or module) level attributes to your project, here is a recommended file-layout to follow:

```
' List Imports statements first(if any…).
' Now list any assembly/module level attributes.
' Enforce CLS compliance for all  Public types in this assembly.
  <Assembly: CLSCompliant(True)>
   ' Now your namespace (if necessary) and types…
```

If you now add a bit of code that falls outside the CLS specification (such as an exposed point of unsigned data):

```
' UInt64 types don't jibe with the CLS.
Public Class Winnebago
  Public notCompliant As UInt64
End Class
```

you are issued a compiler warning.

The Visual Studio 2010 AssemblyInfo.vb File

By default, Visual Studio 2010 projects receive a file named `AssemblyInfo.vb`, which can be viewed by expanding the MyProject of the Solution Explorer (see Figure 15-6).

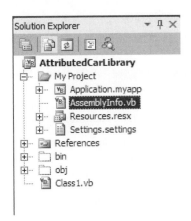

Figure 15-6. The `AssemblyInfo.vb` *file*

This file is a handy place to put attributes that are to be applied at the assembly level. You may recall from Chapter 14, during the examination of .NET assemblies, that the manifest contains assembly-level metadata, much of which comes from the assembly-level attributes shown in Table 15-4.

Table 15-4. *Select Assembly-Level Attributes*

Attribute	Meaning in Life
`<AssemblyCompany()>`	Holds basic company information
`<AssemblyCopyright()>`	Holds any copyright information for the product or assembly
`<AssemblyCulture()>`	Provides information on what cultures or languages the assembly supports
`<AssemblyDescription()>`	Holds a friendly description of the product or modules that make up the assembly
`<AssemblyKeyFile()>`	Specifies the name of the file containing the key pair used to sign the assembly (i.e., establish a strong name)
`<AssemblyProduct()>`	Provides product information
`<AssemblyTrademark()>`	Provides trademark information
`<AssemblyVersion()>`	Specifies the assembly's version information, in the format `<major.minor.build.revision>`

■ **Source Code** The AttributedCarLibrary project is included in the Chapter 15 subdirectory.

Reflecting on Attributes Using Early Binding

Remember that attributes are quite useless until another piece of software reflects over its values. Once a given attribute has been discovered, that piece of software can take whatever course of action necessary. Now, like any application, this "other piece of software" could discover the presence of a custom attribute using either early binding or late binding. If you wish to make use of early binding, you'll require the client application to have a compile-time -definition of the attribute in question (`VehicleDescriptionAttribute` in this case). Given that the `AttributedCarLibrary` assembly has defined this custom attribute as a Public class, early binding is the best option.

To illustrate the process of reflecting on custom attributes, create a new VB 2010 Console Application named VehicleDescriptionAttributeReader. Next, set a reference to the `AttributedCarLibrary` assembly. Finally, update your initial `*.vb` file with the following code:

```vb
Imports AttributedCarLibrary

Module Module1

    Sub Main()
        Console.WriteLine("Value of VehicleDescriptionAttribute" & vbLf)
        ReflectOnAttributesWithEarlyBinding()
        Console.ReadLine()
    End Sub

    Sub ReflectOnAttributesWithEarlyBinding()
        'Get a Type representing the Winnebago.
        Dim t As Type = GetType(Winnebago)

        'Get all attributes on the Winnebago.
        Dim customAtts As Object() = t.GetCustomAttributes(False)

        'Print the description.
        For Each v As VehicleDescriptionAttribute In customAtts
            Console.WriteLine("-> {0}" & vbLf, v.Description)
        Next
    End Sub
End Module
```

The `Type.GetCustomAttributes()` method returns an object array that represents all the attributes applied to the member represented by the `Type` (the Boolean parameter controls whether the search should extend up the inheritance chain). Once you have obtained the list of attributes, iterate over each `VehicleDescriptionAttribute` class and print out the value obtained by the `Description` property.

■ **Source Code** The VehicleDescriptionAttributeReader project is included under the Chapter 15 subdirectory.

Reflecting on Attributes Using Late Binding

The previous example made use of early binding to print out the vehicle description data for the `Winnebago` type. This was possible due to the fact that the `VehicleDescriptionAttribute` class type was defined as a Public member in the `AttributedCarLibrary` assembly. It is also possible to make use of dynamic loading and late binding to reflect over attributes.

Create a new project called VehicleDescriptionAttributeReaderLateBinding and copy `AttributedCarLibrary.dll` to the project's \bin\Debug directory. Now, update your `Module1` Module as follows:

```vb
Imports System.Reflection

Module Module1
   Sub Main()
       Console.WriteLine("*Value of VehicleDescriptionAttribute*" & vbLf)
       ReflectAttributesUsingLateBinding()
       Console.ReadLine()
   End Sub

   Sub ReflectAttributesUsingLateBinding()
      Try
        'Load the local copy of AttributedCarLibrary.
        Dim asm As Assembly = Assembly.Load("AttributedCarLibrary")

        'Get type info of VehicleDescriptionAttribute.
        Dim vehicleDesc As Type =
        asm.GetType("AttributedCarLibrary.VehicleDescriptionAttribute")

        'Get type info of the Description property.
        Dim propDesc As PropertyInfo = vehicleDesc.GetProperty("Description")

        'Get all types in the assembly.
        Dim types As Type() = asm.GetTypes()

        'Iterate over each type and obtain any VehicleDescriptionAttributes.
        For Each t As Type In types
            Dim objs As Object() = t.GetCustomAttributes(vehicleDesc, False)

            'Iterate over each VehicleDescriptionAttribute and print
            'the description using late binding.
            For Each o As Object In objs
                    Console.WriteLine("-> {0}: {1}" & vbLf, t.Name,
                        propDesc.GetValue(o, Nothing))
            Next
        Next

      Catch ex As Exception
            Console.WriteLine(ex.Message)
      End Try
   End Sub
End Module
```

If you were able to follow along with the examples in this chapter, this code should be (more or less) self-explanatory. The only point of interest is the use of the PropertyInfo.GetValue() method, which is used to trigger the property's accessor. Here is the output of the current example:

```
***** Value of VehicleDescriptionAttribute *****


-> Motorcycle: My rocking Harley


-> HorseAndBuggy: The old gray mare, she ain't what she used to be...


-> Winnebago: A very long, slow, but feature rich auto
```

■ **Source Code** The VehicleDescriptionAttributeReaderLateBinding project is included under the Chapter 15 subdirectory.

Putting Reflection, Late Binding, and Custom Attributes in Perspective

Even though you have seen numerous examples of these techniques in action, you may still be wondering when to make use of reflection, dynamic loading, late binding, and custom attributes in your programs? To be sure, these topics can seem a bit on the academic side of programming (which may or may not be a bad thing, depending on your point of view). To help map these topics to a real-world situation, you need a solid example. Assume for the moment that you are on a programming team that is building an application with the following requirement:

- The product must be extendable by the use of additional third-party tools.

What exactly is meant by *extendable*? Well, consider the Visual Studio 2010 IDE. When this application was developed, various "hooks" were inserted into the code base to allow other software vendors to "snap" (or plug-in) custom modules into the IDE. Obviously, the Visual Studio 2010 development team had no way to set references to external .NET assemblies it had not developed yet (thus, no early binding), so how exactly would an application provide the required hooks? Here is one possible way to solve this problem:

- First, an extendable application must provide some input vehicle to allow the user to specify the module to plug in (such as a dialog box or command-line flag). This requires *dynamic loading*.

643

- Second, an extendable application must be able to determine whether the module supports the correct functionality (such as a set of required interfaces) in order to be plugged into the environment. This requires *reflection*.

- Finally, an extendable application must obtain a reference to the required infrastructure (such as a set of interface types) and invoke the members to trigger the underlying functionality. This may require *late binding*.

Simply put, if the extendable application has been preprogrammed to query for specific interfaces, it is able to determine at runtime whether the type can be activated. Once this verification test has been passed, the type in question may support additional interfaces that provide a polymorphic fabric to their functionality. This is the exact approach taken by the Visual Studio 2010 team, and despite what you may be thinking, is not at all difficult!

Building an Extendable Application

In the sections that follow, I will take you through a complete example that illustrates the process of building an extendable Windows Forms application that can be augmented by the functionality of external assemblies. What I will *not* do at this point is comment on the process of building GUI applications with this tried and true desktop API (see Appendix A for an overview of the Windows Forms API).

■ **Note** Windows Forms was the initial desktop API of the .NET platform. However, since the release of .NET 3.0, the Windows Presentation Foundation (WPF) API is quickly becoming preferred GUI framework. While this is true, I will make use of Windows Forms for a number of client UI examples in this text, as the related code is a tad bit more intuitive than the corresponding WPF code.

If you are not familiar with the process of building Windows Forms applications, feel free to simply open up the supplied sample code and follow along. To serve as a road map, our extendable application entails the following assemblies:

- CommonSnappableTypes.dll: This assembly contains type definitions that will be used by each snap-in object and will be directly referenced by the Windows Forms application.

- VbSnapIn.dll: A snap-in written in Visual Basic, which leverages the types of CommonSnappableTypes.dll.

- CSharpSnapIn.dll: A snap-in written in C#, which leverages the types of CommonSnappableTypes.dll.

- MyExtendableApp.exe: This Windows Forms application will be the entity that may be extended by the functionality of each snap-in.

Again, this application will make use of dynamic loading, reflection, and late binding to dynamically gain the functionality of assemblies it has no prior knowledge of.

Building CommonSnappableTypes.dll

The first order of business is to create an assembly that contains the types that a given snap-in must leverage to be plugged into the expandable Windows Forms application. The CommonSnappableTypes Class Library project defines two types:

```
Public Interface IAppFunctionality
    Sub DoIt()
End Interface

<AttributeUsage(AttributeTargets.Class)> _
Public NotInheritable Class CompanyInfoAttribute
    Inherits System.Attribute

    Public Property CompanyName() As String
    Public Property CompanyUrl() As String
End Class
```

The `IAppFunctionality` interface provides a polymorphic interface for all snap-ins that can be consumed by the extendable Windows Forms application. Given that this example is purely illustrative, you supply a single method named `DoIt()`. A more realistic interface (or a set of interfaces) might allow the object to generate scripting code, render an image onto the application's toolbox, or integrate into the main menu of the hosting application.

The `CompanyInfoAttribute` type is a custom attribute that can be applied on any class type that wishes to be snapped into the container. As you can tell by the definition of this class, `<CompanyInfo()>` allows the developer of the snap-in to provide some basic details about the component's point of origin.

Building the VB 2010 Snap-In

Next, you need to create a type that implements the `IAppFunctionality` interface. Again, to focus on the overall design of an extendable application, a trivial type is in order. Assume a new VB 2010 Class Library project named `VbSnapIn`. Given that this class must make use of the types defined in CommonSnappableTypes, be sure to set a reference to the CommonSnappableTypes assembly (as well as `System.Windows.Forms.dll` to display a noteworthy message). This being said, here is the code:

■ **Note** By default, a Visual Basic project will not display the References folder within the Solution Explorer. To add references in a VB project, use the Project ➤ Add Reference… menu option of Visual Studio 2010.

```
Imports CommonSnappableTypes
Imports System.Windows.Forms

<CompanyInfo(CompanyName:="Chucky's Software", CompanyUrl:="www.ChuckySoft.com")>
Public Class VbSnapIn
  Implements IAppFunctionality
```

```
Public Sub DoIt() Implements CommonSnappableTypes.IAppFunctionality.DoIt
    MessageBox.Show("You have just used the VB snap in!")
  End Sub
End Class
```

Building the C# Snap-In

Now, to simulate the role of a third-party vendor who prefers C# over Visual Basic, create a C# Class Library project named CSharpSnapIn. In this project, add a reference to the same external assemblies as in the previous VbSnapIn project, and define a class type named CSharpModule .

The code is (again) intentionally simple:

```csharp
using System;
using System.Collections.Generic;
using System.Linq;
using System.Text;

using CommonSnappableTypes;
using System.Windows.Forms;

namespace CSharpSnapIn
{
  [CompanyInfo(CompanyName = "My Company",
      CompanyUrl = "www.MyCompany.com")]
  public class CSharpModule : IAppFunctionality
  {
    void IAppFunctionality.DoIt()
    {
      MessageBox.Show("You have just used the C# snap in!");
    }
  }
}
```

Notice that I choose to make use of explicit interface implementation (see Chapter 9) when supporting the IAppFunctionality interface. This is not required; however, the idea is that the only part of the system that needs to directly interact with this interface type is the hosting Windows application. By explicitly implementing this interface, the DoIt() method is not directly exposed from the CSharpModule type.

Building an Extendable Windows Forms Application

The final step is to create a new VB 2010 Windows Forms application (MyExtendableApp) that allows the user to select a snap-in using a standard Windows Open dialog box. If you have not created a Windows Forms application before, begin this final project of the chapter by selecting a Windows Forms Application project from the New Project dialog box of Visual Studio 2010 (Figure 15-7).

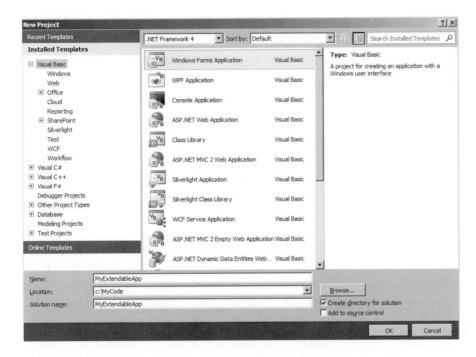

Figure 15-7. Creating a new Windows Forms project with Visual Studio 2010

Now, set a reference to the CommonSnappableTypes.dll assembly, but not the VbSnapIn.dll or CSharpSnapIn.dll code libraries. As well, import the System.Reflection and CommonSnappableTypes namespaces into your form's primary code file (which you can open by right clicking on the form designer and selecting View Code. Remember that the whole goal of this application is to make use of late binding and reflection to determine the "snappability" of independent binaries created by third-party vendors.

Again, I won't bother to examine all the details of Windows Forms development at this point in the text (see Appendix A). However, assuming you have placed a MenuStrip component onto the forms designer, define a topmost menu item named File that provides a single submenu named Snap In Module. As well, the main window will contain a ListBox type (which I renamed as lstLoadedSnapIns) that will be used to display the names of each snap-in loaded by the user. Figure 15-8 shows the final GUI.

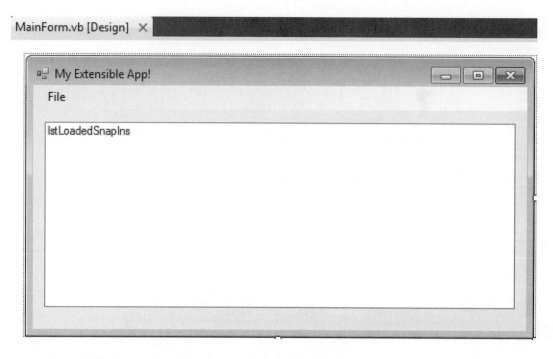

Figure 15-8. *GUI for MyExtendableApp*

The code that handles the **Click** event for the File ➤ Snap In Module menu item (which may be created simply by double-clicking the menu item from the design-time editor) displays a File Open dialog box and extracts the path to the selected file. Assuming the user did not select the **CommonSnappableTypes.dll** assembly (as this is purely infrastructure), the path is then sent into a helper method named **LoadExternalModule()** for processing (implemented next). This method will return **False** when it is unable to find a class implementing **IAppFunctionality**:

```
Private Sub SnapInModuleToolStripMenuItem_Click(ByVal sender As Object, ByVal e As
EventArgs) Handles SnapInModuleToolStripMenuItem.Click

        'Allow user to select an assembly to load.
        Dim dlg As New OpenFileDialog()

        If dlg.ShowDialog() = DialogResult.OK Then
            If dlg.FileName.Contains("CommonSnappableTypes") Then
                MessageBox.Show("CommonSnappableTypes has no snap-ins!")
            ElseIf Not LoadExternalModule(dlg.FileName) Then
                MessageBox.Show("Nothing implements IAppFunctionality!")
            End If
        End If
End Sub
```

The LoadExternalModule() method performs the following tasks:

- Dynamically loads the selected assembly into memory

- Determines whether the assembly contains any types implementing
  IAppFunctionality

- Creates the type using late binding

If a type implementing IAppFunctionality is found, the DoIt() method is called, and the fully
qualified name of the type is added to the ListBox (note that the For Each loop will iterate over all types
in the assembly to account for the possibility that a single assembly has multiple snap-ins).

```
Function LoadExternalModule(ByVal path As String) As Boolean

        Dim foundSnapIn As Boolean = False
        Dim theSnapInAsm As Assembly = Nothing

        Try
            'Dynamically load the selected assembly.
            theSnapInAsm = Assembly.LoadFrom(path)
        Catch ex As Exception
            MessageBox.Show(ex.Message)
            Return foundSnapIn
        End Try

        'Get all IAppFunctionality compatible classes in assembly.
        Dim theClassTypes = From t In theSnapInAsm.GetTypes() _
                            Where t.IsClass AndAlso
                            (t.GetInterface("IAppFunctionality") IsNot Nothing) _
                            Select t

        'Now, create the object and call DoIt() method.
        For Each t As Type In theClassTypes
            foundSnapIn = True

            'Use late binding to create the type.
            Dim itfApp As IAppFunctionality = DirectCast(
                theSnapInAsm.CreateInstance
                (        t.FullName, True),IAppFunctionality)

            itfApp.DoIt()
            lstLoadedSnapIns.Items.Add(t.FullName)
        Next
    Return foundSnapIn
End Function
```

At this point, you can run your application. When you select the VbSnapIn.dll or CSharpSnapIn.dll
assemblies, you should see the correct message displayed. The final task is to display the metadata
provided by the <CompanyInfo()> attribute. To do so, update LoadExternalModule() to call a new helper
method named DisplayCompanyData() before exiting the For Each scope. Notice this method takes a
single System.Type parameter.

```
Function LoadExternalModule(ByVal path As String) As Boolean
        ...
        For Each t As Type In theClassTypes
            ...
            'Show company info.
            DisplayCompanyData(t)
        Next
        Return foundSnapIn
End Function
```

Using the incoming type, simply reflect over the `<CompanyInfo()>` attribute:

```
Sub DisplayCompanyData(ByVal t As Type)
    'Get <CompanyInfo> data.
    Dim compInfo = From ci In t.GetCustomAttributes(False) _
        Where (ci.GetType() = GetType(CompanyInfoAttribute)) _
        Select ci

    'Show data.
    For Each c As CompanyInfoAttribute In compInfo
            MessageBox.Show(c.CompanyUrl, String.Format("More
            info about {0} can be found at", c.CompanyName))
    Next
End Sub
```

Figure 15-9 shows one possible run.

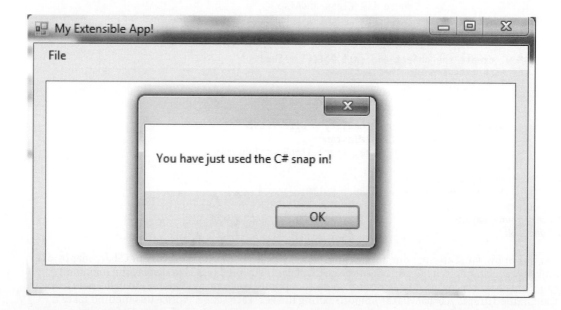

Figure 15-9. Snapping in external assemblies

793_

Excellent! That wraps up the example application. I hope you can see that the topics presented in this chapter can be quite helpful in the real world and are not limited to the tool builders of the world.

■ **Source Code** The ExtendableApp folder under the Chapter 15 subdirectory contains the CommonSnappableTypes, VbSnapIn, CSharpSnapIn, and MyExtendableApp projects.

Summary

Reflection is a very interesting aspect of a robust OO environment. In the world of .NET, the keys to reflection services revolve around the `System.Type` class and the `System.Reflection` namespace. As you have seen, reflection is the process of placing a type under the magnifying glass at runtime to understand the who, what, where, when, why, and how of a given item.

Late binding is the process of creating a type and invoking its members without prior knowledge of the specific names of said members. Late binding is often a direct result of *dynamic loading*, which allows you to load a .NET assembly into memory programmatically. As shown during this chapter's extendable application example, this is a very powerful technique used by tool builders as well as tool consumers. This chapter also examined the role of attribute-based programming. When you adorn your types with attributes, the result is the augmentation of the underlying assembly metadata.

CHAPTER 16

■ ■ ■

Processes, AppDomains, and Object Contexts

In the previous two chapters, you examined the steps taken by the CLR to resolve the location of a referenced external assembly as well as the role of .NET metadata. In this chapter, you'll drill deeper into the details of how an assembly is hosted by the CLR and come to understand the relationship between processes, application domains, and object contexts.

In a nutshell, *application domains* (or simply *AppDomains*) are logical subdivisions within a given process that host a set of related .NET assemblies. As you will see, an AppDomain is further subdivided into *contextual boundaries*, which are used to group together like-minded .NET objects. Using the notion of context, the CLR is able to ensure that objects with special runtime requirements are handled appropriately.

While it is true that many of your day-to-day programming tasks may not involve directly working with processes, app domains, or object contexts, understanding these topics is very important when working with numerous .NET APIs including Windows Communication Foundation (WCF), multithreading and parallel processing and object serialization.

The Role of a Windows Process

The concept of a "process" has existed within Windows-based operating systems well before the release of the .NET platform. In simple terms, a process is a running program. However, formally speaking, a process is an operating system level concept used to describe a set of resources (such as external code libraries and the primary thread) and the necessary memory allocations used by a running application. For each *.exe loaded into memory, the OS creates a separate and isolated process for use during its lifetime.

Using this approach to application isolation, the result is a much more robust and stable runtime environment, given that the failure of one process does not affect the functioning of another. Furthermore, data in one process cannot be directly accessed by another process, unless you make use of a distributed computing programming API such as Windows Communication Foundation. Given these points, you can regard the process as a fixed, safe boundary for a running application.

Now, every Windows process is assigned a unique process identifier (PID) and may be independently loaded and unloaded by the OS as necessary (as well as programmatically). As you may be aware, the Processes tab of the Windows Task Manager utility (activated via the Ctrl+Shift+Esc keystroke combination) allows you to view various statistics regarding the processes running on a given machine, including its PID and image name (see Figure 16-1).

■ **Note** By default, the PID column of the Process tab will not be shown. To enable this feature, activate the View | Select Columns… menu option, and then check the PID (Process Identifier) checkbox.

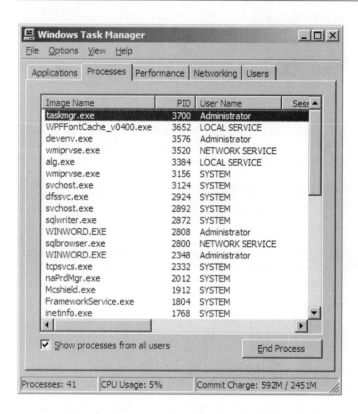

Figure 16-1. The Windows Task Manager

The Role of Threads

Every Windows process contains an initial "thread" that functions as the entry point for the application. Chapter 19 examines the details of building multithreaded applications under the .NET platform; however, to facilitate the topics presented here, you need a few working definitions. First of all, a *thread* is a path of execution within a process. Formally speaking, the first thread created by a process's entry point is termed the *primary thread*. Any .NET executable program (Console Application, Windows Forms application, WPF application, etc.) marks its entry point with the Main() method. When this method is invoked, the primary thread is created automatically.

Processes that contain a single primary thread of execution are intrinsically *thread safe*, given the fact that there is only one thread that can access the data in the application at a given time. However, a single-threaded process (especially one that is GUI-based) will often appear a bit unresponsive to the user if this single thread is performing a complex operation (such as printing out a lengthy text file, performing a mathematically intensive calculation, or attempting to connect to a remote server located thousands of miles away).

Given this potential drawback of single-threaded applications, the Windows API (as well as the .NET platform) makes it possible for the primary thread to spawn additional secondary threads (also termed *worker threads*) using a handful of Windows API functions such as `CreateThread()`. Each thread (primary or secondary) becomes a unique path of execution in the process and has concurrent access to all shared points of data within the process.

As you may have guessed, developers typically create additional threads to help improve the program's overall responsiveness. Multithreaded processes provide the illusion that numerous activities are happening at more or less the same time. For example, an application may spawn a worker thread to perform a labor-intensive unit of work (again, such as printing a large text file). As this secondary thread is churning away, the main thread is still responsive to user input, which gives the entire process the potential of delivering greater performance. However, this may not actually be the case: using too many threads in a single process can actually *degrade* performance, as the CPU must switch between the active threads in the process (which takes time).

On some machines, multithreading is most commonly an illusion provided by the OS. Machines that host a single (non-hyperthreaded) CPU do not have the ability to literally handle multiple threads at the same exact time. Rather, a single CPU will execute one thread for a unit of time (called a *time slice*) based in part on the thread's priority level. When a thread's time slice is up, the existing thread is suspended to allow another thread to perform its business. For a thread to remember what was happening before it was kicked out of the way, each thread is given the ability to write to Thread Local Storage (TLS) and is provided with a separate call stack, as illustrated in Figure 16-2.

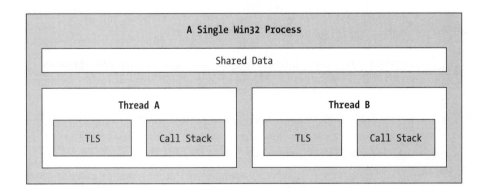

Figure 16-2. The Windows process/thread relationship

If the subject of threads is new to you, don't sweat the details. At this point, just remember that a thread is a unique path of execution within a Windows process. Every process has a primary thread (created via the executable's entry point) and may contain additional threads that have been programmatically created.

Interacting with Processes Under the .NET Platform

Although processes and threads are nothing new, the manner in which you interact with these - primitives under the .NET platform has changed quite a bit (for the better). To pave the way to understanding the world of building multithreaded assemblies (see Chapter 19), let's begin by checking out how to interact with processes using the .NET base class libraries.

The System.Diagnostics namespace defines a number of types that allow you to programmatically interact with processes and various diagnostic-related types such as the system event log and performance counters. In this chapter, you are only concerned with the process-centric types defined in Table 16-1.

Table 16-1. Select Members of the System.Diagnostics Namespace

Process-Centric Types of the System.Diagnostics Namespace	Meaning in Life
Process	The Process class provides access to local and remote processes and also allows you to programmatically start and stop processes.
ProcessModule	This type represents a module (*.dll or *.exe) that is loaded into a particular process. Understand that the ProcessModule type can represent *any* module—COM-based, .NET-based, or traditional C-based binaries.
ProcessModuleCollection	Provides a strongly typed collection of ProcessModule objects.
ProcessStartInfo	Specifies a set of values used when starting a process via the Process.Start() method.
ProcessThread	Represents a thread within a given process. Be aware that ProcessThread is a type used to diagnose a process's thread set and is not used to spawn new threads of execution within a process.
ProcessThreadCollection	Provides a strongly typed collection of ProcessThread objects.

The System.Diagnostics.Process class allows you to analyze the processes running on a given machine (local or remote). The Process class also provides members that allow you to programmatically start and terminate processes, view (or modify) a process's priority level, and obtain a list of active threads and/or loaded modules within a given process. Table 16-2 lists some of the key properties of System.Diagnostics.Process.

Table 16-2. Select Properties of the `Process` *Type*

Property	Meaning in Life
ExitTime	This property gets the timestamp associated with the process that has terminated (represented with a `DateTime` type).
Handle	This property returns the handle (represented by an `IntPtr`) associated to the process by the OS. This can be useful when working building .NET applications which need to communicate with unmanaged code.
Id	This property gets the PID for the associated process.
MachineName	This property gets the name of the computer the associated process is running on.
MainWindowTitle	`MainWindowTitle` gets the caption of the main window of the process (if the process does not have a main window, you receive an empty `string`).
Modules	This property provides access to the strongly typed `ProcessModuleCollection` type, which represents the set of modules (`*.dll` or `*.exe`) loaded within the current process.
ProcessName	This property gets the name of the process (which, as you would assume, is the name of the application itself).
Responding	This property gets a value indicating whether the user interface of the process is responding to user input (or is currently "hung").
StartTime	This property gets the time that the associated process was started (via a `DateTime` type).
Threads	This property gets the set of threads that are running in the associated process (represented via a collection of `ProcessThread` objects).

In addition to the properties just examined, `System.Diagnostics.Process` also defines a few useful methods (Table 16-3).

Table 16-3. Select Methods of the Process Type

Method	Meaning in Life
CloseMainWindow()	This method closes a process that has a user interface by sending a close message to its main window.
GetCurrentProcess()	This Shared method returns a new Process object that represents the currently active process.
GetProcesses()	This Shared method returns an array of new Process objects running on a given machine.
Kill()	This method immediately stops the associated process.
Start()	This method starts a process.

Enumerating Running Processes

To illustrate the process of manipulating **Process** objects (pardon the redundancy), assume you have a VB 2010 Console Application named ProcessManipulator that defines the following Shared helper method within the **Module1** Module (note that the **Process** class is defined in the **System.Diagnostics** namespace, which is one of the default namespaces imported in VB 2010 projects):

```
Sub ListAllRunningProcesses()
        ' Get all the processes on the local machine, ordered by PID.
        Dim runningProcs = From proc In Process.GetProcesses(".") _
                           Order By proc.Id _
                           Select proc

        'Print out PID and name of each process.
        For Each p In runningProcs
                Dim info As String = String.Format("-> PID: {0}" & vbTab & _
                "Name: {1}", p.Id, p.ProcessName)
                Console.WriteLine(info)
        Next
        Console.WriteLine("***********************************" & vbLf)
End Sub
```

The Shared **Process.GetProcesses()** method returns an array of **Process** objects that represent the running processes on the target machine (the dot notation shown here represents the local computer). Once you have obtained the array of **Process** objects, you are able to invoke any of the members seen in Table 16-2 and Table 16-3. Here, you are simply displaying the PID and the name of each process, ordered by PID. Assuming the **Main()** method has been updated to call **ListAllRunningProcesses()**:

```
Sub Main()
    Console.WriteLine("***** Fun with Processes *****" & vbLf)
    ListAllRunningProcesses()
End Sub
```

you will see the names and PIDs for all processes on your local computer. Here is some partial output from my current machine.

```
***** Fun with Processes *****


-> PID: 0       Name: Idle

-> PID: 4       Name: System

-> PID: 108     Name: iexplore

-> PID: 268     Name: smss

-> PID: 432     Name: csrss

-> PID: 448     Name: svchost

-> PID: 472     Name: wininit

-> PID: 504     Name: csrss

-> PID: 536     Name: winlogon

-> PID: 560     Name: services

-> PID: 584     Name: lsass

-> PID: 592     Name: lsm

-> PID: 660     Name: devenv

-> PID: 684     Name: svchost

-> PID: 760     Name: svchost

-> PID: 832     Name: svchost

-> PID: 844     Name: svchost

-> PID: 856     Name: svchost
```

```
-> PID: 900      Name: svchost

-> PID: 924      Name: svchost

-> PID: 956      Name: VMwareService

-> PID: 1116     Name: spoolsv

-> PID: 1136     Name: ProcessManipulator.vshost

***********************************
```

Investigating a Specific Process

In addition to obtaining a full and complete list of all running processes on a given machine, the Shared Process.GetProcessById() method allows you to obtain a single Process object via the associated PID. If you request access to a nonexistent PID, an ArgumentException exception is thrown. For example, if you were interested in obtaining a Process object representing a process with the PID of 987, you could write the following code:

```
' If there is no process with the PID of 987, a
' runtime exception will be thrown.
Sub GetSpecificProcess()
        Dim theProc As Process = Nothing
        Try
            theProc = Process.GetProcessById(987)
        Catch ex As ArgumentException
            Console.WriteLine(ex.Message)
        End Try
End Sub
```

At this point, you have learned how to get a list of all processes, or a specific process on a machine via a PID lookup. While it is somewhat useful to discover PIDs and process names, the Process class also allows you to discover the set of current threads and libraries used within a given process. Let's see how to do so.

Investigating a Process's Thread Set

The set of threads is represented by the strongly typed ProcessThreadCollection collection, which contains some number of individual ProcessThread objects. To illustrate, assume the following additional Shared helper method has been added to your current application:

```vbnet
Sub EnumThreadsForPid(ByVal pID As Integer)
        Dim theProc As Process = Nothing
        Try
            theProc = Process.GetProcessById(pID)
        Catch ex As ArgumentException
            Console.WriteLine(ex.Message)
            Return
        End Try

        'List out stats for each thread in the specified process.
        Console.WriteLine("Here are the threads used by: {0}",theProc.ProcessName)

        Dim theThreads As ProcessThreadCollection = theProc.Threads
        For Each pt As ProcessThread In theThreads

                Dim info As String = String.Format("-> Thread ID: {0}" & vbTab &_
                "StartTime:{1}" & vbTab & "Priority: {2}", pt.Id,pt.StartTime_
                ToShortTimeString(),pt.PriorityLevel)

                Console.WriteLine(info)
        Next
        Console.WriteLine("***********************************" & vbLf)
End Sub
```

As you can see, the `Threads` property of the `System.Diagnostics.Process` type provides access to the `ProcessThreadCollection` class. Here, you are printing out the assigned thread ID, start time, and priority level of each thread in the process specified by the client. Now, update your Module1's `Main()` method to prompt the user for a PID to investigate, as follows:

```vbnet
Sub Main()
        ...
  Console.WriteLine("*** Enter PID of process to investigate ***")
        Console.Write("PID: ")
        Dim pID As String = Console.ReadLine()
        Dim theProcID As Integer = Integer.Parse(pID)
        EnumThreadsForPid(theProcID)
        Console.ReadLine()
End Sub
```

When you run your program, you can now enter the PID of any process on your machine, and see the threads used in the process. The following output shows the threads used by PID 108 on my machine, which happens to be hosting Microsoft Internet Explorer:

```
***** Enter PID of process to investigate *****

PID: 108

Here are the threads used by: iexplore

-> Thread ID: 680       Start Time: 9:05 AM       Priority: Normal

-> Thread ID: 2040      Start Time: 9:05 AM       Priority: Normal

-> Thread ID: 880       Start Time: 9:05 AM       Priority: Normal

-> Thread ID: 3380      Start Time: 9:05 AM       Priority: Normal

-> Thread ID: 3376      Start Time: 9:05 AM       Priority: Normal

-> Thread ID: 3448      Start Time: 9:05 AM       Priority: Normal

-> Thread ID: 3476      Start Time: 9:05 AM       Priority: Normal

-> Thread ID: 2264      Start Time: 9:05 AM       Priority: Normal

-> Thread ID: 2380      Start Time: 9:05 AM       Priority: Normal

-> Thread ID: 2384      Start Time: 9:05 AM       Priority: Normal

-> Thread ID: 2308      Start Time: 9:05 AM       Priority: Normal

-> Thread ID: 3096      Start Time: 9:07 AM       Priority: Highest

-> Thread ID: 3600      Start Time: 9:45 AM       Priority: Normal

-> Thread ID: 1412      Start Time: 10:02 AM      Priority: Normal
```

The `ProcessThread` type has additional members of interest beyond `Id`, `StartTime`, and `PriorityLevel`. Table 16-4 documents some members of interest.

Table 16-4. Select Members of the `ProcessThread` Type

Member	Meaning in Life
CurrentPriority	Gets the current priority of the thread
Id	Gets the unique identifier of the thread
IdealProcessor	Sets the preferred processor for this thread to run on
PriorityLevel	Gets or sets the priority level of the thread
ProcessorAffinity	Sets the processors on which the associated thread can run
StartAddress	Gets the memory address of the function that the operating system called that started this thread
StartTime	Gets the time that the operating system started the thread
ThreadState	Gets the current state of this thread
TotalProcessorTime	Gets the total amount of time that this thread has spent using the processor
WaitReason	Gets the reason that the thread is waiting

Before you read any further, be very aware that the `ProcessThread` type is *not* the entity used to create, suspend, or kill threads under the .NET platform. Rather, `ProcessThread` is a vehicle used to obtain diagnostic information for the active Windows threads within a running process. Again, you will investigate how to build multithreaded applications using the `System.Threading` namespace in Chapter 19.

Investigating a Process's Module Set

Next up, let's check out how to iterate over the number of loaded modules that are hosted within a given process. When talking about processes, a *module* is a general term used to describe a given `*.dll` (or the `*.exe` itself) that is hosted by a specific process. When you access the `ProcessModuleCollection` via the `Process.Modules` property, you are able to enumerate over *all modules* hosted within a process: .NET-based, COM-based, or traditional C-based libraries. Ponder the following additional helper method that will enumerate the modules in a specific process based on the PID:

```
Sub EnumModsForPid(ByVal pID As Integer)
      Dim theProc As Process = Nothing
      Try
          theProc = Process.GetProcessById(pID)
      Catch ex As ArgumentException
          Console.WriteLine(ex.Message)
          Return
      End Try

      Console.WriteLine("Here are the loaded modules for: {0}",
          theProc.ProcessName)

      Dim theMods As ProcessModuleCollection = theProc.Modules
      For Each pm As ProcessModule In theMods
              Dim info As String = String.Format("-> Mod Name: {0}",
                pm.ModuleName)
              Console.WriteLine(info)
      Next
      Console.WriteLine("**********************************" & vbLf)
End Sub
```

To see some possible output, let's check out the loaded modules for the process hosting the current example program (ProcessManipulator). To do so, run the application, identify the PID assigned to ProcessManipulator.exe (via the Task Manager) and pass this value to the EnumModsForPid() method (be sure to update your Main() method accordingly). Once you do, you may be surprised to see the list of *.dlls used for a simple Console Application (GDI32.dll, USER32.dll, ole32.dll, and so forth). Consider the following output:

```
Here are the loaded modules for: ProcessManipulator

-> Mod Name: ProcessManipulator.exe

-> Mod Name: ntdll.dll

-> Mod Name: MSCOREE.DLL

-> Mod Name: KERNEL32.dll

-> Mod Name: KERNELBASE.dll

-> Mod Name: ADVAPI32.dll

-> Mod Name: msvcrt.dll

-> Mod Name: sechost.dll

-> Mod Name: RPCRT4.dll

-> Mod Name: SspiCli.dll
```

```
-> Mod Name: CRYPTBASE.dll

-> Mod Name: mscoreei.dll

-> Mod Name: SHLWAPI.dll

-> Mod Name: GDI32.dll

-> Mod Name: USER32.dll

-> Mod Name: LPK.dll

-> Mod Name: USP10.dll

-> Mod Name: IMM32.DLL

-> Mod Name: MSCTF.dll

-> Mod Name: clr.dll

-> Mod Name: MSVCR100_CLR0400.dll

-> Mod Name: mscorlib.ni.dll

-> Mod Name: nlssorting.dll

-> Mod Name: ole32.dll

-> Mod Name: clrjit.dll

-> Mod Name: System.ni.dll

-> Mod Name: System.Core.ni.dll

-> Mod Name: psapi.dll

-> Mod Name: shfolder.dll

-> Mod Name: SHELL32.dll

***********************************
```

Starting and Stopping Processes Programmatically

The final aspects of the `System.Diagnostics.Process` class examined here are the `Start()` and `Kill()` methods. As you can gather by their names, these members provide a way to programmatically launch and terminate a process, respectively. For example, consider the `StartAndKillProcess()` helper method:

■ **Note** You must be running Visual Studio 2010 with Administrator rights in order to start new processes. If this is not the case, you will receive a runtime error.

```
Sub StartAndKillProcess()
        Dim ieProc As Process = Nothing
        Try
            'Launch Internet Explorer, and go to facebook!
            ieProc = Process.Start("IExplore.exe", "www.facebook.com")

        Catch ex As InvalidOperationException
            Console.WriteLine(ex.Message)
        End Try

        Console.Write("--> Hit enter to kill {0}...", ieProc.ProcessName)
        Console.ReadLine()

        'Kill the iexplore.exe process.
        Try
            ieProc.Kill()
        Catch ex As InvalidOperationException
            Console.WriteLine(ex.Message)
        End Try
End Sub
```

The Shared `Process.Start()` method has been overloaded a few times. At minimum, you will need to specify the friendly name of the process you wish to launch (such as Microsoft Internet Explorer, `iexplore.exe`). This example makes use of a variation of the `Start()` method that allows you to specify any additional arguments to pass into the program's entry point (i.e., the `Main()` method).

Once you call the `Start()` method, you are returned a reference to the newly activated process. When you wish to terminate the process, simply call the instance-level `Kill()` method. Here, you are wrapping the calls to `Start()` and `Kill()` within a Try /Catch block, and handling any `InvalidOperationException` errors. This is especially important when calling the `Kill()` method, as this error will be raised if the process has already been terminated prior to calling `Kill()`.

Controlling Process Startup Using the ProcessStartInfo Class

The `Start()` method also allows you to pass in a `System.Diagnostics.ProcessStartInfo` type to specify additional bits of information regarding how a given process should come to life. Here is a partial definition of `ProcessStartInfo` (see the .NET Framework 4.0 SDK documentation for full details):

```
Public NotInheritable Class ProcessStartInfo
    Inherits Object

    Public Sub New()
    Public Sub New(ByVal fileName As String)
    Public Sub New(ByVal fileName As String, ByVal arguments As String)

    Public Property Arguments() As String
    Public Property CreateNoWindow() As Boolean
    Public ReadOnly Property EnvironmentVariables() As StringDictionary
    Public Property ErrorDialog() As Boolean
    Public Property ErrorDialogParentHandle() As IntPtr
    Public Property FileName() As String
    Public Property LoadUserProfile() As Boolean
    Public Property Password() As SecureString
    Public Property RedirectStandardError() As Boolean
    Public Property RedirectStandardInput() As Boolean
    Public Property RedirectStandardOutput() As Boolean
    Public Property StandardErrorEncoding() As Encoding
    Public Property StandardOutputEncoding() As Encoding
    Public Property UseShellExecute() As Boolean
    Public Property Verb() As String
    Public ReadOnly Property Verbs() As String()
    Public Property WindowStyle() As ProcessWindowStyle
    Public Property WorkingDirectory() As String
End Class
```

To illustrate how to fine-tune your process startup, here is a modified version of
StartAndKillProcess(), which will load Microsoft Internet Explorer, navigate to www.facebook.com, and
show the window in a maximized state:

```
Sub StartAndKillProcess()
        Dim ieProc As Process = Nothing

        ' Launch Internet Explorer, and go to facebook,
        'with maximized window.
        Try
Dim startInfo As New
        ProcessStartInfo("IExplore.exe","www.facebook.com")

            startInfo.WindowStyle = ProcessWindowStyle.Maximized
            ieProc = Process.Start(startInfo)
        Catch ex As InvalidOperationException
            Console.WriteLine(ex.Message)
        End Try
                ...
End Sub
```

Great! Now that you understand the role of Windows processes and how to interact with them from
VB 2010 code, you are ready to investigate the concept of a .NET application domain.

■ **Source Code** The ProcessManipulator project is included under the Chapter 16 subdirectory.

Understanding .NET Application Domains

Under the .NET platform, executables are not hosted directly within a Windows process, as is the case in traditional unmanaged applications. Rather, a .NET executable is hosted by a logical partition within a process termed an *application domain*. As you will see, a single process may contain multiple application domains, each of which is hosting a .NET executable. This additional subdivision of a traditional Windows process offers several benefits, some of which are as follows:

- AppDomains are a key aspect of the OS-neutral nature of the .NET platform, given that this logical division abstracts away the differences in how an underlying OS represents a loaded executable.

- AppDomains are far less expensive in terms of processing power and memory than a full-blown process. Thus, the CLR is able to load and unload application domains much quicker than a formal process, and can drastically improve scalability of server applications.

- AppDomains provide a deeper level of isolation for hosting a loaded application. If one AppDomain within a process fails, the remaining AppDomains remain functional.

As mentioned, a single process can host any number of AppDomains, each of which is fully and completely isolated from other AppDomains within this process (or any other process). Given this fact, be very aware that an application running in one AppDomain is unable to obtain data of any kind (global variables or Shared fields) within another AppDomain unless they make use of a distributed programming protocol (such as Windows Communication Foundation).

While a single process *may* host multiple AppDomains, this is not typically the case. At the very least, an OS process will host what is termed the *default application domain*. This specific application domain is automatically created by the CLR at the time the process launches. After this point, the CLR creates additional application domains on an as-needed basis.

The System.AppDomain Class

The .NET platform allows you to programmatically monitor app domains, create new app domains (or unload them) at runtime, load assemblies into app domains, and a whole slew of additional tasks, using the `AppDomain` class in the `System` namespace of `mscorlib.dll`. Table 16-5 documents some useful methods of the `AppDomain` class (consult the .NET Framework 4.0 SDK documentation for full details).

Table 16-5. Select Methods of AppDomain

Method	Meaning in Life
CreateDomain()	This Shared method allows you to create a new AppDomain in the current process.
CreateInstance()	Creates an instance of a type in an external assembly, after loading said assembly into the calling application domain.
ExecuteAssembly()	This method executes an *.exe assembly within an application domain, given its file name.
GetAssemblies()	This method gets the set of .NET assemblies that have been loaded into this application domain (COM-based or C-based binaries are ignored).
GetCurrentThreadId()	This Shared method returns the ID of the active thread in the current application domain.
Load()	This method is used to dynamically load an assembly into the current application domain.
Unload()	This is another Shared method that allows you to unload a specified AppDomain within a given process.

▪ **Note** The .NET platform does not allow you to unload a specific assembly from memory. The only way to programmatically unload libraries is to tear down the hosting application domain via the Unload() method.

In addition, the AppDomain class also defines a set of properties which can be useful when you wish to monitor activity of a given application domain. Table 16-6 documents some core properties of interest.

Table 16-6. Select Properties of AppDomain

Property	Meaning in Life
BaseDirectory	Gets the directory path that the assembly resolver uses to probe for assemblies.
CurrentDomain	This Shared property gets the application domain for the currently executing thread.
FriendlyName	Gets the friendly name of the current application domain.
MonitoringIsEnabled	Gets or sets a value that indicates whether CPU and memory monitoring of application domains is enabled for the current process. Once monitoring is enabled for a process, it cannot be disabled.
SetupInformation	Gets the configuration details for a given application domain, represented by an AppDomainSetup object.

Last but not least, the AppDomain class supports a set of events that correspond to various aspects of an application domain's life cycle. Table 16-7 shows some of the more useful events you can hook into.

Table 16-7. Select Events of the AppDomain Type

Event	Meaning in Life
AssemblyLoad	Occurs when an assembly is loaded into memory.
AssemblyResolve	This event will fire when the assembly resolver cannot find the location of a required assembly.
DomainUnload	Occurs when an AppDomain is about to be unloaded from the hosting process.
FirstChanceException	This event allows you to be notified that an exception has been thrown from the application domain, before the CLR will begin looking for a fitting catch statement.
ProcessExit	Occurs on the default application domain when the default application domain's parent process exits.
UnhandledException	Occurs when an exception is not caught by an exception handler.

Interacting with the Default Application Domain

Recall that when a .NET executable starts, the CLR will automatically place it into the default app domain o f the hosting process. This is done automatically and transparently, and you never have to author any specific code to do so. However, it is possible for your application to gain access to this default application domain using the Shared `AppDomain.CurrentDomain` property. Once you have this access point, you are able to hook into any events of interest, or make use of the methods and properties of `AppDomain` to perform some runtime diagnostics.

To learn how to interact with the default application domain, begin by creating a new Console Application named `DefaultAppDomainApp`. Now, update your `Module1 Module` with the following logic, which will simply display some details about the default application domain, using a number of members of the `AppDomain` class:

```
Module Module1

    Sub Main()
        Console.WriteLine("Fun with the default app domain" & vbLf)
        DisplayDADStats()
        Console.ReadLine()
    End Sub

    Sub DisplayDADStats()
      'Get access to the app domain for the current thread.
      Dim defaultAD As AppDomain = AppDomain.CurrentDomain

      'Print out various stats about this domain.
      Console.WriteLine("Name of this domain: {0}", defaultAD.FriendlyName)

      Console.WriteLine("ID of domain in this process: {0}", defaultAD.Id)
      Console.WriteLine("Is this the default domain?: {0}", defaultAD.IsDefaultAppDomain())

      Console.WriteLine("Base directory of this domain: {0}", defaultAD.BaseDirectory)
    End Sub
End Module
```

The output of this example can be seen here:

```
***** Fun with the default app domain *****


Name of this domain: DefaultAppDomainApp.exe

ID of domain in this process: 1

Is this the default domain?: True

Base directory of this domain: E:\MyCode\DefaultAppDomainApp\bin\Debug\
```

Notice that the name of the default application domain will be identical to the name of the executable which is contained within it (**DefaultAppDomainApp.exe** in this example). Also notice, that the base directory value, which will be used to probe for externally required private assemblies, maps to the current location of the deployed executable.

Enumerating Loaded Assemblies

It is also possible to discover all of the loaded .NET assemblies within a given application domain using the instance level **GetAssemblies()** method. This method will return to you an array of **Assembly** objects, which as you recall from the previous chapter, is a member of the **System.Reflection** namespace (so don't forget to import this namespace into your VB 2010 code file!)

To illustrate, define a new method named **ListAllAssembliesInAppDomain()** within the **Module1** Module. This helper method will obtain all loaded assemblies, and print out the friendly name and version of each:

```
Sub ListAllAssembliesInAppDomain()

        'Get access to the app domain for the current thread.
        Dim defaultAD As AppDomain = AppDomain.CurrentDomain

        'Now get all loaded assemblies in the default app domain.
        Dim loadedAssemblies As Assembly() = defaultAD.GetAssemblies()

        Console.WriteLine("** Here are the assemblies loaded in {0} **"
                        & vbLf, defaultAD.FriendlyName)

        For Each a As Assembly In loadedAssemblies
            Console.WriteLine("-> Name: {0}", a.GetName().Name)
            Console.WriteLine("-> Version: {0}" &
            vbLf,a.GetName().Version)
        Next
End Sub
```

Assuming you have updated your **Main()** method to call this new member, you will see that the application domain hosting your executable is currently making use of the following .NET libraries:

```
***** Here are the assemblies loaded in DefaultAppDomainApp.exe *****


-> Name: mscorlib

-> Version: 4.0.0.0


-> Name: DefaultAppDomainApp

-> Version: 1.0.0.0
```

Now understand that the list of loaded assemblies can change at any time as you author new VB 2010 code. For example, assume you have updated your ListAllAssembliesInAppDomain() method to make use of a LINQ query, which will order the loaded assemblies by name:

```vb
Sub ListAllAssembliesInAppDomain()
        'Get access to the app domain for the current thread.
        Dim defaultAD As AppDomain = AppDomain.CurrentDomain

        'Now get all loaded assemblies in the default app domain.
        Dim loadedAssemblies = From a In defaultAD.GetAssemblies() _
                               Order By a.GetName().Name _
                               Select a
        Console.WriteLine("*Here are the assemblies loaded in {0}*"
                          & vbLf, defaultAD.FriendlyName)

        For Each a In loadedAssemblies
                Console.WriteLine("-> Name: {0}", a.GetName().Name)
                Console.WriteLine("-> Version: {0}" & vbLf,
                a.GetName().Version)
        Next
End Sub
```

If you were to run the program once again, you will see that System.Core.dll and System.dll have also been loaded into memory, as they are required for the LINQ to Objects API:

```
***** Here are the assemblies loaded in DefaultAppDomainApp.exe *****


-> Name: DefaultAppDomainApp

-> Version: 1.0.0.0


-> Name: mscorlib

-> Version: 4.0.0.0


-> Name: System

-> Version: 4.0.0.0


-> Name: System.Core

-> Version: 4.0.0.0
```

Receiving Assembly Load Notifications

If you wish to be informed by the CLR when a new assembly has been loaded into a given application domain, you may handle the AssemblyLoad event. This event is typed against the AssemblyLoadEventHandler delegate, which can point to any method taking a System.Object as the first parameter, and an AssemblyLoadEventArgs as the second.

Let's add one final method to the current Module1 Module called InitDAD(). As the name suggests, this method will initialize the default application domain, specifically by handling the AssemblyLoad event via a fitting lambda expression:

```
Sub InitDAD()
    'This logic will print out the name of any assembly
    'loaded into the application domain, after it has been created.

    Dim defaultAD As AppDomain = AppDomain.CurrentDomain
    AddHandler defaultAD.AssemblyLoad,Sub(s, e)
                                    Console.WriteLine("{0} has been loaded!",
                                            e.LoadedAssembly.GetName().Name)
                                End Sub
End Sub
```

As you would expect, when you run the modified application, you will be notified when a new assembly has been loaded. Here, you are simply printing out the friendly name of the assembly, using the LoadedAssembly property of the incoming AssemblyLoadedEventArgs parameter.

■ **Source Code** The DefaultAppDomainApp project is included under the Chapter 16 subdirectory.

Creating New Application Domains

Recall that a single process is capable of hosting multiple application domains via the Shared AppDomain.CreateDomain() method. While creating new app domains on the fly is a rather infrequent task for most .NET applications, it is important to understand the basics of doing so. For example, as you will see later in this text, when you build *dynamic assemblies* (see Chapter 17) you will need to install them into a custom app domain. As well, several .NET security APIs require you to understand how to construct new app domains to isolate assemblies based on supplied security credentials.

To investigate how to create new application domains on the fly (and how to load new assemblies into these custom homes), create a new Console Application named CustomAppDomains. The AppDomain.CreateDomain() method has been overloaded a number of times. At minimum, you will specify the friendly name of the new application domain to be constructed. Update your Module1 Module with the following code. Here, you are leveraging the ListAllAssembliesInAppDomain() method from the previous example, however this time you are passing in the AppDomain object to analyze as an incoming argument:

```vb
Imports System.IO

Module Module1
    Sub Main()
        Console.WriteLine("*** Fun with Custom App Domains ***" & vbLf)

        'Show all loaded assemblies in default app domain.
        Dim defaultAD As AppDomain = AppDomain.CurrentDomain
        ListAllAssembliesInAppDomain(defaultAD)

        'Make a new app domain.
        MakeNewAppDomain()
        Console.ReadLine()
    End Sub

    Sub MakeNewAppDomain()

        'Make a new AppDomain in the current process and
        'list loaded assemblies.
        Dim newAD As AppDomain = AppDomain.CreateDomain("SecondAppDomain")

        'List all assemblies.
        ListAllAssembliesInAppDomain(newAD)
    End Sub

    Sub ListAllAssembliesInAppDomain(ByVal ad As AppDomain)

        ' Now get all loaded assemblies in the default app domain.
        Dim loadedAssemblies = From a In ad.GetAssemblies() _
                               Order By a.GetName().Name _
                               Select a

        Console.WriteLine("**Here are the assemblies loaded in {0}**" & _
        vbLf,ad.FriendlyName)

        For Each a In loadedAssemblies
            Console.WriteLine("-> Name: {0}", a.GetName().Name)
            Console.WriteLine("-> Version: {0}" & vbLf,
            a.GetName().Version)
        Next
    End Sub
End Module
```

If you run the current example, you will see that the default application domain (CustomAppDomains.exe) has loaded mscorlib.dll, System.dll, System.Core.dll and CustomAppDomains.exe, given the VB 2010 code base of the current project. However, the new application domain only contains mscorlib.dll, which as you recall is the one .NET assembly which is always loaded by the CLR for each and every application domain:

```
***** Fun with Custom App Domains *****


***** Here are the assemblies loaded in CustomAppDomains.exe *****

-> Name: CustomAppDomains

-> Version: 1.0.0.0


-> Name: mscorlib

-> Version: 4.0.0.0


-> Name: System

-> Version: 4.0.0.0


-> Name: System.Core

-> Version: 4.0.0.0


***** Here are the assemblies loaded in SecondAppDomain *****


-> Name: mscorlib

-> Version: 4.0.0.0
```

■ **Note** If you debug this project (via F5), you will find many additional assemblies are loaded into each AppDomain which are used by the Visual Studio debugging process. Running this project (via Ctrl + F5) will display only the assemblies directly by each app domain.

This may seem counterintuitive if you have a background in traditional Windows (as you might suspect, both application domains have access to the same assembly set). Recall, however, that an assembly loads into an *application domain,* not directly into the process itself.

Loading Assemblies into Custom Application Domains

The CLR will always load assemblies into the default application domain when required. However, if you do ever manually create new app domains, you can load assemblies into said app domain using the `AppDomain.Load()` method. Also, be aware that the `AppDomain.ExecuteAssembly()` method can be called to load an *.exe assembly and execute the `Main()` method.

Assume that you wish to load `CarLibrary.dll` into your new secondary app domain. Provided you have copied this library to the \bin\Debug folder of the current application you could update the `MakeNewAppDomain()` method as so (be sure to import the `System.IO` namespace, to gain access to the `FileNotFoundException` class):

```
Sub MakeNewAppDomain()
        'Make a new AppDomain in the current process.
        Dim newAD As AppDomain = AppDomain.CreateDomain("SecondAppDomain")

        Try
            'Now load CarLibrary.dll into this new domain.
            newAD.Load("CarLibrary")
        Catch ex As FileNotFoundException
            Console.WriteLine(ex.Message)
        End Try

        'List all assemblies.
        ListAllAssembliesInAppDomain(newAD)
End Sub
```

This time, the output of the program would appear as so (note the presence of `CarLibrary.dll`):

```
***** Fun with Custom App Domains *****


***** Here are the assemblies loaded in CustomAppDomains.exe *****


-> Name: CustomAppDomains

-> Version: 1.0.0.0
```

```
-> Name: mscorlib

-> Version: 4.0.0.0


-> Name: System

-> Version: 4.0.0.0


-> Name: System.Core

-> Version: 4.0.0.0


***** Here are the assemblies loaded in SecondAppDomain *****


-> Name: CarLibrary

-> Version: 2.0.0.0


-> Name: mscorlib

-> Version: 4.0.0.0
```

■ **Note** Remember! If you debug this application, you will see many additional libraries loaded into each application domain.

Programmatically Unloading AppDomains

It is important to point out that the CLR does not permit unloading individual .NET assemblies. However, using the `AppDomain.Unload()` method, you are able to selectively unload a given application domain from its hosting process. When you do so, the application domain will unload each assembly in turn.

Recall that the AppDomain type defines the DomainUnload event, which is fired when a custom application domain is unloaded from the containing process. Another event of interest is the ProcessExit event, which is fired when the default application domain is unloaded from the process (which obviously entails the termination of the process itself).

If you wish to programmatically unload newAD from the hosting process, and be notified when the associated application domain is torn down, you could update MakeNewAppDomain() with the following additional logic:

```
Sub MakeNewAppDomain()
        'Make a new AppDomain in the current process.
        Dim newAD As AppDomain = AppDomain.CreateDomain("SecondAppDomain")

        AddHandler newAD.DomainUnload, Sub(o, s)
                        Console.WriteLine("The second app domain has been unloaded!")
                                    End Sub
        Try
            'Now load CarLibrary.dll into this new domain.
            newAD.Load("CarLibrary")
        Catch ex As FileNotFoundException
            Console.WriteLine(ex.Message)
        End Try

        'List all assemblies.
        ListAllAssembliesInAppDomain(newAD)

        'Now tear down this app domain.
        AppDomain.Unload(newAD)
End Sub
```

If you wish to be notified when the default application domain is unloaded, modify your Main() method to handle the ProcessEvent event of the default application domain:

```
Sub Main()
        Console.WriteLine("*** Fun with Custom App Domains ***" & vbLf)

        'Show all loaded assemblies in default app domain.
        Dim defaultAD As AppDomain = AppDomain.CurrentDomain
        AddHandler defaultAD.ProcessExit, Function(o, s)
                                        Console.WriteLine("Default AD unloaded!")
                                        Return o.ToString()
                                    End Function

        ListAllAssembliesInAppDomain(defaultAD)

        MakeNewAppDomain()
        Console.ReadLine()
End Sub
```

That wraps up our look at the .NET application domain. To conclude this chapter, let's look at one further level of partitioning, which is used to group objects into contextual boundaries.

■ **Source Code** The `CustomAppDomains` project is included under the Chapter 16 subdirectory.

Understanding Object Context Boundaries

As you have just seen, AppDomains are logical partitions within a process used to host .NET assemblies. On a related note, a given application domain may be further subdivided into numerous context boundaries. In a nutshell, a .NET context provides a way for a single AppDomain to establish a "specific home" for a given object.

■ **Note** Friendly FYI, while understanding processes and application domains is quite important, most .NET applications will never demand that you work with object contexts. I've included this material just to paint a more complete picture.

Using context, the CLR is able to ensure that objects that have special runtime requirements are handled in an appropriate and consistent manner by intercepting method invocations into and out of a given context. This layer of interception allows the CLR to adjust the current method invocation to conform to the contextual settings of a given object. For example, if you define a VB 2010 class type that requires automatic thread safety (using the `<Synchronization()>` attribute), the CLR will create a "synchronized context" during allocation.

Just as a process defines a default AppDomain, every application domain has a default context. This default context (sometimes referred to as *context 0*, given that it is always the first context created within an application domain) is used to group together .NET objects that have no specific or unique contextual needs. As you may expect, a vast majority of .NET objects are loaded into context 0. If the CLR determines a newly created object has special needs, a new context boundary is created within the hosting application domain. Figure 16-3 illustrates the process/AppDomain/context relationship.

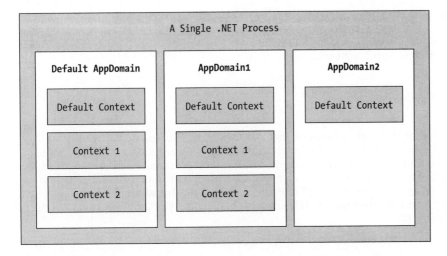

Figure 16-3. Processes, application domains, and context boundaries

Context-Agile and Context-Bound Types

.NET objects that do not demand any special contextual treatment are termed *context-agile* objects. These objects can be accessed from anywhere within the hosting AppDomain without interfering with the object's runtime requirements. Building context-agile objects is very easy, given that you simply do nothing (specifically, you do not adorn the type with any contextual attributes and do not derive from the System.ContextBoundObject base class):

```
'A context-agile object is loaded into context zero.
Public Class SportsCar
End Class
```

On the other hand, objects that do demand contextual allocation are termed *context-bound* objects, and they *must* derive from the System.ContextBoundObject base class. This base class solidifies the fact that the object in question can function appropriately only within the context in which it was created. Given the role of .NET context, it should stand to reason that if a context-bound object were to somehow end up in an incompatible context, bad things would be guaranteed to occur at the most inopportune times.

In addition to deriving from System.ContextBoundObject, a context-sensitive type will also be adorned by a special category of .NET attributes termed (not surprisingly) *context attributes*. All context attributes derive from the ContextAttribute base class. Let's see an example.

Defining a Context-Bound Object

Assume that you wish to define a class (SportsCarTS) that is automatically thread safe in nature, even though you have not hard-coded thread synchronization logic within the member implementations. To do so, derive from ContextBoundObject and apply the <Synchronization()> attribute as follows:

```
Imports System.Runtime.Remoting.Contexts

' This context-bound type will only be loaded into a
'   synchronized (hence thread-safe) context.
<Synchronization()> _
Public Class SportsCarTS
    Inherits ContextBoundObject
End Class
```

Types that are attributed with the `<Synchronization()>` attribute are loaded into a thread-safe context. Given the special contextual needs of the `SportsCarTS` class type, imagine the problems that would occur if an allocated object were moved from a synchronized context into a nonsynchronized context. The object is suddenly no longer thread safe and thus becomes a candidate for massive data corruption, as numerous threads are attempting to interact with the (now thread-volatile) reference object. To ensure the CLR does not move `SportsCarTS` objects outside of a synchronized context, simply derive from `ContextBoundObject`.

Inspecting an Object's Context

Although very few of the applications you will write will need to programmatically interact with context, here is an illustrative example. Create a new Console Application named **ObjectContextApp**. This application defines one context-agile class (**SportsCar**) and a single context-bound type (**SportsCarTS**):

```
'For Context type.
Imports System.Runtime.Remoting.Contexts

'For Thread type.
Imports System.Threading

' SportsCar has no special contextual
' needs and will be loaded into the
' default context of the app domain.

Public Class SportsCar

    Public Sub New()

        'Get context information and print out context ID.
        Dim ctx As Context = Thread.CurrentContext
        Console.WriteLine("{0} object in context {1}", Me.ToString(), ctx.ContextID)

        For Each itfCtxProp As IContextProperty In ctx.ContextProperties
            Console.WriteLine("-> Ctx Prop: {0}", itfCtxProp.Name)
        Next
    End Sub
End Class

' SportsCarTS demands to be loaded in
' a synchronization context.
<Synchronization()> _
```

```
Public Class SportsCarTS
    Inherits ContextBoundObject

    Public Sub New()
        'Get context information and print out context ID.
        Dim ctx As Context = Thread.CurrentContext
        Console.WriteLine("{0} object in context {1}", Me.ToString(), ctx.ContextID)

        For Each itfCtxProp As IContextProperty In ctx.ContextProperties
            Console.WriteLine("-> Ctx Prop: {0}", itfCtxProp.Name)
        Next
    End Sub
End Class
```

Notice that each constructor obtains a `Context` object from the current thread of execution, via the Shared `Thread.CurrentContext` property. Using the `Context` object, you are able to print out statistics about the contextual boundary, such as its assigned ID, as well as a set of descriptors obtained via `Context.ContextProperties`. This property returns an array of objects implementing the `IContextProperty` interface, which exposes each descriptor through the `Name` property. Now, update `Main()` to allocate an instance of each class type:

```
Sub Main()
        Console.WriteLine("***** Fun with Object Context *****" & vbLf)

        'Objects will display contextual info upon creation.
        Dim sport As New SportsCar()
        Console.WriteLine()

        Dim sport2 As New SportsCar()
        Console.WriteLine()

        Dim synchroSport As New SportsCarTS()
        Console.ReadLine()
End Sub
```

As the objects come to life, the class constructors will dump out various bits of context-centric information (the "lease life time service property" printout is a low level aspect of the .NET remoting layer, and can be ignored):

```
***** Fun with Object Context *****


ObjectContextApp.SportsCar object in context 0

-> Ctx Prop: LeaseLifeTimeServiceProperty
```

```
ObjectContextApp.SportsCar object in context 0

-> Ctx Prop: LeaseLifeTimeServiceProperty


ObjectContextApp.SportsCarTS object in context 1

-> Ctx Prop: LeaseLifeTimeServiceProperty

-> Ctx Prop: Synchronization
```

Given that the SportsCar class has not been qualified with a context attribute, the CLR has allocated sport and sport2 into context 0 (i.e., the default context). However, the SportsCarTS object is loaded into a unique contextual boundary (which has been assigned a context ID of 1), given the fact that this context-bound type was adorned with the <Synchronization()> attribute.

■ **Source Code** The ObjectContextApp project is included under the Chapter 16 subdirectory.

Summarizing Processes, AppDomains, and Context

At this point, you hopefully have a much better idea about how a .NET assembly is hosted by the CLR. To summarize the key points:

- A .NET process hosts one to many application domains. Each AppDomain is able to host any number of related .NET assemblies. AppDomains may be independently loaded and unloaded by the CLR (or programmatically via the System.AppDomain type).

- A given AppDomain consists of one to many contexts. Using a context, the CLR is able to place a "special needs" object into a logical container, to ensure that its runtime requirements are honored.

If the previous pages have seemed to be a bit too low level for your liking, fear not. For the most part, the .NET runtime automatically deals with the details of processes, application domains, and contexts on your behalf. The good news, however, is that this information provides a solid foundation for understanding multithreaded programming under the .NET platform.

Summary

The point of this chapter was to examine exactly how a .NET-executable image is hosted by the .NET platform. As you have seen, the long-standing notion of a Windows process has been altered under the hood to accommodate the needs of the CLR. A single process (which can be programmatically manipulated via the `System.Diagnostics.Process` type) is now composed of one or more application domains, which represent isolated and independent boundaries within a process.

As you have seen, a single process can host multiple application domains, each of which is capable of hosting and executing any number of related assemblies. Furthermore, a single application domain can contain any number of contextual boundaries. Using this additional level of type isolation, the CLR can ensure that special-need objects are handled correctly.

CHAPTER 17

■■■

Understanding CIL and the Role of Dynamic Assemblies

When you are building a full-scale .NET application, you will most certainly make use of VB 2010 (or a similar managed language such as C#), given their inherent productivity and ease of use. However, as you learned in the very first chapter, the role of a managed compiler is to translate *.vb code files into terms of CIL code, type metadata and an assembly manifest. As it turns out, CIL is a full-fledged .NET programming language, with its own syntax, semantics, and compiler (ilasm.exe).

In this chapter, you will be given a tour of .NET's mother tongue. Here you will understand the distinction between a CIL *directive*, CIL *attribute*, and CIL *opcode*. You will then learn about the role of round-trip engineering of a .NET assembly and various CIL programming tools. The remainder of the chapter will then walk you through the basics of defining namespaces, types, and members using the grammar of CIL. We wrap up with an examination of the role of the System.Reflection.Emit namespace and examine how it is possible to construct an assembly (with CIL instructions) dynamically at runtime.

Of course, few programmers will ever need to work with raw CIL code on a day-to-day basis. Therefore, I will start up this chapter by examining a few reasons why getting to know the syntax and semantics of this low-level .NET language might be worth your while.

Reasons for Learning the Grammar of CIL

CIL is the true mother tongue of the .NET platform. When you build a .NET assembly using your managed language of choice (VB 2010, C#, F#, COBOL.NET, etc.), the associated compiler translates your source code into terms of CIL. Like any programming language, CIL provides numerous structural and implementation-centric tokens. Given that CIL is just another .NET programming language, it should come as no surprise that it is possible to build your .NET assemblies directly using CIL and the CIL compiler (ilasm.exe) that ships with the .NET Framework 4.0 SDK.

Now while it is true that few programmers would choose to build an entire .NET application directly with CIL, CIL is still an extremely interesting intellectual pursuit. Simply put, the more you understand the grammar of CIL, the better able you are to move into the realm of advanced .NET development. By way of some concrete examples, individuals who possess an understanding of CIL are capable of the following:

- Talking intelligently about how different .NET programming languages map their respective keywords to CIL tokens.

- Disassembling an existing .NET assembly, editing the CIL code, and recompiling the updated code base into a modified .NET binary. For example, there are some scenarios where you might need to modify CIL in order to interoperate with some advanced COM features.

- Building dynamic assemblies using the `System.Reflection.Emit` namespace. This API allows you to generate an in-memory .NET assembly, which can optionally be persisted to disk.

- Leveraging aspects of the CTS that are not supported by higher-level managed languages, but do exist at the level of CIL. To be sure, CIL is the only .NET language that allows you to access each and every aspect of the CTS. For example, using raw CIL, you are able to define global-level members and fields (which are not permissible in VB 2010).

Again, to be perfectly clear, if you choose *not* to concern yourself with the details of CIL code, you are absolutely able to gain mastery of VB 2010 and the .NET base class libraries. In many ways, knowledge of CIL is analogous to a C(++) programmer's understanding of assembly language. Those who know the ins and outs of the low-level "goo" are able to create rather advanced solutions for the task at hand and gain a deeper understanding of the underlying programming (and runtime) environment. So, if you are up for the challenge, let's begin to examine the details of CIL.

■ **Note** Understand that this chapter is not intended to be a comprehensive treatment of the syntax and semantics of CIL. If you require a full examination of the topic, I'd recommend downloading the official ECMA specification (ecma-335.pdf) from the ECMA International web site (http://www.ecma-international.org).

Examining CIL Directives, Attributes, and Opcodes

When you begin to investigate low-level languages such as CIL, you are guaranteed to find new (and often intimidating-sounding) names for very familiar concepts. For example, at this point in the text, if you were shown the following set of items

```
{N, Public, Me, MyBase, Get, Set, Narrowing, Enum, Operator, Partial}
```

you would most certainly understand them to be keywords of the VB 2010 language (which is correct). However, if you look more closely at the members of this set, you may be able to see that while each item is indeed a VB 2010 keyword, it has radically different semantics. For example, the `Enum` keyword defines a `System.Enum`-derived type, while the `Me` and `MyBase` keywords allow you to reference the current object or the object's parent class, respectively. The `Operator` keyword allows you to build a hidden (specially named) method that will be called when you apply a specific VB 2010 operator (such as the plus sign).

In stark contrast to a higher-level language such as VB 2010, CIL does not just simply define a general set of keywords, *per se*. Rather, the token set understood by the CIL compiler is subdivided into three broad categories based on semantics:

- CIL directives
- CIL attributes
- CIL operation codes (opcodes)

Each category of CIL token is expressed using a particular syntax, and the tokens are combined to build a valid .NET assembly.

The Role of CIL Directives

First up, there is a set of well-known CIL tokens that are used to describe the overall structure of a .NET assembly. These tokens are called *directives*. CIL directives are used to inform the CIL compiler how to define the namespaces(s), type(s), and member(s) that will populate an assembly.

Directives are represented syntactically using a single dot (.) prefix (e.g., `.namespace`, `.class`, `.publickeytoken`, `.method`, `.assembly`, etc.). Thus, if your `*.il` file (the conventional extension for a file containing CIL code) has a single `.namespace` directive and three `.class` directives, the CIL compiler will generate an assembly that defines a single .NET namespace containing three .NET class types.

The Role of CIL Attributes

In many cases, CIL directives in and of themselves are not descriptive enough to fully express the definition of a given .NET type or type member. Given this fact, many CIL directives can be further specified with various CIL *attributes* to qualify how a directive should be processed. For example, the `.class` directive can be adorned with the `public` attribute (to establish the type visibility), the `extends` attribute (to explicitly specify the type's base class), and the `implements` attribute (to list the set of interfaces supported by the type).

■ **Note** Don't confuse a ".NET attribute" (see Chapter 15) with that of a "CIL attribute," the two are very different concepts.

The Role of CIL Opcodes

Once a .NET assembly, namespace, and type set have been defined in terms of CIL using various directives and related attributes, the final remaining task is to provide the type's implementation logic. This is a job for *operation codes*, or simply *opcodes*. In the tradition of other low-level languages, many CIL opcodes tend to be cryptic and completely unpronounceable by us mere humans. For example, if you need to load a `string` variable into memory, you don't use a friendly opcode named `LoadString`, but rather `ldstr`.

As you will see, the opcodes of CIL are always used within the scope of a member's implementation, and unlike CIL directives, they are never written with a dot prefix.

The CIL Opcode/CIL Mnemonic Distinction

As just explained, opcodes such as `ldstr` are used to implement the members of a given type. In reality, however, tokens such as `ldstr` are *CIL mnemonics* for the actual *binary CIL opcodes*. To clarify the distinction, assume you have authored the following method in VB 2010:

```
Shared Function Add(ByVal x As Integer, ByVal y As Integer) As Integer
                Return x + y
End Function
```

The act of adding two numbers is expressed in terms of the CIL opcode **0X58**. In a similar vein, subtracting two numbers is expressed using the opcode **0X59**, and the act of allocating a new object on the managed heap is achieved using the **0X73** opcode. Given this reality, understand that the "CIL code" processed by a JIT compiler is actually nothing more than blobs of binary data.

Thankfully, for each binary opcode of CIL, there is a corresponding mnemonic. For example, the **add** mnemonic can be used rather than **0X58**, **sub** rather than **0X59**, and **newobj** rather than **0X73**. Given this opcode/mnemonic distinction, realize that CIL decompilers such as `ildasm.exe` translate an assembly's binary opcodes into their corresponding CIL mnemonics. For example, here would be the CIL presented by `ildasm.exe` for the previous VB 2010 `Add()` method:

```
.method public  static int32 Add(int32 x,
 int32 y) cil managed
{
 // Code size      9 (0x9)
 .maxstack 2
 .locals init ([0] int32 Add)
 IL_0000: nop
 IL_0001: ldarg.0
 IL_0002: ldarg.1
 IL_0003: add.ovf
 IL_0004: stloc.0
 IL_0005: br.s      IL_0007
 IL_0007: ldloc.0
 IL_0008: ret
} //end of method Class1::Add
```

Unless you're building some extremely low-level .NET software (such as a custom managed compiler), you'll never need to concern yourself with the literal numeric binary opcodes of CIL. For all practical purposes, when .NET programmers speak about "CIL opcodes" they're referring to the set of friendly string token mnemonics (as I've done within this text, and will do for the remainder of this chapter) rather than the underlying numerical values.

Pushing and Popping: The Stack-Based Nature of CIL

Higher-level .NET languages (such as VB 2010) attempt to hide low-level CIL grunge from view as much as possible. One aspect of .NET development that is particularly well hidden is the fact that CIL is a stack-based programming language. Recall from the examination of the collection namespaces (see Chapter 10) that the `Stack(Of T)` class can be used to push a value onto a stack as well as pop the topmost value off of the stack for use. Of course, CIL developers do not literally use an object of type

Stack(Of T) to load and unload the values to be evaluated; however, the same pushing and popping mind-set still applies.

Formally speaking, the entity used to hold a set of values to be evaluated is termed the *virtual execution stack*. As you will see, CIL provides a number of opcodes that are used to push a value onto the stack; this process is termed *loading*. As well, CIL defines a number of additional opcodes that transfer the topmost value on the stack into memory (such as a local variable) using a process termed *storing*.

In the world of CIL, it is impossible to access a point of data directly, including locally defined variables, incoming method arguments, or field data of a type. Rather, you are required to explicitly load the item onto the stack, only to then pop it off for later use (keep this point in mind, as it will help explain why a given block of CIL code can look a bit redundant).

■ **Note** Recall that CIL is not directly executed, but compiled on demand. During the compilation of CIL code, many of these implementation redundancies are optimized away. Furthermore, if you enable the code optimization option for your current project (in the Compile tab of the Visual Studio Project Properties window, click the Advanced Compile Options button), the compiler will also remove various CIL redundancies.

To understand how CIL leverages a stack-based processing model, consider a simple VB 2010 method, PrintMessage(), which takes no arguments. Within the implementation of this method, you will simply print out the value of a local string variable to the standard output stream:

```
Public Sub PrintMessage()
        Dim myMessage As String = "Hello."
        Console.WriteLine(myMessage)
End Sub
```

If you were to examine how the VB 2010 compiler translates this method in terms of CIL, you would first find that the PrintMessage() method defines a storage slot for a local variable using the .locals directive. The local string is then loaded and stored in this local variable using the ldstr (load string) and stloc.0 opcodes (which can be read as "store the current value in a local variable at storage slot zero").

The value (again, at index 0) is then loaded into memory using the ldloc.0 ("load the local argument at index 0") opcode for use by the System.Console.WriteLine() method invocation (specified using the call opcode). Finally, the function returns via the ret opcode. Here is the (annotated) CIL code for the PrintMessage() method:

```
.method public  instance void PrintMessage() cil managed
{
  .maxstack  1
  // Define a local string variable (at index 0).
  .locals init ([0] string myMessage)

  // Load a string on to the stack with the value "Hello."
  ldstr  " Hello."

  // Store string value on the stack in the local variable.
  stloc.0
```

```
// Load the value at index 0.
ldloc.0

// Call method with current value.
call   void [mscorlib]System.Console::WriteLine(string)
ret
}
```

■ **Note** As you can see, CIL supports code comments using C# style double-slash syntax (as well as the /*...*/ syntax, for that matter). As in VB 2010, code comments are completely ignored by the CIL compiler.

Now that you have the basics of CIL directives, attributes, and opcodes, let's see a practical use of CIL programming, beginning with the topic of round-trip engineering.

Understanding Round-Trip Engineering

You are aware of how to use `ildasm.exe` to view the CIL code generated by the VB 2010 compiler (see Chapter 1). What you may not know, however, is that `ildasm.exe` allows you to dump the CIL contained within an assembly loaded into `ildasm.exe` to an external file. Once you have the CIL code at your disposal, you are free to edit and recompile the code base using the CIL compiler, `ilasm.exe`.

■ **Note** Also recall that `reflector.exe` can be used to view the CIL code of a given assembly, as well as to translate the CIL code into an approximate VB 2010 code base.

Formally speaking, this technique is termed *round-trip engineering,* and it can be useful under a number of circumstances:

- You need to modify an assembly for which you no longer have the source code.

- You are working with a less-than-perfect .NET language compiler that has emitted ineffective (or flat-out incorrect) CIL code, and you wish to modify the code base.

- You are constructing COM interoperability assemblies and wish to account for some COM IDL attributes that have been lost during the conversion process (such as the COM [`helpstring`] attribute).

To illustrate the process of round-tripping, begin by creating a new VB 2010 code file (`HelloProgram.vb`) using a simple text editor, and define the following class type (you are free to create a new Console Application project using Visual Studio 2010 if you wish. However, be sure to delete the `AssemblyInfo.vb` file to decrease the amount of generated CIL code):

```
'A simple VB 2010 console app.
'Note that we are not wrapping our class in a namespace,
'to help simplify the generated CIL code.
Module Module1
        Sub Main()
                Console.WriteLine("Hello CIL code!")
                Console.ReadLine()
        End Sub
End Module
```

Save your file to a convenient location (for example, `C:\RoundTrip`) and compile your Module using `vbc.exe`:

```
vbc HelloProgram.vb
```

Now, open `HelloProgram.exe` with `ildasm.exe` and, using the File ➤ Dump menu option, save the raw CIL code to a new `*.il` file (`HelloProgram.il`) in the same folder containing your compiled assembly (all of the default values of the resulting dialog box are fine as is).

■ **Note** `ildasm.exe` will also generate a `*.res` file when dumping the contents of an assembly to file. These resource files can be ignored (and deleted) throughout this chapter, as you will not be making use of them.

Now you are able to view this file using your text editor of choice. Here is the (slightly simplified and annotated) result:

```
// Referenced Assemblies.
.assembly extern mscorlib
{
  .publickeytoken = (B7 7A 5C 56 19 34 E0 89 )
  .ver 4:0:0:0
}

// Our assembly.
.assembly HelloProgram
{
  /****   TargetFrameworkAttribute data removed for clarity! ****/

  .hash algorithm 0x00008004
  .ver 0:0:0:0
}
.module HelloProgram.exe
.imagebase 0x00400000
.file alignment 0x00000200
.stackreserve 0x00100000
.subsystem 0x0003
.corflags 0x00000003
```

693

```
// Definition of Module1 Module.
.class private  auto ansi sealed Module1
       extends [mscorlib]System.Object
{
.method public static void  Main() cil managed
  {
     .entrypoint
     .custom instance void [mscorlib]System.STAThreadAttribute::.ctor() = ( 01 00 00 00 )
     // Code size       17 (0x11)
     .maxstack  8
     IL_0000:  ldstr      "Hello CIL code!"
     IL_0005:  call       void [mscorlib]System.Console::WriteLine(string)
     IL_000a:  call       string [mscorlib]System.Console::ReadLine()
     IL_000f:  pop
     IL_0010:  ret
  } // end of method Module1::Main
}
```

First, notice that the *.il file opens by declaring each externally referenced assembly the current assembly is compiled against. Here, you can see a single .assembly extern token set for the always present mscorlib.dll. Of course, if your class library made use of types within other referenced assemblies, you would find additional .assembly extern directives.

Next, you find the formal definition of your HelloProgram.exe assembly, which has been assigned a default version of 0.0.0.0 (given that you did not specify a value using the <AssemblyVersion> attribute). The assembly is further described using various CIL directives (such as .module, .imagebase, and so forth).

After documenting the externally referenced assemblies and defining the current assembly, you find a definition of the Module1 type. Note that the .class directive has various attributes (many of which are actually optional) such as extends, which marks the base class of the type:

```
.class private auto ansi sealed Module1
       extends [mscorlib]System.Object
{ ... }
```

The bulk of the CIL code represents the implementation of the Main() method, which is defined with the .method directive. Once the members have been defined using the correct directives and attributes, they are implemented using various opcodes.

It is critical to understand that when interacting with .NET types (such as System.Console) in CIL, you will *always* need to use the type's fully qualified name. Furthermore, the type's fully qualified name must *always* be prefixed with the friendly name of the defining assembly (in square brackets). Consider the CIL implementation of Main():

```
method public static void  Main() cil managed
  {
     .entrypoint
     .custom instance void [mscorlib]System.STAThreadAttribute::.ctor() = ( 01 00 00 00 )
     // Code size       17 (0x11)
     .maxstack  8
     IL_0000:  ldstr      "Hello CIL code!"
     IL_0005:  call       void [mscorlib]System.Console::WriteLine(string)
```

```
    IL_000a:  call        string [mscorlib]System.Console::ReadLine()
    IL_000f:  pop
    IL_0010:  ret
  } // end of method Module1::Main
```

The Role of CIL Code Labels

One thing you certainly have noticed is that each line of implementation code is prefixed with a token of
the form IL_XXX: (e.g., IL_0000:, IL_0001:, and so on). These tokens are called *code labels* and may be
named in any manner you choose (provided they are not duplicated within the same member scope).
When you dump an assembly to file using ildasm.exe, it will automatically generate code labels that
follow an IL_XXX: naming convention. However, you may change them to reflect a more descriptive
marker:

```
.method public static void  Main() cil managed
  {
    .entrypoint
    .custom instance void [mscorlib]System.STAThreadAttribute::.ctor() = ( 01 00 00 00 )
    // Code size       20 (0x14)
    .maxstack  8
    IL_0000:  nop
    IL_0001:  ldstr       "Hello CIL code!"
    IL_0006:  call        void [mscorlib]System.Console::WriteLine(string)
    IL_000b:  nop
    IL_000c:  call        string [mscorlib]System.Console::ReadLine()
    IL_0011:  pop
    IL_0012:  nop
    IL_0013:  ret
  } // end of method Module1::Main

} // end of class Module1
```

The truth of the matter is that most code labels are completely optional. The only time code labels
are truly mandatory is when you are authoring CIL code that makes use of various branching or looping
constructs, as you can specify where to direct the flow of logic via these code labels. For the current
example, you can remove these autogenerated labels altogether with no ill effect:

```
.method public static void  Main() cil managed
  {
    .entrypoint
    .custom instance void [mscorlib]System.STAThreadAttribute::.ctor() = ( 01 00 00 00 )
    // Code size       20 (0x14)
    .maxstack  8
    IL_0000:  nop
    IL_0001:  ldstr       "Hello CIL code!"
    IL_0006:  call        void [mscorlib]System.Console::WriteLine(string)
    IL_000b:  nop
    IL_000c:  call        string [mscorlib]System.Console::ReadLine()
    IL_0011:  pop
```

```
    IL_0012:  nop
    IL_0013:  ret
  } // end of method Module1::Main

} // end of class Module1
```

Interacting with CIL: Modifying an *.il File

Now that you have a better understanding of how a basic CIL file is composed, let's complete the round-tripping experiment. The goal here is to update the CIL within the existing *.il file as follows:

- Add a reference to the System.Windows.Forms.dll assembly.

- Load a local string within Main().

- Call the System.Windows.Forms.MessageBox.Show() method using the local string variable as an argument.

The first step is to add a new .assembly directive (qualified with the extern attribute) that specifies your assembly requires the System.Windows.Forms.dll assembly. To do so, update the *.il file with the following logic after the external reference to mscorlib:

```
.assembly extern System.Windows.Forms
{
  .publickeytoken = (B7 7A 5C 56 19 34 E0 89)
  .ver 4:0:0:0
}
```

Be aware that the value assigned to the .ver directive may differ depending on which version of the .NET platform you have installed on your development machine. Here, you see that System.Windows.Forms.dll version 4.0.0.0 is used and has the public key token of B77A5C561934E089. If you open the GAC (see Chapter 14) and locate your version of the System.Windows.Forms.dll assembly, you can simply copy the correct version and public key token value.

Next, you need to alter the current implementation of the Main() method. Locate this method within the *.il file and remove the current implementation code (the .maxstack and .entrypoint directives should remain intact):

```
.method public static void Main() cil managed{
  .entrypoint
  .maxstack  8
  // ToDo: Write new CIL code!
}
```

Again, the goal here is to push a new **string** onto the stack and call the MessageBox.Show() method (rather than the Console.WriteLine() method). Recall that when you specify the name of an external type, you must make use of the type's fully qualified name (in conjunction with the friendly name of the assembly). Also notice that in terms of CIL, every method call documents the fully qualified return type. Keeping these things in mind, update the Main() method as follows:

```
.method public static void Main() cil managed
{
  .entrypoint
  .maxstack  8

  ldstr  "CIL is way cool"
  call valuetype [System.Windows.Forms]
    System.Windows.Forms.DialogResult
    [System.Windows.Forms]
    System.Windows.Forms.MessageBox::Show(string)
  pop
  ret
}
```

In effect, you have just updated the CIL code to correspond to the following VB 2010 Module definition:

```
Module Module1
    Sub Main()
        System.Windows.Forms.MessageBox.Show("CIL is way cool")
    End Sub
End Module
```

Compiling CIL Code Using ilasm.exe

Assuming you have saved this modified *.il file, you can compile a new .NET assembly using the ilasm.exe (CIL compiler) utility. While the CIL compiler has numerous command-line options (all of which can be seen by specifying the -? option), Table 17-1 shows the core flags of interest.

Table 17-1. Common ilasm.exe Command-Line Flags

Flag	Meaning in Life
/debug	Includes debug information (such as local variable and argument names, as well as line numbers).
/dll	Produces a *.dll file as output.
/exe	Produces an *.exe file as output. This is the default setting and may be omitted.
/key	Compiles the assembly with a strong name using a given *.snk file.
/output	Specifies the output file name and extension. If you do not make use of the /output flag, the resulting file name (minus the file extension) is the same as the name of the first source file.

To compile your updated `HelloProgram.il` file into a new .NET `*.exe`, you can issue the following command within a Visual Studio 2010 command prompt:

```
ilasm /exe HelloProgram.il /output=NewAssembly.exe
```

Assuming things have worked successfully, you will see the report as shown here in which we have shown the relevant bits and omitted the irrelevant parts.

```
Microsoft (R) .NET Framework IL Assembler.  Version 4.0.30128.1

Copyright (c) Microsoft Corporation.  All rights reserved.

Assembling 'HelloProgram.il'  to EXE --> 'NewAssembly.exe'

Source file is UTF-8


Assembled method My.MyApplication::.ctor

Assembled method My.MyComputer::.ctor

Assembled method My.MyProjectMyWebServices::Equals

Assembled method My.MyProjectMyWebServices::GetHashCode

Assembled method My.MyProjectMyWebServices::GetType

Assembled method My.MyProjectMyWebServices::ToString

Assembled method My.MyProjectMyWebServices::Create__Instance__

Assembled method My.MyProjectMyWebServices::Dispose__Instance__

Assembled method My.MyProjectMyWebServices::.ctor

Assembled method My.MyProjectThreadSafeObjectProvider`1::get_GetInstance

Assembled method My.MyProjectThreadSafeObjectProvider`1::.ctor

Assembled method My.MyProject::.cctor

Assembled method My.MyProject::get_Computer

Assembled method My.MyProject::get_Application

Assembled method My.MyProject::get_User
```

```
Assembled method My.MyProject::get_WebServices

Assembled method My.InternalXmlHelperRemoveNamespaceAttributesClosure::.ctor

Assembled method My.InternalXmlHelperRemoveNamespaceAttributesClosure::ProcessXElement

Assembled method My.InternalXmlHelperRemoveNamespaceAttributesClosure::ProcessObject

Assembled method My.InternalXmlHelper::.ctor

Assembled method My.InternalXmlHelper::get_Value

Assembled method My.InternalXmlHelper::set_Value

Assembled method My.InternalXmlHelper::get_AttributeValue

Assembled method My.InternalXmlHelper::set_AttributeValue

Assembled method My.InternalXmlHelper::get_AttributeValue

Assembled method My.InternalXmlHelper::set_AttributeValue

Assembled method My.InternalXmlHelper::CreateAttribute

Assembled method My.InternalXmlHelper::CreateNamespaceAttribute

Assembled method My.InternalXmlHelper::RemoveNamespaceAttributes

Assembled method My.InternalXmlHelper::RemoveNamespaceAttributes

Assembled method My.InternalXmlHelper::RemoveNamespaceAttributes

Assembled method Module1::Main

Assembled method My.Resources.Resources::get_ResourceManager

Assembled method My.Resources.Resources::get_Culture

Assembled method My.Resources.Resources::set_Culture

Assembled method My.MySettings::.cctor

Assembled method My.MySettings::.ctor
```

Assembled method My.MySettings::get_Default

Assembled method My.MySettingsProperty::get_Settings

Creating PE file

Emitting classes:

Class 1:   My.MyApplication

Class 2:   My.MyComputer

Class 3:   My.MyProject

Class 4:   My.MyProject°MyWebServices

Class 5:   My.MyProject°ThreadSafeObjectProvider`1

Class 6:   Module1

Emitting fields and methods:

Global

Global

Class 1 Methods: 1;

Class 2 Methods: 1;

Class 3 Fields: 4;   Methods: 5;

Class 4 Methods: 7;

Class 5 Fields: 1;   Methods: 2;

Class 6 Methods: 12;

Class 7 Fields: 3;   Methods: 3;

Class 8 Methods: 1;

Class 9 Fields: 2;   Methods: 3;

Class 10   Fields: 1;   Methods: 3;

```
Class 11        Methods: 1;

Resolving local member refs: 50 -> 50 defs, 0 refs, 0 unresolved

Emitting events and properties:

Global

Class 1

Class 2

Class 3 Props: 4;

Class 4

Class 5 Props: 1;

Class 6

Resolving local member refs: 0 -> 0 defs, 0 refs, 0 unresolved

Writing PE file

Operation completed successfully
```

At this point, you can run your new application. Sure enough, rather than showing a message within the console window, you will now see a message box displaying your message. While the output of this simple example are not all that spectacular, it does illustrate one practical use of programming in CIL-round tripping.

Authoring CIL Code Using SharpDevelop

Back in Chapter 2, I made brief mention of the freely available SharpDevelop IDE (http://www.sharpdevelop.com). Beyond supplying a number of VB 2010 and C# project templates, when you access the File ➤ New Solution menu option, you will be happy to see one of your choices is to create a CIL project workspace (see Figure 17-1).

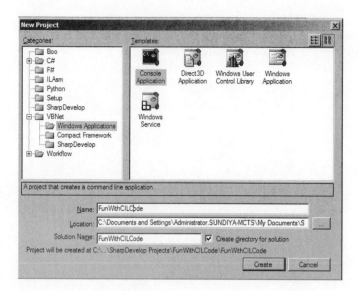

Figure 17-1. The SharpDevelop IDE CIL project template

While SharpDevelop does not have IntelliSense support for CIL projects, CIL tokens are color-coded, and you are able to compile and run your application directly within the IDE (rather than running `ilasm.exe` from a command prompt). When you create this project type, you will be given an initial `*.il` file looking like so (Figure 17-2).

```
MainClass.il                                                    ▼ ×
427
428   .class private auto ansi sealed FunWithCILCode.Program
429          extends [mscorlib]System.Object
430   {
431    .custom instance void [Microsoft.VisualBasic]Microsoft.VisualBasic.Co
432    .method public static void  Main() cil managed
433    {
434      .entrypoint
435      .custom instance void [mscorlib]System.STAThreadAttribute::.ctor()
436      // Code size       32 (0x20)
437      .maxstack  8
438      IL_0000:  nop
439      IL_0001:  ldstr      "Hello World!"
440      IL_0006:  call       void [mscorlib]System.Console::WriteLine(strin
441      IL_000b:  nop
442      IL_000c:  ldstr      "Press any key to continue . . . "
443      IL_0011:  call       void [mscorlib]System.Console::Write(string)
444      IL_0016:  nop
445      IL_0017:  ldc.i4.1
446      IL_0018:  call       valuetype [mscorlib]System.ConsoleKeyInfo [msc
447      IL_001d:  pop
448      IL_001e:  nop
449      IL_001f:  ret
450    } // end of method Program::Main
451
452   } // end of class FunWithCILCode.Program
```

Figure 17-2. The SharpDevelop IDE CIL editor

As you work through the remaining examples of this chapter, I'd recommend using SharpDevelop to author the CIL code. Beyond some color coding functionality, the CIL project workspace will also help you quickly locate the position of coding typos via the Errors window.

■ **Note** The MonoDevelop IDE, a free IDE for building .NET applications under the Mono platform, also supports a CIL project template. See Appendix B for details about MonoDevelop.

The Role of peverify.exe

When you are building or modifying assemblies using CIL code, it is always advisable to verify that the compiled binary image is a well-formed .NET image using the `peverify.exe` command-line tool:

```
peverify NewAssembly.exe
```

This tool will examine all opcodes within the specified assembly for valid CIL code. For example, in terms of CIL code, the evaluation stack must always be empty before exiting a function. If you forget to pop off any remaining values, the `ilasm.exe` compiler will still generate a compiled assembly (given that compilers are concerned only with *syntax*). `peverify.exe`, on the other hand, is concerned with *semantics*. If you did forget to clear the stack before exiting a given function, `peverify.exe` will let you know before you try running your code base.

■ **Source Code** The RoundTrip example is included under the Chapter 17 subdirectory.

Understanding CIL Directives and Attributes

Now that you have seen how `ildasm.exe` and `ilasm.exe` can be used to perform a round-trip, you can get down to the business of checking out the syntax and semantics of CIL itself. The next sections will walk you through the process of authoring a custom namespace containing a set of types. However, to keep things simple, these types will not contain any implementation logic for their members (yet). Once you understand how to create empty types, you can then turn your attention to the process of defining "real" members using CIL opcodes.

Specifying Externally Referenced Assemblies in CIL

Create a new file named `CilTypes.il` using your editor of choice. The first task a CIL project will require is to list the set of external assemblies used by the current assembly. For this example, you will only make use of types found within `mscorlib.dll`. To do so, the `.assembly` directive will be qualified using the `external` attribute. When you are referencing a strongly named assembly, such as `mscorlib.dll`, you'll want to specify the `.publickeytoken` and `.ver` directives as well:

```
.assembly extern mscorlib
{
  .publickeytoken = (B7 7A 5C 56 19 34 E0 89 )
  .ver 4:0:0:0
}
```

■ **Note** Strictly speaking, you are not required to explicitly reference `mscorlib.dll` as an external reference, as `ilasm.exe` will do so automatically. However, for each external .NET library your CIL project requires, you will need to author a similar `.assembly extern` directive.

Defining the Current Assembly in CIL

The next order of business is to define the assembly you are interested in building using the `.assembly` directive. At the simplest level, an assembly can be defined by specifying the friendly name of the binary:

```
// Our assembly.
.assembly CILTypes { }
```

While this indeed defines a new .NET assembly, you will typically place additional directives within the scope of the assembly declaration. For this example, update your assembly definition to include a version number of 1.0.0.0 using the `.ver` directive (note that each numerical identifier is separated by *colons*, not the VB 2010-centric dot notation):

```
// Our assembly.
.assembly CILTypes
{
  .ver 1:0:0:0
}
```

Given that the `CILTypes` assembly is a single-file assembly, you will finish up the assembly -definition using a single `.module` directive, which marks the official name of your .NET binary, `CILTypes.dll`:

```
.assembly CILTypes
{
 .ver 1:0:0:0
}
// The module of our single-file assembly.
.module CILTypes.dll
```

In addition to `.assembly` and `.module` are CIL directives that further qualify the overall structure of the .NET binary you are composing. Table 17-2 lists a few of the more common assembly-level directives.

Table 17-2. Additional Assembly-Centric Directives

Directive	Meaning in Life
.mresources	If your assembly makes use of internal resources (such as bitmaps or string tables), this directive is used to identify the name of the file that contains the resources to be embedded.
.subsystem	This CIL directive is used to establish the preferred UI that the assembly wishes to execute within. For example, a value of 2 signifies that the assembly should run within a GUI application, whereas a value of 3 denotes a console executable.

Defining Namespaces in CIL

Now that you have defined the look and feel of your assembly (and the required external references), you can create a .NET namespace (MyNamespace) using the .namespace directive:

```
// Our assembly has a single namespace.
.namespace MyNamespace {}
```

Like VB 2010, CIL namespace definitions can be nested within further namespaces. There is no need to define a root namespace here; however, for the sake of argument, assume you wish to create a root namespace named MyCompany:

```
.namespace MyCompany
{
  .namespace MyNamespace {}
}
```

Incidentally, CIL allows you to define a nested namespace as follows:

```
// Defining a nested namespace.
.namespace MyCompany.MyNamespace{}
```

Defining Class Types in CIL

Empty namespaces are not very interesting, so let's now check out the process of defining a class type using CIL. Not surprisingly, the .class directive is used to define a new class. However, this simple directive can be adorned with numerous additional attributes, to further qualify the nature of the type. To illustrate, add a public class to your namespace named MyBaseClass. As in VB 2010, if you do not specify an explicit base class, your type will automatically be derived from System.Object.

```
.namespace MyNamespace
{
  // System.Object base class assumed.
  .class public MyBaseClass

      { }
}
```

When you are building a class type that derives from any class other than `System.Object`, you make use of the `extends` attribute. Whenever you need to reference a type defined within the same assembly, CIL demands that you also make use of the fully qualified name (however, if the base type is within the same assembly, you can omit the assembly's friendly name prefix). Therefore, the following attempt to extend `MyBaseClass` results in a compiler error:

```
// This will not compile!
.namespace MyNamespace
{
  .class public MyBaseClass {}

  .class public MyDerivedClass
    extends MyBaseClass {}
}
```

To correctly define the parent class of `MyDerivedClass`, you must specify the full name of `MyBaseClass` as follows:

```
// Better!
.namespace MyNamespace
{
  .class public MyBaseClass {}

  .class public MyDerivedClass
    extends MyNamespace.MyBaseClass {}
}
```

In addition to the `public` and `extends` attributes, a CIL class definition may take numerous additional qualifiers that control the type's visibility, field layout, and so on. Table 17-3 illustrates some (but not all) of the attributes that may be used in conjunction with the `.class` directive.

Table 17-3. Various Attributes Used in Conjunction with the .class Directive

Attributes	Meaning in Life
`public`, `private`, `nested assembly`, `nested famandassem`, `nested family`, `nested famorassem`, `nested public`, `nested private`	CIL defines various attributes that are used to specify the visibility of a given type. As you can see, raw CIL offers numerous possibilities other than those offered by VB 2010. Refer to ECMA 335 for details if you are interested.
`abstract`, `sealed`	These two attributes may be tacked onto a `.class` directive to define an abstract class (e.g., `MustInherit` in VB 2010) or sealed class, (e.g., `NotInheritable` in VB 2010) respectively.
`auto`, `sequential`, `explicit`	These attributes are used to instruct the CLR how to lay out field data in memory. For class types, the default layout flag (`auto`) is appropriate. Changing this default can be helpful if you need to use P/Invoke to call into unmanaged C code.
`extends`, `implements`	These attributes allow you to define the base class of a type (via `extends`) or implement an interface on a type (via `implements`).

Defining and Implementing Interfaces in CIL

As odd as it may seem, interface types are defined in CIL using the `.class` directive. However, when the `.class` directive is adorned with the `interface` attribute, the type is realized as a CTS interface type. Once an interface has been defined, it may be bound to a class or structure type using the CIL `implements` attribute:

```
.namespace MyNamespace
{
  // An interface definition.
  .class public interface IMyInterface {}

  // A simple base class.
  .class public MyBaseClass {}

  // MyDerivedClass now implements IMyInterface,
  // and extends MyBaseClass.
  .class public MyDerivedClass
    extends MyNamespace.MyBaseClass
    implements MyNamespace.IMyInterface {}
}
```

■ **Note** The extends clause must precede the `implements` clause. As well, the `implements` can incorporate a list of interfaces.

As you recall from Chapter 9, interfaces can function as the base interface to other interface types in order to build interface hierarchies. However, contrary to what you might be thinking, the `extends` attribute cannot be used to derive interface A from interface B. The `extends` attribute is used only to qualify a type's base class. When you wish to extend an interface, you will make use of the `implements` attribute yet again:

```
// Extending interfaces in terms of CIL.
.class public interface IMyInterface {}

.class public interface IMyOtherInterface
  implements MyNamespace.IMyInterface {}
```

Defining Structures in CIL

The `.class` directive can be used to define a CTS structure if the type extends `System.ValueType`. Also, the `.class` directive must be qualified with the `sealed` attribute (remember the `sealed` attribute in IL corresponds to the `NotInheritable` keyword in VB 2010) given that structures can never be a base structure to other value types). If you attempt to do otherwise, `ilasm.exe` will issue a compiler error.

```
// A structure definition is always sealed.
.class public sealed MyStruct
  extends [mscorlib]System.ValueType{}
```

Do be aware that CIL provides a shorthand notation to define a structure type. If you use the `value` attribute, the new type will derive the type from `[mscorlib]System.ValueType` automatically. Therefore, you could define `MyStruct` as follows:

```
// Shorthand notation for declaring a structure.
.class public sealed value MyStruct{}
```

Defining Enums in CIL

.NET enumerations (as you recall) derive from `System.Enum`, which is a `System.ValueType` (and therefore must also be sealed). When you wish to define an enum in terms of CIL, simply extend `[mscorlib]System.Enum`:

```
// An enum.
.class public sealed MyEnum
  extends [mscorlib]System.Enum{}
```

Like a structure definition, enumerations can be defined with a shorthand notation using the `enum` attribute:

```
// Enum shorthand.
.class public sealed enum MyEnum{}
```

You'll see how to specify the name/value pairs of an enumeration in just a moment.

■ **Note** The other fundamental .NET type, the delegate, also has a specific CIL representation. See Chapter 11 for details.

Defining Generics in CIL

Generic types also have a specific representation in the syntax of CIL. Recall from Chapter 10 that a given generic type or generic member may have one or more type parameters. For example, the List(Of T) type has a single type parameter, while Dictionary(Of TKey, TValue) has two. In terms of CIL, the number of type parameters is specified using a backward-leaning single tick, `` ` ``, followed by a numerical value representing the number of type parameters. IL uses <T> to represent type parameters, whereas VB 2010 uses (Of T).

■ **Note** On most keyboards, the `` ` `` character can be found on the key above the Tab key (and to the left of the 1 key).

For example, assume you wish to create a List(Of T) variable, where T is of type System.Int32. In CIL, you would author the following (which could appear in any CIL method scope):

```
// In VB 2010:Dim myInts As New List(Of Integer)()
newobj instance void class [mscorlib]
  System.Collections.Generic.List`1<int32>::..ctor()
```

Notice that this generic class is defined as List`1<int32>, as List(Of T) has a single type parameter. However, if you needed to define a Dictionary(Of String, Integer) type, you would do so as the following:

```
// In VB 2010:Dim d As New Dictionary(Of String, Integer)()
newobj instance void class [mscorlib]
  System.Collections.Generic.Dictionary`2<string,int32>::..ctor()
```

As another example, if you have a generic type that uses another generic type as a type parameter, you would author CIL code such as the following:

```
// In VB 2010:Dim myInts As New List(Of List(Of Integer))()
newobj instance void class [mscorlib]
  System.Collections.Generic.List`1<class
  [mscorlib]System.Collections.Generic.List`1<int32>>::..ctor()
```

Compiling the CILTypes.il file

Even though you have not yet added any members or implementation code to the types you have defined, you are able to compile this *.il file into a .NET DLL assembly (which you must do, as you have not specified a Main() method). Open up a command prompt and enter the following command to ilasm.exe:

```
ilasm /dll CilTypes.il
```

Once you have done so, you are able to open your binary into ildasm.exe (see Figure 17-3).

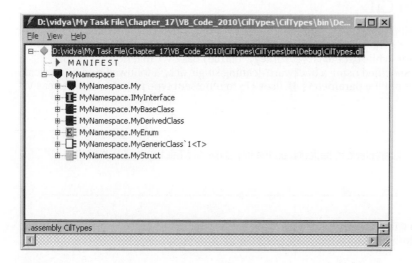

Figure 17-3. The CILTypes.dll assembly

Once you have confirmed the contents of your assembly, run **peverify.exe** against it:

```
peverify CilTypes.dll
```

Notice that you are issued errors, given that all your types are completely empty. Here is some partial output:

```
Microsoft (R) .NET Framework PE Verifier.   Version  4.0.21006.1

Copyright (c) Microsoft Corporation.  All rights reserved.


[MD]: Error: Value class has neither fields nor size parameter. [token:0x02000005]

[MD]: Error: Enum has no instance field. [token:0x02000006]

...
```

To understand how to populate a type with content, you first need to examine the fundamental data types of CIL.

.NET Base Class Library, VB 2010, and CIL Data Type Mappings

Table 17-4 illustrates how a .NET base class type maps to the corresponding VB 2010 keyword, and how each VB 2010 keyword maps into raw CIL. As well, Table 17-4 documents the shorthand constant notations used for each CIL type. As you will see in just a moment, these constants are often referenced by numerous CIL opcodes.

Table 17-4. Mapping .NET Base Class Types to VB 2010 Keywords, and VB 2010 Keywords to CIL

.NET Base Class Type	VB 2010 Keyword	CIL Representation	CIL Constant Notation
System.SByte	SByte	int8	I1
System.Byte	Byte	unsigned int8	U1
System.Int16	Short	int16	I2
System.UInt16	UShort	unsigned int16	U2
System.Int32	Integer	int32	I4
System.UInt32	UInteger	unsigned int32	U4
System.Int64	Long	int64	I8
System.UInt64	ULong	unsigned int64	U8
System.Char	Char	char	CHAR
System.Single	Single	float32	R4
System.Double	Double	float64	R8
System.Boolean	Boolean	bool	BOOLEAN
System.String	String	string	N/A
System.Object	Object	object	N/A
System.Void	Void	void	VOID

■ **Note** The System.IntPtr and System.UIntPtr types map to native integer and native unsigned integer (this is good to know, as many of COM interoperability and P/Invoke scenarios use these extensively).

Defining Type Members in CIL

As you are already aware, .NET types may support various members. Enumerations have some set of name/value pairs. Structures and classes may have constructors, fields, methods, properties, static members, and so on. Over the course of this book's first 16 chapters, you have already seen partial CIL definitions for the items previously mentioned, but nevertheless, here is a quick recap of how various members map to CIL primitives.

Defining Field Data in CIL

Enumerations, structures, and classes can all support field data. In each case, the `.field` directive will be used. For example, let's breathe some life into the skeleton MyEnum enumeration and define three name/value pairs (note the values are specified within parentheses):

```
.class public sealed enum MyEnum
{
.field public static literal valuetype
 MyNamespace.MyEnum A = int32(0)
.field public static literal valuetype
 MyNamespace.MyEnum B = int32(1)
.field public static literal valuetype
 MyNamespace.MyEnum C = int32(2)
}
```

Fields that reside within the scope of a .NET **System.Enum**-derived type are qualified using the **static** and `literal` attributes (the **static** attribute in IL equates to the **Shared** keyword in VB 2010). As you would guess, these attributes set up the field data to be a fixed value accessible from the type itself (e.g., MyEnum.A).

■ **Note** The values assigned to an enum value may also be in hexadecimal with an ox prefix.

Of course, when you wish to define a point of field data within a class or structure, you are not limited to a point of public static literal data. For example, you could update **MyBaseClass** to support two points of private, instance-level field data, set to default values:

```
.class public MyBaseClass
{
  .field private string stringField = "hello!"
  .field private int32 intField = int32(42)
}
```

As in VB 2010, class field data will automatically be initialized to an appropriate default value. If you wish to allow the object user to supply custom values at the time of creation for each of these points of private field data, you (of course) need to create custom constructors.

Defining Type Constructors in CIL

The CTS supports both instance-level and class-level (Shared) constructors. In terms of CIL, instance-level constructors are represented using the `.ctor` token, while a class-level constructor is expressed via `.cctor` (class constructor). Both of these CIL tokens must be qualified using the **rtspecialname** (return type special name) and **specialname** attributes. Simply put, these attributes are used to identify a specific CIL token that can be treated in unique ways by a given .NET language. For example, in VB 2010, constructors do not define a return type; however, in terms of CIL, the return value of a constructor is indeed **void**. The **void** keyword in IL is inspired by the **void** keyword in C#, which means "no return value":

```
.class public MyBaseClass
{
  .field private string stringField
  .field private int32 intField

  .method public hidebysig specialname rtspecialname
    instance void .ctor(string s, int32 i) cil managed
  {
    // TODO: Add implementation code...
  }
}
```

Note that the `.ctor` directive has been qualified with the **instance** attribute (as it is not a Shared constructor). The **cil managed** attributes denote that the scope of this method contains CIL code, rather than unmanaged code, which may be used during platform invocation requests.

Defining Properties in CIL

Properties and methods also have specific CIL representations. By way of an example, if MyBaseClass were updated to support a public property named TheString, you would author the following CIL (note again the use of the specialname attribute):

```
.class public MyBaseClass
{
...
  .method public hidebysig specialname
    instance string  get_TheString() cil managed
  {
    // TODO: Add implementation code...
  }

  .method public hidebysig specialname
    instance void  set_TheString(string 'value') cil managed
  {
    // TODO: Add implementation code...
  }

  .property instance string TheString()
  {
    .get instance string
      MyNamespace.MyBaseClass::get_TheString()
    .set instance void
      MyNamespace.MyBaseClass::set_TheString(string)
  }
}
```

Recall that in terms of CIL, a property maps to a pair of methods that take `get_` and `set_` prefixes. The `.property` directive makes use of the related `.get` and `.set` directives to map property syntax to the correct "specially named" methods.

■ **Note** Notice that the incoming parameter to the `set` method of a property is placed in single-tick quotation marks, which represents the name of the token to use on the right-hand side of the assignment operator within the method scope.

Defining Member Parameters

In a nutshell, specifying arguments in CIL is (more or less) identical to doing so in VB 2010. For example, each argument is defined by specifying its data type followed by the parameter name. Furthermore, like VB 2010, CIL provides a way to define input, output, and pass-by-reference parameters. As well, CIL allows you to define a parameter array argument (aka the VB 2010 `ParamArray` keyword) as well as Optional parameters (which are not supported in C#).

To illustrate the process of defining parameters in raw CIL, assume you wish to build a method that takes an Int32 (by value), an Int32 (by reference), a [mscorlib]System.Collection.ArrayList. In terms of VB 2010, this method would look something like the following:

```
Public Shared Sub MyMethod(ByVal inputInt As Integer,
                           ByRef refInt As Integer,
                           ByVal ar As ArrayList,
                           [Out]ByVal outputInt As Integer)

        outputInt = 0 'Just to satisfy the VB 2010 compiler...
End Sub
```

If you were to map this method into CIL terms, you would find that VB 2010 reference parameters are marked with an ampersand (&) suffixed to the parameter's underlying data type (int32&).

Output parameters also make use of the & suffix, but they are further qualified using the CIL [out] token. Also notice that if the parameter is a reference type (in this case, the [mscorlib]System.Collections.ArrayList type), the class token is prefixed to the data type (not to be confused with the .class directive!):

```
.method public static void MyMethod(int32 inputInt,
  int32& refInt,
  class [mscorlib]System.Collections.ArrayList ar,
  [out] int32& outputInt) cil managed
{
  ...
}
```

Examining CIL Opcodes

The final aspect of CIL code you'll examine in this chapter has to do with the role of various -operational codes (opcodes). Recall that an opcode is simply a CIL token used to build the implementation logic for a given member. The complete set of CIL opcodes (which is fairly large) can be grouped into the following broad categories:

- Opcodes that control program flow

- Opcodes that evaluate expressions

- Opcodes that access values in memory (via parameters, local variables, etc.)

To provide some insight to the world of member implementation via CIL, Table 17-5 defines some of the more useful opcodes that are directly related to member implementation logic, grouped by related functionality.

Table 17-5. Various Implementation-Specific CIL Opcodes

Opcodes	Meaning in Life
add, sub, mul, div, rem	These CIL opcodes allow you to add, subtract, multiply, and divide two values (rem returns the remainder of a division operation).
and, or, not, xor	These CIL opcodes allow you to perform bit-wise operations on two values.
ceq, cgt, clt	These CIL opcodes allow you to compare two values on the stack in various manners, for example: ceq: Compare for equality cgt: Compare for greater than clt: Compare for less than
box, unbox	These CIL opcodes are used to convert between reference types and value types.
ret	This CIL opcode is used to exit a method and return a value to the caller (if necessary).
beq, bgt, ble, blt, switch	These CIL opcodes (in addition to many other related opcodes) are used to control branching logic within a method, for example: beq: Break to code label if equal bgt: Break to code label if greater than ble: Break to code label if less than or equal to blt: Break to code label if less than All of the branch-centric opcodes require that you specify a CIL code label to jump to if the result of the test is true.
call	This CIL opcode is used to call a member on a given type.
newarr, newobj	These CIL opcodes allow you to allocate a new array or new object type into memory (respectively).

The next broad category of CIL opcodes (a subset of which is shown in Table 17-6) are used to load (push) arguments onto the virtual execution stack. Note how these load-specific opcodes take an ld (load) prefix.

Table 17-6. The Primary Stack-Centric Opcodes of CIL

Opcode	Meaning in Life
ldarg (with numerous variations)	Loads a method's argument onto the stack. In addition to the general ldarg (which works in conjunction with a given index that identifies the argument), there are numerous other variations. For example, ldarg opcodes that have a numerical suffix (ldarg_0) hard-code which argument to load. As well, variations of the ldarg opcode allow you to hard-code the data type using the CIL constant notation shown in Table 17-4 (ldarg_I4, for an int32) as well as the data type and value (ldarg_I4_5, to load an int32 with the value of 5).
ldc (with numerous variations)	Loads a constant value onto the stack.
ldfld (with numerous variations)	Loads the value of an instance-level field onto the stack.
ldloc (with numerous variations)	Loads the value of a local variable onto the stack.
ldobj	Obtains all the values gathered by a heap-based object and places them on the stack.
ldstr	Loads a string value onto the stack.

In addition to the set of load-specific opcodes, CIL provides numerous opcodes that explicitly pop the topmost value off the stack. As shown over the first few examples in this chapter, popping a value off the stack typically involves storing the value into temporary local storage for further use (such as a parameter for an upcoming method invocation). Given this, note how many opcodes that pop the current value off the virtual execution stack take an st (store) prefix. Table 17-7 hits the highlights.

Table 17-7. Various Pop-Centric Opcodes

Opcode	Meaning in Life
pop	Removes the value currently on top of the evaluation stack, but does not bother to store the value
starg	Stores the value on top of the stack into the method argument at a specified index
stloc (with numerous variations)	Pops the current value from the top of the evaluation stack and stores it in a local variable list at a specified index
stobj	Copies a value of a specified type from the evaluation stack into a supplied memory address
stsfld	Replaces the value of a static field with a value from the evaluation stack

Do be aware that various CIL opcodes will *implicitly* pop values off the stack to perform the task at hand. For example, if you are attempting to subtract two numbers using the sub opcode, it should be clear that sub will have to pop off the next two available values before it can perform the calculation. Once the calculation is complete, the result of the value (surprise, surprise) is pushed onto the stack once again.

The .maxstack Directive

When you write method implementations using raw CIL, you need to be mindful of a special directive named .maxstack. As its name suggests, .maxstack establishes the maximum number of variables that may be pushed onto the stack at any given time during the execution of the method. The good news is that the .maxstack directive has a default value (8), which should be safe for a vast majority of methods you may be authoring. However, if you wish to be very explicit, you are able to manually calculate the number of local variables on the stack and define this value explicitly:

```
.method public hidebysig instance void
  Speak() cil managed
{
  // During the scope of this method, exactly
  // 1 value (the string literal) is on the stack.
  .maxstack  1
  ldstr "Hello there..."
  call void [mscorlib]System.Console::WriteLine(string)
  ret
}
```

Declaring Local Variables in CIL

Let's first check out how to declare a local variable. Assume you wish to build a Sub in CIL named MyLocalVariables() that takes no arguments. Within the method, you wish to define three local variables of type System.String, System.Int32, and System.Object. In VB 2010, this member would appear as follows (recall that locally scoped variables do not receive a default value and should be set to an initial state before further use):

```
Public Shared Sub MyLocalVariables()
        Dim myStr As String = "CIL code is fun!"
        Dim myInt As Integer = 33
        Dim myObj As New Object()
End Sub
```

If you were to construct MyLocalVariables() directly in CIL, you could author the following:

```
.method public hidebysig static void
  MyLocalVariables() cil managed
{
  .maxstack  8
  // Define three local variables.
  .locals init ([0] string myStr, [1] int32 myInt, [2] object myObj)
```

```
// Load a string onto the virtual execution stack.
ldstr "CIL code is fun!"
// Pop off current value and store in local variable [0].
stloc.0

// Load a constant of type "i4"
// (shorthand for int32) set to the value 33.
ldc.i4 33
// Pop off current value and store in local variable [1].
stloc.1

// Create a new object and place on stack.
newobj instance void [mscorlib]System.Object::.ctor()
// Pop off current value and store in local variable [2].
stloc.2
ret
}
```

As you can see, the first step taken to allocate local variables in raw CIL is to make use of the .locals directive, which is paired with the init attribute. Within the scope of the related parentheses, your goal is to associate a given numerical index to each variable (seen here as [0], [1], and [2]). As you can see, each index is identified by its data type and an optional variable name. Once the local variables have been defined, you load a value onto the stack (using the various load-centric opcodes) and store the value within the local variable (using the various storage-centric opcodes).

Mapping Parameters to Local Variables in CIL

You have already seen how to declare local variables in raw CIL using the .locals init directive; however, you have yet to see exactly how to map incoming parameters to local methods. Consider the following Shared VB 2010 method:

```
Public Shared Function Add(ByVal a As Integer,ByVal b As Integer)↵
  As Integer
        Return a + b
End Function
```

This innocent-looking method has a lot to say in terms of CIL. First, the incoming arguments (a and b) must be pushed onto the virtual execution stack using the ldarg (load argument) opcode. Next, the add opcode will be used to pop the next two values off the stack and find the summation, and store the value on the stack yet again. Finally, this sum is popped off the stack and returned to the caller via the ret opcode. If you were to disassemble this VB 2010 method using ildasm.exe, you would find numerous additional tokens injected by vbc.exe, but the crux of the CIL code is quite simple:

```
.method public hidebysig static int32  Add(int32 a,
  int32 b) cil managed
{
  .maxstack  2
  ldarg.0    // Load "a" onto the stack.
  ldarg.1    // Load "b" onto the stack.
  Add        // Add both values.
  ret
}
```

The Hidden Me Reference

Notice that the two incoming arguments (a and b) are referenced within the CIL code using their indexed position (index 0 and index 1), given that the virtual execution stack begins indexing at position 0.

One thing to be very mindful of when you are examining or authoring CIL code is that every nonshared method that takes incoming arguments automatically receives an implicit additional parameter, which is a reference to the current object (think the VB 2010 Me keyword). Given this, if the Add() method were defined as *non*shared:

```
'No longer Shared
Public Function Add(ByVal a As Integer, ByVal b As Integer) As Integer
        Return a + b
End Function
```

the incoming a and b arguments are loaded using ldarg.1 and ldarg.2 (rather than the expected ldarg.0 and ldarg.1 opcodes). Again, the reason is that slot 0 actually contains the implicit Me reference. Consider the following pseudo-code:

```
// This is JUST pseudo-code!
.method public hidebysig static int32 AddTwoIntParams(
  MyClass_HiddenThisPointer this, int32 a, int32 b) cil managed
{
  ldarg.0    // Load MyClass_HiddenThisPointer onto the stack.
  ldarg.1    // Load "a" onto the stack.
  ldarg.2    // Load "b" onto the stack.
...
}
```

Representing Iteration Constructs in CIL

Iteration constructs in the VB 2010 programming language are represented using the For, For Each, While, and Do constructs, each of which has a specific representation in CIL. Consider the classic For loop:

```
Public Shared Sub CountToTen()
        For i = 0 To 9
        Next
End Sub
```

Now, as you may recall, the **br** opcodes (**br**, **blt**, and so on) are used to control a break in flow when some condition has been met. In this example, you have set up a condition in which the **For** loop should break out of its cycle when the local variable **i** is equal to or greater than the value of 10. With each pass, the value of 1 is added to **i**, at which point the test condition is yet again evaluated.

Also recall that when you make use of any of the CIL branching opcodes, you will need to define a specific code label (or two) that marks the location to jump to when the condition is indeed true. Given these points, ponder the following (augmented) CIL code generated via **ildasm.exe** (including the autogenerated code labels):

```
.method public hidebysig static void CountToTen() cil managed
{
  .maxstack  2
  .locals init ([0] int32 i)   // Init the local integer "i".
  IL_0000:  ldc.i4.0           // Load this value onto the stack.
  IL_0001:  stloc.0            // Store this value at index "0".
  IL_0002:  br.s IL_0008       // Jump to IL_0008.
  IL_0004:  ldloc.0            // Load value of variable at index 0.
  IL_0005:  ldc.i4.1           // Load the value "1" on the stack.
  IL_0006:  add                // Add current value on the stack at index 0.
  IL_0007:  stloc.0
  IL_0008:  ldloc.0            // Load value at index "0".
  IL_0009:  ldc.i4.s    10     // Load value of "10" onto the stack.
  IL_000b:  blt.s IL_0004      // Less than?  If so, jump back to IL_0004
  IL_000d:  ret
}
```

In a nutshell, this CIL code begins by defining the local **int32** and loading it onto the stack. At this point, you jump back and forth between code label **IL_0008** and **IL_0004**, each time bumping the value of **i** by 1 and testing to see whether **i** is still less than the value **10**. If so, you exit the method.

■ **Source Code** The CilTypes example is included under the Chapter 17 subdirectory.

Building a .NET Assembly with CIL

Now that you've taken a tour of the syntax and semantics of raw CIL, it's time to solidify your current understanding by building a .NET application using nothing but **ilasm.exe** and your text editor of choice. Specifically, your application will consist of a privately deployed, single-file *.dll that contains two class type definitions, and a console-based *.exe that interacts with these types.

Building CILCars.dll

The first order of business is to build the *.dll to be consumed by the client. Open a text editor and create a new *.il file named **CILCars.il**. This single-file assembly will make use of two external .NET assemblies. Begin by updating your code file as follows:

```
// Reference mscorlib.dll and
// System.Windows.Forms.dll
.assembly extern mscorlib
{
  .publickeytoken = (B7 7A 5C 56 19 34 E0 89 )
  .ver 4:0:0:0
}
.assembly extern System.Windows.Forms
{
  .publickeytoken = (B7 7A 5C 56 19 34 E0 89 )
  .ver 4:0:0:0
}

// Define the single-file assembly.
.assembly CILCars
{
  .hash algorithm 0x00008004
  .ver 1:0:0:0
}
.module CILCars.dll
```

This assembly will contain two class types. The first type, CILCar, defines two points of field data and a custom constructor. The second type, CarInfoHelper, defines a single Shared Sub named DisplayCarInfo(), which takes CILCar as a parameter and has no return value. Both types are in the CILCars namespace. In terms of CIL, CILCar can be implemented as follows:

```
// Implementation of CILCars.CILCar type.
.namespace CILCars
{
  .class public auto ansi beforefieldinit CILCar
    extends [mscorlib]System.Object
  {
    // The field data of the CILCar.
    .field public string petName
    .field public int32 currSpeed

    // The custom constructor simply allows the caller
    // to assign the field data.
    .method public hidebysig specialname rtspecialname
        instance void .ctor(int32 c, string p) cil managed
    {
      .maxstack  8

      // Load first arg onto the stack and call base class ctor.
      ldarg.0  // "this" object, not the int32!
      call instance void [mscorlib]System.Object::.ctor()

      // Now load first and second args onto the stack.
      ldarg.0  // "this" object
      ldarg.1  // int32 arg
```

```
    // Store topmost stack (int 32) member in currSpeed field.
    stfld int32 CILCars.CILCar::currSpeed

    // Load string arg and store in petName field.
    ldarg.0  // "this" object
    ldarg.2  // string arg
    stfld string CILCars.CILCar::petName
    ret
  }
 }
}
```

Keeping in mind that the real first argument for any nonshared member is the current object reference, the first block of CIL simply loads the object reference and calls the base class constructor. Next, you push the incoming constructor arguments onto the stack and store them into the type's field data using the `stfld` (store in field) opcode.

Now let's implement the second type in this namespace: `CILCarInfo`. The meat of the type is found within the Shared `Display()` method. In a nutshell, the role of this method is to take the incoming `CILCar` parameter, extract the values of its field data, and display it in a Windows Forms message box. Here is the complete implementation of `CILCarInfo` (which should be defined within the `CILCars` namespace) with analysis to follow:

```
.class public auto ansi beforefieldinit CILCarInfo
  extends [mscorlib]System.Object
{
  .method public hidebysig static void
    Display(class CILCars.CILCar c) cil managed
  {
    .maxstack  8

    // We need a local string variable.
    .locals init ([0] string caption)

    // Load string and the incoming CILCar onto the stack.
    ldstr "{0}'s speed is:"
    ldarg.0

    // Now place the value of the CILCar's petName on the
    // stack and call the static String.Format() method.
    ldfld string CILCars.CILCar::petName
    call string [mscorlib]System.String::Format(string, object)
    stloc.0

    // Now load the value of the currSpeed field and get its string
    // representation (note call to ToString() ).
    ldarg.0
    ldflda int32 CILCars.CILCar::currSpeed
    call instance string [mscorlib]System.Int32::ToString()
    ldloc.0
```

```
// Now call the MessageBox.Show() method with loaded values.
call valuetype [System.Windows.Forms]
      System.Windows.Forms.DialogResult
      [System.Windows.Forms]
      System.Windows.Forms.MessageBox::Show(string, string)
  pop
  ret
  }
}
```

Although the amount of CIL code is a bit more than you see in the implementation of CILCar, things are still rather straightforward. First, given that you are defining a Shared method, you don't have to be concerned with the hidden object reference (thus, the ldarg.0 opcode really does load the incoming CILCar argument).

The method begins by loading a string ("{0}'s speed is") onto the stack, followed by the CILCar argument. Once these two values are in place, you load the value of the petName field and call the Shared System.String.Format() method to substitute the curly bracket placeholder with the CILCar's pet name.

The same general procedure takes place when processing the currSpeed field, but note that you use the ldflda opcode, which loads the argument address onto the stack. At this point, you call System.Int32.ToString() to transform the value at said address into a String type. Finally, once both strings have been formatted as necessary, you call the MessageBox.Show() method.

At this point, you are able to compile your new *.dll using ilasm.exe with the following command:

```
ilasm /dll CILCars.il
```

and verify the contained CIL using peverify.exe:

```
peverify CILCars.dll
```

Building CILCarClient.exe

Now you can build a simple *.exe assembly with a Main() method that will

- Make a CILCar object.

- Pass the object into the Shared CILCarInfo.Display() method.

Create a new file named CarClient.il and define external references to mscorlib.dll and CILCars.dll (don't forget to place a copy of this .NET assembly in the client's application directory!). Next, define a single type (Module1) that manipulates the CILCars.dll assembly. Here's the complete code:

```
// External assembly refs.
.assembly extern mscorlib
{
  .publickeytoken = (B7 7A 5C 56 19 34 E0 89)
  .ver 4:0:0:0
}
.assembly extern CILCars
{
  .ver 1:0:0:0
}

// Our executable assembly.
.assembly CarClient
{
  .hash algorithm 0x00008004
  .ver 1:0:0:0
}
.module CarClient.exe

// Implementation of Module1 type
.namespace CarClient
{
  .class private auto ansi beforefieldinit Module1
  extends [mscorlib]System.Object
  {
    .method private hidebysig static void
    Main(string[] args) cil managed
    {
      // Marks the entry point of the *.exe.
      .entrypoint
      .maxstack  8

      // Declare a local CILCar variable and push
      // values on the stack for ctor call.
      .locals init ([0] class
      [CILCars.]CILCar s.CILCar myCilCar)
      ldc.i4.  55
      ldstr "Junior"

      // Make new CilCar; store and load reference.
      newobj instance void
        [CILCars]CILCars.CILCar::.ctor(int32, string)
      stloc.0
      ldloc.0
```

```
// Call Display() and pass in topmost value on stack.
call void [CILCars]
    CILCars.CILCarInfo::Display(
        class [CILCars]CILCars.CILCar)
    ret
  }
 }
}
```

The one opcode that is important to point out is .entrypoint. Recall from the discussion earlier in this chapter that this opcode is used to mark which method of an *.exe functions as the entry point of the module. In fact, given that .entrypoint is how the CLR identifies the initial method to execute, this method can be called anything, although here you are using the standard method name of Main(). The remainder of the CIL code found in the Main() method is your basic pushing and popping of stack-based values.

Do note, however, that the creation of a CILCar object involves the use of the .newobj opcode. On a related note, recall that when you wish to invoke a member of a type using raw CIL, you make use of the double-colon syntax and, as always, make use of the fully qualified name of the type. With this, you can compile your new file with ilasm.exe, verify your assembly with peverify.exe, and execute your program. Issue the following commands within your command prompt:

```
ilasm CarClient.il
peverify CarClient.exe
CarClient.exe
```

Figure 17-4 shows the end result.

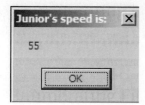

Figure 17-4. Your CILCar in action

■ **Source Code** The CilCars example is included under the Chapter 17 subdirectory.

Understanding Dynamic Assemblies

To be sure, the process of building a complex .NET application in CIL would be quite the labor of love. On the one hand, CIL is an extremely expressive programming language that allows you to interact with all of the programming constructs allowed by the CTS. On the other hand, authoring raw CIL is tedious, error-prone, and painful. While it is true that knowledge is power, you may indeed wonder just how important it is to commit the laws of CIL syntax to memory. The answer is, "It depends." To be sure, most of your .NET programming endeavors will not require you to view, edit, or author CIL code. However, with the CIL primer behind you, you are now ready to investigate the world of dynamic assemblies (as opposed to static assemblies) and the role of the `System.Reflection.Emit` namespace.

The first question you may have is, "What exactly is the difference between static and dynamic assemblies?" By definition, *static assemblies* are .NET binaries loaded directly from disk storage, meaning they are located somewhere on your hard drive in a physical file (or possibly a set of files in the case of a multifile assembly) at the time the CLR requests them. As you might guess, every time you compile your VB 2010 source code, you end up with a static assembly.

A *dynamic assembly*, on the other hand, is created in memory on the fly using the types provided by the `System.Reflection.Emit` namespace. The `System.Reflection.Emit` namespace makes it possible to create an assembly and its modules, type definitions, and CIL implementation logic at *runtime*. Once you have done so, you are then free to save your in-memory binary to disk. This, of course, results in a new static assembly. To be sure, the process of building a dynamic assembly using the `System.Reflection.Emit` namespace does require some level of understanding regarding the nature of CIL opcodes.

Although creating dynamic assemblies is a fairly advanced (and uncommon) programming task, they can be useful under various circumstances:

- You are building a .NET programming tool that needs to generate assemblies on demand based on user input.

- You are building a program that needs to generate proxies to remote types on the fly based on the obtained metadata.

- You wish to load a static assembly and dynamically insert new types into the binary image.

Several aspects of the .NET runtime engine involve generating dynamic assemblies quietly in the background. For example, ASP.NET makes use of this technique to map markup and server-side script code into a runtime object model. LINQ also can generate code on the fly based on various query expressions. This being said, let's check out the types within `System.Reflection.Emit`.

Exploring the System.Reflection.Emit Namespace

Creating a dynamic assembly requires you to have some familiarity with CIL opcodes, but the types of the `System.Reflection.Emit` namespace hide the complexity of CIL as much as possible. For example, rather than directly specifying the necessary CIL directives and attributes to define a class type, you can simply make use of the `TypeBuilder` class. Likewise, if you wish to define a new instance-level constructor, you have no need to emit the `specialname`, `rtspecialname`, or `.ctor` tokens; rather, you can make use of the `ConstructorBuilder`. Table 17-8 documents the key members of the `System.Reflection.Emit` namespace.

Table 17-8. Select Members of the System.Reflection.Emit Namespace

Members	Meaning in Life
AssemblyBuilder	Used to create an assembly (*.dll or *.exe) at runtime. *.exes must call the ModuleBuilder.SetEntryPoint() method to set the method that is the entry point to the module. If no entry point is specified, a *.dll will be generated.
ModuleBuilder	Used to define the set of modules within the current assembly.
EnumBuilder	Used to create a .NET enumeration type.
TypeBuilder	May be used to create classes, interfaces, structures, and delegates within a module at runtime.
MethodBuilder LocalBuilder PropertyBuilder FieldBuilder ConstructorBuilder CustomAttributeBuilder ParameterBuilder EventBuilder	Used to create type members (such as methods, local variables, properties, constructors, and attributes) at runtime.
ILGenerator	Emits CIL opcodes into a given type member.
OpCodes	Provides numerous fields that map to CIL opcodes. This type is used in conjunction with the various members of System.Reflection.Emit.ILGenerator.

In general, the types of the System.Reflection.Emit namespace allow you to represent raw CIL tokens programmatically during the construction of your dynamic assembly. You will see many of these members in the example that follows; however, the ILGenerator type is worth checking out straightaway.

The Role of the System.Reflection.Emit.ILGenerator

As its name implies, the ILGenerator type's role is to inject CIL opcodes into a given type member. However, you cannot directly create ILGenerator objects, as this type has no Public constructors, rather you receive an ILGenerator type by calling specific methods of the builder-centric types (such as the MethodBuilder and ConstructorBuilder types), for example:

```
'Obtain an ILGenerator from a ConstructorBuilder
'object named "myCtorBuilder".
Dim myCtorBuilder As New ConstructorBuilder()
Dim myCILGen As ILGenerator = myCtorBuilder.GetILGenerator()
```

Once you have an `ILGenerator` in your hands, you are then able to emit the raw CIL opcodes using any number of methods. Table 17-9 documents some (but not all) methods of `ILGenerator`.

Table 17-9. Various Methods of ILGenerator

Method	Meaning in Life
BeginCatchBlock()	Begins a `Catch` block
BeginExceptionBlock()	Begins an exception block for a nonfiltered exception
BeginFinallyBlock()	Begins a `Finally` block
BeginScope()	Begins a lexical scope
DeclareLocal()	Declares a local variable
DefineLabel()	Declares a new label
Emit()	Is overloaded numerous times to allow you to emit CIL opcodes
EmitCall()	Pushes a `call` or `callvirt` opcode into the CIL stream
EmitWriteLine()	Emits a call to `Console.WriteLine()` with different types of values
EndExceptionBlock()	Ends an exception block
EndScope()	Ends a lexical scope
ThrowException()	Emits an instruction to throw an exception
UsingNamespace()	Specifies the namespace to be used in evaluating locals and watches for the current active lexical scope

The key method of `ILGenerator` is `Emit()`, which works in conjunction with the `System.Reflection.Emit.OpCodes` class type. As mentioned earlier in this chapter, this type exposes a good number of read-only fields that map to raw CIL opcodes. The full set of these members are all documented within online help, and you will see various examples in the pages that follow.

Emitting a Dynamic Assembly

To illustrate the process of defining a .NET assembly at runtime, let's walk through the process of creating a single-file dynamic assembly named `MyAssembly.dll`. Within this module is a class named `HelloWorld`. The `HelloWorld` class supports a default constructor and a custom constructor that is used to assign the value of a Private member variable (`theMessage`) of type `String`. In addition, `HelloWorld` supports a Public instance method named `SayHello()`, which prints a greeting to the standard I/O stream, and another instance method named GetMsg(), which returns the internal Private String. In effect, you are going to programmatically generate the following class type:

```
'This class will be created at runtime
Public Class HelloWorld

    Private theMessage As String

    Sub New()
    End Sub

    Sub New(ByVal s As String)
        theMessage = s
    End Sub

    Public Function GetMsg() As String
        Return theMessage
    End Function

    Public Sub SayHello()
        System.Console.WriteLine("Hello from the HelloWorld class!")
    End Sub
End Class
```

Assume you have created a new Visual Studio 2010 Console Application project workspace named DynamicAsmBuilder and import the System.Reflection, System.Reflection.Emit, and -System.Threading namespaces. Define a Shared method named CreateMyAsm(). This single method is in charge of the following:

- Defining the characteristics of the dynamic assembly (name, version, etc.)

- Implementing the HelloClass type

- Saving the in-memory assembly to a physical file

Also note that the CreateMyAsm() method takes as a single parameter a System.AppDomain type, which will be used to obtain access to the AssemblyBuilder type associated with the current application domain (see Chapter 17 for a discussion of .NET application domains). Here is the complete code, with analysis to follow:

```
'The caller sends in an AppDomain type.
Public Sub CreateMyAsm(ByVal curAppDomain As AppDomain)

    'Establish general assembly characteristics.
    Dim assemblyName As New AssemblyName()
    assemblyName.Name = "MyAssembly"
    assemblyName.Version = New Version("1.0.0.0")

    'Create new assembly within the current AppDomain.
    Dim assembly As AssemblyBuilder = curAppDomain.DefineDynamicAssembly(assemblyName,
    AssemblyBuilderAccess.Save)
```

```vb
'Given that we are building a single-file
'assembly, the name of the module is the same as the assembly.
Dim theMod As ModuleBuilder = assembly.DefineDynamicModule
        ("MyAssembly", "MyAssembly.dll")

'Define a public class named "MyAssembly.HelloWorld".
Dim helloWorldClass As TypeBuilder = theMod.DefineType
        ("MyAssembly.HelloWorld", TypeAttributes.Public)

'Define a private String member variable named "theMessage".
Dim msgField As FieldBuilder = helloWorldClass.DefineField("theMessage", Type.GetType
        ("System.String"), FieldAttributes.Private)

'Create the custom ctor.
Dim constructorArgs As Type() = New Type(0) {}
constructorArgs(0) = GetType(String)

Dim constructor As ConstructorBuilder =
helloWorldClass.DefineConstructor(MethodAttributes.Public,
            CallingConventions.Standard, constructorArgs)
Dim constructorIL As ILGenerator = constructor.GetILGenerator()
constructorIL.Emit(OpCodes.Ldarg_0)

Dim objectClass As Type = GetType(Object)
Dim superConstructor As ConstructorInfo = objectClass.GetConstructor
            (New Type() {})

constructorIL.Emit(OpCodes.Call, superConstructor)
constructorIL.Emit(OpCodes.Ldarg_0)
constructorIL.Emit(OpCodes.Ldarg_1)
constructorIL.Emit(OpCodes.Stfld, msgField)
constructorIL.Emit(OpCodes.Ret)

'Create the default ctor.
helloWorldClass.DefineDefaultConstructor(MethodAttributes.Public)

'Now create the GetMsg() method.
Dim getMsgMethod As MethodBuilder = helloWorldClass.DefineMethod("GetMsg",
 MethodAttributes.Public
                GetType(String), Nothing)

Dim methodIL As ILGenerator = getMsgMethod.GetILGenerator()
methodIL.Emit(OpCodes.Ldarg_0)
methodIL.Emit(OpCodes.Ldfld, msgField)
methodIL.Emit(OpCodes.Ret)

'Create the SayHello method.
Dim sayHiMethod As MethodBuilder = helloWorldClass.DefineMethod("SayHello",
MethodAttributes.Public
                ,Nothing, Nothing)
```

```
        methodIL = sayHiMethod.GetILGenerator()
        methodIL.EmitWriteLine("Hello from the HelloWorld class!")
        methodIL.Emit(OpCodes.Ret)

        ' 'Bake' the class HelloWorld.
        '(Baking is the formal term for emitting the type)
        helloWorldClass.CreateType()

        '(Optionally) save the assembly to file.
        assembly.Save("MyAssembly.dll")
End Sub
```

Emitting the Assembly and Module Set

The method body begins by establishing the minimal set of characteristics about your assembly, using the `AssemblyName` and `Version` types (defined in the `System.Reflection` namespace). Next, you obtain an `AssemblyBuilder` type via the instance-level `AppDomain.DefineDynamicAssembly()` method (recall the caller will pass in an `AppDomain` reference into the `CreateMyAsm()` method):

```
'Establish general assembly characteristics
'and gain access to the AssemblyBuilder type.
        Public Sub CreateMyAsm(ByVal curAppDomain As AppDomain)

        Dim assemblyName As New AssemblyName()
        assemblyName.Name = "MyAssembly"
        assemblyName.Version = New Version("1.0.0.0")

        'Create new assembly within the current AppDomain.
        Dim assembly As AssemblyBuilder = curAppDomain.
                        DefineDynamicAssembly
                        (assemblyName, AssemblyBuilderAccess.Save)
        ...
End Sub
```

As you can see, when calling `AppDomain.DefineDynamicAssembly()`, you must specify the access mode of the assembly you wish to define, which can be any of the values shown in Table 17-10.

Table 17-10. Values of the AssemblyBuilderAccess Enumeration

Value	Meaning in Life
ReflectionOnly	Represents that a dynamic assembly that can only be reflected over
Run	Represents that a dynamic assembly can be executed in memory but not saved to disk
RunAndSave	Represents that a dynamic assembly can be executed in memory and saved to disk
Save	Represents that a dynamic assembly can be saved to disk but not executed in memory

The next task is to define the module set for your new assembly. Given that the assembly is a single file unit, you need to define only a single module. If you were to build a multi-file assembly using the DefineDynamicModule() method, you would specify an optional second parameter that represents the name of a given module (e.g., myMod.dotnetmodule). However, when creating a single-file assembly, the name of the module will be identical to the name of the assembly itself. In any case, once the DefineDynamicModule() method has returned, you are provided with a reference to a valid ModuleBuilder type:

```
'The single-file assembly.
Dim theMod As ModuleBuilder = assembly.DefineDynamicModule
                ("MyAssembly", "MyAssembly.dll")
```

The Role of the ModuleBuilder Type

ModuleBuilder is the key type used during the development of dynamic assemblies. As you would expect, ModuleBuilder supports a number of members that allow you to define the set of types contained within a given module (classes, interfaces, structures, etc.) as well as the set of embedded resources (string tables, images, etc.) contained within. Table 17-11 describes a few of the creation-centric methods. (Do note that each method will return to you a related type that represents the type you wish to construct.)

Table 17-11. Select Members of the ModuleBuilder Type

Method	Meaning in Life
DefineEnum()	Used to emit a .NET enum definition
DefineResource()	Defines a managed embedded resource to be stored in this module
DefineType()	Constructs a TypeBuilder, which allows you to define value types, interfaces, and class types (including delegates)

The key member of the ModuleBuilder class to be aware of is DefineType(). In addition to specifying the name of the type (via a simple string), you will also make use of the System.Reflection.TypeAttributes enum to describe the format of the type itself. Table 17-12 lists some (but not all) of the key members of the TypeAttributes enumeration.

Table 17-12. Select Members of the `TypeAttributes` *Enumeration*

Member	Meaning in Life
Abstract	Specifies that the type is MustInherit
Class	Specifies that the type is a class
Interface	Specifies that the type is an interface
NestedAssembly	Specifies that the class is nested with assembly visibility and is thus accessible only by methods within its assembly
NestedFamAndAssem	Specifies that the class is nested with assembly and family visibility, and is thus accessible only by methods lying in the intersection of its family and assembly
NestedFamily	Specifies that the class is nested with family visibility and is thus accessible only by methods within its own type and any subtypes
NestedFamORAssem	Specifies that the class is nested with family or assembly visibility, and is thus accessible only by methods lying in the union of its family and assembly
NestedPrivate	Specifies that the class is nested with private visibility
NestedPublic	Specifies that the class is nested with public visibility
NotPublic	Specifies that the class is not public
Public	Specifies that the class is public
Sealed	Specifies that the class is concrete and cannot be extended.
Serializable	Specifies that the class can be serialized

Emitting the HelloClass Type and the String Member Variable

Now that you have a better understanding of the role of the `ModuleBuilder.CreateType()` method, let's examine how you can emit the Public `HelloWorld` class type and the Private String variable:

```
'Define a public class named "MyAssembly.HelloWorld".
Dim helloWorldClass As TypeBuilder = theMod.DefineType
            ("MyAssembly.HelloWorld", TypeAttributes.Public)
```

```
'Define a private String member variable named "theMessage".
Dim msgField As FieldBuilder = helloWorldClass.DefineField
            ("theMessage", Type.GetType("System.String"),
                FieldAttributes.Private)
```

Notice how the `TypeBuilder.DefineField()` method provides access to a `FieldBuilder` type. The `TypeBuilder` class also defines other methods that provide access to other "builder" types. For example, `DefineConstructor()` returns a `ConstructorBuilder`, `DefineProperty()` returns a `PropertyBuilder`, and so forth.

Emitting the Constructors

As mentioned earlier, the `TypeBuilder.DefineConstructor()` method can be used to define a constructor for the current type. However, when it comes to implementing the constructor of `HelloClass`, you need to inject raw CIL code into the constructor body, which is responsible for assigning the incoming parameter to the internal Private String. To obtain an `ILGenerator` type, you call the `GetILGenerator()` method from the respective "builder" type you have reference to (in this case, the `ConstructorBuilder` type).

The `Emit()` method of the `ILGenerator` class is the entity in charge of placing CIL into a member implementation. `Emit()` itself makes frequent use of the `OpCodes` class type, which exposes the opcode set of CIL using read-only fields. For example, `OpCodes.Ret` signals the return of a method call. `OpCodes.Stfld` makes an assignment to a member variable. `OpCodes.Call` is used to call a given method (in this case, the base class constructor). That said, ponder the following constructor logic:

```
'Create the custom constructor taking
'a single System.String argument.
Dim constructorArgs As Type() = New Type(0) {}
constructorArgs(0) = GetType(String)

Dim constructor As ConstructorBuilder = helloWorldClass.
                DefineConstructor(MethodAttributes.Public,
                CallingConventions.Standard, constructorArgs)

' Now emit the necessary CIL into the ctor.
Dim constructorIL As ILGenerator = constructor.GetILGenerator()
                constructorIL.Emit(OpCodes.Ldarg_0)

Dim objectClass As Type = GetType(Object)

Dim superConstructor As ConstructorInfo = objectClass.GetConstructor
                (New Type() {})

'Call base class ctor.
constructorIL.Emit(OpCodes.Call, superConstructor)

'Load the object's "Me" pointer on the stack.
constructorIL.Emit(OpCodes.Ldarg_0)
```

```
'Load incoming argument on virtual stack and store in msgField.
constructorIL.Emit(OpCodes.Ldarg_1)

constructorIL.Emit(OpCodes.Stfld, msgField) 'Assign msgField.
constructorIL.Emit(OpCodes.Ret)              'Return.
```

Now, as you are well aware, as soon as you define a custom constructor for a type, the default constructor is silently removed. To redefine the no-argument constructor, simply call the DefineDefaultConstructor() method of the TypeBuilder type as follows:

```
'Reinsert the default ctor.
helloWorldClass.DefineDefaultConstructor(MethodAttributes.Public)
```

This single call emits the standard CIL code used to define a default constructor:

```
.method public specialname rtspecialname
  instance void  .ctor() cil managed
{
  .maxstack  8
  ldarg.0
  call instance void [mscorlib]System.Object::.ctor()
  ret
}
```

Emitting the SayHello() Method

Last but not least, let's examine the process of emitting the SayHello() method. The first task is to obtain a MethodBuilder type from the helloWorldClass variable. Once you do this, you define the method and obtain the underlying ILGenerator to inject the CIL instructions:

```
'Create the SayHello method.
Dim sayHiMethod As MethodBuilder = helloWorldClass.DefineMethod("SayHello",↵
 MethodAttributes.Public,
                            Nothing, Nothing)
methodIL = sayHiMethod.GetILGenerator()

'write a line to Console
methodIL.EmitWriteLine("Hello from the HelloWorld class!")
methodIL.Emit(OpCodes.Ret)
```

Here you have established a Public method (MethodAttributes.Public) that takes no parameters and returns nothing (marked by the Nothing entries contained in the DefineMethod() call). Also note the EmitWriteLine() call. This helper member of the ILGenerator class automatically writes a line to the standard output with minimal fuss and bother.

Using the Dynamically Generated Assembly

Now that you have the logic in place to create and save your assembly, all that's needed is a class to trigger the logic. To come full circle, assume your current project defines a Module named AsmReader.

The logic in `Main()` obtains the current AppDomain via the `Thread.GetDomain()` method that will be used to host the assembly you will dynamically create. Once you have a reference, you are able to call the `CreateMyAsm()` method.

To make things a bit more interesting, once the call to `CreateMyAsm()` returns, you will exercise some late binding (see Chapter 15) to load your newly created assembly into memory and interact with the members of the `HelloWorld` class. Update your `Main()` method as follows:

```
Sub Main()
        Console.WriteLine("**The Amazing Dynamic Assembly Builder App **")
        'Get the application domain for the current thread.
        Dim curAppDomain As AppDomain = Thread.GetDomain()

        'Create the dynamic assembly using our helper method.
        CreateMyAsm(curAppDomain)
        Console.WriteLine("-> Finished creating MyAssembly.dll.")

        'Now load the new assembly from file.
        Console.WriteLine("-> Loading MyAssembly.dll from file.")
        Dim a As Assembly = Assembly.Load("MyAssembly")

        'Get the HelloWorld type.
        Dim hello As Type = a.GetType("MyAssembly.HelloWorld")

        'Create HelloWorld object and call the correct ctor.
        Console.Write("-> Enter message to pass HelloWorld class: ")
        Dim msg As String = Console.ReadLine()

        Dim ctorArgs As Object() = New Object(0) {}
        ctorArgs(0) = msg
        Dim obj As Object = Activator.CreateInstance(hello, ctorArgs)

        'Call SayHello and show returned string.
        Console.WriteLine("-> Calling SayHello() via late binding.")
        Dim mi As MethodInfo = hello.GetMethod("SayHello")
        mi.Invoke(obj, Nothing)

        'Invoke method.
        mi = hello.GetMethod("GetMsg")
        Console.WriteLine(mi.Invoke(obj, Nothing))
        Console.ReadLine()
End Sub
```

In effect, you have just created a .NET assembly that is able to create and execute .NET assemblies at runtime! That wraps up the examination of CIL and the role of dynamic assemblies. I hope this chapter has deepened your understanding of the .NET type system and the syntax and semantics of CIL.

■ **Source Code** The DynamicAsmBuilder project is included under the Chapter 17 subdirectory.

Summary

This chapter provided an overview of the syntax and semantics of CIL. Unlike higher-level managed languages such as VB 2010, CIL does not simply define a set of keywords, but provides directives (used to define the structure of an assembly and its types), attributes (which further qualify a given directive), and opcodes (which are used to implement type members).

You were introduced to a few CIL-centric programming tools (`ilasm.exe`, SharpDevelop and `peverify.exe`), and learned how to alter the contents of a .NET assembly with new CIL instructions using round-trip engineering. After this point, you spent time learning how to establish the current (and referenced) assembly, namespaces, types and members. I wrapped up with a simple example of building a .NET code library and executable using little more than CIL, command line tools, and a bit of elbow grease.

Finally, you took an introductory look at the process of creating a *dynamic assembly*. Using the `System.Reflection.Emit` namespace, it is possible to define a .NET assembly in memory at runtime. As you have seen firsthand, using this particular API requires you to know the semantics of CIL code in some detail. While the need to build dynamic assemblies is certainly not a common task for most .NET applications, it can be very useful for those of you who need to build support tools and other programming utilities.

CHAPTER 18

■ ■ ■

Dynamic Types and the Dynamic Language Runtime

.NET 4.0 introduces a new concept to the VB 2010 language, specifically, dynamic typing. This allows you to incorporate scripting like behaviors into the strongly typed world of VB 2010. Using this loose typing, you can greatly simplify some complex coding tasks and also gain the ability to interoperate with a number of dynamic languages (such as IronRuby or IronPython) which are .NET savvy.

In this chapter, you will learn all about the dynamic typing, and understand how loosely typed calls are mapped to the correct in memory object using the *Dynamic Language Runtime* (or, DLR). Once you understand the services provided by the DLR, you will see examples of using dynamic types to streamline how you can perform late bound method calls (via reflection services) and to easily communicate with legacy COM libraries.

Basics of Dynamic Typing in VB 2010

Dynamic typing allows you to tell the compiler that the type of an object can be known only at run time, and the compiler doesn't try to interfere. As a result, you can write less code. Dynamic typing is also known as late binding.

The Visual Basic 2010 language compiler performs a process called *binding* when an object is assigned to an object variable. An object is early bound when it is assigned to a variable declared to be of a specific object type. Early bound objects allow the compiler to allocate memory and perform other optimizations before an application executes. For example, the following code fragment declares a variable to be of type `FileStream`:

```
' Create a variable to hold a new object.
Dim fs As New System.IO.FileStream
```

By contrast, an object is *late bound* when it is assigned to a variable declared to be of type `Object`. Objects of this type can hold references to any object, but they lack many of the advantages of early bound objects.

Option Strict plays a key role in VB 2010 for early or late binding. If you want to achieve late binding, then Option Strict Off is recommended. Option Strict On provides *strong typing*, disallows late binding, and improves performance; its use is strongly recommended.

```
' Compile with Option Strict Off to allow late binding.
Dim obj1 As Object
Dim obj2 As Object
```

The VB 2010 compiler default is Option Strict Off. You can always tweak the Option Strict On/Off setting from your project's properties Compile tab, as shown in Figure 18-1.

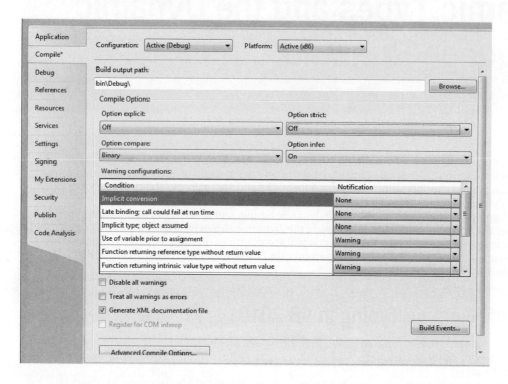

Figure 18-1. Option Strict with VB 2010

The Role of Dynamic Typing in VB 2010

As you learned earlier in the book, VB 2010 supports the concept of implicit types. This mechanism allows you to declare a local variable without specifying its data type. VB 2010 is capable of determining the underlying date type from the initial assignment.

Once this initial assignment has been made, you have a strongly typed variable, and any attempt to assign an incompatible value will result in a compiler error.

To begin your investigation into the **dynamic** typing in VB 2010, create a new Console Application named DynamicType. Now, author the following method in your module, and verify that the final code statement will indeed trigger a compile time error if the statement `'a = "Hello"` is uncommented in the following code:

```
Sub ImplicitlyTypedVariable()

        'a is of type List(Of Integer).
        Dim a = New List(Of Integer)()
        a.Add(90)

        'This would be a compile time error!
        'a = "Hello"
End Sub
```

Using implicit typing simply for the sake of doing so is considered bad style (if you know you need a List(Of Integer), just declare a List(Of Integer)). However, as you have seen in Chapter 13, implicit typing is very useful with LINQ, as many LINQ queries return back enumerations of anonymous class (via projections) which you cannot directly declare in your VB 2010 code. However even in such cases, the implicitly typed variable is, in fact, strongly typed.

On a related note, as you also learned back in Chapter 6, System.Object is the top-most parent class in the .NET framework, and can represent anything at all. Again, if you declare a variable of type Object, you have a strongly typed piece of data, however what it points to in memory can differ based on your assignment of the reference. In order to gain access to the members the object reference is pointing to in memory, you need to perform an explicit cast.

Assume you have a simple class named Person that defines two automatic properties (FirstName and LastName) both encapsulating a String. Now, observer the following code:

```
Sub UseObjectVariable()

        'Assume we have a class named Person.
        Dim o As Object = New Person() With {.FirstName = "Mike", .LastName = "Larson"}

        'Must cast object as Person to gain access TheSansMonoConNormal
        'to the Person properties.
        Console.WriteLine("Person's first name is {0}", (CType(o, Person)).FirstName)
End Sub
```

With the release of .NET 4.0, the VB 2010 language now supports a new concept named dynamic typing. From a high level, you can consider the dynamic typing a specialized form of System.Object, in that any value can be assigned to a dynamic data type. At first glance, this can appear horribly confusing, as it appears you now have three ways to define data whose underlying type is not directly indicated in our code base. For example, this method:

```
Sub PrintThreeStrings()
        Dim s1 = "Greetings"
        Dim s2 As Object = "From"
        Dim s3 As Object = "Minneapolis"

        Console.WriteLine("s1 is of type: {0}", s1.GetType())
        Console.WriteLine("s2 is of type: {0}", s2.GetType())
        Console.WriteLine("s3 is of type: {0}", s3.GetType())
End Sub
```

would print out the following if invoked from `Main()`:

```
s1 is of type: System.String

s2 is of type: System.String

s3 is of type: System.String
```

What makes a dynamic variable much (much) different from a variable declared implicitly or via a `System.Object` reference is that it is *not strongly typed*. Said another way, dynamic data is not *statically typed*. As far as the VB 2010 compiler is concerned, a data point declared as dynamic type can be assigned any initial value at all, and can be reassigned to any new (and possibly unrelated) value during its lifetime. Consider the following method, and the resulting output:

```
Sub ChangeDynamicDataType()

    'Declare a single dynamic data point
    'named 't'.
    Dim t As Object = "Hello!"
    Console.WriteLine("t is of type: {0}", t.GetType())
      t = False
     Console.WriteLine("t is of type: {0}", t.GetType())
     t = New List(Of Integer)()
      Console.WriteLine("t is of type: {0}", t.GetType())
End Sub
```

```
t is of type: System.String

t is of type: System.Boolean

t is of type: System.Collections.Generic.List`1[System.Int32]
```

Now, at this point in your investigation, do be aware that the previous code would compile and execute identically if you were to declare the `t` variable as a `System.Object`. However, as you will soon see, dynamic typing offers many additional features.

Calling Members on Dynamically Declared Data

Now, given that a dynamic data type can take on the identity of any type on the fly (just like a variable of type `System.Object`), the next question on your mind might be about calling members on the dynamic variable (properties, methods, indexers, register with events, etc). Well, syntactically speaking, it will again look no different. Just apply the dot operator to the dynamic data variable, specify a Public member, and supply any arguments (if required).

However (and this is a very big "however"), the validity of the members you specify will not be checked by the compiler! Remember, unlike a variable defined as a `System.Object`, dynamic data is not statically typed. It is not until runtime that you will know if you invoked the dynamic data supports a specified member, if you passed in the correct parameters, spelled the member correctly, and so on. Thus, as strange as it might seem, the following method compiles perfectly:

```
Sub InvokeMembersOnDynamicData()

        Dim textData1 As Object= "Hello"
        Console.WriteLine(textData1.ToUpper())

        'You would expect compiler errors here!
        'But they compile just fine.
        Console.WriteLine(textData1.ToUpper1())
        Console.WriteLine(textData1.Foo(10, "ee", DateTime.Now))
End Sub
```

Notice the second call to WriteLine() attempts to call a method named ToUpper1() on the dynamic data point. As you can see, textData1 is of type String, and therefore you know it does not have a method of this name, which is ToUpper1(). Furthermore, String certainly does not have a method named Foo(), which takes an Integer, String and DataTime Object!

Nevertheless, the VB 2010 compiler is satisfied with Option Strict Off. However, if you invoke this method from within Main(), you will get runtime errors similar to the following output:

```
"Public member 'ToUpper1' on type 'String' not found."
```

The Role of the Microsoft.VisualBasic.dll Assembly

When you create a new Visual Studio 2010 Visual Basic project, you will automatically have a reference set to a new .NET 4.0 assembly named Microsoft.Visual Basic.dll (you can see this for yourself by looking in the project's properties References tab under Imported namespaces). This library contains a namespace (Microsoft.VisualBasic.CompilerServices) as shown in Figure 18-2.

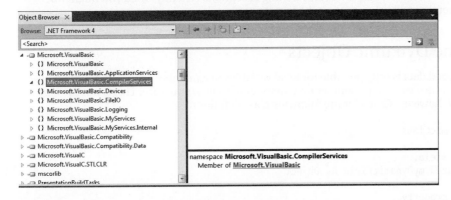

Figure 18-2. The Microsoft.VisualBasic.dll Assembly

This `Microsoft.VisualBasic.CompilerServices` class provides helpers that the Visual Basic compiler uses for late binding calls. Hence, the VB 2010 compiler will be throwing an exception if you attempt to invoke a member on a dynamic data type that does not actually exist (as in the case of the `ToUpper1()` and `Foo()` methods). This same error will be raised if you specify the wrong parameter data to a member which does exist.

Because dynamic data is so volatile, whenever you are invoking members on a variable declared with the VB `Object` keyword, you could wrap the calls within a proper `Try/Catch` block, and handle the error in a graceful manner.

```
Sub InvokeMembersOnDynamicData()
        Dim textData1 As Object = "Hello"

        Try
            Console.WriteLine(textData1.ToUpper())
            Console.WriteLine(textData1.ToUpper1())
            Console.WriteLine(textData1.Foo(10, "ee", Date.Now))
        Catch ex As Exception
            Console.WriteLine(ex.Message)
        End Try
    End Sub
```

If you call this method again, you will find the call to `ToUpper()` works correctly, however you then find the error data displayed to the console:

```
HELLO

Public member 'ToUpper1' on type 'String' not found.
```

Of course, the process of wrapping all dynamic method invocations in a `Try/Catch` block is rather tedious. As long as you watch your spelling for invoking the appropriate method/function and parameter passing, this is not required. However, catching exceptions is handy when you might not know in advance if a member will be present on the target type.

The Scope of the Dynamic Objects

Recall that implicitly typed data is only possible for local variables in a member scope. Implicitly types can never be used as a return value, a parameter or a member of a class/structure. This is not the case with the `Dynamic` object ,however. Consider the following class definition:

```
Public Class VeryDynamicClass

        'A Dynamic field.
        Private Shared myDynamicField As Object

        'A Dynamic property.
        Public Property DynamicProperty() As Object
```

CHAPTER 18 ▪ DYNAMIC TYPES AND THE DYNAMIC LANGUAGE RUNTIME

```vb
        ' A Dynamic return type and a Dynamic paramater type.
        Public Function DynamicMethod(ByVal dynamicParam As Object) As Object

                ' A dynamic local variable.
                Dim dynamicLocalVar As Object = "Local variable"
                Dim myInt As Integer = 10

                If TypeOf dynamicParam Is Integer Then
                    Return dynamicLocalVar
                Else
                    Return myInt
                End If
        End Function
End Class
```

You could now invoke the Public members as expected, however as you are operating on dynamic methods and properties, you cannot be completely sure what the data type will be! To be sure, the VeryDynamicClass definition may not be very useful in a real world application, but it does illustrate the scope of where you can apply dynamic typing.

Limitations of the Dynamic Type

While a great many things can be defined using dynamic typing, there are some limitations regarding its usage. While they are not show stoppers, do know that a dynamic data item cannot make use of lambda expressions or VB 2010 anonymous methods when calling a method. For example, the following code will always result in errors, even if the target method does indeed take a delegate parameter which takes a String value and returns Sub.

```vb
Dim a As Object = GetDynamicObject()

'Error! Dynamic data can't find the Select() extension method!
a.Method(Function(arg) Console.WriteLine(arg))
```

To circumvent this restriction, you will need to work with the underlying delegate directly, using the techniques described in Chapter 11 (anonymous methods and lambda expressions, etc). Another limitation is that a dynamic point of data cannot understand any extension methods (see Chapter 12). Unfortunately, this would also include any of the extension methods which come from the LINQ APIs. Therefore, a variable declared with dynamic typing has very limited use within LINQ to Objects and other LINQ technologies:

```vb
Dim a As Object = GetDynamicObject()

'Error!  Dynamic data can't find the Select() extension method!
Dim data = From d In a _
        Select d
```

Practical Uses of the Dynamic Types

Given the fact that dynamic data is not strongly typed, not checked at compile time, has no ability to trigger IntelliSense and cannot be the target of a LINQ query, you are absolutely correct to assume that using dynamic typing just for the sake of doing so is very poor programming practice.

However, in a few circumstances, dynamic typing can radically reduce the amount of code you need to author by hand. Specifically, if you are building a .NET application which makes heavy use of late binding (via reflection), dynamic typing can save you typing time. As well, if you are building a .NET application that needs to communicate with legacy COM libraries (such as Microsoft Office products), you can greatly simplify your codebase via dynamic typing.

Like any "shortcut," you need to weigh the pros and cons. The use of dynamic typing is a tradeoff between brevity of code, and type safety. While VB 2010 is a strongly typed language at its core, you can opt in (or opt out) dynamic behaviors on a call by call basis. Always remember that you never need to use the dynamic typing. You could always get to the same end result by authoring alternative code by hand (and typically much more of it).

■ **Source Code** The DynamicType project is located under the Chapter 18 subdirectory.

The Role of the Dynamic Language Runtime (DLR)

Now that you better understand what "dynamic data" is all about, let's learn how it is processed. With the release of .NET 4.0, the Common Language Runtime (CLR) has a complementary runtime environment named the Dynamic Language Runtime (DLR). The concept of a 'dynamic runtime' is certainly not new. In fact, many programming languages such as Smalltalk, LISP, Ruby and Python have used them for years. In a nutshell, a dynamic runtime allows a dynamic language the ability to discover types completely at runtime with no compile time checks.

If you have a background in strongly typed languages (including VB 2010, without dynamic types) the very notion of such a runtime may seem undesirable. After all, you typically want to receive compile time errors, not runtime errors, wherever possible. Nevertheless, dynamic languages/runtimes do provide some interesting features including:

- An extremely flexible code base. You can refactor code without making numerous changes to data types.

- A very simple way to interoperate with diverse object types built in different platforms and programming languages.

- A way to add or remove members to a type, in memory, at runtime.

The role of the DLR is to enable various dynamic languages to run with the .NET runtime and give them a way to interoperate with other .NET code. Two popular dynamic languages which make use of the DLR are IronPython and IronRuby. These languages live in a dynamic universe, where type is discovered solely at runtime. And yet, these languages have access to the richness of the .NET base class libraries. Even better, their codebases can interoperate with VB 2010 (or vice versa), thanks to the inclusion of the Object keyword.

The Role of Expression Trees

The DLR makes use of *expression trees* to capture the meaning of a dynamic call in neutral terms. For example, when the DLR encounters some VB 2010 code such as the following:

```
Dim d As Object = GetSomeData()
d.SuperMethod(12)
```

It will automatically build an expression tree which says in effect "Call the method named SuperMethod on Object d, passing in the number 12 as an argument". This information (formally termed the *payload*) is then passed to the correct runtime binder, which again could be the VB 2010 dynamic binder, the IronPython dynamic binder, or even (as explained shortly) legacy COM objects.

From here, the request is mapped into the required call structure for the target Object. The nice thing about these expression trees (beyond the fact that you don't need to manually create them) is that this allows us to write a fixed VB 2010 code statement, and not worry about what the underlying target actually is (COM object, IronPython, or IronRuby codebase, etc). Figure 18-3 illustrates the concept of expression trees from a high level.

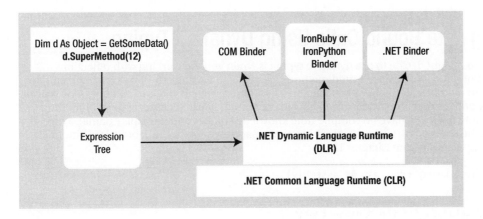

Figure 18-3. Expression trees capture dynamic calls in neutral terms and are processed by binders

The Role of the System.Dynamic Namespace

With the release of .NET 4.0, Microsoft introduced the System.Dynamic namespace within the System.Core.dll assembly. Truth be told, the chances that you will need to ever directly use the types within this namespace are slim to none. However, if you were a language vendor, who wanted to enable their dynamic languages to interact with the DLR, you could make use of System.Dynamic namespace to build a custom runtime binder.

Again, you won't need to directly dig into the types of System.Dynamic in this book, however feel free to check it out using the .NET Framework 4.0 SDK documentation if you are interested. For practical purposes, simply know that this namespace provides the necessary infrastructure to make a dynamic language ".NET aware".

Dynamic Runtime Lookup of Expression Trees

As explained, the DLR will pass the expression trees to a target object, however this dispatching will be influenced by a few factors. If the dynamic data type is pointing in memory to a COM object, the expression tree is sent to a low-level COM interface named IDispatch. As you may know, this interface was COM's way of incorporating its own set of dynamic services. COM objects, however, can be used in a .NET application without the use of the DLR or VB 2010 dynamic typing. Doing so however (as you will see) tends to result in much more complex VB 2010 coding.

If the dynamic data is not pointing to a COM object, the expression tree may be passed to an object implementing the IDynamicObject interface. This interface is used behind the scenes to allow a language such as IronRuby to take a DLR expression tree and map it to Ruby-specifics.

Finally, if the dynamic data is pointing to an object which is *not* a COM object and does *not* implement IDynamicObject, the object is a normal, everyday .NET object. In this case, the expression tree is dispatched to the VB 2010 runtime binder for processing. The process of mapping the expression tree to .NET specifics involves reflection services.

Once the expression tree has been processed by a given binder, the dynamic data will be resolved to the real in-memory data type, after which the correct method is called with any necessary parameters. Now, let's see a few practical uses of the DLR, beginning with the simplification of late bound .NET calls.

Simplifying Late Bound Calls Using Dynamic Typing

One place where you might decide to use dynamic typing is when you are working with reflection services, specifically when making late bound method calls. Back in Chapter 15, you saw a few examples of when this type of method call can be very useful, most commonly when you are building some type of extensible application. At that time, you learned how to use the Activator.CreateInstance() method to create an Object, for which you have no compile time knowledge of (beyond its display name). You can then make use of the types of the System.Reflection namespace to invoke members via late binding. Recall the following example from Chapter 15.

```
Sub CreateUsingLateBinding(ByVal asm As Assembly)

    Try
        'Get metadata for the Minivan type.
        Dim miniVan As Type = asm.GetType("CarLibrary.MiniVan")

        'Create the Minivan on the fly.
        Dim obj As Object = Activator.CreateInstance(miniVan)

        'Get info for TurboBoost.
        Dim mi As MethodInfo = miniVan.GetMethod("TurboBoost")

        'Invoke method ('Nothing' for no parameters).
        mi.Invoke(obj, Nothing)

    Catch ex As Exception
        Console.WriteLine(ex.Message)
    End Try
End Sub
```

While this is code works as expected, you might agree it is a bit clunky. Here, you have to manually make use of the `MethodInfo` class, manually query the metadata, and so forth. The following is a version of this same method, now using VB 2010 dynamic typing and the DLR:

```vb
Sub InvokeMethodWithDynamicKeyword(ByVal asm As Assembly)
     Try
          'Get metadata for the Minivan type.
          Dim miniVan As Type = asm.GetType("CarLibrary.MiniVan")

          'Create the Minivan on the fly and call method!
          Dim obj As Object = Activator.CreateInstance(miniVan)
          obj.TurboBoost()

     Catch ex As Exception
          Console.WriteLine(ex.Message)
     End Try
End Sub
```

By declaring the `obj` variable using the `Object` keyword, the heavy lifting of reflection is done on your behalf courtesy of the DRL!

Leveraging the Dynamic Typing to Pass Arguments

The usefulness of the DLR becomes even more obvious when you need to make late bound calls on methods that take parameters. When you use "longhand" reflection calls, arguments need to be packaged up as an array of `objects` which are passed to the `Invoke()` method of `MethodInfo`.

To illustrate using a fresh example, begin by creating a new VB 2010 Console Application named LateBindingWithDynamic. Next, add a Class Library project to the current solution (using the File | Add | New Project... menu option) named MathLibrary. Rename the initial `Class1.vb` of the MathLibrary project to `SimpleMath.vb`, and implement the class like so:

```vb
Class SimpleMath
        Public Function Add(ByVal x As Integer, ByVal y As Integer) As Integer
              Return x + y
        End Function
End Class
```

Once you have compiled your `MathLibrary.dll` assembly, place a copy of this library in the \bin\Debug folder of the LateBindingWithDynamic project (if you click the Show All Files button for each project of the Solution Explorer, you can simply drag and drop the file between projects). At this point, your Solution Explorer should look something like see Figure 18-4.

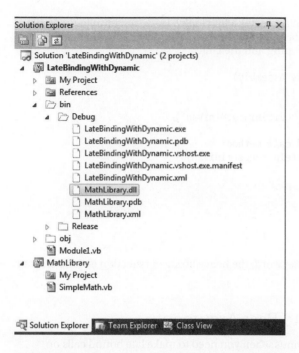

Figure 18-4. The LateBindingWithDynamic project has a private copy of MathLibrary.dll

---

■ **Note** Remember, the whole point of late binding is allowing an application to create an object for which it has no record of it the MANIFEST. This is why you manually copied MathLibrary.dll into the output folder of the Console project, rather than reference the assembly using Visual Studio.

Now, import the `System.Reflection` namespace into the `Module1.vb` file of your Console Application project. Next, add the following method to the module, which invokes the `Add()` method using typical reflection API calls:

```vb
Private Sub AddWithReflection()
    Dim asm As Assembly = Assembly.Load("MathLibrary")
    Try
        'Get metadata for the SimpleMath type.
        Dim math As Type = asm.GetType("MathLibrary.SimpleMath")

        ' Create a SimpleMath on the fly.
        Dim obj As Object = Activator.CreateInstance(math)
```

```
        'Get info for Add.
        Dim mi As MethodInfo = math.GetMethod("Add")

        'Invoke method (with parameters).
        Dim args As Object() = {10, 70}
        Console.WriteLine("Result is: {0}", mi.Invoke(obj, args))

    Catch ex As Exception
        Console.WriteLine(ex.Message)
    End Try
End Sub
```

Now, consider the simplification of the previous logic with dynamic typing:

```
Private Sub AddWithDynamic()

        Dim asm As Assembly = Assembly.Load("MathLibrary")
        Try
            'Get metadata for the SimpleMath type.
            Dim math As Type = asm.GetType("MathLibrary.SimpleMath")

            'Create a SimpleMath on the fly.
            Dim obj As Object = Activator.CreateInstance(math)
            Console.WriteLine("Result is: {0}", obj.Add(10, 70))

        Catch ex As Exception
            Console.WriteLine(ex.Message)
        End Try
End Sub
```

Not too shabby! If you call both methods from the Main() method, you'll see identical output. However, when using dynamic typing, you saved yourself quite a bit of work. With dynamically defined data, you no longer need to manually package up arguments as an array of objects, query the assembly metadata, or other such details.

■ **Source Code** The LateBindingWithDynamic project is included under the Chapter 18 subdirectory.

Simplifying COM Interoperability using Dynamic Data

Let's see another useful case for dynamic typing within the context of a COM interoperability project. Now, if you don't have much background in COM development, do be aware for this next example that a compiled COM library contains metadata, just like a .NET library; however, the format is completely different. Because of this, if a .NET program needs to use a COM object, the first order of business is to generate what is known as an "interop assembly" (described in the following) using Visual Studio 2010. Doing so is quite straightforward. Just activate the Add Reference dialog box, select the COM tab and find the COM library you wish to make use of (see Figure 18-5).

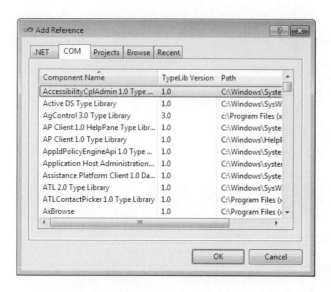

Figure 18-5. The COM tab of the Add Reference dialog box will show you all registered COM libraries on your machine

Once you select a COM library, the IDE will respond by generating a brand new assembly which contains .NET descriptions of COM metadata. Formally speaking, these are termed "interoperability assemblies" (or simply, *interop assemblies*). Interop assemblies do not contain any implementation code, except for a small amount that helps translate COM events to .NET events. However, these interop assemblies are very useful in that they shield your .NET codebase from the complex underbelly of COM internals.

In your VB 2010 code, you can directly program against the interop assembly, allowing the CLR (and if you use dynamic typing, the DLR) to automatically map .NET data types into COM types, and vice versa. Behind the scenes, data is marshaled between the .NET and COM applications using a Runtime Callable Wrapper (RCW), which is basically a dynamically generated proxy. This RCW proxy will marshal and transform .NET data types into COM types, adjust the COM object's reference counter, and map any COM return values into .NET equivalents. Figure 18-6 shows the big picture of .NET to COM interoperability.

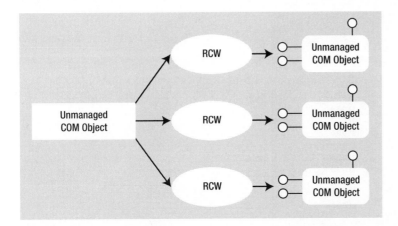

Figure 18-6. .NET programs communicate with COM objects using a proxy termed the RCW

The Role of Primary Interop Assemblies (PIAs)

Many COM libraries created by COM library vendors (such as the Microsoft COM libraries that allow access to the object model of Microsoft Office products) provide an "official" interoperability assembly termed a *primary interop assembly* or PIA. PIAs are optimized interop assemblies, which clean up (and possibly extend) the code typically generated when referencing a COM library using the Add Reference dialog box.

PIAs are typically listed in the .NET tab of the Add Reference dialog box, just like the core .NET libraries. In fact, if you reference a COM library from the COM tab of the Add Reference dialog box, Visual Studio will not generate a new interoperability library as it would normally do, but use the provided PIA instead. Figure 18-7 shows the PIA of the Microsoft Office Excel object model, which you will be using in the next example.

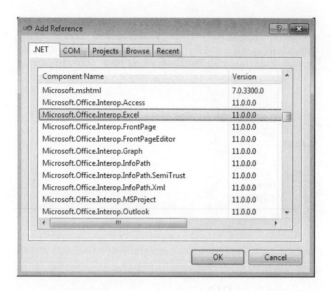

Figure 18-7. PIAs are listed in the .NET tab of the Add Reference dialog box

Embedding Interop Metadata

Before the release of .NET 4.0, when a VB 2010 application made use of a COM library (PIA or not), you needed to ensure the client machine has a copy of the interop assembly on their computer. Not only will this increase the size of your application installer package, but the install script must check that the PIA assemblies are indeed present, and if not, install a copy to the GAC.

However, under .NET 4.0, you can now elect to embed the interoperability data directly within your compiled .NET application. When you do so, you are no longer required to ship a copy of the interoperability assembly along with your .NET application, as the necessary interoperability metadata is hardcoded in the .NET program.

By default, when you select a COM library (PIA or not) using the Add References dialog, the IDE will automatically set the Embed Interop Types property of the library to True. You can see this setting first hand by selecting a referenced interop library in the References folder of the Solution Explorer, and then investigate the Properties window (see Figure 18-8).

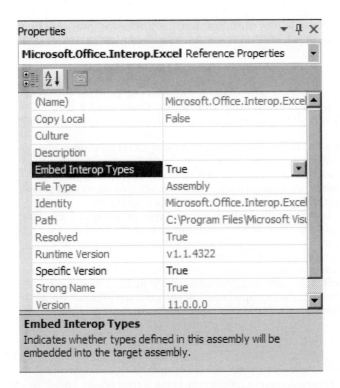

Figure 18-8. .NET 4.0 allows you to embed the parts of an interop assemblies you make use of into your .NET assembly

The VB 2010 compiler will only include the parts of the interop library you are actually making use of. Thus, if the real interop library has .NET descriptions of hundreds of COM objects, you will only bring in the definitions of the subset you are really making use of in your VB 2010 code. Beyond reducing the size of the application you need to ship to the client, you also have an easier installation path, as you don't need to install any missing PIAs on the target machine.

Common COM Interop Pain Points

When you are authoring VB 2010 code that programs against a COM library (via the interop assembly), you were sure to face a number of challenges before the release of .NET 4.0. For example, many COM libraries defined methods which took optional arguments, which were not supported in VB 2010 until the current release. This required you to specify the value `Type.Missing` for every occurrence of the optional argument. For example, if a COM method took five arguments, all of which were Optional, you would need to write the following VB 2010 code in order to accept the default values:

```
myComObj.SomeMethod(Type.Missing, Type.Missing, Type.Missing, Type.Missing, Type.Missing)
```

Thankfully, under .NET 4.0, you are now able to author the following simplified code, given that the `Type.Missing` values will be inserted at compile time if you don't specify a true blue value.

```
myComObj.SomeMethod()
```

On a related note, many COM methods provided support for named arguments, which as you recall from Chapter 4, allows you to pass values to members in any order you require. Given that VB 2010 supports this same feature as of .NET 4.0, it is very simply to "skip' over a set of optional arguments you don't care about, and only set the few you do.

Another common COM interop pain point has to do with the fact that many COM methods were designed to take and return a very particular data type termed the `Variant`. Much like the VB 2010 dynamic type, a `Variant` data type could be assigned to any type of COM data on the fly (strings, interface references, numerical values, etc). Before you had dynamic typing, passing or receiving `Variant` data points required some hoop jumping, typically by way of numerous casting operations.

As of .NET 4.0 and Visual Studio 2010, when you set the Embed Interop Types property to True, all COM variants are automatically mapped to dynamic data. This will not only reduce the need for extraneous casting operations when working with underlying COM `Variant` data types, but will also further hide some COM-complexities, such as working with COM indexers.

To showcase how the use of VB 2010 optional arguments, named arguments and dynamic typing all work together to simplify COM interop, you will now build an application which makes use of the Microsoft Office object model. As you work through the example, you will get a chance to make use of the new features, as well as forgo them, and then compare and contrast the workload.

■ **Note** Previous editions of this book included a detailed examination of how to make use of legacy COM objects in your .NET projects using the `System.Runtime.InteropServices` namespace. In the current edition, I have opted to omit that chapter, as dynamic typing can be used to communicate with COM objects with far fewer pain points. If you wish to see how to communicate with COM objects in a strongly typed (longhand) notation, consult the .NET Framework 4.0 SDK documentation.

COM Interop using VB 2010 Language Features

Assume you have a Windows Form GUI application (named ExportDataToOfficeApp), whose main Form defines a `DataGridView` named `dataGridCars`. This same form has two `Button` controls, one of which will bring up a dialog box to insert a new row of data to the grid, and the other of which needs to export the grid's data to an Excel spreadsheet. Given the fact that the Excel application exposes a programming model via COM, you can hook into this object model using the interoperability layer. Figure 18-9 shows the completed GUI.

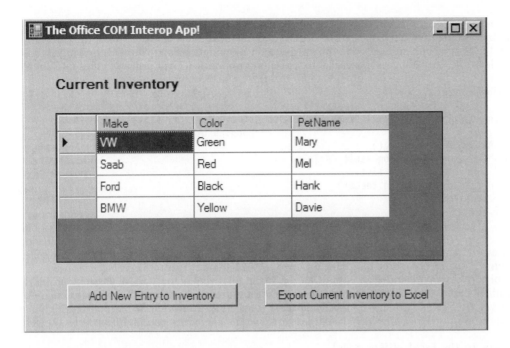

Figure 18-9. The GUI of the COM interop example

You will fill the grid with some initial data by handling the form's **Load** event as so (the **Car** class used as the type parameter for the generic **List(Of T)** is a simple class in the project with **Color**, **Make**, and **PetName** Properties):

```
Public Class MainForm
        Dim carsInStock As List(Of Car) = Nothing

    Private Sub MainForm_Load(ByVal sender As System.Object, ByVal e As System.EventArgs)
    Handles MyBase.Load

        carsInStock = New List(Of Car) From {
            New Car With {.Color = "Green", .Make = "VW", .PetName = "Mary"},
            New Car With {.Color = "Red", .Make = "Saab", .PetName = "Mel"},
            New Car With {.Color = "Black", .Make = "Ford", .PetName = "Hank"},
            New Car With {.Color = "Yellow", .Make = "BMW", .PetName = "Davie"}
                                    }
        UpdateGrid()

    Private Sub UpdateGrid()
                'Reset the source of data.
                dataGridCars.DataSource = Nothing
                dataGridCars.DataSource = carsInStock
        End Sub
End Sub
```

The `Click` event for the "Add" button will launch a custom dialog box to allow the user to enter new data for a `Car` object, and if they click the OK button, the data is added to the grid. I won't bother to show the code behind the dialog box, so please see the provided solution for details. If you are following however, include the `NewCarDialog.vb`, `NewCarDialog.designer.vb` and `NewCarDialog.resx` files into your project (all of which are part of the code download for this text). Once you have done so, implement the "Add" button click hander as so:

```
Private Sub btnAddNewCar_Click(ByVal sender As System.Object, ByVal e As System.EventArgs)
                                                Handles btnAddNewCar.Click

        Dim d As New NewCarDialog()
        If d.ShowDialog() = DialogResult.OK Then
            ' Add new car to list.
            carsInStock.Add(d.theCar)
            UpdateGrid()
        End If
End Sub
```

The `Click` event handler for the "Export" button is the heart of this example. Using the .NET tab of the Add Reference… dialog box, add a reference to the `Microsoft.Office.Interop.Excel.dll` primary interop assembly (as shown previously in Figure 18-7). Add the following namespace alias to the form's primary code file. Be aware that this is not mandatory to define an alias when interacting with COM libraries. However, by doing so, you have a handy qualifier for all of the imported COM objects, which is very handy if some of these COM objects have names which would clash with your .NET types:

```
'Create an alais to the Excel object model.
Imports Excel = Microsoft.Office.Interop.Excel
```

Implement this button `Click` event hander to call a Private method named `ExportToExcel()`:

```
Private Sub btnExportToExcel_Click(ByVal sender As System.Object,
        ByVal e As System.EventArgs)
                                                Handles btnExportToExcel.Click
        ExportToExcel(carsInStock)
End Sub
```

Because you imported the COM library using Visual Studio 2010, the PIA has been automatically configured so that the used metadata will be embedded into the .NET application (recall the role of the Embed Interop Types property). Therefore, all COM `Variants` are realized as `dynamic` data types. Furthermore, because you are compiling your code with VB 2010, you can make use of optional arguments and named arguments. This being said consider the following implementation of `ExportToExcel()`:

```
Shared Sub ExportToExcel(ByVal carsInStock As List(Of Car))
        ' Load up Excel, then make a new empty workbook.
        Dim excelApp As New Excel.Application()
        excelApp.Workbooks.Add()

        ' This example uses a single workSheet.
        Dim workSheet As Excel._Worksheet = excelApp.ActiveSheet
```

```
' Establish column headings in cells.
workSheet.Cells(1, "A") = "Make"
workSheet.Cells(1, "B") = "Color"
workSheet.Cells(1, "C") = "Pet Name"

' Now, map all data in List(Of Car) to the cells of the spread sheet.
Dim row As Integer = 1
For Each c In carsInStock
        row += 1
        workSheet.Cells(row, "A") = c.Make
        workSheet.Cells(row, "B") = c.Color
        workSheet.Cells(row, "C") = c.PetName
Next

' Give our table data a nice look and feel.
workSheet.Range("A1").AutoFormat(Excel.XlRangeAutoFormat.xlRangeAutoFormatClassic2)

' Save the file, quit Excel and display message to user.
workSheet.SaveAs(String.Format("{0}\Inventory.xlsx", Environment.CurrentDirectory))
excelApp.Quit()
MessageBox.Show("The Inventory.xslx file has been saved to your app folder",
                        "Export complete!")
End Sub
```

This method begins by loading Excel into memory, however you won't see it visible on your computer desktop. For this application, you are only interested in using the internal Excel object model. However, if you do want to actually display the UI of Excel, update your method with this additional line of code:

```
Shared Sub ExportToExcel(ByVal carsInStock As List(Of Car))

    'Load up Excel, then make a new empty workbook.
    Dim excelApp As New Excel.Application()
    excelApp.Workbooks.Add()

    'Go ahead and make Excel visible on the computer.
    excelApp.Visible = True
        ...
End Sub
```

Once you create an empty worksheet, you add three columns which are named similar to the properties of the Car class. After this point, you fill the cells with the data of the List(Of Car), and save your file under the (hard coded) name Inventory.xlsx.

At this point if you run your application, add a few new records, and export your data to Excel, you will then be able to open up the Inventory.xlsx file, which will be saved to the \bin\Debug folder of your Windows Forms application. Figure 18-10 shows a possible export.

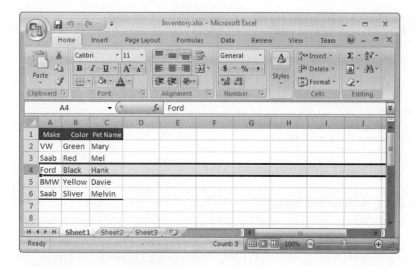

Figure 18-10. Exporting your data to an Excel file

COM Interop without VB 2010 Language Features

Now, if you were to select the `Microsoft.Office.Interop.Excel.dll` assembly (in Solution Explorer), and set its Embed Interop Type Property to False, you would have new compiler errors, as the COM `Variant` data is no longer realized as dynamic data, but as `System.Object` variables. This will require you to update `ExportToExcel()` with a number of casting operations. As well, if this project were compiled under Visual Studio 2010, you no longer have the benefit of optional/named parameters, and must explicitly mark all missing arguments. Here is a version of the `ExportToExcel()` method, which would be required in earlier versions of VB 2010:

```
Shared Sub ExportToExcel2010(ByVal carsInStock As List(Of Car))
    Dim excelApp As New Excel.Application()

    ' Must mark missing params!
    excelApp.Workbooks.Add(Type.Missing)

    ' Must cast Object as _Worksheet!
    Dim workSheet As Excel._Worksheet = CType(excelApp.ActiveSheet, Excel._Worksheet)

    ' Must cast each Object as Range object then call
    ' call low level Value2 property!
    CType(excelApp.Cells(1, "A"), Excel.Range).Value2 = "Make"
    CType(excelApp.Cells(1, "B"), Excel.Range).Value2 = "Color"
    CType(excelApp.Cells(1, "C"), Excel.Range).Value2 = "Pet Name"
```

```
    Dim row As Integer = 1
    For Each c In carsInStock
        row += 1
        ' Must cast each Object as Range and call low level Value2 prop!
        CType(workSheet.Cells(row, "A"), Excel.Range).Value2 = c.Make
        CType(workSheet.Cells(row, "B"), Excel.Range).Value2 = c.Color
        CType(workSheet.Cells(row, "C"), Excel.Range).Value2 = c.PetName
    Next

    ' Must call get_Range method and then specify all missing args!.
    excelApp.get_Range("A1",
            Type.Missing).AutoFormat(Excel.XlRangeAutoFormat.xlRangeAutoFormatClassic2,
            Type.Missing, Type.Missing, Type.Missing, Type.Missing, Type.Missing,
            Type.Missing)

    ' Must specify all missing optional args!
    workSheet.SaveAs(String.Format("{0}\Inventory.xlsx", Environment.CurrentDirectory),
            Type.Missing,
            Type.Missing, Type.Missing, Type.Missing, Type.Missing, Type.Missing,
            Type.Missing, Type.Missing, Type.Missing)

    excelApp.Quit()
    MessageBox.Show("The Inventory.xslx file has been saved to your app folder",
    "Export complete!")
End Sub
```

While the end result is identical, as I am sure you agree, this version of the method is much more verbose. As well, since earlier versions of VB (prior to .NET 4.0, to be specific) don't allow you to embed the COM interop data, you would find that your output directory now contains local copies of a number of interop assemblies, which you would be required to ship to the end user's machine (Figure 18-11).

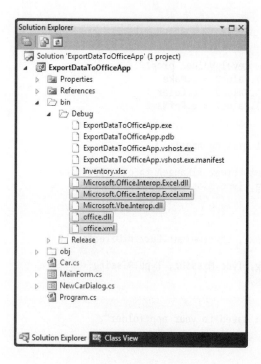

Figure 18-11. Not embedding interop data requires you to ship standalone interoperability assemblies

That wraps up our look at VB 2010 dynamic typing and the DLR. Hopefully you can see how these new .NET 4.0 features can simplify complex programming tasks, and (perhaps more importantly) understand the trade offs. When you opt into dynamic data, you do lose a good amount of type safety, and your code base is prone to many more runtime errors.

■ **Source Code** The ExportDataToOfficeApp project is included under the Chapter 18 subdirectory.

Summary

Dynamic typing in VB 2010 allows you to define data whose true identity is not known until runtime. When processed by the new Dynamic Language Runtime (DLR), the automatically created "expression tree" will be passed to the correct dynamic language binder, where the payload will be unpackaged and sent to the correct object member.

Using dynamic data and the DLR, a number of complex VB 2010 programming tasks can be radically simplified, especially the act of incorporating COM libraries into your .NET applications. As you have also seen in this chapter, .NET 4.0 provides a number of further simplifications to COM interop (which have nothing to do with dynamic data) such as embedding COM interop data into your applications, optional arguments and named arguments.

While these features can certainly simplify your code, always remember that dynamic data makes your VB 2010 code much less type safe, and open to runtime errors. Be sure you weigh the pros and cons of using dynamic data in your VB 2010 projects, and test accordingly!

CHAPTER 19

■■■

Multithreaded and Parallel Programming

Nobody enjoys working with an application which is slow and sluggish during its execution. Moreover, nobody enjoys starting a task in an application (perhaps initiated by the clicking of a toolbar item) which prevents other parts of the program from being as responsive as possible. Before the release of .NET, building applications that had the ability to perform multiple tasks required authoring very complex C++ code and the Windows threading APIs. Thankfully, the .NET platform provides a number of ways for you to build software which can perform complex operations on unique paths of execution, with far less fuss and bother.

This chapter begins by revisiting the .NET delegate type to investigate its intrinsic support for *asynchronous method invocations*. As you'll see, this technique allows you to invoke a method on a secondary thread of execution without needing to manually create or configure the thread itself.

Next, you'll be introduced to the `System.Threading` namespace. Here you'll examine numerous types (`Thread`, `ThreadStart`, etc.) that allow you to easily create additional threads of execution. As well, you will learn about various synchronization primitives that the .NET Framework provides, which helps ensure that multiple threads can share data in a non-volatile manner.

The final part of this chapter will examine the brand new .NET 4.0 Task Parallel Library (TPL) and PLINQ (Parallel LINQ). Using these APIs, you can program against a set of higher level types, which do a good deal to manage thread details on your behalf.

The Process/AppDomain/Context/Thread Relationship

In Chapter 16, a *thread* was defined as a path of execution within an executable application. While many .NET applications can live happy and productive single-threaded lives, an assembly's primary thread (spawned by the CLR when `Main()` executes) may create secondary threads of execution to perform additional units of work. By implementing additional threads, you can build more responsive (but not necessarily faster executing on single-core machines) applications.

■ **Note** These days it is quite common for new computers to make use of multicore processors (or at very least a hyperthreaded single-core processor). Without making use of multiple threads, developers are unable to exploit the full power of multicore machines.

The `System.Threading` namespace contains various types that allow you to create multithreaded applications. The `Thread` class is perhaps the core type, as it represents a given thread. If you wish to programmatically obtain a reference to the thread currently executing a given member, simply call the Shared `Thread.CurrentThread` property:

```
Shared Sub ExtractExecutingThread()
  ' Get the thread currently
  ' executing this method.
  Dim currThread As Thread = Thread.CurrentThread
End Sub
```

Under the .NET platform, there is *not* a direct one-to-one correspondence between application domains and threads. In fact, a given AppDomain can have numerous threads executing within it at any given time. Furthermore, a particular thread is not confined to a single application domain during its lifetime. Threads are free to cross application domain boundaries as the Windows thread scheduler and CLR see fit.

Although active threads can be moved between AppDomain boundaries, a given thread can execute within only a single application domain at any point in time (in other words, it is impossible for a single thread to be doing work in more than one AppDomain at once). When you wish to programmatically gain access to the AppDomain that is hosting the current thread, call the Shared `Thread.GetDomain()` method:

```
Sub ExtractAppDomainHostingThread()
  ' Obtain the AppDomain hosting the current thread.
  Dim ad As AppDomain = Thread.GetDomain()
End Sub
```

A single thread may also be moved into a particular context at any given time, and it may be relocated within a new context at the whim of the CLR. When you wish to obtain the current context a thread happens to be executing in, make use of the Shared `Thread.CurrentContext` property (which returns a `System.Runtime.Remoting.Contexts.Context` object):

```
Sub ExtractCurrentThreadContext()
  ' Obtain the context under which the
  ' current thread is operating.
  Dim ctx As Context = Thread.CurrentContext
End Sub
```

Again, the CLR is the entity that is in charge of moving threads into (and out of) application domains and contexts. As a .NET developer, you can usually remain blissfully unaware where a given thread ends up (or exactly when it is placed into its new boundary). Nevertheless, you should be aware of the various ways of obtaining the underlying primitives.

The Problem of Concurrency

One of the many "joys" (read: painful aspects) of multithreaded programming is that you have little control over how the underlying operating system or the CLR makes use of its threads. For example, if you craft a block of code that creates a new thread of execution, you cannot guarantee that the thread executes immediately. Rather, such code only instructs the OS to execute the thread as soon as possible (which is typically when the thread scheduler gets around to it).

Furthermore, given that threads can be moved between application and contextual boundaries as required by the CLR, you must be mindful of which aspects of your application are *thread-volatile* (e.g., subject to multithreaded access) and which operations are *atomic* (thread-volatile operations are the dangerous ones!).

To illustrate the problem, assume a thread is invoking a method of a specific object. Now assume that this thread is instructed by the thread scheduler to suspend its activity, in order to allow another thread to access the same method of the same object.

If the original thread was not completely finished with its operation, the second incoming thread may be viewing an object in a partially modified state. At this point, the second thread is basically reading bogus data, which is sure to give way to extremely odd (and very hard to find) bugs, which are even harder to replicate and debug.

Atomic operations, on the other hand, are always safe in a multithreaded environment. Sadly, there are very few operations in the .NET base class libraries that are guaranteed to be atomic. Even the act of assigning a value to a member variable is not atomic! Unless the .NET Framework 4.0 SDK documentation specifically says an operation is atomic, you must assume it is thread-volatile and take precautions.

The Role of Thread Synchronization

At this point, it should be clear that multithreaded application domains are in themselves quite volatile, as numerous threads can operate on the shared resources at (more or less) the same time. To protect an application's resources from possible corruption, .NET developers must make use of any number of threading primitives (such as locks, monitors, and the `<Synchronization()>` attribute) to control access among the executing threads.

Although the .NET platform cannot make the difficulties of building robust multithreaded applications completely disappear, the process has been simplified considerably. Using types defined within the `System.Threading` namespace, and the .NET 4.0 Task Parallel Library (TPL), you are able to spawn additional threads with minimal fuss and bother. Likewise, when it is time to lock down shared points of data, you will find additional types that provide the same functionality as the Windows API threading primitives (using a much cleaner object model).

Before diving into the `System.Threading` namespace and the TPL, it is important to note that there is one other useful way to incorporate threads into an application. During the examination of the .NET delegate (see Chapter 11), it was mentioned that all delegates have the ability to invoke members asynchronously. This is a *major* benefit of the .NET platform, given that one of the most common reasons a developer creates threads is for the purpose of invoking methods in a nonblocking (a.k.a. asynchronous) manner.

A Brief Review of the .NET Delegate

Recall that the .NET delegate type is essentially a type-safe, object-oriented, function pointer. When you declare a .NET delegate, the VB 2010 compiler responds by building a NotInheritable class that derives from `System.MulticastDelegate` (which in turn derives from `System.Delegate`). These base classes provide every delegate with the ability to maintain a list of method addresses, all of which may be invoked at a later time. Consider the `BinaryOp` delegate first defined in Chapter 11:

```
' A VB 2010 delegate type.
Public Delegate Function BinaryOp(ByVal x As Integer, ByVal y As Integer) As Integer
```

Based on its definition, `BinaryOp` can point to any method taking two Integers (by value) as arguments and returning an Integer. Once compiled, the defining assembly now contains a full-blown class definition that is dynamically generated when you build your project, based on the delegate declaration. In the case of `BinaryOp`, this class looks more or less like the following (shown in pseudo-code):

```
Public NotInheritable Class BinaryOp
    Inherits System.MulticastDelegate

    Public Sub BinaryOp(ByVal target As Object, ByVal functionAddress
                                    As UInteger)
    Public Sub Invoke(ByVal x As Integer, ByVal y As Integer)
    Public Function BeginInvoke(ByVal x As Integer,
                            ByVal y As Integer,
                            ByVal cb As AsyncCallback,
                            ByVal state As Object) As IAsyncResult
    Public Function EndInvoke(ByVal result As IAsyncResult) As Integer
End Class
```

Recall that the generated `Invoke()` method is used to invoke the methods maintained by a delegate object in a *synchronous manner*. Therefore, the calling thread (such as the primary thread of the application) is forced to wait until the delegate invocation completes. Also recall that in VB 2010, the `Invoke()` method does not need to be directly called in code, but can be triggered indirectly under the hood when applying "normal" method invocation syntax.

Consider the following Console Application program (SyncDelegateReview), which invokes the `Add()` method in a synchronous (a.k.a. blocking) manner (be sure to import the `System.Threading` namespace, as you will be calling the `Thread.Sleep()` method).

```
Public Delegate Function BinaryOp(ByVal x As Integer, ByVal y As Integer)  As Integer

Module Module1
    Sub Main()
        Console.WriteLine("***** Synch Delegate Review *****")

        ' Print out the ID of the executing thread.
        Console.WriteLine("Main() invoked on thread {0}."
                    ,Thread.CurrentThread.ManagedThreadId)

        ' Invoke Add() in a synchronous manner.
        Dim b As New BinaryOp(AddressOf Add)

        ' Could also write b.Invoke(10, 10);
        Dim answer As Integer = b(10, 10)
```

```vb
      ' These lines will not execute until
      'the Add() method has completed.
      Console.WriteLine("Doing more work in Main()!")
      Console.WriteLine("10 + 10 is {0}.", answer)
      Console.ReadLine()
   End Sub

   Private Function Add(ByVal x As Integer, ByVal y As Integer) _
         As Integer
      ' Print out the ID of the executing thread.
      Console.WriteLine("Add() invoked on thread {0}." _
                  ,Thread.CurrentThread.ManagedThreadId)

      ' Pause to simulate a lengthy operation.
      Thread.Sleep(5000)
      Return x + y
   End Function
End Module
```

Within the `Add()` method, you are invoking the Shared `Thread.Sleep()` method to suspend the calling thread for approximately five seconds to simulate a lengthy task. Given that you are invoking the `Add()` method in a *synchronous* manner, the `Main()` method will not print out the result of the operation until the `Add()` method has completed.

Next, note that the `Main()` method is obtaining access to the current thread (via `Thread.CurrentThread`) and printing out the ID of the thread via the `ManagedThreadId` property. This same logic is repeated in the `Add()` method. As you might suspect, given that all the work in this application is performed exclusively by the primary thread, you find the same ID value displayed to the console:

```
***** Synch Delegate Review *****

Main() invoked on thread 1.

Add() invoked on thread 1.

Doing more work in Main()!

10 + 10 is 20.



Press any key to continue . . .
```

When you run this program, you should notice that a five-second delay takes place before you see the final `Console.WriteLine()` logic in `Main()` execute. Although many (if not most) methods may be called synchronously without ill effect, .NET delegates can be instructed to call their methods asynchronously if necessary.

■ **Source Code** The SyncDelegateReview project is located under the Chapter 19 subdirectory.

The Asynchronous Nature of Delegates

If you are new to the topic of multithreading, you may wonder what exactly an *asynchronous* method invocation is all about. As you are no doubt fully aware, some programming operations take time. Although the previous Add() was purely illustrative in nature, imagine that you built a single-threaded application that is invoking a method on a remote object, performing a long-running database query, downloading a large document, or writing 500 lines of text to an external file. While performing these operations, the application will appear to hang for some amount of time. Until the task at hand has been processed, all other aspects of this program (such as menu activation, toolbar clicking, or console output) are unresponsive.

The question therefore is, how can you tell a delegate to invoke a method on a separate thread of execution to simulate numerous tasks performing "at the same time"? The good news is that every .NET delegate type is automatically equipped with this capability. The even better news is that you are *not* required to directly dive into the details of the System.Threading namespace to do so (although these entities can quite naturally work hand in hand).

The BeginInvoke() and EndInvoke() Methods

When the VB 2010 compiler processes the Delegate keyword, the dynamically generated class defines two methods named BeginInvoke() and EndInvoke(). Given the definition of the BinaryOp delegate, these methods are prototyped as follows:

```
Public NotInheritable Class BinaryOp
    Inherits System.MulticastDelegate
    ' Used to invoke a method asynchronously.
    ...
    Public Function BeginInvoke(ByVal x As Integer,
                                ByVal y As Integer,
                                ByVal cb As AsyncCallback,
                                ByVal state As Object) As IAsyncResult

    ' Used to fetch the return value
    ' of the invoked method.
    Public Function EndInvoke(ByVal result As IAsyncResult) As Integer
End Class
```

The first stack of parameters passed into BeginInvoke() will be based on the format of the VB 2010 delegate (two integers in the case of BinaryOp). The final two arguments will always be System.AsyncCallback and System.Object. You'll examine the role of these parameters shortly; for the time being, though, I'll supply Nothing for each. Also note that the return value of EndInvoke() is an Integer, based on the return type of BinaryOp, while the parameter of this method is of type IAsyncResult.

The System.IAsyncResult Interface

The `BeginInvoke()` method always returns an object implementing the `IAsyncResult` interface, while `EndInvoke()` requires an `IAsyncResult`-compatible type as its sole parameter. The `IAsyncResult`-compatible object returned from `BeginInvoke()` is basically a coupling mechanism that allows the calling thread to obtain the result of the asynchronous method invocation at a later time via `EndInvoke()`. The `IAsyncResult` interface (defined in the `System` namespace) is defined as follows:

```
Public Interface IAsyncResult
    ReadOnly Property AsyncState() As Object
    ReadOnly Property AsyncWaitHandle() As WaitHandle
    ReadOnly Property CompletedSynchronously() As Boolean
    ReadOnly Property IsCompleted() As Boolean
End Interface
```

In the simplest case, you are able to avoid directly invoking these members. All you have to do is cache the `IAsyncResult`-compatible object returned by `BeginInvoke()` and pass it to `EndInvoke()` when you are ready to obtain the result of the method invocation. As you will see, you are able to invoke the members of an `IAsyncResult`-compatible object when you wish to become "more involved" with the process of fetching the method's return value.

■ **Note** If you asynchronously invoke a Sub (which returns no value), you can simply "fire and forget." In such cases, you will never need to cache the `IAsyncResult` compatible object or call `EndInvoke()` in the first place (as there is no return value to retrieve).

Invoking a Method Asynchronously

To instruct the `BinaryOp` delegate to invoke `Add()` asynchronously, you will modify the logic in the previous project (feel free to add code to the existing project, however in your lab downloads, you will find a new Console Application named *AsyncDelegate)*. Update the previous `Main()` method as follows:

```
Sub Main()
        Console.WriteLine("***** Async Delegate Invocation *****")

        ' Print out the ID of the executing thread.
        Console.WriteLine("Main() invoked on thread {0}."
                    ,Thread.CurrentThread.ManagedThreadId)

        ' Invoke Add() on a secondary thread.
        Dim b As New BinaryOp(AddressOf Add)
        Dim iftAR As IAsyncResult = b.BeginInvoke(10, 10, Nothing,Nothing)

        ' Do other work on primary thread...
        Console.WriteLine("Doing more work in Main()!")
```

```
        ' Obtain the result of the Add()
        ' method when ready.
        Dim answer As Integer = b.EndInvoke(iftAR)
        Console.WriteLine("10 + 10 is {0}.", answer)
        Console.ReadLine()
End Sub
```

If you run this application, you will find that two unique thread IDs are displayed, given that there are in fact multiple threads working within the current AppDomain:

```
***** Async Delegate Invocation *****

Main() invoked on thread 1.

Doing more work in Main()!

Add() invoked on thread 3.

10 + 10 is 20.
```

In addition to the unique ID values, you will also notice upon running the application that the Doing more work in Main()! message displays immediately, while the secondary thread is occupied attending to its business.

Synchronizing the Calling Thread

If you think carefully about the current implementation of Main(), you might have realized that the time span between calling BeginInvoke() and EndInvoke() is clearly less than five seconds. Therefore, once Doing more work in Main()! prints to the console, the calling thread is now blocked and waiting for the secondary thread to complete before being able to obtain the result of the Add() method. Therefore, you are effectively making yet another *synchronous call*:

```
Sub Main()
        ...
        Dim b As New BinaryOp(Add)

        ' Once the next statement is processed,
        ' the calling thread is now blocked until
        ' BeginInvoke() completes.
        Dim iftAR As IAsyncResult = b.BeginInvoke(10, 10, Nothing,Nothing)
        ' This call takes far less than five seconds!
        Console.WriteLine("Doing more work in Main()!")
        Dim answer As Integer = b.EndInvoke(iftAR)
        ...
End Sub
```

Obviously, asynchronous delegates would lose their appeal if the calling thread had the potential of being blocked under various circumstances. To allow the calling thread to discover if the asynchronously invoked method has completed its work, the IAsyncResult interface provides the IsCompleted property. Using this member, the calling thread is able to determine whether the asynchronous call has indeed completed before calling EndInvoke().

If the method has not completed, IsCompleted returns False, and the calling thread is free to carry on its work. If IsCompleted returns True, the calling thread is able to obtain the result in the "least blocking manner" possible. Ponder the following update to the Main() method:

```
Sub Main()
        ...
        Dim b As New BinaryOp(AddressOf Add)
        Dim iftAR As IAsyncResult = b.BeginInvoke(10, 10, Nothing,Nothing)
        ' This message will keep printing until
        ' the Add() method is finished.
        Do While Not iftAR.IsCompleted
            Console.WriteLine("Doing more work in Main()!")
            Thread.Sleep(1000)
        Loop
        ' Now we know the Add() method is complete.
        Dim answer As Integer = b.EndInvoke(iftAR)
        ...
End Sub
```

Here, you enter a loop that will continue processing the Console.WriteLine() statement until the secondary thread has completed. Once this has occurred, you can obtain the result of the Add() method knowing full well the method has indeed completed. The call to Thread.Sleep(1000) is not necessary for this particular application to function correctly; however, by forcing the primary thread to wait for approximately one second during each iteration, it prevents the same message from printing hundreds of times. Here is the output (your output may differ slightly, based on the speed of your machine and when threads come to life):

```
***** Async Delegate Invocation *****

Main() invoked on thread 1.

Doing more work in Main()!

Add() invoked on thread 3.

Doing more work in Main()!

Doing more work in Main()!

Doing more work in Main()!

Doing more work in Main()!

Doing more work in Main()!
```

```
Doing more work in Main()!

10 + 10 is 20.
```

In addition to the `IsCompleted` property, the `IAsyncResult` interface provides the `AsyncWaitHandle` property for more flexible waiting logic. This property returns an instance of the `WaitHandle` type, which exposes a method named `WaitOne()`. The benefit of `WaitHandle.WaitOne()` is that you can specify the maximum wait time. If the specified amount of time is exceeded, `WaitOne()` returns `False`. Ponder the following updated `While` loop, which no longer makes use of a call to `Thread.Sleep()`:

```
Do While Not iftAR.AsyncWaitHandle.WaitOne(1000, True)
  Console.WriteLine("Doing more work in Main()!")
Loop
```

While these properties of `IAsyncResult` do provide a way to synchronize the calling thread, they are not the most efficient approach. In many ways, the `IsCompleted` property is much like a really annoying manager (or classmate) who is constantly asking, "Are you done yet?" Thankfully, delegates provide a number of additional (and more elegant) techniques to obtain the result of a method that has been called asynchronously.

■ **Source Code** The AsyncDelegate project is located under the Chapter 19 subdirectory.

The Role of the AsyncCallback Delegate

Rather than polling a delegate to determine whether an asynchronously invoked method has completed, it would be more efficient to have the secondary thread inform the calling thread when the task is finished. When you wish to enable this behavior, you will need to supply an instance of the `System.AsyncCallback` delegate as a parameter to `BeginInvoke()`, which up until this point has been `Nothing`. However, when you do supply an `AsyncCallback` object, the delegate will call the specified method automatically when the asynchronous call has completed.

■ **Note** The callback method will be called on the secondary thread not the primary thread. This has important implications when using threads within a graphical user interface (WPF or Windows Forms) as controls have thread-affinity, meaning they can only be manipulated by the thread which created them. You'll see some examples of working the threads from a GUI later in this chapter during the examination of the Task Parallel Library (TPL).

Like any delegate, `AsyncCallback` can only invoke methods that match a specific pattern, which in this case is a method taking `IAsyncResult` as the sole parameter and returning nothing:

```
' Targets of AsyncCallback must match the following pattern.
Sub MyAsyncCallbackMethod(ByVal itfAR As IAsyncResult)
```

Assume you have another Console Application (AsyncCallbackDelegate) making use of the `BinaryOp` delegate. This time, however, you will not poll the delegate to determine whether the `Add()` method has completed. Rather, you will define a method named `AddComplete()` to receive the notification that the asynchronous invocation is finished. Also, this example makes use of a class level `Boolean` field, which will be used to keep the primary thread in `Main()` running a task until the secondary thread is finished.

■ **Note** The use of this Boolean variable in this example is strictly speaking, not thread safe, as there are two different threads which have access to its value. This will be permissible for the current example; however, as a *very* good rule of thumb, you must ensure data that can be shared among multiple threads is locked down. You'll see how to do so later in this chapter.

```vb
Public Delegate Function BinaryOp(ByVal x As Integer, ByVal y As Integer) As Integer

Module Module1
        Private isDone As Boolean = False
    Sub Main()
        Console.WriteLine("*****  AsyncCallbackDelegate Example *****")
        Console.WriteLine("Main() invoked on thread {0}.",
                        Thread.CurrentThread.ManagedThreadId)
        Dim b As New BinaryOp(AddressOf Add)

        Dim iftAR As IAsyncResult = b.BeginInvoke(10, 10,
                New AsyncCallback(AddressOf AddComplete), Nothing)

        'Assume other work is performed here...
        Do While Not isDone
            Thread.Sleep(1000)
            Console.WriteLine("Working....")
        Loop
        Console.ReadLine()
    End Sub

    Private Function Add(ByVal x As Integer, ByVal y As Integer)
                                                    As Integer
        Console.WriteLine("Add() invoked on thread {0}.",
                        Thread.CurrentThread.ManagedThreadId)
        Thread.Sleep(5000)
        Return x + y
    End Function
```

```
      Private Sub AddComplete(ByVal itfAR As IAsyncResult)
          Console.WriteLine("AddComplete() invoked on thread {0}.",
                            Thread.CurrentThread.ManagedThreadId)
          Console.WriteLine("Your addition is complete")
          isDone = True
      End Sub
End Module
```

Again, the AddComplete() method will be invoked by the AsyncCallback delegate when the Add() method has completed. If you run this program, you can confirm that the secondary thread is the thread invoking the AddComplete() callback:

```
***** AsyncCallbackDelegate Example *****

Main() invoked on thread 1.

Add() invoked on thread 3.

Working....

Working....

Working....

Working....

Working....

AddComplete() invoked on thread 3.

Your addition is complete
```

Like other examples in this chapter, your output may be slightly different. In fact, you may see one final "Working…" printout occur after the addition is complete. This is just a byproduct of the forced 1-second delay in Main().

The Role of the AsyncResult Class

Currently, the AddComplete() method is not printing out the actual result of the operation (adding two numbers). The reason is that the target of the AsyncCallback delegate (AddComplete() in this example) does not have access to the original BinaryOp delegate created in the scope of Main(), and therefore you can't call EndInvoke() from within AddComplete()!

While you could simply declare the BinaryOp variable as a member variable in your module to allow both methods to access the same object, a more elegant solution is to use the incoming IAsyncResult parameter.

The incoming IAsyncResult parameter passed into the target of the AsyncCallback delegate is actually an instance of the AsyncResult class (note the lack of an I prefix) defined in the System. Runtime.Remoting.Messaging namespace. The Shared AsyncDelegate property returns a reference to the original asynchronous delegate that was created elsewhere.

Therefore, if you wish to obtain a reference to the BinaryOp delegate object allocated within Main(), simply cast the System.Object returned by the AsyncDelegate property into type BinaryOp. At this point, you can trigger EndInvoke() as expected:

```
'Don't forget to import
'System.Runtime.Remoting.Messaging!
Sub AddComplete(ByVal itfAR As IAsyncResult)
    Console.WriteLine("AddComplete() invoked on thread {0}.", _
                    Thread.CurrentThread.ManagedThreadId)
    Console.WriteLine("Your addition is complete")

    'Now get the result.
    Dim ar As AsyncResult = CType(itfAR, AsyncResult)
    Dim b As BinaryOp = CType(ar.AsyncDelegate, BinaryOp)
    Console.WriteLine("10 + 10 is {0}.", b.EndInvoke(itfAR))
    isDone = True
End Sub
```

Passing and Receiving Custom State Data

The final aspect of asynchronous delegates you need to address is the final argument to the BeginInvoke() method (which has been Nothing up to this point). This parameter allows you to pass additional state information to the callback method from the primary thread. Because this argument is prototyped as a System.Object, you can pass in any type of data whatsoever, as long as the callback method knows what to expect. Assume for the sake of demonstration that the primary thread wishes to pass in a custom text message to the AddComplete() method:

```
Sub Main()
    …
    Dim iftAR As IAsyncResult = b.BeginInvoke(10, 10, New AsyncCallback _
                            (AddressOf AddComplete), _
                            "Main() thanks you for adding these numbers.")
    …
End Sub
```

To obtain this data within the scope of AddComplete(), make use of the AsyncState property of the incoming IAsyncResult parameter. Notice that an explicit cast will be required; therefore the primary and secondary threads must agree on the underlying type returned from AsyncState.

```
Sub AddComplete(ByVal itfAR As IAsyncResult)
    …
    ' Retrieve the informational object and cast it to String.
    Dim msg As String = CStr(itfAR.AsyncState)
    Console.WriteLine(msg)
    isDone = True
End Sub
```

Here is the output of the final iteration:

```
*****  AsyncCallbackDelegate Example *****

Main() invoked on thread 1.

Add() invoked on thread 3.

Working....

Working....

Working....

Working....

Working....

AddComplete() invoked on thread 3.

Your addition is complete

10 + 10 is 20.

Main() thanks you for adding these numbers.

Working....
```

Now that you understand how a .NET delegate can be used to automatically spin off a secondary thread of execution to handle an asynchronous method invocation, let's turn attention to directly interacting with threads using the System.Threading namespace.

■ **Source Code** The AsyncCallbackDelegate project is located under the Chapter 19 subdirectory.

The System.Threading Namespace

Under the .NET platform, the System.Threading namespace provides a number of types that enable the direct construction of multithreaded applications. In addition to providing types that allow you to interact with a particular CLR thread, this namespace defines types that allow access to the CLR maintained thread pool, a simple (non–GUI-based) Timer class, and numerous types used to provide synchronized access to shared resources. Table 19-1 lists some of the core members of this namespace. (Be sure to consult the .NET Framework 4.0 SDK documentation for full details.)

Table 19-1. Select Types of the System.Threading Namespace

Type	Meaning in Life
Interlocked	This type provides atomic operations for variables that are shared by multiple threads.
Monitor	This type provides the synchronization of threading objects using SyncLocks and wait/signals. The VB 2010 SyncLock keyword makes use of a Monitor object under the hood.
Mutex	This synchronization primitive can be used for synchronization between application domain boundaries.
ParameterizedThreadStart	This delegate allows a thread to call methods that take any number of arguments.
Semaphore	This type allows you to limit the number of threads that can access a resource, or a particular type of resource, concurrently.
Thread	This type represents a thread that executes within the CLR. Using this type, you are able to spawn additional threads in the originating AppDomain.
ThreadPool	This type allows you to interact with the CLR-maintained thread pool within a given process.
ThreadPriority	This enum represents a thread's priority level (Highest, Normal, etc.).
ThreadStart	This delegate is used to specify the method to call for a given thread. Unlike the ParameterizedThreadStart delegate, targets of ThreadStart must always have the same prototype.
ThreadState	This enum specifies the valid states a thread may take (Running, Aborted, etc.).
Timer	This type provides a mechanism for executing a method at specified intervals.
TimerCallback	This delegate type is used in conjunction with Timer types.

The System.Threading.Thread Class

The most primitive of all types in the System.Threading namespace is Thread. This class represents an object-oriented wrapper around a given path of execution within a particular AppDomain. This type also defines a number of methods (both Shared and instance level) that allow you to create new threads within the current AppDomain, as well as to suspend, stop, and destroy a particular thread. Consider the list of core Shared members in Table 19-2.

Table 19-2. Key Shared Members of the Thread Type

Shared Member	Meaning in Life
CurrentContext	This read-only property returns the context in which the thread is currently running.
CurrentThread	This read-only property returns a reference to the currently running thread.
GetDomain() GetDomainID()	These methods return a reference to the current AppDomain or the ID of this domain in which the current thread is running.
Sleep()	This method suspends the current thread for a specified time.

The Thread class also supports several instance-level members, some of which are shown in Table 19-3.

Table 19-3. Select Instance-Level Members of the Thread Type

Instance-Level Member	Meaning in Life
IsAlive	Returns a Boolean that indicates whether this thread has been started (and has not yet terminated or aborted).
IsBackground	Gets or sets a value indicating whether or not this thread is a "background thread" (more details in just a moment).
Name	Allows you to establish a friendly text name of the thread.
Priority	Gets or sets the priority of a thread, which may be assigned a value from the ThreadPriority enumeration.
ThreadState	Gets the state of this thread, which may be assigned a value from the ThreadState enumeration.
Abort()	Instructs the CLR to terminate the thread as soon as possible.
Interrupt()	Interrupts (e.g., wakes) the current thread from a suitable wait period.
Join()	Blocks the calling thread until the specified thread (the one on which Join() is called) exits.
Resume()	Resumes a thread that has been previously suspended.
Start()	Instructs the CLR to execute the thread ASAP.
Suspend()	Suspends the thread. If the thread is already suspended, a call to Suspend() has no effect.

▦ **Note** Aborting or suspending an active thread is generally considered a bad idea. When you do so, there is a chance (however small) that a thread could "leak" its workload when disturbed or terminated.

Obtaining Statistics About the Current Thread

Recall that the entry point of an executable assembly (i.e., the `Main()` method) runs on the primary thread of execution. To illustrate the basic use of the `Thread` type, assume you have a new Console Application named `ThreadStats`. As you know, the Shared `Thread.CurrentThread` property retrieves a `Thread` object that represents the currently executing thread. Once you have obtained the current thread, you are able to print out various statistics:

```
' Be sure to import the System.Threading namespace.
Sub Main()
    Console.WriteLine("***** Primary Thread stats *****" & vbLf)

    'Obtain and name the current thread.
    Dim primaryThread As Thread = Thread.CurrentThread
    primaryThread.Name = "ThePrimaryThread"

    'Show details of hosting AppDomain/Context.
    Console.WriteLine("Name of current AppDomain: {0}",
                Thread.GetDomain().FriendlyName)
    Console.WriteLine("ID of current Context: {0}",
                Thread.CurrentContext.ContextID)

    'Print out some stats about this thread.
    Console.WriteLine("Thread Name: {0}", primaryThread.Name)
    Console.WriteLine("Has thread started?: {0}",
                primaryThread.IsAlive)

    Console.WriteLine("Priority Level: {0}", primaryThread.Priority)
    Console.WriteLine("Thread State: {0}", primaryThread.ThreadState)
    Console.ReadLine()
End Sub
```

Here is the current output:

```
***** Primary Thread stats *****


Name of current AppDomain: ThreadStats.exe

ID of current Context: 0

Thread Name: ThePrimaryThread

Has thread started?: True

Priority Level: Normal

Thread State: Running
```

The Name Property

While this code is more or less self-explanatory, do notice that the Thread class supports a property called Name. If you do not set this value, Name will return an empty string. However, once you assign a friendly string moniker to a given Thread object, you can greatly simplify your debugging endeavors. If you are making use of Visual Studio 2010, you may access the Threads window during a debugging session (select Debug ➤ Windows ➤ Threads). As you can see from Figure 19-1, you can quickly identify the thread you wish to diagnose.

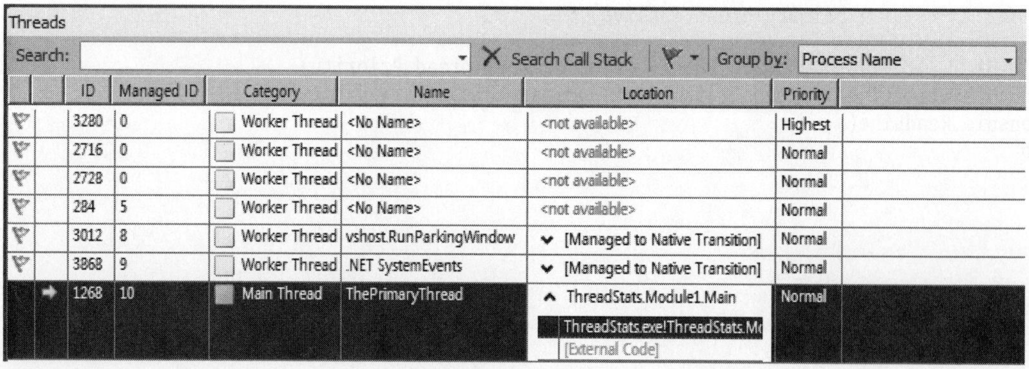

		ID	Managed ID	Category	Name	Location	Priority	
ⵖ		3280	0	☐ Worker Thread	<No Name>	<not available>	Highest	
ⵖ		2716	0	☐ Worker Thread	<No Name>	<not available>	Normal	
ⵖ		2728	0	☐ Worker Thread	<No Name>	<not available>	Normal	
ⵖ		284	5	☐ Worker Thread	<No Name>	<not available>	Normal	
ⵖ		3012	8	☐ Worker Thread	vshost.RunParkingWindow	⌄ [Managed to Native Transition]	Normal	
ⵖ		3868	9	☐ Worker Thread	.NET SystemEvents	⌄ [Managed to Native Transition]	Normal	
	➡	1268	10	■ Main Thread	ThePrimaryThread	⌃ ThreadStats.Module1.Main	Normal	
						ThreadStats.exe!ThreadStats.M(		
						[External Code]		

Figure 19-1. Debugging a thread with Visual Studio 2010

The Priority Property

Next, notice that the `Thread` type defines a property named `Priority`. By default, all threads have a priority level of `Normal`. However, you can change this at any point in the thread's lifetime using the `ThreadPriority` property and the related `System.Threading.ThreadPriority` enumeration:

```
Public Enum ThreadPriority
    Lowest
    BelowNormal
    Normal ' Default value.
    AboveNormal
    Highest
End Enum
```

If you were to assign a thread's priority level to a value other than the default (`ThreadPriority.Normal`), understand that you would have no direct control over when the thread scheduler switches between threads. In reality, a thread's priority level offers a hint to the CLR regarding the importance of the thread's activity. Thus, a thread with the value `ThreadPriority.Highest` is not necessarily guaranteed to be given the highest precedence.

Again, if the thread scheduler is preoccupied with a given task (e.g., synchronizing an object, switching threads, or moving threads), the priority level will most likely be altered accordingly. However, all things being equal, the CLR will read these values and instruct the thread scheduler how to best allocate time slices. Threads with an identical thread priority should each receive the same amount of time to perform their work.

In most cases, you will seldom (if ever) need to directly alter a thread's priority level. In theory, it is possible to jack up the priority level on a set of threads, thereby preventing lower-priority threads from executing at their required levels (so use caution).

■ **Source Code** The ThreadStats project is included under the Chapter 19 subdirectory.

Programmatically Creating Secondary Threads

When you wish to programmatically create additional threads to carry on some unit of work, you will follow a very predictable process:

1. Create a method to be the entry point for the new thread.

2. Create a new `ParameterizedThreadStart` (or `ThreadStart`) delegate, passing the address of the method defined in step 1 to the constructor.

3. Create a `Thread` object, passing the `ParameterizedThreadStart`/`ThreadStart` delegate as a constructor argument.

4. Establish any initial thread characteristics (name, priority, etc.).

5. Call the `Thread.Start()` method. This starts the thread at the method referenced by the delegate created in step 2 as soon as possible.

As stated in step 2, you may make use of two distinct delegate types to "point to" the method that the secondary thread will execute. The ThreadStart delegate has been part of the System.Threading namespace since .NET 1.0, and it can point to any method that takes no arguments and returns nothing. This delegate can be helpful when the method is designed to simply run in the background without further interaction.

The obvious limitation of ThreadStart is that you are unable to pass in parameters for processing. However, the ParameterizedThreadStart delegate type allows a single parameter of type System.Object. Given that anything can be represented as a System.Object, you can pass in any number of parameters via a custom class or structure. Do note, however, that the ParameterizedThreadStart delegate can only point to Subs (i.e., methods that have no return value).

Working with the ThreadStart Delegate

To illustrate the process of building a multithreaded application (as well as to demonstrate the usefulness of doing so), assume you have a Console Application (SimpleMultiThreadApp) that allows the end user to choose whether the application will perform its duties using the single primary thread or split its workload using two separate threads of execution.

Assuming you have imported the System.Threading namespace, your first step is to define a method to perform the work of the (possible) secondary thread. To keep focused on the mechanics of building multithreaded programs, this method will simply print out a sequence of numbers to the console window, pausing for approximately two seconds with each pass. Here is the full definition of the Printer class:

```
Public Class Printer

    Public Sub PrintNumbers()
        'Display Thread info.
        Console.WriteLine("-> {0} is executing PrintNumbers()",
                          Thread.CurrentThread.Name)

        ' Print out numbers.
        Console.Write("Your numbers: ")
        For i As Integer = 0 To 9
            Console.Write("{0}, ", i)
            Thread.Sleep(2000)
        Next
        Console.WriteLine()
    End Sub
End Class
```

Now, within Main(), you will first prompt the user to determine whether one or two threads will be used to perform the application's work. If the user requests a single thread, you will simply invoke the PrintNumbers() method within the primary thread. However, if the user specifies two threads, you will create a ThreadStart delegate that points to PrintNumbers(), pass this delegate object into the constructor of a new Thread object, and call Start() to inform the CLR this thread is ready for processing.

To begin, set a reference to the System.Windows.Forms.dll assembly (and import the System.Windows.Forms namespace) and display a message within Main() using MessageBox.Show() (you'll see the point of doing so once you run the program). Here is the complete implementation of Main():

```vb
Sub Main()
      Console.WriteLine("***** The Amazing Thread App *****" & vbLf)
      Console.Write("Do you want [1] or [2] threads? ")
      Dim threadCount As String = Console.ReadLine()

      ' Name the current thread.
      Dim primaryThread As Thread = Thread.CurrentThread
      primaryThread.Name = "Primary"

      'Display Thread info.
      Console.WriteLine("-> {0} is executing Main()",
                 Thread.CurrentThread.Name)

      ' Make worker class.
      Dim p As New Printer()

      Select Case threadCount
          Case "2"
          ' Now make the thread.
      Dim backgroundThread As New Thread(New ThreadStart
                         (AddressOf p.PrintNumbers))
          backgroundThread.Name = "Secondary"
          backgroundThread.Start()
      Case "1"
      CaseLabel1:

          p.PrintNumbers()
      Case Else
          Console.WriteLine("I don't know what you want...you get 1 thread.")
          GoTo CaseLabel1
   End Select

   ' Do some additional work.
   MessageBox.Show("I'm busy!", "Work on main thread...")
   Console.ReadLine()
End Sub
```

Now, if you run this program with a single thread, you will find that the final message box will not display the message until the entire sequence of numbers has printed to the console. As you are explicitly pausing for approximately two seconds after each number is printed, this will result in a less-than-stellar end-user experience. However, if you select two threads, the message box displays instantly, given that a unique **Thread** object is responsible for printing out the numbers to the console (see Figure 19-2).

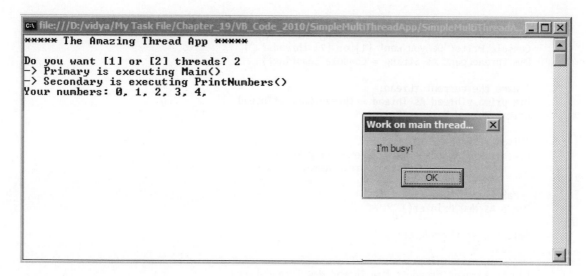

Figure 19-2. Multithreaded applications provide results in more responsive applications

---

■ **Source Code** The SimpleMultiThreadApp project is included under the Chapter 19 subdirectory.

Working with the ParameterizedThreadStart Delegate

Recall that the ThreadStart delegate can point only to Subs(i.e., no return value) and take no arguments. While this may fit the bill in many cases, if you wish to pass data to the method executing on the secondary thread, you will need to make use of the ParameterizedThreadStart delegate type. To illustrate, let's re-create the logic of the AsyncCallbackDelegate project created earlier in this chapter, this time making use of the ParameterizedThreadStart delegate type.

To begin, create a new Console Application named AddWithThreads and import the System.Threading namespace. Now, given that ParameterizedThreadStart can point to any method taking a System.Object parameter, you will create a custom type containing the numbers to be added:

```
Public Class AddParams
    Public a, b As Integer

    Public Sub New(ByVal numb1 As Integer, ByVal numb2 As Integer)
        a = numb1
        b = numb2
    End Sub
End Class
```

Next, create a method in the Module1 Module that will take an AddParams parameter and print out the sum of the two numbers involved:

```
Sub Add(ByVal data As Object)
    If TypeOf data Is AddParams Then
        Console.WriteLine("ID of thread in Add(): {0}",
                    Thread.CurrentThread.ManagedThreadId)
        Dim ap As AddParams = CType(data, AddParams)
        Console.WriteLine("{0} + {1} is {2}", ap.a, ap.b, ap.a + ap.b)
    End If
End Sub
```

The code within Main() is straightforward. Simply use ParameterizedThreadStart rather than ThreadStart:

```
Sub Main()
    Console.WriteLine("***** Adding with Thread objects *****")
    Console.WriteLine("ID of thread in Main(): {0}"
                ,Thread.CurrentThread.ManagedThreadId)

    'Make an AddParams object to pass to the secondary thread.
    Dim ap As New AddParams(10, 10)
    Dim t As New Thread(New ParameterizedThreadStart(AddressOf Add))
    t.Start(ap)

    'Force a wait to let other thread finish.
    Thread.Sleep(5)

    Console.ReadLine()
End Sub
```

The AutoResetEvent Class

In these first few examples, you have made use of a few crude ways to inform the primary thread to wait until the secondary thread has completed. During your examination of asynchronous delegates you used a simple Boolean variable as a toggle; however, this is not a recommended solution, as both threads can access the same point of data, and this can lead to data corruption. A safer, but still undesirable alternative is to call Thread.Sleep() for a fixed amount of time. The problem here is you don't want to wait longer than necessary.

One simple, and thread safe way to force a thread to wait until another is completed is to use the AutoResetEvent class. In the thread which needs to wait (such as a Main() method), create an instance of this class, and pass in False to the constructor in order to signify you have not yet been notified. Then, at the point at which you are willing to wait, call the WaitOne() method. Here is the update to the Module1 Module, which will do this very thing using an AutoResetEvent member variable:

```
Module Module1
    Private waitHandle As New AutoResetEvent(False)

    Sub Main()
        Console.WriteLine("***** Adding with Thread objects *****")
        Console.WriteLine("ID of thread in Main(): {0}",↵
                            Thread.CurrentThread.ManagedThreadId)
        Dim ap As New AddParams(10, 10)
        Dim t As New Thread(New ParameterizedThreadStart(AddressOf Add))
        t.Start(ap)

        ' Wait here until you are notified!
        waitHandle.WaitOne()
        Console.WriteLine("Other thread is done!")

        Console.ReadLine()

    End Sub
    ...
End Module
```

When the other thread is completed with its workload, it will call the Set() method on the same instance of the AutoResetEvent type:

```
Sub Add(ByVal data As Object)
    If TypeOf data Is AddParams Then
        Console.WriteLine("ID of thread in Add(): {0}",
            Thread.CurrentThread.ManagedThreadId)

        Dim ap As AddParams = CType(data, AddParams)
        Console.WriteLine("{0} + {1} is {2}", ap.a, ap.b, ap.a + ap.b)

        ' Tell other thread we are done.
        waitHandle.Set()
    End If
End Sub
```

■ **Source Code** The AddWithThreads project is included under the Chapter 19 subdirectory.

Foreground Threads and Background Threads

Now that you have seen how to programmatically create new threads of execution using the System.Threading namespace, let's formalize the distinction between *foreground threads* and *background threads*.

- *Foreground threads* have the ability to prevent the current application from terminating. The CLR will not shut down an application (which is to say, unload the hosting AppDomain) until all foreground threads have ended.

- *Background threads* (sometimes called *daemon threads*) are viewed by the CLR as expendable paths of execution that can be ignored at any point in time (even if they are currently laboring over some unit of work). Thus, if all foreground threads have terminated, any and all background threads are automatically killed when the application domain unloads.

It is important to note that foreground and background threads are *not* synonymous with primary and worker threads. By default, every thread you create via the `Thread.Start()` method is automatically a foreground thread. Again, this means that the AppDomain will not unload until all threads of execution have completed their units of work. In most cases, this is exactly the behavior you require.

For the sake of argument, however, assume that you wish to invoke `Printer.PrintNumbers()` on a secondary thread that should behave as a background thread. Again, this means that the method pointed to by the `Thread` type (via the `ThreadStart` or `ParameterizedThreadStart` delegate) should be able to halt safely as soon as all foreground threads are done with their work. Configuring such a thread is as simple as setting the `IsBackground` property to `True`:

```
Sub Main()
        Console.WriteLine("***** Background Threads *****" & vbLf)

        Dim p As New Printer()
        Dim bgroundThread As New Thread(New ThreadStart
                        (AddressOf p.PrintNumbers))

        'This is now a background thread.
        bgroundThread.IsBackground = True
        bgroundThread.Start()
End Sub
```

Notice that this `Main()` method is *not* making a call to `Console.ReadLine()` to force the console to remain visible until you press the Enter key. Thus, when you run the application, it will shut down immediately because the `Thread` object has been configured as a background thread. Given that the `Main()` method triggers the creation of the primary *foreground* thread, as soon as the logic in `Main()` completes, the AppDomain unloads before the secondary thread is able to complete its work.

However, if you comment out the line that sets the `IsBackground` property, you will find that each number prints to the console, as all foreground threads must finish their work before the AppDomain is unloaded from the hosting process.

For the most part, configuring a thread to run as a background type can be helpful when the worker thread in question is performing a noncritical task that is no longer needed when the main task of the program is finished. For example, you may build an application which pings an e-mail server every few minutes for new e-mails, updates current weather conditions, or some other non-critical task.

The Issue of Concurrency

When you build multithreaded applications, your program needs to ensure that any piece of shared data is protected against the possibility of numerous threads changing its value. Given that all threads in an AppDomain have concurrent access to the shared data of the application, imagine what might happen if multiple threads were accessing the same point of data. As the thread scheduler will force threads to suspend their work at random, what if thread A is kicked out of the way before it has fully completed its work? Thread B is now reading unstable data.

To illustrate the problem of concurrency, let's build another Console Application project named MultiThreadedPrinting. This application will once again make use of the `Printer` class created previously, but this time the `PrintNumbers()` method will force the current thread to pause for a randomly generated amount of time:

```
Public Class Printer
    Public Sub PrintNumbers()
        …
        For i As Integer = 0 To 9
            ' Put thread to sleep for a random amount of time.
            Dim r As New Random()
            Thread.Sleep(1000 * r.Next(5))
            Console.Write("{0}, ", i)
        Next i
        Console.WriteLine()
    End Sub
End Class
```

The `Main()` method is responsible for creating an array of ten (uniquely named) `Thread` objects, each of which is making calls on the *same instance* of the `Printer` object:

```
Module Module1
  Sub Main()
        Console.WriteLine("*****Synchronizing Threads *****" & vbLf)

        Dim p As New Printer()

        'Make 10 threads that are all pointing to the same
        'method on the same object.
        Dim threads(9) As Thread
        For i As Integer = 0 To 9
          threads(i) = New Thread(New ThreadStart(AddressOf p.PrintNumbers))
          threads(i).Name = String.Format("Worker thread #{0}", i)
        Next i

        'Now start each one.
        For Each t As Thread In threads
          t.Start()
        Next t
        Console.ReadLine()
  End Sub
End Module
```

Before looking at some test runs, let's recap the problem. The primary thread within this AppDomain begins life by spawning ten secondary worker threads. Each worker thread is told to make calls on the PrintNumbers() method on the *same* Printer instance. Given that you have taken no precautions to lock down this object's shared resources (the console), there is a good chance that the current thread will be kicked out of the way before the PrintNumbers() method is able to print out the complete results. Because you don't know exactly when (or if) this might happen, you are bound to get unpredictable results. For example, you might find the output shown here:

```
*****Synchronizing Threads *****


-> Worker thread #1 is executing PrintNumbers()

Your numbers: -> Worker thread #0 is executing PrintNumbers()

-> Worker thread #2 is executing PrintNumbers()

Your numbers: -> Worker thread #3 is executing PrintNumbers()

Your numbers: -> Worker thread #4 is executing PrintNumbers()

Your numbers: -> Worker thread #6 is executing PrintNumbers()

Your numbers: -> Worker thread #7 is executing PrintNumbers()

Your numbers: -> Worker thread #8 is executing PrintNumbers()

Your numbers: -> Worker thread #9 is executing PrintNumbers()

Your numbers: Your numbers: -> Worker thread #5 is executing PrintNumbers()

Your numbers: 0, 0, 0, 0, 1, 0, 0, 1, 1, 1, 2, 2, 2, 3, 3, 3, 2, 1, 0, 0, 4, 3,

4, 1, 2, 4, 5, 5, 5, 6, 6, 6, 2, 7, 7, 7, 3, 4, 0, 8, 4, 5, 1, 5, 8, 8, 9,

2, 6, 1, 0, 9, 1,

6, 2, 7, 9,

2, 1, 7, 8, 3, 2, 3, 3, 9,

8, 4, 4, 5, 9,

4, 3, 5, 5, 6, 3, 6, 7, 4, 7, 6, 8, 7, 4, 8, 5, 5, 6, 6, 8, 7, 7, 9,

8, 9,
```

8, 9,

9,

9,

Now run the application a few more times. Here is another possibility (your results will certainly differ).

```
*****Synchronizing Threads *****

-> Worker thread #0 is executing PrintNumbers()

-> Worker thread #1 is executing PrintNumbers()

-> Worker thread #2 is executing PrintNumbers()

Your numbers: -> Worker thread #4 is executing PrintNumbers()

Your numbers: -> Worker thread #5 is executing PrintNumbers()

Your numbers: Your numbers: -> Worker thread #6 is executing PrintNumbers()

Your numbers: -> Worker thread #7 is executing PrintNumbers()

Your numbers: Your numbers: -> Worker thread #8 is executing PrintNumbers()

Your numbers: -> Worker thread #9 is executing PrintNumbers()

Your numbers: -> Worker thread #3 is executing PrintNumbers()

Your numbers: 0, 0, 0, 0, 0, 0, 0, 0, 0, 0, 1, 1, 1, 1, 1, 1, 1, 1, 1, 1, 2, 2,

2, 2, 2, 2, 2, 2, 2, 2, 3, 3, 3, 3, 3, 3, 3, 3, 3, 3, 4, 4, 4, 4, 4, 4, 4, 4, 4,

 4, 5, 5, 5, 5, 5, 5, 5, 5, 5, 5, 6, 6, 6, 6, 6, 6, 6, 6, 6, 6, 7, 7, 7, 7, 7, 7

, 7, 7, 7, 7, 8, 8, 8, 8, 8, 8, 8, 8, 8, 8, 9,

9,

9,

9,

9,
```

9,

9,

9,

9,

9,

■ **Note** If you are unable to generate unpredictable outputs, increase the number of threads from 10 to 100 (for example) or introduce another call to Thread.Sleep() within your program. Eventually, you will encounter the concurrency issue.

There are clearly some problems here. As each thread is telling the Printer to print out the numerical data, the thread scheduler is happily swapping threads in the background. The result is inconsistent output. What you need is a way to programmatically enforce synchronized access to the shared resources. As you would guess, the System.Threading namespace provides a number of synchronization-centric types. The VB 2010 programming language also provides a particular keyword for the very task of synchronizing shared data in multithreaded applications.

Synchronization Using the VB 2010 SyncLock Keyword

The first technique you can use to synchronize access to shared resources is the VB 2010 SyncLock keyword. This keyword allows you to define a scope of statements that must be synchronized between threads. By doing so, incoming threads cannot interrupt the current thread, preventing it from finishing its work. The SyncLock keyword requires you to specify a *token* (an object reference) that must be acquired by a thread to enter within the lock scope. When you are attempting to lock down a *Private* instance-level method, you can simply pass in a reference to the current type:

```
Private Sub SomePrivateMethod()
    'Use the current object as the thread token.
    SyncLock Me
        ' All code within this scope is thread-safe.
    End SyncLock
End Sub
```

However, if you are locking down a region of code within a *Public* member, it is safer (and a best practice) to declare a private object member variable to serve as the lock token:

```
Public Class Printer
  'SyncLock token.
  Private threadLock As New Object()

  Public Sub PrintNumbers()
      ' Use the lock token.
      SyncLock threadLock
          ...
      End SyncLock
  End Sub
End Class
```

In any case, if you examine the `PrintNumbers()` method, you can see that the shared resource the threads are competing to gain access to is the console window. Therefore, if you scope all interactions with the `Console` type within a SyncLock scope as follows:

```
Public Sub PrintNumbers()

    'Use the Private object lock token.
    SyncLock threadLock
        'Display Thread info.
        Console.WriteLine("-> {0} is executing PrintNumbers()"
                    ,Thread.CurrentThread.Name)

        'Print out numbers.
        Console.Write("Your numbers: ")
        For i = 0 To 9
            Dim r As New Random()
            Thread.Sleep(1000 * r.Next(5))
            Console.Write("{0}, ", i)
        Next
        Console.WriteLine()
    End SyncLock
End Sub
```

you have effectively designed a method that will allow the current thread to complete its task. Once a thread enters into a SyncLock scope, the lock token (in this case, a reference to the current object) is inaccessible by other threads until the lock is released once the lock scope has exited. Thus, if thread A has obtained the lock token, other threads are unable to enter *any scope* that uses the same lock token until thread A relinquishes the lock token.

■ **Note** If you are attempting to lock down code in a Shared method, simply declare a Private Shared object member variable to serve as the lock .

If you now run the application, you can see that each thread has ample opportunity to finish its business:

```
*****Synchronizing Threads *****


-> Worker thread #0 is executing PrintNumbers()

Your numbers: 0, 1, 2, 3, 4, 5, 6, 7, 8, 9,

-> Worker thread #1 is executing PrintNumbers()

Your numbers: 0, 1, 2, 3, 4, 5, 6, 7, 8, 9,

-> Worker thread #3 is executing PrintNumbers()

Your numbers: 0, 1, 2, 3, 4, 5, 6, 7, 8, 9,

-> Worker thread #2 is executing PrintNumbers()

Your numbers: 0, 1, 2, 3, 4, 5, 6, 7, 8, 9,

-> Worker thread #4 is executing PrintNumbers()

Your numbers: 0, 1, 2, 3, 4, 5, 6, 7, 8, 9,

-> Worker thread #5 is executing PrintNumbers()

Your numbers: 0, 1, 2, 3, 4, 5, 6, 7, 8, 9,

-> Worker thread #7 is executing PrintNumbers()

Your numbers: 0, 1, 2, 3, 4, 5, 6, 7, 8, 9,

-> Worker thread #6 is executing PrintNumbers()

Your numbers: 0, 1, 2, 3, 4, 5, 6, 7, 8, 9,

-> Worker thread #8 is executing PrintNumbers()

Your numbers: 0, 1, 2, 3, 4, 5, 6, 7, 8, 9,

-> Worker thread #9 is executing PrintNumbers()

Your numbers: 0, 1, 2, 3, 4, 5, 6, 7, 8, 9,
```

■ **Source Code** The MultiThreadedPrinting project is included under the Chapter 19 subdirectory.

Synchronization Using the System.Threading.Monitor Type

The VB 2010 `SyncLock` statement is really just a shorthand notation for working with the `System.Threading.Monitor` class. Once processed by the VB 2010 compiler, a SyncLock scope actually resolves to the following (which you can verify using `ildasm.exe` or `reflector.exe`):

```
Public Sub PrintNumbers()
    Monitor.Enter(threadLock)
    Try
        'Display Thread info.
        Console.WriteLine("-> {0} is executing PrintNumbers()"
                    ,Thread.CurrentThread.Name)

        'Print out numbers.
        Console.Write("Your numbers: ")
        For i As Integer = 0 To 9
            Dim r As New Random()
            Thread.Sleep(1000 * r.Next(5))
            Console.Write("{0}, ", i)
        Next
         Console.WriteLine()
    Finally
        Monitor.Exit(threadLock)
    End Try
End Sub
```

First, notice that the `Monitor.Enter()` method is the ultimate recipient of the thread token you specified as the argument to the `SyncLock` keyword. Next, all code within a SyncLock scope is wrapped within a `Try` block. The corresponding `Finally` clause ensures that the thread token is released (via the `Monitor.Exit()` method), regardless of any possible runtime exception. If you were to modify the MultiThreadSharedData program to make direct use of the `Monitor` type (as just shown), you will find the output is identical.

Now, given that the `SyncLock` keyword seems to require less code than making explicit use of the `System.Threading.Monitor` type, you may wonder about the benefits of using the `Monitor` type directly. The short answer is control. If you make use of the `Monitor` type, you are able to instruct the active thread to wait for some duration of time (via the Shared `Monitor.Wait()` method), inform waiting threads when the current thread is completed (via the Shared `Monitor.Pulse()` and `Monitor.PulseAll()` methods), and so on.

As you would expect, in a great number of cases, the VB 2010 `SyncLock` keyword will fit the bill. However, if you are interested in checking out additional members of the `Monitor` class, consult the .NET Framework 4.0 SDK documentation.

Synchronization Using the System.Threading.Interlocked Type

Although it always is hard to believe until you look at the underlying CIL code, assignments and simple arithmetic operations are *not atomic*. For this reason, the `System.Threading` namespace provides a type that allows you to operate on a single point of data atomically with less overhead than with the `Monitor` type. The `Interlocked` class defines the following key Shared members shown in Table 19-4.

Table 19-4. Select Members of the System.Threading.Interlocked Type

Member	Meaning in Life
CompareExchange()	Safely tests two values for equality and, if equal, changes one of the values with a third
Decrement()	Safely decrements a value by 1
Exchange()	Safely swaps two values
Increment()	Safely increments a value by 1

Although it might not seem like it from the onset, the process of atomically altering a single value is quite common in a multithreaded environment. Assume you have a method named `AddOne()` that increments an Integer member variable named `intVal`. Rather than writing synchronization code such as the following:

```
Public Sub AddOne()
    SyncLock myLockToken
        intVal += 1
    End SyncLock
End Sub
```

you can simplify your code via the Shared `Interlocked.Increment()` method. Simply pass in the variable to increment by reference. Do note that the `Increment()` method not only adjusts the value of the incoming parameter, but also returns the new value:

```
Public Sub AddOne()
    Dim newVal As Integer = Interlocked.Increment(intVal)
End Sub
```

In addition to `Increment()` and `Decrement()`, the `Interlocked` type allows you to atomically assign numerical and object data. For example, if you wish to assign the value of a member variable to the value 83, you can avoid the need to use an explicit `SyncLock` statement (or explicit `Monitor` logic) and make use of the `Interlocked.Exchange()` method:

```
Public Sub SafeAssignment()
    Interlocked.Exchange(myInt, 83)
End Sub
```

Finally, if you wish to test two values for equality and change the point of comparison in a thread-safe manner, you are able to leverage the `Interlocked.CompareExchange()` method as follows:

```
Public Sub CompareAndExchange()
    ' If the value of i is currently 83, change i to 99.
    Interlocked.CompareExchange(i, 99, 83)
End Sub
```

Synchronization Using the <Synchronization()> Attribute

The final synchronization primitive examined here is the `<Synchronization()>` attribute, which is a member of the `System.Runtime.Remoting.Contexts` namespace. In essence, this class-level attribute effectively locks down *all* instance member code of the object for thread safety. When the CLR allocates objects attributed with `<Synchronization()>`, it will place the object within a synchronized context. As you may recall from Chapter 17, objects that should not be removed from a contextual boundary should derive from `ContextBoundObject`. Therefore, if you wish to make the `Printer` class type thread-safe (without explicitly writing thread-safe code within the class members), you could update the definition as follows:

```
Imports System.Runtime.Remoting.Contexts
...
' All methods of Printer are now thread-safe!
<Synchronization()>
Public Class Printer
    Inherits ContextBoundObject

    Public Sub PrintNumbers()
    ...
    End Sub
End Class
```

In some ways, this approach can be seen as the lazy way to write thread-safe code, given that you are not required to dive into the details about which aspects of the type are truly manipulating thread-sensitive data. The major downfall of this approach, however, is that even if a given method is not making use of thread-sensitive data, the CLR will *still* lock invocations to the method. Obviously, this could degrade the overall functionality of the type, so use this technique with care.

Programming with Timer Callbacks

Many applications have the need to call a specific method during regular intervals of time. For example, you may have an application that needs to display the current time on a status bar via a given helper function. As another example, you may wish to have your application call a helper function every so often to perform noncritical background tasks such as checking for new e-mail messages. For situations such as these, you can use the `System.Threading.Timer` type in conjunction with a related delegate named `TimerCallback`.

To illustrate, assume you have a Console Application (TimerApp) that will print the current time every second until the user presses a key to terminate the application. The first obvious step is to write the method that will be called by the `Timer` type (be sure to import `System.Threading` into your code file):

```
Module Module1
    Private Sub PrintTime(ByVal state As Object)
        Console.WriteLine("Time is: {0}", Date.Now.ToLongTimeString())
    End Sub

    Sub Main()
    End Sub
End Module
```

Notice how this method has a single parameter of type System.Object and has no return value (because it's a Sub). This is not optional, given that the TimerCallback delegate can only call methods that match this signature. The value passed into the target of your TimerCallback delegate can be any bit of information whatsoever (in the case of the e-mail example, this parameter might represent the name of the Microsoft Exchange server to interact with during the process). Also note that given that this parameter is indeed a System.Object, you are able to pass in multiple arguments using a System.Array or custom class/structure.

The next step is to configure an instance of the TimerCallback delegate and pass it into the Timer object. In addition to configuring a TimerCallback delegate, the Timer constructor allows you to specify the optional parameter information to pass into the delegate target (defined as a System.Object), the interval to poll the method, and the amount of time to wait (in milliseconds) before making the first call, for example:

```
Sub Main()
    Console.WriteLine("***** Working with Timer type *****" & vbLf)

    'Create the delegate for the Timer type.
    Dim timeCB As New TimerCallback(AddressOf PrintTime)

    ' Establish timer settings, with these parameters:
    '    timeCB  - The TimerCallBack delegate object.
    '    Nothing - Any info to pass into called method (Nothing for no info).
    '    0       - Amount of the time to wait before starting (in millisecs).
    '    1000    - Interval of time between calls (in millisecs).

    Dim t As New Timer(timeCB, Nothing, 0, 1000)


    Console.WriteLine("Hit key to terminate...")
    Console.ReadLine()
End Sub
```

In this case, the PrintTime() method will be called roughly every second and will pass in no additional information to said method. Here is the output:

```
***** Working with Timer type *****


Hit key to terminate...

Time is: 6:51:48 PM

Time is: 6:51:49 PM

Time is: 6:51:50 PM

Time is: 6:51:51 PM

Time is: 6:51:52 PM

Press any key to continue . . .
```

If you did wish to send in some information for use by the delegate target, simply substitute the `Nothing` value of the second constructor parameter with the appropriate information:

```
'Establish timer settings.
Dim t As New Timer(timeCB, "Hello From Main", 0, 1000)
```

You can then obtain the incoming data as follows:

```
Sub PrintTime(ByVal state As Object)
      Console.WriteLine("Time is: {0}, Param is: {1}",
      DateTime.Now.ToLongTimeString(), state.ToString())
End Sub
```

■ **Source Code** The TimerApp project is included under the Chapter 19 subdirectory.

Understanding the CLR ThreadPool

The next thread-centric topic you will examine in this chapter is the role of the CLR thread pool. When you invoke a method asynchronously using delegate types (via the `BeginInvoke()` method), the CLR does not literally create a brand-new thread. For purposes of efficiency, a delegate's `BeginInvoke()` method leverages a pool of worker threads that is maintained by the runtime. To allow you to interact with this pool of waiting threads, the `System.Threading` namespace provides the `ThreadPool` class type.

If you wish to queue a method call for processing by a worker thread in the pool, you can make use of the `ThreadPool.QueueUserWorkItem()` method. This method has been overloaded to allow you to specify an optional `System.Object` for custom state data in addition to an instance of the `WaitCallback` delegate:

```
Public NotInheritable Class ThreadPool
    ...
    Public Shared QueueUserWorkItem(ByVal callBack As WaitCallback)
                                    As Boolean
    Public Shared QueueUserWorkItem(ByVal callBack As
                WaitCallback,ByVal state As Object) As Boolean
End Class
```

The `WaitCallback` delegate can point to any method that takes a `System.Object` as its sole parameter (which represents the optional state data) and returns nothing. Do note that if you do not provide a `System.Object` when calling `QueueUserWorkItem()`, the CLR automatically passes a Nothing value. To illustrate queuing methods for use by the CLR thread pool, ponder the following program, which makes use of the `Printer` type once again. In this case, however, you are not manually creating an array of `Thread` objects; rather, you are assigning members of the pool to the `PrintNumbers()` method:

```
Module Module1
    Sub Main()
        Console.WriteLine("**** Fun with the CLR Thread Pool ****" & vbLf)

        Console.WriteLine("Main thread started. ThreadID = {0}"
                            ,Thread.CurrentThread.ManagedThreadId)

        Dim p As New Printer()
        Dim workItem As New WaitCallback(AddressOf PrintTheNumbers)

        'Queue the method ten times.
        For i As Integer = 0 To 9
            ThreadPool.QueueUserWorkItem(workItem, p)
        Next
        Console.WriteLine("All tasks queued")
        Console.ReadLine()

    End Sub

    Private Sub PrintTheNumbers(ByVal state As Object)
        Dim task As Printer = CType(state, Printer)
        task.PrintNumbers()
    End Sub
End Module
```

At this point, you may be wondering if it would be advantageous to make use of the CLR-maintained thread pool rather than explicitly creating Thread objects. Consider these benefits of leveraging the thread pool:

- The thread pool manages threads efficiently by minimizing the number of threads that must be created, started, and stopped.

- By using the thread pool, you can focus on your business problem rather than the application's threading infrastructure.

However, using manual thread management is preferred in some cases, for example:

- If you require foreground threads or must set the thread priority. Pooled threads are *always* background threads with default priority (ThreadPriority.Normal).

- If you require a thread with a fixed identity in order to abort it, suspend it, or discover it by name.

■ **Source Code** The ThreadPoolApp project is included under the Chapter 19 subdirectory.

That wraps up your investigation of the System.Threading namespace. While you can use this information to build some responsive applications, the remainder of this chapter will examine a new addition to the base class libraries brought forth with .NET 4.0- The Task Parallel Library.

Parallel Programming under the .NET Platform

If you go shopping at any electronic "super store," you will quickly notice that computers which support two or more CPUs (aka, *cores*) are commonplace. Not only are they commonplace, they are quite cost effective; dual core laptops can be purchased for less than $500.00 USD. When a machine supports multiple CPUs, it has the ability to execute threads in a parallel fashion, which can significantly improve the runtime performance of applications.

Traditionally speaking, if you wanted to build a .NET application which can distribute its workload across multiple cores, you needed to be quite skilled in multithreaded programming techniques (using many of the topics seen in this chapter). While this was certainly possible, doing so was tedious and error prone, given the inherit complexities of building multithreaded applications.

With the release of .NET 4.0, you are provided with a brand new parallel programming library. Using the types of System.Threading.Tasks, you can build fine-grained, scalable parallel code without having to work directly with threads or the thread pool. Furthermore, when you do so, you can make use of strongly typed LINQ queries (via parallel LINQ, or PLINQ) to divide up your workload.

The Task Parallel Library API

Collectively speaking, the types of System.Threading.Tasks (as well as some related types in System.Threading) are referred to as the *Task Parallel Library*, or TPL. The TPL will automatically distribute your application's workload across available CPUs dynamically using the CLR thread pool. The TPL handles the partitioning of the work, thread scheduling, state management, and other low-level details. The end result is that you can maximize the performance of your .NET applications, while being shielded from many of complexities of directly working with threads. Figure 19-3 shows the members of this new .NET 4.0 namespace.

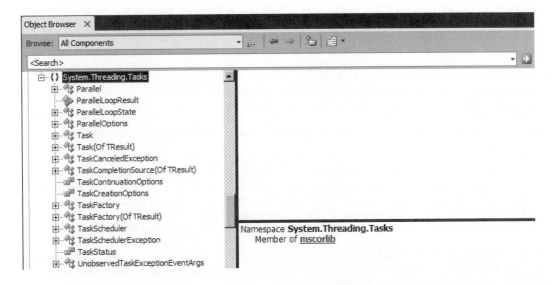

Figure 19-3. Members of the System.Threading.Tasks namespace

Starting with .NET 4.0, use of the TPL is the recommended way to build multithreaded applications. This is certainly not to suggest that having an understanding of traditional multithreading techniques using asynchronous delegates or the classes of `System.Threading` is somehow obsolete. In fact, to effectively use the TPL, you must understand primitive such as threads, locks, and concurrency. Furthermore, many situations that require multiple threads (such as asynchronous calls to remote objects) can be handled without the use of the TPL. Nevertheless, the amount of time you will need to directly work with the `Thread` class decreases significantly.

Finally, be aware that just because you can, does not mean you should. In the same way that creating multiple threads can slow down the execution of your .NET programs, authoring a ton of unnecessary parallel tasks can hurt performance. Use the functionality of the TPL only when you have a workload which truly creates a bottleneck in your programs, such as iterating over hundreds of objects, processing data in multiple files, etc.

■ **Note** The TPL infrastructure is rather intelligent. If it determines that a set of tasks would gain little or no benefit by running in parallel, it will opt to perform them in sequence.

The Role of the Parallel Class

The primary class of the TPL is `System.Threading.Tasks.Parallel`. This class supports a number of methods which allow you to iterate over a collection of data (specifically, an object implementing `IEnumerable(Of T)`) in a parallel fashion. If you were to look up the `Parallel` class in the .NET Framework 4.0 SDK documentation, you'll see that this class supports two primary Shared methods, `Parallel.For()` and `Parallel.ForEach()`, each of which defines numerous overloaded versions.

These methods allow you to author a body of code statements which will be processed in a parallel manner. In concept, these statements are the same sort of logic you would write in a normal looping construct (via the `For` or `For Each` VB 2010 constructs). The benefit however, is that the `Parallel` class will pluck threads from the thread pool (and manage concurrency) on your behalf.

Both of these methods require you to specify an `IEnumerable` or `IEnumerable(Of T)` compatible container that holds the data you need to process in a parallel manner. The container could be a simple array, a non-generic collection (such as `ArrayList`), a generic collection (such as `List(Of T)`), or the results of a LINQ query.

In addition, you will need to make use of the `System.Func(Of T)` and `System.Action(Of T)` delegates to specify the target method which will be called to process the data. You've already encountered the `Func(Of T)` delegate in Chapter 13 during your investigation of LINQ to Objects. Recall that `Func(Of T)` represents a method which can have a given return value and a varied number of arguments. The `Action(Of T)` delegate is very similar to `Func(Of T)`, in that it allows you to point to a method taking some number of parameters. However, `Action(Of T)` specifies a `Sub` (i.e., a method that has no return value).

While you could call the `Parallel.For()` and `Parallel.ForEach()` methods and pass a strongly typed `Func(Of T)` or `Action(Of T)` delegate object, you can simplify your programming by making use of a fitting VB 2010 anonymous method or lambda expression.

Understanding Data Parallelism

The first way to use the TPL is to perform *data parallelism*. Simply put, this term refers to the task of iterating over an array or collection in a parallel manner using the `Parallel.For()` or `Parallel.ForEach()` methods. Assume you need to perform some labor intensive File IO operations. Specifically, you need to load a large number of `*.jpg` files into memory, flip them upside-down, and save the modified image data to a new location.

The .NET Framework 4.0 SDK documentation provides a console based example of this very thing, however we will perform the same overall task using a graphical user interface. To illustrate, create a Windows Forms application named DataParallelismWithForEach, and rename the `Form1.vb` to `MainForm.vb`. Once you do, import the following namespaces in your primary code file:

```
' Need these namespaces!
Imports System.Threading.Tasks
Imports System.Threading
Imports System.IO
```

The GUI of the application consists of a multiline `TextBox` and a single `Button` (named `btnProcessImages`). The purpose of the text area is to allow you to enter data while the work is being performed in the background, thus illustrating the non-blocking nature of the parallel task. The `Click` event of this `Button` will eventually make use of the TPL, but for now, author the following blocking code:

```vbnet
Public Class MainForm

        Private Sub btnProcessImages_Click(ByVal sender As Object,
            ByVal e As EventArgs) Handles btnProcessImages.Click
          ProcessFiles()
        End Sub

        Private Sub ProcessFiles()

            'Load up all *.jpg files, and make a new folder for
            'the modified data.
              Dim files() As String =
            Directory.GetFiles ("C:\Users\AndrewTroelsen\Pictures\My Family",
              "*.jpg",SearchOption.AllDirectories)

            Dim newDir As String = "C:\ModifiedPictures"
            Directory.CreateDirectory(newDir)

            'Process the image data in a blocking manner.
            For Each currentFile As String In files
                Dim filename As String = Path.GetFileName(currentFile)

            Using bmp As New Bitmap(currentFile)
                bmp.RotateFlip(RotateFlipType.Rotate180FlipNone)
            bmp.Save(Path.Combine(newDir, filename))

                Me.Text = String.Format("Processing {0} on thread {1}"
                ,filename, Thread.CurrentThread.ManagedThreadId)
                End Using
            Next
            Me.Text = "All done!"
        End Sub
End Class
```

Notice that the ProcessFiles() method will rotate each *.jpg file under my personal Pictures\My Family subdirectory, which currently contains a total of 37 files (be sure to update the path sent into Directory.GetFiles() as necessary). Currently, all of the work is happening on the primary thread of the executable. Therefore, if the button is clicked, the program will appear to hang. Furthermore, the caption of the window will also report that the same primary thread is processing the file (Figure 19- 4).

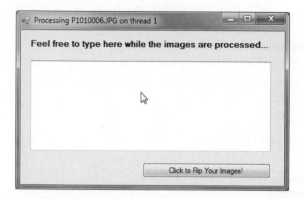

Figure 19-4. Currently, all action is taking place on the primary thread

To process the files on as many CPUs as possible, you can rewrite the current For Each loop to make use of Parallel.ForEach(). Recall that this method has been overloaded numerous times, however in the simplest form, you must specify the IEnumerable(Of T) compatible object that contains the items to process (that would be the files String array) and an Action(Of T) delegate which points to the method that will perform the work. Here is the relevant update, using the VB 2010 lambda operator, in place of a literal Action(Of T) delegate object:

```
Parallel.ForEach(files, _
      Sub(currentFile)
            Dim filename As String = Path.GetFileName(currentFile)
                Using bmp As New Bitmap(currentFile)
                    bmp.RotateFlip(RotateFlipType.Rotate180FlipNone)
                    bmp.Save(Path.Combine(newDir, filename))

                    Me.Text = String.Format("Processing {0} on thread {1}",
                            filename, Thread.CurrentThread.ManagedThreadId)
                End Using
      End Sub)
```

Now, if you run program, the TPL will indeed distribute the workload to multiple threads from the thread pool, using as many CPUs as possible. However, you will not see the window's caption display the name of each unique thread and you won't see anything if you type in the text box, until all the images have been processed! The reason is that the primary UI thread is still blocked, waiting for all of the other threads to finish up their business.

The Task Class

To keep the user interface responsive, you could certainly make use of asynchronous delegates or the members of the System.Threading namespace directly, but the System.Threading.Tasks namespace provides a simpler alternative, via the Task class. Task allows you to easily invoke a method on a secondary thread, and can be used as a simple alternative to working with asynchronous delegates. Update the Click handler of your Button control as so:

```
Private Sub btnProcessImages_Click(ByVal sender As Object,
                                   ByVal e As EventArgs)
                                   Handles btnProcessImages.Click
        'Start a new "task" to process the files.
        Task.Factory.StartNew(Sub() ProcessFiles())
End Sub
```

The Factory property of Task returns a TaskFactory object. When you call its StartNew() method, you pass in an Action(Of T) delegate (here, hidden away with a fitting lambda expression) which points to the method to invoke in an asynchronous manner. With this small update, you will now find that the window's title will show which thread from the thread pool is processing a given file, and better yet, the text area is able to receive input, as the UI thread is no longer blocked.

Handling Cancelation Request

One improvement you can make to the current example is to provide a way for the user to stop the processing of the image data, via a second (aptly named) Cancel button. Thankfully, the Parallel.For() and Parallel.ForEach() methods both support cancellation through the use of *cancellation tokens*. When you invoke methods on Parallel, you can pass in a ParallelOptions object, which in turn contains a CancellationTokenSource object.

First of all, define a new Private member variable in your Form derived class of type CancellationTokenSource named cancelToken:

```
Public Class MainForm
        ' New Form level variable.
        Private cancelToken As New CancellationTokenSource()
        …
End Class
```

Now, assuming you have added a new Button (named btnCancelTask) on your designer, handle the Click event, and implement the handler as so:

```
Private Sub btnCancelTask_Click(ByVal sender As System.Object,
                                ByVal e As System.EventArgs)
                                Handles btnCancelTask.Click
        'This will be used to tell all the worker threads to stop!
        cancelToken.Cancel()
End Sub
```

Now, the real modifications need to occur within the ProcessFiles() method. Consider the final implementation:

```
Private Sub ProcessFiles()
        ' Use ParallelOptions instance to store the CancellationToken
        Dim parOpts As New ParallelOptions()
        parOpts.CancellationToken = cancelToken.Token
        parOpts.MaxDegreeOfParallelism = System.Environment.ProcessorCount
```

```vb
                    'Load up all *.jpg files,and make a
                    ' new folder for the modified data.
                    Dim files() As String = Directory.GetFiles("C:\Users\Public\Pictures\Sample
                            Pictures",
                            "*.jpg", SearchOption.AllDirectories)
                    Dim newDir As String = "C:\ModifiedPictures"
                    Directory.CreateDirectory(newDir)

                    Try
                        'Process the image data in a parallel manner!
                        Parallel.ForEach(files,parOpts,
                            Sub(currentFile)
                                parOpts.CancellationToken.ThrowIfCancellationRequested()
                                    Dim filename As String = Path.GetFileName(currentFile)

                                Using bmp As New Bitmap(currentFile)
                                    bmp.RotateFlip(RotateFlipType.Rotate180FlipNone)
                                    bmp.Save(Path.Combine(newDir, filename))

                                    Me.Text = String.Format("Processing {0} on thread {1}",
                                        filename, Thread.CurrentThread.ManagedThreadId)
                                End Using
                            End Sub)
                        Me.Text = "All done!"
                    Catch ex As OperationCanceledException
                        Me.Text = ex.Message
                    End Try
End Sub
```

Notice that you begin the method by configuring a `ParallelOptions` object, setting the `CancellationToken` property to use the `CancellationTokenSource` token. Also note that when you call the `Parallel.ForEach()` method, you pass in the `ParallelOptions` object as the second parameter.

Within the scope of the looping logic, you make a call to `ThrowIfCancellationRequested()` on the token, which will ensure if the user clicks the Cancel button, all threads will stop and you will be notified via a runtime exception. When you catch the `OperationCanceledException` error, you will set the text of the main window to the error message.

■ **Source Code** The DataParallelismWithForEach project is included under the Chapter 19 subdirectory.

Understanding Task Parallelism

In addition to data parallelism, the TPL can also be used to easily fire off any number of asynchronous tasks using the `Parallel.Invoke()` method. This approach is a bit more straightforward than using delegates or members from `System.Threading`, however if you require more control over the way tasks are executed, you could forgo use of `Parallel.Invoke()` and make use of the `Task` class directly, as you did in the previous example.

To illustrate task parallelism, create a new Windows Forms application called MyEBookReader and import the `System.Threading.Tasks`, `System.Net` and `System.Text` namespaces.

This application is a modification of a useful example in the .NET Framework 4.0 SDK documentation, which will fetch a free e-book from Project Gutenberg (http://www.gutenberg.org), and then perform a set of lengthy tasks in parallel.

The GUI consists of a multi-line `TextBox` control (named `txtBook`) and two `Button` controls (`btnDownload` and `btnGetStats`). Once you have designed the UI, handle the `Click` event for each `Button`, and in the form's code file, declare a class level `String` variable named `theEBook`. Implement the `Click` hander for the `btnDownload` as so:

```
Private Sub btnDownload_Click(ByVal sender As Object,
          ByVal e As EventArgs)Handles btnDownload.Click

    Dim wc As New WebClient()
    AddHandler wc.DownloadStringCompleted, Sub(s, eArgs)
                             theEBook = eArgs.Result
                             txtBook.Text = theEBook
                             End Sub

    'The Project Gutenberg EBook of A Tale of Two Cities,
    'by Charles Dickens
    wc.DownloadStringAsync(New
    Uri("http://www.gutenberg.org/files/98/98-8.txt"))
End Sub
```

The `WebClient` class is a member of `System.Net`. This class provides a number of methods for sending data to and receiving data from a resource identified by a URI. As it turns out, many of these methods have an asynchronous version, such as `DownloadStringAsyn()`. This method will spin up a new thread from the CLR thread pool automatically. When the `WebClient` is done obtaining the data, it will fire the `DownloadStringCompleted` event, which you are handling here using a VB 2010 lambda expression. If you were to call the synchronous version of this method (`DownloadString()`) the form would appear unresponsive for quite some time.

The `Click` event hander for the `btnGetStats` `Button` control is implemented to extract out the individual words contained in `theEBook` variable, and then pass the String array to a few helper methods for processing:

```
Private Sub btnGetStats_Click(ByVal sender As Object,
        ByVal e As EventArgs)Handles btnGetStats.Click
    'Get the words from the e-book.
        Dim words() As String = theEBook.Split(New Char() {
                                  " "c, ControlChars.Lf,
                                  ","c, "."c, ";"c,
                                  "c,", ":"c, "-"c,
                                  "?"c, "/"c},
                          StringSplitOptions.RemoveEmptyEntries)

    'Now, find the ten most common words.
    Dim tenMostCommon() As String = FindTenMostCommon(words)
```

```
    'Get the longest word.
    Dim longestWord As String = FindLongestWord(words)

    'Now that all tasks are complete, build a string to show all
    'stats in a message box.
    Dim bookStats As New StringBuilder("Ten Most Common Words are:"
                                    & vbLf)
    For Each s As String In tenMostCommon
        bookStats.AppendLine(s)
    Next s

    bookStats.AppendFormat("Longest word is: {0}", longestWord)
    bookStats.AppendLine()
    MessageBox.Show(bookStats.ToString(), "Book info")
End Sub
```

The FindTenMostCommon() method uses a LINQ query to obtain a list of String objects which occur most often in the String array, while FindLongestWord() locates, well, the longest word:

```
Private Function FindTenMostCommon(ByVal words() As String) As String()
    Dim frequencyOrder = From word In words
                         Where word.Length > 6
                         Group word By word Into g = Group
                         Order By g.Count() Descending
                         Select word

    Dim commonWords() As String = (frequencyOrder.Take(10)).ToArray()
    Return commonWords
End Function

Private Function FindLongestWord(ByVal words() As String) As String
    Return (
        From w In words
        Order By w.Length Descending
        Select w).First()
End Function
```

If you were to run this project, the amount of time to perform all tasks could take a goodly amount of time, based on the CPU count of your machine and overall processor speed. Eventually, you should see the following output (Figure 19-5).

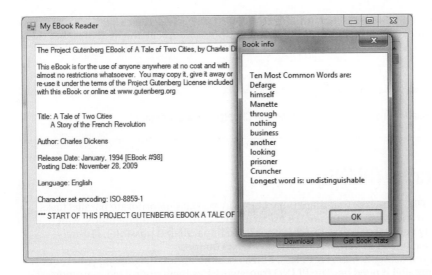

Figure 19-5. Stats about the downloaded EBook

You can help ensure that your application makes use of all available CPUs on the host machine by invoking the `FindTenMostCommon()` and `FindLongestWord()`method in parallel. To do so, modify your `btnGetStats_Click()` method as so:

```
Private Sub btnGetStats_Click(ByVal sender As Object, ByVal e As EventArgs)
                                        Handles btnGetStats.Click

        ' Get the words from the e-book.
        Dim words() As String = theEBook.Split(New Char() {
                                        " "c, ControlChars.Lf,
                                        ","c, "."c, ";"c,
                                        "c,", ":"c, "-"c,
                                        "?"c, "/"c},
                                        StringSplitOptions.RemoveEmptyEntries)
        Dim tenMostCommon() As String = Nothing
        Dim longestWord As String = String.Empty

        ' Now, find the ten most common words.
        ' Get the longest word.
        Parallel.Invoke
                (
                    Sub() tenMostCommon = FindTenMostCommon(words),
        Sub() longestWord = FindLongestWord(words)
                )

        ' Now that all tasks are complete, build a string to show all
        ' stats in a message box.
        ...

End Sub
```

The `Parallel.Invoke()` method expects a parameter array of `Action()` delegates, which you have supplied indirectly using lambda expressions. Again, while the output is identical, the benefit is that the TPL will now make use of all possible processors on the machine to invoke each method in parallel if possible.

■ **Source Code** The MyEBookReader project is included under the Chapter 19 subdirectory.

Parallel LINQ Queries (PLINQ)

To wrap up your look at the TPL, be aware that there is another way you can incorporate parallel tasks into your .NET applications. If you wish, you can make use of a new set of extension methods, which allow you to construct a LINQ query that will perform its workload in parallel (if possible). Fittingly, LINQ queries that are designed to run in parallel are termed PLINQ queries.

Like parallel code authored using the `Parallel` class, PLINQ has the option of ignoring your request to process the collection in parallel if need be. The PLINQ framework has been optimized in numerous ways, which includes determining if a query would in fact perform faster in a synchronous manner.

At run time, PLINQ analyzes the overall structure of the query and if the query is likely to benefit from parallelization, it will run concurrently. However, if parallelizing a query would hurt performance PLINQ just runs the query sequentially. If PLINQ has a choice between a potentially expensive parallel algorithm or an inexpensive sequential algorithm, it chooses the sequential algorithm by default.

The necessary extension methods are found within the `ParallelEnumerable` class of the `System.Linq` namespace. Table 19-5 documents some useful PLINQ extensions.

Table 19-5. Select Members of the ParallelEnumerable Class

Member	Meaning in Life
AsParallel()	Specifies that the rest of the query should be parallelized, if possible.
WithCancellation()	Specifies that PLINQ should periodically monitor the state of the provided cancellation token and cancel execution if it is requested.
WithDegreeOfParallelism()	Specifies the maximum number of processors that PLINQ should use to parallelize the query.
ForAll()	Enables results to be processed in parallel without first merging back to the consumer thread, as would be the case when enumerating a LINQ result using the `For Each` construct.

To see PLINQ in action, create a final Windows Forms application named PLINQDataProcessingWithCancellation and import the `System.Threading` and `System.Threading.Tasks` namespaces. This simple form will only need two `Button` controls named btnExecute and btnCancel. Then the "Execute" button is clicked, you will fire off a new `Task` which executes a LINQ query that investigates a very large array of Integers, looking for only the items x Mod 3 = 0 is True. Here is a *non-parallel* version of the query:

```vb
Public Class MainForm
...
    Private Sub btnExecute_Click(ByVal sender As Object,  ByVal e As EventArgs)
                                                Handles btnExecute.Click
        'Start a new "task" to process the ints.
        Task.Factory.StartNew(Sub() ProcessIntData())
    End Sub

    Private Sub ProcessIntData()
        ' Get a very large array of Integers.
        Dim source() As Integer =
            Enumerable.Range(1,
            10000000).ToArray()

        ' Find the numbers where num Mod 3 = 0 is True, returned
        ' in descending order.
        Dim modThreeIsZero() As Integer = (
                                        From num In source
                                        Where num Mod 3 = 0
                                        Order By num Descending
                                        Select num).ToArray()

        MessageBox.Show(String.Format("Found {0} numbers that match query!",
                                        modThreeIsZero.Count()))
    End Sub
End Class
```

Opting in to a PLINQ Query

If you wish to inform the TPL to execute this query in parallel (if possible), you will want to make use of the AsParallel() extension method as so:

```vb
Dim modThreeIsZero() As Integer = (
                            From num In source.AsParallel()
                            .WithCancellation(cancelToken.Token)

                            Where num Mod 3 = 0
                            Order By num Descending
                            Select num).ToArray()
```

Notice how the overall format of the LINQ query is identical to what you have seen in previous chapters. However, by including a call to AsParallel(), the TPL will attempt to pass the workload off to an available CPU.

Canceling a PLINQ Query

It is also possible to use a `CancellationTokenSource` object to inform a PLINQ query to stop processing under the correct conditions (typically due to user intervention). Declare a form level `CancellationTokenSource` object named `cancelToken` and implement the `Click` handler of the `btnCancel` to call the `Cancel()` method on this object. Here is the relevant code update:

```
Public Class MainForm

        Private cancelToken As New CancellationTokenSource()
        Private Sub btnCancel_Click(ByVal sender As Object,
                    ByVal e As EventArgs)Handles btnCancel.Click
            cancelToken.Cancel()
        End Sub
        ...
End Class
```

Now, inform the PLINQ query that it should be on the lookout for an incoming cancellation request by chaining on the `WithCancellation()` extension method, and passing in the token. In addition, you will want to wrap this PLINQ query in a proper Try/Catch scope, and deal with the possible exception. Here is the final version of the `ProcessIntData()` method.

```
Private Sub ProcessIntData()

        'Get a very large array of Integers.
        Dim source() As Integer = Enumerable.Range(1, 10000000).ToArray()

        'Find the numbers where num Mod 3 = 0 is True, returned
        'in descending order.
        Dim modThreeIsZero() As Integer = Nothing

        Try
            modThreeIsZero = (

                            From num In
                            source.AsParallel().WithCancellation(cancelToken.
                            Token)

                            Where (num Mod 3 = 0)
                            Order By num Descending
                            Select num).ToArray()
        Catch ex As OperationCanceledException
            Me.Text = ex.Message
        End Try

        MessageBox.Show(String.Format("Found {0} numbers that match query!",
            modThreeIsZero.Count()))
End Sub
```

That wraps up the introductory look at the Task Parallel Library and PLINQ. As mentioned, these new .NET 4.0 APIs are quickly becoming the preferred manner to work with multithreaded applications. However, effective use of TPL and PLINQ demand a solid understanding of multithreaded concepts and primitives, which you have been exposed to over the course of this chapter.

If you find these topics interesting, be sure to look up the topic "Parallel Programming in the .NET Framework" in the .NET Framework 4.0 SDK documentation. Here you will find a good number of sample projects which will extend what you have seen here.

■ **Source Code** The PLINQDataProcessingWithCancellation project is included under the Chapter 19 subdirectory.

Summary

This chapter began by examining how .NET delegate types can be configured to execute a method in an asynchronous manner. As you have seen, the `BeginInvoke()` and `EndInvoke()` methods allow you to indirectly manipulate a secondary thread with minimum fuss and bother. During this discussion, you were also introduced to the `IAsyncResult` interface and `AsyncResult` class type. As you learned, these types provide various ways to synchronize the calling thread and obtain possible method return values.

The next part of this chapter examined the role of the `System.Threading` namespace. As you learned, when an application creates additional threads of execution, the result is that the program in question is able to carry out numerous tasks at (what appears to be) the same time. You also examined several manners in which you can protect thread-sensitive blocks of code to ensure that shared resources do not become unusable units of bogus data.

This chapter wrapped up by examining a brand new model for working with multithreaded development under .NET 4.0, the Task Parallel Library and PLINQ. Going forward, these APIs are sure to become the preferred way to author multi-tasked systems, in that they allow us to program against a set of higher level types (many of which reside in the `System.Threading.Tasks` namespace) which hide a good amount of complexity.

■ ■ ■

## CHAPTER 20

File I/O and Object Serialization

When you create desktop applications, the ability to save information between user sessions is imperative. This chapter examines a number of I/O-related topics as seen through the eyes of the .NET Framework. The first order of business is to explore the core types defined in the System.IO namespace and learn how to modify a machine's directory and file structure programmatically. The next task is to explore various ways to read from and write to character-based, binary-based, string-based, and memory-based data stores.

After you learn how to manipulate files and directories using the core I/O types, you will examine the related topic of *object serialization*. You can use object serialization to persist and retrieve the state of an object to (or from) any System.IO.Stream-derived type. The ability to serialize objects is critical when you want to copy an object to a remote machine using various remoting technologies such as Windows Communication Foundation. However, serialization is quite useful in its own right and will likely play a role in many of your .NET applications (distributed or not).

Exploring the System.IO Namespace

In the framework of .NET, the System.IO namespace is the region of the base class libraries devoted to file-based (and memory-based) input and output (I/O) services. Like any namespace, System.IO defines a set of classes, interfaces, enumerations, structures, and delegates, most of which you can find in mscorlib.dll. In addition to the types contained within mscorlib.dll, the System.dll assembly defines additional members of the System.IO namespace. Note that all Visual Studio 2010 projects automatically set a reference to both assemblies.

Many of the types within the System.IO namespace focus on the programmatic manipulation of physical directories and files. However, additional types provide support to read data from and write data to string buffers, as well as raw memory locations. Table 20-1 outlines the core (non-abstract) classes, providing a road map of the functionality in System.IO.

Table 20-1. Key Members of the System.IO Namespace

Non-abstract I/O Class Type	Meaning in Life
BinaryReader BinaryWriter	These classes allow you to store and retrieve primitive data types (Integers, Booleans, Strings, and whatnot) as a binary value.
BufferedStream	This class provides temporary storage for a stream of bytes that you can commit to storage at a later time.
Directory DirectoryInfo	You use these classes to manipulate a machine's directory structure. The Directory type exposes functionality using S*hared members*, while the DirectoryInfo type exposes similar functionality from a valid *object reference*.
DriveInfo	This class provides detailed information regarding the drives that a given machine uses.
File FileInfo	You use these classes to manipulate a machine's set of files. The File type exposes functionality using *Shared members*, while the FileInfo type exposes similar functionality from a valid *object reference*.
FileStream	This class gives you random file access (e.g., seeking capabilities) with data represented as a stream of bytes.
FileSystemWatcher	This class allows you to monitor the modification of external files in a specified directory.
MemoryStream	This class provides random access to streamed data stored in memory rather than a physical file.
Path	This class performs operations on System.String types that contain file or directory path information in a platform-neutral manner.
StreamWriter StreamReader	You use these classes to store (and retrieve) textual information to (or from) a file. These types do not support random file access.
StringWriter StringReader	Like the StreamReader/StreamWriter classes, these classes also work with textual information. However, the underlying storage is a string buffer rather than a physical file.

In addition to these concrete class types, System.IO defines a number of enumerations, as well as a set of MustInherit classes (e.g., Stream, TextReader, and TextWriter), that define a shared polymorphic interface to all descendents. You will read about many of these types in this chapter.

The Directory(Info) and File(Info) Types

System.IO provides four classes that allow you to manipulate individual files, as well as interact with a machine's directory structure. The first two types, Directory and File, expose creation, deletion, copying, and moving operations using various Shared members. The closely related FileInfo and DirectoryInfo types expose similar functionality as instance-level methods (therefore, you must allocate them with the New keyword). In Figure 20-1, the Directory and File classes directly extend System.Object, while DirectoryInfo and FileInfo derive from the MustInherit FileSystemInfo type.

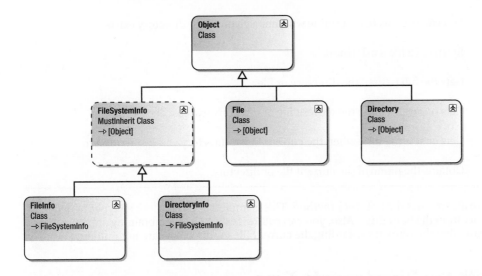

Figure 20-1. The File- and Directory-centric types

FileInfo and DirectoryInfo typically serve as better choices for obtaining full details of a file or directory (e.g., time created, and read/write capabilities) because their members tend to return strongly typed objects. In contrast, the Directory and File class members tend to return simple String values rather than strongly typed objects.

The MustInherit FileSystemInfo Base Class

The DirectoryInfo and FileInfo types receive many behaviors from the MustInherit FileSystemInfo base class. For the most part, you use the members of the FileSystemInfo class to discover general characteristics (such as time of creation, various attributes, and so forth) about a given file or directory. Table 20-2 lists some core properties of interest.

Table 20-2. FileSystemInfo Properties

Property	Meaning in Life
Attributes	Gets or sets the attributes associated with the current file that are represented by the FileAttributes enumeration (e.g., is the file or directory read-only, encrypted, hidden, or compressed?).
CreationTime	Gets or sets the time of creation for the current file or directory.
Exists	You can use this to determine whether a given file or directory exists.
Extension	Retrieves a file's extension.
FullName	Gets the full path of the directory or file.
LastAccessTime	Gets or sets the time the current file or directory was last accessed.
LastWriteTime	Gets or sets the time when the current file or directory was last written to.
Name	Obtains the name of the current file or directory.

FileSystemInfo also defines the Delete() method. This is implemented by derived types to delete a given file or directory from the hard drive. Also, you can call Refresh() prior to obtaining attribute information to ensure that the statistics regarding the current file (or directory) are not outdated.

Working with the DirectoryInfo Type

The first creatable I/O-centric type you will examine is the DirectoryInfo class. This class contains a set of members used for creating, moving, deleting, and enumerating over directories and subdirectories. In addition to the functionality provided by its base class (FileSystemInfo), DirectoryInfo offers the key members in Table 20-3.

Table 20-3. Key Members of the DirectoryInfo Type

Member	Meaning in Life
Create() CreateSubdirectory()	Create a directory (or set of subdirectories) when given a path name.
Delete()	Deletes a directory and all its contents.
GetDirectories()	Returns an array of DirectoryInfo objects that represent all subdirectories in the current directory.

Member	Meaning in Life
GetFiles()	Retrieves an array of FileInfo objects that represent a set of files in the given directory.
MoveTo()	Moves a directory and its contents to a new path.
Parent	Retrieves the parent directory of this directory.
Root	Gets the root portion of a path.

You begin working with the DirectoryInfo type by specifying a particular directory path as a constructor parameter. Use the "." notation if you want to obtain access to the current working directory (the directory of the executing application). Here are some examples:

```
'Bind to the current working directory.
Dim dir1 As New DirectoryInfo(".")

'Bind to C:\Windows,
Dim dir2 As New DirectoryInfo("C:\Windows")
```

In the second example, you make the assumption that the path passed into the constructor (C:\Windows) already exists on the physical machine. However, if you attempt to interact with a nonexistent directory, a System.IO.DirectoryNotFoundException is thrown. Thus, if you specify a directory that is not yet created, you need to call the Create() method before proceeding:

```
'Bind to a nonexistent directory, then create it.
Dim dir3 As New DirectoryInfo("C:\MyCode\Testing")
dir3.Create()
```

Once you create a DirectoryInfo object, you can investigate the underlying directory contents using any of the properties inherited from FileSystemInfo. To see this in action, create a new Console Application named DirectoryApp and update your VB 2010 file to import the System.IO namespace.

Update your module with a new method that creates a new DirectoryInfo object mapped to C:\Windows (adjust your path if need be) that displays a number of interesting statistics:

```
Module Module1
    Sub Main()
        Console.WriteLine("***** Fun with Directory(Info) *****" & vbLf)
        ShowWindowsDirectoryInfo()
        Console.ReadLine()
    End Sub

    Sub ShowWindowsDirectoryInfo()
        'Dump directory information.
        Dim dir As New DirectoryInfo("C:\Windows")
        Console.WriteLine("***** Directory Info *****")
        Console.WriteLine("FullName: {0}", dir.FullName)
        Console.WriteLine("Name: {0}", dir.Name)
```

```
            Console.WriteLine("Parent: {0}", dir.Parent)
            Console.WriteLine("Creation: {0}", dir.CreationTime)
            Console.WriteLine("Attributes: {0}", dir.Attributes)
            Console.WriteLine("Root: {0}", dir.Root)
            Console.WriteLine("*************************" & vbLf)
    End Sub
End Module
```

While your output might differ, you should see something similar to the following:

```
***** Fun with Directory(Info) *****


***** Directory Info *****

FullName: C:\Windows

Name: Windows

Parent:

Creation: 11/15/2009 10:31:24 AM

Attributes: Directory

Root: C:\

*************************
```

Enumerating Files with the DirectoryInfo Type

In addition to obtaining basic details of an existing directory, you can extend the current example to use some methods of the `DirectoryInfo` type. First, you can leverage the `GetFiles()` method to obtain information about all `*.jpg` files located under the `C:\Windows\Web\Wallpaper` directory.

■ **Note** If your machine does not have a `C:\Windows\Web\Wallpaper` directory, retrofit this code to read files of a directory on your machine (e.g., to read all `*.bmp` files from the `C:\Windows` directory).

The GetFiles() method returns an array of FileInfo objects, each of which exposes details of a particular file (you will learn the full details of the FileInfo type later in this chapter). Assume that you have the following method in your module, which you call from Main():

```
Sub DisplayImageFiles()
    Dim dir As New DirectoryInfo("C:\Windows\Web\Wallpaper\")

    'Get all files with a *.jpg extension.
    Dim imageFiles As FileInfo() = dir.GetFiles _
        ("*.jpg", SearchOption.AllDirectories)

    'How many were found?
    Console.WriteLine("Found {0} *.jpg files" & _
        vbLf, imageFiles.Length)

    'Now print out info for each file.
    For Each f As FileInfo In imageFiles
        Console.WriteLine("***************************")
        Console.WriteLine("File name: {0}", f.Name)
        Console.WriteLine("File size: {0}", f.Length)
        Console.WriteLine("Creation: {0}", f.CreationTime)
        Console.WriteLine("Attributes: {0}", f.Attributes)
        Console.WriteLine("***************************" & vbLf)
    Next
End Sub
```

Notice you specify a search option when you call GetFiles(); you do this to look within all subdirectories of the root. Once you run the application, you see a listing of all files that match the search pattern.

Creating Subdirectories with the DirectoryInfo Type

You can programmatically extend a directory structure using the DirectoryInfo.CreateSubdirectory() method. This method can create a single subdirectory, as well as multiple nested subdirectories, in a single function call. This method illustrates how to do so, extending the directory structure of the C: drive with some custom subdirectories:

```
Sub ModifyAppDirectory()
    Dim dir As New DirectoryInfo("C:\")

    'Create \MyFolder off application directory.
    dir.CreateSubdirectory("MyFolder")

    'Create \MyFolder2\Data off application directory.
    dir.CreateSubdirectory("MyFolder2\Data")
End Sub
```

If you call this method from within Main() and examine your C:\ directory using Windows Explorer, you will see that the new subdirectories are present and accounted for (see Figure 20-2).

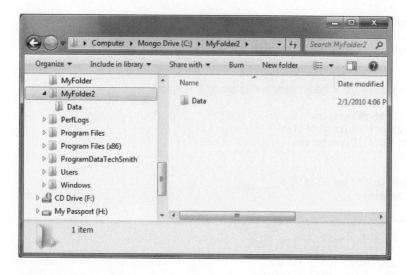

Figure 20-2. Creating subdirectories

You are not required to capture the return value of the CreateSubdirectory() method, but you should be aware that a DirectoryInfo object representing the newly created item is passed back on successful execution. Consider the following update to the previous method:

```
Sub ModifyAppDirectory()
    Dim dir As New DirectoryInfo(".")

    'Create \MyFolder off initial directory.
    dir.CreateSubdirectory("MyFolder")

    'Capture returned DirectoryInfo object.
    Dim myDataFolder As DirectoryInfo = _
        dir.CreateSubdirectory("MyFolder2\Data")

    'Prints path to ..\MyFolder2\Data.
    Console.WriteLine("New Folder is: {0}", myDataFolder)
End Sub
```

Working with the Directory Type

You have seen the DirectoryInfo type in action; now you're ready to learn about the Directory type. For the most part, the Shared members of Directory mimic the functionality provided by the instance-level members defined by DirectoryInfo. Recall, however, that the members of Directory typically return String data rather than strongly typed FileInfo/DirectoryInfo objects.

Now let's look at some functionality of the Directory type; this final helper method displays the names of all drives mapped to the current computer (using the Directory.GetLogicalDrives() method) and uses the Shared Directory.Delete() method to remove the \MyFolder and \MyFolder2\Data subdirectories created previously:

```vbnet
Sub FunWithDirectoryType()

        'List all drives on current computer.
        Dim drives As String() = Directory.GetLogicalDrives()
        Console.WriteLine("Here are your drives:")

        For Each s As String In drives
            Console.WriteLine("--> {0} ", s)
        Next

        'Delete what was created.
        Console.WriteLine("Press Enter to delete directories")
        Console.ReadLine()

        Try
            Directory.Delete("C:\MyFolder")

            'The second parameter specifies whether you
            'wish to destroy any subdirectories.
            Directory.Delete("C:\MyFolder2", True)
        Catch e As IOException
            Console.WriteLine(e.Message)
        End Try
End Sub
```

■ **Source Code** You can find the DirectoryApp project under the Chapter 20 subdirectory.

Working with the DriveInfo Class Type

The System.IO namespace provides a class named DriveInfo. Like Directory.GetLogicalDrives(), the Shared DriveInfo.GetDrives() method allows you to discover the names of a machine's drives. Unlike Directory.GetLogicalDrives(), however, DriveInfo provides numerous other details (e.g., the drive type, available free space, and volume label). Consider the following module defined within a new Console Application named DriveInfoApp (don't forget to import System.IO):

```vbnet
Module Module1
    Sub Main()
        Console.WriteLine("***** Fun with DriveInfo *****" & vbLf)
        'Get info regarding all drives.
        Dim myDrives As DriveInfo() = DriveInfo.GetDrives()

        'Now print drive stats.
        For Each d As DriveInfo In myDrives

            Console.WriteLine("Name: {0}", d.Name)
            Console.WriteLine("Type: {0}", d.DriveType)
```

```
                    'Check to see whether the drive is mounted.
                    If d.IsReady Then
                        Console.WriteLine("Free space: {0}", d.TotalFreeSpace)
                        Console.WriteLine("Format: {0}", d.DriveFormat)
                        Console.WriteLine("Label: {0}", d.VolumeLabel)
                        Console.WriteLine()
                    End If
            Next
            Console.ReadLine()
        End Sub
End Module
```

Here is some possible output:

```
***** Fun with DriveInfo *****


Name: C:\

Type: Fixed

Free space: 587376394240

Format: NTFS

Label: Mongo Drive


Name: D:\

Type: CDRom

Name: E:\

Type: CDRom

Name: F:\

Type: CDRom

Name: H:\
```

```
Type: Fixed

Free space: 477467508736

Format: FAT32

Label: My Passport
```

At this point, you have investigated some core behaviors of the **Directory**, **DirectoryInfo**, and **DriveInfo** classes. Next, you'll learn how to create, open, close, and destroy the files that populate a given directory.

■ **Source Code** You can find the **DriveInfoApp** project under the Chapter 20 subdirectory.

Working with the FileInfo Class

As shown in the previous **DirectoryApp** example, the **FileInfo** class allows you to obtain details regarding existing files on your hard drive (e.g., time created, size, and file attributes) and aids in the creation, copying, moving, and destruction of files. In addition to the set of functionality inherited by **FileSystemInfo**, you can find some core members unique to the **FileInfo** class, which you can see described in Table 20-4.

Table 20-4. FileInfo Core Members

Member	Meaning in Life
AppendText()	Creates a **StreamWriter** object (described later) that appends text to a file.
CopyTo()	Copies an existing file to a new file.
Create()	Creates a new file and returns a **FileStream** object (described later) to interact with the newly created file.
CreateText()	Creates a **StreamWriter** object that writes a new text file.
Delete()	Deletes the file to which a **FileInfo** instance is bound.
Directory	Gets an instance of the parent directory.
DirectoryName	Gets the full path to the parent directory.
Length	Gets the size of the current file.

Continued

Member	Meaning in Life
MoveTo()	Moves a specified file to a new location, providing the option to specify a new file name.
Name	Gets the name of the file.
Open()	Opens a file with various read/write and sharing privileges.
OpenRead()	Creates a read-only FileStream object.
OpenText()	Creates a StreamReader object (described later) that reads from an existing text file.
OpenWrite()	Creates a write-only FileStream object.

Note that a majority of the methods of the FileInfo class return a specific I/O-centric object (e.g., FileStream and StreamWriter) that allows you to begin reading and writing data to (or reading from) the associated file in a variety of formats. You will check out these types in just a moment; however, before you see a working example, you'll find it helpful to examine various ways to obtain a file handle using the FileInfo class type.

The FileInfo.Create() Method

One way you can create a file handle is to use the FileInfo.Create() method:

```
Sub Main()
        'Make a new file on the C drive.
        Dim f As New FileInfo("C:\Test.dat")
        Dim fs As FileStream = f.Create()

        'Use the FileStream object
    ...

        'Close down file stream.
        fs.Close()
End Sub
```

Notice that the FileInfo.Create() method returns a FileStream object, which exposes synchronous and asynchronous write/read operations to/from the underlying file (more details in a moment). Be aware that the FileStream object returned by FileInfo.Create() grants full read/write access to all users.

Also notice that after you finish with the current FileStream object, you must ensure you close down the handle to release the underlying unmanaged stream resources. Given that FileStream implements IDisposable, you can use the VB 2010 Using scope to allow the compiler to generate the teardown logic (see Chapter 8 for details):

```
Sub Main()
        'Defining a 'Using scope' for file I/O
        'types is ideal.
        Dim f As New FileInfo("C:\Test.dat")
        Using fs As FileStream = f.Create()
            'Use the FileStream object...
        End Using
End Sub
```

The FileInfo.Open() Method

You can use the `FileInfo.Open()` method to open existing files, as well as to create new files with far more precision than you can with `FileInfo.Create()`. This works because `Open()` typically takes several parameters to qualify exactly how to iterate the file you want to manipulate. Once the call to `Open()` completes, you are returned a `FileStream` object. Consider the following logic:

```
Sub Main()
        'Make a new file via FileInfo.Open().
        Dim f2 As New FileInfo("C:\Test2.dat")

        Using fs2 As FileStream = f2.Open(FileMode.OpenOrCreate, _
                FileAccess.ReadWrite,FileShare.None)

                'Use the FileStream object...
        End Using
End Sub
```

This version of the overloaded `Open()` method requires three parameters. The first parameter of the `Open()` method specifies the general flavor of the I/O request (e.g., make a new file, open an existing file, and append to a file), which you specify using the **FileMode** enumeration (see Table 20-5 for details):

```
Public Enum FileMode
    CreateNew
    Create
    Open
    OpenOrCreate
    Truncate
    Append
End Enum
```

Table 20-5. *Members of the FileMode Enumeration*

Member	Meaning in Life
CreateNew	Informs the OS to make a new file. If it already exists, an IOException is thrown.
Create	Informs the OS to make a new file. If it already exists, it will be overwritten.
Open	Opens an existing file. If the file does not exist, a FileNotFoundException is thrown.
OpenOrCreate	Opens the file if it exists; otherwise, a new file is created.
Truncate	Opens an existing file and truncates the file to 0 bytes in size.
Append	Opens a file, moves to the end of the file, and begins write operations (you can only use this flag with a write-only stream). If the file does not exist, a new file is created.

You use the second parameter of the Open() method, a value from the FileAccess enumeration, to determine the read/write behavior of the underlying stream:

```
Public Enum FileAccess
    Read
    Write
    ReadWrite
End Enum
```

Finally, the third parameter of the Open() method, FileShare, specifies how to share the file among other file handlers. Here are the core names:

```
Public Enum FileShare
    Delete
    Inheritable
    None
    Read
    ReadWrite
    Write
End Enum
```

The FileInfo.OpenRead() and FileInfo.OpenWrite() Methods

The FileInfo.Open() method allows you to obtain a file handle in a flexible manner, but the FileInfo class also provides members named OpenRead() and OpenWrite(). As you might imagine, these methods return a properly configured read-only or write-only FileStream object, without the need to supply various enumeration values. Like FileInfo.Create() and FileInfo.Open(), OpenRead() and OpenWrite() return a FileStream object (note that the following code assumes you have files named Test3.dat and Test4.dat on your C drive):

```
Sub Main()
        'Get a FileStream object with read-only permissions.
        Dim f3 As New FileInfo("C:\Test3.dat")

        Using readOnlyStream As FileStream = f3.OpenRead()
            'Use the FileStream object...
        End Using

        'Now get a FileStream object with write-only permissions.
        Dim f4 As New FileInfo("C:\Test4.dat")

        Using writeOnlyStream As FileStream = f4.OpenWrite()
            'Use the FileStream object...
        End Using
End Sub
```

The FileInfo.OpenText() Method

Another open-centric member of the FileInfo type is OpenText(). Unlike Create(), Open(), OpenRead(), or OpenWrite(), the OpenText() method returns an instance of the StreamReader type, rather than a FileStream type. Assuming you have a file named boot.ini on your C drive, the following snippet lets you access to its contents:

```
Sub Main()
        'Get a StreamReader object.
        Dim f5 As New FileInfo("C:\boot.ini")
        Using sreader As StreamReader = f5.OpenText()
            'Use the StreamReader object...
        End Using
End Sub
```

As you will see shortly, the StreamReader type provides a way to read character data from the underlying file.

The FileInfo.CreateText() and FileInfo.AppendText() Methods

The final two FileInfo methods of interest at this point are CreateText() and AppendText(). Both return a StreamWriter object, as shown here:

```
Sub Main()
        Dim f6 As New FileInfo("C:\Test6.txt")
        Using swriter As StreamWriter = f6.CreateText()
            'Use the StreamWriter object...
        End Using
```

```vbnet
        Dim f7 As New FileInfo("C:\FinalTest.txt")
        Using swriterAppend As StreamWriter = f7.AppendText()
              'Use the StreamWriter object...
        End Using
End Sub
```

As you might guess, the StreamWriter type provides a way to write character data to the underlying file.

Working with the File Type

The File type uses several Shared members to provide functionality almost identical to that of the FileInfo type. Like FileInfo, File supplies AppendText(), Create(), CreateText(), Open(), OpenRead(), OpenWrite(), and OpenText() methods. In many cases, you can use the File and FileInfo types interchangeably. To see this in action, you can simplify each of the previous FileStream examples by using the File type instead:

```vbnet
Sub Main()
        'Obtain FileStream object via File.Create().
        Using fs As FileStream = File.Create("C:\Test.dat")
        End Using

        'Obtain FileStream object via File.Open().
        Using fs2 As FileStream = File.Open("C:\Test2.dat", ↩
          FileMode.OpenOrCreate, FileAccess.ReadWrite, FileShare.None)
        End Using

        'Get a FileStream object with read-only permissions.
        Using readOnlyStream As FileStream = File.OpenRead("Test3.dat")
        End Using

        'Get a FileStream object with write-only permissions.
        Using writeOnlyStream As FileStream = File.OpenWrite("Test4.dat")
        End Using

        'Get a StreamReader object.
        Using sreader As StreamReader = File.OpenText("C:\boot.ini")
        End Using

        'Get some StreamWriters.
        Using swriter As StreamWriter = File.CreateText("C:\Test6.txt")
        End Using

Using swriterAppend As StreamWriter = File. _
      AppendText("C:\FinalTest.txt")
        End Using
End Sub
```

Additional File-centric Members

The File type also supports a few members shown in Table 20-6, which can greatly simplify the processes of reading and writing textual data.

Table 20-6. Methods of the File Type

Method	Meaning in Life
ReadAllBytes()	Opens the specified file, returns the binary data as an array of bytes, and then closes the file.
ReadAllLines()	Opens a specified file, returns the character data as an array of strings, and then closes the file.
ReadAllText()	Opens a specified file, returns the character data as a System.String, and then closes the file.
WriteAllBytes()	Opens the specified file, writes out the Byte array, and then closes the file.
WriteAllLines()	Opens a specified file, writes out an array of strings, and then closes the file.
WriteAllText()	Opens a specified file, writes the character data from a specified string, and then closes the file.

You can use these methods of the File type to read and write batches of data in only a few lines of code. Even better, each of these members automatically closes down the underlying file handle. For example, the following console program (named SimpleFileIO) persists the String data into a new file on the C: drive (and reads it into memory) with minimal fuss (this example assumes you have imported System.IO):

```
Imports System.IO

Module Module1
    Sub Main()
        Console.WriteLine("*** Simple IO with the File Type *****" & vbLf)
        Dim myTasks As String() = {"Fix bathroom sink", "Call Dave", _
    "Call Mom and Dad", "Play Xbox 360"}

        'Write out all data to file on C drive.
        File.WriteAllLines("C:\tasks.txt", myTasks)

        ' Read it all back and print out.
        For Each task As String In File.ReadAllLines("C:\tasks.txt")
            Console.WriteLine("TODO: {0}", task)
        Next
        Console.ReadLine()
    End Sub
End Module
```

The lesson here: When you wish to obtain a file handle quickly, the `File` type will save you some keystrokes. However, one benefit of creating a `FileInfo` object first is that you can investigate the file using the members of the MustInherit `FileSystemInfo` base class.

■ **Source Code** You can find the `SimpleFileIO` project under the Chapter 20 subdirectory.

The MustInherit Stream Class

At this point, you have seen many ways to obtain `FileStream`, `StreamReader`, and `StreamWriter` objects, but you have yet to read data from or write data to a file using these types. To understand how to do this, you'll need to familiarize yourself with the concept of a stream. In the world of I/O manipulation, a *stream* represents a chunk of data flowing between a source and a destination. Streams provide a common way to interact with *a sequence of bytes*, regardless of what kind of device (e.g., file, network connection, and printer) stores or displays the bytes in question.

The MustInherit `System.IO.Stream` class defines several members that provide support for synchronous and asynchronous interactions with the storage medium (e.g., an underlying file or memory location).

■ **Note** The concept of a stream is not limited to file IO. To be sure, the .NET libraries provide stream access to networks, memory locations, and other stream-centric abstractions.

Again, `Stream` descendents represent data as a raw stream of bytes; therefore, working directly with raw streams can be quite cryptic. Some `Stream`-derived types support *seeking*, which refers to the process of obtaining and adjusting the current position in the stream. Table 20-7 helps you understand the functionality provided by the `Stream` class by describing its core members.

Table 20-7. MustInherit Stream Members

Member	Meaning in Life
CanRead CanWrite CanSeek	Determines whether the current stream supports reading, seeking, and/or writing.
Close()	Closes the current stream and releases any resources (such as sockets and file handles) associated with the current stream. Internally, this method is aliased to the `Dispose()` method; therefore *closing a stream* is functionally equivalent to *disposing a stream*.

Member	Meaning in Life
Flush()	Updates the underlying data source or repository with the current state of the buffer and then clears the buffer. If a stream does not implement a buffer, this method does nothing.
Length	Returns the length of the stream in bytes.
Position	Determines the position in the current stream.
Read() ReadByte()	Reads a sequence of bytes (or a single byte) from the current stream and advances the current position in the stream by the number of bytes read.
Seek()	Sets the position in the current stream.
SetLength()	Sets the length of the current stream.
Write() WriteByte()	Writes a sequence of bytes (or a single byte) to the current stream and advances the current position in this stream by the number of bytes written.

Working with FileStreams

The FileStream class provides an implementation for the MustInherit Stream members in a manner appropriate for file-based streaming. It is a fairly primitive stream; it can read or write only a single byte or an array of bytes. However, you will not often need to interact directly with the members of the FileStream type. Instead, you will probably use various *stream wrappers*, which make it easier to work with textual data or .NET types. Nevertheless, you will find it helpful to experiment with the synchronous read/write capabilities of the FileStream type.

Assume you have a new Console Application named FileStreamApp, and you imported System.IO and System.Text into your VB 2010 code file. Your goal is to write a simple text message to a new file named myMessage.dat. However, given that FileStream can operate only on raw bytes, you will be required to encode the System.String type into a corresponding byte array. Fortunately, the System.Text namespace defines a type named Encoding that provides members that encode and decode strings to (or from) an array of bytes (check out the .NET Framework 4.0 SDK documentation for more details about the Encoding type).

Once encoded, the byte array is persisted to file with the FileStream.Write() method. To read the bytes back into memory, you must reset the internal position of the stream (using the Position property) and call the ReadByte() method. Finally, you display the raw byte array and the decoded string to the console. Here is the complete Main() method:

```
'Don't forget to import the System.Text and System.IO namespaces.
Sub Main()

        Console.WriteLine("***** Fun with FileStreams *****" & vbLf)
        'Obtain a FileStream object.
        Using fStream As FileStream = File.Open _
        ("C:\myMessage.dat",FileMode.Create)

             'Encode a string as an array of Bytes.
             Dim msg As String = "Hello!"
             Dim msgAsByteArray As Byte() = Encoding.Default.GetBytes(msg)

             'Write Byte array to file.
             fStream.Write(msgAsByteArray, 0, msgAsByteArray.Length)

             'Reset internal position of stream.
             fStream.Position = 0

             'Read the types from file and display to console.
             Console.Write("Your message as an array of Bytes: ")
             Dim bytesFromFile As Byte() = New Byte(msgAsByteArray.Length) {}

             For i = 0 To msgAsByteArray.Length - 1
                 bytesFromFile(i) = CByte(fStream.ReadByte())
                 Console.Write(bytesFromFile(i))
             Next

             'Display decoded messages.
             Console.Write(vbLf & "Decoded Message: ")
             Console.WriteLine(Encoding.Default.GetString(bytesFromFile))
        End Using
        Console.ReadLine()
End Sub
```

This example populates the file with data, but it also punctuates the major downfall of working directly with the FileStream type: it demands to operate on raw bytes. Other Stream-derived types operate in a similar manner. For example, if you wish to write a sequence of bytes to a region of memory, you can allocate a MemoryStream. Likewise, if you wish to push an array of bytes through a network connection, you can use the NetworkStream class (in the System.Net.Sockets namespace).

As mentioned previously, the System.IO namespace provides several *reader* and *writer* types that encapsulate the details of working with Stream-derived types.

■ **Source Code** You can find the FileStreamApp project is under the Chapter 20 subdirectory.

Working with StreamWriters and StreamReaders

The StreamWriter and StreamReader classes are useful whenever you need to read or write character-based data (e.g., Strings). Both of these types work by default with Unicode characters; however, you can change this by supplying a properly configured System.Text.Encoding object reference. To keep things simple, assume that the default Unicode encoding fits the bill.

StreamReader derives from a MustInherit type named TextReader, as does the related StringReader type (discussed later in this chapter). The TextReader base class provides a limited set of functionality to each of these descendents; specifically it provides the ability to read and peek into a character stream.

The StreamWriter type (as well as StringWriter, which you will examine later in this chapter) derives from a MustInherit base class named TextWriter. This class defines members that allow derived types to write textual data to a given character stream.

To aid in your understanding of the core writing capabilities of the StreamWriter and StringWriter classes, Table 20-8 describes the core members of the MustInherit TextWriter base class.

Table 20-8. Core Members of TextWriter

Member	Meaning in Life
Close()	This method closes the writer and frees any associated resources. In the process, the buffer is automatically flushed (again, this member is functionally equivalent to calling the Dispose() method).
Flush()	This method clears all buffers for the current writer and causes any buffered data to be written to the underlying device; however, it does not close the writer.
NewLine	This property indicates the newline constant for the derived writer class. The default line terminator for the Windows OS is a carriage return, followed by a line feed.
Write()	This overloaded method writes data to the text stream without a newline constant.
WriteLine()	This overloaded method writes data to the text stream with a newline constant.

■ **Note** The last two members of the TextWriter class probably look familiar to you. If you recall, the System.Console type has Write() and WriteLine() members that push textual data to the standard output device. In fact, the Console.In property wraps a TextWriter, and the Console.Out property wraps a TextReader.

The derived StreamWriter class provides an appropriate implementation for the Write(), Close(), and Flush() methods, and it defines the additional AutoFlush property. When set to True, this property forces StreamWriter to flush all data every time you perform a write operation. Be aware that you can gain better performance by setting AutoFlush to False, provided you always call Close() when you finish writing with a StreamWriter.

Writing to a Text File

To see the `StreamWriter` type in action, create a new Console Application named `StreamWriterReaderApp` and Imports `System.IO`. The following `Main()` method creates a new file named `reminders.txt` using the `File.CreateText()` method. Using the obtained `StreamWriter` object, you can add some textual data to the new file:

```
Sub Main()
    Console.WriteLine("*** Fun with StreamWriter / StreamReader ***" & vbLf)

    ' Get a StreamWriter and write String data.
    Using writer As StreamWriter = File.CreateText("reminders.txt")
        writer.WriteLine("Don't forget Mother's Day this year...")
        writer.WriteLine("Don't forget Father's Day this year...")
        writer.WriteLine("Don't forget these numbers:")

        For i = 0 To 9
            writer.Write(i & " ")
        Next i

        'Insert a new line.
        writer.Write(writer.NewLine)
    End Using

    Console.WriteLine("Created file and wrote some thoughts...")
    Console.ReadLine()
End Sub
```

After you run this program, you can examine the contents of this new file (see Figure 20-3). You will find this file under the bin\Debug folder of your current application because you did not specify an absolute path at the time you called `CreateText()`.

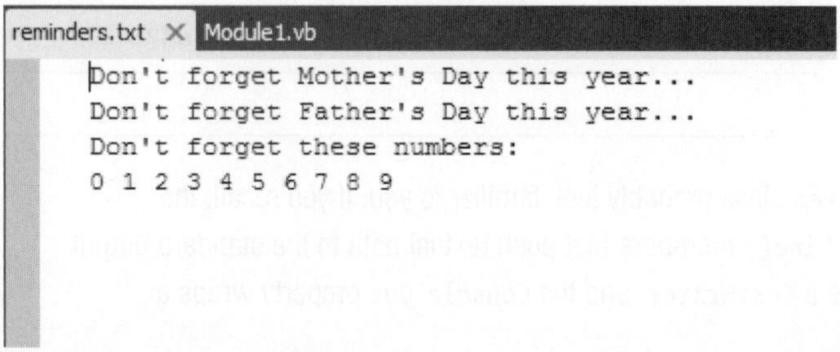

Figure 20-3. *The contents of your *.txt file*

Reading from a Text File

Next, you will learn to read data from a file programmatically by using the corresponding StreamReader type. Recall that this class derives from the MustInherit TextReader, which offers the functionality described in Table 20-9.

Table 20-9. *TextReader Core Members*

Member	Meaning in Life
Peek()	Returns the next available character without actually changing the position of the reader. A value of -1 indicates you are at the end of the stream.
Read()	Reads data from an input stream.
ReadBlock()	Reads a specified maximum number of characters from the current stream and writes the data to a buffer, beginning at a specified index.
ReadLine()	Reads a line of characters from the current stream and returns the data as a String (a Nothing string indicates EOF).
ReadToEnd()	Reads all characters from the current position to the end of the stream and returns them as a single string.

If you now extend the current MyStreamWriterReader sample application to use a StreamReader, you can read in the textual data from the reminders.txt file, as shown here:

```
Sub Main()
    Console.WriteLine("*** Fun with StreamWriter / StreamReader ***" & vbLf)
    ...
    'Now read data from file.
    Console.WriteLine("Here are your thoughts:" & vbLf)

    Using sr As StreamReader = File.OpenText("reminders.txt")
        Dim input As String = Nothing
    input = sr.ReadLine()
        Do While input IsNot Nothing
           Console.WriteLine(input)
           Input = sr.ReadLine()
        Loop
    End Using
Console.ReadLine()
End Sub
```

Once you run the program, you will see the character data in reminders.txt displayed to the console.

Directly Creating StreamWriter/StreamReader Types

One of the confusing aspects of working with the types within System.IO is that you can often achieve an identical result using different approaches. For example, you have already seen that you can use the CreateText() method to obtain a StreamWriter with the File or FileInfo type. It so happens that you can work with StreamWriters and StreamReaders another way: by creating them directly. For example, you could retrofit the current application as follows:

```
Sub Main()
  Console.WriteLine("*** Fun with StreamWriter / StreamReader ***" & vbLf)

  ' Get a StreamWriter and write string data.
  Using writer As New StreamWriter("reminders.txt")
      '...
  End Using

  ' Now read data from file.
  Using sr As New StreamReader("reminders.txt")
      '...
  End Using
End Sub
```

Although it can be a bit confusing to see so many seemingly identical approaches to file I/O, keep in mind that the end result is greater flexibility. In any case, you are now ready to examine the role of the StringWriter and StringReader classes, given that you have seen how to move character data to and from a given file using the StreamWriter and StreamReader types.

■ **Source Code** You can find the StreamWriterReaderApp project under the Chapter 20 subdirectory.

Working with StringWriters and StringReaders

You can use the StringWriter and StringReader types to treat textual information as a stream of in-memory characters. This can prove helpful when you wish to append character-based information to an underlying buffer. The following Console Application (named StringReaderWriterApp) illustrates this by writing a block of String data to a StringWriter object, rather than to a file on the local hard drive:

```
Sub Main()
      Console.WriteLine("Fun with StringWriter / StringReader" & vbLf)

      'Create a StringWriter and emit character data to memory.
      Using strWriter As New StringWriter()
          strWriter.WriteLine("Don't forget Mother's Day this year...")
```

```
                'Get a copy of the contents (stored in a String) and pump
                'to console.
                Console.WriteLine("Contents of StringWriter:" &
                vbLf & "{0}", strWriter)
        End Using
        Console.ReadLine()
End Sub
```

StringWriter and StreamWriter both derive from the same base class (TextWriter), so the writing logic is more or less identical. However, given the nature of StringWriter, you should also be aware that this class allows you to use the GetStringBuilder() method to extract a System.Text.StringBuilder object:

```
Using strWriter As New StringWriter()
        strWriter.WriteLine("Don't forget Mother's Day this year...")
        Console.WriteLine("Contents of StringWriter:" & ↵
          vbLf & "{0}", strWriter)

        'Get the internal StringBuilder.
        Dim sb As StringBuilder = strWriter.GetStringBuilder()
        sb.Insert(0, "Hey!! ")
        Console.WriteLine("-> {0}", sb.ToString())

        sb.Remove(0, "Hey!! ".Length)
        Console.WriteLine("-> {0}", sb.ToString())
End Using
```

When you wish to read from a stream of character data, you can use the corresponding StringReader type, which (as you would expect) functions identically to the related StreamReader class. In fact, the StringReader class does nothing more than override the inherited members to read from a block of character data, rather than from a file, as shown here:

```
Using strWriter As New StringWriter()
        strWriter.WriteLine("Don't forget Mother's Day this year...")
        Console.WriteLine("Contents of StringWriter:" & ↵
                          vbLf & "{0}", strWriter)

        'Read data from the StringWriter.
        Using strReader As New StringReader(strWriter.ToString())
                Dim input As String = Nothing

            Do While input IsNot Nothing
                Console.WriteLine(input)
              input = strReader.ReadLine()
            Loop
        End Using
End Using
```

■ **Source Code** You can find the `StringReaderWriterApp` under the Chapter 20 subdirectory.

Working with BinaryWriters and BinaryReaders

The final writer/reader sets you will examine in this section are `BinaryReader` and `BinaryWriter`. Both derive directly from `System.Object`. These types allow you to read and write discrete data types to an underlying stream in a compact binary format. The `BinaryWriter` class defines a highly overloaded `Write()` method to place a data type in the underlying stream. In addition to the `Write()` member, `BinaryWriter` provides additional members that allow you to get or set the `Stream`-derived type; it also offers support for random access to the data (see Table 20-10).

Table 20-10. `BinaryWriter` Core Members

Member	Meaning in Life
BaseStream	This read-only property provides access to the underlying stream used with the `BinaryWriter` object.
Close()	This method closes the binary stream.
Flush()	This method flushes the binary stream.
Seek()	This method sets the position in the current stream.
Write()	This method writes a value to the current stream.

The `BinaryReader` class complements the functionality offered by `BinaryWriter` with the members described in Table 20-11.

Table 20-11. `BinaryReader` Core Members

Member	Meaning in Life
BaseStream	This read-only property provides access to the underlying stream used with the `BinaryReader` object.
Close()	This method closes the binary reader.
PeekChar()	This method returns the next available character without advancing the position in the stream.
Read()	This method reads a given set of bytes or characters and stores them in the incoming array.
ReadXXXX()	The `BinaryReader` class defines numerous read methods that grab the next type from the stream (e.g., `ReadBoolean()`, `ReadByte()`, and `ReadInt32()`).

The following example (a Console Application named **BinaryWriterReader**) writes a number of data types to a new *.dat* file:

```
Sub Main()
        Console.WriteLine("*** Fun with Binary Writers / Readers ***" & vbLf)

        'Open a binary writer for a file.
        Dim f As New FileInfo("BinFile.dat")

        Using bw As New BinaryWriter(f.OpenWrite())
            'Print out the type of BaseStream.
            '(System.IO.FileStream in this case).
            Console.WriteLine("Base stream is: {0}", bw.BaseStream)

            'Create some data to save in the file
            Dim aDouble As Double = 1234.67
            Dim anInteger As Integer = 34567
            Dim aString As String = "A, B, C"

            'Write the data
            bw.Write(aDouble)
            bw.Write(anInteger)
            bw.Write(aString)
        End Using
         Console.ReadLine()
End Sub
```

Notice how the **FileStream** object returned from **FileInfo.OpenWrite()** is passed to the constructor of the **BinaryWriter** type. Using this technique makes it easy to *layer in* a stream before writing out the data. Note that the constructor of **BinaryWriter** takes any **Stream**-derived type (e.g., **FileStream**, **MemoryStream**, or **BufferedStream**). Thus, writing binary data to memory instead is as simple as supplying a valid **MemoryStream** object.

To read the data out of the **BinFile.dat** file, the **BinaryReader** type provides a number of options. Here, you call various read-centric members to pluck each chunk of data from the file stream:

```
Sub Main()
        ...
        Dim f As New FileInfo("BinFile.dat")
        ...
        'Read the binary data from the stream.
        Using br As New BinaryReader(f.OpenRead())
            Console.WriteLine(br.ReadDouble())
            Console.WriteLine(br.ReadInt32())
            Console.WriteLine(br.ReadString())
        End Using
        Console.ReadLine()
End Sub
```

■ **Source Code** You can find the `BinaryWriterReader` application under the Chapter 20 subdirectory.

Watching Files Programmatically

Now that you have a better handle on the use of various readers and writers, you'll look at the role of the `FileSystemWatcher` class. This type can be quite helpful when you wish to monitor (or "watch") files on your system programmatically. Specifically, you can instruct the `FileSystemWatcher` type to monitor files for any of the actions specified by the `System.IO.NotifyFilters` enumeration (many of these members are self-explanatory, but you should still check the .NET Framework 4.0 SDK documentation for more details):

```
Public Enum NotifyFilters
   Attributes
   CreationTime
   DirectoryName
   FileName
   LastAccess
   LastWrite
   Security
   Size
End Enum
```

To begin working with the `FileSystemWatcher` type, you need to set the `Path` property to specify the name (and location) of the directory that contains the files you want to monitor, as well as the `Filter` property that defines the file extensions of the files you want to monitor.

At this point, you may choose to handle the `Changed`, `Created`, and `Deleted` events, all of which work in conjunction with the `FileSystemEventHandler` delegate. This delegate can call any method matching the following pattern:

```
' The FileSystemEventHandler delegate must point
' to methods matching the following signature.
Sub MyNotificationHandler(ByVal source As Object,
      ByVal e As FileSystemEventArgs)
```

You can also handle the `Renamed` event using the `RenamedEventHandler` delegate type, which can call methods that match the following signature:

```
' The RenamedEventHandler delegate must point
' to methods matching the following signature.
Sub MyRenamedHandler(ByVal source As Object,ByVal e As RenamedEventArgs)
```

Next, let's look at the process of watching a file. Assume you have created a new directory on your `C:` drive named `MyFolder` that contains various `*.txt` files (named whatever you wish). The following Console Application (named `MyDirectoryWatcher`) monitors the `*.txt` files in the `MyFolder` directory and prints out messages when files are created, deleted, modified, or renamed:

```vb
Sub Main()
        Console.WriteLine("****The Amazing File Watcher App****" & vbLf)

        ' Establish the path to the directory to watch.
        Dim watcher As New FileSystemWatcher()
        Try
            watcher.Path = "C:\MyFolder"
        Catch ex As ArgumentException
            Console.WriteLine(ex.Message)
            Return
        End Try

        ' Set up the things to be on the lookout for.
        watcher.NotifyFilter = NotifyFilters.LastAccess Or _
                                NotifyFilters.LastWrite Or __
                                NotifyFilters.FileName Or _
                                NotifyFilters.DirectoryName

        ' Only watch text files.
        watcher.Filter = "*.txt"

        ' Add event handlers.
        AddHandler watcher.Changed, AddressOf OnChanged
        AddHandler watcher.Created, AddressOf OnChanged
        AddHandler watcher.Deleted, AddressOf OnChanged
        AddHandler watcher.Renamed, AddressOf OnRenamed

        ' Begin watching the directory.
        watcher.EnableRaisingEvents = True

        ' Wait for the user to quit the program.
        Console.WriteLine("Press 'q' to quit app.")
        While Console.ReadLine() <> "q"
        End While
End Sub
```

The two event handlers simply print out the current file modification:

```vb
Sub OnChanged(ByVal source As Object, ByVal e As FileSystemEventArgs)
        'Specify what is done when a file is changed, created, or deleted.
        Console.WriteLine("File: {0} {1}!", e.FullPath, e.ChangeType)
End Sub

Sub OnRenamed(ByVal source As Object, ByVal e As RenamedEventArgs)
        'Specify what is done when a file is renamed.
        Console.WriteLine("File: {0} renamed to" & vbLf &
                        "{1}", e.OldFullPath, e.FullPath)
End Sub
```

To test this program, run the application and open Windows Explorer. Try renaming your files, creating a *.txt file, deleting a *.txt file, and so forth. You will see various bits of information generated about the state of the text files within your MyFolder, as in this example:

```
***** The Amazing File Watcher App *****



Press 'q' to quit app.

File: C:\MyFolder\New Text Document.txt Created!

File: C:\MyFolder\New Text Document.txt renamed to

C:\MyFolder\Hello.txt

File: C:\MyFolder\Hello.txt Changed!

File: C:\MyFolder\Hello.txt Changed!

File: C:\MyFolder\Hello.txt Deleted!
```

■ **Source Code** You can find the MyDirectoryWatcher application under the Chapter 20 subdirectory.

That wraps up this chapter's look at fundamental IO operations within the .NET platform. While you will certainly use these techniques in many of your applications, you might also find that *object serialization* services can greatly simplify how you persist large amounts of data.

Understanding Object Serialization

The term *serialization* describes the process of persisting (and possibly transferring) the state of an object into a stream (e.g., file stream and memory stream). The persisted data sequence contains all the necessary information you need to reconstruct (or *deserialize*) the state of the object for use later. Using this technology makes it trivial to save vast amounts of data (in various formats). In many cases, saving application data using serialization services results in less code than using the readers/writers you find in the System.IO namespace.

For example, assume you want to create a GUI-based desktop application that provides a way for end users to save their preferences (e.g., window color and font size). To do this, you might define a class named UserPrefs that encapsulates 20 or so pieces of field data. Now, if you were to use a System.IO.BinaryWriter type, you would need to save each field of the UserPrefs object *manually*. Likewise, if you were to load the data from a file back into memory, you would need to use a

System.IO.BinaryReader and (once again) *manually* read in each value to reconfigure a new UserPrefs object.

This is all doable, but you can save yourself a good amount of time by marking the UserPrefs class with the <Serializable()> attribute:

```
<Serializable()>
Public Class UserPrefs
  Public WindowColor As String
  Public FontSize As Integer
End Class
```

Doing this means that you can persist entire state of the object with only a few lines of code. Without getting hung up on the details for the time being, consider the following Main() method:

```
Sub Main()
Dim userData As New UserPrefs()
userData.WindowColor = "Yellow"
userData.FontSize = "50"

' The BinaryFormatter persists state data in a binary format.
' You would need to import System.Runtime.Serialization.Formatters.Binary
' to gain access to BinaryFormatter.
Dim binFormat As New BinaryFormatter()

' Store object in a local file.
Using fStream As Stream = New FileStream("user.dat", FileMode.Create,
          FileAccess.Write, FileShare.None)

    binFormat.Serialize(fStream, userData)
End Using
Console.ReadLine()
End Sub
```

.NET object serialization makes it easy to persist objects; however, the processes used behind the scenes are quite sophisticated. For example, when an object is persisted to a stream, all associated data (e.g., base class data and contained objects) are automatically serialized, as well. Therefore, if you attempt to persist a derived class, all data up the chain of inheritance comes along for the ride. As you will see, you use an object graph to represent a set of interrelated objects.

.NET serialization services also allow you to persist an object graph in a variety of formats. The previous code example uses the BinaryFormatter type; therefore, the state of the UserPrefs object is persisted as a compact binary format. You can also persist an object graph into SOAP or XML format using other types. These formats can be quite helpful when you wish to ensure that your persisted objects travel well across operating systems, languages, and architectures.

■ **Note** WCF prefers a slightly different mechanism for serializing objects to/from WCF service operations; it uses the <DataContract()> and <DataMember()> attributes. You'll learn more about this in Chapter 25.

Finally, understand that you can persist an object graph into *any* System.IO.Stream-derived type. In the previous example, you use the FileStream type to persist a UserPrefs object into a local file. However, if you would rather store an object to a specific region of memory, you could use a MemoryStream type instead. All that matters is the fact that the sequence of data correctly represents the state of objects within the graph.

The Role of Object Graphs

As mentioned previously, the CLR will account for all related objects to ensure that data is persisted correctly when an object is serialized. This set of related objects is referred to as an *object graph*. Object graphs provide a simple way to document how a set of objects refer to each other, and these relationships do not necessarily map to classic OO relationships (such as the *is-a* or *has-a* relationship), although they do model this paradigm quite well.

Each object in an object graph is assigned a unique numerical value. Keep in mind that the numbers assigned to the members in an object graph are arbitrary and have no real meaning to the outside world. Once you assign all objects a numerical value, the object graph can record each object's set of dependencies.

For example, assume you have created a set of classes that model some automobiles (of course). You have a base class named Car, which *has-a* Radio. Another class named JamesBondCar extends the Car base type. Figure 20-4 shows a possible object graph that models these relationships.

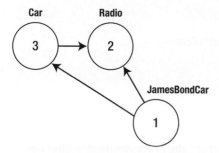

Figure 20-4. A simple object graph

When reading object graphs, you can use the phrase *depends on* or *refers to* when connecting the arrows. Thus, in Figure 20-4, you can see that the Car refers to the Radio class (given the *has-a* relationship). JamesBondCar refers to Car (given the *is-a* relationship), as well as to Radio (it inherits this protected member variable).

Of course, the CLR does not paint pictures in memory to represent a graph of related objects. Rather, the relationship documented in the previous diagram is represented by a mathematical formula that looks something like this:

[Car 3, ref 2], [Radio 2], [JamesBondCar 1, ref 3, ref 2]

If you parse this formula, you can see that object 3 (the Car) has a dependency on object 2 (the Radio). Object 2, the Radio, is a lone wolf and requires nobody. Finally, object 1 (the JamesBondCar) has a dependency on object 3, as well as object 2. In any case, when you serialize or deserialize an instance of JamesBondCar, the object graph ensures that the Radio and Car types also participate in the process.

The beautiful thing about the serialization process is that the graph representing the relationships among your objects is established automatically behind the scenes. As you will see later in this chapter, however, you can become more involved in the construction of a given object graph by customizing the serialization process using attributes and interfaces.

■ **Note** Strictly speaking, the XmlSerializer type (described later in this chapter) does not persist state using object graphs; however, this type still serializes and deserializes related objects in a predictable manner.

Configuring Objects for Serialization

To make an object available to .NET serialization services, all you need to do is decorate each related class (or structure) with the <Serializable()> attribute. If you determine that a given type has some member data that should not (or perhaps cannot) participate in the serialization scheme, you can mark such fields with the <NonSerialized()> attribute. This can be helpful if you wish to reduce the size of the persisted data, and you have member variables in a serializable class that do not need to be remembered (e.g., fixed values, random -values, and transient data).

Defining Serializable Types

To get the ball rolling, create a new Console Application named SimpleSerialize. Insert a new class named Radio, which has been marked <Serializable()>, excluding a single member variable (radioID) that has been marked <NonSerialized()> and will therefore not be persisted into the specified data stream:

```
<Serializable()>
Public Class Radio
        Public hasTweeters As Boolean
        Public hasSubWoofers As Boolean
        Public stationPresets() As Double

        <NonSerialized()>
        Public radioID As String = "XF-552RR6"
End Class
```

Next, insert two additional class types to represent the JamesBondCar and Car base classes, both of which are also marked <Serializable> and define the following pieces of field data:

```
<Serializable()>
Public Class Car
        Public theRadio As New Radio()
        Public isHatchBack As Boolean
End Class
```

```
<Serializable()>
Public Class JamesBondCar
        Inherits Car
        Public canFly As Boolean
        Public canSubmerge As Boolean
End Class
```

Be aware that you cannot inherit the `<Serializable()>` attribute from a parent class. Therefore, if you derive a class from a type marked `<Serializable()>`, the child class must be marked `<Serializable()>` as well, or it cannot be persisted. In fact, all objects in an object graph must be marked with the `<Serializable()>` attribute. If you attempt to serialize a nonserializable object using the `BinaryFormatter` or `SoapFormatter`, you will receive a `SerializationException` at runtime.

Public Fields, Private Fields, and Public Properties

Notice that in each of these classes, you define the field data as Public; this helps keep the example simple. Of course, Private data exposed using Public properties would be preferable from an OO point of view. Also, for the sake of simplicity, this example does not define any custom constructors on these types; therefore, all unassigned field data will receive the expected default values.

OO design principles aside, you might wonder how the various formatters expect a type's field data to be defined in order to be serialized into a stream. The answer is that it depends. If you persist an object's state using the `BinaryFormatter` or `SoapFormatter`, it makes absolutely no difference. These types are programmed to serialize *all* serializable fields of a type, regardless of whether they are Public fields, Private fields, or Private fields exposed through Public properties. Recall, however, that if you have points of data that you do not want to be persisted into the object graph, you can selectively mark Public or Private fields as `<NonSerialized()>`, as you do with the String field of the `Radio` type.

The situation is quite different if you use the `XmlSerializer` type, however. This type will *only* serialize Public data fields or Private data exposed by Public properties. Private data not exposed from properties will be ignored. For example, consider the following serializable `Person` type:

```
<Serializable()>
Public Class Person
  ' A Public field.
  Public isAlive As Boolean = True

  ' A Private field.
  Private personAge As Integer = 21

  ' Public property/Private data.
  Private fName As String = String.Empty
  Public Property FirstName() As String
        Get
            Return fName
        End Get
        Set(ByVal value As String)
            fName = value
        End Set
  End Property
End Class
```

If you processed the preceding with `BinaryFormatter` or `SoapFormatter`, you would find that the `isAlive`, `personAge`, and `fName` fields are saved into the selected stream. However, the `XmlSerializer` would *not* save the value of `personAge` because this piece of Private data is not encapsulated by a Public type property. If you wished to persist the age of the person with the `XmlSerializer`, you would need to define the field publicly or encapsulate the Private member using a Public property.

Choosing a Serialization Formatter

Once you configure your types to participate in the .NET serialization scheme by applying the necessary attributes, your next step is to choose which format (binary, SOAP, or XML) you should use when persisting your object's state. Each possibility is represented by the following classes:

- `BinaryFormatter`
- `SoapFormatter`
- `XmlSerializer`

The `BinaryFormatter` type serializes your object's state to a stream using a compact binary format. This type is defined within the `System.Runtime.Serialization.Formatters.Binary` namespace that is part of `mscorlib.dll`. If you wish to gain access to this type, you can specify the following VB 2010 `Imports` directive:

```
'Gain access to the BinaryFormatter in mscorlib.dll.
Imports System.Runtime.Serialization.Formatters.Binary
```

The `SoapFormatter` type persists an object's state as a SOAP message (the standard XML format for passing messages to/from a web service). This type is defined within the `System.Runtime.Serialization.Formatters.Soap` namespace, which is defined in a *separate assembly*. Thus, to format your object graph into a SOAP message, you must first set a reference to `System.Runtime.Serialization.Formatters.Soap.dll` using the Visual Studio 2010 Add Reference dialog box and then specify the following VB 2010 `Imports` directive:

```
'Must reference System.Runtime.Serialization.Formatters.Soap.dll.
Imports System.Runtime.Serialization.Formatters.Soap
```

Finally, if you wish to persist a tree of objects as an XML document, you can use the `XmlSerializer` type. To use this type, you need to specify that you are using the `System.Xml.Serialization` namespace and set a reference to the assembly `System.Xml.dll`. As luck would have it, all Visual Studio 2010 project templates automatically reference `System.Xml.dll`; therefore, all you need to do is use the following namespace:

```
'Defined within System.Xml.dll.
Imports System.Xml.Serialization
```

The IFormatter and IRemotingFormatter Interfaces

Regardless of which formatter you choose to use, be aware that all of them derive directly from `System.Object`, so they do *not* share a common set of members from a serialization-centric base class. However, the `BinaryFormatter` and `SoapFormatter` types do support common members through the implementation of the IFormatter and IRemotingFormatter interfaces (strange as it might seem, the XmlSerializer implements neither).

System.Runtime.Serialization.IFormatter defines the core Serialize() and Deserialize() methods, which do the grunt work to move your object graphs into and out of a specific stream. Beyond these members, IFormatter defines a few properties that the implementing type uses behind the scenes:

```
Public Interface IFormatter
    Property Binder() As SerializationBinder
    Property Context() As StreamingContext
    Property SurrogateSelector() As ISurrogateSelector
    Function Deserialize(ByVal serializationStream As Stream) As Object
    Sub Serialize(ByVal serializationStream As Stream, ByVal graph As Object)
End Interface
```

The System.Runtime.Remoting.Messaging.IRemotingFormatter interface (which is leveraged internally by the .NET remoting layer) overloads the Serialize() and Deserialize() members into a manner more appropriate for distributed persistence. Note that IRemotingFormatter derives from the more general IFormatter interface:

```
Public Interface IRemotingFormatter
  Inherits IFormatter

  Function Deserialize(ByVal serializationStream As Stream,
          ByVal handler As HeaderHandler) As Object

  Sub Serialize(ByVal serializationStream As Stream,
            ByVal graph As Object,
            ByVal headers() As Header)
End Interface
```

Although you might not need to interact directly with these interfaces for most of your serialization endeavors, recall that interface-based polymorphism allows you to hold an instance of BinaryFormatter or SoapFormatter using an IFormatter reference. Therefore, if you wish to build a method that can serialize an object graph using either of these classes, you could write the following:

```
Sub SerializeObjectGraph(ByVal itfFormat As IFormatter,
                         ByVal destStream As Stream,
                         ByVal graph As Object)
  itfFormat.Serialize(destStream, graph)
End Sub
```

Type Fidelity Among the Formatters

The most obvious difference among the three formatters is how the object graph is persisted to the stream (binary, SOAP, or XML). You should also be aware of a few more subtle points of distinction; specifically, how the formatters contend with *type fidelity*. When you use the BinaryFormatter type, it will persist not only the field data of the objects in the object graph, but also each type's fully qualified name and the full name of the defining assembly (name, version, public key token, and culture). These extra points of data make the BinaryFormatter an ideal choice when you wish to transport objects by value (e.g., as a full copy) across machine boundaries for .NET-centric applications.

The SoapFormatter persists traces of the assembly of origin through the use of an XML namespace. For example, recall the Person type earlier in this chapter. If this type were persisted as a SOAP message, you would find that the opening element of Person is qualified by the generated xmlns. Consider this partial definition, paying special attention to the a1 XML namespace:

```
<a1:Person id="ref-1" xmlns:a1=
  "http://schemas.microsoft.com/clr/nsassem/SimpleSerialize/MyApp%2C%20
  Version%3D1.0.0.0%2C%20Culture%3Dneutral%2C%20PublicKeyToken%3Dnull">
  <isAlive>true</isAlive>
  <personAge>21</personAge>
  <fName id="ref-3"></fName>
</a1:Person>
```

However, the XmlSerializer does *not* attempt to preserve full type fidelity; therefore, it does not record the type's fully qualified name or assembly of origin. This might seem like a limitation at first glance, but XML serialization is used by classic .NET web services, which can be called from clients on any platform (not just .NET). This means that there is no point serializing full .NET type metadata. Here is a possible XML representation of the Person type:

```
<?xml version="1.0"?>
<Person xmlns:xsi="http://www.w3.org/2001/XMLSchema-instance"
        xmlns:xsd="http://www.w3.org/2001/XMLSchema">
  <isAlive>true</isAlive>
  <PersonAge>21</PersonAge>
  <FirstName />
</Person>
```

If you wish to persist an object's state in a manner that can be used by any operating system (e.g., Windows 7, Mac OS X, and various Linux distributions), application framework (e.g., .NET, Java Enterprise Edition, and COM), or programming language, you do not want to maintain full type fidelity because you cannot assume all possible recipients can understand .NET-specific data types. Given this, SoapFormatter and XmlSerializer are ideal choices when you wish to ensure as broad a reach as possible for the persisted tree of objects.

Serializing Objects Using the BinaryFormatter

You can use the BinaryFormatter type to illustrate how easy it is to persist an instance of the JamesBondCar to a physical file. Again, the two key methods of the BinaryFormatter type to be aware of are Serialize() and Deserialize():

- Serialize(): Persists an object graph to a specified stream as a sequence of bytes.
- Deserialize(): Converts a persisted sequence of bytes to an object graph.

Assume you have created an instance of JamesBondCar, modified some state data, and want to persist your spy mobile into a *.dat file. Begin by creating the *.dat file itself. You can achieve this by creating an instance of the System.IO.FileStream type. At this point, you can create an instance of the BinaryFormatter and pass in the FileStream and object graph to persist. Consider the following Main() method:

```
' Be sure to import the System.Runtime.Serialization.Formatters.Binary
' and System.IO namespaces.
Sub Main()
    Console.WriteLine("***** Fun with Object Serialization *****" & vbLf)

    ' Make a JamesBondCar and set state.
    Dim jbc As New JamesBondCar()
        jbc.canFly = True
        jbc.canSubmerge = False
        jbc.theRadio.stationPresets = New Double(){89.3, 105.1, 97.1}
        jbc.theRadio.hasTweeters = True

        ' Now save the car to a specific file in a binary format.
        SaveAsBinaryFormat(jbc, "CarData.dat")
        Console.ReadLine()
End Sub
```

You implement the SaveAsBinaryFormat() method like this:

```
Sub SaveAsBinaryFormat(ByVal objGraph As Object,
                       ByVal fileName As String)

    'Save object to a file named CarData.dat in binary.
    Dim binFormat As New BinaryFormatter()

    Using fStream As Stream = New FileStream(fileName, FileMode. _
        Create,FileAccess.Write, FileShare.None)

        binFormat.Serialize(fStream, objGraph)
End Using
Console.WriteLine("=> Saved car in binary format!")
End Sub
```

The BinaryFormatter.Serialize() method is the member responsible for composing the object graph and moving the byte sequence to some Stream-derived type. In this case, the stream happens to be a physical file. You could also serialize your object types to any Stream-derived type, such as a memory location or network stream.

Once you run your program, you can view the contents of the CarData.dat file that represents this instance of the JamesBondCar by navigating to the \bin\Debug folder of the current project. Figure 20-5 shows this file opened within Visual Studio 2010.

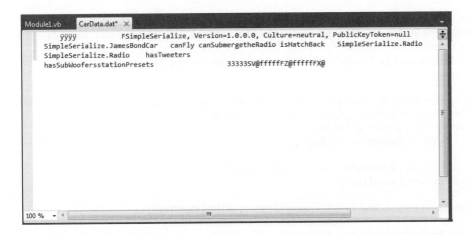

Figure 20-5. JamesBondCar serialized using a BinaryFormatter

Deserializing Objects Using the BinaryFormatter

Now suppose you want to read the persisted JamesBondCar from the binary file back into an object variable. Once you open CarData.dat programmatically (with the File.OpenRead() method), you can call the Deserialize() method of the BinaryFormatter. Be aware that Deserialize() returns a general System.Object type, so you need to impose an explicit cast, as shown here:

```
Sub LoadFromBinaryFile(ByVal fileName As String)
    Dim binFormat As New BinaryFormatter()

    'Read the JamesBondCar from the binary file.
    Using fStream As Stream = File.OpenRead(fileName)

        Dim carFromDisk As JamesBondCar = CType(binFormat.Deserialize
                                    (fStream), JamesBondCar)

        Console.WriteLine("Can this car fly? :{0}",carFromDisk.canFly)
    End Using
End Sub
```

Notice that when you call Deserialize(), you pass the Stream-derived type that represents the location of the persisted object graph. Once you cast the object back into the correct type, you will find the state data has been retained from the point at which you saved the object.

Serializing Objects Using the SoapFormatter

Your next choice of formatter is the SoapFormatter type, which serializes data in a proper SOAP envelope. In a nutshell, the Simple Object Access Protocol (SOAP) defines a standard process in which you can invoke methods in a platform- and OS-neutral manner.

Assuming you have set a reference to the System.Runtime.Serialization.Formatters.Soap.dll assembly (and imported the System.Runtime.Serialization.Formatters.Soap namespace), you can persist and retrieve a JamesBondCar as a SOAP message simply by replacing each occurrence of BinaryFormatter with SoapFormatter. Consider the following new method of your module, which serializes an object to a local file:

```
'Be sure to import System.Runtime.Serialization.Formatters.Soap
'and reference System.Runtime.Serialization.Formatters.Soap.dll.
Sub SaveAsSoapFormat(ByVal objGraph As Object,
                     ByVal fileName As String)

    'Save object to a file named CarData.soap in SOAP format.
    Dim soapFormat As New SoapFormatter()

        Using fStream As Stream = New FileStream(fileName, FileMode.Create,
                                    FileAccess.Write, FileShare.None)
            soapFormat.Serialize(fStream, objGraph)
        End Using
            Console.WriteLine("=> Saved car in SOAP format!")
End Sub
```

As before, you use Serialize() and Deserialize() to move the object graph into and out of the stream. If you call this method from Main() and run the application, you can open the resulting *.soap file. Here you can locate the XML elements that mark the stateful values of the current JamesBondCar, as well as the relationship between the objects in the graph by using the #ref tokens (see Figure 20-6).

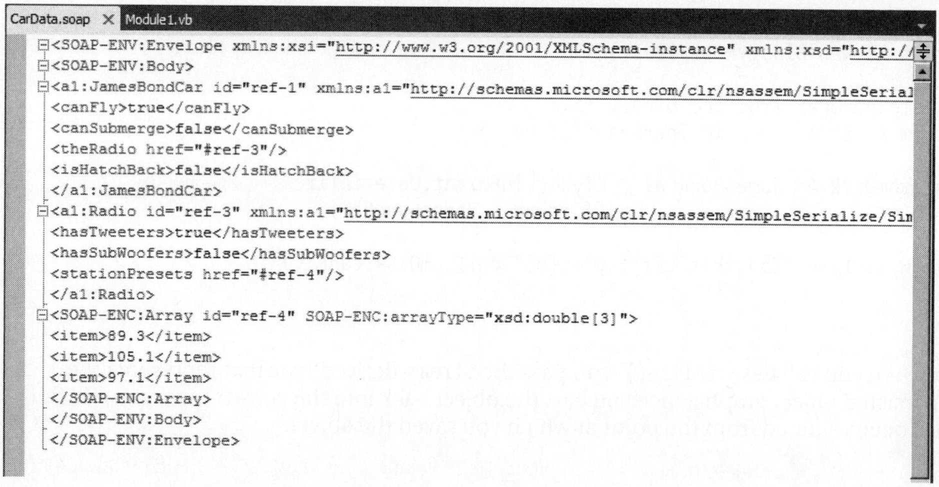

Figure 20-6. JamesBondCar serialized using a SoapFormatter

Serializing Objects Using the XmlSerializer

In addition to the SOAP and binary formatters, the System.Xml.dll assembly provides a third formatter, System.Xml.Serialization.XmlSerializer. You can use this formatter to persist the *Public* state of a given object as pure XML, as opposed to XML data wrapped within a SOAP message. Working with this type is a bit different from working with the SoapFormatter or BinaryFormatter type. Consider the following code, which assumes you have imported the System.Xml.Serialization namespace:

```
Sub SaveAsXmlFormat(ByVal objGraph As Object, ByVal fileName As String)
        'Save object to a file named CarData.xml in XML format.
        Dim xmlFormat As New XmlSerializer(GetType(JamesBondCar))

        Using fStream As Stream = New FileStream(fileName, FileMode.Create,
                            FileAccess.Write, FileShare.None)
                xmlFormat.Serialize(fStream, objGraph)
        End Using
        Console.WriteLine("=> Saved car in XML format!")
End Sub
```

The key difference is that the XmlSerializer type requires you to specify type information that represents the class you want to serialize. If you were to look within the newly generated XML file (assuming you call this new method from within Main()), you would find the XML data shown here:

```
<?xml version="1.0"?>
<JamesBondCar xmlns:xsi="http://www.w3.org/2001/XMLSchema-instance"
xmlns:xsd="http://www.w3.org/2001/XMLSchema">
  <theRadio>
    <hasTweeters>true</hasTweeters>
    <hasSubWoofers>false</hasSubWoofers>
    <stationPresets>
      <double>89.3</double>
      <double>105.1</double>
      <double>97.1</double>
    </stationPresets>
    <radioID>XF-552RR6</radioID>
  </theRadio>
  <isHatchBack>false</isHatchBack>
  <canFly>true</canFly>
  <canSubmerge>false</canSubmerge>
</JamesBondCar>
```

■ **Note** The XmlSerializer demands that all serialized types in the object graph support a default constructor (so be sure to add it back if you define custom constructors). If this is not the case, you will receive an InvalidOperationException at runtime.

Controlling the Generated XML Data

If you have a background in XML technologies, you know that it is often critical to ensure the data within an XML document conforms to a set of rules that establish the *validity* of the data. Understand that a *valid* XML document does not have anything to do with the syntactic well-being of the XML elements (e.g., all opening elements must have a closing element). Rather, valid documents conform to agreed-upon formatting rules (e.g., field X must be expressed as an attribute and not a sub-element), which are typically defined by an XML schema or document-type definition (DTD) file.

By default, XmlSerializer serializes all Public fields/properties as XML elements, rather than as XML attributes. If you wish to control how the XmlSerializer generates the resulting XML document, you can decorate types with any number of additional .NET attributes from the System.Xml.Serialization namespace. Table 20-12 documents some (but not all) of the .NET attributes that influence how XML data is encoded to a stream.

Table 20-12. Select Attributes of the System.Xml.Serialization Namespace

.NET Attribute	Meaning in Life
<XmlAttribute()>	You can use this .NET attribute on a Public field or property in a class to tell XmlSerializer to serialize the data as an XML attribute (rather than as a sub-element).
<XmlElement()>	The field or property will be serialized as an XML element named as you so choose.
<XmlEnum()>	This attribute provides the element name of an enumeration member.
<XmlRoot()>	This attribute controls how the root element will be constructed (namespace and element name).
<XmlText()>	The property or field will be serialized as XML text (i.e. the content between the start tag and the end tag of the root element).
<XmlType()>	This attribute provides the name and namespace of the XML type.

This simple example illustrates how the field data of JamesBondCar is currently persisted as XML:

```
<?xml version="1.0" encoding="utf-8"?>
<JamesBondCar xmlns:xsi="http://www.w3.org/2001/XMLSchema-instance"
              xmlns:xsd="http://www.w3.org/2001/XMLSchema">
...
  <canFly>true</canFly>
  <canSubmerge>false</canSubmerge>
</JamesBondCar>
```

If you wish to specify a custom XML namespace that qualifies the `JamesBondCar` and encodes the `canFly` and `canSubmerge` values as XML attributes, you can do so by modifying the VB 2010 definition of `JamesBondCar`:

```
<XmlRoot(Namespace := "http://www.MyCompany.com")>
Public Class JamesBondCar
    Inherits Car

    <XmlAttribute()>
    Public canFly As Boolean
    <XmlAttribute>
    Public canSubmerge As Boolean
End Class
```

This yields the following XML document (note the opening `<JamesBondCar>` element):

```
<?xml version="1.0"""?>
<JamesBondCar xmlns:xsi="http://www.w3.org/2001/XMLSchema-instance"
              xmlns:xsd="http://www.w3.org/2001/XMLSchema"
  canFly="true" canSubmerge="false"
  xmlns="http://www.MyCompany.com">
...
</JamesBondCar>
```

Of course, you can use many other attributes to control how the `XmlSerializer` generates the resulting XML document. For full details, look up the `System.Xml.Serialization` namespace in the .NET Framework 4.0 SDK documentation.

Serializing Collections of Objects

Now that you have seen how to persist a single object to a stream, you're ready to examine how to save a set of objects. As you might have noticed, the `Serialize()` method of the `IFormatter` interface does not provide a way to specify an arbitrary number of objects as input (only a single `System.Object`). On a related note, the return value of `Deserialize()` is, again, a single `System.Object` (the same basic limitation holds true for `XmlSerializer`):

```
Public Interface IFormatter
...
  Function Deserialize(ByVal serializationStream As Stream) As Object
  Sub Serialize(ByVal serializationStream As Stream, ByVal graph As Object)
End Interface
```

Recall that the `System.Object` represents a complete tree of objects. Given this, if you pass in an object that has been marked as `,<Serializable()>` and contains other `<Serializable()>` objects, the entire set of objects is persisted in a single method call. As luck would have it, most of the types you find in the `System.Collections` and `System.Collections.Generic` namespaces have already been marked as `<Serializable()>`. Therefore, if you wish to persist a set of objects, simply add the desired set to the container (such as an `ArrayList` or a `List(Of T)`) and serialize the object to your stream of choice.

Now assume that you want to update the `JamesBondCar` class with a two-argument constructor, so you can set a few pieces of state data (note that you add back the default constructor as required by the `XmlSerializer`):

```
<Serializable, XmlRoot(Namespace := "http://www.MyCompany.com")>
Public Class JamesBondCar
  Inherits Car
    Public Sub New(ByVal skyWorthy As Boolean, ByVal seaWorthy As Boolean)
        canFly = skyWorthy
        canSubmerge = seaWorthy
    End Sub

    ' The XmlSerializer demands a default constructor!
    Public Sub New()
End Sub
...
End Class
```

With this, you can now persist any number of `JamesBondCar`s:

```
Sub SaveListOfCars()
    ' Now persist a List(Of T) of JamesBondCars.
    Dim myCars As New List(Of JamesBondCar)()
    myCars.Add(New JamesBondCar(True, True))
    myCars.Add(New JamesBondCar(True, False))
    myCars.Add(New JamesBondCar(False, True))
    myCars.Add(New JamesBondCar(False, False))

    Using fStream As Stream = New FileStream("CarCollection.xml",FileMode
                        .Create, FileAccess.Write, FileShare.None)

        Dim xmlFormat As New XmlSerializer(GetType(List(Of JamesBondCar)))
        xmlFormat.Serialize(fStream, myCars)
    End Using
    Console.WriteLine("=> Saved list of cars!")
End Sub
```

You use `XmlSerializer` here, so you are required to specify type information for each of the sub-objects within the root object (`List(Of JamesBondCar)`, in this case). However, the logic would be even more straightforward if you were to use the `BinaryFormatter` or `SoapFormatter` type, instead:

```
Sub SaveListOfCarsAsBinary()
    'Save ArrayList object (myCars) as binary.
    Dim myCars As New List(Of JamesBondCar)()

    Dim binFormat As New BinaryFormatter()
    Using fStream As Stream = New FileStream("AllMyCars.dat",
            FileMode.Create, FileAccess.Write, FileShare.None)
        binFormat.Serialize(fStream, myCars)
    End Using
```

```
        Console.WriteLine("=> Saved list of cars in binary!")
End Sub
```

■ **Source Code** You can find the SimpleSerialize application under the Chapter 20 subdirectory.

Customizing the Soap/Binary Serialization Process

In a majority of cases, the default serialization scheme provided by the .NET platform will be exactly what you require. Simply apply the <Serializable()> attribute to your related types and pass the tree of objects to your formatter of choice for processing. In some cases, however, you might wish to become more involved with how a tree is constructed and handled during the serialization process. For example, perhaps you have a business rule that says all field data must be persisted using a particular format, or perhaps you wish to add additional bits of data to the stream that do not map directly to fields in the object being persisted (e.g., timestamps and unique identifiers).

When you wish to become more involved with the process of object serialization, the System.Runtime.Serialization namespace provides several types that allow you to do so. Table 20-13 describes some of the core types you should be aware of.

Table 20-13. System.Runtime.Serialization Namespace Core Types

Type	Meaning in Life
ISerializable	You can implement this interface on a <Serializable()> type to control its serialization and deserialization.
ObjectIDGenerator	This type generates IDs for members in an object graph.
<OnDeserialized()>	This attribute allows you to specify a method that will be called immediately after the object has been deserialized.
<OnDeserializing()>	This attribute allows you to specify a method that will be called before the deserialization process.
<OnSerialized()>	This attribute allows you to specify a method that will be called immediately after the object has been serialized.
<OnSerializing()>	This attribute allows you to specify a method that will be called before the serialization process.
<OptionalField()>	This attribute allows you to define a field on a type that can be missing from the specified stream.
<SerializationInfo()>	In essence, this class is a *property bag* that maintains name/value pairs representing the state of an object during the serialization process.

A Deeper Look at Object Serialization

Before you examine various ways that you can customize the serialization process, you will find it helpful to take a deeper look at what takes place behind the scenes. When the `BinaryFormatter` serializes an object graph, it is in charge of transmitting the following information into the specified stream:

- The fully qualified name of the objects in the graph (e.g., `MyApp.JamesBondCar`)

- The name of the assembly defining the object graph (e.g., `MyApp.exe`)

- An instance of the `SerializationInfo` class that contains all stateful data maintained by the members in the object graph

During the deserialization process, the `BinaryFormatter` uses this same information to build an identical copy of the object, using the information extracted from the underlying stream. `SoapFormatter` uses a quite similar process.

> ■ **Note** Recall that the `XmlSerializer` does not persist a type's fully qualified name or the name of the defining assembly; this behavior helps keep the state of the object as mobile as possible. This type is concerned only with persisting exposed public data.

Beyond moving the required data into and out of a stream, formatters also analyze the members in the object graph for the following pieces of infrastructure:

- A check is made to determine whether the object is marked with the `<Serializable()>` attribute. If the object is not, a `SerializationException` is thrown.

- If the object is marked `<Serializable()>`, a check is made to determine whether the object implements the `ISerializable` interface. If this is the case, `GetObjectData()` is called on the object.

- If the object does not implement `ISerializable`, the default serialization process is used, serializing all fields not marked as `<NonSerialized()>`.

In addition to determining whether the type supports `ISerializable`, formatters are also responsible for discovering whether the types in question support members that have been adorned with the `<OnSerializing()>`, `<OnSerialized()>`, `<OnDeserializing()>`, or `<OnDeserialized()>` attributes. You'll examine the role of these attributes in momentarily, but first you need to look at the role of `ISerializable`.

Customizing Serialization Using ISerializable

Objects that are marked `<Serializable()>` have the option of implementing the `ISerializable` interface. Doing so lets you get "involved" with the serialization process and perform any pre- or post-data formatting.

■ **Note** Since the release of .NET 2.0, the preferred way to customize the serialization process is to use the serialization attributes (described next). However, knowledge of `ISerializable` is important for the purpose of maintaining existing systems.

The `ISerializable` interface is quite simple, given that it defines only a single method, `GetObjectData()`:

```
' When you wish to tweak the serialization process,
' implement ISerializable.
Public Interface ISerializable

        Sub GetObjectData(ByVal info As SerializationInfo,
                          ByVal context As StreamingContext)
End Interface
```

The `GetObjectData()` method is called automatically by a given formatter during the serialization process. The implementation of this method populates the incoming `SerializationInfo` parameter with a series of name/value pairs that (typically) map to the field data of the object being persisted. `SerializationInfo` defines numerous variations on the overloaded `AddValue()` method, as well as a small set of properties that allow the type to get and set the type's name, defining assembly, and member count. Here is a partial snapshot:

```
Public NotInheritable Class SerializationInfo
        Public Sub New(ByVal mytype As Type, ByVal converter As
                                    IFormatterConverter)
        Public Property AssemblyName() As String
        Public Property FullTypeName() As String
        Public ReadOnly Property MemberCount() As Integer

        Public Sub AddValue(ByVal name As String, ByVal value As Short)
        Public Sub AddValue(ByVal name As String, ByVal value As UShort)
        Public Sub AddValue(ByVal name As String, ByVal value As Integer)
...
End Class
```

Types that implement the `ISerializable` interface must also define a special constructor that takes the following signature:

```
' You must supply a custom constructor with this signature
' to allow the runtime engine to set the state of your object.
<Serializable()>
Public Class SomeClass
        Implements ISerializable
```

```
        Protected Sub New(ByVal si As SerializationInfo,
                          ByVal ctx As StreamingContext)
                ...
        End Sub
    ...
End Class
```

Notice that the visibility of this constructor is set as *Protected*. This is permissible because the formatter will have access to this member, regardless of its visibility. These special constructors tend to be marked as Protected (or Private for that matter) to ensure that the casual object user can never create an object in this manner. The first parameter of this constructor is an instance of the `SerializationInfo` type (which you've seen previously).

The second parameter of this special constructor is a `StreamingContext` type, which contains information regarding the source of the bits. The most informative member of `StreamingContext` is the `State` property, which represents a value from the `StreamingContextStates` enumeration. The values of this enumeration represent the basic composition of the current stream.

Unless you intend to implement some low-level custom remoting services, you will seldom need to deal with this enumeration directly. Nevertheless, here are the possible names of the `StreamingContextStates` Enum (consult the .NET Framework 4.0 SDK documentation for full details):

```
Public Enum StreamingContextStates
    CrossProcess
    CrossMachine
    File
    Persistence
    Remoting
    Other
    Clone
    CrossAppDomain
    All
End Enum
```

Now let's look at how to customize the serialization process using `ISerializable`. Assume you have a new Console Application project (named `CustomSerialization`) that defines a class type containing two points of `string` data. Also assume that you must ensure that the `String` objects are serialized to the stream all uppercase and deserialized from the stream in lowercase. To account for such rules, you could implement `ISerializable` like this (be sure to import the `System.Runtime.Serialization` namespace):

```
<Serializable()>
Public Class StringData
        Implements ISerializable

        Private dataItemOne As String = "First data block"
        Private dataItemTwo As String = "More data"

        Public Sub New()
        End Sub
```

```
    Protected Sub New(ByVal si As SerializationInfo,
                      ByVal ctx As StreamingContext)
        ' Rehydrate member variables from stream.
        dataItemOne = si.GetString("First_Item").ToLower()
        dataItemTwo = si.GetString("dataItemTwo").ToLower()
    End Sub

    Private Sub GetObjectData(ByVal info As SerializationInfo,
                              ByVal ctx As StreamingContext)
                    Implements ISerializable.GetObjectData

        ' Fill up the SerializationInfo object with the formatted data.
        info.AddValue("First_Item", dataItemOne.ToUpper())
        info.AddValue("dataItemTwo", dataItemTwo.ToUpper())
    End Sub
End Class
```

Notice that when you fill the SerializationInfo type with the GetObjectData() method, you are *not* required to name the data points identically to the type's internal member variables. This can obviously be helpful if you need to further decouple the type's data from the persisted format. Be aware, however, that you will need to obtain the values from the special, Protected constructor using the same names assigned within GetObjectData().

To test your customization, assume that you want to persist an instance of MyStringData using a SoapFormatter (so update your assembly references and imports accordingly):

```
Sub Main()
  Console.WriteLine("***** Fun with Custom Serialization *****")

  ' Recall that this type implements ISerializable.
  Dim myData As New StringData()

  ' Save to a local file in SOAP format.
  Dim soapFormat As New SoapFormatter()

  Using fStream As Stream = New FileStream("MyData.soap", FileMode.Create
                                    ,FileAccess.Write, FileShare.None)
          soapFormat.Serialize(fStream, myData)
  End Using
  Console.ReadLine()
End Sub
```

When you view the resulting *.soap file, you will see that the String fields have been persisted in uppercase (see Figure 20-7).

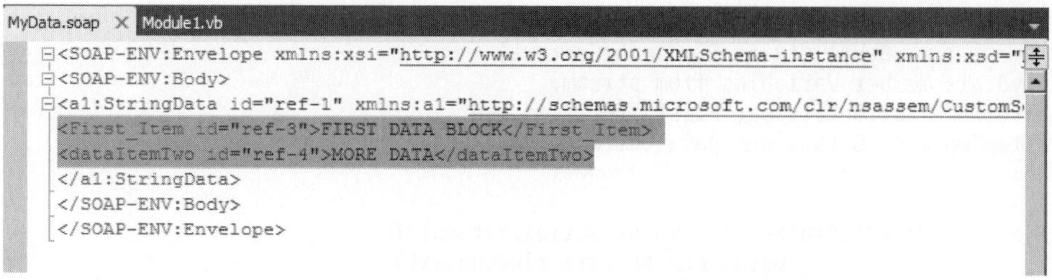

```
MyData.soap  X  Module1.vb
 ⊟<SOAP-ENV:Envelope xmlns:xsi="http://www.w3.org/2001/XMLSchema-instance" xmlns:xsd="
 ⊟<SOAP-ENV:Body>
 ⊟<a1:StringData id="ref-1" xmlns:a1="http://schemas.microsoft.com/clr/nsassem/CustomS
   <First_Item id="ref-3">FIRST DATA BLOCK</First_Item>
   <dataItemTwo id="ref-4">MORE DATA</dataItemTwo>
   </a1:StringData>
   </SOAP-ENV:Body>
   </SOAP-ENV:Envelope>
```

Figure 20-7. *Customizing your serialization with ISerializable*

Customizing Serialization Using Attributes

Although implementing the ISerializable interface is one way to customize the serialization process, the preferred way to customize the serialization process since the release of .NET 2.0 is to define methods that are attributed with any of the new serialization-centric attributes: <OnSerializing()>, <OnSerialized()>, <OnDeserializing()>, or <OnDeserialized()>. Using these attributes is less cumbersome than implementing ISerializable because you do not need to interact manually with an incoming SerializationInfo parameter. Instead, you can modify your state data directly, while the formatter operates on the type.

■ **Note** You can find these serialization attributes defined in the System.Runtime.Serialization namespace.

When you define method decorated with these attributes, you must define the methods so they receive a StreamingContext parameter and don't return anything (otherwise, you will receive a runtime exception). Note that you are not required to account for each of the serialization-centric attributes, and you can simply contend with the stages of serialization you want to intercept. The following snippet illustrates this. Here, a new <Serializable()> type has the same requirements as StringData, but this time you account for using the <OnSerializing()> and <OnDeserialized()> attributes:

```vb
<Serializable()>
Public Class MoreData
  Private dataItemOne As String = "First data block"
  Private dataItemTwo As String= "More data"

  <OnSerializing()>
  Private Sub OnSerializing(ByVal context As StreamingContext)
          'Called during the serialization process.
          dataItemOne = dataItemOne.ToUpper()
          dataItemTwo = dataItemTwo.ToUpper()
  End Sub
```

```
<OnDeserialized()>
Private Sub OnDeserialized(ByVal context As StreamingContext)
        'Called once the deserialization process is complete.
        dataItemOne = dataItemOne.ToLower()
        dataItemTwo = dataItemTwo.ToLower()
    End Sub
End Class
```

If you were to serialize this new type, you would again find that the data has been persisted as uppercase and deserialized as lowercase.

■ **Source Code** You can find the CustomSerialization project under the Chapter 20 subdirectory.

With this example behind you, your exploration of the core details of object serialization services, including various ways to customize the process, is complete. As you have seen, the serialization and deserialization process makes it easy to persist large amounts of data, and it can be less labor-intensive than working with the various reader/writer classes of the System.IO namespace.

Summary

You began this chapter by examining the use of the Directory(Info) and File(Info) types. As you learned, these classes allow you to manipulate a physical file or directory on your hard drive. Next, you examined a number of classes derived from the MustInherit Stream class. Given that Stream-derived types operate on a raw stream of bytes, the System.IO namespace provides numerous reader/writer types (e.g., StreamWriter, StringWriter, and BinaryWriter) that simplify the process. Along the way, you also checked out the functionality provided by DriveType, learned how to monitor files using the FileSystemWatcher type, and saw how to interact with streams in an asynchronous manner.

This chapter also introduced you to the topic of object serialization services. As you have seen, the .NET platform uses an object graph to account for the full set of related objects that you want to persist to a stream. As long as each member in the object graph has been marked with the <Serializable()> attribute, the data is persisted using your format of choice (binary or SOAP).

You also learned that it is possible to customize the out-of-the-box serialization process using two possible approaches. First, you learned how to implement the ISerializable interface (and support a special Private constructor), which enables you to become more involved with how formatters persist the supplied data. Second, you learned about a set of .NET attributes that simplify the process of custom serialization. All you need to do is apply the <OnSerializing()>, <OnSerialized()>, <OnDeserializing()>, or <OnDeserialized()> attribute on members that take a StreamingContext parameter, and the formatters will invoke them accordingly.

CHAPTER 21

■ ■ ■

ADO.NET
Part I: The Connected Layer

As you might expect, the .NET platform defines a number of namespaces that allow you to interact directly with machine local and remote relational databases. Collectively speaking, these namespaces are known as *ADO.NET*. In this chapter, you'll learn about the overall role of ADO.NET, then move on to the topic of ADO.NET data providers. The .NET platform supports numerous data providers, each of which is optimized to communicate with a specific database management system (e.g., Microsoft SQL Server, Oracle, and MySQL).

After you understand the common functionality provided by various data providers, you will then look at the data provider factory pattern. As you will see, using types within the `System.Data.Common` namespace (and a related `App.config` file), you can build a single code base that can dynamically pick and choose the underlying data provider without the need to recompile or redeploy the application's code base.

Perhaps most importantly, this chapter will give you the chance to build a custom data access library assembly (`AutoLotDAL.dll`) that encapsulates various database operations performed on a custom database named `AutoLot`. You will expand this library in Chapters 23 and 24 and leverage it over many of this book's remaining chapters. Finally, you will wrap things up by examining the topic of database transactions.

A High-Level Definition of ADO.NET

If you have a background in Microsoft's previous COM-based data access model (ActiveX Data Objects, or ADO), you need to understand that ADO.NET has little to do with ADO beyond the letters *A, D,* and *O*. While it is true that there is some relationship between the two systems (e.g., each has the concept of connection and command objects), some familiar ADO types (e.g., the `Recordset`) no longer exist. Furthermore, you can find many new ADO.NET types that have no direct equivalent under classic ADO (e.g., the data adapter).

Unlike classic ADO, which was primarily designed for tightly coupled client/server systems, ADO.NET was built with the disconnected world in mind, using `DataSets`. This type represents a local copy of any number of related data tables, each of which contains a collection of rows and column. Using the `DataSet`, the calling assembly (such as a web page or desktop executable) is able to manipulate and update a `DataSet`'s contents while disconnected from the data source and send any modified data back for processing using a related *data adapter*.

Perhaps the most fundamental difference between classic ADO and ADO.NET is that ADO.NET is a managed library of code; therefore, it plays by the same rules as any other managed library. The types that make up ADO.NET use the CLR memory management protocol, adhere to the same type system (e.g., classes, interfaces, enums, structures, and delegates), and can be accessed by any .NET language.

From a programmatic point of view, the bulk of ADO.NET is represented by a core assembly named System.Data.dll. Within this binary, you find a good number of namespaces (see Figure 21-1), many of which represent the types of a particular ADO.NET data provider (defined momentarily).

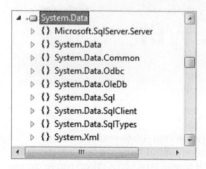

Figure 21-1. System.Data.dll is the core ADO.NET assembly.

It turns out most Visual Studio 2010 project templates automatically reference this key data access assembly. However, you do need to update your code files to import the namespaces you wish to use, as in this example:

```
' Bring in some ADO.NET namespaces!
Imports System.Data
Imports System.Data.SqlClient

Module Module1
        Sub Main()
        End Sub
End Module
```

You should also understand that there are other ADO.NET-centric assemblies beyond System.Data.dll (e.g., System.Data.OracleClient.dll and System.Data.Entity.dll) that you might need to reference manually in your current project using the Add Reference dialog box.

The Three Faces of ADO.NET

You can use the ADO.NET libraries in three conceptually unique manners: connected, disconnected, or through the Entity Framework. When you use the *connected layer* (the subject of this chapter), your code base explicitly connects to and disconnects from the underlying data store. When you use ADO.NET in this manner, you typically interact with the data store using connection objects, command objects, and data reader objects.

The disconnected layer (you will learn more about this in Chapter 22) allows you to manipulate a set of DataTable objects (contained within a DataSet) that functions as a client-side copy of the external data. When you obtain a DataSet using a related data adapter object, the connection is automatically opened and closed on your behalf. As you would guess, this approach helps free up connections for other callers quickly and goes a long way toward increasing the scalability of your systems.

Once a caller receives a DataSet, it is able to traverse and manipulate the contents without incurring the cost of network traffic. Also, if the caller wishes to submit the changes back to the data store, the data adapter (in conjunction with a set of SQL statements) is used to update the data source; at this point the connection is reopened for the database updates to occur, and then closed again immediately.

With the release of .NET 3.5 SP1, ADO.NET was enhanced to support a new API termed the Entity Framework (or simply, EF). Using EF, you will find that many of the low-level database specifics (such as complex SQL queries) are hidden from view and authored on your behalf when you generate a fitting LINQ query (e.g., LINQ to Entities). You will examine this aspect of ADO.NET in Chapter 23.

Understanding ADO.NET Data Providers

Unlike other database APIs you might have used in the past, ADO.NET does not provide a single set of types that communicate with multiple database management systems (DBMSs). Rather, ADO.NET supports multiple *data providers*, each of which is optimized to interact with a specific DBMS. The first benefit of this approach is that you can program a specific data provider to access any unique features of a particular DBMS. The second benefit is that a specific data provider can connect directly to the underlying engine of the DBMS in question without an intermediate mapping layer standing between the tiers.

Simply put, a *data provider* is a set of types defined in a given namespace that understand how to communicate with a specific type of data source. Regardless of which data provider you use, each defines a set of class types that provide core functionality. Table 21-1 documents some of the core common types, their base class (all defined in the System.Data.Common namespace), and the key interfaces (each is defined in the System.Data namespace) they implement.

Table 21-1. *The Core Objects of an ADO.NET Data Provider*

Type of Object	Base Class	Relevant Interfaces	Meaning in Life
Connection	DbConnection	IDbConnection	Provides the ability to connect to and disconnect from the data store. Connection objects also provide access to a related transaction object.
Command	DbCommand	IDbCommand	Represents a SQL query or a stored procedure. Command objects also provide access to the provider's data reader object.
DataReader	DbDataReader	IDataReader, IDataRecord	Provides forward-only, read-only access to data using a server-side cursor.
DataAdapter	DbDataAdapter	IDataAdapter, IDbDataAdapter	Transfers DataSets between the caller and the data store. Data adapters contain a connection and a set of four internal command objects used to select, insert, update, and delete information from the data store.
Parameter	DbParameter	IDataParameter, IDbDataParameter	Represents a named parameter within a parameterized query.
Transaction	DbTransaction	IDbTransaction	Encapsulates a database transaction.

Although the specific names of these core classes will differ among data providers (e.g., SqlConnection vs. OracleConnection vs. OdbcConnection vs. MySqlConnection), each class derives from the same base class (DbConnection, in the case of connection objects) that implements identical interfaces (e.g., IDbConnection). Given this, you would be correct to assume that once you learn how to work with one data provider, the remaining providers prove quite straightforward.

■ **Note** When you refer to a connection object under ADO.NET, you're actually referring to a specific DbConnection-derived type; there is no class literally named *Connection*. The same idea holds true for a *command object*, *data adapter object*, and so forth. As a naming convention, the objects in a specific data provider are prefixed with the name of the related DBMS (e.g., SqlConnection, OracleConnection, and SqlDataReader).

Figure 21-2 shows the big picture behind ADO.NET data providers. Note how the diagram illustrates that the *Client Assembly* can literally be any type of .NET application: console program, Windows Forms application, WPF application, ASP.NET web page, WCF service, a .NET code library, and so on.

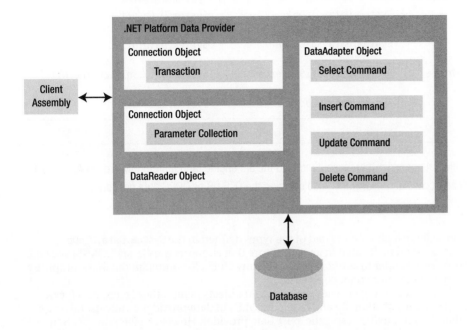

Figure 21-2. ADO.NET data providers provide access to a given DBMS

A data provider will supply you with other types beyond the objects shown in Figure 21-2; however, these core objects define a common baseline across all data providers.

The Microsoft-Supplied ADO.NET Data Providers

Microsoft's .NET distribution ships with numerous data providers, including a provider for Oracle, SQL Server, and OLE DB/ODBC-style connectivity. Table 21-2 documents the namespace and containing assembly for each Microsoft ADO.NET data provider.

Table 21-2. Microsoft ADO.NET Data Providers

Data Provider	Namespace	Assembly
OLE DB	System.Data.OleDb	System.Data.dll
Microsoft SQL Server	System.Data.SqlClient	System.Data.dll
Microsoft SQL Server Mobile	System.Data.SqlServerCe	System.Data.SqlServerCe.dll
ODBC	System.Data.Odbc	System.Data.dll

■ **Note** There is no specific data provider that maps directly to the Jet engine (and therefore Microsoft Access). If you wish to interact with an Access data file, you can do so using the OLE DB or ODBC data provider.

The OLE DB data provider, which is composed of the types defined in the `System.Data.OleDb` namespace, allows you to access data located in any data store that supports the classic COM-based OLE DB protocol. You can use this provider to communicate with any OLE DB–compliant database simply by tweaking the `Provider` segment of your connection string.

However, the OLE DB provider interacts with various COM objects behind the scenes, which can affect the performance of your application. By and large, the OLE DB data provider is only useful if you interact with a DBMS that does not define a specific .NET data provider. However, given the fact that these days any DBMS worth its salt should have a custom ADO.NET data provider for download, you should consider `System.Data.OleDb` a legacy namespace that has little use in the .NET 4.0 world (this is even more the case with the advent of the data provider factory model introduced under .NET 2.0, which you will learn about shortly).

■ **Note** There is one case in which using the types of `System.Data.OleDb` is necessary: when you need to communicate with Microsoft SQL Server version 6.5 or earlier. The `System.Data.SqlClient` namespace can only communicate with Microsoft SQL Server version 7.0 or higher.

The Microsoft SQL Server data provider offers direct access to Microsoft SQL Server data stores—and *only* SQL Server data stores (version 7.0 and greater). The `System.Data.SqlClient` namespace contains the types used by the SQL Server provider and offers the same basic functionality as the OLE DB provider. The key difference is that the SQL Server provider bypasses the OLE DB layer and gives numerous performance benefits. The Microsoft SQL Server data provider also allows you to gain access to the unique features of this particular DBMS.

The remaining Microsoft-supplied providers (`System.Data.Odbc` and `System.Data.SqlClientCe`) provide access to ODBC connections, and the SQL Server Mobile edition DBMS (commonly used by handheld devices, such as Windows Mobile). The ODBC types defined within the `System.Data.Odbc` namespace are typically only useful if you need to communicate with a given DBMS for which there is no custom .NET data provider. This is true because ODBC is a widespread model that provides access to a number of data stores.

A Word Regarding System.Data.OracleClient.dll

Earlier versions of the .NET platform shipped with an assembly named `System.Data.OracleClient.dll`, which as the name suggests, offered a data provider to communicate with Oracle databases. As of .NET 4.0, however, this assembly has been marked as *obsolete* and will eventually be *deprecated*.

At first glance, this might cause you to fear that ADO.NET is slowly becoming focused squarely on Microsoft-centric data stores; however, this is not the case. Oracle provides its own custom .NET assembly, which follows the same overall design guidelines as the data providers provided by Microsoft. If you need to obtain this .NET assembly, you can visit the downloads section of Oracle's web site at `www.oracle.com/technology/tech/windows/odpnet/index.html`.

Obtaining Third-Party ADO.NET Data Providers

In addition to the data providers that ship from Microsoft (as well as Oracle's custom .NET library), numerous third-party data providers exist for various open source and commercial databases. While you will most likely be able to obtain an ADO.NET data provider directly from the database vendor, you should be aware of the following site: `www.sqlsummit.com/DataProv.htm`.

This web site is one of many sites that document each known ADO.NET data provider and provide links for more information and downloads. Here you will find numerous ADO.NET providers, including SQLite, IBM DB2, MySQL, PostgreSQL, TurboDB, Sybase, and many others.

Given the large number of ADO.NET data providers, the examples in this book will use the Microsoft SQL Server data provider (`System.Data.SqlClient.dll`). Recall that this provider allows you to communicate with Microsoft SQL Server version 7.0 and higher, including SQL Server Express Edition. If you intend to use ADO.NET to interact with another DBMS, you should have no problem doing so once you understand the material presented in the pages that follow.

Additional ADO.NET Namespaces

In addition to the .NET namespaces that define the types of a specific data provider, the .NET base class libraries provide a number of additional ADO.NET-centric namespaces, some of which you can see in Table 21-3 (again, Chapter 24 will address the assemblies and namespaces specific to Entity Framework).

Table 21-3. Select Additional ADO.NET-Centric Namespaces

Namespace	Meaning in Life
`Microsoft.SqlServer.Server`	This namespace provides types that facilitate CLR and SQL Server 2005 and later integration services.
`System.Data`	This namespace defines the core ADO.NET types used by all data providers, including common interfaces and numerous types that represent the disconnected layer (e.g., `DataSet` and `DataTable`).
`System.Data.Common`	This namespace contains types shared between all ADO.NET data providers, including the common MustInherit base classes.
`System.Data.Sql`	This namespace contains types that allow you to discover Microsoft SQL Server instances installed on the current local network.
`System.Data.SqlTypes`	This namespace contains native data types used by Microsoft SQL Server. You can always use the corresponding CLR data types, but the `SqlTypes` are optimized to work with SQL Server (e.g., if your SQL Server database contains an integer value, you can represent it using either `Integer` or `SqlTypes.SqlInt32`).

Note that this chapter does not examine every type within every ADO.NET namespace (that task would require a large book all by itself); however, it is quite important that you understand the types within the `System.Data` namespace.

The Types of the System.Data Namespace

Of all the ADO.NET namespaces, `System.Data` is the lowest common denominator. You cannot build ADO.NET applications without specifying this namespace in your data access applications. This namespace contains types that are shared among all ADO.NET data providers, regardless of the underlying data store. In addition to a number of database-centric exceptions (e.g., `NoNullAllowedException`, `RowNotInTableException`, and `MissingPrimaryKeyException`), `System.Data` contains types that represent various database primitives (e.g., tables, rows, columns, and constraints), as well as the common interfaces implemented by data provider objects. Table 21-4 lists some of the core types you should be aware of.

Table 21-4. Core Members of the System.Data Namespace

Type	Meaning in Life
Constraint	Represents a constraint for a given `DataColumn` object.
DataColumn	Represents a single column within a `DataTable` object.
DataRelation	Represents a parent/child relationship between two `DataTable` objects.
DataRow	Represents a single row within a `DataTable` object.
DataSet	Represents an in-memory cache of data consisting of any number of interrelated `DataTable` objects.
DataTable	Represents a tabular block of in-memory data.
DataTableReader	Allows you to treat a `DataTable` as a fire-hose cursor (forward only, read-only data access).
DataView	Represents a customized view of a `DataTable` for sorting, filtering, searching, editing, and navigation.
IDataAdapter	Defines the core behavior of a data adapter object.
IDataParameter	Defines the core behavior of a parameter object.
IDataReader	Defines the core behavior of a data reader object.
IDbCommand	Defines the core behavior of a command object.
IDbDataAdapter	Extends `IDataAdapter` to provide additional functionality of a data adapter object.
IDbTransaction	Defines the core behavior of a transaction object.

You use the vast majority of the classes within **System.Data** when programming against the disconnected layer of ADO.NET. In the next chapter, you will get to know the details of the **DataSet** and its related cohorts (e.g., **DataTable**, **DataRelation**, and **DataRow**) and how to use them (and a related data adapter) to represent and manipulate client-side copies of remote data.

However, your next task is to examine the core interfaces of **System.Data** at a high level; this can help you understand the common functionality offered by any data provider. You will also learn specific details throughout this chapter; however, for now it's best to focus on the overall behavior of each interface type.

The Role of the IDbConnection Interface

The **IDbConnection** type is implemented by a data provider's *connection object*. This interface defines a set of members used to configure a connection to a specific data store. It also allows you to obtain the data provider's transaction object. Here is the formal definition of **IDbConnection**:

```
Public Interface IDbConnection
    Inherits IDisposable

    Property ConnectionString() As String
    ReadOnly Property ConnectionTimeout() As Integer
    ReadOnly Property Database() As String
    ReadOnly Property State() As ConnectionState

    Function BeginTransaction() As IDbTransaction
    Function BeginTransaction(ByVal il As IsolationLevel)
        As IDbTransaction
    Sub ChangeDatabase(ByVal databaseName As String)
    Sub Close()
    Function CreateCommand() As IDbCommand
    Sub Open()
End Interface
```

■ **Note** Like many other types in the .NET base class libraries, the Close() method is functionally equivalent to calling the Dispose() method directly or indirectly within VB 2010 by using scope (see Chapter 8).

The Role of the IDbTransaction Interface

The overloaded **BeginTransaction()** method defined by **IDbConnection** provides access to the provider's *transaction object*. You can use the members defined by **IDbTransaction** to interact programmatically with a transactional session and the underlying data store:

```
Public Interface IDbTransaction
        Inherits IDisposable

            ReadOnly Property Connection() As IDbConnection
            ReadOnly Property IsolationLevel() As IsolationLevel

            Sub Commit()
            Sub Rollback()
End Interface
```

The Role of the IDbCommand Interface

Next up is the IDbCommand interface, which will be implemented by a data provider's *command object*. Like other data access object models, command objects allow programmatic manipulation of SQL statements, stored procedures, and parameterized queries. Command objects also provide access to the data provider's data reader type through the overloaded ExecuteReader() method:

```
Public Interface IDbCommand
      Inherits IDisposable

      Property CommandText() As String
      Property CommandTimeout() As Integer
      Property CommandType() As CommandType
      Property Connection() As IDbConnection
      ReadOnly Property Parameters() As IDataParameterCollection
      Property Transaction() As IDbTransaction
      Property UpdatedRowSource() As UpdateRowSource

      Sub Cancel()
      Function CreateParameter() As IDbDataParameter
      Function ExecuteNonQuery() As Integer
      Function ExecuteReader() As IDataReader
      Function ExecuteReader(ByVal behavior As CommandBehavior) As IDataReader
      Function ExecuteScalar() As Object
      Sub Prepare()
End Interface
```

The Role of the IDbDataParameter and IDataParameter Interfaces

Notice that the Parameters property of IDbCommand returns a strongly typed collection that implements IDataParameterCollection. This interface provides access to a set of IDbDataParameter-compliant class types (e.g., parameter objects):

```
Public Interface IDbDataParameter
      Inherits IDataParameter

      Property Precision() As Byte
      Property Scale() As Byte
      Property Size() As Integer
End Interface
```

IDbDataParameter extends the IDataParameter interface to obtain the following additional behaviors:

```
Public Interface IDataParameter
      Property DbType() As DbType
      Property Direction() As ParameterDirection
      ReadOnly Property IsNullable() As Boolean
      Property ParameterName() As String
      Property SourceColumn() As String
```

```
        Property SourceVersion() As DataRowVersion
        Property Value() As Object
End Interface
```

As you will see, the functionality of the IDbDataParameter and IDataParameter interfaces allows you to represent parameters within a SQL command (including stored procedures) through specific ADO.NET parameter objects, rather than through hard-coded string literals.

The Role of the IDbDataAdapter and IDataAdapter Interfaces

You use *data adapters* to push and pull DataSets to and from a given data store. The IDbDataAdapter interface defines a set of properties that you can use to maintain the SQL statements for the related select, insert, update, and delete operations:

```
Public Interface IDbDataAdapter
        Inherits IDataAdapter

        Property DeleteCommand() As IDbCommand
        Property InsertCommand() As IDbCommand
        Property SelectCommand() As IDbCommand
        Property UpdateCommand() As IDbCommand
End Interface
```

In addition to these four properties, an ADO.NET data adapter also picks up the behavior defined in the base interface, IDataAdapter. This interface defines the key function of a data adapter type: the ability to transfer DataSets between the caller and underlying data store using the Fill() and Update() methods. The IDataAdapter interface also allows you to map database column names to more user-friendly display names with the TableMappings property:

```
Public Interface IDataAdapter
        Property MissingMappingAction() As MissingMappingAction
        Property MissingSchemaAction() As MissingSchemaAction
        ReadOnly Property TableMappings() As ITableMappingCollection

        Function Fill(ByVal ds As DataSet) As Integer
        Function FillSchema(ByVal ds As DataSet, ByVal st  As SchemaType)
                                     As DataTable()
        Function GetFillParameters() As IDataParameter()
        Function Update(ByVal ds As DataSet) As Integer
End Interface
```

The Role of the IDataReader and IDataRecord Interfaces

The next key interface to be aware of is IDataReader, which represents the common behaviors supported by a given data reader object. When you obtain an IDataReader-compatible type from an ADO.NET data provider, you can iterate over the result set in a forward-only, read-only manner:

```
Public Interface IDataReader
    Inherits IDisposable, IDataRecord

    ReadOnly Property Depth() As Integer
    ReadOnly Property IsClosed() As Boolean
    ReadOnly Property RecordsAffected() As Integer

    Sub Close()
    Function GetSchemaTable() As DataTable
    Function NextResult() As Boolean
    Function Read() As Boolean
End Interface
```

Finally, **IDataReader** extends **IDataRecord**, which defines many members that allow you to extract a strongly typed value from the stream, rather than casting the generic **System.Object** retrieved from the data reader's overloaded indexer method. Here is a partial listing of the various **GetXXX()** methods defined by **IDataRecord** (see the .NET Framework 4.0 SDK documentation for a complete listing):

```
Public Interface IDataRecord
    ReadOnly Property FieldCount() As Integer
    Default ReadOnly Property Item(ByVal name As String) As Object
    Default ReadOnly Property Item(ByVal i As Integer) As Object
    Function GetBoolean(ByVal i As Integer) As Boolean
    Function GetByte(ByVal i As Integer) As Byte
    Function GetChar(ByVal i As Integer) As Char
    Function GetDateTime(ByVal i As Integer) As DateTime
    Function GetDecimal(ByVal i As Integer) As Decimal
    Function GetFloat(ByVal i As Integer) As Single
    Function GetInt16(ByVal i As Integer) As Short
    Function GetInt32(ByVal i As Integer) As Integer
    Function GetInt64(ByVal i As Integer) As Long
    ...
    Function IsDBNull(ByVal i As Integer) As Boolean
End Interface
```

■ **Note** You can use the IDataReader.IsDBNull() method to discover programmatically whether a specified field is set to Nothing before obtaining a value from the data reader (to avoid triggering a runtime exception). Also recall that VB 2010 supports nullable data types (see Chapter 4), which are ideal for interacting with data columns that could be NULL in the database table.

Abstracting Data Providers Using Interfaces

At this point, you should have a better idea of the common functionality found among all .NET data providers. Recall that even though the exact names of the implementing types will differ among data providers, you can program against these types in a similar manner—that's the beauty of interface-based polymorphism. For example, if you define a method that takes an IDbConnection parameter, you can pass in any ADO.NET connection object:

```
Public Sub OpenConnection(ByVal cn As IDbConnection)
    ' Open the incoming connection for the caller.
    cn.Open()
End Sub
```

■ **Note** Interfaces are not strictly required; you can achieve the same level of abstraction using MustInherit base classes (such as DbConnection) as parameters or return values.

The same holds true for member return values. For example, consider the following simple VB 2010 Console Application project (named **MyConnectionFactory**), which allows you to obtain a specific connection object based on the value of a custom enumeration. For diagnostic purposes, you simply print out the underlying connection object using reflection services, and then enter the following code:

```
'Need these to get definitions of common interfaces,
'and various connection objects for our test.
Imports System.Data
Imports System.Data.SqlClient
Imports System.Data.OleDb
Imports System.Data.Odbc

'A list of possible providers.
Enum DataProvider
    SqlServer
    OleDb
    Odbc
    None
End Enum

Module Module1
    Sub Main()
        Console.WriteLine("*** Very Simple Connection Factory ***" & vbLf)

        ' Get a specific connection.
        Dim myCn As IDbConnection = GetConnection(DataProvider.SqlServer)
        Console.WriteLine("Your connection is a {0}",
                          myCn.GetType().Name)

        ' Open, use and close connection...
        Console.ReadLine()
    End Sub
```

```
' This method returns a specific connection object
' based on the value of a DataProvider Enum.
Private Function GetConnection(ByVal dp As DataProvider)
                              As IDbConnection

    Dim conn As IDbConnection = Nothing
    Select Case dp
        Case DataProvider.SqlServer
            conn = New SqlConnection()
        Case DataProvider.OleDb
            conn = New OleDbConnection()
        Case DataProvider.Odbc
            conn = New OdbcConnection()
    End Select
    Return conn
End Function
End Module
```

The benefit of working with the general interfaces of `System.Data` (or for that matter, the MustInherit base classes of `System.Data.Common`) is that you have a much better chance of building a flexible code base that can evolve over time. For example, today you might be building an application that targets Microsoft SQL Server; however, it's possible your company could switch to Oracle months down the road. If you build a solution that hard-codes the MS SQL Server–specific types of `System.Data.SqlClient`, you would obviously need to edit, recompile, and redeploy the assembly should the back-end database management system change.

Increasing Flexibility Using Application Configuration Files

To increase the flexibility of your ADO.NET applications, you could incorporate a client-side `*.config` file that uses custom key/value pairs within the `<appSettings>` element. Recall from Chapter 14 that you can obtain the custom data stored within a `*.config` file programmatically by using types within the `System.Configuration` namespace. For example, assume you have specified a data provider value within a configuration file, as in this example:

```
<?xml version="1.0" encoding="utf-8" ?>
<configuration>
  <appSettings>
    <!-- This key value maps to one of our enum values-->
    <add key="provider" value="SqlServer"/>
  </appSettings>
...
```

With this, you could update `Main()` to obtain the underlying data provider programmatically. Doing this essentially builds a *connection object factory* that allows you to change the provider, but without requiring you to recompile your code base (you simply change the `*.config` file). Here are the relevant updates to `Main()`:

```vb
Sub Main()
    Console.WriteLine("*** Very Simple Connection Factory ***" & vbLf)

    ' Read the provider key.
    Dim dataProvString As String = ConfigurationManager.
                                       AppSettings("provider")

    ' Transform string to Enum.
    Dim dp As DataProvider = DataProvider.None
    If System.Enum.IsDefined(GetType(DataProvider), dataProvString) Then

        dp = CType(System.Enum.Parse(GetType(DataProvider),
            dataProvString), DataProvider)
    Else
        Console.WriteLine("Sorry, no provider exists!")
    End If

    ' Get a specific connection.
    Dim myCn As IDbConnection = GetConnection(dp)

    If myCn IsNot Nothing Then
        Console.WriteLine("Your connection is a {0}",
                            myCn.GetType().Name)
    End If

    'Open, use, and close connection...

    Console.ReadLine()
End Sub
```

■ **Note** To use the `ConfigurationManager` type, be sure to set a reference to the `System.Configuration.dll` assembly and import the `System.Configuration` namespace.

At this point, you have authored some ADO.NET code that allows you to specify the underlying connection dynamically. One obvious problem, however, is that this abstraction is only used within the `MyConnectionFactory.exe` application. If you were to rework this example within a .NET code library (e.g., `MyConnectionFactory.dll`), you would be able to build any number of clients that could obtain various connection objects using layers of abstraction.

However, obtaining a connection object is only one aspect of working with ADO.NET. To make a worthwhile data provider factory library, you would also have to account for command objects, data readers, data adapters, transaction objects, and other data-centric types. Building such a code library would not necessarily be difficult, but it would require a considerable amount of code and time.

Since the release of .NET 2.0, the kind folks in Redmond have built this exact functionality directly into the .NET base class libraries. You will examine this formal API in just a moment; however, first you need to create a custom database to use throughout this chapter (and for many chapters to come).

■ **Source Code** You can find the MyConnectionFactory project under the Chapter 21 subdirectory.

Creating the AutoLot Database

As you work through this chapter, you will execute queries against a simple SQL Server test database named **AutoLot**. In keeping with the automotive theme used throughout this book, this database will contain three interrelated tables (**Inventory**, **Orders**, and **Customers**) that contain various bits of data representing order information for a fictional automobile sales company.

The assumption in this book is that you have a copy of Microsoft SQL Server (7.0 or higher) or a copy of Microsoft SQL Server 2008 Express Edition (**www.microsoft.com/express/Database**). This lightweight database server is perfect for your needs in this book: it is free, it provides a GUI front end (the SQL Server Management Tool) to create and administer your databases, and it integrates with Visual Studio 2010/Visual VB 2010 Express Edition.

To illustrate the last point, the remainder of this section will walk you through the construction of the **AutoLot** database using Visual Studio 2010. If you use Visual Basic 2010 Express, you can perform operations similar to what is explained here by using the Database Explorer window (you can load this from the View ➤ Other Windows menu option).

■ **Note** You will use the **AutoLot** database throughout the rest of this book.

Creating the Inventory Table

To begin building your testing database, launch Visual Studio 2010 and open the Server Explorer using the View menu of the IDE. Next, right-click the Data Connections node and select the Create New SQL Server Database menu option. In the resulting dialog box, connect to the SQL Server installation on your local machine (with the **(local)** token) and specify AutoLot as the database name (Windows Authentication should be fine; see Figure 21-3).

■ **Note** If you use SQL Server Express, you will need to enter (local)\SQLEXPRESS in the Server name text box.

Figure 21-3. *Creating a new SQL Server 2008 Express database with Visual Studio 2010*

At this point, the `AutoLot` database is empty of any database objects (e.g., tables and stored procedures). To insert a new database table, right-click the Tables node and select Add New Table (see Figure 21-4).

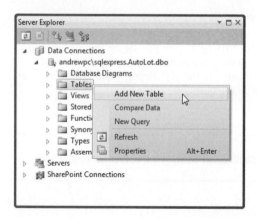

Figure 21-4. *Adding the Inventory table*

Use the table editor to add four columns (`CarID`, `Make`, `Color`, and `PetName`). Ensure that the `CarID` column has been set to the Primary Key (do this by right-clicking the `CarID` row and selecting Set Primary Key). Figure 21-5 shows the final table settings (you don't need to change anything in the Column Properties editor, but you should notice the data types for each column).

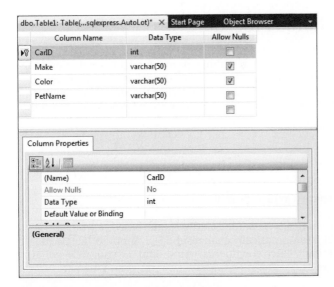

Figure 21-5. Designing the Inventory table

Save (and then close) your new table; also, be sure you name this new database object Inventory. At this point, you should see the Inventory table under the Tables node of the Server Explorer. Right-click the Inventory table icon and select Show Table Data. Enter a handful of new automobiles of your choosing (to make it interesting, be sure to include some cars that have identical colors and makes). Figure 21-6 shows one possible list of inventory.

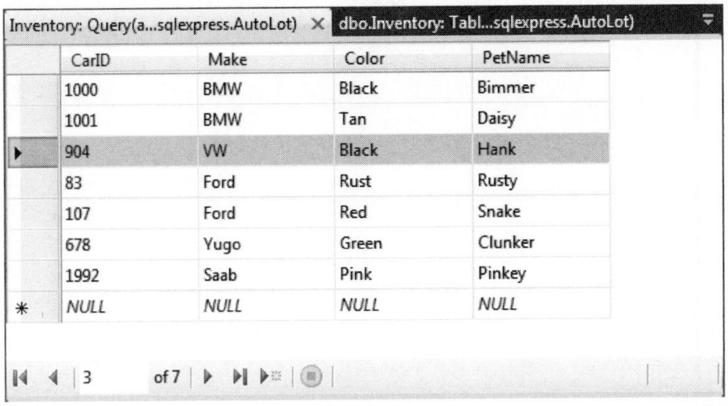

CarID	Make	Color	PetName
1000	BMW	Black	Bimmer
1001	BMW	Tan	Daisy
904	VW	Black	Hank
83	Ford	Rust	Rusty
107	Ford	Red	Snake
678	Yugo	Green	Clunker
1992	Saab	Pink	Pinkey
NULL	*NULL*	*NULL*	*NULL*

Figure 21-6. Populating the Inventory table

Authoring the GetPetName() Stored Procedure

Later in this chapter in the chapter, you will learn how to use ADO.NET to invoke stored procedures. As you might already know, stored procedures are routines stored within a particular database that operate often on table data to yield a return value. you will add a single stored procedure that will return an automobile's pet name, based on the supplied **CarID** value. To do so, right-click the Stored Procedures node of the **AutoLot** database within the Server Explorer and select Add New Stored Procedure. Enter the following in the editor that pops up:

```
CREATE PROCEDURE GetPetName
@carID int,
@petName char(10) output
AS
SELECT @petName = PetName from Inventory where CarID = @carID
```

When you save your procedure, it will automatically be named GetPetName, based on your **CREATE PROCEDURE** statement (note that Visual Studio 2010 automatically changes the SQL Script to "**ALTER PROCEDURE...**" as soon as you save it for the first time). Once you do this, you should see your new stored procedure within the Server Explorer (see Figure 21-7).

■ **Note** Stored procedures do not have to return data using output parameters, as shown here; however, doing things this way sets the stage for talking about the **Direction** property of the **SqlParameter** later in this chapter.

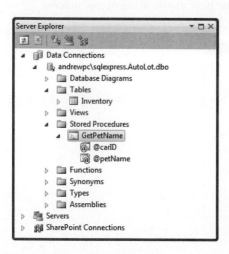

Figure 21-7. The GetPetName stored procedure

Creating the Customers and Orders Tables

Your testing database will have two additional tables: Customers and Orders. The Customers table (as the name suggests) will contain a list of customers; these which will be represented by three columns: CustID (which should be set as the primary key), FirstName, and LastName. You can create the Customers table by following the same steps you used to create the Inventory table; be sure to create the Customers table using the schema shown in Figure 21-8.

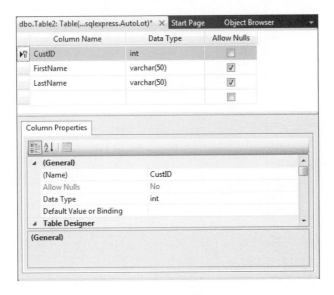

Figure 21-8. Designing the Customers table

After you save your table, add a handful of customer records (see Figure 21-9).

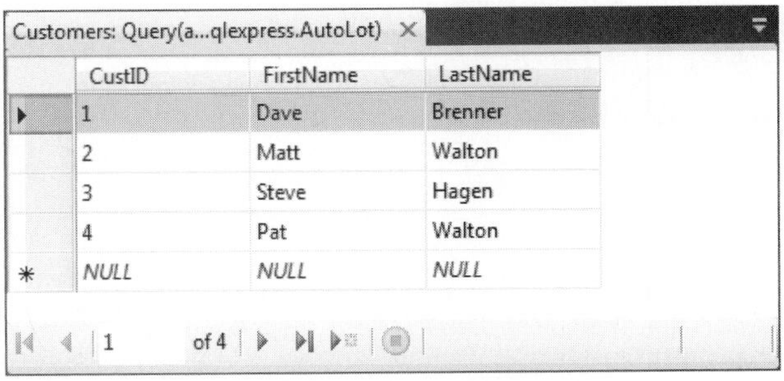

CustID	FirstName	LastName
1	Dave	Brenner
2	Matt	Walton
3	Steve	Hagen
4	Pat	Walton
NULL	NULL	NULL

Figure 21-9. Populating the Customers table

You will use your final table, Orders, to represent the automobile a given customer is interested in purchasing. Do this by mapping OrderID values to CarID/CustID values. Figure 21-10 shows the structure of your final table (again, note that OrderID is the primary key).

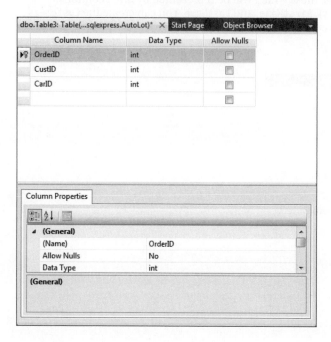

Figure 21-10. Designing the Orders table

Now add data to your Orders table. Assuming that the OrderID value begins at 1000, select a unique CarID for each CustID value (see Figure 21-11).

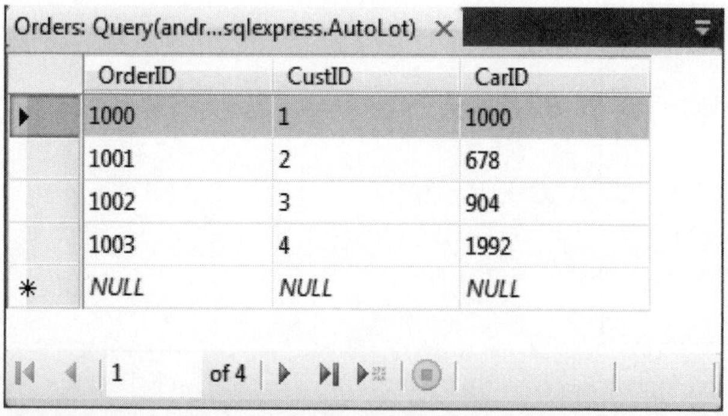

OrderID	CustID	CarID
1000	1	1000
1001	2	678
1002	3	904
1003	4	1992
NULL	NULL	NULL

Figure 21-11. Populating the Orders table

For example, the entries used in this text indicate that Dave Brenner (CustID = 1) is interested in the black BMW (CarID = 1000), while Pat Walton (CustID = 4) has her eye on the pink Saab (CarID = 1992).

Visually Creating Table Relationships

The final task is to establish parent/child table relationships between the Customers, Orders, and Inventory tables. It is easy to do this using Visual Studio 2010 because you can elect to insert a new database diagram at design time. Using the Server Explorer, right-click the Database Diagrams node of the AutoLot database and select the Add New Diagram menu option. This brings up a dialog box that lets you pick which tables to add to the diagram. Be sure to select each of the tables from the AutoLot database (Figure 21-12).

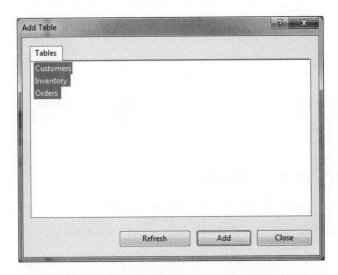

Figure 21-12. Selecting tables for your diagram

You can begin establishing the relationships between the tables by clicking the CarID key of the Inventory table and (while holding down the mouse button) drag it to the CarID field of the Orders table. Once you release the mouse, accept all defaults from the resulting dialog boxes.

Now repeat the same process to map the CustID key of the Customers table to the CustID field of the Orders table. Once you do this, you should see the class dialog box shown in Figure 21-13 (note that you enable the display of the table relationship labels by right-clicking the designer and selecting Show Relationship Labels).

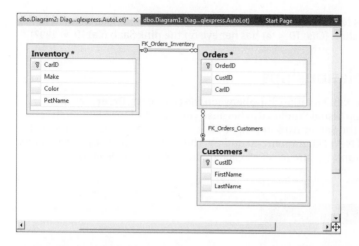

Figure 21-13. The interconnected Orders, Inventory, and Customers tables

With this, the AutoLot database is complete! This is a far cry from a real-world corporate database, but it will serve your needs over the remainder of this book. Now that you have a database to test with, you can dive into the details of the ADO.NET data provider factory model.

The ADO.NET Data Provider Factory Model

The .NET data provider factory pattern allows you to build a single code base using generalized data access types. Furthermore, using application configuration files (and the <connectionStrings> subelement), you can obtain providers and connection strings declaratively, without the need to recompile or redeploy the assembly that uses the ADO.NET APIs.

To understand the data provider factory implementation, recall from Table 21-1 that the classes within a data provider each derive from the same base classes defined within the System.Data.Common namespace:

- DbCommand: The MustInherit base class for all command classes

- DbConnection: The MustInherit base class for all connection classes

- DbDataAdapter: The MustInherit base class for all data adapter classes

- DbDataReader: The MustInherit base class for all data reader classes

- DbParameter: The MustInherit base class for all parameter classes

- DbTransaction: The MustInherit base class for all transaction classes

Each of the Microsoft-supplied data providers contains a class type that derives from `System.Data.Common.DbProviderFactory`. This base class defines several methods that retrieve provider-specific data objects. Here is a snapshot of the relevant members of `DbProviderFactory`:

```
Public MustInherit Class DbProviderFactory
    ...
    Public Overridable Function CreateCommand() As DbCommand
    Public Overridable Function CreateCommandBuilder() As DbCommandBuilder
    Public Overridable Function CreateConnection() As DbConnection
    Public Overridable Function CreateConnectionStringBuilder() _
                                            As DbConnectionStringBuilder
    Public Overridable Function CreateDataAdapter() As DbDataAdapter
    Public Overridable Function CreateDataSourceEnumerator() As DbDataSourceEnumerator
    Public Overridable Function CreateParameter() As DbParameter
End Class
```

To obtain the `DbProviderFactory`-derived type for your data provider, the `System.Data.Common` namespace provides a class type named `DbProviderFactories` (note the plural in this type's name). You can use the Shared `GetFactory()` method to obtain the specific `DbProviderFactory` object of the specified data provider; do this by specifying a string name that represents the .NET namespace containing the provider's functionality:

```
Sub Main()
    ' Get the factory for the SQL data provider.
    Dim sqlFactory As DbProviderFactory =DbProviderFactories.GetFactory

("System.Data.SqlClient")
    ...
End Sub
```

Of course, rather than obtaining a factory using a hard-coded string literal, you could instead read in this information from a client-side `*.config` file (much like the earlier `MyConnectionFactory` example). You will learn how to do this shortly; for the moment, you can obtain the associated provider-specific data objects (e.g., connections, commands, and data readers) once you obtain the factory for your data provider.

■ **Note** For all practical purposes, you can regard the argument sent to `DbProviderFactories.GetFactory()` as the name of the data provider's .NET namespace. In reality, the `machine.config` value uses this string value to load the correct library dynamically from the Global Assembly Cache.

A Complete Data Provider Factory Example

For a complete example, you can create a new VB 2010 Console Application (named DataProviderFactory) that prints out the automobile inventory of the `AutoLot` database. For this initial example, you will hard-code the data access logic directly within the `DataProviderFactory.exe` assembly (to keep things simple for the time being). However, once you begin to dig into the details of the

ADO.NET programming model, you will isolate your data logic to a specific .NET code library that you will use for the remainder of this book.

Begin by adding a reference to the `System.Configuration.dll` assembly and importing the `System.Configuration` namespace. Next, insert an `App.config` file to the current project and define an empty `<appSettings>` element. Add a new key-named `provider` that maps to the namespace name of the data provider you wish to obtain (`System.Data.SqlClient`). Also, define a connection string that represents a connection to the `AutoLot` database (on the local instance of SQL Server Express):

```
<?xml version="1.0" encoding="utf-8" ?>
<configuration>
  <appSettings>
    <!-- Which provider? -->
    <add key="provider" value="System.Data.SqlClient" />

    <!-- Which connection string? -->
    <add key="cnStr" value= "Data Source=(local)\SQLEXPRESS;
            Initial Catalog=AutoLot;Integrated Security=True"/>
  </appSettings>
...
</configuration>
```

■ **Note** You will learn about connection strings in more detail momentarily; however, if you select your `AutoLot` database icon within the Server Explorer, you can copy-and-paste the correct connection string from the Connection String property of the Visual Studio 2010 Properties Window.

Now that you have a proper `*.config` file, you can read in the `provider` and `cnStr` values using the `ConfigurationManager.AppSettings` indexer. The `provider` value will be passed to `DbProviderFactories.GetFactory()` to obtain the data provider-specific factory type. You will use the `cnStr` value to set the `ConnectionString` property of the `DbConnection`-derived type.

Assuming you have imported the `System.Data` and `System.Data.Common` namespaces, you can update your `Main()` method like this:

```
Sub Main()
    Console.WriteLine("***** Fun with Data Provider Factories *****" & vbLf)

    ' Get Connection string/provider from *.config.
    Dim dp As String = ConfigurationManager.AppSettings("provider")
    Dim cnStr As String = ConfigurationManager.AppSettings("cnStr")

    ' Get the factory provider.
    Dim df As DbProviderFactory = DbProviderFactories.GetFactory(dp)
```

```vb
    ' Now get the connection object.
    Using cn As DbConnection = df.CreateConnection()
            Console.WriteLine("Your connection object is a: {0}", cn.GetType().Name)
            cn.ConnectionString = cnStr
            cn.Open()

            ' Make command object.
            Dim cmd As DbCommand = df.CreateCommand()
            Console.WriteLine("Your command object is a: {0}", cmd.GetType().Name)
            cmd.Connection = cn
            cmd.CommandText = "Select * From Inventory"

            ' Print out data with data reader.
            Using dr As DbDataReader = cmd.ExecuteReader()
                    Console.WriteLine("Your data reader object is a: {0}", ←
                                    dr.GetType().Name)

                    Console.WriteLine(vbLf & "***** Current Inventory *****")

                    Do While dr.Read()
                            Console.WriteLine("-> Car #{0} is a {1}.", dr("CarID"),
                                            dr("Make").ToString())
                    Loop
            End Using
    End Using
    Console.ReadLine()
End Sub
```

Notice that, for diagnostic purposes, you use reflection services to print the name of the underlying connection, command, and data reader. If you run this application, you will find the current data in the Inventory table of the AutoLot database printed to the console:

```
***** Fun with Data Provider Factories *****


Your connection object is a: SqlConnection

Your command object is a: SqlCommand

Your data reader object is a: SqlDataReader


***** Current Inventory *****

-> Car #83 is a Ford.

-> Car #107 is a Ford.
```

-> Car #678 is a Yugo.

-> Car #904 is a VW.

-> Car #1000 is a BMW.

-> Car #1001 is a BMW.

-> Car #1992 is a Saab.

Now change the *.config file to specify System.Data.OleDb as the data provider (and update your connection string with a Provider segment):

```
<configuration>
 <appSettings>
  <!-- Which provider? -->
  <add key="provider" value="System.Data.OleDb" />

  <!-- Which connection string? -->
  <add key="cnStr" value=
  "Provider=SQLOLEDB;Data Source=(local)\SQLEXPRESS;
    Integrated Security=SSPI;Initial Catalog=AutoLot"/>
 </appSettings>
</configuration>
```

Doing this indicates that the System.Data.OleDb types are used behind the scenes:

```
***** Fun with Data Provider Factories *****


Your connection object is a: OleDbConnection

Your command object is a: OleDbCommand

Your data reader object is a: OleDbDataReader


***** Current Inventory *****

-> Car #83 is a Ford.

-> Car #107 is a Ford.

-> Car #678 is a Yugo.
```

-> Car #904 is a VW.

-> Car #1000 is a BMW.

-> Car #1001 is a BMW.

-> Car #1992 is a Saab.

Of course, based on your experience with ADO.NET, you might be a bit unsure exactly what the connection, command, and data reader objects actually *do*. Don't sweat the details for the time being (quite a few pages remain in this chapter, after all!). At this point, it's enough to know that you can use the ADO.NET data provider factory model to build a single code base that can consume various data providers in a declarative manner.

A Potential Drawback with the Provide Factory Model

Although this is a powerful model, you must make sure that the code base uses only types and methods common to all providers through the members of the MustInherit base classes. Therefore, when authoring your code base, you are limited to the members exposed by DbConnection, DbCommand, and the other types of the System.Data.Common namespace.

Given this, you might find that this generalized approach prevents you from directly accessing some of the bells and whistles of a particular DBMS. If you must be able to invoke specific members of the underlying provider (e.g., SqlConnection), you can do so using an explicit cast, as in this example:

```
Using cn As DbConnection = df.CreateConnection()
     Console.WriteLine("Your connection object is a: {0}", cn.GetType().Name)
     cn.ConnectionString = cnStr
     cn.Open()
     If TypeOf cn Is SqlConnection Then
       ' Print out which version of SQL Server is used.
       Console.WriteLine((CType(cn, SqlConnection)).ServerVersion)
     End If
     ...
End Using
```

When doing this, however, your code base becomes a bit harder to maintain (and less flexible) because you must add a number of runtime checks. Nevertheless, if you need to build data access libraries in the most flexible way possible, the data provider factory model provides a great mechanism for doing so.

The <connectionStrings> Element

Currently your connection string data is in the <appSettings> element of your *.config file. Application configuration files might define an element named <connectionStrings>. Within this element, you can define any number of name/value pairs that can be programmatically read into memory using the ConfigurationManager.ConnectionStrings indexer. One advantage of this approach (as opposed to using the <appSettings> element and the ConfigurationManager.AppSettings indexer) is that you can define multiple connection strings for a single application in a consistent manner.

To see this in action, update your current **App.config** file as follows (note that each connection string is documented using the name and connectionString attributes rather than the key and value attributes you find in <appSettings>):

```
<configuration>
 <appSettings>
  <!-- Which provider? -->
  <add key="provider" value="System.Data.SqlClient" />
 </appSettings>

 <!-- Here are the connection strings -->
 <connectionStrings>
  <add name ="AutoLotSqlProvider" connectionString =
      "Data Source=(local)\SQLEXPRESS;
       Integrated Security=SSPI;Initial Catalog=AutoLot"/>

  <add name ="AutoLotOleDbProvider" connectionString =
      "Provider=SQLOLEDB;Data Source=(local)\SQLEXPRESS;
       Integrated Security=SSPI;Initial Catalog=AutoLot"/>
 </connectionStrings>
</configuration>
```

You can now update your Main() method as follows:

```
Sub Main()
     Console.WriteLine("***** Fun with Data Provider Factories *****" & vbLf)
     Dim dp As String = ConfigurationManager.AppSettings("provider")

     Dim cnStr As String = ConfigurationManager.ConnectionStrings
                 ("AutoLotSqlProvider").ConnectionString
...
End Sub
```

At this point, you have an application that can display the results of the **Inventory** table of the AutoLot database using a neutral code base. Offloading the provider name and connection string to an external *.config file, means that the data provider factory model can dynamically load the correct provider in the background. With this first example behind you, you can now dive into the details of working with the connected layer of ADO.NET.

■ **Note** Now that you understand the role of ADO.NET data provider factories, the remaining examples in this book will focus on the task at hand by explicitly using the types within the System.Data.SqlClient namespace. If you use a different database management system (such as Oracle), you need to update your code base accordingly.

■ **Source Code** You can find the DataProviderFactory project under the Chapter 21 subdirectory.

Understanding the Connected Layer of ADO.NET

Recall that the *connected layer* of ADO.NET allows you to interact with a database using the connection, command, and data reader objects of your data provider. You have already used these objects in the previous DataProviderFactory application, now you'll walk through the process again, this time using an expanded example. You need to perform the following steps when you wish to connect to a database and read the records using a data reader object:

1. Allocate, configure, and open your connection object.

2. Allocate and configure a command object, specifying the connection object as a constructor argument or with the Connection property.

3. Call ExecuteReader() on the configured command class.

4. Process each record using the Read() method of the data reader.

To get the ball rolling, create a new Console Application named AutoLotDataReader and import the System.Data and System.Data.SqlClient namespaces. Here is the complete code within Main(); an analysis will follow:

```
Module Module1
    Sub Main()
        Console.WriteLine("***** Fun with Data Readers *****" & vbLf)

        ' Create and open a connection.
        Using cn As New SqlConnection()
            cn.ConnectionString = "Data Source=(local)\SQLEXPRESS;Integrated Security=SSPI;" & _
                                    "Initial Catalog=AutoLot"
            cn.Open()

            ' Create a SQL command object.
            Dim strSQL As String = "Select * From Inventory"
            Dim myCommand As New SqlCommand(strSQL, cn)

            ' Obtain a data reader a la ExecuteReader().
            Using myDataReader As SqlDataReader = myCommand.ExecuteReader()

                ' Loop over the results.
                Do While myDataReader.Read()
                    Console.WriteLine("-> Make: {0}, PetName: {1}, Color: {2}.", _
                        myDataReader("Make").ToString(), _
                        myDataReader("PetName").ToString(), _
                        myDataReader("Color").ToString())
                Loop
            End Using
        End Using
        Console.ReadLine()
    End Sub
End Module
```

Working with Connection Objects

The first step to take when working with a data provider is to establish a session with the data source using the connection object (which, as you recall, derives from DbConnection). .NET connection objects are provided with a formatted *connection string*; this string contains a number of name/value pairs, separated by semicolons. You use this information to identify the name of the machine you wish to connect to, required security settings, the name of the database on that machine, and other data provider–specific information.

As you can infer from the preceding code, the Initial Catalog name refers to the database you want to establish a session with. The Data Source name identifies the name of the machine that maintains the database. Here, (local) allows you to define a single token to specify the current local machine (regardless of the literal name of said machine), while the \SQLEXPRESS token informs the SQL server provider that you are connecting to the default SQL Server Express edition installation (if you created AutoLot on a full version of Microsoft SQL Server on your local computer, specify Data Source=(local)).

Beyond this, you can supply any number of tokens that represent security credentials. Here, you set the Integrated Security to SSPI (equivalent to True), which uses the current Windows account credentials for user authentication.

■ **Note** Look up the ConnectionString property of your data provider's connection object in the .NET Framework 4.0 SDK documentation to learn more about each name/value pair for your specific DBMS.

Once you establish your construction string, you can use a call to Open() to establish a connection with the DBMS. In addition to the ConnectionString, Open(), and Close() members, a connection object provides a number of members that let you configure additional settings regarding your connection, such as timeout settings and transactional information. Table 21-5 lists some (but not all) members of the DbConnection base class.

Table 21-5. Members of the DbConnection Type

Member	Meaning in Life
BeginTransaction()	You use this method to begin a database transaction.
ChangeDatabase()	You use this method to change the database on an open connection.
ConnectionTimeout	This read-only property returns the amount of time to wait while establishing a connection before terminating and generating an error (the default value is 15 seconds). If you wish to change the default, specify a Connect Timeout segment in the connection string (e.g., Connect Timeout=30).
Database	This read-only property gets the name of the database maintained by the connection object.

Member	Meaning in Life
DataSource	This read-only property gets the location of the database maintained by the connection object.
GetSchema()	This method returns a DataTable object that contains schema information from the data source.
State	This read-only property gets the current state of the connection, which is represented by the ConnectionState enumeration.

The properties of the DbConnection type are typically read-only in nature and are only useful when you wish to obtain the characteristics of a connection at runtime. When you wish to override default settings, you must alter the connection string itself. For example, the connection string sets the connection timeout setting from 15 seconds to 30 seconds:

```
Sub Main()
    Console.WriteLine("***** Fun with Data Readers *****" & vbLf)

    Using cn As New SqlConnection()
        cn.ConnectionString = "Data Source=(local)\SQLEXPRESS;" & "Integrated Security=SSPI;
                Initial Catalog=AutoLot;Connect Timeout=30"
        cn.Open()

            ' New helper method (see below).
            ShowConnectionStatus(cn)
            ...
    End Using
End Sub
```

In the preceding code, you pass your connection object as a parameter to a new helper method named ShowConnectionStatus(), which you implement as follows:

```
Sub ShowConnectionStatus(ByVal cn As SqlConnection)
    ' Show various stats about current connection object.
    Console.WriteLine("***** Info about your connection *****")
    Console.WriteLine("Database location: {0}", cn.DataSource)
    Console.WriteLine("Database name: {0}", cn.Database)
    Console.WriteLine("Timeout: {0}", cn.ConnectionTimeout)
    Console.WriteLine("Connection state: {0}" & vbLf, cn.State.ToString())
End Sub
```

While most of these properties are self-explanatory, the State property is worth special mention. You can assign this property any value of the ConnectionState enumeration:

```
Public Enum ConnectionState
    Broken
    Closed
    Connecting
    Executing
```

```
        Fetching
        Open
End Enum
```

However, the only valid `ConnectionState` values are `ConnectionState.Open` and `ConnectionState.Closed` (the remaining members of this Enum are reserved for future use). Also, it is always safe to close a connection where connection state is currently `ConnectionState.Closed`.

Working with ConnectionStringBuilder Objects

Working with connection strings programmatically can be cumbersome because they are often represented as string literals, which are difficult to maintain and error-prone at best. The Microsoft-supplied ADO.NET data providers support *connection string builder objects,* which allow you to establish the name/value pairs using strongly typed properties. Consider the following update to the current `Main()` method:

```
Sub Main()
        Console.WriteLine("***** Fun with Data Readers *****" & vbLf)

        ' Create a connection string via the builder object.
        Dim cnStrBuilder As New SqlConnectionStringBuilder()
        cnStrBuilder.InitialCatalog = "AutoLot"
        cnStrBuilder.DataSource = "(local)\SQLEXPRESS"
        cnStrBuilder.ConnectTimeout = 30
        cnStrBuilder.IntegratedSecurity = True

        Using cn As New SqlConnection()
                cn.ConnectionString = cnStrBuilder.ConnectionString
                cn.Open()

                ShowConnectionStatus(cn)
                ...
        End Using
        Console.ReadLine()
End Sub
```

In this iteration, you create an instance of `SqlConnectionStringBuilder`, set the properties accordingly, and obtain the internal string using the `ConnectionString` property. Also note that you use the default constructor of the type. If you so choose, you can also create an instance of your data provider's connection string builder object by passing in an existing connection string as a starting point (this can be helpful when you read these values dynamically from an `App.config` file). Once you have hydrated the object with the initial string data, you can change specific name/value pairs using the related properties, as in this example:

```
Sub Main()
    Console.WriteLine("***** Fun with Data Readers *****" & vbLf)

    ' Assume you really obtained the cnStr value from a *.config file.
    Dim cnStr As String = "Data Source=(local)\SQLEXPRESS; Integrated Security=SSPI;
                                    Initial Catalog=AutoLot"

    Dim cnStrBuilder As New SqlConnectionStringBuilder(cnStr)

    ' Change timeout value.
    cnStrBuilder.ConnectTimeout = 5
    ...
End Sub
```

Working with Command Objects

Now that you understand better the role of the connection object, the next order of business is to check out how to submit SQL queries to the database in question. The SqlCommand type (which derives from DbCommand) is an OO representation of a SQL query, table name, or stored procedure. You specify the type of command using the CommandType property, which can take any value from the CommandType Enum:

```
Public Enum CommandType
      StoredProcedure
      TableDirect
      Text ' Default value.
End Enum
```

When you create a command object, you can establish the SQL query as a constructor parameter or directly by using the CommandText property. Also when you create a command object, you need to specify the connection you want to use. Again, you can do so as a constructor parameter or by using the Connection property. Consider this code snippet:

```
' Create command object via ctor args.
Dim strSQL As String = "Select * From Inventory"
Dim myCommand As New SqlCommand(strSQL, cn)

' Create another command object via properties.
Dim testCommand As New SqlCommand()
testCommand.Connection = cn
testCommand.CommandText = strSQL
```

Realize that at this point that you have not literally submitted the SQL query to the AutoLot database, but instead prepared the state of the command object for future use. Table 21-6 highlights some additional members of the DbCommand type.

Table 21-6. Members of the DbCommand Type

Member	Meaning in Life
CommandTimeout	Gets or sets the time to wait while executing the command before terminating the attempt and generating an error. The default is 30 seconds.
Connection	Gets or sets the DbConnection used by this instance of the DbCommand.
Parameters	Gets the collection of DbParameter objects used for a parameterized query.
Cancel()	Cancels the execution of a command.
ExecuteReader()	Executes a SQL query and returns the data provider's DbDataReader object, which provides forward-only, read-only access for the result of the query.
ExecuteNonQuery()	Executes a SQL non-query (e.g., an insert, update, delete, or create table).
ExecuteScalar()	A lightweight version of the ExecuteReader() method that was designed specifically for singleton queries (e.g., obtaining a record count).
Prepare()	Creates a prepared (or compiled) version of the command on the data source. As you might know, a *prepared query* executes slightly faster and is useful when you wish to execute the same query multiple times (typically with different parameters each time).

Working with Data Readers

Once you establish the active connection and SQL command, the next step is to submit the query to the data source. As you might guess, you have a number of ways to do this. The DbDataReader type (which implements IDataReader) is the simplest and fastest way to obtain information from a data store. Recall that data readers represent a read-only, forward-only stream of data returned one record at a time. Given this, data readers are useful only when submitting SQL selection statements to the underlying data store.

Data readers are useful when you need to iterate over large amounts of data quickly and you do not need to maintain an in-memory representation. For example, if you request 20,000 records from a table to store in a text file, it would be rather memory-intensive to hold this information in a DataSet (because a DataSet holds the entire result of the query in memory at the same time).

A better approach is to create a data reader that spins over each record as rapidly as possible. Be aware, however, that data reader objects (unlike data adapter objects, which you'll examine later) maintain an open connection to their data source until you explicitly close the connection.

You obtain data reader objects from the command object using a call to ExecuteReader().The data reader represents the current record it has read from the database. The data reader has an indexer method (e.g., () syntax in VB 2010) that allows you to access a column in the current record. You can access the column either by name or by zero-based integer.

The following use of the data reader leverages the **Read()** method to determine when you have reached the end of your records (using a **False** return value). For each incoming record that you read from the database, you use the type indexer to print out the make, pet name, and color of each automobile. Also note that you call **Close()** as soon as you finish processing the records; this frees up the connection object:

```
Sub Main()
    ...
    ' Obtain a data reader via ExecuteReader().
    Using myDataReader As SqlDataReader = myCommand.ExecuteReader()
        ' Loop over the results.
        Do While myDataReader.Read()
          Console.WriteLine("-> Make: {0}, PetName: {1}, Color: {2}.", ↵
                            myDataReader("Make").ToString(), ↵
                            myDataReader("PetName").ToString(), ↵
                            myDataReader("Color").ToString())
        Loop
    End Using
    Console.ReadLine()
End Sub
```

In the preceding snippet, you overload the indexer of a data reader object to take either a **String** (representing the name of the column) or an **Integer** (representing the column's ordinal position). Thus, you can clean up the current reader logic (and avoid hard-coded string names) with the following update (note the use of the **FieldCount** property):

```
Do While myDataReader.Read()
    Console.WriteLine("***** Record *****")
    For i As Integer = 0 To myDataReader.FieldCount - 1
        Console.WriteLine("{0} = {1} ", myDataReader.GetName(i)
                                      , myDataReader.GetValue(i).ToString())
    Next
    Console.WriteLine()
Loop
```

If you compile and run your project at this point, you should see a list of all automobiles in the **Inventory** table of the **AutoLot** database. The following output shows the initial few records from my own version of **AutoLot**:

```
***** Fun with Data Readers *****



***** Info about your connection *****

Database location: (local)\SQLEXPRESS

Database name: AutoLot
```

```
Timeout: 30

Connection state: Open


***** Record *****

CarID = 83

Make = Ford

Color = Rust

PetName = Rusty


***** Record *****

CarID = 107

Make = Ford

Color = Red

PetName = Snake
```

Obtaining Multiple Result Sets Using a Data Reader

Data reader objects can obtain multiple result sets using a single command object. For example, if you want to obtain all rows from the Inventory table, as well as all rows from the Customers table, you can specify both SQL select statements using a semicolon delimiter:

```
Dim strSQL As String = "Select * From Inventory;Select * from Customers"
```

Once you obtain the data reader, you can iterate over each result set using the NextResult() method. Note that you are always returned the first result set automatically. Thus, if you wish to read over the rows of each table, you can build the following iteration construct:

```
Do
    Do While myDataReader.Read()

        Console.WriteLine("***** Record *****")
        For i As Integer = 0 To myDataReader.FieldCount - 1
```

```
            Console.WriteLine("{0} = {1}", myDataReader.GetName(i)
                                , myDataReader.GetValue(i).ToString())
        Next
        Console.WriteLine()
    Loop
Loop While myDataReader.NextResult()
```

At this point, you should be more aware of the functionality data reader objects bring to the table. Always remember that a data reader can only process SQL Select statements; you cannot use them to modify an existing database table using Insert, Update, or Delete requests. Modifying an existing database requires additional investigation of command objects.

■ **Source Code** You can find the AutoLotDataReader project under the Chapter 21 subdirectory.

Building a Reusable Data Access Library

The ExecuteReader() method extracts a data reader object that allows you to examine the results of a SQL Select statement using a forward-only, read-only flow of information. However, when you wish to submit SQL statements that result in the modification of a given table (or any other non-query SQL statement, such as creating tables or granting permissions), you call the ExecuteNonQuery() method of your command object. This single method performs inserts, updates, and deletes based on the format of your command text.

■ **Note** Technically speaking, a *nonquery* is a SQL statement that does not return a result set. Thus, Select statements are queries, while Insert, Update, and Delete statements are not. Given this, ExecuteNonQuery() returns an Integer that represents the number of rows affected, not a new set of records.

Next, you will learn how to modify an existing database using nothing more than a call to ExecuteNonQuery(); your next goal is to build a custom data access library that can encapsulate the process of operating upon the AutoLot database. In a production-level environment, your ADO.NET logic will almost always be isolated to a .NET *.dll assembly for one simple reason: code reuse! The first examples of this chapter have not done, simply so you can keep focused on the task at hand; however, it would be a waste of time to author the *same* connection logic, the *same* data reading logic, and the *same* command logic for every application that needs to interact with the AutoLot database.

Isolating data access logic to a .NET code library means that multiple applications using any sort of front end (e.g., console-based, desktop-based, and web based) can reference the library at hand in a language-independent manner. Thus, if you author your data library using VB 2010, other .NET programmers can build a UI in the language of their choice (e.g., C# or C++/CLI).

In this chapter, your data library (AutoLotDAL.dll) will contain a single namespace (AutoLotConnectedLayer) that interacts with AutoLot using the connected types of ADO.NET. In the next chapter, you will add a new namespace (AutoLotDisconnectionLayer) to this same *.dll that contains types to communicate with AutoLot using the disconnected layer. Multiple applications will take advantage of this library throughout the remainder of this book.

Begin by creating a new VB 2010 Class Library project named AutoLotDAL (short for AutoLot Data Access Layer) and renaming your initial VB 2010 code file to AutoLotConnDAL.vb. Next, change the name of the class to InventoryDAL. This class will define various members to interact with the Inventory table of the AutoLot database.

Enclose your class in a namespace named AutoLotConnectedLayer (also, in the Project Properties window, set the Root Namespace to be nothing – we'll take care of defining namespaces explicitly in our application). Finally, import the following .NET namespaces:

```
' You will use the SQL server
' provider; however, it would also be
' permissible to use the ADO.NET
' factory pattern for greater flexibility.
Imports System.Data
Imports System.Data.SqlClient

Namespace AutoLotConnectedLayer

        Public Class InventoryDAL

        End Class

End Namespace
```

■ **Note** You might recall from Chapter 8 that when objects use types that manage raw resources (e.g., a database connection), it is a good practice to implement IDisposable and author a proper finalizer. In a production environment, classes such as InventoryDAL would do the same; however, you won't do that here, so you can stay focused on the particulars of ADO.NET.

Adding the Connection Logic

The first task you must attend to is to define some methods that allow the caller to connect to and disconnect from the data source using a valid connection string. You will hard-code your AutoLotDAL.dll assembly to use of the types of System.Data.SqlClient, so you need to define a Private member variable of SqlConnection that is allocated at the time the InventoryDAL object is created. Also, define a method named OpenConnection() and another named CloseConnection() to interact with this member variable:

```
Public Class InventoryDAL

        ' This member will be used by all methods.
        Private sqlCn As SqlConnection = Nothing
```

```
    Public Sub OpenConnection(ByVal connectionString As String)
      sqlCn = New SqlConnection()
      sqlCn.ConnectionString = connectionString
      sqlCn.Open()
    End Sub

    Public Sub CloseConnection()
      sqlCn.Close()
    End Sub
End Class
```

For the sake of brevity, your **InventoryDAL** type will not test for possible exceptions, nor will it throw custom exceptions under various circumstances (e.g., a malformed connection string). If you were to build an industrial-strength data access library, you would absolutely want to use structured exception handling techniques to account for any runtime anomalies.

Adding the Insertion Logic

Inserting a new record into the **Inventory** table is as simple as formatting the SQL **Insert** statement (based on user input) and calling the **ExecuteNonQuery()** using your command object. You can see this in action by adding a Public method to your **InventoryDAL** type named **InsertAuto()** that takes four parameters that map to the four columns of the **Inventory** table (**CarID**, **Color**, **Make**, and **PetName**). You use these arguments to format a String type to insert the new record. Finally, use your **SqlConnection** object to execute the SQL statement:

```
Public Sub InsertAuto(ByVal id As Integer, ByVal color As String, ByVal make As String,
                           ByVal petName As String)

    ' Format and execute SQL statement.
        Dim sql As String = String.Format("Insert Into Inventory " &
                                    "(CarID, Make, Color, PetName)  " &
                                    "Values'{0}', '{1}', '{2}', '{3}')",
                                     id, make, color, petName)

    ' Execute using our connection.
    Using cmd As New SqlCommand(sql, Me.sqlCn)
        cmd.ExecuteNonQuery()
    End Using
End Sub
```

This method is syntactically fine, but you could supply an overloaded version that allows the caller to pass in a strongly typed class that represents the data for the new row. Define a new **NewCar** class, which represents a new row in the **Inventory** table:

```
Public Class NewCar
        Public Property CarID() As Integer
        Public Property Color() As String
        Public Property Make() As String
        Public Property PetName() As String
End Class
```

Now add the following version of `InsertAuto()` to your `InventoryDAL` class:

```
Public Sub InsertAuto(ByVal car As NewCar)
    ' Format and execute SQL statement.
        Dim sql As String = String.Format("Insert Into Inventory" &
                                        "(CarID, Make, Color, PetName) " &
                                        "Values ('{0}', '{1}', '{2}', '{3}')",
                                        car.CarID, car.Make, car.Color, car.PetName)

    ' Execute using our connection.
    Using cmd As New SqlCommand(sql, Me.sqlCn)
        cmd.ExecuteNonQuery()
    End Using
End Sub
```

Defining classes that represent records in a relational database is a common way to build a data access library. In fact, as you will see in Chapter 23, the ADO.NET Entity Framework automatically generates strongly typed classes that allow you to interact with database data. On a related note, the *disconnected layer* of ADO.NET (see Chapter 22) generates strongly typed **DataSet** objects to represent data from a given table in a relational database.

■ **Note** As you might know, building a SQL statement using string concatenation can be risky from a security point of view (think: SQL injection attacks). The preferred way to build command text is to use a parameterized query, which you will learn about shortly.

Adding the Deletion Logic

Deleting an existing record is as simple as inserting a new record. Unlike when you created the code listing for `InsertAuto()`, this time you will learn about an important **Try/Catch** scope that handles the possibility of attempting to delete a car that is currently on order for an individual in the **Customers** table. Add the following method to the **InventoryDAL** class type:

```
Public Sub DeleteCar(ByVal id As Integer)

    ' Get ID of car to delete, then do so.
    Dim sql As String = String.Format("Delete from Inventory where CarID = '{0}'", id)

    Using cmd As New SqlCommand(sql, Me.sqlCn)
        Try
            cmd.ExecuteNonQuery()
        Catch ex As SqlException
            Dim [err ] As New Exception("Sorry! That car is on order!", ex)
            Throw [err]
        End Try
    End Using
End Sub
```

Adding the Update Logic

When it comes to the act of updating an existing record in the **Inventory** table, the first thing you must decide is what you want to allow the caller to change, whether it's the car's color, the pet name, the make, or all of the above. One way to give the caller complete flexibility is to define a method that takes a **String** type to represent any sort of SQL statement, but that is risky at best.

Ideally, you want to have a set of methods that allow the caller to update a record in a variety of ways. However, for this simple data access library, you will define a single method that allows the caller to update the pet name of a given automobile:

```
Public Sub UpdateCarPetName(ByVal id As Integer, ByVal newPetName As String)
    ' Get ID of car to modify and new pet name.
    Dim sql As String = String.Format("Update Inventory Set PetName = '{0}' " &
                            "Where CarID = '{1}'", newPetName, id)

    Using cmd As New SqlCommand(sql, Me.sqlCn)
        cmd.ExecuteNonQuery()
    End Using
End Sub
```

Adding the Selection Logic

Next, you need to add a selection method. As you saw earlier in this chapter, a data provider's data reader object allows for a selection of records using a read-only, forward-only server-side cursor. As you call the **Read()** method, you can process each record in a fitting manner. While this is all well and good, you need to contend with the issue of how to return these records to the calling tier of your application.

One approach would be to populate and return a multidimensional array (or other such return value, such as a generic **List(Of NewCar)** object) with the data obtained by the **Read()** method. Here is a second way to obtain data from the **Inventory** table that uses the latter approach:

```
Public Function GetAllInventoryAsList() As List(Of NewCar)
    ' This will hold the records.
    Dim inv As New List(Of NewCar)()

    ' Prep command object.
    Dim sql As String = "Select * From Inventory"
    Using cmd As New SqlCommand(sql, Me.sqlCn)
        Dim dr As SqlDataReader = cmd.ExecuteReader()
        Do While dr.Read()
            inv.Add(New NewCar With
            {
              .CarID = CInt(dr("CarID")),
              .Color = CStr(dr("Color")),
              .Make = CStr(dr("Make")),
              .PetName = CStr(dr("PetName"))
            })
        Loop
        dr.Close()
```

```
      End Using
      Return inv
End Function
```

Still another approach is to return a `System.Data.DataTable` object, which is actually part of the disconnected layer of ADO.NET. You will find complete coverage of the disconnected layer in the next chapter; however, for the time being, you should understand that a `DataTable` is a class type that represents a tabular block of data (e.g., a grid on a spreadsheet).

Internally, the `DataTable` class represents data as a collection of rows and columns. While you can fill these collections programmatically, the `DataTable` type provides a method named `Load()` that automatically populates these collections using a data reader object! Consider the following methods, which return data from `Inventory` as a `DataTable`:

```
Public Function GetAllInventoryAsDataTable() As DataTable
      ' This will hold the records.
      Dim inv As New DataTable()

      ' Prep command object.
      Dim sql As String = "Select * From Inventory"
      Using cmd As New SqlCommand(sql, Me.sqlCn)
        Dim dr As SqlDataReader = cmd.ExecuteReader()
        ' Fill the DataTable with data from the reader and clean up.
        inv.Load(dr)
        dr.Close()
      End Using
      Return inv
End Function
```

Working with Parameterized Command Objects

Currently, the insert, update, and delete logic for the `InventoryDAL` type uses hard-coded string-literals for each SQL query. As you might know, you can use a *parameterized query* to treat SQL parameters as objects, rather than as a simple blob of text. Treating SQL queries in a more object-oriented manner helps reduce the number of typos (given strongly typed properties); plus, parameterized queries typically execute much faster than a literal SQL string because they are parsed exactly once (rather than each time the SQL string is assigned to the `CommandText` property). Parameterized queries also help protect against SQL injection attacks (a well-known data access security issue).

To support parameterized queries, ADO.NET command objects maintain a collection of individual parameter objects. By default, this collection is empty, but you can insert any number of parameter objects that map to a *placeholder parameter* in the SQL query. When you wish to associate a parameter within a SQL query to a member in the command object's parameters collection, you can prefix the SQL text parameter with the @ symbol (at least when using Microsoft SQL Server; not all DBMSs support this notation).

Specifying Parameters Using the DbParameter Type

Before you build a parameterized query, you need to familiarize yourself with the `DbParameter` type (which is the base class to a provider's specific parameter object). This class maintains a number of properties that allow you to configure the name, size, and data type of the parameter, as well as other characteristics, including the parameter's direction of travel. Table 21-7 describes some key properties of the DbParameter type.

Table 21-7. Key Members of the DbParameter Type

Property	Meaning in Life
DbType	Gets or sets the native data type of the parameter, represented as a CLR data type.
Direction	Gets or sets whether the parameter is input-only, output-only, bidirectional, or a return value parameter.
IsNullable	Gets or sets whether the parameter accepts Nothing values.
ParameterName	Gets or sets the name of the DbParameter.
Size	Gets or sets the maximum parameter size of the data in bytes; this is only useful for textual data.
Value	Gets or sets the value of the parameter.

Now let's look at how to populate a command object's collection of DBParameter-compatible objects by reworking the following version of the InsertAuto() method to leverage parameter objects (you could perform a similar reworking for your remaining methods; however, that's not necessary for this example):

```
Public Sub InsertAuto(ByVal id As Integer, ByVal color As String, ByVal make As String,
                      ByVal petName As String)

    ' Note the "placeholders" in the SQL query.
    Dim sql As String = String.Format("Insert Into Inventory " &
                        "(CarID, Make, Color, PetName)" &
                        "Values (@CarID, @Make, @Color, @PetName)")

    ' This command will have internal parameters.
    Using cmd As New SqlCommand(sql, Me.sqlCn)
        ' Fill params collection.
        Dim param As New SqlParameter()
        param.ParameterName = "@CarID"
        param.Value = id
        param.SqlDbType = SqlDbType.Int
        cmd.Parameters.Add(param)

        param = New SqlParameter()
        param.ParameterName = "@Make"
        param.Value = make
        param.SqlDbType = SqlDbType.Char
        param.Size = 10
        cmd.Parameters.Add(param)
```

```
        param = New SqlParameter()
        param.ParameterName = "@Color"
        param.Value = color
        param.SqlDbType = SqlDbType.Char
        param.Size = 10
        cmd.Parameters.Add(param)

        param = New SqlParameter()
        param.ParameterName = "@PetName"
        param.Value = petName
        param.SqlDbType = SqlDbType.Char
        param.Size = 10
        cmd.Parameters.Add(param)

        cmd.ExecuteNonQuery()
    End Using
End Sub
```

Again, notice that your SQL query consists of four embedded placeholder symbols, each of which is prefixed with the @ token. You can use the `SqlParameter` type to map each placeholder using the `ParameterName` property and specify various details (e.g., its value, data type, and size) in a strongly typed matter. Once each parameter object is hydrated, it is added to the command object's collection through a call to `Add()`.

■ **Note** This example uses various properties to establish a parameter object. Note, however, that parameter objects support a number of overloaded constructors that allow you to set the values of various properties (which will result in a more compact code base). Also be aware that Visual Studio 2010 provides many graphical designers that will generate a good deal of this grungy parameter-centric code on your behalf (see Chapters 22 and 23).

While building a parameterized query often requires more code, the end result is a more convenient way to tweak SQL statements programmatically, as well as to achieve better overall performance. While you are free to use this technique whenever a SQL query is involved, parameterized queries prove most helpful when you wish to trigger a stored procedure.

Executing a Stored Procedure

Recall that a *stored procedure* is a named block of SQL code stored in the database. You can construct stored procedures so they return a set of rows or scalar data types or do anything else that makes sense (e.g., insert, update, or delete); you can also have them take any number of optional parameters. The end result is a unit of work that behaves like a typical function, except that it is located on a data store rather than a binary business object. Currently, your `AutoLot` database defines a single stored procedure named `GetPetName`, which you formatted as follows:

```
GetPetName
@carID int,
@petName char(10) output
AS
SELECT @petName = PetName from Inventory where CarID = @carID
```

Now consider the following final method of the **InventoryDAL** type, which invokes your stored procedure:

```
Public Function LookUpPetName(ByVal carID As Integer) As String
    Dim carPetName As String = String.Empty

    ' Establish name of stored proc.
    Using cmd As New SqlCommand("GetPetName", Me.sqlCn)
        cmd.CommandType = CommandType.StoredProcedure

        ' Input param.
        Dim param As New SqlParameter()
        param.ParameterName = "@carID"
        param.SqlDbType = SqlDbType.Int
        param.Value = carID

        ' The default direction is in fact Input, but to be clear:
        param.Direction = ParameterDirection.Input
        cmd.Parameters.Add(param)

        ' Output param.
        param = New SqlParameter()
        param.ParameterName = "@petName"
        param.SqlDbType = SqlDbType.Char
        param.Size = 10
        param.Direction = ParameterDirection.Output
        cmd.Parameters.Add(param)

        ' Execute the stored proc.
        cmd.ExecuteNonQuery()

        ' Return output param.
        carPetName = CStr(cmd.Parameters("@petName").Value)
    End Using
    Return carPetName
End Function
```

One important aspect of invoking a stored procedure is to keep in mind that a command object can represent a SQL statement (the default) *or* the name of a stored procedure. When you wish to inform a command object that it will be invoking a stored procedure, you pass in the name of the procedure (as a constructor argument or by using the **CommandText** property) and must set the **CommandType** property to the value **CommandType.StoredProcedure** (if you fail to do this, you will receive a runtime exception because the command object is expecting a SQL statement by default):

```
Dim cmd As New SqlCommand("GetPetName", Me.sqlCn)
cmd.CommandType = CommandType.StoredProcedure
```

Next, notice that the **Direction** property of a parameter object allows you to specify the direction of travel for each parameter passed to the stored procedure (e.g., input parameter, output parameter, in/out parameter, or return value). As before, you add each parameter object to the command object's parameters collection:

```
' Input param.
Dim param As New SqlParameter()
param.ParameterName = "@carID"
param.SqlDbType = SqlDbType.Int
param.Value = carID
param.Direction = ParameterDirection.Input
cmd.Parameters.Add(param)
```

After the stored procedure completes with a call to **ExecuteNonQuery()**, you can obtain the value of the output parameter by investigating the command object's parameter collection and casting accordingly:

```
' Return output param.
carPetName = CStr(cmd.Parameters("@petName").Value)
```

At this point, your initial iteration of the **AutoLotDAL.dll** data access library is complete! You can use this assembly to build any sort of front end to display and edit your data you want (e.g., console based, Windows Forms based, Windows Presentation Foundation based, or an HTML-based web application). You have not yet examined how to build graphical user interfaces, so next you will test your data library from a new console application.

■ **Source Code** You can find the AutoLotDAL project under the Chapter 21 subdirectory.

Creating a Console UI–Based Front End

Create a new Console Application named **AutoLotCUIClient**. After you create your new project, be sure to add a reference to your **AutoLotDAL.dll** assembly, as well as **System.Configuration.dll**. Next, add the following **Imports** statements to your VB 2010 code file:

```
Imports AutoLotConnectedLayer
Imports System.Configuration
Imports System.Data
```

Now insert a new **App.config** file into your project that contains a **<connectionStrings>** element, which you will use to connect to your instance of the **AutoLot** database, as in this example:

```xml
<?xml version="1.0" encoding="utf-8" ?>
<configuration>
  <connectionStrings>
    <add name ="AutoLotSqlProvider" connectionString =
    "Data Source=(local)\SQLEXPRESS;
     Integrated Security=SSPI;Initial Catalog=AutoLot"/>
  </connectionStrings>
  ...
</configuration>
```

Implementing the Main() Method

The Main() method is responsible for prompting the user for a specific course of action and executing that request using a Select statement. This program allows the user to enter the following commands:

- I: Inserts a new record into the Inventory table.

- U: Updates an existing record in the Inventory table.

- D: Deletes an existing record from the Inventory table.

- L: Displays the current inventory using a data reader.

- S: Shows these options to the user.

- P: Looks up pet name from car ID.

- Q: Quits the program.

Each possible option is handled by a unique method within the Module1 Module. The next snippet shows the complete implementation of Main(). Notice that each method invoked from the Do/While loop (with the exception of the ShowInstructions() method) takes an InventoryDAL object as its sole parameter:

```vb
Sub Main()
    Console.WriteLine("***** The AutoLot Console UI *****" & vbLf)

    ' Get connection string from App.config.
    Dim cnStr As String = ConfigurationManager.ConnectionStrings("AutoLotSqlProvider").
                              ConnectionString
    Dim userDone As Boolean = False
    Dim userCommand As String = ""

    ' Create our InventoryDAL object.
    Dim invDAL As New InventoryDAL()
    invDAL.OpenConnection(cnStr)

    ' Keep asking for input until user presses the Q key.
    Try
      ShowInstructions()
      Do
        Console.Write(vbLf & "Please enter your command: ")
        userCommand = Console.ReadLine()
```

```
        Console.WriteLine()
        Select Case userCommand.ToUpper()
            Case "I"
            InsertNewCar(invDAL)
            Case "U"
            UpdateCarPetName(invDAL)
            Case "D"
            DeleteCar(invDAL)
            Case "L"
            ListInventory(invDAL)
            Case "S"
            ShowInstructions()
            Case "P"
            LookUpPetName(invDAL)
            Case "Q"
            userDone = True
            Case Else
            Console.WriteLine("Bad data!  Try again")
        End Select
    Loop While Not userDone
    Catch ex As Exception
      Console.WriteLine(ex.Message)
    Finally
      invDAL.CloseConnection()
    End Try
End Sub
```

Implementing the ShowInstructions() Method

The ShowInstructions() method does what you would expect:

```
Private Sub ShowInstructions()
        Console.WriteLine("I: Inserts a new car.")
        Console.WriteLine("U: Updates an existing car.")
        Console.WriteLine("D: Deletes an existing car.")
        Console.WriteLine("L: Lists current inventory.")
        Console.WriteLine("S: Shows these instructions.")
        Console.WriteLine("P: Looks up pet name.")
        Console.WriteLine("Q: Quits program.")
End Sub
```

Implementing the ListInventory() Method

You could implement the ListInventory() method in either of two ways, based on how you constructed your data access library. Recall that the GetAllInventoryAsDataTable() method of InventoryDAL returns a DataTable object. You could implement this approach like this:

```vb
Private Sub ListInventory(ByVal invDAL As InventoryDAL)
        'Get the list of inventory.
                Dim dt As DataTable = invDAL.GetAllInventoryAsDataTable()

        'Pass DataTable to helper method to display.
        DisplayTable(dt)
End Sub
```

The DisplayTable() helper method displays the table data using the Rows and Columns properties of the incoming DataTable (again, you will learn the full details of the DataTable object the next chapter, so don't fret over the details):

```vb
Private Sub DisplayTable(ByVal dt As DataTable)
        ' Print out the column names.
        For curCol As Integer = 0 To dt.Columns.Count - 1
                Console.Write(dt.Columns(curCol).ColumnName & vbTab)
        Next
        Console.WriteLine(vbLf & "--------------------------------")

        ' Print the DataTable.
        For curRow As Integer = 0 To dt.Rows.Count - 1
                For curCol As Integer = 0 To dt.Columns.Count - 1
                        Console.Write(dt.Rows(curRow)(curCol).ToString() & vbTab)
                Next l
                Console.WriteLine()
        Next
End Sub
```

If you would prefer to call the GetAllInventoryAsList() method of InventoryDAL, you could implement a method named ListInventoryViaList():

```vb
Private Sub ListInventoryViaList(ByVal invDAL As InventoryDAL)
        ' Get the list of inventory.
        Dim record As List(Of NewCar) = invDAL.GetAllInventoryAsList()

        For Each c As NewCar In record
                Console.WriteLine("CarID: {0}, Make: {1}, Color: {2}, PetName: {3}", c.CarID,
                                c.Make, c.Color, c.PetName)

        Next
End Sub
```

Implementing the DeleteCar() Method

Deleting an existing automobile is as simple as asking the user for the ID of the car and passing this to the DeleteCar() method of the InventoryDAL type:

```
Private Sub DeleteCar(ByVal invDAL As InventoryDAL)
    ' Get ID of car to delete.
    Console.Write("Enter ID of Car to delete: ")
    Dim id As Integer = Integer.Parse(Console.ReadLine())

    ' Just in case you have a referential integrity
    ' violation!
    Try
       invDAL.DeleteCar(id)
    Catch ex As Exception
       Console.WriteLine(ex.Message)
    End Try
End Sub
```

Implementing the InsertNewCar() Method

Inserting a new record into the Inventory table is a simple matter of asking the user for the new bits of data (using Console.ReadLine() calls) and passing this data into the InsertAuto() method of InventoryDAL:

```
Private Sub InsertNewCar(ByVal invDAL As InventoryDAL)
    ' First get the user data.
    Dim newCarID As Integer
    Dim newCarColor, newCarMake, newCarPetName As String

    Console.Write("Enter Car ID: ")
    newCarID = Integer.Parse(Console.ReadLine())

    Console.Write("Enter Car Color: ")
    newCarColor = Console.ReadLine()

    Console.Write("Enter Car Make: ")
    newCarMake = Console.ReadLine()

    Console.Write("Enter Pet Name: ")
    newCarPetName = Console.ReadLine()

    ' Now pass to data access library.
    invDAL.InsertAuto(newCarID, newCarColor, newCarMake, newCarPetName)
End Sub
```

Recall that you overloaded InsertAuto() to take a NewCar object, rather than a set of independent arguments. Thus, you could have implemented InsertNewCar() like this:

```vbnet
Private Sub InsertNewCar(ByVal invDAL As InventoryDAL)
        ' First get the user data.

        …
        ' Now pass to data access library.
        Dim c As NewCar = New NewCar With {.CarID = newCarID, .Color = newCarColor,
                                        .Make = newCarMake, .PetName = newCarPetName}

        invDAL.InsertAuto(c)
End Sub
```

Implementing the UpdateCarPetName() Method

The implementation of UpdateCarPetName() looks similar:

```vbnet
Private Sub UpdateCarPetName(ByVal invDAL As InventoryDAL)
        ' First get the user data.
        Dim carID As Integer
        Dim newCarPetName As String

        Console.Write("Enter Car ID: ")
        carID = Integer.Parse(Console.ReadLine())
        Console.Write("Enter New Pet Name: ")
        newCarPetName = Console.ReadLine()

        ' Now pass to data access library.
        invDAL.UpdateCarPetName(carID, newCarPetName)
End Sub
```

Implementing LookUpPetName()

Obtaining the pet name of a given automobile works similarly to the previous methods; this is so because the data access library encapsulates all of the lower-level ADO.NET calls:

```vbnet
Private Sub LookUpPetName(ByVal invDAL As InventoryDAL)
        ' Get ID of car to look up.
        Console.Write("Enter ID of Car to look up: ")
        Dim id As Integer = Integer.Parse(Console.ReadLine())
        Console.WriteLine("Petname of {0} is {1}.", id, invDAL.LookUpPetName(id))
End Sub
```

With this, your console-based front end is finished! It's time to run your program and test each method. Here is some partial output that tests the L, P, and Q commands:

```
***** The AutoLot Console UI *****



I: Inserts a new car.

U: Updates an existing car.

D: Deletes an existing car.

L: Lists current inventory.

S: Shows these instructions.

P: Looks up pet name.

Q: Quits program.



Please enter your command: L


CarID   Make    Color   PetName

----------------------------------

83      Ford    Rust    Rusty

107     Ford    Red     Snake

678     Yugo    Green   Clunker

904     VW      Black   Hank

1000    BMW     Black   Bimmer

1001    BMW     Tan     Daisy

1992    Saab    Pink    Pinkey
```

```
Please enter your command: P



Enter ID of Car to look up: 904

Petname of 904 is Hank.



Please enter your command: Q



Press any key to continue . . .
```

■ **Source Code** You can find the `AutoLotCUIClient` application under the Chapter 21 subdirectory.

Understanding Database Transactions

Let's wrap up this examination of the connected layer of ADO.NET by taking a look at the concept of a database transaction. Simply put, a *transaction* is a set of database operations that must either *all* work or *all* fail as a collective unit. As you might imagine, transactions are quite important to ensure that table data is safe, valid, and consistent.

Transactions are important when a database operation involves interacting with multiple tables or multiple stored procedures (or a combination of database atoms). The classic transaction example involves the process of transferring monetary funds between two bank accounts. For example, if you were to transfer $500.00 from your savings account into your checking account, the following steps should occur in a transactional manner:

- The bank should remove $500.00 from your savings account.

- The bank should add $500.00 to your checking account.

It would be an extremely bad thing if the money were removed from the savings account, but not transferred to the checking account (due to some error on the bank's part) because then you would be out $500.00! However, if these steps are wrapped up into a database transaction, the DBMS ensures that all related steps occur as a single unit. If any part of the transaction fails, the entire operation is *rolled back* to the original state. On the other hand, if all steps succeed, the transaction is *committed*.

■ **Note** You might be familiar with the acronym ACID from looking at transactional literature. This represents the four key properties of a prim-and-proper transaction: *Atomic* (all or nothing); *Consistent* (data remains stable throughout the transaction); *Isolated* (transactions do not step on each other's feet); and Durable (transactions are saved and logged).

It turns out that the .NET platform supports transactions in a variety of ways. This chapter will look at the transaction object of your ADO.NET data provider (`SqlTransaction`, in the case of `System.Data.SqlClient`). The .NET base class libraries also provide transactional support within numerous APIs, including the following:

- `System.EnterpriseServices`: This namespace (located in the `System.EnterpriseServices.dll` assembly) provides types that allow you to integrate with the COM+ runtime layer, including its support for distributed transactions.

- `System.Transactions`: This namespace (located in the `System.Transactions.dll` assembly) contains classes that allow you to write your own transactional applications and resource managers for a variety of services (e.g., MSMQ, ADO.NET, and COM+).

- `Windows Communication Foundation`: The WCF API provides services to facilitate transactions with various distributed binding classes.

- `Windows Workflow Foundations`: The WF API provides transactional support for workflow activities.

In addition to the baked-in transactional support found within the .NET base class libraries, it is also possible to use the SQL language of your database management system. For example, you could author a stored procedure that uses the `BEGIN TRANSACTION`, `ROLLBACK`, and `COMMIT` statements.

Key Members of an ADO.NET Transaction Object

While transactional-aware types exist throughout the base class libraries, you will focus on transaction objects found within an ADO.NET data provider, all of which derive from `DBTransaction` and implement the `IDbTransaction` interface. Recall from the beginning of this chapter that -`IDbTransaction` defines a handful of members:

```
Public Interface IDbTransaction
        Inherits IDisposable
        ReadOnly Property Connection() As IDbConnection
        ReadOnly Property IsolationLevel() As IsolationLevel

        Sub Commit()
        Sub Rollback()
End Interface
```

Notice the Connection property, which returns a reference to the connection object that initiated the current transaction (as you'll see, you obtain a transaction object from a given connection object). You call the Commit() method when each of your database operations have succeeded. Doing this causes each of the pending changes to be persisted in the data store. Conversely, you can call the Rollback() method in the event of a runtime exception, which informs the DMBS to disregard any pending changes, leaving the original data intact.

■ **Note** The IsolationLevel property of a transaction object allows you to specify how aggressively a transaction should be guarded against the activities of other parallel transactions. By default, transactions are isolated completely until committed. Consult the .NET Framework 4.0 SDK documentation for full details regarding the values of the IsolationLevel enumeration.

Beyond the members defined by the IDbTransaction interface, the SqlTransaction type defines an additional member named Save(), which allows you to define *save points*. This concept allows you to roll back a failed transaction up until a named point, rather than rolling back the entire transaction. Essentially, when you call Save() using a SqlTransaction object, you can specify a friendly string moniker. When you call Rollback(), you can specify this same moniker as an argument to perform an effective *partial rollback*. Calling Rollback() with no arguments causes all of the pending changes to be rolled back.

Adding a CreditRisks Table to the AutoLot Database

Now let's look at how you use ADO.NET transactions. Begin by using the Server Explorer of Visual Studio 2010 to add a new table named CreditRisks to the AutoLot database, which has the same exact columns as the Customers table you created earlier in this chapter: CustID, which is the primary key; FirstName; and LastName. As its name suggests, CreditRisks is where you banish the undesirable customers who fail a credit check. Assuming you have added this new table to your database diagram, you should now see the AutoLot implementation shown in Figure 21-14.

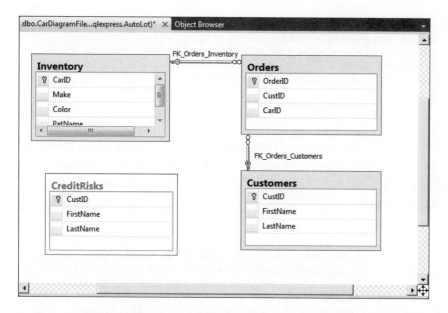

Figure 21-14. The interconnected Orders, Inventory, and Customers tables

Like the earlier savings-to-checking money transfer example, this example, where you move a risky customer from the `Customers` table into the `CreditRisks` table, should occur under the watchful eye of a transactional scope (after all, you will want to remember the ID and names of those who are not creditworthy). Specifically, you need to ensure that *either* you successfully delete the current credit risks from the `Customers` table and add them to the `CreditRisks` table, *or* you need to ensure that neither of these database operations occurs.

■ **Note** In a production environment, you would not need to build a whole new database table to capture high risk customers; instead, you could add a Boolean column named `IsCreditRisk` to the existing Customers table. However, this new table lets you play with a simple transaction.

Adding a Transaction Method to InventoryDAL

Now let's look at how you work with ADO.NET transactions programmatically. Begin by opening the `AutoLotDAL Code Library` project you created earlier and add a new Public method named `ProcessCreditRisk()` to the `InventoryDAL` class to deal with perceived a credit risks (note that this example avoids using a parameterized query to keep the implementation simple; however, you'd want use such a query for a production-level method):

```vbnet
' A new member of the InventoryDAL class.
    Public Sub ProcessCreditRisk(ByVal throwEx As Boolean, ByVal custID As Integer)

        ' First, look up current name based on customer ID.
        Dim fName As String = String.Empty
        Dim lName As String = String.Empty
        Dim cmdSelect As New SqlCommand(String.Format("Select * from Customers where CustID =
                                            {0}", custID), sqlCn)
        Using dr As SqlDataReader = cmdSelect.ExecuteReader()
          If dr.HasRows Then
            dr.Read()
            fName = CStr(dr("FirstName"))
            lName = CStr(dr("LastName"))
          Else
            Return
          End If
        End Using


        ' Create command objects that represent each step of the operation.
        Dim cmdRemove As New SqlCommand(String.Format("Delete from Customers where CustID =
                                            {0}", custID), sqlCn)

        Dim cmdInsert As New SqlCommand(String.Format("Insert Into CreditRisks" &
                                            "(CustID, FirstName , LastName) Values" &
                                            "({0}, '{1}', '{2}')", custID, fName,
                                            lName), sqlCn)

        ' You will get this from the connection object.
        Dim tx As SqlTransaction = Nothing
        Try
          tx = sqlCn.BeginTransaction()

          ' Enlist the commands into this transaction.
          cmdInsert.Transaction = tx
          cmdRemove.Transaction = tx

          ' Execute the commands.
          cmdInsert.ExecuteNonQuery()
          cmdRemove.ExecuteNonQuery()

          ' Simulate error.
          If throwEx Then
            Throw New Exception("Sorry!  Database error! Tx failed...")
          End If

          ' Commit it!
          tx.Commit()
```

```
    Catch ex As Exception
      Console.WriteLine(ex.Message)
      ' Any error will roll back transaction.
      tx.Rollback()
    End Try
  End Sub
End Sub
```

Here, you use an incoming **Boolean** parameter to represent whether you will throw an arbitrary exception when you attempt to process the offending customer. This allows you to simulate an unforeseen circumstance that will cause the database transaction to fail. Obviously, you do this here only for illustrative purposes; a true database transaction method would not want to allow the caller to force the logic to fail on a whim!

Note that you use two **SqlCommand** objects to represent each step in the transaction you will kick off. Once you obtain the customer's first and last name based on the incoming **custID** parameter, you can obtain a valid **SqlTransaction** object from the connection object using **BeginTransaction()**. Next, and most importantly, you must *enlist each command object* by assigning the **Transaction** property to the transaction object you have just obtained. If you fail to do so, the Insert/Delete logic will not be under a transactional context.

After you call **ExecuteNonQuery()** on each command, you throw an exception if (and only if) the value of the **Boolean** parameter is **True**. In this case, all pending database operations are rolled back. If you do not throw an exception, both steps will be committed to the database tables once you call **Commit()**. Now compile your modified **AutoLotDAL** project to ensure you do not have any typos.

Testing Your Database Transaction

You could update your previous **AutoLotCUIClient** application with a new option to invoke the **ProcessCreditRisk()** method; instead, however, you will create a new Console Application named **AdoNetTransaction** to accomplish this. Set a reference to your **AutoLotDAL.dll** assembly and import the **AutoLotConnectedLayer** namespace.

Next, open your Customers table for data entry by right-clicking the table icon from the Server Explorer and selecting Show Table Data. Now add a new customer who will be the victim of a low credit score:

- **CustID**: 333

- **FirstName**: Homer

- **LastName**: Simpson

Finally, update your **Main()** method as follows:

```
Sub Main()
    Console.WriteLine("***** Simple Transaction Example *****" & vbLf)

    ' A simple way to allow the tx to succeed or not.
    Dim throwEx As Boolean = True
    Dim userAnswer As String = String.Empty
```

```
Console.Write("Do you want to throw an exception (Y or N): ")
userAnswer = Console.ReadLine()
If userAnswer.ToLower() = "n" Then
  throwEx = False
End If

Dim dal As New InventoryDAL()
dal.OpenConnection("Data Source=(local)\SQLEXPRESS;Integrated Security=SSPI;" &
                   "Initial Catalog=AutoLot")

' Process customer 333.
dal.ProcessCreditRisk(throwEx, 333)

Console.WriteLine("Check CreditRisk table for results")
Console.ReadLine()
End Sub
```

If you were to run your program and elect to throw an exception, you would find that Homer is *not* removed from the Customers table because the entire transaction has been rolled back. However, if you did not throw an exception, you would find that Customer ID 333 is no longer in the Customers table and has been placed in the CreditRisks table instead.

■ **Source Code** You can find the AdoNetTransaction project under the Chapter 21 subdirectory.

Summary

ADO.NET is the native data access technology of the .NET platform, and you can use it in three distinct manners: connected, disconnected, or through the Entity Framework. In this chapter, you examined the connected layer and learned the role of data providers, which are essentially concrete implementations of several MustInherit base classes (in the System.Data.Common) namespace and interface types (in the System.Data namespace). You also saw that it is possible to build a provider-neutral code base using the ADO.NET data provider factory model.

You also learned that you can use connection objects, transaction objects, command objects, and data reader objects of the connected layer to select, update, insert, and delete records. Also, recall that command objects support an internal parameter collection, which you can use to add some type safety to your SQL queries; these also prove quite helpful when triggering stored procedures.

■ ■ ■

## CHAPTER 22

ADO.NET
Part II: The Disconnected Layer

The previous chapter gave you a chance to examine the *connected layer* of ADO.NET, which allows you to submit SQL statements to a database using the connection, command, and data reader objects of your data provider. In this chapter, you will learn about the *disconnected layer* of ADO.NET. Using this facet of ADO.NET lets you model database data in memory within the calling tier by leveraging numerous members of the `System.Data` namespace (most notably: `DataSet`, `DataTable`, `DataRow`, `DataColumn`, `DataView`, and `DataRelation`). By doing so, you can provide the illusion that the calling tier is continuously connected to an external data source; the reality is that the caller is operating on a local copy of relational data.

While it is possible to use this *disconnected* aspect of ADO.NET without ever making a literal connection to a relational database, you will most often obtain populated `DataSet` objects using the data adapter object of your data provider. As you will see, data adapter objects function as a bridge between the client tier and a relational database. Using these objects, you can obtain `DataSet` objects, manipulate their contents, and send modified rows back for processing. The end result is a highly scalable data-centric .NET application.

This chapter will also illustrate some data-binding techniques, using the context of a Windows Forms GUI desktop application, and examine the role of a *strongly typed DataSet*. You will also update the `AutoLotDAL.dll` data library you created in Chapter 21 with a new namespace that uses the disconnected layer of ADO.NET. Last but not least, you will learn about the role of LINQ to DataSet, which allows you to apply LINQ queries to your in-memory data cache.

■ **Note** You will learn about data-binding techniques for Windows Presentation Foundation and ASP.NET applications later in this book.

Understanding the Disconnected Layer of ADO.NET

As you saw in the previous chapter, working with the connected layer allows you to interact with a database using the primary connection, command, and data reader objects. You can use this handful of classes to select, insert, update, and delete records to your heart's content (as well as invoke stored procedures or perform other data operations [e.g., DDL to create table and DCL to grant permissions]). However, you have seen only part of the ADO.NET story. Recall that you can use the ADO.NET object model in a disconnected manner.

Using the disconnected layer, it is possible to model relational data using an in-memory object model. Far beyond simply modeling a tabular block of rows and columns, the types within System.Data allow you to represent table relationships, column constraints, primary keys, views, and other database primitives. Once you model the data, you can apply filters, submit in-memory queries, and persist (or load) your data in XML and binary formats. You can do all of this without ever making a literal connection to a DBMS (hence the term, *disconnected layer*) by loading data from a local XML file or manually building a DataSet in code.

You could use the disconnected types without ever connecting to a database, but you will typically still use connection and command objects. In addition, you will leverage a specific object, the *data adapter* (which extends the MustInherit DbDataAdapter class), to fetch and update data. Unlike the connected layer, data obtained with a data adapter is not processed using data reader objects. Rather, data adapter objects use DataSet objects to move data between the caller and data source. The DataSet type is a container for any number of DataTable objects, each of which contains a collection of DataRow and DataColumn objects.

The data adapter object of your data provider handles the database connection automatically. In an effort to increase scalability, data adapters keep the connection open for the shortest amount of time possible. Once the caller receives the DataSet object, the calling tier is completely disconnected from the database and left with a local copy of the remote data. The caller is free to insert, delete, or update rows from a given DataTable, but the physical database is not updated until the caller explicitly passes the DataSet to the data adapter for updating. In a nutshell, DataSets allow the clients to pretend they are always connected; however, they actually operate on an in-memory database (see Figure 22-1).

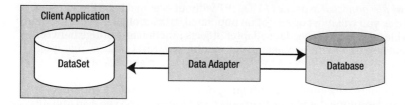

Figure 22-1. Data adapter objects move DataSets to and from the client tier

Given that the centerpiece of the disconnected layer is the DataSet class, the first task of this chapter is to learn how to manipulate a DataSet manually. Once you can do this, you will have no problem manipulating the contents of a DataSet retrieved from a data adapter object.

Understanding the Role of the DataSet

As noted previously, a DataSet is an in-memory representation of relational data. More specifically, a DataSet is a class type that internally maintains three strongly typed collections (see Figure 22-2).

Figure 22-2. The anatomy of a DataSet

The `Tables` property of the `DataSet` allows you to access the `DataTableCollection` that contains the individual `DataTables`. Another important collection used by the `DataSet`: `DataRelationCollection`. Given that a `DataSet` is a disconnected version of a database schema, you can use it to represent the parent/child relationships programmatically between its tables. For example, you can create a relation between two tables to model a foreign key constraint using the `DataRelation` type. You can add this object to the `DataRelationCollection` with the `Relations` property. At this point, you can navigate between the related tables as you search for data. You will see how to do this later in the chapter.

The `ExtendedProperties` property provides access to the `PropertyCollection` object, which allows you to associate any extra information to the `DataSet` as name/value pairs. This information can be literally anything, even if it has no bearing on the database data itself. For example, you can associate your company's name to a `DataSet`, which can then function as in-memory metadata. Other examples of extended properties might include time stamps, an encrypted password that must be supplied to access the contents of the `DataSet`, a number representing a data refresh rate, and so forth.

■ **Note** The `DataTable` and `DataColumn` classes also support the `ExtendedProperties` property.

Key Properties of the DataSet

Before exploring too many other programmatic details, let's take a look at some core members of the `DataSet`. Table 22-1 describes some additional properties of interest beyond the `Tables`, `Relations`, and `ExtendedProperties` properties.

Table 22-1. Properties of the DataSet

Property	Meaning in Life
CaseSensitive	Indicates whether string comparisons in DataTable objects are case sensitive (or not). The default is False (string comparisons are not case sensitive by default).
DataSetName	Represents the friendly name of this DataSet. Typically, you establish this value as a constructor parameter.
EnforceConstraints	Gets or sets a value indicating whether constraint rules are followed when attempting any update operations (the default is True).
HasErrors	Gets a value indicating whether there are errors in any of the rows in any of the DataTables of the DataSet.
RemotingFormat	Allows you to define how the DataSet should serialize its content (binary or XML, which is the default).

Key Methods of the DataSet

The methods of the DataSet work in conjunction with some of the functionality provided by the aforementioned properties. In addition to interacting with XML streams, the DataSet provides methods that allow you to copy the contents of your DataSet, navigate between the internal tables, and establish the beginning and ending points of a batch of updates. Table 22-2 describes some core methods.

Table 22-2. Select Methods of the DataSet

Methods	Meaning in Life
AcceptChanges()	Commits all the changes made to this DataSet since it was loaded or the last time AcceptChanges() was called.
Clear()	Completely clears the DataSet data by removing every row in each DataTable.
Clone()	Clones the structure, but not the data, of the DataSet, including all DataTables, as well as all relations and any constraints.
Copy()	Copies both the structure and data for this DataSet.
GetChanges()	Returns a copy of the DataSet containing all changes made to it since it was last loaded or since AcceptChanges() was called. This method is overloaded, so that you can get just the new rows, just the modified rows, or just the deleted rows.
HasChanges()	Gets a value indicating whether the DataSet has changes, including new, deleted, or modified rows.

Methods	Meaning in Life
Merge()	Merges this DataSet with a specified DataSet.
ReadXml()	Allows you to define the structure of a DataSet object and populate it with data, based on XML schema and data read from a stream.
RejectChanges()	Rolls back all the changes made to this DataSet since it was created or since the last time AcceptChanges() was called.
WriteXml()	Allow you to write out the contents of a DataSet into a valid stream.

Building a DataSet

Now that you have a better understanding of the role of the DataSet (and some idea of what you can do with one), create a new Console Application named SimpleDataSet. VB 2010 applications import the System.Data namespace automatically, so there's no need to add an Imports System.Data statement in your code. Within the Main() method, define a new DataSet object that contains three extended properties that represent a time stamp, a unique identifier (represented as a System.Guid type), and your company's name:

```
Sub Main()
    Console.WriteLine("***** Fun with DataSets *****" & vbLf)

    'Create the DataSet object and add a few properties.
    Dim carsInventoryDS As New DataSet("Car Inventory")

    carsInventoryDS.ExtendedProperties("TimeStamp") = Date.Now
    carsInventoryDS.ExtendedProperties("DataSetID") = Guid.NewGuid()
    carsInventoryDS.ExtendedProperties("Company") = "Mikko's Hot Tub Super Store"
    Console.ReadLine()
End Sub
```

You might be unfamiliar with the concept of a globally unique identifier (GUID); all you need to know is that it is a statically unique 128-bit number. While GUIDs are used throughout the COM framework to identify numerous things (e.g., classes, interfaces, and applications), the System.Guid type remains helpful under .NET when you need to generate a unique identifier quickly.

In any case, a DataSet object is not interesting until you insert any number of DataTables. Therefore, the next task is to examine the internal composition of the DataTable, beginning with the DataColumn type.

Working with DataColumns

The DataColumn type represents a single column within a DataTable. Collectively speaking, the set of all DataColumn types bound to a given DataTable represents the foundation of a table's *schema* information. For example, if you were to model the Inventory table of the AutoLot database (see Chapter 21), you would create four DataColumns, one for each column (CarID, Make, Color, and PetName). Once you create your DataColumn objects, you typically add them into the columns collection of the DataTable type (using the Columns property).

Based on your background, you might know that you can assign a given column in a database table a set of constraints (e.g., configured as a primary key, assigned a default value, or configured to contain read-only information). Also, every column in a table must map to an underlying data type. For example, the Inventory table's schema requires that the CarID column map to an integer, while Make, Color, and PetName map to an array of characters. The DataColumn class has numerous properties that allow you to configure precisely these things. Table 22-3 provides a rundown of some core properties.

Table 22-3. Properties of the DataColumn

Properties	Meaning in Life
AllowDBNull	You use this property to indicate whether a row can specify null values in this column. The default value is True.
AutoIncrement AutoIncrementSeed AutoIncrementStep	You use these properties to configure the autoincrement behavior for a given column. This can be helpful when you wish to ensure unique values in a given DataColumn (such as a primary key). By default, a DataColumn does not support autoincrement behavior.
Caption	This property gets or sets the caption you want to display for this column. This allows you to define a user-friendly version of a literal database column name.
ColumnMapping	This property determines how a DataColumn is represented when a DataSet is saved as an XML document using the DataSet.WriteXml() method. You can specify that the data column should be written out as an XML element, an XML attribute, simple text content, or ignored altogether.
ColumnName	This property gets or sets the name of the column in the Columns collection (meaning how it is represented internally by the DataTable). If you do not set the ColumnName explicitly, the default values are Column with (*n*+1) numerical suffixes (e.g., Column1, Column2, and Column3).
DataType	This property defines the data type (e.g., Boolean, String, or Double) stored in the column.
DefaultValue	This property gets or sets the default value assigned to this column when you insert new rows.
Expression	This property gets or sets the expression used to filter rows, calculate a column's value, or create an aggregate column.
Ordinal	This property gets the numerical position of the column in the Columns collection maintained by the DataTable.
ReadOnly	This property determines whether this column is read only once a row has been added to the table. The default is False.

Properties	Meaning in Life
Table	This property gets the DataTable that contains this DataColumn.
Unique	This property gets or sets a value indicating whether the values in each row of the column must be unique or if repeating values are permissible. If you assign a column a primary key constraint, then you must set the Unique property to True.

Building a DataColumn

To continue with the SimpleDataSet project (and illustrate the use of the DataColumn), assume you wish to model the columns of the Inventory table. Given that the CarID column will be the table's primary key, you will configure this DataColumn object as read-only, unique, and non-null (using the ReadOnly, Unique, and AllowDBNull properties). Next, update the Module1 Module with a new method named FillDataSet(), which you use to build four DataColumn objects. Note this method takes a DataSet object as its only parameter:

```
Sub FillDataSet(ByVal ds As DataSet)
    'Create data columns that map to the
    ''real' columns in the Inventory table
    'of the AutoLot database.
    Dim carIDColumn As New DataColumn("CarID", GetType(Integer))
    carIDColumn.Caption = "Car ID"
    carIDColumn.ReadOnly = True
    carIDColumn.AllowDBNull = False
    carIDColumn.Unique = True

    Dim carMakeColumn As New DataColumn("Make", GetType(String))
    Dim carColorColumn As New DataColumn("Color", GetType(String))
    Dim carPetNameColumn As New DataColumn("PetName", GetType(String))
    carPetNameColumn.Caption = "Pet Name"
End Sub
```

Notice that when you configure the carIDColumn object, you assign a value to the Caption property. This property is helpful because it allows you to define a String value for display purposes, which can be distinct from the literal database table column name (column names in a literal database table are typically better suited for programming purposes [e.g., au_fname] than display purposes [e.g., Author First Name]). Here, you set the caption for the PetName column for the same reason, because *Pet Name* looks nicer than *PetName* to the end user.

Enabling Autoincrementing Fields

One aspect of the DataColumn you can choose to configure is its ability to *autoincrement*. You use an autoincrementing column to ensure that when a new row is added to a given table, the value of this column is assigned automatically, based on the current step of the increase. This can be helpful when you wish to ensure that a column has no repeating values (e.g., a primary key).

You control this behavior using the `AutoIncrement`, `AutoIncrementSeed`, and `AutoIncrementStep` properties. You use the seed value to mark the starting value of the column; you use the step value to identify the number to add to the seed when incrementing. Consider the following update to the construction of the `carIDColumn DataColumn`:

```
Sub FillDataSet(ByVal ds As DataSet)
    Dim carIDColumn As New DataColumn("CarID", GetType(Integer))
    carIDColumn.ReadOnly = True
    carIDColumn.Caption = "Car ID"
    carIDColumn.AllowDBNull = False
    carIDColumn.Unique = True
    carIDColumn.AutoIncrement = True
    carIDColumn.AutoIncrementSeed = 0
    carIDColumn.AutoIncrementStep = 1
    ...
End Sub
```

Here, you configure the `carIDColumn` object to ensure that, as rows are added to the respective table, the value for this column is incremented by 1. You set the seed at 0, so this column would be numbered 0, 1, 2, 3, and so forth.

Adding DataColumn Objects to a DataTable

The `DataColumn` type does not typically exist as a stand-alone entity; however, you do typically insert it into a related `DataTable`. For example, create a new `DataTable` object (fully detailed in a moment) and insert each `DataColumn` object in the columns collection using the `Columns` property:

```
Sub FillDataSet(ByVal ds As DataSet)
    ...
    ' Now add DataColumns to a DataTable.
    Dim inventoryTable As New DataTable("Inventory")
    inventoryTable.Columns.AddRange(New DataColumn()
            { carIDColumn, carMakeColumn, carColorColumn, carPetNameColumn })
End Sub
```

At this point, the `DataTable` object contains four `DataColumn` objects that represent the schema of the in-memory Inventory table. However, the table is currently devoid of data, and the table is currently outside of the table collection maintained by the `DataSet`. You will deal with both of these shortcomings, beginning by populating the table with data using a `DataRow` objects.

Working with DataRows

As you have seen, a collection of `DataColumn` objects represents the schema of a `DataTable`. In contrast, a collection of `DataRow` objects represents the actual data in the table. Thus, if you have 20 rows in the `Inventory` table of the `AutoLot` database, you can represent these records using 20 `DataRow` objects. Table 22-4 documents some (but not all) of the members of the `DataRow` type.

Table 22-4. Key Members of the DataRow Type

Members	Meaning in Life
HasErrors GetColumnsInError() GetColumnError() ClearErrors() RowError	The HasErrors property returns a Boolean value indicating whether there are errors in a DataRow. If so, you can use the GetColumnsInError() method to obtain the offending columns and GetColumnError()to obtain the error description. Similarly, you can use the ClearErrors() method to remove each error listing for the row. The RowError property allows you to configure a textual description of the error for a given row.
ItemArray	This property gets or sets all of the column values for this row using an array of objects.
RowState	You use this property to pinpoint the current *state* of the DataRow in the DataTable containing the DataRow, using values of the RowState enumeration (e.g., a row can be flagged as new, modified, unchanged, or deleted).
Table	You use this property to obtain a reference to the DataTable containing this DataRow.
AcceptChanges() RejectChanges()	These methods commit or reject all changes made to this row since the last time AcceptChanges() was called.
BeginEdit() EndEdit() CancelEdit()	These methods begin, end, or cancel an edit operation on a DataRow object.
Delete()	This method marks a row you want to remove when the AcceptChanges() method is called.
IsNull()	This method gets a value indicating whether the specified column contains a null value.

Working with a DataRow is a bit different from working with a DataColumn; you cannot create a direct instance of this type because there is no Public constructor:

```
' Error! No public constructor!
Dim r As New DataRow()
```

Instead, you obtain a new DataRow object from a given DataTable. For example, assume you wish to insert two rows in the Inventory table. The DataTable.NewRow() method allows you to obtain the next slot in the table, at which point you can fill each column with new data using the type indexer. When doing so, you can specify either the string name assigned to the DataColumn or its (zero-based) ordinal position:

```
Sub FillDataSet(ByVal ds As DataSet)
    ...
    ' Now add some rows to the Inventory Table.
    Dim carRow As DataRow = inventoryTable.NewRow()
    carRow("Make") = "BMW"
    carRow("Color") = "Black"
    carRow("PetName") = "Hamlet"
    inventoryTable.Rows.Add(carRow)

    carRow = inventoryTable.NewRow()
    ' Column 0 is the autoincremented ID field,
    ' so start at 1.
    carRow(1) = "Saab"
    carRow(2) = "Red"
    carRow(3) = "Sea Breeze"
    inventoryTable.Rows.Add(carRow)
End Sub
```

■ **Note** If you pass the DataRow's indexer method an invalid column name or ordinal position, you will receive a runtime exception.

At this point, you have a single DataTable containing two rows. Of course, you can repeat this general process to create a number of DataTables to define the schema and data content. Before you insert the inventoryTable object into your DataSet object, you should check out the all-important RowState property.

Understanding the RowState Property

The RowState property is useful when you need to identify programmatically the set of all rows in a table that have changed from their original value, have been newly inserted, and so forth. You can assign this property any value from the DataRowState enumeration, as shown in Table 22-5.

Table 22-5. Values of the DataRowState Enumeration

Value	Meaning in Life
Added	The row has been added to a DataRowCollection, and AcceptChanges() has not been called.
Deleted	The row has been marked for deletion using the Delete() method of the DataRow, and AcceptChanges() has not been called.
Detached	The row has been created but is not part of any DataRowCollection. A DataRow is in this state immediately after it has been created, but before it is added to a collection. It is also in this state if it has been removed from a collection.

Value	Meaning in Life
Modified	The row has been modified, and AcceptChanges() has not been called.
Unchanged	The row has not changed since AcceptChanges() was last called.

When you manipulate the rows of a given DataTable programmatically, the RowState property is set automatically. For example, add a new method to your Module1 Module, which operates on a local DataRow object, printing out its row state along the way:

```
Private Sub ManipulateDataRowState()
    ' Create a temp DataTable for testing.
    Dim temp As New DataTable("Temp")
    temp.Columns.Add(New DataColumn("TempColumn", GetType(Integer)))

    ' RowState = Detached (i.e. not part of a DataTable yet)
    Dim row As DataRow = temp.NewRow()
    Console.WriteLine("After calling NewRow(): {0}", row.RowState)

    ' RowState = Added.
    temp.Rows.Add(row)
    Console.WriteLine("After calling Rows.Add(): {0}", row.RowState)

    ' RowState = Added.
    row("TempColumn") = 10
    Console.WriteLine("After first assignment: {0}", row.RowState)

    ' RowState = Unchanged.
    temp.AcceptChanges()
    Console.WriteLine("After calling AcceptChanges: {0}", row.RowState)

    ' RowState = Modified.
    row("TempColumn") = 11
    Console.WriteLine("After first assignment: {0}", row.RowState)

    ' RowState = Deleted.
    temp.Rows(0).Delete()
    Console.WriteLine("After calling Delete: {0}", row.RowState)
End Sub
```

The ADO.NET DataRow is smart enough to remember its current state of affairs. Given this, the owning DataTable is able to identify which rows have been added, updated, or deleted. This is a key feature of the DataSet because, when it comes time to send updated information to the data store, only the modified data is submitted.

Understanding the DataRowVersion Property

Beyond maintaining the current state of a row with the RowState property, a DataRow object maintains three possible versions of the data it contains using the DataRowVersion property. When a DataRow object is first constructed, it contains only a single copy of data, represented as the current version. However, as you programmatically manipulate a DataRow object (using various method calls), additional versions of the data spring to life. Specifically, you can set the DataRowVersion to any value of the related DataRowVersion enumeration (see Table 22-6).

Table 22-6. *Values of the DataRowVersion Enumeration*

Value	Meaning in Life
Current	This represents the current value of a row, even after changes have been made.
Default	This is the default version of DataRowState. For a DataRowState value of Added, Modified, or Deleted, the default version is Current. For a DataRowState value of Detached, the version is Proposed.
Original	This represents the value first inserted into a DataRow or the value the last time AcceptChanges() was called.
Proposed	This is the value of a row currently being edited due to a call to BeginEdit().

As suggested in Table 22-6, the value of the DataRowVersion property is dependent on the value of the DataRowState property in many cases. As mentioned previously, the DataRowVersion property will be changed behind the scenes when you invoke various methods on the DataRow (or, in some cases, the DataTable) object. Here is a breakdown of the methods that can affect the value of a row's DataRowVersion property:

- If you call the DataRow.BeginEdit() method and change the row's value, the Current and Proposed values become available.

- If you call the DataRow.CancelEdit() method, the Proposed value is deleted.

- After you call DataRow.EndEdit(), the Proposed value becomes the Current value.

- After you call the DataRow.AcceptChanges() method, the Original value becomes identical to the Current value. The same transformation occurs when you call DataTable.AcceptChanges().

- After you call DataRow.RejectChanges(), the Proposed value is discarded, and the version becomes Current.

Yes, this is a bit convoluted, not least because a DataRow might or might not have all versions at any given time (you'll receive runtime exceptions if you attempt to obtain a row version that is not currently tracked). Regardless of the complexity, given that the DataRow maintains three copies of data, it becomes simple to build a front end that allows an end user to alter values, change his or her mind and roll back values, or commit values permanently. You'll see various examples of manipulating these methods over the remainder of this chapter.

Working with DataTables

The DataTable type defines many members, many of which are identical in name and functionality to those of the DataSet. Table 22-7 describes some core members of the DataTable type beyond Rows and Columns.

Table 22-7. *Key Members of the DataTable Type*

Member	Meaning in Life
CaseSensitive	Indicates whether string comparisons within the table are case sensitive. The default value is False.
ChildRelations	Returns the collection of child relations for this DataTable (if any).
Constraints	Gets the collection of constraints maintained by the table.
Copy()	A method that copies the schema and data of a given DataTable into a new instance.
DataSet	Gets the DataSet that contains this table (if any).
DefaultView	Gets a customized view of the table that might include a filtered view or a cursor position.
ParentRelations	Gets the collection of parent relations for this DataTable.
PrimaryKey	Gets or sets an array of columns that function as primary keys for the data table.
RemotingFormat	Allows you to define how the DataSet should serialize its content (binary or XML) for the .NET remoting layer.
TableName	Gets or sets the name of the table. This same property might also be specified as a constructor parameter.

To continue with the current example, you can set the PrimaryKey property of the DataTable to the carIDColumn DataColumn object. Be aware that the PrimaryKey property is assigned a collection of DataColumn objects to account for a multicolumned key. In this case, however, you need to specify only the CarID column (being the first ordinal position in the table):

```
Sub FillDataSet(ByVal ds As DataSet)
    ...
    ' Mark the primary key of this table.
    inventoryTable.PrimaryKey = New DataColumn() { inventoryTable.Columns(0) }
End Sub
```

Inserting DataTables into DataSets

At this point, your DataTable object is complete. The final step is to insert the DataTable into the carsInventoryDS DataSet object using the Tables collection:

```
Sub FillDataSet(ByVal ds As DataSet)
    ...
    ' Finally, add our table to the DataSet.
    ds.Tables.Add(inventoryTable)
End Sub
```

Now update your Main() method to call FillDataSet(), passing in your local DataSet object as an argument. Next, pass the same object into a new (yet to be written) helper method named PrintDataSet():

```
Sub Main(ByVal args() As String)
    Console.WriteLine("***** Fun with DataSets *****" & vbLf)

    ...
    FillDataSet(carsInventoryDS)
    PrintDataSet(carsInventoryDS)
    Console.ReadLine()
End Sub
```

Obtaining Data in a DataSet

The PrintDataSet() method simply iterates over the DataSet metadata (using the ExtendedProperties collection) and each DataTable in the DataSet, printing out the column names and row values using the type indexers:

```
Sub PrintDataSet(ByVal ds As DataSet)

    ' Print out the DataSet name and any extended properties.
    Console.WriteLine("DataSet is named: {0}", ds.DataSetName)

    For Each de As System.Collections.DictionaryEntry In ds.ExtendedProperties
        Console.WriteLine("Key = {0}, Value = {1}", de.Key, de.Value)
    Next
    Console.WriteLine()

    ' Print out each table.
    For Each dt As DataTable In ds.Tables
    Console.WriteLine("=> {0} Table:", dt.TableName)

        ' Print out the column names.
        For curCol As Integer = 0 To dt.Columns.Count - 1
            Console.Write(dt.Columns(curCol).ColumnName & vbTab)
        Next
        Console.WriteLine(vbLf & "---------------------------------")
```

```
        ' Print the DataTable.
        For curRow As Integer = 0 To dt.Rows.Count - 1
            For curCol As Integer = 0 To dt.Columns.Count - 1
                Console.Write(dt.Rows(curRow)(curCol).ToString() & vbTab)
            Next
            Console.WriteLine()
        Next
    Next
End Sub
```

If you run your program now, you'll see the following output (your time stamp and GUID value will differ of course):

```
***** Fun with DataSets *****


DataSet is named: Car Inventory

Key = TimeStamp, Value = 7/26/2010 9:42:22 AM

Key = DataSetID, Value = 11c533ed-d1aa-4c82-96d4-b0f88893ab21

Key = Company, Value = Mikko's Hot Tub Super Store


=> Inventory Table:

CarID   Make    Color    PetName

----------------------------------

0          BMW    Black   Hamlet

1          Saab    Red     Sea Breeze
```

Processing DataTable Data Using DataTableReader Objects

Given your work in the previous chapter, you should notice that the manner in which you process data using the connected layer (e.g., data reader objects) and the disconnected layer (e.g., DataSet objects) is quite different. Working with a data reader typically involves establishing a while loop, calling the Read() method, and using an indexer to pluck out the name/value pairs. On the other hand, DataSet processing typically involves a series of iteration constructs to drill into the data within the tables, rows, and columns (remember that DataReader requires an open database connection so that it can read the data from the actual database).

DataTables support a method named CreateDataReader(). This method allows you to obtain the data within a DataTable using a data reader–like navigation scheme (the data reader will now read data from the in-memory DataTable, not from the actual database, so there's no database connection involved here). The major benefit of this approach is that you now use a single model to process data, regardless of which layer of ADO.NET you use to obtain it. Assume you have authored a new method in your Module1 Module named PrintTable():

```vb
Sub PrintTable(ByVal dt As DataTable)
    ' Get the DataTableReader type.
    Dim dtReader As DataTableReader = dt.CreateDataReader()

    ' The DataTableReader works just like the DataReader.
    Do While dtReader.Read()
        For i As Integer = 0 To dtReader.FieldCount - 1
            Console.Write("{0}" & vbTab, dtReader.GetValue(i).ToString().Trim())
        Next
        Console.WriteLine()
    Loop
    dtReader.Close()
End Sub
```

Notice that the DataTableReader works identically to the data reader object of your data provider. A DataTableReader can be an ideal choice when you wish to pump out the data within a DataTable quickly, without needing to traverse the internal row and column collections. Now assume you have updated the previous PrintDataSet() method to invoke PrintTable(), rather than drilling into the Rows and Columns collections:

```vb
Sub PrintDataSet(ByVal ds As DataSet)

    ' Print out the DataSet name, plus any extended properties.
    Console.WriteLine("DataSet is named: {0}", ds.DataSetName)
    For Each de As System.Collections.DictionaryEntry In ds.ExtendedProperties
        Console.WriteLine("Key = {0}, Value = {1}", de.Key, de.Value)
    Next
    Console.WriteLine()

    For Each dt As DataTable In ds.Tables
        Console.WriteLine("=> {0} Table:", dt.TableName)

        ' Print out the column names.
        For curCol As Integer = 0 To dt.Columns.Count - 1
          Console.Write(dt.Columns(curCol).ColumnName.Trim() & vbTab)
        Next
        Console.WriteLine(vbLf & "---------------------------------")

        ' Call our new helper method.
        PrintTable(dt)
    Next
End Sub
```

When you run the application, the output is identical to that shown previously. The only difference is how you access the DataTable's contents internally.

Serializing DataTable/DataSet Objects As XML

DataSets and DataTables both support the WriteXml() and ReadXml() methods. WriteXml() allows you to persist an object's content to a local file (as well as into any System.IO.Stream-derived type) as an XML document. ReadXml() allows you to hydrate the state of a DataSet (or DataTable) from a given XML document. In addition, DataSets and DataTables both support WriteXmlSchema() and ReadXmlSchema() for saving or loading an *.xsd file.

To test this out for yourself, update your Main() method to call the following helper function (notice that you pass a DataSet as the sole parameter):

```
Sub SaveAndLoadAsXml(ByVal carsInventoryDS As DataSet)
    ' Save this DataSet as XML.
    carsInventoryDS.WriteXml("carsDataSet.xml")
    carsInventoryDS.WriteXmlSchema("carsDataSet.xsd")

    ' Clear out DataSet.
    carsInventoryDS.Clear()

    ' Load DataSet from XML file.
    carsInventoryDS.ReadXml("carsDataSet.xml")
End Sub
```

If you open the carsDataSet.xml file (which you will find under the \bin\Debug folder of your project), you will find that each column in the table has been encoded as an XML element:

```
<?xml version="1.0" standalone="yes"?>
<Car_x0020_Inventory>
  <Inventory>
    <CarID>0</CarID>
    <Make>BMW</Make>
    <Color>Black</Color>
    <PetName>Hamlet</PetName>
  </Inventory>
  <Inventory>
    <CarID>1</CarID>
    <Make>Saab</Make>
    <Color>Red</Color>
    <PetName>Sea Breeze</PetName>
  </Inventory>
</Car_x0020_Inventory>
```

If you were to double click on the generated *.xsd file (also found under your \bin\Debug folder) within Visual Studio, you will open the IDE's XML schema editor (Figure 22-3).

Figure 22-3. *The XSD editor of Visual Studio 2010*

■ **Note** Chapter 24 will introduce you to the LINQ to XML API, which is the preferred manner for manipulating XML data in the .NET platform.

Serializing DataTable/DataSet Objects in a Binary Format

It is also possible to persist the contents of a `DataSet` (or an individual `DataTable`) as a compact binary format. This can be especially helpful when a `DataSet` object needs to be passed across a machine boundary (in the case of a distributed application); one drawback of XML data representation is that its descriptive nature can result in a good deal of overhead.

To persist `DataTables` or `DataSets` in a binary format, set the `RemotingFormat` property to `SerializationFormat.Binary`. At this point, you can use the `BinaryFormatter` type (see Chapter 20) as expected. Consider the following final method of the SimpleDataSet project (don't forget to import the `System.IO` and `System.Runtime.Serialization.Formatters.Binary` namespaces):

```
Sub SaveAndLoadAsBinary(ByVal carsInventoryDS As DataSet)
    ' Set binary serialization flag.
    carsInventoryDS.RemotingFormat = SerializationFormat.Binary

    ' Save this DataSet as binary.
    Dim fs As New FileStream("BinaryCars.bin", FileMode.Create)
    Dim bFormat As New BinaryFormatter()
    bFormat.Serialize(fs, carsInventoryDS)
    fs.Close()

    ' Clear out DataSet.
    carsInventoryDS.Clear()
```

```vb
' Load DataSet from binary file.
fs = New FileStream("BinaryCars.bin", FileMode.Open)
Dim data As DataSet = CType(bFormat.Deserialize(fs), DataSet)
End Sub
```

If you call this method from Main(), you can find the *.bin file in your bin\Debug folder. Figure 22-4 shows the contents of the BinaryCars.bin file.

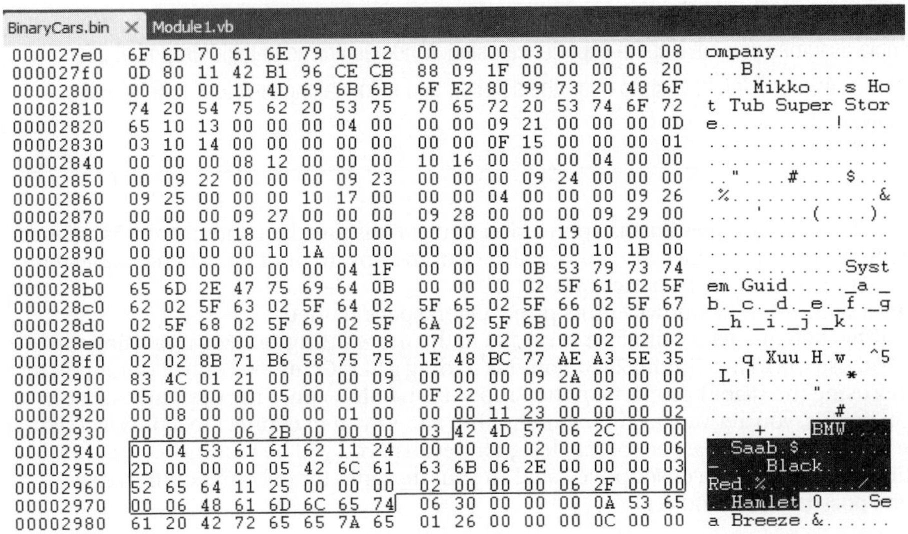

Figure 22-4. A DataSet saved to a binary format

■ **Source Code** You can find the SimpleDataSet application under the Chapter 22 subdirectory.

Binding DataTable Objects to Windows Forms GUIs

So far, you have examined how to create, hydrate, and iterate over the contents of a DataSet object manually using the inherit object model of ADO.NET. While understanding how to do so is quite important, the .NET platform ships with numerous APIs that have the ability to *bind* data to user interface elements automatically.

For example, the original GUI toolkit of .NET, Windows Forms, supplies a control named `DataGridView` that includes the built-in ability to display the contents of a `DataSet` or `DataTable` object using only a few lines of code. ASP.NET (.NET's web development API) and the Windows Presentation Foundation API (a supercharged GUI API introduced with .NET 3.0) also support the notion of data binding. You will learn to bind data to WPF and ASP.NET GUI elements later in this book; however, in this chapter, you will use Windows Forms because it is a fairly simple and straightforward programming model.

■ **Note** The next example assumes you have some experience using Windows Forms to build graphical user interfaces. If this is not the case, you might wish to open the solution and follow along or return to this section once you have read Appendix A.

Your next task is to build a Windows Forms application that will display the contents of a `DataTable` object within its user interface. Along the way, you will also examine how to filter and change table data. You will also learn about the role of the `DataView` object.

Begin by creating a brand-new Windows Forms project workspace named `WindowsFormsDataBinding`. Rename your initial `Form1.vb` file to the more fitting `MainForm.vb` using the Solution Explorer. Next, use the Visual Studio 2010 Toolbox to drag a `DataGridView` control (renamed to `carInventoryGridView` using the `(Name)` property of the Properties window) onto the designer surface. Notice that when you do this, you activate a context menu that allows you to connect to a physical data source. For the time being, ignore this aspect of the designer because you will be binding your `DataTable` object programmatically. Finally, add a descriptive `Label` to your designer for information purposes. Figure 22-5 shows one possible look-and-feel.

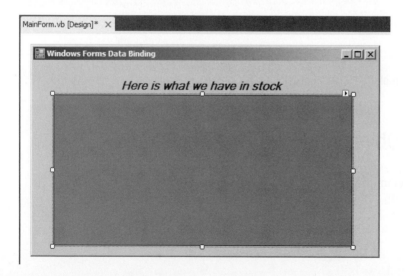

Figure 22-5. The initial GUI of your Windows Forms application

Hydrating a DataTable from a Generic List(Of T)

Similar to the previous SimpleDataSet example, the WindowsFormsDataBinding application will construct a `DataTable` that contains a set of `DataColumns` representing various columns and rows of data. This time, however, you will fill the rows using a generic `List(Of T)` member variable. First, insert a new VB 2010 class into your project (named `Car`), which you define as follows:

```
Public Class Car
     Public Property ID() As Integer
     Public Property PetName() As String
     Public Property Make() As String
     Public Property Color() As String
End Class
```

We're now going to add some code to the `MainForm` class. To do this, right-click MainForm in Solution Explorer, and then click View Code. Within the default constructor of your main form, populate a `List(Of T)` member variable (named `listCars`) with a set of new `Car` objects:

```
Public Class MainForm
    ' A collection of Car objects.
    Dim listCars As List(Of Car) = Nothing

    Public Sub New()
        InitializeComponent()

        ' Fill the list with some cars.
        listCars = New List(Of Car) From {
                New Car With {.ID = 100, .PetName = "Chucky", .Make = "BMW", ↵
                            .Color = "Green"},
                New Car With {.ID = 101, .PetName = "Tiny", .Make = "Yugo", ↵
                            .Color = "White"},
                New Car With {.ID = 102, .PetName = "Ami", .Make = "Jeep", .Color = "Tan"},
                New Car With {.ID = 103, .PetName = "Pain Inducer", .Make = "Caravan",↵
                            .Color = "Pink"},
                New Car With {.ID = 104, .PetName = "Fred", .Make = "BMW", ↵
                            .Color = "Green"},
                New Car With {.ID = 105, .PetName = "Sidd", .Make = "BMW", ↵
                            .Color = "Black"},
                New Car With {.ID = 106, .PetName = "Mel", .Make = "Firebird", ↵
                            .Color = "Red"},
                New Car With {.ID = 107, .PetName = "Sarah", .Make = "Colt", ↵
                            .Color = "Black"}}

    End Sub
End Class
```

Next, add a new member variable named **inventoryTable** of type **DataTable** to your **MainForm** class type:

```
Public Class MainForm
    ' A collection of Car objects.
    Private listCars As List(Of Car) = Nothing

    ' Inventory information
    Private inventoryTable As New DataTable()
    …
End Class
```

Now add a new helper method to your class named **CreateDataTable()** and call this method within the default constructor of the **MainForm** class:

```
Private Sub CreateDataTable()

    ' Create table schema.
    Dim carIDColumn As New DataColumn("ID", GetType(Integer))
    Dim carMakeColumn As New DataColumn("Make", GetType(String))
    Dim carColorColumn As New DataColumn("Color", GetType(String))
    Dim carPetNameColumn As New DataColumn("PetName", GetType(String))

    carPetNameColumn.Caption = "Pet Name"
    inventoryTable.Columns.AddRange(New DataColumn() _
            { carIDColumn, carMakeColumn, carColorColumn, carPetNameColumn })

    ' Iterate over the List(Of T) to make rows.
    For Each c As Car In listCars
        Dim newRow As DataRow = inventoryTable.NewRow()
        newRow("ID") = c.ID
        newRow("Make") = c.Make
        newRow("Color") = c.Color
        newRow("PetName") = c.PetName
        inventoryTable.Rows.Add(newRow)
    Next

    ' Bind the DataTable to the carInventoryGridView.
    carInventoryGridView.DataSource = inventoryTable
End Sub
```

The method implementation begins by creating the schema of the **DataTable** by creating four **DataColumn** objects (for the sake of simplicity, you don't need to bother autoincrementing the ID field or set it as a primary key). After you do this, you can add them to the column collection of the **DataTable** member variable. You map the row data from your **List(Of Car)** collection into the **DataTable** using a **For Each** iteration construct and the native ADO.NET object model.

However, notice that the final code statement within the CreateDataTable() method assigns the inventoryTable to the DataSource property of the DataGridView object. This single property is all you need to set to bind a DataTable to a Windows Forms DataGridView object. Under the hood, this GUI control reads the row and column collections internally, much like what happens with the PrintDataSet() method of the SimpleDataSet example. At this point, you should be able to run your application and see the DataTable within the DataGridView control, as shown in Figure 22-6.

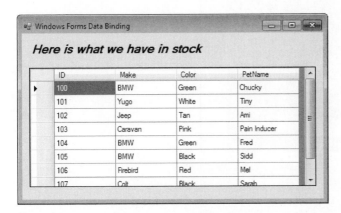

Figure 22-6. Binding a DataTable to a Windows Forms DataGridView

Deleting Rows from a DataTable

Now, assume you wish to update your graphical interface to allow the user to delete a row from the in-memory DataTable that is bound to the DataGridView. One approach is to call the Delete() method of the DataRow object that represents the row to terminate. In this case, you specify the index (or DataRow object) representing the row to remove. To allow the user to specify which row to delete, add a TextBox (named txtCarToRemove) and a Button control (named btnRemoveCar) to the current designer. Figure 22-7 shows one possible UI update (note this example wraps the two controls in a GroupBox control, illustrating how they are related).

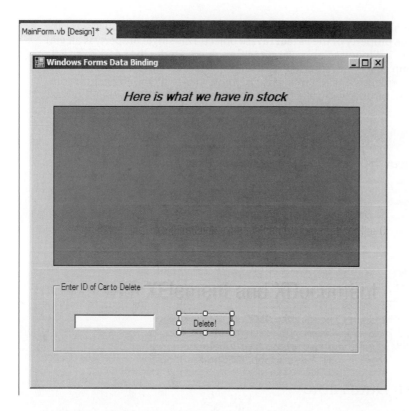

Figure 22-7. Updating the UI to enable removal of rows from the underlying DataTable

The following logic behind the new **Button**'s **Click** event handler removes the user-specified row, based on the ID of a car, from your in-memory **DataTable**. The **Select()** method of the **DataTable** class allows you to specify a search criteria, which is modeled after normal SQL syntax. The return value is an array of **DataRow** objects that matches the search criteria:

```
' Remove this row from the DataRowCollection.
Private Sub btnRemoveCar_Click(ByVal sender As Object, ByVal e As EventArgs)
        Handles btnRemoveCar.Click
    Try
        ' Find the correct row to delete.
        Dim rowToDelete() As DataRow = inventoryTable.Select _
                    (String.Format("ID={0}", Integer.Parse(txtCarToRemove.Text)))

        ' Delete it!
        rowToDelete(0).Delete()
        inventoryTable.AcceptChanges()
```

```
    Catch ex As Exception
        MessageBox.Show(ex.Message)
    End Try
End Sub
```

You should now be able to run your application and specify a car ID to delete from the DataTable. As you remove DataRow objects from the DataTable, you will notice that the grid's UI is updated immediately; this occurs because it is bound to the state of the DataTable object.

Selecting Rows Based on Filter Criteria

Many data-centric applications require the need to view a small subset of a DataTable's data, as specified by some sort of filtering criteria. For example, assume you wish to see only a certain make of automobile from the in-memory DataTable (e.g., only BMWs). You've already seen how the Select() method of the DataTable class allows you to find a row to delete; however you can also use this method to grab a subset of records for display purposes.

To see this in action, update your UI again, this time allowing users to specify a string that represents the make of the automobile they want to see (see Figure 22-8) using a new TextBox (named txtMakeToView) and a new Button (named btnDisplayMakes).

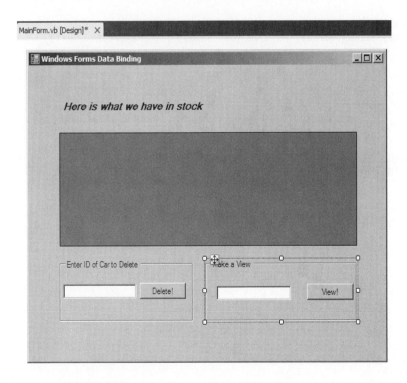

Figure 22-8. Updating the UI to enable row filtering

The Select() method has been overloaded a number of times to provide different selection semantics. At its most basic level, the parameter sent to Select() is a String that contains some conditional operation. To begin, observe the following logic for the Click event handler of your new button:

```
Private Sub btnDisplayMakes_Click(ByVal sender As Object, ByVal e As EventArgs)
        Handles btnDisplayMakes.Click
    ' Build a filter based on user input.
    Dim filterStr As String = String.Format("Make= '{0}'", txtMakeToView.Text)

    ' Find all rows matching the filter.
    Dim makes() As DataRow = inventoryTable.Select(filterStr)

    If makes.Length = 0 Then
        MessageBox.Show("Sorry, no cars...", "Selection error!")
    Else
        Dim strMake As String = ""
        For i As Integer = 0 To makes.Length - 1
        ' From the current row, get the PetName value.
        strMake &= makes(i)("PetName") & vbLf
        Next

        ' Show the names of call cars matching the specified Make.
        MessageBox.Show(strMake, String.Format("We have {0}s named:", txtMakeToView.Text))
    End If
End Sub
```

Here, you begin by building a simple filter based on the value in the associated **TextBox**. If you specify BMW, your filter looks like this:

```
Make = 'BMW'
```

When you send this filter to the Select() method, you get back an array of **DataRow** types that represent each row that matches the filter (see Figure 22-9).

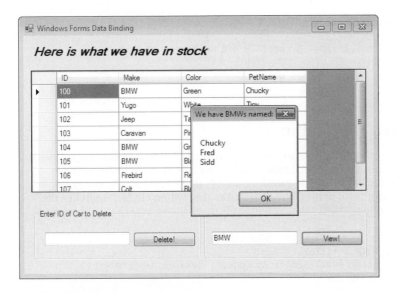

Figure 22-9. *Displaying filtered data*

Again, the filtering logic is based on standard SQL syntax. For example, assume you wish to obtain the results of the previous Select() invocation alphabetically, based on the pet name. In terms of SQL, this translates into a sort based on the PetName column. Fortunately, the Select() method has been overloaded to send in a sort criterion:

```
' Sort by PetName.
makes = inventoryTable.Select(filterStr, "PetName")
```

Call Select() as seen here if you want the results in descending order:

```
' Return results in descending order.
makes = inventoryTable.Select(filterStr, "PetName DESC")
```

In general, the sort string contains the column name, followed by ASC (ascending, which is the default) or DESC (descending). If necessary, you can separate multiple columns by commas. Finally, understand that a filter string can be composed of any number of relational operators. For example, assume you want to find all cars with an ID greater than 5. This helper method lets you accomplish that:

```
Private Sub ShowCarsWithIdGreaterThanFive()

    ' Now show the pet names of all cars with ID greater than 5.
    Dim properIDs() As DataRow
    Dim newFilterStr As String = "ID > 5"
    properIDs = inventoryTable.Select(newFilterStr)
    Dim strIDs As String = Nothing
```

```
    For i As Integer = 0 To properIDs.Length - 1
      Dim temp As DataRow = properIDs(i)
      strIDs &= temp("PetName") & " is ID " & temp("ID") & vbLf
    Next
    MessageBox.Show(strIDs, "Pet names of cars where ID > 5")
End Sub
```

Updating Rows Within a DataTable

The final aspect of the DataTable you should be aware of is the process of updating an existing row with new values. One approach is to first obtain the row(s) that match a given filter criterion using the Select() method. Once you obtain the DataRow(s) in question, modify them accordingly. For example, assume you have a new Button on your form named btnChangeMakes that (when clicked) searches the DataTable for all rows where Make is equal to BMW. Once you identify these items, you change the Make from BMW to Yugo:

```
' Find the rows you want to edit with a filter.
    Private Sub btnChangeMakes_Click(ByVal sender As Object, ByVal e As EventArgs)
            Handles btnChangeMakes.Click
      ' Confirm selection.
    If DialogResult.Yes = MessageBox.Show("Are you sure?? BMWs are much nicer than Yugos!",
                        "Please Confirm!", MessageBoxButtons.YesNo) Then
      ' Build a filter.
    Dim filterStr As String = "Make='BMW'"
    Dim strMake As String = String.Empty

      ' Find all rows matching the filter.
    Dim makes() As DataRow = inventoryTable.Select(filterStr)

      ' Change all Beemers to Yugos!
    For i As Integer = 0 To makes.Length - 1
      makes(i)("Make") = "Yugo"
    Next
    End If
End Sub
```

Working with the DataView Type

A *view object* is an alternative representation of a table (or set of tables). For example, you can use Microsoft SQL Server to create a view for your Inventory table that returns a new table containing automobiles only of a given color. In ADO.NET, the DataView type allows you to extract a subset of data programmatically from the DataTable into a stand-alone object.

One great advantage of holding multiple views of the same table is that you can bind these views to various GUI widgets (such as the DataGridView). For example, one DataGridView might be bound to a DataView showing all autos in the Inventory, while another might be configured to display only green automobiles.

To see this in action, update the current UI with an additional DataGridView type named dataGridYugosView and a descriptive Label. Next, define a member variable named yugosOnlyView of type DataView:

```
Public Class MainForm
    ' View of the DataTable.
    Private yugosOnlyView As DataView
    ...
End Class
```

Now create a new helper method named CreateDataView() and call this method within the form's default constructor immediately after the DataTable has been fully constructed, as shown here:

```
Public Sub New()
    ...
    ' Make a data table.
    CreateDataTable()

    ' Make a view.
    CreateDataView()
End Sub
```

Here is the implementation of this new helper method. Notice that the constructor of each DataView has been passed the DataTable that you will use to build the custom set of data rows:

```
Private Sub CreateDataView()
    ' Set the table that is used to construct this view.
    yugosOnlyView = New DataView(inventoryTable)

    ' Now configure the views using a filter.
    yugosOnlyView.RowFilter = "Make = 'Yugo'"

    ' Bind to the new grid.
    dataGridYugosView.DataSource = yugosOnlyView
End Sub
```

As you can see, the DataView class supports a property named RowFilter, which contains the String representing the filtering criteria used to extract matching rows. Once you establish your view, set the grid's DataSource property accordingly. Figure 22-10 shows the completed Windows Forms data-binding application in action.

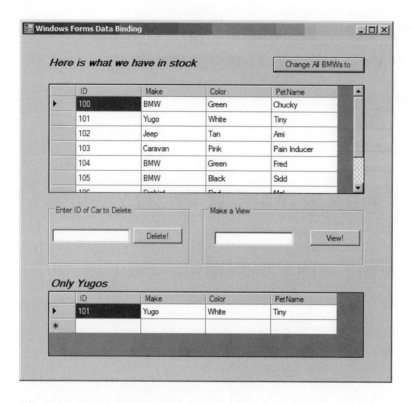

Figure 22-10. Displaying a unique view of your data

■ **Source Code** You can find the WindowsFormsDataBinding project under the Chapter 22 subdirectory.

Working with Data Adapters

Now that you understand the ins-and-outs of manipulating ADO.NET DataSets manually, it's time to turn your attention to the topic of *data adapter objects*. A data adapter is a class used to fill a DataSet with DataTable objects; this class can also send modified DataTables back to the database for processing. Table 22-8 documents the core members of the DbDataAdapter base class, the common parent to every data adapter object (e.g., SqlDataAdapter and OdbcDataAdapter).

Table 22-8. Core Members of the DbDataAdapter Class

Members	Meaning in Life
Fill()	Executes a SQL SELECT command (as specified by the SelectCommand property) to query the database for data and loads the data into a DataTable.
SelectCommand InsertCommand UpdateCommand DeleteCommand	Establishes the SQL commands that you will issue to the data store when the Fill() and Update() methods are called.
Update()	Executes SQL INSERT, UPDATE, and DELETE commands (as specified by the InsertCommand, UpdateCommand, and DeleteCommand properties) to persist DataTable changes to the database.

Notice that a data adapter defines four properties: SelectCommand, InsertCommand, UpdateCommand, and DeleteCommand. When you create the data adapter object for your particular data provider (e.g., SqlDataAdapter), you can pass in a String that represents the command text used by the SelectCommand's command object.

Assuming each of the four command objects has been properly configured, you can then call the Fill() method to obtain a DataSet (or a single DataTable, if you wish). To do so, you have the data adapter execute the SQL SELECT statement specified by the SelectCommand property.

Similarly, if you wish to persist a modified DataSet (or DataTable) object back to the database, you can call the Update() method, which will use any of the remaining command objects, based on the state of each row in the DataTable (you'll learn more about this in a bit).

One of the strangest aspects of working with a data adapter object is the fact that you are never required to open or close a connection to the database. Rather, the underlying connection to the database is managed on your behalf. However, you will still need to supply the data adapter with a valid connection object or a connection string (which you will use to build a connection object internally) to inform the data adapter exactly which database you wish to communicate with.

■ **Note** A data adapter is agnostic by nature. You can plug in different connection objects and command objects on the fly and fetch data from a diverse variety of databases. For example, a single DataSet could contain table data obtained from SQL server, Oracle, and MySQL database providers.

A Simple Data Adapter Example

The next step is to add new functionality to the data access library assembly (AutoLotDAL.dll) you created in Chapter 21. Begin by creating a simple example that fills a DataSet with a single table using an ADO.NET data adapter object.

Create a new Console Application named FillDataSetUsingSqlDataAdapter and import the System.Data.SqlClient namespace (remember, the System.Data namespace is imported automatically in a VB 2010 project) into your initial VB 2010 code file. Now update your Main() method as follows (you might need to change the connection string, based on how you created the AutoLot database in the previous chapter):

```
Sub Main()
      Console.WriteLine("***** Fun with Data Adapters *****" & vbLf)

      ' Hard-coded connection string.
      Dim cnStr As String = "Integrated Security = SSPI;Initial Catalog=AutoLot;"
                & "Data Source=(local)\SQLEXPRESS"

      ' Caller creates the DataSet object.
      Dim ds As New DataSet("AutoLot")

      ' Inform adapter of the Select command text and connection string.
      Dim dAdapt As New SqlDataAdapter("Select * From Inventory", cnStr)

      ' Fill our DataSet with a new table, named Inventory.
      dAdapt.Fill(ds, "Inventory")

      ' Display contents of DataSet.
      PrintDataSet(ds)
      Console.ReadLine()
End Sub
```

Notice that you construct the data adapter by specifying a string literal that will map to the SQL Select statement. You will use this value to build a command object internally, which you can obtain later using the SelectCommand property.

Next, notice that it is the job of the caller to create an instance of the DataSet type, which is passed into the Fill() method. Optionally, you can pass the Fill() method as a second argument a String name that you use to set the TableName property of the new DataTable (if you do not specify a table name, the data adapter will simply name the table, Table). In most cases, the name you assign a DataTable will be identical to the name of the physical table in the relational database; however, this is not required.

■ **Note** The Fill() method returns an integer that represents the number of rows returned by the SQL query.

Finally, notice that you do not explicitly open or close the connection to the database anywhere in the Main() method. You preprogram the Fill() method of a given data adapter to open and then close the underlying connection before returning from the Fill() method. Therefore, when you pass the DataSet to the PrintDataSet() method (implemented earlier in this chapter), you are operating on a local copy of disconnected data, incurring no round-trips to fetch the data.

Mapping Database Names to Friendly Names

As mentioned previously, database administrators tend to create table and column names that are less than friendly to end users (e.g., au_id, au_fname, and au_lname). The good news is that data adapter objects maintain an internal strongly typed collection (named DataTableMappingCollection) of System.Data.Common.DataTableMapping objects. You can access this collection using the TableMappings property of your data adapter object.

If you so choose, you can manipulate this collection to inform a DataTable which *display names* it should use when asked to print its contents. For example, assume that you wish to map the table name Inventory to Current Inventory for display purposes. For example, assume you wish to display the CarID column name as Car ID (note the extra space) and the PetName column name as Name of Car. To do so, add the following code before calling the Fill() method of your data adapter object (be sure to import the System.Data.Common namespace to gain the definition of the DataTableMapping type):

```
Sub Main()
    ...
    ' Now map DB column names to user-friendly names.
    Dim custMap As DataTableMapping = dAdapt.TableMappings.Add("Inventory", ↵
                                  "Current Inventory")
    custMap.ColumnMappings.Add("CarID", "Car ID")
    custMap.ColumnMappings.Add("PetName", "Name of Car")
    dAdapt.Fill(ds, "Inventory")
    ...
End Sub
```

If you were to run this program again, you would find that the PrintDataSet() method now displays the friendly names of the DataTable and DataRow objects, rather than the names established by the database schema:

```
***** Fun with Data Adapters *****


DataSet is named: AutoLot


=> Current Inventory Table:

Car ID  Make    Color   Name of Car

----------------------------------

83      Ford    Rust    Rusty

107     Ford    Red     Snake

678     Yugo    Green   Clunker
```

904	VW	Black	Hank
1000	BMW	Black	Bimmer
1001	BMW	Tan	Daisy
1992	Saab	Pink	Pinkey
2003	Yugo	Rust	Mel

■ **Source Code** You can find the `FillDataSetUsingSqlDataAdapter` project under the Chapter 22 subdirectory.

Adding Disconnection Functionality to AutoLotDAL.dll

To illustrate the process of using a data adapter to push changes in a `DataTable` back to the database for processing, you will now update the `AutoLotDAL.dll` assembly created back in Chapter 21 to include a new namespace (named `AutoLotDisconnectedLayer`). This namespace contains a new class, `InventoryDALDisLayer`, that uses a data adapter to interact with a `DataTable`.

A good way to begin is by copying the entire `AutoLotDAL` project folder you created in Chapter 21 to a new location on your hard drive and rename this folder to `AutoLot (Version Two)`. Now use Visual Studio 2010 to activate the File ➤ Open Project/Solution... menu option, and then open the `AutoLotDAL.sln` file in your `AutoLot (Version Two)` folder.

Defining the Initial Class Type

Insert a new class named `InventoryDALDisLayer` using the Project ➤ Add Class menu option. Next, ensure you have a `public` class type in your new code file. Wrap the `InventoryDALDisLayer` class in a namespace named `AutoLotDisconnectedLayer` and import the `System.Data.SqlClient` namespace.

Unlike the connection-centric `InventoryDAL` type, this new class doesn't need to provide custom open/close methods because the data adapter handles the details automatically.

Begin by adding a custom constructor that sets a Private `String` variable representing the connection string. Also, define a Private `SqlDataAdapter` member variable, which you configure by calling a (yet to be created) helper method called `ConfigureAdapter()`, which takes a `SqlDataAdapter` parameter by reference:

```
Namespace AutoLotDisconnectedLayer
    Public Class InventoryDALDisLayer
            ' Field data.
            Private cnString As String = String.Empty
            Private dAdapt As SqlDataAdapter = Nothing
```

```
        Public Sub New(ByVal connectionString As String)
                cnString = connectionString

                'Configure the SqlDataAdapter.
                ConfigureAdapter(dAdapt)
        End Sub
    End Class
End Namespace
```

Configuring the Data Adapter Using the SqlCommandBuilder

When you use a data adapter to modify tables in a DataSet, the first order of business is to assign the UpdateCommand, DeleteCommand, and InsertCommand properties with valid command objects (until you do so, these properties return Nothing references).

Configuring the command objects manually for the InsertCommand, UpdateCommand, and DeleteCommand properties can entail a significant amount of code, especially if you use parameterized queries. Recall from Chapter 21 that a parameterized query allows you to build a SQL statement using a set of parameter objects. Thus, if you were to take the long road, you could implement ConfigureAdapter() to create three new SqlCommand objects manually, each of which contains a set of SqlParameter objects. At this point, you could set each object to the UpdateCommand, DeleteCommand, and InsertCommand properties of the adapter.

Visual Studio 2010 provides several designer tools to take care of this mundane and tedious code on your behalf. These designers differ a bit based on which API you use (e.g., Windows Forms, WPF, or ASP.NET), but their overall functionality is similar. You'll see examples of using these designers throughout this book, including some Windows Forms designers later in this chapter.

You won't need to author the numerous code statements to configure a data adapter fully at this time; instead, you can take a massive shortcut by implementing ConfigureAdapter() like this:

```
Private Sub ConfigureAdapter(ByRef dAdapt As SqlDataAdapter)
    ' Create the adapter and set up the SelectCommand.
    dAdapt = New SqlDataAdapter("Select * From Inventory", cnString)

    ' Obtain the remaining Command objects dynamically at runtime
    ' using the SqlCommandBuilder.
    Dim builder As New SqlCommandBuilder(dAdapt)
End Sub
```

To simplify the construction of data adapter objects, each of the Microsoft-supplied ADO.NET data providers provides a *command builder* type. The SqlCommandBuilder automatically generates the values contained within the SqlDataAdapter's InsertCommand, UpdateCommand, and DeleteCommand properties, based on the initial SelectCommand. The benefit here is that you do not need to build all the SqlCommand and SqlParameter types by hand.

Here's an obvious question at this point: how is a command builder able to build these SQL command objects on the fly? The short answer is metadata. When you call the Update() method of a data adapter at runtime, the related command builder will read the database's schema data to autogenerate the underlying insert, delete, and update command objects.

Obviously, doing so requires additional roundtrips to the remote database; this means it will hurt performance if you use the SqlCommandBuilder numerous times in a single application. Here, you minimize the negative effect by calling your ConfigureAdapter() method at the time the

InventoryDALDisLayer object is constructed, retaining the configured SqlDataAdapter for use throughout the object's lifetime.

In the previous code snippet, you did not use the command builder object (SqlCommandBuilder, in this case) beyond passing in the data adapter object as a constructor parameter. As odd as this might seem, this is all you must do (at a minimum). Under the hood, this type configures the data adapter with the remaining command objects.

While you might love the idea of getting something for nothing, you should understand that command builders come with some critical restrictions. Specifically, a command builder is only able to autogenerate SQL commands for use by a data adapter if all of the following conditions are true:

- The SQL Select command interacts with only a single table (e.g., no joins).

- The single table has been attributed with a primary key.

- The table must have a column or columns representing the primary key that you include in your SQL Select statement.

Based on the way you constructed your AutoLot database, these restrictions pose no problem. However, in a more industrial-strength database, you will need to consider whether this type is at all useful (if not, remember that Visual Studio 2010 will autogenerate a good deal of the required code using various database designer tools, as you will see later).

Implementing GetAllInventory()

Now that your data adapter is ready to go, the first method of your new class type will use the Fill() method of the SqlDataAdapter object to fetch a DataTable representing all records in the Inventory table of the AutoLot database:

```
Public Function GetAllInventory() As DataTable
    Dim inv As New DataTable("Inventory")
    dAdapt.Fill(inv)
    Return inv
End Function
```

Implementing UpdateInventory()

The UpdateInventory() method is simple:

```
Public Sub UpdateInventory(ByVal modifiedTable As DataTable)
    dAdapt.Update(modifiedTable)
End Sub
```

Here, the data adapter object examines the RowState value of each row of the incoming DataTable. Based on this value (e.g., RowState.Added, RowState.Deleted, or RowState.Modified), the correct command object is leveraged behind the scenes.

Setting Your Version Number

Great! At this point, the logic of the second version of your data access library is complete. You are not required to do so, but set the version number of this library to 2.0.0.0, just for good housekeeping. As described in Chapter 14, you can change the version of a .NET assembly by double-clicking your project's MyProject node in Solution Explorer, and then clicking the Assembly Information... button located in the Application tab. In the resulting dialog box, set the Major number of the Assembly Version to the value of **2** (see Chapter 14 for more details). Once you do this, recompile your application to update the assembly manifest.

■ **Source Code** You can find the AutoLotDAL (Version 2) project under the Chapter 22 subdirectory.

Testing the Disconnected Functionality

At this point, you can build a front end to test your new InventoryDALDisLayer class. Once again, you will use the Windows Forms API to display your data on a graphical user interface. Create a new Windows Forms application named InventoryDALDisconnectedGUI and change your initial **Form1.vb** file to **MainForm.vb** using the Solution Explorer. Once you create the project, set a reference to your updated **AutoLotDAL.dll** assembly (be sure you pick version 2.0.0.0!) and import the following namespace:

```
Imports AutoLotDisconnectedLayer
```

The design of the form consists of a single Label, DataGridView (named inventoryGrid), and Button control (named btnUpdateInventory), which you configure to handle the Click event. Here is the definition of the form:

```
Public Class MainForm
    Private dal As InventoryDALDisLayer = Nothing

    Public Sub New()
      InitializeComponent()

      Dim cnStr As String = "Data Source=(local)\SQLEXPRESS;Initial Catalog=AutoLot;" _
                  & "Integrated Security=True;Pooling=False"

      ' Create our data access object.
      dal = New InventoryDALDisLayer(cnStr)

      ' Fill up our grid!
      inventoryGrid.DataSource = dal.GetAllInventory()
    End Sub

    Private Sub btnUpdateInventory_Click(ByVal sender As Object, ByVal e As EventArgs)
        Handles btnUpdateInventory.Click
      ' Get modified data from the grid.
      Dim changedDT As DataTable = CType(inventoryGrid.DataSource, DataTable)
```

```
        Try
                ' Commit our changes.
                dal.UpdateInventory(changedDT)
        Catch ex As Exception
                MessageBox.Show(ex.Message)
        End Try
    End Sub
End Class
```

Once you create the `InventoryDALDisLayer` object, you can bind the `DataTable` returned from `GetAllInventory()` to the `DataGridView` object. When the user clicks the Update button, you extract the modified `DataTable` from the grid (with the `DataSource` property) and pass it into your `UpdateInventory()` method.

That's it! After you run this application, add a set of new rows to the grid and update/delete a few others. Assuming you click the `Button` control, you will see your changes have persisted into the `AutoLot` database.

■ **Source Code** You can find the updated InventoryDALDisconnectedGUI project under the Chapter 22 subdirectory.

Multitabled DataSet Objects and Data Relationships

So far, all of this chapter's examples have operated on a single `DataTable` object. However, the power of the disconnected layer shines through when a `DataSet` object contains numerous interrelated `DataTable`s. In this case, you can define any number of `DataRelation` objects in the `DataSet`'s `DataRelation` collection to account for the interdependencies of the tables. The client tier can use these objects to navigate between the table data without incurring network roundtrips.

■ **Note** Rather than updating `AutoLotDAL.dll` to account for the `Customers` and `Orders` tables, this example isolates all of the data access logic within a new Windows Forms project. However, intermixing UI and data logic in a production-level application is not recommended. The final examples of this chapter leverage various database design tools to decouple the UI logic from the data logic code.

Begin this example by creating a new Windows Forms application named `MultitabledDataSetApp`. The GUI is simple enough. In Figure 22-11, you can see three `DataGridView` widgets (`dataGridViewInventory`, `dataGridViewCustomers`, and `dataGridViewOrders`) that hold the data retrieved from the `Inventory`, `Orders`, and `Customers` tables of the `AutoLot` database. In addition, the initial `Button` (named `btnUpdateDatabase`) submits any and all changes entered within the grids back to the database for processing using data adapter objects.

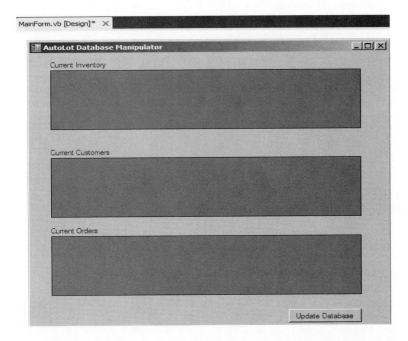

Figure 22-11. The initial UI will display data from each table of the AutoLot database

Prepping the Data Adapters

To keep the data access code as simple as possible, the MainForm will make use of command builder objects to autogenerate the SQL commands for each of the three SqlDataAdapters (one for each table). Here is the initial update to the Form-derived type (don't forget to import the System.Data.SqlClient namespace):

```
Public Class MainForm
    ' Form wide DataSet.
    Private autoLotDS As New DataSet("AutoLot")

    ' Make use of command builders to simplify data adapter configuration.
    Private sqlCBInventory As SqlCommandBuilder
    Private sqlCBCustomers As SqlCommandBuilder
    Private sqlCBOrders As SqlCommandBuilder

    ' Our data adapters (for each table).
    Private invTableAdapter As SqlDataAdapter
    Private custTableAdapter As SqlDataAdapter
    Private ordersTableAdapter As SqlDataAdapter
```

```
        ' Form wide connection string.
        Private cnStr As String = String.Empty
            …
End Class
```

The constructor does the grunt work of creating your data-centric member variables and filling the DataSet. This example assumes you have authored an App.config file that contains the correct connection string data (and that you have referenced System.Configuration.dll and imported the System.Configuration namespace), as in this example:

```
<?xml version="1.0" encoding="utf-8" ?>
<configuration>
  <connectionStrings>
    <add name ="AutoLotSqlProvider"  connectionString =
  "Data Source=(local)\SQLEXPRESS;Integrated Security=SSPI;Initial Catalog=AutoLot"/>
  </connectionStrings>
    …
</configuration>
```

Also note that you include a call to a Private helper method, BuildTableRelationship():

```
Public Sub New()
    InitializeComponent()

    ' Get connection string from *.config file.
    cnStr = ConfigurationManager.ConnectionStrings("AutoLotSqlProvider").ConnectionString

    ' Create adapters.
    invTableAdapter = New SqlDataAdapter("Select * from Inventory", cnStr)
    custTableAdapter = New SqlDataAdapter("Select * from Customers", cnStr)
    ordersTableAdapter = New SqlDataAdapter("Select * from Orders", cnStr)

    ' Autogenerate commands.
    sqlCBInventory = New SqlCommandBuilder(invTableAdapter)
    sqlCBOrders = New SqlCommandBuilder(ordersTableAdapter)
    sqlCBCustomers = New SqlCommandBuilder(custTableAdapter)

    ' Fill tables in DS.
    invTableAdapter.Fill(autoLotDS, "Inventory")
    custTableAdapter.Fill(autoLotDS, "Customers")
    ordersTableAdapter.Fill(autoLotDS, "Orders")

    ' Build relations between tables.
    BuildTableRelationship()

    ' Bind to grids
    dataGridViewInventory.DataSource = autoLotDS.Tables("Inventory")
    dataGridViewCustomers.DataSource = autoLotDS.Tables("Customers")
    dataGridViewOrders.DataSource = autoLotDS.Tables("Orders")
End Sub
```

Building the Table Relationships

The BuildTableRelationship() helper method does the grunt work to add two DataRelation objects into the autoLotDS object. Recall from Chapter 21 that the AutoLot database expresses a number of parent/child relationships, which you can account for with the following code:

```
Private Sub BuildTableRelationship()

    ' Create CustomerOrder data relation object.
    Dim dr As New DataRelation("CustomerOrder",
    autoLotDS.Tables("Customers").Columns("CustID"),

    autoLotDS.Tables("Orders").Columns("CustID"))
    autoLotDS.Relations.Add(dr)

    ' Create InventoryOrder data relation object.
    dr = New DataRelation("InventoryOrder", autoLotDS.Tables("Inventory").Columns("CarID"),
    autoLotDS.Tables("Orders").Columns("CarID"))
    autoLotDS.Relations.Add(dr)

End Sub
```

Note that you establish a friendly string moniker with the first parameter when you create a DataRelation object (you'll see the usefulness of doing so in just a minute). You also establish the keys used to build the relationship itself. Notice that the parent table (the second constructor parameter) is specified before the child table (the third constructor parameter).

Updating the Database Tables

Now that the DataSet has been filled with data from the data source, you can manipulate each DataTable locally. To do so, run the application and insert, update, or delete values from any of the three DataGridViews. When you are ready to submit the data back for processing, click the Update button. You should find it easy to follow along with the code behind the related Click event at this point:

```
Private Sub btnUpdateDatabase_Click(ByVal sender As Object, ByVal e As EventArgs)
        Handles btnUpdateDatabase.Click
    Try
        invTableAdapter.Update(autoLotDS, "Inventory")
        custTableAdapter.Update(autoLotDS, "Customers")
        ordersTableAdapter.Update(autoLotDS, "Orders")
    Catch ex As Exception
        MessageBox.Show(ex.Message)
    End Try
End Sub
```

Now run your application and perform various updates. When you rerun the application, you should find that your grids are populated with the recent changes.

Navigating Between Related Tables

Now let's look at how a DataRelation allows you to move between related tables programmatically. Extend your UI to include a new Button (named btnGetOrderInfo), a related TextBox (named txtCustID), and a descriptive Label (you can group these controls within a GroupBox for more visual appeal). Figure 22-12 shows one possible UI of the application.

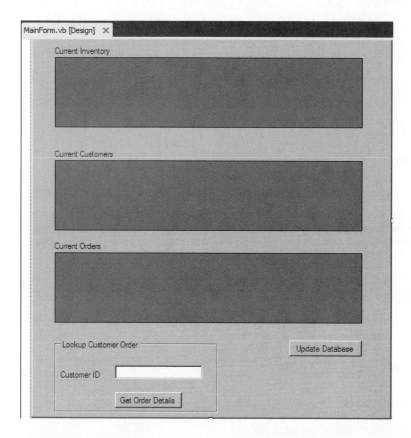

Figure 22-12. The updated UI allows the user to look up customer order information

This updated UI lets the user enter the ID of a customer and retrieve all the relevant information about that customer's order (e.g., name, order ID, and car order). This information will be formatted into a String type that is eventually displayed within a message box. Consider the code behind the new Button's Click event handler:

```vb
Private Sub btnGetOrderInfo_Click(ByVal sender As Object, ByVal e As System.EventArgs)
                                        Handles btnGetOrderInfo.Click
    Dim strOrderInfo As String = String.Empty
    Dim drsCust() As DataRow = Nothing
    Dim drsOrder() As DataRow = Nothing

    ' Get the customer ID in the text box.
Dim custID As Integer = Integer.Parse(Me.txtCustID.Text)

    ' Now based on custID, get the correct row in Customers table.
    drsCust = autoLotDS.Tables("Customers").Select(String.Format("CustID = {0}", custID))
    strOrderInfo &= String.Format("Customer {0}: {1} {2}" & vbLf,
                            drsCust(0)("CustID").ToString(),
                            drsCust(0)("FirstName").ToString(),
                            drsCust(0)("LastName").ToString())

    ' Navigate from Customers table to Orders table.
    drsOrder = drsCust(0).GetChildRows(autoLotDS.Relations("CustomerOrder"))

    ' Loop through all orders for this customer.
    For Each order As DataRow In drsOrder
        strOrderInfo &= String.Format("----" & vbLf & "Order Number: {0}" & vbLf,
    order("OrderID"))

        ' Get the car referenced by this order.
        Dim drsInv() As DataRow = order.GetParentRows(autoLotDS.Relations("InventoryOrder"))

        ' Get info for (SINGLE) car info for this order.
        Dim car As DataRow = drsInv(0)
        strOrderInfo &= String.Format("Make: {0}" & vbLf, car("Make"))
        strOrderInfo &= String.Format("Color: {0}" & vbLf, car("Color"))
        strOrderInfo &= String.Format("Pet Name: {0}" & vbLf, car("PetName"))
Next

MessageBox.Show(strOrderInfo, "Order Details")
End Sub
```

Figure 22-13 shows one possible output when specifying a customer ID with the value of 3 (this is Steve Hagen in my copy of the AutoLot database, who currently has two orders pending).

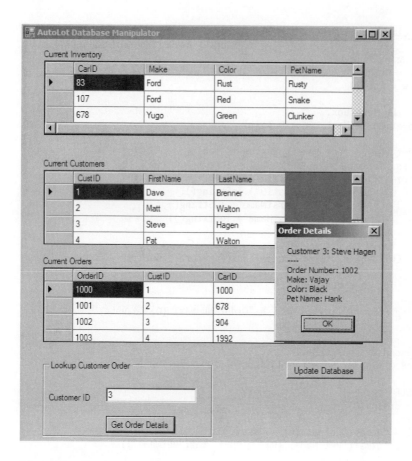

Figure 22-13. Navigating data relations

This last example should probably convince you of the usefulness of the **DataSet** class. Given that a **DataSet** is completely disconnected from the underlying data source, you can work with an in-memory copy of data and navigate around each table to make any necessary updates, deletes, or inserts without incurring any roundtrips to the database. Once you finish this, you can submit your changes to the data store for processing. The end result is a scalable and robust application.

■ **Source Code** You can find the `MultitabledDataSetApp` project under the Chapter 22 subdirectory.

The Windows Forms Database Designer Tools

All of the examples thus far have involved a fair amount of elbow grease in the sense that you had to author all data access logic by hand. While you did offload a good amount of this code to a .NET code library (`AutoLotDAL.dll`) for reuse in later chapters of the book, you still had to create the various objects of your data provider manually before interacting with the relational database. The next task in this chapter is to look at how you use various Windows Forms database designer tools, which can produce a good deal of data access code on your behalf.

■ **Note** Windows Presentation Foundation and ASP.NET web projects have similar database designer tools; you'll look at some of these later in this chapter.

One way you can use these integrated tools is to use the designers supported by the Windows Forms `DataGridView` control. The problem with this approach is that the database designer tools will embed all of the data access code directly into your GUI code base! Ideally, you want to isolate all of this designer generated code in a dedicated .NET code library, so you can easily reuse your database access logic across multiple projects.

Nevertheless, it might be helpful to begin with an examination of how you can use the `DataGridView` control to generate the required data access code, given that this approach does have some usefulness in small-scale projects and application prototypes. Next, you will learn how to isolate the same designer generated code into a third version of `AutoLot.dll`.

Visually Designing the DataGridView

The `DataGridView` control has an associated wizard that can generate data access code on your behalf. Begin by creating a brand-new Windows Forms application project named `DataGridViewDataDesigner`. Rename the initial form to `MainForm.vb` using the Solution Explorer, and then add an instance of the `DataGridView` control (named `inventoryDataGridView`) to your initial form. Note that an inline editor opens to the right-hand side of the control when you do this. From the Choose Data Source drop-down box, select the Add Project Data Source link (see Figure 22-14).

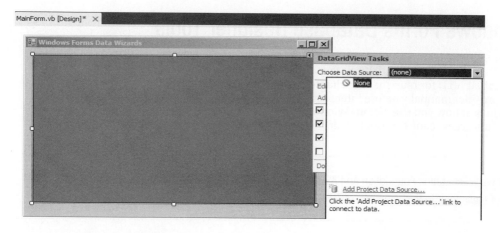

Figure 22-14. The DataGridView editor

This launches the Data Source Configuration Wizard. This tool guides you through a series of steps that allow you to select and configure a data source, which you can then bind to the `DataGridView`. The first step of the wizard asks you to identify the type of data source you wish to interact with. Select Database (see Figure 22-15) and click the Next button.

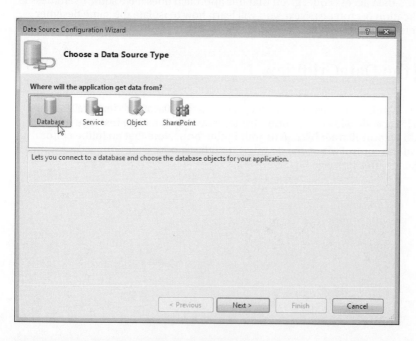

Figure 22-15. Selecting the type of data source

The next step (which will differ slightly based on your selection in step 1) asks whether you wish to use the DataSet database model or the Entity data model. Be sure you pick the DataSet database model (see Figure 22-16) because you have not yet looked at the Entity Framework (you'll learn more about this in the next chapter).

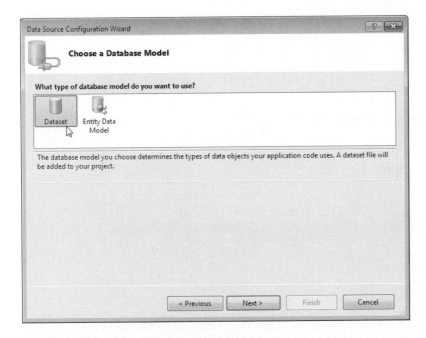

Figure 22-16. Choosing the database model

The next step allows you to configure your database connection. If you have a database currently added to Server Explorer, you should find it listed automatically in the dropdown list. If this is not the case (or if you ever need to connect to a database you have not previously added to Server Explorer), click the New Connection button. Figure 22-17 shows the result of selecting the local instance of AutoLot (notice that this tool will also generate the required connection string).

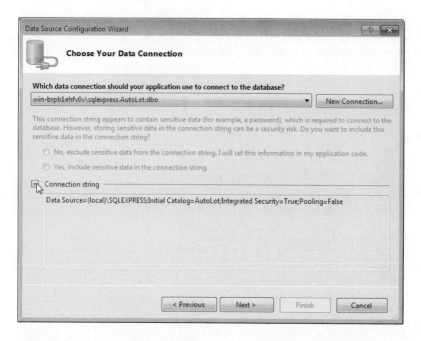

Figure 22-17. Choosing the database

After clicking on the Next button, the wizard will show you another screen asking, "Do you want to save the connection string?" Select the "Yes" option and accept the default name, and then click Next.

In the wizard's final step, you select the database objects that will be accounted for by the autogenerated DataSet and related data adapters. While you could select each of the data objects of the AutoLot database, here you concern yourself only with the Inventory table. Given this, change the suggested name of the DataSet to InventoryDataSet (see Figure 22-18), check the Inventory table, and click the Finish button.

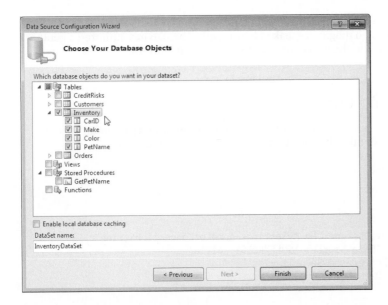

Figure 22-18. Selecting the Inventory table

Once you do this, you will see that the visual designer has been updated in many ways. The most noticeable change is the fact that the `DataGridView` displays the schema of the Inventory table, as illustrated by the column headers. Also, you will see three components on the bottom of the form designer (in a region dubbed the *component tray*): a `DataSet` component, a `BindingSource` component, and a `TableAdapter` component (see Figure 22-19).

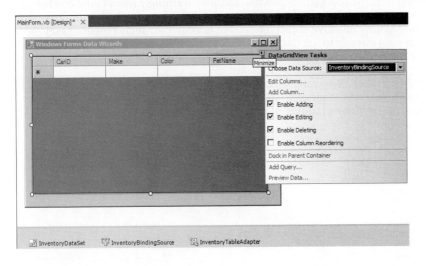

Figure 22-19. Your Windows Forms project, after running the Data Source Configuration Wizard

At this point, you can run your application, and lo and behold, the grid is filled with the records of the Inventory table! Of course, there is no magic to speak of in this case. The IDE has authored a good amount of code on your behalf and set up the grid control to use it. Let's dig into some of this autogenerated code.

The Generated app.config File

If you examine your Solution Explorer, you will find your project now contains an `app.config` file that contains a `<connectionStrings>` element that has been given a somewhat peculiar name:

```
<?xml version="1.0" encoding="utf-8" ?>
<configuration>
    <configSections>
    </configSections>
    <connectionStrings>
        <add name="DataGridViewDataDesigner.My.MySettings.AutoLotConnectionString"
                connectionString="Data Source=.\SQLEXPRESS;Initial
                Catalog=AutoLot;Integrated Security=True"
            providerName="System.Data.SqlClient" />
    </connectionStrings>
    ..,
</configuration>
```

The autogenerated data adapter object (which you will learn more about momentarily) uses the lengthy value, `"DataGridViewDataDesigner.My.MySettings.AutoLotConnectionString"`.

Examining the Strongly Typed DataSet

In addition to your configuration file, the IDE generates what is termed a *strongly typed DataSet*. This term describes a custom class that extends `DataSet` and exposes a number of members that allow you to interact with the database using a more intuitive object model. For example, strongly typed `DataSet` objects contain properties that map directly to the database tables names. Thus, you can use the `Inventory` property to nab the rows and columns directly, rather than having to drill into the collection of tables using the `Tables` property.

If you insert a new class diagram file into your project (by selecting the project icon in Solution Explorer and clicking the View Class Diagram button), you'll notice that the wizard has created a class named `InventoryDataSet`. This class defines a handful of members, the most important of which is a property named `Inventory` (see Figure 22-20).

Figure 22-20. The Data Source Configuration Wizard created a strongly typed DataSet

If you double-click the `InventoryDataSet.xsd` file within Solution Explorer, you will load the Visual Studio 2010 Dataset Designer (you'll learn more details about this designer momentarily). If you right-click anywhere within this designer and select the View Code option, you will notice a fairly empty partial class definition:

```
Partial Class InventoryDataSet
End Class
```

If necessary, you can add custom members to this partial class definition; however, the real action takes place within the designer-maintained file, `InventoryDataSet.Designer.vb` (to see this file in Solution Explorer, click the Show All Files icon). If you open this file using Solution Explorer, you will see that `InventoryDataSet` extends the `DataSet` parent class. Consider the following partial code, with comments added for clarity:

```
' This is all designer-generated code!
Partial Public Class InventoryDataSet
    Inherits Global.System.Data.DataSet

    ' A member variable of type InventoryDataTable.
    Private tableInventory As InventoryDataTable

    ' Each constructor calls a helper method named InitClass().
    Public Sub New()

       …
       Me.InitClass
    End Sub


    ' InitClass() preps the DataSet and adds the InventoryDataTable
    ' to the Tables collection.
    Private Sub InitClass()
       Me.DataSetName = "InventoryDataSet"
       Me.Prefix = ""
```

```
        Me.Namespace = "http://tempuri.org/InventoryDataSet.xsd"
        Me.EnforceConstraints = true
        Me.SchemaSerializationMode = Global.System.Data.SchemaSerializationMode↵
                            .IncludeSchema
        Me.tableInventory = New InventoryDataTable()
        MyBase.Tables.Add(Me.tableInventory)
    End Sub


    ' The read-only Inventory property returns
    ' the InventoryDataTable member variable.
    Public ReadOnly Property Inventory() As InventoryDataTable
        Get
            Return Me.tableInventory
        End Get
    End Property
End Class
```

Notice that your strongly typed `DataSet` has a member variable that is a *strongly typed DataTable*; in this case, the class is named `InventoryDataTable`. The constructor of the strongly typed `DataSet` class makes a call to a private initialization method named `InitClass()`, which adds an instance of this strongly typed `DataTable` to the `Tables` collection of the `DataSet`. Last but not least, notice that the implementation of the `Inventory` property returns the `InventoryDataTable` member variable.

Examining the Strongly Typed DataTable

Now return to the class diagram file and open up the Nested Types node on the InventoryDataSet icon. Here you will see the strongly typed `DataTable` class named InventoryDataTable and a *strongly typed DataRow* class named InventoryRow.

The `InventoryDataTable` class (which is the same type as the member variable of the strongly typed `DataSet` you examined) defines a set of properties that are based on the column names of the physical `Inventory` table (`CarIDColumn`, `ColorColumn`, `MakeColumn`, and `PetNameColumn`), as well as a custom indexer and a `Count` property to obtain the current number of records.

More interestingly, this strongly typed `DataTable` class defines a set of methods that allow you to insert, locate, and delete rows within the table using strongly typed members (an attractive alternative to navigating the `Rows` and `Columns` indexers manually). For example, `AddInventoryRow()` lets you add a new record row to the table in memory, `FindByCarID()` lets you do a look up based on the primary key of the table, and `RemoveInventoryRow()` lets you remove a row from the strongly typed table (see Figure 22-21).

Figure 22-21. The strongly typed DataTable is nested in the strongly typed DataSet

Examining the Strongly Typed DataRow

The strongly typed `DataRow` class, which is also nested in the strongly typed DataSet, extends the `DataRow` class and exposes properties that map directly to the schema of the `Inventory` table. Also, the data designer tool has created a method (`IsPetNameNull()`) that will perform a check on whether this column has a value (see Figure 22-22).

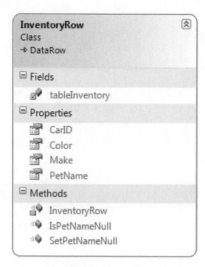

Figure 22-22. *The strongly typed DataRow*

Examining the Strongly Typed Data Adapter

Strong typing for your disconnected types is a solid benefit of using the Data Source Configuration Wizard, given that creating these classes by hand would be tedious (but entirely possible). This same wizard was kind enough to generate a custom data adapter object that can fill and update the `InventoryDataSet` and `InventoryDataTable` objects in a strongly typed manner. Locate the InventoryTableAdapter on the visual class designer and examine the generated members in Figure 22-23.

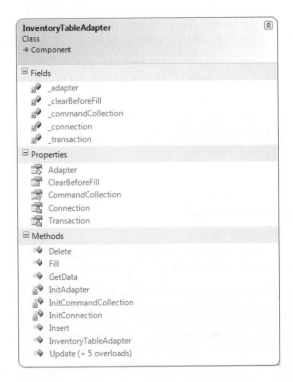

Figure 22-23. A customized data adapter that operates on the strongly typed DataSet and DataTable

The autogenerated `InventoryTableAdapter` type maintains a collection of `SqlCommand` objects (which you can access using the `CommandCollection` property), each of which has a fully populated set of `SqlParameter` objects. Furthermore, this custom data adapter provides a set of properties to extract the underlying connection, transaction, and data adapter objects, as well as a property to obtain an array representing each command type.

Completing the Windows Forms Application

If you examine the `Load` event handler of the form-derived type (in other words, if you view the code for `MainForm.vb` and locate the `MainForm_Load()` method) you will find that the `Fill()` method of the custom table adapter is called upon startup, passing in the custom `DataTable` maintained by the custom `DataSet`:

```
Private Sub MainForm_Load(ByVal sender As Object, ByVal e As EventArgs)
        Handles MyBase.Load
    Me.inventoryTableAdapter.Fill(Me.inventoryDataSet.Inventory)
End Sub
```

You can use this same custom data adapter object to update changes to the grid. Update the UI of your form with a single Button control (named btnUpdateInventory). Next, handle the Click event and author the following code within the event handler:

```
Private Sub btnUpdateInventory_Click(ByVal sender As Object, ByVal e As EventArgs)
      Handles btnUpdateInventory.Click
    Try
    ' Save changes with the Inventory table back to the database.
    Me.inventoryTableAdapter.Update(Me.inventoryDataSet.Inventory)
    Catch ex As Exception
    MessageBox.Show(ex.Message)
    End Try

    ' Get fresh copy for grid.
    Me.inventoryTableAdapter.Fill(Me.inventoryDataSet.Inventory)
End Sub
```

Run your application again; add, delete, or update the records displayed in the grid; and click the Update button. When you run the program again, you will find your changes are present and accounted for.

Great! This example shows how helpful the DataGridView control designer can be. It lets you work with strongly typed data generates a majority of the necessary database logic on your behalf. The obvious problem is that this code is tightly connected to the window that uses it. Ideally, this sort of code belongs in your AutoLotDAL.dll assembly (or some other data access library). However, you might wonder how to harvest the code generated using the DataGridView's associated wizard in a Class Library project, given that there is no form designer by default.

■ **Source Code** You can find the DataGridViewDataDesigner project under the Chapter 22 subdirectory.

Isolating Strongly Typed Database Code into a Class Library

Fortunately, you can activate the data design tools of Visual Studio 2010 from any sort of project (UI-based or otherwise) without the need to copy-and-paste massive amounts of code between projects. You can see this in action by adding more functionality to AutoLot.dll.

This time, try copying the entire AutoLot (Version two) project folder you created earlier in this chapter to a new location on your hard drive and rename this folder to AutoLot (Version Three). Next, activate the Visual Studio 2010 File ➤ Open Project/Solution... menu option, and open the AutoLotDAL.sln file in your new AutoLot (Version Three) folder.

Now, insert a new strongly typed DataSet class (named AutoLotDataSet.xsd) into your new project using the Project ➤ Add New Item menu option (see Figure 22-24).

Figure 22-24. Inserting a new strongly typed DataSet

This opens a blank Dataset Designer surface. At this point, you can use the Server Explorer to connect to a given database (you should already have a connection to AutoLot), and drag-and-drop each table and stored procedure you wish to generate onto the surface. In Figure 22-25, you can see each of the custom aspects of AutoLot are accounted for, and their relationships are realized automatically (this example does not drag over the CreditRisk table).

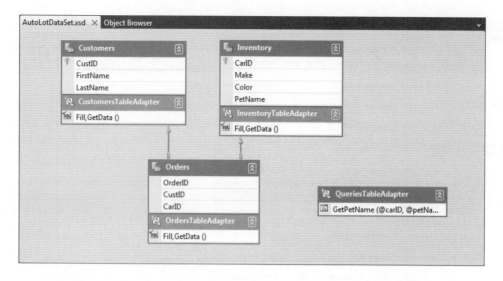

Figure 22-25. Your custom strongly typed types, this time within a Class Library project

Viewing the Generated Code

The DataSet designer created the exact same sort of code that the `DataGridView` wizard did in the previous Windows Forms example. However, this time you account for the `Inventory`, `Customers`, and `Orders` tables, as well as the `GetPetName` stored procedure, so you have many more generated classes. Basically, each database table you drag onto the designer surface gives you a strongly typed `DataSet`, `DataTable`, `DataRow`, and data adapter class.

The strongly typed `DataSet`, `DataTable`, and `DataRow` classes will be placed into the root namespace of the project (`AutoLotDAL`). The custom table adapters will be placed within a nested namespace. You can view all of the generated types most easily by using the Class View tool, which you open from the Visual Studio View menu (see Figure 22-26).

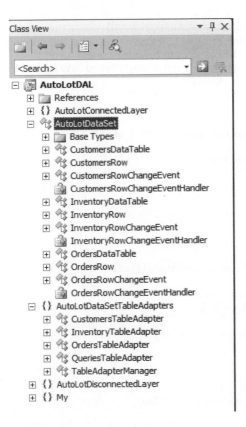

Figure 22-26. The autogenerated strongly typed data of the AutoLot database

For the sake of completion, you might want use the Visual Studio 2010 Properties editor (see Chapter 14 for details) to set the version of this latest incarnation of `AutoLot.dll` to `3.0.0.0`.

■ **Source Code** You can find the `AutoLotDAL (Version 3)` project under the Chapter 22 subdirectory.

Selecting Data with the Generated Code

At this point, you can use your strongly typed data within any .NET application that needs to communicate with the AutoLot database. To make sure you understand the basic mechanics, create a Console application named `StronglyTypedDataSetConsoleClient`. Next, add a reference to your latest-and-greatest version of `AutoLot.dll` and import the `AutoLotDataSetTableAdapters` namespace into your initial VB 2010 code file.

Here is a `Main()` method that uses the `InventoryTableAdapter` object to retrieve all data in the `Inventory` table. Notice that you do not need to specify a connection string because that information is now part of the strongly typed object model. Once you fill the table, you print out the results using a helper method named `PrintInventory()`. Note that you can manipulate the strongly typed `DataTable` just as you do a "normal" `DataTable` using the `Rows` and `Columns` collections:

```
Module Module1
    Sub Main()
      Console.WriteLine("***** Fun with Strongly Typed DataSets *****" & vbLf)

      Dim table As New AutoLotDataSet.InventoryDataTable()
      Dim dAdapt As New InventoryTableAdapter()
      dAdapt.Fill(table)

      PrintInventory(table)
      Console.ReadLine()
    End Sub

    Private Sub PrintInventory(ByVal dt As AutoLotDataSet.InventoryDataTable)
      ' Print out the column names.
      For curCol As Integer = 0 To dt.Columns.Count - 1
        Console.Write(dt.Columns(curCol).ColumnName & vbTab)
      Next curCol
      Console.WriteLine(vbLf & "----------------------------------")

      ' Print the data.
      For curRow As Integer = 0 To dt.Rows.Count - 1
        For curCol As Integer = 0 To dt.Columns.Count - 1
            Console.Write(dt.Rows(curRow)(curCol).ToString() & vbTab)
        Next
        Console.WriteLine()
      Next
  End Sub
End Module
```

Inserting Data with the Generated Code

Now assume you want to insert new records using this strongly typed object model. The following helper method adds two new rows to the current `InventoryDataTable`, then updates the database using the data adapter. You add the first row manually by configuring a strongly typed `DataRow`; you add the second row by passing in the needed column data, which allows the `DataRow` to be created in the background automatically:

```
Public Sub AddRecords(ByVal tb As AutoLotDataSet.InventoryDataTable,
                                ByVal dAdapt As InventoryTableAdapter)

    ' Get a new strongly typed row from the table.
    Dim newRow As AutoLotDataSet.InventoryRow = tb.NewInventoryRow()
```

```
    ' Fill row with some sample data.
    newRow.CarID = 999
    newRow.Color = "Purple"
    newRow.Make = "BMW"
    newRow.PetName = "Saku"

    ' Insert the new row.
    tb.AddInventoryRow(newRow)

    ' Add one more row, using overloaded Add method.
    tb.AddInventoryRow(888, "Yugo", "Green", "Zippy")

    ' Update database.
    dAdapt.Update(tb)
End Sub
```

The Main() method can invoke this method; doing so updates the database table with these new records:

```
Sub Main()
    ...
    ' Add rows, update and reprint.
    AddRecords(table, dAdapt)
    table.Clear()
    dAdapt.Fill(table)
    PrintInventory(table)
    Console.ReadLine()
End Sub
```

Deleting Data with the Generated Code

Deleting records with this strongly typed object model is also simple. The autogenerated FindByXXXX() method (where *XXXX* is the name of the primary key column) of the strongly typed DataTable returns the correct (strongly typed) DataRow using the primary key. Here is another helper method that deletes the two records you just created:

```
Private Sub RemoveRecords(ByVal tb As AutoLotDataSet.InventoryDataTable,
                          ByVal dAdapt As InventoryTableAdapter)

    Dim rowToDelete As AutoLotDataSet.InventoryRow = tb.FindByCarID(999)
    dAdapt.Delete(rowToDelete.CarID, rowToDelete.Make, rowToDelete.Color,
    rowToDelete.PetName)
    rowToDelete = tb.FindByCarID(888)
    dAdapt.Delete(rowToDelete.CarID, rowToDelete.Make, rowToDelete.Color,
    rowToDelete.PetName)
End Sub
```

If you call this from your Main() method and reprint the table, you should find these two test records are no longer displayed.

■ **Note** If you run this app twice and call the AddRecord() method each time, you get a VIOLATION CONSTRAINT ERROR because the AddRecord() method tries to insert the same CarID primary key value each time. If you wish to make this example more flexible, you can gather data from the user.

Invoking a Stored Procedure using the Generated Code

Let's look at one more example of using the strongly typed object model. In this case, you create a final method that invokes the GetPetName stored procedure. When the data adapters for the AutoLot database were created, there was a special class created named QueriesTableAdapter, which as the name implies, encapsulates the process of invoking stored procedures in the relational database. This final helper method displays the name of the specified car when called from Main():

```
Public Sub CallStoredProc()
    Dim q As New QueriesTableAdapter()
    Console.Write("Enter ID of car to look up: ")
    Dim carID As String = Console.ReadLine()
    Dim carName As String = ""
    q.GetPetName(Integer.Parse(carID), carName)
    Console.WriteLine("CarID {0} has the name of {1}", carID, carName)
End Sub
```

At this point, you know how to use strongly typed database types, and package them up into a dedicated class library. You can find more aspects of this object model to play around with, but you should be in a perfect position to dig deeper if that interests you. To wrap things up for this chapter, you will learn how to apply LINQ queries to an ADO.NET DataSet object.

■ **Source Code** You can find the StronglyTypedDataSetConsoleClient project under the Chapter 22 subdirectory.

Programming with LINQ to DataSet

You have seen in this chapter that you can manipulate the data within a DataSet in three distinct manners:

- By using the Tables, Rows, and Columns collections

- By using data table readers

- By using strongly typed data classes

When you use the various indexers of the DataSet and DataTable type, you can interact with the contained data in a straightforward but loosely typed manner. Recall that this approach requires you to treat the data as a tabular block of cells, as in this example:

```
Sub PrintDataWithIndxers(ByVal dt As DataTable)
      ' Print the DataTable.
      For curRow As Integer = 0 To dt.Rows.Count - 1

        For curCol As Integer = 0 To dt.Columns.Count - 1
          Console.Write(dt.Rows(curRow)(curCol).ToString() & vbTab)
        Next
        Console.WriteLine()
      Next
End Sub
```

The `CreateDataReader()` method of the `DataTable` type offers a second approach, where you can treat the data in the `DataSet` as a linear set of rows to be processed in a sequential manner. This allows you to apply a connected data reader programming model to a disconnected `DataSet`:

```
Sub PrintDataWithDataTableReader(ByVal dt As DataTable)
      ' Get the DataTableReader type.
      Dim dtReader As DataTableReader = dt.CreateDataReader()
      Do While dtReader.Read()
        For i As Integer = 0 To dtReader.FieldCount - 1
          Console.Write("{0}" & vbTab, dtReader.GetValue(i))
        Next
        Console.WriteLine()
      Loop
      dtReader.Close()
End Sub
```

Finally, you can use a strongly typed `DataSet` to yield a code base that allows you to interact with data in the object using properties that map to the column names in the relational database. Using strongly typed objects allows you to author code such as the following:

```
Sub AddRowWithTypedDataSet()
      Dim invDA As New InventoryTableAdapter()
      Dim inv As AutoLotDataSet.InventoryDataTable = invDA.GetData()
      inv.AddInventoryRow(999, "Ford", "Yellow", "Sal")
      invDA.Update(inv)
End Sub
```

While all of these approaches have their place, the LINQ to DataSet API provides yet another option to manipulate `DataSet` data using LINQ query expressions.

■ **Note** You only use the LINQ to DataSet to apply LINQ queries to DataSet objects returned by a data adapter, but this has nothing to do with applying LINQ queries directly to the database engine itself. Chapter 23 will introduce you to LINQ to Entities and the ADO.NET Entity Framework, which provide a way to represent SQL queries as LINQ queries.

The Role of the DataSet Extensions Library

The `System.Data.DataSetExtensions.dll` assembly, which is referenced by default in all Visual Studio 2010 projects, augments the `System.Data` namespace with a handful of new types (see Figure 22-27).

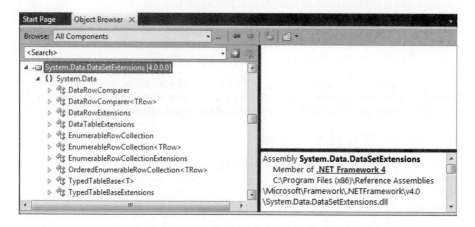

Figure 22-27. The System.Data.DataSetExtensions.dll assembly

The two most useful types by far are `DataTableExtensions` and `DataRowExtensions`. These classes extend the functionality of `DataTable` and `DataRow` by using a set of extension methods (see Chapter 12). The other key class is `TypedTableBaseExtensions`, which defines extension methods that you can apply to strongly typed `DataSet` objects to make the internal `DataTable` objects LINQ aware. All of the remaining members within the `System.Data.DataSetExtensions.dll` assembly are pure infrastructure, and they are not intended to be used directly in your code base.

Obtaining a LINQ-Compatible DataTable

Now let's look at how you use the DataSet extensions. Assume you have a new VB 2010 Console Application named `LinqToDataSetApp`. Add a reference to the latest and greatest version (`3.0.0.0`) of the `AutoLotDAL.dll` assembly and update your initial code file with the following logic:

```vb
' Location of strongly typed data adapters.
Imports AutoLotDataSetTableAdapters

Module Module1
    Sub Main()
        Console.WriteLine("***** LINQ over DataSet *****" & vbLf)

        ' Get a strongly typed DataTable containing the current Inventory
        ' of the AutoLot database.
        Dim dal As New AutoLotDataSet()
        Dim da As New InventoryTableAdapter()
        Dim data As AutoLotDataSet.InventoryDataTable = da.GetData()
```

```vbnet
    ' Invoke the methods that follow here!

    Console.ReadLine()
  End Sub
End Module
```

When you wish to transform an ADO.NET DataTable (including a strongly typed DataTable) into a LINQ-compatible object, you must call the AsEnumerable() extension method defined by the DataTableExtensions type. This returns an EnumerableRowCollection object that contains a collection of DataRows.

You can then use the EnumerableRowCollection type to operate on each row using basic DataRow syntax (e.g., indexer syntax). Consider the following new method in your application, which takes a strongly typed DataTable, obtains an enumerable copy of the data, and prints out each CarID value:

```vbnet
Sub PrintAllCarIDs(ByVal data As DataTable)
    ' Get enumerable version of DataTable.
    Dim enumData As EnumerableRowCollection = data.AsEnumerable()

    ' Print the car ID values.
    For Each r As DataRow In enumData
        Console.WriteLine("Car ID = {0}", r("CarID"))
    Next
End Sub
```

At this point, you have not applied a LINQ query; however, the point here is that the enumData object can now be the target of a LINQ query expression. Again, notice that the EnumerableRowCollection contains a collection of DataRow objects because you are applying a type indexer against each sub-object to print out the value of the CarID column.

In most cases, you do not need to declare a variable of type EnumerableRowCollection to hold the return value of AsEnumerable(). Rather, you can invoke this method from within the query expression itself. Here is a more interesting method for your application, which obtains a projection of CarID + Makes from all entries in the DataTable where the color is red (if you don't have any red autos in your Inventory table, you update this LINQ query as necessary):

```vbnet
Sub ShowRedCars(ByVal data As DataTable)
    ' Project a new result set containing
    ' the ID/color for rows where Color = Red.
    Dim cars = From car In data.AsEnumerable()
          Where CStr(car("Color")) = "Red"
                Select New With {Key .ID = car.Field(Of Integer)("CarID"),
                Key .Make = car.Field(Of String)("Make")}
    Console.WriteLine("Here are the red cars we have in stock:")
    For Each item In cars
        Console.WriteLine("-> CarID = {0} is {1}", item.ID, item.Make)
    Next
End Sub
```

The Role of the DataRowExtensions.Field(Of T)() Extension Method

One undesirable aspect of the current LINQ query expression is that you use numerous casting operations and `DataRow` indexers to gather the result set, which could result in runtime exceptions if you attempt to cast to an incompatible data type. To inject some strong typing into your query, you can use the `Field(Of T)()` extension method of the `DataRow` type. Doing so lets you increase the type safety of your query because the compatibility of data types is checked at compile time. Consider the following update:

```
Dim cars = From car In data.AsEnumerable()
           Where car.Field(Of String)("Color").Trim() = "Red"
           Select New With {
               .ID = car.Field(Of Integer)("CarID"),
               .Make = car.Field(Of String)("Make")}
```

In this case, you can invoke `Field(Of T)()` and specify a type parameter to represent the underlying data type of the column. As an argument to this method, you pass in the column name itself. Given the additional compile-time checking, you should consider it a best practice to use `Field(Of T)()` (rather than the `DataRow` indexer) when you process the roles of an `EnumerableRowCollection`.

Beyond the fact that you call the `AsEnumerable()` method, the overall format of the LINQ query is identical to what you have already seen in Chapter 13. Given this, there is no reason to repeat the details of the various LINQ operators here. If you wish to see additional examples, you can look up the topic "LINQ to DataSet Examples" in the .NET Framework 4.0 SDK documentation.

Hydrating New DataTables from LINQ Queries

It is also possible to populate the data of a new `DataTable` easily, based on the results of a LINQ query and provided that you are *not* using projections. When you have a result set where the underlying type can be represented as `IEnumerable(Of T)`, you can call the `CopyToDataTable(Of T)()` extension method on the result, as in this example:

```
Sub BuildDataTableFromQuery(ByVal data As DataTable)
    Dim cars = From car In data.AsEnumerable()
               Where car.Field(Of Integer)("CarID") > 5
               Select car

    ' Use this result set to build a new DataTable.
    Dim newTable As DataTable = cars.CopyToDataTable()

    ' Print the DataTable.
    For curRow As Integer = 0 To newTable.Rows.Count - 1
      For curCol As Integer = 0 To newTable.Columns.Count - 1
        Console.Write(newTable.Rows(curRow)(curCol).ToString().Trim() & vbTab)
      Next
      Console.WriteLine()
    Next
End Sub
```

■ **Note** It is also possible to transform a LINQ query to a DataView type by using the AsDataView(Of T)() extension method.

You might find this technique helpful when you wish to use the result of a LINQ query as the source of a data binding operation. Recall that the DataGridView of Windows Forms (as well as an ASP.NET or WPF grid control) supports a property named DataSource. You could bind a LINQ result to the grid as follows:

```
' Assume myDataGrid is a GUI-based grid object.
myDataGrid.DataSource = (
        From car In data.AsEnumerable()
        Where car.Field(Of Integer)("CarID") > 5
        Select car).CopyToDataTable()
```

This wraps up the examination of the disconnected layer of ADO.NET. Using this aspect of the API, you can fetch data from a relational database, munch on the data, and return it for processing while keeping the database connection open for the shortest possible amount of time.

■ **Source Code** You can find the LinqOverDataSet example under the Chapter 22 subdirectory.

Summary

This chapter dove into the details of the disconnected layer of ADO.NET. As you have seen, the centerpiece of the disconnected layer is the DataSet. This type is an in-memory representation of any number of tables and any number of optional interrelationships, constraints, and expressions. The beauty of establishing relations on your local tables is that you can programmatically navigate between them while disconnected from the remote data store.

You also examined the role of the data adapter type in this chapter. Using this type (and the related SelectCommand, InsertCommand, UpdateCommand, and DeleteCommand properties), the adapter can resolve changes in the DataSet with the original data store. You also learned how to navigate the object model of a DataSet using the brute-force manual approach, as well as with strongly typed objects, which the Dataset Designer tools of Visual Studio 2010 typically generate.

You wrapped up by looking at one aspect of the LINQ technology set named LINQ to DataSet. This allows you to obtain a queryable copy of the DataSet, which can receive well formatted LINQ queries.

## CHAPTER 23

ADO.NET Part III: The Entity Framework

The previous two chapters examined the fundamental ADO.NET programming models—the connected and disconnected layers, specifically. These approaches have enabled .NET programmers to work with relational data (in a relatively straightforward manner) since the initial release of the platform. However, Microsoft introduced a brand new component of the ADO.NET API called the *Entity Framework* (or simply, *EF)* in .NET 3.5 Service Pack 1.

The overarching goal of EF is to allow you to interact with relational databases using an object model that maps directly to the business objects in your application. For example, rather than treating a batch of data as a collection of rows and columns, you can operate on a collection of strongly typed objects termed *entities*. These entities are also natively LINQ aware, and you can query against them using the same LINQ grammar you learned about in Chapter 13. The EF runtime engine translates your LINQ queries into proper SQL queries on your behalf.

This chapter will introduce you to the EF programming model. You will learn about various bits of infrastructure, including object services, entity client, LINQ to Entities, and Entity SQL. You will also learn about the format of the all-important `*.edmx` file and its role in the Entity Framework API. Next, you will learn how to generate `*.edmx` files using Visual Studio 2010 and at the command line using the EDM generator utility (`edmgen.exe`).

By the time you complete this chapter, you will have the final version of `AutoLotDAL.dll`, and you will learn how to bind entity objects to a Windows Forms desktop application.

Understanding the Role of Entity Framework

The connected and disconnected layers of ADO.NET provide you with a fabric that lets you select, insert, update, and delete data with connections, commands, data readers, data adapters, and `DataSet` objects. While this is all well and good, these aspects of ADO.NET force you to treat the fetched data in a manner that is tightly coupled to the physical database schema. Recall for example, that when you use the connected layer, you typically iterate over each record by specifying column names to a data reader. On the other hand, if you opt to use the disconnected layer, you find yourself traversing the rows and columns collections of a `DataTable` object within a `DataSet` container.

If you use the disconnected layer in conjunction with strongly typed `DataSet`s/data adapters, you end up with a programming abstraction that provides some helpful benefits. First, the strongly typed `DataSet` class exposes table data using class properties. Second, the strongly typed table adapter supports methods that encapsulate the construction of the underlying SQL statements. Recall the `AddRecords()` method from Chapter 22:

```
Public Sub AddRecords(ByVal tb As AutoLotDataSet.InventoryDataTable,
                      ByVal dAdapt As InventoryTableAdapter)
    ' Get a new strongly typed row from the table.
    Dim newRow As AutoLotDataSet.InventoryRow = tb.NewInventoryRow()

    ' Fill row with some sample data.
    newRow.CarID = 999
    newRow.Color = "Purple"
    newRow.Make = "BMW"
    newRow.PetName = "Saku"

    ' Insert the new row.
    tb.AddInventoryRow(newRow)

    ' Add one more row, using overloaded Add method.
    tb.AddInventoryRow(888, "Yugo", "Green", "Zippy")

    ' Update database.
    dAdapt.Update(tb)
End Sub
```

Things get even better if you combine the disconnected layer with LINQ to DataSet. In this case, you can apply LINQ queries to your in-memory data to obtain a new result set, which you can then optionally map to a standalone object such as a new `DataTable`, a `List(Of T)`, `Dictionary(Of K,V)`, or array of data, as follows:

```
Sub BuildDataTableFromQuery(ByVal data As DataTable)
    Dim cars = From car In data.AsEnumerable()
               Where car.Field(Of Integer)("CarID") > 5
               Select car
    ' Use this result set to build a new DataTable.
    Dim newTable As DataTable = cars.CopyToDataTable()

    ' Work with DataTable...
End Sub
```

LINQ to DataSet is useful; however, you need to remember that the target of your LINQ query is the *data returned from the database*, not the database engine itself. Ideally, you could build a LINQ query that you send directly to the database engine for processing, and get back some strongly typed data in return (which is exactly what the ADO.NET Entity Framework lets you accomplish).

When you use either the connected or disconnected layer of ADO.NET, you must always be mindful of the physical structure of the back-end database. You must know the schema of each data table, author complex SQL queries to interact with said table data, and so forth. This can force you to author some fairly verbose VB 2010 code because as VB 2010 itself does not speak the language of database schema directly.

To make matters worse, the way in which a physical database is constructed (by your friendly DBA) is squarely focused on database constructs such as foreign keys, views, and stored procedures. The databases constructed by your friendly DBA can grow quite complex as the DBA endeavors to account for security and scalability. This also complicates the sort of VB 2010 code you must author in order to interact with the data store.

The ADO.NET Entity Framework (EF) is a programming model that attempts to lessen the gap between database constructs and object-oriented programming constructs. Using EF, you can interact with a relational database without ever seeing a line of SQL code (if you so choose). Rather, when you apply LINQ queries to your strongly typed classes, the EF runtime generates proper SQL statements on your behalf.

■ **Note** *LINQ to Entities* is the term that describes the act of applying LINQ queries to ADO.NET EF entity objects.

Another possible approach: Rather than updating database data by finding a row, updating the row, and sending the row back for processing with a batch of SQL queries, you can simply change properties on an object and save its state. Again, the EF runtime updates the database automatically.

As far as Microsoft is concerned, the ADO.NET Entity Framework is a new member of the data access family, and it is not intended to replace the connected or disconnected layers. However, once you spend some time working with EF, you might quickly find yourself preferring this rich object model over the more primitive world of SQL queries and row/column collections.

Nevertheless, chances are you will find uses for all three approaches in your .NET projects; in some cases, the EF model might complicate your code base. For example, if you want to build an in-house application that needs to communicate only with a single database table, you might prefer to use the connected layer to hit a batch of related stored procedures. Larger applications can particularly benefit from EF, especially if the development team is comfortable working with LINQ. As with any new technology, you will need to determine how (and when) ADO.NET EF is appropriate for the task at hand.

■ **Note** You might recall a database programming API introduced with .NET 3.5 called LINQ to SQL. This API is close in concept (and fairly close in terms of programming constructs) to ADO.NET EF. While LINQ to SQL is not formally dead, the official word from those kind folks in Redmond is that you should put your efforts into EF, not LINQ to SQL.

The Role of Entities

The strongly typed classes mentioned previously are called *entities*. Entities are a conceptual model of a physical database that maps to your business domain. Formally speaking, this model is termed *an Entity Data Model* (*EDM*). The EDM is a client-side set of classes that map to a physical database, but you should understand that the entities need not map directly to the database schema in so far as naming conventions go. You are free to restructure your entity classes to fit your needs, and the EF runtime will map your unique names to the correct database schema.

For example, you might recall that you created the simple `Inventory` table in the `AutoLot` database using the database schema shown in Figure 23-1.

Figure 23-1. *Structure of the Inventory table of the AutoLot database*

If you were to generate an EDM for the `Inventory` table of the `AutoLot` database (you'll see how to do so momentarily), the entity will be called *Inventory* by default. However, you could rename this class to `Car` and define uniquely named properties of your choosing, which will be mapped to the columns of the `Inventory` table. This loose coupling means that you can shape the entities so they closely model your business domain. Figure 23-2 shows such an entity class.

Figure 23-2. *The Car entity is a client-side reshaping of the Inventory schema*

■ **Note** In many cases, the client-side entity class will be identically named to the related database table. However, remember that you can always reshape the entity to match your business situation.

Now, consider the following module, which uses the `Car` entity class (and a related class named `AutoLotEntities`) to add a new row to the `Inventory` table of `AutoLot`. This class is termed an *object context*; the job of this class it is to communicate with the physical database on your behalf (you will learn more details soon):

```
Module Module1
    Sub Main()
        ' Connection string automatically read from
        ' generated config file.
        Using context As New AutoLotEntities()
```

```
            ' Add a new record to Inventory table, using our entity.
            context.Cars.AddObject(New Car() With {.AutoIDNumber = 987,
           .CarColor = "Black",.MakeOfCar = "Pinto",
           .NicknameOfCar = "Pete"})
            context.SaveChanges()
        End Using
    End Sub
End Module
```

It is up to the EF runtime to take the client-side representation of the `Inventory` table (here, a class named `Car`) and map it back to the correct columns of the `Inventory` table. Notice that you see no trace of any sort of SQL INSERT statement; you simply add a new `Car` object to the collection maintained by the aptly named `Cars` property of the context object and save your changes. Sure enough, if you view the table data using the Server Explorer of Visual Studio 2010, you will see a brand new record (see Figure 23-3).

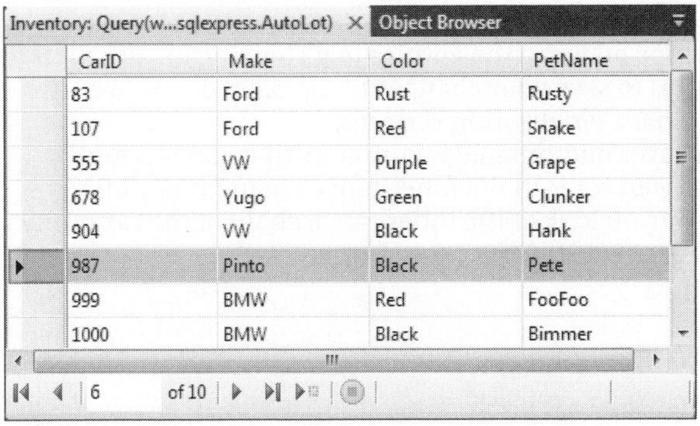
Inventory: Query(w...sqlexpress.AutoLot)
Object Browser
CarID Make Color PetName
83 Ford Rust Rusty
107 Ford Red Snake
555 VW Purple Grape
678 Yugo Green Clunker
904 VW Black Hank
987 Pinto Black Pete
999 BMW Red FooFoo
1000 BMW Black Bimmer
6 of 10

Figure 23-3. *The result of saving the context*

There is no magic in the preceding example. Under the covers, a connection to the database is made, a proper SQL statement is generated, and so forth. The benefit of EF is that these details are handled on your behalf. Now let's look at the core services of EF that make this possible.

The Building Blocks of the Entity Framework

The EF API sits on top of the existing ADO.NET infrastructure you have already examined in the previous two chapters. Like any ADO.NET interaction, the entity framework uses an ADO.NET data provider to communicate with the data store. However, the data provider must be updated so it supports a new set of services before it can interact with the EF API. As you might expect, the Microsoft SQL Server data provider has been updated with the necessary infrastructure, which is accounted for when using the `System.Data.Entity.dll` assembly.

■ **Note** Many third party databases (e.g., Oracle and MySQL) provide EF-aware data providers. Consult your database vendor for details or log onto www.sqlsummit.com/dataprov.htm for a list of known ADO.NET data providers.

In addition to adding the necessary bits to the Microsoft SQL Server data provider, the System.Data.Entity.dll assembly contains various namespaces that account for the EF services themselves. The two key pieces of the EF API to concentrate on for the time being are *object services* and *entity client.*

The Role of Object Services

Object services is the name given to the part of EF that manages the client-side entities as you work with them in code. For example, object services track the changes you make to an entity (e.g., changing the color of a car from green to blue), manage relationships between the entities (e.g., looking up all orders for a customer named Steve Hagen), and provide ways to save your changes to the database, as well as ways to persist the state of an entity with XML and binary serialization services.

Programmatically speaking, the object services layer micromanages any class that extends the EntityObject base class. As you might suspect, EntityObject is in the inheritance chain for all entity classes in the EF programming model. For example, if you look at the inheritance chain of the Car entity class used in the previous example, you see that Car *Is-A* EntityObject (see Figure 23-4).

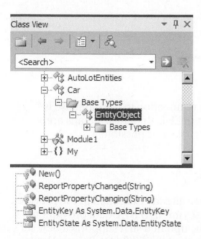

Figure 23-4. EF's object service layer can manage any class that extends EntityObject

The Role of the Entity Client

Another major aspect of the EF API is the entity client layer. This part of the EF API is in charge of working with the underlying ADO.NET data provider to make connections to the database, generate the necessary SQL statements based on the state of your entities and LINQ queries, map fetched database data into the correct shape of your entities, and manage other details you would normally perform by hand if you were not using the Entity Framework.

You can find the functionality of the entity client layer in the `System.Data.EntityClient` namespace. This namespace includes a set of classes that map EF concepts (such as LINQ to Entity queries) to the underlying ADO.NET data provider. These classes (e.g., `EntityCommand` and `EntityConnection`) are eerily similar to the classes you find in an ADO.NET data provider; for example, Figure 23-5 illustrates how the classes of the entity client layer extend the same MustInherit base classes of any other provider (e.g., `DbCommand` and `DbConnection`; you can also see Chapter 22 for more details on this subject).

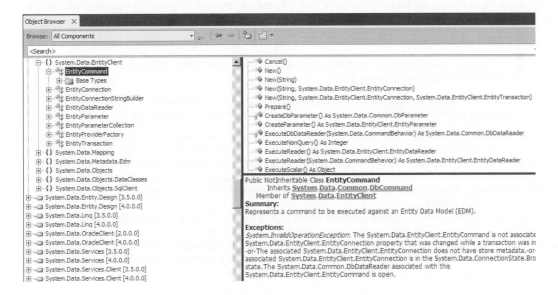

Figure 23-5. *The entity client layer maps entity commands to the underlying ADO.NET data provider*

The entity client layer typically works behind the scenes, but it is entirely possible to work directly with an entity client if you require full control over how it performs its duties (most notably, how it generates the SQL queries and handles the returned database data).

If you require greater control over how the entity client builds a SQL statement based on the incoming LINQ query, you can use *Entity SQL*. Entity SQL is a database-independent dialect of SQL that works directly with entities. Once you build an entity SQL query, it can be sent directly to entity client services (or if you wish, to object services), where it will be formatted into a proper SQL statement for the underlying data provider. You will not work with Entity SQL to any significant extent in this chapter, but you will see a few examples of this new SQL-based grammar later in the chapter.

If you require greater control over how a fetched result set is manipulated, you can forego the automatic mapping of database results to entity objects and manually process the records using the `EntityDataReader` class. Unsurprisingly, the `EntityDataReader` allows you to process fetched data using a forward only, read only stream of data, just as `SqlDataReader` does. You will see a working example of this approach later in the chapter.

The Role of the *.edmx File (and Friends)

Recapping the story thus far, entities are client-side classes, which function as an Entity Data Model. While the client side entities will eventually be mapped to the correct database table, there is no tight coupling between the property names of your entity classes and the column names on the data table.

For the Entity Framework API to map entity class data to database table data correctly, you need a proper definition of the mapping logic. In any data model-driven system, the entities, the real database, and the mapping layers are separated into three related parts: a *conceptual model*, a *logical model*, and a *physical model*.

- The conceptual model defines the entities and their relationships (if any).

- The logical model maps the entities and relationships into tables with any required foreign key constraints.

- The physical model represents the capabilities of a particular data engine by specifying storage details, such table schema, partitioning, and indexing.

In the world of EF, each of these three layers is captured in an XML-based file format. When you use the integrated Entity Framework designers of Visual Studio 2010, you end up with a file that takes an *.edmx file extension (remember, EDM = entity data model). This file includes XML descriptions of the entities, the physical database, and instructions on how to map this information between the conceptual and physical models. You will examine the format of the *.edmx file in the first example of this chapter (which you will see in a moment).

When you compile your EF-based projects using Visual Studio 2010, the *.edmx file is used to generate three standalone XML files: one for the conceptual model data (*.csdl), one for the physical model (*.ssdl), and one for the mapping layer (*.msl). The data of these three XML-based files is then bundled into your application in the form of binary resources. Once compiled, your .NET assembly has all the necessary data for the EF API calls you make in your code base.

The Role of the ObjectContext and ObjectSet(Of T) Classes

The final part of the EF puzzle is the `ObjectContext` class, which is a member of the `System.Data.Objects` namespace. When you generate your *.edmx file, you get the entity classes that map to the database tables and a class that extends `ObjectContext`. You typically use this class to interact with object services and entity client functionality indirectly.

`ObjectContext` provides a number of core services to child classes, including the ability to save all changes (which results in a database update), tweak the connection string, delete objects, call stored procedures, and handle other fundamental details. Table 23-1 describes some of the core members of the `ObjectContext` class (be aware that a majority of these members stay in memory until you call `SaveChanges()`).

Table 23-1. Common Members of ObjectContext

Member of ObjectContext	Meaning in Life
AcceptAllChanges()	Accepts all changes made to entity objects within the object context.
AddObject()	Adds an object to the object context.
DeleteObject()	Marks an object for deletion.
ExecuteFunction(Of T)()	Executes a stored procedure in the database.
ExecuteStoreCommand()	Allows you to send a SQL command to the data store directly.
GetObjectByKey()	Locates an object within the object context by its key.
SaveChanges()	Sends all updates to the data store.
CommandTimeout	This property gets or sets the timeout value in seconds for all object context operations.
Connection	This property returns the connection string used by the current object context.
SavingChanges	This event fires when the object context saves changes to the data store.

The `ObjectContext` derived class serves as a container that manages entity objects, which are stored in a collection of type `ObjectSet(Of T)`. For example, if you generate an `*.edmx` file for the `Inventory` table of the `AutoLot` database, you end up with a class named (by default) `AutoLotEntities`. This class supports a property named `Inventories` (note the plural name) that encapsulates an `ObjectSet(Of Inventory)` data member. If you create an EDM for the `Orders` table of the `AutoLot` database, the `AutoLotEntities` class will define a second property named `Orders` that encapsulates an `ObjectSet(Of Order)` member variable. Table 23-2 defines some common members of `System.Data.Objects.ObjectSet(Of T)`.

Table 23-2. Common Members of ObjectSet(Of T)

Member of ObjectSet(Of T)	Meaning in Life
AddObject()	Allows you to insert a new entity object into the collection.
CreateObject(Of T)()	Creates a new instance of the specified entity type.
DeleteObject	Marks an object for deletion.

Once you drill into the correct property of the object context, you can call any member of ObjectSet(Of T). Consider again the sample code shown in the first few pages of this chapter:

```
Using context As New AutoLotEntities()
    ' Add a new record to Inventory table, using our entity.
    context.Cars.AddObject(New Car() With {.AutoIDNumber = 987,
    .CarColor = "Black",.MakeOfCar = "Pinto", .NicknameOfCar = "Pete"})

    context.SaveChanges()
End Using
```

Here, AutoLotEntities is-a ObjectContext. The Cars property gives you access to the ObjectSet(Of Car) variable. You use this reference to insert a new Car entity object and tell the ObjectContext to save all changes to the database.

ObjectSet(Of T) is typically the target of LINQ to Entity queries; as such, ObjectSet(Of T) supports the same extension methods you learned about in Chapter 13. Moreover, ObjectSet(Of T) gains a good deal of functionality from its direct parent class, ObjectQuery(Of T), which is a class that represents a strongly typed LINQ (or Entity SQL) query.

All Together Now!

Before you build your first Entity Framework example, take a moment to ponder Figure 23-6, which shows you how the EF API is organized.

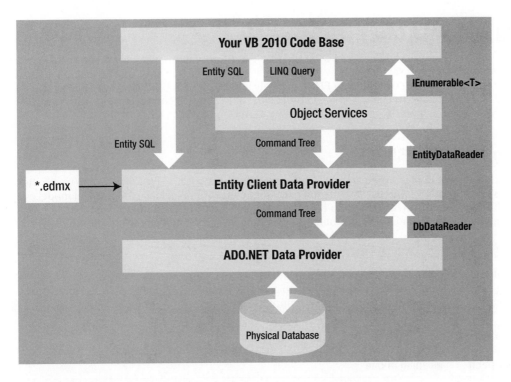

Figure 23-6. The major components of the ADO.NET Entity Framework

The moving parts illustrated by Figure 23-6 are not as complex as they might seem at first glance. For example, consider this common scenario. You author some VB 2010 code that applies a LINQ query to an entity you received from your context. This query is passed into object services, where it formats the LINQ command into a tree entity client can understand. In turn, the entity client formats this tree into a proper SQL statement for the underlying ADO.NET provider. The provider returns a data reader (e.g., a DbDataReader derived object) that client services use to stream data to object services using an EntiryDataReader. What your VB 2010 code base gets back is an enumeration of entity data (IEnumerable(Of T)).

Here is another scenario to consider. Your VB 2010 code base wants more control over how client services constructs the eventual SQL statement to send to the database. Thus, you author some VB 2010 code using Entity SQL that can be passed directly to entity client or object services. The end result returns as an IEnumerable(Of T).

In either of these scenarios, you must make the XML data of the *.edmx file known to client services; this enables it to understand how to map database atoms to entities. Finally, remember that the client (e.g., your VB 2010 code base) can also nab the results sent from entity client by using the EntityDataReader directly.

Building and Analyzing your First EDM

Now that you have a better understanding of what the ADO.NET Entity Framework is attempting to accomplish, as well as a high-level idea of how it all works, it's time to look at your first full example. To keep things simple for now, you will build an EDM that only allow access to the Inventory table of AutoLot. Once you understand the basics, you will build a new EDM that accounts for the entire AutoLot database, and then display your data in a graphical user interface.

Generating the *.edmx File

Begin by creating a new Console Application named InventoryEDMConsoleApp. When you wish to use the Entity Framework, your first step is to generate the necessary conceptual, logical, and physical model data defined by the *.edmx file. One way to do this is to use the .NET 4.0 SDK command line tool, EdmGen.exe. Open a Visual Studio 2010 Command Prompt and enter the following instruction:

EdmGen.exe -?

You should see a list of options that you can supply to the tool to generate the necessary files based on an existing database; you should also see options to generate a brand new database based on existing entity files! Table 23-3 documents some common options of EdmGen.exe.

Table 23-3. Common Command-Line Flags of EdmGen.exe

EdmGen.exe Option	Meaning in Life
/mode:FullGeneration	Generate the *.ssdl, *.msl, *.csdl files and client entities from a specified database.
/project:	This is the base name to be used for the generated code and files. Typically, this is the name of the database you pull data from (it can use the short form, /p:).
/connectionstring:	This is the connection string you use to interact with the database (it can use the short form, /c:).
/language:	Allows you to specify whether you wish to use VB 2010 or C# syntax for the generated code.
/pluralize	Automatically pluralize or singularize the entity set name, entity type name, and navigation property name using English language rules.

As of .NET 4.0, the EF programming model supports *domain first* programming, which allows you to create your entities (with typical object-oriented techniques) and use them to generate a brand new database. In this introductory look at ADO.NET EF, you will not use this model-first mentality, nor will you use EdmGen.exe to generate your client-side entity model. Instead, you will use the graphical EDM designers of Visual Studio 2010.

Now activate the Project ➤ Add New Item... menu option and insert a new ADO.NET Entity Data Model item (see Figure 23-7) named `InventoryEDM.edmx`.

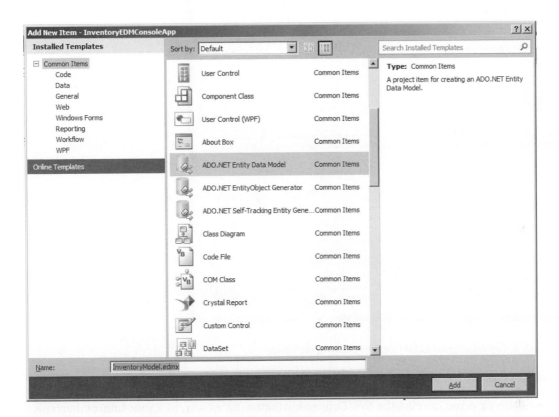

Figure 23-7. Inserting a new ADO.NET EDM project item

Clicking the Add button launches the Entity Model Data Wizard. The wizard's first step allows you to select whether you wish to generate an EDM from an existing database or define an empty model (for model-first development). Select the Generate from database option and click the Next button (see Figure 23-8).

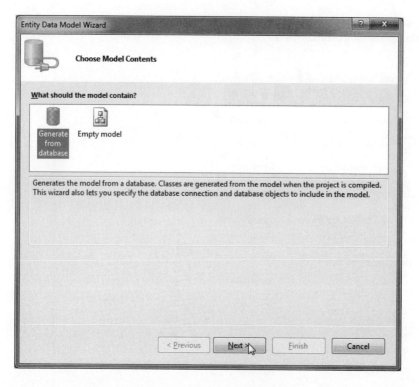

Figure 23-8. *Generating an EDM from an existing database*

You can select your database in the wizard's second step. If you already have a connection to a database within the Visual Studio 2010 Server Explorer, you will see it listed in the dropdown combo box. If this is not the case, you can click the New Connection button. Either way, pick your `AutoLot` database, and then make certain you save the connection string data in the (autogenerated) `App.config` file (Figure 23-9).

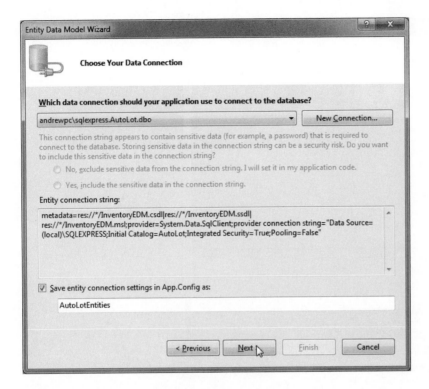

Figure 23-9. Selecting the database to generate the EDM from

Before you click the Next button, take a moment to examine the format of your connection string:

```
metadata=res://*/InventoryEDM.csdl|res://*/InventoryEDM.ssdl|res://*/
        InventoryEDM.msl; provider=System.Data.SqlClient;
        provider connection string="Data Source=(local)\SQLEXPRESS;
        Initial Catalog=AutoLot;Integrated Security=True;Pooling=False"
```

The point of interest here is the **metadata** flag, which you use to denote the names of the embedded XML resource data for your conceptual, physical, and mapping files (recall that the single *.edmx file will be broken into three separate files at compile time, and the data in these files takes the form of binary resources embedded in your assembly).

In the wizard's final step, you can select the items from the database you wish to use to generate the EDM. Again, you are only concerned with the **Inventory** table in this example (Figure 23-10).

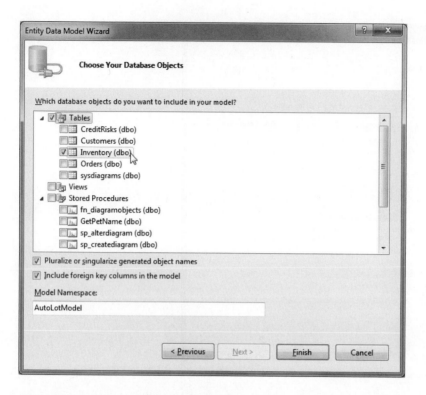

Figure 23-10. Selecting the database items

Now, click the Finish button to generate your EDM data.

Reshaping the Entity Data

Once you complete the wizard, you will see the EDM designer open within the IDE, where you should see a single entity named *Inventory*. You can view the composition of any entity on the designer using the Entity Data Model Browser window (you open this using the View ➤ Other Windows menu option). Now look at the format of your conceptual model for the **Inventory** database table under the Entity Types folder (see Figure 23-11). You can see the physical model of the database under the Store node, where the name of your store will be based on the name of the database itself (**AutoLotModel.Store**, in this case).

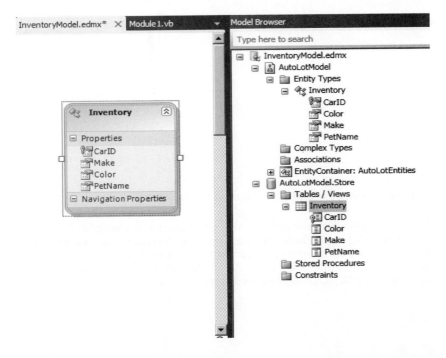

Figure 23-11. The Entity designer and Model Browser window

By default, the names of your entities will be based on the original database object names; however, recall that the names of entities in your conceptual model can be anything you choose. You can change the entity name, as well as property names of the entity, by selecting an item on the designer and renaming it using the Name property in the Visual Studio 2010 Properties window. Next, rename the Inventory entity to Car and the PetName property to CarNickname (see Figure 23-12).

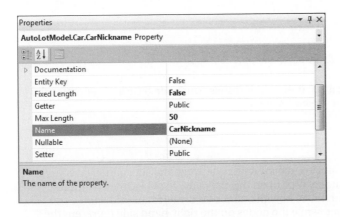

Figure 23-12. Reshaping entities using the Properties window

At this point, your conceptual model should look similar to what is shown in Figure 23-13.

Figure 23-13. The client side model, reshaped to match your business domain

Now select the entire `Car` entity on the designer and look at the Properties window again. You should see that the Entity Set Name field has also been renamed from `Inventories` to `Cars` (see Figure 23-14). The Entity Set value is important because this corresponds to the name of the property on the data context class, which you will use to modify the database. Recall that this property encapsulates an `ObjectSet(Of T)` member variable in the `ObjectContext` derived class.

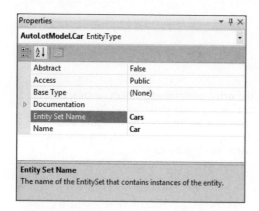

Figure 23-14. The name of the ObjectSet(Of T) property wrapper

Before moving on, compile your application; doing so refreshes your code base and generates the `*.csdl`, `*.msl`, and `*.ssdl` files based on your `*.edmx` file data.

Viewing the Mappings

Now that you have reshaped the data, you can view the mappings between the conceptual layer and the physical layer using the Mapping Details window (you open this using the View ➤ Other Windows... menu option). Next, look at Figure 23-15 and notice how the nodes on the left-hand side of the tree represent the data names in the physical layer, while the nodes on the right-hand side represent the names of your conceptual model.

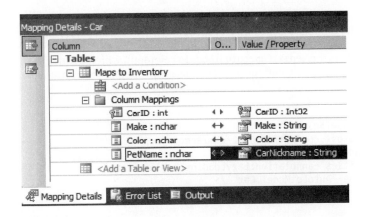

Figure 23-15. *The Mapping Details window shows the mappings of your conceptual and physical models*

Viewing the Generated *.edmx File Data

Now, let's see exactly what the EDM Wizard generated for you. Right-click the **InventoryEDM.edmx** file in the Solution Explorer and select the Open With... menu option. From the resulting dialog box, pick the XML Editor option. This allows you to see the underlying XML data seen in the EDM designer. The structure of this XML document is broken down into four parts; you can find all of them in the **<edmx:Edmx>** root element.

The **<edmx:Runtime>** sub-elements define the XML data for your conceptual, physical, and mapping layer models. First, you have the definition of the physical **Inventory** database table:

```
<edmx:StorageModels>
  <Schema Namespace="AutoLotModel.Store" Alias="Self" Provider="System.Data.SqlClient"
ProviderManifestToken="2008"
xmlns:store="http://schemas.microsoft.com/ado/2007/12/edm/EntityStoreSchemaGenerator"
xmlns="http://schemas.microsoft.com/ado/2009/02/edm/ssdl">
    <EntityContainer Name="AutoLotModelStoreContainer">
      <EntitySet Name="Inventory" EntityType="AutoLotModel.Store.Inventory"
store:Type="Tables" Schema="dbo" />
    </EntityContainer>
    <EntityType Name="Inventory">
      <Key>
        <PropertyRef Name="CarID" />
      </Key>
      <Property Name="CarID" Type="int" Nullable="false" />
      <Property Name="Make" Type="nchar" Nullable="false" MaxLength="10" />
      <Property Name="Color" Type="nchar" Nullable="false" MaxLength="10" />
      <Property Name="PetName" Type="nchar" MaxLength="10" />
    </EntityType>
  </Schema>
</edmx:StorageModels>
```

Note that the `<Schema>` node defines the name of the ADO.NET data provider that will use this information when communicating with the database (`System.Data.SqlClient`). The `<EntityType>` node marks the name of the physical database table, as well as each column in the table.

The next major chunk of the *.edmx file is the `<edmx:ConceptualModels>` element, which defines the shaped client-side entities. Notice that the `Cars` entity defines the `CarNickname` property, which you change using the designer:

```
<edmx:ConceptualModels>
  <Schema Namespace="AutoLotModel" Alias="Self"
xmlns:annotation="http://schemas.microsoft.com/ado/2009/02/edm/annotation"
xmlns="http://schemas.microsoft.com/ado/2008/09/edm">
    <EntityContainer Name="AutoLotEntities" annotation:LazyLoadingEnabled="true">
      <EntitySet Name="Cars" EntityType="AutoLotModel.Car" />
    </EntityContainer>
    <EntityType Name="Car">
      <Key>
        <PropertyRef Name="CarID" />
      </Key>
      <Property Name="CarID" Type="Int32" Nullable="false" />
      <Property Name="Make" Type="String" Nullable="false" MaxLength="10" Unicode="true"
FixedLength="true" />
      <Property Name="Color" Type="String" Nullable="false" MaxLength="10" Unicode="true"
FixedLength="true" />
      <Property Name="CarNickname" Type="String" MaxLength="10" Unicode="true"
FixedLength="true" />
    </EntityType>
  </Schema>
</edmx:ConceptualModels>
```

That brings you to the mapping layer, which the Mapping Details window (and the EF runtime) uses to connect names in the conceptual model to the physical model:

```
<edmx:ConceptualModels>
  <Schema Namespace="AutoLotModel" Alias="Self"
xmlns:annotation="http://schemas.microsoft.com/ado/2009/02/edm/annotation"
xmlns="http://schemas.microsoft.com/ado/2008/09/edm">
    <EntityContainer Name="AutoLotEntities" annotation:LazyLoadingEnabled="true">
      <EntitySet Name="Cars" EntityType="AutoLotModel.Car" />
    </EntityContainer>
    <EntityType Name="Car">
      <Key>
        <PropertyRef Name="CarID" />
      </Key>
      <Property Name="CarID" Type="Int32" Nullable="false" />
      <Property Name="Make" Type="String" Nullable="false" MaxLength="10" Unicode="true"
FixedLength="true" />
      <Property Name="Color" Type="String" Nullable="false" MaxLength="10" Unicode="true"
FixedLength="true" />
```

```
    <Property Name="CarNickname" Type="String" MaxLength="10" Unicode="true"
FixedLength="true" />
    </EntityType>
  </Schema>
</edmx:ConceptualModels>
```

The last part of the *.edmx file is the `<Designer>` element, which is not used by the EF runtime. If you view this data, you will see it contains instructions used by Visual Studio to display your entities on the visual designer surface.

Again, ensure that you have compiled your project at least once and click the Show All Files button of the Solution Explorer. Next, begin by drilling into the **obj\x86\Debug** folder; and then drill into the **edmxResourcesToEmbed** subdirectory. Here you will find three XML files that are based on the entirety of your *.edmx file (see Figure 23-16).

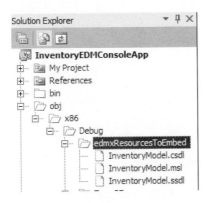

*Figure 23-16. You use the *.edmx file to generate three seperate XML files*

The data in these files will be embedded as binary resources in your assembly. Thus, your .NET application has all the information it needs to understand the conceptual, physical, and mapping layers of the EDM.

Viewing the Generated Source Code

You are almost ready to author some code to use your EDM; before you do, however, you should check out the generated VB 2010 code base. Open the Class View window and expand your default namespace. You will see that, in addition to the Module1 Module, the EDM Wizard generated an entity class (which you renamed to **Car**) and another class named **AutoLotEntities**.

If you go to the Solution Explorer and expand the **InventoryEDM.edmx** node, you will see an IDE-maintained file named **InventoryEDM.Designer.vb**. As with any IDE-maintained file, you should not directly edit this file because the IDE will recreate it each time you compile. However, you can open this file for viewing by double-clicking it.

The **AutoLotEntities** class extends the **ObjectContext** class, which (as you probably recall) is your entry point to the EF programming model. The constructors of **AutoLotEntities** provide various ways for you to feed in connection string data. The default constructor has been configured to read the connection string data automatically from the wizard-generated **App.config** file:

```
Public Partial Class AutoLotEntities
      Inherits ObjectContext
    Public Sub New()
          MyBase.New("name=AutoLotEntities", "AutoLotEntities")
          MyBase.ContextOptions.LazyLoadingEnabled = True
          OnContextCreated()
    End Sub
    …
End Class
```

Next, notice that the `Cars` property of the `AutoLotEntities` class encapsulates the `ObjectSet(Of Car)` data member. You can use this property to work with the EDM model to modify the physical back-end database indirectly:

```
Public Partial Class AutoLotEntities
    Inherits ObjectContext

    Public ReadOnly Property Cars() As ObjectSet(Of Car)
        Get
            If (_Cars Is Nothing) Then
                _Cars = MyBase.CreateObjectSet(Of Car)("Cars")
            End If
            Return _Cars
        End Get
    End Property

    Private _Cars As ObjectSet(Of Car)
End Class
```

■ **Note** You will also see various methods in your `ObjectContext`-derived classes that begin with `AddTo`. While you can use them to add new entities to the `ObjectSet(Of T)` member variables, the preferred way to do this is with the `ObjectSet(Of T)` member obtained from the strongly typed properties.

The last item of interest in the designer code file is the `Car` entity class. The bulk of the code for each entity class is a collection of properties that model the shape of your conceptual model. Each of these properties implement its Set logic using a call to the Shared `StructuralObject.SetValidValue()` method of the EF API.

Also, the Set logic includes code that informs the EF runtime that the state of an entity has changed, which is important because the `ObjectContext` must know about these changes to push updates to the physical database.

In addition, the Set logic makes calls on two Partial methods. Recall that a VB 2010 Partial method provides a simple way to deal with change notifications in your applications. If you don't implement a Partial method, it is ignored by the compiler and stripped away. Here is the implementation of the `CarNickname` property of the `Car` entity class:

```vb
Public Partial Class Car
        Inherits EntityObject
    ….
    Public Property CarNickname() As Global.System.String
        Get
            Return _CarNickname
        End Get

        Set
            OnCarNicknameChanging(value)
            ReportPropertyChanging("CarNickname")
            _CarNickname = StructuralObject.SetValidValue(value, True)
            ReportPropertyChanged("CarNickname")
            OnCarNicknameChanged()
        End Set
    End Property

    Private _CarNickname As Global.System.String

    Private Partial Sub OnCarNicknameChanging(ByVal value As
            Global.System.String)
    End Sub

    Private Partial Sub OnCarNicknameChanged()
    End Sub
End Class
```

Enhancing the Generated Source Code

All of the designer generated classes have been declared with the **Partial** keyword, which as you recall allows you to implement a class across multiple VB 2010 code files. This is especially useful when working with the EF programming model because it means you can add "real" methods to your entity classes that help you model your business domain better.

In this example, you override the **ToString()** method of the **Car** entity class to return the state of the entity with a well formatted **string**. You also complete the definitions of the Partial **OnCarNicknameChanging()** and **OnCarNicknameChanged()** methods to serve as simple diagnostic notifications. You define the following Partial Class declaration in a new **Car.vb** file:

```vb
Public Class Car
    Public Overrides Function ToString() As String
        ' Since the PetName column could be empty, supply
        ' the default name of **No Name**.
        Return String.Format("{0} is a {1} {2}
        with ID {3}.",
          If(Me.CarNickname, "**No Name**"),
        Me.Color,
        Me.Make,
        Me.CarID)
    End Function
```

```
    Private Sub OnCarNicknameChanging(ByVal value As Global.System.String)
        Console.WriteLine(vbTab & "-> Changing name to: {0}", value)
    End Sub

    Private Sub OnCarNicknameChanged()
        Console.WriteLine(vbTab & "-> Name of car has been changed!")
    End Sub
End Class
```

A friendly reminder: When you provide implementations to these Partial methods, you can receive notifications if the properties of the *entity classes* have changed or are being changed, but not when the physical database has changed. If you need to know when the physical database has changed, you can handle the SavingChanges event on your ObjectContext derived class.

Programming Against the Conceptual Model

Now you can author some code that interacts with your EDM. Begin by updating your Module Module1 to call a helper method from Main(), which will print out each item in the Inventory database using your conceptual model, and another which will insert a new record to the Inventory table:

```
Module Module1
    Sub Main()
        Console.WriteLine("***** Fun with ADO.NET EF *****")
        AddNewRecord()
        PrintAllInventory()
        Console.ReadLine()
    End Sub

    Private Sub AddNewRecord()
        ' Add record to the Inventory table of the AutoLot
        ' database.
        Using context As New AutoLotEntities()
            Try
                ' Hard code data for a new record, for testing.
                context.Cars.AddObject(New Car() With {.CarID = 2222,
                                    .Make = "Yugo", .Color="Brown"})
                context.SaveChanges()
            Catch ex As Exception
                Console.WriteLine(ex.InnerException.Message)
            End Try
        End Using
    End Sub

    Private Sub PrintAllInventory()
        ' Select all items from the Inventory  table of AutoLot,
        ' and print out the data using our custom ToString()
        ' of the Car entity class.
```

```
        Using context As New AutoLotEntities()
            For Each c As Car In context.Cars
                Console.WriteLine(c)
            Next
        End Using
    End Sub
End Module
```

You have seen code similar to this earlier in the chapter, but now you should have a much better idea about how it works. Each helper method creates an instance of the ObjectContext derived class (AutoLotEntities), and uses the strongly typed Cars property to interact with the ObjectSet(Of Car) field. Enumerating each item exposed by the Cars property enables you to submit a SQL SELECT statement indirectly to the underlying ADO.NET data provider. By inserting a new Car object with the AddObject() method of ObjectSet(Of Car), and then calling SaveChanges() on the context, you have preformed a SQL INSERT.

Deleting a Record

When you wish to remove a record from the database, you will first need to locate the correct item in the ObjectSet(Of T), which you can find by passing an EntityKey object (which is a member of the System.Data namespace) to the GetObjectByKey() method. The System.Data namespace is automatically imported into VB projects by default, so you can now author the following helper method:

```
Private Sub RemoveRecord()
    ' Find a car to delete by primary key.
    Using context As New AutoLotEntities()
        ' Define a key for the entity we are looking for.
        Dim key As New EntityKey("AutoLotEntities.Cars", "CarID", 2222)

        ' See if we have it, and delete it if we do.
        Dim carToDelete As Car = CType(context.GetObjectByKey(key), Car)
        If carToDelete IsNot Nothing Then
            context.DeleteObject(carToDelete)
            context.SaveChanges()
        End If
    End Using
End Sub
```

■ **Note** For better or for worse, calling GetObjectByKey() requires a roundtrip to the database before you can delete the object.

Notice that when you are creating an EntityKey object, you need use a String object to inform it which ObjectSet(Of T) to evaluate in a given ObjectContext derived class. The second argument is another String; this one represents the property name on the entity class that is marked as the key, and the final constructor argument is the value of the primary key. Once you find the object in question, you can call DeleteObject() off your context and save the changes.

Updating a Record

Updating a record is also straightforward; locate the object you wish to change, set new property values on the returned entity, and save the changes:

```
Private Sub UpdateRecord()
        ' Find a car to delete by primary key.
    Using context As New AutoLotEntities()
        ' Define a key for the entity we are looking for.
        Dim key As New EntityKey("AutoLotEntities.Cars", "CarID", 2222)

        ' Grab the car, change it, save!
        Dim carToUpdate As Car = CType(context.GetObjectByKey(key), Car)
        If carToUpdate IsNot Nothing Then
          carToUpdate.Color = "Blue"
          context.SaveChanges()
        End If
    End Using
End Sub
```

The preceding method might seem a bit off, at least until you remember that the entity object returned from GetObjectByKey() is a reference to an existing object in the ObjectSet(Of T) field. Thus, when you set properties to change the state, you are changing the same object in memory.

■ **Note** Much like an ADO.NET DataRow object (see Chapter 22), any descendent of EntityObject (meaning, all of your entity classes) has a property named EntityState, which is used by the object context to determine whether the item has been modified, deleted, is detached, and so forth. This is set on your behalf as you work with the programming model; however, you can change this manually as required.

Querying with LINQ to Entities

So far, you have been working with a few simple methods on the object context and entity objects to perform selections, inserts, updates, and deletes. This is useful all by itself; however, EF becomes much more powerful when you incorporate LINQ queries. If you wish to use LINQ to update or delete records, you don't need to make an EntityKey object manually. Consider the following update to the RemoveRecord() method, which will *not work* as expected at this point:

```
Private Sub RemoveRecord()
        ' Find a car to delete by primary key.
    Using context As New AutoLotEntities()
            ' See if we have it?
        Dim carToDelete = From c In context.Cars
                          Where c.CarID = 2222
                          Select c
```

```
      If carToDelete IsNot Nothing Then
        context.DeleteObject(carToDelete)
        context.SaveChanges()
      End If
   End Using
End Sub
```

This code compiles, but you will receive a runtime exception when you attempt to call the DeleteObject() method. The reason: This particular LINQ query returns an ObjectQuery(Of T) object, not a Car object. Always remember that when you build a LINQ query that attempts to locate a single entity, you will get back an ObjectQuery(Of T) representing a query that is capable of bringing back the data you are looking for. To execute the query (and bring back the Car entity), you must execute a method such as FirstOrDefault() on the query object, as in the following example:

```
   Dim carToDelete = (
      From c In context.Cars
      Where c.CarID = 2222
      Select c).FirstOrDefault()
```

By calling FirstOrDefault() on the ObjectQuery(Of T), you find the item you want; or, if there is no Car with the ID of 2222, a default value of null.

Given that you have already worked with many LINQ expressions in Chapter 13, a few more examples will suffice for the time being:

```
Private Sub FunWithLINQQueries()
   Using context As New AutoLotEntities()
      ' Get a projection of new data.
      Dim colorsMakes = From item In context.Cars
                        Select New With {Key item.Color, Key item.Make}

      For Each item In colorsMakes
        Console.WriteLine(item)
      Next

      ' Get only items where CarID < 1000
      Dim idsLessThan1000 = From item In context.Cars
                            Where item.CarID < 1000
                            Select item
      For Each item In idsLessThan1000
        Console.WriteLine(item)
      Next
   End Using
End Sub
```

While the syntax of these queries is simple enough, remember that you are hitting a database each time you apply a LINQ query to the object context! Recall that when you wish to obtain an independent copy of data, which can be the target of new LINQ queries, you want to use immediate execution with the ToList(Of T)(), ToArray(Of T)() or ToDictionary(Of K,V)() extension methods (among others). Here is an update of the previous method, which performs the equivalent of a SELECT *, caches the entities as an array, and manipulates the array data using LINQ to Objects:

```vb
Using context As New AutoLotEntities()
    ' Get all data from the Inventory table.
    ' could also write:
    ' Dim allData = (From item in context.Cars Select item).ToArray()
    Dim allData = context.Cars.ToArray()

    ' Get a projection of new data.
    Dim colorsMakes = From item In allData
                      Select New With {Key item.Color, Key item.Make}

    ' Get only items where CarID < 1000
    Dim idsLessThan1000 = From item In allData
                          Where item.CarID < 1000
                          Select item
End Using
```

Working with LINQ to Entities is much more enticing when your EDM contains multiple related tables. You'll see some example that illustrate this in a moment; however, let's wrap up this current example by looking at two other ways you can interact with your object context.

Querying with Entity SQL

To be sure, you will be querying and `ObjectSet<(Of T)` with LINQ a majority of the time. The entity client will break down your LINQ query into a fitting SQL statement, passing it onto the database for processing. However, you can use Entity SQL if you wish to have more control over how the query is formatted.

Entity SQL is a SQL-like query language that can be applied to entities. While the format of an Entity SQL statement is similar to a traditional SQL statement, it is not identical. Entity SQL has a unique syntax because the entities receive the query, not the physical database. Like a LINQ to Entities query, an Entity SQL query is used to pass a "real" SQL query to the database.

This chapter will not dive into the details of building Entity SQL commands, so please consult the .NET Framework 4.0 SDK documentation if you want more information. However, one example might be helpful. Consider the following method, which builds an Entity SQL statement that finds all black cars in the `ObjectSet(Of Car>)` collection:

```vb
Private Sub FunWithEntitySQL()
    Using context As New AutoLotEntities()
        ' Build a string containing Entity SQL syntax.
        Dim query As String = "SELECT VALUE car" &
                              "FROM AutoLotEntities.Cars AS car" &
                              "WHERE car.Color='black'"

        ' Now build a ObjectQuery(Of T) based on the string.
        Dim blackCars = context.CreateQuery(Of Car)(query)
        For Each item In blackCars
            Console.WriteLine(item)
        Next
    End Using
End Sub
```

Notice that you pass in the formatted Entity SQL statement as an argument to the `CreateQuery(Of T)` method of your object context.

Working with the Entity Client Data Reader Object

When you use LINQ to Entities or Entity SQL, the fetched data is mapped back to your entity classes automatically, thanks to the entity client service. Typically this is exactly what you require; however, you can intercept the result set before it makes its way to your entity objects and process it manually using the `EntityDataReader`.

Here is a final helper method for this example, which uses several members of the `System.Data.EntityClient` namespace to build a connection manually through a command object and data reader. This code should look familiar due to your previous work in Chapter 21; the major difference is that you use Entity SQL, rather than "normal" SQL:

```
Private Sub FunWithEntityDataReader()
    ' Make a connection object, based on our *.config file.
    Using cn As New EntityConnection("name=AutoLotEntities")
        cn.Open()

        ' Now build an Entity SQL query.
        Dim query As String = "SELECT VALUE car "&
                              "FROM AutoLotEntities.Cars AS car"

        ' Create a command object.
        Using cmd As EntityCommand = cn.CreateCommand()
          cmd.CommandText = query

          ' Finally, get the data reader and process records.
          Using dr As EntityDataReader =
              cmd.ExecuteReader(CommandBehavior.SequentialAccess)
                  Do While dr.Read()
                          Console.WriteLine("***** RECORD *****")
                          Console.WriteLine("ID: {0}", dr("CarID"))
                          Console.WriteLine("Make: {0}", dr("Make"))
                          Console.WriteLine("Color: {0}", dr("Color"))
                          Console.WriteLine("Pet Name: {0}", dr("CarNickname"))
                          Console.WriteLine()
                  Loop
              End Using
        End Using
    End Using
End Sub
```

Great! This initial example should go a long way toward helping you understand the nuts and bolts of working with the Entity Framework. As mentioned previously, things become much more interesting when your EDM contains interrelated tables, which you will learn about next.

■ **Source Code** You can find the InventoryEDMConsoleApp example under the Chapter 23 subdirectory.

AutoLotDAL Version 4.0, Now with Entities

Next, you will learn how to build an EDM that captures the bulk of the AutoLot database, including your GetPetName stored procedure. I strongly suggest that you make a copy of the AutoLotDAL (Version 3) project you created in Chapter 22 and rename this copy to AutoLotDAL (Version 4).

Open the latest version of the AutoLotDAL project in Visual Studio 2010 and insert a new ADO.NET Entity Data Model project item named AutoLotDAL_EF.edmx. On step three of the wizard, you should select the Inventory, Orders, and Customers tables (there's no need to nab the CreditRisks table at this time), as well as the custom stored procedure (see Figure 23-17).

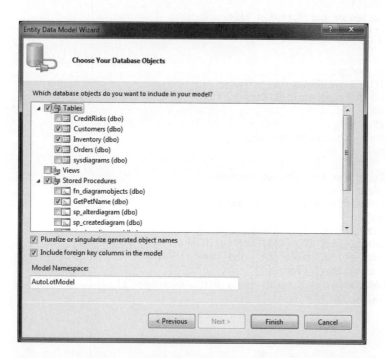

Figure 23-17. The *.edmx file for a majority of the AutoLot database

In contrast to the first EDM example, this time you don't bother renaming your entity class names or their properties.

Mapping the Stored Procedure

Here's one aspect of the EDM Wizard that is quite odd: even when you check off the name of a stored procedure to include in your conceptual model, your work is not done. At this point all you have done is make the IDE aware of the physical stored procedure; to make it materialize in code, you need to import the function into the conceptual layer. Open the Model browser (using the View ➤ Other Windows ➤ Entity Data Model Browser menu) and notice that you can see GetPetName in the physical database (located under AutoLotModel.Store); however, the Function Imports folder (highlighted in Figure 23-18) is currently empty.

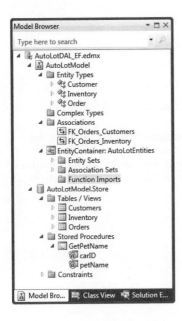

Figure 23-18. Stored procedures must be imported before you can call them!

You can begin mapping this to your conceptual layer by right-clicking on the Function Imports folder and selecting the Add Function Import... menu option (see Figure 23-19).

Figure 23-19. *Choosing to import a stored procedure into your conceptual model*

In the resulting dialog box, you want to pick the name of the physical stored procedure (from the Stored Procedure Name dropdown box), and then supply a name of the method to map to in your conceptual model. In this case, the names will map directly. Now recall that your stored procedure does not literally return a set of records; however, it does return an output parameter. Thus, you need to make sure that you check the None radio button (see Figure 23-20).

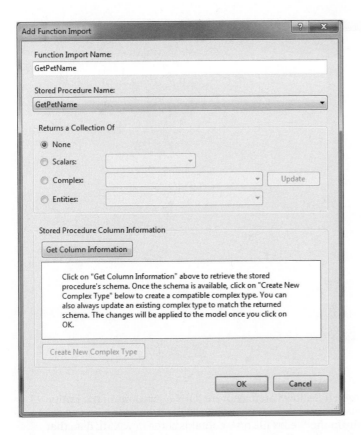

Figure 23-20. Mapping the physical stored procedure to the conceptual model

The Role of Navigation Properties

If you look at the EDM designer now, you will see each table is accounted for, including new entries in the Navigation Properties section of a given entity class (see Figure 23-21).

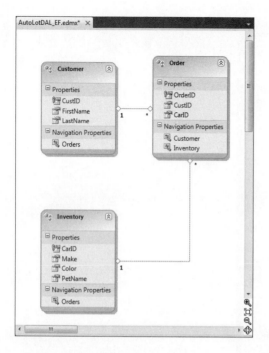

Figure 23-21. Navigation properties

As the name suggests, *navigation properties* allow you to capture JOIN operations in the Entity Framework programming model (without the need to author complex SQL statements). To account for these foreign key relationships, each entity in the *.edmx file now contains some new XML data that shows how entities are connected through key data. Feel free to open the *.edmx file using the XML editor if you wish to see the markup directly; however, you can see this same information in the Model Browser window, under the Associations folder (see Figure 23-22).

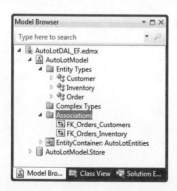

Figure 23-22. Viewing your entity relationships

If you wish, change the version number of this new library to 4.0.0.0 (using the Assembly Information button within Applications tab of Properties window). Now compile your modified `AutoLot.dll` assembly before moving to the first client application.

■ **Source Code** You can find the `AutoLotDAL` (Version 4) project under the Chapter 23 subdirectory.

Using Navigation Properties within LINQ to Entity Queries

Next, you will learn how to use these navigation properties within the context of LINQ to Entity queries (you could also use them with Entity SQL; however, this book doesn't delve into that aspect of this topic). Before you bind your data to a Windows Forms GUI, you make one final Console Application named `AutoLotEDMClient`. Once you create the project, set a reference to `System.Data.Entity.dll` and the latest and greatest version of `AutoLotDAL.dll`.

Next, insert the `App.config` file from your `AutoLotDAL` project (using the Project ➤ Add Existing Item menu option) and import the `AutoLotDAL` namespace. Recall that the `App.Config` file generated by the EDM tools defines the correct connection string required by the Entity Framework.

Next, you will update the physical Orders table with a few new records. Specifically, you want to ensure that a single customer has multiple orders. Using the Visual Studio 2010 Server Explorer, update the `Orders` table with one or two new records to ensure that a single customer has two or more orders. For example, in Figure 23-23, customer #4 has two pending orders, for cars #1992 and #83.

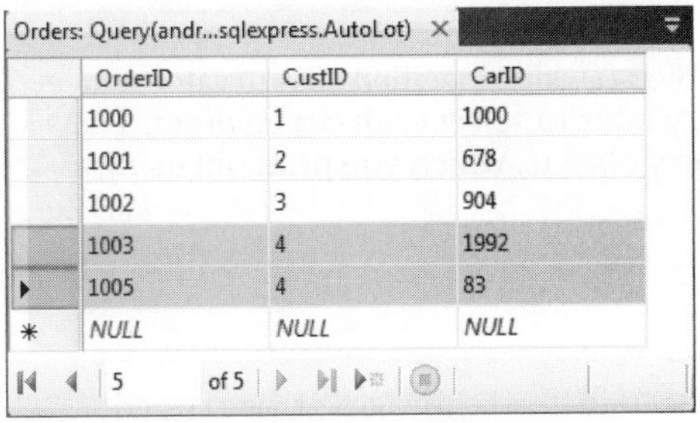

Figure 23-23. A single customer with multiple orders

Now update your `Module1` Module with a new helper method (called from `Main()`). This method uses the navigation properties to select each `Inventory` object on order for a given customer:

```
Private Sub PrintCustomerOrders(ByVal custID As String)

    Dim id As Integer = Integer.Parse(custID)

    Using context As New AutoLotEntities()
        Dim carsOnOrder = From o In context.Orders
                          Where o.CustID = id
                          Select o.Inventory
```

```
                    Console.WriteLine(vbLf & "Customer has {0} orders pending:",
                                        carsOnOrder.Count())
                    For Each item In carsOnOrder
                        Console.WriteLine("-> {0} {1} named {2}.",
                                        item.Color, item.Make, item.PetName)
                    Next
            End Using

    End Sub
```

When you run your application, you see something similar to the following output (notice that you specify a customer ID of four when you call PrintCustomerOrders() from Main()):

```
***** Navigation Properties *****

Please enter customer ID: 4


Customer has 2 orders pending:

-> Pink Saab named Pinky.

-> Rust Ford named Rusty.
```

Here, you find a single Customer entity in the context, which has the specified CustID value. Once you find the given customer, you can navigate to the Inventory table to select each car on order. The return value of your LINQ query is an enumeration of Inventory objects, which you print out using a standard For Each loop.

Invoking a Stored Procedure

In the AutoLotDAL EMD, you now have the information you need to invoke the GetPetName stored procedure. You can do this using either of two approaches:

```
Private Sub CallStoredProc()
    Using context As New AutoLotEntities()
        Dim input As New ObjectParameter("carID", 83)
        Dim output As New ObjectParameter("petName", GetType(String))

        ' Call ExecuteFunction off the context....
        context.ExecuteFunction("GetPetName", input, output)

        ' ....or use the strongly typed method on the context.
        context.GetPetName(83, output)
```

```
        Console.WriteLine("Car #83 is named {0}", output.Value)
    End Using
End Sub
```

The first approach is to call the `ExecuteFunction()` method of your object context. In this case, the stored procedure is identified by a string name, and each parameter is represented by an object of type `ObjectParameter`, which is in the `System.Data.Objects` namespace (don't forget to import this into your VB 2010 code file!).

The second approach is to use the strongly typed name in your object context. This approach proves a tad simpler because you can send input parameters (such as the `car` ID) as typed data, rather than as an `ObjectParameter` object.

■ **Source Code** You can find the `AutoLotEDMClient` example under the Chapter 23 subdirectory.

Data Binding Entities to Windows Forms GUIs

To conclude this introductory examination of the ADO.NET Entity Framework, you will create a simple example where you bind entity objects to a Windows Forms GUI. As mentioned earlier in this chapter, you will examine data-binding operations in WPF and ASP.NET projects.

Create a new Windows Forms application named AutoLotEDM_GUI and rename your initial form to `MainForm`. After you create the project (and similar to the previous client application you created), you set a reference to `System.Data.Entity.dll` and the latest and greatest version of `AutoLotDAL.dll`. Next, insert the `App.config` file from your AutoLotDAL project (using the Project ➤ Add Existing Item menu option)to replace the existing app.config in your project and import the `AutoLotModel` namespace into your Form's primary code file.

Now add a `DataGridView` object to the form designer and rename the control to `gridInventory`. Once you place this control on the designer, select the inline grid editor (the tiny arrow on the upper right of the widget). From the Choose Data Source dropdown box, add a project data source (see Figure 23-24).

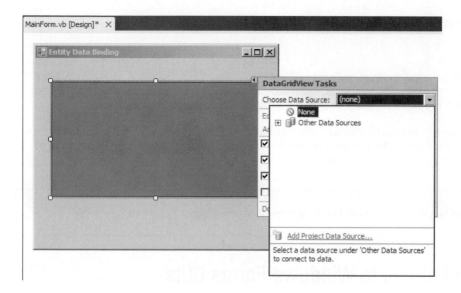

Figure 23-24. Designing the Windows Forms DataGridView control

In this case, you do not bind directly to the database; instead, you bind to an entity class, so pick the Object option (see Figure 23-25).

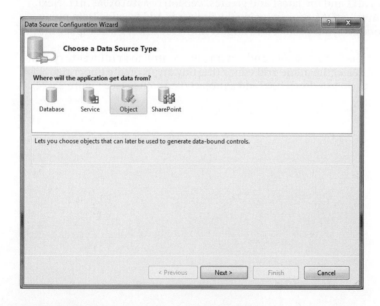

Figure 23-25. Binding to a strongly typed object

In the final step, check off the **Inventory** table of `AutoLotDAL.dll` as shown in Figure 23-26 (if you don't see it listed, you probably forgot to reference this library).

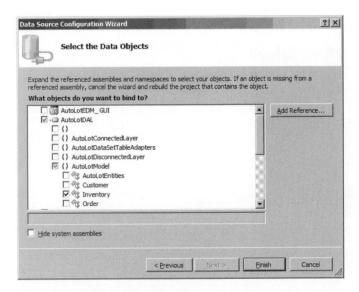

Figure 23-26. Selecting the Inventory table

Once you click the Finish button, you'll see that the grid displays each property of the **Inventory** entity class, including the navigation properties! To remove them from the grid, activate the inline editor again (that tiny little arrow) and this time click the Edit Columns... link. Select the `Orders` column in the Edit Columns dialog and remove it from view (see Figure 23-27).

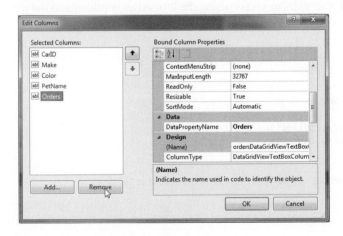

Figure 23-27. Cleaning up the grid's UI

To finish the UI, add a single Button control and rename it to btnUpdate. At this point, your designer should look something like what you see in Figure 23-28.

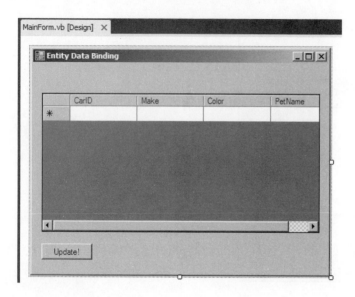

Figure 23-28. The final UI

Adding the Data Binding Code

At this point, you have a grid that can display any number of Inventory objects; however, you need to write the code to do so. Thanks to the runtime engine of the EF, the code could not be simpler. Begin by handling the FormClosed and Load events of your MainForm class (using the Properties window) and the Click event of the Button control. Once you do this, update your code file with the following snippet:

```vb
Public Class MainForm
        Inherits Form
    Private context As New AutoLotEntities()

    Private Sub MainForm_Load(ByVal sender As Object, ByVal e As EventArgs)
      Handles MyBase.Load
        ' Bind the ObjectSet(Of Inventory) collection to the grid.
        gridInventory.DataSource = context.Inventories
    End Sub

    Private Sub btnUpdate_Click(ByVal sender As Object, ByVal e As EventArgs)
      Handles btnUpdate.Click
        context.SaveChanges()
        MessageBox.Show("Data saved!")
    End Sub
```

```
    Private Sub MainForm_FormClosed(ByVal sender As Object,
                                     ByVal e As FormClosedEventArgs)
        Handles MyBase.FormClosed
            context.Dispose()
    End Sub
End Class
```

This is all you need to do! If you run your application, you can now add new records to the grid, select a row and delete it, and modify existing rows. When you click your Update button, the **Inventory** database is updated automatically because the object context has been kind enough to generate all the necessary SQL statements for selecting, updating, deleting, and inserting automatically. Figure 23-29 shows the completed Windows Forms application.

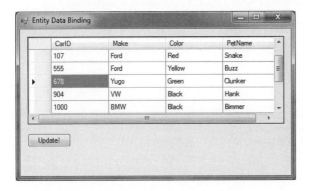

Figure 23-29. *The completed application*

Here are some key takeaways from this preceding example:

- The context remains allocated throughout the application.

- The call to **context.Inventories** executes SQL to fetch all rows from the **Inventory** table into memory.

- The context tracks *dirty* entities, so it knows what SQL to execute upon **SaveChanges()**.

- After **SaveChanges()**, the entities are considered *clean* again.

That wraps up this chapter's examination of the ADO.NET Entity Framework. While there is so much more to this programming model than this chapter can address, you should now have a solid understanding about what problems EF attempts to solve and how to work with the overall programming model. Be sure to consult the .NET Framework 4.0 SDK documentation for more details of this slick data programming API.

Summary

This chapter wrapped up your formal investigation of database programming using ADO.NET by examining the role of the Entity Framework. EF allows you to program against a conceptual model that closely maps to your business domain. While you can reshape your entities in any way you choose, the EF runtime ensures that the changed data is mapped to the correct physical table data.

You learned about the role of (and composition of) `*.edmx` files and how to generate them using the Visual Studio 2010 IDE. Along the way, you also learned how to map stored procedures to functions in your conceptual layer, how to apply LINQ queries to the object model, the role of Entity SQL, and how to consume fetched data at the lowest level using the `EntityDataReader`.

You wrapped up this chapter with a simple example of binding entity classes to graphical user interfaces within the context of a Windows Forms application. You'll see other examples of binding entities to GUI applications when you examine Windows Presentation Foundation and ASP.NET.

■ ■ ■

## CHAPTER 24

Introducing LINQ to XML

As a .NET developer, you are bound to encounter XML-based data in numerous places. Application and web-based configuration files store information as XML. ADO.NET **DataSet**s can easily save out (or load in) data as XML. Windows Presentation Foundation, Silverlight, and Windows Workflow Foundation all make use of an XML-based grammar (XAML) to represent desktop UIs browser-based UIs, and workflows respectively. Even Windows Communication Foundation (as well as the original .NET remoting APIs) also stores numerous settings as the well-formatted string called XML.

Although XML is indeed everywhere, programming with XML has historically been very tedious, very verbose, and very complex if one is not well versed in a great number of XML technologies (XPath, XQuery, XSLT, DOM, SAX, etc.). Since the inception of the .NET platform, Microsoft has provided a specific assembly devoted to programming with XML documents named **System.Xml.dll**. Within this binary are a number of namespaces and types to various XML programming techniques, as well as a few .NET-specific XML APIs such as the **XmlReader/XmlWriter** classes.

These days, most .NET programmers prefer to interact with XML data using the LINQ to XML API. As you will see in this chapter, the LINQ to XML programming model allows you to capture the structure of an XML data in code, and provides a much simpler way to create, manipulate, load, and save XML data. While you could use LINQ to XML as little more than a simpler way to create XML documents, you can also easily incorporate LINQ query expressions into the mix, to quickly query a document for information.

A Tale of Two XML APIs

When the .NET platform was first introduced, programmers were able to manipulate XML documents using the types within the **System.Xml.dll** assembly. Using the contained namespaces and types, you were able to generate XML data in memory and save it to disk storage. As well, the **System.Xml.dll** assembly provided types allowing you to load XML documents into memory, search an XML document for specific nodes, validate a document against a given schema, and other common programming tasks.

While this original library has been used successfully in many .NET projects, working with these types was a tad bit cumbersome (to put it politely), as the programming model bore no relationship to the structure of the XML document itself. For example, assume you needed to build an XML file in memory and save it to the file system. If you were to use the types of **System.Xml.dll**, you might author code like the following (if you want to follow along, create a new Console Application project named LinqToXmlFirstLook, and import the System.Xml namespace):

```
Private Sub BuildXmlDocWithDOM()
    ' Make a new XML document in memory.
    Dim doc As New XmlDocument()

    ' Fill this document with a root element
    ' named <Inventory>.
    Dim inventory As XmlElement = doc.CreateElement("Inventory")

    ' Now, make a sub element named <Car> with
    ' an ID attribute.
    Dim car As XmlElement = doc.CreateElement("Car")
    car.SetAttribute("ID", "1000")

    ' Build the data within the <Car> element.
    Dim name As XmlElement = doc.CreateElement("PetName")
    name.InnerText = "Jimbo"
    Dim color As XmlElement = doc.CreateElement("Color")
    color.InnerText = "Red"
    Dim make As XmlElement = doc.CreateElement("Make")
    make.InnerText = "Ford"

    ' Add <PetName>, <Color> and <Make> to the <Car>
    ' element.
    car.AppendChild(name)
    car.AppendChild(color)
    car.AppendChild(make)

    ' Add the <Car> element to the <Inventory> element.
    inventory.AppendChild(car)

    ' Insert the complete XML into the XmlDocument object,
    ' and save to file.
    doc.AppendChild(inventory)
    doc.Save("Inventory.xml")
End Sub
```

If you were to call this method, you could be able to see that the Inventory.xml file (located in the bin\Debug folder) contains the following data:

```
<Inventory>

  <Car ID="1000">

    <PetName>Jimbo</PetName>

    <Color>Red</Color>

    <Make>Ford</Make>
```

```
    </Car>

</Inventory>
```

While this method works as expected, a few observations are in order. First, the programming model of System.Xml.dll is Microsoft's implementation of the W3C Document Object Model (DOM) specification. Under this model, an XML document is created from the bottom up. First you create a document, then you create sub-elements, and finally you add the elements to the document. To account for this in code, you need to author quite a bit of function calls off the XmlDocument, and XmlElement classes (among others).

For this example, it took 16 lines of code (not including code comments) to build even this very simple XML document. If you needed to build a more complex document with the System.Xml.dll assembly, you could end up with a great deal of code. While you could certainly streamline this code, by building nodes via various looping or decision constructs, the fact remains that the body of code has little visual indicators regarding the final XML tree.

LINQ to XML As a Better DOM

The LINQ to XML API is an alternative manner to create, manipulate, and query XML documents, which uses a much more functional approach than the System.Xml DOM model. Rather than building an XML document by assembling elements individually and updating the XML tree through a set of function calls, you can author top-down code such as the following:

```
Private Sub BuildXmlDocWithLINQToXml()
    ' Create a XML document in a more 'functional' manner.
    Dim doc As New XElement("Inventory",
      New XElement("Car", New XAttribute("ID", "1000"),
      New XElement("PetName", "Jimbo"),
      New XElement("Color", "Red"),
      New XElement("Make", "Ford")))

      ' Save to file.
    doc.Save("InventoryWithLINQ.xml")
End Sub
```

Here, you are using a new set of types from the System.Xml.Linq namespace, specifically XElement and XAttribute. If you were to call this method, you will find the same XML data has been created, this time with much less fuss and bother. Notice how, through some careful indentation, your source code has the same overall structure of the resulting XML document. This is very useful in and of itself, but also notice that you have a much smaller body of code than the previous example (based on how you space your code, you saved about 10 lines!)

Here, you have not made use of any LINQ query expressions, but have simply used the types of the System.Xml.Linq namespace to generate an in-memory XML document which is then saved to file. Effectively, you have used LINQ to XML as a better DOM. As you will see later in this chapter, the classes of System.Xml.Linq are LINQ-aware, and can be the target for the same sort of LINQ queries you learned about in Chapter 13.

As you learn more about LINQ to XML, you will most likely find it much easier to work with than the initial XML libraries of .NET. However, this is not to say you will never use the namespaces of the original `System.Xml.dll` library. But chances are the times you will opt to use `System.Xml.dll` for new projects will be significantly reduced.

VB 2010 Literal Syntax As a Better LINQ to XML

Before you begin your formal examination into LINQ to XML as seen through VB 2010, I do want to briefly mention that the Visual Basic language takes the functional approach of this API to the next level. In VB 2010, you can define *XML literals*, which allow you to assign an `XElement` to a stream of inline XML markup, directly in code. Assuming you had a VB 2010 project, you could build the following method:

```
Public Class XmlLiteralExample
  Public Sub MakeXmlFileUsingLiterals()
    ' Notice that we can inline XML data
    ' to an XElement.
    Dim doc As XElement = _
      <Inventory>
        <Car ID="1000">
          <PetName>Jimbo</PetName>
          <Color>Red</Color>
          <Make>Ford</Make>
        </Car>
      </Inventory>

    ' Save to file.
    doc.Save("InventoryVBStyle.xml")
  End Sub
End Class
```

Once the VB 2010 compiler processes the XML literal, it will map the XML data into the correct underlying LINQ to XML object model. In fact, when you are working with LINQ to XML within a VB 2010 project, the IDE already understands that your XML literal syntax is just a shorthand notation for the related code. In Figure 24-1, notice how you can apply the dot operator to the `</Inventory>` end tag and see the same members as you would find if you apply the dot operator to a strongly typed `XElement`.

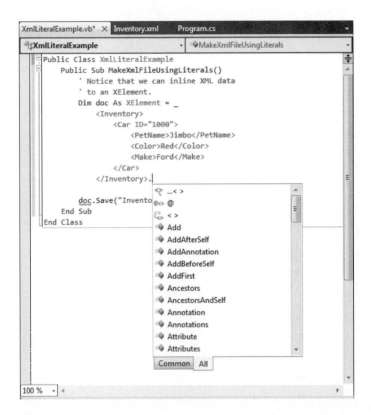

Figure 24-1. VB 2010 XML literal syntax is a shorthand notation for working with the LINQ to XML object model

Members of the System.Xml.Linq Namespace

Somewhat surprisingly, the core LINQ to XML assembly (System.Xml.Linq.dll) defines a very small number of types in three distinct namespaces, specifically System.Xml.Linq, System.Xml.Schema, and System.Xml.XPath (see Figure 24-2).

Figure 24-2. The namespaces of `System.Xml.Linq.dll`

The core namespace, `System.Xml.Linq`, contains a very manageable set of classes that represent various aspects of an XML document (its elements and their attributes, XML namespaces, XML comments, and processing instructions, etc.). Table 24-1 documents the core members of `System.Xml.Linq`.

Table 24-1. Select Members of the System.Xml.Linq Namespace

Member of System.Xml.Linq	Meaning in Life
XAttribute	Represents an XML attribute on a given XML element.
XCData	Represents a CDATA section in the XML document. Information in a CDATA section represents data in an XML document which must be included, but does not conform to the rules of XML grammars (for example, script code).
XComment	Represents an XML comment.
XDeclaration	Represents the opening declaration of an XML document.
XDocument	Represents the entirety of an XML document.

Member of System.Xml.Linq	Meaning in Life
XElement	Represents a given element within an XML document, including the root element.
XName	Represents the name of an XML element or XML attribute.
XNamespace	Represents an XML namespace.
XNode	Represents the abstract concept of a node (element, comment, document type, processing instruction, or text node) in the XML tree.
XProcessingInstruction	Represents an XML processing instruction.
XStreamingElement	Represents elements in an XML tree that supports deferred streaming output.

Figure 24-3 shows how the inheritance chain of the key class types.

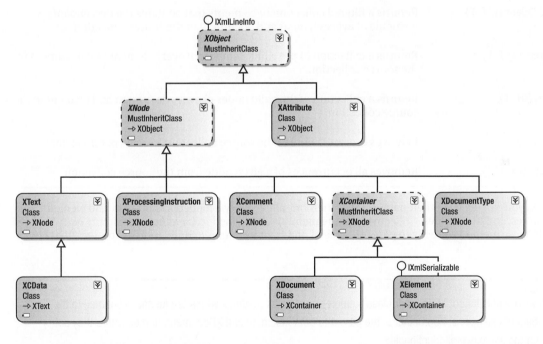

Figure 24-3. The LINQ to XML core class hierarchy

The LINQ to XML Axis Methods

In addition to the X* classes, System.Xml.Linq defines a class named Extensions, which (of course) defines a set of extension methods which typically extend IEnumerable(Of T), where T is some descendent of XNode or XContainer. Table 24-2 documents some of the important extension methods to be aware of (as you will see, these are very useful when you wish to work with LINQ queries).

Table 24-2. Select Members of the LINQ to XML Extensions Class

Member of Extensions	Meaning in Life
Ancestors(Of T)()	Returns a filtered collection of elements that contains the ancestors of every node in the source collection.
Attributes()	Returns a filtered collection of the attributes of every element in the source collection.
DescendantNodes(Of T)()	Returns a collection of the descendant nodes of every document and element in the source collection.
Descendants(Of T)	Returns a filtered collection of elements that contains the descendant elements of every element and document in the source collection.
Elements(Of T)	Returns a collection of the child elements of every element and document in the source collection.
Nodes(Of T)	Returns a collection of the child nodes of every document and element in the source collection.
Remove()	Removes every attribute in the source collection from its parent element.
Remove(Of T)()	Removes all occurrences of a given node from the source collection.

As you can tell from their names, these methods allow query a loaded XML tree to find elements, attributes, and their values. Collectively, these methods are termed *axis methods,* or simply *axes.* You can apply these methods directly to parts of a tree of nodes, or use them to build more elaborate LINQ queries.

■ **Note** The MustInherit XContainer class support a number of methods which are identically named to the members of Extensions. XContainer is the parent to both XElement and XDocument, and therefore they both support the same overall functionality.

You'll see examples of using some of these axis methods over the chapter. However, here is a quick example:

```
Private Sub DeleteNodeFromDoc()
Dim doc As New XElement("Inventory",
   New XElement("Car", New XAttribute("ID", "1000"),
   New XElement("PetName", "Jimbo"),
   New XElement("Color", "Red"),
   New XElement("Make", "Ford")))

' Delete the PetName element from the tree.
doc.Descendants("PetName").Remove()
Console.WriteLine(doc)
End Sub
```

If you invoke this method, you'd see the following "pruned" XML tree:

```
<Inventory>

  <Car ID="1000">

    <Color>Red</Color>

    <Make>Ford</Make>

  </Car>

</Inventory>
```

The Oddness of XName (and XNamespace)

If you examine the signatures of the LINQ to XML axis methods (or the identically named members of XContainer), you'll notice that they typically require you to specify what looks to be an XName object. Consider the signature of the Descendants() method defined by XContainer:

```
Public Function Descendants(ByVal name As XName) As IEnumerable(Of XElement)
```

XName is "odd" in that you will never really directly make use of it in your code. In fact, since this class has no Public constructor, you cannot make an XName object:

```
' Error!  Can't make XName objects!
doc.Descendants(New XName("PetName")).Remove()
```

If you were to view the formal definition of XName, you will see that this class defines a custom implicit conversion operator (see Chapter 12 for information of defining custom conversion operators), which will map a simple System.String to the correct XName object:

```
' We really make an XName in the background!
doc.Descendants("PetName").Remove()
```

■ **Note** The XNamespace class also supports the same flavor of implicit string conversion.

The good news is that you can use textual values to represent the names of elements or attributes when you work with these axis methods, and allow the LINQ to XML API to map your String data to the necessary object types.

■ **Source Code** The LinqToXmlFirstLook example can be found under the Chapter 24 subdirectory.

Working with XElement and XDocument

Let's continue the investigation of LINQ to XML with a new Console Application named ConstructingXmlDocs. As you have already seen, **XDocument** represents the entirety of an XML document in the LINQ to XML programming model, as it can be used to define a root element, and all contained elements, processing instructions and XML declarations. Here is another example of building XML data using **XDocument**:

```
Sub CreateFullXDocument()
    Dim inventoryDoc As New XDocument(New XDeclaration("1.0", "utf-8", "yes"),
        New XComment("Current Inventory of cars!"),
        New XProcessingInstruction("xml-stylesheet",
                                    "href='MyStyles.css' title='Compact' type='text/css'"),
        New XElement("Inventory",
            New XElement("Car", New XAttribute("ID", "1"),
            New XElement("Color", "Green"),
            New XElement("Make", "BMW"),
            New XElement("PetName", "Stan")),
            New XElement("Car", New XAttribute("ID", "2"),
            New XElement("Color", "Pink"),
            New XElement("Make", "Yugo"),
            New XElement("PetName", "Melvin"))))

    ' Save to disk.
    inventoryDoc.Save("SimpleInventory.xml")
End Sub
```

Again, notice that the constructor of the **XDocument** object is in fact a tree of additional LINQ to XML objects. The constructor called here takes as the first parameter an **XDeclaration**, followed by a parameter array of **object**s (recall, VB 2010 ParamArrays allow you to pass in a comma delimited list of arguments, which are packaged as an array on your behalf):

```
Public Sub New(ByVal declaration As System.Xml.Linq.XDeclaration,
                       ByVal ParamArray content() As Object)
```

If you were to invoke this method from Main(), you'd see the following data in the SimpleInventory.xml file:

```xml
<?xml version="1.0" encoding="utf-8" standalone="yes"?>

<!--Current Inventory of cars!-->

<?xml-stylesheet href='MyStyles.css' title='Compact' type='text/css'?>

<Inventory>

  <Car ID="1">

    <Color>Green</Color>

    <Make>BMW</Make>

    <PetName>Stan</PetName>

  </Car>

  <Car ID="2">

    <Color>Pink</Color>

    <Make>Yugo</Make>

    <PetName>Melvin</PetName>

  </Car>

</Inventory>
```

As it turns out, the default XML declaration for any XDocument is to use utf-8 encoding, XML version 1.0, as a standalone document. Therefore, you could completely delete the creation of the XDeclaration object and end up with the same data; given that just about every document requires this same declaration, use of XDeclaration is typically not that common.

If you do not need to define processing instructions or a custom XML declaration, you can avoid the use of XDocument all together, and simply use XElement. Remember, XElement can be used to represent the root element of the XML document and all sub-objects. Thus, you could generate a commented list of inventory items as so:

```
Sub CreateRootAndChildren()
Dim inventoryDoc As New XElement("Inventory",
```

```
    New XComment("Current Inventory of cars!"),
    New XElement("Car", New XAttribute("ID", "1"),
        New XElement("Color", "Green"),
        New XElement("Make", "BMW"),
        New XElement("PetName", "Stan")),
        New XElement("Car", New XAttribute("ID", "2"),
        New XElement("Color", "Pink"),
        New XElement("Make", "Yugo"),
        New XElement("PetName", "Melvin")))

    ' Save to disk.
    inventoryDoc.Save("SimpleInventory.xml")
End Sub
```

The output is more or less identical, sans the custom processing instruction for a hypothetical style sheet:

```
<?xml version="1.0" encoding="utf-8"?>

<Inventory>

  <!--Current Inventory of cars!-->

  <Car ID="1">

    <Color>Green</Color>

    <Make>BMW</Make>

    <PetName>Stan</PetName>

  </Car>

  <Car ID="2">

    <Color>Pink</Color>

    <Make>Yugo</Make>

    <PetName>Melvin</PetName>

  </Car>

</Inventory>
```

Generating Documents from Arrays and Containers

So far you have been building XML documents using fixed hard coded constructor values. More commonly, you will need to generate XElements (or XDocuments) by reading data from arrays, ADO.NET objects, file data, or whatnot One way to map in-memory data to a new XElement is by using a set of standard "For loops" to move data into the LINQ to XML object model. While this is certainly doable, it is more streamlined to embed a LINQ query within the construction of the XElement directly.

Assume you have an anonymous array of anonymous classes (just to avoid the amount of code for this example; any array, List(Of T) or other container would do here). You could map this data into an XElement as so:

```
Sub MakeXElementFromArray()
    ' Create an anonymous array of anonymous types.
    Dim people = { New With  {Key .FirstName = "Mandy", Key .Age = 32},
                             New With {Key .FirstName = "Andrew", Key .Age = 40},
                             New With {Key .FirstName = "Dave", Key .Age = 41},
                             New With {Key .FirstName = "Sara", Key .Age = 31}
                        }

    Dim peopleDoc As New XElement("People",
            From c In people  Select New XElement("Person",
                                              New XAttribute("Age", c.Age),
                                              New XElement("FirstName", c.FirstName)))

            Console.WriteLine(peopleDoc)
End Sub
```

Here, the peopleDoc object defines the root <People> element with the results of a LINQ query. This LINQ query creates new XElements based on each item in the people array. If this embedded query is a bit hard on the eyes, you could break things down into explicit steps, like so:

```
Sub MakeXElementFromArray()
    ' Create an anonymous array of anonymous types.
    Dim people =
    {
        New With {Key .FirstName = "Mandy", Key .Age = 32},
        New With {Key .FirstName = "Andrew", Key .Age = 40},
        New With {Key .FirstName = "Dave",  Key .Age = 41},
        New With {Key .FirstName = "Sara", Key .Age = 31}
    }

    Dim peopleDoc As New XElement("People",
            From c In people Select New XElement("Person",
                                              New XAttribute("Age", c.Age),
                                              New XElement("FirstName", c.FirstName))

            Console.WriteLine(peopleDoc)
End Sub
```

Either way, the output is the same:

```
<People>

  <Person Age="32">

    <FirstName>Mandy</FirstName>

  </Person>

  <Person Age="40">

    <FirstName>Andrew</FirstName>

  </Person>

  <Person Age="41">

    <FirstName>Dave</FirstName>

  </Person>

  <Person Age="31">

    <FirstName>Sara</FirstName>

  </Person>

</People>
```

Loading and Parsing XML Content

The XElement and XDocument types both support Load() and Parse() methods, which allow you to hydrate an XML object model from String objects containing XML data or external XML files. Consider the following method, which illustrates both approaches:

```
Sub ParseAndLoadExistingXml()
    ' Build an XElement from String.
    Dim myElement As String = "<Car ID ='3'>" & vbLf &
                                "<Color>Yellow</Color>" & vbLf &
                                "<Make>Yugo</Make>" & vbLf &
                                "</Car>"
    Dim newElement As XElement = XElement.Parse(myElement)
    Console.WriteLine(newElement)
    Console.WriteLine()
```

```vb
        ' Load the SimpleInventory.xml file.
        Dim myDoc As XDocument = XDocument.Load("SimpleInventory.xml")
        Console.WriteLine(myDoc)
End Sub
```

■ **Source Code** The ConstructingXmlDocs example can be found under the Chapter 24 subdirectory.

Manipulating an in Memory XML Document

So, that this point you have seen various ways in which LINQ to XML can be used to create, save, parse, and load XML data. The next aspect of LINQ to XML you need to examine is how to navigate a given document to locate and change specific items in the tree using LINQ queries and the LINQ to XML axis methods.

To do so, you will build a Windows Forms application which will display the data within a XML document saved on the hard drive. The GUI will allow the user to enter data for a new node, which will be added to the same XML document. Finally, you will provide a few ways for the user to perform searches on the document, via a handful of LINQ queries.

■ **Note** Given that you have already built a number of LINQ queries in Chapter 13, I won't bother to relist numerous queries. If you are interested in seeing some additional LINQ to XML specific examples, look up the topic "Querying XML Trees" in the .NET Framework 4.0 SDK documentation.

Building the UI of the LINQ to XML App

Create a Windows Forms application named LinqToXmlWinApp and change the name of your initial **Form1.vb** file to **MainForm.vb** (using the Solution Explorer). The GUI of this window is quite simple. On the left of the window, you have a **TextBox** control (named **txtInventory**), which has the **Multiline** property set to **True**, and the **ScrollBars** property set to **Both**.

Beyond that, you have one group of simple **TextBox** controls (**txtMake**, **txtColor** and **txtPetName**) and a Button **btnAddNewItem**, which will allow the user to add a new entry to the XML document. Finally, you have another group of controls (a **TextBox** named **txtMakeToLookUp** and a final **Button** named **btnLookUpColors**) which allows the user to query the XML document for a set of specified nodes. Figure 24-4 shows one possible layout.

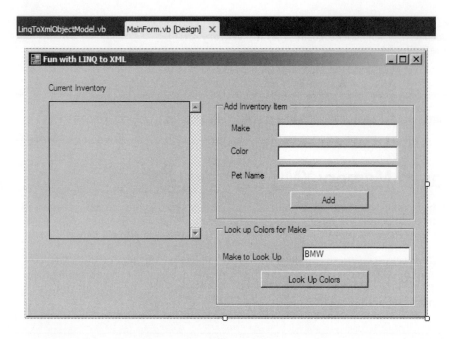

Figure 24-4. The GUI of the LINQ to XML application

Handle the Click event for each button to generate the event handler methods. Also handle the Load event of the Form itself. You will implement these handlers in a bit.

Import the Inventory.xml File

The downloadable code for this book contains a file named **Inventory.xml** within the solution code for this example. It supports a set of entries within the root **<Inventory>** element. Import this file into your project by selecting the Project ➤ Add Existing Item menu option. As you look at the data, you will see the root element defines a set of **<Car>** elements, each of which is defined similar to the following:

```
<Car carID ="0">
  <Make>Ford</Make>
  <Color>Blue</Color>
  <PetName>Chuck</PetName>
</Car>
```

Before you continue on, be sure you select this file in the Solution Explorer, and then, using the Properties window, set the Copy to Output Directory property to Copy Always. This will ensure the data is deployed to your \bin\Debug folder when you compile the application.

Defining a LINQ to XML Helper Class

To isolate the LINQ to XML data, insert a new class to your project named `LinqToXmlObjectModel`. This class will define a set of Shared methods which encapsulate some LINQ to XML logic. First of all, define a method which returns a populated `XDocument` based on the contents of the `Inventory.xml` file (be sure to import the `System.Windows.Forms` namespace into this new file):

```
Public Shared Function GetXmlInventory() As XDocument
    Try
        Dim inventoryDoc As XDocument = XDocument.Load("Inventory.xml")
        Return inventoryDoc
    Catch ex As System.IO.FileNotFoundException
        MessageBox.Show(ex.Message)
        Return Nothing
    End Try
End Function
```

The `InsertNewElement()` method (shown in the following) receives the values of the "Add Inventory Item" `TextBox` controls to place a new node into the `<Inventory>` element using the `Descendants()` axis method. After this is done, you will save the document.

```
Public Shared Sub InsertNewElement(ByVal make As String, ByVal color As String,
                                              ByVal petName As String)
    ' Load current document.
    Dim inventoryDoc As XDocument = XDocument.Load("Inventory.xml")

    ' Generate a random number for the ID.
    Dim r As New Random()

    ' Make new XElement based on incoming parameters.
    Dim newElement As New XElement("Car", New XAttribute("ID", r.Next(50000)),
                                New XElement("Color", color),
                                New XElement("Make", make),
                                New XElement("PetName", petName))

    ' Add to in-memory object.
    inventoryDoc.Descendants("Inventory").First().Add(newElement)

    ' Save changes to disk.
    inventoryDoc.Save("Inventory.xml")
End Sub
```

The final method, `LookUpColorsForMake()` will receive the data in the final `TextBox` to build a string that contains the colors of a specified make, using a LINQ query. Consider the following implementation:

```
Public Shared Sub LookUpColorsForMake(ByVal make As String)
    ' Load current document.
    Dim inventoryDoc As XDocument = XDocument.Load("Inventory.xml")

    ' Find the colors for a given make.
```

```
    Dim makeInfo = From car In inventoryDoc.Descendants("Car")
                              Where CStr(car.Element("Make")) = make
                              Select car.Element("Color").Value

    ' Build a string representing each color.
    Dim data As String = String.Empty
    For Each item In makeInfo.Distinct()
        data &= String.Format("- {0}" & vbLf, item)
    Next

    ' Show colors.
    MessageBox.Show(data, String.Format("{0} colors:", make))
End Sub
```

Rigging up the UI to Your Helper Class

All you need to do at this point is fill in the details of your event handlers. Doing so is as simple as making calls to your helper methods:

```
Public Class MainForm

    Private Sub MainForm_Load(ByVal sender As Object,
                 ByVal e As EventArgs) Handles MyBase.Load
        ' Display current XML inventory document in TextBox control.
        txtInventory.Text = LinqToXmlObjectModel.GetXmlInventory().ToString()
    End Sub

    Private Sub btnAddNewItem_Click(ByVal sender As System.Object,
                 ByVal e As System.EventArgs) Handles btnAddNewItem.Click
        ' Add new item to doc.
        LinqToXmlObjectModel.InsertNewElement(txtMake.Text,
                                      txtColor.Text, txtPetName.Text)
        ' Display current XML inventory document in TextBox control.
        txtInventory.Text = LinqToXmlObjectModel.GetXmlInventory().ToString()
    End Sub

    Private Sub btnLookUpColors_Click(ByVal sender As Object,
                 ByVal e As EventArgs) Handles btnLookUpColors.Click
        LinqToXmlObjectModel.LookUpColorsForMake(txtMakeToLookUp.Text)
    End Sub
End Class
```

Figure 24-5 shows the end result.

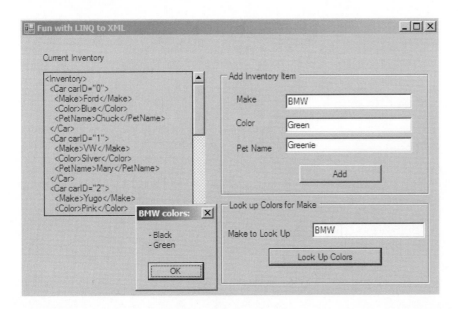

Figure 24-5. The completed LINQ to XML application

That wraps up the introductory look at LINQ to XML and your investigation of LINQ. You first encountered LINQ in Chapter 13, where you learned about LINQ to Objects. Chapter 19 showed various examples using PLINQ, while Chapter 23 showcased how you can apply LINQ queries to ADO.NET Entity objects. Using all of this information, you are in good shape to dig deeper, which you should. Microsoft has made it very clear that LINQ will continue to evolve as the .NET platform grows.

■ **Source Code** The LinqToXmlWinApp to XML example can be found under the Chapter 24 subdirectory.

Summary

This chapter examined the role of LINQ to XML. As you have seen, this API is an alternative to the initial XML manipulation library which shipped with the .NET platform, System.Xml.dll. Using System.Xml.Linq.dll, you are able to generate new XML documents using a top down approach, where the structure of your code has a striking resemblance to the final XML data. In this light, LINQ to XML is a better DOM. You also learned how to build XDocument and XElement objects in a variety of ways (parsing, loading from file, mapping from in-memory objects) and how to navigate and manipulate data using LINQ queries.

CHAPTER 25

■■■

Introducing Windows Communication Foundation

.NET 3.0 introduced an API designed specifically for the process of building distributed systems: Windows Communication Foundation (WCF). Unlike other distributed APIs you might have used in the past (e.g., DCOM, .NET remoting, XML web services, message queuing), WCF provides a single, unified, and extendable programming object model that you can used to interact with a number of previously diverse distributed technologies.

This chapter begins by framing the need for WCF and examining the problems it intends to solve by way of a quick review of previous distributed computing APIs. After you look at the services provided by WCF, you'll turn your attention to examining the key .NET assemblies, namespaces, and types that represent this programming model.

Over the remainder of this chapter, you'll build several WCF services, hosts, and clients using various WCF development tools. You'll also learn about a few helpful simplifications and shortcuts that .NET 4.0 provides. You'll also build one simple example under .NET 4.0 that walks you through how the task of building hosting configuration files becomes much easier (if you are not sure what a *configuration file* is at this point, you'll see many examples of such files in the pages to come).

A Potpourri of Distributed Computing APIs

The Windows operating system has historically provided many APIs for building distributed systems. While it is true that most people consider a *distributed system* to involve at least two networked computers, this term in the broader sense can refer to two executables that need to exchange data, even if they happen to be running on the same physical machine. Using this definition, selecting a distributed API for your current programming task typically involves asking the following pivotal question:

> *Will this system be used exclusively in house, or will external users require access to the application's functionality?*

If you build a distributed system for in-house use, you have a far greater chance of ensuring that each connected computer is running the same operating system and using the same programming framework (e.g., .NET, COM, or the Java platform). Running in-house systems also means that you can leverage your existing security system for purposes of authentication, authorization, and so forth. In this situation, you might be willing to select a particular distributed API that will tie you to a specific operating system/programming framework for the purposes of performance.

In contrast, if you build a system that others must reach from outside of your walls, you have a whole other set of issues to contend with. First, you will most likely *not* be able to dictate to external users which operating system/s they can use, which programming framework/s they can use, or how they configure their security settings.

Second, if you happen to work for a larger company or in a university setting that uses numerous operating systems and programming technologies, an in-house application suddenly faces the same challenges as an outward-facing application. In either of these cases, you need to limit yourself to a more flexible distributed API to ensure the furthest reach of your application.

Based on your answer to this key distributed computing question, the next task is to pinpoint exactly which API (or set of APIs) to use. The following sections provide a quick recap of some of the major distributed APIs historically used by Windows software developers. Once you finish this brief history lesson, you will be able to see the usefulness of Windows Communication Foundation quite easily.

■ **Note** To ensure we are on the same page here, I feel compelled to point out that WCF (and the technologies it encompasses) has nothing to do with building an HTML-based web site. While it is true that web applications can be considered distributed because two machines are typically involved in the exchange, WCF is about establishing connections between machines to share the functionality of remote components—not for displaying HTML in a web browser. Chapter 32 will initiate your examination of building websites with the .NET platform.

The Role of DCOM

Prior to the release of the .NET platform, the Distributed Component Object Model (DCOM) was the remoting API of choice for Microsoft-centric development endeavors. Using DCOM, it was possible to build distributed systems using COM objects, the system registry, and a good amount of elbow grease. One benefit of DCOM was that it allowed for *location transparency* of components. Simply put, this allowed you to program client software in such a way that the physical locations of the remote objects were not hard-coded in the application. Regardless of whether the remote object was on the same machine or a secondary networked machine, the code base could remain neutral because the actual location was recorded externally in the system registry.

While DCOM did enjoy some degree of success, for all practical purposes it was a Windows-centric API. DCOM alone did not provide a fabric to build comprehensive solutions involving multiple operating systems (e.g., Windows, Unix, and Mac) or promote sharing of data between diverse architectures (e.g., COM, Java, or CORBA).

■ **Note** There were some attempts to port DCOM to various flavors of Unix/Linux, but the end results were lackluster and eventually became technology footnotes.

By and large, DCOM was best suited for in-house application development because exposing COM objects outside company walls entailed a set of additional complications (firewalls and so forth). With the release of the .NET platform, DCOM quickly became a legacy programming model; and unless you maintain legacy DCOM systems, you can consider it a deprecated technology.

The Role of COM+/Enterprise Services

DCOM alone did little more than define a way to establish a communication channel between two pieces of COM-based software. To fill in the missing pieces required for building a feature-rich distributed computing solution, Microsoft eventually released Microsoft Transaction Server (MTS), which was later renamed to COM+.

Despite its name, COM+ is not used only by COM programmers—it is completely accessible to .NET professionals, as well. Since the first release of the .NET platform, the base class libraries provided a namespace named `System.EnterpriseServices`. Here, .NET programmers could build managed libraries that could be installed into the COM+ runtime to access the same set of services as a traditional COM+-aware COM server. In either case, once a COM+-aware library was installed into the COM+ runtime, it was termed a *serviced component*.

COM+ provides a number of features that serviced components can leverage, including transaction management, object lifetime management, pooling services, a role-based security system, a loosely coupled event model, and so on. This was a major benefit at the time, given that most distributed systems require the same set of services. Rather than forcing developers to code them by hand, COM+ provided an out-of-the-box solution.

One of the compelling aspects of COM+ was the fact that all of these settings could be configured in a declarative manner using administrative tools. Thus, if you wished to ensure an object was monitored under a transactional context or belonged to a particular security role, you simply selected the correct check boxes.

While COM+/Enterprise Services is still in use today, this technology is a Windows-only solution that is best suited for in-house application development or as a back-end service indirectly manipulated by more agonistic front ends (e.g., a public website that makes calls on serviced components [aka COM+ objects] in the background).

■ **Note** WCF does not provide a way to build serviced components. However, it does provide a manner for WCF services to communicate with existing COM+ objects. If you need to build serviced components using VB 2010, you will need to make direct use of the `System.EnterpriseServices` namespace. Consult the .NET Framework 4.0 SDK documentation for details.

The Role of MSMQ

The Microsoft Message Queuing (MSMQ) API allows developers to build distributed systems that need to ensure reliable delivery of message data on the network. As developers know all too well, in any distributed system there is the risk that a network server is down, a database is offline, or connections are inexplicably lost. Furthermore, you must construct many applications in such a way that they hold message data for delivery at a later time (this process is known as *queuing data*).

Microsoft initially packaged MSMQ as a set of low-level C-based APIs and COM objects. With the release of the .NET platform, VB 2010 programmers could use `System.Messaging` namespace to hook into MSMQ and build software that communicated with intermittently connected applications in a dependable fashion.

On a related note, the COM+ layer incorporated MSMQ functionality into the runtime (in a simplified format) using a technology termed Queued Components (QC). This manner of communicating with MSMQ was packaged up into the `System.EnterpriseServices` namespace mentioned in the previous section.

Regardless of which programming model you used to interact with the MSMQ runtime, the end result ensured that applications could deliver messages in a reliable and timely fashion. Like COM+, MSMQ is still part of the fabric of building distributed software on the Windows operating system.

The Role of .NET Remoting

As mentioned previously, DCOM quickly became a legacy distributed API after the release of the .NET platform. In its place, the .NET base class libraries shipped with the .NET remoting layer, represented by the `System.Runtime.Remoting` namespace. This API allows multiple computers to distribute objects, provided they all run the applications under the .NET platform.

The .NET remoting APIs provided a number of useful features. Most important was the use of XML-based configuration files to define declaratively the underlying plumbing used by the client and the server software. Using `*.config` files, it was easy to alter the functionality of your distributed system radically simply by changing the content of the configuration files and restarting the application.

Also, given that only .NET applications can use this API is usable, you can gain various performance benefits because data can be encoded in a compact binary format, and you can use the Common Type System (CTS) when defining parameters and return values. While it is possible to use.NET remoting to build distributed systems that span multiple operating systems (using Mono, which was briefly mentioned in Chapter 1 and detailed in Appendix B), interoperability between other programming architectures (e.g., Java) was still not directly possible.

The Role of XML Web Services

Each of the previous distributed APIs provided little (if any) support to allow external callers to access the supplied functionality in an *agnostic manner*. When you need to expose the services of remote objects to *any* operating system and *any* programming model, XML web services provide the most straightforward way of doing so.

Unlike a traditional browser-based web application, a web service provides a way to expose the functionality of remote components using standard web protocols. Since the initial release of .NET, programmers have been provided with superior support for building and consuming XML web services with the `System.Web.Services` namespace. In many cases, building a feature-complete web service is no more complicated than applying the `<WebMethod()>` attribute to each Public method you wish to provide access to. Furthermore, Visual Studio 2010 allows you to connect to a remote web service with the click of a button (or two).

Web services allow developers to build .NET assemblies containing types that can be accessed using simple HTTP. Furthermore, a web service encodes its data as simple XML. Given the fact that web services are based on open industry standards (e.g., HTTP, XML, and SOAP) rather than proprietary type systems and proprietary wire formats (as is the case with DCOM or .NET remoting), they allow for a high degree of interoperability and data exchange. Figure 25-1 illustrates the agnostic nature of XML web services.

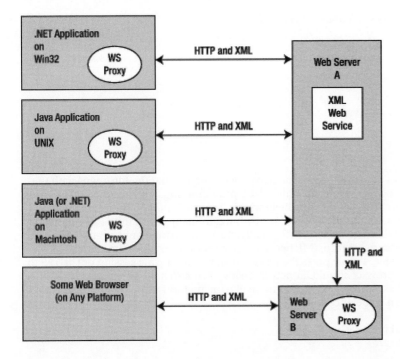

Figure 25-1. XML web services allow for a high degree of interoperability

Of course, no distributed API is perfect. One potential drawback of web services is the fact that they can suffer from some performance issues (given the use of HTTP and XML data representation); another drawback is that they might not be an ideal solution for in-house applications where you could use a TCP-based protocol and binary formatting of data without incurring a penalty.

A .NET Web Service Example

For many years, .NET programmers have created web services using the ASP.NET Web Service project template of Visual Studio, which can be accessed using the File ➤ New ➤ Web Site dialog box. This particular project template creates a commonly used directory structure and a handful of initial files to represent the web service itself. While this project template is helpful in getting you up and running, you can build a .NET XML web service with a simple text editor and test it immediately with the ASP.NET development web server (Chapter 32 examines this utility in more detail).

For example, assume you have authored the following programming logic in a new file named `HelloWebService.asmx` (`*.asmx` is the default file extension for a .NET XML web service file). Once you do this, save it into a folder such as `C:\HelloWebService`:

```
<%@ WebService Language="vb" Class="HelloWebService" %>

Imports System
Imports System.Web.Services

Public Class HelloWebService
    <WebMethod()> _
    Public Function HelloWorld() As String
        Return "Hello World"
    End Function
End Class
```

While this simple service doesn't do anything particularly useful, notice that the file opens with the `<%@WebService%>` directive, which you use to specify which .NET programming language the file uses and the name of the class type that represents the service. Beyond this, the only point of interest is that you decorate the `HelloWorld()` method with the `<WebMethod()>` attribute. In many cases, this is all you need to do to expose a method to external callers using HTTP. Finally, notice that you do not need to do anything special to encode the return value into XML because the runtime does this automatically.

If you wish to test this web service, simply press the F5 key to start a debugging session or Ctrl+F5 to run the project. At this point, your browser should launch, showing each *web method* exposed from this endpoint. At this point, you can click the `HelloWorld` link to invoke the method using HTTP. Once you do this, the browser displays the return value encoded as XML:

```
<?xml version="1.0" encoding="utf-8" ?>
<string xmlns="http://tempuri.org/">
  Hello World
</string>
```

Simple stuff, right? Even better, when you wish to build a "real" client to communicate with the service, you can generate a client-side proxy that you can use to invoke web methods. As you might know, a *proxy* is a class that encapsulates the low-level details of communicating with another object; in this case, that is the service itself.

You can generate proxies for a classic XML web service in two ways. First, you can use the command-line tool, `wsdl.exe`, which is useful when you want full control over how the proxy is generated. Second, you can simplify matters by using Visual Studio's Add Web Reference option under the Project menu. Both of these approaches also generate a required client-side `*.config` file, which contains various configuration settings for the proxy (such as the web service location).

Assuming you have generated a proxy for this simple web service (you don't need to do so here), the client application can invoke the web method in a simple manner:

```
Sub Main()
    ' The proxy type contains code to read the *.config file
    ' to resolve the location of the web service.
    Dim proxy As New HelloWebServiceProxy()
    Console.WriteLine(proxy.HelloWorld())
    Console.ReadLine()
End Sub
```

While it remains possible to build this traditional flavor of XML web service under .NET 4.0, most new service projects will benefit from using the WCF templates instead. In fact, WCF is the preferred manner to build service-oriented systems since the release of .NET 3.0.

■ **Source Code** You can find the HelloWorldWebService project under the Chapter 25 subdirectory.

Web Service Standards

A major problem that web services faced early on was the fact that all of the big industry players (e.g., Microsoft, IBM, and Sun Microsystems) created web service implementations that were not 100-percent compatible with other web service implementations. Obviously, this was an issue because the whole point of web services is to achieve a high degree of interoperability across platforms and operating systems!

To ensure the interoperability of web services, groups such as the World Wide Web Consortium (W3C: `www.w3.org`) and the Web Services Interoperability Organization (WS-I: `www.ws-i.org`) began to author several specifications that laid out how a software vendor (e.g., IBM, Microsoft, or Sun Microsystems) should build web service–centric software libraries to ensure compatibility.

Collectively, all of these specifications are given the blanket name WS-*, and they cover such issues as security, attachments, the description of web services (using the *Web Service Description Language*, or *WSDL*), policies, SOAP formats, and a slew of other important details.

Microsoft's implementation of most of these standards (for both managed and unmanaged code) is embodied in the Web Services Enhancements (WSE) toolkit, which you can download for free from the supporting website: `http://msdn2.microsoft.com/en-us/webservices`.

When you build WCF service applications, you do not need to use the assemblies that are part of the WSE toolkit directly. Rather, if you build a WCF service that uses an HTTP-based binding (you'll learn more details about this later in the chapter), these same WS-* specifications are given to you out of the box (exactly which ones depend on the binding you choose).

Named Pipes, Sockets, and P2P

As if choosing from DCOM, .NET remoting, web services, COM+, and MSMQ were not challenging enough, the list of distributed APIs continues. Programmers can also use additional interprocess communication APIs such as named pipes, sockets, and peer-to-peer (P2P) services. These lower-level APIs typically provide better performance (especially for machines on the same LAN); however, using these APIs becomes more complex (if not impossible) for outward-facing applications.

If you build a distributed system involving a set of applications running on the same physical machine, you can use the named pipes API with the `System.IO.Pipes` namespace. This approach can provide the absolute fastest way to push data between applications on the same machine.

Also, if you build an application that requires absolute control over how network access is obtained and maintained, you can implement sockets and P2P functionality under the .NET platform using the `System.Net.Sockets` and `System.Net.PeerToPeer` namespaces, respectively.

The Role of WCF

The wide array of distributed technologies makes it difficult to pick the right tool for the job. This is further complicated by the fact that several of these technologies overlap in the services they provide (most notably in the areas of transactions and security).

Even when a .NET developer has selected what appear to be the correct technologies for the task at hand, building, maintaining, and configuring such an application is complex, at best. Each API has its own programming model, its own unique set of configuration tools, and so forth.

Prior to .NET 3.0, this meant that it was difficult to *plug and play* distributed APIs without authoring a considerable amount of custom infrastructure. For example, if you build your system using the .NET remoting APIs, and you later decide that XML web services are a more appropriate solution, you need to reengineer your code base.

WCF is a distributed computing toolkit introduced with .NET 3.0 that integrates these previously independent distributed technologies into a streamlined API represented primarily by the `System.ServiceModel` namespace. Using WCF, you can expose services to callers using a wide variety of techniques. For example, if you build an in-house application where all connected machines are Windows based, you can use various TCP protocols to ensure the fastest-possible performance. You can also expose this same service with the XML web service–based protocol to allow external callers to leverage its functionality, regardless of the programming language or operating system.

Given the fact that WCF allows you to pick the correct protocol for the job (using a common programming model), you will find that it becomes quite easy to plug and play the underlying plumbing of your distributed application. In most cases, you can do so without having to recompile or redeploy the client/service software because the grungy details are often relegated to application configuration files (much like the older .NET remoting APIs).

An Overview of WCF Features

Interoperability and integration of diverse APIs are only two (important) aspects of WCF. WCF also provides a rich software fabric that complements the remoting technologies it exposes. Consider the following list of major WCF features:

- Support for strongly typed as well as untyped messages. This approach allows .NET applications to share custom types efficiently, while software created using other platforms (such as Java) can consume streams of loosely typed XML.

- Support for several bindings (e.g., raw HTTP, TCP, MSMQ, and named pipes) allows to choose the most appropriate plumbing to transport message data.

- Support for the latest and greatest web service specifications (WS-*).

- A fully integrated security model encompassing both native Windows/.NET security protocols and numerous neutral-security techniques built on web service standards.

- Support for session-like state management techniques, as well as support for one-way or stateless messages.

As impressive as this list of features might be, it only scratches the surface of the functionality WCF provides. WCF also offers tracing and logging facilities, performance counters, a publish-and-subscribe event model, and transactional support, among other features.

An Overview of Service-Oriented Architecture

Yet another benefit of WCF is that it is based on the design principles established by *service-oriented architecture* (SOA). To be sure, SOA is a major buzzword in the industry; and like most buzzwords, SOA can be defined in numerous ways. Simply put, SOA is a way to design a distributed system where several autonomous *services* work in conjunction by passing *messages* across boundaries (either networked machines or two processes on the same machine) using well-defined *interfaces*.

In the world of WCF, you typically create these well-defined interfaces using CLR interface types (see Chapter 9). In a more general sense, however, the interface of a service simply describes the set of members that might be invoked by external callers.

The team that designed WCF observed the four tenets of SOA design principles. While these tenets are typically honored automatically simply by building a WCF application, understanding these four cardinal design rules of SOA can help you understand WCF better. The sections that follow provide a brief overview of each tenet.

Tenet 1: Boundaries Are Explicit

This tenet reiterates the fact that the functionality of a WCF service is expressed using well-defined interfaces (e.g., descriptions of each member, its parameters, and its return values). The only way that an external caller can communicate with a WCF service is through the interface, and the external caller remains blissfully unaware of the underlying implementation details.

Tenet 2: Services Are Autonomous

The term *autonomous entities* refers to the fact that a given WCF service is (as much as possible) an island unto itself. An autonomous service should be independent with regard to version, deployment, and installation issues. To help promote this tenet, you can fall back on a key aspect of interface-based programming. Once an interface is in production, it should never be changed (or you will risk breaking existing clients). When you need to extend the functionality of your WCF service, you author new interfaces that model the desired functionality.

Tenet 3: Services Communicate via Contract, Not Implementation

The third tenet is yet another byproduct of interface-based programming. The implementation details of a WCF service (e.g., the language it was written in how it gets accomplishes its work, etc.) are of no concern to the external caller. WCF clients interact with services solely through their exposed public interfaces. Furthermore, if the members of a service interface expose custom complex types, they need to be fully detailed as a *data contract* to ensure that all callers can map the content to a particular data structure.

Tenet 4: Service Compatibility Is Based on Policy

Because CLR interfaces provide strongly typed contracts for all WCF clients (and can also be used to generate a related WSDL document based on your choice of binding), it is important to realize that interfaces and WSDL alone are not expressive enough to detail aspects of what the service is capable of doing. Given this, SOA allows you to define *policies* that further qualify the semantics of the service (e.g., the expected security requirements used to talk to the service). Using these policies, you can basically separate the low-level syntactic description of your service (the exposed interfaces) from the semantic details of how they work and how they need to be invoked.

WCF: The Bottom Line

The preceding short history lesson explains why WCF is the preferred approach for building distributed applications under .NET 3.0 and later. WCF is the recommended API whether you want to build an in-house application using TCP protocols, move data between programs on the same machine using named pipes, or expose data to the world at large using web service protocols.

This is not to say that you cannot use the original .NET distributed-centric namespaces (e.g., `System.Runtime.Remoting`, `System.Messaging`, `System.EnterpriseServices`, and `System.Web.Services`) in new development efforts. In some cases (e.g., if you need to build COM+ objects), you must do so. In any case, if you have used these APIs in previous projects, you will find learning WCF straightforward. Like the technologies that preceded it, WCF makes considerable use of XML-based configuration files, .NET attributes, and proxy generation utilities.

With this introductory foundation behind you, you can concentrate on the topic of building WCF applications. Again, you should understand that full coverage of WCF would require an entire book because each of the supported services (e.g., MSMQ, COM+, P2P, and named pipes) could be a chapter unto itself. Here, you will learn the overall process of building WCF programs using both TCP- and HTTP-based (e.g., web service) protocols. This should put you in a good position to study these topics further, as you see fit.

Investigating the Core WCF Assemblies

As you might expect, the programming fabric of WCF is represented by a set of .NET assemblies installed into the GAC. Table 25-1 describes the overall role of the core WCF assemblies you need to use in just about any WCF application.

Table 25-1. Core WCF Assemblies

Assembly	Meaning in Life
`System.Runtime.Serialization.dll`	Defines namespaces and types that you can use for serializing and deserializing objects in the WCF framework.
`System.ServiceModel.dll`	This core assembly contains the types used to build any sort of WCF application.

These two assemblies define many new namespaces and types. You should consult the .NET Framework 4.0 SDK documentation for complete details; however, Table 25-2 documents the roles of some of the important namespaces.

Table 25-2. Core WCF Namespaces

Namespace	Meaning in Life
System.Runtime.Serialization	Defines many types you use to control how data is serialized and deserialized within the WCF framework.
System.ServiceModel	This primary WCF namespace defines binding and hosting types, as well as basic security and transactional types.
System.ServiceModel.Configuration	Defines numerous types that provide programmatic access to WCF configuration files.
System.ServiceModel.Description	Defines types that provide an object model to the addresses, bindings, and contracts defined within WCF configuration files.
System.ServiceModel.MsmqIntegration	Contains types to integrate with the MSMQ service.
System.ServiceModel.Security	Defines numerous types to control aspects of the WCF security layers.

A BRIEF WORD REGARDING CARDSPACE

In addition to System.ServiceModel.dll and System.Runtime.Serialization.dll, WCF provides a third assembly named System.IdentityModel.dll. This assembly contains many additional namespaces and types that support the CardSpace API. This technology allows you to establish and manage digital identities within a WCF application. Essentially, the CardSpace API provides a unified programming model to account for various security-related details for WCF applications, such as caller identity, user authentication/authorization services, and so on.

You will not examine CardSpace further in this edition of the book, so be sure to consult the .NET Framework 4.0 SDK documentation if you want to learn more.

The Visual Studio WCF Project Templates

As will be explained in more detail later in this chapter, a WCF application is typically represented by three interrelated assemblies, one of which is a *.dll that contains the types that external callers can communicate with (in other words, the WCF service itself). When you wish to build a WCF service, it is perfectly permissible to select a standard Class Library project template (see Chapter 14) as a starting point and manually reference the WCF assemblies.

Alternatively, you can create a new WCF service by selecting the WCF Service Library project template of Visual Studio 2010 (see Figure 25-2). This project type automatically sets references to the required WCF assemblies; however, it also generates a good deal of starter code, which you will more likely than not delete.

Figure 25-2. The Visual Studio 2010 WCF Service Library project template

One benefit of selecting the WCF Service Library project template is that it also supplies you with an `App.config` file, which might seem strange because you are building a .NET `*.dll`, not a .NET `*.exe`. However, this file is useful because, when you debug or run your WCF Service Library project, the Visual Studio 2010 IDE will automatically launch the WCF Test Client application. This program (`WcfTestClient.exe`) will look up the settings in the `App.config` file, so it can host your service for testing purposes. You'll learn more about the WCF Test Client later in this chapter.

■ **Note** The `App.config` file of the WCF Service Library project is also useful because it shows you the bare-bones settings used to configure a WCF host application. In fact, you can copy and paste much of this code into your host's actual configuration file.

In addition to the basic WCF Service Library template, the WCF project category of the New Project dialog box defines two WCF library projects that integrate Windows Workflow Foundation (WF) functionality into a WCF service, as well as a template to build an RSS library (see Figure 25-2). The next chapter will introduce you to the Windows Workflow Foundation, so you'll ignore these particular WCF project templates for the time being (I'll leave it to the interested reader to dig into the RSS feed project template).

The WCF Service Website Project Template

You can find yet another Visual Studio 2010 WCF-centric project template in the New Web Site dialog box, which you activate using the File ➤ New ➤ Web Site menu option (see Figure 25-3).

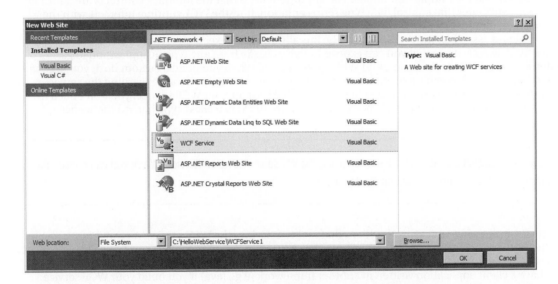

Figure 25-3. The Visual Studio 2010 web-based WCF Service project template.

This WCF Service project template is useful when you know from the outset that your WCF service will use web service–based protocols rather than, for example, TCP or named pipes. This option can automatically create a new Internet Information Services (IIS) virtual directory to contain your WCF program files, create a proper `Web.config` file to expose the service through HTTP, and author the necessary `*.svc` file (you'll learn more about `*.svc` files later in this chapter). Thus, the web-based WCF Service project is a time-saver because the IDE automatically sets up the required IIS infrastructure.

In contrast, if you build a new WCF service using the WCF Service Library option, you have the ability to host the service in a variety of ways (e.g., custom host, Windows service, or manually built IIS virtual directory). This option is more appropriate when you wish to build a custom host for your WCF service that can work with any number of WCF bindings.

The Basic Composition of a WCF Application

When you build a WCF distributed system, you will typically do so by creating three interrelated assemblies:

- *The WCF Service assembly:* This ***.dll** contains the classes and interfaces that represent the overall functionality you want to expose to external callers.

- *The WCF Service host:* This software module is the entity that hosts your WCF service assembly.

- *The WCF client:* This is the application that accesses the service's functionality through an intervening proxy.

As mentioned previously, the WCF service assembly is a .NET class library that contains a number of WCF contracts and their implementations. The key difference is that the interface contracts are adorned with various attributes that control data type representation, how the WCF runtime interacts with the exposed types, and so forth.

The second assembly, the WCF host, can be literally any .NET executable. As you will see later in this chapter, WCF was set up so that you can exposed services easily from any type of application (e.g., Windows Forms, a Windows service, and WPF applications). When you build a custom host, you use the **ServiceHost** type and possibly a related ***.config** file. The latter contains details regarding the server-side plumbing you wish to use. However, if you use as the host for your WCF service, you don't need to build a custom host programmatically because IIS will use the **ServiceHost** type behind the scenes.

■ **Note** It is also possible to host a WCF service using the Windows Activation Service (WAS); you can consult the .NET Framework 4.0 SDK documentation for details.

The final assembly represents the client that makes calls into the WCF service. As you might expect, this client can be any type of .NET application. Similar to the host, client applications typically use a client-side ***.config** file that defines the client-side plumbing. You should also be aware that you can easily have a client application written in another framework (e.g., Java) if you build your WCF service using HTTP-based bindings.

Figure 25-4 illustrates the relationship between these three interrelated WCF assemblies(from a high level). Behind the scenes, several lower-level details are used to represent the required plumbing (e.g., factories, channels, and listeners). These low-level details are usually hidden from view; however, they can be extended or customized if required. In most cases, the default plumbing fits the bill sufficiently.

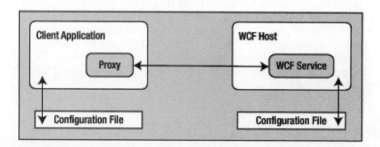

Figure 25-4. A high-level look at a typical WCF application

It is also worth pointing out that using a server-side or client-side `*.config` file is technically optional. If you wish, you can hard-code the host (as well as the client) to specify the necessary plumbing (e.g., endpoints, binding, and addresses). The obvious problem with this approach is that if you need to change the plumbing details, you will need to recode, recompile, and redeploy a number of assemblies. Using a `*.config` file keeps your code base much more flexible because changing the plumbing is as simple as updating the file's content and restarting the application. On the other hand, programmatic configuration allows an application more dynamic flexibility—it can choose how to configure the plumbing based on *if-tests*, for example.

The ABCs of WCF

Hosts and clients communicate with each other by agreeing on the ABCs, a friendly mnemonic for remembering the core building blocks of a WCF application *address*, *binding*, and *contract*:

- *Address*: Describes the location of the service. In code, you represent this with a `System.Uri` type; however, you typically store the value in `*.config` files.

- *Binding*: WCF ships with a many different bindings that specify network protocols, encoding mechanisms, and the transport layer.

- *Contract*: Provides a description of each method exposed from the WCF service.

You should realize that the ABC abbreviation does not imply that a developer must define the address first, followed by binding, and ending with the contract. In many cases, a WCF developer begins by defining a contract for the service, followed by establishing an address and bindings (any order will do, as long as each aspect is accounted for). Before you build your first WCF application, you will take a more detailed walk through of the ABCs.

Understanding WCF Contracts

Understanding the notion of a *contract* is the key to building a WCF service. While not mandatory, the vast majority of your WCF applications will begin by defining a set of .NET interface types that are used to represent the set of members a given WCF service will support. Specifically, interfaces that represent a WCF contract are called *service contracts*. The classes (or structures) that implement them are called *service types*.

WCF service contracts are adorned with various attributes, the most common of which are defined in the `System.ServiceModel` namespace. When the members of a service contract (the methods in the interface) contain only simple data types (e.g., numerical data, Booleans, and String data), you can build a complete WCF service using nothing more than the `<ServiceContract()>` and `<OperationContract()>` attributes.

However, if your members expose custom types, you will need to use types in the `System.Runtime.Serialization` namespace (see Figure 25-5) of the `System.Runtime.Serialization.dll` assembly. Here you will find additional attributes (e.g., `<DataMember()>` and `<DataContract()>`) to fine-tune the process of defining how your composite types are serialized to and from XML when they are passed to and from service operations.

Strictly speaking, you are not required to use CLR interfaces to define a WCF contract. Many of these same attributes can be applied on Public members of a Public class (or structure). However, given the many benefits of interface-based programming (e.g., polymorphism and elegant versioning), it is safe to consider using CLR interfaces to describe a WCF contract a best practice.

Figure 25-5. *System.Runtime.Serialization defines a number of attributes used when building WCF data contracts*

Understanding WCF Bindings

Once you define and implement a contract (or a set of contracts) in your service library, the next logical step is to build a hosting agent for the WCF service itself. As mentioned previously, you have a variety of possible hosts to choose from, all of which must specify the *bindings* used by remote callers to gain access to the service type's functionality.

Choosing a set of bindings is one area that makes WCF development quite different from .NET remoting and/or XML web service development. WCF ships with many of binding choices, each of which is tailored to a specific need. If none of the out-of-the-box bindings fits the bill, you can create your own by extending the `CustomBinding` type (something you will not do in this chapter). A WCF binding can specify the following characteristics:

- The transport layer used to move data (HTTP, MSMQ, named pipes, and TCP)

- The channels used by the transport (one-way, request-reply, and duplex)

- The encoding mechanism used to deal with the data itself (e.g., XML and binary)

- Any supported web service protocols (if permitted by the binding), such as WS-Security, WS-Transactions, WS-Reliability, and so on

Let's take a look at your basic choices.

HTTP-Based Bindings

The BasicHttpBinding, WSHttpBinding, WSDualHttpBinding, and WSFederationHttpBinding options are geared toward exposing contract types through XML web service protocols. If you require the furthest reach possible for your service (e.g., multiple operating systems and multiple programming architectures), you want to focus on these bindings because all of these binding types encode data based on XML representation and use HTTP on the wire.

Table 25-3 shows note how you can represent a WCF binding in code (using class types within the System.ServiceModel namespace) or as XML attributes defined within *.config files.

Table 25-3. The HTTP-Centric WCF Bindings

Binding Class	Binding Element	Meaning in Life
BasicHttpBinding	<basicHttpBinding>	You use this to build a WS-Basic Profile–conformant (WS-I Basic Profile 1.1) WCF service. This binding uses HTTP as the transport and Text/XML as the default message encoding.
WSHttpBinding	<wsHttpBinding>	This is similar to BasicHttpBinding, but provides more web service features. This binding adds support for transactions, reliable messaging, and WS-Addressing.
WSDualHttpBinding	<wsDualHttpBinding>	This is similar to WSHttpBinding, but intended for use with duplex contracts (e.g., the service and client can send messages back and forth). This binding supports only SOAP security and requires reliable messaging.
WSFederationHttpBinding	<wsFederationHttpBinding>	This is a secure and interoperable binding that supports the WS-Federation protocol, enabling organizations that are in a federation to authenticate and authorize users efficiently.

As its name suggests, BasicHttpBinding is the simplest of all web service–centric protocols. Specifically, this binding ensures that your WCF service conforms to a specification named WS-I Basic Profile 1.1 (defined by WS-I). The main reason to use this binding is for maintaining backward compatibility with applications that were previously built to communicate with ASP.NET web services (which have been part of the .NET libraries since version 1.0).

The WSHttpBinding protocol not only incorporates support for a subset of the WS-* specification (transactions, security, and reliable sessions), but also supports the ability to handle binary data encoding using Message Transmission Optimization Mechanism (MTOM).

The main benefit of WSDualHttpBinding is that it adds the ability to allow the caller and sender to communicate using *duplex messaging,* which is a fancy way of saying they can engage in a two-way conversation. When selecting WSDualHttpBinding, you can hook into the WCF publish/subscribe event model.

Finally, `WSFederationHttpBinding` is the web service–based protocol you might wish to consider when security among a group of organizations is of the utmost importance. This binding supports the WS-Trust, WS-Security, and WS-SecureConversation specifications, which are represented by the WCF CardSpace APIs.

TCP-Based Bindings

If you build a distributed application involving machines that are configured with the .NET 4.0 libraries (in other words, all machines are running the Windows operating system), you can gain performance benefits by bypassing web service bindings and opting for a TCP binding, which ensures that all data is encoded in a compact binary format, rather than XML. Again, when you use the bindings shown in Table 25-4, the client and host must be .NET applications.

Table 25-4. The TCP-Centric WCF Bindings

Binding Class	Binding Element	Meaning in Life
NetNamedPipeBinding	<netNamedPipeBinding>	Serves as a secure, reliable, optimized binding for on-the-same-machine communication between .NET applications.
NetPeerTcpBinding	<netPeerTcpBinding>	Provides a secure binding for P2P network applications.
NetTcpBinding	<netTcpBinding>	Serves as a secure and optimized binding suitable for cross-machine communication between .NET applications.

The `NetTcpBinding` class uses TCP to move binary data between the client and WCF service. As mentioned previously, this will result in higher performance than the web service protocols, but limits you to an in-house Windows solution. On the plus side, `NetTcpBinding` supports transactions, reliable sessions, and secure communications.

Like `NetTcpBinding`, `NetNamedPipeBinding` supports transactions, reliable sessions, and secure communications; however, it has no ability to make cross-machine calls. If you want to find the fastest way to push data between WCF applications on the same machine (e.g., cross-application domain communications), `NetNamedPipeBinding` is the binding choice of champions. For more information on `NetPeerTcpBinding`, consult the .NET Framework 4.0 documentation for details regarding P2P networking.

MSMQ-Based Bindings

Finally, the `NetMsmqBinding` and `MsmqIntegrationBinding` bindings are of immediate interest if you want to integrate with a Microsoft MSMQ server. This chapter will not examine the details of using MSMQ bindings, but Table 25-5 documents the basic role of each.

Table 25-5. The MSMQ-Centric WCF Bindings

Binding Class	Binding Element	Meaning in Life
MsmqIntegrationBinding	<msmqIntegrationBinding>	You can use this binding to enable WCF applications to send and receive messages to and from existing MSMQ applications that use COM, native C++, or the types defined in the System. Messaging namespace.
NetMsmqBinding	<netMsmqBinding>	You can use this queued binding for cross-machine communication between .NET applications. This is the preferred approach among the MSMQ-centric bindings.

Understanding WCF Addresses

Once you establish the contracts and bindings, the final piece of the puzzle is to specify an *address* for the WCF service. This is important because remote callers will be unable to communicate with the remote types if they cannot locate them! Like most aspects of WCF, an address can be hard-coded in an assembly (using the System.Uri type) or offloaded to a *.config file.

In either case, the exact format of the WCF address will differ based on your choice of binding (HTTP based, named pipes, TCP based, or MSMQ based). From a high level, WCF addresses can specify the following bits of information:

- Scheme: The transport protocol (e.g., HTTP)
- MachineName: The fully qualified domain of the machine
- Port: This is optional in many cases; for example, the default for HTTP bindings is port 80.
- Path: The path to the WCF service

This information can be represented by the following generalized template (the Port value is optional because some bindings don't use them):

scheme://<MachineName>[:Port]/Path

When you use a web service–based binding (e.g., basicHttpBinding, wsHttpBinding, wsDualHttpBinding, or wsFederationHttpBinding), the address breaks down like this (recall that HTTP-based protocols default to port 80 if you do not specify a port number):

http://localhost:8080/MyWCFService

If you use TCP-centric bindings (e.g., NetTcpBinding or NetPeerTcpBinding), the URI takes the following format:

net.tcp://localhost:8080/MyWCFService

The MSMQ-centric bindings (`NetMsmqBinding` and `MsmqIntegrationBinding`) are unique in their URI format because MSMQ can use public or private queues (which are available only on the local machine), and port numbers have no meaning in an MSMQ-centric URI. Consider the following URI, which describes a private queue named `MyPrivateQ`:

```
net.msmq://localhost/private$/MyPrivateQ
```

Last but not least, the address format used for the named-pipe binding, `NetNamedPipeBinding`, breaks down like this (recall that named pipes allow for interprocess communication for applications on the same physical machine):

```
net.pipe://localhost/MyWCFService
```

While a single WCF service might expose only a single address (based on a single binding), it is possible to configure a collection of unique addresses (with different bindings). You can do this in a `*.config` file by defining multiple `<endpoint>` elements. Here, you can specify any number of ABCs for the same service. This approach can be helpful when you want to allow callers to select which protocol they would like to use when communicating with the service.

Building a WCF Service

Now that you have a better understanding about the building blocks of a WCF application, it's time to create your first sample application and see how the ABCs are accounted for in code and configuration. This first example avoids using the Visual Studio 2010 WCF project templates, so you can focus on the specific steps involved in making a WCF service.

Begin by creating a new VB 2010 Class Library project named `MagicEightBallServiceLib`. Next, rename your initial file from `Class1.vb` to `MagicEightBallService.vb`, and then add a reference to the `System.ServiceModel.dll` assembly. In the initial code file, specify that you are using the `System.ServiceModel` namespace. At this point, your VB 2010 file should look like this:

```vb
' The key WCF namespace.
Imports System.ServiceModel

Public Class MagicEightBallService
End Class
```

Your class type implements a single WCF service contract represented by a strongly typed CLR interface named `IEightBall`. As you most likely know, the Magic 8-Ball is a toy that allows you to view one of a handful of fixed answers to a question you might ask. Your interface here will define a single method that allows the caller to pose a question to the Magic 8-Ball to obtain a random answer.

WCF service interfaces are adorned with the `<ServiceContract()>` attribute, while each interface member is decorated with the `<OperationContract()>` attribute (you'll learn more details regarding these two attributes in just a moment). Here is the definition of the `IEightBall` interface:

```
<ServiceContract () >
Public Interface IEightBall

    ' Ask a question, receive an answer!
    <OperationContract()>
    Function ObtainAnswerToQuestion(ByVal userQuestion As String) As String
End Interface
```

▪ **Note** It is permissible to define a service contract interface that contains methods not adorned with the
<OperationContract()> attribute; however, such members will not be exposed through the WCF runtime.

As you know from your study of the interface type (see Chapter 9), interfaces are quite useless until
they are implemented by a class or structure that fleshes out their functionality. Like a real Magic 8-Ball,
the implementation of your service type (MagicEightBallService) will randomly return a canned answer
from an array of strings. Also, your default constructor will display an information message that will be
(eventually) displayed within the host's console window (for diagnostic purposes):

```
Public Class MagicEightBallService
        Implements IEightBall

        ' Just for display purposes on the host.
        Public Sub New()
                Console.WriteLine("The 8-Ball awaits your question...")
        End Sub

    Public Function ObtainAnswerToQuestion(ByVal userQuestion As String) As String
            Implements IEightBall.ObtainAnswerToQuestion

            Dim answers() As String = { "Future Uncertain", "Yes", "No", "Hazy",
                                        "Ask again later", "Definitely" }
            ' Return a random response.
            Dim r As New Random()
            Return answers(r.Next(answers.Length))
    End Function
End Class
```

At this point, your WCF service library is complete. However, before you construct a host for this
service, you need to examine some additional details of the <ServiceContract()> and
<OperationContract()> attributes.

The <ServiceContract()> Attribute

For a CLR interface to participate in the services provided by WCF, it must be adorned with the
<ServiceContract()> attribute. Like many other .NET attributes, the ServiceContractAttribute type
supports many properties that further qualify its intended purpose. You can set two properties, Name and
Namespace, to control the name of the service type and the name of the XML namespace that defines the

service type. If you use a web service–specific binding, you use these values to define the `<portType>` elements of the related WSDL document.

Here, you do not bother to assign a `Name` value because the default name of the service type is directly based on the VB 2010 class name. However, the default name for the underlying XML namespace is simply `http://tempuri.org` (you should change this for all of your WCF services).

When you build a WCF service that will send and receive custom data types (which you are not currently doing), it is important that you establish a meaningful value to the underlying XML namespace because this ensures that your custom types are unique. As you might know from your experience building XML web services, XML namespaces provide a way to wrap your custom types in a unique container to ensure that your types do not clash with types in another organization.

For this reason, you can update your interface definition with a more fitting definition, which, much like the process of defining an XML namespace in a .NET Web Service project, is typically the URI of the service's point of origin, as in the following example:

```
<ServiceContract(Namespace := "http://MyCompany.com")>
Public Interface IEightBall
    ...
End Interface
```

Beyond `Namespace` and `Name`, the `<ServiceContract()>` attribute can be configured with the additional properties shown in Table 25-6. Be aware that some of these settings will be ignored, depending on your binding selection.

Table 25-6. Various Named Properties of the <ServiceContract()> Attribute

Property	Meaning in Life
CallbackContract	Establishes whether this service contract requires callback functionality for two-way message exchange (e.g., duplex bindings).
ConfigurationName	You use this name to locate the service element in an application configuration file. The default is the name of the service implementation class.
ProtectionLevel	Allows you to specify the degree to which the contract binding requires encryption, digital signatures, or both for endpoints that expose the contract.
SessionMode	You use this to establish whether sessions are allowed, not allowed, or required by this service contract.

The <OperationContract()> Attribute

Methods that you wish to use within the WCF framework must be attributed with the `<OperationContract()>` attribute, which can also be configured with various named properties. You can use the properties shown in Table 25-7 to declare that a given method is intended to be one-way in nature, supports asynchronous invocation, requires encrypted message data, and so forth (again, many of these values might be ignored based on your binding selection).

Table 25-7. Various Named Properties of the <OperationContract()> Attribute

Property	Meaning in Life
AsyncPattern	Indicates whether the operation is implemented asynchronously using a Begin/End method pair on the service. This allows the service to offload processing to another server-side thread; this has nothing to do with the client calling the method asynchronously!
IsInitiating	Specifies whether this operation can be the initial operation in a session.
IsOneWay	Indicates whether the operation consists of only a single input message (and no associated output).
IsTerminating	Specifies whether the WCF runtime should attempt to terminate the current session after the operation completes.

For the initial example, you don't need to configure the ObtainAnswerToQuestion() method with additional traits; this means you can use the <OperationContract()> attribute as currently defined.

Service Types As Operational Contracts

Finally, recall that the use of interfaces is not required when building WCF service types. In fact, it is possible to apply the <ServiceContract()> and <OperationContract()> attributes directly to the service type itself:

```
' This is only for illustrative purposes
' and not used for the current example.
<ServiceContract(Namespace := "http://MyCompany.com")>
Public Class ServiceTypeAsContract
    <OperationContract()>
    Private Sub SomeMethod()
    End Sub

    <OperationContract()>
    Private Sub AnotherMethod()
    End Sub
End Class
```

You can take this approach; however, you receive many benefits if you explicitly define an interface type to represent the service contract. The most obvious benefit is that you can apply a given interface to multiple service types (authored in a variety of languages and architectures) to achieve a high degree of polymorphism. Another benefit: You can use a service contract interface as the basis of new contracts (using interface inheritance), without having to carry any implementation baggage.

In any case, your first WCF service library is now complete. Compile your project to ensure you do not have any typos.

Hosting the WCF Service

You are now ready to define a host. Although you would host a production-level service from a Windows service or an IIS virtual directory, you will make your first host a simple console named MagicEightBallServiceHost.

Once you create this new Console Application project, add a reference to the System.ServiceModel.dll and MagicEightBallServiceLib.dll assemblies, and then update your initial code file by importing the System.ServiceModel and MagicEightBallServiceLib namespaces:

```
Imports System.ServiceModel
Imports MagicEightBallServiceLib

Module Module1
    Sub Main()
            Console.WriteLine("***** Console Based WCF Host *****")
            Console.ReadLine()
    End Sub
End Module
```

The first step you must take when building a host for a WCF service type is to decide whether you want to define the necessary hosting logic completely in code or to relegate several low-level details to an application configuration file. As mentioned previously, the benefit of *.config files is that the host can change the underlying plumbing without requiring you to recompile and redeploy the executable. However, always remember this is strictly optional because you can hard-code the hosting logic using the types within the System.ServiceModel.dll assembly.

This console-based host will use an application configuration file, so insert a new Application Configuration File into your current project using the Project ➤ Add New Item menu option.

Establishing the ABCs Within an App.config File

When you build a host for a WCF service type, you follow a predictable set of steps—some that rely on configuration and some that rely on code:

- Define the *endpoint* for the WCF service being hosted within the host's configuration file.

- Programmatically use the ServiceHost type to expose the service types available from this endpoint.

- Ensure the host remains running to service incoming client requests. Obviously, this step is not required if you host your service types using a Windows service or IIS.

In the world of WCF, the term *endpoint* represents the address, binding, and contract rolled together in a nice, tidy package. In XML, an endpoint is expressed using the `<endpoint>` element and the `address`, `binding`, and `contract` elements. Update your `*.config` file to specify a single endpoint (reachable through port 8080) exposed by this host:

```xml
<?xml version="1.0" encoding="utf-8" ?>
<configuration>
  <system.serviceModel>
    <services>
      <service name="MagicEightBallServiceLib.MagicEightBallService">
        <endpoint address ="http://localhost:8080/MagicEightBallService"
                  binding="basicHttpBinding"
                  contract="MagicEightBallServiceLib.IEightBall"/>
      </service>
    </services>
  </system.serviceModel>
  ...
</configuration>
```

Notice that the `<system.serviceModel>` element is the root for all of a host's WCF settings. Each service exposed by the host is represented by a `<service>` element that is wrapped by the `<services>` base element. Here, your single `<service>` element uses the (optional) `name` attribute to specify the friendly name of the service type.

The nested `<endpoint>` element handles the task of defining the address, the binding model (`basicHttpBinding`, in this example), and the fully qualified name of the interface type defining the WCF service contract (`IEightBall`). Because you are using an HTTP-based binding, you use the `http://` scheme, specifying an arbitrary port ID.

Coding Against the ServiceHost Type

With the current configuration file in place, the actual programming logic required to complete the host is simple. When your executable starts up, you will create an instance of the `ServiceHost` class and inform it which WCF service it is responsible for hosting. At runtime, this object will automatically read the data within the scope of the `<system.serviceModel>` element of the host's `*.config` file to determine the correct address, binding, and contract. It will then create the necessary plumbing:

```vb
Sub Main()
    Console.WriteLine("***** Console Based WCF Host *****")

    Using svcHost As New ServiceHost(GetType(MagicEightBallService))
        ' Open the host and start listening for incoming messages.
        svcHost.Open()

        ' Keep the service running until the Enter key is pressed.
        Console.WriteLine("The service is ready.")
        Console.WriteLine("Press the Enter key to terminate service.")
        Console.ReadLine()
    End Using
End Sub
```

If you run this application now, you will find that the host is alive in memory, ready to take incoming requests from remote clients.

■ **Note** If you get a System.ServiceModel.AddressAccessDeniedException when you try to run the application, close Visual Studio and restart it as an Administrator (i.e., on the Windows Start menu, right-click Microsoft Visual Studio 2010 and select "Run as administrator" from the pop-up menu).

Specifying Base Addresses

Currently, you create your ServiceHost using a constructor that requires only the service's type information. However, it is also possible to pass in an array of System.Uri types as a constructor argument to represent the collection of addresses this service is accessible from. Currently, you find the address using the *.config file. However, assume that you were to update the Using scope like this:

```
Using svcHost As New ServiceHost(
    GetType(MagicEightBallService),
    New Uri() {New Uri("http://localhost:8080/MagicEightBallService")})
```

If you did, you could now define your endpoint like this:

```
<endpoint address =""
        binding="basicHttpBinding"
        contract="MagicEightBallServiceLib.IEightBall"/>
```

Of course, too much hard-coding within a host's code base decreases flexibility. Therefore, the current host example assumes you create the service host simply by supplying the type information, as you did before:

```
Using svcHost As New ServiceHost(GetType(MagicEightBallService))
    ...
End Using
```

One of the (slightly frustrating) aspects of authoring host *.config files is that you have several ways to construct the XML descriptors, based on the amount of hard-coding you have in the code base (as you have just seen in the case of the optional Uri array). Here's a reworking that shows yet another way to author *.config files:

```
<?xml version="1.0" encoding="utf-8" ?>
<configuration>
  <system.serviceModel>
    <services>
      <service name="MagicEightBallServiceLib.MagicEightBallService">
```

```
<!-- Address obtained from <baseAddresses> -->
<endpoint address =""
          binding="basicHttpBinding"
          contract="MagicEightBallServiceLib.IEightBall"/>

<!-- List all of the base addresses in a dedicated section-->
<host>
  <baseAddresses>
    <add baseAddress ="http://localhost:8080/MagicEightBallService"/>
  </baseAddresses>
</host>
    </service>
  </services>
</system.serviceModel>

</configuration>
```

In this case, the `address` attribute of the `<endpoint>` element is still empty; regardless of the fact that you do not specify an array of `Uri` objects in code when creating the `ServiceHost`, the application runs as before because the value is pulled from the `baseAddresses` scope. The benefit of storing the base address in a `<host>`'s `<baseAddresses>` region is that other parts of a `*.config` file (such as, which you'll learn about shortly) also need to know the address of the service's endpoint. Thus, rather than having to copy and pass address values within a single `*.config` file, you can isolate the single value, as shown in the preceding snippet.

■ **Note** In a later example, you'll be introduced to a graphical configuration tool that allows you to author configuration files in a less tedious manner.

In any case, you have a bit more work to do before you build a client application to communicate with your service. Specifically, you will dig a bit deeper into the role of the `ServiceHost` class type and `<service.serviceModel>` element, as well as the role of metadata exchange (MEX) services.

Details of the ServiceHost Type

You use the `ServiceHost` class type to configure and expose a WCF service from the hosting executable. However, be aware that you will only use this type directly when building a custom `*.exe` to host your services. If you use IIS (or the Vista and Windows 7 specific WAS) to expose a service, the `ServiceHost` object is created automatically on your behalf.

As you have seen, this type requires a complete service description, which is obtained dynamically through the configuration settings of the host's `*.config` file. While this happens automatically when you create a `ServiceHost` object, it is possible to configure the state of your `ServiceHost` object manually using a number of members. In addition to `Open()` and `Close()` (which communicate with your service in a synchronous manner), Table 25-8 illustrates some further members of interest.

Table 25-8. Select Members of the ServiceHost Type

Members	Meaning in Life
Authorization	This property gets the authorization level for the service being hosted.
AddDefaultEndpoints()	This method is new to .NET 4.0, and you can use it to configure a WCF service host programmatically so it uses any number of prebuilt endpoints supplied by the framework.
AddServiceEndpoint()	This method allows you to register an endpoint to the host programmatically.
BaseAddresses	This property obtains the list of registered base addresses for the current service.
BeginOpen() BeginClose()	These methods allow you to open and close a ServiceHost object asynchronously, using the standard asynchronous .NET delegate syntax.
CloseTimeout	This property allows you to set and get the time allowed for the service to close down.
Credentials	This property obtains the security credentials used by the current service.
EndOpen() EndClose()	These methods are the asynchronous counterparts to BeginOpen() and BeginClose().
OpenTimeout	This property allows you to set and get the time allowed for the service to start up.
State	This property gets a value that indicates the current state of the communication object, which is represented by the CommunicationState enum (e.g., opened, closed, and created).

You can see some additional aspects of **ServiceHost** in action by updating your **Module1** Module with a new method that prints out the ABCs of each endpoint used by the host:

```
Sub DisplayHostInfo(ByVal svcHost As ServiceHost)
    Console.WriteLine()
    Console.WriteLine("***** Host Info *****")

    For Each se As System.ServiceModel.Description.ServiceEndpoint In
            svchost.Description.Endpoints
        Console.WriteLine("Address: {0}", se.Address)
        Console.WriteLine("Binding: {0}", se.Binding.Name)
        Console.WriteLine("Contract: {0}", se.Contract.Name)
        Console.WriteLine()
```

```
    Next
    Console.WriteLine("********************")
End Sub
```

Now assuming that you call this new method from within `Main()` after opening your host:

```
Using svcHost As New ServiceHost(GetType(MagicEightBallService))
    ' Open the host and start listening for incoming messages.
    svcHost.Open()
    DisplayHostInfo(svcHost)
    …
End Using
```

Doing this will generate the statistics shown in the following output:

```
***** Console Based WCF Host *****


***** Host Info *****

Address: http://localhost:8080/MagicEightBallService

Binding: BasicHttpBinding

Contract: IEightBall

********************

The service is ready.

Press the Enter key to terminate service.
```

Details of the <system.serviceModel> Element

Like any XML element, `<system.serviceModel>` can define a set of sub-elements, each of which can be qualified using various attributes. While you should consult the .NET Framework 4.0 SDK documentation for full details regarding the set of possible attributes, here is a skeleton that lists the critical sub-elements:

```
<system.serviceModel>
  <behaviors>
  </behaviors>
  <client>
  </client>
  <commonBehaviors>
  </commonBehaviors>
```

```
    <diagnostics>
    </diagnostics>
    <comContracts>
    </comContracts>
    <services>
    </services>
    <bindings>
    </bindings>
</system.serviceModel>
```

You'll see more exotic configuration files as you move through the chapter; however, you can see the crux of each sub-element in Table 25-9.

Table 25-9. Sub-elements of <service.serviceModel>

Sub-element	Meaning in Life
behaviors	WCF supports various endpoint and service behaviors. In a nutshell, a *behavior* allows you to qualify further the functionality of a host, service, or client.
bindings	This element allows you to fine-tune each of the WCF-supplied bindings (e.g., basicHttpBinding and netMsmqBinding), as well as to specify any custom bindings used by the host.
client	This element contains a list of endpoints a client uses to connect to a service. Obviously, this is not particularly useful in a host's *.config file.
comContracts	This element defines COM contracts enabled for WCF and COM interoperability.
commonBehaviors	This element can only be set within a machine.config file. You can use it to define all of the behaviors used by each WCF service on a given machine.
diagnostics	This element contains settings for the diagnostic features of WCF. The user can enable/disable tracing, performance counters, and the WMI provider; the user can also add custom message filters.
services	This element contains a collection of WCF services exposed by the host.

Enabling Metadata Exchange

Recall that WCF client applications communicate with the WCF service through an intervening proxy type. While you could author the proxy code completely by hand, doing so would be tedious and error-prone. Ideally, you could use a tool to generate the necessary grunge code (including the client-side *.config file). Thankfully, the .NET Framework 4.0 SDK provides a command-line tool (svcutil.exe) for this purpose. Also, Visual Studio 2010 provides similar functionality through its Project ➤ Add Service Reference menu option.

For these tools to generate the necessary proxy code/`*.config` file, however, they must be able to discover the format of the WCF service interfaces and any defined data contracts (e.g., the method names and type of parameters).

Metadata exchange (MEX) is a WCF *service behavior* that you can use to fine-tune how the WCF runtime handles your service. Simply put, each `<behavior>` element can define a set of activities a given service can subscribe to. WCF provides numerous behaviors out of the box, and it is possible to build your own.

The MEX behavior (which is disabled by default) will intercept any metadata requests sent through HTTP GET. You must enable MEX if you want to allow `svcutil.exe` or Visual Studio 2010 to automate the creation of the required client-side proxy `*.config` file.

Enabling MEX is a matter of tweaking the host's `*.config` file with the proper settings (or authoring the corresponding VB 2010 code). First, you must add a new `<endpoint>` just for MEX. Second, you need to define a WCF behavior to allow HTTP GET access. Third, you need to associate this behavior by name to your service using the `behaviorConfiguration` attribute on the opening `<service>` element. Finally, you need to add a `<host>` element to define the base address of this service (MEX will look here to figure out the locations of the types to describe).

■ **Note** You can bypass this final step if you pass in a `System.Uri` object to represent the base address as a parameter to the `ServiceHost` constructor.

Consider the following updated host `*.config` file, which creates a custom `<behavior>` element (named `EightBallServiceMEXBehavior`) that is associated to your service through the `behaviorConfiguration` attribute within the `<service>` definition:

```
<?xml version="1.0" encoding="utf-8" ?>
<configuration>
  <system.serviceModel>
    <services>
      <service name="MagicEightBallServiceLib.MagicEightBallService"
               behaviorConfiguration = "EightBallServiceMEXBehavior">
        <endpoint address =""
                  binding="basicHttpBinding"
                  contract="MagicEightBallServiceLib.IEightBall"/>

        <!-- Enable the MEX endpoint -->
        <endpoint address="mex"
                  binding="mexHttpBinding"
                  contract="IMetadataExchange" />
```

```
    <!-- Need to add this so MEX knows the address of our service -->
    <host>
      <baseAddresses>
        <add baseAddress ="http://localhost:8080/MagicEightBallService"/>
      </baseAddresses>
    </host>
  </service>
</services>

<!-- A behavior definition for MEX -->
<behaviors>
  <serviceBehaviors>
    <behavior name="EightBallServiceMEXBehavior" >
      <serviceMetadata httpGetEnabled="true" />
    </behavior>
  </serviceBehaviors>
</behaviors>
</system.serviceModel>
...
</configuration>
```

You can now restart the service and view its metadata description using the web browser of your choice. To do so, enter the address as the URL while the host is still running:

```
http://localhost:8080/MagicEightBallService
```

Once you are at the homepage for your WCF service (see Figure 25-6), you are provided with basic details regarding how to interact with this service programmatically, as well as a way to view the WSDL contract by clicking the hyperlink at the top of the page. Recall that Web Service Description Language (WSDL) is a grammar that describes the structure of web services at a given endpoint.

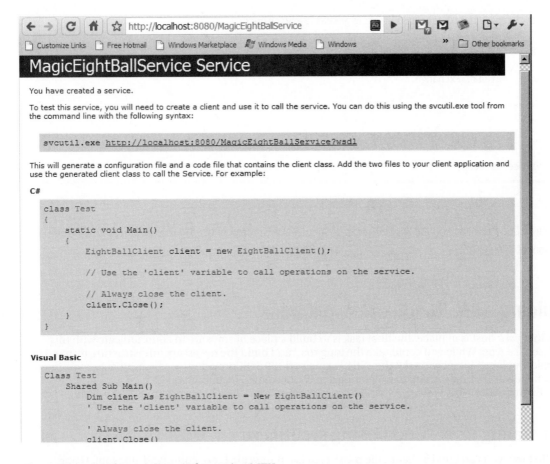

Figure 25-6. *Ready to view metadata using MEX*

Your host now exposes two different endpoints (one for the service and one for MEX), so your host's console output will appear like this:

```
***** Console Based WCF Host *****


***** Host Info *****

Address: http://localhost:8080/MagicEightBallService

Binding: BasicHttpBinding

Contract: IEightBall
```

```
Address: http://localhost:8080/MagicEightBallService/mex

Binding: MetadataExchangeHttpBinding

Contract: IMetadataExchange

**********************


The service is ready.
```

■ **Source Code** You can find the `MagicEightBallServiceHost` project under the `MagicEightBallServiceHTTP` directory of Chapter 25.

Building the WCF Client Application

Now that your host is in place, the final task is to build a piece of software to communicate with this WCF service type. While you could take the long road and build the necessary infrastructure by hand (a feasible, but labor-intensive task), the .NET Framework 4.0 SDK provides several approaches to generate a client-side proxy quickly. Begin by creating a new Console Application named `MagicEightBallServiceClient`.

Generating Proxy Code Using svcutil.exe

The first way you can build a client-side proxy is to use the `svcutil.exe` command-line tool. Using `svcutil.exe`, you can generate a new VB 2010 language file that represents the proxy code itself, as well as a client-side configuration file. You can do this by specifying the service's endpoint as the first parameter. You use the `/out:` flag to define the name of the `*.vb` file containing the proxy, and you use the `/config:` option to specify the name of the generated client-side `*.config` file.

Assuming your service is currently running, the following command set passed into `svcutil.exe` will generate two new files in the working directory (which should, of course, be entered as a single line within a Visual Studio 2010 command prompt). Also, note that the /l:vb flag means you want the proxy class to be generated in the VB language; the default in C#):

```
svcutil http://localhost:8080/MagicEightBallService
        /l:vb/out:myProxy.vb /config:app.config
```

If you open the `myProxy.vb` file, you will find a client-side representation of the `IEightBall` interface, as well as a new class named `EightBallClient`, which is the proxy class itself. This class derives from the generic class, `System.ServiceModel.ClientBase(Of T)`, where `T` is the registered service interface.

In addition to a number of custom constructors, each method of the proxy (which is based on the original interface methods) will be implemented to use the inherited `Channel` property to invoke the correct service method. Here is a partial snapshot of the proxy type:

```
<System.Diagnostics.DebuggerStepThroughAttribute(),
 System.CodeDom.Compiler.GeneratedCodeAttribute("System.ServiceModel", "4.0.0.0")>
Partial Public Class EightBallClient
    Inherits System.ServiceModel.ClientBase(Of IEightBall)
    Implements IEightBall

    ...
    Public Function ObtainAnswerToQuestion(ByVal userQuestion As String) As String
        Implements IEightBall.ObtainAnswerToQuestion
            Return MyBase.Channel.ObtainAnswerToQuestion(userQuestion)
    End Function
End Class
```

When you create an instance of the proxy type in your client application, the base class will establish a connection to the endpoint using the settings specified in the client-side application configuration file. Much like the server-side configuration file, the generated client-side `App.config` file contains an `<endpoint>` element and details about the `basicHttpBinding` used to communicate with the service.

You will also find the following `<client>` element, which (again) establishes the ABCs from the client's perspective:

```
<client>
  <endpoint
    address="http://localhost:8080/MagicEightBallService"
    binding="basicHttpBinding" bindingConfiguration="BasicHttpBinding_IEightBall"
    contract="IEightBall" name="BasicHttpBinding_IEightBall" />
</client>
```

At this point, you could include these two files into a client project (and reference the `System.ServiceModel.dll` assembly), and then use the proxy type to communicate with the remote WCF service. However, you'll take a different approach here, looking at how Visual Studio can help you further automate the creation of client-side proxy files.

Generating Proxy Code Using Visual Studio 2010

Like any good command-line tool, `svcutil.exe` provides a great number of options that you can use to control how the client proxy is generated. If you do not require these advanced options, you can generate the same two files using the Visual Studio 2010 IDE. For the client project, simply select the Add Service Reference option from the Project menu.

Once you activate this menu option, you will be prompted to enter the service URI. At this point, click the Go button to see the service description (see Figure 25-7).

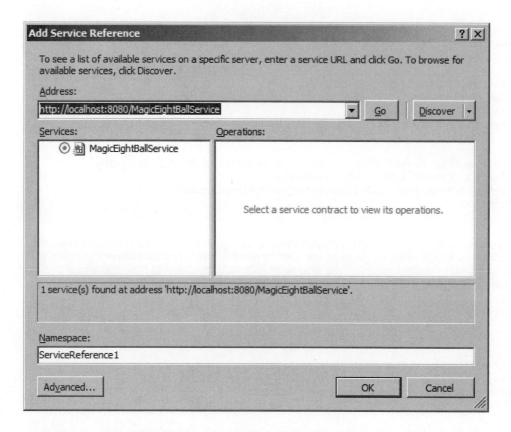

Figure 25-7. Generating the proxy files using Visual Studio 2010

Beyond creating and inserting the proxy files into your current project, this tool is kind enough to reference the WCF assemblies automatically on your behalf. In accordance with a naming convention, the proxy class is defined within a namespace called **ServiceReference1**, which is nested in the client's namespace (to avoid possible name clashes). Here is the complete client code:

```
' Location of the proxy.
Imports MagicEightBallServiceClient.ServiceReference1

Module Module1
    Sub Main()
        Console.WriteLine("***** Ask the Magic 8 Ball *****" & vbLf)
```

```
        Using ball As New EightBallClient()
            Console.Write("Your question: ")
            Dim question As String = Console.ReadLine()
            Dim answer As String = ball.ObtainAnswerToQuestion(question)
            Console.WriteLine("8-Ball says: {0}", answer)
        End Using
        Console.ReadLine()
    End Sub
End Module
```

Now assume your WCF console host is running, so you can execute the client. Here is one possible response to a question I've been asking quite a bit during the authoring of this edition of the book (with apologies to fine folks at Apress!)

```
***** Ask the Magic 8 Ball *****


Your question: Will I get this book done soon?

8-Ball says: No


Press any key to continue . . .
```

■ **Source Code** You can find the `MagicEightBallServiceClient` project located under the `MagicEightBallServiceHTTP` directory of Chapter 25.

Configuring a TCP-Based Binding

At this point, the host and client applications are both configured to use the simplest of the HTTP-based bindings, `basicHttpBinding`. Recall that the benefit of offloading settings to configuration files is that you can change the underlying plumbing in a declarative manner and expose multiple bindings for the same service.

To illustrate this, you can try a little experiment. Create a new folder on your `C:` drive (or wherever you happen to be saving your code) named `EightBallTCP`; in this new folder, create two subdirectories named `Host` and `Client`.

Next, use Windows Explorer to navigate to the `\bin\Debug` folder of the host project and copy `MagicEightBallServiceHost.exe`, `MagicEightBallServiceHost.exe.config`, and `MagicEightBallServiceLib.dll` to the `C:\EightBallTCP\Host` folder. Now use a simple text editor to open the `*.config` file for editing and modify the existing contents as follows:

```xml
<?xml version="1.0" encoding="utf-8" ?>
<configuration>
  <system.serviceModel>
    <services>
      <service name="MagicEightBallServiceLib.MagicEightBallService">
        <endpoint address =""
                  binding="netTcpBinding"
                  contract="MagicEightBallServiceLib.IEightBall"/>
        <host>
          <baseAddresses>
            <add baseAddress ="net.tcp://localhost:8090/MagicEightBallService"/>
          </baseAddresses>
        </host>
      </service>
    </services>
  </system.serviceModel>
</configuration>
```

Essentially, this host's `*.config` file strips out all the MEX settings (because you already built the proxy) and establishes that it is using the `netTcpBinding` binding type through a unique port. Now run the application by double-clicking the `*.exe`. If all is well, you should see the host output shown here:

```
***** Console Based WCF Host *****



***** Host Info *****

Address: net.tcp://localhost:8090/MagicEightBallService

Binding: NetTcpBinding

Contract: IEightBall



*********************

The service is ready.

Press the Enter key to terminate service.
```

To complete the test, copy the `MagicEightBallServiceClient.exe` and `MagicEightBallServiceClient.exe.config` files from the `\bin\Debug` folder of the client application into the `C:\EightBallTCP\Client` folder. Update the client configuration file like this:

```xml
<?xml version="1.0" encoding="utf-8" ?>
<configuration>
  <system.serviceModel>
    <client>
      <endpoint address="net.tcp://localhost:8090/MagicEightBallService"
                binding="netTcpBinding"
                contract="ServiceReference1.IEightBall"
                name="netTcpBinding_IEightBall" />
    </client>
  </system.serviceModel>
</configuration>
```

This client-side configuration file is a massive simplification compared to what the Visual Studio proxy generator authored. Notice how you have completely removed the existing <bindings> element. Originally, the *.config file contained a <bindings> element with a <basicHttpBinding> sub-element that supplied numerous details of the client's binding settings (e.g., timeouts).

The truth is you never needed that detail for this example because you automatically obtain the default values of the underlying BasicHttpBinding object. If you needed to, you could of course update the existing <bindings> element to define details of the <netTcpBinding> sub-element; however, doing so is not required if you are happy with the default values of the NetTcpBinding object.

In any case, you should now be able to run your client application. Assuming the host is still running in the background, you will be able to move data between your assemblies using TCP.

■ **Source Code** You can find the MagicEightBallTCP project under the Chapter 25 subdirectory.

Simplifying Configuration Settings with WCF 4.0

As you were working through the first example of the chapter, you might have noticed that the hosting configuration logic is quite verbose. For example, your host's *.config file (for the original basic HTTP binding) needed to define an <endpoint> element for the service, a second <endpoint> element for MEX, a <baseAddresses> element (technically optional) to reduce redundant URIs, and then a <behaviors> section to define the runtime nature of metadata exchange.

To be sure, learning how to author hosting *.config files can be a major hurdle when building WCF services. To make matters more frustrating, a good number of WCF services tend to require the same basic settings in a host configuration file. For example, if you were to make a brand new WCF service and a brand new host, and you wanted to expose this service using <basicHttpBinding> with MEX support, the required *.config file would look almost identical to the one you previously authored.

Thankfully, under .NET 4.0, the Windows Communication Foundation API ships with a number of simplifications, including default settings (and other shortcuts) that make the process of building host configuration files much easier.

Default Endpoints in WCF 4.0

Under .NET 3.5, if you call Open() on the ServiceHost object, and you have not yet specified at least one <endpoint> element in your configuration file, the runtime will thrown an exception. And you get a similar result if you call `AddServiceEndpoint()` in code to specify an endpoint. However, with the release of .NET 4.0, every WCF service is automatically provided with *default endpoints* that capture commonplace configuration details for each supported protocol.

If you were to open the `machine.config` file for .NET 4.0, you would find a new element named `<protocolMapping>`. This element documents which WCF bindings to use by default, if you do not specify any:

```
<system.serviceModel>
...
  <protocolMapping>
    <add scheme="http" binding="basicHttpBinding"/>
    <add scheme="net.tcp" binding="netTcpBinding"/>
    <add scheme="net.pipe" binding="netNamedPipeBinding"/>
    <add scheme="net.msmq" binding="netMsmqBinding"/>
  </protocolMapping>
  ...
</system.serviceModel>
```

To use these default bindings, all you need to do is specify base addresses in your host configuration file. To see this in action, open the HTTP-based `MagicEightBallServiceHost` project in Visual Studio. Now update your hosting `*.config` file by completely removing the `<endpoint>` element for your WCF service and all MEX-specific data. Your configuration file should now look like this:

```
<configuration>
  <system.serviceModel>
    <services>
      <service name="MagicEightBallServiceLib.MagicEightBallService" >
        <host>
          <baseAddresses>
            <add baseAddress="http://localhost:8080/MagicEightBallService"/>
          </baseAddresses>
        </host>
      </service>
    </services>
  </system.serviceModel>
</configuration>
```

Because you specified a valid HTTP `<baseAddress>`, your host will automatically use `basicHttpBinding`. If you run your host again, you will see the same listing of ABC data:

```
***** Console Based WCF Host *****


***** Host Info *****

Address: http://localhost:8080/MagicEightBallService

Binding: BasicHttpBinding
```

```
Contract: IEightBall

*********************

The service is ready.

Press the Enter key to terminate service.
```

You have not yet enabled MEX, but you will do so in a moment using another .NET 4.0 simplification known as *default behavior configurations*. First, however, you will learn how to expose a single WCF service using multiple bindings.

Exposing a Single WCF Service Using Multiple Bindings

Since its first release, WCF has had the ability to allow a single host to expose a WCF service using multiple endpoints. For example, you could expose the MagicEightBallService using HTTP, TCP, and named pipe bindings simply by adding new endpoints to your configuration file. Once you restart the host, all of the necessary plumbing is created automatically.

This is a huge benefit for many reasons. Before WCF, it was difficult to expose a single service using multiple bindings because each type of binding (e.g., HTTP and TCP) had its own programming model. Nevertheless, the ability to allow a caller to pick the most appropriate binding is extremely useful. In-house callers might like to use TCP bindings that an outwardly facing client (outside of your company firewall) would need to use HTTP to access, while clients on the same machine might wish to use a named pipe.

To do this before .NET 4.0, your hosting configuration file would need to define multiple <endpoint> elements manually. It would also have to define multiple <baseAddress> elements for each protocol. However, today you can simply author the following configuration file:

```xml
<configuration>
  <system.serviceModel>
    <services>
      <service name="MagicEightBallServiceLib.MagicEightBallService" >
        <host>
          <baseAddresses>
            <add baseAddress="http://localhost:8080/MagicEightBallService"/>
            <add baseAddress=
                "net.tcp://localhost:8099/MagicEightBallService"/>
          </baseAddresses>
        </host>
      </service>
    </services>
  </system.serviceModel>
</configuration>
```

If you compile your project (to refresh the deployed *.config file) and restart the host, you would now see the following endpoint data:

```
***** Console Based WCF Host *****


***** Host Info *****

Address: http://localhost:8080/MagicEightBallService

Binding: BasicHttpBinding

Contract: IEightBall

Address: net.tcp://localhost:8099/MagicEightBallService

Binding: NetTcpBinding

Contract: IEightBall


*********************

The service is ready.

Press the Enter key to terminate service.
```

Now that your WCF service can be reachable from two unique endpoints, you might wonder how the caller is able to select between them. When you generate a client-side proxy, the Add Service reference tool will give each exposed endpoint a string name in the client side *.config file. In code, you can pass in the correct string name to the proxy's constructor, and sure enough, the correct binding will be used. Before you can do this, however, you need to reestablish MEX for this modified hosting configuration file and learn how to tweak the settings of a default binding.

Changing Settings for a WCF Binding

If you specify the ABCs of a service in VB 2010 code (which you will do later in this chapter), it becomes obvious how you change the default settings of a WCF binding; you simply change the property values of the object! For example, if you want to use BasicHttpBinding, but also want to change the timeout settings, you could do so as follows:

```
Private Sub ConfigureBindingInCode()
    Dim binding As New BasicHttpBinding()
    binding.OpenTimeout = TimeSpan.FromSeconds(30)
    ...
End Sub
```

It has always been possible to configure settings for a binding in a declarative manner. For example,.NET 3.5 let you build a host configuration file that changes the `OpenTimeout` property of `BasicHttpBinding`:

```
<configuration>
  <system.serviceModel>

    <bindings>
      <basicHttpBinding>
        <binding name = "myCustomHttpBinding"
                 openTimeout = "00:00:30" />
      </basicHttpBinding>
    </bindings>

    <services>
      <service name = "WcfMathService.MyCalc">
        <endpoint address = "http://localhost:8080/MyCalc"
                  binding = "basicHttpBinding"
                  bindingConfiguration = "myCustomHttpBinding"
                  contract = "WcfMathService.IBasicMath" />
      </service>
    </services>
  </system.serviceModel>
</configuration>
```

Here, you have a configuration file for a service named `WcfMathService.MyCalc`, which supports a single interface named `IBasicMath`. Note how the `<bindings>` section allows you to define a named `<binding>` element, which tweaks settings for a given binding. Within the `<endpoint>` of the service, you can connect your specific settings using the `bindingConfiguration` attribute.

This sort of hosting configuration still works as expected under .NET 4.0; however if you leverage a default endpoint, you can't connect the `<binding>` to the `<endpoint>`! As luck would have it, you can control the settings of a default endpoint simply by omitting the `name` attribute of the `<binding>` element. For example, this snippet changes some properties of the default `BasicHttpBinding` and `NetTcpBinding` objects used in the background:

```
<configuration>
  <system.serviceModel>
    <services>
      <service name="MagicEightBallServiceLib.MagicEightBallService" >
        <host>
          <baseAddresses>
            <add baseAddress="http://localhost:8080/MagicEightBallService"/>
            <add baseAddress=
              "net.tcp://localhost:8099/MagicEightBallService"/>
          </baseAddresses>
        </host>
      </service>
    </services>
```

```
    <bindings>
      <basicHttpBinding>
        <binding openTimeout = "00:00:30" />
      </basicHttpBinding>
      <netTcpBinding>
        <binding closeTimeout="00:00:15"/>
      </netTcpBinding>
    </bindings>

  </system.serviceModel>
</configuration>
```

The WCF 4.0 Default MEX Behavior Configuration

A proxy generation tool must discover the composition of a service at runtime before it can do its work. In WCF, you allow this runtime discovery to occur by enabling MEX. Again, most host configuration files need to enable MEX (at least during development); fortunately, the way you configure MEX seldom changes, so .NET 4.0 provides a few handy shortcuts.

The most useful shortcut is out-of-the-box MEX support. You don't need to add a MEX endpoint, define a named MEX service behavior, and then connect the named binding to the service (as you did in the HTTP version of the MagicEightBallServiceHost); instead, you can now simply add the following:

```
<configuration>
  <system.serviceModel>
    <services>
      <service name="MagicEightBallServiceLib.MagicEightBallService" >
        <host>
          <baseAddresses>
            <add baseAddress="http://localhost:8080/MagicEightBallService"/>
            <add baseAddress=
              "net.tcp://localhost:8099/MagicEightBallService"/>
          </baseAddresses>
        </host>
      </service>
    </services>

    <bindings>
      <basicHttpBinding>
        <binding openTimeout = "00:00:30" />
      </basicHttpBinding>
      <netTcpBinding>
        <binding closeTimeout="00:00:15"/>
      </netTcpBinding>
    </bindings>
```

```
    <behaviors>
      <serviceBehaviors>
        <behavior>
          <!-- To get default MEX,
               don't name your <serviceMetadata> element-->
          <serviceMetadata httpGetEnabled="true"/>
        </behavior>
      </serviceBehaviors>
    </behaviors>

  </system.serviceModel>
...
</configuration>
```

The trick is that the <serviceMetadata> element no longer has a name attribute (also notice the <service> element no longer needs the behaviorConfiguration attribute). With this adjustment, you get free MEX support at runtime. To test this, you can run your host (after you compile to refresh the configuration file) and type in the following URL in a browser:

```
http://localhost:8080/MagicEightBallService
```

Once you do this, you can click the wsdl link at the top of the web page to see the WSDL description of the service (see Figure 25-6 for a refresher). Note that you do not see the host's console window print out data for the MEX endpoint because you have not explicitly defined an endpoint for IMetadataExchange in your configuration file. Nevertheless, MEX is enabled, and you can start to build client proxies.

Refreshing the Client Proxy and Selecting the Binding

Assuming your updated host has been compiled and is running in the background, you will now want to open the client application and refresh the current service reference. Begin by opening the Service References folder found in the Solution Explorer. Next, right-click the current ServiceReference and pick the Update Service Reference menu option (see Figure 25-8).

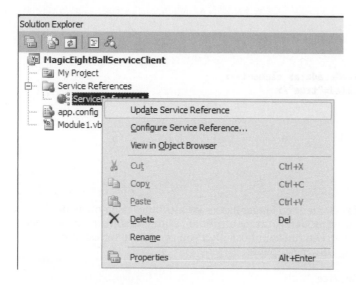

Figure 25-8. Refreshing the proxy and client side *.config file

Once you done this, you will see that the client side `*.config` file has two bindings to select from: one for HTTP and one for TCP. As you can see, you give each binding a fitting name. Here is a partial listing of the refreshed configuration file:

```
<configuration>
  <system.serviceModel>

    <bindings>
      <basicHttpBinding>
        <binding name="BasicHttpBinding_IEightBall" ... />
      </basicHttpBinding>

      <netTcpBinding>
        <binding name="NetTcpBinding_IEightBall" ... />
      </netTcpBinding>
    </bindings>
...
  </system.serviceModel>
</configuration>
```

The client can use these names when it creates the proxy object to select the binding it wishes to use. Thus, if your client would like to use TCP, you could update the client side VB 2010 code as follows:

```
Sub Main()
      Console.WriteLine("***** Ask the Magic 8 Ball *****" & vbLf)

      Using ball As New EightBallClient("NetTcpBinding_IEightBall")
       ...
      End Using
      Console.ReadLine()
End Sub
```

If a client would rather use the HTTP binding, you could write:

```
Using ball As New EightBallClient("BasicHttpBinding_IEightBall")
   ...
End Using
```

That wraps up the current example, which showcased a number of WCF 4.0's useful features. These features simplify how you can author hosting configuration files. Next up, you will see how to use the WCF Service Library Project template.

■ **Source Code** You can find the `MagicEightBallServiceHTTPDefaultBindings` project located under the Chapter 25 subdirectory.

Using the WCF Service Library Project Template

You need to do one more thing before you build a more exotic WCF service that communicates with the `AutoLot` database you created in Chapter 21. The next example will illustrate a number of important topics, including the benefits of the WCF Service Library project template, the WCF Test Client, the WCF configuration editor, hosting WCF services within a Windows service, and asynchronous client calls. To stay focused on these new concepts, this WCF service will be kept intentionally simple.

Building a Simple Math Service

To begin, create a brand-new WCF Service Library project named `MathServiceLibrary`, making sure you select the correct option under the WCF node of the New Project dialog box (see Figure 25-2 if you need a nudge). Now change the name of the initial `IService1.vb` file to `IBasicMath.vb`. Once you do so, *delete* all of the example code in IBasicMath.vb and replace it with the following code:

```
<ServiceContract(Namespace:="http://MyCompany.com")>
Public Interface IBasicMath
      <OperationContract()>
      Function Add(ByVal x As Integer, ByVal y As Integer) As Integer
End Interface
```

Next, change the name of the `Service1.vb` file to `MathService.vb`, delete all the example code in MathService.vb, and implement your service contract as follows:

```
Public Class MathService
    Implements IBasicMath

    Public Function Add(ByVal x As Integer, ByVal y As Integer) As Integer
            Implements IBasicMath.Add

            ' To simulate a lengthy request.
            System.Threading.Thread.Sleep(5000)
            Return x + y
    End Function
End Class
```

Finally, open the supplied `App.config` file and verify all occurrences of `IService1` have been changed to `IBasicMath`. Also, change any remaining occurrences of `Service1` to `MathService`. Also take a moment to notice that this `*.config` file has already been enabled to support MEX; by default, your service endpoint uses the `wsHttpBinding` protocol.

Testing the WCF Service with WcfTestClient.exe

One benefit of using the WCF Service Library project is that when you debug or run your library, it will read the settings in the `*.config` file and use them to load the WCF Test Client application (`WcfTestClient.exe`). This GUI-based application allows you to test each member of your service interface as you build the WCF service; this means you don't have to build a host/client manually simply for testing purposes, as you did previously.

Figure 25-9 shows the testing environment for `MathService`. Notice that when you double-click an interface method, you can specify input parameters and invoke the member.

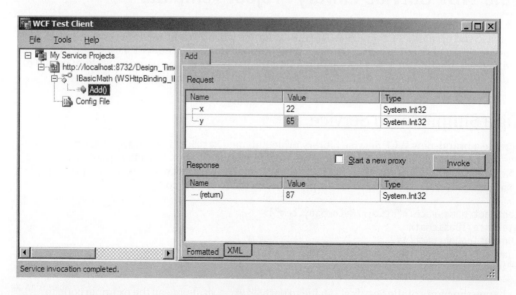

Figure 25-9. Testing the WCF service using WcfTestClient.exe

This utility works out of the box when you have created a WCF Service Library project; however, be aware that you can use this tool to test any WCF service when you start it at the command line by specifying a MEX endpoint. For example, if you were to start the MagicEightBallServiceHost.exe application, you could specify the following command at a Visual Studio 2010 command prompt:

```
wcftestclient http://localhost:8080/MagicEightBallService
```

Once you do this, you can invoke ObtainAnswerToQuestion() in a similar manner.

Altering Configuration Files Using SvcConfigEditor.exe

Another benefit of making use of the WCF Service Library project is that you are able to right-click on the App.config file within the Solution Explorer to activate the GUI-based Service Configuration Editor, SvcConfigEditor.exe (see Figure 25-10). This same technique can be used from a client application that has referenced a WCF service.

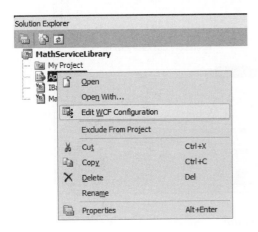

*Figure 25-10. GUI-based *.config file editing starts here*

Once you activate this tool, you can change the XML-based data using a friendly user interface. Using a tool such as this to maintain your *.config files provides many benefits. First (and foremost), you can rest assured that the generated markup conforms to the expected format and is typo-free. Second, it is a great way to see the valid values that could be assigned to a given attribute. Finally, you no longer need to author tedious XML data manually.

Figure 25-11 shows the overall look-and-feel of the Service Configuration Editor. Truth be told, an entire chapter could be devoted to describing all of the interesting options SvcConfigEditor.exe supports (e.g., COM+ integration and creation of new *.config files). Be sure to take time to investigate this tool; also be aware that you can access a fairly detailed help system by pressing F1.

■ **Note** The `SvcConfigEditor.exe` utility can edit (or create) configuration files, even if you do not select an initial WCF Service Library project. Use a Visual Studio 2010 command window to launch the tool, and then use the File ➤ Open menu option to load an existing `*.config` file for editing.

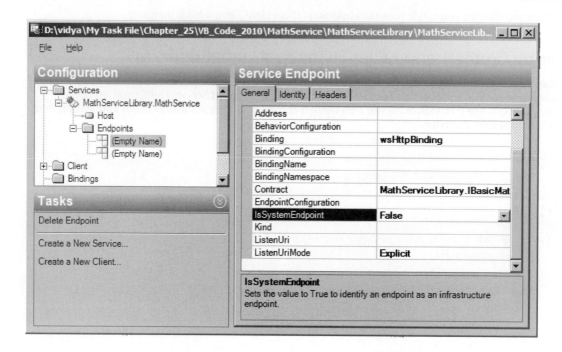

Figure 25-11. Working with the WCF Service Configuration Editor

You have no need to further configure your WCF `MathService`; at this point, you can move on to the task of building a custom host.

Hosting the WCF Service within a Windows Service

Hosting a WCF service from within a console application (or within a GUI desktop application, for that matter) is not an ideal choice for a production-level server, given that the host must remain running visibly in the background to service clients. Even if you were to minimize the hosting application to the Windows taskbar, it would still be far too easy to accidentally shut down the host, thereby terminating the connection with any client applications.

■ **Note** While it is true that a desktop Windows application does not *have* to show a main window, a typical *.exe does require user interaction to load the executable. However, you can configure a Windows service (described next) to run even if no users are currently logged on to the workstation.

If you build an in-house WCF application, another alternative you have is to host your WCF service library from within a dedicated Windows service. One benefit of doing so is that you can configure a Windows service to start automatically when the target machine boots up. Another benefit is that Windows services run invisibly in the background (unlike your console application) and do not require user interactivity.

Next, you will learn how to build such a host. Begin by creating a new Windows service project named MathWindowsServiceHost (see Figure 25-12). Once you do this, rename your initial **Service1.vb** file to MathWinService.vb using Solution Explorer.

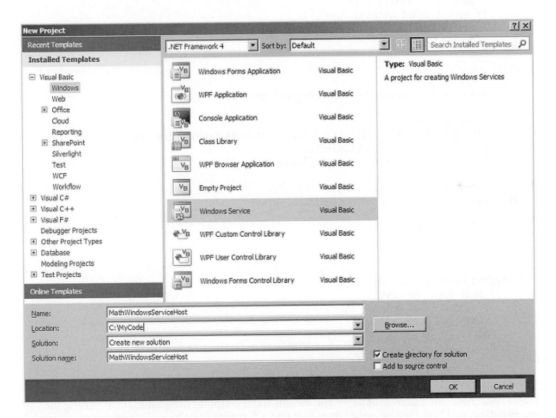

Figure 25-12. Creating a Windows service to host your WCF service

Specifying the ABCs in Code

Now assume you have set a reference to your `MathServiceLibrary.dll` and `System.ServiceModel.dll` assemblies. All you need to do is use the `ServiceHost` type in the `OnStart()` and `OnStop()` methods of your Windows service type. Open the code file for your service host class (by right-clicking the designer and selecting View Code) and add the following logic:

```vb
' Be sure to import these namespaces:
Imports MathServiceLibrary
Imports System.ServiceModel

Public Class MathWinService
        ' A member variable of type ServiceHost.
        Private myHost As ServiceHost

        Protected Overrides Sub OnStart(ByVal args() As String)
                ' Just to be really safe.
                If myHost IsNot Nothing Then
                    myHost.Close()
                    myHost = Nothing
                End If

                ' Create the host.
                myHost = New ServiceHost(GetType(MathService))

                ' The ABCs in code!
                Dim address As New Uri("http://localhost:8080/MathServiceLibrary")
                Dim binding As New WSHttpBinding()
                Dim contract As Type = GetType(IBasicMath)

                ' Add this endpoint.
                myHost.AddServiceEndpoint(contract, binding, address)

                ' Open the host.
                myHost.Open()
        End Sub

        Protected Overrides Sub OnStop()
                ' Shut down the host.
                If myHost IsNot Nothing Then
                    myHost.Close()
                End If
        End Sub
End Class
```

While nothing prevents you from using a configuration file when building a Windows service host for a WCF service, here (for a change of pace) you establish the endpoint programmatically using the `Uri`, `WSHttpBinding`, and `Type` classes, rather than by using a `*.config` file. Once you create each aspect of the ABCs, you inform the host programmatically by calling `AddServiceEndpoint()`.

If you wish to inform the runtime that you want to gain access to each of the default endpoint bindings stored in the .NET 4.0 `machine.config` file, you can simplify your programming logic by specifying base addresses when you invoke the constructor of `ServiceHost`. In this case, you do not need to specify the ABCs manually in code or call `AddServiceEndpoint()`; instead, you call `AddDefaultEndpoints()`. Consider the following update:

```
Protected Overrides Sub OnStart(ByVal args() As String)
        If myHost IsNot Nothing Then
            myHost.Close()
        End If

        ' Create the host and specify a URL for an HTTP binding.
        myHost = New ServiceHost(GetType(MathService),
                        New Uri("http://localhost:8080/MathServiceLibrary"))

        ' Opt in for the default endpoints!
        myHost.AddDefaultEndpoints()

        ' Open the host.
        myHost.Open()
End Sub
```

Enabling MEX

While you could enable MEX programmatically as well, here you will opt for a WCF 4.0 configuration file. Insert a new `App.config` file into your Windows service project that contains the following default MEX settings:

```
<?xml version="1.0" encoding="utf-8" ?>
<configuration>
  <system.serviceModel>
    <services>
      <service name="MathServiceLibrary.MathService">
      </service>
    </services>

    <behaviors>
      <serviceBehaviors>
        <behavior>
          <serviceMetadata httpGetEnabled="true"/>
        </behavior>
      </serviceBehaviors>
    </behaviors>

  </system.serviceModel>
...
</configuration>
```

Creating a Windows Service Installer

To register your Windows service with the operating system, you need to add an installer to your project that contains the necessary code to allow you to register the service. To do so, right-click the Windows service designer surface and select Add Installer (see Figure 25-13).

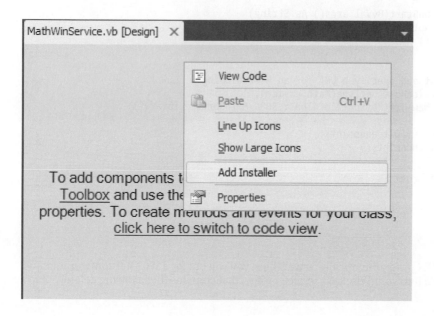

Figure 25-13. Adding an installer for the Windows service

Once you do this, you can see two components have been added to a new designer surface representing the installer. The first component (named `ServiceProcessInstaller1` by default) represents an item that can install a new Windows service on the target machine. Select this item on the designer and use the Properties window to set the `Account` property to `LocalSystem` (see Figure 25-14).

Figure 25-14. Be sure to run the Windows service as a local system account

The second component (named **ServiceInstaller1**) represents a type that will install your particular Windows service. Again, use the Properties window to change the **ServiceName** property to **MathService** (as you might have guessed, this represents the friendly display name of the registered Windows service), set the **StartType** property to **Automatic**, and add a friendly description of your Windows service using the **Description** property (see Figure 25-15).

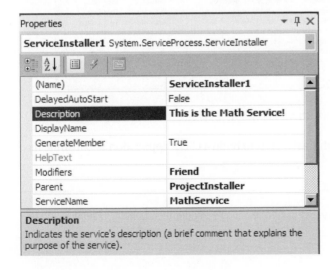

Figure 25-15. Configuring installer details

At this point, you can compile your application.

Installing the Windows Service

A Windows service can be installed on the host machine using a traditional setup program (such as an *.msi installer) or via the installutil.exe command-line tool. Using a Visual Studio 2010 command prompt (as an Administrator), change into the \bin\Debug folder of your MathWindowsServiceHost project. Now, enter the following command:

```
installutil MathWindowsServiceHost.exe
```

Assuming the installation succeeded, you can now open the Services applet located under the Administrative Tools folder of your Control Panel. You should see the friendly name of your Windows service listed alphabetically. Once you locate it, make sure you start the service on your local machine using the Start link (see Figure 25-16).

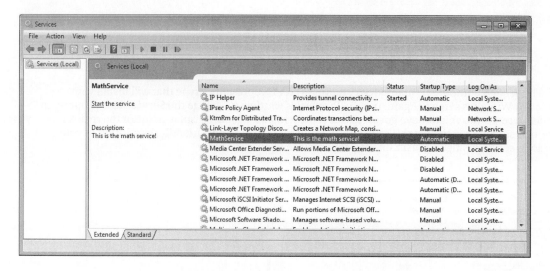

Figure 25-16. Viewing your Windows service, which hosts your WCF service

Now that the service is alive and kicking, the last step is to build a client application to consume its services.

■ **Source Code** You can find the MathWindowsServiceHost project located under the Chapter 25 subdirectory.

Invoking a Service Asynchronously from the Client

Create a new Console Application named MathClient and set a Service Reference to your running WCF
service (that is current hosted by the Windows service running in the background) using the Add Service
Reference option of Visual Studio (you'll need to type the URL in the Addresses box). Don't click the OK
button yet, however! Notice that the Add Service Reference dialog box has an Advanced button in the
lower-left corner (see Figure 25-17).

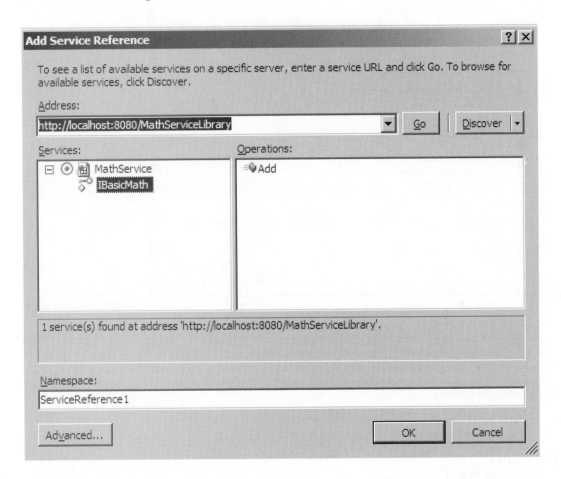

Figure 25-17. Referencing your MathService and getting ready to configure advanced settings

Click this button now to view the additional proxy configuration settings (see Figure 25-18). You can
use this dialog box to generate code that allows you to call the remote methods in an asynchronous
manner, provided you check the Generate Asynchronous Operators check box. Go ahead and check this
option for the time being.

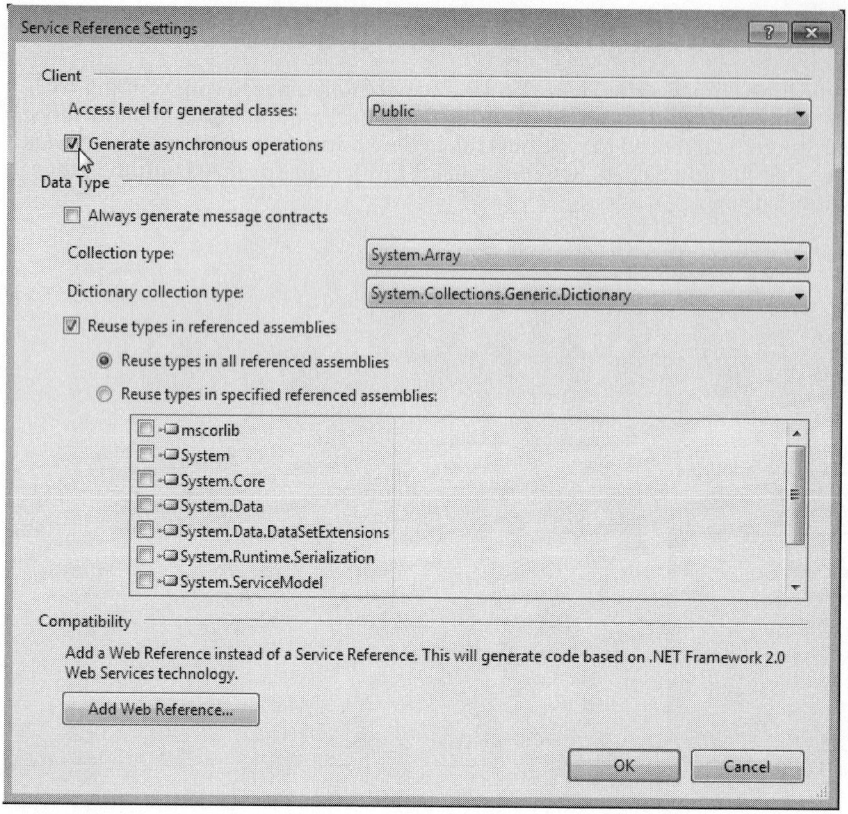

Figure 25-18. Advanced client-side proxy configuration options

At this point, the proxy code contains additional methods that allow you to invoke each member of the service contract using the expected **Begin**/**End** asynchronous invocation pattern described in Chapter 19. Here is a simple implementation that uses a lambda expression rather than a strongly typed **AsyncCallback** delegate:

```
Imports MathClient.ServiceReference1
Imports System.Threading

Module Module1
        Sub Main()
            Console.WriteLine("***** The Async Math Client *****" & vbLf)

            Using proxy As New BasicMathClient()
                proxy.Open()
                ' Add numbers in an async manner, using a lambda expression.
```

```
            Dim result As IAsyncResult =
                proxy.BeginAdd(2, 3,
                                Sub(ar) Console.WriteLine ("2 + 5 = {0}",
                    proxy.EndAdd(ar)), Nothing)

            While Not result.IsCompleted
                    Thread.Sleep(200)
                    Console.WriteLine("Client working...")
            End While
        End Using
        Console.ReadLine()
    End Sub
End Module
```

■ **Source Code** You can find the MathClient project located under the Chapter 25 subdirectory.

Designing WCF Data Contracts

This chapter's final example shows you how to construct WCF *data contracts*. The previous WCF services defined simple methods that operate on primitive CLR data types. When you use of any of the HTTP binding types (e.g., basicHttpBinding and wsHttpBinding), incoming and outgoing simple data types are automatically formatted into XML elements. On a related note, if you use a TCP-based binding (such as netTcpBinding), the parameters and return values of simple data types are transmitted using a compact binary format.

■ **Note** The WCF runtime will also automatically encode any type marked with the <Serializable()> attribute; however, this is not the preferred way to define WCF contracts, and it is only included for backwards compatibility.

However, when you define service contracts that use custom classes as parameters or return values, you must define these types using a data contract. Simply put, a data contract is a type adorned with the <DataContract()> attribute. Likewise, you must mark each field you expect to be used as part of the proposed contract with the <DataMember()> attribute.

■ **Note** If a data contract contains fields not marked with the <DataMember()> attribute, those fields will not be serialized by the WCF runtime.

Next you'll see how to construct data contracts. Begin by creating a brand-new WCF service that interacts with the `AutoLot` database you created in Chapter 21. Also, you will create this final WCF service using the web-based WCF Service template. Recall that this type of WCF service will automatically be placed into an IIS virtual directory, and it will function in a similar fashion to a traditional .NET XML web service. Once you understand the composition of such a WCF service, you should have little problem porting an existing WCF service into a new IIS virtual directory.

■ **Note** This example assumes you are somewhat comfortable with the structure of an IIS virtual directory (and IIS itself). If this is not the case, see Chapter 32 for details on this subject.

Using the Web-Centric WCF Service Project Template

Use the File ➤ New ➤ Web Site menu option to create a new WCF service named `AutoLotWCFService`, and then expose this service from the following URI: `http://localhost/AutoLotWCFService` (see Figure 25-19). Also, make sure the Location dropdown list has HTTP as the active selection.

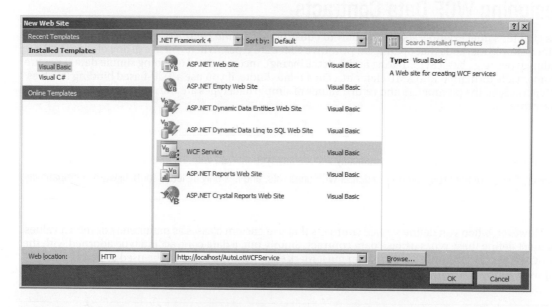

Figure 25-19. Creating a web-centric WCF service

After you done this, set a reference to the `AutoLotDAL.dll` assembly you created in Chapter 21 (using the Website ➤ Add Reference menu option). You have been given some example starter code (located under the App_Code folder), which you will want to delete. Begin by renaming the initial `IService.vb` file to `IAutoLotService.vb`, and then define the initial service contract within your newly named file:

```
<ServiceContract()>
Public Interface IAutoLotService
    <OperationContract()>
    Sub InsertCar(ByVal id As Integer, ByVal make As String,
                          ByVal color As String, ByVal petname As String)

    <OperationContract()>
    Sub InsertCar(ByVal car As InventoryRecord)

    <OperationContract()>
    Function GetInventory() As InventoryRecord()
End Interface
```

This interface defines three methods, one of which returns an array of the (yet-to-be-created) InventoryRecord type. You might recall that the GetInventory() method of InventoryDAL simply returned a DataTable object, and this might make you wonder why your service's GetInventory() method does not do the same.

While it would work to return a DataTable from a WCF service method, recall that WCF was built to honor the use of SOA principles, one of which is to program against contracts, not implementations. Therefore, you won't return the .NET-specific DataTable type to an external caller; instead you will return a custom data contract (InventoryRecord) that will be correctly expressed in the contained WSDL document in an agnostic manner.

Also note that the interface listed previously defines an overloaded method named InsertCar(). The first version takes four incoming parameters, while the second version takes an InventoryRecord type as input. You can define the InventoryRecord data contract as follows:

```
<DataContract()>
Public Class InventoryRecord
        <DataMember()>
        Public ID As Integer

        <DataMember()>
        Public Make As String

        <DataMember()>
        Public Color As String

        <DataMember()>
        Public PetName As String
End Class
```

If you were to implement this interface as it now stands, and then build a host and attempt to call these methods from a client, you might be surprised to see you'll get a runtime exception. The reason: One of the requirements of a WSDL description is that each method exposed from a given endpoint must be *uniquely named*. Thus, while method overloading works just fine as far as VB 2010 is concerned, the current web service specifications do not permit two identically named InsertCar() methods.

Fortunately, the <OperationContract()> attribute supports a named property (Name) that allows you to specify how the VB 2010 method will be represented within a WSDL description. Given this, you can update the second version of InsertCar() as follows:

```vb
Public Interface IAutoLotService
    ….
    <OperationContract(Name := "InsertCarWithDetails")>
    Sub InsertCar(ByVal car As InventoryRecord)
End Interface
```

Implementing the Service Contract

Now rename Service.vb to AutoLotService.vb. The AutoLotService type implements this interface as follows (be sure to import the AutoLotConnectedLayer and System.Data namespaces into this code file):

```vb
Imports AutoLotConnectedLayer
Imports System.Data

Public Class AutoLotService
    Implements IAutoLotService

    Private Const ConnString As String = "Data Source=.\SQLEXPRESS;↵
            Initial Catalog=AutoLot" & ";Integrated Security=True"

    Public Sub InsertCar(ByVal id As Integer, ByVal make As String,
        ByVal color As String, ByVal petname As String) Implements IAutoLotService.InsertCar
        Dim d As New InventoryDAL()
        d.OpenConnection(ConnString)
        d.InsertAuto(id, color, make, petname)
        d.CloseConnection()
    End Sub

    Public Sub InsertCar(ByVal car As InventoryRecord)
        Implements IAutoLotService.InsertCar
        Dim d As New InventoryDAL()
        d.OpenConnection(ConnString)
        d.InsertAuto(car.ID, car.Color, car.Make, car.PetName)
        d.CloseConnection()
    End Sub

    Public Function GetInventory() As InventoryRecord()
        Implements IAutoLotService.GetInventory
        ' First, get the DataTable from the database.
        Dim d As New InventoryDAL()
        d.OpenConnection(ConnString)
        Dim dt As DataTable = d.GetAllInventoryAsDataTable()
        d.CloseConnection()

        ' Now make a List(Of T) to contain the records.
        Dim records As New List(Of InventoryRecord)()

        ' Copy the data table into List() of custom contracts.
        Dim reader As DataTableReader = dt.CreateDataReader()
        Do While reader.Read()
```

```
            Dim r As New InventoryRecord()
            r.ID = CInt(reader("CarID"))
            r.Color = CStr(reader("Color"))
            r.Make = CStr(reader("Make"))
            r.PetName = (CStr(reader("PetName")))
            records.Add(r)
        Loop

        ' Transform List(Of T) to array of InventoryRecord types.
        Return CType(records.ToArray(), InventoryRecord())
    End Function
End Class
```

There isn't too much to say about the preceding code. For the sake of simplicity, you hard-code the connection string value (which you might need to adjust based on your machine settings), rather than store it in your Web.config file. Given that your data access library does all the real work of communicating with the AutoLot database, all you need to do is pass the incoming parameters to the InsertAuto() method of the InventoryDAL class type. The only other point of interest is the act of mapping the DataTable object's values into a generic list of InventoryRecord types (using a DataTableReader), and then transforming the List(Of T) into an array of InventoryRecord types.

The Role of the *.svc File

When you create a web-centric WCF service, you will find your project contains a specific file with a *.svc file extension. This particular file is required for any WCF service hosted by IIS; it describes the name and location of the service implementation within the install point. Because you have changed the names of your starter files and WCF types, you must now update the contents of the Service.svc file as follows:

```
<%@ ServiceHost Language="VB" Debug="true"
  Service="AutoLotService" CodeBehind="~/App_Code/AutoLotService. vb" %>
```

■ **Note** Under .NET 4.0, it is now possible to deploy a WCF service to an IIS virtual directory without a *.svc file. However, doing this means that your entire service can be nothing more than a collection of VB 2010 code files. Your service will also look highly similar to a traditional ASP.NET XML Web Service! To see more details, look up the following topic in the .NET Framework 4.0 SDK documentation: "What's new in Windows Communication Foundation."

Examining the Web.config File

The Web.config file of a WCF Service created under HTTP will use a number of the .NET 4.0 simplifications examined earlier in this chapter. As will be described in more detail during your examination of ASP.NET later in this book, the Web.config file serves a similar purpose to an executable's

`*.config` file; however, it also controls a number of web-specific settings. For this example, notice that MEX is enabled, and you do not have to specify a custom `<endpoint>` manually:

```
<configuration>

  <system.web>
    <compilation debug="false" targetFramework="4.0" />
  </system.web>

  <system.serviceModel>
    <behaviors>
      <serviceBehaviors>
        <behavior>
          <!-- To avoid disclosing metadata information,
               set the value below to false and remove the
               metadata endpoint above before deployment -->
          <serviceMetadata httpGetEnabled="true"/>
          <!-- To receive exception details in faults for debugging purposes,
               set the value below to true.
               Set to false before deployment to avoid
               disclosing exception information -->
          <serviceDebug includeExceptionDetailInFaults="false"/>
        </behavior>
      </serviceBehaviors>
    </behaviors>
  </system.serviceModel>

  <system.webServer>
    <modules runAllManagedModulesForAllRequests="true"/>
  </system.webServer>

</configuration>
```

Testing the Service

Now you are free to build any sort of client to test your service, including passing in the endpoint of the `*.svc` file to the `WcfTestClient.exe` application:

```
WcfTestClient http://localhost/AutoLotWCFService/Service.svc
```

If you wish to build a custom client application, you can use the Add Service Reference dialog box, as you did for the `MagicEightBallServiceClient` and `MathClient` project examples earlier in this chapter.

■ **Source Code** You can find the AutoLotService project located under the Chapter 25 subdirectory.

That wraps up your look at the Windows Communication Foundation API. Of course, there is much more to WCF than could be covered in this introductory chapter; however if you understand the materials presented here, you are in great shape to seek out more details as you see fit. Be sure to consult the .NET Framework 4.0 SDK documentation if you want to learn more about WCF.

Summary

This chapter introduced you to the Windows Communication Foundation (WCF) API, which has been part of the base class libraries since .NET 3.0. As explained in this chapter, the major motivation behind WCF was to provide a unified object model that exposes a number of (previously unrelated) distributed computing APIs under a single umbrella. Furthermore, a WCF service is represented by specified addresses, bindings, and contracts (which you can remember easily by the friendly abbreviation, *ABC*).

You also learned that a typical WCF application involves the use of three interrelated assemblies. The first assembly defines the service contracts and service types that represent the service's functionality. This assembly is then hosted by a custom executable, an IIS virtual directory, or a Windows service. Finally, the client assembly uses a generated code file that defines a proxy type (and settings within the application configuration file) to communicate with the remote type.

The chapter also examined how to use a number of WCF programming tools, such as SvcConfigEditor.exe (which allows you to modify *.config files), the WcfTestClient.exe application (to test a WCF service quickly), and various Visual Studio 2010 WCF project templates. You also learned about a number of WCF 4.0 simplifications, including default endpoints and behaviors.

CHAPTER 26

■■■

Introducing Windows Workflow Foundation 4.0

A few years back, Microsoft shipped an API named Windows Workflow Foundation (WF) with the release of NET 3.0. This API allowed you to model, configure, monitor, and execute the *workflows* (which are used to model a business process) used internally by a given .NET program. The out-of-the-box functionality provided by the first release of WF was very a welcomed step in the right direction, as we were no longer required to manually develop complex infrastructure to support workflow-enabled applications.

As intriguing a technology as the first release of WF was, it was not without its warts. A number of developers felt the designer experience provided by Visual Studio 2008 was lackluster and that it was too cumbersome to navigate complex workflow during development. As well, the initial release of WF required a good deal of boilerplate code to get a workflow up and running, and even the act of building the workflow itself was a bit clunky, given the fact that your VB 2010 code base and the related workflow designer representation did not mesh together as seamlessly as hoped.

.NET 4.0 gives us a complete reboot of the entire WF API. Going forward, workflows are modeled (by default) using a declarative XML-based grammar named XAML where data used by the workflow is treated as a first class citizen. As well, the Visual Studio 2010 WF designers have been completely overhauled and rewritten using Windows Presentation Foundation (WPF) technologies. So, if you used the previous version of the WF API and were a tad dissatisfied, I encourage you to read on with a fresh set of eyes.

If you are new to the topic of WF, this chapter begins by defining the role of business processes and describes how they relate to the WF API. As well, you will be exposed to the concept of a WF activity, the two major flavors of workflows under 4.0 (flowchart and sequential), and various project templates and programming tools. Once we've covered the basics, we'll build several example programs that illustrate how to leverage the WF programming model to establish business processes that execute under the watchful eye of the WF runtime engine.

■ **Note** The entirety of WF 4.0 cannot be covered in a single introductory chapter. If you require a deeper treatment of the topic than presented here, check out *Pro WF: Windows Workflow in .NET 4.0* by Bruce Bukovics (Apress, 2010).

Defining a Business Process

Any real-world application must be able to model various *business processes*. Simply put, a business process is a conceptual grouping of tasks that logically work as a collective whole. For example, assume you are building an application that allows a user to purchase an automobile online. Once the user submits the order, a large number of activities are set in motion. You might begin by performing a credit check. If the user passes the credit verification, you might start a database transaction in order to remove the entry from an Inventory table, add a new entry to an Orders table, and update the customer account information. After the database transaction has completed, you still might need to send a confirmation e-mail to the buyer, and then invoke a remote service to place the order at the car dealership. Collectively, all of these tasks could represent a single business process.

Historically speaking, modeling a business process was yet another detail that programmers had to account for, often by authoring custom code to ensure that a business process was not only modeled correctly but also executed correctly within the application itself. For example, you may need to author code to account for points of failure, tracing, and logging support (to see what a given business process is up to); persistence support (to save the state of long-running processes); and whatnot. As you may know firsthand, building this sort of infrastructure from scratch entails a great deal of time and manual labor.

Assuming that a development team did, in fact, build a custom business process framework for their applications, their work was not yet complete. Simply put, a raw VB 2010 code base cannot be easily explained to nonprogrammers on the team who *also* need to understand the business process. The truth of the matter is that subject matter experts (SMEs), managers, salespeople, and members of a graphical design team often do not speak the language of code. Given this, as programmers, we were required to make use of other modeling tools (such as Microsoft Visio, the office whiteboard, etc) to graphically represent our processes using skill set–neutral terms. The obvious problem here is we now have two entities to keep in sync: If we change the code, we need to update the diagrams. If we change the diagrams, we need to update the code.

Furthermore, when building a sophisticated software application using the *100% code approach*, the code base has very little trace of the internal "flow" of the application. For example, a typical .NET program might be composed of hundreds of custom types (not to mention the numerous types used within the base class libraries). While programmers may have a feel for which objects are making calls on other objects, the code itself is a far cry from a living document that explains the overall sequence of activity. While the development team may build external documentation and workflow charts, again there is the problem of multiple representations of the same process.

The Role of WF 4.0

In essence, the Windows Workflow Foundation 4.0 API allows programmers to declaratively design business processes using a prefabricated set of *activities*. Thus, rather than only using a set custom of assemblies to represent a given business activity and the necessary infrastructure, we can make use of the WF designers of Visual Studio 2010 to create our business process at design time. In this respect, WF allows us to build the skeleton of a business process, which can be fleshed out through code where required.

When programming with the WF API, a single entity can then be used to represent the overall business process as well as the code that defines it. In addition to being a friendly visual representation of the process, since a single WF document is used to represent the code driving the process, we no longer need to worry about multiple documents falling out of sync. Better yet, this WF document will clearly illustrate the process itself. With a little bit of guidance, even the most non-technical of staff members should be able to get a grip on what your WF designer is modeling.

Building a (Painfully) Simple Workflow

As you build a workflow-enabled application, you will undoubtedly notice that it "feels different" from building a typical .NET application. For example, up until this point in the text, every code example began by creating a new project workspace (most often a Console Application project) and involved authoring code to represent the program at large. A WF application also consists of custom code; however, in addition, you are building *directly into the assembly* a model of the business process itself.

Another aspect of WF which is quite different from other sorts of .NET applications is that a vast majority of your workflows will be modeled in a declarative manner, using an XML-based grammar named XAML. Much of the time, you will not need to directly author this markup, as the Visual Studio 2010 IDE will do so automatically as you work with the WF designer tools. This is a big change in direction from the previous version of the WF API, which favored using VB 2010 code as the standard way to model a workflow.

■ **Note** Be aware that the XAML dialect used within WF is not identical to the XAML dialect used for WPF. You will learn about the syntax and semantics of WPF XAML in Chapter 27, as unlike WF XAML, it is quite common to directly edit designer-generated WPF XAML.

To get you into the workflow mindset, open Visual Studio 2010. From the New Project dialog box, pick a new Workflow Console Application project named FirstWorkflowExampleApp (see Figure 26-1).

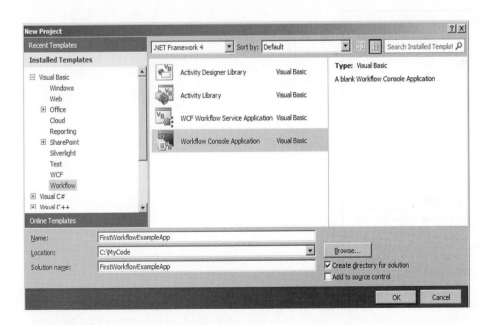

Figure 26-1. Creating a new console based workflow application

Now, consider Figure 26-2, which illustrates the initial workflow diagram generated by Visual Studio 2010. As you can see, there is not too much happening at this point, just a message telling you to drop activities on the designer.

Figure 26-2. A workflow designer is a container for activities that model your business process

For this first simple test workflow, open the Visual Studio 2010 Toolbox, and locate the `WriteLine` activity under the Primitives section (Figure 26-3).

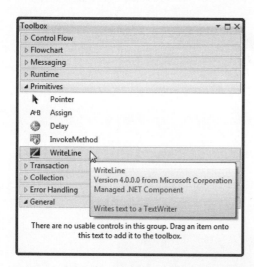

Figure 26-3. The Toolbox will show you all the default activities of WF 4.0

Once you have located this activity, drag it onto of the designer's drop target (be sure you drag it directly onto the area which says *Drop activity here*), and enter a friendly double quoted string message into the **Text** edit box Figure 26-4 shows one possible workflow.

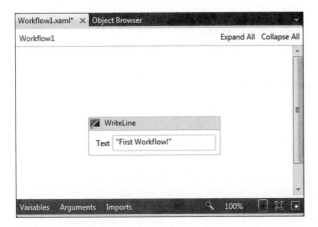

Figure 26-4. The WriteLine activity will display text to a TextWriter, the console in this case

Viewing the Underlying XAML

Now, if you close the workflow designer, you can right click on `Workflow1.xaml` using the Solution Explorer and pick the "View code" menu option. This will display the underlying XAML representation of your workflow. As you can see, the root node of this XML-based document is `<Activity>`. In the opening declaration of the root element, you will find a large number of XML namespace definitions, almost all of which have the token `clr-namespace` embedded within.

As explained in more detail in Chapter 27, when a XAML file needs to reference the definitions of .NET types contained in external assemblies (or a different namespace in the current assembly), you are required to build a .NET to XAML mapping using the `clr-namespace` token:

```
<Activity mc:Ignorable="sap"
         x:Class="Workflow1"
         sap:VirtualizedContainerService.HintSize="251,240"
         mva:VisualBasic.Settings="Assembly references and imported namespaces for internal
implementation"
         xmlns="http://schemas.microsoft.com/netfx/2009/xaml/activities"
         xmlns:mc="http://schemas.openxmlformats.org/markup-compatibility/2006"
         xmlns:mv="clr-namespace:Microsoft.VisualBasic;assembly=System"
         xmlns:mva="clr-
namespace:Microsoft.VisualBasic.Activities;assembly=System.Activities"
         xmlns:s="clr-namespace:System;assembly=mscorlib"
         xmlns:s1="clr-namespace:System;assembly=System"
         xmlns:s2="clr-namespace:System;assembly=System.Xml"
         xmlns:s3="clr-namespace:System;assembly=System.Core"
         xmlns:sad="clr-namespace:System.Activities.Debugger;assembly=System.Activities"
         xmlns:sap="http://schemas.microsoft.com/netfx/2009/xaml/activities/presentation"
         xmlns:scg="clr-namespace:System.Collections.Generic;assembly=System"
         xmlns:scg1="clr-namespace:System.Collections.Generic;assembly=System.ServiceModel"
         xmlns:scg2="clr-namespace:System.Collections.Generic;assembly=System.Core"
         xmlns:scg3="clr-namespace:System.Collections.Generic;assembly=mscorlib"
```

```
                xmlns:sd="clr-namespace:System.Data;assembly=System.Data"
                xmlns:sl="clr-namespace:System.Linq;assembly=System.Core"
                xmlns:st="clr-namespace:System.Text;assembly=mscorlib"
                xmlns:x="http://schemas.microsoft.com/winfx/2006/xaml">
  <WriteLine sad:XamlDebuggerXmlReader.FileName="D:\OSL\Apress\VB 2010\Code\Ch
26\FirstWorkflowExampleApp\FirstWorkflowExampleApp\Workflow1.xaml"
            sap:VirtualizedContainerService.HintSize="211,200" Text="First Workflow!" />
</Activity>
```

The `<Activity>` element is the container of all other tasks which represent your workflow. Here, we have only one other sub-activity, `<WriteLine>`. Notice that the `Text` attribute has been set based on the data you entered in the workflow designer.

Now remember that when you are building workflows using Visual Studio 2010, you will typically not be required to manually modify this markup. Using this designer (and the various WF-centric tools integrated into Visual Studio 2010), you are able to model your process while the markup is generated by the IDE. Because of this fact, this chapter will not dive into the details of WF XAML to any great degree. However, feel free to view the markup generated by the IDE as you drag and drop activities onto the designer (this will get you in the proper mindset for your examination of WPF).

In any case, the markup found in a XAML file always maps to "real" types in a .NET assembly. For example, each element in a XAML file (such as `<Activity>`) is a declarative way to define a .NET object (such as `System.Activities.Activity`). Attributes which appear in the opening element definition map to properties or events on the related class type. At runtime, your markup will be fed into a runtime object model, where each element description will be used to set the state of the related .NET object.

Allowing us to define the structure of a workflow in a declarative manner using XAML has a number of benefits, most notably tool support. For example, it is possible to host the same Visual Studio 2010 designer tools in a custom GUI application. By doing so, you can build a simple tool which can be used by the non-programmers on your team to create the business processes they wish to have you implement in your products. Their design can be saved as a `*.xaml` file and imported into your .NET projects.

Another compelling benefit of using markup to define a workflow is that it now becomes possible to (easily) load in external XAML files into memory on the fly and thereby change how your business process operates. For example, you could author code that reads a `*.xaml` file on the fly and hydrates the related object model. Since your workflow logic is not hard-coded into your assembly, changing the functionality of the business process could be as simple as changing the markup and restarting your application.

Do understand that WF is far more than a pretty designer that allows you to model the activities of a business process. As you are building your WF diagram, your markup can always be extended using code to represent the runtime behavior of your process. In fact, if you wanted to do so, you could avoid the use of XAML all together and author the workflow using nothing but VB 2010. If you were to this, however, you would be back to the same basic issue of having a body of code that is not readily understandable to non-technical staff.

If you were to run your application at this point, you would see your message display to the console window:

```
First Workflow!

Press any key to continue . . .
```

Fair enough; however, what started this workflow? And how were you able to ensure that the console application stayed running long enough for the workflow to complete? The answers to these questions require an understanding of the workflow runtime engine.

The WF 4.0 Runtime

The next thing to understand is that the WF API also consists of a runtime engine to load, execute, unload, and in other ways manipulate a workflow which you have defined. The WF runtime engine can be hosted within any .NET application domain; however, be aware that a single application domain can only have one running instance of the WF engine.

Recall from Chapter 16 that an AppDomain is a partition within a Windows process that plays host to a .NET application and any external code libraries. As such, the WF engine can be embedded within a simple console program, a GUI desktop application (Windows Forms or WPF), or exposed from a Windows Communication Foundation (WCF) service.

■ **Note** The WCF Workflow Service Application project template is a great starting point if you wish to build a WCF service (see Chapter 25) that makes use of workflows internally.

If you are modeling a business process that needs to be used by a wide variety of systems, you also have the option of authoring your WF within a VB 2010 Class Library project of a Workflow Activity Library project. In this way, new applications can simply reference your *.dll to reuse a predefined collection of business processes. This is obviously helpful in that you would not want to have to re-create the same workflows multiple times.

Hosting a Workflow using WorkflowInvoker

The host process of the WF runtime can interact with said runtime using a few different techniques. The simplest way to do so is to use the WorkflowInvoker class of the System.Activities namespace. This class allows you to start a workflow using a single line of code. If you were to open up the Module1.vb file of your current Workflow Console Application project, you will see the following Main() method:

```
Sub Main()
        WorkflowInvoker.Invoke(New Workflow1())
End Sub
```

Using the WorkflowInvoker is very useful when you simply want a workflow to kick off and don't care to monitor it any further. The Invoke() method will execute the workflow is a *synchronous blocking manner*. The calling thread is blocked until the entire workflow has finished or has been terminated abruptly. Because the Invoke() method is a synchronous call, you are guaranteed that the entire workflow will indeed complete before Main() is terminated. In fact, if you were to add any code after the call to WorkflowInvoker.Invoke(), it will only execute when the workflow is completed (or in a worse case situation, terminated abruptly):

```
Sub Main()
        WorkflowInvoker.Invoke(New Workflow1())
        Console.WriteLine("Thanks for playing")
End Sub
```

Passing Arguments to your Workflow using WorkflowInvoker

When a host process kicks off a workflow, it is very common for the host to send custom startup arguments. For example, assume that you wish to let the user of your program specify which message to display in the `WriteLine` activity in place of the currently hard-coded text message. In normal VB 2010 code, you might create a custom constructor on a class to receive such arguments. However, a workflow is always created using the default constructor! Moreover, most workflows are defined only using XAML, not procedural code.

As it turns out, the `Invoke()` method has been overloaded multiple times, one version of which allows you to pass in arguments to the workflow when it starts. These arguments are represented using a `Dictionary(Of String, Object)` variable that contains a set of name/value pairs that will be used to set identically named (and typed) argument variables in the workflow itself.

Defining Arguments Using the Workflow Designer

To define the arguments that will capture the incoming dictionary data, you will make use of the workflow designer. In Solution Explorer, right-click `Workflow1.xaml` and select `View Designer`. Notice on the bottom of the designer there is a button named Arguments. Click this button now, and from the resulting UI, add an input argument of type `String` named `MessageToShow` (no need to assign a default value for this new argument). As well, delete your initial message from the `WriteLine` activity. Figure 26-5 shows the end result.

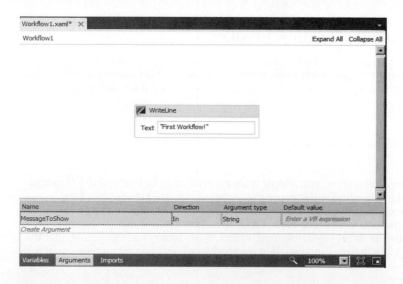

Figure 26-5. *Workflow arguments can be used to receive host supplied arguments*

Now, in the Text property of the WriteLine activity, you can simply enter MessageToShow as the evaluation expression. As you are typing in this token, you'll notice IntelliSense will kick in (Figure 26-6).

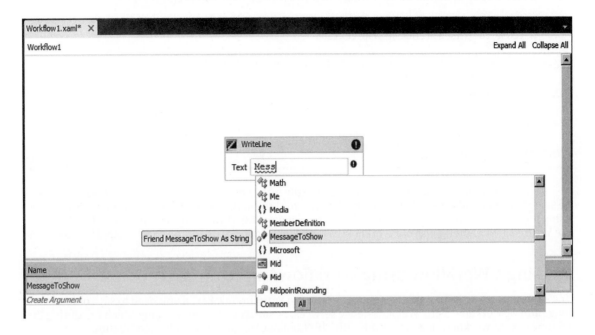

Figure 26-6. Using a custom argument as input to an activity

Now that you have the correct infrastructure in place, consider the following update to the Main() method of the Module1 Module.

```vb
Sub Main()
    Console.WriteLine("***** Welcome to this amazing WF application *****")

    ' Get data from user, to pass to workflow.
    Console.Write("Please enter the data to pass the workflow: ")
    Dim wfData As String = Console.ReadLine()

    ' Package up the data as a dictionary.
    Dim wfArgs As New Dictionary(Of String, Object)()
    wfArgs.Add("MessageToShow", wfData)

    ' Pass to the workflow.
    WorkflowInvoker.Invoke(New Workflow1(), wfArgs)

    Console.WriteLine("Thanks for playing")
End Sub
```

Again, it is important to point out that the string values for each member of your `Dictionary()` variable will need to be identically named to the related argument variable in your workflow. In any case, you will find output similar to the following when you run the modified program:

```
***** Welcome to this amazing WF application *****

Please enter the data to pass the workflow: Hello Mr. Workflow!

Hello Mr. Workflow!

Thanks for playing

Press any key to continue . . .
```

Beyond the `Invoke()` method, the only other really interesting members of `WorkflowInvoker` would be `BeginInvoke()` and `EndInvoke()`, which allow you to start up the workflow on a secondary thread using the .NET asynchronous delegate pattern (see Chapter 19). If you require more control over how the WF runtime manipulates your workflow, you can instead make use of the `WorkflowApplication` class.

Hosting a Workflow using WorkflowApplication

You'll want to use `WorkflowApplication` (as opposed to `WorkflowInvoker`) if you need to save or load a long running workflow using WF persistence services, be notified of various events which fire during the lifetime of your workflow instance, work with WF "bookmarks," and other advanced features.

If you have a background in the previous version of the WF API, use of `WorkflowApplication` will look familiar to using the .NET 3.5 WF `WorkflowRuntime` class, in that you will need to call the `Run()` method to start the workflow instance.

When you do call `Run()`, a new background thread will be plucked from the CLR thread pool. Therefore, if you do not add additional support to ensure the main thread waits for the secondary thread to complete, the workflow instance may not have a chance to finish its work!

One way to make sure the calling thread waits long enough for the background thread to finish its work is to use an `AutoResetEvent` object of the `System.Threading` namespace. (In fact, this is what the .NET 3.5 workflow starter code made use of.) Here is an update to the current example, which now uses `WorkflowApplication` rather than `WorkflowInvoker`:

```
Sub Main()
    Console.WriteLine("***** Welcome to this amazing WF application *****")

    ' Get data from user, to pass to workflow.
    Console.Write("Please enter the data to pass the workflow: ")
    Dim wfData As String = Console.ReadLine()

    ' Package up the data as a dictionary.
    Dim wfArgs As New Dictionary(Of String, Object)()
    wfArgs.Add("MessageToShow", wfData)
```

```
' Used to inform primary thread to wait!
Dim waitHandle As New AutoResetEvent(False)

' Pass to the workflow.
Dim app As New WorkflowApplication(New Workflow1(), wfArgs)

' Hook up an event with this app.
' When I'm done, notifiy other thread I'm done,
' and print a message.
app.Completed =
    Sub(completedArgs)
      waitHandle.Set()
      Console.WriteLine("The workflow is done!")
    End Sub

' Start the workflow!
app.Run()

' Wait until I am notified the workflow is done.
waitHandle.WaitOne()

Console.WriteLine("Thanks for playing")
End Sub
```

The output will be similar to the previous iteration of the project:

```
***** Welcome to this amazing WF application *****

Please enter the data to pass the workflow: Hey again!

Hey again!

The workflow is done!

Thanks for playing

Press any key to continue . . .
```

The benefit of using WorkflowApplication is you can hook into events (as you have done indirectly using the Completed property here) and can also tap into more sophisticated services (persistence, bookmarks, etc).

For this introductory look at WF 4.0, we will not dive into the details of these runtime services. Be sure to check out the .NET Framework 4.0 SDK documentation for details regarding the runtime behaviors and services of the Windows Workflow Foundation 4.0 runtime environment.

> ■ **Note** In addition to WorkflowInvoker and WorkflowApplication, you can also start and monitor a workflow instance using WorkflowServiceHost. This class supports features like messaging activities, multi-instancing, and configuration. If your workflow-enabled WCF service is under IIS, WorkflowServiceHost is used automatically.

Recap of your First Workflow

That wraps up your first look at WF 4.0. While this example was very trivial, you did learn a few interesting (and useful) tasks. First, you learned that you can pass in a `Dictionary` object which contains name/value pairs that will be passed to identically named arguments in your workflow. This is really useful when you need to gather user input (such as a customer ID number, SSN, name of a Doctor, etc) which will be used by the workflow to process its activities.

You also learned that a .NET 4.0 workflow is defined in a declarative manner (by default) using an XML-based grammar named XAML. Using XAML, you can specify which activities your workflow contains. At runtime, this data will be used to create the correct in-memory object model. Last but not least, you looked at two different approaches to kick off a workflow using the `WorkflowInvoker` and `WorkflowApplicaion` classes.

> ■ **Source Code** The FirstWorkflowExampleApp project is included under the Chapter 26 subdirectory.

Examining the Workflow 4.0 Activities

Recall that the purpose of WF is to allow you to model a business process in a declarative manner, which is then executed by the WF runtime engine. In the vernacular of WF, a business process is composed of any number of *activities*. Simply put, a WF activity is an atomic "step" in the overall process. When you create a new workflow application, you will find the Toolbox contains iconic representations of the built-in activities grouped by category.

These out-of-the-box activities are used to model your business process. Each activity in the Toolbox maps to a real class within the `System.Activities.dll` assembly (most often contained within the `System.Activities.Statements` namespace). You'll make use of several of these baked-in activities over the course of this chapter; however, here is a walkthrough of many of these default activities. As always, consult the .NET Framework 4.0 SDK documentation for full details.

Control Flow Activities

The first category of activities in the toolbox allow you to represent looping and decision tasks in a larger workflow. Their usefulness should be easy to understand, given that we do similar tasks in VB 2010 code quite often. In Table 26-1, notice that some of these control flow activities allow for parallel processing of activities using the Task Parallel Library behind the scenes (see Chapter 19).

Table 26-1. The Control Flow Activities of WF 4.0

Activities	Meaning in Life
DoWhile	A looping activity that executes contained activities at least once, until a condition is no longer true.
ForEach<T>	Executes an activity action once for each value provided in the ForEach<T>.Values collection.
If	Models an If-Then-Else condition.
Parallel	An activity that executes all child activities simultaneously and asynchronously.
ParallelForEach<T>	Enumerates the elements of a collection and executes each element of the collection in parallel.
Pick	Provides event-based control flow modeling.
PickBranch	A potential path of execution within a parent Pick activity.
Sequence	Executes a set of child activities sequentially.
Switch<T>	Selects one choice from a number of activities to execute, based on the value of a given expression of the type specified in this object's type parameter.
While	Executes a contained workflow element while a condition evaluates to true.

Flowchart Activities

Next are the flowchart activities, which are actually quite important given that the Flowchart activity will very often be the first item you place on your WF designer. The concept of a *flow chart workflow* is new with .NET 4.0. It allows you to build a workflow using the well known flow chart model, where the execution of the workflow is based on numerous branching paths, each of which is based on the truth or falsity of some internal condition. Table 26-2 documents each member of this activity set.

Table 26-2. The Flowchart Activities of WF 4.0

Activities	Meaning in Life
Flowchart	Models workflows using the familiar flowchart paradigm. This is often the very first activity you will place on a new designer.
FlowDecision	A node that provides the ability to model a conditional node with two possible outcomes.
FlowSwitch<T>	A node that allows modeling a switch construct, with one expression and one outcome for each match.

Messaging Activities

A workflow can easily invoke members of an external XML web service or WCF service, as well as be notified by an external service using *messaging activities*. Because these activities are very closely related to WCF development, they have been packaged up in a dedicated .NET assembly, System. ServiceModel.Activities.dll. Within this library, you will find an identically named namespace defining the core activities seen in Table 26-3.

Table 26-3. The Messaging Activities of WF 4.0

Activities	Meaning in Life
CorrelationScope	Used to manage child message activities.
InitializeCorrelation	Initializes correlation without sending or receiving a message.
Receive	Receives a message from a WCF service.
Send	Sends a message to a WCF service.
SendAndReceiveReply	Sends a message to a WCF service and captures the return value.
TransactedReceiveScope	An activity that enables you to flow a transaction into a workflow or dispatcher-created server side transactions.

The most common messaging activities are **Send** and **Receive**, which allow you to communicate with external XML web services or WCF services.

The Runtime and Primitives Activities

The next two categories in the toolbox, Runtime and Primitives, allow you to build a workflow which makes calls to the workflow runtime (in the case of `Persist` and `TerminateWorkflow`) and performs common operations such as push text to an output stream or invoke a method on a .NET object. Consider Table 26-4.

Table 26-4. The Runtime and Primitive Activities of WF 4.0

Activities	Meaning in Life
Persist	Requests that a workflow instance persist its state into a database using the WF persistence service.
TerminateWorkflow	Terminates the running workflow instance, raises the `WorkflowApplication.Completed` event in the host, and reports error information. Once the workflow is terminated, it cannot be resumed.
Assign	Allows you to set properties on an activity using the assignment values you defined via the workflow designer.
Delay	Forces a workflow to stop for a fixed amount of time.
InvokeMethod	Calls a method of a specified object or type.
WriteLine	Writes a specified string to a specified `TextWriter` derived type. By default, this will be the standard output stream (a.k.a. the console); however, you can configure other streams , such as a `FileStream`.

InvokeMethod is maybe the most interesting and useful activity of this set because it allows you to call methods of .NET classes in a declarative manner. You can also configure `InvokeMethod` to hold onto any return value send from the method you call. `TerminateWorkflow` can also be helpful when you need to account for a *point of no return*. If the workflow instance hits this activity, it will raise the `Competed` event which can be caught in the host, just like you did in the first example.

The Transaction Activities

When you are building a workflow, you might need to ensure that a group of activities work in an atomic manner, meaning they must *all* succeed or *all* fail as a collective group. Even if the activities in question are not directly working with a relational database, the core activities seen in Table 26-5 allow you to add a transactional scope into a workflow.

Table 26-5. The Transaction Activities of WF 4.0

Activities	Meaning in Life
CancellationScope	Associates cancellation logic within a main path of execution.
CompensableActivity	An activity that supports compensation of its child activities.
TransactionScope	An activity that demarcates a transaction boundary.

The Collection and Error Handling Activities

The final two categories to consider in this introductory chapter allow you to declaratively manipulate generic collections and respond to runtime exceptions. The collection activities are great when you need to manipulate objects which represent business data (such as purchase orders, medical information objects, or order tracking) on the fly in XAML. Error activities, on the other hand, allow you to essentially author try/catch/throw logic within a workflow. Table 26-6 documents this final set of WF 4.0 activities.

Table 26-6. The Collection and Error Handling Activities of WF 4.0

Activities	Meaning in Life
AddToCollection<T>	Adds an item to a specified collection.
ClearCollection<T>	Clears a specified collection of all items.
ExistsInCollection<T>	Indicates whether a given item is present in a given collection.
RemoveFromCollection<T>	Removes an item from a specified collection.
Rethrow	Throws a previously thrown exception from within a Catch activity.
Throw	Throws an exception.
TryCatch	Contains workflow elements to be executed by the workflow runtime within an exception handling block.

OK! Now that we have seen many of the default activities at a high level, we can start to build some more interesting workflows that make use of them. Along the way, you will learn about the two key activities that typically function as the root of your workflow, Flowchart and Sequence.

Building a Flowchart Workflow

In the first example, I had you drag a WriteLine activity directly on the workflow designer. While it is true that any activity seen in the Visual Studio 2010 Toolbox can be the first item placed on the designer, only a few of them are able to contain sub-activities (which is obviously very important!). When you are building a new workflow, the chances are very good that the first item you will place on your designer will be a `Flowchart` or `Sequence` activity.

Both of these built in activities have the ability to contain any number of internal child activities (including additional `Flowchart` or `Sequence` activities) to represent the entirety of your business process. To begin, let's create a brand new Workflow Console Application named EnumerateMachineDataWF. Once you have done so, rename your initial *.xaml file to `MachineInfoWF.xaml`.

Now, under the Flowchart section of your Toolbox, drag a `Flowchart` activity onto the designer. Next, using the Properties window, change the `DisplayName` property to something a tad more catchy, such as *Show Machine Data Flowchart* (as I am sure you can guess, the `DisplayName` property controls how the item is named on the designer). At this point, your workflow designer should look something like Figure 26-7.

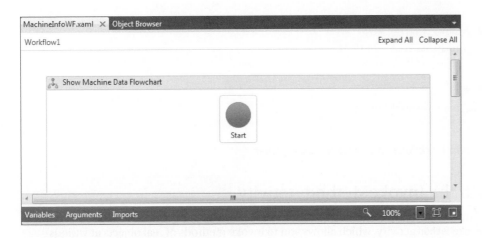

Figure 26-7. The initial Flowchart activity

Be aware that there is a grab-handle on the lower right of the `Flowchart` activity, which can be used to increase or decrease the size of the flowchart designer space. You'll need to increase the size as you add more and more activities.

Connecting Activities in a Flowchart

The large Start icon represents the entry point to the Flowchart activity, which in this example is the first activity in our entire workflow and will be triggered when you execute the workflow using the `WorkflowInvoker` or `WorkflowApplication` classes. This icon can be positioned anywhere on your designer, and I'd suggest you move it to the upper left, just to make some more space.

Your goal is to assembly your flowchart by connecting any number of additional activities together, typically making use of the `FlowDecision` activity during the process. To start, drag a `WriteLine` activity on the designer, changing the `DisplayName` to *Greet User*. Now, if you hover your mouse over the Start icon, you will see one docking tab on each side. Click and hold the docking tab closest to the `WriteLine` activity, and drag it to the docking tab of the `WriteLine` activity. Once you have done so, you should see a connection between these first two items, signifying that the first activity which will be executed in your workflow will be Greet User.

Now, similar to the first example, add a workflow argument (via the Arguments button) named UserName of type string with no default value. This will be passed in dynamically via the custom Dictionary() object in just a bit. Finally, set the Text property of the WriteLine activity to the following code statement:

```
"Hello" & UserName
```

Note that whenever you enter code into a workflow activity, you always use VB 2010 syntax (not C#). This is true even in a C# project! This is because the WF 4.0 API is making use of a helper assembly that has been coded to process VB 2010 statements rather than C# statements (strange but true).

Add a second WriteLine activity to your designer, which is connected to the previous. This time, define a hard coded string value of "Do you want me to list all machine drives?" for the Text property, and change the DisplayName property to *Ask User*. Figure 26-8 shows the connections between current workflow activities.

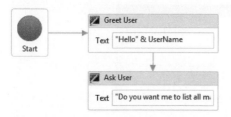

Figure 26-8. Flowchart workflows connect activities together

Working with the InvokeMethod Activity

Because the majority of a workflow is defined in a declarative manner using XAML, you are sure to make good use of the InvokeMethod activity, which allows you to invoke methods of real objects at various points in your workflow. Drag one of these items to your designer, change the DisplayName property to *Get Y or N*, and make a connection between it and the *Ask User* WriteLine activity.

The first property to configure for an InvokeMethod activity is the TargetType property, which represents the name of the class that defines a Shared member you wish to invoke. Using the dropdown list box for the TargetType of the InvokeMethod activity, pick the Browse for Types... option (Figure 26-9).

Figure 26-9. Specifying a target for InvokeMethod

From the resulting dialog box, pick the System.Console class of mscorlib.dll (if you enter the name of the type within the Type Name edit area, the dialog will automatically find the type). Once you have found the System.Console class, click the OK button.

Now, using the InvokeMethod activity on the designer, enter *ReadLine* as the value for the MethodName property. This will configure your InvokeMethod activity to invoke the Console.ReadLine() method when this step of the workflow is reached.

As you know, Console.ReadLine() will return a String value that contains the keystrokes entered on the keyboard before the Enter key is pressed; however, you need to have a way to capture the return value! You will do this next.

Defining Workflow Wide Variables

Defining a workflow variable in XAML is almost identical to defining an argument, in that you can do so directly on the designer (this time with the Variables button). The difference is that *arguments* are used to capture data passed in by the host, whereas *variables* are simply points of data in the workflow which will be used to influence its runtime behavior.

Using the Variables aspect of the designer, add a new String variable named YesOrNo. Notice that if you have multiple parent containers in your workflow (for example, a Flowchart containing another Sequence), you can pick the scope of the variable. Here, your only choice is the root Flowchart. Next, select the InvokeMethod activity on the designer, and using the Properties window of Visual Studio 2010, set the Result property to your new variable (Figure 26-10).

Figure 26-10. The fully configured InvokeMethod

Now that you can grab a piece of data from an external method call, you can use it to make a runtime decision in your flow chart using the FlowDecision activity.

Working with the FlowDecision Activity

A FlowDecision activity is used to take two possible courses of action, based on the truth or falsity of a Boolean variable, or a statement which resolves to a Boolean value. Drag one of these activities onto your designer, and connect it to the InvokeMethod activity (Figure 26-11).

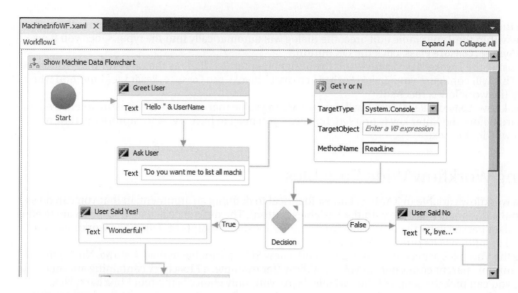

Figure 26-11. A FlowDecision can branch two directions

■ **Note** If you need to respond to multiple branching conditions within a flowchart, make use of the FlowSwitch<T> activity. This allows you to define any number of paths, which will be entered based on the value of a defined workflow variable.

Set the `Condition` property (using the Properties window) of your `FlowDecision` activity to the following code statement, which you can type directly into the editor:

```
YesOrNo.ToUpper() = "Y"
```

Here you are testing an upper case version of your `YesOrNo` variable against the value "Y". You are entering VB 2010 code here with the VB 2010 equality operator (=).

Working with the TerminateWorkflow Activity

You now need to build the activities which will occur on each side of the `FlowDecision` activity. On the "False" side, connect a final `WriteLine` activity which prints out a hard coded message of your choosing, followed by a `TerminateWorkflow` activity (Figure 26-12).

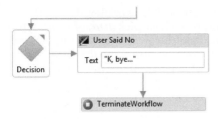

Figure 26-12. The "false" branch

Strictly speaking, you don't need to use the `TerminateWorkflow` activity, as this workflow would simply end once you reach the end of the false branch. However, by using this activity type, you can throw back an exception to the workflow host, informing them exactly why you are stopping. This exception can be configured in the Properties window.

Assuming you have selected the `TerminateWorkflow` activity on the designer, use the Properties window, and click on the ellipse button for the `Exception` property. This will open up an editor which allows you to throw back an exception, just like if you were doing so in code (VB 2010 code that is; see Figure 26-13).

Figure 26-13. Configuring an exception to throw when the TerminateWorkflow activity is encountered

Complete the configuration of this activity by setting the `Reason` property to "YesOrNo was False".

Building the "True" Condition

To begin building the "True" condition of the `FlowDecision`, connect a `WriteLine` activity, which simply displays a hard coded string confirming the user has agreed to proceed. From here, connect to a new `InvokeMethod` activity, which will call the `GetLogicalDrives()` method of the `System.Environment` class. To do so, set the `TargetType` property to `System.Environment` and the `MethodName` property to `GetLogicalDrives`.

Next, add a new workflow level variable (using the Variables button of the workflow designer) named **DriveNames** of a **String** array. To specify you want an array of **strings**, pick *Array of [T]* from the Variable Type drop down list, and pick **String** from the resulting dialog box. Visual Studio displays the variable type as **String[]**; this is reminiscent of the C# syntax for arrays (C# uses [ ] to denote an array, rather than (), as we have in Visual Basic). Figure 26-14 shows the first part of the "True" condition.

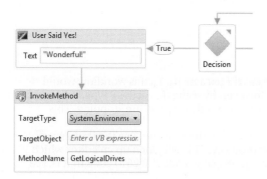

Figure 26-14. *The "True" branch of the FlowDecision activity*

Now, set the **Result** property of this new **InvokeMethod** activity to your **DriveNames** variable.

Working with the ForEach<T> Activity

The next part of your workflow will be to print out the names of each drive to the console window, which is to say you need to loop over the data exposed by the **DriveNames** variable, which has been configured as an array of **String** objects. The **ForEach<T>** activity is the WF XAML equivalent of the VB 2010 **For Each** construct, and it is configured in a very similar manner (at least conceptually).

Drag one of these activities on your designer and connect it to the previous **InvokeMethod** activity. You will configure the **ForEach<T>** activity in just a minute, but to complete the True condition branch, place one final **WriteLine** activity on your designer to close things off. Here is the final top-level look at your workflow (Figure 26-15).

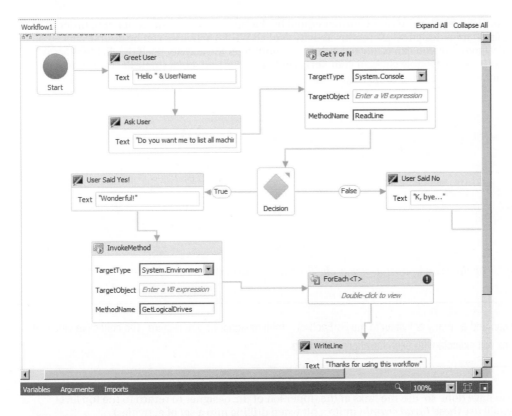

Figure 26-15. The completed top-level workflow

To get rid of the current designer error, you need to finish the configuration of the ForEach<T> activity. First, use the Properties window to specify the type parameter to the generic, which in this example will be a String type. The Values property is where the data is coming from, which will be your DriveNames variable (Figure 26-16).

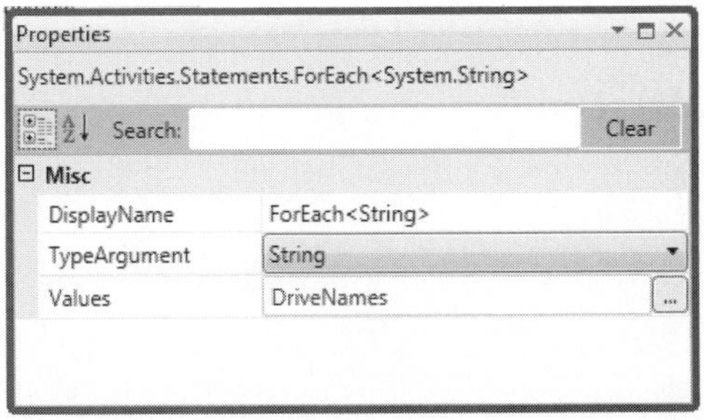

Properties	▼ □ ×
System.Activities.Statements.ForEach<System.String>	

Search:		Clear
⊟ Misc		
DisplayName	ForEach<String>	
TypeArgument	String	▼
Values	DriveNames	...

Figure 26-16. Setting the type of for-each enumeration

This particular activity needs to be further edited by double clicking on the designer in order to open a brand new mini designer just for this activity. Not all WF 4.0 activities can be double clicked on to yield a new designer, but you can easily tell if this is an option on the activity itself (it will literally say "Double-click to view"). Double click on your ForEach<T> activity, and add a single WriteLine activity, which will print out each String value (Figure 26-17).

Figure 26-17. The final configuration step of the ForEach<T> activity

---

■ **Note** You can add as many activities to the ForEach<T> mini designer as you require. The collective whole of these activities will execute with each iteration of the loop.

Once you have done so, use the links at the upper left of the designer to return to the top level workflow (you'll use these *bread crumbs* quite a bit when drilling into a set of activities).

Completing the Application

You are just about done with this example! All you need to do is update the Main() method of the module to catch the exception that will be raised if the user says "NO" and thereby triggers the Exception object. Update your code as the following:

```
Sub Main()
        Try
        Dim wfArgs As New Dictionary(Of String, Object)()
        wfArgs.Add("UserName", "Andrew")
        WorkflowInvoker.Invoke(New Workflow1(), wfArgs)
        Catch ex As Exception
        Console.WriteLine(ex.Message)
        Console.WriteLine(ex.Data("Reason"))
        End Try
End Sub
```

Notice that the "Reason" for the exception can be obtained using the `Data` property of `System.Exception`. So, if you run the program and enter "Y" when asked to enumerate your drives, you'll see the following type of output:

```
Hello Andrew

Do you want me to list all machine drives?

y

Wonderful!

C:\

D:\

E:\

F:\

G:\

H:\

I:\

Thanks for using this workflow
```

However, if you enter "N" (or any other value other than "Y" or "y"), you will see the following:

```
Hello Andrew

Do you want me to list all machine drives?

n

K, bye...

YesOrNo was False
```

Reflecting on What We Have Done

Now, if you are new to working with a workflow environment, you might be wondering what you have gained by authoring this very simple business process using WF XAML rather than good-old VB 2010 code. After all, you could have avoided Windows Workflow Foundation all together and simply built the following VB 2010 module:

```vbnet
Module Module1
    Sub Main()

            Try
                    ExecuteBusinessProcess()
            Catch ex As Exception
                    Console.WriteLine(ex.Message)
                    Console.WriteLine(ex.Data("Reason"))
            End Try
    End Sub

    Private Sub ExecuteBusinessProcess()
            Dim UserName As String = "Andrew"
            Console.WriteLine("Hello {0}", UserName)
            Console.WriteLine("Do you want me to list all machine drives?")

            Dim YesOrNo As String = Console.ReadLine()
            If YesOrNo.ToUpper() = "Y" Then
               Console.WriteLine("Wonderful!")
               Dim DriveNames() As String = Environment.GetLogicalDrives()

               For Each item As String In DriveNames
                    Console.WriteLine(item)
               Next
               Console.WriteLine("Thanks for using this workflow")
            Else
               Console.WriteLine("K, Bye...")
               Dim ex As New Exception("User Said No!")
               ex.Data("Reason") = "YesOrNo was false"
            End If
    End Sub
End Module
```

The output of the program would be absolutely identical to the previous XAML based workflow. So, why bother tinkering with all these activities in the first place? First of all, remember that not everyone is comfortable reading VB 2010 code. Be honest: If you had to explain this business process to a room full of sales people and non-technical managers, would you rather try to explain this VB 2010 code or show them the flowchart? I know my answer...

More importantly, remember that the WF API has a whole slew of additional runtime services, including persistence of long running workflows to a database, automatic tracking of workflow events, and so on (alas, I don't have time to cover them here). When you think of the amount of work you would need to do in order to replicate this functionality in a new project, the utility of WF is even clearer.

Finally, by allowing us a declarative way to generate workflows using designers and XAML, we can offload the construction of a workflow to higher level subject matter experts and managers, while we incorporate the XAML into our VB 2010 projects.

All of this being said, the WF API is not necessarily the correct tool of choice for all .NET programs. However, for most traditional business applications, the ability to define, host, execute and monitor workflows in this manner is a very good thing indeed. Like any new technology, you will need to determine if this is useful for your current project. Let's see another example of working with the WF API, this time by packaging up a workflow in a dedicated *.dll.

■ **Source Code** The EnumerateMachineInfoWF project is included under the Chapter 26 subdirectory.

Isolating Workflows into Dedicated Libraries

While making a Workflow Console Application is great for experimenting with the WF API, a production-ready workflow will certainly need to be packaged up into a custom .NET *.dll assembly. By doing so, you can reuse your workflows at a binary level across multiple projects.

While you could begin using a VB 2010 Class Library project as a starting point, the easiest way to build a workflow library is to start with the Activity Library project, under the Workflow node of the New Project dialog. The benefits of this project type are that it will set the required WF assembly references automatically and give you a *.xaml file to create your initial workflow.

This workflow will model the process of querying the AutoLot database to see if a given car of the correct make and color is in the Inventory table. If the requested car is in stock, you will build a nicely formatted response to the host via an *output parameter*. If the item in not in stock, you will generate a memo to the head of the sales division requesting that they find a car of the correct color.

Defining the Initial Project

Create a new Activity Library project named CheckInventoryWorkflowLib (Figure 26-18). Once the project is created, rename the initial `Activity1.xaml` file to `CheckInventory.xaml`.

Figure 26-18. Building an Activity Library

Now, before you continue, close down the visual workflow designer, and view the underlying XAML definition by right clicking on your XAML file and selecting the View Code menu option. Make sure that the `x:Class` attribute in the root `<Activity>` element has been updated as so (if not, replace *Activity1* with *CheckInventory*):

```
<Activity x:Class="CheckInventoryWorkflowLib.CheckInventory" ... >
```

■ **Note** It is always a good idea to check the x:Class value of your root activity when making a workflow library, as client programs will use this name to create an instance of the workflow.

This workflow will make use of a `Sequence` activity as the primary activity, rather than `Flowchart`. Drag a new `Sequence` activity onto your designer (you'll find it under the Control Flow area of your Toolbox) and change the `DisplayName` property to *Look Up Product*.

As the name suggests, a `Sequence` activity allows you to easily create sequential tasks, which occur one after the other. This does not necessarily mean the children activities must follow a strict linear path, however. Your sequence could contain flow charts, other sequences, parallel processing of data, `If Then/Else` branches and whatever else might make good sense for the business process you are designing.

Importing Assemblies and Namespaces

Because your workflow will be communicating with the AutoLot database, the next step is to reference your `AutoLot.dll` assembly using the Add Reference dialog box of Visual Studio 2010. This example will make use of the disconnected layer, so I'd suggest you reference the final version of this assembly created in Chapter 22 (if you set a reference to the final version created in Chapter 23, you'll also need to set a reference to `System.Data.Entity.dll`, as this is required by the ADO.NET Entity Framework).

This workflow will also be making use of LINQ to DataSet to query the returned `DataTable` in order to discover if you have the requested item in stock. Therefore, you should also set a reference to `System.Data.DataSetExtensions.dll`.

Once you have referenced these assemblies, click on the Imports button located at the bottom of the workflow designer. Here you will see a listing of all of the .NET namespaces that you can make use of in your workflow designer (think of this area as a declarative version of the VB 2010 `Imports` keyword).

You can add namespaces from any referenced assembly by typing in the text box mounted on the top of the Imports editor. For convenience, import `AutoLotDisconnectedLayer` and `System.Data.DataSetExtensions`. By doing so, you can reference the contained types without needing to use fully qualified names. Figure 26-19 shows some new listings of the Imports area once you are finished.

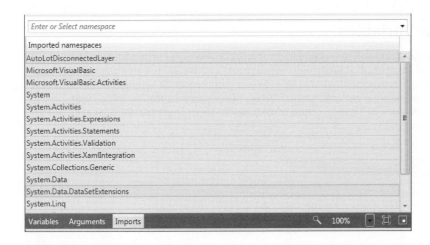

Figure 26-19. Similar to the VB 2010 Imports keyword, the Imports area allows you to include .NET namespaces

Defining the Workflow Arguments

Next, define two new workflow wide input arguments, named `RequestedMake` and `RequestedColor`, both of which will be of type `String`. Like the previous example, the host of the workflow will create a `Dictionary` object that contains data that maps to these arguments, so there is no need to assign a default value to these items using the Arguments editor. As you might guess, the workflow will use these values to perform the database query.

As well, you can use this same Arguments editor to define an *output argument* named `FormattedResponse` of type `String`. When you need to return data from the workflow back to the host, you can create any number of output arguments which can be enumerated by the host when the workflow has completed. Figure 26-20 shows the current workflow designer.

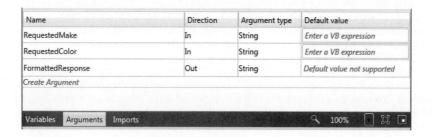

Name	Direction	Argument type	Default value
RequestedMake	In	String	*Enter a VB expression*
RequestedColor	In	String	*Enter a VB expression*
FormattedResponse	Out	String	*Default value not supported*
Create Argument			

Figure 26-20. Recall that workflow arguments provide a way send data to and return data from the workflow

Defining Workflow Variables

At this point, you need to declare a member variable in your workflow which corresponds to the `InventoryDALDisLayer` class of `AutoLot.dll`. You might recall from Chapter 22 that this class allows you to get all data from the Inventory returned as a `DataTable`. Select your `Sequence` activity on the designer, and using the Variables button, create a variable named `AutoLotInventory`. In the Variable Type dropdown list box, pick the Browse For Types... menu option, and type in `InventoryDALDisLayer` (Figure 26-21).

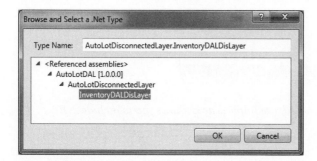

Figure 26-21. Recall that workflow variables provide a way to declarativly define variables within a scope

Now, making sure your new variable is selected, go to the Visual Studio 2010 Properties window and click on the ellipse button of the `Default` property. This will open up a code editor which you can resize as you see fit (very helpful when entering lengthy code). This editor is much easier to use when entering complex code for a variable assignment. Enter the following (VB) code, which allocates your `InventoryDALDisLayer` variable:

```
New InventoryDALDisLayer("Data Source=(local)\SQLEXPRESS;" &
                         "Initial Catalog=AutoLot;Integrated Security=True")
```

Declare a second workflow variable of type System.Data.DataTable named Inventory, again using the Browse For Types... menu option (set the default value of this variable to Nothing). You will be assigning the Inventory variable to the result of calling GetAllInventory() on the InventoryDALDisLayer variable in a later step.

Working with the Assign Activity

The Assign activity allows you to set a variable to a value, which can be the result of any sort of valid code statements. Drag an Assign activity (located in the Primitives area of your Toolbox) into your Sequence activity. In the To edit box, specify your Inventory variable. Using the Properties window, click on the ellipse button of the Value property and enter the following code:

```
AutoLotInventory.GetAllInventory()
```

Once the Assign activity has been encountered in your workflow, you will have a DataTable that contains all records of the Inventory table. However, you need to discover if the correct item is in stock using the values of the RequestedMake and RequestedColor arguments sent by the host. To determine if this is the case, you will make use of LINQ to DataSet. Once you know if you have the item in stock, you will use an If activity to perform the XAML equivalent of an if/else/then statement.

Working with the If and Switch Activities

Drag an If activity onto your Sequence node directly under the Assign activity. Because this activity is the XAML based way to make a simple runtime decision, you first need to configure the If activity to test against a Boolean expression. In the Condition editor, enter the following check LINQ to DataSet query:

```
(From car In Inventory.AsEnumerable()
   Where CType(car("Color"), String) = RequestedColor And
   CType(car("Make"), String) = RequestedMake Select car).Any()
```

This query will use the host supplied RequestedColor and RequestedMake data to fetch all records in the DataTable of the correct make and color. The call to the Any() extension method will return a True or False value based on if the result of the query contains any results.

Your next task is to configure the set of activities that will execute when the specified condition is True or False. Recall that your ultimate goal here is to send a formatted message to the user if you do indeed have the car in question. However, to spice things up a tad, you will return a unique message based on which make of automobile the caller has requested (BMW, Yugo, or anything else).

Drag a Switch<T> activity (located in the Flow Control area of the Toolbox) into the Then area of the If activity. As soon as you drop this activity, Visual Studio displays a dialog box asking for the type of the generic type parameter-specify String here. In the Expression area of your Switch activity, type RequestedMake.

You will see that a default option for the switch is already in place and is inviting you to add an activity to represent how to respond. You only need a single Assign activity; however, if you wanted to perform more complex actions, your default area might very well be a new Sequence or Flowchart.

Once you have added the Assign activity to the Default edit area (by clicking "Add Activity"), assign the FormattedResponse argument to the following code statement:

```
String.Format("Yes, we have a {0} {1} you can purchase",
              RequestedColor, RequestedMake)
```

At this point, your **Switch** editor will look like this (Figure 26-22).

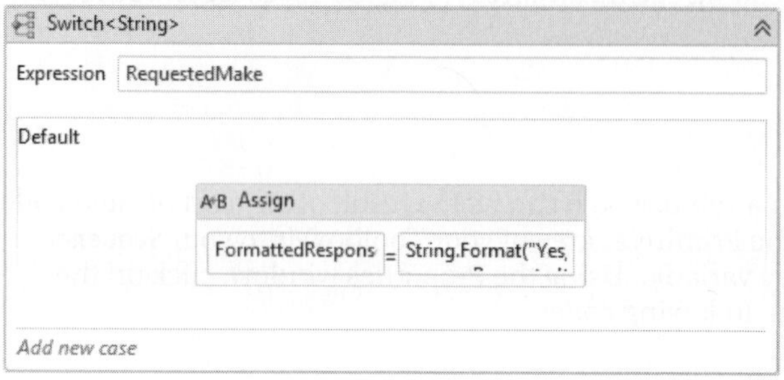

Figure 26-22. Defining the default task for a Switch activity

Now, click on the "Add New Case" link and enter **BMW** (without any double quotes) for the first case, and once again for a final case of **Yugo** (again, no double quotes). Within each of these case areas, drop an **Assign** activity, both of which assign a value to the **FormattedResponse** variable. For the case of BMW, assign a value such as:

```
String.Format("Yes sir! We can send you {0} {1} as soon as {2}!", _
              RequestedColor, RequestedMake, DateTime.Now)
```

For the case of the Yugo, use the following expression:

```
String.Format("Please, we will pay you to get this {0} off our lot!", _
              RequestedMake)
```

The **Switch** activity will now look something like the following (Figure 26-23).

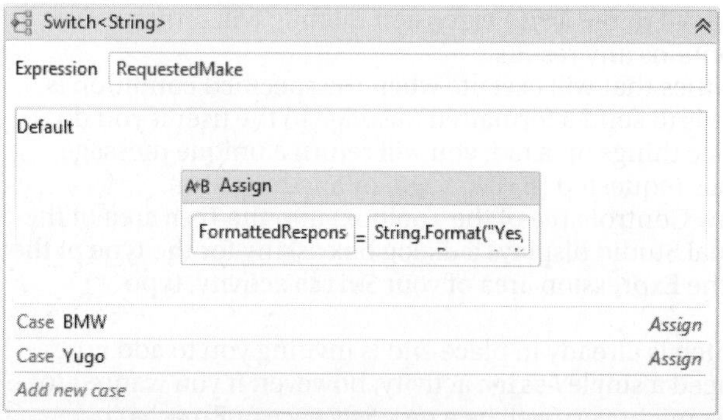

Figure 26-23. The final Switch activity

Building a Custom Code Activity

As expressive as the workflow designer experience is with its ability to embed complex code statements (and LINQ queries) in your XAML file, there will certainly be times when you just need to write code in a dedicated class. There are a number of ways to do so with the WF API, but the most straightforward way is to create a class extending **CodeActivity**, or if your activity needs to return a value, **CodeActivity<T>** (where T is the type of return value).

Here, you will make a simple custom activity which will dump out data to a text file, informing the sales staff that a request has come in for a car that is currently not in the inventory system. First, activate the Project | Add New Item menu option and insert a new Code Activity named **CreateSalesMemoActivity.vb** (Figure 26-24).

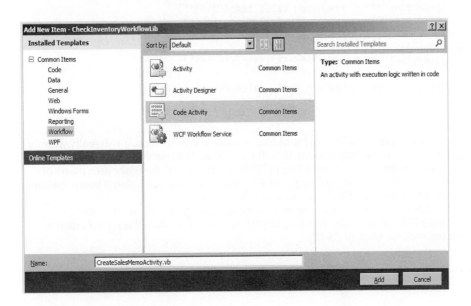

Figure 26-24. Inserting a new Code Activity

If your custom activity requires inputs to process, they will each be represented by a property encapsulating an **InArgument(Of T)** object. The **InArgument(Of T)** class type is a WF API specific entity, which provides a way to pass through data supplied by a workflow to the custom activity class itself. Your activity will need two such properties representing the make and color of the item not in stock.

As well, a custom code activity will need to override the **Execute()** method, which will be called by the WF runtime when this activity is encountered. Typically, this method will use the **InArgument()** properties to get the workload accomplished. To get the real underlying value, you will need to do so indirectly using the **GetValue()** method of the incoming **CodeActivityContext**.

Here then is the code for your custom activity, which generates a new *.txt file describing the situation to the sales team:

```
Public NotInheritable Class CreateSalesMemoActivity
    Inherits CodeActivity

    ' Two properties for the custom activity
    Public Property Make() As InArgument(Of String)
    Public Property Color() As InArgument(Of String)

    ' If the activity returns a value, derive from CodeActivity(Of TResult)
    ' and return the value from the Execute method.
    Protected Overrides Sub Execute(ByVal context As CodeActivityContext)
        ' Dump a message to a local text file.
        Dim salesMessage As New StringBuilder()
        salesMessage.AppendLine("***** Attention sales team! *****")
        salesMessage.AppendLine("Please order the following ASAP!")
        salesMessage.AppendFormat("1 {0} {1}" & vbLf, context.GetValue(Color),
        context.GetValue(Make))
        salesMessage.AppendLine("*******************************")

        System.IO.File.WriteAllText("SalesMemo.txt", salesMessage.ToString())
    End Sub
End Class
```

Now that you have a custom code activity, how should you make use of it? Well, if you really wanted to deliver a polished activity, WF 4.0 does allow a way to build a custom designer for your custom code activities. However, doing so requires an understanding of WPF, as the custom designer uses many of the same techniques as you would use when building a WPF **Window** or **UserControl**. You'll begin learning about WPF in the next chapter, so for now I'll show you a simpler approach.

First, compile your workflow assembly. Ensuring your workflow designer is the active window within the Visual Studio 2010 IDE, examine the top area of your toolbox. You should see your custom activity is present and accounted for (Figure 26-25).

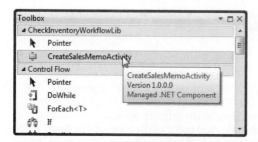

Figure 26-25. *Custom code activities appear in the Visual Studio 2010 toolbox*

First, drag a new **Sequence** activity into the **Else** branch of your **If** activity. Next, drag your custom activity into the **Sequence**. At this point, you can assign values to each of the exposed properties using the Properties window. Using your **RequestedMake** and **RequestedMake** variables, set the **Make** and **Color** properties of your activity as shown in Figure 26-26.

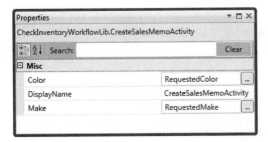

Figure 26-26. Setting the properties of your custom code activity

To complete this workflow, drag a final **Assign** activity into the **Sequence** activity of the **Else** branch, and set the **FormattedResponse** to the string value "Sorry, out of stock". Figure 26-27 shows the final workflow design.

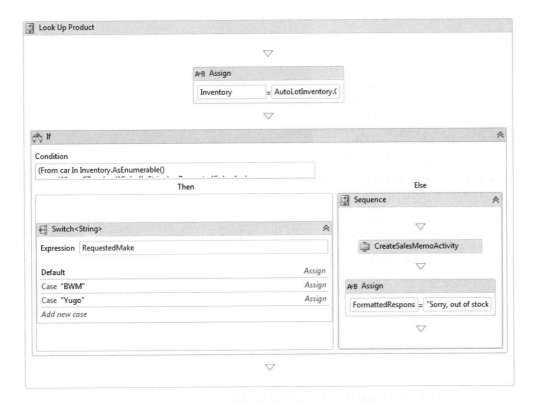

Figure 26-27. The completed sequential workflow

Compile your project and move onto the final part of this chapter, where you will build a client host to make use of the workflow.

■ **Source Code** The CheckInventoryWorkflowLib project is included under the Chapter 26 subdirectory.

Consuming the Workflow Library

Any sort of application can make use of a workflow library; however, here you will opt for simplicity and build a simple Console Application named WorkflowLibraryClient. Once you make the project, you will need to set a reference not only to your `CheckInventoryWorkflowLib.dll` and `AutoLot.dll` assemblies, but also the key WF 4.0 library, `System.Activities.dll`, which can be found in the .NET tab of the Visual Studio 2010 Add Reference dialog.

Once each assembly reference has been set, update your `Module1.vb` file with the following logic:

```
Imports System.Activities
Imports CheckInventoryWorkflowLib

Module Module1
    Sub Main()
        Console.WriteLine("**** Inventory Look up ****")

        ' Get user preferences.
        Console.Write("Enter Color: ")
        Dim color As String = Console.ReadLine()
        Console.Write("Enter Make: ")
        Dim make As String = Console.ReadLine()

        ' Package up data for workflow.
        Dim wfArgs As New Dictionary(Of String, Object)() From
        {{"RequestedColor", color}, {"RequestedMake", make}}

        Try
            ' Send data to workflow!
            WorkflowInvoker.Invoke(New CheckInventory(), wfArgs)
        Catch ex As Exception
            Console.WriteLine(ex.Message)
        End Try
    End Sub
End Module
```

As you have done in other examples, you are using the `WorkflowInvoker` to spin off the workflow in a synchronous manner. While this is all well and good, how are you to get back the return value of the workflow? Remember, once the workflow terminates, you should get back a formatted response!

Retrieving the Workflow Output Argument

The `WorkflowInvoker.Invoke()` method will return an object implementing the `IDictionary(Of String, Object)` interface. Because a workflow can return back any number of output arguments, you will need to specify the name of a given output argument as a string value to the type indexer. Update your Try/Catch logic as so:

```
Try
  ' Send data to workflow!
  Dim outputArgs As IDictionary(Of String, Object) = WorkflowInvoker.Invoke(
                                            New CheckInventory(), wfArgs)

  ' Print out the output message.
  Console.WriteLine(outputArgs("FormattedResponse"))
  Catch ex As Exception
  Console.WriteLine(ex.Message)
End Try
```

Now, run your program and enter a make and color which is currently in your copy of the Inventory table of the AutoLot database. You'll see output such as the following:

```
**** Inventory Look up ****

Enter Color: Black

Enter Make: BMW

Yes sir! We can send you Black BMW as soon as 7/30/2010 6:22:31 AM!

Press any key to continue . . .
```

However, if you enter information for an item not currently in stock, you will not only see output such as:

```
**** Inventory Look up ****

Enter Color: Pea Soup Green

Enter Make: Viper

Sorry, out of stock

Press any key to continue . . .
```

You will also find a new ***.txt** file in the \bin\Debug folder of the client application. If you open this in any text editor, you'll find the "sales memo":

```
***** Attention sales team! *****

Please order the following ASAP!

1 Pea Soup Green Viper

*******************************
```

That wraps up your introductory look at the brand new WF 4.0 API. As mentioned at the opening of this chapter, if you have worked with the previous version of the Windows Workflow Foundation API, you can clearly see the entire programming model has been overhauled completely (for the better, in my opinion).

While this chapter has only touched on some of the key aspects of this .NET 4.0 API, I do hope you feel confident that you can dive into the topic further if you are interested.

■ **Source Code** The WorkflowLibraryClientproject is included under the Chapter 26 subdirectory.

Summary

In essence, WF allows you to model an application's internal business processes directly within the application itself. Beyond simply modeling the overall workflow, however, WF provides a complete runtime engine and several services that round out this API's overall functionality (persistence and tracking services, etc.). While this introductory chapter did not examine these services directly, do remember that a production-level WF application will most certainly make use of these facilities.

.NET 4.0 completely changes the entire WF programming mode originally introduced in .NET 3.0. Going forward, we are able to model our workflows in a completely declarative manner using an XML-based grammar named XAML. Not only can we use XAML to define the state of each activity in our workflow, we can also embed "real code" into a XAML document indirectly when we make use of the WF designers.

In this introduction to the topic, you learned about two key top level activities, namely **Flowchart** and **Sequence**. While each of these types control the flow of logic in unique manners, they both can contain the same sort of child activities and are executed by the host in the same manner (via **WorkflowInvoker** or **WorkflowApplication**). You also learned how to pass host arguments *to* a workflow using a generic **Dictionary** object and how to retrieve output arguments *from* a workflow using a generic **IDictionary** compatible object.

■ ■ ■

## CHAPTER 27

Introducing Windows Presentation Foundation and XAML

When version 1.0 of the .NET platform was released, programmers who needed to build graphical desktop applications made use of two APIs named Windows Forms and GDI+, packaged up primarily in the `System.Windows.Forms.dll` and `System.Drawing.dll` assemblies. While Windows Forms/GDI+ are excellent APIs for building traditional desktop GUIs, Microsoft shipped an alternative GUI desktop API named Windows Presentation Foundation (WPF) beginning with the release of .NET 3.0.

This initial WPF chapter begins by examining the motivation behind this new GUI framework, which will help you see the differences between the Windows Forms/GDI+ and WPF programming models. Next, we will examine the different types of WPF applications supported by the API, and come to know the role of the several important classes including `Application`, `Window`, `ContentControl`, `Control`, `UIElement`, and `FrameworkElement`. During this time, you will learn to intercept keyboard and mouse activities, define application wide data, and other common WPF tasks using nothing but VB 2010 code.

This chapter will then introduce you to an XML-based grammar named *Extensible Application Markup Language* (XAML). Here, you will learn the syntax and semantics of XAML, including attached property syntax, the role of type converters, markup extensions, and understanding how to generate, load and parse XAML at runtime. As well, you will learn how to integrate XAML data into a VB 2010 WFP-code base (and the benefits of doing so).

This chapter wraps up by the integrated WPF designers of Visual Studio 2010. Here, you will build your own custom XAML editor/parser, which illustrates how XAML can be manipulated at runtime to build dynamic user interfaces.

■ **Note** The remaining WPF chapters of this book will introduce you to Microsoft Expression Blend, which is a WPF-centric tool dedicated to the generation of XAML on your behalf.

The Motivation Behind WPF

Over the years, Microsoft has created numerous graphical user interface toolkits (VB6, raw C/C++/Windows API development, MFC, etc.) to build desktop executables. Each of these APIs provided a code base to represent the basic aspects of a GUI application, including main windows, dialog boxes, controls, menu systems, and other basic necessities. With the initial release of the .NET platform, the Windows Forms API quickly became the preferred model for UI development, given its simple yet very powerful object model.

While many full-featured desktop applications have been successfully created using Windows Forms, the fact of the matter is that this programming model is rather *asymmetrical*. Simply put, `System.Windows.Forms.dll` and `System.Drawing.dll` do not provide direct support for many additional technologies required to build a feature-rich desktop application. To illustrate this point, consider the ad hoc nature of GUI development before the release of WPF (e.g., .NET 2.0; see Table 27-1).

Table 27-1. .NET 2.0 Solutions to Desired Functionalities

Desired Functionality	.NET 2.0 Solution
Building windows with controls	Windows Forms
2D graphics support	GDI+ (`System.Drawing.dll`)
3D graphics support	DirectX APIs
Support for streaming video	Windows Media Player APIs
Support for flow-style documents	Programmatic manipulation of PDF files

As you can see, a Windows Forms developer must pull in types from a number of unrelated APIs and object models. While it is true that making use of these diverse APIs may look similar syntactically (it is just VB 2010 code, after all), you may also agree that each technology requires a radically different mind-set. For example, the skills required to create a 3D rendered animation using DirectX are completely different from those used to bind data to a grid. To be sure, it is very difficult for a Windows Forms programmer to master the diverse nature of each API.

■ **Note** Appendix A provides an introduction to Windows Forms and GDI+ application development.

Unifying Diverse APIs

WPF (introduced with .NET 3.0) was purposely created to merge these previously unrelated programming tasks into a single unified object model. Thus, if you need to author a 3D animation, you have no need to manually program against the DirectX API (although you could), as 3D functionality is baked directly into WPF. To see how well things have cleaned up, consider Table 27-2, which illustrates the desktop development model ushered in as of .NET 3.0.

Table 27-2. .NET 3.0 Solutions to Desired Functionalities

Desired Functionality	.NET 3.0 and Higher Solution
Building forms with controls	WPF
2D graphics support	WPF
3D graphics support	WPF
Support for streaming video	WPF
Support for flow-style documents	WPF

The obvious benefit here is that .NET programmers now have a single, symmetrical API for all common GUI programming needs. Once you become comfortable with the functionality of the key WPF assemblies and the grammar of XAML, you'll be amazed how quickly you can create very sophisticated UIs.

Providing a Separation of Concerns via XAML

Perhaps one of the most compelling benefits is that WPF provides a way to cleanly separate the look and feel of a Windows application from the programming logic that drives it. Using XAML, it is possible to define the UI of an application via XML *markup*. This markup (ideally generated using tools such as Microsoft Expression Blend) can then be connected to a managed code base to provide the guts of the program's functionality.

■ **Note** XAML is not limited to WPF applications! Any application can use XAML to describe a tree of .NET objects, even if they have nothing to do with a visible user interface. For example, the Windows Workflow Foundation API uses a XAML-based grammar to define business processes and custom activities.

As you dig into WPF, you may be surprised how much flexibility "desktop markup" provides. XAML allows you to define not only simple UI elements (buttons, grids, list boxes, etc.) in markup, but also 2D and 3D graphical data, animations, data binding logic, and multimedia functionality (such as video playback). For example, defining a circular button control that animates a company logo requires just a few lines of markup.

As shown in Chapter 31, WPF controls can be modified through styles and templates, which allow you to change the overall look and feel of an application with minimum fuss and bother. Unlike Windows Forms development, the only compelling reason to build a custom WPF control library is if you need to change the *behaviors* of a control (e.g., add custom methods, properties, or events; subclass an existing control to override Overridable members). If you simply need to change the *look and feel* of a control (again, such as a circular animated button), you can do so entirely through markup.

Providing an Optimized Rendering Model

GUI toolkits such as Windows Forms, VB6, or MFC preformed all graphical rendering requests (including the rendering of UI elements such as buttons and list boxes) using a low level, API (GDI), which has been part of the Windows OS for years. GDI provides adequate performance for typical business applications or simple graphical programs; however, if a UI application needed to tap into high performance graphics, DirectX was required.

The WPF programming model is quite different in that GDI is *not* used when rendering graphical data. All rendering operations (e.g., 2D graphics, 3D graphics, animations, UI widget renderings buttons, list boxes) now make use of the DirectX API. The first obvious benefit is that your WPF applications will automatically take advantage of hardware and software optimizations. As well, WPF applications can tap into very rich graphical services (blur effects, anti-aliasing, transparency, etc.) without the complexity of programming directly against the DirectX API.

■ **Note** Although WPF does push all rendering requests to the DirectX layer, I don't want to suggest that a WPF application will perform as fast as building an application using unmanaged C++ and DirectX directly. If you are build a desktop application that requires the fastest possible execution speed (such as a 3D video game), unmanaged C++ and DirectX are still the best approach.

Simplifying Complex UI Programming

To recap the story thus far, Windows Presentation Foundation (WPF) is an API to build desktop applications that integrates various desktop APIs into a single object model and provides a clean separation of concerns via XAML. In addition to these major points, WPF applications also benefit from a very simple way to integrate services into your programs, which historically were quite complex to account for. Here is a quick rundown of the core WPF features:

- A number of layout managers (far more than Windows Forms) to provide extremely flexible control over placement and reposition of content.

- Use of an enhanced data-binding engine to bind content to UI elements in a variety of ways.

- A built-in style engine, which allows you to define "themes" for a WPF application.

- Use of vector graphics, which allows content to be automatically resized to fit the size and resolution of the screen hosting the application.

- Support for 2D and 3D graphics, animations, and video and audio playback.

- A rich typography API, such as support for XML Paper Specification (XPS) documents, fixed documents (WYSIWYG), flow documents, and document annotations (e.g., a Sticky Notes API).

- Support for interoperating with legacy GUI models (e.g., Windows Forms, ActiveX, and Win32 HWNDs). For example, you can incorporate custom Windows Forms controls into a WPF application, and vice versa.

Now that you have some idea of what WPF brings to the table, let's turn our attention to the various types of applications that can be created using this API.

The Various Flavors of WPF

The WPF API can be used to build a variety of GUI-centric applications that basically differ in their navigational structure and deployment models. The sections that follow present a high-level walk through each option.

Traditional Desktop Applications

The first (and most familiar) option is to use WPF to build a traditional executable assembly that runs on a local machine. For example, you could use WPF to build a text editor, painting program, or multimedia program such as a digital music player, photo viewer, and so forth. Like any other desktop applications, these *.exe files can be installed using traditional means (setup programs, Windows Installer packages, etc.) or via ClickOnce technology to allow desktop applications to be distributed and installed via a remote web server.

Programmatically speaking, this type of WPF application will make use (at a minimum) of the Window and Application types, in addition to the expected set of dialog boxes, toolbars, status bars, menu systems, and other UI elements.

Now, you can certainly use WPF to build your basic, bland business application that does not support any bells and whistles, but WPF really shines when you *do* incorporate such features. Consider Figure 27-1, which shows a WPF sample desktop application for viewing patient records in a medical environment.

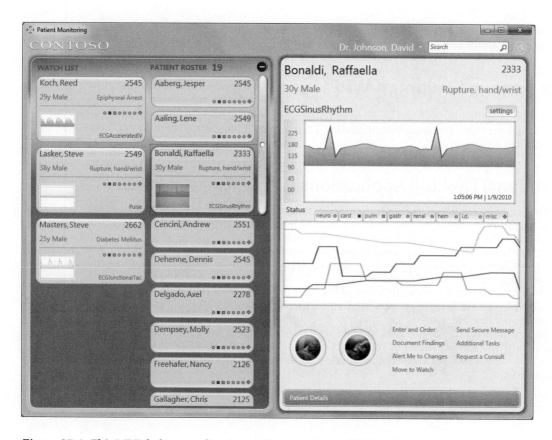

Figure 27-1. This WPF desktop application makes use of several WPF APIs

Sadly, the printed page does not show the full feature set of this window. Note that the upper right of the main window is displaying a real time graph of the patient's sinus rhythm. If you click on Patient Details button on the lower right, several animations take place to flip, rotate and transform the UI to the following look and feel (Figure 27-2).

Figure 27-2. Transformations and animations are very simple under WPF

Could you build this same application without WPF? Absolutely. However, the amount of code—and the complexity of the code—would be much higher.

■ **Note** This example application can be downloaded (with source code) from the office WPF web site, `http://windowsclient.net`. Here you will find numerous WPF (and Windows Forms) sample projects, technology walkthroughs and forums.

Navigation-Based WPF Applications

WPF applications can optionally choose to make use of a navigation-based structure, which makes a traditional desktop application take on the basic behavior of a web browser application. Using this model, you can build a desktop *.exe that provides a "forward" and "back" button that allows the end user to move back and forth between various UI displays called *pages*.

The application itself maintains a list of each page and provides the necessary infrastructure to navigate between them, pass data across pages (similar to a web-based application variable), and maintain a history list. By way of a concrete example, consider Windows Explorer (see Figure 27-3), which makes use of such functionality. Notice the navigation buttons (and history list) mounted on the upper-left corner of the window.

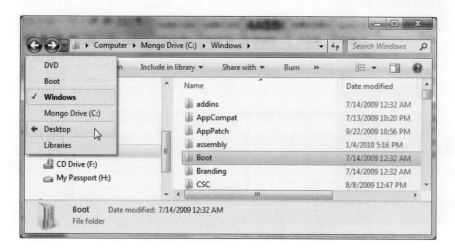

Figure 27-3. A navigation-based desktop program

Regardless of the fact that a WPF desktop application can take on a weblike navigational structure, understand that this is simply a UI design issue. The application itself is still little more than a local executable assembly running on a desktop machine, and it has little to do with a web application beyond a slightly similar look and feel. Programmatically speaking, this type of WPF application is constructed using classes such as Application, Page, NavigationWindow, and Frame.

XBAP Applications

WPF also allows you to build applications that can be hosted *within* a web browser. This flavor of WPF application is termed an XAML browser application, or XBAP. Under this model, the end user navigates to a given URL, at which point the XBAP (which is essentially a collection of Page objects) is transparently downloaded and installed to the local machine. Unlike a traditional ClickOnce installation for an executable application, however, the XBAP program is hosted directly within the browser and adopts the browser's intrinsic navigational system. Figure 27-4 illustrates an XBAP program in action (specifically, the ExpenseIt WPF sample program that ships with the .NET Framework 4.0 SDK).

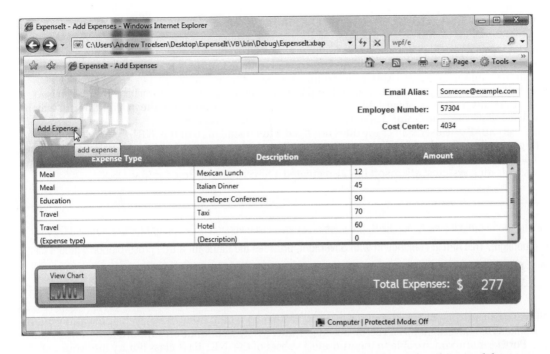

Figure 27-4. XBAP programs are downloaded to a local machine and hosted within a web browser

The benefit of an XBAP is that it allows you to create sophisticated UIs which are much more expressive than a typical web page built with HTML and JavaScript. An XBAP Page object can make use of the same WPF services as a desktop WPF application, including animations, 2D and 3D graphics, themes and whatnot. In effect, the web browser is just a container for WPF Page objects, and is *not* displaying ASP.NET web pages.

However, given that these Page objects are deployed to a remote web server, XBAPs can be easily versioned and updated without the need to redeploy executables to the user's desktop. Like a traditional web program, you can simply update the Page objects in the web server, and the user will get the 'latest and greatest' when they access the URL.

One downside to this flavor of WPF is that XBAPs must be hosted within Microsoft Internet Explorer or Firefox web browsers. If you are deploying XBAPs across a company intranet, browser compatibility should not be a problem, given that system administrators can play dictator regarding which browser should be installed on users' machines. However, if you want the outside world to make use of your XBAP, it is not possible to ensure each end user is making use of Internet Explorer/Firefox, and therefore some external users may not be able to view your WPF XBAP.

Another issue to be aware of is the machine which is viewing an XBAP must have a local installation of the .NET framework, as the Page objects will be using the same .NET assemblies as an application running natively on the machine. Given this particular point, XBAPs are limited to Windows operating systems and thus cannot be viewed on a system running Mac OS X or Linux.

The WPF/Silverlight Relationship

WPF and XAML also provide the foundation for a cross-platform, cross-browser WPF-based technology termed Silverlight. From a high level, you can consider Silverlight as a competitor to Adobe Flash, with the benefit of using VB 2010 and XAML rather than a new set of tools and languages. Silverlight is a subset of WPF functionality, which is used to build highly interactive plug-ins for a larger HTML-based web page. In reality, however, Silverlight is a completely unique distribution of the .NET platform, which ships with a "mini" CLR and "mini" version of the .NET base class libraries.

Unlike an XBAP, the user's machine does not need a full installation of the .NET Framework. As long as the target machine has the Silverlight runtime installed, the browser will load the Silverlight runtime and display the Silverlight application automatically. Best of all, Silverlight plug-ins are not limited to the Windows operating systems! Microsoft has also created a Silverlight runtime for Mac OS X.

■ **Note** The Mono project (see Appendix B) provides an open source version of Silverlight for Linux based OSs named Moonlight. This API, in conjunction with Silverlight, provides the fabric for a true cross-platform model for extremely rich web pages.

With Silverlight, you are able to build extremely feature-rich (and interactive) web applications. For example, like WPF, Silverlight has a vector-based graphical system, animation support, and multimedia support. Furthermore, you are able to incorporate a subset of the .NET base class library into your applications. This subset includes a number of WPF controls, LINQ support, generic collection types, web service support, and a healthy subset of `mscorlib.dll` (file I/O, XML manipulation, etc.).

■ **Note** This edition of the text does not address Silverlight; however, a majority of your WPF knowledge will map directly to the construction of Silverlight web plug-ins. If you are interested in learning more about this API, check out `www.silverlight.net`.

Investigating the WPF Assemblies

Regardless of which type of WPF application you wish to build, WPF is ultimately little more than a collection of types bundled within .NET assemblies. Table 27-3 describes the core assemblies used to build WPF applications, each of which must be referenced when creating a new project (as you would hope, Visual Studio 2010 and Expression Blend WPF projects automatically reference the required assemblies).

Table 27-3. Core WPF Assemblies

Assembly	Meaning in Life
`PresentationCore.dll`	This assembly defines numerous types that constitute the foundation of the WPF GUI layer. For example, this assembly contains support for the WPF Ink API (for programming against stylus input for Pocket PCs and Tablet PCs), several animation primitives, and numerous graphical rendering types.
`PresentationFramework.dll`	This assembly contains a majority of the WPF controls, the `Application` and `Window` classes, and support for interactive 2D geometries. As well, this library provides basic functionality to read and write XAML documents at runtime.
`System.Xaml.dll`	This assembly provides namespaces which allow you to program against a XAML document at runtime. By and large, this library is only useful if you are authoring WPF support tools or need absolute control over XAML at runtime.
`WindowsBase.dll`	This assembly defines types that constitute the infrastructure of the WPF API., including those representing WPF threading types, security types, various type converters, and support for *dependency properties* and *routed events* (described in Chapter 29).

Collectively, these assemblies define a number of new namespaces and hundreds of new .NET classes, interfaces, structures, enumerations, and delegates. While you should consult the .NET Framework 4.0 SDK documentation for complete details, Table 27-4 describes the role of some (but certainly not all) of the namespaces you should be aware of.

Table 27-4. Core WPF Namespaces

Namespace	Meaning in Life
`System.Windows`	This is the root namespace of WPF. Here you will find core classes (such as `Application` and `Window`) that are required by any WPF desktop project.
`System.Windows.Controls`	Contains all of the expected WPF widgets, including types to build menu systems, tool tips, and numerous layout managers.
`System.Windows.Data`	Types to work with the WPF data binding engine, as well as support for data binding templates.
`System.Windows.Documents`	Contains types to work with the documents API, which allows you to integrate PDF style functionality into your WPF applications, via the XML Paper Specification (XPS) protocol.

Continued

Namespace	Meaning in Life
System.Windows.Ink	Support for the Ink API, which allows you to capture input from a stylus or mouse, respond to input gestures, and so forth. Very useful for Tablet PC program; however, any WPF can make use of this API.
System.Windows.Markup	This namespace defines a number of types that allow XAML markup (and the equivalent binary format, BAML) to be parsed and processed programmatically.
System.Windows.Media	This is the root namespace to several media-centric namespaces. Within these namespaces you will find types to work with animations, 3D rendering, text rendering, and other multimedia primitives.
System.Windows.Navigation	This namespace provides types to account for the navigation logic employed by XAML browser applications (XBAPs) as well as standard desktop applications that require a navigational page model.
System.Windows.Shapes	Defines classes which allow you to render interactive 2D graphics that automatically respond to mouse input.

To begin your journey into the WPF programming model, you'll examine two members of the System.Windows namespace that are commonplace to any traditional desktop development effort: Application and Window.

■ **Note** If you are new to the development of desktop applications using the .NET platform, be aware that the System.Windows.Forms.* and System.Drawing.* assemblies are not related to WPF! These libraries represent the original .NET GUI toolkit, Windows Forms (see Appendix A).

The Role of the Application Class

The System.Windows.Application class represents a global instance of a running WPF application. This class supplies a Run() method (to start the application), a series of events that you are able to handle in order to interact with the application's lifetime (such as Startup and Exit), and a number of events that are specific to XAML browser applications (such as events that fire as a user navigates between pages). Table 27-5 details some of the key properties to be aware of.

Table 27-5. Key Properties of the Application Type

Property	Meaning in Life
Current	This Shared property allows you to gain access to the running `Application` object from anywhere in your code. This can be very helpful when a window or dialog box needs to gain access to the `Application` object that created it, typically to access application wide variables and functionality.
MainWindow	This property allows you to programmatically get or set the main window of the application.
Properties	This property allows you to establish and obtain data that is accessible throughout all aspects of a WPF application (windows, dialog boxes, etc.).
StartupUri	This property gets or sets a URI that specifies a window or page to open automatically when the application starts.
Windows	This property returns a `WindowCollection` type, which provides access to each window created from the thread that created the `Application` object. This can be very helpful when you wish to iterate over each open window of an application and alter its state (such as minimizing all windows).

Constructing an Application Class

Any WPF application will need to define a class that extends `Application`. Within this class, you will define your program's entry point (the `Main()` method), which creates an instance of this subclass and typically handles the `Startup` and `Exit` events. You will build a full example project in just a moment, but here is a quick example:

```
'Define the global application object
'for this WPF program.
Class MyApp
    Inherits Application
        <STAThread()> _
        Shared Sub Main(ByVal args As String())
            ' Create the application object.
            Dim app As New MyApp()

            ' Register the Startup / Exit events.
            AddHandler app.Startup, AddressOf AppStartUp
            AddHandler app.Exit, AddressOf AppExit
        End Sub
End Class
```

Within the Startup handler, you will most often process any incoming command line arguments and launch the main window of the program. The Exit handler, as you would expect, is where you can author any necessary shut down logic for the program (e.g., save user preferences, write to the Windows registry).

Enumerating the Application.Windows collection

Another interesting property exposed by Application is Windows, which provides access to a collection representing each window loaded into memory for the current WPF application. Recall that as you create new Window objects, they are automatically added into the Application.Windows collection. Here is an example method that will minimize each window of the application (perhaps in response to a given keyboard gesture or menu option triggered by the end user):

```
Private Shared Sub MinimizeAllWindows()
    For Each wnd As Window In Application.Current.Windows
        wnd.WindowState = WindowState.Minimized
    Next
End Sub
```

You'll build a complete Application-derived type in an upcoming example. Until then, let's check out the core functionality of the Window type and learn about a number of important WPF base classes in the process.

The Role of the Window Class

The System.Windows.Window class represents a single window owned by the Application-derived class, including any dialog boxes displayed by the main window. Not surprisingly, Window has a series of parent classes, each of which brings more functionality to the table. Consider Figure 27-5, which shows the inheritance chain (and implemented interfaces) for System.Windows.Window as seen through the Visual Studio 2010 object browser.

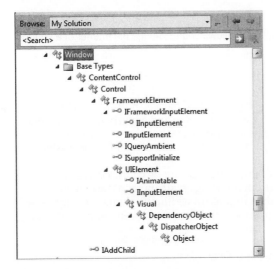

Figure 27-5. The hierarchy of the Window class

You'll come to understand the functionality provided by many of these base classes as you progress through this chapter and the chapters to come. However, to whet your appetite, the following sections present a breakdown of the functionality provided by each base class (consult the .NET Framework 4.0 SDK documentation for full details).

The Role of System.Windows.Controls.ContentControl

The direct parent of Window is ContentControl, which is quite possibly the most enticing of all WPF classes. This base class provides derived types with the ability to host a single piece of *content*, which, simply put, refers to the data placed within the interior of the control's surface area via the Content property. The WPF content model makes it very simple to customize the basic look and feel of a content control.

For example, when you think of a typical "button" control, you tend to assume that the content is a basic string literal (OK, Cancel, Abort, etc). If you are using XAML to describe a WPF control, and the value you wish to assign to the Content property can be captured as a simple string, you may set the Content property within the element's opening definition as so (don't fret over the exact markup at this point):

```
<!-- Setting the Content value in the opening element -->
<Button Height="80" Width="100" Content="OK"/>
```

■ **Note** The Content property can also be set in VB 2010 code, which allows you to change the interior of a control at runtime.

However, content can be anything. For example, let's say you wish to have a "button" that has something more interesting than a simple string, perhaps a custom graphic and a blurb of text. In other UI frameworks such as Windows Forms, you would be required to build a custom control, which could entail quite a bit of code and a whole new class to maintain. With the WPF content model, there is no need to do so.

When you wish to assign to the `Content` property to a value which cannot be captured as a simple array of characters, you are unable to assign the `Content` property using an attribute in the control's opening definition. Rather, you must define the content data *implicitly*, within the element's scope. For example, this `<Button>` contains a `<StackPanel>` as content, which itself contains some unique data (an `<Ellipse>` and `<Label>`, to be exact):

```
<!-- Implicitly setting the Content property with complex data -->
<Button Height="80" Width="100">
  <StackPanel>
    <Ellipse Fill="Red" Width="25" Height="25"/>
    <Label Content ="OK!"/>
  </StackPanel>
</Button>
```

You can also make use of XAML's *property-element syntax* to set complex content. Consider the following functionally equivalent `<Button>` definition, which sets the `Content` property explicitly using property-element syntax (again, you'll find more information on XAML later in this chapter, so don't sweat the details just yet):

```
<!-- Setting the Content property using property element syntax -->
<Button Height="80" Width="100">
  <Button.Content>
    <StackPanel>
      <Ellipse Fill="Red" Width="25" Height="25"/>
      <Label Content ="OK!"/>
    </StackPanel>
  <Button.Content>
</Button>
```

Do be aware that not every WPF control derives from `ContentControl`, and therefore not all controls supports this unique content model. As well, some WPF controls add a few refinements to the basic content model you have just examined. Chapter 28 will examine the role of WPF content in much more detail.

The Role of System.Windows.Controls.Control

Unlike ContentControl, all WPF controls share the Control base class as a common parent. This base class provides numerous core members that account for basic UI functionality. For example, Control defines properties to establish the control's size, opacity, tab order logic, the display cursor, background color, and so forth. Furthermore, this parent class provides support for *templating services*. As explained in Chapter 31, WPF controls can completely change the way they render their appearance using templates and styles. Table 27-6 documents some key members of the Control type, grouped by related functionality.

Table 27-6. Key Members of the Control Type

Members	Meaning in Life
Background, Foreground, BorderBrush, BorderThickness, Padding, HorizontalContentAlignment, VerticalContentAlignment	These properties allow you to set basic settings regarding how the control will be rendered and positioned.
FontFamily, FontSize, FontStretch, FontWeight	These properties control various font-centric settings.
IsTabStop, TabIndex	These properties are used to establish tab order among controls on a window.
MouseDoubleClick, PreviewMouseDoubleClick	These events handle the act of double-clicking a widget.
Template	This property allows you to get and set the control's template, which can be used to change the rendering output of the widget.

The Role of System.Windows.FrameworkElement

This base class provides a number of members that are used throughout the WPF framework, such as support for storyboarding (used within animations) and support for data binding, as well as the ability to name a member (via the Name property), obtain any resources defined by the derived type, and establish the overall dimensions of the derived type. Table 27-7 hits the highlights.

Table 27-7. Key Members of the FrameworkElement Type

Members	Meaning in Life
`ActualHeight, ActualWidth, MaxHeight, MaxWidth, MinHeight, MinWidth, Height, Width`	These properties control the size of the derived type.
`ContextMenu`	Gets or sets the pop-up menu associated with the derived type.
`Cursor`	Gets or sets the mouse cursor associated with the derived type.
`HorizontalAlignment, VerticalAlignment`	Gets or sets how the type is positioned within a container (such as a panel or list box).
`Name`	Allows to you assign a name to the type, in order to access its functionality in a code file.
`Resources`	Provides access to any resources defined by the type (see Chapter 30 for an examination of the WPF resource system).
`ToolTip`	Gets or sets the tool tip associated with the derived type.

The Role of System.Windows.UIElement

Of all the types within a `Window`'s inheritance chain, the `UIElement` base class provides the greatest amount of functionality. The key task of `UIElement` is to provide the derived type with numerous events to allow the derived type to receive focus and process input requests. For example, this class provides numerous events to account for drag-and-drop operations, mouse movement, keyboard input, and stylus input (for Pocket PCs and Tablet PCs).

Chapter 29 digs into the WPF event model in detail; however, many of the core events will look quite familiar (`MouseMove`, `KeyUp`, `MouseDown`, `MouseEnter`, `MouseLeave`, etc.). In addition to defining dozens of events, this parent class provides a number of properties to account for control focus, enabled state, visibility, and hit testing logic, as shown in Table 27-8.

Table 27-8. Key Members of the UIElement Type

Members	Meaning in Life
Focusable, IsFocused	These properties allow you to set focus on a given derived type.
IsEnabled	This property allows you to control whether a given derived type is enabled or disabled.
IsMouseDirectlyOver, IsMouseOver	These properties provide a simple way to perform hit-testing logic.
IsVisible, Visibility	These properties allow you to work with the visibility setting of a derived type.
RenderTransform	This property allows you to establish a transformation that will be used to render the derived type.

The Role of System.Windows.Media.Visual

The Visual class type provides core rendering support in WPF, which includes hit testing of rendered data, coordinate transformation, and bounding box calculations. In fact, the Visual class interacts with the underlying DirectX subsystem to actually draw data on the screen. As examined in Chapter 29, WPF provides three possible manners in which you can render graphical data, each of which differs in terms of functionality and performance. Use of the Visual type (and its children, such as DrawingVisual) provides the most lightweight way to render graphical data, but it also entails the greatest amount of manual code to account for all the required services. Again, more details to come in Chapter 29.

The Role of System.Windows.DependencyObject

WPF supports a particular flavor of .NET properties termed *dependency properties*. Simply put, this approach allows a type to compute the value of a property based on the value of other properties. In order for a type to participate in this new property scheme, it will need to derive from the DependencyObject base class. In addition, DependencyObject allows derived types to support *attached properties*, which are a form of dependency property very useful when programming against the WPF data-binding model as well as when laying out UI elements within various WPF panel types.

The DependencyObject base class provides two key methods to all derived types: GetValue() and SetValue(). Using these members, you are able to establish the property itself. Other bits of infrastructure allow you to "register" who can use the dependency/attached property in question. While dependency properties are a key aspect of WPF development, much of the time their details are hidden from view. Chapter 29 dives further into the details of the "new" property type.

The Role of System.Windows.Threading.DispatcherObject

The final base class of the Window type (beyond System.Object, which I assume needs no further explanation at this point in the book) is DispatcherObject. This type provides one property of interest, Dispatcher, which returns the associated System.Windows.Threading.Dispatcher object. The Dispatcher class is the entry point to the event queue of the WPF application, and it provides the basic constructs for dealing with concurrency and threading. By and large, this is a lower-level class that can be ignored by the majority of your WPF applications.

Building a WPF Application without XAML

Given all of the functionality provided by the parent classes of the `Window` type, it is possible to represent a window in your application by either directly creating a `Window` object or using this class as the parent to a strongly typed descendent. Let's examine both approaches in the following code example. Although most WPF applications will make use of XAML, doing so is entirely optional. Anything that can be expressed in XAML can be expressed in code and (for the most part) vice versa. If you wish, it is possible to build a complete WPF project using the underlying object model and procedural code.

To illustrate, let's create a minimal but complete application *without* the use of XAML using the `Application` and `Window` classes directly. Begin by creating a new Console Application named WpfAppAllCode (don't worry, you will use the Visual Studio WPF project template later in this chapter). Next, access the Project | Add Reference dialog box and add a reference to `WindowsBase.dll`, `PresentationCore.dll`, `System.Xaml.dll` and `PresentationFramework.dll`.

Now, update your initial VB 2010 file with the following code, which creates a window of modest functionality:

```vb
' A simple WPF application, written without XAML.
Imports System.Windows
Imports System.Windows.Controls

' In this first example, you are defining a single class type to
' represent the application itself and the main window.
Class Program
    Inherits Application

    <STAThread()> _
    Public Shared Sub Main(ByVal args As String())
        ' Handle the Startup and Exit events, and then run the application.
        Dim app As New Program()
        AddHandler app.Startup, AddressOf AppStartUp
        AddHandler app.Exit, AddressOf AppExit

        ' Fires the Startup event.
        app.Run()
    End Sub

    Private Shared Sub AppExit(ByVal sender As Object, ByVal e As ExitEventArgs)
        MessageBox.Show("App has exited")
    End Sub

    Private Shared Sub AppStartUp(ByVal sender As Object, ByVal e As StartupEventArgs)
        ' Create a Window object and set some basic properties.
        Dim mainWindow As New Window()
        mainWindow.Title = "My First WPF App!"
        mainWindow.Height = 200
        mainWindow.Width = 300
```

```
        mainWindow.WindowStartupLocation = WindowStartupLocation.CenterScreen
        mainWindow.Show()
    End Sub
End Class
```

■ **Note** The Main() method of a WPF application must be attributed with the <STAThread()> attribute, which ensures any legacy COM objects used by your application are thread-safe. If you do not annotate Main() in this way, you will encounter a runtime exception.

Note that the Program class extends the System.Windows.Application class. Within the Main() method, you create an instance of the application object and handle the Startup and Exit events using method group conversion syntax. Recall from Chapter 11 that this shorthand notation removes the need to manually specify the underlying delegates used by a particular event.

Of course, if you wish, you can specify the underlying delegates directly by name. In the following modified Main() method, notice that the Startup event works in conjunction with the StartupEventHandler delegate, which can only point to methods taking an Object as the first parameter and a StartupEventArgs as the second. The Exit event, on the other hand, works with the ExitEventHandler delegate, which demands that the method pointed to take an ExitEventArgs type as the second parameter:

```
<STAThread()> _
Public Shared Sub Main(ByVal args As String())
    ' This time, specify the underlying delegates.
    Dim app As New Program()
    AddHandler app.Startup, AddressOf AppStartUp
    AddHandler app.Exit, AddressOf AppExit

    ' Fires the Startup event.
    app.Run()
End Sub
```

In any case, the AppStartUp() method has been configured to create a Window object, establish some very basic property settings, and call Show() to display the window on the screen in a modeless fashion (the ShowDialog() method can be used to launch a modal dialog). The AppExit() method simply makes use of the WPF MessageBox class to display a diagnostic message when the application is being terminated.

Before you compile and run the project, you may want to set the entry point of the application. To do so, go to the project's properties and then select the Application tab. Select the Startup object drop-down, choose Sub Main from the list, and save the changes. Now if you run the project you will find a very simple main window that can be minimized, maximized, and closed. To spice things up a bit, you need to add some user interface elements. Before you do, however, you should refactor your code base to account for a strongly typed and well-encapsulated Window-derived class.

Creating a Strongly Typed Window

Currently, the `Application`-derived class directly creates an instance of the `Window` type upon application startup. Ideally, you would create a class deriving from `Window` in order to encapsulate its appearance and functionality. Assume that you have created the following class definition within your current `WpfAppAllCode` application (if you place this class in a new VB 2010 file, be sure to import the `System.Windows` namespace):

```vb
Class MainWindow
    Inherits Window

    Public Sub New(ByVal windowTitle As String, ByVal windowHeight As Integer, _
      ByVal windowWidth As Integer)
        Me.Title = windowTitle
        Me.WindowStartupLocation = WindowStartupLocation.CenterScreen
        Me.Height = windowHeight
        Me.Width = windowWidth
    End Sub
End Class
```

You can now update your `Startup` event handler to simply directly create an instance of `MainWindow`:

```vb
Private Shared Sub AppStartUp(ByVal sender As Object, ByVal e As StartupEventArgs)
    ' Create a MainWindow object.
    Dim wnd As New MainWindow("My better WPF App!", 200, 300)
    wnd.Show()
End Sub
```

Once the program is recompiled and executed, the output is identical. The obvious benefit is that you now have a strongly typed window class to build upon.

■ **Note** When you create a `Window` (or `Window`-derived) object, it will automatically be added to the windows collection of the `Application` class (via some constructor logic found in the `Window` class itself). You can use the `Application.Windows` property to iterate over the list of Window objects currently in memory.

Creating a Simple User Interface

Adding a UI element to a `Window` in VB 2010 code will involve the following basic steps:

1. Define a member variable to represent the control.

2. Configure the control's look and feel upon `Window` construction.

3. Assign the control to the inherited `Content` property, or alternatively, as a parameter to the inherited `AddChild()` method.

Recall that the WPF control content model demands that the **Content** property is set only once. Of course, a Window that only contained a single UI control would be quite useless. Therefore, in almost every case, the "single piece of content" that is assigned to the **Content** property is, in reality, a layout manager, such as **DockPanel**, **Grid**, **Canvas**, or **StackPanel**. Within the layout manager, you can have any combination of internal controls, including other nested layout managers. (Read more on this aspect of WPF development in Chapter 28.)

For now, you will add a single **Button** control to your **Window** derived class. When you click the button, you will close the current window, which will indirectly terminate the application, as you have no other windows in memory. Ponder the following update to the **MainWindow** class (be sure you have imported **System.Windows.Controls** to gain access to the **Button** class):

```
Class MainWindow
    Inherits Window

    ' Our UI element.
    Private btnExitApp As New Button()

    Public Sub New(ByVal windowTitle As String, ByVal windowHeight As Integer,
      ByVal windowWidth As Integer)
        ' Configure button and set the child control.
        AddHandler btnExitApp.Click, AddressOf btnExitApp_Clicked
        btnExitApp.Content = "Exit Application"
        btnExitApp.Height = 25
        btnExitApp.Width = 100

        ' Set the content of this window to a single button.
        Me.Content = btnExitApp

        ' Configure the window.
        Me.Title = windowTitle
        Me.WindowStartupLocation = WindowStartupLocation.CenterScreen
        Me.Height = windowHeight
        Me.Width = windowWidth
        Me.Show()
    End Sub

    Private Sub btnExitApp_Clicked(ByVal sender As Object, ByVal e As RoutedEventArgs)
        ' close the window
        Me.Close()
    End Sub
End Class
```

Notice that the **Click** event of the WPF **Button** works in conjunction with a delegate named **RoutedEventHandler**, which begs the question, what is a routed event? You'll examine the details of the WPF event model in the next chapter; for the time being, simply understand that targets of the **RoutedEventHandler** delegate must supply an **Object** as the first parameter and a **RoutedEventArgs** as the second.

In any case, once you recompile and run this application, you will find the customized window shown in Figure 27-6. Notice that your button is automatically placed in the dead center of the window's client area; this is the default behavior when content is not placed within a WPF panel type.

Figure 27-6. *A Simple WPF application writen in 100% VB 2010 code*

Interacting with Application Level Data

Recall that the `Application` class defines a property named `Properties`, which allows you to define a collection of name/value pairs via a type indexer. Because this indexer has been defined to operate on type `System.Object`, you are able to store any sort of item within this collection (including your custom classes), to be retrieved at a later time using a friendly moniker. Using this approach, it is simple to share data across all windows in a WPF application.

To illustrate, you will update the current `Startup` event handler to check the incoming command-line arguments for a value named `/GODMODE` (a common cheat code for many PC video games). If you find this token, you will establish a `Boolean` value set to `True` within the properties collection of the same name (otherwise you will set the value to `False`).

Sounds simple enough, but how are you going to pass the incoming command-line arguments (typically obtained from the `Main()` method) to your `Startup` event handler? One approach is to call the Shared `Environment.GetCommandLineArgs()` method. However, these same arguments are automatically added to the incoming `StartupEventArgs` parameter and can be accessed via the `Args` property. That being said, here is the first update to the current code base:

```
Private Shared Sub AppStartUp(ByVal sender As Object, ByVal e As StartupEventArgs)
    ' Check the incoming command-line arguments and see if they
    ' specified a flag for /GODMODE.
    Application.Current.Properties("GodMode") = False

    For Each arg As String In e.Args
        If arg.ToLower() = "/godmode" Then
            Application.Current.Properties("GodMode") = True
            Exit For
        End If
    Next
    ' Create a MainWindow object.
    Dim wnd As New MainWindow("My better WPF App!", 200, 300)
End Sub
```

Application-wide data can be accessed from anywhere within the WPF application. All you are required to do is obtain an access point to the global application object (via `Application.Current`) and investigate the collection. For example, you could update the `Click` event handler of the `Button` as so:

```
Private Sub btnExitApp_Clicked(ByVal sender As Object, ByVal e As
    RoutedEventArgs)
    ' Did user enable /godmode?
    If CBool(Application.Current.Properties("GodMode")) Then
        MessageBox.Show("Cheater!")
    End If

    Me.Close()
End Sub
```

With this, if the end user launches our program as follows:

```
WpfAppAllCode.exe /godmode
```

he or she will see our shameful message box displayed when terminating the application.

■ **Note** Recall that you can supply command line arguments within Visual Studio. Simply double click on the Properties icon within Solution Explorer, click the Debug tab from the resulting editor, and enter /godmode within the "Command line arguments" editor.

Handling the Closing of a Window Object

End users can shut down a window using numerous built-in system-level techniques (e.g., clicking the "X" close button on the window's frame) or by indirectly calling the Close() method in response to some user interaction element (e.g., File ➤ Exit). In either case, WPF provides two events that you can intercept to determine if the user is *truly* ready to shut down the window and remove it from memory. The first event to fire is Closing, which works in conjunction with the CancelEventHandler delegate.

This delegate expects target methods to take System.ComponentModel.CancelEventArgs as the second parameter. CancelEventArgs provides the Cancel property, which when set to True will prevent the window from actually closing (this is handy when you have asked the user if he really wants to close the window or if perhaps he would like to save his work first).

If the user did indeed wish to close the window, CancelEventArgs.Cancel can be set to False. This will then cause the Closed event to fire (which works with the System.EventHandler delegate), making it the point at which the window is about to be closed for good.

Update the MainWindow class to handle these two events by adding these code statements to the current constructor:

```
Public Sub New(ByVal windowTitle As String, ByVal windowHeight As Integer,
  ByVal windowWidth As Integer)
    ...
    AddHandler Me.Closing, AddressOf MainWindow_Closing
    AddHandler Me.Closed, AddressOf MainWindow_Closed
End Sub
```

Now, implement the corresponding event handlers as so:

```
Private Sub MainWindow_Closing(ByVal sender As Object, ByVal e As
  System.ComponentModel.CancelEventArgs)
    ' See if the user really wants to shut down this window.
    Dim msg As String = "Do you want to close without saving?"
    Dim result As MessageBoxResult = MessageBox.Show(msg, "My App",
     MessageBoxButton.YesNo, MessageBoxImage.Warning)

    If result = MessageBoxResult.No Then
        ' If user doesn't want to close, cancel closure.
        e.Cancel = True
    End If
End Sub


Private Sub MainWindow_Closed(ByVal sender As Object, ByVal e As EventArgs)
    MessageBox.Show("See ya!")
End Sub
```

Now, run your program and attempt to close the window, either by clicking the "X" icon on the upper right of the window or by clicking the button control. You should see the following confirmation dialog (Figure 27-7).

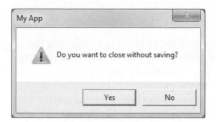

Figure 27-7. Trapping the Closing event of a Window

If you click the Yes button, the application will terminate; however, clicking the No button will keep the window in memory.

Intercepting Mouse Events

The WPF API provides a number of events you can capture in order to interact with the mouse. Specifically, the UIElement base class defines a number of mouse-centric events such as MouseMove, MouseUp, MouseDown, MouseEnter, MouseLeave, and so forth.

Consider, for example, the act of handling the MouseMove event. This event works in conjunction with the System.Windows.Input.MouseEventHandler delegate, which expects its target to take a System.Windows.Input.MouseEventArgs type as the second parameter. Using MouseEventArgs (like a Windows Forms application), you are able to extract out the (*x*, *y*) position of the mouse and other relevant details. Consider the following partial definition:

```
Public Class MouseEventArgs
    Inherits InputEventArgs

    ...
    Public Function GetPosition(ByVal relativeTo As IInputElement) As Point
    Public ReadOnly Property LeftButton() As MouseButtonState
    Public ReadOnly Property MiddleButton() As MouseButtonState
    Public ReadOnly Property MouseDevice() As MouseDevice
    Public ReadOnly Property RightButton() As MouseButtonState
    Public ReadOnly Property StylusDevice() As StylusDevice
    Public ReadOnly Property XButton1() As MouseButtonState
    Public ReadOnly Property XButton2() As MouseButtonState
End Class
```

■ **Note** The XButton1 and XButton2 properties allow you to interact with "extended mouse buttons" (such as the "next" and "previous" buttons found on some mouse controls). These are often used to interact with a browser's history list to navigate between visited pages.

The GetPosition() method allows you to get the (*x, y*) value relative to a UI element on the window. If you are interested in capturing the position relative to the activated window, simply pass in this. Handle the MouseMove event in the constructor of your MainWindow class like so:

```
Public Sub New(windowTitle As String, windowHeight As Integer,
 windowWidth As Integer)
    ...
AddHandler Me.MouseMove, AddressOf MainWindow_MouseMove
End Sub
```

Here is an event handler for MouseMove that will display the location of the mouse in the window's title area (notice you are translating the returned Point type into a text value via ToString()):

```
Private Sub MainWindow_MouseMove(ByVal sender As Object, ByVal e As
 System.Windows.Input.MouseEventArgs)
    ' Set the title of the window to the current X,Y of the mouse.
    Me.Title = e.GetPosition(Me).ToString()
End Sub
```

Intercepting Keyboard Events

Processing keyboard input is also very straightforward. UIElement defines a number of events that you can capture to intercept keypresses from the keyboard on the active element (e.g., KeyUp, KeyDown). The KeyUp and KeyDown events both work with the System.Windows.Input.KeyEventHandler delegate, which expects the target's second event handler to be of type KeyEventArgs, which defines several public properties of interest:

```
Public Class KeyEventArgs
    Inherits KeyboardEventArgs

    ...
    Public ReadOnly Property IsDown() As Boolean
    Public ReadOnly Property IsRepeat() As Boolean
    Public ReadOnly Property IsToggled() As Boolean
    Public ReadOnly Property IsUp() As Boolean
    Public ReadOnly Property Key() As Key
    Public ReadOnly Property KeyStates() As KeyStates
    Public ReadOnly Property SystemKey() As Key
End Class
```

To illustrate, handle the **KeyDown** event in the constructor of **MainWindow** (just like you did for the previous events) and implement the following event handler that changes the content of the button with the currently pressed key, use this code:

```
Private Sub MainWindow_KeyDown(sender As Object, e As
 System.Windows.Input.KeyEventArgs)
    ' Display key press on the button.
    btnExitApp.Content = e.Key.ToString()
End Sub
```

As a finishing touch, double click on the Properties icon of the Solution Explorer, and under the Application tab, set the Output Type setting to Windows Application. This will prevent the console window from launching in the background of your WPF application. Figure 27-8 shows the final product of your first WPF program.

Figure 27-8. Your first WPF program, 100% XAML free

At this point in the chapter, WPF might look like nothing more than yet another GUI framework that is providing (more or less) the same services as Windows Forms, VB6, or MFC. If this were in fact the case, you might question the need for yet another UI toolkit. To truly see what makes WPF so unique requires an understanding of the XML-based grammar, XAML.

■ **Source Code** The WpfAppAllCode project is included under the Chapter 27 subdirectory.

Building a WPF Application using Only XAML

A typical WPF application will *not* be composed exclusively of code, as you did in this first example. Rather, your VB 2010 code files will be paired with a related XAML source file, and together they represent the entirety of a given `Window` or `Application`, as well as other class types we have not yet examined such as `UserControl` and `Page`.

This approach is termed the *code file* approach to building a WPF application, and you will make use of this technique extensively throughout the remainder of the books WPF coverage. However, before you do, the next example will illustrate how to build a WPF application using nothing but XAML files. While this "100% XAML" approach is not recommended, it will help you clearly understand how blobs of markup are transformed into a corresponding VB 2010 code base, and ultimately, a .NET assembly.

■ **Note** This next example will make use of a number of XAML techniques we have not yet formally examined, so don't sweat the details. You may wish to simply load the solution files into a text editor and follow along; however, don't use Visual Studio 2010 to do so! Some of the markup in this sample contains markup that cannot be displayed in the Visual Studio XAML designers.

In general, XAML files will contain markup that describes the look and feel of the window , while the related VB 2010 code files contain the implementation logic. For example, the XAML file for a `Window` might describe the overall layout system, the controls within that layout system, and specify the names of various event handlers. The related VB 2010 file would contain the implementation logic of these event handlers and any custom code required by the application.

Extensible Application Markup Language, or XAML, is an XML-based grammar that allows you to define the state (and, to some extent, the functionality) of a tree of .NET objects through markup. While XAML is frequently used when building UIs with WPF, in reality it can be used to describe any tree of *nonabstract* .NET types (including your own custom types defined in a custom .NET assembly), provided each supports a default constructor. As you will see, the markup within a `*.xaml` file is transformed into a full-blown object model.

Because XAML is an XML-based grammar, we gain all the benefits and drawbacks XML affords us. On the plus side, XAML files are very self-describing (as any XML document should be). By and large, each element in an XAML file represents a type name (such as `Button`, `Window`, or `Application`) within a given .NET namespace. Attributes within the scope of an opening element map to properties (`Height`, `Width`, etc.) and events (`Startup`, `Click`, etc.) of the specified type.

Given the fact that XAML is simply a declarative way to define the state of an object, it is possible to define a WPF widget via markup or procedural code. For example, the following XAML

```
<!-- Defining a WPF Button in XAML -->
<Button Name = "btnClickMe" Height = "40" Width = "100" Content = "Click Me" />
```

can be represented programmatically as follows:

```
' Defining the same WPF Button in VB 2010 code.
Dim btnClickMe As New Button()
btnClickMe.Height = 40
btnClickMe.Width = 100
btnClickMe.Content = "Click Me"
```

On the downside, XAML can be verbose and is (like any XML document) case sensitive, thus complex XAML definitions can result in a good deal of markup. Most developers will not need to manually author a complete XAML description of their WPF applications. Rather, the majority of this task will (thankfully) be relegated to development tools such as Visual Studio 2010, Microsoft Expression Blend, or any number of third-party products. Once the tools generate the basic markup, you can go in and fine-tune the XAML definitions by hand if necessary.

Defining MainWindow in XAML

While tools can generate a good deal of XAML on your behalf, it is important for you to understand the basic workings of XAML syntax and how this markup is eventually transformed into a valid .NET assembly. To illustrate XAML in action, in the next example you'll build a WPF application using nothing more than a pair of *.xaml files.

The first Window-derived class (MainWindow) was defined in VB 2010 as a class type that extends the System.Windows.Window base class. This class contains a single Button object that calls a registered event handler when clicked. Defining this same Window type in the grammar of XAML can be achieved as so (assume this markup has been defined in a file named MainWindow.xaml):

```xml
<!-- Here is your Window definition -->
<Window x:Class="SimpleXamlApp.MainWindow"
  xmlns="http://schemas.microsoft.com/winfx/2006/xaml/presentation"
  xmlns:x="http://schemas.microsoft.com/winfx/2006/xaml"
  Title="A Window built using 100% XAML"
  Height="200" Width="300"
  WindowStartupLocation ="CenterScreen">

  <!--This window has a single button as content -->
  <Button x:Name="btnExitApp" Width="133" Height="24"
          Content = "Close Window" Click ="btnExitApp_Clicked"/>

  <!--The implementation of your button's Click event handler! -->
<x:Code>
  <![CDATA[
  Sub btnExitApp_Clicked(ByVal sender As Object, ByVal e As RoutedEventArgs)
    ' Get a handle to the current app and shut it down.
    Me.Close()
  End Sub
  ]]>
</x:Code>
</Window>
```

First of all, notice that the root element `<Window>` makes use of the `Class` attribute, which is used to specify the name of the VB 2010 class that will be generated when this XAML file is processed. Also notice that the `Class` attribute is prefixed with the `x:` tag prefix. If you look within the opening `<Window>` element, you'll see that this XML tag prefix is assigned to the string `"http://schemas.microsoft.com/winfx/2006/xaml"` to build an XML namespace declaration. You will understand the details of these XML namespace definitions a bit later in the chapter, but for now, just be aware that any time you want to make reference to an item defined by the `"http://schemas.microsoft.com/winfx/2006/xaml"` XAML namespace, you must prefix the `x:` token.

Within the scope of the `<Window>` start tag, you have specified values for the `Title`, `Height`, `Width`, and `WindowsStartupLocation` attributes, which are a direct mapping to properties of the same name supported by the `System.Windows.Window` class in the `PresentationFramework.dll` assembly.

Next up, notice that within the scope of the window's definition, you have authored markup to describe the look and feel of a `Button` object that will be used to implicitly set the `Content` property of the window. Beyond setting up the variable name (using the `x:Name` XAML token) and its overall dimensions, you have also handled the `Click` event of the `Button` type by assigning the method to delegate to when the `Click` event occurs.

The final aspect of this XAML file is the `<x:Code>` element, which allows you to author event handlers and other methods of this class directly within an `*.xaml` file. As a safety measure, the code itself is wrapped within a `CDATA` scope to prevent XML parsers from attempting to directly interpret the data (although this is not strictly required for the current example).

It is important to point out that authoring functionality within a `<Code>` element is not recommended. Although this "single-file approach" isolates all the action to one location, inline code does not provide a clear separation of concerns between UI markup and programming logic. In most WPF applications, implementation code will be found within a related VB 2010 file (which you will do eventually).

Defining the Application Object in XAML

Remember that XAML can be used to define in markup any nonabstract .NET class that supports a default constructor. Given this, you could most certainly define your application object in markup as well. Consider the following content within a new file, `MyApp.xaml`:

```
<!-- The Main() method seems to be missing!
     However, the StartupUri attribute is the
     functional equivalent -->
<Application x:Class="SimpleXamlApp.MyApp"
  xmlns="http://schemas.microsoft.com/winfx/2006/xaml/presentation"
  xmlns:x="http://schemas.microsoft.com/winfx/2006/xaml"
  StartupUri="MainWindow.xaml">
</Application>
```

Here, you might agree, the mapping between the `Application`-derived VB 2010 class type and its XAML description is not as clear-cut as was the case for our `MainWindow`'s XAML definition. Specifically, there does not seem to be any trace of a `Main()` method. Given that any .NET executable must have a program entry point, you are correct to assume it is generated at compile time, based in part on the `StartupUrl` property. The value assigned to `StartupUrl` represents which XAML resource to display when the application starts up.

Although the `Main()` method is automatically created at compile time, you are free to use the `<x:Code>` element to capture other VB 2010 code blocks. For example, if you wanted to display a message when your program shuts down, you could handle the `Exit` event and implement it as so:

```
<Application x:Class="SimpleXamlApp.MyApp"
  xmlns="http://schemas.microsoft.com/winfx/2006/xaml/presentation"
  xmlns:x="http://schemas.microsoft.com/winfx/2006/xaml"
  StartupUri="MainWindow.xaml" Exit ="AppExit">
  <x:Code>
    <![CDATA[
Sub AppExit(ByVal Sender As Object, ByVal e As ExitEventArgs)
    MessageBox.Show("App has exited")
End Sub

    ]]>
  </x:Code>
</Application>
```

Processing the XAML Files using msbuild.exe

At this point, you are ready to transform our markup into a valid .NET assembly. However, you cannot directly use the VB 2010 compiler to do so! To date, the VB 2010 compiler does not have a native understanding of XAML markup. However, the msbuild.exe command-line utility does understand how to transform XAML into VB 2010 code and compile this code on the fly when it is informed of the correct *.targets files.

Msbuild.exe is a tool that will compile .NET code based on the instructions contained within an XML based build script. As it turns out, these build script files contain the exact same sort of data that is found in the *.vbproj file generated by Visual Studio! Therefore, it is possible to compile a .NET program at the command-line using msbuild.exe or using Visual Studio 2010 itself.

■ **Note** A full examination of the msbuild.exe utility is beyond the scope of this chapter. If you'd like to learn more, perform a search for the topic "MSBuild" in the .NET Framework 4.0 SDK documentation.

Here is a very simple build script, SimpleXamlApp.vbproj, which contains just enough information to inform msbuild.exe how to transform your XAML files into a related VB 2010 code base:

```
<Project DefaultTargets="Build"
  xmlns="http://schemas.microsoft.com/developer/msbuild/2003">
  <PropertyGroup>
    <RootNamespace>SimpleXamlApp</RootNamespace>
    <AssemblyName>SimpleXamlApp</AssemblyName>
    <OutputType>winexe</OutputType>
  </PropertyGroup>
  <ItemGroup>
    <Reference Include="System" />
    <Reference Include="WindowsBase" />
    <Reference Include="PresentationCore" />
    <Reference Include="PresentationFramework" />
  </ItemGroup>
  <ItemGroup>
```

```
        <ApplicationDefinition Include="MyApp.xaml" />
        <Page Include="MainWindow.xaml" />
    </ItemGroup>
    <Import Project="$(MSBuildBinPath)\Microsoft.VisualBasic.targets" />
    <Import Project="$(MSBuildBinPath)\Microsoft.WinFX.targets" />
</Project>
```

■ **Note** This *.vbproj file cannot be loaded directly into Visual Studio 2010, as it only contains the minimal instructions necessary to build our application at the command line.

The `<PropertyGroup>` element is used to specify some basic aspects of the build, such as the root namespace, the name of the resulting assembly, and the output type (the equivalent of the `/target:winexe` option of vbc.exe).

The first `<ItemGroup>` specifies the set of external assemblies to reference with the current build, which, as you can see, are the core WPF assemblies examined earlier in this chapter.

The second `<ItemGroup>` is much more interesting. Notice that the `<ApplicationDefinition>` element's `Include` attribute is assigned to the *.xaml file that defines our application object. The `<Page>`'s `Include` attribute can be used to list each of the remaining *.xaml files that define the windows (and pages, which are often used when building XAML browser applications) processed by the application object.

However, the "magic" of this build script is the final `<Import>` elements. Here, you are referencing two *.targets files, each of which contains numerous other instructions used during the build process. The `Microsoft.WinFX.targets` file contains the necessary build settings to transform the XAML definitions into equivalent VB 2010 code files, while `Microsoft.VisualBasic` contains data to interact with the VB 2010 compiler itself.

In any case, at this point you can use a Visual Studio 2010 Command Prompt to process your XAML data with `msbuild.exe`. To do so, change to the directory containing your `MainWindow.xaml`, `MyApp.xaml` and `SimpleXamlApp.vbproj` files, and enter the following command:

```
msbuild SimpleXamlApp.vbproj
```

Once the build process has completed, you will find that your working directory now contains a \bin and \obj subdirectory (just like a Visual Studio project). If you were to open the \bin\Debug folder, sure enough, you will find a new .NET assembly named `SimpleXamlApp.exe`. If you open this assembly into `ildasm.exe`, you can see that (somehow) your XAML has been transformed into a valid executable application (see Figure 27-9).

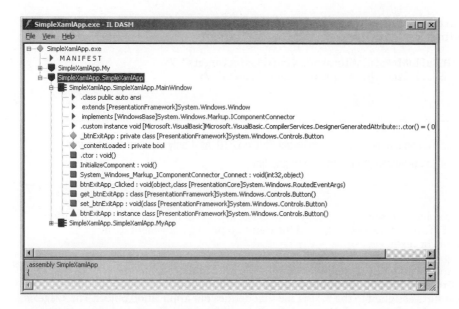

Figure 27-9. Transforming XAML markup into a .NET assembly? Interesting . . .

And if you run your program by double clicking on the executable, you will see your main window launch on the screen.

Transforming Markup into a .NET Assembly

To understand exactly *how* your markup was transformed into a .NET assembly, you need to dig a bit deeper into the `msbuild.exe` process and examine a number of compiler-generated files, including a particular binary resource embedded within the assembly at compile time. The first task is to learn how your `*.xaml` files are transformed into a corresponding VB 2010 code base.

Mapping the Window XAML Data to VB 2010 Code

The `*.targets` files specified in a msbuild script contain numerous instructions to translate XAML elements into VB 2010 code. When `msbuild.exe` processed your `*.vbproj` file, it produced two files with the form `*.g.vb` (where g denotes auto*generated*) that were saved into the `\obj\Debug` directory. Based on the names of your `*.xaml` file names, the VB 2010 files in question are `MainWindow.g.vb` and `MyApp.g.vb`.

If you open the `MainWindow.g.vb` file into a text editor, you will find a class named `MainWindow`, which extends the `Window` base class. The name of this class is a direct result of the `x:Class` attribute in the `<Window>` start tag. This class also contains a member variable of type `System.Windows.Controls.Button`, named `btnExitApp`. In this case, the name of the control is based on the `x:Name` attribute value within the opening `<Button>` declaration. This class also contains the handler for the button's `Click` event, `btnExitApp_Clicked()`. Here is a partial listing of this compiler generated file:

```
Partial Public Class MainWindow
    Inherits System.Windows.Window
    Implements System.Windows.Markup.IComponentConnector

    Friend WithEvents btnExitApp As System.Windows.Controls.Button

    Sub btnExitApp_Clicked(ByVal sender As Object, ByVal e As
      RoutedEventArgs)
        Me.Close()
    End Sub
    ...
End Class
```

This class defines a private member variable of type Boolean (named _contentLoaded), which was not directly accounted for in the XAML markup. This data member is used to determine (and ensure) the content of the window is assigned only once:

```
Public Partial Class MainWindow
    Inherits System.Windows.Window
    Implements System.Windows.Markup.IComponentConnector

    ' This member variable will be explained soon enough.
    Private _contentLoaded As Boolean
    ...
End Class
```

Notice that the compiler generated class also explicitly implements the WPF IComponentConnector interface defined in the System.Windows.Markup namespace. This interface defines a single method called Connect(), which has been implemented to prep each control defined in the markup and rig up the event logic as specified within the original MainWindow.xaml file. Before the method completes, the _contentLoaded member variable is set to True. Here is the crux of the method:

```
Sub System_Windows_Markup_IComponentConnector_Connect(ByVal connectionId As Integer, ByVal
target As Object) Implements System.Windows.Markup.IComponentConnector.Connect

    If (connectionId = 1) Then
        Me.btnExitApp = CType(target, System.Windows.Controls.Button)

    #ExternalSource("..\..\MainWindow.xaml",11)
        AddHandler Me.btnExitApp.Click, New
        System.Windows.RoutedEventHandler(AddressOf Me.btnExitApp_Clicked)

    #End ExternalSource
        Return
    End If
    Me._contentLoaded = True
End Sub
```

Last but not least, the MainWindow class also defines and implements a method named InitializeComponent(). You might expect that this method contains code that sets up the look and feel of each control by setting various properties (Height, Width, Content, etc). However, this is not the case!

How then do the controls take on the correct UI? The logic with `InitializeComponent()` resolves the location of an embedded assembly resource that is named identical to the original `*.xaml` file:

```
Public Sub InitializeComponent()
 Implements System.Windows.Markup.IComponentConnector.InitializeComponent
    If _contentLoaded Then
        Return
    End If
    _contentLoaded = True
    Dim resourceLocater As New
     System.Uri("/SimpleXamlApp;component/mainwindow.xaml",
     System.UriKind.Relative)
     System.Windows.Application.LoadComponent(Me, resourceLocater)
End Sub
```

At this point, the question becomes, *what exactly is this embedded resource?*

The Role of BAML

When `msbuild.exe` processed our `*.vbproj` file, it generated a file taking a `*.baml` file extension. The full name of this file is named based on the initial `MainWindow.xaml` file, therefore you should see a file called `MainWindow.baml` in the \obj\Debug folder. As you might have guessed from the name, Binary Application Markup Language (BAML) is a compact, binary representation of the original XAML data.

This `*.baml` file is embedded as a resource (via a generated `*.g.resources` file) into the compiled assembly. You can verify this for yourself by opening your assembly using `reflector.exe`, as shown in Figure 27-10.

Figure 27-10. Viewing the embedded *.baml resource using Reflector

This BAML resource contains all of the data needed to establish the look and feel of the UI widgets (again, such as the `Height` and `Width` properties). In fact, if you open the `*.baml` file into Visual Studio 2010, you can see traces of the initial XAML attributes (see Figure 27-11).

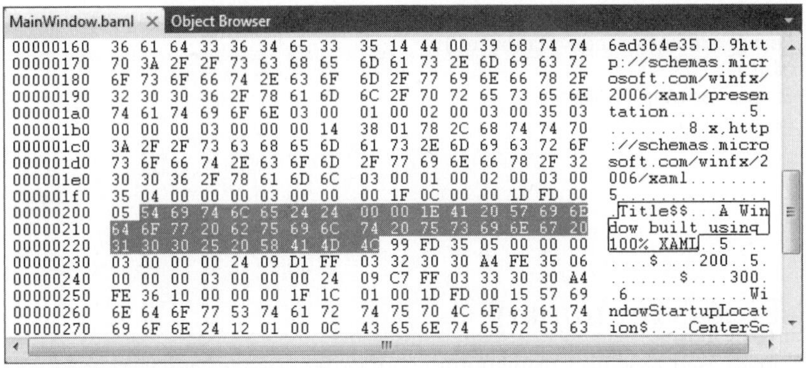

Figure 27-11. BAML is a compact, binary version of the initial XAML markup

The important take-away here is to understand that a WPF application contains within itself a binary representation (the BAML) of the markup. At runtime, this BAML will be plucked out of the resource container and used to make sure all windows and controls are initialized to the correct look and feel.

Also, remember that the name of these binary resources are *identical* to the name of the standalone *.xaml files you authored. However, this does not imply in any way that you must distribute the loose *.xaml files with your compiled WPF program! Unless you build a WPF application that will dynamically load and parse *.xaml files at runtime, you will never need to ship the original markup.

Mapping the Application XAML Data to VB 2010 Code

The final piece of the autogenerated code to examine is the MyApp.g.vb file. Here, you see your Application-derived class with a proper Main() entry point method. The implementation of this method calls InitializeComponent() on the Application-derived type, which, in turn, sets the StartupUri property, allowing each of the objects to establish its correct property settings based on the binary XAML definition.

```
Namespace SimpleXamlApp

    Partial Public Class MyApp
        Inherits System.Windows.Application

        Sub AppExit(ByVal sender As Object, ByVal e As ExitEventArgs)
            MessageBox.Show("App has exited")
        End Sub

        <System.Diagnostics.DebuggerNonUserCodeAttribute()> _
        Public Sub InitializeComponent()
            AddHandler [Exit], New System.Windows.ExitEventHandler(AddressOf
            Me.AppExit)
            Me.StartupUri = New System.Uri("MainWindow.xaml",
            System.UriKind.Relative)
        End Sub
```

```vb
        <System.STAThreadAttribute(), _
        System.Diagnostics.DebuggerNonUserCodeAttribute()>_
        Public Shared Sub Main()
            Dim app As New SimpleXamlApp.MyApp()
            app.InitializeComponent()
            app.Run()
        End Sub
    End Class
End Namespace
```

XAML-to-Assembly Process Summary

So far, you have created a full-blown .NET assembly using nothing but two XAML files and a related build script. As you have seen, `msbuild.exe` leverages auxiliary settings defined within the `*.targets` file to process the XAML files (and generate the `*.baml`) for the build process. While these gory details happen behind the scenes, Figure 27-12 illustrates the overall picture regarding the compile-time processing of `*.xaml` files.

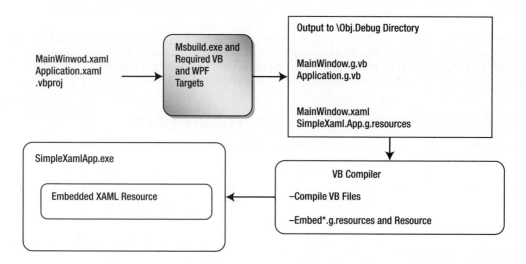

Figure 27-12. The XAML-to-assembly compile-time process

Hopefully you now have a much better idea how XAML data is used to build a .NET application. At this point, you are ready to take a look at the syntax and semantics of XAML itself.

■ **Source Code** The WpfAppAllXaml project can be found under the Chapter 27 subdirectory.

Understanding The Syntax of WPF XAML

Production level WPF applications will typically make use of dedicated tools to generate the necessary XAML. As helpful as these tools are, it is a very good idea to have an understanding of the overall structure of XAML markup.

Introducing Kaxaml

When you are first learning the grammar of XAML, it can be very helpful to use a free tool named *kaxaml*. You can obtain this popular WPF XAML editor/parser from the following web site:

```
http://www.kaxaml.com
```

Kaxaml is helpful in that it has no clue about VB 2010 source code, event handlers or implementation logic and is a much more straightforward way to test XAML snippets than using a full-blown Visual Studio 2010 WPF project template. As well, kaxaml has a number of integrated tools, such as a color chooser, XAML snippet manager, and even a "XAML scrubber" option that will format your XAML based on your settings.

When you first open kaxaml, you will find simple markup for a `<Page>` control:

```
<Page
  xmlns="http://schemas.microsoft.com/winfx/2006/xaml/presentation"
  xmlns:x="http://schemas.microsoft.com/winfx/2006/xaml">
  <Grid>
    <!-- Add your XAML here! -->
  </Grid>
</Page>
```

Like a `Window`, a `Page` contains various layout managers and controls. However, unlike a `Window`, `Page` objects cannot run as standalone entities. Rather, they must be placed inside of a suitable host such as a `NavigationWindow`, `Frame` or a web browser (and in that case, you have just made an XBAP!). The good news is that you can type identical markup within a `<Page>` or `<Window>` scope.

■ **Note** If you change the <Page> and </Page> elements in the kaxaml markup window to <Window> and </Window>, you can press the F5 key to load a new window onto the screen.

As an initial test, enter the following markup into the XAML pane at the bottom of the tool:

```
<Page
  xmlns="http://schemas.microsoft.com/winfx/2006/xaml/presentation"
  xmlns:x="http://schemas.microsoft.com/winfx/2006/xaml">
  <Grid>
    <!-- A button with custom content -->
```

```
    <Button Height="100" Width="100">
      <Ellipse Fill="Green" Height="50" Width="50"/>
    </Button>
  </Grid>
</Page>
```

You should now see your page render at the upper part of the kaxaml editor (Figure 27-13).

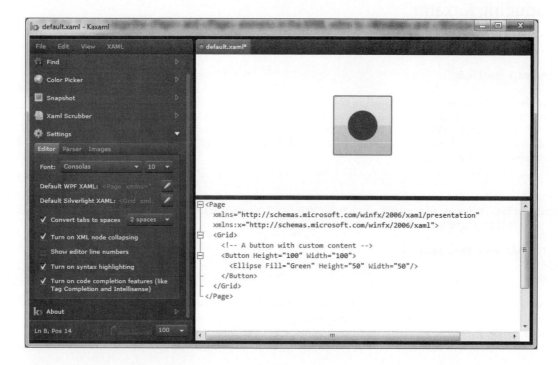

Figure 27-13. Kaxaml is a very helpful (and free) tool used to learn the grammar of XAML

As you work with kaxaml, remember that this tool does not allow you to author any markup that entails code compilation (however, using x:Name is allowed). This includes defining a x:Class attribute (for specifying a code file), entering event handler names in markup, or using any XAML keywords that also entail code compilation (such as FieldModifier or ClassModifier). Any attempt to do so will result in a markup error.

XAML XML Namespaces and XAML "Keywords"

The root element of a WPF XAML document (such as a <Window>, <Page>, <UserControl> or <Application> definition) will almost always make reference to two predefined XML namespaces:

```
<Page
  xmlns="http://schemas.microsoft.com/winfx/2006/xaml/presentation"
  xmlns:x="http://schemas.microsoft.com/winfx/2006/xaml">
  <Grid>

  </Grid>
</Page>
```

The first XML namespace, `http://schemas.microsoft.com/winfx/2006/xaml/presentation`, maps a slew of WPF .NET namespaces for use by the current `*.xaml` file (`System.Windows`, `System.Windows.Controls`, `System.Windows.Data`, `System.Windows.Ink`, `System.Windows.Media`, `System.Windows.Navigation`, etc.).

This one-to-many mapping is actually hard-coded within the WPF assemblies (`WindowsBase.dll`, `PresentationCore.dll`, and `PresentationFramework.dll`) using the assembly-level `<XmlnsDefinition()>` attribute. Here is one such listing, which essentially imports `System.Windows`:

```
<Assembly: XmlnsDefinition("http://schemas.microsoft.com/winfx/2006/xaml/presentation",
                           "System.Windows")>
```

If you load these WPF assemblies into `reflector.exe`, you can view these mappings firsthand. For example, if you select the `PresentationCore.dll` assembly (see Figure 27-14), and press the Space key, you will see numerous instances of the `<XmlnsDefinition>` attribute.

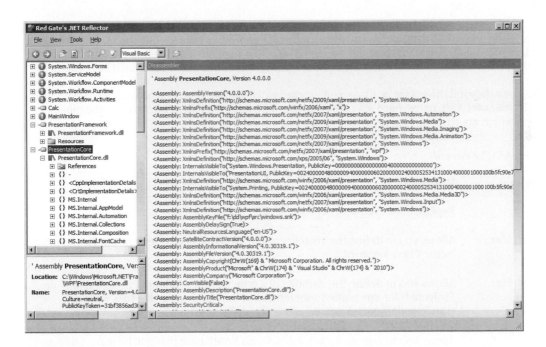

Figure 27-14. *The http://schemas.microsoft.com/winfx/2006/xaml/presentation namespace maps to the core WPF namespaces*

The second XML namespace, http://schemas.microsoft.com/winfx/2006/xaml, is used to include XAML-specific "keywords" (for lack of a better term) as well as the inclusion of the System.Windows.Markup namespace:

```
<Assembly: XmlnsDefinition("http://schemas.microsoft.com/winfx/2006/xaml",
                           "System.Windows.Markup")>
```

One rule of any well-formed XML document (remember, XAML is an XML-based grammar) is that the opening root element designates one XML namespace as the *primary namespace*, which typically is the namespace that contains the most commonly used items. If a root element requires the inclusion of additional secondary namespaces (as seen here), they must be defined using a unique tag prefix (to resolve any possible name clashes). As a convention, the prefix is simply x; however, this can be any unique token you require, such as XamlSpecificStuff:

```
<Page
  xmlns="http://schemas.microsoft.com/winfx/2006/xaml/presentation"
  xmlns:XamlSpecificStuff="http://schemas.microsoft.com/winfx/2006/xaml">
  <Grid>
    <!-- A button with custom content -->
    <Button XamlSpecificStuff:Name="button1" Height="100" Width="100">
      <Ellipse Fill="Green" Height="50" Width="50"/>
    </Button>
  </Grid>
</Page>
```

The obvious downside of defining wordy XML namespace prefixes is you would be required to type XamlSpecificStuff each time your XAML file needs to refer to one of the items defined within this XAML-centric XML namespace . Given that XamlSpecificStuff requires many additional keystrokes, just stick with x.

In any case, beyond the x:Name, x:Class and x:Code keywords, the http://schemas.microsoft.com/winfx/2006/xaml XML namespace also provides access to additional XAML keywords, the most common of which are shown in Table 27-9.

Table 27-9. XAML Keywords

XAML Keyword	Meaning in Life
x:Array	Represents a .NET array type in XAML.
x:ClassModifier	Allows you to define the visibility of the VB 2010 class (Friend or Public) denoted by the Class keyword.
x:FieldModifier	Allows you to define the visibility of a type member (Friend, Public, Private, or Protected) for any named subelement of the root (e.g., a <Button> within a <Window> element). A *named element* is defined using the Name XAML keyword.
x:Key	Allows you to establish a key value for an XAML item that will be placed into a dictionary element.

XAML Keyword	Meaning in Life
x:Name	Allows you to specify the generated VB 2010 name of a given XAML element.
x:Null	Represents a null reference (i.e., Nothing in VB 2010).
x:Static	Allows you to make reference to a Shared member of a type.
x:Type	The XAML equivalent of the VB GetType operator (it will yield a System.Type based on the supplied name).
x:TypeArguments	Allows you to establish an element as a generic type with a specific type parameter (e.g., List(Of Integer) vs. List(Of Boolean)).

In addition to these two necessary XML namespace declarations, it is possible, and sometimes necessary, to define additional tag prefixes in the opening element of a XAML document. You will typically do so whenever you need to describe in XAML a .NET class defined in an external assembly. For example, say you have built a few custom WPF controls and packaged them in a library named MyControls.dll.

Now, if you wish to create a new Window that uses these controls, you can establish a custom XML namespace that maps to your library using the clr-namespace and assembly tokens. Here is some example markup that creates a tag prefix named myCtrls, which can be used to access members in your library:

```
<Window x:Class="WpfApplication1.MainWindow"
  xmlns="http://schemas.microsoft.com/winfx/2006/xaml/presentation"
  xmlns:x="http://schemas.microsoft.com/winfx/2006/xaml"
  xmlns:myCtrls="clr-namespace:MyControls;assembly=MyControls"
  Title="MainWindow" Height="350" Width="525">
  <Grid>
    <myCtrls:MyCustomControl />
  </Grid>
</Window>
```

The clr-namespace token is assigned to the name of the .NET namespace in the assembly, while the assembly token is set to the friendly name of the external *.dll assembly. You can use this syntax for any external .NET library you wish to manipulate in markup.

Controlling Class and Member Variable Declarations

You will see many of these keywords in action where required in the chapters to come; however, by way of a simple example, consider the following XAML <Window> definition that makes use of the ClassModifier and FieldModifier keywords as well as x:Name and x:Class (remember that kaxaml.exe will not allow you to make use of any XAML keyword that entails code compilation, such as x:Code, x:FieldModifier, or x:ClassModifier):

```
<!-- This class will now be declared Friend in the *.g.vb file -->
<Window x:Class="MyWPFApp.MainWindow" x:ClassModifier="Friend"
    xmlns="http://schemas.microsoft.com/winfx/2006/xaml/presentation"
    xmlns:x="http://schemas.microsoft.com/winfx/2006/xaml">

    <!-- This button will be Public in the *.g.vb file -->
    <Button x:Name ="myButton" x:FieldModifier = "Public" Content = "OK"/>
</Window>
```

By default, all VB 2010/XAML type definitions are Public, while members default to Friend. However, based on your XAML definition, the resulting autogenerated file contains a Friend class type with a Public Button type:

```
Partial Friend Class MainWindow
    Inherits System.Windows.Window
    Implements System.Windows.Markup.IComponentConnector

    Public WithEvents myButton As System.Windows.Controls.Button
    ...
End Class
```

XAML Elements, XAML Attributes and Type Converters

Once you have established your root element and any required XML namespaces, your next task is to populate the root with a *child element*. In a real-world WPF application, the child will be a layout manager (such as a Grid or StackPanel) which contains, in turn, any number of additional UI elements that describe the user interface. The next chapter examines these layout managers in detail, so for now just assume that your <Window> type will contain a single Button element.

As you have already seen over the course of this chapter, XAML *elements* map to a class or structure type within a given .NET namespace, while the *attributes* within the opening element tag map to properties or events of the type.

To illustrate, enter the following <Button> definition into kaxaml:

```
<Page
  xmlns="http://schemas.microsoft.com/winfx/2006/xaml/presentation"
  xmlns:x="http://schemas.microsoft.com/winfx/2006/xaml">
  <Grid>
    <!-- Configure the look and feel of a Button -->
    <Button Height="50" Width="100" Content="OK!"
            FontSize="20" Background="Green" Foreground="Yellow"/>
  </Grid>
</Page>
```

Notice that the values assigned to each property have been captured as a simple text value. This may seem like a complete mismatch of data types because if you were to make this Button in VB 2010 code, you would *not* assign string objects to these properties but would make use of specific data types. For example, here is the same button authored in code:

```vb
Public Sub MakeAButton()
    Dim myBtn As New Button()
    myBtn.Height = 50
    myBtn.Width = 100
    myBtn.FontSize = 20
    myBtn.Content = "OK!"
    myBtn.Background = New SolidColorBrush(Colors.Green)
    myBtn.Foreground = New SolidColorBrush(Colors.Yellow)
End Sub
```

As it turns out, WPF ships with a number of *type converter* classes, which will be used to transform simple text values into the correct underlying data type. This process happens transparently (and automatically).

While this is all well and good, there will be many times when you need to assign a much more complex value to a XAML attribute, which cannot be captured as a simple string. For example, let's say you want to build a custom brush to set the `Background` property of the `Button`. If you are building the brush in code, it is quite straightforward:

```vb
Public Sub MakeAButton()
    ...
    ' A fancy brush for the background.
    Dim fancyBrush As New LinearGradientBrush(Colors.DarkGreen,
      Colors.LightGreen, 45)
    myBtn.Background = fancyBrush
    myBtn.Foreground = New SolidColorBrush(Colors.Yellow)
End Sub
```

How, however, can you represent your complex brush as a string? Well, you can't! Thankfully XAML provides a special syntax that can be used whenever you need to assign a property value to a complex object, termed property-element syntax.

Understanding XAML Property-Element Syntax

Property-element syntax allows you to assign complex objects to a property. Here is an XAML description for a Button that makes use of a `LinearGradientBrush` to set its `Background` property:

```xml
<Button Height="50" Width="100" Content="OK!"
        FontSize="20" Foreground="Yellow">
  <Button.Background>
    <LinearGradientBrush>
      <GradientStop Color="DarkGreen" Offset="0"/>
      <GradientStop Color="LightGreen" Offset="1"/>
    </LinearGradientBrush>
  </Button.Background>
</Button>
```

Notice that within the scope of the `<Button>` and `</Button>` tags, you have defined a sub-scope named `<Button.Background>`. Within this scope, you have defined a custom `<LinearGradientBrush>`. (Don't worry about the exact code for the brush; you'll learn about WPF graphics in Chapter 30.)

1209

Generally speaking, any property can be set using property-element syntax, that always breaks down to the following pattern:

```
<DefiningClass>
  <DefiningClass.PropertyOnDefiningClass>
    <!-- Value for Property here! -->
  </DefiningClass.PropertyOnDefiningClass>
</DefiningClass>
```

While any property *could* be set using this syntax, if you can capture a value as a simple string, you will save yourself typing time. For example, here would be a much more verbose way to set the Width of your Button:

```
<Button Height="50" Content="OK!"
        FontSize="20" Foreground="Yellow">
...
  <Button.Width>
    100
  </Button.Width>
</Button>
```

Understanding XAML Attached Properties

In addition to property-element syntax, XAML defines a special syntax used to set a value to an *attached property*. Essentially, an attached property allows a child element to set the value for a property that is actually defined in a parent element. The general template to follow looks like this:

```
<ParentElement>
  <ChildElement ParentElement.PropertyOnParent = "Value">
</ParentElement>
```

The most common use of attached property syntax is to position UI elements within one of the WPF layout managers classes (Grid, DockPanel, etc.). The next chapter dives into these panels in some detail; for now, enter the following in kaxaml:

```
<Page
  xmlns="http://schemas.microsoft.com/winfx/2006/xaml/presentation"
  xmlns:x="http://schemas.microsoft.com/winfx/2006/xaml">
  <Canvas Height="200" Width="200" Background="LightBlue">
    <Ellipse Canvas.Top="40" Canvas.Left="40" Height="20" Width="20" Fill="DarkBlue"/>
  </Canvas>
</Page>
```

Here, you have defined a Canvas layout manager that contains an Ellipse. Notice that the Ellipse is able to inform its parent (the Canvas) where to position its top/left position using attached property syntax.

There are a few items to be aware of regarding attached properties. First and foremost, this is not an all-purpose syntax that can be applied to *any* property of *any* parent. For example, the following XAML cannot be parsed without error:

```
<!-- Error! Set Background property on Canvas via attached property? -->
<Canvas Height="200" Width="200">
  <Ellipse Canvas.Background="LightBlue"
           Canvas.Top="40" Canvas.Left="90"
           Height="20" Width="20" Fill="DarkBlue"/>
</Canvas>
```

In reality, attached properties are a specialized form of a WPF-specific concept termed a *dependency property*. Unless a property was implemented in a very specific manner, you cannot set its value using attached property syntax. You will explore dependency properties in a detail in Chapter 31.

■ **Note** Kaxaml, Visual Studio 2010, and Expression Blend all have IntelliSense, which will show you valid attached properties that can be set by a given element.

Understanding XAML Markup Extensions

As explained, property values are most often represented using a simple string or via property-element syntax. There is, however, another way to specify the value of a XAML attribute, using *markup extensions*. Markup extensions allow a XAML parser to obtain the value for a property from a dedicated, external class. This can be very beneficial, given that some property values require a number of code statements to execute to figure out the value.

Markup extensions provide a way to cleanly extend the grammar of XAML with new functionality. A markup extension is represented internally as a class that derives from `MarkupExtension`. Note that the chances of your ever needing to build a custom markup extension will be slim to none. However, a subset of XAML keywords (such as `x:Array`, `x:Null`, `x:Static`, and `x:Type`) are markup extensions in disguise!

A markup extension is sandwiched between curly brackets, like so:

```
<Element PropertyToSet = "{MarkUpExtension}"/>
```

To see a markup extension in action, author the following into kaxaml:

```
<Page
  xmlns="http://schemas.microsoft.com/winfx/2006/xaml/presentation"
  xmlns:x="http://schemas.microsoft.com/winfx/2006/xaml"
  xmlns:CorLib="clr-namespace:System;assembly=mscorlib">

  <StackPanel>
    <!-- The Static markup extension lets us obtain a value
         from a static member of a class -->
    <Label Content ="{x:Static CorLib:Environment.OSVersion}"/>
    <Label Content ="{x:Static CorLib:Environment.ProcessorCount}"/>
```

```
<!-- The Type markup extension is a XAML verion of
     the VB 2010 GetType()function -->
<Label Content ="{x:Type Button}" />
<Label Content ="{x:Type CorLib:Boolean}" />

<!-- Fill a ListBox with an array of strings! -->
<ListBox Width="200" Height="50">
  <ListBox.ItemsSource>
    <x:Array Type="CorLib:String">
      <CorLib:String>Sun Kil Moon</CorLib:String>
      <CorLib:String>Red House Painters</CorLib:String>
      <CorLib:String>Besnard Lakes</CorLib:String>
    </x:Array>
  </ListBox.ItemsSource>
</ListBox>
</StackPanel>
</Page>
```

First of all, notice that the `<Page>` definition has a new XML namespace declaration, which allows you to gain access to the `System` namespace of `mscorlib.dll`. With this XML namespace established, you first make use of the x:Static markup extension and grab values from `OSVersion` and `ProcessorCount` of the `System.Environment` class.

▪ **Note** As you know, class-level members are called shared members in the vernacular of VB 2010. In terms of XAML, however, shared members are called *static*, and, therefore, we must use the `{x:Static}` token.

The `x:Type` markup extension allows you to gain access to the metadata description of the specified item. Here, you are simply assigning the fully qualified names of the WPF Button and `System.Boolean` types.

The most interesting part of this markup is the `ListBox`. Here, you are setting the `ItemsSource` property to an array of strings declared entirely in markup! Notice how the `x:Array` markup extension allows you to specify a set of sub-items within its scope:

```
<x:Array Type="CorLib:String">
  <CorLib:String>Sun Kil Moon</CorLib:String>
  <CorLib:String>Red House Painters</CorLib:String>
  <CorLib:String>Besnard Lakes</CorLib:String>
</x:Array>
```

▪ **Note** The previous XAML example is only used to illustrate a markup extension in action. As you will see in Chapter 28, there are much easier ways to populate `ListBox` controls!

Figure 27-15 shows the mark up of this `<Page>` in kaxaml.

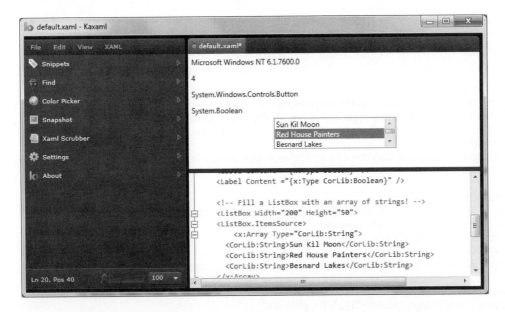

Figure 27-15. Markup extensions allow you to set values via the functionality of a dedicated class

So! At this point, you have seen numerous examples that showcase each of the core aspects of XAML syntax. As you might agree, XAML is very interesting in that it allows you to describe a tree of .NET objects in a declarative manner. While this is extremely helpful when configuring graphical user interfaces, do remember that XAML can describe *any* type from *any* assembly provided it is a nonabstract type containing a default constructor.

Building a WPF Application using Code-Behind Files

The first two examples of this chapter illustrated the extreme ends of building a WPF application, using all code or using all XAML. The recommended way to build any WPF application, however, is to use the *code file* approach. Under this model, the XAML files of your project contain nothing but the markup that describes the general state of your classes, while the code file contains the implementation details.

Adding a Code File for the MainWindow Class

To illustrate, you will update the WpfAppAllXaml example to use code files. If you are following along, copy this entire folder and give it the name WpfAppCodeFiles. Now, create a new VB 2010 code file in this folder named `MainWindow.xaml.vb` (by convention, the name of a VB 2010 code-behind file takes the form `*.xaml.vb`). Add the following code to this new file:

```
' MainWindow.xaml.vb
Class MainWindow

    Private Sub btnExitApp_Clicked(ByVal sender As System.Object, ByVal e As
System.Windows.RoutedEventArgs)
        Me.Close()
    End Sub
End Class
```

Here, you have defined a partial class to contain the event handling logic that will be merged with the partial class definition of the same type in the `*.g.vb` file. Given that `InitializeComponent()` is defined within the `MainWindow.g.vb` file, your window's constructor makes a call in order to load and process the embedded BAML resource.

The `MainWindow.xaml` file will also need to be updated; this simply involves gutting all traces of the previous VB 2010 code:

```
<Window x:Class="MainWindow"
  xmlns="http://schemas.microsoft.com/winfx/2006/xaml/presentation"
  xmlns:x="http://schemas.microsoft.com/winfx/2006/xaml"
  Title="A Window built using Code Files!"
  Height="200" Width="300"
  WindowStartupLocation ="CenterScreen">

  <!--The event handler is now in your code file -->
  <Button x:Name="btnExitApp" Width="133" Height="24"
          Content = "Close Window" Click ="btnExitApp_Clicked"/>
</Window>
```

Adding a Code File for the MyApp Class

If desired, you could also build a code-behind file for your `Application`-derived type. Because most of the action takes place in the `MyApp.g.vb` file, the code within `MyApp.xaml.vb` is little more than the following:

```
' MyApp.xaml.vb
Imports System.Windows
Imports System.Windows.Controls

Namespace SimpleXamlApp

    Partial Public Class Application

      Private Sub AppExit(ByVal sender As Object, ByVal e As ExitEventArgs)
          MessageBox.Show("App has exited")
      End Sub

    End Class

End Namespace
```

The `MyApp.xaml` file now looks like so:

```
<Application x:Class="SimpleXamlApp.MyApp"
  xmlns="http://schemas.microsoft.com/winfx/2006/xaml/presentation"
  xmlns:x="http://schemas.microsoft.com/winfx/2006/xaml"
  StartupUri="MainWindow.xaml"
  Exit ="AppExit">
</Application>
```

Processing the Code Files with msbuild.exe

Before you recompile your files using `msbuild.exe`, you need to update our `*.vbproj` file to account for the new VB 2010 files to include in the compilation process, via the `<Compile>` elements (shown in bold):

```
<Project DefaultTargets="Build" xmlns=
  "http://schemas.microsoft.com/developer/msbuild/2003">

  <PropertyGroup>
    <RootNamespace>SimpleXamlApp</RootNamespace>
    <AssemblyName>SimpleXamlApp</AssemblyName>
    <OutputType>winexe</OutputType>
  </PropertyGroup>
  <ItemGroup>
    <Reference Include="System" />
    <Reference Include="WindowsBase" />
    <Reference Include="PresentationCore" />
    <Reference Include="PresentationFramework" />
  </ItemGroup>
  <ItemGroup>
    <ApplicationDefinition Include="MyApp.xaml" />
    <Compile Include = "MainWindow.xaml.vb" />
    <Compile Include = "MyApp.xaml.vb" />
    <Page Include="MainWindow.xaml" />
  </ItemGroup>
  <Import Project="$(MSBuildBinPath)\Microsoft.VisualBasic.targets" />
  <Import Project="$(MSBuildBinPath)\Microsoft.WinFX.targets" />
</Project>
```

Once you pass our build script into `msbuild.exe`, you find once again the same executable assembly as the WpfAppAllXaml application. However, as far as development is concerned, you now have a clean partition of presentation (XAML) from programming logic (VB 2010).

Given that this is the preferred method for WPF development, you'll be happy to know that WPF applications created using Visual Studio 2010 always make use of the code-behind model just presented.

■ **Source Code** The WpfAppCodeFiles project can be found under the Chapter 27 subdirectory.

Building WPF Applications Using Visual Studio 2010

Over the course of this chapter you created examples using no-frills text editors, the command-line compiler, and `kaxaml.exe`. The reason for doing so, of course, was to focus on the core syntax of WPF applications without getting distracted by the bells and whistles of a graphical designer. Now that you have seen how to build WPF applications in the raw, let's examine how Visual Studio 2010 can simplify the construction of WPF applications.

■ **Note** While Visual Studio 2010 does have some support for authoring complex XAML using the integrated designers, Expression Blend is a far better alternative to build the UI of your WPF applications. You will begin to examine Expression Blend in Chapter 28.

The WPF Project Templates

The New Project dialog box of Visual Studio 2010 defines a set of WPF project workspaces, all of which are contained under the Window node of the Visual Basic root. Here, you can choose from a WPF Application, WPF User Control Library, WPF Custom Control Library, and WPF Browser Application (i.e., XBAP). To begin, create a new WPF Application named MyXamlPad (Figure 27-16).

Figure 27-16. The WPF project templates of Visual Studio 2010

Beyond setting references to each of the WPF assemblies (`PresentationCore.dll`, `PresentationFramework.dll`, and `WindowsBase.dll`), you will also be provided with initial `Window` and `Application` derived classes, making use of code files and a related XAML file. Consider Figure 27-17, which shows the Solution Explorer for this new WPF project.

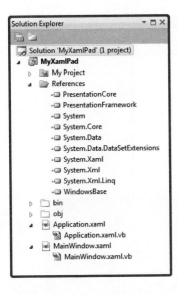

Figure 27-17. The initial files of a WPF Application project

Exploring the WPF Designer Tools

Visual Studio 2010 provides a Toolbox (which you can open via the View menu) that contains numerous WPF controls (Figure 27-18).

Figure 27-18. The Toolbox contains the WPF controls that can be placed on the designer surface

Using a standard mouse drag and drop, you can place any of these controls onto the Window's designer surface. As you do, the underlying XAML will be authored on your behalf. However, you can also manually type in your markup using the integrated XAML editor. As you can see in Figure 27-19, you do get IntelliSense support, which can help simplify the authoring of the markup.

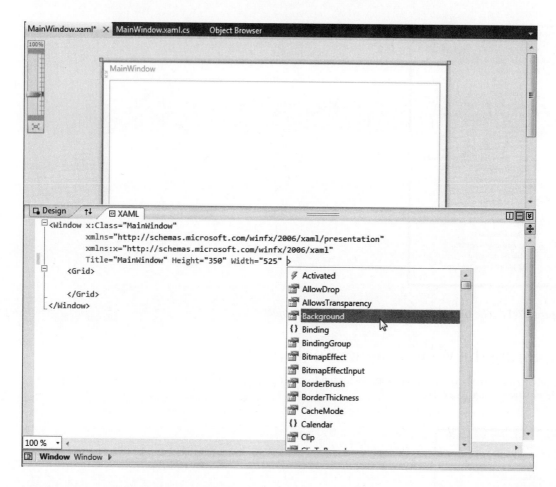

Figure 27-19. The WPF Window designer

■ **Note** You can reposition the display panes of the visual designer using the buttons embedded within the splitter window, such as the Swap Panes button (indicated by the up/down arrows), the Horizontal and Vertical split buttons, and so on. Take a moment to find a configuration you are comfortable with.

Once you have placed controls onto your designer (which you will do in a moment), you can then make use of the Properties window to set property values for the selected control, as well as rig up event handlers for the selected control. By way of a simple test, drag a button control anywhere on your visual designer. Once you do, you will see that Visual Studio authored XAML similar to the following:

```
<Button Content="Button" Height="23" HorizontalAlignment="Left"
        Margin="12,12,0,0" Name="button1" VerticalAlignment="Top" Width="75" />
```

Now, use the Properties window to change the Background color of the Button using the integrated brush editor (Figure 27-20).

___

■ **Note** The Brush Editor of Expression Blend is very similar to the Visual Studio brush editor and will be examined in detail in Chapter 29.

___

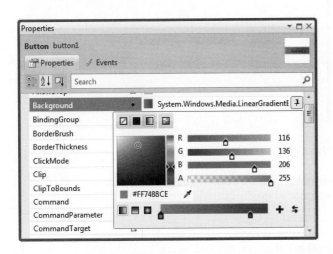

Figure 27-20. *The Properties window can be used to configure the UI of a WPF control*

Once you have finished tinkering with the brush editor, check out the generated markup. It might look something like this:

```
<Button Content="Button" Height="23" HorizontalAlignment="Left" Margin="12,12,0,0"
        Name="button1" VerticalAlignment="Top" Width="75">
  <Button.Background>
    <LinearGradientBrush EndPoint="1,0.5" StartPoint="0,0.5">
      <GradientStop Color="#FF7488CE" Offset="0" />
      <GradientStop Color="#FFC11E1E" Offset="0.837" />
    </LinearGradientBrush>
  </Button.Background>
</Button>
```

If you wish to handle events for a given control, you can also make use of the Properties window, but this time you need to click on the Events tab. Ensure that the button is selected on your designer, click on the Events tab, and locate the Click event. Once you do, double click directly on the Click event entry. This will cause Visual Studio 2010 to automatically build an event handler that takes the form:

```
NameOfControl_NameOfEvent
```

Since you did not rename your button, the Properties window shows it generated an event handler named **button1_Click** (see Figure 27-21).

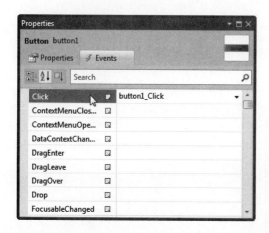

Figure 27-21. *Handling events using the visual designer*

As well, Visual Studio 2010 generated the corresponding VB 2010 code in your window's code file. Here, you can add any sort of code that must execute when the button is clicked:

```
Class MainWindow
    Private Sub button1_Click(ByVal sender As System.Object,
      ByVal e As System.Windows.RoutedEventArgs) Handles button1.Click

    End Sub
End Class
```

You can also handle events directly in the XAML editor. By way of an example, place your mouse within the <Button> element and type in the MouseEnter event, followed by the equals sign. Once you do, you will see Visual Studio displays any compatible handlers in your code file, as well as the <New Event Handler> option. If you double click <New Event Handler>, the IDE will generate a fitting handler in your VB 2010 code file.

Now that you have seen the basic tools used within Visual Studio 2010 to create WPF applications, let's leverage this IDE to build an example program that illustrates the process of parsing XAML at runtime.

Before you start, completely delete the markup describing the **Button** you just created and also delete the VB 2010 event handler code.

Designing the GUI of our Window

The WPF API supports the ability to load, parse, and save XAML descriptions programmatically. Doing so can be quite useful in a variety of situations. For example, assume you have five different XAML files that describe the look and feel of a Window type. As long as the names of each control (and any necessary event handlers) are identical within each file, it would be possible to dynamically apply "skins" to the window (perhaps based on a startup argument passed into the application).

Interacting with XAML at runtime revolves around the XamlReader and XamlWriter types, both of which are defined within the System.Windows.Markup namespace. To illustrate how to programmatically hydrate a Window object from an external *.xaml file, you will build an application that mimics the basic functionality of the kaxaml.

While your application will certainly not be as feature-rich as kaxaml.exe, it will provide the ability to enter XAML markup, view the results, and save the XAML to an external file. To begin, update the initial XAML definition of your <Window> as:

■ **Note** The next chapter will dive into the details of working with controls and panels, so don't fret over the details of the control declarations.

```
<Window x:Class="MainWindow"
  xmlns="http://schemas.microsoft.com/winfx/2006/xaml/presentation"
  xmlns:x="http://schemas.microsoft.com/winfx/2006/xaml"
  Title="My Custom XAML Editor"
  Height="338" Width="1041"
  Loaded="Window_Loaded" Closed="Window_Closed"
  WindowStartupLocation="CenterScreen">

  <!-- You will use a DockPanel, not a Grid -->
  <DockPanel LastChildFill="True" >

    <!-- This button will launch a window with defined XAML -->
    <Button DockPanel.Dock="Top" Name = "btnViewXaml" Width="100" Height="40"
            Content ="View Xaml" Click="btnViewXaml_Click" />

    <!-- This will be the area to type within -->
    <TextBox AcceptsReturn ="True" Name ="txtXamlData"
            FontSize ="14" Background="Black" Foreground="Yellow"
            BorderBrush ="Blue" VerticalScrollBarVisibility="Auto"
            AcceptsTab="True"/>
  </DockPanel>
</Window>
```

First of all, notice that you have replaced the initial <Grid> with a <DockPanel> type that contains a Button (named btnViewXaml) and a TextBox (named txtXamlData), and that the Click event of the Button type has been handled. Also notice that the Loaded and Closed events of the Window itself have been handled within the opening <Window> element. If you have used the designer to handle your events, you should find the following code in your MainWindow.xaml.vb file:

```
Partial Public Class MainWindow
    Private Sub btnViewXaml_Click(ByVal sender As Object, ByVal e As
        RoutedEventArgs)
    End Sub

    Private Sub Window_Closed(ByVal sender As Object, ByVal e As EventArgs)
    End Sub

    Private Sub Window_Loaded(ByVal sender As Object, ByVal e As RoutedEventArgs)
    End Sub
End Class
```

Before continuing, be sure to import the following namespaces into your `MainWindow.xaml.vb` fMainWindow.xaml.vb file:

```
Imports System.IO
Imports System.Windows.Markup
```

Implementing the Loaded Event

The Loaded event of your main window is in charge of determining if there is currently a file named `YourXaml.xaml` in the folder containing the application. If this file does exist, you will read in the data and place it into the TextBox on the main window. If not, you will fill the TextBox with an initial default XAML description of an empty window (this description is the exact same markup as an initial window definition, except that you are using a `<StackPanel>` rather than a `<Grid>`).

■ **Note** The string you are building to represent the key XML namespaces is a bit cumbersome to type, given the escape characters required for the embedded quotations, so type carefully.

```
Private Sub Window_Loaded(ByVal sender As System.Object, ByVal e As
System.Windows.RoutedEventArgs)
    ' When the main window of the app loads,
    ' place some basic XAML text into the text block.
    If (File.Exists(System.Environment.CurrentDirectory + "\YourXaml.xaml")) Then
        txtXamlData.Text = File.ReadAllText("YourXaml.xaml")
    Else
        txtXamlData.Text = "<Window
xmlns=""http://schemas.microsoft.com/winfx/2006/xaml/presentation""" & vbLf &
" xmlns:x=""http://schemas.microsoft.com/winfx/2006/xaml""" & vbLf &
" Height =""400"" Width =""500""
```

```
WindowStartupLocation=""CenterScreen"">" & vbLf &
                     "<StackPanel>" & vbLf &
                     "</StackPanel>" & vbLf &
                     "</Window>"
    End If
End Sub
```

Using this approach, your application will be able to load the XAML entered in a previous session or supply a default block of markup if necessary. At this point, you should be able to run your program and find the display shown in Figure 27-22 within the **TextBox** type.

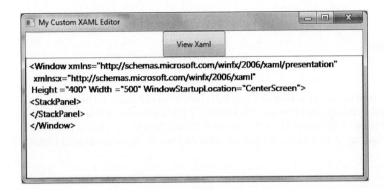

Figure 27-22. The first run of MyXamlPad.exe

Implementing the Button's Click Event

When you click the **Button**, you will first save the current data in the **TextBox** into the **YourXaml.xaml** file. At this point, you will read in the persisted data via **File.Open()** to obtain a **Stream**-derived type. This is necessary, as the **XamlReader.Load()** method requires a **Stream**-derived type (rather than a simple **System.String**) to represent the XAML to be parsed.

Once you have loaded the XAML description of the **<Window>** you wish to construct, create an instance of **System.Windows.Window** based on the in-memory XAML and display the **Window** as a modal dialog:

```
Private Sub btnViewXaml_Click(ByVal sender As System.Object, ByVal e As
 System.Windows.RoutedEventArgs)
    ' Write out the data in the text block to a local *.xaml file.
    File.WriteAllText("YourXaml.xaml", txtXamlData.Text)

    ' This is the window that will be dynamically XAML-ed.
    Dim myWindow As Window = Nothing
```

```
    ' Open local *.xaml file.
    Try
        Using sr As Stream = File.Open("YourXaml.xaml", FileMode.Open)

            ' Connect the XAML to the Window object.
            myWindow = DirectCast(XamlReader.Load(sr), Window)

            'Show window as a dialog and clean up
            myWindow.ShowDialog()
            myWindow.Close()
            myWindow = Nothing
        End Using

    Catch ex As Exception
        MessageBox.Show(ex.Message)
    End Try
End Sub
```

Note that you are wrapping much of our logic within a **Try/Catch** block. In this way, if the **YourXaml.xaml** file contains ill-formed markup, you can see the error of your ways within the resulting message box. For example, run your program, and purposely misspell **<StackPanel>** by adding an extra letter P in the opening element or whatnot. If you click the button, you will see an error similar to Figure 27-23.

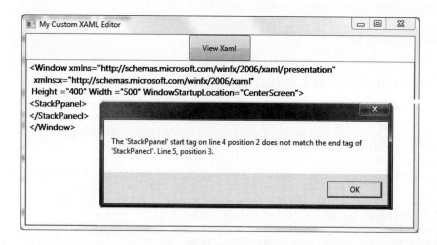

Figure 27-23. Catching markup errors

Implementing the Closed Event

Finally, the **Closed** event of your **Window** type will ensure that the latest and greatest data in the **TextBox** is persisted to the **YourXaml.xaml** file:

```
Private Sub Window_Closed(ByVal sender As System.Object, ByVal e As System.EventArgs)
    ' Write out the data in the text block to a local *.xaml file.
    File.WriteAllText("YourXaml.xaml", txtXamlData.Text)
End Sub
```

Testing the Application

Now fire up your program and enter some XAML into your text area. Do be aware that (like kaxaml.exe) this program does not allow you to specify any code generation–centric XAML attributes (such as Class or any event handlers). As a test, enter the following XAML within your <Window> scope:

```
<StackPanel>
    <Rectangle Fill = "Green" Height = "40" Width = "200" />
    <Button Content = "OK!" Height = "40" Width = "100" />
    <Label Content ="{x:Type Label}" />
</StackPanel>
```

Once you click the button, you will see a window appear that renders your XAML definitions (or possibly you'll see a parsing error in the message box—watch your typing!). Figure 27-24 shows possible output.

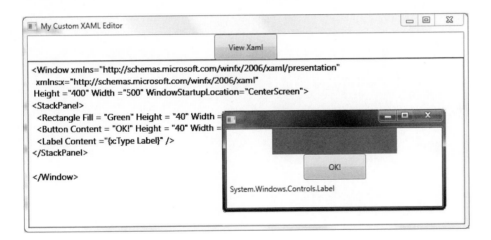

Figure 27-24. MyXamlPad.exe in action

Great! I am sure you can think of many possible enhancements to this application, but to do so you need to be aware of how to work with WPF controls and the panels that contain them. You will do so starting in the next chapter.

■ **Source Code** The MyXamlPad project can be found under the Chapter 27 subdirectory.

Summary

Windows Presentation Foundation (WPF) is a user interface toolkit introduced since the release of .NET 3.0. The major goal of WPF is to integrate and unify a number of previously unrelated desktop technologies (2D graphics, 3D graphics, window and control development, etc.) into a single unified programming model. Beyond this point, WPF programs typically make use of Extendable Application Markup Language (XAML), which allows you to declare the look and feel of your WPF elements via markup.

Recall that XAML allows you to describe trees of .NET objects using a declarative syntax. During this chapter's investigation of XAML, you were exposed to several new bits of syntax including property-element syntax and attached properties, as well as the role of type converters and XAML markup extensions.

While XAML is a key aspect for any production level WPF application, your first example of this chapter illustrated how you can build a WPF program using nothing but VB 2010 code. Next, you discovered how you could build a WPF program using nothing but XAML (this is not recommended; however, it was a useful learning exercise!). Finally, you learned about the use of "code files" which allow you to partition look-and-feel from functionality.

The final example of this chapter gave you a chance to build a WPF application that allowed you to programmatically interact with XAML definitions using the `XamlReader` and `XamlWriter` classes. Along the way, you took a tour of the WPF designers of Visual Studio 2010.

■ ■ ■

## CHAPTER 28

Programming with WPF Controls

The previous chapter provided a foundation for the WPF programming model, including an examination of the Window and Application classes, the grammar of XAML, and the use of code files. Chapter 27 also introduced you to the process of building WPF applications using the designers of Visual Studio 2010. In this chapter you will dig into the construction of more sophisticated graphical user interfaces using several new controls and layout managers.

This chapter will also examine some related WPF control topics such as the data binding programming model and the use of control commands. You will also learn how to use the Ink and Documents APIs, which allow you to capture stylus (or mouse) input and build rich text documents using the XML Paper Specification, respectively.

Finally, this chapter will show you how to use Expression Blend to build the UI of a WPF application. Using Blend in a WPF project is technically optional, but this IDE can greatly simplify your development because it can generate the necessary XAML using a number of integrated designers, editors, and wizards.

A Survey of the Core WPF Controls

Unless you are new to the concept of building graphical user interfaces (which is fine), the general role of the WPF controls should not raise too many issues. Regardless of which GUI toolkit you might have used in the past (e.g., Windows Forms, VB 6.0, MFC, Java AWT/Swing, Mac OS X [Cocoa], or GTK+/GTK#), the core WPF controls listed in Table 28-1 are likely to look familiar.

Table 28-1. The Core WPF Controls

WPF Control Category	Example Members	Meaning in Life
Core user input controls	Button, RadioButton, ComboBox, CheckBox, Calendar, DatePicker, Expander, DataGrid, ListBox, ListView, Slider, ToggleButton, TreeView, ContextMenu, ScrollBar, Slider, TabControl, TextBlock, TextBox, RepeatButton, RichTextBox, Label	WPF provides an entire family of controls you can use to build the crux of a user interface.
Window and control adornments	Menu, ToolBar, StatusBar, ToolTip, ProgressBar	You use these UI elements to decorate the frame of a Window object with input devices (such as the Menu) and user informational elements (e.g., StatusBar and ToolTip).
Media controls	Image, MediaElement, SoundPlayerAction	These controls provide support for audio/video playback and image display.
Layout controls	Border, Canvas, DockPanel, Grid, GridView, GridSplitter, GroupBox, Panel, TabControl, StackPanel, Viewbox, WrapPanel	WPF provides numerous controls that allow you to group and organize other controls for the purpose of layout management.

A majority of these standard WPF controls have been packaged up in the System.Windows.Controls namespace of the PresentationFramework.dll assembly. When you build a WPF application using Visual Studio 2010, you will find most of these common controls contained in the Toolbox, provided you have a WPF designer open as the active window (see Figure 28-1).

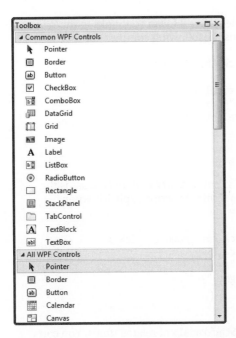

Figure 28-1. The Visual Studio 2010 Toolbox exposes the intrinsic WPF controls

Much as you can with a Windows Forms application, you can drag these controls onto the WPF window designer and configure them using the Properties window (which you learned about in the previous chapter). While Visual Studio 2010 will generate a good amount of the XAML on your behalf, it is not uncommon to edit the markup yourself manually. Let's review the basics.

Working with WPF Controls Using Visual Studio 2010

You might recall from Chapter 27 that when you place a WPF control onto the Visual Studio 2010 designer, you want to set the x:Name property through the Properties window because this allows you to access the object in your related VB 2010 code file. You might also recall that you can use the Events tab of the Properties window to generate event handlers for a selected control. Thus, you could use Visual Studio to generate the following markup for a simple Button control:

```
<Button x:Name="btnShowDlg" Content="Click Me!" Height="23" Width="140"
        Click="btnShowDlg_Click" />
```

Here, you set the Content property of the Button to a simple string. However, thanks to the WPF control content model, you could fashion a Button that contains the following complex content:

```
<Button x:Name="btnShowDlg" Height="121" Width="156" Click="btnShowDlg_Click">
  <Button.Content>
    <StackPanel Height="95" Width="128" Orientation="Vertical">
      <Ellipse Fill="Red" Width="52" Height="45" Margin="5"/>
      <Label Width="59" FontSize="20" Content="Click!" Height="36" />
    </StackPanel>
  </Button.Content>
</Button>
```

You might also recall that the immediate child element of a ContentControl-derived class is the implied content; therefore, you do not need to define a <Button.Context> scope explicitly when specifying complex content. You could simply author the following:

```
<Button x:Name="btnShowDlg" Height="121" Width="156" Click="btnShowDlg_Click">
  <StackPanel Height="95" Width="128" Orientation="Vertical">
    <Ellipse Fill="Red" Width="52" Height="45" Margin="5"/>
    <Label Width="59" FontSize="20" Content="Click!" Height="36" />
  </StackPanel>
</Button>
```

In either case, you set the button's Content property to a <StackPanel> of related items. You can author this sort of complex content using the Visual Studio 2010 designer, as well. Once you define the layout manager, you can select it on the design to serve as a drop target for the internal controls. At this point, you can edit each using the Properties window.

You should also be aware that the Document Outline window of Visual Studio 2010 (which you can open using the View ➤ Other Windows menu) is useful when designing a WPF control that has complex content. Notice in Figure 28-2 how the logical tree of XAML is displayed for the Window you are building. If you click any of these nodes, you can get a preview of the selected item.

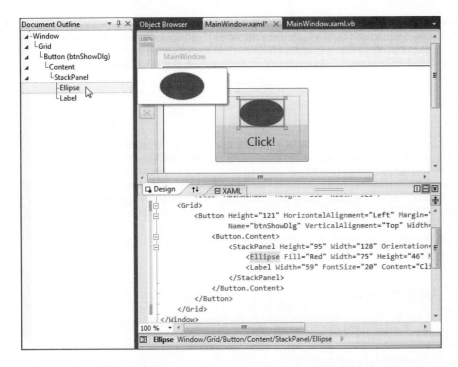

Figure 28-2. *The Visual Studio 2010 Document Outline window can help you navigate complex content*

In any case, once you define the initial markup, you are free to open the related VB 2010 code file to add your implementation logic:

```vb
Private Sub btnShowDlg_Click(ByVal sender As Object, ByVal e As RoutedEventArgs)
        Handles btn ShowDlg.Click
        MessageBox.Show("You clicked the button!")
End Sub
```

The first part of this chapter uses Visual Studio 2010 to build the UIs of the example projects. The chapter will point out additional features as necessary, but make sure you take some time to explore the options of the Properties window and designer functionality. Later in this chapter, you will use Expression Blend to build your UIs. As you will see, Blend has many integrated tools that generate a majority of the required XAML automatically.

The WPF Ink Controls

In addition to the common WPF controls listed in Table 28-1, WPF defines additional controls for working with the digital Ink API. This aspect of WPF development is useful during tablet PC development because it lets you capture input from the stylus. However, this is not to say a standard desktop application cannot leverage the Ink API because the same controls can capture input using the mouse.

The `System.Windows.Ink` namespace of `PresentationCore.dll` contains various Ink API support types (e.g., `Stroke` and `StrokeCollection`); however, a majority of the Ink API controls (e.g., `InkCanvas` and `InkPresenter`) are packaged up with the common WPF controls under the `System.Windows.Controls` namespace in the `PresentationFramework.dll` assembly. You'll work with the Ink API later in this chapter.

The WPF Document Controls

WPF also provides controls for advanced document processing, allowing you to build applications that incorporate Adobe PDF-style functionality. Using the types within the `System.Windows.Documents` namespace (also in the `PresentationFramework.dll` assembly), you can create print-ready documents that support zooming, searching, user annotations (sticky notes), and other rich text services.

Under the covers, however, the document controls do not use Adobe PDF APIs; rather, they use the XML Paper Specification (XPS) API. To the end user, there will really appear to be no difference because PDF documents and XPS documents have an almost identical look-and-feel. In fact, you can find many free utilities that allow you to convert between the two file formats on the fly. You'll work with some aspects of the document controls in an upcoming example.

WPF Common Dialog Boxes

WPF also provides you with a few common dialog boxes such as `OpenFileDialog` and `SaveFileDialog`. These dialog boxes are defined within the `Microsoft.Win32` namespace of the `PresentationFramework.dll` assembly. Working with either of these dialog boxes is a matter of creating an object and invoking the `ShowDialog()` method:

```
Imports Microsoft.Win32

    Class MainWindow
      Private Sub btnShowDlg_Click(ByVal sender As Object,ByVal e As RoutedEventArgs)↵
              Handles btnShowDlg.Click
              ' Show a file save dialog.
              Dim saveDlg As New SaveFileDialog()
              saveDlg.ShowDialog()
      End Sub
    End Class
End Namespace
```

As you would hope, these classes support various members that allow you to establish file filters and directory paths, and gain access to user-selected files. You will put these file dialogs to use in later examples; you will also learn how to build custom dialog boxes to gather user input.

The Details Are in the Documentation

Despite what you might be thinking, the intent of this chapter is *not* to walk through each and every member of each and every WPF control. Rather, you will receive an overview of the various controls with an emphasis on the underlying programming model and key services common to most WPF controls. You will also learn how to build UIs with Expression Blend and Visual Studio 2010.

To round out your understanding of the particular functionality of a given control, be sure to consult the .NET Framework 4.0 SDK documentation—specifically, the Control Library section of the help system, which you can find under Windows Presentation Foundation ➤ Controls (see Figure 28-3).

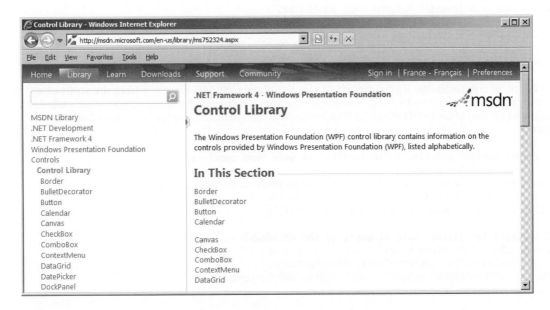

Figure 28-3. The full details of each WPF control are just a keypress away (F1)

Here you will find full details of each control, various code samples (in XAML, as well as VB 2010), and information regarding a control's inheritance chain, implemented interfaces, and applied attributes.

Controlling Content Layout Using Panels

A WPF application invariably contains a good number of UI elements (e.g., user input controls, graphical content, menu systems, and status bars) that need to be well organized within various windows. Once you place the UI elements, you need to make sure they behave as intended when the end user resizes the window or possibly a portion of the window (as in the case of a splitter window). To ensure your WPF controls retain their position within the hosting window, you can take advantage of a good number of *panel* types.

When you declare a control directly inside a window that doesn't use panels, the control is positioned dead-center in the container. Consider the following simple window declaration, which contains a single Button control. Regardless of how you resize the window, the UI widget is always equidistant from all four sides of the client area:

```
<!-- This button is in the center of the window at all times-->
<Window x:Class="MainWindow"
  xmlns="http://schemas.microsoft.com/winfx/2006/xaml/presentation"
  xmlns:x="http://schemas.microsoft.com/winfx/2006/xaml"
  Title="Fun with Panels!" Height="285" Width="325">

  <Button x:Name="btnOK" Height = "100"
          Width="80" Content="OK"/>
</Window>
```

You might also recall that if you attempt to place multiple elements directly within the scope of a <Window>, you will receive markup and compile-time errors. The reason for these errors is that a window (or any descendant of ContentControl for that matter) can assign only a single object to its Content property:

```
<!-- Error! Content property is implicitly set more than once!-->
<Window x:Class=" MainWindow"
  xmlns="http://schemas.microsoft.com/winfx/2006/xaml/presentation"
  xmlns:x="http://schemas.microsoft.com/winfx/2006/xaml"
  Title="Fun with Panels!" Height="285" Width="325">

  <!-- Error! Two direct child elements of the <Window>! -->
  <Label x:Name="lblInstructions" Width="328" Height="27"
          FontSize="15" Content="Enter Information"/>
  <Button x:Name="btnOK" Height = "100" Width="80" Content="OK"/>
</Window>
```

Obviously a window that can only contain a single control is of little use. When a window needs to contain multiple elements, those elements must be arranged within any number of panels. The panel will contain all of the UI elements that represent the window, after which the panel itself is used as the single object assigned to the Content property.

The System.Windows.Controls namespace provides numerous panels, each of which controls how sub-elements are maintained. You can use panels to establish how the controls behave if the end user resizes the window, if the controls remain exactly where they were placed at design time, if the controls reflow horizontally from left-to-right or vertically from top-to-bottom, and so forth.

You can also intermix panel controls within other panels (e.g., a DockPanel that contains a StackPanel of other items) to provide a great deal of flexibility and control. Table 28-2 documents the role of some commonly used WPF panel controls.

Table 28-2. Core WPF Panel Controls

Panel Control	Meaning in Life
Canvas	Provides a classic mode of content placement. Items stay exactly where you put them at design time.
DockPanel	Locks content to a specified side of the panel (Top, Bottom, Left, or Right).
Grid	Arranges content within a series of cells, maintained within a tabular grid.
StackPanel	Stacks content in a vertical or horizontal manner, as dictated by the Orientation property.
WrapPanel	Positions content from left-to-right, breaking the content to the next line at the edge of the containing box. Subsequent ordering happens sequentially from top-to-bottom or from right-to-left, depending on the value of the Orientation property.

In the next few sections, you will learn how to use these commonly used panel types by copying some predefined XAML data into the MyXamlPad.exe application you created in Chapter 27 (you could also load this data into kaxaml.exe, if you wish). You can find all these loose XAML files contained inside the PanelMarkup subfolder of your Chapter 28 code download folder (Figure 28-4).

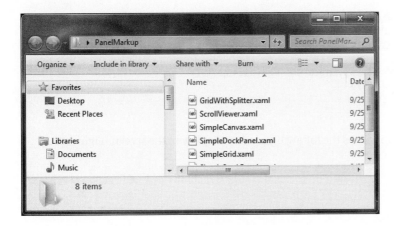

Figure 28-4. You will be loading the supplied XAML data into your MyXamlPad.exe appliction to test various layouts

Positioning Content Within Canvas Panels

You will probably feel most at home with the Canvas panel because it allows for absolute positioning of UI content. If the end user resizes the window to an area that is smaller than the layout maintained by the Canvas panel, the internal content will not be visible until the container is stretched to a size equal to or larger than the Canvas area.

To add content to a Canvas, you begin by defining the required controls within the scope of the opening <Canvas> and closing </Canvas> tags. Next, specify the upper-left corner for each control; this is where the rendering should begin using the Canvas.Top and Canvas.Left properties. You can specify the bottom-right area indirectly in each control by setting its Height and Width properties, or directly by using the Canvas.Right and Canvas.Bottom properties.

To see Canvas in action, open the provided SimpleCanvas.xaml file using a text editor and copy the content into MyXamlPad.exe (or kaxaml.exe). You should see the following Canvas definition:

```
<Window
  xmlns="http://schemas.microsoft.com/winfx/2006/xaml/presentation"
  xmlns:x="http://schemas.microsoft.com/winfx/2006/xaml"
  Title="Fun with Panels!" Height="285" Width="325">
  <Canvas Background="LightSteelBlue">
    <Button x:Name="btnOK" Canvas.Left="212" Canvas.Top="203"
          Width="80" Content="OK"/>
    <Label x:Name="lblInstructions" Canvas.Left="17" Canvas.Top="14"
          Width="328" Height="27" FontSize="15"
          Content="Enter Car Information"/>
    <Label x:Name="lblMake" Canvas.Left="17" Canvas.Top="60"
          Content="Make"/>
    <TextBox x:Name="txtMake" Canvas.Left="94" Canvas.Top="60"
          Width="193" Height="25"/>
    <Label x:Name="lblColor" Canvas.Left="17" Canvas.Top="109"
          Content="Color"/>
    <TextBox x:Name="txtColor" Canvas.Left="94" Canvas.Top="107"
          Width="193" Height="25"/>
    <Label x:Name="lblPetName" Canvas.Left="17" Canvas.Top="155"
          Content="Pet Name"/>
    <TextBox x:Name="txtPetName" Canvas.Left="94" Canvas.Top="153"
          Width="193" Height="25"/>
  </Canvas>
</Window>
```

Clicking your View Xaml button causes the following window display on the screen (Figure 28-5).

Figure 28-5. The Canvas layout manager allows for absolute positioning of content

Note that the order you declare content within a Canvas is not used to calculate placement; instead, placement is based on the control's size and the Canvas.Top, Canvas.Bottom, Canvas.Left, and Canvas.Right properties.

■ **Note** If sub-elements within a Canvas do not define a specific location using attached property syntax (e.g. Canvas.Left and Canvas.Top), they automatically attach to the extreme upper-left corner of Canvas.

Using the Canvas type might seem like the preferred way to arrange content (because it feels so familiar), but this approach does suffer from some limitations. First, items within a Canvas do not dynamically resize themselves when applying styles or templates (e.g., their font sizes are unaffected). Second, the Canvas will not attempt to keep elements visible when the end user resizes the window to a smaller surface.

Perhaps the best use of the Canvas type is for positioning *graphical content*. For example, if you were building a custom image using XAML, you certainly would want the lines, shapes, and text to remain in the same location, rather than see them dynamically repositioned as the user resizes the window! You'll revisit Canvas in the next chapter when you examine WPF's graphical rendering services.

Positioning Content Within WrapPanel Panels

A WrapPanel allows you to define content that will flow across the panel as the window is resized. When positioning elements in a WrapPanel, you do not specify top, bottom, left, and right docking values as you typically do with Canvas. However, each sub-element is free to define a Height and Width value (among other property values) to control its overall size in the container.

Because content within a WrapPanel does not dock to a given side of the panel, the order in which you declare the elements is important (content is rendered from the first element to the last). If you were to load the XAML data found within the SimpleWrapPanel.xaml file, you would find it contains the following markup (enclosed within a <Window> definition):

```
<WrapPanel Background="LightSteelBlue">
  <Label x:Name="lblInstruction" Width="328"
        Height="27" FontSize="15" Content="Enter Car Information"/>
  <Label x:Name="lblMake" Content="Make"/>
  <TextBox x:Name="txtMake" Width="193" Height="25"/>
  <Label x:Name="lblColor" Content="Color"/>
  <TextBox x:Name="txtColor" Width="193" Height="25"/>
  <Label x:Name="lblPetName" Content="Pet Name"/>
  <TextBox x:Name="txtPetName" Width="193" Height="25"/>
  <Button x:Name="btnOK" Width="80" Content="OK"/>
</WrapPanel>
```

When you load this markup, the content looks out of sorts as you resize the width because it flows from left-to-right across the window (see Figure 28-6).

Figure 28-6. Content in a WrapPanel behaves much like a traditional HTML page

By default, content within a `WrapPanel` flows from left-to-right. However, if you change the value of the `Orientation` property to `Vertical`, you can have content wrap in a top-to-bottom manner:

```
<WrapPanel Orientation ="Vertical">
```

You can declare a `WrapPanel` (as well as some other panel types) by specifying `ItemWidth` and `ItemHeight` values, which control the default size of each item. If a sub-element does provide its own `Height` and/or `Width` value, it will be positioned relative to the size established by the panel. Consider the following markup:

```
<WrapPanel ItemWidth ="200" ItemHeight ="30">
  <Label x:Name="lblInstruction"
         FontSize="15" Content="Enter Car Information"/>
  <Label x:Name="lblMake" Content="Make"/>
  <TextBox x:Name="txtMake"/>
  <Label x:Name="lblColor" Content="Color"/>
  <TextBox x:Name="txtColor"/>
  <Label x:Name="lblPetName" Content="Pet Name"/>
  <TextBox x:Name="txtPetName"/>
  <Button x:Name="btnOK" Width ="80" Content="OK"/>
</WrapPanel>
```

When you see this code rendered, you find the output shown in Figure 28-7 (notice the size and position of the `Button` control, which has specified a unique `Width` value).

Figure 28-7. A WrapPanel can establish the width and height of a given item

As you might agree after looking at Figure 28-7, a WrapPanel is not typically the best choice for arranging content directly in a window because its elements can become scrambled as the user resizes the window. In most cases, a WrapPanel will be a sub-element to another panel type, allowing a small area of the window to wrap its content when resized (e.g., a Toolbar control).

Positioning Content Within StackPanel Panels

Like a WrapPanel, a StackPanel control arranges content into a single line that can be oriented horizontally or vertically (the default), based on the value assigned to the Orientation property. The difference, however, is that the StackPanel will *not* attempt to wrap the content as the user resizes the window. Rather, the items in the StackPanel will simply stretch (based on their orientation) to accommodate the size of the StackPanel itself. For example, the SimpleStackPanel.xaml file contains markup that results in the output shown in Figure 28-8:

```
<StackPanel Background="LightSteelBlue">
  <Label x:Name="lblInstruction"
         FontSize="15" Content="Enter Car Information"/>
  <Label x:Name="lblMake" Content="Make"/>
  <TextBox Name="txtMake"/>
  <Label x:Name="lblColor" Content="Color"/>
  <TextBox x:Name="txtColor"/>
  <Label x:Name="lblPetName" Content="Pet Name"/>
  <TextBox x:Name="txtPetName"/>
  <Button x:Name="btnOK" Width ="80" Content="OK"/>
</StackPanel>
```

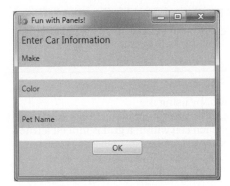

Figure 28-8. Vertical stacking of content

If you assign the Orientation property to Horizontal as follows, the rendered output will match that shown in Figure 28-9:

```
<StackPanel Orientation ="Horizontal">
```

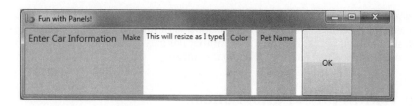

Figure 28-9. Horizontal stacking of content

Again, as is the case with the WrapPanel, you will seldom want to use a StackPanel to arrange content directly within a window. Instead, you'll be better off using StackPanel as a subpanel to a master panel.

Positioning Content Within Grid Panels

Of all the panels provided with the WPF APIs, Grid is far and away the most flexible. Like an HTML table, the Grid can be carved up into a set of cells, each one of which provides content. When defining a Grid, you perform three steps:

1. Define and configure each column.

2. Define and configure each row.

3. Assign content to each cell of the grid using attached property syntax.

■ **Note** If you do not define any rows or columns, the `<Grid>` defaults to a single cell that fills the entire surface of the window. Furthermore, if you do not assign a cell value for a sub-element within a `<Grid>`, it automatically attaches to column 0, row 0.

You achieve the first two steps (defining the columns and rows) by using the `<Grid.ColumnDefinitions>` and `<Grid.RowDefinitions>` elements, which contain a collection of `<ColumnDefinition>` and `<RowDefinition>` elements, respectively. Each cell within a grid is indeed a true .NET object, so you can configure the look–and–feel and behavior of each cell as you see fit.

Here is a `<Grid>` definition (that you can find in the SimpleGrid.xaml file) that arranges your UI content as shown in Figure 28-10:

```
<Grid ShowGridLines ="True" Background ="AliceBlue">
  <!-- Define the rows/columns -->
  <Grid.ColumnDefinitions>
    <ColumnDefinition/>
    <ColumnDefinition/>
  </Grid.ColumnDefinitions>
  <Grid.RowDefinitions>
    <RowDefinition/>
    <RowDefinition/>
  </Grid.RowDefinitions>
```

```
<!-- Now add the elements to the grid's cells-->
<Label x:Name="lblInstruction" Grid.Column ="0" Grid.Row ="0"
        FontSize="15" Content="Enter Car Information"/>
<Button x:Name="btnOK"  Height ="30" Grid.Column ="0"
        Grid.Row ="0" Content="OK"/>
<Label x:Name="lblMake" Grid.Column ="1"
        Grid.Row ="0" Content="Make"/>
<TextBox x:Name="txtMake" Grid.Column ="1"
        Grid.Row ="0" Width="193" Height="25"/>
<Label x:Name="lblColor" Grid.Column ="0"
        Grid.Row ="1" Content="Color"/>
<TextBox x:Name="txtColor" Width="193" Height="25"
        Grid.Column ="0" Grid.Row ="1" />

<!-- Just to keep things interesting, add some color to the pet name cell -->
<Rectangle Fill ="LightGreen" Grid.Column ="1" Grid.Row ="1" />
<Label x:Name="lblPetName" Grid.Column ="1" Grid.Row ="1" Content="Pet Name"/>
<TextBox x:Name="txtPetName" Grid.Column ="1" Grid.Row ="1"
        Width="193" Height="25"/>
</Grid>
```

Notice that each element (including a light green Rectangle element thrown in for good measure) connects itself to a cell in the grid using the Grid.Row and Grid.Column attached properties. By default, the ordering of cells in a grid begins at the upper left, which you specify using Grid.Column="0" Grid.Row="0". Given that your grid defines a total of four cells, you can identify the bottom-right cell using Grid.Column="1" Grid.Row="1".

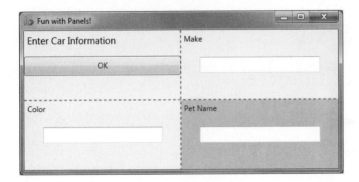

Figure 28-10. *The Grid panel in action*

Grids with GridSplitter Types

Grid objects can also support *splitters*. As you might know, splitters allow the end user to resize rows or columns of a grid type. As this is done, the content within each resizable cell will reshape itself based on how the items have been contained. Adding splitters to a Grid is easy to do; you simply define the <GridSplitter> control, using attached property syntax to establish which row or column it affects.

1241

Be aware that you must assign a `Width` or `Height` value (depending on vertical or horizontal splitting) for the splitter to be visible on the screen. Consider the following simple `Grid` type with a splitter on the first column (`Grid.Column = "0"`). The contents of the provided `GridWithSplitter.xaml` file look like this:

```
<Grid Background ="AliceBlue">
  <!-- Define columns -->
  <Grid.ColumnDefinitions>
    <ColumnDefinition Width ="Auto"/>
    <ColumnDefinition/>
  </Grid.ColumnDefinitions>

  <!-- Add this label to cell 0 -->
  <Label x:Name="lblLeft" Background ="GreenYellow"
         Grid.Column="0" Content ="Left!"/>

  <!-- Define the splitter -->
  <GridSplitter Grid.Column ="0" Width ="5"/>

  <!-- Add this label to cell 1 -->
  <Label x:Name="lblRight" Grid.Column ="1" Content ="Right!"/>
</Grid>
```

First and foremost, notice that the column that will support the splitter has a `Width` property of `Auto`. Next, notice that the `<GridSplitter>` uses attached property syntax to establish which column it is working with. If you were to view this output, you would find a five-pixel splitter that allows you to resize each `Label`. Note that the content fills up the entire cell because you have not specified `Height` or `Width` properties for either `Label` (see Figure 28-11).

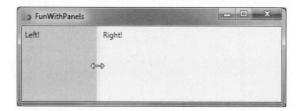

Figure 28-11. Grid types containing splitters

Positioning Content Within DockPanel Panels

`DockPanel` is typically used as a master panel that contains any number of additional panels for grouping related content. `DockPanels` use attached property syntax (as seen with the `Canvas` or `Grid` types) to control where each item docks itself within the `DockPanel`.

The `SimpleDockPanel.xaml` file defines a simple `DockPanel` definition that results in the output shown in Figure 28-12:

```
<DockPanel LastChildFill ="True">
  <!-- Dock items to the panel -->
  <Label x:Name="lblInstruction" DockPanel.Dock ="Top"
         FontSize="15" Content="Enter Car Information"/>
  <Label x:Name="lblMake" DockPanel.Dock ="Left" Content="Make"/>
  <Label x:Name="lblColor" DockPanel.Dock ="Right" Content="Color"/>
  <Label x:Name="lblPetName" DockPanel.Dock ="Bottom" Content="Pet Name"/>
  <Button x:Name="btnOK" Content="OK"/>
</DockPanel>
```

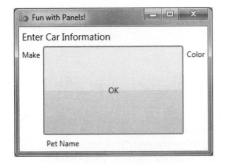

Figure 28-12. *A simple DockPanel*

■ **Note** If you add multiple elements to the same side of a DockPanel, they will stack along the specified edge in the order that they are declared.

The benefit of using DockPanel types is that, as the user resizes the window, each element remains connected to the specified side of the panel (through DockPanel.Dock). Also notice that the opening <DockPanel> tag sets the LastChildFill attribute to True. Given that the Button control has not specified any DockPanel.Dock value, it will therefore be stretched within the remaining space.

Enabling Scrolling for Panel Types

It is worth pointing out the WPF supplies a ScrollViewer class, which provides automatic scrolling behaviors for data within panel objects. The ScrollViewer.xaml file defines the following:

```
<ScrollViewer>
  <StackPanel>
    <Button Content ="First" Background = "Green" Height ="40"/>
    <Button Content ="Second" Background = "Red" Height ="40"/>
    <Button Content ="Third" Background = "Pink" Height ="40"/>
```

```
      <Button Content ="Fourth" Background = "Yellow" Height ="40"/>
      <Button Content ="Fifth" Background = "Blue" Height ="40"/>
    </StackPanel>
</ScrollViewer>
```

You can see the result of the previous XAML definition in Figure 28-13.

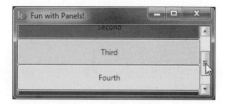

Figure 28-13. Working with the ScrollViewer type

As you would expect, each panel provides numerous members that allow you to fine-tune content placement. On a related note, many WPF controls support two properties of interest (`Padding` and `Margin`) that allow the control itself to inform the panel how it wishes to be treated. Specifically, the `Padding` property controls how much extra space should surround the interior control, while `Margin` controls the extra space around the exterior of a control.

This wraps up this chapter's look at the major panel types of WPF, as well as the various ways they position their content. Next, you will see an example that uses nested panels to create a layout system for a main window.

Building a Window's Frame Using Nested Panels

As mentioned previously, a typical WPF window will not use a single panel control, but instead will nest panels within other panels to gain the desired layout system. The next step is to learn how to nest panels, as well as how to use a number of new WPF controls. You will learn this by building a simple WPF word processor application. Begin by opening Visual Studio 2010 and creating a new WPF Application named `MyWordPad`.

Your goal is to construct a layout where the main window has a topmost menu system, a toolbar under the menu system, and a status bar mounted on the bottom of the window. The status bar will contain a pane to hold text prompts that are displayed when the user selects a menu item (or toolbar button), while the menu system and toolbar will offer UI triggers to close the application and display spelling suggestions in an `Expander` widget. Figure 28-14 shows the initial layout you are shooting for; it also displays spelling suggestions for *XAML*.

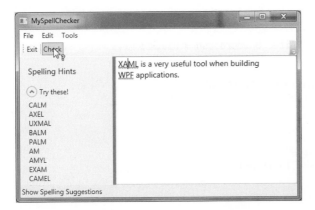

Figure 28-14. Using nested panels to establish a window's UI

Notice that the two toolbar buttons are not supporting an expected image, but a simple text value. This would not be sufficient for a production-level application, but assigning images to toolbar buttons typically involves using embedded resources, a topic that you will examine in Chapter 30 (so text data will do for now). Also note that, as the mouse button is placed over the Check button, the mouse cursor changes and the single pane of the status bar displays a useful UI message.

To begin building this UI, update the initial XAML definition for your `Window` type so it uses a `<DockPanel>` child element, rather than the default `<Grid>`:

```
<Window x:Class="MainWindow"
  xmlns="http://schemas.microsoft.com/winfx/2006/xaml/presentation"
  xmlns:x="http://schemas.microsoft.com/winfx/2006/xaml"
  Title="MySpellChecker" Height="331" Width="508"
  WindowStartupLocation ="CenterScreen" >

  <!-- This panel establishes the content for the window -->
  <DockPanel>
  </DockPanel>

</Window>
```

Building the Menu System

Menu systems in WPF are represented by the `Menu` class, which maintains a collection of `MenuItem` objects. When building a menu system in XAML, you can have each `MenuItem` handle various events. The most notable of these events is `Click`, which occurs when the end user selects a sub-item. In this example, you begin by building the two topmost menu items (File and Tools; you will build the Edit menu later in this example), which expose Exit and Spelling Hints sub-items, respectively.

In addition to handling the `Click` event for each sub-item, you also need to handle the `MouseEnter` and `MouseExit` events, which you will use to set the status bar text in a later step. Add the following markup within your `<DockPanel>` scope (feel free to use Properties window of Visual Studio 2010 to help minimize the amount of markup you need to type by hand):

```
<!--Dock menu system on the top-->
<Menu DockPanel.Dock ="Top"
      HorizontalAlignment="Left" Background="White" BorderBrush ="Black">
  <MenuItem Header="_File">
    <Separator/>
    <MenuItem Header ="_Exit" MouseEnter ="MouseEnterExitArea"
              MouseLeave ="MouseLeaveArea" Click ="FileExit_Click"/>
    </MenuItem>
    <MenuItem Header="_Tools">
      <MenuItem Header ="_Spelling Hints"
          MouseEnter ="MouseEnterToolsHintsArea"
          MouseLeave ="MouseLeaveArea" Click ="ToolsSpellingHints_Click"/>
  </MenuItem>
</Menu>
```

Notice that you dock the menu system to the top of the **DockPanel**. Also, you use the `<Separator>` element to insert a thin horizontal line in the menu system, directly before the Exit option. Also notice that the **Header** values for each **MenuItem** contain an embedded underbar token (e.g., **_Exit**). You use this token to establish which letter will be underlined when the end user presses the Alt key (for keyboard shortcuts).

So far you've implemented the complete the menu system definition; next, you need to implement the various event handlers. First, you have the File ➤ Exit handler, **FileExit_Click()**, which simply closes the window, which in turn terminates the application because this is your topmost window. The **MouseEnter** and **MouseExit** event handlers for each sub-item will eventually update your status bar; however, for now, you will simply provide shells. Finally, the **ToolsSpellingHints_Click()** handler for the Tools ➤ Spelling Hints menu item will also remain a shell for the time being. Here are the current updates to your code-behind file:

```
Class MainWindow
        Protected Sub FileExit_Click(ByVal sender As Object, ByVal args As RoutedEventArgs)
                ' Close this window.
                Me.Close()
        End Sub

        Protected Sub ToolsSpellingHints_Click(ByVal sender As Object,
                ByVal args As RoutedEventArgs)
        End Sub

        Protected Sub MouseEnterExitArea(ByVal sender As Object,
                ByVal args As RoutedEventArgs)
        End Sub

        Protected Sub MouseEnterToolsHintsArea(ByVal sender As Object,
                ByVal args As RoutedEventArgs)
        End Sub

        Protected Sub MouseLeaveArea(ByVal sender As Object, ByVal args As RoutedEventArgs)
        End Sub
End Class
```

Building the ToolBar

Toolbars (represented by the `ToolBar` class in WPF) typically provide an alternative manner for activating a menu option. Add the following markup directly after the closing scope of your `<Menu>` definition:

```
<!-- Put Toolbar under the Menu -->
<ToolBar DockPanel.Dock ="Top" >
  <Button Content ="Exit" MouseEnter ="MouseEnterExitArea"
          MouseLeave ="MouseLeaveArea" Click ="FileExit_Click"/>
  <Separator/>
  <Button Content ="Check" MouseEnter ="MouseEnterToolsHintsArea"
          MouseLeave ="MouseLeaveArea" Click ="ToolsSpellingHints_Click"
          Cursor="Help" />
</ToolBar>
```

Your `ToolBar` control consists of two `Button` controls, which just so happen to handle the same events and are handled by the same methods in your code file. Using this technique, you can double-up your handlers to serve both menu items and toolbar buttons. Although this toolbar uses the typical push buttons, you should appreciate that the `ToolBar` type "is-a" `ContentControl`; therefore, you are free to embed any types into its surface (e.g., drop-down lists, images, and graphics). The only other point of interest here is that the Check button supports a custom mouse cursor through the `Cursor` property.

■ **Note** You can optionally wrap the `ToolBar` element within a `<ToolBarTray>` element, which controls layout, docking, and drag-and-drop operations for a set of `ToolBar` objects. Consult the .NET Framework 4.0 SDK documentation for details.

Building the StatusBar

A `StatusBar` control will be docked to the lower portion of the `<DockPanel>` and contain a single `<TextBlock>` control, which you have not used prior to this point in the chapter. You can use a `TextBlock` to hold text that supports numerous textual annotations, such as bold text, underlined text, line breaks, and so forth. Add the following markup directly after the previous `ToolBar` definition:

```
<!-- Put a StatusBar at the bottom -->
<StatusBar DockPanel.Dock ="Bottom" Background="Beige" >
  <StatusBarItem>
    <TextBlock Name="statBarText" Text="Ready"/>
  </StatusBarItem>
</StatusBar>
```

Finalizing the UI Design

The final aspect of your UI design is to define a splittable `Grid` that defines two columns. On the left you place an `Expander` control that will display a list of spelling suggestions, wrapped within a `<StackPanel>`. On the right, you place a `TextBox` control that supports multiple lines and scrollbars, and includes enabled spell checking. You mount the entire `<Grid>` to the left of the parent `<DockPanel>`. Add the following XAML markup directly under the markup describing the `StatusBar` to complete the definition of our Window's UI:

```
<Grid DockPanel.Dock ="Left" Background ="AliceBlue">
  <!-- Define the rows and columns -->
  <Grid.ColumnDefinitions>
    <ColumnDefinition />
    <ColumnDefinition />
  </Grid.ColumnDefinitions>

  <GridSplitter Grid.Column ="0" Width ="5" Background ="Gray" />
  <StackPanel Grid.Column="0" VerticalAlignment ="Stretch" >
    <Label Name="lblSpellingInstructions" FontSize="14" Margin="10,10,0,0">
     Spelling Hints
    </Label>

    <Expander Name="expanderSpelling" Header ="Try these!"
              Margin="10,10,10,10">
      <!-- This will be filled programmatically -->
      <Label Name ="lblSpellingHints" FontSize ="12"/>
    </Expander>
  </StackPanel>

  <!-- This will be the area to type within -->
  <TextBox  Grid.Column ="1"
            SpellCheck.IsEnabled ="True"
            AcceptsReturn ="True"
            Name ="txtData"  FontSize ="14"
            BorderBrush ="Blue"
            VerticalScrollBarVisibility="Auto"
            HorizontalScrollBarVisibility="Auto">
  </TextBox>
</Grid>
```

Implementing the MouseEnter/MouseLeave Event Handlers

At this point, the UI of your window is complete. The only remaining tasks are to provide an implementation for the remaining event handlers. Begin by updating your VB 2010 code file so that each of the MouseEnter and MouseLeave handlers set the text pane of the status bar with a fitting message to help the end user:

```
Class MainWindow
...
        Protected Sub MouseEnterExitArea(ByVal sender As Object,
              ByVal args As RoutedEventArgs)
              statBarText.Text = "Exit the Application"
        End Sub
```

```
        Protected Sub MouseEnterToolsHintsArea(ByVal sender As Object,
                ByVal args As RoutedEventArgs)
                statBarText.Text = "Show Spelling Suggestions"
        End Sub

        Protected Sub MouseLeaveArea(ByVal sender As Object, ByVal args As RoutedEventArgs)
                statBarText.Text = "Ready"
        End Sub
End Class
```

At this point, you can run your application. You should see your status bar change its text, based on which menu item/toolbar button you have selected.

Implementing the Spell Checking Logic

The WPF API ships with built-in spell checker support, which is independent of Microsoft Office products. This means you don't need to use the COM interop layer to use the spell checker of Microsoft Word; instead, you can easily add the same type of support with only a few lines of code.

You might recall that when you defined the <TextBox> control, you set the SpellCheck.IsEnabled property to True. When you do this, misspelled words are underlined in a red squiggle, just as they are in Microsoft Office. Even better, the underlying programming model gives you access to the spell-checker engine, which allows you to get a list of suggestions for misspelled words. Add the following code to your ToolsSpellingHints_Click() method:

```
Protected Sub ToolsSpellingHints_Click(ByVal  sender As Object, ByVal args As
RoutedEventArgs)
        Dim spellingHints As String = String.Empty

        ' Try to get a spelling error at the current caret location.
        Dim err As SpellingError = txtData.GetSpellingError(txtData.CaretIndex)
        If err IsNot Nothing Then
                ' Build a String of spelling suggestions.
                For Each s As String In err.Suggestions
                spellingHints &= String.Format("{0}" & vbLf, s)
                Next

                ' Show suggestions and expand the expander.
                lblSpellingHints.Content = spellingHints
                expanderSpelling.IsExpanded = True
        End If
End Sub
```

The preceding code is quite simple. You simply figure out the current location of the caret in the text box by using the CaretIndex property to extract a SpellingError object. If there is an error at said location (meaning the value is not Nothing), you loop over the list of suggestions using the aptly named Suggestions property. Once you have all of the suggestions for the misspelled word, you connect the data to the Label in the Expander.

So there you have it! With only a few lines of procedural code (and a healthy dose of XAML), you have the beginnings of a functioning word processor. An understanding of *control commands* can help you add a bit more pizzazz.

Understanding WPF Control Commands

Windows Presentation Foundation provides support for what might be considered *control-agnostic events* with *control commands*. A typical .NET event is defined within a specific base class and can only be used by that class or a derivative thereof. Therefore, normal .NET events are tightly coupled to the class in which they are defined.

In contrast, WPF control commands are event-like entities that are independent from a specific control and, in many cases, can be successfully applied to numerous (and seemingly unrelated) control types. By way of a few examples, WPF supports Copy, Paste, and Cut commands, which you can apply to a wide variety of UI elements (e.g., menu items, toolbar buttons, and custom buttons), as well as keyboard shortcuts (e.g., Ctrl+C, and Ctrl+V).

While other UI toolkits (such as Windows Forms) provided standard events for such purposes, using them typically left you with redundant and hard to maintain code. Under the WPF model, you can use commands as an alternative. The end result typically yields a smaller and more flexible code base.

The Intrinsic Control Command Objects

WPF ships with numerous built-in control commands, all of which you can configure with associated keyboard shortcuts (or other input gestures). Programmatically speaking, a WPF control command is any object that supports a property (often called *Command*) that returns an object implementing the ICommand interface, as shown here:

```
Public Interface ICommand
        ' Occurs when changes occur that affect whether
        ' or not the command should execute.
        Event CanExecuteChanged As EventHandler

        ' Defines the method that determines whether the command
        ' can execute in its current state.
        Function CanExecute(ByVal parameter As Object) As Boolean

        ' Defines the method to be called when the command is invoked.
        Sub Execute(ByVal parameter As Object)
End Interface
```

While you could provide your own implementation of this interface to account for a control command, the chances that you will need to do so are slim, given that the functionality provided by the five WPF classes contains close to 100 command objects out-of-the-box. These classes define numerous properties that expose specific command objects, each of which implements ICommand.

Table 28-3 documents some of the standard command objects available (be sure to consult the .NET Framework 4.0 SDK documentation for complete details).

Table 28-3. *The Intrinsic WPF Control Command Objects*

WPF Class	Command Objects	Meaning in Life
ApplicationCommands	Close, Copy, Cut, Delete, Find, Open, Paste, Save, SaveAs, Redo, Undo	Various application-level commands
ComponentCommands	MoveDown, MoveFocusBack, MoveLeft, MoveRight, ScrollToEnd, ScrollToHome	Various commands common to UI components
MediaCommands	BoostBase, ChannelUp, ChannelDown, FastForward, NextTrack, Play, Rewind, Select, Stop	Various media-centric commands
NavigationCommands	BrowseBack, BrowseForward, Favorites, LastPage, NextPage, Zoom	Various commands relating to the WPF navigation model
EditingCommands	AlignCenter, CorrectSpellingError, DecreaseFontSize, EnterLineBreak, EnterParagraphBreak, MoveDownByLine, MoveRightByWord	Various commands relating to the WPF document API

Connecting Commands to the Command Property

If you wish to connect any of these command properties to a UI element that supports the Command property (such as a Button or MenuItem), you have little work to do. You can see how to do this by updating the current menu system so it supports a new topmost menu item named Edit and three sub-items to account for copying, pasting, and cutting of textual data:

```
<Menu DockPanel.Dock ="Top"
     HorizontalAlignment="Left"
     Background="White" BorderBrush ="Black">
  <MenuItem Header="_File" Click ="FileExit_Click" >
    <Separator/>
    <MenuItem Header ="_Exit" MouseEnter ="MouseEnterExitArea"
              MouseLeave ="MouseLeaveArea" Click ="FileExit_Click"/>
  </MenuItem>

  <!-- New menu item with commands! -->
  <MenuItem Header="_Edit">
    <MenuItem Command ="ApplicationCommands.Copy"/>
    <MenuItem Command ="ApplicationCommands.Cut"/>
    <MenuItem Command ="ApplicationCommands.Paste"/>
  </MenuItem>
```

```
<MenuItem Header="_Tools">
    <MenuItem Header ="_Spelling Hints"
              MouseEnter ="MouseEnterToolsHintsArea"
              MouseLeave ="MouseLeaveArea"
              Click ="ToolsSpellingHints_Click"/>
</MenuItem>
</Menu>
```

Notice that each of the sub-items on the Edit menu has a value assigned to the **Command** property. Doing this means that the menu items automatically receive the correct name and shortcut key (e.g., Ctrl+C for a cut operation) in the menu item UI; it also means that the application is now *copy, cut, and paste* aware with no procedural code!

If you were to run the application and select some of your text, you would be able to use your new menu items out-of-the-box. As a bonus, your application is also equipped to respond to a standard *right-click* operation to present the user with the same options (Figure 28-15).

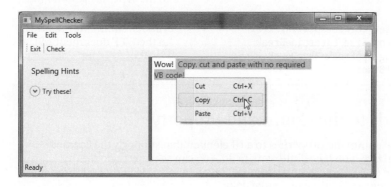

Figure 28-15. *Command objects provide a good deal of built-in functionality for free*

Connecting Commands to Arbitrary Actions

If you wish to connect a command object to an arbitrary (application-specific) event, you will need to drop down to procedural code. Doing so is not complex, but it does involve a bit more logic than you see in XAML. For example, assume that want to have the entire window respond to the F1 key, so that when the end user presses this key, he will activate an associated help system.

Also, assume your code file for the main window defines a new method named `SetF1CommandBinding()`, which you call within the constructor after a call to `InitializeComponent()`:

```
Public Sub New()
      InitializeComponent()
      SetF1CommandBinding()
End Sub
```

This new method will programmatically create a new **CommandBinding** object, which you can use whenever you wish to bind a command object to a given event handler in your application. Here, you configure your `CommandBinding` object to operate with the `ApplicationCommands.Help` command, which is automatically F1-aware:

```
Private Sub SetF1CommandBinding()
        Dim helpBinding As New CommandBinding(ApplicationCommands.Help)
        AddHandler helpBinding.CanExecute, AddressOf CanHelpExecute
        AddHandler helpBinding.Executed, AddressOf HelpExecuted
        CommandBindings.Add(helpBinding)
End Sub
```

Most `CommandBinding` objects will want to handle the `CanExecute` event (which allows you to specify whether the command occurs based on the operation of your program) and the `Executed` event (which is where you can author the content that should occur once the command occurs). Add the following event handlers to your `Window`-derived type (note the format of each method, as required by the associated delegates):

```
Private Sub CanHelpExecute(ByVal sender As Object, ByVal e As CanExecuteRoutedEventArgs)
        ' Here, you can set CanExecute to False if you wish to prevent the
        ' command from executing.
        e.CanExecute = True
End Sub

Private Sub HelpExecuted(ByVal sender As Object, ByVal e As ExecutedRoutedEventArgs)
    MessageBox.Show("Look, it is not that difficult.  Just type something!", "Help!")
End Sub
```

In the preceding snippet, you implemented `CanHelpExecute()` so it always allows F1 help to launch; you do this by simply returning `True`. However, if you have certain situations where the help system should not display, you can account for this and return `False` when necessary. Your "help system" displayed within `HelpExecuted()` is little more than a message box. At this point, you can run your application. When you press the F1 key on your keyboard, you will see your (less than helpful, if not a bit insulting) user-guidance system (see Figure 28-16).

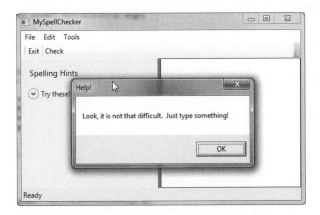

Figure 28-16. Your custom help system (which is not quite as helpful as the user would hope)

Working with the Open and Save Commands

To complete the current example, you will add functionality to save your text data to an external file and open up *.txt files for editing. If you want to take the long road, you can manually add programming logic that enables or disables new menu items based on whether your TextBox has data inside it. Once again, however, you can use commands to decrease your burden.

Begin by updating the <MenuItem> element that represents your topmost File menu by adding two new submenus that use the Save and Open ApplicationCommands objects:

```
<MenuItem Header="_File">
  <MenuItem Command ="ApplicationCommands.Open"/>
  <MenuItem Command ="ApplicationCommands.Save"/>
  <Separator/>
  <MenuItem Header ="_Exit"
            MouseEnter ="MouseEnterExitArea"
            MouseLeave ="MouseLeaveArea" Click ="FileExit_Click"/>

</MenuItem>
```

Again, remember that all command objects implement the ICommand interface, which defines two events (CanExecute and Executed). Now you need to enable the entire window, so it can check whether it is currently OK to fire these commands; if so, you can define an event handler to execute the custom code.

You do this by populating the CommandBindings collection maintained by the window. To do so in XAML requires that you use property element syntax to define a <Window.CommandBindings> scope in which you place two <CommandBinding> definitions. Update your <Window> like this:

```
<Window x:Class="MainWindow"
  xmlns="http://schemas.microsoft.com/winfx/2006/xaml/presentation"
  xmlns:x="http://schemas.microsoft.com/winfx/2006/xaml"
  Title="MySpellChecker" Height="331" Width="508"
  WindowStartupLocation ="CenterScreen" >

  <!-- This will inform the Window which handlers to call,
       when testing for the Open and Save commands. -->
  <Window.CommandBindings>
    <CommandBinding Command="ApplicationCommands.Open"
                    Executed="OpenCmdExecuted"
                    CanExecute="OpenCmdCanExecute"/>
    <CommandBinding Command="ApplicationCommands.Save"
                    Executed="SaveCmdExecuted"
                    CanExecute="SaveCmdCanExecute"/>
  </Window.CommandBindings>

  <!-- This panel establishes the content for the window -->
  <DockPanel>
  ...
  </DockPanel>
</Window>
```

Now right-click each of the Executed and CanExecute attributes in your XAML editor and pick the Navigate to Event Handler menu option. As you might recall from Chapter 27, this will automatically generate stub code for the event itself. At this point, you should have four empty handlers in the VB 2010 code file for the window.

The implementation of CanExecute event handlers will tell the window that it is OK to fire the corresponding Executed events at any time by setting the CanExecute property of the incoming CanExecuteRoutedEventArgs object:

```vb
Private Sub OpenCmdCanExecute(ByVal sender As Object, ByVal e As CanExecuteRoutedEventArgs)
        e.CanExecute = True
End Sub

Private Sub SaveCmdCanExecute(ByVal sender As Object, ByVal e As CanExecuteRoutedEventArgs)
        e.CanExecute = True
End Sub
```

The corresponding Executed handlers perform the actual work of displaying the open and save dialog boxes; they also send the data in your TextBox to a file. Begin by making sure that you import the System.IO and Microsoft.Win32 namespaces into your code file. The completed code is straightforward:

```vb
Private Sub OpenCmdExecuted(ByVal sender As Object, ByVal e As ExecutedRoutedEventArgs)
        ' Create an open file dialog box and only show XAML files.
        Dim openDlg As New OpenFileDialog()
        openDlg.Filter = "Text Files |*.txt"

        ' Did they click on the OK button?
        If True = openDlg.ShowDialog() Then
            ' Load all text of selected file
            Dim dataFromFile As String = File.ReadAllText(openDlg.FileName)

            ' Show string in TextBox.
            txtData.Text = dataFromFile
        End If
End Sub

Private Sub SaveCmdExecuted(ByVal sender As Object, ByVal e As ExecutedRoutedEventArgs)
        Dim saveDlg As New SaveFileDialog()
        saveDlg.Filter = "Text Files |*.txt"

        ' Did they click on the OK button?
        If True = saveDlg.ShowDialog() Then
            ' Save data in the TextBox to the named file.
            File.WriteAllText(saveDlg.FileName, txtData.Text)
        End If
End Sub
```

That wraps up this example and your initial look at working with WPF controls. Here, you learned how to work with menu systems, status bars, tool bars, nested panels, and a few basic UI controls, such as TextBox and Expander. The next example will work with some more exotic controls, while examining several important WPF services at the same time. As an added bonus, you will build the interface using Expression Blend.

■ **Source Code** You can find the MyWordPad project under the Chapter 28 subdirectory.

Building a WPF User Interface with Expression Blend

Visual Studio 2010 provides a solid WPF-editing experience; and, if you so choose, you can use the IDE for all of your XAML editing. However, for complex applications, your work load will often decrease considerably if you use Blend to generate the markup, and then open the same project in Visual Studio to tweak the markup (if needed) and author code.

On a related node, Blend ships with a simple code editor; while it is not anywhere near as powerful as Visual Studio, you can use this built-in VB 2010 editor to add code quickly to the UI event handlers during development.

Getting to know the Key Aspects of the Blend IDE

To begin learning about Blend, load the product and click the New Project button from the Welcome dialog (if you don't see the dialog, you can activate it from the File ➤ New project menu command). In the New Project dialog (see Figure 28-17), create a new WPF Application named WpfControlsAndAPIs.

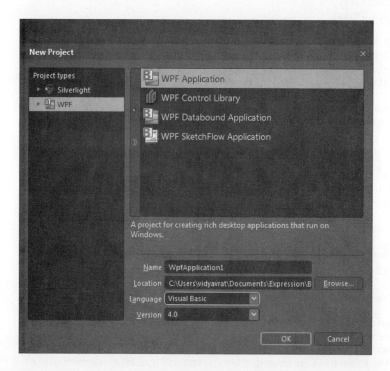

Figure 28-17. Creating a new WPF Application with Expression Blend

Once you open the project, activate the Projects tab mounted on the upper-left area of the IDE (if you don't see it, activate the Window ➤ Projects menu option). As you can see in Figure 28-18, a WPF Application generated with Blend is identical to a WPF project generated with Visual Studio.

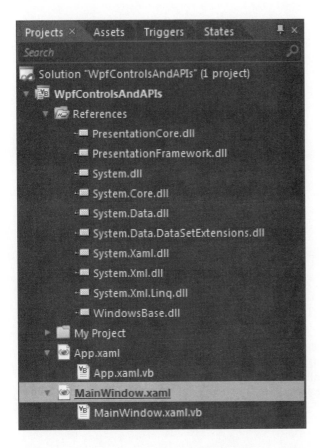

Figure 28-18. An Expression Blend WPF project is identical to a Visual Studio WPF project

Now locate the Properties tab on the right-hand side of the Blend IDE. Similar to Visual Studio 2010, this aspect of the tool allows you to assign property values to an item selected on the designer. However, it looks quite different from its Visual Studio 2010 counterpart. For example, notice that similar properties are grouped together in collapsible panes (see Figure 28-19).

Figure 28-19. The Blend Properties editor

Perhaps the most obvious part of the Blend IDE is its window designer, which takes up a majority of the real estate. Notice that you can see three small buttons in the upper-right area of the window designer; these buttons allow you to open the designer itself, the underlying XAML, or a split view. Figure 28-20 shows the designer in split view.

Figure 28-20. *The Blend Designer allows you to view the underlying XAML*

The XAML editor is quite feature-rich. For example, as you start typing, you will activate IntelliSense and find support for auto completion, as well as a useful help system. You won't have to enter much XAML manually in this example, but you can see the editor at work in Figure 28-21.

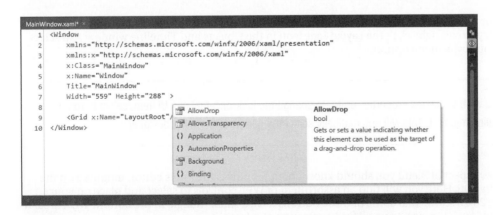

Figure 28-21. *The Blend XAML editor is as rich as the editor in Visual Studio*

Another key aspect of Blend to be aware of is the Objects and Timeline area (located in the bottom-left area of the Blend window). As you will learn in Chapter 30, the timeline aspect of this tool allows you to capture animation sequences. For now, suffice it to say that this aspect of the IDE allows you to view the logical tree of markup, much as the Document Viewer in Visual Studio 2010 does. Currently, your Objects and Timeline window should look like what you see in Figure 28-22.

Figure 28-22. You can view the tree of XAML using the Objects and Timeline editor

Here, you can see that your top-most node is the Window itself, which has an item named LayoutRoot as content. If you view the XAML of your initial window, you see this is the name given to the default `<Grid>` layout manager:

```
<Window
  xmlns="http://schemas.microsoft.com/winfx/2006/xaml/presentation"
  xmlns:x="http://schemas.microsoft.com/winfx/2006/xaml"
  x:Class="MainWindow"
  x:Name="Window"
  Title="MainWindow"
  Width="559" Height="288" >
  <Grid x:Name="LayoutRoot"/>
</Window>
```

If you do not want to use a Grid as your default layout manager, you can edit the XAML file directly. Or, if you prefer, you can right-click the LayoutRoot icon in the Objects and Timeline window and select the Change Layout Type menu option.

■ **Note** When you wish to use the Properties editor to change the look-and-feel of a UI item, select it from the Objects and Timeline tree first. This will automatically select the correct item on the designer.

One final key aspect of Blend you should know about for now is the Tools editor, mounted on the far-left side of the IDE. Here you will find an assortment of WPF controls to select and place on your designer. Figure 28-23 shows that some of these buttons have a small triangle in the bottom-right area. If you click and hold such buttons, you will find a selection of related choices.

■ **Note** I have my Tools window mounted at the top of the Blend IDE, so my controls appear in a horizontal, rather than vertical strip. You can dock almost any Blend window using a standard mouse drag-and-drop command. Also, the Window ➤ Reset Current Workspace menu option automatically restores the default location of each Blend window.

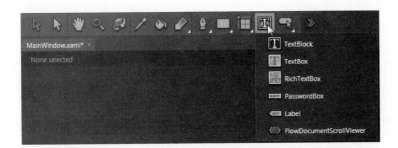

Figure 28-23. The Tools editor allows you to select a WPF control to place on the designer

Also notice that one of the buttons on the Tools window looks like a double greater-than sign (>>). Clicking this button opens up the Assets Library (see Figure 28-24). Here you will find many additional WPF controls that don't appear on the Tools window by default. Selecting items from the Assets Library moves them into the Tools area for use.

Figure 28-24. The Assets Library gives you access to additional WPF controls

Another important topic related to the Tools window is a common point of confusion for people who work with Blend for the first time; specifically, people are often confused about the difference between the Selection and Direct Selection buttons.

When you want to select an item on the designer (such as a Button) to change its size or relocate it in the container, you do so using the Selection button, which is the black arrow button (see Figure 28-25).

Figure 28-25. *A Selection allows you to resize and reposition content on the designer*

You use the Direct Selection arrow button (white in color) to drill into the content of a content control. Thus, if you direct select a Button, you can drill into its interior to build complex content visually (e.g., add a StackPanel and graphical items). You will revisit direct selection in Chapter 31 when you look at building custom controls. For this chapter, make sure you choose Select items, rather than Direct Select, when you build your GUIs.

Using the TabControl

Your window will contain a TabControl with four different tabs, each of which shows off a set of related controls and/or WPF APIs. Begin by ensuring that LayoutRoot is the selected node in your Objects and Timeline editor; this ensures that the control will be added to the panel. Next, use the Assets Library (the >> button) to locate the TabControl control. Now select the new item on your Tools window and draw the control onto the window designer so it takes up the majority of the surface. You should now see a tab system on your window with two default tabs.

Select your new TabControl in the Objects and Timeline editor, and then use the Properties window to name your new control myTabSystem using the Name edit area at the top of the property editor. Next, right-click the TabControl in the Objects and Timeline editor and select Add TabItem (see Figure 28-26).

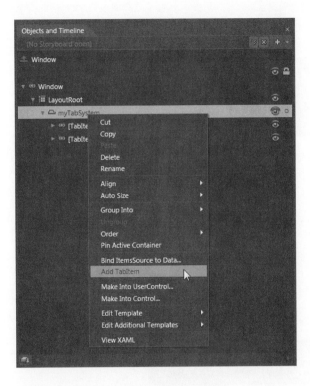

Figure 28-26. Visually adding TabItems

Add another tab to your control and use the Properties editor to locate the Common Properties area of the Properties window. Next, change the `Header` property for each tab, naming them `Ink API`, `Documents`, `Data Binding`, and `DataGrid` (see Figure 28-27).

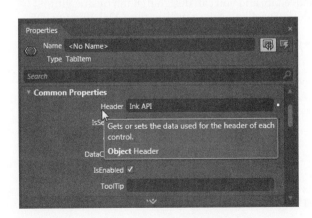

Figure 28-27. Visually editing the TabItem controls

At this point, your window designer should look like what you see in Figure 28-28.

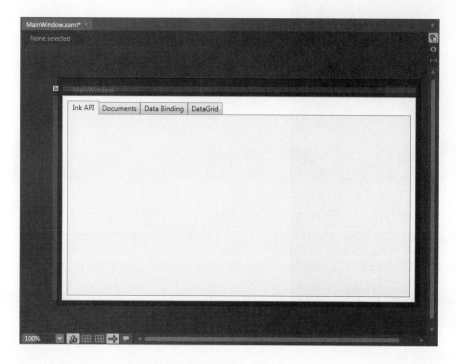

Figure 28-28. *The initial layout of the tab system*

Now click each tab again and use the Properties window to give each tab a unique, proper name (you can also select each tab item using the Objects and Timeline editor). Be aware that when you click a tab using either approach, that tab becomes the active tab, and you can design that tab by dragging controls from the Tools area. Before you begin to design each tab, take a peek at the XAML that the IDE generates on your behalf by clicking the XAML button. You should see markup similar to the following (your markup might differ based on the properties you set):

```
<Window
  xmlns="http://schemas.microsoft.com/winfx/2006/xaml/presentation"
  xmlns:x="http://schemas.microsoft.com/winfx/2006/xaml"
  x:Class="MainWindow"
  x:Name="Window"
  Title="MainWindow"
  Width="628" Height="383" >

  <Grid x:Name="LayoutRoot">
    <TabControl x:Name="myTabSystem" Margin="8">
      <TabItem x:Name="tabInk" Header="Ink API">
        <Grid/>
      </TabItem>
```

```
    <TabItem x:Name="tabDocuments" Header="Documents">
      <Grid/>
    </TabItem>
    <TabItem x:Name="tabDataBinding" Header="Data Binding">
      <Grid/>
    </TabItem>
    <TabItem x:Name="tabDataGrid" Header="DataGrid">
      <Grid/>
    </TabItem>
  </TabControl>
 </Grid>
</Window>
```

Building the Ink API Tab

The first tab shows the overall role of WPF's digital ink API, which allows you to incorporate painting functionality into a program easily. Of course, the application does not literally need to be a paining application; you can use this API for a wide variety of purposes, including capturing hand-writing input with a stylus for a TabletPC.

Begin by locating the node that represents the Ink API tab in your Objects and Timeline area and expand it. You should see that the default layout manager for this TabItem is a <Grid>. Right-click this and change it to a StackPanel (see Figure 28-29).

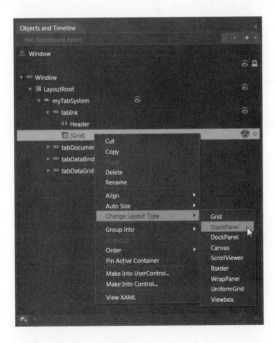

Figure 28-29. Changing the layout manager

Designing the ToolBar

You can ensure that the StackPanel is the currently selected node in the Objects and Timeline editor by using the Assets Library to insert a new ToolBar control named inkToolbar. Next, select the inkToolbar node in the Objects and Timeline editor, locate the Layout section of the Properties window, and set the Height of the Toolbar control to 60 (leave the Width set to Auto).

Now find the Common Properties section of your Properties window and click the ellipse button for the Items (Collection) property (see Figure 28-30).

Figure 28-30. The first step in adding controls to a ToolBar with the Blend Properties window

After you click this button, you are presented with a dialog box that allows you to select the controls you want to add to the ToolBar. Click the dropdown area of the Add another item button, then add three RadioButton controls (Figure 28-31).

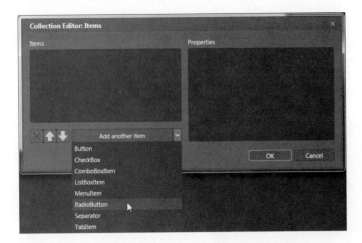

Figure 28-31. Adding three RadioButtons to the ToolBar

You can use the embedded Properties editor of this dialog to give each `RadioButton` a `Height` of `50` and a `Width` of `100` (again, you can find these properties in the Layout area). Also, set the `Content` property (located in the Common Properties area) of each `RadioButton` to the values `Ink Mode!`, `Erase Mode!`, and `Select Mode!` (see Figure 28-32).

Figure 28-32. Configuring each RadioButton

Once you add your three **RadioButton** controls, add a **Separator** control using the Add another item dropdown list. Now you need to add the final **ComboBox** (not **ComboBoxItem**) control; however, you will *not* see this control listed in the Add another item dropdown. When you need to insert non-standard controls using the Items (Collection) dialog, just click the Add another item area as if it were a push button. This opens the Select Object editor, where you can type in the name of the control you want (see Figure 28-33).

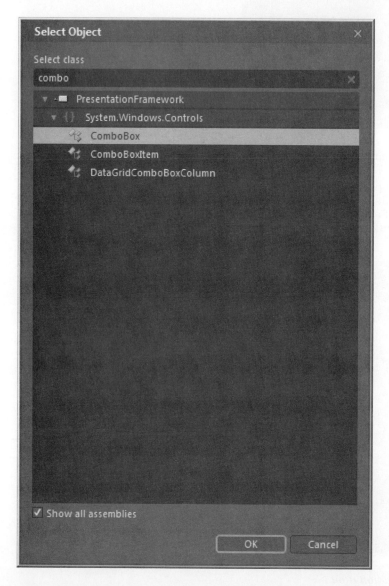

Figure 28-33. Using the Select Object editor to add unique items to the Toolbar

Set the Width property of the ComboBox to 100 and add three ComboBoxItem objects to the ComboBox using the Items (Collection) property (again) in the Common Properties section of the property editor. Set the Content property of each ComboBoxItem to the strings Red, Green, and Blue.

Once you do this, close the editor to return to the window designer. The last task for this section is to use the Name property to assign variable names to your new items. Name your three RadioButton controls inkRadio, selectRadio, and eraseRadio. Also, name your ComboBox control comboColors.

▥ **Note** As you built your toolbar using Blend, you might have thought to yourself how much quicker your task would be if you could simply edit the XAML by hand... and you're right! You might remember that Expression Blend is targeted at graphical artists who might not feel comfortable manually entering markup or code. As a VB 2010 programmer, you can always use the integrated XAML editor of Blend as you work through these chapters; however, it is useful to know how to work within the IDE, especially when you need to explain how to use the tool to designers!

The RadioButton Control

In this example, you want these three RadioButton controls to be mutually exclusive. In other GUI frameworks, ensuring that a group of related controls (such as radio buttons) were mutually exclusive required that you place them in the same group box. You don't need to do this under WPF. Instead, you can simply assign them all to the same *group name*. This is helpful because the related items do not need to be physically collected in the same area, but can be anywhere in the window.

Do this by selecting each RadioButton on the designer (you can select all three using a Shift-Click operation), and then setting the GroupName property (located in the Common Properties area of the Properties window) to InkMode.

When a RadioButton control is not placed inside of a parent panel control, it will take on a UI identical to a Button control! However, unlike a Button, the RadioButton class includes an IsChecked property, which toggles between True and False when the end user clicks the UI element. Furthermore, RadioButton provides two events (Checked and Unchecked) that you can use to intercept this state change.

To configure your RadioButton controls to look like typical radio buttons, select each control on the designer using a Shift+Click operation, then right-click the selection and pick the Group Into ➤ Border menu option (see Figure 28-34).

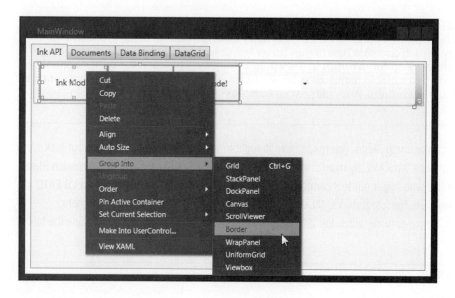

Figure 28-34. Grouping items in a Border control

At this point, you're ready to test the program, which you can do by pressing the F5 key. You should now see three mutually exclusive radio buttons and a combo box with three selections (see Figure 28-35).

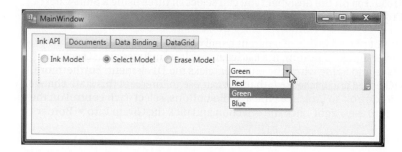

Figure 28-35. The completed toolbar system

Before you finish the UI of your Ink API tab, you need to handle the Click event for each RadioButton control. Similar to Visual Studio, the Blend Properties window has a Lightning Bolt button to enter the names of event handlers (you can see it mounted next to the Name property). Use this tool to route the Click event for each button to the same handler, named RadioButtonClicked (see Figure 28-36).

Figure 28-36. Handling the Click event for each RadioButton

Doing this brings up the Blend code editor. Once you handle all three `Click` events, handle the `SelectionChanged` event of the `ComboBox` using a handler named `ColorChanged`. When you finish, you should have the following VB 2010 code:

```
Class MainWindow

        Private Sub RadioButtonClicked(ByVal sender As Object,
            ByVal e As RoutedEventArgs)
            ' TODO: Add event handler implementation here.
        End Sub

        Private Sub ColorChanged(ByVal sender As Object,
            ByVal e As SelectionChangedEventArgs)
            ' TODO: Add event handler implementation here.
        End Sub
End Class
```

You will implement these handlers in a later step, so leave them empty for the time being.

The InkCanvas Control

To finish the UI of this tab, you need to place an `InkCanvas` control into the `StackPanel`, so it appears below the `Toolbar` you have just created. Select the `StackPanel` for the `tabInk` object in the Objects and Timeline editor, and then use the Assets Library to add an `InkCanvas` named `myInkCanvas`. Next, click the Selection tool on your Tools window (you can also press the V key on your keyboard as a shortcut) and stretch the ink canvas so it takes up a majority of the tab area.

Also, you might wish to use the Brushes editor to give your InkCanvas a unique background color (you'll learn much more about the brush editor in the next chapter). Once you do this, run your program by pressing the F5 key. You will see the canvas is already able to draw data when you click-and-drag the left-mouse button (see Figure 28-37).

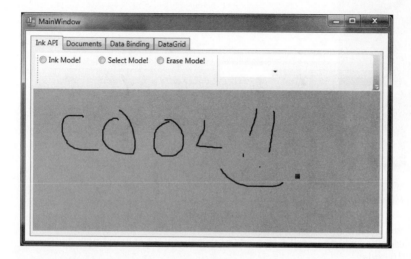

Figure 28-37. *The InkCanvas in action*

The InkCanvas does more than draw mouse (or stylus) strokes; it also supports a number of unique editing modes, controlled by the EditingMode property. You can assign this property any value from the related InkCanvasEditingMode enumeration. For this example, you are interested in Ink mode, which is the default option you just witnessed; Select mode, which allows the user to select a region with the mouse to move or resize; and EraseByStoke, which will delete the previous mouse stroke.

■ **Note** A *stroke* is the rendering that takes place during a single mouse down/mouse up operation. The InkCanvas stores all strokes in a StrokeCollection object, which you can access using the Strokes property.

Update your RadioButtonClicked() hander with the following logic, which places the InkCanvas in the correct mode, based on the selected RadioButton:

```
Private Sub RadioButtonClicked(ByVal sender As Object,
            ByVal e As RoutedEventArgs)
    ' Based on which button sent the event, place the InkCanvas in a unique
    ' mode of operation.
    Select Case TryCast(sender, RadioButton).Content.ToString()
        ' These strings must be the same as the Content values for each
        ' RadioButton.
        Case "Ink Mode!"
```

```
            Me.myInkCanvas.EditingMode = InkCanvasEditingMode.Ink
        Case "Erase Mode!"
            Me.myInkCanvas.EditingMode = InkCanvasEditingMode.EraseByStroke
        Case "Select Mode!"
            Me.myInkCanvas.EditingMode = InkCanvasEditingMode.[Select]
    End Select
End Sub
```

Also, add a constructor to your Main Window class to set the mode to Ink by default. And while you are at it, set a default selection for the ComboBox (more details on this control in the next section):

```
Public Sub New()

' First must call InitializeComponent().
    Me.InitializeComponent()

    ' Be in Ink mode by default.
    Me.myInkCanvas.EditingMode = InkCanvasEditingMode.Ink
    Me.inkRadio.IsChecked = True
    Me.comboColors.SelectedIndex = 0

End Sub
```

Now run your program again by pressing F5. Enter Ink mode and draw some data. Next, enter Erase mode and remove the previous mouse stroke you entered (you'll notice the mouse icon automatically looks like an erasure). Finally, enter Select mode and select some strokes by using the mouse as a lasso. After you circle the item, you can move it around the canvas and resize its dimensions. Figure 28-38 shows your edit modes at work.

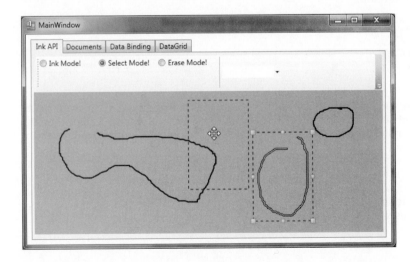

Figure 28-38. The InkCanvas in action, with edit modes!

The ComboBox Control

Once you populate a ComboBox control (or a ListBox), you have three ways to determine the selected item. First, if you wish to find the numerical index of the item selected, you can use the SelectedIndex property (which is zero-based; a value of -1 represents no selection). Second, if you wish to obtain the object within the list that has been selected, the SelectedItem property fits the bill. Third, the SelectedValue allows you to obtain the value of the selected object (typically obtained using a call to ToString()).

You need to add the last bit of code for this tab to change the color of the strokes entered on the InkCanvas. The DefaultDrawingAttributes property of InkCanvas returns a DrawingAttributes object that allows you to configure numerous aspect of the pen nib, including its size and color (among other settings). Update your VB 2010 code with this implementation of the ColorChanged() method:

```
Private Sub ColorChanged(ByVal sender As Object,
                              ByVal e As
SelectionChangedEventArgs)

    ' Get the Tag of the selected StackPanel.
    Dim colorToUse As String =
    TryCast(Me.comboColors.SelectedItem, ComboBoxItem).Content.ToString()

  ' Change the color used to render the strokes.
  Me.myInkCanvas.DefaultDrawingAttributes.Color =
      DirectCast(ColorConverter.ConvertFromString(colorToUse), Color)

End Sub
```

Now recall that the ComboBox has a collection of ComboBoxItems. If you were to view the generated XAML, you'd see the following definition:

```
<ComboBox x:Name="comboColors" Width="100" SelectionChanged="ColorChanged">
  <ComboBoxItem Content="Red"/>
  <ComboBoxItem Content="Green"/>
  <ComboBoxItem Content="Blue"/>
</ComboBox>
```

When you call SelectedItem, you grab the selected ComboBoxItem, which is stored as a general Object. Once you cast the Object as a ComboBoxItem, you pluck out the value of the Content, which will be the String Red, Green, or Blue. This String is then converted to a Color object using the handy ColorConverter utility class. Now run your program again. You should be able to change between colors as you render your image.

Note that the ComboBox and ListBox controls can contain complex content as well, rather than a list of text data. You can get a sense of some of the things that are possible by opening the XAML editor for your window and changing the definition of your ComboBox so it contains a set of <StackPanel> elements, each of which contains an <Ellipse> and a <Label> (notice that the Width of the ComboBox is 200):

```
<ComboBox x:Name="comboColors" Width="200" SelectionChanged="ColorChanged">
  <StackPanel Orientation ="Horizontal" Tag="Red">
    <Ellipse Fill ="Red" Height ="50" Width ="50"/>
    <Label FontSize ="20" HorizontalAlignment="Center"
           VerticalAlignment="Center" Content="Red"/>
  </StackPanel>

  <StackPanel Orientation ="Horizontal" Tag="Green">
    <Ellipse Fill ="Green" Height ="50" Width ="50"/>
    <Label FontSize ="20" HorizontalAlignment="Center"
           VerticalAlignment="Center" Content="Green"/>
  </StackPanel>

  <StackPanel Orientation ="Horizontal" Tag="Blue">
    <Ellipse Fill ="Blue" Height ="50" Width ="50"/>
    <Label FontSize ="20" HorizontalAlignment="Center"
           VerticalAlignment="Center" Content="Blue"/>
  </StackPanel>
</ComboBox>
```

Notice that each StackPanel assigns a value to its Tag property, which is a simple, fast, and convenient way to discover which stack of items has been selected by the user (there are better ways to do this, but this will do for now). With this adjustment, you need to change the implementation of your ColorChanged() method, like this:

```
Private Sub ColorChanged(ByVal sender As Object,
                ByVal e As SelectionChangedEventArgs)
    ' Get the Tag of the selected StackPanel.
    Dim colorToUse As String = TryCast(
                Me.comboColors.SelectedItem, ComboBoxItem).Content.ToString()
    ...
End Sub
```

Now run your program again and take note of your unique ComboBox (see Figure 28-39).

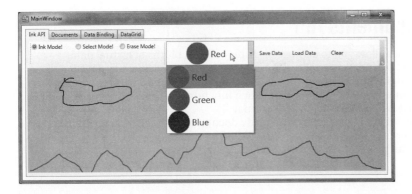

Figure 28-39. A custom ComboBox, thanks to the WPF content model

Saving, Loading, and Clearing InkCanvas Data

The last part of this tab will enable you to save and load your canvas data, as well as clear it of all content. At this point in the chapter, you might feel a bit more comfortable designing a UI with Blend, so the instructions will be short and sweet.

Begin by importing the `System.IO` and `System.Windows.Ink` namespaces to your code file. Now add three more `Button` controls to your `ToolBar` named `btnSave`, `btnLoad`, and `btnClear`. Next, handle the `Click` event for each control, then Implement the handlers, like this:

```
Private Sub SaveData(ByVal sender As Object, ByVal e As RoutedEventArgs)
    ' Save all data on the InkCanvas to a local file.
    Using fs As New FileStream("StrokeData.bin", FileMode.Create)
        Me.myInkCanvas.Strokes.Save(fs)
        fs.Close()
    End Using
End Sub

Private Sub LoadData(ByVal sender As Object, ByVal e As RoutedEventArgs)
    ' Fill StrokeCollection from file.
    Using fs As New FileStream("StrokeData.bin", FileMode.Open, FileAccess.Read)
        Dim strokes As New StrokeCollection(fs)
        Me.myInkCanvas.Strokes = strokes
    End Using
End Sub

Private Sub Clear(ByVal sender As Object, ByVal e As RoutedEventArgs)
    ' Clear all strokes.
    Me.myInkCanvas.Strokes.Clear()
End Sub
```

You should now be able to save your data to a file, load it from the file, and clear the `InkCanvas` of all data. That wraps up the first tab of the `TabControl`, as well as your examination of the WPF digital Ink API. To be sure, there is more to say about this technology; however, you should be in a good position to dig into the topic further if that interests you. Next, you will learn how to use the WPF Documents API.

Introducing the Documents API

WPF ships with many controls that allow you to capture or display simple blurbs of textual data, including `Label`, `TextBox`, `TextBlock`, and `PasswordBox`. These controls are useful, but some WPF applications require the use of sophisticated, highly formatted text data, similar to what you might find in an Adobe PDF file. The Documents API of WPF provides such functionality; however, it uses the XML Paper Specification (XPS) format rather than the PDF file format .

You can use the Documents API to construct a print-ready document by leveraging several classes from the `System.Windows.Documents` namespace. Here you will find a number of types that represent pieces of a rich XPS document, such as `List`, `Paragraph`, `Section`, `Table`, `LineBreak`, `Figure`, `Floater`, and `Span`.

Block Elements and Inline Elements

Formally speaking, the items you add to a XPS document belong to one of two broad categories: *block elements* and *inline elements*. This first category, *block elements*, consists of classes that extend the `System.Windows.Documents.Block` base class. Examples of block elements include `List`, `Paragraph`, `BlockUIContainer`, `Section`, and `Table`. You use classes from this category to group together other content (e.g., a list containing paragraph data, and a paragraph containing sub paragraphs for different text formatting).

The second category, *inline elements*, consists of classes that extend the `System.Windows.Documents.Inline` base class. You nest inline elements within another block item (or possibly within another inline element inside a block element). Some common inline elements include `Run`, `Span`, `LineBreak`, `Figure`, and `Floater`.

These classes possess names that you might encounter when building a rich document with a professional editor. As with any other WPF control, you can configure these classes in XAML or through code. Therefore, you can declare an empty `<Paragraph>` element that is populated at runtime (you'll see how to do such tasks in this example).

Document Layout Managers

You might think you can simply place inline and block elements directly into a panel container such as a `Grid`; however, you need to wrap them in a `<FlowDocument>` element or a `<FixedDocument>` element.

It is ideal to place items in a `FlowDocument` when you wish to let your end user change the way the data is presented on the computer screen. The user can do this by zooming text or changing how the data is presented (e.g., a single long page or a pair of columns). You're better off using `FixedDocument` for true print-ready (WYSIWYG), unchangeable document data.

For this example, you will only concern yourself with the `FlowDocument` container. Once you insert inline and block items to your `FlowDocument`, the `FlowDocument` object is placed in one of four specialized XPS-aware layout managers, listed in Table 28-4.

Table 28-4. XPS Control Layout Managers

Panel Control	Meaning in Life
`FlowDocumentReader`	Displays data in a `FlowDocument` and adds support for zooming, searching, and content layout in various forms.
`FlowDocumentScrollViewer`	Displays data in a `FlowDocument`; however, the data is presented as a single document viewed with scrollbars. This container does not support zooming, searching, or alternative layout modes.
`RichTextBox`	Displays data in a `FlowDocument` and adds support for user editing.
`FlowDocumentPageViewer`	Displays the document page-by-page, one page at a time. Data can also be zoomed, but not searched.

The most feature-rich way to display a FlowDocument is to wrap it within a FlowDocumentReader manager. When you do this, the user can alter the layout, search for words in the document, and zoom in on the data using the provided UI. The one limitation of this container (as well as of FlowDocumentScrollViewer and FlowDocumentPageViewer) is that the content you display with it is read only. However, if you do want to allow the end user to enter new information to the FlowDocument, you can wrap it in a RichTextBox control.

Building the Documents Tab

Click on the Documents tab of your TabItem and use the Blend editor to open this control for editing. You should already have a default <Grid> control as the direct child of the TabItem control; however, change it to a StackPanel here using the Objects and Timeline window. This tab will display a FlowDocument that allows the user to highlight selected text, as well as add annotations using the Sticky Notes API.

Begin by defining the following ToolBar control, which has three simple (and unnamed!) Button controls. You will be rigging up a few new commands to these controls later on, so you do not need to refer to them in code:

```
<TabItem x:Name="tabDocuments" Header="Documents" VerticalAlignment="Bottom"
        Height="20">
  <StackPanel>
    <ToolBar>
      <Button BorderBrush="Green" Content="Add Sticky Note"/>
      <Button BorderBrush="Green" Content="Delete Sticky Notes"/>
      <Button BorderBrush="Green" Content="Highlight Text"/>
    </ToolBar>
  </StackPanel>
</TabItem>
```

Next, open the Assets Library and locate the FlowDocumentReader control from the All category of the Controls node. Place this control into your StackPanel, rename it to myDocumentReader, and stretch it out over the surface of your StackPanel (make sure you have clicked the Selection tool). At this point, your layout should look similar to what you see in Figure 28-40.

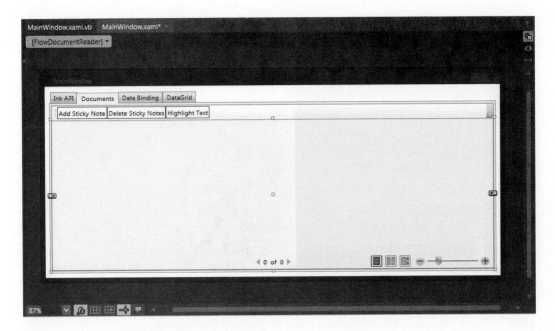

Figure 28-40. *The layout of the Documents tab*

Now select your `FlowDocumentReader` control in the Objects and Timeline editor and locate the Miscellaneous category of the Properties window. Next, click the New button next to the Document property. Doing this updates your XAML with an empty `<FlowDocument>`:

```
<FlowDocumentReader x:Name="myDocumentReader" Height="269.4">
  <FlowDocument/>
</FlowDocumentReader>
```

At this point, you can add document classes (e.g., `List`, `Paragraph`, `Section`, `Table`, `LineBreak`, `Figure`, `Floater`, and `Span`) to the element.

Populating a FlowDocument using Blend

As soon as you add a new document to a document container, the Document property in the Properties window becomes expandable, displaying a *ton* of new properties that allow you to build the design of your document. For this example, the only property you care about is the `Blocks` (`Collection`) property (see Figure 28-41).

Figure 28-41. You can populate a FlowDocument using the Blocks (Collection) property

Click the ellipse button (...) to the right of `Blocks (Collection)`, and then use the Add another item button of the resulting dialog box to insert a `Section`, `List`, and `Paragraph`. You can edit each one of these further using the Blocks editor; furthermore, a given block can contain related sub-blocks. For example, if you select your `Section`, you can add a `Paragraph` sub-block. In my case, I configured my `Section` with a specific background color, foreground color, and font size. I also inserted a sub-`Paragraph`.

Go ahead and configure your `Section` as you wish; however, leave the `List` and original `Paragraph` empty because you will drive these through code. Here is one possible way to configure the `FlowDocument`:

```
<FlowDocumentReader x:Name="myDocumentReader" Height="269.4">
  <FlowDocument>
    <Section Foreground = "Yellow" Background = "Black">
      <Paragraph FontSize = "20">
        Here are some fun facts about the WPF Document API!
      </Paragraph>
    </Section>
    <List/>
    <Paragraph/>
  </FlowDocument>
</FlowDocumentReader>
```

If you run your program now (hit the F5 key), you should already be able to zoom your document (using the lower-right slider bar), search for a keyword (using the lower-left search editor) and display the data in one of three manners (using the layout buttons). Figure 28-42 shows a search for the text *WPF*; note too that the content shown in this figure has been zoomed in on.

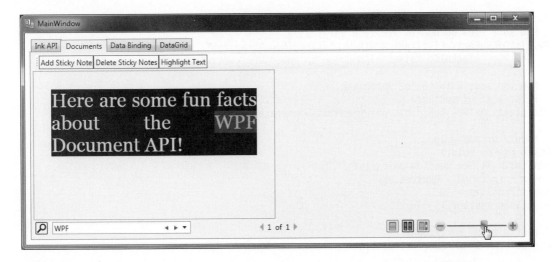

Figure 28-42. Manipulating the FlowDocument with the FlowDocumentReader

Before moving to the next step, you might want to edit your XAML to use a different FlowDocument container, such as the FlowDocumentScrollViewer or a RichTextBox, rather than the FlowDocumentReader. Once you done this, run the application again and notice the different ways the document data is handled. Be sure to roll back to the FlowDocumentReader type when you finish this task.

Populating a FlowDocument Using Code

Now, let's build the List block and the remaining Paragraph block in code. This is important because you might need to populate a FlowDocument based on user input, external files, database information, or what have you. Before you do so, use the XAML editor of Blend to give the List and Paragraph elements proper names, so you can access them in code:

```
<List x:Name="listOfFunFacts"/>
<Paragraph x:Name="paraBodyText"/>
```

In your code file, define a new Private method named PopulateDocument(). This method first adds a set of new ListItems to the List, each of which has a Paragraph with a single Run. Also, your helper method dynamically builds a formatted paragraph using three separate Run objects, as in the following example:

```
Private Sub PopulateDocument()
    ' Add some data to the List item.
    Me.listOfFunFacts.FontSize = 14
    Me.listOfFunFacts.MarkerStyle = TextMarkerStyle.Circle
    Me.listOfFunFacts.ListItems.Add(New ListItem(New Paragraph(
      New Run("Fixed documents are for WYSIWYG print ready docs!"))))
    Me.listOfFunFacts.ListItems.Add(New ListItem(New Paragraph(
      New Run("The API supports tables and embedded figures!"))))
```

```
        Me.listOfFunFacts.ListItems.Add(New ListItem(New Paragraph(
          New Run("Flow documents are read only!"))))
        Me.listOfFunFacts.ListItems.Add(New ListItem(New Paragraph(
          New Run("BlockUIContainer allows you to embed WPF controls in the document!"))))

        ' Now add some data to the Paragraph.
        ' First part of sentence.
        Dim prefix As New Run("This paragraph was generated ")

        ' Middle of paragraph.
        Dim b As New Bold()
        Dim infix As New Run("dynamically")
        infix.Foreground = Brushes.Red
        infix.FontSize = 30
        b.Inlines.Add(infix)

        ' Last part of paragraph.
        Dim suffix As New Run(" at runtime!")

        ' Now add each piece to the collection of inline elements
        ' of the Paragraph.
        Me.paraBodyText.Inlines.Add(prefix)
        Me.paraBodyText.Inlines.Add(infix)
        Me.paraBodyText.Inlines.Add(suffix)
    End Sub
```

Make sure you call this method from your window's constructor. Once you do this, you can run the application and see your new, dynamically generated document content.

Enabling Annotations and Sticky Notes

So far, so good. You can now build a document with interesting data using XAML and VB 2010 code; however, you still need to address the three buttons on your toolbar for the Documents tab. WPF ships with a set of commands that are used specifically with the Documents API. You can use these commands to allow the user to select a part of a document for highlighting or to add sticky note annotations. Best of all, you can add all of this with a few lines of code (and a tad of markup).

You can find the command objects for the Documents API bundled in the System.Windows.Annotations namespace of PresentationFramework.dll. Thus, you need to define a custom XML namespace in the opening element of the <Window> to use such objects in XAML (notice that the tag prefix is *a*):

```
<Window
...
  xmlns:a=
  "clr-namespace:System.Windows.Annotations;assembly=PresentationFramework"
  x:Class="MainWindow"
  x:Name="Window"
  Title="MainWindow"
```

```
 Width="856" Height="383"
   WindowStartupLocation="CenterScreen" >
...
</Window>
```

Now update your three <Button> definitions to set the Command property to three of the supplied annotation commands:

```
<ToolBar>
  <Button BorderBrush="Green" Content="Add Sticky Note"
          Command="a:AnnotationService.CreateTextStickyNoteCommand"/>
  <Button BorderBrush="Green" Content="Delete Sticky Notes"
          Command="a:AnnotationService.DeleteStickyNotesCommand"/>
  <Button BorderBrush="Green" Content="Highlight Text"
          Command="a:AnnotationService.CreateHighlightCommand"/>
</ToolBar>
```

The last thing you need to do is to enable annotation services for the FlowDocumentReader object, which you named myDocumentReader. Add another Private method in your class named EnableAnnotations(), which is called from the constructor of the window. Now import the following namespaces:

```
Imports System.Windows.Annotations
Imports System.Windows.Annotations.Storage
```

Next, implement this method:

```
Private Sub EnableAnnotations()
    ' Create the AnnotationService object that works
    ' with our FlowDocumentReader.
    Dim anoService As New AnnotationService(myDocumentReader)

    ' Create a MemoryStream which will hold the annotations.
    Dim anoStream As New MemoryStream()

    ' Now, create a XML-based store based on the MemoryStream.
    ' You could use this object to programmatically add, delete
    ' or find annotations.
    Dim store As AnnotationStore = New XmlStreamStore(anoStream)

    ' Enable the annotation services.
    anoService.Enable(store)
End Sub
```

The AnnotationService class allows a given document layout manger to opt in to annotation support. Before you call the Enable() method of this object, you need to provide a location for the object to store annotation data, which in this example is a chunk of memory represented by a MemoryStream object. Notice that you connect the AnnotationService object with the Stream using the AnnotationStore.

Now, run your application. When you select some text, you can click the Add Sticky Note button and type in some information. Also, when you select some text, you can highlight data (the color is yellow by default). Finally, you can delete created notes once you select them and click the Delete Sticky Note button. Figure 28-43 shows a test run.

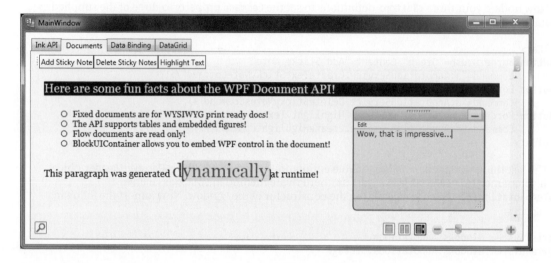

Figure 28-43. Sticky notes!

Saving and Loading a Flow Document

Let's wrap up this look at the Documents API by looking at how simple it is to save a document out to a file, as well as read a document in from a file. Recall that, unless you wrap your FlowDocument object in a RichTextBox, the end user cannot edit the document; however, part of the document was created dynamically at runtime, so you might like to save it for later use. The ability to load an XPS style document could also be useful in many WPF applications because you might wish to define a blank document and load it all on the fly.

This next snippet assumes you will add two new Buttons to the Toolbar of the Documents tab, which you declare like this (note that you did not handle any events in your markup):

```
<Button x:Name="btnSaveDoc" HorizontalAlignment="Stretch"
        VerticalAlignment="Stretch" Width="75" Content="Save Doc"/>
<Button x:Name="btnLoadDoc" HorizontalAlignment="Stretch"
        VerticalAlignment="Stretch" Width="75" Content="Load Doc"/>
```

Add the following code to your Window class, to save and load the FlowDocument data (you'll need to import the System.Windows.Markup namespace to gain access to the XamlReader and XamlWriter classes):

```vbnet
Public Sub New()
    ...
    ' Rig up some Click handlers for the save / load of the flow doc.
    AddHandler btnSaveDoc.Click, AddressOf SaveFlowDoc
    AddHandler btnLoadDoc.Click, AddressOf LoadFlowDoc
End Sub

Private Sub SaveFlowDoc()
    Using fStream As FileStream = File.Open("documentData.xaml", FileMode.Create)
        XamlWriter.Save(Me.myDocumentReader.Document, fStream)
    End Using
End Sub

Private Sub LoadFlowDoc()
    Using fStream As FileStream = File.Open("documentData.xaml", FileMode.Open)
        Try
            Dim doc As FlowDocument = TryCast(XamlReader.Load(fStream), FlowDocument)
            Me.myDocumentReader.Document = doc
        Catch ex As Exception
            MessageBox.Show(ex.Message, "Error Loading Doc!")
        End Try
    End Using
End Sub
```

That is all you need to do to save the document (note that you did not save any annotations; however, you can also accomplish that using annotation services). If you click your Save button, you will see a new *.xaml file in your \bin\Debug folder. This file contains the current document data.

That wraps up your look at the WPF Documents API. To be sure, there is more to this API than you have seen here; but at this point, you know a good deal about the basics. To wrap up this chapter, you will look at a handful of data-binding topics and complete the current application.

Introducing the WPF Data-Binding Model

Controls are often the target of various data-binding operations. Simply put, *data binding* is the act of connecting control properties to data values that might change over the course of your application's lifetime. Doing so lets a user interface element display the state of a variable in your code. For example, you might use data binding to accomplish the following:

- Check a CheckBox control based on a Boolean property of a given object.

- Display data in DataGrid objects from a relational database table.

- Connect a Label to an integer that represents the number of files in a folder.

When you use the intrinsic WPF data-binding engine, you must be aware of the distinction between the *source* and the *destination* of the binding operation. As you might expect, the source of a data-binding operation is the data itself (e.g., a Boolean property or relational data), while the destination (target) is the UI control property that uses the data content (e.g., a CheckBox or TextBox).

Truth be told, using the WPF data-binding infrastructure is always optional. If you were to roll your own data-binding logic, the connection between a source and destination typically would involve handling various events and authoring procedural code to connect the source and destination. For example, if you had a ScrollBar on a window that needed to display its value on a Label type, you might handle the ScrollBar's ValueChanged event and update the Label's content accordingly.

However, you can use WPF data binding to connect the source and destination directly in XAML (or use VB 2010 code in your code file) without the need to handle various events or hard-code the connections between the source and destination. Also, based on how you set up your data-binding logic, you can ensure that the source and destination stay in sync if either of their values changes.

Building the Data Binding Tab

Using the Objects and Timeline editor, change the Grid of your third tab to a StackPanel. Now, use the Assets Library and the Properties editor of Blend to build the following initial layout:

```
<TabItem x:Name="tabDataBinding" Header="Data Binding">
  <StackPanel Width="250">
    <Label Content="Move the scroll bar to see the current value"/>

    <!-- The scrollbar's value is the source of this data bind -->
    <ScrollBar x:Name="mySB" Orientation="Horizontal" Height="30"
          Minimum = "1" Maximum = "100" LargeChange="1" SmallChange="1"/>

    <!-- The label's content will be bound to the scroll bar! -->
    <Label x:Name="labelSBThumb" Height="30" BorderBrush="Blue"
          BorderThickness="2" Content = "0"/>
  </StackPanel>
</TabItem>
```

Notice that the <ScrollBar> object (named mySB here) has been configured with a range between 1 and 100. The goal is to ensure that, as you reposition the thumb of the scrollbar (or click the left or right arrow), the Label will automatically update with the current value.

Establishing Data Bindings using Blend

The glue that makes it possible to define a binding in XAML is the {Binding} markup extension. If you wish to establish a binding between controls using Blend, you can do so easily. For this example, locate the Content property of the Label object (in the Common Properties area of the Properties window) and click the (very) small white square next to the property to open the Advanced Property options. From here, select Data Binding (see Figure 28-44).

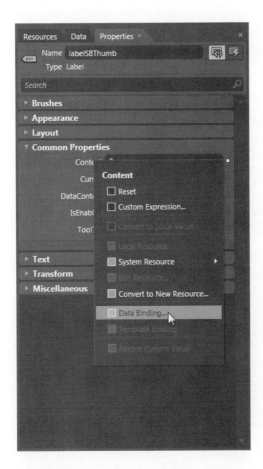

Figure 28-44. Configuring a data binding operation with Blend

You are interested in the Element Property tab here because this will give you a list of all items in your XAML file, which you can select as the source of the data-binding operation. Select this tab, and in the Scene elements list box, find your ScrollBar object (named mySB). In the Properties list box, find the Value property (see Figure 28-45). Click the OK button once you do this.

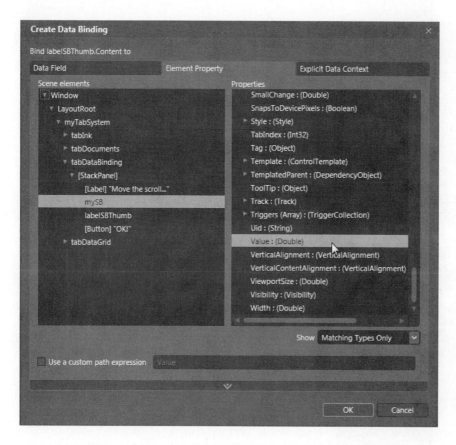

Figure 28-45. *Selecting the source object and the property on the object*

If you run your program again, you will find that the content of the label updates as you move the thumb! Now look at the XAML the data binding tool generated on your behalf:

```
<Label x:Name="labelSBThumb" Height="30" BorderBrush="Blue" BorderThickness="2"
        Content = "{Binding Value, ElementName=mySB, Mode=Default}"/>
```

Note the value assigned to the **Label**'s **Content** property. Here, the **ElementName** value represents the source of the data-binding operation (the **ScrollBar** object), while the first item after the Binding keyword (**Value**) represents (in this case) the property of the element to obtain.

If you have worked with WPF data binding previously, you might expect to see the use of the Path token to set the property to observe on the object. For example, the following markup would also update the **Label** correctly:

```
<Label x:Name="labelSBThumb" Height="30" BorderBrush="Blue"
        BorderThickness="2" Content = "{Binding Path=Value,
        ElementName=mySB, Mode=Default}"/>
```

By default, Blend omits the `Path=` aspect of the data-binding operation unless the property is a sub-property of another object (e.g., `myObject.MyProperty.Object2.Property2`).

The DataContext Property

You can define a data-binding operation in XAML using an alternative format, where it is possible to break out the values specified by the `{Binding}` markup extension by explicitly setting the `DataContext` property to the source of the binding operation, as follows:

```
<!-- Breaking object/value apart via DataContext -->
<Label x:Name="labelSBThumb" Height="30" BorderBrush="Blue"
       BorderThickness="2"
       DataContext = "{Binding ElementName=mySB}"
       Content = "{Binding Path=Value}" />
```

In the current example, the output would be identical if you were to modify the markup in this way. Given this, you might wonder when you would want to set the `DataContext` property explicitly. Doing so can be helpful because sub-elements can inherit its value in a tree of markup.

In this way, you can easily set the same data source to a family of controls, rather than having to repeat a bunch of redundant `"{Binding ElementName=X, Path=Y}"` XAML values to multiple controls. For example, assume you have added a new `Button` to the `<StackPanel>` of this tab (you'll see why it is so large in just a moment):

```
<Button Content="Click" Height="140"/>
```

You could use Blend to generate data bindings for multiple controls, but instead try entering the modified markup manually using the XAML editor:

```
<!-- Note the StackPanel sets the DataContext property -->
<StackPanel Width="250" DataContext = "{Binding ElementName=mySB}">
  <Label Content="Move the scroll bar to see the current value"/>

  <ScrollBar Orientation="Horizontal" Height="30" Name="mySB"
             Maximum = "100" LargeChange="1" SmallChange="1"/>

  <!-- Now both UI elements use the scrollbar's value in unique ways. -->
  <Label x:Name="labelSBThumb" Height="30" BorderBrush="Blue" BorderThickness="2"
         Content = "{Binding Path=Value}"/>

  <Button Content="Click" Height="200"
          FontSize = "{Binding Path=Value}"/>
</StackPanel>
```

Here, you set the `DataContext` property on the `<StackPanel>` directly. Therefore, as you move the thumb, you see not only the current value on the `Label`, but also see the font size of the `Button` grow and shrink accordingly, based on the same value (see Figure 28-46 shows for one possible output).

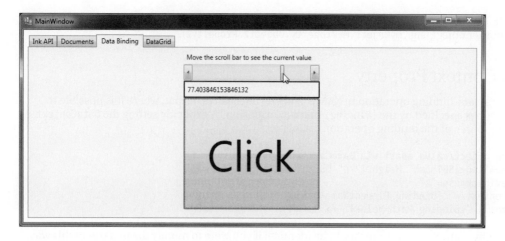

Figure 28-46. Binding the ScrollBar value to a Label and a Button

Data Conversion Using IValueConverter

The ScrollBar type uses a Double to represent the value of the thumb, rather than an expected whole number (e.g., an Integer). Therefore, as you drag the thumb, you will find various floating-point numbers displayed within the Label (e.g., 61.0576923076923). The end user would find this rather unintuitive because he is most likely expecting to see whole numbers (e.g., 61, 62, and 63).

If you wish to convert the value of a data-binding operation into an alternative format, you could create a custom class that implements the IValueConverter interface of the System.Windows.Data namespace. This interface defines two members that allow you to perform the conversion to and from the target and destination (in the case of a two-way data binding). Once you define this class, you can use it to qualify further the processing of your data-binding operation.

Assuming that you wish to display whole numbers within the Label control, you can build the following class using Expression Blend. Activate the Project ➤ Add New Item menu and insert a class named MyDoubleConverter. Next, add the following:

```
Class MyDoubleConverter
  Implements IValueConverter
    Public Function Convert(
              ByVal value As Object,
              ByVal targetType As Type,
              ByVal parameter As Object,
              ByVal culture As System.Globalization.CultureInfo) As Object _
              Implements IValueConverter.Convert

          ' Convert the double to an Integer.
              Dim v As Double = CDbl(value)
              Return CInt(Math.Truncate(v))

    End Function
```

```
        Public Function ConvertBack(
                ByVal value As Object,
                ByVal targetType As Type,
                ByVal parameter As Object,
                ByVal culture As System.Globalization.CultureInfo) As Object _
                Implements IValueConverter.ConvertBack

                ' We won't worry about "two way" bindings
                        ' here, so just return the value.
                        Return value
        End Function
End Class
```

The `Convert()` method is called when the value is transferred from the source (the `ScrollBar`) to the destination (the `Text` property of the `TextBox`). You receive many of incoming arguments, but you only need to manipulate the incoming `object` for this conversion, which is the value of the current `Double`. You can use this type to cast the type into an Integer and return the new number.

The `ConvertBack()` method will be called when the value is passed from the destination to the source (if you have enabled a two-way binding mode). Here, you simply return the value straightaway. Doing so lets you type a floating-point value into the `TextBox` (e.g., `99.9`) and have it automatically convert to a whole number value (e.g., `99`) when the user tabs off the control. This "free" conversion happens due to the fact that the `Convert()` method is called again, after a call to `ConvertBack()`. If you were simply to return `Nothing` from `ConvertBack()`, your binding would appear to be out of sync because the text box would still be displaying a floating-point number!

Establishing Data Bindings in Code

With this class in place, you are ready to register your custom converter with any control that wishes to use it. You could accomplish this exclusively in XAML; however, to do so, you would need to define some custom object resources, which you will not learn how to do until the next chapter. For now, you can register your data conversion class in code. Begin by cleaning up the current definition of the <Label> control in your data binding tab, so that it no longer uses the `{Binding}` markup extension:

```
<Label x:Name="labelSBThumb" Height="30" BorderBrush="Blue"
        BorderThickness="2" Content = "0"/>
```

In your window's constructor, call a new Private helper Method called `SetBindings()`. In this method, add the following code:

```
Private Sub SetBindings()
    ' Create a Binding object.
    Dim b As New Binding()

    ' Register the converter, source and path.
    b.Converter = New MyDoubleConverter()
    b.Source = Me.mySB
    b.Path = New PropertyPath("Value")
```

```
    ' Call the SetBinding method on the Label.
    Me.labelSBThumb.SetBinding(Label.ContentProperty, b)
End Sub
```

The only part of this function that probably looks a bit off is the call to SetBinding(). Notice that the first parameter calls a Shared, read-only field of the Label class named ContentProperty.

As you will learn about in Chapter 31, you are specifying what is known as a *dependency property*. For the time being, just know that when you set bindings in code, the first argument will nearly always require you to specify the name of the class that wants the binding (the Label, in this case), followed by a call to the underlying property with the -Property suffix (again, you'll learn more about this in Chapter 31). In any case, running the application illustrates that the Label only prints out whole numbers.

Building the DataGrid Tab

You have built an interesting example so far using nothing but Expression Blend. For the remainder of this project, however, you will use Visual Studio 2010, which will give you some firsthand experience regarding how Blend and Visual Studio can work hand-in-hand. So, save your project and close down Blend. Next, open the same project in Visual Studio 2010 using the File ➤ Open ➤ Project/Solution... menu option.

The previous data-binding example illustrated how to configure two (or more) controls to participate in a data-binding operation. While this is helpful, it is also possible to bind data from XML files, database data, and in-memory objects. To complete this example, you will design the final tab of your tab control, so it displays data obtained from the Inventory table of the AutoLot database.

As with the other tabs, you begin by changing the current Grid to a StackPanel. Do this by directly updating the XAML using Visual Studio. Now define a DataGrid control in your new StackPanel named gridInventory:

```
<TabItem x:Name="tabDataGrid" Header="DataGrid">
  <StackPanel>
    <DataGrid x:Name="gridInventory" Height="288"/>
  </StackPanel>
</TabItem>
```

Next, reference the AutoLotDAL.dll assembly you created in Chapter 23 (where you used the Entity Framework), as well as System.Data.Entity.dll. You will use the Entity Framework, so you need to ensure that your project has the required connection string data in an App.config file. You should probably begin by copying the App.config file from your AutoLotEDM_GUI project from Chapter 23 into this project using the Project ➤ Add Existing Item menu option.

Open the code file for your window and add a final helper Method called ConfigureGrid();make sure you call this from your constructor. Assuming that you did import the AutoLotDAL namespace, all you need to do is add a few lines of code:

```
Private Sub ConfigureGrid()
    Using context As New AutoLotEntities()
        ' Build a LINQ query that gets back some data from the Inventory table.
        Dim dataToShow = From c In context.Inventories _
         Select New With{ _
          c.CarID, _
          c.Make, _
```

```
        c.Color, _
        c.PetName}
    Me.gridInventory.ItemsSource = dataToShow
    End Using
End Sub
```

Notice that you do not directly bind `context.Inventories` to the grid's `ItemsSource` collection; instead, you build a LINQ query that appears to ask for the same data in the entities. The reason for this approach: The Inventory object set *also* contains additional EF properties that would appear on the grid, but which don't map to the physical database.

If we were to run the project as-is, you would see an extremely plain grid. To make the grid a bit less of an eye sore, use the Visual Studio 2010 Properties window to edit the Rows category of the `DataGrid`. At a minimum, set the `AlternationCount` property to `2` and pick a custom brush using the integrated editor for the `AlternatingRowBackground` and `RowBackground` properties (see Figure 28-47 for some possible values).

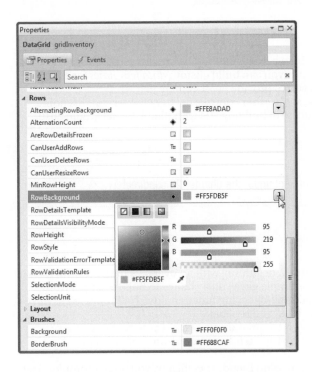

Figure 28-47. Applying some eye candy to the grid

You can see the final tab for this example in Figure 28-48.

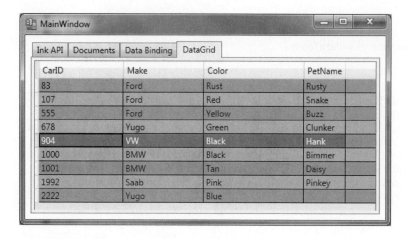

Figure 28-48. The final tab of your project

To be sure, you can configure the WPF `DataGrid` in a huge number of ways, so you'll want to consult the .NET Framework 4.0 SDK for details. For example, you can build custom *data templates* for the DataGrid using WPF graphical types; this enables you to provide an extremely rich UI.

That wraps up the current example. You'll use some other controls in later chapters; at this point, however, you should feel comfortable with the process of building UIs with Blend, Visual Studio 2010, and manually using XAML and VB 2010 code.

■ **Source Code** You can find the WpfControlsAndAPIs project under the Chapter 28 subdirectory.

Summary

This chapter examined several aspects of WPF controls, beginning with an overview of the control toolkit and the role of layout managers (panels). The first example gave you a chance to build a simple word processor application that illustrated the integrated spell-checking functionality of WPF, as well as how to build a main window with menu systems, status bars, and tool bars.

More importantly, you examined how to use WPF commands. Recall that you can attach these control-agnostic events to a UI element or an input gesture to inherit out-of-the-box services automatically (e.g., clipboard operations).

You also learned quite a bit about Microsoft Expression Blend. Specifically, you built a complex user interface using numerous aspects of the tool, and you learned about the WPF `Ink` and `Document` APIs at the same time. You also received an introduction to WPF data binding operations, including how to use the .NET 4.0 WPF `DataGrid` class to display data from your custom AutoLot database.

■ ■ ■

## CHAPTER 29

WPF Graphics Rendering Services

In this chapter we'll examine the graphical rendering capabilities of Windows Presentation Foundation (WPF). As you'll see, WPF provides three separate ways to render graphical data—shapes, drawings and visuals. Once you understand the pros and cons of each approach, you will start learning about the world of interactive 2D graphics using the classes within System.Windows.Shapes. After this, you'll see how drawings and geometries allow you to render 2D data in a more lightweight manner. And last but not least, you'll learn how the visual layer gives you the greatest level of power and performance.

Along the way, you will explore a number of related topics, such as the creation of custom brushes and pens, how to apply graphical transformations to your renderings, and how to perform hit-test operations. In particular, you'll see how the integrated tools of Visual Studio 2010, Expression Blend and Expression Design, can help simplify your graphical coding endeavors.

■ **Note** Graphics are a key aspect of WPF development. Even if you are not building a graphics-heavy application (such as a video game or multimedia application), the topics in this chapter are critical when you work with services such as control templates, animations, and data binding customization.

Understanding WPF's Graphical Rendering Services

WPF uses a particular flavor of graphical rendering that goes by the term *retained-mode graphics*. Simply put, this means that as you are using XAML or procedural code to generate graphical renderings, it is the responsibility of WPF to persist these visual items and ensure they are correctly redrawn and refreshed in an optimal manner. Thus, when you render graphical data, it is always present, even when the end user hides the image by resizing or minimizing the window, by covering the window with another, and so forth.

In stark contrast, previous Microsoft graphical rendering APIs (including Windows Form's GDI+) were *immediate-mode* graphical systems. In this model, it was up to the programmer to ensure that rendered visuals were correctly "remembered" and updated during the life of the application. For example, in a Windows Forms application, rendering a shape such as a rectangle involves handling the Paint event (or overriding the OnPaint() method), obtaining a Graphics object to draw the rectangle and, most important, adding the infrastructure to ensure that the image was persisted when the user resized the window (for example, creating member variables to represent the position of the rectangle and calling Invalidate() throughout your program).

The shift from immediate-mode to retained-mode graphics is indeed a good thing, as programmers have far less grungy graphics code to author and maintain. However, I'm not suggesting that the WPF graphics API is *completely* different from earlier rendering toolkits. For example, like GDI+, WPF supports various brush types and pen objects, techniques for hit-testing, clipping regions, graphical transformations, and so on. So, if you currently have a background in GDI+, you already know a good deal about how to perform basic renderings under WPF.

WPF Graphical Rendering Options

As with other aspects of WPF development, you have a number of choices regarding how to perform your graphical rendering, beyond the decision to do so via XAML or procedural VB 2010 code (or perhaps a combination of both). Specifically, WPF provides three distinct ways to render graphical data:

- **Shapes**: WPF provides the `System.Windows.Shapes` namespace, which defines a small number of classes for rendering 2D geometric objects (rectangles, ellipses, polygons, etc.). While these types are very simple to use, and very powerful, they do come with a fair amount of memory overhead if used with reckless abandon.

- **Drawings and Geometries**: The WPF API provides a second way to render graphical data, using descendants from the `System.Windows.Media.Drawing` MustInherit class. Using classes such as `GeometryDrawing` or `ImageDrawing` (in addition to various *geometry objects*) you can render graphical data in a more lightweight (but less feature-rich) manner.

- **Visuals**: The fastest and most lightweight way to render graphical data under WPF is using the visual layer, which is accessible only through VB 2010 code. Using descendants of `System.Windows.Media.Visual`, you can speak directly to the WPF graphical subsystem.

The reason for offering different ways to do the exact same thing (i.e., render graphical data) has to do with memory use and ultimately application performance. Because WPF is such a graphically intensive system, it is not unreasonable for an application to render hundreds or even thousands of different images on a window's surface, and the choice of implementation (shapes, drawings, or visuals) could have a huge impact.

Do understand that when you build a WPF application, chances are good you'll use all three options. As a rule of thumb, if you need a modest amount of *interactive* graphical data that can be manipulated by the user (receive mouse input, display tooltips, etc), you'll want to use members in the `System.Windows.Shapes` namespace.

In contrast, drawings and geometries are more appropriate when you need to model complex, generally non-interactive, vector-based graphical data using XAML or VB 2010. While drawings and geometries can still respond to mouse events, hit-testing, and drag-and-drop operations, you will typically need to author more code to do so.

Last but not least, if you require the fastest possible way to render massive amounts of graphical data, the visual layer is the way to go. For example, let's say you are using WPF to build a scientific application that can plot out thousands of points of data. Using the visual layer, you can render the plot points in the most optimal way possible. As you will see later in this chapter, the visual layer is only accessible via VB 2010 code, and is not XAML-friendly.

No matter which approach you take (shapes, drawings and geometries, or visuals) you will make use of common graphical primitives such as brushes (which fill interiors), pens (which draw exteriors) and transformation objects (which, well, transform the data). To begin the journey, we will begin working with the classes of `System.Windows.Shapes`.

■ **Note** WPF also ships with a full-blown API that can be used to render and manipulate 3D graphics, which is not addressed in this edition of the text. Please consult the .NET Framework 4.0 SDK documentation if you are interested in incorporating 3D graphics in your applications.

Rendering Graphical Data Using Shapes

Members of the `System.Windows.Shapes` namespace provide the most straightforward, most interactive, yet most memory-intensive way to render a two-dimensional image. This namespace (defined in the `PresentationFramework.dll` assembly) is quite small and consists of only six NonInheritable classes that extend the MustInherit `Shape` base class: `Ellipse`, `Rectangle`, `Line`, `Polygon`, `Polyline`, and `Path`.

Create a new WPF Application named RenderingWithShapes. Now, if you locate the MustInherit `Shape` class in the Visual Studio 2010 object browser (see Figure 29-1) and expand each of the parent nodes, you can see that each descendent of `Shape` receives a great deal of functionality up the inheritance chain.

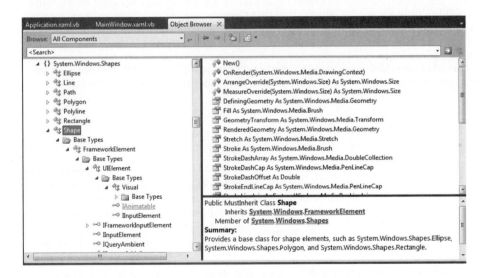

Figure 29-1. The Shape base class receives a good deal of functionality from its parent classes

Now, given your work in the previous two chapters, some of these parent classes may ring a bell. Recall, for example, that `UIElement` defines numerous methods to receive mouse input and deal with drag-and-drop events, while `FrameworkElement` defines members to deal with sizing, tooltips, mouse cursors, and whatnot. Given this inheritance chain, be aware that when you render graphical data using `Shape` derived classes, the objects are just about as functional (as far as user interactivity is concerned) as a WPF control!

For example, determining if the user has clicked on your rendered image is no more complicated than handling the MouseDown event. By way of a simple example, if you authored the following XAML of a Rectangle object:

```
<Rectangle x:Name="myRect" Height="30" Width="30"
          Fill="Green" MouseDown="myRect_MouseDown"/>
```

you could implement a VB 2010 event handler for the MouseDown event that changes the rectangle's background color when clicked:

```
Private Sub myRect_MouseDown(ByVal sender As Object, ByVal e As MouseButtonEventArgs)
    ' Change color of Rectangle when clicked.
    myRect.Fill = Brushes.Pink
End Sub
```

Unlike with other graphical toolkits you may have used, you do *not* need to author a ton of infrastructure code that manually maps mouse coordinates to the geometry, manually calculates hit-testing, renders to an off-screen buffer, and so forth. The members of System.Windows.Shapes simply respond to the events you register with, just like a typical WPF control (Button, etc.).

The downside of all this out-of-the-box functionality is that the shapes do take up a fair amount of memory. Again, if you're building a scientific application that plots thousands of points on the screen, using shapes would be a poor choice (essentially, it would be about as memory-intensive as rendering thousands of Button objects!). However, when you need to generate an interactive 2D vector image, shapes are a wonderful choice.

Beyond the functionality inherited from the UIElement and FrameworkElement parent classes, Shape defines a number of members for each of the children; some of the more useful ones are shown in Table 29-1.

Table 29-1. *Key Properties of the Shape Base Class*

Properties	Meaning in Life
DefiningGeometry	Returns a Geometry object that represents the overall dimensions of the current shape. This object *only* contains the plot points that are used to render the data, and has no trace of the functionality from UIElement or FrameworkElement.
Fill	Allows you to specify a "brush object" to render the interior portion of a shape.
GeometryTransform	Allows you to apply transformations to a shape, *before* it is rendered on the screen. The inherited RenderTransform property (from UIElement) applies the transformation *after* it has been rendered on the screen.
Stretch	Describes how to fill a shape within its allocated space, such as its position within a layout manager. This is controlled using the corresponding System.Windows.Media.Stretch enumeration.

Properties	Meaning in Life
Stroke	Defines a brush object, or in some cases, a pen object (which is really a brush in disguise) that is used to paint the border of a shape.
StrokeDashArray, StrokeEndLineCap, StrokeStartLineCap StrokeThickness	These (and other) stroke-related properties control how lines are configured when drawing the border of a shape. In a majority of cases, these properties will configure the brush used to draw a border or line.

■ **Note** If you forget to set the Fill and Stroke properties, WPF will give you "invisible" brushes and therefore the shape will not be visible on the screen!

Adding Rectangles, Ellipses, and Lines to a Canvas

Later in this chapter, you will learn to use Expression Blend and Expression Design to generate XAML descriptions of graphical data. For now, we will build a WPF application that can render shapes using XAML and VB 2010, and while doing so, learn a bit about the process of hit-testing. First of all, update the initial XAML of the <Window> to define a <DockPanel>, containing a (now empty) <ToolBar> and a <Canvas>. Note that we have given each contained item a fitting name via the Name property.

```
<DockPanel LastChildFill="True">
  <ToolBar DockPanel.Dock="Top" Name="mainToolBar" Height="50">
  </ToolBar>
  <Canvas Background="LightBlue" Name="canvasDrawingArea"/>
</DockPanel>
```

Now, populate the <ToolBar> with a set of <RadioButton> objects, each of which contains a specific Shape derived class as content. Notice that each <RadioButton> is assigned to the same GroupName (to ensure mutual exclusivity) and is also given a fitting name:

```
<ToolBar DockPanel.Dock="Top" Name="mainToolBar" Height="50">
  <RadioButton Name="circleOption" GroupName="shapeSelection">
    <Ellipse Fill="Green" Height="35" Width="35" />
  </RadioButton>

  <RadioButton Name="rectOption" GroupName="shapeSelection">
    <Rectangle Fill="Red" Height="35"
               Width="35" RadiusY="10" RadiusX="10" />
  </RadioButton>
```

```
<RadioButton Name="lineOption" GroupName="shapeSelection">
    <Line  Height="35" Width="35"
           StrokeThickness="10" Stroke="Blue"
           X1="10" Y1="10" Y2="25" X2="25"
           StrokeStartLineCap="Triangle" StrokeEndLineCap="Round" />
    </RadioButton>
</ToolBar>
```

As you can see, declaring **Rectangle**, **Ellipse**, and **Line** objects in XAML is quite straightforward and requires little comment. Recall that the **Fill** property is used to specify a *brush* to paint the interior of a shape. When you require a solid-colored brush, you can simply specify a hard-coded string of known values and the underlying type converter (see Chapter 28) will generate the correct object. One interesting feature of the **Rectangle** type is that it defines **RadiusX** and **RadiusY** properties to allow you to render curved corners if you require.

Line represents its starting and end points using the **X1**, **X2**, **Y1**, and **Y2** properties (given that *height* and *width* make little sense when describing a line). Here we are setting up a few additional properties that control how to render the starting and ending points of the **Line**, as well as how to configure the stroke settings. Figure 29-2 shows the rendered toolbar, as seen through the Visual Studio 2010 WPF designer:

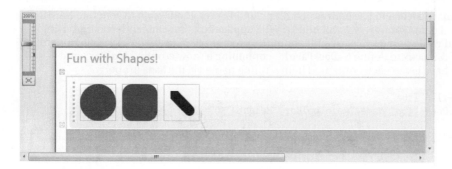

Figure 29-2. Using Shapes as content for a set of RadioButtons

Now, using the Properties window of Visual Studio 2010, handle the **MouseLeftButtonDown** event for the **Canvas**, and the **Click** event for each **RadioButton**. In your VB 2010 file, your goal is to render the selected shape (a circle, square, or line) when the user clicks within the **Canvas**. First, define the following nested Enum (and corresponding member variable) within your **Window** derived class:

```
Class MainWindow
    Private Enum SelectedShape
        Circle
        Rectangle
        Line
    End Enum

    Private currentShape As SelectedShape
...
End Class
```

Within each Click event handler, set the **currentShape** member variable to the correct SelectedShape value. For example, here is the implementation code for the **Click** event of the circleOption RadioButton. Implement the remaining two **Click** handlers in a similar manner:

```
Private Sub circleOption_Click(ByVal sender As Object, ByVal e As RoutedEventArgs) Handles
circleOption.Click
    currentShape = SelectedShape.Circle
End Sub
```

With the MouseLeftButtonDown event handler of the **Canvas**, you will render out the correct shape (of a predefined size), using the X,Y position of the mouse cursor as a starting point. Here is the complete implementation, with analysis to follow:

```
Private Sub canvasDrawingArea_MouseLeftButtonDown(ByVal sender As Object,
    ByVal e As MouseButtonEventArgs) _
 Handles canvasDrawingArea.MouseLeftButtonDown
    Dim shapeToRender As Shape = Nothing

    ' configure the correct shape to draw.
    Select Case currentShape
        Case SelectedShape.Circle
            shapeToRender = New Ellipse() With {
            .Fill = Brushes.Green,
            .Height = 35, _
            .Width = 35 _
            }


        Case SelectedShape.Rectangle
            shapeToRender = New Rectangle() With { _
            .Fill = Brushes.Red, _
            .Height = 35, _
            .Width = 35, _
            .RadiusX = 10, _
            .RadiusY = 10 _
            }

        Case SelectedShape.Line
            shapeToRender = New Line() With { _
            .Stroke = Brushes.Blue, _
            .StrokeThickness = 10, _
            .X1 = 0, _
            .X2 = 50, _
            .Y1 = 0, _
            .Y2 = 50, _
            .StrokeStartLineCap = PenLineCap.Triangle, _
            .StrokeEndLineCap = PenLineCap.Round _
            }
```

1301

```
        Case Else
              Return
    End Select



    ' Set top / left to draw in the canvas.
    Canvas.SetLeft(shapeToRender, e.GetPosition(canvasDrawingArea).X)
    Canvas.SetTop(shapeToRender, e.GetPosition(canvasDrawingArea).Y)

    ' Draw shape!
    canvasDrawingArea.Children.Add(shapeToRender)
End Sub
```

■ **Note** You may notice that the Ellipse, Rectangle, and Line objects being created in this method have the same property settings as the corresponding XAML definitions! As you might hope, we can streamline this code—but that requires an understanding of the WPF object resources, which we will examine in Chapter 30.

As you can see, we are testing the **currentShape** member variable to create the correct **Shape** derived object. After this point, we set the top-left value within the **Canvas** using the incoming **MouseButtonEventArgs**. Last but not least, we add the new **Shape** derived type to the collection of **UIElement** objects maintained by the **Canvas**. If you run your program now, you should be able to click anywhere in the canvas and see the selected shape rendered at the location of the left mouse-click.

Removing Rectangles, Ellipses, and Lines from a Canvas

With the **Canvas** maintaining a collection of objects, you may wonder how you can dynamically remove an item, perhaps in response to the user right-clicking on a shape. You can certainly do this, using a class in the **System.Windows.Media** namespace called the **VisualTreeHelper**. In Chapter 31, you will come to know the role of "visual trees" and "logical trees" in some detail. Until then, handle the **MouseRightButtonDown** event on your **Canvas** object, and implement the corresponding event handler like so:

```
Private Sub canvasDrawingArea_MouseRightButtonDown(ByVal sender As Object,
   ByVal e As MouseButtonEventArgs)
   Handles canvasDrawingArea.MouseRightButtonDown
        ' First, get the X,Y location of where the user clicked.
        Dim pt As Point = e.GetPosition(DirectCast(sender, Canvas))

        ' Use the HitTest() method of VisualTreeHelper to see if the user clicked
        ' on an item in the canvas.
        Dim result As HitTestResult = VisualTreeHelper.HitTest(canvasDrawingArea, pt)
```

```
        ' If the result is not Nothing, they DID click on a shape!
        If result IsNot Nothing Then
                ' Get the underlying shape clicked on, and remove it from
                ' the canvas.
                canvasDrawingArea.Children.Remove(TryCast(result.VisualHit, Shape))
        End If
End Sub
```

This method begins by obtaining the exact X,Y location the user clicked in the **Canvas**, and performs a hit-test operation via the Shared **VisualTreeHelper.HitTest()** method. The return value, a **HitTestResult** object, will be set to Nothing if the user does not click on a **UIElement** within the **Canvas**. If **HitTestResult** is *not* Nothing, we can obtain the underlying **UIElement** that was clicked via the **VisualHit** property, which we are casting into a **Shape** derived object (remember, a **Canvas** can hold any **UIElement**, not just shapes!) Again, you'll get more details on exactly what a "visual tree" is in the next chapter.

■ **Note** By default, VisualTreeHelper.HitTest() returns the top-most UIElement clicked on, and does not provide information on other objects below that item (e.g., objects overlapping by Z-order).

With this modification, you should be able to add a shape to the canvas with a left mouse-click, and delete an item from the canvas with a right mouse-click! Figure 29-3 shows the functionality of the current example:

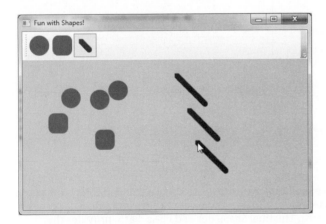

Figure 29-3. Fun with shapes

So far so good. At this point, you have used **Shape** derived objects to render content on **RadioButtons** using XAML and populate a **Canvas** using VB 2010. We will add a bit more functionality to this example when we examine the role of brushes and graphical transformations. On a related note, a different example in this chapter will illustrate drag-and-drop techniques on **UIElement** objects. Until then, we will examine the remaining members of **System.Windows.Shapes**.

Working with Polylines and Polygons

The current example used only three of the Shape derived classes. The remaining child classes (Polyline, Polygon, and Path) are extremely tedious to render correctly without the use of a tool like Expression Blend, simply because they require a large number of plot points to represent their output. You'll use Blend in just a moment, but until then, here is an overview of the remaining Shapes types.

The Polyline type lets you define a collection of (x, y) coordinates (via the Points property) to draw a series of line segments that do not require connecting ends. The Polygon type is similar; however, it is programmed so that it will always close the starting and ending points and fill the interior with the specified brush. Assume you have authored the following <StackPanel> in the kaxaml editor, or better yet, in the custom XAML editor you created in Chapter 27:

```
<!-- Polylines do not automatically connect the ends -->
<Polyline Stroke ="Red" StrokeThickness ="20" StrokeLineJoin ="Round"
          Points ="10,10  40,40  10,90  300,50"/>

<!-- A Polygon always closes the end points-->
<Polygon Fill ="AliceBlue" StrokeThickness ="5" Stroke ="Green"
         Points ="40,10 70,80 10,50" />
```

Figure 29-4 shows the rendered output.

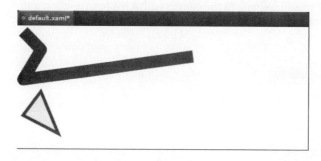

Figure 29-4. *Polygons and polylines*

Working with Paths

Using the Rectangle, Ellipse, Polygon, Polyline, and Line types alone to draw a detailed 2Dvector image would be extremely complex, as these primitives do not allow you to easily capture graphical data such as curves, unions of overlapping data, and so forth. The final Shape derived class, Path, provides the ability to define complex 2D graphical data represented as a collection of independent *geometries*. Once you have defined a collection of such geometries, you can assign them to the Data property of the Path class, where this information will be used to render your complex 2D image.

The Data property takes a System.Windows.Media.Geometry derived class, which contains the key members described in Table 29-2.

Table 29-2. Select Members of the System.Windows.Media.Geometry Type

Member	Meaning in Life
Bounds	Establishes the current bounding rectangle containing the geometry.
FillContains()	Determines if a given Point (or other Geometry object) is within the bounds of a particular Geometry-derived class. This is useful for hit-testing calculations.
GetArea()	Returns the entire area a Geometry-derived type occupies.
GetRenderBounds()	Returns a Rect that contains the smallest possible rectangle that could be used to render the Geometry-derived class.
Transform	Assigns a Transform object to the geometry to alter the rendering.

The classes that extend Geometry (see Table 29-3) look very much like their Shape-derived counterparts. For example, EllipseGeometry has similar members to Ellipse. The big distinction is that Geometry derived classes *do not know* how to render themselves directly, as they are not UIElements. Rather, Geometry derived classes represent little more than a collection of plot-point data, which say in effect "If a Path uses my data, this is how I would render myself."

■ **Note** Path is not the only class in WPF that can use a collection of geometries. For example, DoubleAnimationUsingPath, DrawingGroup, GeometryDrawing and even UIElement can all use geometries for rendering, using the PathGeometry, ClipGeometry, Geometry, and Clip properties, respectively.

Table 29-3. Geometry Derived Classes

Geometry Class	Meaning in Life
LineGeometry	Represents a straight line.
RectangleGeometry	Represents a rectangle.
EllipseGeometry	Represents an ellipse.
GeometryGroup	Allows you to group together several Geometry objects.
CombinedGeometry	Allows you to merge two different Geometry objects into a single shape.
PathGeometry	Represents a figure composed of lines and curves.

Here is a `Path` defined in kaxaml that makes use of a few `Geometry`-derived types. Notice that we are setting the `Data` property of `Path` to a `GeometryGroup` object that contains other `Geometry`-derived objects such as `EllipseGeometry`, `RectangleGeometry,` and `LineGeometry`. Figure 29-5 shows the output.

```
<!--A Path contains a set of geometry objects,
    set with the Data property -->
<Path Fill = "Orange" Stroke = "Blue" StrokeThickness = "3">
  <Path.Data>
    <GeometryGroup>
      <EllipseGeometry Center = "75,70"
        RadiusX = "30" RadiusY = "30" />
      <RectangleGeometry Rect = "25,55 100 30" />
      <LineGeometry StartPoint="0,0" EndPoint="70,30" />
      <LineGeometry StartPoint="70,30" EndPoint="0,30" />
    </GeometryGroup>
  </Path.Data>
</Path>
```

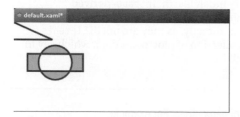

Figure 29-5. *A Path containing various Geometries objects*

The image in Figure 29-5 could have been rendered using the `Line`, `Ellipse`, and `Rectangle` classes shown earlier. However, this would have put various `UIElement` objects in memory. When you use geometries to model the plot points of what to draw, and then place the geometry collection into a container that can render the data (`Path`, in this case), you reduce the memory overhead.

Now recall that `Path` has the same inheritance chain as any other member of `System.Windows.Shapes`, and therefore has the ability to send the same event notifications as other `UIElements`. Thus, if you were to define this same `<Path>` element in a Visual Studio 2010 project, you could determine if the user clicked anywhere in the sweeping line simply by handling a mouse event (remember, kaxaml does not allow you to handle events for the markup you have authored).

The Path "Modeling Mini Language"

Of all the classes listed in Table 29-2, `PathGeometry` is the most complex to configure in terms of XAML or code. This has to do with the fact that each *segment* of the `PathGeometry` is composed of objects that contain various segments and figures (for example, `ArcSegment`, `BezierSegment`, `LineSegment`, `PolyBezierSegment`, `PolyLineSegment`, `PolyQuadraticBezierSegment`, etc). Here is an example of a `Path` object whose `Data` property has been set to a `<PathGeometry>` composed of various figures and segments.

```
<Path Stroke="Black" StrokeThickness="1" >
  <Path.Data>
    <PathGeometry>
      <PathGeometry.Figures>
        <PathFigure StartPoint="10,50">
          <PathFigure.Segments>
            <BezierSegment
              Point1="100,0"
              Point2="200,200"
              Point3="300,100"/>
            <LineSegment Point="400,100" />
            <ArcSegment
              Size="50,50" RotationAngle="45"
              IsLargeArc="True" SweepDirection="Clockwise"
              Point="200,100"/>
          </PathFigure.Segments>
        </PathFigure>
      </PathGeometry.Figures>
    </PathGeometry>
  </Path.Data>
</Path>
```

Now, to be perfectly honest, very few programmers will ever need to manually build complex 2D images by directly describing Geometry or PathSegment derived classes. In reality, complex paths will be composed on your behalf when you are working with Expression Blend or Expression Design.

Even with the assistance of these tools, the amount of XAML required to define a complex Path object would be ghastly, as the data consists of full descriptions of various Geometry or PathSegment derived classes. In order to produce more concise and compact markup, the Path class has been designed to understand a specialized "mini-language."

For example, rather than setting the Data property of Path to a collection of Geometry and PathSegment derived types, you can set the Data property to a single string literal containing a number of known symbols and various values that define the shape to be rendered. In fact, when you use the Expression tools to build a Path object, the mini-language is used automatically. Here is a simple example, and the resulting output (see Figure 29-6).

```
<Path Stroke="Black" StrokeThickness="3"
      Data="M 10,75 C 70,15 250,270 300,175 H 240" />
```

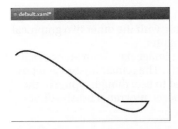

Figure 29-6. *The path mini-language allows you to compactly describe a Geometry/PathSegment object model*

The M command (short for *move*) takes an X,Y position that represents the starting point of the drawing. The C command takes a series of plot points to render a curve (a cubic Bézier curve to be exact) while H draws a horizontal line.

Now, to be perfectly honest, the chances that you will ever need to manually build or parse a string literal containing path mini-language instructions are slim to none. However, at the very least, you will no longer be surprised when you view XAML generated by Expression Blend. If you are interested in examining the details of this particular grammar, look up "Path Markup Syntax" in the .NET Framework 4.0 SDK documentation.

WPF Brushes and Pens

Each of SDK the WPF graphical rendering options (shape, drawing and geometries, and visuals) makes extensive use of *brushes*, which allow you to control how the interior of a 2D surface is filled. WPF provides six different brush types, all of which extend System.Windows.Media.Brush. While Brush is abstract, the descendents described in Table 29-4 can be used to fill a region with just about any conceivable option.

Table 29-4. WPF Brush-Derived Types

Brush Type	Meaning in Life
DrawingBrush	Paints an area with a Drawing derived object (GeometryDrawing, ImageDrawing, or VideoDrawing)
ImageBrush	Paints an area with an image (represented by an ImageSource object)
LinearGradientBrush	Paints an area with a linear gradient
RadialGradientBrush	Paints an area with a radial gradient
SolidColorBrush	Paints a single color, set with the Color property
VisualBrush	Paints an area with a Visual derived object (DrawingVisual, Viewport3DVisual, and ContainerVisual)

The DrawingBrush and VisualBrush classes allow you to build a brush based on an existing Drawing or Visual derived class. These brush classes are used when you are working with the other two graphical options of WPF (drawings or visuals) and will be examined later in this chapter.

ImageBrush, as the name suggests, lets you build a brush that displays image data from an external file or embedded application resource, by setting the ImageSource property. The remaining brush types (LinearGradientBrush and RadialGradientBrush) are quite straightforward to use, though typing in the required XAML can be a tad verbose. Thankfully, Visual Studio 2010 supports integrated brush editors that make it simple to generate stylized brushes.

Configuring Brushes Using Visual Studio 2010

Let's update our WPF drawing program, RenderingWithShapes to use some more interesting brushes. The three shapes we've employed so far to render data on our toolbar use simple, solid colors, so we can capture their values using simple string literals. To spice things up a tad, we will now use the integrated brush editor. Ensure that the XAML editor of your initial window is the open window within the IDE, and select the Ellipse element. Now, locate the Fill property in the Properties window, and click the drop-down list. You should now see the following brush editor (Figure 29-7).

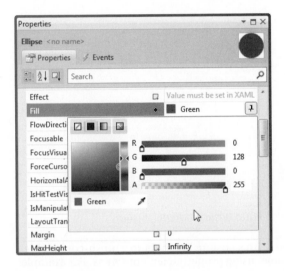

Figure 29-7. Any property that requires a brush can be configured with the integrated brush editor

As you can see, this editor contains four slider controls, which allow you to set the ARGB (alpha, red, green and blue, where "alpha" controls transparency) of the current brush. Using these sliders and the related color selection area, you can create any sort of solid color. Go ahead and use these tools to change the color of your Ellipse, and view the resulting XAML. You'll notice the color is stored as a hexadecimal value, for example:

```
<Ellipse Fill="#FF47CE47" Height="35" Width="35" />
```

More interestingly, this same editor allows you to configure gradient brushes, which are used to define a series of colors and transition points. On the upper-left of the brush editor, you will see four small buttons, the first of which lets you set a *null brush* for no rendered output. The other three allow you to set up a solid color brush (what we just examined), gradient brush, or image brush.

Click the gradient brush button and the editor will display a few new options (see Figure 29-8). The three buttons on the lower left allow you to pick a vertical, horizontal, or radial gradient. The bottom-most strip will show you the current color of each gradient stop, each of which is marked by a "thumb" on the strip. As you drag these thumbs around the gradient strip, you can control the gradient offset. Furthermore, when you click on a given thumb, you can change the color for that particular gradient stop via the color selector. Finally, if you click directly on the gradient strip, you can add additional gradient stops.

Take a few minutes to play around this editor to build a radial gradient brush containing three gradient stops, set to your colors of choice. Figure 29-8 shows the brush I just constructed, using three different shades of green.

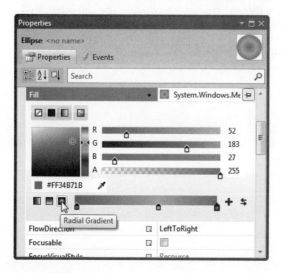

Figure 29-8. *The Visual Studio brush editor allows you to build basic gradient brushes*

Once you are done, the IDE will update your XAML with a custom brush set to a brush-compatible property (the `Fill` property of the `Ellipse` in our example) using property-element syntax. For example:

```
<Ellipse Height="35" Width="35">
  <Ellipse.Fill>
    <RadialGradientBrush>
      <GradientStop Color="#FF87E71B" Offset="0.589" />
      <GradientStop Color="#FF2BA92B" Offset="0.013" />
      <GradientStop Color="#FF34B71B" Offset="1" />
    </RadialGradientBrush>
  </Ellipse.Fill>
</Ellipse>
```

Configuring Brushes in Code

Now that we have built a custom brush for the XAML definition of our `Ellipse`, the corresponding VB 2010 code is out of date, in that it will still render a solid green circle. To sync things back up, update the correct Case statement to use the same brush you just created. Here is the necessary update, which looks more complex than you might expect, just because we are converting the hexadecimal value to a proper `Color` object via the `System.Windows.Media.ColorConverter` class (see Figure 29-9 for the modified output):

```
Case SelectedShape.Circle
    shapeToRender = New Ellipse() With {
    .Height = 35, _
    .Width = 35 _
    }

    ' Make a RadialGradientBrush in code!
    Dim brush As New RadialGradientBrush()
    brush.GradientStops.Add(New GradientStop(
        DirectCast(ColorConverter.ConvertFromString("#FF87E71B"), Color), 0.589))
    brush.GradientStops.Add(New GradientStop(
        DirectCast(ColorConverter.ConvertFromString("#FF2BA92B"), Color), 0.013))
    brush.GradientStops.Add(New GradientStop(
        DirectCast(ColorConverter.ConvertFromString("#FF34B71B"), Color), 1))
    shapeToRender.Fill = brush
```

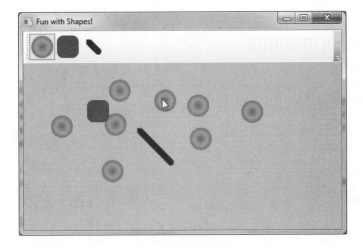

Figure 29-9. Drawing circles with a bit more pizzazz!

By the way, you can build GradientStop objects by specifying a simple color as the first constructor parameter using the Colors enumeration, which returns a configured Color object:

```
Dim g As New GradientStop(Colors.Aquamarine, 1)
```

Or, if you require even finer control, you can pass in a configured Color object. For example:

```
Dim myColor As New Color() With { .R = 200, .G = 100, .B = 20, .A = 40 }
Dim g As New GradientStop(myColor, 34)
```

Of course, the Colors enum and Color class are not limited to gradient brushes. You can use them anytime you need to represent a color value in code.

Configuring Pens

In comparison with brushes, a *pen* is an object for drawing borders of geometries, or in the case of the Line or PolyLine class, the line geometry itself. Specifically, the Pen class allows you to draw a specified thickness, represented by a Double value. In addition, a Pen can be configured with the same sort of properties seen in the Shape class, such as starting and stopping pen caps, dot-dash patterns, and so forth. For example:

```
<Pen Thickness="10" LineJoin="Round" EndLineCap="Triangle" StartLineCap="Round" />
```

In many cases, you won't need to directly create a Pen object, as this will be done indirectly when you assign a value to properties, such as StrokeThickness to a Shape derived type (as well as other UIElements). However, building a custom Pen object is very handy when working with Drawing derived types (described later in the chapter). Visual Studio 2010 does not have a pen editor, *per se*, but it does allow you to configure all of the stroke-centric properties of a selected item using the Properties Window.

Applying Graphical Transformations

To wrap up our discussion of using shapes, let's address the topic of *transformations*. WPF ships with numerous classes that extend the System.Windows.Media.Transform MustInherit base class. Table 29-5 documents many of the key out-of-the-box Transform derived classes.

Table 29-5. Key Descendents of the System.Windows.Media.Transform Type

Type	Meaning in Life
MatrixTransform	Creates an arbitrary matrix transformation that is used to manipulate objects or coordinate systems in a 2D plane
RotateTransform	Rotates an object clockwise about a specified point in a 2D (*x, y*) coordinate system
ScaleTransform	Scales an object in the 2D (*x, y*) coordinate system
SkewTransform	Skews an object in the 2D (*x, y*) coordinate system
TranslateTransform	Translates (moves) an object in the 2-D x-y coordinate system.
TransformGroup	Represents a composite Transform composed of other Transform objects

Transformations can be applied to any UIElement (e.g., descendents of Shape as well as controls such as Buttons, TextBoxes, and the like). Using these transformation classes, you can render graphical data at a given angle, skew the image across a surface, and expand, shrink, or flip the target item in a variety of ways.

■ **Note** While transformation objects can be used anywhere, you will find them most useful when working with WPF animations and custom control templates. As you will see later in the text, you can use WPF animations to incorporate visual cues to the end user for a custom control.

Transformation objects (or a whole set of them) can be assigned to a target object (Button, Path, etc.) using two common properties. The LayoutTransform property is helpful in that the transformation occurs *before* elements are rendered into a layout manager, and therefore the transformation will not affect z-ordering operations (in other words, the transformed image data will not overlap).

The RenderTransform property, on the other hand, occurs after the items are in their container, and therefore it is quite possible that elements can be transformed in such a way that they could overlap each other, based on how they were arranged in the container.

A First Look at Transformations

We will add some transformational logic to our RenderingWithShapes project in just a moment. However, to see transformation objects in action, open kaxaml (or your custom XAML editor) and define a simple <StackPanel> in the root <Page> or <Window>, and set the Orientation property to Horizontal. Now, add the following <Rectangle>, which will be drawn at a 45-degree angle using a RotateTransform object.

```
<!-- A Rectangle with a rotate transformation -->
<Rectangle Height ="100" Width ="40" Fill ="Red">
  <Rectangle.LayoutTransform>
    <RotateTransform Angle ="45"/>
  </Rectangle.LayoutTransform>
</Rectangle>
```

Here is a <Button> that is skewed across the surface by 20 percent, using a <SkewTransform>:

```
<!-- A Button with a skew transformation -->
<Button Content ="Click Me!" Width="95" Height="40">
  <Button.LayoutTransform>
    <SkewTransform AngleX ="20" AngleY ="20"/>
  </Button.LayoutTransform>
</Button>
```

And for good measure, here is an <Ellipse> that is scaled by 20 percent with a ScaleTransform, (note the values set to the initial Height and Width), as well as a <TextBox> that has a group of transformation objects applied to it.

```
<!-- An Ellipse that has been scaled by 20% -->
<Ellipse Fill ="Blue" Width="5" Height="5">
  <Ellipse.LayoutTransform>
    <ScaleTransform ScaleX ="20" ScaleY ="20"/>
  </Ellipse.LayoutTransform>
</Ellipse>
```

```
<!-- A textbox that has been rotated and skewed -->
<TextBox Text ="Me Too!" Width="50" Height="40">
  <TextBox.LayoutTransform>
    <TransformGroup>
      <RotateTransform Angle ="45"/>
      <SkewTransform AngleX ="5" AngleY ="20"/>
    </TransformGroup>
  </TextBox.LayoutTransform>
</TextBox>
```

Note that when a transformation is applied, you are not required to perform any manual calculations to correctly respond to hit-testing, input focus, or whatnot. The WPF graphics engine handles such tasks on your behalf. For example, in Figure 29-10, you can see that the **TextBox** is still responsive to keyboard input.

Figure 29-10. The results of graphical transformation objects

Transforming our Canvas Data

Now, let's see how we can incorporate some transformational logic into our RenderingWithShapes example. In addition to applying a transformation object to a single item (**Rectangle**, **TextBox**, etc.), you can also apply transformation objects to a layout manager, to transform all of the internal data. You could, for example, render the entire **<DockPanel>** of the main window at an angle like so:

```
<DockPanel LastChildFill="True">
  <DockPanel.LayoutTransform>
    <RotateTransform Angle="45"/>
  </DockPanel.LayoutTransform>
...
</DockPanel>
```

This is a bit extreme for this example, so let's add a final (less aggressive) feature that allows the user to flip the entire **Canvas** and all contained graphics. Begin by adding a final **<ToggleButton>** to your **<ToolBar>**, defined as:

```
<ToggleButton Name="flipCanvas" Content="Flip Canvas!"/>
```

Within the `Click` event handler, you create a `RotateTransform` object and connect it to the `Canvas` object via the `LayoutTransform` property if this new `ToggleButton` is clicked. If the `ToggleButton` is not clicked, you remove the transformation by setting the same property to `null`:

```
Private Sub flipCanvas_Click(ByVal sender As Object, ByVal e As RoutedEventArgs) ↵
        Handles flipcanvas.Click
    If flipCanvas.IsChecked = True Then
        Dim rotate As New RotateTransform(-180)
        canvasDrawingArea.LayoutTransform = rotate
    Else
        canvasDrawingArea.LayoutTransform = Nothing
    End If
End Sub
```

Run your application and add a bunch of graphics throughout the canvas area. If you click your new button, you will find that the shape data flows outside of the boundaries of the canvas! This is because we have not defined a clipping region (see Figure 29-11).

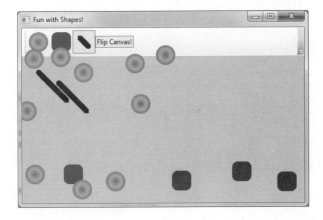

Figure 29-11. Oops! Our data is flowing outside of the canvas after the transformation!

Fixing this is trivial. Rather than manually authoring complex clipping-logic code, simply set the `ClipToBounds` property of the `<Canvas>` to `True`, which prevents child elements from being rendered outside the parent's boundaries. If you run your program again, you'll find the data will not bleed off the canvas boundary.

```
<Canvas ClipToBounds = "True" ... >
```

The last tiny modification to make has to do with the fact that when you flip the canvas by pressing your toggle button, and then click on the canvas to draw a new shape, the point at which you click is *not* the point where the graphical data is applied. Rather the data is rendered above the mouse cursor.

To resolve this issue, check out the solution code for this example where I have added one final Boolean member variable (`isFlipped`), which will apply the same transformation object to the shape being drawn before the rendering occurs (via `RenderTransform`). Here is the crux of the code:

```
Private Sub canvasDrawingArea_MouseLeftButtonDown(ByVal sender As Object, ByVal e As↩
  MouseButtonEventArgs) Handles DrawingArea.MouseLeftButtonDown
    Dim shapeToRender As Shape = Nothing
    ...

    ' isFlipped is a Private Boolean field. This is toggled when the
    ' toggle button is clicked.
    If isFlipped Then
        Dim rotate As New RotateTransform(-180)
        shapeToRender.RenderTransform = rotate
    End If

    ' Set top / left to draw in the canvas.
    Canvas.SetLeft(shapeToRender, e.GetPosition(canvasDrawingArea).X)
    Canvas.SetTop(shapeToRender, e.GetPosition(canvasDrawingArea).Y)

    ' Draw shape!
    canvasDrawingArea.Children.Add(shapeToRender)
End Sub
```

This wraps up our examination of `System.Windows.Shapes`, brushes, and transformations. Before turning our attending to the role of rendering graphics using drawings and geometries, let's see how Expression Blend can be used to simplify how we work with primitive graphics.

■ **Source Code** The RenderingWithShapes project can be found under the Chapter 29 subdirectory.

Working with Shapes using Expression Blend

Although Visual Studio 2010 does give you a few IDE tools that let you work with shapes, Expression Blend provides many more features, including a graphical transformation editor. If you'd like to try things out first hand, launch Expression Blend and create a new WPF application. (We are not going to do much beyond trying out a few features of the IDE, so you can name this project whatever you wish.)

Selecting a Shape to Render from the Tool Palette

Look at your tool palette and you'll see an area that lets you select an Ellipse, Rectangle, or Line (recall, you click-and-hold on buttons that have a small triangle on the lower-right to pop-up any available choices; see Figure 29-12).

Figure 29-12. Rendering basic shapes with Blend

Go ahead and draw a few overlapping shapes—you'll see why in just a moment. Now, locate the area of the Blend tool palette where you can select the Pen and Pencil tools, as shown in Figure 29-13.

Figure 29-13. Working with pens and pencils

The Pencil tool allows you to render completely free-form polygons, similar to a scribble program. The Pen tool is better suited for rendering swooping arcs or straight lines. To draw lines with the Pen, simply click at the desired starting point, then click at the desired ending point on the designer. Be aware that both of these tools will generate a `Path` definition, with the `Data` property set using the path mini language mentioned earlier.

Play around with these tools and render some new graphics on the designer. Note that if you perform a Direct Select on any `Path` (such as the `Path` created by the Pencil tool) you can tweak the overall connecting segments, as seen in Figure 29-14.

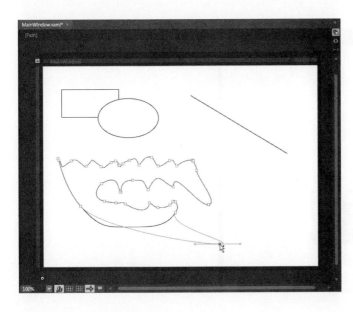

Figure 29-14. Editing a Path

Converting Shapes to Paths

When you use the Ellipse, Rectangle, or Line tools, the XAML will indeed use the `<Ellipse>`, `<Rectangle>` and `<Line>` elements. For example:

```
<Rectangle Stroke="Black" StrokeThickness="1" HorizontalAlignment="Left"
  Margin="44,42,0,0" VerticalAlignment="Top" Width="137" Height="35"/>
```

If you right-click on one of these primitive types on your designer, you can select the Path-> Convert to Path menu option. When you select this operation, the original shape declaration is transformed into a Path containing a set of geometries, via the path mini language. Here is the previous `<Rectangle>` after conversion:

```
<Path Stretch="Fill" Stroke="Black" StrokeThickness="1" HorizontalAlignment="Left"
  Margin="44,42,0,0" VerticalAlignment="Top" Width="137"
  Height="35" Data="M0.5,0.5 L136.5,0.5 L136.5,34.5 L0.5,34.5 z"/>
```

While you might not need to convert a single shape into a Path containing geometries, it is common to combine multiple shapes into new paths.

Combining Shapes

Now try this. Select two or more shapes on the designer (via a mouse click-and-drag operation) and then right-click on the set of selected items. You'll see that you have a number of options under the Combine menu that allow you to generate new Path objects based on a set of selections and a combine operation (Figure 29-15).

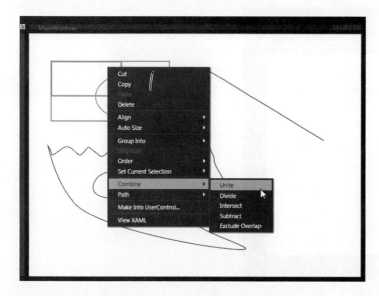

Figure 29-15. Combining Paths to generate new Paths

Essentially, the options under the Combine menu are basic Venn diagramming operations. Try a few and then view the generated XAML (and remember, just as in Visual Studio 2010, Ctrl + z will undo the previous operation!)

The Brush and Transformation Editors

Like Visual Studio 2010, Blend supports a brush editor. When you select an item on the designer (such as one of your shapes), you can then go to the Brushes area of the Properties window. At the very top of the Brushes editor, you'll find all properties on the selected object that can be assigned a Brush type. Below, you'll find the same basic editing features you saw earlier in this chapter. Figure 29-16 shows one possible brush configuration.

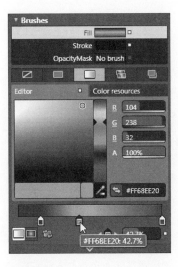

Figure 29-16. The Blend brush editor

The only major difference between the Blend and Visual Studio 2010 brush editors is that with Blend you can remove a gradient stop by clicking on the offending thumb marker and dragging it off the gradient slider (literally anywhere off the gradient slider will do; right-clicking won't work!).

Another nice feature of the Blend brush editor is that when you have selected an item that makes use of a gradient brush, you can press the G key on your keyboard or click the Gradient Tool icon on the tool palette to change the origin of the gradient (Figure 29-17).

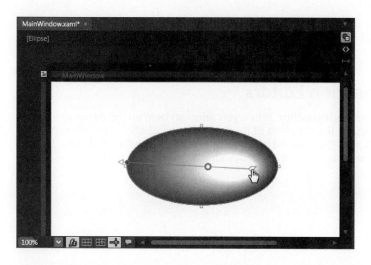

Figure 29-17. Changing the origin of a gradient

Finally, Blend also supports an integrated transformation editor. First, select a shape on your designer (of course, the transformation editor works for any item selected in the Objects and Timeline window). Now, on your Properties window, locate the Transform pane (Figure 29-18).

Figure 29-18. The Blend transformation editor

As you experiment with the transformation editor, be sure to take some time to examine the resulting XAML. Also note that many transformations can be applied directly on the designer, by hovering the mouse over a resizing node of the selected object. For example, if you place the mouse next to a node on the side of a selected item, you can apply a skew. (Personally speaking, however, I tend to use the transformation editor, rather than trying to get the mouse positioned just so.)

> ■ **Note** Recall that members of the System.Windows.Shapes namespace are UIElements and have numerous events you can respond to. Given this, you can handle events on your drawings using Blend, just as you would when handling an event for a typical control (see Chapter 29).

That wraps up our first look at the graphical rendering services of WPF and our whirlwind tour of using Blend to generate simple graphical data. While you could use this information to build a number of graphical applications, our next step is to examine the second way to render out graphical data, using drawings and geometries.

Rendering Graphical Data Using Drawings and Geometries

While the Shape types allow you to generate any sort of interactive two-dimensional surface, they entail quite a bit of memory overhead due to their rich inheritance chain. And though the Path class can help remove some of this overhead using contained geometries (rather than a large collection of other shapes), WPF provides a sophisticated drawing and geometry programming interface that renders even more lightweight 2D vector images.

The entry point into this API is the MustInherit System.Windows.Media.Drawing class (in PresentationCore.dll), which on its own does little more than define a bounding rectangle to hold the rendering. Notice in Figure 29-19, the inheritance chain of the Drawing class is significantly more lightweight than Shape, given that neither UIElement nor FrameworkElement is in the inheritance chain.

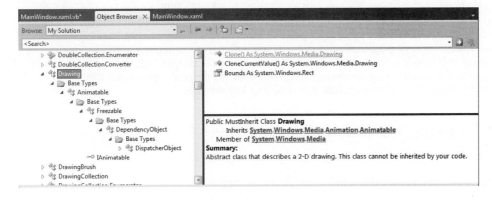

Figure 29-19. The Drawing class is more lightwight than Shape

WPF provides various classes that extend Drawing, each of which represents a particular way of drawing the content, as described in Table 29-6.

Table 29-6. WPF Drawing Derived Types

Type	Meaning in Life
DrawingGroup	Used to combine a collection of separate Drawing derived objects into a single composite rendering.
GeometryDrawing	Used to render 2D shapes in a very lightweight manner.
GlyphRunDrawing	Used to render textual data using WPF graphical rendering services.
ImageDrawing	Used to render an image file, or geometry set, into a bounding rectangle.
VideoDrawing	Used to play an audio file or video file. This type can only be fully exploited using procedural code. If you wish to play videos via XAML, the MediaPlayer type is a better choice.

Because they are more lightweight, Drawing derived types do not have intrinsic support for handling input events as they are not UIElements or FrameworkElements (although it is possible to programmatically perform hit-testing logic); however, they can be animated due to the fact that they extend Animatable (Chapter 30 will examine the animation features of WPF).

Another key difference between Drawing derived types and Shape derived types is that Drawing derived types have no ability to render themselves, as they do not derive from UIElement! Rather, derived types must be placed within a hosting object (specifically, DrawingImage, DrawingBrush, or DrawingVisual) to display their content.

DrawingImage allows you to place drawing and geometries inside of a WPF Image control, which typically is used to display data from an external file. DrawingBrush allows you to build a brush based on a drawing and its geometries, in order to set a property that requires a brush. Finally, DrawingVisual is used only in the "visual" layer of graphical rendering, which is driven completely via VB 2010 code.

Although using drawings is a bit more complex than using simple shapes, this decoupling of graphical composition from graphical rendering makes the Drawing derived types much more lightweight than the Shape derived types, while still retaining key services.

Building a DrawingBrush using Geometries

Earlier in this chapter, we filled a Path with a group of geometries like so:

```
<Path Fill = "Orange" Stroke = "Blue" StrokeThickness = "3">
  <Path.Data>
    <GeometryGroup>
      <EllipseGeometry Center = "75,70"
        RadiusX = "30" RadiusY = "30" />
      <RectangleGeometry Rect = "25,55 100 30" />
      <LineGeometry StartPoint="0,0" EndPoint="70,30" />
      <LineGeometry StartPoint="70,30" EndPoint="0,30" />
    </GeometryGroup>
  </Path.Data>
</Path>
```

By doing this, we gain interactivity from Path but are still fairly lightweight given our geometries. However, if you want to render the same output and have no need for any (out-of-the-box) interactivity, you can place the same `<GeometryGroup>` inside a `DrawingBrush`, like this:

```
<DrawingBrush>
  <DrawingBrush.Drawing>
    <GeometryDrawing>
      <GeometryDrawing.Geometry>
        <GeometryGroup>
          <EllipseGeometry Center = "75,70"
                           RadiusX = "30" RadiusY = "30" />
          <RectangleGeometry Rect = "25,55 100 30" />
          <LineGeometry StartPoint="0,0" EndPoint="70,30" />
          <LineGeometry StartPoint="70,30" EndPoint="0,30" />
        </GeometryGroup>
      </GeometryDrawing.Geometry>
      <!-- A custom pen to draw the borders -->
      <GeometryDrawing.Pen>
        <Pen Brush="Blue" Thickness="3"/>
      </GeometryDrawing.Pen>
      <!-- A custom brush to fill the interior -->
      <GeometryDrawing.Brush>
        <SolidColorBrush Color="Orange"/>
      </GeometryDrawing.Brush>
    </GeometryDrawing>
  </DrawingBrush.Drawing>
</DrawingBrush>
```

When you place a group of geometries into a `DrawingBrush`, you also need to establish the `Pen` object used to draw the boundaries, as we no longer inherit a `Stroke` property from the `Shape` base class. Here, I created a `<Pen>` with the same settings used in the `Stroke` and `StrokeThickness` values of the previous `Path` example.

Furthermore, since we no longer inherit a `Fill` property from `Shape`, we also need to use property element syntax to define a brush object to use for the `<DrawingGeometry>`, which here is a solid colored orange brush, just like the previous `Path` settings.

Painting with the DrawingBrush

Now that you have a `DrawingBrush`, you can use it to set the value of any property requiring a brush object. For example, if you are authoring this markup in kaxaml, you could use property-element syntax to paint your drawing over the entire surface of a `Page`:

```
<Page
  xmlns="http://schemas.microsoft.com/winfx/2006/xaml/presentation"
  xmlns:x="http://schemas.microsoft.com/winfx/2006/xaml">
```

```
    <Page.Background>
      <!-- Same DrawingBrush as seen above -->
      <DrawingBrush>
        ...
      </DrawingBrush>
    </Page.Background>
  </Page>
```

Or, you can use this `<DrawingBrush>` to set a different brush-compatible property, such as the Background property of a Button:

```
<Page
  xmlns="http://schemas.microsoft.com/winfx/2006/xaml/presentation"
  xmlns:x="http://schemas.microsoft.com/winfx/2006/xaml">

  <Button Height="100" Width="100">
    <Button.Background>
      <!-- Same DrawingBrush as seen above -->
      <DrawingBrush>
        ...
      </DrawingBrush>
    </Button.Background>
  </Button>

</Page>
```

No matter which brush-compatible property you set with your custom `<DrawingBrush>`, the bottom line is you are rendering a 2D vector image with much less overhead than the same 2D image rendered with shapes.

Containing Drawing Types in a DrawingImage

The DrawingImage type allows you to plug your drawing geometry into a WPF `<Image>` control. Consider the following:

```
<Page
  xmlns="http://schemas.microsoft.com/winfx/2006/xaml/presentation"
  xmlns:x="http://schemas.microsoft.com/winfx/2006/xaml">
  <Image Height="100" Width="100">
    <Image.Source>
      <DrawingImage>
        <DrawingImage.Drawing>
          <GeometryDrawing>
            <GeometryDrawing.Geometry>
              <GeometryGroup>
                <EllipseGeometry Center = "75,70"
                                 RadiusX = "30" RadiusY = "30" />
                <RectangleGeometry Rect = "25,55 100 30" />
                <LineGeometry StartPoint="0,0" EndPoint="70,30" />
```

```
            <LineGeometry StartPoint="70,30" EndPoint="0,30" />
          </GeometryGroup>
        </GeometryDrawing.Geometry>

        <!-- A custom pen to draw the borders -->
        <GeometryDrawing.Pen>
          <Pen Brush="Blue" Thickness="3"/>
        </GeometryDrawing.Pen>

        <!-- A custom brush to fill the interior -->
        <GeometryDrawing.Brush>
          <SolidColorBrush Color="Orange"/>
        </GeometryDrawing.Brush>
      </GeometryDrawing>
    </DrawingImage.Drawing>
  </DrawingImage>
 </Image.Source>
 </Image>
</Page>
```

In this case, our `<GeometryDrawing>` has been placed into a `<DrawingImage>`, rather than a `<DrawingBrush>`. Using this `<DrawingImage>`, we can set the `Source` property of the `Image` control.

Generating Complex Vector Graphics using Expression Design

To be sure, manually authoring XAML that represents a complex set of geometries, segments, figures, and paths would be a nightmare, and nobody would expect us to do so. As we have already seen, Expression Blend does contain a few IDE features that allow us to work with basic graphics; however when you need to generate professional, compelling vector graphics, Expression Design is the tool of champions.

■ **Note** If you do not have a copy of Expression Design, you can download a trial edition of the product from the official web site: `http://www.microsoft.com/expression`.

Expression Design has features similar to those you might find in a professional graphical design tool such as Adobe Photoshop or Adobe Illustrator. In the hands of a talented graphical artist, Design can be used to create very sophisticated 2D and 3D images, which can be exported in a variety of file formats—including XAML!

The ability to export a graphical image as XAML is very compelling, in that we (as programmers) can incorporate the markup into our applications, name objects, and manipulate them in code. For example, a graphical artist could use Design to create a 3D cube image. Once the image is exported to XAML, we could add the `x:Name` attribute to the items we wish to interact with, and gain access to the generated object in our VB 2010 codebase.

Exporting a Design Document to XAML

Now, in the spirit of full disclosure, I must admit that I am in no way, shape, or form, a graphical artist. Therefore, I am not going to walk through using Expression Design to render complex graphical data; rather we will view and manipulate some standard sample documents that ship with the product.

To begin, launch Expression Design and activate the Help ➤ Samples menu selection. In the resulting dialog box, double-click one of the sample drawings. For this example, I'll assume you clicked the bear_paper.design file that ships with Expression Design.

Now, select the File ➤ Export menu option. Here you will find a dialog box that allows you to save the selected image data to a variety of common file formats, including .png, .jpeg, .gif, .tif, .bmp and .wdp (for HD photos). If you use Design simply to make professional static images, these file formats should fit the bill. However, if you want to add interactivity to your vector art, you can save the file in a XAML description.

Select XAML Silverlight 4 / WPF Canvas from the Format drop-down list in the Export dialog box. Notice the other options in Figure 29-20, including the ability to give each item a default name (via the x:Name attribute) and to save any text data as a Path object. You can leave the default settings, but be sure to save the XAML file to an easily found location and then click the Export All button.

Figure 29-20. Expression Design files can be exported as XAML

At this point, you can copy the generated XAML `Canvas` object into any Visual Studio 2010 or Expression Blend WPF application. Or, for an even easier test, you could copy the generated markup into a `<Page>` or `<Window>` scope within the kaxaml editor (or the custom XAML editor you created in Chapter 27).

In any case, if you view the generated XAML, you'll see that `Path` objects are the default format. At this point, you can handle events on the parts of the image you wish to manipulate, and author the related VB 2010 code. While I won't walk you through the process (you should already be in pretty good shape by this point in the chapter), you might want to import the "teddy bear" data into a new WPF application and see if you can handle the `MouseDown` event for one of eyeball objects. In the event handler, try to apply a transformation object or change the color (I have to admit I did make my bear's eye blood-red when clicked upon...).

■ **Note** We will not use Expression Design anymore in this book. If you're interested in the product, however, Design ships with its own dedicated help system, which can be activated via the F1 key.

Rendering Graphical Data Using the Visual Layer

The final option for rendering graphical data with WPF is termed the *visual layer*. As mentioned, you can only gain access to this layer through code (it is not XAML-friendly). While a vast majority of your WPF applications will work just fine using shapes, drawings, and geometries, the visual layer does provide the fastest possible way to render huge amounts of graphical data. Oddly, this very low-level graphical layer can also be useful when you need render to single image over a very large area. For example, if you need to fill the background of a window with a plain static image, the visual layer will be the fastest way to do so, and it may be useful if you need to change between window backgrounds very quickly, based on user input or whatnot.

While we won't spend too much time delving into the details of this aspect of WPF programming, let's build a small sample program that illustrates the basics.

The Visual Base Class and Derived Child Classes

The MustInherit `System.Windows.Media.Visual` class type supplies a minimal set of services (rendering, hit testing, transformations) to render graphics, but it does not provide support for additional non-visual services, which can lead to code bloat (input events, layout services, styles, and data binding). Notice the simple inheritance chain of the `Visual` type, as shown in Figure 29-21.

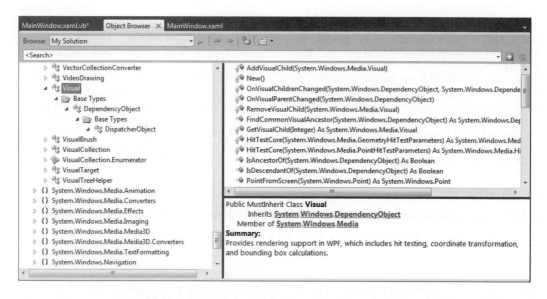

Figure 29-21. The Visual type provides basic hit testing, coordinate transformation, and bounding box calculations

Given that Visual is a MustInherit base class, we need to use one of the derived types to perform actual rendering operations. WPF provides a handful of subclasses, including `DrawingVisual`, `Viewport3DVisual,` and `ContainerVisual`.

In this example, we will focus only on `DrawingVisual`, a lightweight drawing class that is used to render shapes, images, or text.

A First Look at using the DrawingVisual Class

To render data onto a surface using a `DrawingVisual`, you need to take the following basic steps:

- Obtain a `DrawingContext` object from the `DrawingVisual.`

- Use the `DrawingContext` to render the graphical data.

These two steps represent the bare minimum necessary for rendering some data to a surface. However, if you want the graphical data you've rendered to be responsive to hit-testing calculations (which would be important for adding user interactivity), you will also need to perform these additional steps:

- Update the logical and visual trees maintained by the container you are rendering on top of.

- Override two methods from the `FrameworkElement` class, allowing the container to obtain the visual data you have created.

We will examine these final two steps in a bit. First, to illustrate how you can use the `DrawingVisual` class to render 2D data, create a new WPF application with Visual Studio named RenderingWithVisuals. Our first goal is to use a `DrawingVisual` to dynamically assign data to a WPF Image control. Begin by updating the XAML of your window like so:

```
<Window x:Class="MainWindow"
        xmlns="http://schemas.microsoft.com/winfx/2006/xaml/presentation"
        xmlns:x="http://schemas.microsoft.com/winfx/2006/xaml"
        Title=" Fun with the Visual Layer" Height="350" Width="525"
        WindowStartupLocation="CenterScreen">
    <StackPanel Background="AliceBlue" Name="myStackPanel">
        <Image Name="myImage" Height="80"/>
    </StackPanel>
</Window>
```

Notice that our `<Image>` control does not yet have a **Source** value, as that will happen at runtime. Now let's handle the `Loaded` event of the window, to do the work of building the in-memory graphical data using a `DrawingBrush` object:

```
Private Sub Window_Loaded(ByVal sender As Object, ByVal e As RoutedEventArgs)
  Handles MyBase.Loaded
    Const TextFontSize As Integer = 30

    ' Make a System.Windows.Media.FormattedText object.
    Dim text As New FormattedText("Hello Visual Layer!",
      New System.Globalization.CultureInfo("en-us"),
      FlowDirection.LeftToRight,
       New Typeface (Me.FontFamily, FontStyles.Italic, _
      FontWeights.DemiBold, FontStretches.UltraExpanded),
      TextFontSize,
      Brushes.Green)

    ' Create a DrawingVisual, and obtain the DrawingContext.
    Dim drawingVisual As New DrawingVisual()
    Using drawingContext As DrawingContext = drawingVisual.RenderOpen()
        ' Now, call any of the methods of DrawingContext to render data.
        drawingContext.DrawRoundedRectangle(
            Brushes.Yellow,
            New Pen (Brushes.Black, 5),
            New Rect(5, 5, 450, 100), 20, 20)
        drawingContext.DrawText(text, New Point(20, 20))
    End Using

    ' Dynamically make a bitmap, using the data in the DrawingVisual.
    Dim bmp As New RenderTargetBitmap(500, 100, 100, 90, PixelFormats.Pbgra32)
    bmp.Render(drawingVisual)

    ' Set the source of the Image control!
    myImage.Source = bmp
End Sub
```

This code introduces a number of new WPF classes, which I will briefly comment on here (be sure to check the .NET Framework 4.0 SDK documentation for full details if you are interested). The method begins by creating a new `FormattedText` object that represents the textual portion of the in-memory image we are constructing. As you can see, the constructor allows us to specify numerous attributes such as font size, font family, foreground color, and the text itself.

Next, we obtain the necessary `DrawingContext` object via a call to `RenderOpen()` on the `DrawingVisual` instance. Here, we are rendering a colored, rounded rectangle into the `DrawingVisual`, followed by our formatted text. In both cases, we are placing the graphical data into the `DrawingVisual` using hard-coded values, which is not necessarily a great idea for production, but fine for our simple test.

■ **Note** Be sure to look up the DrawingContext class within the .NET Framework 4.0 SDK documentation to view all rendering members. If you have worked with the Windows Forms Graphics object in the past, DrawingContext should look very similar.

The last few statements map the `DrawingVisual` into a `RenderTargetBitmap` object, which is a member of the `System.Windows.Media.Imaging` namespace. This class will take a visual object, and transform it into an in-memory bitmap image. After this point, we set the `Source` property of the `Image` control, and sure enough, we see the output in Figure 29-22.

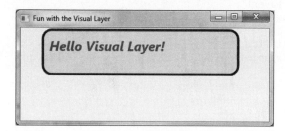

Figure 29-22. Using the visual layer to render an in-memory bitmap

---

■ **Note** The System.Windows.Media.Imaging namespace contains a number of additional encoding classes that let you save the in-memory RenderTargetBitmap object to a physical file in a variety of formats. Check out the JpegBitmapEncoder class (and friends) for more information.

Rendering Visual Data to a Custom Layout Manager

While it is interesting to use `DrawingVisual` to paint onto the background of a WPF control, it is perhaps more common to build a custom layout manager (`Grid`, `StackPanel`, `Canvas`, etc) that uses the visual layer internally to render its content. Once you have created such a custom layout manager, you can plug it into a normal Window (or Page, or UserControl) and have a part of the UI using a highly optimized rendering agent, while the non-critical aspects of the hosting Window use shapes and drawings for the remainder of the graphical data.

If you don't require the extra functionality provided by a dedicated layout manager, you could opt to simply extend FrameworkElement, which does have the necessary infrastructure to also contain visual items. To illustrate how this could be done, insert a new class to your project named CustomVisualFrameworkElement. Extend this class from FrameworkElement and import the System.Windows, System.Windows.Input and System.Windows.Media namespaces.

This class will maintain a member variable of type VisualCollection, which contains two fixed DrawingVisual objects (of course, you could add new members to this collection via a mouse operation, but this example will keep it simple). Update your class with the following new functionality:

```
Public Class CustomVisualFrameworkElement
    Inherits FrameworkElement

    ' A collection of all the visuals we are building.
    Private theVisuals As VisualCollection

    Public Sub New()
        ' Fill the VisualCollection with a few DrawingVisual objects.
        theVisuals = New VisualCollection(Me)
        theVisuals.Add(AddRect())
        theVisuals.Add(AddCircle())

    End Sub

    Private Function AddCircle() As Visual
        Dim drawingVisual As New DrawingVisual()

        ' Retrieve the DrawingContext in order to create new drawing content.
        Using drawingContext As DrawingContext = drawingVisual.RenderOpen()
            ' Create a circle and draw it in the DrawingContext.
            Dim rect As New Rect(New Point(160, 100), New Size(320, 80))
            drawingContext.DrawEllipse(Brushes.DarkBlue, Nothing, New Point(70, 90), 40, 50)
        End Using
        Return drawingVisual
    End Function

    Private Function AddRect() As Visual
        Dim drawingVisual As New DrawingVisual()

        ' Retrieve the DrawingContext in order to create new drawing content.
        Using drawingContext As DrawingContext = drawingVisual.RenderOpen()
            ' Create a rectangle and draw it in the DrawingContext.
            Dim rect As New Rect(New Point(160, 100), New Size(320, 80))
            drawingContext.DrawRectangle(Brushes.Tomato, Nothing, rect)
        End Using
        Return drawingVisual
    End Function
End Class
```

Now, before we can use this custom FrameworkElement in our Window, we must override two key methods mentioned previously, both of which are called internally by WPF during the rendering process. The GetVisualChild() method returns a child at the specified index from the collection of child elements. The read-only VisualChildrenCount property returns the number of visual child elements within this visual collection. Both methods are easy to implement, as we can delegate the real work to the VisualCollection member variable:

```
Protected Overrides ReadOnly Property VisualChildrenCount() As Integer
    Get
        Return theVisuals.Count
    End Get
End Property

Protected Overrides Function GetVisualChild(ByVal index As Integer) As Visual
    ' Value must be creater than zero, so do a sanity check.
    If index < 0 OrElse index >= theVisuals.Count Then
        Throw New ArgumentOutOfRangeException()
    End If

    Return theVisuals(index)
End Function
```

We now have just enough functionality to test our custom class. Update the XAML description of the Window to add one of your CustomVisualFrameworkElement objects to the existing StackPanel. Doing so will require you to build a custom XML namespace that maps to your .NET namespace (see Chapter 28):

```
<Window x:Class="MainWindow"
  xmlns="http://schemas.microsoft.com/winfx/2006/xaml/presentation"
  xmlns:x="http://schemas.microsoft.com/winfx/2006/xaml"
  xmlns:custom="clr-namespace:RenderingWithVisuals"
  Title="Fun with the Visual Layer" Height="350" Width="525"
  Loaded="Window_Loaded" WindowStartupLocation="CenterScreen">
    <StackPanel Background="AliceBlue" Name="myStackPanel">
        <Image Name="myImage" Height="80"/>
        <custom:CustomVisualFrameworkElement/>
    </StackPanel>
</Window>
```

If all is well, you should see something similar to Figure 29-23 when you run your program.

Figure 29-23. Using the visual layer to render data to a custom FrameworkElement

Responding to Hit Test Operations

Because DrawingVisual does not have any of the infrastructure of UIElement or FrameworkElement, you will need to programmatically add in the ability to calculate hit-test operations. Thankfully, this is fairly easy to do in the visual layer because of the concept of *logical* and *visual* trees. As it turns out, when you author a blob of XAML, you are essentially building a logical tree of elements. However, behind every logical tree is a much richer description known as the visual tree, which contains lower-level rendering instructions.

Chapter 32 will delve into these trees in more detail but for now, just understand that until you register your custom visuals with these data structures, you will not be able to perform hit-testing operations. Luckily, the VisualCollection container does this on your behalf (which explains why we needed to pass in a reference to the custom FrameworkElement as a constructor argument).

First, update the CustomVisualFrameworkElement class to handle the MouseDown event in the class constructor using standard VB 2010 syntax:

```
AddHandler Me.MouseDown, AddressOf MyVisualHost_MouseDown
```

The implementation of this handler will call the VisualTreeHelper.HitTest() method to see if the mouse is within the boundaries of one of the rendered visuals. To do this, we specify as a parameter to HitTest(), a HitTestResultCallback delegate that will perform the calculations. If we did click on a visual, we will toggle between a skewed rendering of the visual and the original rendering. Add the following methods to your CustomVisualFrameworkElement class:

```
Private Sub MyVisualHost_MouseDown(ByVal sender As Object, ByVal e As MouseButtonEventArgs)
    ' Figure out where the user clicked.
    Dim pt As Point = e.GetPosition(DirectCast(sender, UIElement))

    ' Call helper function via delegate to see if we clicked on a visual.
    VisualTreeHelper.HitTest(
        Me,
        Nothing,
```

```
            New HitTestResultCallback(AddressOf myCallback),
            New PointHitTestParameters(pt))
End Sub

Public Function myCallback(ByVal result As HitTestResult) As HitTestResultBehavior
    ' Toggle between a skewed rendering and normal rendering,
    ' if a visual was clicked.
    If result.VisualHit.GetType() = GetType(DrawingVisual) Then
        If DirectCast(result.VisualHit, DrawingVisual).Transform Is Nothing Then
            DirectCast(result.VisualHit, DrawingVisual).Transform = New SkewTransform(7, 7)
        Else
            DirectCast(result.VisualHit, DrawingVisual).Transform = Nothing
        End If
    End If

    ' Tell HitTest() to stop drilling into the visual tree.
    Return HitTestResultBehavior.Stop
End Function
```

Now, run your program once again. You should now be able to click on either rendered visual and see the transformation in action! While this is just a very simple example of working with the visual layer of WPF, remember that you make use of the same brushes, transformations, pens, and layout managers as you would when working with XAML. As a result, you already know quite a bit about working this **Visual** derived classes.

■ **Source Code** The RenderingWithVisuals project can be found under the Chapter 29 subdirectory.

That wraps up our investigation of the graphical rendering services of Windows Presentation Foundation. While we covered a number of interesting topics, the reality is that we have only scratched the surface of WPF's graphical capabilities. I will leave it in your hands to dig deeper into the topics of shapes, drawings, brushes, transformations, and visuals (and, to be sure, you will see some additional details of these topics in the remaining WPF chapters).

Summary

Since Windows Presentation Foundation is such a graphically intensive GUI API, it comes as no surprise that we are given a number of ways to render graphical output. This chapter began by examining each of three ways a WPF application can do so (shapes, drawings, and visuals), and along the way discussed various rendering primitives such as brushes, pens, and transformations.

Remember that when you need to build interactive 2D renderings, shapes make the process very simple. However, static, non-interactive renderings can be rendered in a more optimal manner by using drawings and geometries, while the visual layer (accessible only in code) gives you maximum control and performance.

■ ■ ■

## CHAPTER 30

WPF Resources, Animations, and Styles

This chapter introduces you to three important (and interrelated) topics that will deepen your understanding of the Windows Presentation Foundation (WPF) API. The first order of business is to learn the role of *logical resources*. As you will see, the logical resource (also known as an *object resource*) system is a way to name and refer to commonly used objects within a WPF application. While logical resources are often authored in XAML, they can also be defined in procedural code.

Next, you will learn how to define, execute, and control an animation sequence. Despite what you may think, WPF animations are not limited to video game or multimedia applications. Under the WPF API, animations can be as subtle as making a button appear to glow when it receives focus, or expanding the size of a selected row in a `DataGrid`. Understanding animations is a key aspect of building custom control templates (as you'll see in Chapter 31).

We wrap up by exploring the role of WPF styles. Much like a web page that uses CSS or the ASP.NET theme engine, a WPF application can define a common look and feel for a set of controls. You can define these styles in markup and store them as object resources for later use, and you can also apply them dynamically at runtime.

Understanding the WPF Resource System

Our first task is to examine the topic of embedding and accessing application resources. WPF supports two flavors of resources. The first is a *binary resource,* and this category typically includes items most programmers consider a resource in the traditional sense (embedded image files or sound clips, icons used by the application, and so on).

The second flavor, termed *object resources* or *logical resources*, represents a named .NET object that can be packaged and reused throughout the application. While any .NET object can be packaged as an object resource, logical resources are particularly helpful when working with graphical data of any sort, given that you can define commonly used graphic primitives (brushes, pens, animations, etc.) and refer to them when required.

Working with Binary Resources

Before we get to the topic of object resources, let's quickly examine how to package up *binary resources* such as icons or image files (e.g., company logos and images for an animation) into your applications. If you'd like to follow along, create a new WPF application named BinaryResourcesApp using Visual Studio 2010. Update the markup for your initial window to use a DockPanel as the layout root:

```
<Window x:Class="MainWindow"
  xmlns="http://schemas.microsoft.com/winfx/2006/xaml/presentation"
  xmlns:x="http://schemas.microsoft.com/winfx/2006/xaml"
  Title="Fun with Binary Resources" Height="500" Width="649">

  <DockPanel LastChildFill="True">
  </DockPanel>

</Window>
```

Now, let's say your application needs to display one of three image files inside part of the window, based on user input. The WPF Image control can be used to not only display a typical image file (*.bmp, *.gif, *.ico, *.jpg, *.png, *.wdp, and *.tiff) but also data in a DrawingImage (as you saw in Chapter 29). You might build a UI for your window that supports a DockPanel containing a simple toolbar with Next and Previous buttons. Below this toolbar you can place an Image control, which currently does not have a value set to the Source property, as we will do this in code:

```
<Window x:Class="MainWindow"
  xmlns="http://schemas.microsoft.com/winfx/2006/xaml/presentation"
  xmlns:x="http://schemas.microsoft.com/winfx/2006/xaml"
  Title="Fun with Binary Resources" Height="500" Width="649">

  <DockPanel LastChildFill="True">
    <ToolBar Height="60" Name="picturePickerToolbar" DockPanel.Dock="Top">
      <Button x:Name="btnPreviousImage" Height="40" Width="100" BorderBrush="Black"
              Margin="5" Content="Previous" />
      <Button x:Name="btnNextImage" Height="40" Width="100" BorderBrush="Black"
              Margin="5" Content="Next" />
    </ToolBar>

    <!-- We will fill this Image in code -->
    <Border BorderThickness="2" BorderBrush="Green">
      <Image x:Name="imageHolder" Stretch="Fill" />
    </Border>
  </DockPanel>

</Window>
```

In the Designer, handle the Click event for each button. How can we code these Click handlers to cycle through the image data? More importantly, do we want to have the image data located on the user's hard drive or embedded in our compiled assembly? Let's examine our options.

Including Loose Resource Files in a Project

Let's assume you wish to ship your image files as a set of loose files in a subdirectory of the application install path. Using the Solution Explorer window of Visual Studio, you can right-click on your project node and select the Add ➤ New Folder menu option to create such a subdirectory, which I have called Images.

Now, when you right-click on this folder, you can select the Add ➤ Existing Item menu option, to copy the image files into the new subdirectory. In the downloadable source code for this project, you will find three image files named `Welcome.jpg`, `Dogs.jpg` and `Deer.jpg` that you can include in this project, or simply add three image files of your choice. Figure 30-1 shows the current setup.

Figure 30-1. A new subdirectory in our WPF project containing image data

Configuring the Loose Resources

When you want Visual Studio 2010 to copy project content to your output directory, you need to adjust a few settings using the Properties window. To ensure that the content of your \Images folder is copied to the \bin\Debug folder, begin by selecting each image in the Solution Explorer. Now, with these images still selected, use the Properties window to set the Build Action property to Content, and the Copy to Output Directory property to Copy always (see Figure 30-2).

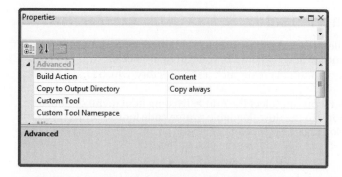

Figure 30-2. Configuring the image data to be copied to our output directory

If you recompile your program, you can now click on the Show all Files button of the Solution Explorer and view the copied Image folder under your \bin\Debug directory (you might need to click the refresh button). See Figure 30-3.

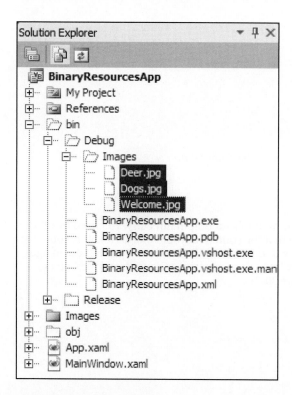

Figure 30-3. The copied data

Programmatically Loading an Image

WPF provides a class named `BitmapImage`, which is part of the `System.Windows.Media.Imaging` namespace. This class allows you to load data from an image file whose location is represented by a `System.Uri` object. If you handle the `Loaded` event of your window, you might fill a `List(Of T)` of `BitmapImages` like so:

```
Class MainWindow
      ' A List of BitmapImage files.
      Private images As New List(Of BitmapImage)()

      ' Current position in the list.
      Private currImage As Integer = 0
      Private Const MAX_IMAGES As Integer = 2

      Private Sub Window_Loaded(ByVal sender As Object, ByVal e As RoutedEventArgs)
            Handles MyBase.Loaded
        Try
        Dim path As String = Environment.CurrentDirectory

        ' Load these images when the window loads.
        images.Add(New BitmapImage(New Uri(String.Format("{0}\Images\Deer.jpg", path))))
        images.Add(New BitmapImage(New Uri(String.Format("{0}\Images\Dogs.jpg", path))))
        images.Add(New BitmapImage(New Uri(String.Format("{0}\Images\Welcome.jpg",
        path))))

        ' Show first image in the List(Of BitmapImage)
        imageHolder.Source = images(currImage)
        Catch ex As Exception
        MessageBox.Show(ex.Message)
      End Try
    End Sub
    ...
End Class
```

Notice that this class also defines an `Integer` member variable (`currImage`) that will allow the `Click` event handlers to loop through each item in the `List(Of T)` and display it in the `Image` control by setting the `Source` property. (Here, our `Loaded` event handler sets the `Source` property to the first image in the `List(Of T)`.) In addition, our `MAX_IMAGES` constant will let us test for upper and lower limits as we iterate over the list. Here are the `Click` handlers that do exactly this:

```
Private Sub btnPreviousImage_Click(ByVal sender As Object, ByVal e As RoutedEventArgs)
        Handles btnPreviousImage.Click
      currImage -= 1
      If currImage < 0 Then
       currImage = MAX_IMAGES
      End If
      imageHolder.Source = images(currImage)
End Sub
```

```
Private Sub btnNextImage_Click(ByVal sender As Object, ByVal e As RoutedEventArgs)
        Handles btnNextImage.Click
    currImage += 1
    If currImage > MAX_IMAGES Then
     currImage = 0
    End If
    imageHolder.Source = images(currImage)
End Sub
```

At this point, you can run your program and flip through each picture.

Embedding Application Resources

If you'd rather configure your image files to be compiled directly into your .NET assembly as binary resources, select the image files in Solution Explorer (in the \Images folder, not in the \bin\Debug\Images folder). Then change the Build Action property to Resource and the Copy to Output Directory property to Do not copy (Figure 30-4).

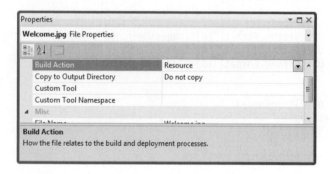

Figure 30-4. Configuring the images to be embedded resources

Now, using Visual Studio 2010's Build menu, select the Clean Solution option to wipe out the current contents of \bin\Debug\Images, then rebuild your project. Refresh the Solution Explorer, and observe the absence of \bin\Debug\Images in your \bin\Debug directory.

With the current build options, your graphical data is no longer copied to the output folder and is now embedded within the assembly itself. Assuming you have recompiled your project, you can open the assembly into **reflector.exe**, and see the embedded image data (Figure 30-5).

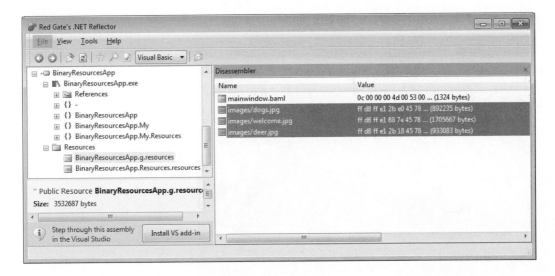

Figure 30-5. The embedded image data

With this adjustment, we will now need to modify our code to load these images by extracting them from the compiled assembly:

```
Private Sub Window_Loaded(ByVal sender As Object, ByVal e As RoutedEventArgs)
        Handles MyBase.Loaded
    Try
        images.Add(New BitmapImage(New Uri("/Images/Deer.jpg", UriKind.Relative)))
        images.Add(New BitmapImage(New Uri("/Images/Dogs.jpg", UriKind.Relative)))
        images.Add(New BitmapImage(New Uri("/Images/Welcome.jpg", UriKind.Relative)))
        imageHolder.Source = images(currImage)
    Catch ex As Exception
        MessageBox.Show(ex.Message)
    End Try
End Sub
```

Notice in this case, we no longer need to determine the installation path and can simply list the resources by name, which takes into account the name of the original subdirectory. Also notice, when we create our Uri objects, we specify a UriKind value of Relative. In any case, at this point our executable is a standalone entity that can be run from any location on the machine, as all compiled data is within the binary. Figure 30-6 shows the completed application.

Figure 30-6. *Our simple picture viewer*

■ **Source Code** The BinaryResourcesApp can be found under the Chapter 30 subdirectory.

Working with Object (Logical) Resources

When you are building a WPF application, it is very common to define a blurb of XAML to use in multiple locations within a window, or perhaps across multiple windows or projects. For example, say you are using Expression Blend to build the *perfect* linear gradient brush, which consists of 10 lines of markup. Now, you want to use that brush as the background color for every `Button` control in the project...which consists of 8 windows...for a total of 16 `Buttons`.

The worst thing you could do is to copy and paste the XAML to each and every control. Clearly, this would be a nightmare to maintain, as you would need to make numerous changes anytime you wanted to tweak the look and feel of the brush.

Thankfully, *object resources* allow us to define a blob of XAML, give it a name, and store it in a fitting dictionary for later use. Like a binary resource, object resources are often compiled into the assembly that requires them. However, you don't need to tinker with the Build Action property to do so. As long as you place your XAML into the correct location, the compiler will take care of the rest.

Working with object resources is a big part of WPF development. As you will see, object resources can be far more complex than a custom brush. You could define a XAML-based animation, a 3D rendering, a custom control style, data template, control template, and more, and package each one as a reusable resource.

The Role of the Resources Property

As mentioned, object resources must be placed in a fitting dictionary object in order to be used across an application. As it stands, every descendent of FrameworkElement supports a Resources property. This property encapsulates a ResourceDictionary object that contains the defined object resources. The ResourceDictionary can hold any type of item as it operates on System.Object types and may be manipulated via XAML or procedural code.

In WPF, all controls, Windows, Pages (used when building navigation applications or XBAP programs) and UserControls extend FrameworkElement, so just about all widgets provide access to a ResourceDictionary. Furthermore, the Application class, while not extending FrameworkElement, supports an identically named Resources property for the same purpose.

Defining Window-Wide Resources

To begin exploring the role of object resources, create a new WPF application named ObjectResourcesApp using Visual Studio 2010 and change the initial Grid to a horizontally aligned StackPanel layout manager. Into this StackPanel, define two Button controls (we really don't need much to illustrate the role of object resources, so this will do):

```
<Window x:Class="MainWindow"
  xmlns="http://schemas.microsoft.com/winfx/2006/xaml/presentation"
  xmlns:x="http://schemas.microsoft.com/winfx/2006/xaml"
  Title="Fun with Object Resources" Height="350" Width="525">

  <StackPanel Orientation="Horizontal">
    <Button Margin="25" Height="200" Width="200" Content="OK" FontSize="20"/>
    <Button Margin="25" Height="200" Width="200" Content="Cancel" FontSize="20"/>
  </StackPanel>

</Window>
```

Now, select the OK button and set the Background color property to a custom brush type using the integrated brush editor (discussed in Chapter 29). Once you've done so, notice how the brush is embedded within the scope of the <Button> and </Button> tags:

```
<Button Margin="25" Height="200" Width="200" Content="OK" FontSize="20">
  <Button.Background>
    <RadialGradientBrush>
      <GradientStop Color="#FFC44EC4" Offset="0" />
      <GradientStop Color="#FF829CEB" Offset="1" />
      <GradientStop Color="#FF793879" Offset="0.669" />
    </RadialGradientBrush>
  </Button.Background>
</Button>
```

To allow the Cancel button to use this brush as well, we should promote the scope of our <RadialGradientBrush> to a parent element's resource dictionary. For example, if we move it to the <StackPanel>, both buttons can use the same brush, as they are child elements of the layout manager. Even better, we could package the brush into the resource dictionary of the window itself, so all aspects of the window's content (nested panels, etc.) can freely make use of it.

When you need to define a resource, you use property element syntax to set the Resources property of the owner. You also give the resource item an x:Key value, which will be used by other parts of the window when they want to refer to the object resource. Be aware that x:Key and x:Name are not the same! The x:Name attribute allows you to gain access to the object as a member variable in your code file, while the x:Key attribute allows you to refer to an item in a resource dictionary.

Visual Studio 2010 and Expression Blend both allow you to promote a resource to a higher scope using their respective Properties windows. In Visual Studio 2010, first identify the property that has the complex object you wish to package as a resource (the Background property in our example). Next to the property, you'll see a small diamond button that, when clicked, will open a pop-up menu. From here, select the "Extract value to Resource..." option (Figure 30-7).

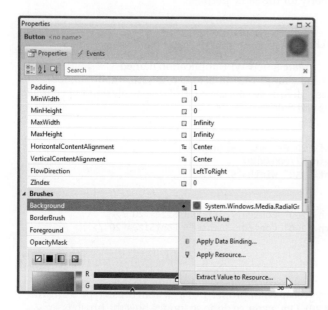

Figure 30-7. Moving a complex object into a resource container

You are now asked to name your resource (myBrush), and specify where to place it. For this example, leave the default selection of MainWindow.xaml (Figure 30-8).

Figure 30-8. Naming the object resource

When you're done, the markup will be restructured like this:

```
<Window x:Class=" MainWindow"
  xmlns="http://schemas.microsoft.com/winfx/2006/xaml/presentation"
  xmlns:x="http://schemas.microsoft.com/winfx/2006/xaml"
  Title="Fun with Object Resources" Height="350" Width="525">

  <Window.Resources>
    <RadialGradientBrush x:Key="myBrush">
      <GradientStop Color="#FFC44EC4" Offset="0" />
      <GradientStop Color="#FF829CEB" Offset="1" />
      <GradientStop Color="#FF793879" Offset="0.669" />
    </RadialGradientBrush>
  </Window.Resources>

  <StackPanel Orientation="Horizontal">
    <Button Margin="25" Height="200" Width="200" Content="OK"
            FontSize="20" Background="{StaticResource myBrush}"></Button>
    <Button Margin="25" Height="200" Width="200" Content="Cancel" FontSize="20"/>
  </StackPanel>

</Window>
```

Notice the new `<Window.Resources>` scope, which now contains the `RadialGradientBrush` object, which has a key value of `myBrush`.

The {StaticResource} Markup Extension

The other change that took place when we extracted our object resource was that the property that was the target of the extraction (again, `Background`) now makes use of the `{StaticResource}` markup extension. As you can see, the key name is specified as an argument. Now, if the Cancel button wishes to use the same brush to paint its background, it is free to do so. Or, if the Cancel button had some complex content, any sub-element of that Button could also use the window-level resource—for example, the `Fill` property of an `Ellipse`:

```
<StackPanel Orientation="Horizontal">
  <Button Margin="25" Height="200" Width="200" Content="OK" FontSize="20"
          Background="{StaticResource myBrush}">
  </Button>

  <Button Margin="25" Height="200" Width="200" FontSize="20">
    <StackPanel>
      <Label HorizontalAlignment="Center" Content= "No Way!"/>
      <Ellipse Height="100" Width="100" Fill="{StaticResource myBrush}"/>
    </StackPanel>
  </Button>
</StackPanel>
```

Changing a Resource after Extraction

After you have extracted a resource to the scope of a window, you can locate it in your Document Outline window, which can be opened via the View ➤ Other Windows ➤ Document Outline menu (Figure 30-9).

Figure 30-9. Viewing our resource in the Document Outline

If you select any aspect of the object resource in the Document Outline window, you can change values using the Properties window. Thus, you could change the individual gradient stops, the origin offset, and other aspects of the brush.

The {DynamicResource} Markup Extension

It is also possible for a property to use the {DynamicResource} markup extension when connecting to a keyed resource. To understand the difference, name your OK button btnOK and handle the Click event. In this event handler, use the Resources property to obtain the custom brush, and then change some aspect of it:

```
Private Sub btnOK_Click(ByVal sender As Object, ByVal e As RoutedEventArgs)
            Handles btnOK.Click
        ' Get the brush and make a change.
        Dim b As RadialGradientBrush = CType(Resources("myBrush"), RadialGradientBrush)
        b.GradientStops(1) = New GradientStop(Colors.Black, 0.0)
End Sub
```

■ **Note** We are using the Resources indexer to locate a resource by name here. Be aware, however, that this will throw a runtime exception if the resource can't be found. You could also use the TryFindResource() method, which will not throw a runtime error but simply return Nothing if the specified resource can't be located.

If you run this application and click the OK button, you will see the brush's change is accounted for and each button updates to render the modified brush. However, what if you completely changed the type of brush specified by the myBrush key? For example:

```
Private Sub btnOK_Click(ByVal sender As Object, ByVal e As RoutedEventArgs) ↩
                        Handles btn.Click
' Put a totally new brush into the myBrush slot.
Resources("myBrush") = New SolidColorBrush(Colors.Red)
End Sub
```

This time, when you click the button, neither updates as expected. This is because the {StaticResource} markup extension applies the resource only once and stays "connected" to the original object during the life of the application. However, if we change each occurrence of {StaticResource} to {DynamicResource} in our markup, we find our custom brush has been replaced with the expected solid red brush.

Essentially, the {DynamicResource} markup extension is able to detect whether the underlying keyed object has been replaced with a new object. As you might guess, this requires some extra runtime infrastructure, so you should typically stick to using {StaticResource} unless you know you have an object resource that will be swapped with a different object at runtime, and you want all items using that resource to be informed.

Application-Level Resources

When you have object resources in a window's resource dictionary, all items in the window are free to make use of it, but other windows in the application cannot. Give your Cancel button a name of btnCancel and handle the Click event. Insert a new window into your current project (named TestWindow.xaml) that contains a single Button, which, when clicked, will close the window:

```
Public Class TestWindow
        Private Sub btnClose_Click(ByVal sender As Object, ByVal e As RoutedEventArgs)
            Handles btnClose.Click
          Me.Close()
        End Sub
End Class
```

Now, in the Click handler of the Cancel button on your first window, just load and display this new window, like so:

```
Private Sub btnCancel_Click(ByVal sender As Object, ByVal e As RoutedEventArgs)
        Handles btnCancel.Click
    Dim w As New TestWindow()
    w.Owner = Me
    w.WindowStartupLocation = WindowStartupLocation.CenterOwner
    w.ShowDialog()
End Sub
```

So, if the new window wants to use `myBrush`, it currently won't be able to as it is not within the correct "scope." The solution is to define the object resource at the application level, rather than at the level of a specific window. There is no way to automate this within Visual Studio 2010, so simply cut the current brush object out of the `<Windows.Resources>` scope, and place it in the `<Application.Resources>` scope in your `App.xaml` file:

```
<Application x:Class="Application"
  xmlns="http://schemas.microsoft.com/winfx/2006/xaml/presentation"
  xmlns:x="http://schemas.microsoft.com/winfx/2006/xaml"
  StartupUri="MainWindow.xaml">

  <Application.Resources>
    <RadialGradientBrush x:Key="myBrush">
      <GradientStop Color="#FFC44EC4" Offset="0" />
      <GradientStop Color="#FF829CEB" Offset="1" />
      <GradientStop Color="#FF793879" Offset="0.669" />
    </RadialGradientBrush>
  </Application.Resources>

</Application>
```

Now your `TestWindow` is free to use this same brush to paint its background. If you find the `Background` property for this new `Window`, click the "Advanced properties" square and you can activate the Apply Resource... menu option. You can then search for your application-level brush by typing its name into the Search box (Figure 30-10).

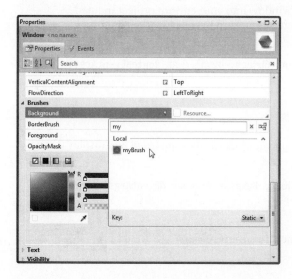

Figure 30-10. Applying application-level resources

Defining Merged Resource Dictionaries

Application-level resources are a good starting point, but what if you need to define a set of complex (or not so complex) resources that need to be reused across multiple WPF projects? In this case, you want to define what is known as a "merged resource dictionary." This is nothing more than a `.xaml` file that contains nothing but a collection of object resources. A single project can have as many of these files as required (one for brushes, one for animations, and so forth), each of which can be inserted using the Add New Item dialog box activated via the Project menu (Figure 30-11).

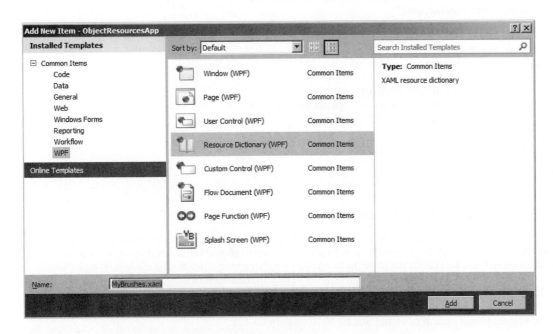

Figure 30-11. Inserting a new merged resource dictionary

In the new `MyBrushes.xaml` file, we will want to cut the current resources in the `Application.Resources` scope and move them into our dictionary, like so:

```
<ResourceDictionary xmlns="http://schemas.microsoft.com/winfx/2006/xaml/presentation"
                    xmlns:x="http://schemas.microsoft.com/winfx/2006/xaml">

  <RadialGradientBrush x:Key="myBrush">
    <GradientStop Color="#FFC44EC4" Offset="0" />
    <GradientStop Color="#FF829CEB" Offset="1" />
    <GradientStop Color="#FF793879" Offset="0.669" />
  </RadialGradientBrush>

</ResourceDictionary>
```

Now, even though this resource dictionary is part of our project, we will get runtime errors. The reason is that all resource dictionaries must be merged (typically at the application level) into an existing resource dictionary. To do this, use the following format (note that multiple resource dictionaries can be merged by adding multiple <ResourceDictionary> elements within the <ResourceDictionary.MergedDictionaries> scope).

```
<Application x:Class="Application"
  xmlns="http://schemas.microsoft.com/winfx/2006/xaml/presentation"
  xmlns:x="http://schemas.microsoft.com/winfx/2006/xaml"
  StartupUri="MainWindow.xaml">

  <!-- Bring in the logical resources
       from the MyBrushes.xaml file. -->
  <Application.Resources>
    <ResourceDictionary>
      <ResourceDictionary.MergedDictionaries>
        <ResourceDictionary Source = "MyBrushes.xaml"/>
      </ResourceDictionary.MergedDictionaries>
    </ResourceDictionary>
  </Application.Resources>

</Application>
```

Defining a Resource-Only Assembly

Last but not least, it is possible to create .NET class libraries that contain nothing but dictionaries of object resources. This can be useful if you have defined a set of themes that need to be used on a machine-wide level. You could package up the object resource into a dedicated assembly, and then applications that wish to make use of them could load them into memory.

The easiest way to build a resource-only assembly is to actually begin with a WPF User Control Library project. Add such as project (named MyBrushesLibrary) to your current solution, using the Add ➤ New Project menu option of Visual Studio 2010 (Figure 30-12).

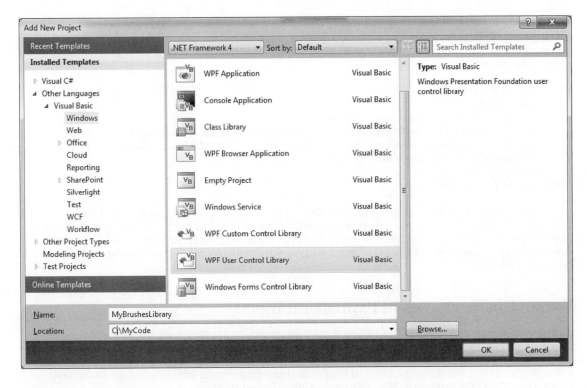

Figure 30-12. Adding a User Control library as a starting point for a resource-only library

Now, completely delete the `UserControl1.xaml` file from the project (the only items we really want are the referenced WPF assemblies). Next, drag and drop the `MyBrushes.xaml` file into your MyBrushesLibrary project and delete it from the ObjectResourcesApp project. Your Solution Explorer should now look like Figure 30-13.

Figure 30-13. Moving the MyBrushes.xaml file into our new library project

Compile your code library project. Next, reference this library from the ObjectResourcesApp project using the Add Reference dialog box. Now, you will want to merge these binary resources into the application-level resource dictionary of the ObjectResourcesApp project. Doing so, however, requires some rather funky syntax, shown here:

```
<Application.Resources>
  <ResourceDictionary>
    <ResourceDictionary.MergedDictionaries>
      <!--The syntax is /NameOfAssembly;Component/NameOfXamlFileInAssembly.xaml -->
      <ResourceDictionary Source = "/MyBrushesLibrary;Component/MyBrushes.xaml"/>
    </ResourceDictionary.MergedDictionaries>
  </ResourceDictionary>
</Application.Resources>
```

First, be aware that this string is space-sensitive. If you have extra white space around your semicolon or forward slashes, you will generate runtime errors. The first part of the string is the friendly name of the external library (no file extension). After the semicolon, you type in the word *Component* followed by the name of the compiled binary resource, which will be identical to the original XAML resource dictionary.

Extracting Resources in Expression Blend

As mentioned, Expression Blend has similar ways to promote local resources to window-level, application-level, and even resource-dictionary-level. Assume you have defined a custom brush for the Background property of the main window and wish to package it as a new resource. Using the Brush editor, click on the (ever so tiny) Advanced Properties button (the small white dot) of the Background property to access the Convert to New Resource option (Figure 30-14).

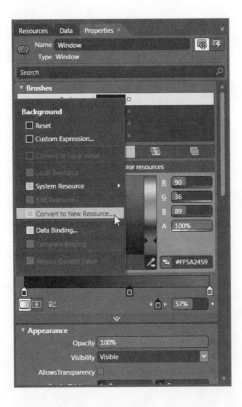

Figure 30-14. Extracting a new resource using Blend

From the resulting dialog box, you can give your object resource a name and specify where Blend should store it (the current window, the application, or a new merged resource dictionary). Here I have placed myNewBrush at the application level (Figure 30-15).

Figure 30-15. Defining a new application-level resource with Blend

Once you've done this, you will see that your `App.xaml` file has been updated as expected. Also, using the Resources tab (opened via the Window menu) you can modify existing resources using the appropriate editor (Figure 30-16).

Figure 30-16. Modifying existing resources with Blend

That wraps up our examination of WPF's resource management system. You will make good use of these techniques for most of your applications, as well as during the remainder of the WPF chapters of this text. Next up, let's investigate the integrated animation API of Windows Presentation Foundation.

■ **Source Code** The ObjectResourcesApp project can be found under the Chapter 30 subdirectory.

Understanding WPF's Animation Services

In addition to the graphical rendering services you examined in Chapter 29, WPF supplies a programming interface to support animation services. The term *animation* may bring to mind visions of spinning company logos, a sequence of rotating image resources (to provide the illusion of movement), text bouncing across the screen, or specific types of programs such as video games or multimedia applications.

While WPF's animation APIs could certainly be used for such purposes, animation can be used any time you wish to give an application additional flair. For example, you could build an animation for a button on a screen that magnifies slightly when the mouse cursor hovers within its boundaries (and shrinks back once the mouse cursor moves beyond the boundaries). Or you could animate a window so that it closes using a particular visual appearance, such as slowly fading into transparency. In fact, WPF's animation support can be used within any sort of application (a business application, multimedia programs, video games, etc.) whenever you wish to provide a more engaging user experience.

As with many other aspects of WPF, the notion of building animations is nothing new. What is new is that, unlike other APIs you may have used in the past (including Windows Forms), developers are not required to author the necessary infrastructure by hand. Under WPF, there's no need to create the background threads or timers used to advance the animation sequence, define custom types to represent the animation, erase and redraw images, or bother with tedious mathematical calculations.

Like other aspects of WPF, we can build an animation entirely using XAML, entirely using VB 2010 code, or using a combination of the two. Furthermore, we can use Microsoft Expression Blend to design an animation using integrated tools and wizards—without seeing a bit of VB 2010 or XAML in the foreground. You will see how to use Blend to author animations in the next chapter during our discussion of control templates. For now, let's get to know the overall role of the animation API.

■ **Note** Visual Studio 2010 has no support for authoring animations using GUI animation tools. If you author an animation with Visual Studio, you will do so by typing in the XAML directly.

The Role of the Animation Class Types

To understand WPF's animation support, we must begin by examining the animation classes within the `System.Windows.Media.Animation` namespace of `PresentationCore.dll`. Here you will find over 100 different class types that are named using the `Animation` token.

All of these classes can be placed into one of three broad categories. First of all, any class that follows the name convention `DataTypeAnimation` (`ByteAnimation`, `ColorAnimation`, `DoubleAnimation`, `In32Animation`, etc.) allows you to work with linear interpolation animations. This enables you to change a value smoothly over time from a start value to a final value.

Next, the classes that follow the naming convention `DataTypeAnimationUsingKeyFrames` (`StringAnimationUsingKeyFrames`, `DoubleAnimationUsingKeyFrames`, `PointAnimationUsingKeyFrames`, etc.) represent "key frame animations," which allow you to cycle through a set of defined values over a period of time. For example, you could use keyframes to change the caption of a button by cycling through a series of individual characters.

Finally, classes that follow the `DataTypeAnimationUsingPath` naming convention (`DoubleAnimationUsingPath`, `PointAnimationUsingPath`, among others) are path-based animations that allow you to animate objects to move along a path you define. By way of an example, if you were building a GPS application, you could use a path-based animation to move an item along the quickest travel route to the user's destination.

Now, obviously, these classes are *not* used to somehow provide an animation sequence directly to a variable of a particular data type (after all, how exactly could we animate the value "9" using an `Int32Animation`?).

For example, consider the `Label` type's `Height` and `Width` properties, both of which are dependency properties wrapping a `Double`. If you wish to define an animation that would increase the height of a label over a time span, you could connect a `DoubleAnimation` object to the `Height` property and allow WPF to take care of the details of performing the actual animation itself. By way of another example, if you wish to transition the color of a brush type from green to yellow over a period of 5 seconds, you could do so using the `ColorAnimation` type.

To be very clear, these Animation classes can be connected to any *dependency property* of a given object that matches the underlying types. As explained in Chapter 31, dependency properties are a specialized form of property required by many WPF services including animation, data binding, and styles.

By convention, a dependency property is defined as a Shared read-only field of the class, and is named by suffixing the word Property to the normal property name. For example, the dependency property for the Height property of a Button would be accessed in code using Button.HeightProperty.

The To, From, and By Properties

All Animation classes define a handful of key properties that control the starting and ending values used to perform the animation:

- To: This property represents the animation's ending value.

- From: This property represents the animation's starting value.

- By: This property represents the total amount by which the animation changes its starting value.

Despite the fact that all Animation classes support the To, From, and By properties, they do not receive them via Overridable members of a base class. The reason for this is that the underlying types wrapped by these properties vary greatly (integers, colors, Thickness objects, etc.), and representing all possibilities using a single base class would result in very complex coding constructs.

On a related note, you might also wonder why .NET generics were not used to define a single generic animation class with a single type parameter (e.g., Animate(Of T)). Again, given that there are so many underlying data types (colors, vectors, integers, strings, etc.) used to animated dependency properties, it would not be as clean a solution as you might expect (not to mention XAML has only limited support for generic types).

The Role of the Timeline Base Class

Although a single base class was not used to define To, From, and By properties, the Animation classes do share a common base class: System.Windows.Media.Animation.Timeline. This type provides a number of additional properties that control the pacing of the animation, as described in Table 30-1.

Table 30-1. Key Members of the Timeline Base Class

Properties	Meaning in Life
AccelerationRatio, DecelerationRatio, SpeedRatio	These properties can be used to control the overall pacing of the animation sequence.
AutoReverse	This property gets or sets a value that indicates whether the timeline plays in reverse after it completes a forward iteration (the default value is False).

Properties	Meaning in Life
BeginTime	This property gets or sets the time at which this timeline should begin. The default value is 0, which begins the animation immediately.
Duration	This property allows you to set a duration of time to play the timeline.
FillBehavior, RepeatBehavior	These properties are used to control what should happen once the timeline has completed (repeat the animation, do nothing, etc.).

Authoring an Animation in VB 2010 Code

The chances are quite good that a majority of your WPF animation projects will be authored using the Expression Blend animation editor, and will therefore be represented as markup. However, our first look at WPF's animation services will use nothing but VB 2010 code, as I feel it is a tad more straightforward.

Specifically, we will build a Window that contains a `Button`, which has the odd behavior of spinning in a circle (based on the upper left corner) whenever the mouse enters its surface area. Begin by creating a new WPF application named SpinningButtonAnimationApp, using Visual Studio 2010. Update the initial markup like the following (and handle the button's MouseEnter event):

```
<Window x:Class=".MainWindow"
  xmlns="http://schemas.microsoft.com/winfx/2006/xaml/presentation"
  xmlns:x="http://schemas.microsoft.com/winfx/2006/xaml"
  Title="Animations in VB 2010 code" Height="350"
  Width="525" WindowStartupLocation="CenterScreen">
  <Grid>
    <Button x:Name="btnSpinner" Height="50" Width="100" Content="I Spin!"
/>
  </Grid>
</Window>
```

Now, import the `System.Windows.Media.Animation` namespace and add the following code in the window's VB 2010 code file:

```
Class MainWindow

    Private isSpinning As Boolean = False

    Private Sub btnSpinner_MouseEnter(ByVal sender As Object, ByVal e As MouseEventArgs)
        Handles btnSpinner.MouseEnter
        If Not isSpinning Then
            isSpinning = True

            ' Make a Double animation object, and register
            ' with the Completed event.
            Dim dblAnim As New DoubleAnimation()
            AddHandler dblAnim.Completed, Sub(o, s) isSpinning = False
```

```
                ' Set the start value and end value.
                dblAnim.From = 0
                dblAnim.To = 360

                ' Now, create a RotateTransform object, and set
                ' it to the RenderTransform property of our
                ' button.
                Dim rt As New RotateTransform()
                btnSpinner.RenderTransform = rt

                ' Now, animation the RotateTransform object.
                rt.BeginAnimation(RotateTransform.AngleProperty, dblAnim)
            End If
    End Sub
End Class
```

The first major task of this method is to configure a `DoubleAnimation` object, which will start at the value `0` and end at the value `360`. Notice that we are handling the `Completed` event on this object as well, to toggle a class-level `Boolean` variable that is used to ensure that if an animation is currently being performed, we don't "reset" it to start again.

Next, we create a `RotateTransform` object that is connected to the `RenderTransform` property of our `Button` control (`btnSpinner`). Last but not least, we inform the `RenderTransform` object to begin animating its `Angle` property using our `DoubleAnimation` object. When you are authoring animations in code, you typically do so by calling `BeginAnimation()`, and pass in the underlying *dependency property* you wish to animate (remember, by convention, this is a Shared field on the class), followed by a related animation object.

Let's add another animation to the program, which will cause the button to fade into invisibility when clicked. First, handle the `Click` event of the `btnSpinner` object, then add the following code in the resulting event handler:

```
Private Sub btnSpinner_Click(ByVal sender As Object, ByVal e As RoutedEventArgs)
        Handles btnSpinner.Click
    Dim dblAnim As New DoubleAnimation()
    dblAnim.From = 1.0
    dblAnim.To = 0.0
    btnSpinner.BeginAnimation(Button.OpacityProperty, dblAnim)
End Sub
```

Here, we are changing the Opacity property value to fade the button out of view. Currently, however, this is hard to do, as the button is spinning very fast! How, then, can we control the pace of an animation? Glad you asked.

Controlling the Pacing of an Animation

By default, an animation will take approximately one second to transition between the values assigned to the `From` and `To` properties. Therefore, our button has one second to spin around a full 360 degree angle, while the button will fade away to invisibility (when clicked) over the course of one second.

If you wish to define a custom amount of time for an animation's transition, you may do so via the animation object's **Duration** property, which can be set to an instance of a **Duration** object. Typically, the time span is established by passing a **TimeSpan** object to the **Duration**'s constructor. Consider the following update that will give the button a full 4 seconds to rotate:

```
Private Sub btnSpinner_MouseEnter(ByVal sender As Object, ByVal e As MouseEventArgs)
        Handles btnSpinner.MouseEnter
    If Not isSpinning Then
        isSpinning = True

        ' Make a Double animation object, and register
        ' with the Completed event.
        Dim dblAnim As New DoubleAnimation()
        AddHandler dblAnim.Completed, Sub(o, s) isSpinning = False

        ' Button has 4 seconds to finish the spin!
        dblAnim.Duration = New Duration(TimeSpan.FromSeconds(4))
        ...
    End If
End Sub
```

With this adjustment, you should have a fighting chance to click the button while it is spinning, at which point it will fade away.

■ **Note** The BeginTime property of an Animation class also takes a TimeSpan object. Recall that this property can be set to establish a wait time before starting an animation sequence.

Reversing and Looping an Animation

You can also tell **Animation** objects to play an animation in reverse at the completion of the animation sequence by setting the **AutoReverse** property to **True**. For example, if you wish to have the button come back into view after it has faded away, you could author the following:

```
Private Sub btnSpinner_Click(ByVal sender As Object, ByVal e As RoutedEventArgs)
        Handles btnSpinner.Click
    Dim dblAnim As New DoubleAnimation()
    dblAnim.From = 1.0
    dblAnim.To = 0.0

    ' Reverse when done.
    dblAnim.AutoReverse = True
    btnSpinner.BeginAnimation(Button.OpacityProperty, dblAnim)
End Sub
```

If you'd like to have an animation repeat some number of times (or to never stop once activated), you can do so using the **RepeatBehavior** property, which is common to all **Animation** classes. If you pass in a simple numerical value to the constructor, you can specify a hard-coded number of times to repeat.

On the other hand, if you pass in a `TimeSpan` object to the constructor, you can establish an amount of time the animation should repeat. Finally, if you wish an animation to loop ad infinitum, you can simply specify `RepeatBehavior.Forever`. Consider the following ways we could change the repeat behaviors of either of the `DoubleAnimation` objects used in this example:

```
' Loop forever.
dblAnim.RepeatBehavior = RepeatBehavior.Forever

' Loop three times.
dblAnim.RepeatBehavior = New RepeatBehavior(3)

' Loop for 30 seconds.
dblAnim.RepeatBehavior = New RepeatBehavior(TimeSpan.FromSeconds(30))
```

That wraps up our investigation about how to animate aspects of an object using VB 2010 code and the WPF animation API. Next, we will learn how to do the same using XAML.

──

■ **Source Code** The SpinningButtonAnimationApp project can be found under the Chapter 30 subdirectory.

──

Authoring Animations in XAML

Authoring animations in markup is similar to authoring them in code, at least for simple, straightforward animation sequences. When you need to capture more complex animations, which may involve changing the values of numerous properties at once, the amount of markup can grow considerably. Thankfully, the Expression Blend animation editors can take care of the details for us. Even so, it is important to know the basics of how an animation is represented in XAML, as this will make it easier for you to modify and tweak tool-generated content.

──

■ **Note** You will find a number of XAML files in the XamlAnimations folder of the downloadable source code. As you go through the next several pages, copy these markup files into your custom XAML editor, or into the kaxaml editor, to see the results.

──

For the most part, creating an animation is similar to what you have already seen. You still configure an `Animation` object and associate it to an object's property. One big difference, however, is that WPF is not function-call-friendly. As a result, instead of calling `BeginAnimation()`, you use a *storyboard* as a layer of indirection.

Let's walk through a complete example of an animation defined in terms of XAML, followed by a detailed breakdown. The following XAML definition will display a window that contains a single label. As soon as the `Label` object loads into memory, it begins an animation sequence in which the font size increases from 12 points to 100 over a period of four seconds. The animation will repeat for as long as the Window object is loaded in memory. You can find this markup in the `GrowLabelFont.xaml` file, so copy it into your MyXamlPad.exe application and observe the behavior.

```
<Window
  xmlns="http://schemas.microsoft.com/winfx/2006/xaml/presentation"
  xmlns:x="http://schemas.microsoft.com/winfx/2006/xaml"
  Height="200" Width="600" WindowStartupLocation="CenterScreen" Title="Growing Label Font!">
  <StackPanel>
    <Label Content = "Interesting...">
      <Label.Triggers>
        <EventTrigger RoutedEvent = "Label.Loaded">
          <EventTrigger.Actions>
            <BeginStoryboard>
              <Storyboard TargetProperty = "FontSize">
                <DoubleAnimation From = "12" To = "100" Duration = "0:0:4"
                                 RepeatBehavior = "Forever"/>
              </Storyboard>
            </BeginStoryboard>
          </EventTrigger.Actions>
        </EventTrigger>
      </Label.Triggers>
    </Label>
  </StackPanel>
</Window>
```

Now, let's break this example down bit-by-bit.

The Role of Storyboards

Working from the innermost element outward, we first encounter the `<DoubleAnimation>` element, which makes use of the same properties we set in procedural code (`To`, `From`, `Duration`, and `RepeatBehavior`):

```
<DoubleAnimation From = "12" To = "100" Duration = "0:0:4"
                 RepeatBehavior = "Forever"/>
```

As mentioned, `Animation` elements are placed within a `<Storyboard>` element, which is used to map the animation object to a given property on the parent type via the `TargetProperty` property—which in this case is `FontSize`. A `<Storyboard>` is always wrapped in a parent element named `<BeginStoryboard>`, which is little more than a way to denote a storyboard's location:

```
<BeginStoryboard>
  <Storyboard TargetProperty = "FontSize">
    <DoubleAnimation From = "12" To = "100" Duration = "0:0:4"
                     RepeatBehavior = "Forever"/>
  </Storyboard>
</BeginStoryboard>
```

The Role of Event Triggers

Once the `<BeginStoryboard>` element has been defined, we need to specify some sort of action that will cause the animation to begin executing. WPF has a few different ways to respond to runtime conditions in markup, one of which is termed a *trigger*. From a high level, you can consider a trigger a way of responding to an event condition in XAML, without the need for procedural code.

Typically, when you respond to an event in VB 2010, you author custom code that will execute when the event occurs. A trigger, however, is just a way to be notified that some event condition has happened ("I'm loaded into memory", "The mouse is over me!", "I have focus!").

Once you've been notified that an event condition has occurred, you can start the storyboard. In this example, we are responding to the `Label` being loaded into memory. Because it is the `Label`'s `Loaded` event we are interested in, the `<EventTrigger>` is placed in the `Label`'s trigger collection:

```
<Label Content = "Interesting...">
  <Label.Triggers>
    <EventTrigger RoutedEvent = "Label.Loaded">
      <EventTrigger.Actions>
        <BeginStoryboard>
          <Storyboard TargetProperty = "FontSize">
            <DoubleAnimation From = "12" To = "100" Duration = "0:0:4"
                             RepeatBehavior = "Forever"/>
          </Storyboard>
        </BeginStoryboard>
      </EventTrigger.Actions>
    </EventTrigger>
  </Label.Triggers>
</Label>
```

Let's see another example of defining an animation in XAML, this time using a *key frame* animation.

Animation Using Discrete Key Frames

Unlike the linear interpolation animation objects, which can only move between a starting point and an ending point, the *key frame* counterparts allow us to create a collection of specific values for an animation that should take place at specific times.

To illustrate the use of a discrete key frame type, assume you wish to build a `Button` control that animates its content so that over the course of three seconds, the value "OK!" appears, one character at a time. You'll find the following markup in the `StringAnimation.xaml` file. Copy this markup into your `MyXamlPad.exe` program and view the results:

```
<Window xmlns="http://schemas.microsoft.com/winfx/2006/xaml/presentation"
  xmlns:x="http://schemas.microsoft.com/winfx/2006/xaml"
  Height="100" Width="300"
  WindowStartupLocation="CenterScreen" Title="Animate String Data!">
  <StackPanel>
    <Button Name="myButton" Height="40"
            FontSize="16pt" FontFamily="Verdana" Width = "100">
      <Button.Triggers>
        <EventTrigger RoutedEvent="Button.Loaded">
          <BeginStoryboard>
```

```
        <Storyboard>
          <StringAnimationUsingKeyFrames RepeatBehavior = "Forever"
              Storyboard.TargetName="myButton"
              Storyboard.TargetProperty="Content"
              Duration="0:0:3">
            <DiscreteStringKeyFrame Value="" KeyTime="0:0:0" />
            <DiscreteStringKeyFrame Value="O" KeyTime="0:0:1" />
            <DiscreteStringKeyFrame Value="OK" KeyTime="0:0:1.5" />
            <DiscreteStringKeyFrame Value="OK!" KeyTime="0:0:2" />
          </StringAnimationUsingKeyFrames>
        </Storyboard>
      </BeginStoryboard>
    </EventTrigger>
  </Button.Triggers>
  </Button>
 </StackPanel>
</Window>
```

Notice first of all that we have defined an event trigger for our button to ensure that our storyboard executes when the button has loaded into memory. The `StringAnimationUsingKeyFrames` class is in charge of changing the content of the button, via the `Storyboard.TargetName` and `Storyboard.TargetProperty` values.

Within the scope of the `<StringAnimationUsingKeyFrames>` element, we defined four `DiscreteStringKeyFrame` elements, which change the button's `Content` property over the course of two seconds (note that the duration established by `StringAnimationUsingKeyFrames` is a total of three seconds, so we will see a slight pause between the final "!" and looping "O").

Now that you have a better feel for how to build animations in VB 2010 code and XAML, let's turn our attention of the role of WPF styles, which make heavy use of graphics, object resources, and animations.

■ **Source Code** These loose XAML files can be found under the XamlAnimations subdirectory of Chapter 30.

Understanding the Role of WPF Styles

When you are building the UI of a WPF application, it is not uncommon for a family of controls to require a shared look and feel. For example, you may want all button types have the same height, width, background color, and font size for their string content. Though you could handle this by setting each button's individual properties to identical values, such an approach makes it difficult to implement changes down the road, as you'd need to reset the same set of properties on multiple objects for every change.

Thankfully, WPF offers a simple way to constrain the look and feel of related controls using *styles*. Simply put, a WPF style is an object that maintains a collection of property/value pairs. Programmatically speaking, an individual style is represented using the `System.Windows.Style` class. This class has a property named `Setters`, which exposes a strongly typed collection of `Setter` objects. It is the `Setter` object that allows you to define the property/value pairs.

In addition to the Setters collection, the Style class also defines a few other important members that allow you to incorporate triggers, restrict where a style can be applied, and even create a new style based on an existing style (think of it as "style inheritance"). In particular, be aware of the following members of the Style class:

- **Triggers**: Exposes a collection of trigger objects, which allow you to capture various event conditions within a style.

- **BasedOn**: Allows you to build a new style based on an existing style.

- **TargetType**: Allows you to constrain where a style can be applied.

Defining and Applying a Style

In almost every case, a Style object will be packaged as an object resource. Like any object resource, you can package it at the window or application level, as well as within a dedicated resource dictionary (this is great, because it makes the Style object easily accessible throughout your application). Now recall that the goal is to define a Style object that fills (at minimum) the Setters collection with a set of property/value pairs.

Create a new WPF application named WpfStyles using Visual Studio 2010. Let's build a style that captures the basic font characteristics of a control in our application. Open your **Application.xaml** file and define the following named style:

```
<Application x:Class="Application"
  xmlns="http://schemas.microsoft.com/winfx/2006/xaml/presentation"
  xmlns:x="http://schemas.microsoft.com/winfx/2006/xaml"
  StartupUri="MainWindow.xaml">

  <Application.Resources>
    <Style x:Key ="BasicControlStyle">
      <Setter Property = "Control.FontSize" Value ="14"/>
      <Setter Property = "Control.Height" Value = "40"/>
      <Setter Property = "Control.Cursor" Value = "Hand"/>
    </Style>
  </Application.Resources>

</Application>
```

Notice that our "BasicControlStyle" adds three Setter objects to the internal collection. Now, let's apply this style to a few controls in our main window. Because this style is an object resource, the controls that wish to use it still need to use the {StaticResource} or {DynamicResource} markup extension to locate the style. When they find the style, they will set the resource item to the identically named Style property. Consider the following <Window> definition:

```
<Window x:Class="MainWindow"
  xmlns="http://schemas.microsoft.com/winfx/2006/xaml/presentation"
  xmlns:x="http://schemas.microsoft.com/winfx/2006/xaml"
  Title="A Window with Style!" Height="229"
  Width="525" WindowStartupLocation="CenterScreen">
```

```
<StackPanel>
  <Label x:Name="lblInfo" Content="This style is boring..."
         Style="{StaticResource BasicControlStyle}" Width="150"/>
  <Button x:Name="btnTestButton" Content="Yes, but we are reusing settings!"
         Style="{StaticResource BasicControlStyle}" Width="250"/>
</StackPanel>

</Window>
```

If you run this application, you'll find that both controls support the same cursor, height, and font size.

Overriding Style Settings

Here we have a Button and Label that have both opted in to the constraints enforced by our style. Of course, if a control wishes to apply a style and then change some of the defined settings, that's fine. For example, the Button will now use the Help cursor (rather than the Hand cursor defined in the style):

```
<Button x:Name="btnTestButton" Content="Yes, but we are reusing settings!"
        Cursor="Help" Style="{StaticResource BasicControlStyle}" Width="250" />
```

Styles are processed before the individual property settings of the control using the style; therefore controls can "override" settings on a case-by-case basis.

Automatically Applying a Style with TargetType

Currently, our style is defined in such a way that any control can adopt it (and has to do so explicitly by setting the control's Style property), given that each property is qualified by the Control class. For a program that defines dozens of settings, this would entail a good amount of repeated code. One way to clean this style up a bit is to use the TargetType attribute. When you add this attribute to a Style's opening element, you can mark exactly once where it can be applied:

```
<Style x:Key ="BasicControlStyle" TargetType="Control">
  <Setter Property = "FontSize" Value ="14"/>
  <Setter Property = "Height" Value = "40"/>
  <Setter Property = "Cursor" Value = "Hand"/>
</Style>
```

■ **Note** When you are building a style that is using a base class type, you needn't be concerned if you assign a value to a dependency property not supported by derived types. If the derived type does not support a given dependency property, it is ignored.

This is somewhat helpful, but we still have a style that can apply to any control. The `TargetType` attribute is more useful when you wish to define a style that can only be applied to a particular type of control. Add the following new style to the application's resource dictionary:

```
<Style x:Key ="BigGreenButton" TargetType="Button">
  <Setter Property = "FontSize" Value ="20"/>
  <Setter Property = "Height" Value = "100"/>
  <Setter Property = "Width" Value = "100"/>
  <Setter Property = "Background" Value = "DarkGreen"/>
  <Setter Property = "Foreground" Value = "Yellow"/>
</Style>
```

This style will work only on `Button` controls (or a sub-class of `Button`) and if you apply it on an incompatible element, you will get markup and compiler errors. If the `Button` uses this new style like so:

```
<Button x:Name="btnTestButton" Content="This Style ROCKS!"
        Cursor="Help" Style="{StaticResource BigGreenButton}" Width="250"  />
```

you'd see the output like that shown in Figure 30-17.

Figure 30-17. *Controls with different styles*

Subclassing Existing Styles

You can also build new styles using an existing style, via the `BasedOn` property. The style you are extending must have been given a proper x:Key in the dictionary, as the derived style will reference it by name using the `{StaticResource}` markup extension. Here is a new style based on "BigGreenButton", which rotates the button element by 20 degrees:

```
<!-- This style is based on BigGreenButton -->
<Style x:Key ="TiltButton" TargetType="Button" BasedOn = "{StaticResource BigGreenButton}">
  <Setter Property = "Foreground" Value = "White"/>
  <Setter Property = "RenderTransform">
    <Setter.Value>
      <RotateTransform Angle = "20"/>
    </Setter.Value>
  </Setter>
</Style>
```

This time, the output appears as in Figure 30-18.

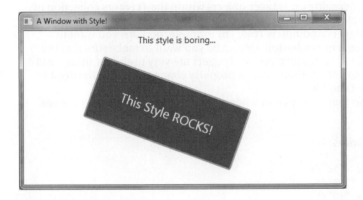

Figure 30-18. Using a derived style

The Role of Unnamed Styles

Assume you need to ensure that all TextBox controls have the same look and feel. Now assume you have defined a style as an application-level resource, so all windows in the program have access to it. While this is a step in the right direction, if you have numerous windows with numerous TextBox controls, you'll need to set the Style property numerous times!

WPF styles can be implicitly applied to all controls within a given XAML scope. To create such a style, you use the TargetType property but you don't assign the Style resource an x:Key value. This "unnamed style" now applies to all controls of the correct type. Here is another application-level style that will apply automatically to all TextBox controls in the current application.

```
<!-- The default style for all text boxes -->
<Style TargetType="TextBox">
  <Setter Property = "FontSize" Value ="14"/>
  <Setter Property = "Width" Value = "100"/>
  <Setter Property = "Height" Value = "30"/>
  <Setter Property = "BorderThickness" Value = "5"/>
  <Setter Property = "BorderBrush" Value = "Red"/>
  <Setter Property = "FontStyle" Value = "Italic"/>
</Style>
```

We can now define any number of **TextBox** controls and they will automatically get the defined look. If a given **TextBox** does not want this default look and feel, it can opt out by setting the Style property to **{x:Null}**. For example, **txtTest** will get the default unnamed style, while **txtTest2** is doing things its own way:

```
<TextBox x:Name="txtTest"/>
<TextBox x:Name="txtTest2" Style="{x:Null}" BorderBrush="Black"
                BorderThickness="5" Height="60" Width="100" Text="Ha!"/>
```

Defining Styles with Triggers

WPF styles can also contain triggers, by packaging up **Trigger** objects within the **Triggers** collection of the **Style** object. Using triggers in a style allows you to define certain **<Setter>** elements in such a way that they will be applied only if a given trigger condition is **True**. For example, perhaps you want to increase the size of a font when the mouse is over a button. Or maybe you want to make sure that the text box with the current focus is highlighted with a given color. Triggers are very useful for these sorts of situations, in that they allow you to take specific actions when a property changes without the need to author explicit VB 2010 code in a code-behind file.

Here is an update to the **TextBox** style that ensures that when a **TextBox** has the input focus, it will receive a yellow background:

```
<!-- The default style for all text boxes -->
<Style TargetType="TextBox">
  <Setter Property = "FontSize" Value ="14"/>
  <Setter Property = "Width" Value = "100"/>
  <Setter Property = "Height" Value = "30"/>
  <Setter Property = "BorderThickness" Value = "5"/>
  <Setter Property = "BorderBrush" Value = "Red"/>
  <Setter Property = "FontStyle" Value = "Italic"/>
  <!-- The following setter will only be applied when the text box is
       in focus. -->
  <Style.Triggers>
    <Trigger Property = "IsFocused" Value = "True">
      <Setter Property = "Background" Value = "Yellow"/>
    </Trigger>
  </Style.Triggers>
</Style>
```

If you test this style, you'll find that as you tab between various **TextBox** objects, the currently selected **TextBox** has a bright yellow background (provided it has not opted out by assigning **{x:Null}** to the **Style** property).

Property triggers are also very smart, in that when the trigger's condition is *not True*, the property automatically receives the default assigned value. Therefore, as soon as a **TextBox** loses focus, it also automatically becomes the default color without any work on your part. In contrast, event triggers (examined when we looked at WPF animations) do not automatically revert to a previous condition.

Defining Styles with Multiple Triggers

Triggers can also be designed in such a way that the defined `<Setter>` elements will be applied when *multiple conditions* are True (similar to building an `if` statement for multiple conditions). Let's say we want to set the background of a `TextBox` to Yellow only if it has the active focus and the mouse is hovering within its boundaries. To do so, we can make use of the `<MultiTrigger>` element to define each condition:

```
<!-- The default style for all text boxes -->
<Style TargetType="TextBox">
  <Setter Property = "FontSize" Value ="14"/>
  <Setter Property = "Width" Value = "100"/>
  <Setter Property = "Height" Value = "30"/>
  <Setter Property = "BorderThickness" Value = "5"/>
  <Setter Property = "BorderBrush" Value = "Red"/>
  <Setter Property = "FontStyle" Value = "Italic"/>
  <!-- The following setter will only be applied when the text box is
  in focus AND the mouse is over the text box. -->
  <Style.Triggers>
    <MultiTrigger>
      <MultiTrigger.Conditions>
          <Condition Property = "IsFocused" Value = "True"/>
          <Condition Property = "IsMouseOver" Value = "True"/>
      </MultiTrigger.Conditions>
      <Setter Property = "Background" Value = "Yellow"/>
    </MultiTrigger>
  </Style.Triggers>
</Style>
```

Animated Styles

Styles can also incorporate triggers that kick off an animation sequence. Here is one final style that, when applied to `Button` controls, will cause the control to grow and shrink in size when the mouse is inside the button's surface area:

```
<!-- The growing button style! -->
<Style x:Key = "GrowingButtonStyle" TargetType="Button">
  <Setter Property = "Height" Value = "40"/>
  <Setter Property = "Width" Value = "100"/>
  <Style.Triggers>
    <Trigger Property = "IsMouseOver" Value = "True">
      <Trigger.EnterActions>
        <BeginStoryboard>
          <Storyboard TargetProperty = "Height">
            <DoubleAnimation From = "40" To = "200"
                             Duration = "0:0:2" AutoReverse="True"/>
          </Storyboard>
        </BeginStoryboard>
      </Trigger.EnterActions>
    </Trigger>
```

```
    </Style.Triggers>
</Style>
```

Here, our triggers collection is on the lookout for the IsMouseOver property to return True. When this occurs, we define a <Trigger.EnterActions> element to execute a simple storyboard that forces the button to grow to a Height value of 200 (and then return to a Height of 40) over 2 seconds. If you wish to perform other property changes, you could also define a <Trigger.ExitActions> scope to define any custom actions to take when IsMouseOver is False.

Assigning Styles Programmatically

Recall that a style can be applied at runtime as well. This can be helpful if you want to let end users choose how their UI looks and feels, or if you need to enforce a look and feel based on security settings (e.g., the "DisableAllButton" style) or what have you.

During this project, you have defined a number of styles, many of which can apply to Button controls. So, let's retool the UI of our main window to allow the user to pick from some of these styles by selecting names in a ListBox. Based on the user's selection, we will apply the appropriate style. Here is the new (and final) markup for the <Window> element:

```
<Window x:Class="MainWindow"
  xmlns="http://schemas.microsoft.com/winfx/2006/xaml/presentation"
  xmlns:x="http://schemas.microsoft.com/winfx/2006/xaml"
  Height="350" Title="A Window with Style!"
  Width="525" WindowStartupLocation="CenterScreen">

  <DockPanel >
    <StackPanel Orientation="Horizontal" DockPanel.Dock="Top">
      <Label Content="Please Pick a Style for this Button" Height="50"/>
      <ListBox x:Name ="lstStyles" Height ="80" Width ="150" Background="LightBlue"
             />
    </StackPanel>
    <Button x:Name="btnStyle" Height="40" Width="100" Content="OK!"/>
  </DockPanel>

</Window>
```

The ListBox control (named lstStyles) will be filled dynamically within the window's constructor like so:

```
Public Sub New()
        InitializeComponent()

        ' Fill the list box with all the Button
        ' styles.
        lstStyles.Items.Add("GrowingButtonStyle")
        lstStyles.Items.Add("TiltButton")
        lstStyles.Items.Add("BigGreenButton")
        lstStyles.Items.Add("BasicControlStyle")
End Sub
```

The final task is to handle the ListBox's SelectionChanged event. Notice in the following code how we are able to extract the current resource by name, using the inherited TryFindResource() method:

```
Private Sub lstStyles_Changed(ByVal sender As Object, ByVal e As SelectionChangedEventArgs)
        Handles lstStyles.SelectionChanged
    ' Get the selected style name from the list box.
    Dim currStyle As Style = CType(TryFindResource(lstStyles.SelectedValue), Style)
    If currStyle IsNot Nothing Then
        ' Set the style of the button type.
        Me.btnStyle.Style = currStyle
    End If
End Sub
```

When you run this application, you can pick from one of these four button styles on the fly. Figure 30-19 shows our completed application.

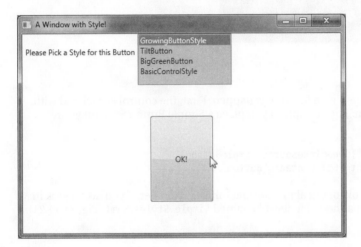

Figure 30-19. Controls with different styles

■ **Source Code** The WpfStyles project can be found under the Chapter 30 subdirectory.

Generating Styles with Expression Blend

To wrap up our examination of WPF styles, let's take a quick tour of how Blend can help automate the process of style construction. Again, however, I'll hold off discussing the animation editor (and related topics, such as triggers and control templates) until the next chapter. Here I want to point out the default "Simple Styles" of the Assets Library.

Working with Default Visual Styles

Blend ships with a number of default styles for common controls, referred to as the *Simple Styles*. If you open the Assets Library, you can locate the Styles in the tree view on the left-hand side (Figure 30-20).

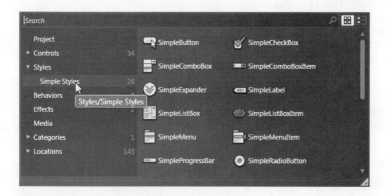

Figure 30-20. Blend's default styles

When you select one of these simple styles, a few things happen. First, the control is declared with the {DynamicResource} markup extension. For example, if you place a Simple Button Style on your designer, you'll find XAML similar to:

```
<Button Margin="116,49,220,0" Style="{DynamicResource SimpleButton}"
        VerticalAlignment="Top" Height="63" Content="Button"/>
```

Strangely enough, the control will look identical to a normal Button. However, if you take a look in your Project window, you will see Blend has added a new file named **Simple Styles.xaml** (Figure 30-21).

Figure 30-21. This is a resource dictionary!

If you double-click on this item and open the XAML editor, you will see it is a very large `<ResourceDictionary>` of default control styles. Furthermore, if you open the Blend Resources window, you'll see each item is listed and can be edited by clicking a given entry (Figure 30-22).

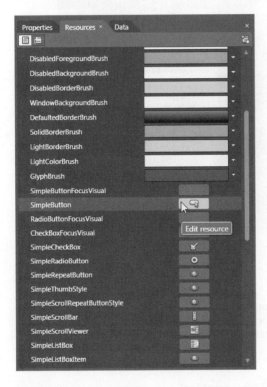

Figure 30-22. Selecting a default style for editing

If you click on the `SimpleButton` icon in the Resources view, a new designer will open that you can use to change the style to your heart's content using Blend's standard editing tools (the Properties window, animation editor, etc). Consider Figure 30-23.

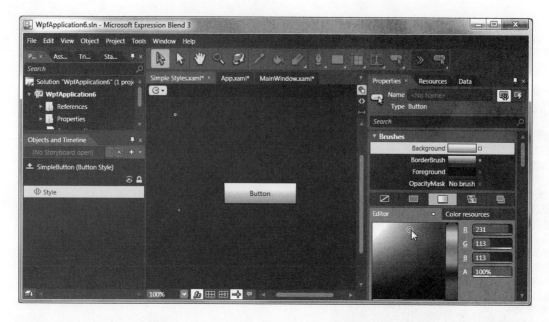

Figure 30-23. *Editing a default style*

The beauty of this approach is that the `Simple Styles.xaml` file is merged with your application resources and, therefore, all of your local edits will automatically be compiled into your application. Taking advantage of default simple styles essentially allows you to use starter markup for a control's normal look and feel, and customize it on a per-project basis. Here's the markup that would be in your `App.xaml` file:

```
<Application
  xmlns="http://schemas.microsoft.com/winfx/2006/xaml/presentation"
  xmlns:x="http://schemas.microsoft.com/winfx/2006/xaml"
  x:Class="WpfApplication6.App"
  StartupUri="MainWindow.xaml">
  <Application.Resources>
    <!-- Resources scoped at the Application level should be defined here. -->
    <ResourceDictionary>
      <ResourceDictionary.MergedDictionaries>
        <ResourceDictionary Source="Simple Styles.xaml"/>
      </ResourceDictionary.MergedDictionaries>
    </ResourceDictionary>
  </Application.Resources>
</Application>
```

Well, that wraps up this chapter. The next chapter will complete our examination of WPF by looking at the role of control templates and custom `UserControl` classes. Along the way, I'll also illustrate several new aspects of working with Expression Blend.

Summary

The first part of this chapter examined the resource management system of WPF. We began by looking at how to work with binary resources, then quickly turned our attention of the role of object resources. As you learned, object resources are named blobs of XAML that can be stored at various locations, in order to reuse content.

Next, you learned about WPF's animation framework. Here you had a chance to create some animations using VB 2010 code, as well as with XAML. You learned that if you define an animation in markup, you use Storyboard elements and triggers to control execution.

We wrapped up by looking at the WPF style mechanism, which makes heavy use of graphics, object resources, and animations. Along the way, you learned about how you can use Blend to simplify the creation of styles using default simple styles as a starting point.

WPF Control Templates and UserControls

This chapter concludes your investigation of the Windows Presentation Foundation (WPF) programming model by introducing you to the process of building customized controls. While it is true that the content model and style mechanism do allow you to add unique bits to a standard WPF control, the process of building custom templates and UserControls allows you to fully define how a control should render its output, respond to state transitions, and integrate into the WPF APIs.

This chapter begins by examining two topics that are important when creating a custom control, specifically *dependency properties* and *routed events*. Once you understand these topics, you will then learn about the role of a *default template* and how to view them programmatically at runtime.

Once this foundation has been laid, the remainder of this chapter will examine how to build custom UserControl classes using Visual Studio 2010 and Expression Blend. Along the way, you will learn more about the WPF trigger framework (first introduced in Chapter 30), as well as the new .NET 4.0 Visual State Manager (VSM). Finally, you will learn how to use the animation editor of Expression Blend to define state transitions and see how to incorporate your custom controls into larger WPF applications.

Understanding the Role of Dependency Properties

Like any .NET API, WPF makes use of each member of the .NET type system (classes, structures, interfaces, delegates, enumerations) and each type member (properties, methods, events, constant data, read-only fields, etc.) within its implementation. However, WPF also supports a unique programming concept termed a *dependency property*.

■ **Note** Dependency properties are also part of the Windows Workflow Foundation (WF) API. While a WF dependency property is constructed in a similar manner as a WPF dependency property, WF uses a different technology stack to implement them.

Like a "normal" .NET property (often termed a *CLR property* in the WPF literature), dependency properties can be set declaratively using XAML or programmatically within a code file. Furthermore, dependency properties (like CLR properties) ultimately exist to encapsulate data fields of a class and can be configured as read-only, write-only or read-write.

To make matters more interesting, in almost every case you will be blissfully unaware that you have actually set (or accessed) a dependency property as opposed to a CLR property! For example, the `Height` and `Width` properties that WPF controls inherit from `FrameworkElement`, as well as the `Content` member inherited from `ControlContent`, are all, in fact, dependency properties:

```
<!-- Set three dependency properties! -->
<Button x:Name = "btnMyButton" Height = "50" Width = "100" Content = "OK"/>
```

Given all of these similarities, why does WPF defines a new term for such a familiar concept? The answer lies in how a dependency property is implemented within the class. You'll see a coding example in just a little bit; however, from a high level, all dependency properties are created in the following manner:

- First, the class that defined a dependency property must have `DependencyObject` in its inheritance chain.

- A single dependency property is represented as a Public, Shared, Read-Only field in the class of type `DependencyProperty`. By convention, this field is named by suffixing the word `Property` to the name of the CLR wrapper (see final bullet point).

- The `DependencyProperty` variable is registered via a Shared call to `DependencyProperty.Register()`, which typically occurs in a Shared constructor or inline when the variable is declared.

- Finally, the class will define a XAML-friendly CLR property, which makes calls to methods provided by `DependencyObject` to get and set the value.

Once implemented, dependency properties provide a number of powerful features that are used by various WPF technologies including data binding, animation services, styles, and so forth. In a nutshell, the motivation of dependency properties is to provide a way to compute the value of a property based on the value of other inputs. Here is a list of some of these key benefits, which go well beyond those of the simple data encapsulation found with a CLR property:

- Dependency properties can inherit their values from a parent element's XAML definition. For example, if you defined a value for the `FontSize` attribute in the opening tag of a `<Window>`, all controls in that `Window` would have the same font size by default.

- Dependency properties support the ability to have values set by elements contained within their XAML scope, such as a `Button` setting the `Dock` property of a `DockPanel` parent. (Recall from Chapter 28 that *attached properties* do this very thing, as attached properties are a form of dependency properties.)

- Dependency properties allow WPF to compute a value based on multiple external values, which can be very important for animation and data binding services.

- Dependency properties provide infrastructure support for WPF triggers (also used quite often when working with animation and data binding).

Now remember, in many cases you will interact with an existing dependency property in a manner identical to a normal CLR property (thanks to the XAML wrapper). However, when I covered data binding in Chapter 28, you learned that if you need to establish a data binding in code, you must call the SetBinding() method on the object that is the destination of the operation and specify the *dependency property* it will operate on:

```
Private Sub SetBindings()
    Dim b As New Binding()
    b.Converter = New MyDoubleConverter()
    b.Source = Me.mySB
    b.Path = New PropertyPath("Value")

    ' Specify the dependency property!
    Me.labelSBThumb.SetBinding(Label.ContentProperty, b)
End Sub
```

You also saw similar code when you examined how to start an animation in code, back in the previous chapter:

```
' Specify the dependency property!
rt.BeginAnimation(RotateTransform.AngleProperty, dblAnim)
```

The only time when you would need to build your own custom dependency property is when you are authoring a custom WPF control. For example, if you are building a UserControl which defines four custom properties and you want these properties to integrate well within the WPF API, you should author them using dependency property logic.

Specifically, if your properties need to be the target of a data binding or animation operation, if the property must broadcast when it has changed, if it must be able to work as a Setter in a WPF style, or if it must be able to receive their values from a parent element, a normal CLR property will *not* be enough. If you were to use a normal CLR property, other programmers may indeed be able to get and set a value; however, if they attempt to use your properties within the context of a WPF service, things will not work as expected. Because you can never know how others might want to interact with the properties of your custom UserControl classes, you should get in the habit of *always* defining dependency properties when building custom controls.

Examining an Existing Dependency Property

Before you learn how to build a custom dependency property, let's take a look at how the Height property of the FrameworkElement class has been implemented internally. The relevant code is shown here (with my included comments); however, you can view the same code yourself if you make use of reflector.exe (just use the View | Search option).

```
' FrameworkElement is-a DependencyObject.
Public Class FrameworkElement
    Inherits UIElement
    Implements IFrameworkInputElement, IInputElement,
                    ISupportInitialize, IHaveResources, IQueryAmbient

    ….
    ' A Shared ReadOnly field of type DependencyProperty.
    Public Shared ReadOnly HeightProperty As DependencyProperty
```

```
' The DependencyProperty field is often registered
' in the Shared constructor of the class.
Shared Sub New()
    …
    HeightProperty = DependencyProperty.Register(
                    "Height", GetType(Double),
                    GetType(FrameworkElement),
                    New FrameworkPropertyMetadata(CDbl(1.0) / CDbl(0.0),
                    FrameworkPropertyMetadataOptions.AffectsMeasure,
                    New PropertyChangedCallback(AddressOf FrameworkElement↵
                    .OnTransformDirty)),
                    New ValidateValueCallback(AddressOf FrameworkElement↵
                    .IsWidthHeightValid))
End Sub

' The CLR wrapper, which is implemented using
' the inherited GetValue()/SetValue() methods.
Public Property Height() As Double
    Get
        Return CDbl(MyBase.GetValue(HeightProperty))
    End Get
    Set(ByVal value As Double)
        MyBase.SetValue(HeightProperty, value)
    End Set
End Property
End Class
```

As you can see, dependency properties require quite a bit of additional code from a normal CLR property! And in reality, a dependency can be even more complex than what you see here (thankfully, many implementations are simpler than Height).

First and foremost, remember that if a class wants to define a dependency property, it must have DependencyObject in the inheritance chain, as this is the class which defines the GetValue() and SetValue() methods used in the CLR wrapper. Since FrameworkElement is-a DependencyObject, this requirement is satisfied.

Next, recall that the entity which will hold the actual value of the property (a Double in the case of Height) is represented as a Public, Shared ReadOnly field of type DependencyProperty. The name of this field should, by convention, always be named by suffixing the word Property to the name of the related CLR wrapper, like so:

```
Public Shared ReadOnly HeightProperty As DependencyProperty
```

Given that dependency properties are declared as Shared fields, they are typically created (and registered) within the Shared constructor of the class. The DependencyProperty object is created via a call to the Shared DependencyProperty.Register() method. This method has been overloaded many times; however, in the case of Height, DependencyProperty.Register() is invoked as follows:

```
HeightProperty = DependencyProperty.Register("Height",
            GetType(Double), GetType(FrameworkElement),
            New FrameworkPropertyMetadata(CDbl(0.0),
                FrameworkPropertyMetadataOptions.AffectsMeasure,
```

```
        New PropertyChangedCallback(AddressOf  FrameworkElement.OnTransformDirty)),
        New ValidateValueCallback(AddressOf FrameworkElement.IsWidthHeightValid))
```

The first argument to `DependencyProperty.Register()` is the name of the normal CLR property on the class (`Height` in this case), while the second argument is the type information of the underlying data type it is encapsulating (a `Double`). The third argument specifies the type information of the class that this property belongs to (`FrameworkElement` in this case). While this might seem redundant (after all, the `HeightProperty` field is already defined within the `FrameworkElement` class), this is a very clever aspect of WPF in that it allows one class to register properties on another (even if the class definition has been declared as `NotInheritable`!).

The fourth argument passed to `DependencyProperty.Register()` in this example is what really gives dependency properties their own unique flavor. Here a `FrameworkPropertyMetadata` object is passed that describes various details regarding how WPF should handle this property with respect to callback notifications (if the property needs to notify others when the value changes) and various options (represented by the `FrameworkPropertyMetadataOptions` enum) that control what is effected by the property in question (Does it work with data binding?, Can it be inherited?, etc.). In this case, the constructor arguments of `FrameworkPropertyMetadata` break down as so:

```
Dim TempFrameworkPropertyMetadata As FrameworkPropertyMetadata =
' Default value of property.
New FrameworkPropertyMetadata(CDbl(0.0),

' Metadata options.
FrameworkPropertyMetadataOptions.AffectsMeasure,

' Delegate pointing to method called when property changes
New PropertyChangedCallback(
AddressOf FrameworkElement.OnTransformDirty))
```

Because the final argument to the `FrameworkPropertyMetadata` constructor is a delegate, note that its constructor parameter is pointing to a Shared method on the `FrameworkElement` class named `OnTransformDirty()`. I won't bother to show the code behind this method, but be aware that any time you are building a custom dependency property, you can specify a `PropertyChangedCallback` delegate to point to a method that will be called when your property value has been changed.

This brings me to the final parameter passed to the `DependencyProperty.Register()` method, a second delegate of type `ValidateValueCallback`, which points to a method on the `FrameworkElement` class, which is called to ensure the value assigned to the property is valid:

```
New ValidateValueCallback(AddressOf FrameworkElement.IsWidthHeightValid)
```

This method contains logic you might normally expect to find in the Set block of a property (more information on this point in the next section):

```
Private Shared Function IsWidthHeightValid(ByVal value As Object) As Boolean
    Dim num As Double = CDbl(value)
    Return (((Not DoubleUtil.IsNaN(num)) AndAlso (num >= 0.0)) AndAlso
            (Not Double.IsPositiveInfinity(num)))
End Function
```

Once the `DependencyProperty` object has been registered, the final task is to wrap the field within a normal CLR property (`Height` in this case). Notice, however, that the Get and Set scopes do not simply return or set a class-level Double-member variable, but do so indirectly using the `GetValue()` and `SetValue()` methods from the `System.Windows.DependencyObject` base class:

```
Public Property Height() As Double
    Get
        Return CDbl(MyBase.GetValue(HeightProperty))
    End Get
    Set(ByVal value As Double)
        MyBase.SetValue(HeightProperty, value)
    End Set
End Property
```

Important Notes Regarding CLR Property Wrappers

So, just to recap the story thus far, dependency properties look like a normal every day property when you get or set their values in XAML or code, but behind the scenes they are implemented with much more elaborate coding techniques. Remember, the whole reason to go through this process is to build a custom control that has custom properties that need to integrate with WPF services that demand communication with a dependency property (e.g., animation, data binding, and styles).

Even though part of the implementation of a dependency property includes defining a CLR wrapper, *you should never put validation logic in the Set block*. For that matter, the CLR wrapper of a dependency property *should never do anything other than call GetValue() or SetValue()*.

The reason is that the WPF runtime has been constructed in such a way that when you write XAML that seems to set a property, such as

```
<Button x:Name="myButton" Height="100" .../>
```

the runtime will completely bypass the Set block of the `Height` property and directly call `SetValue()`! The reason for this odd behavior has to do with a simple optimization technique. If the WPF runtime were to directly call the Set block of the `Height` property, it would have to perform runtime reflection to figure out where the `DependencyProperty` field (specified by the first argument to `SetValue()`) is located, reference it in memory, and so forth. The same story holds true if you were write XAML which retrieves the value of the `Height` property; `GetValue()` is called directly.

Since this is the case, why do you need to build this CLR wrapper at all? Well, WPF XAML does not allow you to call functions in markup, so the following markup would be an error:

```
<!-- Nope!  Can't call methods in WPF XAML! -->
<Button x:Name="myButton" this.SetValue("100") .../>
```

In effect, when you set or get a value in markup using the CLR wrapper, think of it as a way to tell the WPF runtime, "Hey! Go call `GetValue()` / `SetValue()` for me, since I can't do it in markup!"

Now, what if you call the CLR wrapper in code like so:

```
Dim b As New Button()
b.Height = 10
```

In this case, if the Set block of the `Height` property contained code other than a call to `SetValue()`, it would execute as the WPF XAML parser optimization is not involved. The short answer is that when registering a dependency property, use a `ValidateValueCallaback` delegate to point to a method that performs the data validation. This ensures that the correct behavior will occur, regardless of whether you use XAML or code to get/set a dependency property.

Building a Custom Dependency Property

If you have a slight headache at this point in the chapter, this is a perfectly normal response. Building dependency properties can take some time to get used to. However, for better or worse, it is part of the process of building many custom WPF controls, so let's take a look at how to build a dependency property.

Begin by creating a new WPF Application named CustomDepPropApp. Now, using the Project menu, activate the Add UserControl menu option, and create a control named `ShowNumberControl.xaml` (Figure 31-1).

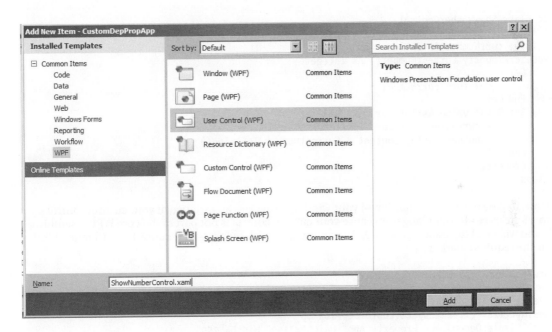

Figure 31-1. Inserting a new custom UserControl

■ **Note** You will learn more details about the WPF `UserControl` later in this chapter, so just following along as shown for now.

Just like a window, WPF `UserControl` types have a XAML file and a related code file. Update the XAML of your user control to define a single `Label` control in the `Grid`:

```
<UserControl x:Class="ShowNumberControl"
  xmlns="http://schemas.microsoft.com/winfx/2006/xaml/presentation"
  xmlns:x="http://schemas.microsoft.com/winfx/2006/xaml"
  xmlns:mc="http://schemas.openxmlformats.org/markup-compatibility/2006"
  xmlns:d="http://schemas.microsoft.com/expression/blend/2008"
  mc:Ignorable="d"
  d:DesignHeight="300" d:DesignWidth="300">
  <Grid>
    <Label x:Name="numberDisplay" Height="50" Width="200" Background="LightBlue"/>
  </Grid>
</UserControl>
```

In the code file of this custom control, create a normal, everyday .NET property which wraps an `Integer` and sets the `Content` property of the `Label` with the new value:

```
Public Class ShowNumberControl
    ' A normal, everyday .NET property
    Private currNumber As Integer = 0
    Public Property CurrentNumber() As Integer
        Get
                Return currNumber
        End Get
        Set(ByVal value As Integer)
                currNumber = value
                numberDisplay.Content = CurrentNumber.ToString()
        End Set
    End Property
End Class
```

Now, update the XAML definition of your window to declare an instance of your custom control within a `StackPanel` layout manger. Because your custom control is not part of the core WPF assembly stack, you will need to define a custom XML namespace which maps to your control (see Chapter 27). Here is the required markup:

```
<Window x:Class="MainWindow"
  xmlns="http://schemas.microsoft.com/winfx/2006/xaml/presentation"
  xmlns:x="http://schemas.microsoft.com/winfx/2006/xaml"
  xmlns:myCtrls="clr-namespace:CustomDepPropApp"
  Title="Simple Dependency Property App" Height="150" Width="250"
  WindowStartupLocation="CenterScreen">

  <StackPanel>
    <myCtrls:ShowNumberControl x:Name="myShowNumberCtrl" CurrentNumber="100"/>
  </StackPanel>
</Window>
```

As you can see, the Visual Studio 2010 designer appears to correctly display the value that you set in the `CurrentNumber` property (Figure 31-2).

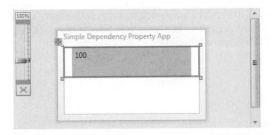

Figure 31-2. It appears your property works as expected...

However, what if you want to apply an animation object to the **CurrentNumber** property so that the value changes from **100** to **200** over the period of **10** seconds? If you wanted to do so in markup, you might update your **<myCtrls:ShowNumberControl>** scope as so:

```
<myCtrls:ShowNumberControl x:Name="myShowNumberCtrl" CurrentNumber="100">
  <myCtrls:ShowNumberControl.Triggers>
    <EventTrigger RoutedEvent = "myCtrls:ShowNumberControl.Loaded">
      <EventTrigger.Actions>
        <BeginStoryboard>
          <Storyboard TargetProperty = "CurrentNumber">
            <Int32Animation From = "100" To = "200" Duration = "0:0:10"/>
          </Storyboard>
        </BeginStoryboard>
      </EventTrigger.Actions>
    </EventTrigger>
  </myCtrls:ShowNumberControl.Triggers>
</myCtrls:ShowNumberControl>
```

Here's the simplest implementation of a **CurrentNumber** dependency property in the ShowNumberControl class:

```
Public Class ShowNumberControl

    Public Property CurrentNumber() As Integer
        Get
                Return CInt(GetValue(CurrentNumberProperty))
        End Get
        Set(ByVal value As Integer)
                SetValue(CurrentNumberProperty, value)
        End Set
    End Property

Public Shared ReadOnly CurrentNumberProperty As DependencyProperty =
            DependencyProperty.Register(
                    "CurrentNumber", GetType(Integer), GetType(ShowNumberControl),
                    New UIPropertyMetadata(0))

    ...
End Class
```

This is similar to what you saw in the implementation of the `Height` property; however, the code snippet registers the property inline rather than within a Shared constructor (which is fine). Also notice that a `UIPropertyMetadata` object is used to define the default value of the integer (0) rather than the more complex `FrameworkPropertyMetadata` object.

Adding a Data Validation Routine

Although you now have a dependency property named `CurrentNumber`, you still won't see your animation take hold. The next adjustment you might want to make is to specify a method to call to perform some data validation logic. For this example, assume that you need to ensure that the value of `CurrentNumber` is between 0 and 500.

To do so, add a final argument to the `DependencyProperty.Register()` method of type `ValidateValueCallback`, which points to a method named `ValidateCurrentNumber`.

`ValidateValueCallback` is a delegate that can only point to methods returning `Boolean` and take an `Object` as the only argument. This `Objectparameter` represents the new value that is being assigned. Implement `ValidateCurrentNumber` to return `True` or `False`, if the incoming value is within the expected range:

```
Public Shared ReadOnly CurrentNumberProperty As DependencyProperty =
        DependencyProperty.Register(
                        "CurrentNumber", GetType(Integer),
                        GetType(ShowNumberControl),
                        New UIPropertyMetadata(100),
                        New ValidateValueCallback(
                                AddressOf ValidateCurrentNumber))

Public Shared Function ValidateCurrentNumber(ByVal value As Object) As Boolean
    ' Just a simple business rule.  Value must be between 0 and 500.
    If Convert.ToInt32(value) >= 0 AndAlso Convert.ToInt32(value) <= 500 Then
        Return True
    Else
        Return False
    End If
End Function
```

Responding to the Property Change

OK, so now you have a valid number, but still no animation. The final change you need to make is to specify a second argument to the constructor of `UIPropertyMetadata`, which is a `PropertyChangedCallback` object. This delegate can point to any method that takes a `DependencyObject` as the first parameter and a `DependencyPropertyChangedEventArgs` as the second. First, update your code as so:

```
' Note the second param of UIPropertyMetadata construtor.
Public Shared ReadOnly CurrentNumberProperty As DependencyProperty =
        DependencyProperty.Register(
                        "CurrentNumber", GetType(Integer),
                        GetType(ShowNumberControl),
                        New UIPropertyMetadata(100,
```

```
                                          New PropertyChangedCallback(AddressOf↵
CurrentNumberChanged)),
                                          New ValidateValueCallback(AddressOf↵
ValidateCurrentNumber))
```

Within the `CurrentNumberChanged()` method, your ultimate goal is to change the `Content` of the `Label` to the new value assigned by the `CurrentNumber` property. You have one big problem, however: the `CurrentNumberChanged()` method is Shared, as it must be to work with the Shared `DependencyProperty` object. So how are you supposed to gain access to the Label for the current instance of `ShowNumberControl`? That reference is contained in the first `DependencyObject` parameter. You can find the new value using the incoming event arguments. Here is the necessary code which will change the `Content` property of the `Label`:

```vb
Private Shared Sub CurrentNumberChanged(ByVal depObj As DependencyObject,
                             ByVal args As DependencyPropertyChangedEventArgs)
    ' Cast the DependencyObject into ShowNumberControl
    Dim c As ShowNumberControl = CType(depObj, ShowNumberControl)

    ' Get the Label control in the ShowNumberControl.
    Dim theLabel As Label = c.numberDisplay

    ' Set the label with the new value.
    theLabel.Content = args.NewValue.ToString()
End Sub
```

Whew! That was a long way to go just to change the output of a label. The benefit is that your `CurrentNumber` dependency property can now be the target of a WPF style, an animation object, the target of a data binding operation, and so forth. Figure 31-3 shows your completed application (and yes, it really is changing the value while running).

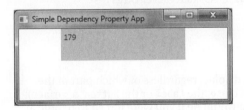

Figure 31-3. Animation at last!

That wraps up your look at WPF dependency properties. While I hope you have a much better idea about what these constructs allow you to do and have a better idea of how to make your own, please be aware that there are many details I have not covered here.

If you find yourself in a position where you are building a number of custom controls which support custom properties, please look up the topic "Properties" under the "WPF Fundamentals" node of the .NET Framework 4.0 SDK documentation. Here, you will find many more examples of building dependency properties, attached properties, various ways to configure property metadata, and a slew of other details.

■ **Source Code** The CustomDepPropApp project is included under the Chapter 31 subdirectory.

Understanding Routed Events

Properties are not the only .NET programming construct to be given a facelift in order to work well within the WPF API. The standard CLR event model has also been refined just a bit to ensure that events can be processed in a manner that is fitting for XAML's description of a tree of objects. Assume you have a new WPF Application project named WPFRoutedEvents. Now, update the XAML description of the initial window by adding the following `<Button>` control which defines some complex content:

```
<Button Name="btnClickMe" Height="75" Width = "250">
  <StackPanel Orientation ="Horizontal">
    <Label Height="50" FontSize ="20">Fancy Button!</Label>
    <Canvas Height ="50" Width ="100" >
    <Ellipse Name = "outerEllipse" Fill ="Green" Height ="25"
             Width ="50" Cursor="Hand" Canvas.Left="25" Canvas.Top="12"/>
    <Ellipse Name = "innerEllipse" Fill ="Yellow" Height = "15" Width ="36"
             Canvas.Top="17" Canvas.Left="32"/>
    </Canvas>
  </StackPanel>
</Button>
```

Now handle the button's `Click` event The `Click` event works with the `RoutedEventHandler` delegate, which expects an event handler that takes an `object` as the first parameter and a `System.Windows.RoutedEventArgs` as the second. Implement this handler as so:

```
Public Sub btnClickMe_Click(ByVal sender As Object, ByVal e As RoutedEventArgs) ↵
                           Handles btnClickMe.Click
    ' Do something when button is clicked.
    MessageBox.Show("Clicked the button")
End Sub
```

If you run your application, you will see this message box display, regardless of which part of the button's content you click on (the green `Ellipse`, the yellow `Ellipse`, the `Label` or the `Button's` surface). This is a good thing. Imagine how tedious WPF event handling would be if you were forced to handle a `Click` event for each and every one of these sub-elements. Not only would the creation of separate event handlers for each aspect of the `Button` be labor intensive, you would end up with some mighty nasty code to maintain down the road.

Thankfully, WPF *routed events* take care of ensuring that your single `Click` event handler will be called regardless of which part of the button is clicked automatically. Simply put, the routed events model automatically propagates an event up (or down) a tree of objects, looking for an appropriate handler.

Specifically speaking, a routed event can make use of three *routing strategies*. If an event is moving from the point of origin up to other defining scopes within the object tree, the event is said to be a *bubbling event*. Conversely, if an event is moving from the outermost element (e.g., a `Window`) down to the point of origin, the event is said to be a *tunneling event*. Finally, if an event is raised and handled only by the originating element (which is what could be described as a normal CLR event), it is said to be a *direct event*.

The Role of Routed Bubbling Events

In the current example, if the user clicks the inner yellow oval, the `Click` event bubbles out to the next level of scope (the `Canvas`), then to the `StackPanel`, and finally to the `Button` where the `Click` event handler is handled. In a similar way, if the user clicks the `Label`, the event is bubbled to the `StackPanel` and then finally to the `Button` element.

Given this bubbling routed event pattern, you have no need to worry about registering specific `Click` event handlers for all members of a composite control. However, if you wished to perform custom clicking logic for multiple elements within the same object tree, you can do so.

By way of illustration, assume you need to handle the clicking of the `outerEllipse` control in a unique manner. First, handle the `MouseDown` event for this subelement (graphically rendered types such as the `Ellipse` do not support a click event; however, they can monitor mouse button activity via `MouseDown`, `MouseUp`, etc.).

Here's a possible implementation for the `MouseDown` event handler, which for illustrative purposes will simply change the `Title` property of the main window:

```
Private Sub outerEllipse_MouseDown(ByVal sender As Object, ByVal e As MouseButtonEventArgs)
    Handles outerEllipse.MouseDown
        ' Change title of window.
        Me.Title = "You clicked the outer ellipse!"
End Sub
```

With this, you can now take different courses of action depending on where the end user has clicked (which boils down to the outer ellipse and everywhere else within the button's scope). ·

■ **Note** Routed bubbling events always move from the point of origin to the *next defining scope*. Thus, in this example, if you were to click the `innerEllipse` object, the event would be bubbled to the `Canvas`, *not* to the `outerEllipse`, as they are both `Ellipse` types within the scope of `Canvas`.

Continuing or Halting Bubbling

Currently, if the user clicks the `outerEllipse` object, it will trigger the registered `MouseDown` event handler for this `Ellipse` object, at which point the event bubbles to the button's `Click` event. If you wish to inform WPF to stop bubbling up the tree of objects, you can set the `Handled` property of the `RoutedEventArgs` parameter to `True`:

```
Private Sub outerEllipse_MouseDown(ByVal sender As Object, ByVal e As↵
MouseButtonEventArgs) Handles outerEllipse.MouseDown
    ' Change title of window.
    Me.Title = "You clicked the outer ellipse!"

    ' Stop bubbling!
    e.Handled = True
End Sub
```

In this case, you would find that the title of the window is changed, but you will not see the **MessageBox** displayed by the **Click** event handler of the **Button**. In a nutshell, routed bubbling events make it possible to allow a complex group of content to act either as a single logical element (e.g., a **Button**) or as discrete items (e.g., an **Ellipse** within the **Button**).

The Role of Routed Tunneling Events

Strictly speaking, routed events can be *bubbling* (as just described) or *tunneling* in nature. Tunneling events (which all begin with the **Preview** suffix—e.g., **PreviewMouseDown**) drill down from the topmost element into the inner scopes of the object tree. By and large, each bubbling event in the WPF base class libraries is paired with a related tunneling event that fires *before* the bubbling counterpart. For example, before the bubbling **MouseDown** event fires, the tunneling **PreviewMouseDown** event fires first.

Handling a tunneling event looks just like the processing of handling any other events; simply define a handler for the appropriate **PreviewXXX** event for your control, and implement the handler in the code file. Just to illustrate the interplay of tunneling and bubbling events, handle the **PreviewMouseDown** event for the **outerEllipse** object:

Next, retrofit the current VB 2010 class definition by updating each event handler (for all objects) to append data about the current event into a **String** member variable named **mouseActivity**, using the incoming event args object. This will allow you to observe the flow of events firing in the background:

```
Class MainWindow

    Private mouseActivity As String = String.Empty

    Private Sub btnClickMe_Clicked(ByVal sender As Object,
            ByVal e As RoutedEventArgs) Handles btnClickMe.Click
    AddEventInfo(sender, e)
    MessageBox.Show(mouseActivity, "Your Event Info")

    ' Clear string for next round.
    mouseActivity = ""
End Sub

Private Sub AddEventInfo(ByVal sender As Object, ByVal e As RoutedEventArgs)
    mouseActivity &= String.Format("{0} sent a {1} event named {2}." & vbLf, sender,
    e.RoutedEvent.RoutingStrategy, e.RoutedEvent.Name)
End Sub
```

```
    Private Sub outerEllipse_MouseDown(ByVal sender As Object,
        ByVal e As MouseButtonEventArgs) Handles outerEllipse.MouseDown
      AddEventInfo(sender, e)
    End Sub

    Private Sub outerEllipse_PreviewMouseDown(ByVal sender As Object,
        ByVal e As MouseButtonEventArgs) outerEllipse.PreviewMouseDown
      AddEventInfo(sender, e)
    End Sub
End Class
```

Notice that you are not halting the bubbling of an event for any event handler. If you run this application, you will see a unique message box display based on where you click the button. Figure 31-4 shows the result of clicking on the outer `Ellipse` object:

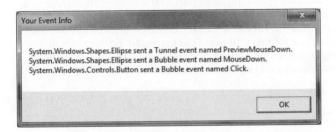

Figure 31-4. Tunneling first, bubbling second

So, why do WPF events typically tend to come in pairs (one tunneling and one bubbling)? The answer is that by previewing events, you have the power to perform any special logic (data validation, disable bubbling action, etc.) before the bubbling counterpart fires. By way of an example, assume you have a `TextBox` that should only contain numerical data. You could handle the `PreviewKeyDown` event, and if you see the user has entered non-numerical data, you could cancel the bubbling event by setting the `Handled` property to `True`.

As you would guess, when you are building a custom control that contains custom events, you could author the event in such a way that it can bubble (or tunnel) through a tree of XAML. For the purpose of this chapter, I will not be examining how to build custom routed events (however, the process is not that different from building a custom dependency property). If you are interested, check out the topic "Routed Events Overview" within the .NET Framework 4.0 SDK documentation. Here, you will find a number of tutorials which will help you on your way.

■ **Source Code** The WPFRoutedEvents project is included under the Chapter 31 subdirectory.

Logical Trees, Visual Trees and Default Templates

There are a few more preparatory topics to investigate before you begin learning how to build custom controls. Specifically, you need to learn the distinction between a *logical tree*, a *visual tree* and a *default template*. When you are typing XAML into Visual Studio 2010, Expression Blend, or a tool such as kaxaml.exe, your markup is the *logical view* of the XAML document. As well, if you author VB 2010 code that adds new items to a `StackPanel` control, you are inserting new items into the logical tree. Essentially, a logical view represents how your content will be positioned within the various layout managers for a main `Window` (or another root element, such as `Page` or `NavigationWindow`).

However, behind every logical tree, there is a much more verbose representation termed a *visual tree*, which is used internally by WPF to correctly render out elements onto the screen. Within any visual tree, there will be full details of the templates and styles used to render out each object, including any necessary drawings, shapes, visuals and animations.

It is useful to understand the distinction between logical and visual trees because when you are building a custom control template, you are essentially replacing all or part of the default visual tree of a control and inserting your own. Therefore, if you want a `Button` control to be rendered as a star shape, you could define a new star template and plug it into the `Button`'s visual tree. Logically, the `Button` is still of type `Button`, and it supports all of the properties, methods and events as expected. But visually, it has taken on a whole new appearance. This fact alone makes WPF an extremely useful API, given that other toolkits would require you to build a brand new class to make a star shaped button. With WPF, you simply need to define new markup.

■ **Note** WPF controls are often described as *lookless*. This refers to the fact that the look and feel of a WPF control is completely independent (and customizable) from its behavior.

Programmatically Inspecting a Logical Tree

While analyzing a window's logical tree at runtime is not a tremendously common WPF programming activity, it is worth mentioning that the `System.Windows` namespace defines a class named `LogicalTreeHelper` that allows you to inspect the structure of a logic tree at runtime. To illustrate the connection between logic trees, visual trees and control templates, create a new WPF Application named TreesAndTemplatesApp.

Update the markup for your window so that it contains two `Button` controls and a large read-only `TextBox` with scroll bars enabled. Make sure you use the IDE to handle the `Click` event of each button. The following XAML will do nicely:

```
<Window x:Class="MainWindow"
  xmlns="http://schemas.microsoft.com/winfx/2006/xaml/presentation"
  xmlns:x="http://schemas.microsoft.com/winfx/2006/xaml"
  Title="Fun with Trees and Templates" Height="518"
  Width="836" WindowStartupLocation="CenterScreen">

<DockPanel LastChildFill="True">
  <Border Height="50"  DockPanel.Dock="Top" BorderBrush="Blue">
    <StackPanel Orientation="Horizontal">
      <Button x:Name="btnShowLogicalTree" Content="Logical Tree of Window"
```

```
                    Margin="4" BorderBrush="Blue" Height="40"/>
            <Button x:Name="btnShowVisualTree" Content="Visual Tree of Window"
                    BorderBrush="Blue" Height="40"/>
        </StackPanel>
      </Border>
      <TextBox x:Name="txtDisplayArea" Margin="10" Background="AliceBlue" IsReadOnly="True"
               BorderBrush="Red" VerticalScrollBarVisibility="Auto"
               HorizontalScrollBarVisibility="Auto" />
   </DockPanel>

</Window>
```

Within your VB 2010 code file, define a String member variable named dataToShow. Now, within the Click handler for the btnShowLogicalTree object, call a helper method which calls itself recursively in order to populate the String variable with the logical tree of the Window. To do so, you will call the Shared GetChildren() method of LogicalTreeHelper. Here is the code:

```
Private Sub btnShowLogicalTree_Click(ByVal sender As Object, ByVal e As RoutedEventArgs)↩
 Handles btnShowLogicalTree.Click
    dataToShow = ""
    BuildLogicalTree(0, Me)
    Me.txtDisplayArea.Text = dataToShow
End Sub

Private Sub BuildLogicalTree(ByVal depth As Integer, ByVal obj As Object)
    ' Add the type name to the dataToShow member variable.
    dataToShow &= New String(" "c, depth) & obj.GetType().Name & vbLf

    ' If an item is not a DependencyObject, skip it.
    If Not(TypeOf obj Is DependencyObject) Then
        Return
    End If

    ' Make a recursive call for each logical child
    For Each child As Object In LogicalTreeHelper.GetChildren(TryCast(obj,↩
DependencyObject))
        BuildLogicalTree(depth + 5, child)
    Next
End Sub
```

If you run your application and click this first button, you will see a tree print out in the text area, which is just about an exact replica of the original XAML (Figure 31-5).

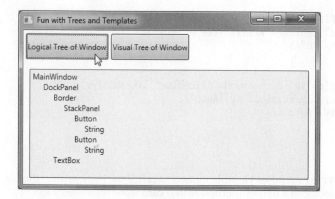

Figure 31-5. Viewing a logical tree at runtime

Programmatically Inspecting a Visual Tree

A Window's visual tree can also be inspected at runtime using the VisualTreeHelper class of System.Windows.Media. Here is a Click implementation of the second Button control (btnShowVisualTree), which performs similar recursive logic to build a textual representation of the visual tree:

```
Private Sub btnShowVisualTree_Click(ByVal sender As Object, ByVal e As RoutedEventArgs)↵
 Handles btnShowVisualTree.Click
        dataToShow = ""
        BuildVisualTree(0, Me)
        Me.txtDisplayArea.Text = dataToShow
End Sub

Private Sub BuildVisualTree(ByVal depth As Integer, ByVal obj As DependencyObject)
        ' Add the type name to the dataToShow member variable.
        dataToShow &= New String(" "c, depth) & obj.GetType().Name & vbLf

        ' Make a recursive call for each visual child
        For i As Integer = 0 To VisualTreeHelper.GetChildrenCount(obj) - 1
          BuildVisualTree(depth + 1, VisualTreeHelper.GetChild(obj, i))
        Next
End Sub
```

As you can see in Figure 31-6, the visual tree exposes a number of lower-level rendering agents such as ContentPresenter, AdornerDecorator, TextBoxLineDrawingVisual, and so forth.

Figure 31-6. Viewing a visual tree at runtime

Programmatically Inspecting a Control's Default Template

Recall that a visual tree is used by WPF to understand how to render a `Window` and all contained elements. Every WPF control stores its own set of rendering commands within its default template. Programmatically speaking, any template can represented as an instance of the `ControlTemplate` class. As well, you can obtain a control's default template by using the aptly named Template property:

```
' Get the default template of the Button.
Dim myBtn As New Button()
Dim template As ControlTemplate = myBtn.Template
```

Likewise, you could create a new `ControlTemplate` object in code and plug it into a control's Template property:

```
' Plug in a new template for the button to use.
Dim myBtn As New Button()
Dim customTemplate As New ControlTemplate()

' Assume this method adds all the code for a star template
MakeStarTemplate(customTemplate)
myBtn.Template = customTemplate
```

While you could build a new template in code, it is far more common to do so in XAML. In fact, Expression Blend has a large number of tools which can be used to define a template with minimal fuss and bother.

However, before you start building your own templates, let's finish the current example and add the ability to view the default template of a WPF control at runtime. This can be a really useful way to take a look at the overall composition of a template. First, update the markup of your window with a new StackPanel of controls docked to the left side of the master DockPanel, defined as so:

```
<Border DockPanel.Dock="Left" Margin="10" BorderBrush="DarkGreen"
        BorderThickness="4" Width="358">
  <StackPanel>
    <Label Content="Enter Full Name of WPF Control" Width="340" FontWeight="DemiBold" />
    <TextBox x:Name="txtFullName" Width="340" BorderBrush="Green"
             Background="BlanchedAlmond" Height="22"
             Text="System.Windows.Controls.Button" />
    <Button x:Name="btnTemplate" Content="See Template" BorderBrush="Green"
             Height="40" Width="100" Margin="5"
             HorizontalAlignment="Left" />
    <Border BorderBrush="DarkGreen" BorderThickness="2" Height="260"
             Width="301" Margin="10" Background="LightGreen" >
      <StackPanel x:Name="stackTemplatePanel" />
    </Border>
  </StackPanel>
</Border>
```

Do take note of the empty StackPanel, stackTemplatePanel, as you will refer to it in code. Anyway, your window should now look something like Figure 31-7.

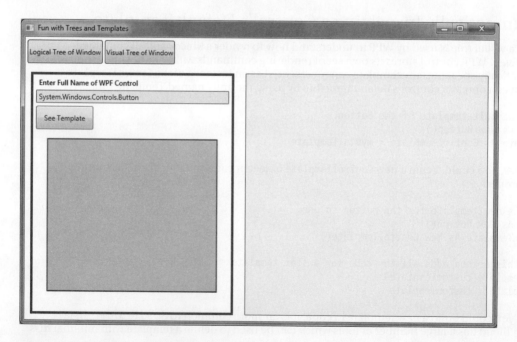

Figure 31-7. The updated UI of your window

The upper left text area allows you to enter in the fully qualified name of a WPF control located the `PresentationFramework.dll` assembly. Once the library is loaded, you will dynamically create an instance of the object and display it in the large square in the bottom left. Last but not least, the control's default template will be displayed in the right hand text area. First, add a new member variable to your VB 2010 class of type `Control`:

Private ctrlToExamine As Control = Nothing

Here is the implementation of the btnTemplate's `Click` event handler, plus a helper method to show a control template. You'll have to import the `System.Reflection`, `System.Xml`, `System.Text`, and `System.Windows.Markup` namespaces for this code:

```vb
Private Sub btnTemplate_Click(ByVal sender As Object, ByVal e As RoutedEventArgs)↵
 Handles btnTemplate.Click
    dataToShow = ""
    ShowTemplate()
    Me.txtDisplayArea.Text = dataToShow
End Sub

Private Sub ShowTemplate()
    ' Remove the control which is currently in the preview area.
    If ctrlToExamine IsNot Nothing Then
        stackTemplatePanel.Children.Remove(ctrlToExamine)
    End If

    Try
        ' Load PresentationFramework, and create an instance of the
        'specified control.  Give it a size for display purposes, then add the
        ' empty StackPanel.
        Dim asm As Assembly =Assembly.Load("PresentationFramework, Version=4.0.0.0," &↵
        "Culture=neutral, PublicKeyToken=31bf3856ad364e35")
        ctrlToExamine = CType(asm.CreateInstance(txtFullName.Text), Control)
        ctrlToExamine.Height = 200
        ctrlToExamine.Width = 200
        ctrlToExamine.Margin = New Thickness(5)
        stackTemplatePanel.Children.Add(ctrlToExamine)

        ' Define some XML settings to preserve indentation.
        Dim xmlSettings As New XmlWriterSettings()
        xmlSettings.Indent = True

        ' Create a StringBuilder to hold the XAML.
        Dim strBuilder As New StringBuilder()

        ' Create an XmlWriter based on our settings.
        Dim xWriter As XmlWriter = XmlWriter.Create(strBuilder, xmlSettings)

        ' Now save the XAML into the XmlWriter object based on the ControlTemplate.
        XamlWriter.Save(ctrlToExamine.Template, xWriter)
```

```
        ' Display XAML in the text box.
        dataToShow = strBuilder.ToString()
    Catch ex As Exception
        dataToShow = ex.Message
    End Try
End Sub
```

The bulk of the work is just tinkering with the compiled BAML resource to map it into a XAML string. Figure 31-8 shows your final application in action, displaying the default template of the DatePicker control.

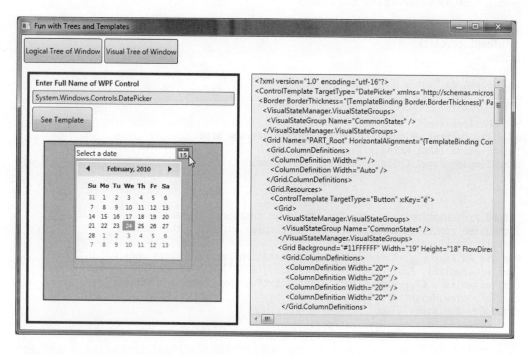

Figure 31-8. Investigating a ControlTemplate at runtime

Great! Hopefully you have a better idea about how logical trees, visual trees, and control templates work together. Now you can spend the remainder of this chapter learning how to build custom templates and user controls.

■ **Source Code** The TreesAndTemplatesApp project is included under the Chapter 31 subdirectory.

Building a Custom Control Template with Visual Studio 2010

When you are building a custom template for a control, you could do so with nothing but VB 2010 code. Using this approach, you would be adding data to a `ControlTemplate` object and then assigning it to a control's `Template` property. Most of the time, however, you will define the look and feel of a `ControlTemplate` using XAML, and to help in the endeavor, you will typically want to use Expression Blend to do so. You will use Expression Blend for this very thing in the final example of this chapter, but for now, you will build a simple template using Visual Studio 2010. Although this IDE does not include as many template design tools as Expression Blend, using Visual Studio 2010 is a good way to learn the nuts and bolts of template construction.

Create a brand new WPF Application named ButtonTemplate. For this project, you are more interested in the mechanics of creating and using templates, so the markup for this main window is very simple:

```
<Window x:Class=" MainWindow"
  xmlns="http://schemas.microsoft.com/winfx/2006/xaml/presentation"
  xmlns:x="http://schemas.microsoft.com/winfx/2006/xaml"
  Title="Fun with Templates" Height="350" Width="525">
  <StackPanel>
    <Button x:Name="myButton" Width="100" Height="100"/>
  </StackPanel>
</Window>
```

To handle the button's `Click` event, simply display a message box (via `MessageBox.Show()`) which displays a message confirming the clicking of the control. Remember, when you build custom templates, the *behavior* of the control is constant but the *look* may vary.

Currently, this `Button` is rendered using the default template, which, as the last example illustrated, is a BAML resource within a given WPF assembly. When you wish to define your own template, you are essentially replacing this default visual tree with your own creation. To begin, update the definition of the `<Button>` element to specify a new template using property element syntax. This template will give the control a round appearance:

```
<Button x:Name="myButton" Width="100" Height="100">
  <Button.Template>
    <ControlTemplate>
      <Grid x:Name="controlLayout">
        <Ellipse  x:Name="buttonSurface" Fill = "LightBlue"/>
        <Label x:Name="buttonCaption" VerticalAlignment = "Center"
              HorizontalAlignment = "Center"
              FontWeight = "Bold" FontSize = "20" Content = "OK!"/>
      </Grid>
    </ControlTemplate>
  </Button.Template>
</Button>
```

Here, you have defined a template which consists of a named `Grid` control containing a named `Ellipse` and a `Label`. Because your `Grid` has no defined rows or columns, each child stacks on top of the previous control, allowing you to have centering of content. Now, if you run your application, you will notice that the `Click` event will *only* fire when the mouse cursor is within the bounds of the `Ellipse` (i.e. not in the corners around the edges of the ellipse)! This is a great feature of the WPF template architecture: you do not need to recalculate hit-testing, bounds checking, or any other low level detail. So, if your template used a Polygon object to render some oddball geometry, you can rest assured that the mouse hit testing details are relative to the shape of the control, not the larger bounding rectangle.

Templates as Resources

Currently, your template is embedded to a specific Button control, which limits your reuse options. Ideally, you would place your template into a resource dictionary, so you can reuse your round button template between projects, or at minimum, move it into the application resource container for reuse within this project. Let's move the local Button resource to the application level using Visual Studio 2010. First, locate the Template property for your Button in the Properties editor. Now, click on the small black diamond icon and select "Extract Value to Resource…" (see Figure 31-9).

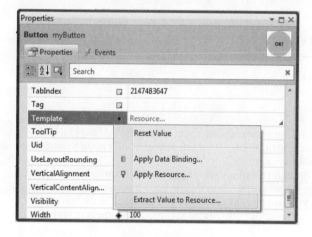

Figure 31-9. *Extracting a local resource*

From the resulting dialog box, define a new template named RoundButtonTemplate, which is stored in Application.xaml (Figure 31-10).

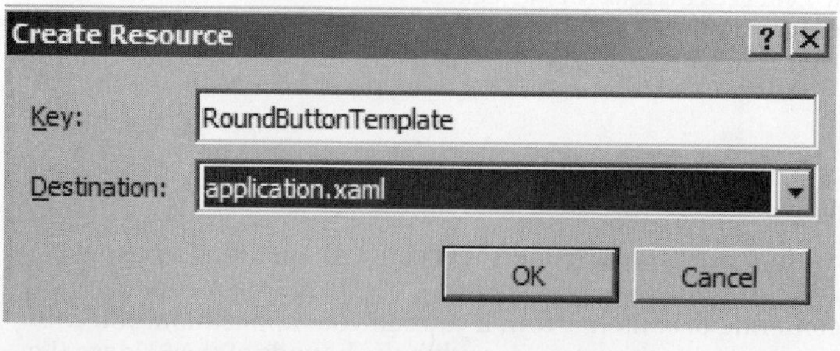

Figure 31-10. *Placing your resource into Application.xaml*

1400

At this point, you will find the following data in your `Application` object's markup:

```xml
<Application x:Class="Application"
    xmlns="http://schemas.microsoft.com/winfx/2006/xaml/presentation"
    xmlns:x="http://schemas.microsoft.com/winfx/2006/xaml"
    StartupUri="MainWindow.xaml">
    <Application.Resources>
    <ControlTemplate x:Key="RoundButtonTemplate">
      <Grid x:Name="controlLayout">
        <Ellipse   x:Name="buttonSurface" Fill = "LightBlue"/>
        <Label x:Name="buttonCaption" VerticalAlignment = "Center"
               HorizontalAlignment = "Center"
               FontWeight = "Bold" FontSize = "20" Content = "OK!"/>
      </Grid>
    </ControlTemplate>
  </Application.Resources>
</Application>
```

You may wish to constrain where this template can be applied. Like a WPF style, you can add the `TargetType` attribute to any `<ControlTemplate>`. Update the `<ControlTemplate>` start tag to ensure that only `Button` controls can use this template:

```xml
<ControlTemplate x:Key="RoundButtonTemplate" TargetType ="Button">
```

Now, because this resource is available for the entire application, you can define any number of round buttons. Go ahead and create two additional `Button` controls which use this template for testing purposes (no need to handle the `Click` event for these new items).

```xml
<StackPanel>
   <Button x:Name="myButton" Width="100" Height="100"
           Template="{StaticResource RoundButtonTemplate}"></Button>
   <Button x:Name="myButton2" Width="100" Height="100"
           Template="{StaticResource RoundButtonTemplate}"></Button>
   <Button x:Name="myButton3" Width="100" Height="100"
           Template="{StaticResource RoundButtonTemplate}"></Button>
</StackPanel>
```

Incorporating Visual Cues using Triggers

When you define a custom template, all of the visual cues of the default template are removed as well. For example, the default button template contains markup which informs the control how to look when certain UI events occur, such as when it receives focus, when it is clicked with the mouse, when it is enabled (or disabled), and so on. Users are quite accustomed to these sort of visual cues, as it gives the control somewhat of a tactile response. However, your RoundButtonTemplate does not define any such markup, so the look of the control is identical regardless of the mouse activity. Ideally, your control should look slightly different when clicked (maybe via a color change or drop shadow) to let the user know the visual state has changed.

When WPF was first released, the way to add in such visual cues was to add to the template any number of triggers which would typically change values of object properties or start a storyboard animation (or both) when the trigger condition was True. By way of example, update your

RoundButtonTemplate with the following markup, which will change the color of the control to blue and the Foreground color to yellow when the mouse is over the surface:

```
<ControlTemplate x:Key="RoundButtonTemplate" TargetType="Button" >
  <Grid x:Name="controlLayout">
    <Ellipse x:Name="buttonSurface" Fill="LightBlue" />
    <Label x:Name="buttonCaption" Content="OK!" FontSize="20" FontWeight="Bold"
           HorizontalAlignment="Center" VerticalAlignment="Center" />
  </Grid>
    <ControlTemplate.Triggers>
      <Trigger Property = "IsMouseOver" Value = "True">
        <Setter TargetName = "buttonSurface" Property = "Fill" Value = "Blue"/>
        <Setter TargetName = "buttonCaption" Property = "Foreground"
                Value = "Yellow"/>
      </Trigger>
    </ControlTemplate.Triggers>
  </ControlTemplate>
```

If you run the program yet again, you should find the color does toggle based on whether or not the mouse is within the Ellipse area. Here is another trigger, which will shrink the size of the Grid (and therefore all child elements) when the control is pressed via the mouse. Add this to your <ControlTemplate.Triggers> collection:

```
<Trigger Property = "IsPressed" Value="True">
  <Setter TargetName="controlLayout"
          Property="RenderTransformOrigin" Value="0.5,0.5"/>
  <Setter TargetName="controlLayout" Property="RenderTransform">
    <Setter.Value>
      <ScaleTransform ScaleX="0.8" ScaleY="0.8"/>
    </Setter.Value>
  </Setter>
</Trigger>
```

At this point, you have a custom template with a few visual cues incorporated using WPF triggers. As you will see in the next (and final) example of this chapter, .NET 4.0 introduces an alternative way to incorporate visual cues using the Visual State Manager. Before you get to that point, let's talk about the role of the {TemplateBinding} markup extension and the ContentPresenter class.

The Role of {TemplateBinding} Markup Extension

Your template can only be applied to Button controls, and therefore it would stand to reason that you could set properties on the <Button> element that will cause the template to render itself in a unique manner. For example, right now, the Fill property of the Ellipse is hard coded to be blue and the Content of the Label is always set to the string value "OK". Of course, you might want buttons of different colors and text values, so you might try to define the following buttons in your main window:

```
<StackPanel>
  <Button x:Name="myButton" Width="100" Height="100"
          Background="Red" Content="Howdy!"
          Template="{StaticResource RoundButtonTemplate}" />
  <Button x:Name="myButton2" Width="100" Height="100"
          Background="LightGreen" Content="Cancel!"
          Template="{StaticResource RoundButtonTemplate}" />
  <Button x:Name="myButton3" Width="100" Height="100"
          Background="Yellow" Content="Format"
          Template="{StaticResource RoundButtonTemplate}" />
</StackPanel>
```

However, regardless of the fact that each Button is setting a unique Background and Content value, you still end up with three blue buttons which contain the text "OK". The problem is that the properties of the control using the template (Button) have properties which do not match identically with the items on the template (such as the Fill property of the Ellipse). As well, although the Label does have a Content property, the value defined in the <Button> scope is not automatically routed to the internal child of the template.

You can solve these issues by using the {TemplateBinding} markup extension when you build your template. This allows you to capture property settings defined by the control using your template and use them to set values in the template itself. Here is a reworked version of RoundButtonTemplate, which now uses this markup extension to map the Background property of the Button to the Fill property of the Ellipse; it also makes sure the Content of the Button is indeed passed to the Content property of the Label:

```
<ControlTemplate x:Key="RoundButtonTemplate" TargetType="Button">
  <Grid x:Name="controlLayout">
    <Ellipse x:Name="buttonSurface" Fill="{TemplateBinding Background}"/>
    <Label x:Name="buttonCaption" Content="{TemplateBinding Content}"
           FontSize="20" FontWeight="Bold"
           HorizontalAlignment="Center" VerticalAlignment="Center" />
  </Grid>
  <ControlTemplate.Triggers>
    ...
  </ControlTemplate.Triggers>
</ControlTemplate>
```

With this update, you can now create buttons of various colors and textual values (Figure 31-11).

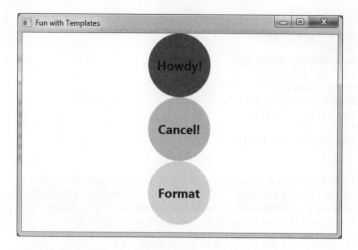

Figure 31-11. *Template bindings allow values to pass through to the internal controls*

The Role of ContentPresenter

When you designed your template, you used a Label to display the textual value of the control. Like the Button, the Label supports a Content property. Therefore, given your use of {TemplateBinding}, you could define a Button which contained complex content beyond that of a simple string. For example:

```
<Button x:Name="myButton4" Width="100" Height="100" Background="Yellow"
        Template="{StaticResource RoundButtonTemplate}">
  <Button.Content>
    <ListBox Height="50" Width="75">
      <ListBoxItem>Hello</ListBoxItem>
      <ListBoxItem>Hello</ListBoxItem>
      <ListBoxItem>Hello</ListBoxItem>
    </ListBox>
  </Button.Content>
</Button>
```

For this particular control, things work just as hoped. However, what if you need to pass in complex content to a template member that does *not* have a Content property? When you wish to define a generalized *content display area* in a template, you can use the ContentPresenter class as opposed to a specific type of control (Label or TextBlock). You have no need to do so for this example; however, here is some simple markup which illustrates how you could build a custom template that uses ContentPresenter to show the value of the Content property of the control using the template:

```
<!-- This button template will display whatever is set
     to the Content of the hosting button -->
<ControlTemplate x:Key="NewRoundButton" TargetType="Button">
```

```
<Grid>
    <Ellipse Fill="{TemplateBinding Background}"/>
    <ContentPresenter HorizontalAlignment="Center"
                      VerticalAlignment="Center"/>
  </Grid>
</ControlTemplate>
```

Incorporating Templates into Styles

Currently, your template simply defines a basic look and feel of the Button control. However, the process of establishing the basic properties of the control (content, font size, font weight, etc.) is the responsibility of the Button itself:

```
<!-- Currently the Button must set basic property values, not the template -->
<Button x:Name ="myButton" Foreground ="Black" FontSize ="20" FontWeight ="Bold"
        Template ="{StaticResource RoundButtonTemplate />
```

If you wish, you could establish these values *in the template*. By doing so, you can effectively create a default look and feel. As you may have already realized, this is a job for WPF styles. When you build a style (to account for basic property settings), you can define a template *within the style*! Here is your updated application resource in the application resources in Application.xaml, which has been rekeyed as RoundButtonStyle:

```
<!-- A style containing a template -->
<Style x:Key ="RoundButtonStyle" TargetType ="Button">
  <Setter Property ="Foreground" Value ="Black"/>
  <Setter Property ="FontSize" Value ="14"/>
  <Setter Property ="FontWeight" Value ="Bold"/>
  <Setter Property="Width" Value="100"/>
  <Setter Property="Height" Value="100"/>
  <!-- Here is the template! -->
  <Setter Property ="Template">
    <Setter.Value>
      <ControlTemplate TargetType ="Button">
        <Grid x:Name="controlLayout">
          <Ellipse x:Name="buttonSurface" Fill="{TemplateBinding Background}"/>
          <Label x:Name="buttonCaption" Content ="{TemplateBinding Content}"
                 HorizontalAlignment="Center" VerticalAlignment="Center" />
        </Grid>
        <ControlTemplate.Triggers>
          <Trigger Property = "IsMouseOver" Value = "True">
            <Setter TargetName = "buttonSurface" Property = "Fill" Value = "Blue"/>
            <Setter TargetName = "buttonCaption" Property = "Foreground" Value = "Yellow"/>
          </Trigger>
          <Trigger Property = "IsPressed" Value="True">
            <Setter TargetName="controlLayout"
                    Property="RenderTransformOrigin" Value="0.5,0.5"/>
```

```
        <Setter TargetName="controlLayout" Property="RenderTransform">
          <Setter.Value>
            <ScaleTransform ScaleX="0.8" ScaleY="0.8"/>
          </Setter.Value>
        </Setter>
      </Trigger>
    </ControlTemplate.Triggers>
  </ControlTemplate>
  </Setter.Value>
  </Setter>
</Style>
```

With this update, you can now create button controls by setting the **Style** property as so:

```
<Button x:Name="myButton" Background="Red" Content="Howdy!"
        Style="{StaticResource RoundButtonStyle}"/>
```

While the rendering and behavior of the button is identical, the benefit of nesting templates within styles is that you are able to provide a canned set of values for common properties.

That wraps up your look at how to use Visual Studio 2010 to build custom templates for a control. However, before you conclude this chapter and move onto the world of web development using ASP.NET, you will look at how Expression Blend can be used to not only generate control templates but to create custom UserControls.

■ **Source Code** The ButtonTemplate project can be found under the Chapter 31 subdirectory.

Building Custom UserControls with Blend

During your examination of dependency properties, you were briefly introduced to the concept of a **UserControl**. In some ways, a **UserControl** is the next logical step after a control template. Recall that when you build a control template, you are essentially applying a *skin* which changes the physical appearance of a WPF control. A custom **UserControl**, however, allows you to literally build a new class type that may contain unique members (methods, events, properties, etc.). As well, many custom **UserControls** use templates and styles; however, it is also just fine if the control's tree of markup is defined directly within the <UserControl> scope.

Recall that you can add a **UserControl** project item to any Visual Studio 2010 WPF application, including creating a **UserControl** library project, which is a *.dll that contains nothing but a collection of **UserControls** to make use of across projects.

In this final section of the chapter, I will make use of Expression Blend to show you a few very interesting development techniques, including creating a new control from a geometry, working with the animation editor, and incorporating visual cues using the .NET 4.0 Visual State Manager (VSM). While going through these topics, remember that you can certainly achieve the same end result if you make use of Visual Studio 2010; it will just require more manually typing for the markup.

Creating a UserControl Library Project

The goal for this final example of the chapter is to build a WPF application that represents a simple jackpot game. While you could bundle all of the logic in a new WPF executable, you will instead place your custom controls in a dedicated library project. Begin by launching Expression Blend, and from the File | New Project menu create a new WPF Control Library project named MyCustomControl (Figure 31-12).

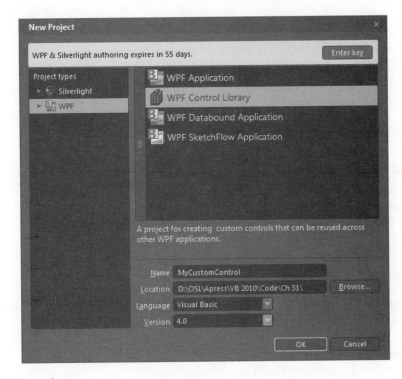

Figure 31-12. A new Blend WPF Control Library project

Renaming the Initial UserControl

This project type will provide you with an initial UserControl named MainControl. Let's rename this control to SpinControl. To do so, begin by changing the name of the MainControl.xaml file to SpinControl.xaml via the Projects tab. Next, open the XAML editor for your initial control, and change the x:Class attribute as shown here (also, delete the x:Name attribute completely). Then, set the Height and Width of the UserControl to 150 each:

```
<UserControl
  xmlns="http://schemas.microsoft.com/winfx/2006/xaml/presentation"
  xmlns:x="http://schemas.microsoft.com/winfx/2006/xaml"
  xmlns:d="http://schemas.microsoft.com/expression/blend/2008"
  xmlns:mc="http://schemas.openxmlformats.org/markup-compatibility/2006"
  mc:Ignorable="d"
  x:Class="SpinControl"
  Width="150" Height="150">
  <Grid/>
</UserControl>
```

Last but not least, open the VB 2010 code file that is paired to your XAML document, and change the name of this class to SpinControl:

```
Class SpinControl
End Class
```

Now, just for a sanity check, build your entire project just to ensure you don't have any typos.

Designing the SpinControl

The purpose of the custom SpinControl is to cycle through three image files in a random manner whenever the Spin() method is called. The downloadable code for this book includes three image files (Cherries.png, Jackpot.jpg and Limes.jpg) which represent the possible images that could be displayed, so feel free to add them to your current project using the Project | Add Existing Item… menu option. When you add these images to your Blend project, they will automatically be configured to be embedded into the resulting assembly.

The visual design of the SpinControl is quite simple. Using the Assets Library, include a Border control which uses a BorderThickness value of 5, and using the Brushes editor, select a BorderBrush color of your liking. Next, place an Image control (named imgDisplay) within the Grid, and set the Stretch property to the value Fill. When you are done, the Grid should be configured similar to the following:

```
<Grid x:Name="LayoutRoot">
  <Border BorderBrush="#FFD51919" BorderThickness="5"/>
  <Image x:Name="imgDisplay" Margin="8" Stretch="Fill"/>
</Grid>
```

Finally, set the Source property of the Image control to one of your three images. Your designer should now look something like Figure 31-13.

Figure 31-13. The UI of the SpinControl

Adding the Initial VB 2010 Code

Now that the markup is complete, use the Events tab of the Blend Properties window to handle the Loaded event for your control, and specify a method named SpinControl_Loaded. In your code window, declare an array of three BitmapImage objects that are filled with the embedded binary image files when the Loaded event fires:

```
Class SpinControl
        ' An array of BitmapImage objects.
        Private images(2) As BitmapImage

        Private Sub SpinControl_Loaded(ByVal sender As Object,
                                    ByVal e As System.Windows.RoutedEventArgs)
            ' Fill the ImageSource array with each image.
            images(0) = New BitmapImage(New Uri("Cherries.png", UriKind.Relative))
            images(1) = New BitmapImage(New Uri("Jackpot.jpg", UriKind.Relative))
            images(2) = New BitmapImage(New Uri("Limes.jpg", UriKind.Relative))
        End Sub
End Class
```

Next, define a Public method named Spin(), which is implemented to randomly show one of the three BitmapImage objects in the Image control and return the value of the random number:

```
Public Function Spin() As Integer
    'Randomly put one of the images into the Image control.
    Dim r As New Random(Date.Now.Millisecond)
    Dim randomNumber As Integer = r.Next(3)
    Me.imgDisplay.Source = images(randomNumber)
    Return randomNumber
End Function
```

Defining an Animation using Blend

Your SpinControl is almost complete; however, to make things more visual appealing to the user, you will now use Blend to define an animation that will make the Image control appear to flip in a rotation in order to give the illusion that the graphical image has spun. You could author some VB 2010 code which preformed the animation logic; however, in this example, you will make use of the integrated animation editor of Blend to define a XAML storyboard.

Ensure that the designer of your SpinControl is the active window in your project. Now, using the Objects and Timeline editor, select your Image control, and then click on the "New Storyboard" button (Figure 31-14).

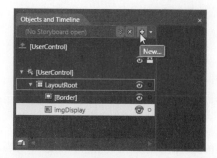

Figure 31-14. Creating a new Storyboard using Expression Blend

From the resulting dialog box, name your storyboard SpinImageStoryboard. Once you have clicked the OK button, you will notice that the Objects and Timeline editor has changed its appearance. Specifically, you'll see a time line editor, which can be more easily viewed by pressing the F6 key to arrange the IDE into *animation editor mode* (press F6 again to toggle back to the previous IDE layout).

This editor allows you to capture how an object will change over units of time called *keyframes*. To begin, click the yellow arrow of the timeline and drag it to the 0.5 second mark. Once you have done so, click the Record Keyframe button, which is located right above the zero second mark. When you are done, your time line editor should look like Figure 31-15.

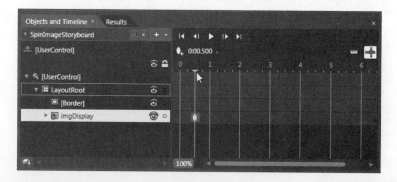

Figure 31-15. Defining a new keyframe

You will also notice that your visual editor is now in *record mode*, signified by the red border around the visual designer. You are free to now change any property of an object using the Properties editor. While you are making changes, these are being recorded by the IDE and are written out as XAML animation instructions. For this animation, locate the Transform editor in the Properties window of Expression Blend, and pick the Flip Y Access option (Figure 31-16).

Figure 31-16. Applying a transformation to the Image control

Now, go back to the Objects and Timeline editor, and click on your `SpinImageStoryboard` story board resource (Figure 31-17).

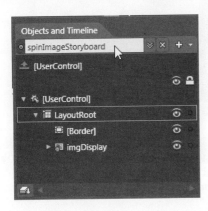

Figure 31-17. Selecting the SpinImageStoryboard for editing

Once you select a story board for editing, you can configure various settings on the storyboard itself, such as auto-reversing or repeat behaviors using the Properties editor. For your animation storyboard, click the AutoReverse checkbox (Figure 31-18).

Figure 31-18. Auto reversing your animation

At this point, you can test your animation! Just click the Play button (Figure 31-19). You should see your image flip and then reverse back to the original upright display.

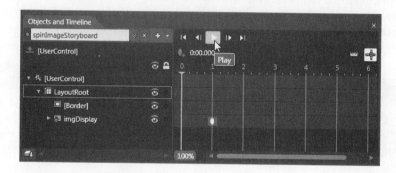

Figure 31-19. Testing your animation

In summary, you have defined a simple animation which will take place over a total of 1 second (1/2 a second for the flipping of the image and an additional 1/2 a second to reverse the transformation). You can now exit the animation editor by clicking on the recording button on your visual designer (Figure 31-20).

Figure 31-20. Exiting the animation editor

■ **Note** Your animation only changed a single property of a single object. Note that a storyboard can change any number of properties (for any number of objects) over various key frames. To do so, simply drag the yellow timeline to a new unit of time, click the Add Keyframe button, and change properties on the object selected in Objects and Timeline.

If you were to view the underlying XAML, you will see that Blend has added a new **<Storyboard>** to your **UserControl's** resource dictionary:

```
<UserControl.Resources>
    <Storyboard x:Key="SpinImageStoryboard" AutoReverse="True">
        <PointAnimationUsingKeyFrames Storyboard.TargetProperty=
"(UIElement.RenderTransformOrigin)" Storyboard.TargetName="imgDisplay">
            <EasingPointKeyFrame KeyTime="0:0:0.5" Value="0.5,0.5"/>
        </PointAnimationUsingKeyFrames>
        <DoubleAnimationUsingKeyFrames Storyboard.TargetProperty=
"(UIElement.RenderTransform).(TransformGroup.Children)[0].(ScaleTransform.ScaleY)"
    Storyboard.TargetName="imgDisplay">
            <EasingDoubleKeyFrame KeyTime="0:0:0.5" Value="-1"/>
        </DoubleAnimationUsingKeyFrames>
    </Storyboard>
</UserControl.Resources>
```

Programmatically Starting our Storyboard

Before you move onto the construction of the WPF Application that will make use of your custom button, you have a final task to attend to. By default, when you use the Blend animation editor, it will add a trigger that will start your storyboard when the UserControl (or Window, in the case of a WPF application project) loads into memory:

```
<UserControl.Triggers>
  <EventTrigger RoutedEvent="FrameworkElement.Loaded">
    <BeginStoryboard Storyboard="{StaticResource SpinImageStoryboard}"/>
  </EventTrigger>
</UserControl.Triggers>
```

You can verify this by clicking on the Triggers editor (which can be opened via the Windows menu of Expression Blend; see Figure 31-21).

Figure 31-21. Deleting the automatically added trigger

In addition to spinning when the control loads, you will also spin when the Spin() method is called. Import the System.Windows.Media.Animation namespace in your VB 2010 code file, and update your Spin() method to invoke the story board like so:

```
Public Function Spin() As Integer
    ' Randomly put of the images into the Image control.
    Dim r As New Random(Date.Now.Millisecond)
    Dim randomNumber As Integer = r.Next(3)
    Me.imgDisplay.Source = images(randomNumber)

    ' Start the storyboard animation!
    CType(Resources("SpinImageStoryboard"), Storyboard).Begin()

    Return randomNumber
End Function
```

That completes your custom control library! Go ahead and build your project to ensure you don't have any errors. Now let's make use of this control from within a WPF Application.

■ **Source Code** The MyCustomControl project can be found under the Chapter 31 subdirectory.

Creating the Jackpot Deluxe WPF Application

Create a brand new WPF Application project named JackpotDeluxe using Expression Blend, and set a reference to MyCustomControl.dll using the Project | Add Reference… menu option. Because your control is defined in an external assembly, update the opening element of the Window to define a new XML namespace named custom that maps to your MyCustomControl namespace:

```
<Window
  xmlns="http://schemas.microsoft.com/winfx/2006/xaml/presentation"
  xmlns:x="http://schemas.microsoft.com/winfx/2006/xaml"
  xmlns:custom="clr-namespace:MyCustomControl;assembly=MyCustomControl"
  x:Class="MainWindow"
  x:Name="Window"
  Title="MainWindow"
  Width="640" Height="438">
  <Grid/>
</Window>
```

You will build your complete UI of this window in just a few moments; however, before you do, you will make one additional custom control.

Extracting a UserControl from a Drawing Geometry

Expression Blend has a number of very useful shortcuts that can make the process of building custom controls very simple. When you stop to think about it, the chances are very good that many custom controls begin life as a simple graphic created by a graphic artist. To illustrate, select your Grid in the Objects and Timeline editor, and then pick the Pencil tool in your Toolbox (which can be seen if you click and hold the Pen button). Use this tool to draw an interesting image of your liking. In Figure 31-22, you can see my (somewhat sad) attempt at rendering a star shaped image, with the Fill property set to an orange colored brush and the Stroke property set to a blue brush.

Figure 31-22. Using the Pencil control to render a unique shape

Now, if you look at the XAML which was generated on your behalf, you will see that Expression Blend defined a `Path` object. So let's say that you would like to use this geometry as the starting point for a custom control. To so do, simply right click on the Path object on the designer, and select the Make Into UserControl... option (Figure 31-23).

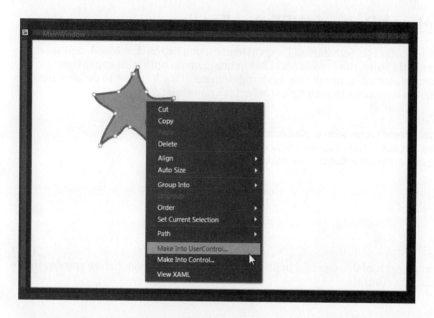

Figure 31-23. Transforming a geometry into a new UserControl

As soon as you select this option, you will be asked to name your control, which I will assume is `StarButton` (you can leave all other settings of this dialog to their default values). Expression Blend will then create a brand new `UserControl` derived class with a corresponding XAML and VB 2010 code file! As well, the original `Path` object on the `Window` has been replaced with an instance of the new control, which is mapped to a new XML namespace in the `MainWindow.xaml` file:

```
<Window
  xmlns="http://schemas.microsoft.com/winfx/2006/xaml/presentation"
  xmlns:x="http://schemas.microsoft.com/winfx/2006/xaml"
  xmlns:custom="clr-namespace:MyCustomControl;assembly=MyCustomControl"
  xmlns:local="clr-namespace:JackpotDeluxe"
  x:Class="MainWindow"
  x:Name="Window"
  Title="MainWindow"
  Width="640" Height="438">
```

```
<Grid>
  <local:StarButton HorizontalAlignment="Left"
        Margin="102,41,0,0" VerticalAlignment="Top"
        Width="136" Height="131"/>
</Grid>
</Window>
```

You will build the real UI of your Window in just a moment, but leave this control in place for the time being.

The Role of .NET 4.0 Visual States

Recall that one of the important tasks of custom control development is adding in visual cues for the end user. In an earlier example of this chapter, you added a few visual cues to a custom Button template by using WPF triggers. You could certainly use triggers for StarButton as well; however, as of .NET 4.0, WPF supports an alternative way to do so via *visual state groups*.

■ **Note** The concept of visual states was first introduced in the Silverlight API. Many felt that the use of visual states (and the related Visual State Manager) was a simpler alternative to WPF triggers, and therefore WPF incorporated this alternative approach into the API beginning with .NET 4.0.

Using WPF visual states, you are able to define a group of related states that your control could be in at any given time. Think of a visual state group as little more than a named container for related UI cues. Ultimately, the names of the groups you define are completely up to you; however, some common group names might include MouseStateGroup, FocusedStateGroup, or EnabledStateGroup.

Once you have defined a set of visual state groups, you then define the individual states for a specific group. For example, MouseStateGroup could define three possible mouse-centric states named MouseEnterStar, MouseExitStar, and MouseDownStar. The FocusedStateGroup might define two states named GainFocusStar and LoseFocusStar.

After you have defined the states for a group, you will then define storyboards that represent the UI cues that will occur when your control transitions into a given state. For example, you could create a storyboard for the MouseEnterStar state which causes the control to change color. Maybe you have a second storyboard for the MouseDownStar state, which causes the control to shrink (or grow) in size. You can use the integrated animation editor of Blend to quickly define each storyboard.

Once you have all of your states defined, you can then force your control to move into any given state using two approaches. If you wish to move between states in code, you can call the static GoToState() method of the VisualStateManager class. Simply specify the name of a state and the related storyboard will execute.

■ **Note** If you wish to transition between states using only markup, you can define triggers which will move between states using the GoToStateAction XAML element.

Defining Visual States for the StarButton Control

To add visual states to the StarButton control, first ensure that the visual editor for your StarButton UserControl is the active window in the Blend IDE. Now, locate the States tab (which can be opened via the Windows menu of Expression Blend) and click the Add State Group button (Figure 31-24).

Figure 31-24. Adding a new visual state group

Now, change the name of the generated group (currently named VisualStateGroup) to the more fitting name, MouseStateGroup. Once you do, notice the Add State button (Figure 31-25).

Figure 31-25. The MouseStateGroup

Using the Add State button, add three states to the MouseStateGroup, named MouseEnterStar, MouseExitStar and MouseDownStar (Figure 31-26).

Figure 31-26. The states of the MouseStateGroup

Each one of your states can now be defined in terms of a storyboard. First, select the MouseEnterStar state. Now, using the Properties window, pick a new color for the Fill property (I made mine a darker shade of orange). Feel free to change properties of other aspects of your control if you wish, such as changing the shape of your control by moving the control points on the visual editor or changing the StrokeThickness property.

Next, select the MouseExitStar state, and notice it will set the Fill color back to the original value, which is perfect for this example. Pick the MouseDownStar state, and use the Properties window to apply a simple transformation to the control (I elected to apply a slight skew to the control).

Defining State Transition Timings

At this point, you have successfully defined a single visual state group with three states. By default, when you transition between states, it will happen immediately because the Default transition value is set to zero seconds (you'll see this listed directly under the name of each state group within the States tab). If you wish, you can define custom amounts of time that should transpire as a control moves between states.

Let's configure the MouseDownStar state in such a way that it will execute the storyboard over a period of 2 seconds. To do so, first click the Add Transition button. Here, you will see a listing of all the possible transitions for the current state. Pick the first listing, which represents the act of moving from the current state into the MouseDownStar state (Figure 31-27).

Figure 31-27. Changing the timing for this state transition

Once you pick this option, define a 1 second amount of time for this transition (Figure 31-28).

Figure 31-28. Defining a one second amount of time for this transition to occur

Viewing the Generated XAML

That is all you need to do for your visual state group. If you click on the XAML tab for your control, you will see the markup which was created by the IDE. Based on how many properties you changed, you could be looking at a good amount of XAML. However, the basic skeleton will look something like so:

```
<VisualStateManager.VisualStateGroups>
  <VisualStateGroup x:Name="MouseStateGroup">
    <VisualStateGroup.Transitions>
      <VisualTransition GeneratedDuration="00:00:01" To="MouseDownStar"/>
    </VisualStateGroup.Transitions>
    <VisualState x:Name="MouseEnterStar">
      <Storyboard>
        < !-- Storyboard for MouseEnterStar -->
      </Storyboard>
    </VisualState>
    <VisualState x:Name="MouseExitStar"/>
    <VisualState x:Name="MouseDownStar">
      <Storyboard>
        < !-- Storyboard for MouseDownStar -->
      </Storyboard>
    </VisualState>
  </VisualStateGroup>
</VisualStateManager.VisualStateGroups>
```

Now that you have all of your states in place, all you need to do is to move between them when appropriate.

Changing Visual States in Code using the VisualStateManager Class

To complete your StarButton, you will use the VisualStateManager class to move between your states. Using the Events tab of the Properties window, handle the MouseDown, MouseEnter and MouseLeave events on your custom UserControl. Implement each handler to move into the related state as so:

```
Partial Public Class StarButton
        Inherits UserControl
...
            Private Sub StarControl_MouseDown(ByVal sender As Object,
                                ByVal e As System.Windows.Input.MouseButtonEventArgs)
              ' Parameter 1 : Which control am I working with?
              ' Parameter 2 : Which state do I want to transition to?
              ' Parameter 3 : Do I want to use transition times?
              VisualStateManager.GoToState(Me, "MouseDownStar", True)
            End Sub

            Private Sub StarControl_MouseEnter(ByVal sender As Object,
                                ByVal e As System.Windows.Input.MouseEventArgs)
              VisualStateManager.GoToState(Me, "MouseEnterStar", True)
            End Sub

            Private Sub StarControl_MouseLeave(ByVal sender As Object,
                                ByVal e As System.Windows.Input.MouseEventArgs)
              VisualStateManager.GoToState(Me, "MouseExitStar", True)
            End Sub
End Class
```

That completes the construction of your second custom control for this project! If you run your project, you should be able to test that your visual states are working correctly by interacting with the StarButton on your initial window.

Finalizing the Jackpot Deluxe Application

Now that you have your custom controls in place, you can wrap things up quite rapidly. Delete the current StarControl that is on your Window, and redefine the layout root to be a StackPanel rather than the current Grid. Here is one possible layout for your window (Figure 31-29).

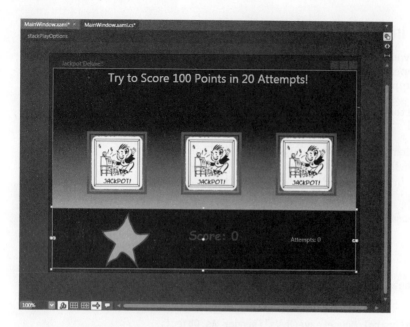

Figure 31-29. The layout of the Jackpot Deluxe window

The key aspects of this markup are the definition of three custom **SpinControl** objects (named **imgFirst**, **imgSecond,** and **imgThird**) and an instance of the **StarButton** control (named **btnSpin**), which has handled the **MouseDown** event.

In addition, you will make use of three **TextBlock** controls (named **txtInstructions**, **txtScore** and **txtAttempts**) which will be used to inform the user about their current score, current number of attempts, and a general text message. Here is the full markup for the root **StackPanel**, which maintains a few nested **StackPanel** objects to boot:

```
<StackPanel x:Name="LayoutRoot" Background="#FF0F0202" Orientation="Vertical">
  <TextBlock  x:Name="txtInstructions" Width="639"  Height="96" Foreground="Yellow"
              HorizontalAlignment="Left" FontSize="24"
              TextAlignment="Center" Text="Try to Score 100 Points in 20 Attempts!"/>

  <StackPanel Height="184" Width="639" Orientation="Horizontal">
    <StackPanel.Background>
      <LinearGradientBrush EndPoint="0.5,1" StartPoint="0.5,0">
        <GradientStop Color="#FF000000"/>
        <GradientStop Color="#FFB08282" Offset="1"/>
      </LinearGradientBrush>
    </StackPanel.Background>
```

```
<!-- The SpinControls -->
<custom:SpinControl x:Name="imgFirst" Height="125" Margin="70,0,0,0" Width="125"/>
<custom:SpinControl x:Name="imgSecond" Height="125" Margin="70,0,0,0" Width="125"/>
<custom:SpinControl x:Name="imgThird" Height="125" Margin="70,0,0,0" Width="125"/>
</StackPanel>

<StackPanel Height="120" Orientation="Horizontal">
  <!-- The StarButton -->
  <local:StarButton x:Name="btnSpin" HorizontalAlignment="Left" Margin="102,8,0,0"
       VerticalAlignment="Top" Width="100" Height="108" MouseDown="btnSpin_MouseDown"/>
  <TextBlock x:Name="txtScore" Text="Score: 0" FontFamily="Comic Sans MS" Width="140"
            Height="50" FontWeight="Bold" FontSize="24"
            Foreground="#FF6F0269" Margin="80,0,0,0"  />
  <TextBlock x:Name="txtAttempts" Text="Attempts: 0" Height="19" Width="82"
            Foreground="#FF28EA16" Margin="70,0,0,0"/>
</StackPanel>

</StackPanel>
```

Within the VB 2010 code file, define three Private member variables to keep track of the player's point total, the current number of attempts, and the maximum number of allowed spins:

```
Class MainWindow
    Private totalPoints As Integer = 0
    Private totalAttempts As Integer = 0
    Private MaxAttempts As Integer = 20
    ...
End Class
```

Now, define two Private helper methods, which will be called if the user wins (defined as getting 100 points in 20 tries or less) or loses:

```
Private Sub DoLosingCondition()
    ' Change text for losing!
    Me.txtInstructions.Text = "YOU LOSE!"
    Me.txtInstructions.FontSize = 80
    Me.txtInstructions.Foreground = New SolidColorBrush(Colors.Gray)

    ' Disable button, game over dude!
    Me.btnSpin.IsEnabled = False
End Sub

Private Sub DoWinningCondition()
    ' Change text for winning!
    Me.txtInstructions.Text = "YOU WIN!"
    Me.txtInstructions.FontSize = 80
    Me.txtInstructions.Foreground = New SolidColorBrush(Colors.Orange)

    ' Disable button, game over dude!
    Me.btnSpin.IsEnabled = False
End Sub
```

As you can see, both of these methods will change the Text property of txtInstructions to a fitting message and disable your spin button.

The remaining bit of code is the logic behind the clicking of your StarButton. Consider the following implementation of the MouseDown event handler:

```
Private Sub btnSpin_MouseDown(ByVal sender As Object,
                            ByVal e As System.Windows.Input.MouseButtonEventArgs)
    ' Add 1 to number of tries.
    totalAttempts += 1
    Me.txtAttempts.Text = String.Format("Attempts: {0}", (totalAttempts).ToString())

    ' Last attempt??
    If totalAttempts >= MaxAttempts Then
        DoLosingCondition()
    End If

    ' Spin each control.
    Dim randomOne As Integer = Me.imgFirst.Spin()
    Dim randomTwo As Integer = Me.imgSecond.Spin()
    Dim randomThree As Integer = Me.imgThird.Spin()

    ' Calculate the new score. To make things simple, players only get
    ' points if all three images are identical.
    If randomOne = randomTwo AndAlso randomTwo = randomThree Then
        ' Adjust points.
        totalPoints += 10
        Me.txtScore.Text = String.Format("Score: {0}", totalPoints.ToString())

        ' Did they get 100 or more points?
        If totalPoints >= 100 Then
            DoWinningCondition()
        End If
    End If
End Sub
```

This logic is very simple. Each time they click the custom StarButton, you check if they have reached the maximum number of attempts, and if so, display the losing condition. If they still have some attempts remaining, you spin each SpinControl object and check if each image is identical. If so, you add some points to the player total and check for the winning condition. Figure 31-30 shows the final end result:

Figure 31-30. The completed Jackpot Deluxe application!

That concludes the examination of building desktop applications using the Windows Presentation Foundation API. Over these last five chapters, you have learned quite a bit about this aspect of .NET development; however, there is much more to learn. As well, you have used Expression Blend to build a number of example applications.

Just like Visual Studio 2010, Expression Blend has a dedicated documentation system. If you are serious about learning the ins-and-outs of Expression Blend, be sure to consult the integrated help system. (If Expression Blend is loaded on your desktop, just press the F1 key.) Here, you will find dozens of excellent tutorials which will deepen your understanding of this key aspect of WPF (and Silverlight) application development (Figure 31-31).

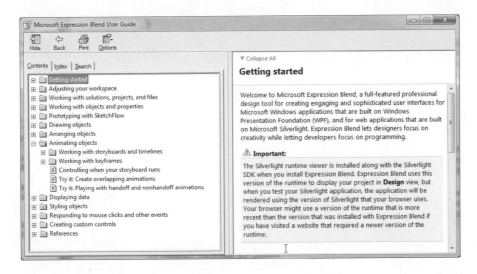

Figure 31-31. Be kind to yourself and be sure to examing the help system of Expression Blend

Summary

This chapter examined a number of related WPF topics, all of which are focused on the construction of custom user controls. You started by investigating how WPF places a unique spin on traditional .NET programming primitives, specifically properties and events. As you have seen, a *dependency property* allows you to build a property which can integrate within the WPF set of services (animations, data bindings, styles and so on). On a related note, *routed events* provide a way for an event to flow up or down a tree of markup.

You then examined the relationship between a *logical tree* and *visual tree*. The logical tree is basically a one-to-one correspondence of the markup you would author to describe a WPF root element. Behind this logic tree is a much deeper visual tree that contains detailed rendering instructions.

The role of a *default template* was then examined. Remember, when you are building custom templates, you are essentially ripping out all (or part) of a control's visual tree and replacing it with your own custom implementation. From here, you learned a number of ways to build custom UserControl classes, including the use of the .NET 4.0 Visual State Manager, Expression Blend, and the integrated animation editor.

CHAPTER 32

■ ■ ■

Building ASP.NET Web Pages

Until now, all of the examples in this book have focused on console-based and desktop graphical user interfaces created using the WPF API. The remainder of the text will explore how the .NET platform facilitates the construction of browser-based presentation layers using a technology named ASP.NET. To begin, you'll quickly review a number of key web development concepts (HTTP, HTML, client-side scripting, postbacks) and examine the role of Microsoft's commercial web server (IIS) as well as that of the ASP.NET development web server.

With this brief web primer out of the way, the remainder of this chapter concentrates on the structure of ASP.NET web pages (including the single-page and code-behind model) and examines the functionality of the Page base class. Along the way, you'll be introduced to the role of ASP.NET web controls, the directory structure of an ASP.NET web site, and how to use a Web.config file to control the runtime operation of your web sites via XML instructions.

■ **Note** If you wish to load any of the ASP.NET web site projects found within this book's downloadable source code, launch Visual Studio 2010 and select File ➤ Open ➤ Web Site... menu option. From the resulting dialog box, click on the File System button (mounted on the left hand side), and select the folder containing the web project files. This will load all content for the current web application into the Visual Studio IDE.

The Role of HTTP

Web applications are very different animals from graphical desktop applications. The first obvious difference is that a production-level web application involves at least two networked machines: one hosting the web site and the other viewing data within a web browser. Of course, during development it is entirely possible to have a single machine play the role of both the browser-based client and the hosting web server that serves up content. Given the nature of web applications, the networked machines in question must agree upon a particular wire protocol to determine how to send and receive data. The wire protocol that connects the computers in question is the Hypertext Transfer Protocol (HTTP).

The HTTP Request/Response Cycle

When a client machine launches a web browser (such as Opera, Mozilla Firefox, Apple Safari or Microsoft Internet Explorer), an HTTP *request* is made to access a particular resource (typically a web page) on the remote server machine. HTTP is a text-based protocol that is built upon a standard request/ response paradigm. For example, if you navigate to www.facebook.com, the browser software leverages a web technology termed *Domain Name Service* (DNS) that converts the registered URL into a numerical value termed an *IP address*. At this point, the browser opens a socket connection (typically via port 80 for a nonsecure connection) and sends the HTTP request for processing to the target site.

The web server receives the incoming HTTP request and may choose to process out any client-supplied input values (such as values within a text box, check box, or list box) in order to format a proper HTTP *response*. Web programmers may leverage any number of technologies (CGI, ASP, ASP.NET, JSP, etc.) to dynamically generate the content to be emitted into the HTTP response. At this point, the client-side browser renders the returned HTML sent from the web server. Figure 32-1 illustrates the basic HTTP request/response cycle.

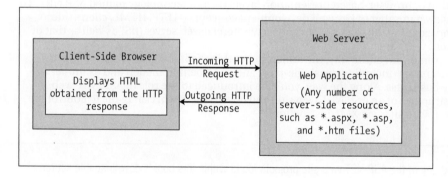

Figure 32-1. The HTTP request/response cycle

HTTP Is a Stateless Protocol

Another aspect of web development that is markedly different from traditional desktop programming is the fact that HTTP is essentially a *stateless* wire protocol. As soon as the web server sends a response to the client browser, everything about the previous interaction is forgotten. This is certainly not the case in a traditional desktop application, where the state of the executable is most often alive and kicking until the user shuts down the main window of the application.

Given this point, as a web developer, it is up to you take specific steps to "remember" information (such as items in a shopping cart, credit card numbers, and home addresses) about the users who are currently logged on to your site. As you will see in Chapter 34, ASP.NET provides numerous ways to handle state, using techniques such as session variables, cookies, and the application cache as well as the ASP.NET profile management API.

Understanding Web Applications and Web Servers

A *web application* can be understood as a collection of files (e.g., *.htm, *.aspx, image files, XML-based file data) and related components (such as a .NET code library) stored within a particular set of directories on a web server. As shown in Chapter 34, ASP.NET web applications have a specific life cycle and provide numerous events (such as initial startup or final shutdown) that you can hook into to perform specialized processing during your website's operation.

A *web server* is a software product in charge of hosting your web applications; it typically provides a number of related services such as integrated security, File Transfer Protocol (FTP) support, mail exchange services, and so forth. Internet Information Services (IIS) is the Microsoft enterprise-level web server product, and it offers intrinsic support for classic ASP as well as ASP.NET web applications.

Assuming you have IIS properly installed on your workstation, you can interact with IIS from the Administrative Tools folder (located in the Control Panel folder) by double-clicking the Internet Information Services applet. Figure 32-2 shows the Default Web Site node of IIS 7 where a majority of the configuration details occur (if you are running earlier versions of IIS, your UI will look different).

Figure 32-2. The IIS applet can be used to configure the runtime behavior of Microsoft IIS

The Role of IIS Virtual Directories

A single IIS installation is able to host numerous web applications, each of which resides in a *virtual directory*. Each virtual directory is mapped to a physical directory on the machine's hard drive. For example, if you create a new virtual directory named CarsAreUs, the outside world can navigate to this site using a URL such as http://www.MyDomain.com/CarsAreUs (assuming your site's IP address has been registered with a DNS of www.MyDomain.com). Under the hood, this virtual directory maps to a physical root directory on the web server which contains the content of the CarsAreUs web application.

As you will see later in this chapter, when you create ASP.NET web applications using Visual Studio 2010, you have the option of having the IDE generate a new virtual directory for the current website automatically. However, if required, you are certainly able to manually create a virtual directory by hand by right-clicking the Default Web Site node of IIS and selecting Add Virtual Directory from the context menu.

The ASP.NET Development Web Server

Prior to .NET 2.0, ASP.NET developers were required to make use of IIS virtual directories during the development and testing of their web applications. In many cases, this tight dependency on IIS made team development more complex than necessary, not to mention that many network administrators frowned upon installing IIS on every developer's machine.

Happily, there is the option of a lightweight web server named the ASP.NET Development Web Server. This utility allows developers to host an ASP.NET web application outside the bounds of IIS. Using this tool, you can build and test your web pages from any folder on your machine. This is quite helpful for team development scenarios and for building ASP.NET web applications on versions of Windows that do not support IIS installations.

Most of the examples in this book will make use of the ASP.NET Development Web Server (via the correct Visual Studio 2010 project option) rather than hosting web content under an IIS virtual directory. While this approach can simplify the development of your web application, be aware that this web server is *not* intended to host production-level web applications. It is intended purely for development and testing purposes. Once a web application is ready for prime time, your site will need to be copied to an IIS virtual directory.

■ **Note** The Mono project (see Appendix B) provides a free ASP.NET plug-in for the Apache web server. This makes it possible to build and host ASP.NET web applications on operating systems other than Microsoft Windows. Check out `www.mono-project.com/ASP.NET` for details.

The Role of HTML

Once you have configured a directory to host your web application and you have chosen a web server to serve as the host, you need to create the content itself. Recall that a web application is simply a set of files that constitute the functionality of the site. To be sure, many of these files will contain Hypertext Markup Language (HTML) statements. HTML is a standard markup language used to describe how literal text, images, external links, and various HTML controls are to be rendered within the client-side browser.

While it is true that modern IDEs (including Visual Studio 2010) and web development platforms (such as ASP.NET) generate much of the HTML automatically, you will do well to have a working knowledge of HTML as you work with ASP.NET.

■ **Note** Recall from Chapter 2 that Microsoft has released a number of free IDEs under the Express family of products (such as Visual Basic 2010 Express). If you are interested in web development, you may wish to also download Visual Web Developer Express. This free IDE is geared exclusively towards the construction of ASP.NET web applications.

While this section will most certainly not cover all aspects of HTML, it will touch on some basics. This will help you better understand the markup generated on your behalf by the ASP.NET programming model.

HTML Document Structure

An HTML file consists of a set of tags that describe the look and feel of a given web page. The basic structure of an HTML document tends to remain the same. For example, *.htm files (or, equivalently, *.html files) open and close with <html> and </html> tags, typically define a <body> section, and so forth. Keep in mind that traditional HTML is *not* case sensitive. Therefore, in the eyes of the hosting browser, <HTML>, <html>, and <HtmL> are identical.

To illustrate some HTML basics, open Visual Studio 2010 and create empty HTML Page file via the File ➤ New ➤ File menu selection (notice that you are not making a web project at this point, you are just opening a blank HTML file for editing). Once you have done so, save it as **default.htm** in a convenient location. You should see the following initial markup:

```
<!DOCTYPE html PUBLIC "-//W3C//DTD XHTML 1.0 Transitional//EN"
          "http://www.w3.org/TR/xhtml1/DTD/xhtml1-transitional.dtd">
<html xmlns="http://www.w3.org/1999/xhtml" >
  <head>
    <title>Untitled Page</title>
  </head>
  <body>

  </body>
</html>
```

First of all, notice that this HTML file opens with a **DOCTYPE** processing instruction. This informs the IDE that the contained HTML tags should be validated against the XHTML standard. As mentioned, traditional HTML was very *loose* in its syntax. Beyond the case insensitivity issue, it was permissible to define an opening element (such as <br> for a line break) that did not have a corresponding closing break (</br> in this case). The XHTML standard is a W3C specification that adds some much-needed rigor to the basic HTML markup language.

■ **Note** By default, Visual Studio 2010 validates all HTML documents against the XHTML 1.0 Transitional validation scheme to ensure the markup is in sync with the XHTML standard. If you wish to specify an alternative validation scheme (such as HTML 4.01), activate the Tools ➤ Options dialog box, expand the Text Editor node, expand the HTML node, and then select the Validation node. On a related note, if you would rather not see validation warnings, simply uncheck the Show Errors check box found in the same location.

The `<html>` and `</html>` tags are used to mark the beginning and end of your document. Notice that the opening `<html>` tag is further qualified with an `xmlns` (XML namespace) attribute that qualifies the various tags that may appear within this document (again, by default these tags are based on the XHTML standard). Web browsers use these particular tags to understand where to begin applying the rendering formats specified in the body of the document. The `<body>` scope is where the vast majority of the actual content is defined. To spruce things up just a bit, update the title of your page as so:

```
<head>
  <title>This is my simple web page</title>
</head>
```

Not surprisingly, the `<title>` tags are used to specify the text string that should be placed in the title bar of the calling web browser.

The Role of an HTML Form

The real meat of most `*.htm` files occurs within the scope of the `<form>` elements. An *HTML form* is simply a named group of related UI elements typically used to gather user input. Do not confuse an HTML form with the entire display area shown by a given browser. In reality, an HTML form is more of a *logical grouping* of widgets placed in the `<form>` and `</form>` tag set:

```
<html xmlns="http://www.w3.org/1999/xhtml" >
<head>
  <title>This is my simple web page</title>
</head>
<body>
  <form id="defaultPage">
    <!-- Insert web UI content here -->
  </form>
</body>
</html>
```

This form has been assigned the ID of `"defaultPage"`. Typically, the opening `<form>` tag supplies an `action` attribute that specifies the URL to which to submit the form data, as well as the method of transmitting that data itself (POST or GET). For the time being, let's look at the sorts of items that can be placed in an HTML form (beyond simple literal text).

The Visual Studio 2010 HTML Designer Tools

Visual Studio 2010 provides an HTML tab on the Toolbox that allows you to select an HTML control that you wish to place on your HTML designer (see Figure 32-3).

Figure 32-3. *The HTML tab of the Toolbox*

■ **Note** When you are building ASP.NET web pages, you will *not* be using these HTML controls to create the user interface! Rather, you will use the ASP.NET web controls, which will render back the correct HTML on your behalf.

Similar to the process of building a Windows Forms or WPF application, these HTML controls can be dragged onto the HTML designer surface. If you click on the Split button on the bottom of the HTML editor, the bottom pane of the HTML editor will display the HTML visual layout and the upper pane will show the related markup. Another benefit of this editor is that as you select markup or an HTML UI element, the corresponding representation is highlighted (Figure 32-4).

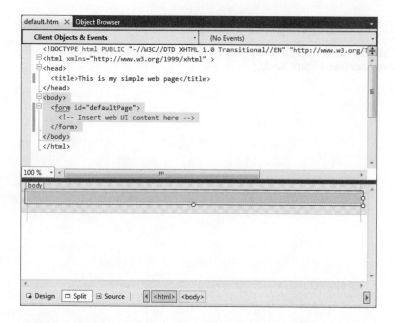

Figure 32-4. *The Visual Studio 2010 HTML designer*

Visual Studio 2010 also allows you to edit the overall look and feel of the *.htm file or a given HTML control in the <form> using the Properties window. For example, if you select DOCUMENT from the drop-down list of the Properties window, you are able to configure various aspects of the HTML page, such as the background color, background image (if any), title, and so forth (Figure 32-5).

Figure 32-5. *The Visual Studio Properties window can be used to configure the HTML markup*

As you use the Properties window to configure an aspect of your web page, the IDE will update the HTML accordingly. Here is a minor change to your page that now sets the background color of the overall document:

```
<html xmlns="http://www.w3.org/1999/xhtml" >
<head>
  <title>This is my simple web page</title>
</head>
<body bgcolor="#ffffcc">
  <form id="defaultPage">
    <!-- Insert web UI content here -->
  </form>
</body>
</html>
```

Building an HTML Form

Update the <body> of the default.htm file to display some literal text that prompts the user to enter a message (be aware that you can enter and format literal textual content by typing directly in the HTML designer). Here you are using the <h1> tag to set a header weight, <p> for a paragraph block and <i> for italic text:

```
<html xmlns="http://www.w3.org/1999/xhtml" >
<head>
  <title>This is my simple web page</title>
</head>
<body bgcolor="ffffcc">
  <!-- Prompt for user input-->
  <h1 align="center">Simple HTML Page</h1>
  <p align="center">
    <br/>
    <i>Please enter a message</i>.
  </p>

  <form id="defaultPage">
  </form>

</body>
</html>
```

Now let's build the HTML form itself. In general, each HTML control is described using an id attribute (used to identify the item programmatically) and a type attribute (used to specify which UI element you are interested in placing in the <form> declaration). Depending on which UI widget you have declared, you will find additional attributes specific to the control that can be modified using the Properties window.

The UI you will build here will contain one text field and two button types. The first button will be used to run a client side script and the other to reset the form input fields to the default values. Update your HTML form as so:

```html
<!-- Build a form to get user info -->
<form id="defaultPage">
  <p align="center">
    Your Message:
    <input id="txtUserMessage" type="text"/></p>
  <p align="center">
    <input id="btnShow" type="button" value="Show!"/>
    <input id="btnReset" type="reset" value="Reset"/>
  </p>
</form>
```

Notice that you have assigned relevant IDs to each control (txtUserMessage, btnShow, and btnReset) and that each input item has an extra attribute named type that marks these input controls as UI items that automatically clear all fields to their initial values (type="reset"), receive text input (type="text"), or function as a simple client side button which does not post back to the web server (type="button").

Save your file, then right click on the designer and select the View in Browser menu option. Figure 32-6 shows the current page with Google Chrome.

Figure 32-6. Your simple default.htm page

■ **Note** When you select the View in Browser option, Visual Studio 2010 will automatically launch the ASP.NET Development web server to host your content.

The Role of Client-Side Scripting

In addition to HTML UI elements, a given *.htm file may contain blocks of script code that will be processed by the requesting browser. There are two major reasons why client-side scripting is used:

- To validate user input in the browser before posting back to the web server
- To interact with the Document Object Model (DOM) of the browser

Regarding the first point, understand that the inherent evil of a web application is the need to make frequent round-trips (termed *postbacks*) to the server machine to update the HTML to be rendered into the browser. While postbacks are unavoidable, you should always be mindful of ways to minimize travel across the wire. One technique that saves postbacks is to use client-side scripting to validate user input before submitting the form data to the web server. If an error is found, such as not supplying data within a required field, you can alert the user to the error without incurring the cost of posting back to the web server. (After all, nothing is more annoying to users than posting back on a slow connection, only to receive instructions to address input errors!)

■ **Note** Be aware that even when performing client-side validation (for improved response time), validation should *also* occur on the web server itself. This will ensure that the data has not been tampered with as it was sent across the wire. The ASP.NET validation controls will automatically perform client- and server-side validation (more on this in the following chapter).

Client-side scripts can also be used to interact with the underlying object model (the Document Object Model or DOM) of the web browser itself. Most commercial browsers expose a set of objects that can be leveraged to control how the browser should behave.

When a browser parses an HTML page, it builds an object tree in memory, representing all the contents of the Web page (forms, input controls, etc). Browsers provide an API called DOM that exposes the object tree and allows you to modify its contents programmatically. For example, you can write JavaScript that executes in the browser to get the values from specific controls, change the color of a control, add new controls to the page dynamically, etc.

One major annoyance is the fact that different browsers tend to expose similar, *but not identical*, object models. Thus, if you emit a block of client-side script code that interacts with the DOM, it may not work identically on all browsers (thus, testing is always a must!).

ASP.NET provides the `HttpRequest.Browser` property, which allows you to determine at runtime the capacities of the browser and device that sent the current request. You can use this information to stylize how to emit back the HTTP response in the most optimal manner. But you rarely need to worry about this, unless you are implementing custom controls, because all the standard Web controls in ASP.NET automatically know how to render themselves appropriately based on the browser type. This remarkable capability is known as *adaptive rendering*, and it's implemented out-of-the-box for all standard ASP.NET controls.

There are many scripting languages that can be used to author client-side script code. Two of the more popular ones are VBScript and JavaScript. VBScript is a subset of the Visual Basic 6.0 programming language. Be aware that Microsoft Internet Explorer is the only web browser that has built-in support for client-side VBScript support (other browsers may or may not provide optional plug-ins). Note that if you wish your HTML pages to work correctly in any commercial web browser, do *not* use VBScript for your client-side scripting logic.

The other popular scripting language is JavaScript. It's important to note that JavaScript is in no way, shape, or form the same as the Java language. While JavaScript and Java have a somewhat similar syntax, JavaScript is not a full-fledged OOP language, and thus it is far less powerful than Java. The good news is that all modern-day web browsers support JavaScript, which makes it a natural candidate for client-side scripting logic.

A Client-Side Scripting Example

To illustrate the role of client-side scripting, let's first examine how to intercept events sent from client-side HTML GUI widgets. To capture the Click event for the Show button, select btnShow from the upper-left drop-down list of the HTML form designer and select the onclick event from the right drop-down list. This will add an onclick attribute to the definition of the Show button:

```
<input id="btnShow" type="button" value="Show!"
       onclick="return btnShow_onclick()" />
```

Visual Studio 2010 will also create an empty JavaScript function that will be called when the user clicks the button. Within this stub, use the alert() method to display a client-side message box containing the value in the text box via the value property:

```
<script language="javascript" type="text/javascript">
// <![CDATA[
  function btnShow_onclick() {
    alert(defaultPage.txtUserMessage.value);
  }
// ]]>
</script>
```

Note that the scripting block has been wrapped within a CDATA section. The reason for this is simple. If your page ends up on a browser that does not support JavaScript, the code will be treated as a comment block and ignored. Of course, your page may be less functional, but the upside is that your page will not blow up when rendered by the browser.

In any case, if you view your page in a browser once again, you should be able to type a message and see it pop up in a client side message box (Figure 32-7).

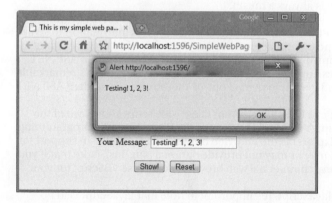

Figure 32-7. Invoking a client side JavaScript function

As well, when you click on the Reset button, you should find that the text area is cleared of data, as this particular button has been created by specifying type="reset".

Posting Back to the Web Server

This simple HTML page is executing all functionality within the hosting browser. A *real* web page needs to post back to a resource on the web server, passing all of the input data at the same time. Once the server side resource receives this data, it can use it to build a proper HTTP response.

The `action` attribute on the opening `<form>` tag specifies the recipient of the incoming form data. Possible receivers include mail servers, other HTML files on the web server, a classic (COM-based) Active Server Pages (ASP) file, an ASP.NET web page, and so forth.

Beyond the `action` attribute, you will also likely have a *submit button*, which when clicked, will transmit the form data to the web application via an HTTP request. You have no need to do so for this example; however, here is an update to the `default.htm` file, specifying the following attribute in the opening `<form>` tag:

```
<form id="defaultPage"
      action="http://localhost/Cars/ClassicAspPage.asp" method="GET">
  <input id="btnPostBack" type="submit" value="Post to Server!"/>
...
</form>
```

When the submit button for this form is clicked, the form data is sent to the `ClassicAspPage.asp` at the specified URL. When you specify `method="GET"` as the mode of transmission, the form data is appended to the query string as a set of name/value pairs separated by ampersands. You may have seen this sort of data in your browser before, for example:

```
http://www.google.com/search?hl=en&source=hp&q=vikings&cts=1264370773666&aq=
f&aql=&aqi=g1g-z1g1g-z1g1g-z1g4&oq=
```

The other method of transmitting form data to the web server is to specify `method="POST"`:

```
<form id="defaultPage"
      action="http://localhost/Cars/ClassicAspPage.asp" method = "POST">
...
</form>
```

In this case, the form data is not appended to the query string. Using POST, the form data is not directly visible to the outside world. More important, POST data does not have a character-length limitation; many browsers have a limit for GET queries.

Postbacks under ASP.NET

When you are building ASP.NET based web sites, the framework will take care of the posting mechanics on your behalf. One of the many benefits of building a web site using ASP.NET is that the programming model layers on top of standard HTTP Request/Response an event driven system. Thus, rather than manually setting an `action` attribute and defining an HTML `submit` button, you can simply handle events on the ASP.NET web controls using standard VB 2010 syntax.

Using this event driven model, you can very easily post back to the web server using a large number of controls. If you require, you can post back to the web server if the user clicks on a radio button, an item in a list box, a day on a calendar control, and so on. In each case, you simply handle the correct event, and the ASP.NET runtime will automatically emit back the correct HTML posting data.

■ **Source Code** The SimpleWebPage website is included under the Chapter 32 subdirectory.

The Feature Set of the ASP.NET API

At this point, your whirlwind review of classic web application development is complete, and you are ready to dive into ASP.NET itself. Before you create your first web application, let me set the stage regarding the major features of .NET's web development API, as seen from the major versions of the framework.

Major Features of ASP.NET 1.0-1.1

The first release of ASP.NET (version 1.x) contained a number of features that allow developers to build web applications in a strongly typed and object oriented matter. Here are some key features which are supported in all versions of the .NET platform:

- ASP.NET provides a model termed *code-behind*, which allows you to separate presentation logic (HTML) from business logic (VB 2010 code).

- ASP.NET pages are coded using .NET programming languages, rather than server side scripting languages. The code files are compiled into valid .NET *.dll assemblies (which translates into much faster execution).

- Web controls allow programmers to build the GUI of a web application in a manner similar to building a Windows Forms/WPF application.

- By default, ASP.NET web controls automatically maintain their state during postbacks using a hidden form field named __VIEWSTATE.

- ASP.NET web applications can make use of any of the assemblies within the .NET base class libraries (of course, it makes little sense to make use of desktop GUI APIs such as Windows Forms within the context of a web app).

- ASP.NET web applications can be easily configured using standard IIS settings *or* using a web application configuration file (Web.config).

The first point I want to elaborate on here is the fact that the UI of an ASP.NET web page is built using any number of *web controls*. Unlike a typical HTML control, web controls are executed on the web server and will emit back to the HTTP response their correct HTML tags. This alone is a huge benefit of ASP.NET in that the amount of HTML you must manually author by hand diminishes greatly. By way of a quick example, assume you have defined the following ASP.NET web control in an ASP.NET web page:

```
<asp:Button ID="btnMyButton" runat="server" Text="Button" BorderColor="Blue"
        BorderStyle="Solid" BorderWidth="5px" />
```

You'll learn the details of declaring ASP.NET web controls soon enough, but for right now, notice that many attributes of the `<asp:Button>` control look very similar to the properties you have encountered in the Windows Forms and WPF examples (`BorderColor`, `Text`, `BorderStyle`, etc.). The same is true for all ASP.NET web controls because when Microsoft built the web control toolkit, these widgets were purposely designed to look and feel like their desktop counterparts.

Now, if a browser makes a call to the `*.aspx` file containing this control, the control responds by emitting into the output stream the following HTML declaration:

```
<input type="submit" name="btnMyButton" value="Button" id="btnMyButton"
       style="border-color:Blue;border-width:5px;border-style:Solid;" />
```

Notice how the web control emits back standard HTML (or XHTML, based on your settings) that can be rendered in any browser. Given this, understand that using ASP.NET web controls in no way ties you to the Microsoft family of operating systems or to Microsoft Internet Explorer. Any operating system or browser (including those on handheld devices such as the Apple iPhone or BlackBerry devices) can view an ASP.NET web page.

Next, note from the previous list of features that an ASP.NET web application will be compiled into a .NET assembly. Thus, your web projects are no different than any .NET `*.dll` built during this book. The compiled web application will be composed of CIL code, an assembly MANIFEST, and type metadata. This has a number of huge benefits, most notably performance gains, strong typing, and the ability to be micromanaged by the CLR (e.g., garbage collection, etc.).

Finally, ASP.NET web applications provide a programming model whereby you can partition your page's markup from its related VB 2010 code base using *code files*. You'll learn about this topic in just a bit, but know that this feature addresses a common complaint found when building classic (COM-based) ASP pages, where a typical `*.asp` file was a confused mismatch of HTML and script code. Using code files, the markup you type will map to a full-blown object model that is merged with your VB 2010 code file via Partial Class declarations.

Major Features of ASP.NET 2.0

ASP.NET 1.x was a major step in the right direction, and ASP.NET 2.0 provided many additional bells and whistles that helped ASP.NET move from a way to build dynamic *web pages* to a way to build feature rich *web sites*. Consider this partial list of key features:

- Introduction of the ASP.NET Development web server (which means developers no longer need IIS installed on their development computers).

- A large number of new web controls that handle many complex situations (navigation controls, security controls, new data binding controls, etc.).

- The introduction of *master pages*, which allow developers to attach a common UI frame to a set of related pages.

- Support for *themes*, which offer a declarative manner to change the look and feel of the entire web application on the web server.

- Support for *Web Parts*, which allow end users to customize the look and feel of a web page and store their settings for later use (a la portals).

- Introduction of a web-based configuration and management utility that maintains the various `Web.config` files.

Beyond the ASP.NET Development web server, one of the biggest additions brought forth with ASP.NET 2.0 was the introduction of *master pages*. As you are aware, most web sites have a look and feel which is common to all pages on the site. Consider a commercial web site such as www.amazon.com. Every page has the same elements, such as a common header, common footer, common navigation menus and so on.

Using a master page, you can model this common functionality and define *placeholders* that other `*.aspx` files can plug into. This makes it very easy to quickly reshape the overall look and feel of your site (reposition the navigation bar, change the header logo, and so on) by simply changing the master page, leaving the other `*.aspx` files unmodified.

■ **Note** Master pages are so useful that as of Visual Studio 2010, all new ASP.NET web projects will include a master page by default.

ASP.NET 2.0 also added many new web controls into the mix, including controls that automatically incorporate common security features (log in controls, password recovery controls, etc), controls that allow you to layer a navigational structure on top of a set of related `*.aspx` files, and even more controls for performing complex data binding operations, where the necessary SQL queries could be generated using a set of ASP.NET web controls.

Major Features of ASP.NET 3.5 (and .NET 3.5 SP1)

.NET 3.5 added the ability for ASP.NET web applications to make use of the LINQ programming model (also introduced in .NET 3.5) and the following web-centric features:

- New controls to support Silverlight development (recall that this is a WPF-based API for designing rich media content for a website).

- Support for data binding against ADO.NET entity classes (see Chapter 23).

- Support for ASP.NET Dynamic Data. This is a Ruby on Rails-inspired web framework that can be used to build data driven web applications. It exposes tables in a database by encoding it in the URI of the ASP.NET web service, and the data in the table is automatically rendered to HTML.

- Integrated support for Ajax-style development, which essentially allows for micro-postbacks to refresh part of a web page as quickly as possible.

One of the most welcomed features in ASP.NET 3.5 was a new set of controls that allow for Ajax development. This web-centric API makes it possible to refresh a small portion of a larger web page in the most efficient manner possible. While Ajax can be used by any web development API, doing so within an ASP.NET site is very simple because the Ajax controls do all of the heavy lifting by emitting back the necessary client side JavaScript code on your behalf.

The ASP.NET Dynamic Data project templates, introduced with .NET 3.5 Service Pack 1, provide a new model to build sites that are driven heavily by a relational database. Of course, most web sites will need to communicate with databases to some extent, but the ASP.NET Dynamic Data projects are tightly connected to the ADO.NET Entity Framework and are squarely focused on the rapid development of data-driven sites (similar to what one might build when using Ruby).

Major Features of ASP.NET 4.0

And this brings me to the web features that ship with the current version of the framework, .NET 4.0. Beyond allowing you to leverage the overall .NET 4.0 features, here is a hit list of some of the key web-centric features:

- The ability to compress "view state" data using the GZIP standard.

- Updated browser definitions to ensure that ASP.NET pages render correctly on new browsers and devices (Google Chrome, Apple IPhone, BlackBerry devices, etc.).

- Ability to customize the output of validation controls using a cascading style sheet (CSS).

- Inclusion of the ASP.NET Chart control, which allows for building ASP.NET pages that include intuitive charts for complex statistical or financial analysis.

- Official support for the ASP.NET Model View Controller project template, which decreases the dependency among application layers by using the Model-View-Controller (MVC) pattern.

Note that this list of ASP.NET 1.0-4.0 features is in no way all inclusive, but it does accentuate just how feature-rich this web API truly is. Truth be told, if I were to cover every possible feature of ASP.NET, this book would easily double in size (triple, perhaps). Since this is not realistic, the goal for the remainder of text is to examine the core features of ASP.NET that you will likely use on a day-to-day basis. Be sure to make use of the .NET Framework 4.0 SDK documentation to check out the features not covered here.

■ **Note** If you require a comprehensive treatment of building web applications using ASP.NET, I suggest picking up a copy of *Pro ASP.NET 4.0 in VB 2010, Third Edition* by Dan Mabbutt and Matthew MacDonald (Apress, 2010).

Building a Single File ASP.NET Web Page

As it turns out, an ASP.NET web page can be constructed using one of two approaches, the first of which is to build a single `*.aspx` file that contains a blend of server-side code and HTML. Using this *single-file page model* approach, the server-side code is placed within a `<script>` scope, but the code itself is *not* script code proper (e.g., VBScript/JavaScript). Rather, the code within a `<script>` block are written in your .NET language of choice (VB 2010, C#, etc.).

If you are building a web page that contains very little code (but a good deal of static HTML), a single-file page model may be easier to work with, as you can see the code and the markup in one unified `*.aspx` file. In addition, placing your procedural code and HTML markup into a single `*.aspx` file provides a few other advantages:

- Pages written using the single-file model are slightly easier to deploy or to send to another developer.

- Because there is no dependency between multiple files, a single-file page is easier to rename.

- Managing files in a source code control system is slightly easier, as all the action is taking place in a single file.

On the downside, the single file page model can lead to the same problems you had under classic COM-based ASP: a single file that is doing too much (defining UI markup and programming logic in one place). Nevertheless, you'll begin your journey of ASP.NET by examining the single-file page model.

Your goal is to build an *.aspx file that displays the Inventory table of the AutoLot database (created in Chapter 21) using the connected layer (but, as you would guess, you could also use the disconnected layer or the Entity Framework). To begin, launch Visual Studio 2010 and create a new Web Form using the File ➤ New ➤ File menu option (see Figure 32-8).

Figure 32-8. Creating a new single file ASP.NET page

Once you have done so, save this file as Default1.aspx under a new directory on your hard drive that you can easily find later (for example, C:\MyCode\SinglePageModel).

Referencing AutoLotDAL.dll

Next, use Windows Explorer to create a subdirectory under the SinglePageModel folder named *bin*. The specially named bin subdirectory is a registered name with the ASP.NET runtime engine. Into the \bin folder of a website's root, you are able to deploy any private assemblies used by the web application. For this example, place a copy of AutoLotDAL.dll (see Chapter 21) into the C:\MyCode\ SinglePageModel\bin folder.

■ **Note** As shown later in this chapter, when you use Visual Studio 2010 to create an ASP.NET web project, the IDE will maintain the \bin folder on your behalf.

Designing the UI

Now, using the Visual Studio 2010 Toolbox, select the Standard tab and drag and drop a Button, Label, and GridView control (the GridView widget can be found under the Data tab of the Toolbox) onto the page designer between the opening and closing form elements. Feel free to make use of the Properties window to set various visual properties settings as you choose. Also, be sure to give each web widget a proper name via the ID attribute. Figure 32-9 shows one possible design. (I kept the example's look and feel intentionally bland to minimize the amount of control markup, but feel free to spruce things up to your liking.)

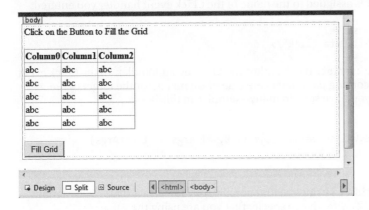

Figure 32-9. The Default.aspx GUI

Now, locate the <form> section of your page. Notice how each web control has been defined using an <asp:> tag. After this tag prefix, you will find the name of an ASP.NET web control (Label, GridView and Button). Before the closing tag of a given element, you will find a series of name/value pairs that correspond to the settings you made in the Properties window, for example:

```
<form id="form1" runat="server">
<div>
  <asp:Label ID="lblInfo" runat="server"
    Text="Click on the Button to Fill the Grid">
  </asp:Label>
  <br />
  <br />
  <asp:GridView ID="carsGridView" runat="server">
  </asp:GridView>
  <br />
  <asp:Button ID="btnFillData" runat="server" Text="Fill Grid" />
</div>
</form>
```

You will dig into the full details of ASP.NET web controls later in Chapter 33. Until then, recall that web controls are objects processed on the web server that emit back their HTML representation into the outgoing HTTP response automatically. Beyond this major benefit, ASP.NET web controls mimic a desktop-like programming model in that the names of the properties, methods, and events typically echo a Windows Forms/WPF counterpart.

Adding the Data Access Logic

Handle the Click event for the Button type using either the Visual Studio Properties window (via the lightning bolt icon) or the drop-down boxes mounted at the top of the designer window (like you did for this chapter's HTML review section). Once you do, you will find your Button's definition has been updated with an OnClick attribute that is assigned to the name of the Click event handler you entered:

```
<asp:Button ID="btnFillData" runat="server"
    Text="Fill Grid" OnClick="btnFillData_Click"/>
```

Now, within the *.aspx server side <script> block author the Click event handler. In the Click event handler code below, notice that the incoming parameters are a dead-on match for the target of the System.EventHandler delegate, which you have seen in many examples in this book:

```
<script runat="server">
  Protected Sub btnFillData_Click(ByVal sender As Object, ByVal args As EventArgs)
  End Sub
</script>
```

The next step is to populate the GridView using the functionality of your AutoLotDAL.dll assembly. To do so, you must use the <%@ Import %> directive to specify that you are using the AutoLotConnectedLayer namespace.

■ **Note** You will only need to use the <%@ Import %> directive if you are building a page with the single file code model. If you are using the default code file approach, you will simply use the Imports keyword of VB 2010 to include namespaces in your code file. The same is true for the <%@ Assembly %> directive, described next.

In addition, you need to inform the ASP.NET runtime that this single-file page is referencing the `AutoLotDAL.dll` assembly via the `<%@ Assembly %>` directive (more details on directives in just a moment). Here is the remaining relevant page logic of the `Default1.aspx` file (modify your connection string as required):

```
<%@ Page Language="VB" %>
<%@ Import Namespace = "AutoLotConnectedLayer" %>
<%@ Assembly Name ="AutoLotDAL" %>

<!DOCTYPE html PUBLIC "-//W3C//DTD XHTML 1.0 Transitional//EN"
  "http://www.w3.org/TR/xhtml1/DTD/xhtml1-transitional.dtd">

<script runat="server">
      Protected Sub btnFillData_Click(ByVal sender As Object, ByVal args As EventArgs)
        Dim dal As New InventoryDAL()
        dal.OpenConnection("Data Source=(local)\SQLEXPRESS;" &
                           "Initial Catalog=AutoLot;Integrated Security=True")

        carsGridView.DataSource = dal.GetAllInventoryAsList()
        carsGridView.DataBind()
        dal.CloseConnection()
      End Sub
</script>
<html xmlns="http://www.w3.org/1999/xhtml" >
...
</html>
```

Before you dive into the details behind the format of this `*.aspx` file, let's try a test run. First, save your `*.aspx` file. Now, right click anywhere on the `*.aspx` designer and select the View in Browser menu option, which will launch the ASP .NET Development web server, which, in turn, hosts your page.

When the page is served, you will initially see your `Label` and `Button` controls. However, when you click your button control, a postback occurs to the web server, at which point the web controls render back their corresponding HTML tags. Figure 32-10 shows the output once you click the Fill Grid button.

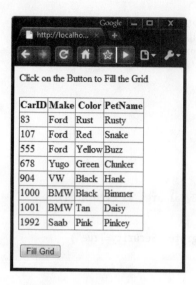

Figure 32-10. *ASP.NET provides a declarative data binding model*

Given, the current UI is quite bland. To spice up the current example, select the `GridView` control on the designer, and using the context menu (that tiny arrow on the upper left of the control), select the Auto Format option (Figure 32-11).

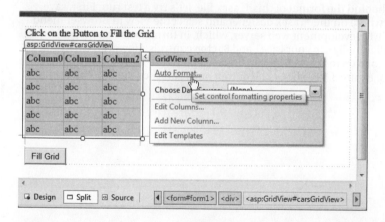

Figure 32-11. *A richer GridView control!*

From the resulting dialog box, pick a template that suits your fancy (I picked "Slate"). Once you click OK, view the generated control declaration, which is quite a bit richer than before:

```
<asp:GridView ID="carsGridView" runat="server" BackColor="White"
    BorderColor="#E7E7FF" BorderStyle="None" BorderWidth="1px" CellPadding="3"
    GridLines="Horizontal">
  <AlternatingRowStyle BackColor="#F7F7F7" />
  <FooterStyle BackColor="#B5C7DE" ForeColor="#4A3C8C" />
  <HeaderStyle BackColor="#4A3C8C" Font-Bold="True" ForeColor="#F7F7F7" />
  <PagerStyle BackColor="#E7E7FF" ForeColor="#4A3C8C" HorizontalAlign="Right" />
  <RowStyle BackColor="#E7E7FF" ForeColor="#4A3C8C" />
  <SelectedRowStyle BackColor="#738A9C" Font-Bold="True" ForeColor="#F7F7F7" />
  <SortedAscendingCellStyle BackColor="#F4F4FD" />
  <SortedAscendingHeaderStyle BackColor="#5A4C9D" />
  <SortedDescendingCellStyle BackColor="#D8D8F0" />
  <SortedDescendingHeaderStyle BackColor="#3E3277" />
</asp:GridView>
```

If you view your application again and click on your button, you will now see a more interesting UI (Figure 32-12), shown via Apple Safari on my Windows 7 install.

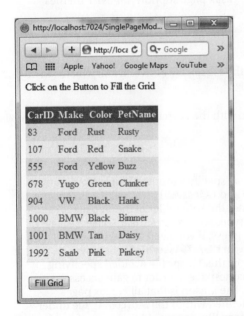

Figure 32-12. Your simple web page in Apple Safari

That was simple, yes? Of course, as they say, the devil is in the details, so let's dig a bit deeper into the composition of this *.aspx file, beginning with examining the role of the <%@Page... %> directive. Do be aware that the topics you examine will apply directly to the more preferred *code file* model examined next.

The Role of ASP.NET Directives

A given *.aspx file will typically open with a set of *directives*. ASP.NET directives are always denoted with <%@ ... %> markers and may be qualified with various attributes to inform the ASP.NET runtime how to process the attribute in question.

Every *.aspx file must have at minimum a <%@Page%> directive that is used to define the managed language used within the page (via the language attribute). Also, the <%@Page%> directive may define the name of the related code-behind file (examined soon), and so on. Table 32-1 documents some of the more interesting <%@Page%>-centric attributes.

Table 32-1. Select Attributes of the <%@Page%> Directive

Attribute	Meaning in Life
CodePage	Specifies the name of the related code-behind file
EnableTheming	Establishes whether the controls on the *.aspx page support ASP.NET themes
EnableViewState	Indicates whether view state is maintained across page requests (more details on this property in Chapter 33)
Inherits	Defines a class in the code-behind page the *.aspx file derives from, which can be any class derived from System.Web.UI.Page
MasterPageFile	Sets the master page used in conjunction with the current *.aspx page
Trace	Indicates whether tracing is enabled

In addition to the <%@Page%> directive, a given *.aspx file may specify various <%@Import%> directives to explicitly state the namespaces required by the current page and <%@Assembly%> directives to specify the external code libraries used by the site (typically placed under the \bin folder of the website).

In this example, you specified you were making use of the types within the AutoLotConnectedLayer namespace within the AutoLotDAL.dll assembly. As you would guess, if you need to make use of additional .NET namespaces, you simply specify multiple <%@Import%>/<%@Assembly%> directives.

Given your current knowledge of .NET, you may wonder how this *.aspx file avoided specifying additional <%@Import%> directives to gain access to the System namespace in order to gain access to the System.Object and System.EventHandler types (among others). The reason is that all *.aspx pages automatically have access to a set of key namespaces that are defined within the web.config file under your installation path of the .NET platform. Within this XML-based file, you would find a number of autoimported namespaces, including the following:

```
<pages>
  <namespaces>
    <add namespace="System"/>
    <add namespace="System.Collections"/>
    <add namespace="System.Collections.Generic"/>
    <add namespace="System.Collections.Specialized"/>
    <add namespace="System.Configuration"/>
```

```
<add namespace="System.Data.Entity.Design" />
<add namespace="System.Data.Linq" />
<add namespace="System.Linq" />
<add namespace="System.Text"/>
<add namespace="System.Text.RegularExpressions"/>
<add namespace="System.Web"/>
<add namespace="System.Web.Caching"/>
<add namespace="System.Web.SessionState"/>
<add namespace="System.Web.Security"/>
<add namespace="System.Web.Profile"/>
<add namespace="System.Web.UI"/>
<add namespace="System.Web.UI.WebControls"/>
<add namespace="System.Web.UI.WebControls.WebParts"/>
<add namespace="System.Web.UI.HtmlControls"/>
...
  </namespaces>
</pages>
```

To be sure, ASP.NET does define a number of other directives that may appear in an *.aspx file above and beyond <%@Page%>, <%@Import%>, and <%@Assembly%>; however, I'll reserve commenting on those for the time being. You'll see examples of other directives as you progress through the remaining chapters.

Analyzing the "Script" Block

Under the single-file page model, an *.aspx file may contain server-side scripting logic that executes on the web server. In this case, it is *critical* that all of your server-side code blocks are defined to execute at the server, using the runat="server" attribute. If the runat="server" attribute is not supplied, the runtime assumes you have authored a block of *client-side* script to be emitted into the outgoing HTTP response, and it will throw an exception. That being said, here is a proper server side <script> block:

■ **Note** All ASP.NET web controls will need to have the runat="server" attribute in their opening declaration. If not, they will not render their HTML into the outbound HTTP response.

```
<script runat="server">
    Protected Sub btnFillData_Click(ByVal sender As Object, ByVal args As EventArgs)
        Dim dal As New InventoryDAL()
        dal.OpenConnection("Data Source=(local)\SQLEXPRESS;" &
                            "Initial Catalog=AutoLot;Integrated Security=True")
        carsGridView.DataSource = dal.GetAllInventoryAsList()
        carsGridView.DataBind()
        dal.CloseConnection()
    End Sub
</script>
```

The signature of this helper method should look strangely familiar. Recall that a given control event handler must match the pattern defined by a related .NET delegate. The delegate in question is `System.EventHandler` that can only call methods that take `System.Object` as the first parameter and `System.EventArgs` as the second.

Analyzing the ASP.NET Control Declarations

The final point of interest in this first example is the declaration of the `Button`, `Label`, and `GridView` web controls. Like classic ASP and raw HTML, ASP.NET web widgets are scoped within `<form>` elements. This time, however, the opening `<form>` element is marked with the `runat="server"` attribute and is qualified with the `asp:` tag prefix. Any control which takes this prefix is a member of the ASP.NET control library and has a corresponding VB 2010 class representation in a given .NET namespace of the .NET base class libraries. Here you find:

```
<form id="form1" runat="server">
<div>
  <asp:Label ID="lblInfo" runat="server"
    Text="Click on the Button to Fill the Grid">
  </asp:Label>
  <br />
  <br />
  <asp:GridView ID="carsGridView" runat="server">
    ...
  </asp:GridView>
  <br />
  <asp:Button ID="btnFillData" runat="server" Text="Fill Grid" OnClick="btnFillData_Click"/>
</div>
</form>
```

The `System.Web.UI.WebControls` namespace of the `System.Web.dll` assembly contains a majority of the ASP.NET web controls. If you were to open the Visual Studio 2010 Object Browser, you could, for example, locate the `Label` control (Figure 32-13).

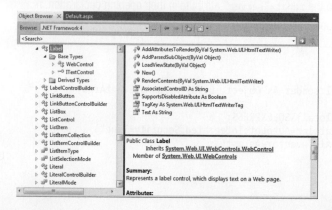

Figure 32-13. All ASP.NET control declarations map to a .NET class type

1452

As you can see, an ASP.NET web control has an inheritance chain with `System.Object` at the very top. The `WebControl` parent class is a common base to all ASP.NET controls and defines all the common UI properties you would expect (`BackColor`, `Height`, etc.). The `Control` class is also very common within the framework; however, it defines more infrastructure-centric members (data binding, view state, etc) rather than a child's graphical look and feel. You'll learn more about these classes in Chapter 33.

Compilation Cycle for Single-File Pages

If you are making use of the single-file page model, the HTML markup, server side `<script>` blocks, and web control definitions are dynamically compiled into a class type deriving from `System.Web.UI.Page` when the first request is made. The name of this class is based on the name of the `*.aspx` file and takes an `_aspx` suffix (e.g., a page named `MyPage.aspx` becomes a class named `MyPage_aspx`). Figure 32-14 illustrates the basic process.

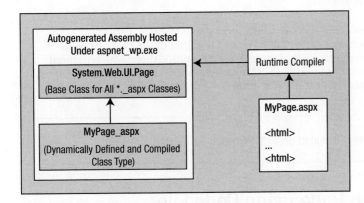

Figure 32-14. The compilation model for single-file pages

This dynamically compiled assembly is deployed to a runtime-defined subdirectory under the C:\Windows\Microsoft.NET\Framework\v4.0\Temporary ASP.NET Files root directory. The path beneath this root will differ based on a number of factors (hash codes, etc.), but if you are determined, eventually you will find the `*.dll` (and supporting files) in question. Figure 32-15 shows the generated assembly for the SinglePageModel example shown earlier in this chapter.

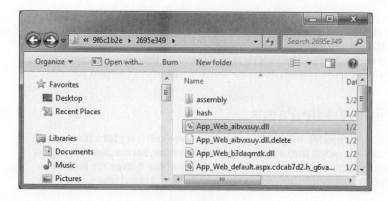

Figure 32-15. The ASP.NET autogenerated assembly

If you were to open this assembly into a tool such as ildasm.exe or reflector.exe, sure enough you will find a class extending Page, which each web control defined as a member of the class. Now, do be aware that you will typically never need to manually find, or in any way modify, these autogenerated assemblies. However, it is important to point out that if you change any aspect of your *.aspx file, it will be dynamically recompiled when a browser request the web page.

■ **Source Code** The SinglePageModel website is included under the Chapter 32 subdirectory.

Building an ASP.NET Web Page using Code Files

While the single file code model can be helpful at times, the default approach taken by Visual Studio 2010 (when creating a new web project) is to make use of a technique known as *code-behind*, which allows you to separate your programming code from your HTML presentation logic using two distinct files. This model works quite well when your pages contain a significant amount of code or when multiple developers are working on the same website. The code-behind model offers other benefits as well:

- Because code-behind pages offer a clean separation of HTML markup and code, it is possible to have designers working on the markup while programmers author the VB 2010 code.

- Code is not exposed to page designers or others who are working only with the page markup (as you might guess, HTML folks are not always interested in viewing reams of VB 2010 code).

- Code files can be used across multiple *.aspx files.

Regardless of which approach you take, there is *no* difference in terms of performance. In fact, many ASP.NET web applications will benefit from building sites that make use of both approaches.

To illustrate the code-behind page model, let's recreate the previous example using a blank Visual Studio 2010 Web Site template (note that Visual Studio 2010 is not required to build pages using code-behind). Activate the File ➤ New ➤ Web Site menu option and select the ASP.NET Empty Web Site template, as shown in Figure 32-16.

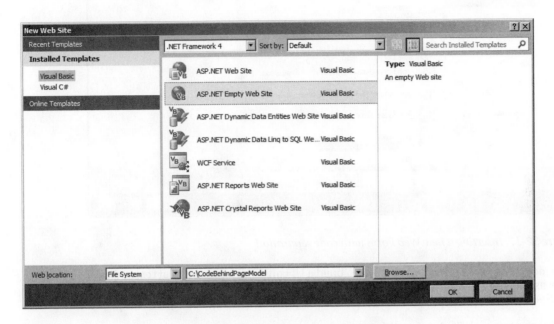

Figure 32-16. The ASP.NET Empty Web Site template

Notice in Figure 32-16 that you are able to select the location of your new site. If you select File System, your content files will be placed within a local directory and pages will be served via the ASP.NET development web server. If you select FTP or HTTP, your site will be hosted within a new virtual directory maintained by IIS. For this example, it makes no difference which option you select, but for simplicity I suggest selecting the File System option and specifying a new folder named C:\CodeBehindPageModel.

■ **Note** The Empty Web Site project template will automatically include a web.config file, which is similar to an App.config file for a desktop executable. You'll learn about the format of this file later in the chapter.

Now, using Website ➤ Add New Item... menu option, insert a new Web Form item named `Default.aspx`. You'll notice that, by default, the Place code in separate file checkbox is checked automatically, which is exactly what you want (Figure 32-17).

Figure 32-17. Inserting a new Web Form with code separation

Once again, make use of the designer to build a UI consisting of a `Label`, `Button`, and `GridView`, and make use of the Properties window to build a UI of your liking.

Note that the `<%@Page%>` directive has been updated with a few new attributes:

```
<%@ Page Language="VB" AutoEventWireup="False"
        CodeFile="Default.aspx.vb" Inherits="_Default" %>
```

The `CodeFile` attribute is used to specify the related external file that contains this page's coding logic. By default, these code-behind files are named by adding the suffix `.vb` to the name of the `*.aspx` file (`Default.aspx.vb` in this example). If you examine Solution Explorer, you will see this code-behind file is visible via a subnode on the Web Form icon (see Figure 32-18).

Figure 32-18. The associated code-behind file for a given `*.aspx` file

If you were to open your code-behind file, you would find a Partial class deriving from `System.Web.UI.Page`. Notice that the name of this class (`_Default`) is identical to the `Inherits` attribute within the `<%@Page%>` directive:

```
Partial Class _Default
    Inherits System.Web.UI.Page

End Class
```

Referencing the AutoLotDAL.dll Assembly

As previously mentioned, when creating web application projects using Visual Studio 2010, you do not need to manually build a \bin subdirectory and copy private assemblies by hand. For this example, activate the Add Reference dialog box using the Website menu option and reference `AutoLotDAL.dll`. When you do so, you will see the new \bin folder within Solution Explorer, as shown in Figure 32-19.

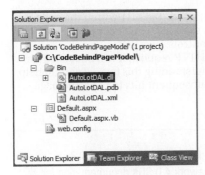

Figure 32-19. Visual Studio typically maintains special ASP.NET folders

Updating the Code File

Handle the `Click` event for the `Button` type by double-clicking the `Button` placed on the designer. As before, the `Button` definition has been updated with an `OnClick` attribute. However, the server-side event handler is no longer placed within a `<script>` scope of the `*.aspx` file but as a method of the `_Default` class type.

To complete this example, add a `using` statement for `AutoLotConnectedLayer` inside your code-behind file and implement the handler using the previous logic:

```
Imports AutoLotConnectedLayer

Partial Class _Default
        Inherits System.Web.UI.Page

    Protected Sub btnFillData_Click(ByVal sender As Object, ByVal e As EventArgs)
        Handles btnFillData.Click
```

```
        Dim dal As New InventoryDAL()
        dal.OpenConnection("Data Source=(local)\SQLEXPRESS;" & "Initial Catalog=AutoLot;" &
                                                              "Integrated Security=True")

        carsGridView.DataSource = dal.GetAllInventoryAsList()
        carsGridView.DataBind()
        dal.CloseConnection()
    End Sub
End Class
```

At this point, you can run your web site by pressing the Ctrl+F5 key combination. Once again, the ASP.NET development web server will fire up, serving your page into your hosting browser.

Compilation Cycle for Multifile Pages

The compilation process of a page making use of the code-behind model is similar to that of the single-file model. However, the type deriving from `System.Web.UI.Page` is composed of three files rather than the expected two.

Recall that the `Default.aspx` file was connected to a Partial class named `_Default` within the code-behind file. In addition, a third aspect of the Partial class generated in memory, which contains in-memory code that correctly sets properties and events on your web controls.

In any case, once the assembly has been created upon the initial HTTP request, it will be reused for all subsequent requests, and thus will not have to be recompiled. Understanding this factoid should help explain why the first request of an `*.aspx` page takes the longest and subsequent hits to the same page are extremely efficient.

■ **Note** Under ASP.NET, it is possible to precompile all pages (or a subset of pages) of a website using a command-line tool named `aspnet_compiler.exe`. Check out the .NET Framework 4.0 SDK documentation for details.

Debugging and Tracing ASP.NET Pages

When you are building ASP.NET web projects, you can use the same debugging techniques as you would with any other sort of Visual Studio 2010 project type. Thus, you can set breakpoints in your code-behind file (as well as embedded "script" blocks in an `*.aspx` file), start a debug session (via the F5 key, by default), and step through your code.

However, to debug your ASP.NET web applications, your site must contain a properly configured `Web.config` file. By default, all Visual Studio 2010 web projects will automatically have a `Web.config` file. However, debugging support is initially disabled (as debugging would degrade performance). When you start a debugging session, the IDE will prompt you whether you would like to modify `Web.config` to enable debugging. Once you have opted to do so, the `<compilation>` element of the `Web.config` file is updated like so:

```
<compilation debug="true" strict="false" explicit="true" targetFramework="4.0"/>
```

On a related note, you are also able to enable *tracing support* for an *.aspx file by setting the Trace attribute to true within the <%@Page%> directive (it is also possible to enable tracing for your entire site by modifying the Web.config file):

```
<%@ Page Language="VB" AutoEventWireup="false"
        CodeFile="Default.aspx.vb" Inherits="_Default" Trace="true" %>
```

Once you do, the emitted HTML contains numerous details regarding the previous HTTP request/response (server variables, session and application variables, request/response, etc.). To insert your own trace messages into the mix, you can use the Trace property inherited from System.Web.UI.Page.

Anytime you wish to log a custom message (from a script block or VB 2010 source code file), simply call the Shared Trace.Write() method. The first argument represents the name of your custom category, the second argument specifies the trace message. To illustrate, update the Click handler of your Button with the following code statement:

```
Protected Sub btnFillData_Click(ByVal sender As Object, ByVal e As EventArgs)
    Handles btnFillData.Click
        Trace.Write("CodeFileTraceInfo!", "Filling the grid!")
...
End Sub
```

Run your project once again and click the button. You will find your custom category and custom message are present and accounted for. In Figure 32-20, take note of the highlighted message that displays the trace information.

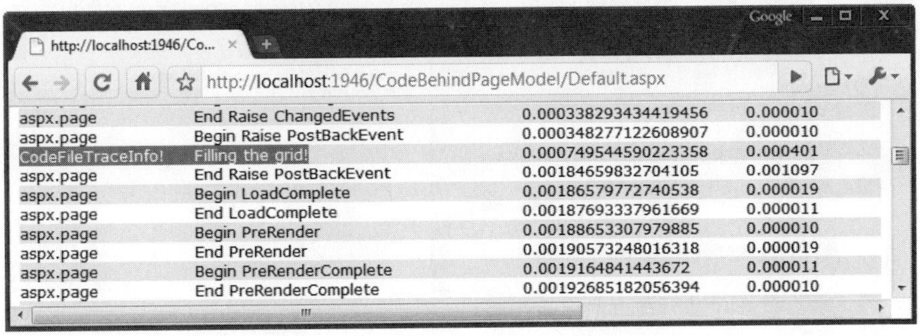

Figure 32-20. Logging custom trace messages

At this point, you have seen how to build a single ASP.NET web page using the single-file and code-file approach. The remaining topics of this chapter will take a deeper look into the composition of an ASP.NET web project, as well as ways to interact with the HTTP request/response and the life cycle of a Page derived class. Before you dive in, I need to clarify the distinction between an ASP.NET Web Site and an ASP.NET Web Application.

■ **Source Code** The CodeBehindPageModel website is included under the Chapter 32 subdirectory.

ASP.NET Web Sites and ASP.NET Web Applications

When you are about to build a new ASP.NET web application, you will need to make a choice regard which of two project formats you will make use of, specifically an *ASP.NET Web Site* or an *ASP.NET Web Application*. Your choice of web project will control the way in which Visual Studio organizes and processes your web application starter files, the type of initial project files that are created, and how much control you have over the resulting composition of the compiled .NET assembly.

When ASP.NET was first released with .NET 1.0, the only option was to build what is now termed a *web application*. Under this model, you have direct control over the name and location of the compiled output assembly. As well, under this model, the in-memory Partial class which contains control declarations and configurations is *not* in memory but rather found within another physical VB 2010 code file.

Web applications are useful when you are migrating older .NET 1.1 web sites into .NET 2.0 and higher projects. Web applications are also helpful when you wish to build a single Visual Studio 2010 Solution that can contain multiple projects (for example, the web application and three related .NET code libraries). To build an ASP.NET Web Application, you activate the File ➤ New Project... menu item and pick a template from the Web category (Figure 32-21).

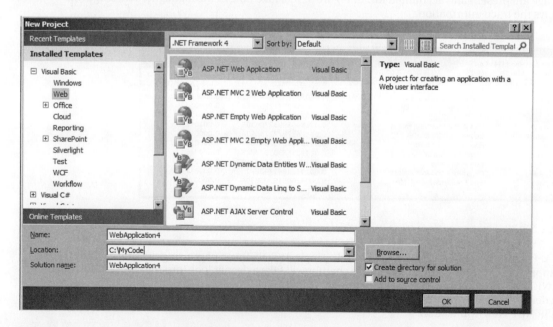

Figure 32-21. The Visual Studio Web Application Templates

You have no need to do so now; however, assume you did create a new ASP.NET Web Application project. You will find a large number of starter files (which will make sense as you work through the chapters to come), but most importantly note that each ASP.NET web page is composed of three files; the `*.aspx` file (for markup), the `*.Designer.vb` file (for designer-generated VB 2010 code), and the primary VB 2010 code file (for your event handlers, custom methods and whatnot). See Figure 32-22.

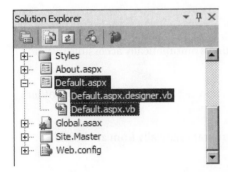

Figure 32-22. Under the Web Application model, each web page is composed of three files

In stark contrast, the Visual Studio 2010 ASP.NET Web Site project templates (found under the File ➤ New Web Site... menu option) hides the `*.Designer.vb` file in favor of an in-memory Partial class. Moreover, ASP.NET Web Site projects support a number of specially named folders, such as App_Code. Within this folder, you can place any VB 2010 (or C#) code files that are not directly mapped to your web pages, and the runtime compiler will dynamically compile them as required. This is a great simplification to the normal act of building a dedicated .NET code library and referencing it in new projects. On a related note, a Web Site project can be pushed as-is to a production web server without the need to precompile the site as you would need to do with an ASP.NET Web Application.

In this book, I'll make use of ASP.NET Web Site project types, as they do offer some simplifications to the process of building web applications under the .NET platform. However, regardless of which approach you take, you will have access to the same overall programming model.

■ **Note** Because the Visual Studio 2010 ASP.NET project templates generate a great deal of starter code (master pages, content pages, script libraries, a log in page, etc), this book will opt to use the Blank web site template. However, once you have completed reading the ASP.NET chapters of this text, make sure you create a new ASP.NET web site project and examine this starter code first hand.

The ASP.NET Web Site Directory Structure

When you create a new ASP.NET Web Site project, your project may contain any number of specifically named subdirectories, each of which has a special meaning to the ASP.NET runtime. Table 32-2 documents these special subdirectories.

Table 32-2. Special ASP.NET Subdirectories

Subfolder	Meaning in Life
App_Browsers	Folder for browser definition files that are used to identify individual browsers and determine their capabilities
App_Code	Folder for source code for components or classes that you want to compile as part of your application. ASP.NET compiles the code in this folder when pages are requested. Code in the App_Code folder is automatically accessible by your application
App_Data	Folder for storing Access *.mdb files, SQL Express *.mdf files, XML files, or other data stores
App_GlobalResources	Folder for *.resx files that are accessed programmatically from application code
App_LocalResources	Folder for *.resx files that are bound to a specific page
App_Themes	Folder that contains a collection of files that define the appearance of ASP.NET web pages and controls
App_WebReferences	Folder for proxy classes, schemas, and other files associated with using a web service in your application
Bin	Folder for compiled private assemblies (*.dll files). Assemblies in the Bin folder are automatically referenced by your application

If you are interested in adding any of these known subfolders to your current web application, you may do so explicitly using the Website ➤ Add Folder menu option. However, in many cases, the IDE will automatically do so as you naturally insert related files into your site. For example, inserting a new class file into your project will automatically add an App_Code folder to your directory structure if one does not currently exist.

Referencing Assemblies

Although the Web Site templates do generate an *.sln file to load your *.aspx files into the IDE, there is no longer a related *.vbproj file. However, an ASP.NET Web Application projects records all external assemblies within *.vbproj. So where are the external assemblies recorded under ASP.NET?

As you have seen, when you reference a private assembly, Visual Studio 2010 will automatically create a \bin directory within your directory structure to store a local copy of the binary. When your code base makes use of types within these code libraries, they are automatically loaded on demand.

If you reference a shared assembly located in the Global Assembly Cache, Visual Studio 2010 will automatically insert a Web.config file into your current web solution (if one is not currently in place) and record the external reference within the <assemblies> element. For example, if you again activate the

Web Site ➤ Add Reference menu option and this time select a shared assembly (such as System.Data.OracleClient.dll), you will find that your Web.config file has been updated as follows:

```
<assemblies>
  <add assembly="System.Data.OracleClient, Version=4.0.0.0,
       Culture=neutral, PublicKeyToken=B03F5F7F11D50A3A"/>
</assemblies>
```

As you can see, each assembly is described using the same information required for a dynamic load via the Assembly.Load() method (see Chapter 15).

The Role of the App_Code Folder

The App_Code folder is used to store source code files that are not directly tied to a specific web page (such as a code-behind file) but are to be compiled for use by your website. Code within the App_Code folder will be automatically compiled on the fly on an as-needed basis. After this point, the assembly is accessible to any other code in the website. To this end, the App_Code folder is much like the Bin folder, except that you can store source code in it instead of compiled code. The major benefit of this approach is that it is possible to define custom types for your web application without having to compile them independently.

A single App_Code folder can contain code files from multiple languages. At runtime, the appropriate compiler kicks in to generate the assembly in question. If you would rather partition your code, however, you can define multiple subdirectories that are used to hold any number of managed code files (*.vb, *.cs, etc.).

For example, assume you have added an App_Code folder to the root directory of a website application that has two subfolders, MyVbNetCode and MyCSharpCode, that contain language-specific files. Once you do, you are able to update your Web.config file to specify these subdirectories using a <codeSubDirectories> element nested within the <configuration> element:

```
<compilation debug="false" strict="false" explicit="true"targetFramework="4.0">
  <codeSubDirectories>
        <add directoryName="MyVbNetCode" />
        <add directoryName="MyCSharpCode" />
  </codeSubDirectories>
...
</compilation>
```

■ **Note** The App_Code directory will also be used to contain files that are not language files but are useful nonetheless (*.xsd files, *.wsdl files, etc.).

Beyond Bin and App_Code, the App_Data and App_Themes folders are two additional special subdirectories that you should be familiar with, both of which will be detailed in the next several chapters. As always, consult the .NET Framework 4.0 SDK documentation for full details of the remaining ASP.NET subdirectories if you require further information.

The Inheritance Chain of the Page Type

As you have just seen, all .NET web pages eventually derive from System.Web.UI.Page. Like any base class, this type provides a polymorphic interface to all derived types. However, the Page type is not the only member in your inheritance hierarchy. If you were to locate the System.Web.UI.Page class (within the System.Web.dll assembly) using the Visual Studio 2010 object browser, you would find that Page is-a TemplateControl, which is-a Control, which is-a Object (see Figure 32-23).

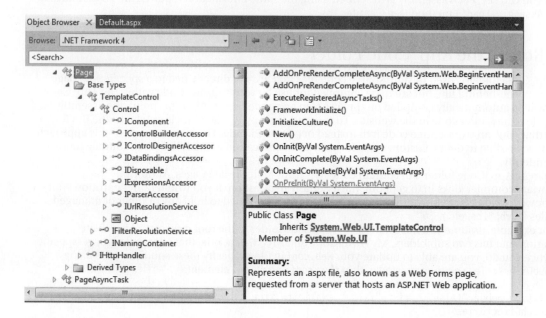

Figure 32-23. The inheritance chain of Page

Each of these base classes brings a good deal of functionality to each and every *.aspx file. For the majority of your projects, you will make use of the members defined within the Page and Control parent classes. The functionality gained from the System. Web.UI.TemplateControl class is only of interest if you are building custom Web Form controls or interacting with the rendering process.

The first parent class of interest is Page itself. Here you will find numerous properties that enable you to interact with various web primitives such as application and session variables, the HTTP request/response, theme support, and so forth. Table 32-3 describes some (but by no means all) of the core properties.

Table 32-3. Select Properties of the Page Type

Property	Meaning in Life
Application	Allows you to interact with data that can be accessed across the entire website for all users
Cache	Allows you to interact with the cache object for the current website
ClientTarget	Allows you to specify how this page should render itself based on the requesting browser
IsPostBack	Gets a value indicating whether the page is being loaded in response to a client postback or whether it is being loaded and accessed for the first time
MasterPageFile	Establishes the master page for the current page
Request	Provides access to the current HTTP request
Response	Allows you to interact with the outgoing HTTP response
Server	Provides access to the HttpServerUtility object, which contains various server-side helper methods
Session	Allows you to interact with the session data for the current caller
Theme	Gets or sets the name of the theme used for the current page
Trace	Provides access to a TraceContext object, which allows you to log custom messages during debugging sessions

Interacting with the Incoming HTTP Request

As you saw earlier in this chapter, the basic flow of a web application begins with a client requesting a web page, possibly filling in user information, and clicking a "Submit button" to post back the HTML form data to a given web page for processing. In most cases, the opening tag of the form statement specifies an action attribute and a method attribute that indicates the file on the web server that will be sent the data in the various HTML widgets, as well as the method of sending this data (GET or POST):

```
<form name="defaultPage" id="defaultPage"
      action="http://localhost/Cars/ClassicAspPage.asp" method = "GET">
...
</form>
```

All ASP.NET pages support the System.Web.UI.Page.Request property, which provides access to an instance of the HttpRequest class type (see Table 32-4 for some common members of this class).

Table 32-4. Members of the HttpRequest Type

Member	Meaning in Life
ApplicationPath	Gets the ASP.NET application's virtual application root path on the server
Browser	Provides information about the capabilities of the client browser
Cookies	Gets a collection of cookies sent by the client browser
FilePath	Indicates the virtual path of the current request
Form	Gets a collection of HTTP form variables
Headers	Gets a collection of HTTP headers
HttpMethod	Indicates the HTTP data transfer method used by the client (GET, POST)
IsSecureConnection	Indicates whether the HTTP connection is secure (i.e., HTTPS)
QueryString	Gets the collection of HTTP query string variables
RawUrl	Gets the current request's raw URL
RequestType	Indicates the HTTP data transfer method used by the client (GET, POST)
ServerVariables	Gets a collection of web server variables
UserHostAddress	Gets the IP host address of the remote client
UserHostName	Gets the DNS name of the remote client

In addition to these properties, the HttpRequest type has a number of useful methods, including the following:

- MapPath(): Maps the virtual path in the requested URL to a physical path on the server for the current request

- SaveAs(): Saves details of the current HTTP request to a file on the web server, which can prove helpful for debugging purposes.

- ValidateInput(): If the validation feature is enabled via the Validate attribute of the page directive, this method can be called to check all user input data (including cookie data) against a predefined list of potentially dangerous input data.

Obtaining Brower Statistics

The first interesting aspect of the `HttpRequest` type is the `Browser` property, which provides access to an underlying `HttpBrowserCapabilities` object. `HttpBrowserCapabilities,` in turn, exposes numerous members that allow you to programmatically investigate statistics regarding the browser that sent the incoming HTTP request.

Create a new ASP.NET website named `FunWithPageMembers` (again, elect to use the File System option). Your first task is to build a UI that allows users to click a `Button` web control (named `btnGetBrowserStats`) to view various statistics about the calling browser. These statistics will be generated dynamically and attached to a `Label` type (named `lblOutput`). The button's `Click` event handler is as follows:

```
Protected Sub btnGetBrowserStats_Click(ByVal sender As Object, ByVal e As EventArgs)
    Handles btnGetBrowserStats.Click
    Dim theInfo As String = ""
    theInfo &= String.Format("<li>Is the client AOL? {0}</li>", Request.Browser.AOL),
    theInfo &= String.Format("<li>Does the client support ActiveX? {0}</li>"
                                        Request.Browser.ActiveXControls)
    theInfo &= String.Format("<li>Is the client a Beta? {0}</li>", Request.Browser.Beta)
    theInfo &= String.Format("<li>Does the client support Java Applets? {0}</li>"
                                        Request.Browser.JavaApplets),
    theInfo &= String.Format("<li>Does the client support Cookies? {0}</li>",
    Request.Browser.Cookies)
    theInfo &= String.Format("<li>Does the client support VBScript? {0}</li>",
                                        Request.Browser.VBScript)

    lblOutput.Text = theInfo
End Sub
```

Here you are testing for a number of browser capabilities. As you would guess, it is (very) helpful to discover a browser's support for ActiveX controls, Java applets, and client-side VBScript code. If the calling browser does not support a given web technology, your `*.aspx` page will be able to take an alternative course of action.

Access to Incoming Form Data

Other aspects of the `HttpResponse` type are the `Form` and `QueryString` properties. These two properties allow you to examine the incoming form data using name/value pairs. While you could make use of the `HttpRequest.Form` and `HttpRequest.QueryString` properties to access client-supplied form data on the web server, ASP.NET provides a more elegant, object-oriented approach. Given that ASP.NET supplies you with server-side web controls, you are able to treat HTML UI elements as true objects. Therefore, rather than obtaining the value within a text box as follows

```
Protected Sub btnGetFormData_Click(ByVal sender As Object, ByVal e As EventArgs)
    Handles btnGetFormData.Click
        ' Get value for a widget with ID txtFirstName.
        Dim firstName As String = Request.Form("txtFirstName")

        ' Use this value in your page ...
End Sub
```

you can simply ask the server-side widget directly via the Text property for use in your program, like so

```
Protected Sub btnGetFormData_Click(ByVal sender As Object, ByVal e As EventArgs)
    Handles btnGetFormData.Click
        ' Get value for a widget with ID txtFirstName.
        Dim firstName As String = txtFirstName.Text

        ' Use this value in your page ...
End Sub
```

Not only does this approach lend itself to solid OO principles, but also you do not need to concern yourself with how the form data was submitted (GET or POST) before obtaining the values. Furthermore, working with the widget directly is much more type-safe, given that typing errors are discovered at compile time rather than runtime. Of course, this is not to say that you will *never* need to make use of the Form or QueryString property in ASP.NET; rather, the need to do so has greatly diminished and is usually optional.

The IsPostBack Property

Another very important member of HttpRequest is the IsPostBack property. Recall that "postback" refers to a web page posting back to the same URL at the Web server. Given this definition, understand that the IsPostBack property will return True if the current HTTP request has been sent by a user currently in session, and False if this is the user's first interaction with the page.

Typically, the need to determine whether the current HTTP request is indeed a postback is most helpful when you wish to execute a block of code only the first time the user accesses a given page. For example, you may wish to populate an ADO.NET DataSet when the user first accesses an *.aspx file and cache the object for later use. When the caller returns to the page, you can avoid the need to hit the database unnecessarily (of course, some pages may require that the DataSet always be updated upon each request, but that is another issue). Assuming your *.aspx file has handled the page's Load event (described in detail later in this chapter), you could programmatically test for postback conditions as follows:

```
Protected Sub Page_Load(ByVal sender As Object, ByVal e As System.EventArgs)
    Handles Me.Load
        ' Fill DataSet only the very first time
        ' the user comes to this page.
        If Not IsPostBack Then
            ' Populate DataSet and cache it!
        End If
        ' Use cached DataSet.
End Sub
```

Interacting with the Outgoing HTTP Response

Now that you have a better understanding of how the Page type allows you to interact with the incoming HTTP request, the next step is to see how to interact with the outgoing HTTP response. In ASP.NET, the Response property of the Page class provides access to an instance of the HttpResponse type. This type defines a number of properties that allow you to format the HTTP response sent back to the client browser. Table 32-5 lists some core properties.

Table 32-5. Properties of the HttpResponse Type

Property	Meaning in Life
Cache	Returns the caching semantics of the web page (see Chapter 34)
ContentEncoding	Gets or sets the HTTP character set of the output stream
ContentType	Gets or sets the HTTP MIME type of the output stream
Cookies	Gets the HttpCookie collection that will be returned to the browser
Output	Enables text output to the outgoing HTTP content body
OutputStream	Enables binary output to the outgoing HTTP content body
StatusCode	Gets or sets the HTTP status code of output returned to the client
StatusDescription	Gets or sets the HTTP status string of output returned to the client
SuppressContent	Gets or sets a value indicating that HTTP content will not be sent to the client

Also, consider the partial list of methods supported by the HttpResponse type described in Table 32-6.

Table 32-6. Methods of the HttpResponse Type

Method	Meaning in Life
Clear()	Clears all headers and content output from the buffer stream
End()	Sends all currently buffered output to the client and then closes the socket connection
Flush()	Sends all currently buffered output to the client
Redirect()	Redirects a client to a new URL
Write()	Writes values to an HTTP output content stream
WriteFile()	Writes a file directly to an HTTP content output stream

Emitting HTML Content

Perhaps the most well-known aspect of the HttpResponse type is the ability to write content directly to the HTTP output stream. The HttpResponse.Write() method allows you to pass in any HTML tags and/or text literals. The HttpResponse.WriteFile() method takes this functionality one step further, in that you can specify the name of a physical file on the web server whose contents should be rendered to the output stream (this is quite helpful to quickly emit the contents of an existing *.htm file).

To illustrate, assume you have added another Button type to your current *.aspx file that implements the server-side Click event handler like so:

```
Protected Sub btnHttpResponse_Click(ByVal sender As Object, ByVal e As EventArgs)
    Handles btnHttpResponse.Click
        Response.Write("<b>My name is:</b><br>")
        Response.Write(Me.ToString())
        Response.Write("<br><br><b>Here was your last request:</b><br>")
        Response.WriteFile("MyHTMLPage.htm")
End Sub
```

The role of this helper method is quite simple. The only point of interest is the fact that the HttpResponse.WriteFile() method is now emitting the contents of a server-side *.htm file within the root directory of the website.

Again, while you can always take this old-school approach and render HTML tags and content using the Write() method, this approach is far less common under ASP.NET than with classic ASP. The reason is (once again) due to the advent of server-side web controls. Thus, if you wish to render a block of textual data to the browser, your task is as simple as assigning a string to the Text property of a Label widget.

Redirecting Users

Another aspect of the HttpResponse type is the ability to redirect the user to a new URL:

```
Protected Sub btnWasteTime_Click(ByVal sender As Object, ByVal e As EventArgs)
    Handles btnWasteTime.Click
        Response.Redirect("http://www.facebook.com")
End Sub
```

If this event handler is invoked via a client-side postback, the user will automatically be redirected to the specified URL.

■ **Note** The HttpResponse.Redirect() method will always entail a trip back to the client browser. If you simply wish to transfer control to an *.aspx file in the same virtual directory, the HttpServerUtility.Transfer() method, accessed via the inherited Server property, is more efficient.

So much for investigating the functionality of `System.Web.UI.Page`. I will examine the role of the `System.Web.UI.Control` base class in the next chapter. Next up, let's examine the life and times of a **Page**-derived object.

■ **Source Code** The FunWithPageMembers website is included under the Chapter 32 subdirectory.

The Life Cycle of an ASP.NET Web Page

Every ASP.NET web page has a fixed life cycle. When the ASP.NET runtime receives an incoming request for a given `*.aspx` file, the associated `System.Web.UI.Page`-derived type is allocated into memory using the type's default constructor. After this point, the framework will automatically fire a series of events. By default, the **Load** event is automatically accounted for, where you can add your custom code:

```
Partial Class _Default
    Inherits System.Web.UI.Page

        Protected Sub Page_Load(ByVal sender As Object, ByVal e As EventArgs)
                Handles Me.Load
                Response.Write("Load event fired!")
        End Sub
End Class
```

Beyond the **Load** event, a given **Page** is able to intercept any of the core events in Table 32-7, which are listed in the order in which they are encountered (consult the .NET Framework 4.0 SDK documentation for details on all possible events that may fire during a page's lifetime).

Table 32-7. Select Events of the Page Type

Event	Meaning in Life
PreInit	The framework uses this event to allocate any web controls, apply themes, establish the master page, and set user profiles. You may intercept this event to customize the process.
Init	The framework uses this event to set the properties of web controls to their previous values via postback or view state data.
Load	When this event fires, the page and its controls are fully initialized, and their previous values are restored. At this point, it is safe to interact with each web widget.
"Event that triggered the postback"	There is, of course, no event of this name. This "event" simply refers to whichever event caused the browser to perform the postback to the web server (such as a **Button** click).

Continued

Event	Meaning in Life
PreRender	All control data binding and UI configuration has occurred and the controls are ready to render their data into the outbound HTTP response.
Unload	The page and its controls have finished the rendering process, and the page object is about to be destroyed. At this point, it is a runtime error to interact with the outgoing HTTP response. You may, however, capture this event to perform any page-level cleanup (close file or database connections, perform any form of logging activity, dispose of objects, etc.).

When a VB 2010 programmer needs to handle events beyond Load, There are combo boxes in the top of the code editor window, where you can author a method in your code file taking the name Page_*NameOfEvent*. For example, here is how you can handle the Unload event:

```
Partial Class _Default
    Inherits System.Web.UI.Page

    Protected Sub Page_Load(ByVal sender As Object, ByVal e As EventArgs)
    Handles Me.Load
    Response.Write("Load event fired!")
    End Sub

    Protected Sub Page_Unload(ByVal sender As Object, ByVal e As EventArgs)
    Handles Me.UnLoad
        ' No longer possible to emit data to the HTTP
        ' response, so we will write to a local file.
        System.IO.File.WriteAllText("C:\MyLog.txt", "Page unloading!")
    End Sub
End Class
```

■ **Note** Each event of the Page type works in conjunction with the System.EventHandler delegate; therefore, the methods that handle these events always take an Object as the first parameter and an EventArgs as the second parameter.

The Error Event

Another event that may occur during your page's life cycle is Error. This event will be fired if a method on the Page-derived type triggered an exception that was not explicitly handled. Assume that you have handled the Click event for a given Button on your page, and within the event handler (which I named btnGetFile_Click), you attempt to write out the contents of a local file to the HTTP response.

Also assume you have *failed* to test for the presence of this file via standard structured exception handling. If you have defined a handler for the Page's Error event, you have one final chance to deal with the problem on this page before the end user finds an ugly error. Consider the following code:

```
Partial Class _Default
    Inherits System.Web.UI.Page

Protected Sub Page_Error(ByVal sender As Object, ByVal e As EventArgs) Handles Me.Error
        Response.Clear()
        Response.Write("I am sorry...I can't find a required file.<br>")
        Response.Write(String.Format("The error was: <b>{0}</b>",
        Server.GetLastError().Message))
        Server.ClearError()
    End Sub

    Protected Sub Page_Load(ByVal sender As Object, ByVal e As EventArgs) Handles Me.Load
        Response.Write("Load event fired!")
    End Sub

    Protected Sub Page_Unload(ByVal sender As Object, ByVal e As EventArgs)
        Handles Me.UnLoad
        ' No longer possible to emit data to the HTTP
        ' response at this point, so we will write to a local file.
        System.IO.File.WriteAllText("C:\MyLog.txt", "Page unloading!")
    End Sub

    Protected Sub btnPostback_Click(ByVal sender As Object, ByVal e As EventArgs)
        Handles btnPostBack.Click
        ' Nothing happens here, this is just to ensure a
        ' postback to the page.
    End Sub

    Protected Sub btnTriggerError_Click(ByVal sender As Object, ByVal e As EventArgs)
        Handles btnTriggerError.Click
        System.IO.File.ReadAllText("C:\IDontExist.txt")
    End Sub
End Class
```

Notice that your `Error` event handler begins by clearing out any content currently within the HTTP response and emits a generic error message. If you wish to gain access to the specific `System.Exception` object, you may do so using the `HttpServerUtility.GetLastError()` method exposed by the inherited `Server` property:

```
Dim e As Exception = Server.GetLastError()
```

Finally, note that before exiting this generic error handler, you are explicitly calling the `HttpServerUtility.ClearError()` method via the `Server` property. This is required, as it informs the runtime that you have dealt with the issue at hand and require no further processing. If you forget to do so, the end user will be presented with the runtime's error page. Figure 32-24 shows the result of this error-trapping logic.

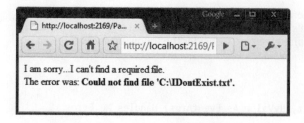

Figure 32-24. *Page-level error handling*

At this point, you should feel confident with the composition of an ASP.NET **Page** type. Now that you have such a foundation, you can turn your attention to the role of ASP.NET web controls, themes, and master pages, all of which are the subject of remaining chapters. To wrap up this chapter, however, let's examine the role of the **Web.config** file.

■ **Source Code** The PageLifeCycle website is included under the Chapter 32 subdirectory.

The Role of the Web.config File

By default, all VB 2010 ASP.NET web applications created with Visual Studio 2010 are automatically provided with a **Web.config** file. However, if you ever need to manually insert a **Web.config** file into your site (e.g., when you are working with the single-page model and have not created a web solution), you may do so using the using the Website ➤ Add New Item menu option. In either case, within this scope of a **Web.config** file you are able to add settings that control how your web application will function at runtime.

Recall during your examination of .NET assemblies (in Chapter 15) that you learned client applications can leverage an XML-based configuration file to instruct the CLR how it should handle binding requests, assembly probing, and other runtime details. The same holds true for ASP.NET web applications, with the notable exception that web-centric configuration files are always named **Web.config** (unlike *.exe configuration files, which are named based on the related client executable).

The full structure of a **Web.config** file is rather verbose. However, Table 32-8 outlines some of the more interesting subelements that can be found within a **Web.config** file.

Table 32-8. Select Elements of a `Web.config` *File*

Element	Meaning in Life
`<appSettings>`	This element is used to establish custom name/value pairs that can be programmatically read in memory for use by your pages using the `ConfigurationManager` type.
`<authentication>`	This security-related element is used to define the authentication mode for this web application.
`<authorization>`	This is another security-centric element used to define which users can access which resources on the web server.
`<connectionStrings>`	This element is used to hold external connection strings used within this website.
`<customErrors>`	This element is used to tell the runtime exactly how to display errors that occur during the functioning of the web application.
`<globalization>`	This element is used to configure the globalization settings for this web application.
`<namespaces>`	This element documents all of the namespaces to include if your web application has been precompiled using the new `aspnet_compiler.exe` command-line tool.
`<sessionState>`	This element is used to control how and where session state data will be stored by the .NET runtime.
`<trace>`	This element is used to enable (or disable) tracing support for this web application.

A `Web.config` file may contain additional subelements above and beyond the set presented in Table 32-8. The vast majority of these items are security related, while the remaining items are useful only during advanced ASP.NET scenarios such as creating with custom HTTP headers or custom HTTP modules (topics that are not covered here).

The ASP.NET Website Administration Utility

Although you are always free to modify the content of a `Web.config` file directly using Visual Studio 2010, ASP.NET web projects can make use of a handy web-based editor that will allow you to graphically edit numerous elements and attributes of your project's `Web.config` file. To launch this tool, activate the Website ➤ ASP.NET Configuration menu option.

If you were to click the tabs located on the top of the page, you would quickly notice that most of this tool's functionality is used to establish security settings for your website. However, this tool also makes it possible to add settings to your `<appSettings>` element, define debugging and tracing settings, and establish a default error page.

You'll see more of this tool in action where necessary; however, do be aware that this utility will *not* allow you to add all possible settings to a `Web.config` file. There will most certainly be times when you will need to manually update this file using your text editor of choice.

Summary

Building web applications requires a different frame of mind than is used to assemble traditional desktop applications. In this chapter, you began with a quick and painless review of some core web topics, including HTML, HTTP, the role of client-side scripting, and server-side scripts using classic ASP. The bulk of this chapter was spent examining the architecture of an ASP.NET page. As you have seen, each `*.aspx` file in your project has an associated `System.Web.UI.Page`-derived class. Using this OO approach, ASP.NET allows you to build more reusable and OO-aware systems.

After examining some of the core functionality of a page's inheritance chain, this chapter then discussed how your pages are ultimately compiled into a valid .NET assembly. We wrapped up by exploring the role of the `Web.config` file and overviewed the ASP.NET Web Site Administration tool.

CHAPTER 33

ASP.NET Web Controls, Master Pages, and Themes

The previous chapter concentrated on the composition and behavior of ASP.NET **Page** objects. This chapter will dive into the details of the *web controls* that make up a page's user interface. After examining the overall nature of an ASP.NET web control, you will come to understand how to make use of several UI elements including the validation controls and various data binding controls.

The bulk of this chapter will examine the role of *master pages* and show how they provide a simplified manner to define a common UI skeleton that will be replicated across the pages in your website. Closely related to the topic of master pages is the use of site navigation controls (and a related ***.sitemap** file) that allow you to define the navigational structure of a multi-paged site via a server side XML file.

To wrap things up, you will learn about the role of ASP.NET themes. Conceptually, themes serve the same purpose as a cascading style sheet; however, ASP.NET themes are applied on the web server (as opposed to within the client side browser) and therefore have access to server side resources.

Understanding the Nature of Web Controls

A major benefit of ASP.NET is the ability to assemble the UI of your pages using the types defined in the **System.Web.UI.WebControls** namespace. As you have seen, these controls (which go by the names *server controls*, *web controls*, or *Web Form controls*) are extremely helpful in that they automatically generate the necessary HTML for the requesting browser and expose a set of events that may be processed on the web server. Furthermore, because each ASP.NET control has a corresponding class in the **System.Web.UI.WebControls** namespace, it can be manipulated in an object-oriented manner.

When you configure the properties of a web control using the Visual Studio 2010 Properties window, your edits are recorded in the opening control declaration of a given element in the ***.aspx** file as a series of name/value pairs. Thus, if you add a new **TextBox** to the designer of a given ***.aspx** file and change the **ID**, **BorderStyle**, **BorderWidth**, **BackColor**, and **Text** properties, the opening **<asp:TextBox>** tag is modified accordingly (however, note that the **Text** value becomes the inner text of the **TextBox** scope):

```
<asp:TextBox ID="txtNameTextBox" runat="server" BackColor="#C0FFC0"
    BorderStyle="Dotted" BorderWidth="3px">Enter Your Name</asp:TextBox>
```

Given that the declaration of a web control eventually becomes a member variable from the `System.Web.UI.WebControls` namespace (via the dynamic compilation cycle examined in Chapter 32), you are able to interact with the members of this type within a server-side `<script>` block or the page's code-behind file. If you add a new `Button` control to an `*.aspx` file, you can handle the `Click` event and write a server side handler that changes the background color of the `TextBox`:

```
Patial Class _Default
        Inherits System.Web.UI.Page

    Protected Sub btnChangeTextBoxColor_Click(ByVal sender As Object,
        ByVal e As EventArgs) Handles btnChangeTextBoxColor.Click
        ' Change color of text box object in code.
        Me.txtNameTextBox.BackColor = System.Drawing.Color.DarkBlue
    End Sub
End Class
```

All ASP.NET web controls ultimately derive from a common base class named `System.Web.UI.WebControls.WebControl`. In turn, `WebControl` derives from `System.Web.UI.Control` (which derives from `System.Object`). `Control` and `WebControl` each define a number of properties common to all server-side controls. Before I examine the inherited functionality, let's formalize what it means to handle a server-side event.

Understanding Server-Side Event Handling

Given the current state of the World Wide Web, it is impossible to avoid the fundamental nature of browser/web server interaction. Whenever these two entities communicate, there is always an underlying, stateless HTTP request-and-response cycle. While ASP.NET server controls do a great deal to shield you from the details of the raw HTTP protocol, always remember that treating the Web as an event-driven entity is just a magnificent smoke-and-mirrors show provided by the CLR, and it is not identical to the event-driven model of a Windows-based UI.

For example, although the `System.Windows.Forms`, `System.Windows.Controls`, and `System.Web.UI.WebControls` namespaces define types with the same simple names (`Button`, `TextBox`, `Label`, and so on), they do not expose an identical set of events. For example, there is no way to handle a server-side `MouseMove` event when the user moves the cursor over a Web Form `Button` control. Obviously, this is a good thing. (Who wants to post back to the server each time the user mouse moves in the browser?)

The bottom line is that a given ASP.NET web control will expose a limited set of events, all of which ultimately result in a postback to the web server. Any necessary client-side event processing will require you to author blurbs of *client-side* JavaScript/VBScript script code to be processed by the requesting browser's scripting engine. Given that ASP.NET is primarily a server-side technology, I will not be addressing the topic of authoring client-side scripts.

■ **Note** Handling an event for a given web control using Visual Studio 2010 can be done in an identical manner as doing so for a Windows Forms control. Simply select the widget from the designer and click the lightning bolt icon on the Properties window.

The AutoPostBack Property

It is also worth pointing out that many of the ASP.NET web controls support a property named
AutoPostBack (most notably, the **CheckBox**, **RadioButton**, and **TextBox** controls, as well as any widget that
derives from the **ListControl** type). By default, this property is set to **False**, which disables an immediate
postback to the server (even if you have indeed rigged up the event in the code-behind file). In most
cases, this is the exact behavior you require, given that UI elements such as check boxes typically don't
require postback functionality. In other words, you don't want to post back to the server immediately
after the user checks or unchecks a checkbox, as the page object can obtain the state of the widget within
a more natural **Button Click** event handler.

However, if you wish to cause any of these widgets to post back to a server-side event handler
immediately, simply set the value of **AutoPostBack** to **True**. This technique can be helpful if you wish to
have the state of one widget automatically populate another value within another widget on the same
page. To illustrate, assume you have a web page that contains a single **TextBox** (named **txtAutoPostback**)
and a single **ListBox** control (named **lstTextBoxData**). Here is the relevant markup:

```
<form id="form1" runat="server">
  <asp:TextBox ID="txtAutoPostback" runat="server"></asp:TextBox>
  <br/>
  <asp:ListBox ID="lstTextBoxData" runat="server"></asp:ListBox>
</form>
```

Now, handle the **TextChanged** event of the **TextBox**, and within the server-side event handler,
populate the **ListBox** with the current value in the **TextBox**:

```
Partial Class _Default
      Inherits System.Web.UI.Page

    Protected Sub txtAutoPostback_TextChanged(ByVal sender As Object,
        ByVal e As EventArgs) Handles txtAutoPostback.TextChanged
        lstTextBoxData.Items.Add(txtAutoPostback.Text)
    End Sub
End Class
```

If you run the application as is, you will find that as you type in the **TextBox**, nothing happens.
Furthermore, if you type in the **TextBox** and tab to the next control, nothing happens. The reason is that
the **AutoPostBack** property of the **TextBox** is set to **False** by default. However, if you set this property to

```
true
<asp:TextBox ID="txtAutoPostback"
    runat="server" AutoPostBack="true" ... >
</asp:TextBox>
```

you will find that when you tab away from the **TextBox** (or press the Enter key), the **ListBox** is
automatically populated with the current value in the **TextBox**. To be sure, beyond the need to populate
the items of one widget based on the value of another widget, you will typically not need to alter the state
of a widget's **AutoPostBack** property (and even then, sometimes this can be accomplished purely in client
script, removing the need for server interaction at all).

The Control and WebControl Base Classes

The `System.Web.UI.Control` base class defines various properties, methods, and events that allow the ability to interact with core (typically non-GUI) aspects of a web control. Table 33-1 documents some, but not all, members of interest.

Table 33-1. Select Members of `System.Web.UI.Control`

Member	Meaning in Life
Controls	This property gets a `ControlCollection` object that represents the child controls within the current control.
DataBind()	This method binds a data source to the invoked server control and all its child controls.
EnableTheming	This property establishes whether the control supports theme functionality (the default is true).
HasControls()	This method determines whether the server control contains any child controls.
ID	This property gets or sets the programmatic identifier assigned to the server control.
Page	This property gets a reference to the `Page` instance that contains the server control.
Parent	This property gets a reference to the server control's parent control in the page control hierarchy.
SkinID	This property gets or sets the *skin* to apply to the control, which allows you to set the look and feel using server side resources.
Visible	This property gets or sets a value that indicates whether a server control is rendered as a UI element on the page.

Enumerating Contained Controls

The first aspect of `System.Web.UI.Control` we will examine is the fact that all web controls (including `Page` itself) inherit a custom controls collection (accessed via the `Controls` property). Much like in a Windows Forms application, the `Controls` property provides access to a strongly typed collection of `WebControl` derived types. Like any .NET collection, you have the ability to add, insert, and remove items dynamically at runtime.

While it is technically possible to add web controls directly to a `Page`-derived type, it is easier (and more robust) to make use of a `Panel` control. The `Panel` class represents a container of widgets that may or may not be visible to the end user (based on the value of its `Visible` and `BorderStyle` properties).

To illustrate, create a new Empty Web Site named DynamicCtrls and add a new web page to your project. Using the Visual Studio 2010 page designer, add a Panel control (named myPanel) that contains a TextBox, Button, and HyperLink widget named whatever you choose (be aware that the designer requires that you drag internal items within the UI of the Panel type). Next, place a Label widget outside the scope of the Panel (named lblControlInfo) to hold the rendered output. Here is one possible HTML description:

```
<html xmlns="http://www.w3.org/1999/xhtml">
<head runat="server">
  <title>Dynamic Control Test</title>
</head>
<body>
  <form id="form1" runat="server">
    <div>
    <hr />
    <h1>Dynamic Controls</h1>
    <asp:Label ID="lblTextBoxText" runat="server"></asp:Label>
    <hr />
    </div>

    <!-- The Panel has three contained controls -->
    <asp:Panel ID="myPanel" runat="server" Width="200px"
        BorderColor="Black" BorderStyle="Solid" >
      <asp:TextBox ID="TextBox1" runat="server"></asp:TextBox><br/>
      <asp:Button ID="Button1" runat="server" Text="Button"/><br/>
      <asp:HyperLink ID="HyperLink1" runat="server">HyperLink
      </asp:HyperLink>
    </asp:Panel>
  <br />
  <br />
  <asp:Label ID="lblControlInfo" runat="server"></asp:Label>
</form>
</body>
</html>
```

With this markup, your page designer will look something like that of Figure 33-1.

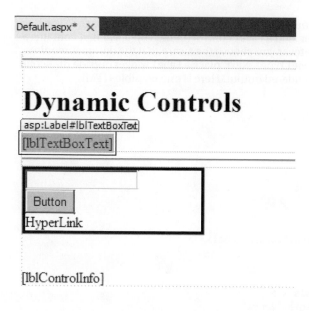

Figure 33-1. The UI of the Dynamic Controls web page

Assume in the Page_Load() event you wish to obtain details regarding the controls contained within the Panel and assign this information to the Label control (named lblControlInfo). Consider the following VB 2010 code:

```
Partial Class _Default
    Inherits System.Web.UI.Page

    Private Sub ListControlsInPanel()
        Dim theInfo As String = ""
        theInfo = String.Format("<b>Does the panel have controls? {0} </b><br/>",
                                        myPanel.HasControls())

        ' Get all controls in the panel.
        For Each c As Control In myPanel.Controls
            If Not Object.ReferenceEquals(c.GetType(),
            GetType(System.Web.UI.LiteralControl))
            Then theInfo &= "*************************<br/>"
                theInfo &= String.Format("Control Name? {0} <br/>", c.ToString())
                theInfo &= String.Format("ID? {0} <br>", c.ID)
```

```
                theInfo &= String.Format("Control Visible? {0} <br/>", c.Visible)
                theInfo &= String.Format("ViewState? {0} <br/>", c.EnableViewState)
            End If
        Next
        lblControlInfo.Text = theInfo
End Sub

Protected Sub Page_Load(ByVal sender As Object, ByVal e As EventArgs)
    Handles Me.Load
        ListControlsInPanel()
    End Sub
End Class
```

Here, you iterate over each `WebControl` maintained on the `Panel` and perform a check to see whether the current type is of type `System.Web.UI.LiteralControl`, and if so, we skip over it. This class is used to represent literal HTML tags and content (such as `<br>`, text literals, etc.). If you do not do this sanity check, you might be surprised to find many more controls in the scope of the `Panel` (given the `*.aspx` declaration seen previously). Assuming the control is not literal HTML content, you then print out some various statistics about the widget. Figure 33-2 shows the output.

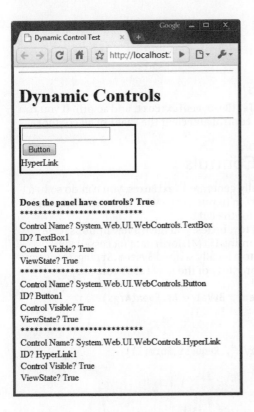

Figure 33-2. Enumerating controls at runtime

1483

Dynamically Adding and Removing Controls

Now, what if you wish to modify the contents of a Panel at runtime? Let's update the current page to support an additional Button (named btnAddWidgets) that dynamically adds three new TextBox controls to the Panel and another Button (named btnClearPanel) that clears the Panel widget of all controls. The Click event handlers for each are shown here:

```
Protected Sub btnClearPanel_Click(ByVal sender As Object, ByVal e As EventArgs)
    Handles btnClearPanel.Click
        ' Clear all content from the panel, then re-list items.
        myPanel.Controls.Clear()
        ListControlsInPanel()
End Sub

Protected Sub btnAddWidgets_Click(ByVal sender As Object, ByVal e As EventArgs)
    Handles btnAddWidgets.Click
        For i As Integer= 0 To 2
        ' Assign an ID so we can get
        ' the text value out later
        ' using the incoming form data.
        Dim t As New TextBox()
        t.ID = String.Format("newTextBox{0}", i)
        myPanel.Controls.Add(t)
        ListControlsInPanel()
        Next
End Sub
```

Notice that you assign a unique ID to each TextBox (e.g., newTextBox0, newTextBox1, and so on). If you run your page, you should be able to add new items to the Panel control and clear the Panel of all content.

Interacting with Dynamically Created Controls

Now, if you want to obtain the values within these dynamically generated TextBoxes, you can do so in a variety of ways. First, update your UI with one additional Button (named btnGetTextData), a final Label control named lblTextBoxData, and handle the Click event for the Button.

To get access to the data within the dynamically created text boxes, you have a few options. One approach is to loop over each item contained within the incoming HTML form data (accessed via HttpRequest.Form) and concatenate the textual information to a locally scoped System.String. Once you have exhausted the collection, assign this string to the Text property of the new Label control:

```
Protected Sub btnGetTextData_Click(ByVal sender As Object, ByVal e As EventArgs)
    Handles btnGetTextData.Click
    Dim textBoxValues As String = ""
    For i = 0 To Request.Form.Count - 1
        textBoxValues &= String.Format("<li>{0}</li><br/>", Request.Form(i))
    Next
    lblTextBoxData.Text = textBoxValues
End Sub
```

When you run the application, you will find that you are able to view the content of each text box, including some rather long (unreadable) string data. This string contains the *view state* for each control on the page. You'll learn about the role of view state in Chapter 35.

To clean up the output, you could instead pluck out the textual data for your uniquely named items (newTextBox0, newTextBox1 and newTextBox2). Consider the following update:

```
Protected Sub btnGetTextData_Click(ByVal sender As Object, ByVal e As EventArgs)
    Handles btnGetTextData.Click
    ' Get teach text box by name.
    Dim lableData As String = String.Format("<li>{0}</li><br/>",
    Request.Form.Get("newTextBox0"))
    lableData &= String.Format("<li>{0}</li><br/>", Request.Form.Get("newTextBox1"))
    lableData &= String.Format("<li>{0}</li><br/>", Request.Form.Get("newTextBox2"))
    lblTextBoxData.Text = lableData
End Sub
```

Using either approach, you will notice that once the request has been processed, the text boxes disappear. Again, the reason has to do with the stateless nature of HTTP. If you wish to maintain these dynamically created TextBoxes between postbacks, you need to persist these objects using ASP.NET state programming techniques (again, see Chapter 35).

■ **Source Code** The DynamicCtrls website is included under the Chapter 33 subdirectory.

Functionality of the WebControl Base Class

As you can tell, the Control type provides a number of non–GUI-related behaviors (the controls collection, autopostback support, etc.). On the other hand, the WebControl base class provides a graphical polymorphic interface to all web widgets, as suggested in Table 33-2.

Table 33-2. Select Properties of the WebControl Base Class

Property	Meaning in Life
BackColor	Gets or sets the background color of the web control.
BorderColor	Gets or sets the border color of the web control.
BorderStyle	Gets or sets the border style of the web control.
BorderWidth	Gets or sets the border width of the web control.
Enabled	Gets or sets a value indicating whether the web control is enabled.

Continued

Property	Meaning in Life
CssClass	Allows you to assign a class defined within a Cascading Style Sheet to a web widget.
Font	Gets font information for the web control.
ForeColor	Gets or sets the foreground color (typically the color of the text) of the web control.
Height, Width	Get or set the height and width of the web control.
TabIndex	Gets or sets the tab index of the web control.
ToolTip	Gets or sets the tool tip for the web control to be displayed when the cursor is over the control.

Almost all of these properties are self-explanatory, so rather than drill through the use of them one by one, let's instead check out a number of ASP.NET Web Form controls in action.

Major Categories of ASP.NET Web Controls

The ASP.NET web control library can be broken down into several broad categories, all of which can be viewed within the Visual Studio 2010 Toolbox (provided you have an ***.aspx** page open for design!). See Figure 33-3.

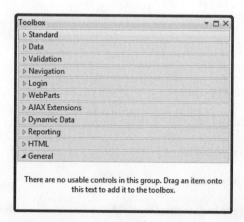

Figure 33-3. The categories of ASP.NET web controls

Under the Standard area of the Toolbox, you will find the most frequently used controls, including `Button`, `Label`, `TextBox` and `ListBox`. In addition to these vanilla-flavored UI elements, the Standard area also lists more exotic web controls such as `Calendar`, `Wizard`, and `AdRotator` (Figure 33-4).

Figure 33-4. The Standard ASP.NET web controls

The Data section is where you can find a set of controls used for data binding operations, including the new ASP.NET `Chart` control, which allows you to render out graphical chart data (pie charts, line charts) typically as the result of a data binding operation (see Figure 33-5).

Figure 33-5. Data centric ASP.NET web controls

The ASP.NET validation controls (found in the Validation area of the toolbox) are very interesting in that they can be configured to emit back blocks of client side JavaScript that will test input fields for valid data. If a validation error occurs, the user will see an error message and will not be allowed to post back to the web server until the error is corrected.

The Navigation node of the Toolbox is where you will find a small set of controls (`Menu`, `SiteMapPath` and `TreeView`) which typically work in conjunction with a `*.sitemap` file. As briefly mentioned earlier in this chapter, these navigation controls allow you to describe the structure of a multi-paged site using XML descriptions.

The *really* exotic set of ASP.NET web controls would have to be the Login controls (Figure 33-6).

Figure 33-6. Security ASP.NET web controls

These controls can radically simplify how to incorporate basic security features (password recovery, login screens, etc.) into your web applications. In fact, these controls are so powerful, they will even dynamically create a dedicated database to store credentials (saved under the App_Data folder of your website) if you do not already have a specific security database.

■ **Note** The remaining categories of web controls shown in the Visual Studio toolbox (such as WebParts, AJAX Extensions and Dynamic Data) are for more specialized programming needs and will not be examined here.

A Brief Word Regarding System.Web.UI.HtmlControls

Truth be told, there are two distinct web control toolkits that ship with ASP.NET. In addition to the ASP.NET web controls (within the `System.Web.UI.WebControls` namespace), the base class libraries also provides the `System.Web.UI.HtmlControls` control library.

The HTML controls are a collection of types that allow you to make use of traditional HTML controls on a web forms page. However, unlike simple HTML tags, HTML controls are object-oriented entities that can be configured to run on the server and thus support server-side event handling. Unlike ASP.NET web controls, HTML controls are quite simplistic in nature and offer little functionality beyond standard HTML tags (`HtmlButton`, `HtmlInputControl`, `HtmlTable`, etc.).

The HTML controls can be useful if your team has a clear division between those who build HTML UIs and .NET developers. HTML folks can make use of their web editor of choice using familiar markup tags and pass the HTML files to the development team. At this point, developers can configure these

HTML controls to run as server controls (by right-clicking an HTML widget within Visual Studio 2010). This will allow developers to handle server-side events and work with the HTML widget programmatically.

The HTML controls provide a public interface that mimics standard HTML attributes. For example, to obtain the information within an input area, you make use of the `Value` property rather than the web control–centric `Text` property. Given that the HTML controls are not as feature-rich as the ASP.NET web controls, I won't make further mention of them in this text.

Web Control Documentation

You will get a chance to work with a number of ASP.NET web controls during the remainder of this book; however, you should certainly take a moment to search the .NET Framework 4.0 SDK documentation for the `System.Web.UI.WebControls` Namespace. Here you will find explanations and code examples for each member of the namespace (Figure 33-7).

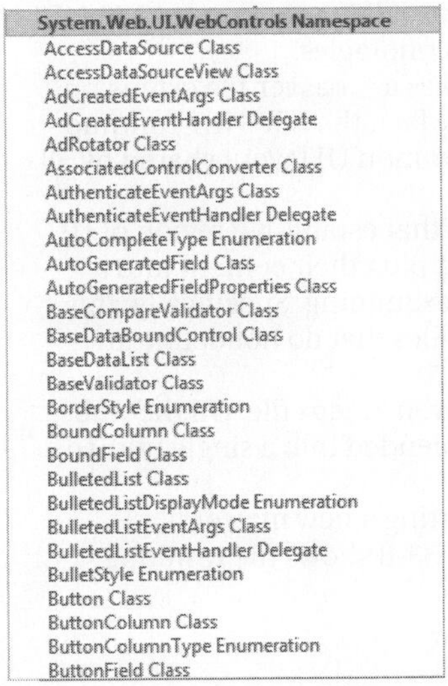

System.Web.UI.WebControls Namespace
- AccessDataSource Class
- AccessDataSourceView Class
- AdCreatedEventArgs Class
- AdCreatedEventHandler Delegate
- AdRotator Class
- AssociatedControlConverter Class
- AuthenticateEventArgs Class
- AuthenticateEventHandler Delegate
- AutoCompleteType Enumeration
- AutoGeneratedField Class
- AutoGeneratedFieldProperties Class
- BaseCompareValidator Class
- BaseDataBoundControl Class
- BaseDataList Class
- BaseValidator Class
- BorderStyle Enumeration
- BoundColumn Class
- BoundField Class
- BulletedList Class
- BulletedListDisplayMode Enumeration
- BulletedListEventArgs Class
- BulletedListEventHandler Delegate
- BulletStyle Enumeration
- Button Class
- ButtonColumn Class
- ButtonColumnType Enumeration
- ButtonField Class

Figure 33-7. All ASP.NET web controls are documented in the .NET Framework 4.0 SDK documentation

Building the ASP.NET Cars Web Site

Given that many of the "simple" controls look and feel so close to their Windows Forms counterparts, I won't bother to enumerate the details of the basic widgets (`Buttons`, `Labels`, `TextBoxes`, etc.). Rather, let's build a new website that illustrates working with several of the more exotic controls as well as the ASP.NET master page model and aspects of the data binding engine. Specifically, this next example will illustrate the following techniques:

- Working with master pages

- Working with site map navigation

- Working with the `GridView` control

- Working with the `Wizard` control

To begin, create an Empty ASP.NET Web Site project named AspNetCarsSite. Note that we are not yet creating a (fully populated) ASP.NET Web Site project, as this will add a number of starter files to the mix which we have not yet examined. For this project, we will add what we need manually.

Working with ASP.NET Master Pages

Many websites provide a consistent look and feel across multiple pages (a common menu navigation system, common header and footer content, company logo, etc.). Under ASP.NET 1.*x*, developers made extensive use of `UserControls` and custom web controls to define web content that was to be used across multiple pages. While `UserControls` and custom web controls are still a very valid option under ASP.NET, we are also provided with *master pages* that complement these existing technologies.

Simply put, a master page is little more than an ASP.NET page that takes a `*.master` file extension. On their own, master pages are not viewable from a client-side browser (in fact, the ASP.NET runtime will not serve this flavor of web content). Rather, master pages define a common UI layout shared by all pages (or a subset of pages) in your site.

As well, a `*.master` page will define various content placeholder areas that establish a region of UI real estate other `*.aspx` files may plug into. As you will see, `*.aspx` files that plug their content into a master file look and feel a bit different from the `*.aspx` files we have been examining. Specifically, this flavor of an `*.aspx` file is termed a *content page*. Content pages are `*.aspx` files that do not define an HTML `<form>` element (that is the job of the master page).

However, as far as the end user is concerned, a request is made to a given `*.aspx` file. On the web server, the related `*.master` file and any related `*.aspx` content pages are blended into a single unified HTML page declaration.

To illustrate the use of master pages and content pages, begin by inserting a new master page into your website via the Website ➤ Add New Item menu selection (Figure 33-8 shows the resulting dialog box).

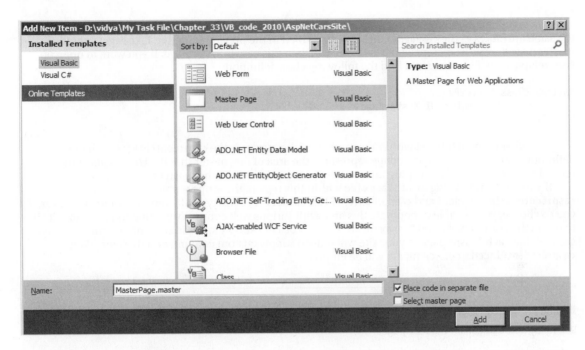

Figure 33-8. Inserting a new *.master *file*

The initial markup of the MasterPage.master file looks like the following:

```
<%@ Master Language="VB"
    CodeFile="MasterPage.master.vb" Inherits="MasterPage" %>

<!DOCTYPE html PUBLIC "-//W3C//DTD XHTML 1.0 Transitional//EN"
  "http://www.w3.org/TR/xhtml1/DTD/xhtml1-transitional.dtd">

<html xmlns="http://www.w3.org/1999/xhtml">
<head runat="server">
  <title>Untitled Page</title>
  <asp:ContentPlaceHolder id="head" runat="server">
  </asp:ContentPlaceHolder>
</head>
<body>
  <form id="form1" runat="server">
  <div>
    <asp:ContentPlaceHolder id="ContentPlaceHolder1" runat="server">
    </asp:ContentPlaceHolder>
  </div>
  </form>
</body>
</html>
```

The first point of interest is the new `<%@Master%>` directive. For the most part, this directive supports the same attributes as the `<%@Page%>` directive described in the previous chapter. Like `Page` types, a master page derives from a specific base class, which in this case is `MasterPage`. If you were to open up your related code file, you would find the following class definition:

```
Partial Class MasterPage
    Inherits System.Web.UI.MasterPage
End Class
```

The other point of interest within the markup of the master is the `<asp:ContentPlaceHolder>` definition. This region of a master page represents the area of the master that the UI widgets of the related `*.aspx` content file may plug into, not the content defined by the master page itself.

If you do intend to plug in an `*.aspx` file within this region, the scope within the `<asp:ContentPlaceHolder>` and `</asp:ContentPlaceHolder>` tags will typically remain empty. However, if you so choose, you are able to populate this area with various web controls that function as a default UI to use in the event that a given `*.aspx` file in the site does not supply specific content. For this example, assume that each `*.aspx` page in your site will indeed supply custom content, and therefore your `<asp:ContentPlaceHolder>` elements will be empty.

■ **Note** A `*.master` page may define as many content placeholders as necessary. As well, a single `*.master` page may nest additional `*.master` pages.

You are able to build a common UI of a `*.master` file using the same Visual Studio 2010 designers used to build `*.aspx` files. For this site, you will add a descriptive `Label` (to serve as a common welcome message), an `AdRotator` control (which will randomly display one of two image files), and a `TreeView` control (to allow the user to navigate to other areas of the site). Here is some possible markup:

```
<html xmlns="http://www.w3.org/1999/xhtml">
<head runat="server">
    <title>Untitled Page</title>
    <asp:ContentPlaceHolder id="head" runat="server">
    </asp:ContentPlaceHolder>
</head>
<body>
    <form id="form1" runat="server">
    <div>
      <hr />
      <asp:Label ID="Label1" runat="server" Font-Size="XX-Large"
        Text="Welcome to the ASP.NET Cars Super Site!"></asp:Label>
      <asp:AdRotator ID="myAdRotator" runat="server"/>
       <br />
      <br />
      <asp:TreeView ID="navigationTree" runat="server">
      </asp:TreeView>
      <hr />
    </div>
    <div>
```

```
            <asp:ContentPlaceHolder id="ContentPlaceHolder1" runat="server">
            </asp:ContentPlaceHolder>
        </div>
        </form>
</body>
</html>
```

Figure 33-9 shows the design time view of the current master page.

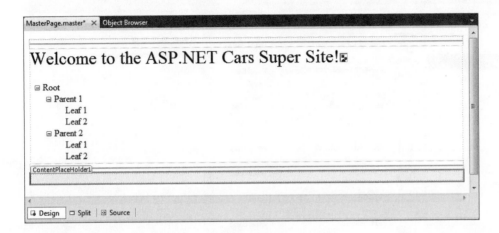

*Figure 33-9. The *.master file's shared UI*

Feel free to enhance the look of your TreeView control by using the inline editor of the control and selecting the Auto Format... link. For my example, I selected the Arrow theme from the resulting dialog and ended up with the following control markup:

```
<asp:TreeView ID="navigationTree" runat="server"
        ImageSet="Arrows">
  <HoverNodeStyle Font-Underline="True" ForeColor="#5555DD" />
  <NodeStyle Font-Names="Verdana" Font-Size="8pt" ForeColor="Black"
             HorizontalPadding="5px" NodeSpacing="0px" VerticalPadding="0px" />
  <ParentNodeStyle Font-Bold="False" />
  <SelectedNodeStyle Font-Underline="True" ForeColor="#5555DD"
                     HorizontalPadding="0px" VerticalPadding="0px" />
</asp:TreeView>
```

Working with the TreeView Control Site Navigation Logic

ASP.NET ships with several web controls that allow you to handle site navigation: SiteMapPath, TreeView, and Menu. As you would expect, these web widgets can be configured in multiple ways. For example, each of these controls can dynamically generate its nodes via an external XML file (or an XML-based *.sitemap file), programmatically generate nodes in code, or through markup using the designers of Visual Studio 2010.

Your navigation system will be dynamically populated using a *.sitemap file. The benefit of this approach is that we can define the overall structure of our website in an external file and then bind it to a TreeView (or Menu) control on the fly. This way, if the navigational structure of your website changes, we simply need to modify the *.sitemap file and reload the page. To begin, insert a new Web.sitemap file into your project using the Website ➤ Add New Item menu option to bring up the dialog box shown in Figure 33-10.

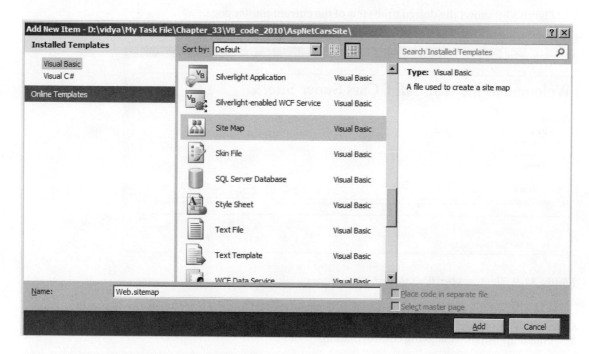

Figure 33-10. Inserting a new Web.sitemap *file*

As you can see, the initial Web.sitemap file defines a topmost item with two subnodes:

```
<?xml version="1.0" encoding="utf-8" ?>
<siteMap xmlns="http://schemas.microsoft.com/AspNet/SiteMap-File-1.0" >
  <siteMapNode url="" title="" description="">
    <siteMapNode url="" title="" description="" />
    <siteMapNode url="" title="" description="" />
  </siteMapNode>
</siteMap>
```

If we were to bind this structure to a Menu control, we would find a topmost menu item with two submenus. Therefore, when you wish to define subitems, simply define new <siteMapNode> elements within the scope of an existing <siteMapNode>. In any case, the goal is to define the overall structure of your website within a Web.sitemap file using various <siteMapNode> elements. Each one of these elements can define a title and URL attribute. The URL attribute represents which *.aspx file to navigate to when the user clicks a given menu item (or node of a TreeView). Your site map will contain three site map nodes (underneath the top-level site map node), as follows:

- *Home*: Default.aspx

- *Build a Car*: BuildCar.aspx

- *View Inventory*: Inventory.aspx

Your menu system has a single topmost Welcome item with three subelements. Therefore, you can update the Web.sitemap file as follows, but be aware that each url value must be unique (if not, you will receive a runtime error):

```
<?xml version="1.0" encoding="utf-8" ?>
<siteMap xmlns="http://schemas.microsoft.com/AspNet/SiteMap-File-1.0" >
  <siteMapNode url="" title="Welcome!" description="">
    <siteMapNode url="~/Default.aspx" title="Home"
      description="The Home Page" />
    <siteMapNode url="~/BuildCar.aspx" title="Build a car"
      description="Create your dream car" />
    <siteMapNode url="~/Inventory.aspx" title="View Inventory"
      description="See what is in stock" />
  </siteMapNode>
</siteMap>
```

■ **Note** The ~/ prefix before each page in the url attribute is a notation that represents the root of the website.

Now, despite what you may be thinking, you do not associate a Web.sitemap file directly to a Menu or TreeView control using a given property. Rather, the *.master or *.aspx file that contains the UI widget that will display the Web.sitemap file must contain a SiteMapDataSource component. This type will automatically load the Web.sitemap file into its object model when the page is requested. The Menu and TreeView types then set their DataSourceID property to point to the SiteMapDataSource instance.

To add a new SiteMapDataSource to your *.master file and automatically set the DataSourceID property, you can make use of the Visual Studio 2010 designer. Activate the inline editor of the TreeView control (i.e., click the tiny arrow in the top-right corner of the TreeView) and select New Data Source, as shown in Figure 33-11.

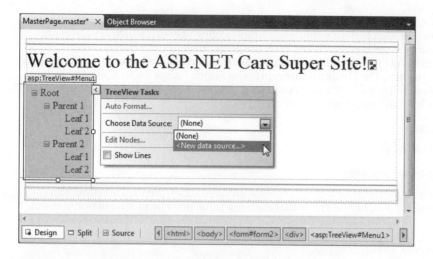

Figure 33-11. Adding a new SiteMapDataSource

From the resulting dialog box, select the SiteMap icon. This will set the DataSourceID property of the Menu item as well as add a new SiteMapDataSource component to your page. This is all you need to do to configure your TreeView control to navigate to the additional pages on your site. If you wish to perform additional processing when the user selects a given menu item, you may do so by handling the SelectedNodeChanged event. There is no need to do so for this example, but be aware that you are able to determine which menu item was selected using the incoming event arguments.

Establishing Bread Crumbs with the SiteMapPath Type

Before moving on to the AdRotator control, add a SiteMapPath type (located in the Navigation tab in the toolbox) onto your *.master file, beneath the content placeholder element. This widget will automatically adjust its content based on the current selection of the menu system. As you may know, this can provide a helpful visual cue for the end user (formally, this UI technique is termed *breadcrumbs*). Once you complete this example, you will notice that when you select the Welcome ➤ Build a Car menu item, the SiteMapPath widget updates accordingly automatically.

Working with the AdRotator

The role of the ASP.NET AdRotator widget is to randomly display a given image at some position in the browser. Go ahead and add an AdRotator widget to the designer. Once you do, it is displayed as an empty placeholder. Functionally, this control cannot do its magic until you assign the AdvertisementFile property to point to the source file that describes each image. For this example, the data source will be a simple XML file named Ads.xml.

To add the XML file to the Web site, go to the Website ➤ Add New Item menu option and select XML file. Name the file Ads.xml and specify a unique <Ad> element for each image you wish to display. At minimum, each <Ad> element specifies the image to display (ImageUrl), the URL to navigate to if the image is selected (TargetUrl), mouseover text (AlternateText), and the weight of the ad (Impressions):

<Advertisements>

```
<Ad>
  <ImageUrl>SlugBug.jpg</ImageUrl>
  <TargetUrl>http://www.Cars.com</TargetUrl>
  <AlternateText>Your new Car?</AlternateText>
  <Impressions>80</Impressions>
</Ad>
<Ad>
  <ImageUrl>car.gif</ImageUrl>
  <TargetUrl>http://www.CarSuperSite.com</TargetUrl>
  <AlternateText>Like this Car?</AlternateText>
  <Impressions>80</Impressions>
</Ad>
</Advertisements>
```

Here you have specified two image files (`car.gif` and `slugbug.jpg`). As a result, you will need to ensure that these files are in the root of your website (these files have been included with this book's code download). To add them to your current project, select the Website ➤ Add Existing Item menu option. At this point, you can associate your XML file to the `AdRotator` control via the `AdvertisementFile` property (in the Properties window):

```
<asp:AdRotator ID="myAdRotator" runat="server"
               AdvertisementFile="~/Ads.xml"/>
```

Later when you run this application and post back to the page, you will be randomly presented with one of two image files.

Defining the Default Content Page

Now that you have a master page established, you can begin designing the individual `*.aspx` pages that will define the UI content to merge within the `<asp:ContentPlaceHolder>` tag of the master page. The `*.aspx` files that are merged within a master page are called *content pages* and have a few key differences from a normal, standalone ASP.NET web page.

In a nutshell, the `*.master` file defines the `<form>` section of the final HTML page. Therefore, the existing `<form>` area within the `*.aspx` file will need to be replaced with an `<asp:Content>` scope. While you could update the markup of your initial `*.aspx` file by hand, you can insert a new content page to your project; simply right-click anywhere on the designer surface of the `*.master` file and select the Add Content Page menu option. This will generate a new `*.aspx` file with the following initial markup:

```
<%@ Page Language="VB" MasterPageFile="~/MasterPage.master"
        AutoEventWireup="False" CodeFile="Default.aspx.vb"
        Inherits="_Default" Title="Untitled Page" %>

<asp:Content ID="Content1"
  ContentPlaceHolderID="head" Runat="Server">
</asp:Content>
<asp:Content ID="Content2"
  ContentPlaceHolderID="ContentPlaceHolder1" Runat="Server">
</asp:Content>
```

First, notice that the <%@Page%> directive has been updated with a new MasterPageFile attribute that is assigned to your *.master file. Also note that rather than having a <form> element, we have an <asp:Content> scope (currently empty) that has set the ContentPlaceHolderID value identical to the <asp:ContentPlaceHolder> component in the master file.

Given these associations, the content page understands where to plug in its content, while the master's content is displayed in a read-only nature on the content page. There is no need to build a complex UI for your Default.aspx content area. For this example, simply add some literal text that provides some basic site instructions, as you see in Figure 33-12 (also notice on the upper right of the content page that there is a link to switch to the related master file).

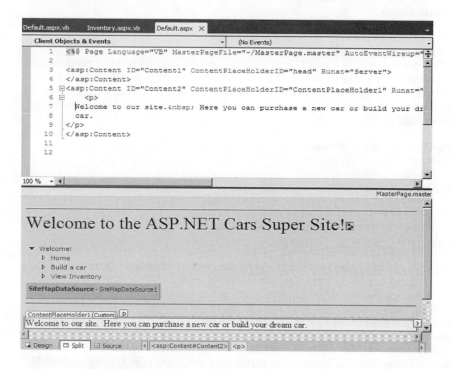

Figure 33-12. Authoring the first content page

Now, if you run your project, you will find that the UI content of the *.master and Default.aspx files have been merged into a single stream of HTML. As you can see from Figure 33-13, the end user is unaware that the master page even exists. Also, as you refresh the page (via the F5 key), you should see the AdRotator randomly displaying one of two images.

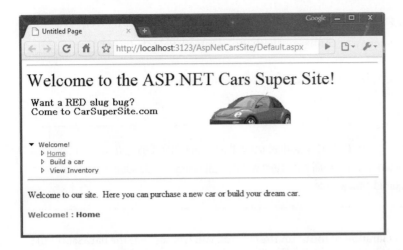

Figure 33-13. At runtime, master files and content pages render back a single form

---

■ **Note** Do be aware that a Page object's master page can be assigned programmatically within the PreInit event of a Page derived type using the inherited Master property.

Designing the Inventory Content Page

To insert the Inventory.aspx content page into your current project, open the *.master page in the IDE, select Website ➤ Add Content Page, and rename this file to Inventory.aspx. The role of the Inventory content page is to display the contents of the Inventory table of the AutoLot database within a GridView control.

The ASP.NET GridView control has the ability to represent connection string data and SQL Select, Insert, Update, and Delete statements (or alternatively stored procedures) *in markup*. Therefore, rather than authoring all of the necessary ADO.NET code by hand, you can allow the SqlDataSource class to generate the markup for you. Using the visual designers, you are able to assign the DataSourceID property of the GridView to the SqlDataSource component.

With a few simple mouse clicks, you can configure the GridView to automatically select, update, and delete records of the underlying data store. While this zero-code mindset greatly simplifies the amount of boilerplate code, understand that this simplicity comes with a loss of control and may not be the best approach for an enterprise-level application. This model can be wonderful for low-trafficked pages, prototyping a website, or smaller in-house applications.

To illustrate how to work with the GridView (and the data access logic) in a declarative manner, begin by updating the Inventory.aspx content page with a descriptive Label control. Next, open the Server Explorer tool (via the View menu) and make sure you have added a data connection to the AutoLot database created during your examination of ADO.NET (see Chapter 21 for a walkthrough of the process of adding a data connection). Now, select the Inventory table in Server Explorer and drag it onto the content area of the Inventory.aspx file. Once you have done so, the IDE responds by performing the following steps:

1. Your web.config file was updated with a new <connectionStrings> element.

2. A SqlDataSource component was configured with the necessary Select, Insert, Update, and Delete logic.

3. The DataSourceID property of the GridView has been set to the new SqlDataSource component.

■ **Note** As an alternative, you can configure a GridView widget using the inline editor. Select New Data Source from the Choose Data Source drop-down box. This will activate a wizard that walks you through a series of steps to connect this component to the required data source.

If you examine the opening declaration of the GridView control, you will see that the DataSourceID property has been set to the SqlDataSource you just defined:

```
<asp:GridView ID="GridView1" runat="server" AutoGenerateColumns="False"
    DataKeyNames="CarID" DataSourceID="SqlDataSource1"
    EmptyDataText="There are no data records to display.">
  <Columns>
    <asp:BoundField DataField="CarID" HeaderText="CarID" ReadOnly="True"
        SortExpression="CarID" />
    <asp:BoundField DataField="Make" HeaderText="Make" SortExpression="Make" />
    <asp:BoundField DataField="Color" HeaderText="Color" SortExpression="Color" />
    <asp:BoundField DataField="PetName" HeaderText="PetName"
                    SortExpression="PetName" />
  </Columns>
</asp:GridView>
```

The SqlDataSource type is where a majority of the action is taking place. In the markup that follows, notice that this type has recorded the necessary SQL statements (with parameterized queries, no less) to interact with the Inventory table of the AutoLot database. As well, using the $ syntax of the ConnectionString property, this component will automatically read the <connectionStrings> value from web.config:

```
<asp:SqlDataSource ID="SqlDataSource1" runat="server"
  ConnectionString="<%$ ConnectionStrings:AutoLotConnectionString1 %>"
  DeleteCommand="DELETE FROM [Inventory] WHERE [CarID] = @CarID"
  InsertCommand="INSERT INTO [Inventory] ([CarID], [Make], [Color], [PetName])
    VALUES (@CarID, @Make, @Color, @PetName)"
  ProviderName="<%$ ConnectionStrings:AutoLotConnectionString1.ProviderName %>"
  SelectCommand="SELECT [CarID], [Make], [Color], [PetName] FROM [Inventory]"
  UpdateCommand="UPDATE [Inventory] SET [Make] = @Make,
    [Color] = @Color, [PetName] = @PetName WHERE [CarID] = @CarID">
  <DeleteParameters>
    <asp:Parameter Name="CarID" Type="Int32" />
  </DeleteParameters>
  <UpdateParameters>
```

```
      <asp:Parameter Name="Make" Type="String" />
      <asp:Parameter Name="Color" Type="String" />
      <asp:Parameter Name="PetName" Type="String" />
      <asp:Parameter Name="CarID" Type="Int32" />
    </UpdateParameters>
    <InsertParameters>
      <asp:Parameter Name="CarID" Type="Int32" />
      <asp:Parameter Name="Make" Type="String" />
      <asp:Parameter Name="Color" Type="String" />
      <asp:Parameter Name="PetName" Type="String" />
    </InsertParameters>
</asp:SqlDataSource>
```

At this point, you are able to run your web program, click the View Inventory menu item, and view your data, as shown in Figure 33-14. (Note that I updated my DataView grid with a unique look and feel using the inline designer.)

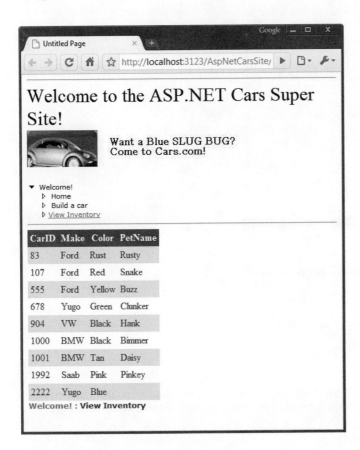

Figure 33-14. The zero-code model of the SqlDataSource *component*

Enabling Sorting and Paging

The `GridView` control can easily be configured for sorting (via column name hyperlinks) and paging (via numeric or next/previous hyperlinks). To do so, activate the inline editor and check the appropriate options, as shown in Figure 33-15.

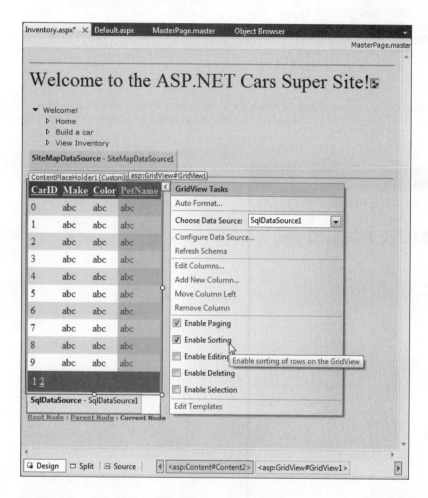

Figure 33-15. Enabling sorting and paging

When you run your page again, you will be able to sort your data by clicking the column names and scrolling through your data via the paging links (provided you have enough records in the Inventory table!).

Enabling In-Place Editing

The final detail of this page is to enable the GridView control's support for in-place activation. Given that your SqlDataSource already has the necessary Delete and Update logic, all you need to do is check the Enable Deleting and Enable Editing check boxes of the GridView (see Figure 33-15 for a reference point). Sure enough, when you navigate back to the Inventory.aspx page, you are able to edit and delete records (as shown in Figure 33-16) and update the underlying Inventory table of the AutoLot database.

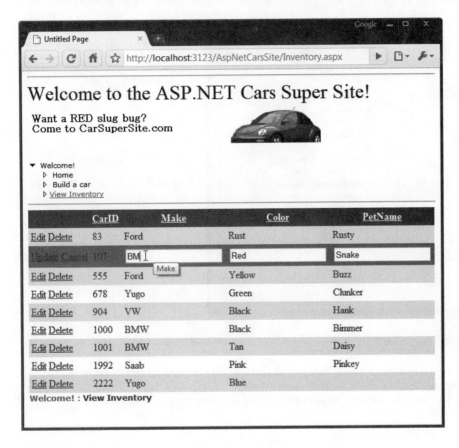

Figure 33-16. Editing and deleting functionality

■ **Note** Enabling in-place editing for a GridView requires that the database table be assigned a primary key. If you do not see these options enabled, chances are you forgot to set CarID as the primary key of the Inventory table within the AutoLot database.

Designing the Build-a-Car Content Page

The final task for this example is to design the `BuildCar.aspx` content page. Insert this file into the current project (via the Website ➤ Add Content Page menu option). This new page will make use of the ASP.NET `Wizard` web control, which provides a simple way to walk the end user through a series of related steps. Here, the steps in question will simulate the act of building an automobile for purchase.

Place a descriptive `Label` and `Wizard` control onto the content area. Next, activate the inline editor for the `Wizard` and click the Add/Remove WizardSteps link. Add a total of four steps, as shown in Figure 33-17.

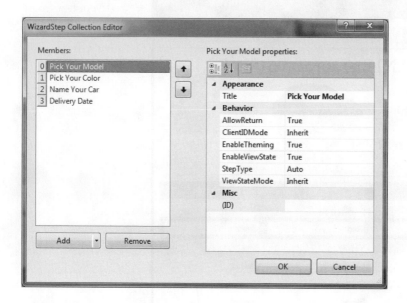

Figure 33-17. *Configuring our wizard*

Once you have defined these steps, you will notice that the `Wizard` defines an empty content area where you can now drag and drop controls for the currently selected step. For this example, update each step with the following UI elements (be sure to provide a fitting ID value for each item using the Properties window):

- *Pick Your Model*: A `TextBox` control

- *Pick Your Color*: A `ListBox` control

- *Name Your Car*: A `TextBox` control

- *Delivery Date*: A `Calendar` control

The `ListBox` control is the only UI element of the `Wizard` that requires additional steps. Select this item on the designer (making sure you first select the Pick Your Color link) and fill this widget with a set of colors using the `Items` property of the Properties window. Once you do, you will find markup much like the following within the scope of the `Wizard` definition:

```
<asp:ListBox ID="ListBoxColors" runat="server" Width="237px">
  <asp:ListItem>Purple</asp:ListItem>
  <asp:ListItem>Green</asp:ListItem>
  <asp:ListItem>Red</asp:ListItem>
  <asp:ListItem>Yellow</asp:ListItem>
  <asp:ListItem>Pea Soup Green</asp:ListItem>
  <asp:ListItem>Black</asp:ListItem>
  <asp:ListItem>Lime Green</asp:ListItem>
</asp:ListBox>
```

Now that you have defined each of the steps, you can handle the `FinishButtonClick` event for the autogenerated Finish button. Be aware, however, that you won't see this Finish button until you select the final step of the wizard on the designer. Once you have selected the final step, simply double click on the Finish button to generate the event handler. Within the server-side event handler, obtain the selections from each UI element and build a description string that is assigned to the `Text` property of an additional `Label` type named `lblOrder`:

```
Partial Class Default2
        Inherits System.Web.UI.Page

    Protected Sub carWizard_FinishButtonClick(ByVal sender As Object,
        ByVal e As System.Web.UI.WebControls.WizardNavigationEventArgs)
        Handles carWizard.FinishButtonClick
        ' Get each value.
        Dim order As String = String.Format("{0}, your {1} {2} will arrive on {3}.",
                                    txtCarPetName.Text,
                                    ListBoxColors.SelectedValue,
                                    txtCarModel.Text,
                                    carCalendar.SelectedDate.ToShortDateString())

        ' Assign to label
        lblOrder.Text = order
    End Sub
End Class
```

At this point, your AspNetCarsSite web application is complete! Figure 33-18 shows the `Wizard` in action.

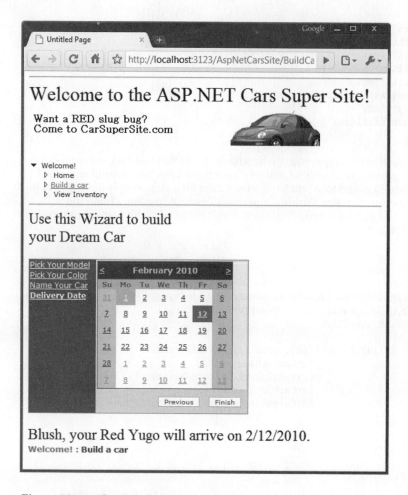

Figure 33-18. The `Wizard` *control in action*

That wraps up your first look of various ASP.NET web controls, master pages, content pages and site map navigation. Next up, let's look at the functionality of the ASP.NET validation controls.

■ **Source Code** The AspNetCarsSite website is included under the Chapter 33 subdirectory.

The Role of the Validation Controls

The next set of Web Form controls we will examine are known collectively as *validation controls*. Unlike the other Web Form controls we've examined, validation controls are not used to emit HTML for rendering purposes, but are used to emit client-side JavaScript (and possibly related server-side code) for the purpose of form validation. As illustrated at the beginning of this chapter, client-side form validation is quite useful because you can ensure that various constraints are in place before posting back to the web server, thereby avoiding expensive round-trips. Table 33-3 gives a rundown of the ASP.NET validation controls.

Table 33-3. ASP.NET Validation Controls

Control	Meaning in Life
CompareValidator	Validates that the value of an input control is equal to a given value of another input control or a fixed constant.
CustomValidator	Allows you to build a custom validation function that validates a given control.
RangeValidator	Determines that a given value is in a predetermined range.
RegularExpressionValidator	Checks whether the value of the associated input control matches the pattern of a regular expression.
RequiredFieldValidator	Ensures that a given input control contains a value (i.e., is not empty).
ValidationSummary	Displays a summary of all validation errors of a page in a list, bulleted list, or single-paragraph format. The errors can be displayed inline and/or in a pop-up message box.

All of the validation controls ultimately derive from a common base class named System.Web.UI.WebControls.BaseValidator, and therefore they have a set of common features. Table 33-4 documents the key members.

Table 33-4. Common Properties of the ASP.NET Validators

Member	Meaning in Life
ControlToValidate	Gets or sets the input control to validate.
Display	Gets or sets the display behavior of the error message in a validation control.
EnableClientScript	Gets or sets a value indicating whether client-side validation is enabled.
ErrorMessage	Gets or sets the text for the error message.
ForeColor	Gets or sets the color of the message displayed when validation fails.

To illustrate working with these validation controls, create a new ASP.NET Empty Web Site project named ValidatorCtrls and insert a new Web Form named `Default.aspx`. To begin, place four (well-named) `TextBox` controls (with four corresponding and descriptive `Labels`) onto your page. Next, place a `RequiredFieldValidator`, `RangeValidator`, `RegularExpressionValidator`, and `CompareValidator` type adjacent to each respective input field. Last of all, add a single `Button` and final `Label` (see Figure 33-19).

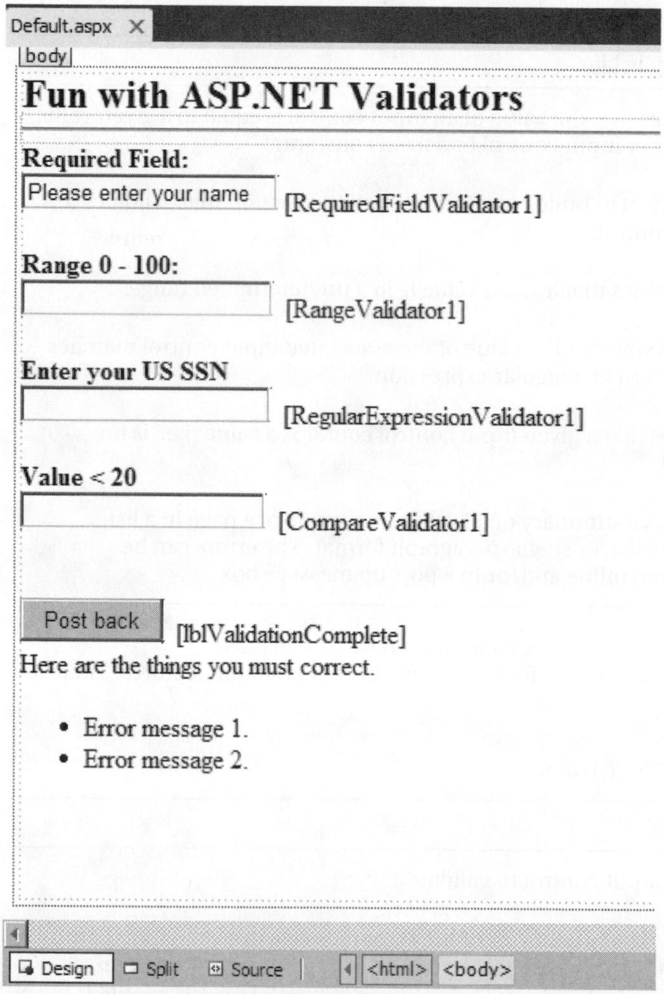

Figure 33-19. ASP.NET validation controls will ensure your form data is correct before allowing postback

Now that you have an initial UI, let's walk through the process of configuring each validator.

The RequiredFieldValidator

Configuring the `RequiredFieldValidator` is straightforward. Simply set the `ErrorMessage` and `ControlToValidate` properties accordingly using the Visual Studio 2010 Properties window. Here is the resulting markup that ensures the `txtRequiredField` text box is not empty:

```
<asp:RequiredFieldValidator ID="RequiredFieldValidator1"
  runat="server" ControlToValidate="txtRequiredField"
  ErrorMessage="Oops!  Need to enter data.">
</asp:RequiredFieldValidator>
```

The `RequiredFieldValidator` supports an `InitialValue` property. You can use this property to ensure that the user enters any value other than the initial value in the related `TextBox`. For example, when the user first posts to a page, you may wish to configure a `TextBox` to contain the value "Please enter your name". Now, if you did not set the `InitialValue` property of the `RequiredFieldValidator`, the runtime would assume that the string "Please enter your name" is valid. Thus, to ensure a required `TextBox` is valid only when the user enters anything other than "Please enter your name", configure your widgets as follows:

```
<asp:RequiredFieldValidator ID="RequiredFieldValidator1"
  runat="server" ControlToValidate="txtRequiredField"
  ErrorMessage="Oops!  Need to enter data."
  InitialValue="Please enter your name">
</asp:RequiredFieldValidator>
```

The RegularExpressionValidator

The `RegularExpressionValidator` can be used when you wish to apply a pattern against the characters entered within a given input field. To ensure that a given `TextBox` contains a valid US Social Security number, you could define the widget as follows:

```
<asp:RegularExpressionValidator ID="RegularExpressionValidator1"
  runat="server" ControlToValidate="txtRegExp"
  ErrorMessage="Please enter a valid US SSN."
  ValidationExpression="\d{3}-\d{2}-\d{4}">
</asp:RegularExpressionValidator>
```

Notice how the `RegularExpressionValidator` defines a `ValidationExpression` property. If you have never worked with regular expressions before, all you need to be aware of for this example is that they are used to match a given string pattern. Here, the expression `"\d{3}-\d{2}-\d{4}"` is capturing a standard US Social Security number of the form xxx-xx-xxxx (where x is any digit).

This particular regular expression is fairly self-explanatory; however, assume you wish to test for a valid Japanese phone number. The correct expression now becomes much more complex: `"(0\d{1,4}-|\(0\d{1,4}\)?)?\d{1,4}-\d{4}"`. The good news is that when you select the `ValidationExpression` property using the Properties window, you can pick from a predefined set of common regular expressions by clicking the ellipse button.

■ **Note** If you are interested in regular expressions, you will be happy to know that the .NET platform supplies two namespaces (`System.Text.RegularExpressions` and `System.Web.RegularExpressions`) devoted to the programmatic manipulation of such patterns.

The RangeValidator

In addition to a `MinimumValue` and `MaximumValue` property, `RangeValidators` have a property named `Type`. Because you are interested in testing the user-supplied input against a range of whole numbers, you need to specify `Integer` (which is *not* the default!):

```
<asp:RangeValidator ID="RangeValidator1"
  runat="server" ControlToValidate="txtRange"
  ErrorMessage="Please enter value between 0 and 100."

  MaximumValue="100" MinimumValue="0" Type="Integer">
</asp:RangeValidator>
```

The `RangeValidator` can also be used to test whether a given value is between a currency value, date, floating-point number, or string data (the default setting).

The CompareValidator

Finally, notice that the `CompareValidator` supports an `Operator` property:

```
<asp:CompareValidator ID="CompareValidator1" runat="server"
  ControlToValidate="txtComparison"
  ErrorMessage="Enter a value less than 20." Operator="LessThan"
  ValueToCompare="20" Type="Integer">
</asp:CompareValidator>
```

Given that the role of this validator is to compare the value in the text box against another value using a binary operator, it should be no surprise that the `Operator` property may be set to values such as `LessThan`, `GreaterThan`, `Equal`, and `NotEqual`. Also note that the `ValueToCompare` is used to establish a value to compare against. Do notice here that we have set the `Type` attribute to `Integer`. By default, the `CompareValidator` will be testing against string values!

■ **Note** The `CompareValidator` can also be configured to compare a value within another Web Form control (rather than a hard-coded value) using the `ControlToValidate` property.

To finish up the code for this page, handle the `Click` event for the `Button` control and inform the user that he or she has succeeded in the validation logic:

```
Partial Class _Default
    Inherits System.Web.UI.Page

    Protected Sub btnPostback_Click(ByVal sender As Object, ByVal e As EventArgs)
        Handles btnPostBack.Click
        lblValidationComplete.Text = "You passed validation!"
    End Sub
End Class
```

Now, navigate to this page using your browser of choice. At this point, you should not see any noticeable changes. However, when you attempt to click the Submit button after entering bogus data, your error message is suddenly visible. Once you enter valid data, the error messages are removed and postback occurs.

If you look at the HTML rendered by the browser, you see that the validation controls generate a client-side JavaScript function that makes use of a specific library of JavaScript functions that is automatically downloaded to the user's machine. Once the validation has occurred, the form data is posted back to the server, where the ASP.NET runtime will perform the *same* validation tests on the web server (just to ensure that no along-the-wire tampering has taken place).

On a related note, if the HTTP request was sent by a browser that does not support client-side JavaScript, all validation will occur on the server. In this way, you can program against the validation controls without being concerned with the target browser; the returned HTML page redirects the error processing back to the web server.

Creating Validation Summaries

The next validation-centric topic we will examine here is the use of the `ValidationSummary` widget. Currently, each of your validators displays its error message at the exact place in which it was positioned at design time. In many cases, this may be exactly what you are looking for. However, on a complex form with numerous input widgets, you may not want to have random blobs of red text pop up. Using the `ValidationSummary` type, you can instruct all of your validation types to display their error messages at a specific location on the page.

The first step is to simply place a `ValidationSummary` on your `*.aspx` file. You may optionally set the `HeaderText` property of this type as well as the `DisplayMode`, which by default will list all error messages as a bulleted list.

```
<asp:ValidationSummary id="ValidationSummary1"
  runat="server" Width="353px"
  HeaderText="Here are the things you must correct.">
</asp:ValidationSummary>
```

Next, you need to set the `Display` property to `None` for each of the individual validators (e.g., `RequiredFieldValidator`, `RangeValidator`) on the page. This will ensure that you do not see duplicate error messages for a given validation failure (one in the summary pane and another at the validator's location). Figure 33-20 shows the summary pane in action.

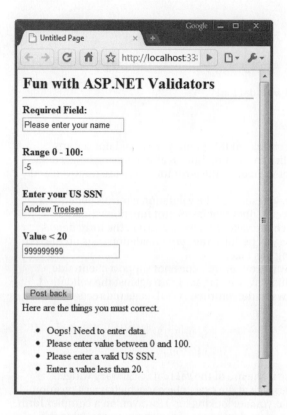

Figure 33-20. Using a validation summary

Last but not least, if you would rather have the error messages displayed using a client-side `MessageBox`, set the `ValidationSummary` control's `ShowMessageBox` property to `True` and the `ShowSummary` property to `False`.

Defining Validation Groups

It is also possible to define *groups* for validators to belong to. This can be very helpful when you have regions of a page that work as a collective whole. For example, you may have one group of controls in a `Panel` object to allow the user to enter his or her mailing address and another `Panel` containing UI elements to gather credit card information. Using groups, you can configure each group of controls to be validated independently.

Insert a new page into your current project named `ValidationGroups.aspx` that defines two `Panels`. The first `Panel` object expects a `TextBox` to contain some form of user input (via a `RequiredFieldValidator`) and the second `Panel` expects a US SSN value (via a `RegularExpressionValidator`). Figure 33-21 shows one possible UI.

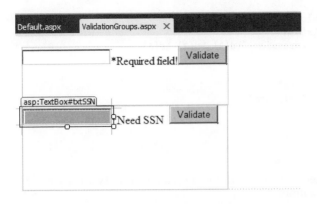

Figure 33-21. These Panel objects will independently configure their input areas

To ensure that the validators function independently, simply assign each validator and the control being validated to a uniquely named group using the ValidationGroup property. In the following possible markup, note that the Click event handlers used here are essentially empty stubs in the code file, and they are only used to allow postback to occur to the web server:

```
<form id="form1" runat="server">

  <asp:Panel ID="Panel1" runat="server" Height="83px" Width="296px">
    <asp:TextBox ID="txtRequiredData" runat="server"
              ValidationGroup="FirstGroup">
    </asp:TextBox>
    <asp:RequiredFieldValidator ID="RequiredFieldValidator1" runat="server"
        ErrorMessage="*Required field!" ControlToValidate="txtRequiredData"
        ValidationGroup="FirstGroup">
    </asp:RequiredFieldValidator>
    <asp:Button ID="bntValidateRequired" runat="server"
        OnClick="bntValidateRequired_Click"
        Text="Validate" ValidationGroup="FirstGroup" />
  </asp:Panel>

  <asp:Panel ID="Panel2" runat="server" Height="119px" Width="295px">
    <asp:TextBox ID="txtSSN" runat="server"
        ValidationGroup="SecondGroup">
    </asp:TextBox>
```

```
    <asp:RegularExpressionValidator ID="RegularExpressionValidator1"
        runat="server" ControlToValidate="txtSSN"
        ErrorMessage="*Need SSN" ValidationExpression="\d{3}-\d{2}-\d{4}"
        ValidationGroup="SecondGroup">
    </asp:RegularExpressionValidator> 
    <asp:Button ID="btnValidateSSN" runat="server"
        OnClick="btnValidateSSN_Click" Text="Validate"
        ValidationGroup="SecondGroup" />
</asp:Panel>
```

```
</form>
```

Now, right-click this page's designer and select the View In Browser menu option to verify each panel's widgets operate in a mutually exclusive manner.

■ **Source Code** The ValidatorCtrls website is included under the Chapter 33 subdirectory.

Working with Themes

At this point, you have had the chance to work with numerous ASP.NET web controls. As you have seen, each control exposes a set of properties (many of which are inherited by `System.Web.UI.WebControls.WebControl`) that allow you to establish a given UI look and feel (background color, font size, border style, and whatnot). Of course, on a multipaged website, it is quite common for the site as a whole to define a common look and feel for various types of widgets. For example, all `TextBox`es might be configured to support a given font, all `Button`s have a custom image, and all `Calendar`s have a light blue border.

Obviously, it would be very labor intensive (and error prone) to establish the *same* property settings for *every* widget on *every* page within your website. Even if you were able to manually update the properties of each UI widget on each page, imagine how painful it would be when you now need to change the background color for each `TextBox` yet again. Clearly, there must be a better way to apply sitewide UI settings.

One approach to simplifying the application of a common UI look and feel is to define *style sheets*. If you have a background in web development, you are aware that style sheets define a common set of UI-centric settings that are applied on the browser. As you would hope, ASP.NET web controls can be assigned a given style by assigning the `CssStyle` property.

However, ASP.NET ships with a complementary technology to define a common UI termed *themes*. Unlike a style sheet, themes are applied on the web server (rather than the browser) and can be done so programmatically or declaratively. Given that a theme is applied on the web server, it has access to all the server-side resources on the website. Furthermore, themes are defined by authoring the same markup you would find within any `*.aspx` file (as you may agree, the syntax of a style sheet is a bit on the terse side).

Recall from Chapter 32 that ASP.NET web applications may define any number of special subdirectories, one of which is App_Themes. This single subdirectory may be further partitioned with additional subdirectories, each of which represents a possible theme on your site. For example, consider Figure 33-22, which illustrates a single App_Themes folder containing three subdirectories, each of which has a set of files that make up the theme itself.

Figure 33-22. A single App_Theme folder may define numerous themes

Understanding *.skin Files

The one file that every theme subdirectory is sure to have is a *.skin file. These files define the look and feel for various web controls. To illustrate, create a new website named FunWithThemes. Next, insert a new *.skin file (using the Website ➤ Add New Item menu option) named BasicGreen.skin, as shown in Figure 33-23.

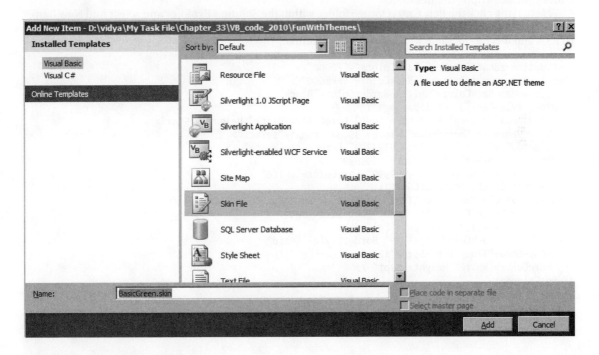

*Figure 33-23. Inserting *.skin files*

Visual Studio 2010 will prompt you to confirm this file can be added into an App_Themes folder (which is exactly what we want). If you were now to look in your Solution Explorer, you would indeed find your App_Themes folder has a subfolder named BasicGreen containing your new `BasicGreen.skin` file.

A `*.skin` file is where you are able to define the look and feel for various widgets using ASP.NET control declaration syntax. Sadly, the IDE does not provide designer support for `*.skin` files. One way to reduce the amount of typing time is to insert a temporary `*.aspx` file into your program (`temp.aspx`, for example) that can be used to build up the UI of the widgets using the Visual Studio 2010 page designer.

The resulting markup can then be copied and pasted into your `*.skin` file. When you do so, however, you *must* delete the ID attribute for each web control! This should make sense, given that we are not trying to define a UI look and feel for a particular Button (for example) but *all* Buttons.

This being said, here is the markup for `BasicGreen.skin` that defines a default look and feel for the Button, TextBox, and Calendar types:

```
<asp:Button runat="server" BackColor="#80FF80"/>
<asp:TextBox runat="server" BackColor="#80FF80"/>
<asp:Calendar runat="server" BackColor="#80FF80"/>
```

Notice that each widget still has the `runat="server"` attribute (which is mandatory), and none of the widgets have been assigned an ID attribute.

Now, let's define a second theme named CrazyOrange. Using the Solution Explorer, right-click your App_Themes folder and add a new theme named CrazyOrange. This will create a new subdirectory under your site's App_Themes folder.

Next, right-click the new CrazyOrange folder within the Solution Explorer and select Add New Item. From the resulting dialog box, add a new `*.skin` file. Update the `CrazyOrange.skin` file to define a unique UI look and feel for the same web controls. For example:

```
<asp:Button runat="server" BackColor="#FF8000"/>
<asp:TextBox runat="server" BackColor="#FF8000"/>
<asp:Calendar BackColor="White" BorderColor="Black"
  BorderStyle="Solid" CellSpacing="1"
  Font-Names="Verdana" Font-Size="9pt" ForeColor="Black" Height="250px"
  NextPrevFormat="ShortMonth" Width="330px" runat="server">
  <SelectedDayStyle BackColor="#333399" ForeColor="White" />
  <OtherMonthDayStyle ForeColor="#999999" />
  <TodayDayStyle BackColor="#999999" ForeColor="White" />
  <DayStyle BackColor="#CCCCCC" />
  <NextPrevStyle Font-Bold="True" Font-Size="8pt" ForeColor="White" />
  <DayHeaderStyle Font-Bold="True" Font-Size="8pt"
    ForeColor="#333333" Height="8pt" />
  <TitleStyle BackColor="#333399" BorderStyle="Solid"
    Font-Bold="True" Font-Size="12pt"
    ForeColor="White" Height="12pt" />
</asp:Calendar>
```

At this point, your Solution Explorer should like Figure 33-24.

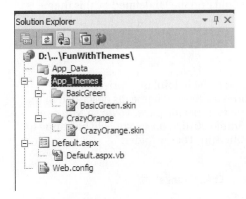

Figure 33-24. A single website with multiple themes

Now that your site has a few themes defined, the next logical question is how to apply them to your pages? As you might guess, there are many ways to do so.

■ **Note** To be sure, these example themes are quite bland by design (in order to reduce the amount of markup on the printed page). Feel free to spruce things up to your liking.

Applying Sitewide Themes

If you wish to make sure that every page in your site adheres to the same theme, the simplest way to do so is to update your `web.config` file. Open your current `web.config` file and define a `<pages>` element within the scope of your `<system.web>` root element. If you add a theme attribute to the `<pages>` element, this will ensure that every page in your website is assigned the selected theme (which is, of course, the name of one of the subdirectories under App_Theme). Here is the core update:

```
<configuration>
  <system.web>
    ...
    <pages theme="BasicGreen">
    </pages>
  </system.web>
</configuration>
```

If you were to now place various Buttons, Calendars, and TextBoxes onto your Default.aspx file and run the application, you would find each widget has the UI of BasicGreen. If you were to update the theme attribute to CrazyOrange and run the page again, you would find the UI defined by this theme is used instead.

Applying Themes at the Page Level

It is also possible to assign themes on a page-by-page level. This can be helpful in a variety of circumstances. For example, perhaps your web.config file defines a sitewide theme (as described in the previous section); however, you wish to assign a different theme to a specific page. To do so, you can simply update the <%@Page%> directive. If you are using Visual Studio 2010 to do so, you will be happy to find that IntelliSense will display each defined theme within your App_Theme folder.

```
<%@ Page Language="VB" AutoEventWireup="False"
    CodeFile="Default.aspx.vb" Inherits="_Default" Theme ="CrazyOrange" %>
```

Because you assigned the CrazyOrange theme to this page, but the Web.config file specified the BasicGreen theme, all pages *but this page* will be rendered using BasicGreen.

The SkinID Property

Sometimes you wish to define a set of possible UI look and feel scenarios for a single widget. For example, assume you want to define two possible UIs for the Button type within the CrazyOrange theme. When you wish do so, you may differentiate each look and feel using the SkinID property of a control within the *.skin file:

```
<asp:Button runat="server" BackColor="#FF8000"/>
<asp:Button runat="server" SkinID = "BigFontButton"
            Font-Size="30pt" BackColor="#FF8000"/>
```

Now, if you have a page that makes use of the CrazyOrange theme, each Button will, by default, be assigned the unnamed Button skin. If you wish to have various buttons within the *.aspx file make use of the BigFontButton skin, simply specify the SkinID property within the markup:

```
<asp:Button ID="Button2" runat="server"
            SkinID="BigFontButton" Text="Button" /><br />
```

Assigning Themes Programmatically

Last but not least, it is possible to assign a theme in code. This can be helpful when you wish to provide a way for end users to select a theme for their current session. Of course, we have not yet showed you how to build stateful web applications, so the current theme selection will be forgotten between postbacks. In a production-level site, you may wish to store the user's current theme selection within a session variable, or persist the theme selection to a database.

To illustrate how to assign a theme programmatically, update the UI of your `Default.aspx` file with three new `Button` controls as shown in Figure 33-25. Once you have done so, handle the `Click` event for each `Button` type.

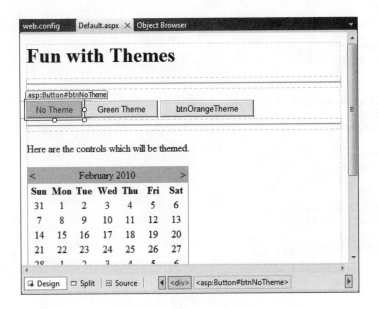

Figure 33-25. The updated UI of the themes example

Now be aware that you can only assign a theme programmatically during specific phases of your page's life cycle. Typically, this will be done within the `Page_PreInit` event. This being said, update your code file as follows:

```
Partial Class _Default
    Inherits System.Web.UI.Page

    Protected Sub btnNoTheme_Click(ByVal sender As Object, ByVal e As EventArgs)
        Handles btnNoTheme.Click
        ' Empty strings result in no theme being applied.
        Session("UserTheme") = ""

        ' Triggers the PreInit event again.
        Server.Transfer(Request.FilePath)
    End Sub

    Protected Sub btnGreenTheme_Click(ByVal sender As Object, ByVal e As EventArgs)
        Handles btnGreenTheme.Click
        Session("UserTheme") = "BasicGreen"

        ' Triggers the PreInit event again.
        Server.Transfer(Request.FilePath)
    End Sub

    Protected Sub btnOrangeTheme_Click(ByVal sender As Object, ByVal e As EventArgs)
        Handles btnOrangeTheme.Click
        Session("UserTheme") = "CrazyOrange"

        ' Triggers the PreInit event again.
        Server.Transfer(Request.FilePath)
    End Sub

    Protected Sub Page_PreInit(ByVal sender As Object,
    ByVal e As System.EventArgs) Handles Me.PreInit
        Try
            Theme = Session("UserTheme").ToString()
        Catch
            Theme = ""
        End Try
    End Sub
End Class
```

Notice that we are storing the selected theme within a session variable (see Chapter 33 for details) named UserTheme, which is formally assigned within the Page_PreInit() event handler. Also note that when the user clicks a given Button, we programmatically force the PreInit event to fire by calling Server.Transfer() and requesting the current page once again. If you were to run this page, you would now find that you can establish your theme via various Button clicks.

■ **Source Code** The FunWithThemes web site is included under the Chapter 33 subdirectory.

Summary

This chapter examined how to make use of various ASP.NET web controls. We began by examining the role of the `Control` and `WebControl` base classes, and you learned how to dynamically interact with a panel's internal controls collection. Along the way, you were exposed to the new site navigation model (`*.sitemap` files and the `SiteMapDataSource` component), the new data binding engine (via the `SqlDataSource` component and the `GridView` control), and various validation -controls.

The latter half of this chapter examined the role of master pages and themes. Recall that master pages can be used to define a common layout for a set of pages on your site. Also recall that the `*.master` file defines any number of content placeholders to which content pages plug in their custom UI content. Finally, as you were shown, the ASP.NET theme engine allows you to declaratively or programmatically apply a common UI look and feel to your widgets on the web server.

■ ■ ■

## CHAPTER 34

ASP.NET State Management Techniques

The previous two chapters concentrated on the composition and behavior of ASP.NET pages and the web controls they contain. This chapter builds on that information by examining the role of the `Global.asax` file and the underlying `HttpApplication` type. As you will see, the functionality of `HttpApplication` allows you to intercept numerous events that enable you to treat your web application as a cohesive unit, rather than a set of stand-alone `*.aspx` files driven by a master page.

In addition to investigating the `HttpApplication` type, this chapter also addresses the all-important topic of state management. Here you will learn the role of view state, session and application variables (including the application cache), cookie data, and the ASP.NET Profile API.

The Issue of State

At the beginning of the Chapter 32, I pointed out that HTTP on the Web results in a *stateless* wire protocol. This very fact makes web development extremely different from the process of building an executable assembly. For example, when you are building a Windows Forms application, you can rest assured that any member variables defined in the `Form`-derived class will typically exist in memory until the user explicitly shuts down the executable:

```
Public Class MainWindow
          ' State data!
          Private userFavoriteCar As String = "Yugo"
End Class
```

In the World Wide Web environment, however, you are not afforded the same luxurious assumption. To prove the point, create a new ASP.NET Empty Web Site project named SimpleStateExample and insert a new Web Form. In the code-behind file of your `*.aspx` file, define a page-level String variable named `userFavoriteCar`:

```
Partial Class _Default
    Inherits System.Web.UI.Page
        ' State data?
        Private userFavoriteCar As String = "Yugo"

End Class
```

Next, construct the web UI as shown in Figure 34-1.

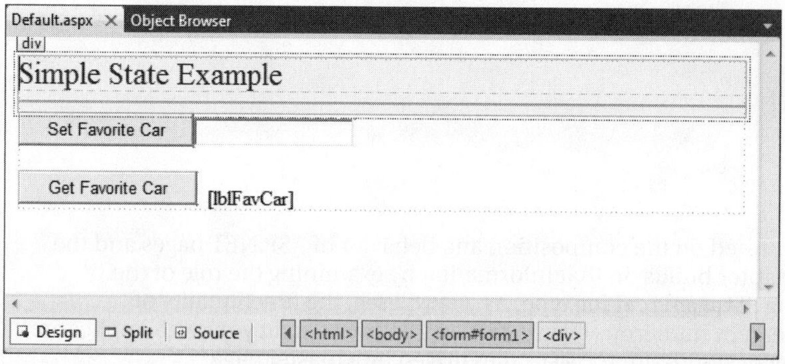

Figure 34-1. *The UI for the simple state page*

The server-side **Click** event handler for the Set button (named **btnSetCar**) allows the user to assign the **string** member variable to the value within the **TextBox** (named **txtFavCar**):

```
Protected Sub btnSetCar_Click(ByVal sender As Object, ByVal e As EventArgs)
    Handles btnSetCar.Click
    ' Store fave car in member variable.
    userFavoriteCar = txtFavCar.Text
End Sub
```

The **Click** event handler for the Get button (**btnGetCar**) displays the current value of the member variable within the page's **Label** widget (**lblFavCar**):

```
Protected Sub btnGetCar_Click(ByVal sender As Object, ByVal e As EventArgs)
    Handles btnGetCar.Click
    ' Show value of member variable.
    lblFavCar.Text = userFavoriteCar
End Sub
```

Now, if you were building a Windows Forms application, you would be right to assume that once the user sets the initial value, it would be remembered throughout the life of the desktop application. Sadly, when you run this web application, you find that each time you post back to the web server (by clicking either button), the value of the **userFavoriteCar** String variable is set back to the initial value of "Yugo"; therefore, the **Label**'s text is continuously fixed.

Again, given that HTTP has no clue how to automatically remember data once the HTTP response has been sent, it stands to reason that the Page object is destroyed almost instantly. As a result, when the client posts back to the *.aspx file, a new Page object is constructed that will reset any page-level member variables. This is clearly a major issue. Imagine how useless online shopping would be if every time you posted back to the web server, any and all information you previously entered (such as the items you wished to purchase) were discarded. When you wish to remember information regarding the users who are logged on to your site, you need to make use of various state management techniques.

■ **Note** This issue is in no way limited to ASP.NET. Java web applications, CGI applications, classic ASP applications, and PHP applications all must contend with the thorny issue of state management.

To remember the value of the userFavoriteCar String type between postbacks, one approach is to store the value of this String type in a *session variable*. We will examine the details of session state in the pages that follow. For the sake of completion, however, here are the necessary updates for the current page (note that you are no longer using the Private String member variable, so feel free to comment out or remove the definition altogether):

```
Partial Class _Default
    Inherits System.Web.UI.Page
    ' State data?
    ' Private userFavoriteCar As String = "Yugo"

    Protected Sub btnSetCar_Click(ByVal sender As Object, ByVal e As EventArgs)
        Handles btnSetCar.Click
        ' Store value to be remembered in session variable.
        Session("UserFavCar") = txtFavCar.Text
    End Sub

    Protected Sub btnGetCar_Click(ByVal sender As Object, ByVal e As EventArgs)
        Handles btnGetCar.Click
        ' Get session variable value.
        lblFavCar.Text = CStr(Session("UserFavCar"))
    End Sub
End Class
```

If you now run the application, the value of your favorite automobile will be preserved across postbacks, thanks to the HttpSessionState object manipulated indirectly by the inherited Session property.

■ **Source Code** The SimpleStateExample web site is included under the Chapter 34 subdirectory.

ASP.NET State Management Techniques

ASP.NET provides several mechanisms you can use to maintain stateful information in your web applications. Specifically, you can:

- Use ASP.NET view state.

- Use ASP.NET control state.

- Define application-level data.

- Use the cache object.

- Define session-level data.

- Define cookie data.

In addition to these techniques, if you want to persist user data in a permanent manner, ASP.NET provides an out-of-the-box Profile API. We'll examine the details of each approach in turn, beginning with the topic of ASP.NET view state.

Understanding the Role of ASP.NET View State

The term *view state* has been thrown out a few times here and in the previous two chapters without a formal definition, so let's demystify this term once and for all. Under classic (COM-based) ASP, web developers were required to manually repopulate the values of the incoming form widgets during the process of constructing the outgoing HTTP response. For example, if the incoming HTTP request contained five text boxes with specific values, the `*.asp` file required script code to extract the current values (via the `Form` or `QueryString` collections of the `Request` object) and manually place them back into the HTTP response stream. Needless to say, this was a drag. If the developer failed to do so, the caller was presented with a set of five empty text boxes!

Under ASP.NET, we no longer have to manually scrape out and repopulate the values in the HTML widgets because the ASP.NET runtime automatically embeds a hidden form field (named `__VIEWSTATE`), which will flow between the browser and a specific page. The data assigned to this field is a Base64-encoded string that contains a set of name/value pairs representing the values of each GUI widget on the page at hand.

The `System.Web.UI.Page` base class's `Init` event handler is the entity in charge of reading the incoming values in the `__VIEWSTATE` field to populate the appropriate member variables in the derived class. (This is why it is risky at best to access the state of a web widget within the scope of a page's `Init` event handler.)

Also, just before the outgoing response is emitted back to the requesting browser, the `__VIEWSTATE` data is used to repopulate the form's widgets. Clearly, the best thing about this aspect of ASP.NET is that it just happens without any work on your part. Of course, you are always able to interact with, alter, or disable this default functionality if you so choose. To understand how to do this, let's see a concrete view state example.

Demonstrating View State

First, create a new ASP.NET Empty Web Site called ViewStateApp and insert a new Web Form. On your .aspx page, add a single ASP.NET ListBox web control named myListBox and a single Button control named btnPostback. Handle the Click event for the Button to provide a way for the user to post back to the web server:

```
Partial Class _Default
   Inherits System.Web.UI.Page

      Protected Sub btnPostback_Click(ByVal sender As Object, ByVal e As EventArgs)
      Handles btnPostBack.Click
       ' No-op. This is just here to allow a postback.
      End Sub
End Class
```

Now, using the Visual Studio 2010 Properties window, access the Items property and add four ListItems to the ListBox using the associated dialog box. The resulting markup looks like this:

```
<asp:ListBox ID="myListBox" runat="server">
  <asp:ListItem>Item One</asp:ListItem>
  <asp:ListItem>Item Two</asp:ListItem>
  <asp:ListItem>Item Three</asp:ListItem>
  <asp:ListItem>Item Four</asp:ListItem>
</asp:ListBox>
```

Note that you are hard-coding the items in the ListBox directly within the *.aspx file. As you already know, all <asp:> definitions in an HTML form will automatically render back their HTML representation before the final HTTP response (provided they have the runat="server" attribute).

The <%@Page%> directive has an optional attribute called EnableViewState that by default is set to True. To disable this behavior, simply update the <%@Page%> directive as follows:

```
<%@ Page Language="VB" AutoEventWireup="false"
  CodeFile="Default.aspx.vb" Inherits="_Default"
  EnableViewState ="false" %>
```

So, what exactly does it mean to disable view state? The answer is, it depends. Given the previous definition of the term, you would think that if you disable view state for an *.aspx file, the values in your ListBox would not be remembered between postbacks to the web server. However, if you were to run this application as is, you might be surprised to find that the information in the ListBox is retained regardless of how many times you post back to the page.

In fact, if you examine the source HTML returned to the browser (by right-clicking the page within the browser and selecting View Source), you may be further surprised to see that the hidden __VIEWSTATE field is *still present*:

```
<input type="hidden" name="__VIEWSTATE" id="__VIEWSTATE"
  value="/wEPDwUKLTM4MTM2MDM4NGRkqGC6gjEV25JnddkJiRmoIc1oSIA=" />
```

However, assume that your ListBox is dynamically populated within the code-behind file rather than within the HTML <form> definition. First, remove the <asp:ListItem> declarations from the current *.aspx file:

```
<asp:ListBox ID="myListBox" runat="server">
</asp:ListBox>
```

Next, fill the list items within the Load event handler in your code-behind file:

```
Protected Sub Page_Load(ByVal sender As Object, ByVal e As EventArgs) Handles Me.Load
    If Not IsPostBack Then
        ' Fill ListBox dynamically!
        myListBox.Items.Add("Item One")
        myListBox.Items.Add("Item Two")
        myListBox.Items.Add("Item Three")
        myListBox.Items.Add("Item Four")
    End If
End Sub
```

If you post to this updated page, you'll find that the first time the browser requests the page, the values in the ListBox are present and accounted for. However, on postback, the ListBox is suddenly empty. The first rule of ASP.NET view state is that its effect is only realized when you have widgets whose values are dynamically generated through code. If you hard-code values within the *.aspx file's <form> tags, the state of these items is always remembered across postbacks (even when you set EnableViewState to false for a given page).

If the idea of disabling view state for the entire *.aspx file seems a bit too aggressive, know that every descendent of the System.Web.UI.Control base class inherits the EnableViewState property, which makes it very simple to disable view state on a control-by-control basis:

```
<asp:GridView id="myHugeDynamicallyFilledGridOfData" runat="server"
 EnableViewState="false">
</asp:GridView>
```

■ **Note** Under .NET 4.0, large view state data values are automatically compressed, to help reduce the size of this hidden form field.

Adding Custom View State Data

In addition to the EnableViewState property, the System.Web.UI.Control base class provides a Protected property named ViewState. Under the hood, this property provides access to a System.Web.UI.StateBag type, which represents all the data contained within the __VIEWSTATE field. Using the indexer of the StateBag type, you can embed custom information within the hidden __VIEWSTATE form field using a set of name/value pairs. Here's a simple example:

```
Protected Sub btnAddToVS_Click(ByVal sender As Object, ByVal e As EventArgs)
    Handles btnAddToVS.Click
        ViewState("CustomViewStateItem") = "Some user data"
        lblVSValue.Text = CStr(ViewState("CustomViewStateItem"))
End Sub
```

Because the `System.Web.UI.StateBag` type has been designed to operate on `System.Object` types, when you wish to access the value of a given key, you should explicitly cast it into the correct underlying data type (in this case, a `System.String`). Be aware, however, that values placed within the `__VIEWSTATE` field cannot literally be any object. Specifically, the only valid types are `String`s, `Integer`s, `Boolean`s, `ArrayList`s, `Hashtable`s, or an array of these types.

So, given that `.aspx` pages can insert custom bits of information into the `__VIEWSTATE` string, the next logical question is when you would want to do so. Most of the time, custom view-state data is best suited for user-specific preferences. For example, you may establish view-state data that specifies how a user wishes to view the UI of a `GridView` (such as a sort order). However, view-state data is not well-suited for full-blown user data, such as items in a shopping cart or cached `DataSet`s. When you need to store this sort of complex information, you must work with session or application data. Before we get to that point, though, you need to understand the role of the `Global.asax` `Global.asax` file.

■ **Source Code** The ViewStateApp web site is included under the Chapter 34 subdirectory.

The Role of the Global.asax File

At this point, an ASP.NET application may seem little more than a set of `.aspx` files and their respective web controls. While you could build a web application by simply linking a set of related web pages, you will most likely need a way to interact with the web application as a whole. To this end, an ASP.NET application may choose to include an optional `Global.asax` file via the Web Site ➤ Add New Item menu option, as shown in Figure 34-2 (notice you are selecting the Global Application Class icon).

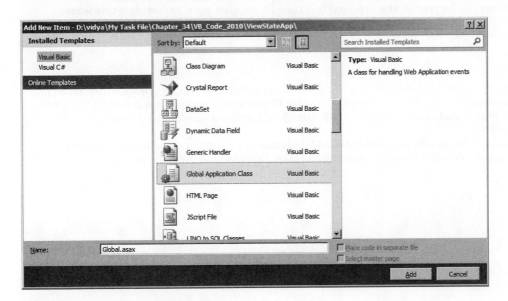

Figure 34-2. The Global.asax file

Simply put, `Global.asax` is just about as close to a traditional double-clickable `*.exe` as you can get in the world of ASP.NET, meaning this type represents the runtime behavior of the web site itself. When you insert a `Global.asax` file into a web project, you'll see it's little more than a `<script>` block containing a set of event handlers:

```vb
<%@ Application Language="VB" %>

<script runat="server">

    Sub Application_Start(ByVal sender As Object, ByVal e As EventArgs)
        ' Code that runs on application startup.
    End Sub

    Sub Application_End(ByVal sender As Object, ByVal e As EventArgs)
        ' Code that runs on application shutdown
    End Sub

    Sub Application_Error(ByVal sender As Object, ByVal e As EventArgs)
        ' Code that runs when an unhandled error occurs
    End Sub

    Sub Session_Start(ByVal sender As Object, ByVal e As EventArgs)
        ' Code that runs when a new session is started
    End Sub

    Sub Session_End(ByVal sender As Object, ByVal e As EventArgs)
        ' Code that runs when a session ends.
        ' Note: The Session_End event is raised only when the sessionstate mode
        ' is set to InProc in the Web.config file. If session mode is set to StateServer
        ' or SQLServer, the event is not raised.
    End Sub

</script>
```

Looks can be deceiving, however. At runtime, the code within this `<script>` block is assembled into a class type deriving from `System.Web.HttpApplication` (if you have a background in ASP.NET 1.x, you may recall that the `Global.asax` code-behind file literally did define a class deriving from `HttpApplication`).

As mentioned, the members defined inside `Global.asax` are event handlers that allow you to interact with application-level (and session-level) events. Table 34-1 documents the role of each member.

Table 34-1. Core Types of the System.Web Namespace

Event Handler	Meaning in Life
Application_Start()	This event handler is called the very first time the web application is launched. Thus, this event will fire exactly once over the lifetime of a web application. It is an ideal place to define application-level data used throughout your web application.
Application_End()	This event handler is called when the application is shutting down. This will occur when the last user times out or if you manually shut down the application via IIS.
Session_Start()	This event handler is fired when a new user reaches your application. Here you can establish any user-specific data points you want to preserve across postbacks.
Session_End()	This event handler is fired when a user's session has terminated (typically through a predefined timeout).
Application_Error()	This is a global error handler that will be called when an unhandled exception is thrown by the web application.

The Global Last-Chance Exception Event Handler

First, let me point out the role of the Application_Error() event handler. Recall that a specific page may handle the Error event to process any unhandled exception that occurred within the scope of the page itself. In a similar light, the Application_Error() event handler is the final place to handle an exception that was not handled by a given page. As with the page-level Error event, you are able to access the specific System.Exception using the inherited Server property:

```
Sub Application_Error(ByVal sender As Object, ByVal e As EventArgs)
    ' Obtain the unhandled error.
    Dim ex As Exception = Server.GetLastError()

    ' Process error here...

    ' Clear error when finished.
    Server.ClearError()
End Sub
```

Given that the Application_Error() event handler is the last-chance exception handler for your web application, it is quite common to implement this method in such a way that the user is transferred to a predefined error page on the server. Other common duties may include sending an e-mail to the web administrator or writing to an external error log.

The HttpApplication Base Class

As mentioned, the `Global.asax` script is dynamically generated as a class deriving from the `System.Web.HttpApplication` base class, which supplies some of the same sort of functionality as the `System.Web.UI.Page` type (without a visible user interface). Table 34-2 documents the key members of interest.

Table 34-2. Key Members Defined by the System.Web.HttpApplication Type

Property	Meaning in Life
Application	This property allows you to interact with application-level data, using the exposed `HttpApplicationState` type.
Request	This property allows you to interact with the incoming HTTP request, using the underlying `HttpRequest` object.
Response	This property allows you to interact with the incoming HTTP response, using the underlying `HttpResponse` object.
Server	This property gets the intrinsic server object for the current request, using the underlying `HttpServerUtility` object.
Session	This property allows you to interact with session-level data, using the underlying `HttpSessionState` object.

Again, given that the `Global.asax` file does not explicitly document that `HttpApplication` is the underlying base class, it is important to remember that all of the rules of the "is-a" relationship do indeed apply. For example, if you were to apply the dot operator to the `MyBase` keyword (or if you prefer, the `Me` keyword) within any of the members in `Global.asax`, you would find you have immediate access to all members of the chain of inheritance, as you see in Figure 34-3.

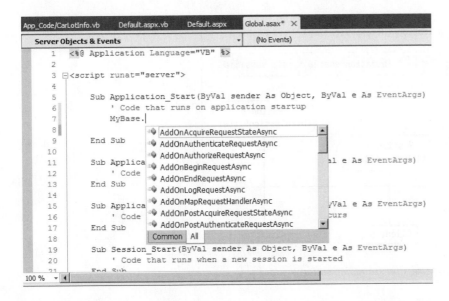

Figure 34-3. Remember that HttpApplication is the parent of the type lurking within Global.asax.

Understanding the Application/Session Distinction

Under ASP.NET, application state is maintained by an instance of the HttpApplicationState type. This class enables you to share global information across all users (and all pages) using your ASP.NET application. Not only can application data be shared by all users on your site, but also if the value of an application-level data point changes, the new value is seen by all users on their next postback.

On the other hand, session state is used to remember information for a specific user (again, such as items in a shopping cart). Physically, a user's session state is represented by the HttpSessionState class type. When a new user reaches an ASP.NET web application, the runtime will automatically assign that user a new session ID, which by default will expire after 20 minutes of inactivity. Thus, if 20,000 users are logged on to your site, you have 20,000 distinct HttpSessionState objects, each of which is automatically assigned a unique session ID. The relationship between a web application and web sessions is shown in Figure 34-4.

If you have ever worked with classic ASP, you might recall that application- and session-state data is represented using distinct COM objects (e.g., Application and Session). Under ASP.NET, Page-derived types as well as the HttpApplication type use identically named properties (i.e., Application and Session), which expose the underlying HttpApplicationState and HttpSessionState types.

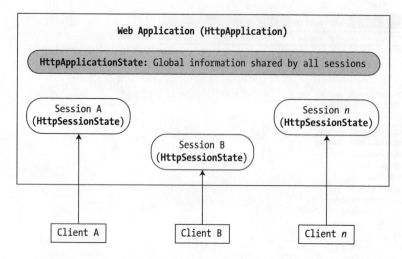

Figure 34-4. The application/session state distinction

Maintaining Application-Level State Data

The **HttpApplicationState** type enables developers to share global information across multiple users in an ASP.NET application. Table 34-3 describes some core members of this type.

Table 34-3. Members of the HttpApplicationState Type

Members	Meaning in Life
Add()	This method allows you to add a new name/value pair to the **HttpApplicationState** object. Do note that this method is typically *not* used in favor of the indexer of the **HttpApplicationState** class.
AllKeys	This property returns an array of **String** objects that represent all the names in the **HttpApplicationState** type.
Clear()	This method deletes all items in the **HttpApplicationState** object. This is functionally equivalent to the **RemoveAll()** method.
Count	This property gets the number of item objects in the **HttpApplicationState** type.
Lock(), UnLock()	These two methods are used when you wish to alter a set of application variables in a thread-safe manner.
RemoveAll(), Remove(), RemoveAt()	These methods remove a specific item (by String name) within the **Http ApplicationState** object. **RemoveAt()** removes the item via a numerical indexer.

To illustrate working with application state, create a new ASP.NET Empty Web Site project named AppState (and insert a new Web Form). Next, insert a new `Global.asax` file. When you create data members that can be shared among all users, you need to establish a set of name/value pairs. In most cases, the most natural place to do so is within the `Application_Start()` event handler in `Global.asax`, for example:

```
Sub Application_Start(ByVal sender As Object, ByVal e As EventArgs)
    ' Set up some application variables.
    Application("SalesPersonOfTheMonth") = "Chucky"
    Application("CurrentCarOnSale") = "Colt"
    Application("MostPopularColorOnLot") = "Black"
End Sub
```

During the lifetime of your web application (which is to say, until the web application is manually shut down or until the final user times out), any user on any page may access these values as necessary. Assume you have a page that will display the current discount car within a `Label` via a button `Click` event handler:

```
Protected Sub btnShowCarOnSale_Click(ByVal sender As Object, ByVal arg As EventArgs)
    Handles btnShowCarOnSale.Click
        lblCurrCarOnSale.Text = String.Format("Sale on {0}'s today!",
            CStr(Application("CurrentCarOnSale")))
End Sub
```

As with the `ViewState` property, notice how you should cast the value returned from the `HttpApplicationState` object into the correct underlying type because the `Application` property operates on general `System.Object` types.

Now, given that the `Application` property can hold any type, it should stand to reason that you can place custom types (or any .NET object) within your site's application state. Assume you'd rather maintain the three current application variables within a strongly typed class named `CarLotInfo` (located in the App_Code folder in your web site):

```
Public Class CarLotInfo
    Public Sub New(ByVal s As String, ByVal c As String, ByVal m As String)
        salesPersonOfTheMonth = s
        currentCarOnSale = c
        mostPopularColorOnLot = m
    End Sub

    ' Public for easy access, could also make use of automatic
    ' property syntax.
    Public salesPersonOfTheMonth As String
    Public currentCarOnSale As String
    Public mostPopularColorOnLot As String
End Class
```

With this helper class in place, you could modify the `Application_Start()` event handler as follows:

```
Sub Application_Start(ByVal sender As Object, ByVal e As EventArgs)
    ' Place a custom object in the application data sector.
    Application("CarSiteInfo") = New CarLotInfo("Chucky", "Colt", "Black")
End Sub
```

and then access the information using the Public field data within a server-side `Click` event handler for a `Button` control named `btnShowAppVariables`:

```
Protected Sub btnShowAppVariables_Click(ByVal sender As Object, ByVal e As EventArgs)
    Handles btnShowAppVariables.Click
        Dim appVars As CarLotInfo = (CType(Application("CarSiteInfo"), CarLotInfo))
        Dim appState As String = String.Format("<li>Car on sale: {0}</li>",
                                        appVars.currentCarOnSale)
        appState &= String.Format("<li>Most popular color: {0}</li>",
                                        appVars.mostPopularColorOnLot)
        appState &= String.Format("<li>Big shot SalesPerson: {0}</li>",
                                        appVars.salesPersonOfTheMonth)
        lblAppVariables.Text = appState
End Sub
```

Given that the current car-on-sale data is now exposed from a custom class type, your `btnShowCarOnSale Click` event handler would also need to be updated, like so:

```
Protected Sub btnShowCarOnSale_Click(ByVal sender As Object, ByVal e As EventArgs)
    Handles btnShowCarOnSale.Click
        lblCurrCarOnSale.Text = String.Format(
            "Sale on {0}'s today!",
            (CType(Application("CarSiteInfo"), CarLotInfo)).currentCarOnSale)
End Sub
```

Modifying Application Data

You may programmatically update or delete any or all application-wide data items using members of the `HttpApplicationState` type during the execution of your web application. For example, to delete a specific item, simply call the `Remove()` method. If you wish to destroy all application-level data, call `RemoveAll()`:

```
Private Sub CleanAppData()
    ' Remove a single item via string name.
    Application.Remove("SomeItemIDontNeed")

    ' Destroy all application data!
    Application.RemoveAll()
End Sub
```

If you want to change the value of an existing application-level data item, you need only make a new assignment to the data item in question. Assume your page now has a **Button** that allows your user to change the current hotshot salesperson by reading in a value from a **TextBox** named **txtNewSP**. The **Click** event handler is as you'd expect:

```
Protected Sub btnSetNewSP_Click(ByVal sender As Object, ByVal e As EventArgs)
    Handles btnSetNewSP.Click
        ' Set the new Salesperson.
        CType(Application("CarSiteInfo"), CarLotInfo).salesPersonOfTheMonth = txtNewSP.Text
End Sub
```

If you run the web application, you'll find that the application-level data item has been updated. Furthermore, given that application variables are accessible by any user on any page in the Web application, if you launched three or four instances of your web browser, you'd find that if one instance changes the current hotshot salesperson, each of the other browsers displays the new value on postback. Figure 34-5 shows some possible output.

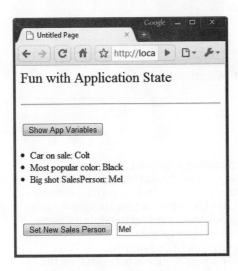

Figure 34-5. Displaying application data

Understand that if you have a situation where a set of application-level variables must be updated as a unit, you risk the possibility of data corruption (since it is technically possible that an application-level data point may be changed while another user is attempting to access it!). You could take the long road and manually lock down the logic using threading primitives of the **System.Threading** namespace, but the **HttpApplicationState** type has two methods, **Lock()** and **Unlock()**, that automatically ensure thread safety:

```
' Safely access related application data.
Application.Lock()
Application("SalesPersonOfTheMonth") = "Maxine"
Application("CurrentBonusedEmployee") = Application("SalesPersonOfTheMonth")
Application.UnLock()
```

Handling Web Application Shutdown

The HttpApplicationState type is designed to maintain the values of the items it contains until one of two situations occurs: the last user on your site times out (or manually logs out) or someone manually shuts down the web site via IIS. In either case, the Application_End() method of the HttpApplication-derived type will automatically be called. Within this event handler, you are able to perform whatever sort of cleanup is necessary:

```
Sub Application_End(ByVal sender As Object, ByVal e As EventArgs)
            ' Write current application variables
            ' to a database or whatever else you need to do...
End Sub
```

■ **Source Code** The AppState web site is included under the Chapter 34 subdirectory.

Working with the Application Cache

ASP.NET provides a second and more flexible way to handle application-wide data. As you recall, the values within the HttpApplicationState object remain in memory as long as your web application is alive and kicking. Sometimes, however, you may want to maintain a piece of application data only for a specific period of time. For example, you may wish to obtain an ADO.NET DataSet that is valid for only five minutes. After that time, you may want to obtain a fresh DataSet to account for possible database updates. While it's technically possible to build this infrastructure using HttpApplicationState and some sort of handcrafted monitor, the ASP.NET application cache greatly simplifies your task.

As its name suggests, the ASP.NET System.Web.Caching.Cache object (which is accessible via the Context.Cache property) allows you to define objects that are accessible by all users from all pages for a fixed amount of time. In its simplest form, interacting with the cache looks identical to interacting with the HttpApplicationState type:

```
' Add an item to the cache.
' This item will *not* expire.
Context.Cache("SomeStringItem") = "This is the string item"

' Get item from the cache.
Dim s As String = CStr(Context.Cache("SomeStringItem"))
```

■ **Note** If you wish to access the cache from within Global.asax, you need to use the Context property. However, if you are within the scope of a System.Web.UI.Page-derived type, you can access the Cache object directly via the page's Cache property.

The System.Web.Caching.Cache class defines only a small number of members beyond the type's indexer. You can use the Add() method to insert a new item into the cache that is not currently defined (if the specified item is already present, Add() effectively does nothing). The Insert() method will also place a member into the cache. If the item is currently defined, however, Insert() will replace the current item with the new object. Since this is generally the behavior you'll desire, I'll focus on the Insert() method exclusively.

Fun with Data Caching

Let's see an example. To begin, create a new ASP.NET Empty Web Site named CacheState and insert a Web Form and a Global.asax file. Like an application-level data item maintained by the HttpApplicationState type, the cache may hold any System.Object-derived type and is often populated within the Application_Start() event handler. For this example, the goal is to automatically update the contents of a DataSet every 15 seconds. The DataSet in question will contain the current set of records from the Inventory table of the AutoLot database created during our discussion of ADO.NET.

Given these design notes, set a reference to AutoLotDAL.dll (see Chapter 21) and update your Global.asax like so (code analysis to follow):

```vb
<%@ Application Language="VB" %>
<%@ Import Namespace = "AutoLotConnectedLayer" %>
<%@ Import Namespace = "System.Data" %>

<script runat="server">
    ' Define a Shared Cache member variable.
    Private Shared theCache As Cache

    Sub Application_Start(ByVal sender As Object, ByVal e As EventArgs)
        ' First assign the Shared 'theCache' variable.
        theCache = Context.Cache

        ' When the application starts up,
        ' read the current records in the
        ' Inventory table of the AutoLot DB.
        Dim dal As New InventoryDAL()
        dal.OpenConnection("Data Source=(local)\SQLEXPRESS;" &
                        "Initial Catalog=AutoLot;Integrated Security=True")
        Dim theCars As DataTable = dal.GetAllInventoryAsDataTable()
        dal.CloseConnection()
```

```
    ' Now store DataTable in the cache.
    theCache.Insert("AppDataTable",
        theCars,
        Nothing,
        Date.Now.AddSeconds(15),
        Cache.NoSlidingExpiration,
        CacheItemPriority.Default,
        New CacheItemRemovedCallback(AddressOf UpdateCarInventory))
    End Sub

    ' The target for the CacheItemRemovedCallback delegate.
    Shared Sub UpdateCarInventory(ByVal key As String, ByVal item As Object,
                            ByVal reason As CacheItemRemovedReason)
    Dim dal As New InventoryDAL()
    dal.OpenConnection("Data Source=(local)\SQLEXPRESS;" &
                    "Initial Catalog=AutoLot;Integrated Security=True")
    Dim theCars As DataTable = dal.GetAllInventoryAsDataTable()
    dal.CloseConnection()

    ' Now store in the cache.
    theCache.Insert("AppDataTable",
        theCars,
        Nothing,
        Date.Now.AddSeconds(15),
        Cache.NoSlidingExpiration,
        CacheItemPriority.Default,
        New CacheItemRemovedCallback(AddressOf UpdateCarInventory))
        End Sub
...
</script>
```

First, notice we've defined a Shared Cache member variable. The reason is that you've defined two Shared members that need to access the Cache object. Recall that Shared methods do not have access to inherited members, so you can't use the Context property!

Inside the Application_Start() event handler, you fill a DataTable and insert it into the application cache. As you would guess, the Context.Cache.Insert() method has been overloaded a number of times. Here, you supply a value for each possible parameter. Consider the following commented call to Insert():

```
theCache.Insert("AppDataTable",    'Name used to identify item in the cache.
theCars,                            'Object to put in the cache.
Nothing,                            'Any dependencies for this object?
Date.Now.AddSeconds(15),            'Absolute timeout value.
Cache.NoSlidingExpiration,           'Don't use sliding expiration (see below)
CacheItemPriority.Default,          'Priority level of cache item.
'Delegate for CacheItemRemove event.
New CacheItemRemovedCallback(AddressOf UpdateCarInventory))
```

The first two parameters simply make up the name/value pair of the item. The third parameter allows you to define a `CacheDependency` object (which is `Nothing` in this case, as the `DataTable` does not depend on anything).

The `DateTime.Now.AddSeconds(15)` parameter specifies an absolute expiration time. It means the cache item will definitely be evicted from the cache after 15 seconds. Absolute expiration is useful for data items that need to be constantly refreshed (such as a stock ticker).

The `Cache.NoSlidingExpiration` parameter specifies that the cache item doesn't use sliding expiration. Sliding expiration is a way of keeping an item in the cache for at least a certain amount of time. For example, if you set a sliding expiration of 60 seconds for a cache item, it will live in the cache for at least 60 seconds. If any web page accesses the cache item within that time, the clock is reset and the cache item has a fresh 60 seconds to live. If no web page accesses the cache item in 60 seconds, the item is removed from the cache. Sliding expiration is useful for data that might be expensive (time-wise) to generate, but which might not be used very frequently by web pages.

Note that you can't specify both an absolute expiration and a sliding expiration for a given cache item. You set either an absolute expiration (and use `Cache.NoSlidingExpiration`) or a sliding expiration (and use `Cache.NoAbsoluteExpiration`).

Finally, as you can see from the signature of the `UpdateCarInventory()` method, the `CacheItemRemovedCallback` delegate can only call methods that match the following signature:

```
Sub UpdateCarInventory(ByVal key As String, ByVal item As Object,
                       ByVal reason As CacheItemRemovedReason)
End Sub
```

So, at this point, when the application starts up, the `DataTable` is populated and cached. Every 15 seconds, the `DataTable` is purged, updated, and reinserted into the cache. To see the effects of doing this, you need to create a page that allows for some degree of user interaction.

Modifying the *.aspx File

Update the UI of your initial `*.aspx` file as shown in Figure 34-6.

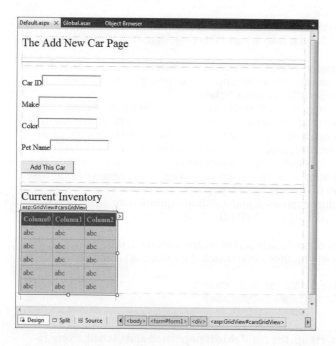

Figure 34-6. The cache application GUI

In the page's **Load** event handler, configure your **GridView** to display the current contents of the cached **DataTable** the first time the user posts to the page (be sure to import the **System.Data** and **AutoLotConnectedLayer** namespaces within your code file):

```
Protected Sub Page_Load(ByVal sender As Object, ByVal e As EventArgs) Handles Me.Load
    If Not IsPostBack Then
        carsGridView.DataSource = CType(Cache("AppDataTable"), DataTable)
        carsGridView.DataBind()
    End If
End Sub
```

In the **Click** event handler of the Add This Car button, insert the new record into the AutoLot database using the **InventoryDAL** type. Once the record has been inserted, call a helper function named **RefreshGrid()**, which will update the UI:

```
Protected Sub btnAddCar_Click(ByVal sender As Object, ByVal e As EventArgs)
        Handles btnAddCar.Click
    ' Update the Inventory table
    ' and call RefreshGrid().
    Dim dal As New InventoryDAL()
    dal.OpenConnection("Data Source=(local)\SQLEXPRESS;" &
                    "Initial Catalog=AutoLot;Integrated Security=True")
    dal.InsertAuto(Integer.Parse(txtCarID.Text), txtCarColor.Text, txtCarMake.Text,
                                        txtCarPetName.Text)
```

```
        dal.CloseConnection()
        RefreshGrid()
End Sub

Private Sub RefreshGrid()
    Dim dal As New InventoryDAL()
    dal.OpenConnection("Data Source=(local)\SQLEXPRESS;" &
                    "Initial Catalog=AutoLot;Integrated Security=True")
    Dim theCars As DataTable = dal.GetAllInventoryAsDataTable()
    dal.CloseConnection()

    carsGridView.DataSource = theCars
    carsGridView.DataBind()
End Sub
```

Now, to test the use of the cache, begin by running the current program (Ctrl+F5) and copy the URL appearing in the browser to your clipboard. Next, launch a second instance of your browser (using the Start button) and paste the URL into this instance. At this point you should have two instances of your web browser, both viewing Default.aspx and showing identical data.

In one instance of the browser, add a new automobile entry. Obviously, this results in an updated GridView viewable from the browser that initiated the postback.

In the second browser instance, click the Refresh button (F5). You should not see the new item, since the Page_Load event handler is reading directly from the cache. (If you did see the value, the 15 seconds had already expired. Either type faster or increase the amount of time the DataTable will remain in the cache.) Wait a few seconds and click the Refresh button from the second browser instance one more time. Now you should see the new item, given that the DataTable in the cache has expired and the CacheItemRemovedCallback delegate target method has automatically updated the cached DataTable.

As you can see, the major benefit of the Cache type is that you can ensure that when an item is removed, you have a chance to respond. In this example, you certainly could avoid using the Cache and simply have the Page_Load() event handler always read directly from the AutoLot database (but this would potentially be much slower than the caching approach). Nevertheless, the point should be clear: the cache allows you to automatically refresh data using the cache mechanism.

■ **Source Code** The CacheState web site is included under the Chapter 34 subdirectory.

Maintaining Session Data

So much for our examination of application-level and cached data. Next, let's check out the role of per-user data. As mentioned earlier, a *session* is little more than a given user's ongoing interaction with a web application, which is represented via a unique HttpSessionState object. To maintain stateful information for a particular user, you can use the Session property in your web page class or in Global.asax. The classic example of the need to maintain per-user data is an online shopping cart. Again, if 10 people all log on to an online store, each individual will have a unique set of items that she (may) intend to purchase, and that data needs to be maintained.

When a new user joins to your web application, the .NET runtime automatically assigns the user a unique session ID, which is used to identify that user. Each session ID identifies a custom instance of the HttpSessionState type to hold on to user-specific data. Inserting or retrieving session data is syntactically identical to manipulating application data, for example:

```
' Add/retrieve session data for current user.
Session("DesiredCarColor") = "Green"
Dim color As String = CStr(Session("DesiredCarColor"))
```

In Global.asax, you can intercept the beginning and end of a session via the Session_Start() and Session_End() event handlers. Within Session_Start(), you can freely create any per-user data items, while Session_End() allows you to perform any work you may need to do when the user's session has terminated:

```
<%@ Application Language="VB" %>
...
Sub Session_Start(ByVal sender As Object, ByVal e As EventArgs)
 ' New session! Prep if required.
End Sub

Private Sub Session_End(ByVal sender As Object, ByVal e As EventArgs)
 ' User logged off/timed out. Tear down if needed.
End Sub
```

Like application state, session state may hold any System.Object-derived type, including your custom classes. For example, assume you have a new ASP.NET Empty Web Site project (named SessionState) that defines a class named UserShoppingCart:

```
Public Class UserShoppingCart
        Public desiredCar As String
        Public desiredCarColor As String
        Public downPayment As Single
        Public isLeasing As Boolean
        Public dateOfPickUp As Date

        Public Overrides Function ToString() As String
                Return String.Format ("Car: {0}<br>Color: {1}<br>$ Down: {2}<br>Lease:↵
                                    {3}<br>
                                Pick-up Date: {4}", desiredCar, desiredCarColor,
                                    downPayment, isLeasing,
                                    dateOfPickUp.ToShortDateString())
        End Function
End Class
```

Now, insert a Global.asax file. Within the Session_Start() event handler, you can now assign each user a new instance of the UserShoppingCart class:

```
Sub Session_Start(ByVal sender As Object, ByVal e As EventArgs)
        Session("UserShoppingCartInfo") = New UserShoppingCart()
End Sub
```

As the user traverses your web pages, you are able to pluck out the UserShoppingCart instance and fill the fields with user-specific data. For example, assume you have a simple *.aspx page that defines a set of input controls that correspond to each field of the UserShoppingCart type, a Button for setting the values, and two Labels that will be used to display the user's session ID and session information (see Figure 34-7).

Figure 34-7. The session application GUI

The server-side Click event handler for the Button control is straightforward (scrape out values from TextBoxes and display the shopping cart data on a Label control):

```
Protected Sub btnSubmit_Click(ByVal sender As Object, ByVal e As EventArgs) ↵
                        Handles btnSubmit.Click
    ' Set current user prefs.
    Dim cart As UserShoppingCart = CType(Session("UserShoppingCartInfo"),↵
                                UserShoppingCart)
    cart.dateOfPickUp = myCalendar.SelectedDate
    cart.desiredCar = txtCarMake.Text
    cart.desiredCarColor = txtCarColor.Text
    cart.downPayment = Single.Parse(txtDownPayment.Text)
    cart.isLeasing = chkIsLeasing.Checked
    lblUserInfo.Text = cart.ToString()
    Session("UserShoppingCartInfo") = cart
End Sub
```

1545

Within Session_End(), you may wish to persist the fields of the UserShoppingCart to a database or whatnot (however, as you will see at the conclusion of this chapter, the ASP.NET Profile API will do so automatically). As well, you may wish to implement Session_Error() to trap any faulty input (or perhaps make use of various validation controls on the Default.aspx page to account for such user errors).

In any case, if you were to launch two or three instances of your browser of choice all posting to the same URL (via a copy/paste operation as you did for the data cache example), you would find that each user is able to build a custom shopping cart that maps to his unique instance of HttpSessionState.

Additional Members of HttpSessionState

The HttpSessionState class defines a number of other members of interest beyond the type indexer. First, the SessionID property will return the current user's unique ID. If you wish to view the automatically assigned session ID for this example, handle the Load event of your page as follows:

```
Protected Sub Page_Load(ByVal sender As Object, ByVal e As EventArgs) Handles Me.Load
        lblUserID.Text = String.Format("Here is your ID: {0}", Session.SessionID)
End Sub
```

The Remove() and RemoveAll() methods may be used to clear items out of the user's instance of HttpSessionState:

```
Session.Remove("SomeItemWeDontNeedAnymore")
```

The HttpSessionState type also defines a set of members that control the expiration policy of the current session. Again, by default each user has 20 minutes of inactivity before the HttpSessionState object is destroyed. Thus, if a user enters your web application (and therefore obtains a unique session ID), but then does not return to the site within 20 minutes, the runtime assumes the user is no longer interested and destroys all session data for that user. You are free to change this default 20-minute expiration value on a user-by-user basis using the Timeout property. The most common place to do so is within the scope of your Session_Start() method:

```
Sub Session_Start(ByVal sender As Object, ByVal e As EventArgs)
    ' Each user has 5 minutes of inactivity.
    Session.Timeout = 5
    Session("UserShoppingCartInfo") = New UserShoppingCart()
End Sub
```

■ **Note** If you do not need to tweak each user's Timeout value, you can alter the 20-minute default for all users via the Timeout attribute of the <sessionState> element within the Web.config file (examined at the end of this chapter).

The benefit of the Timeout property is that you have the ability to assign specific timeout values separately for each user. For example, imagine you have created a web application that allows users to pay cash for a given membership level. You may say that Gold members should time out within one hour, while Wood members should get only 30 seconds. This possibility begs the question, how can you remember user-specific information (such as the current membership level) if users close the browser and come back at a later time? One possible answer is through the use of the HttpCookie type. (And speaking of cookies . . .)

■ **Source Code** The SessionState web site is included under the Chapter 34 subdirectory.

Understanding Cookies

The next state management technique we'll examine is the persisting of data within a *cookie*, which is often realized as a text file (or set of files) on the user's machine. When a user joins a given site, the browser checks to see whether the user's machine has a cookie file for the URL in question and, if so, appends this data to the HTTP request.

The receiving server-side web page can then read the cookie data to create a GUI based on the current user preferences. I'm sure you've noticed that when you visit certain of your favorite web sites, they somehow "just know" the sort of content you wish to see. The reason (in part) may have to do with a cookie stored on your computer that contains information relevant to a given web site.

■ **Note** The exact location of your cookie files will depend on which browser and operating system you happen to be using.

The contents of a given cookie file will obviously vary among URLs, but keep in mind that they are ultimately text files. Thus, cookies are a horrible choice for maintaining sensitive information about the current user (such as a credit card number, password, and the like). Even if you take the time to encrypt the data, a crafty hacker could decrypt the value and use it for evil purposes. In any case, cookies do play a role in the development of web applications, so let's check out how ASP.NET handles this particular state management technique.

Creating Cookies

First of all, understand that ASP.NET cookies can be configured to be either persistent or temporary. A *persistent* cookie is typically regarded as the classic definition of cookie data, in that the set of name/value pairs is physically saved to the user's hard drive. A *temporary* cookie (also termed a *session cookie*) contains the same data as a persistent cookie, but the name/value pairs are never saved to the user's hard drive; rather, they exist *only* while the browser is open. Once the user shuts down the browser, all data contained in the session cookie is destroyed.

The System.Web.HttpCookie type is the class that represents the server side of the cookie data (persistent or temporary). When you wish to create a new cookie in your web page code, you access the Response.Cookies property. Once the new HttpCookie is inserted into the internal collection, the name/value pairs flow back to the browser within the HTTP header.

To check out cookie behavior firsthand, create a new ASP.NET Empty Web Site (named CookieStateApp) and create the UI of the first Web Form (which you will need to insert) displayed in Figure 34-8.

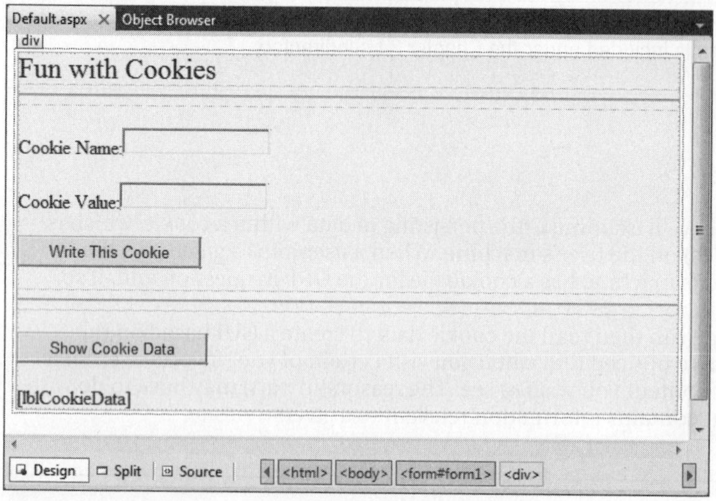

Figure 34-8. The UI of CookieStateApp

Within the first button's `Click` event handler, build a new `HttpCookie` and insert it into the `Cookie` collection exposed from the `HttpRequest.Cookies` property. Be very aware that the data will not persist itself to the user's hard drive unless you explicitly set an expiration date using the `HttpCookie.Expires` property. Thus, the following implementation will create a temporary cookie that is destroyed when the user shuts down the browser:

```
Protected Sub btnCookie_Click(ByVal sender As Object, ByVal e As EventArgs) ↵
                          Handles btnCookie.Click
    ' Make a temp cookie.
    Dim theCookie As New HttpCookie(txtCookieName.Text, txtCookieValue.Text)
    Response.Cookies.Add(theCookie)
End Sub
```

However, the following generates a persistent cookie that will expire three months from today:

```
Protected Sub btnCookie_Click(ByVal sender As Object, ByVal e As EventArgs)
        Handles btnCookie.Click
    Dim theCookie As New HttpCookie(txtCookieName.Text, txtCookieValue.Text)
    theCookie.Expires = Date.Now.AddMonths(3)
    Response.Cookies.Add(theCookie)
End Sub
```

Reading Incoming Cookie Data

Recall that the browser is the entity in charge of accessing persisted cookies when navigating to a previously visited page. If a browser decides to send a cookie to the server, you can access the incoming data in your *.aspx page via the HttpRequest.Cookies property. To illustrate, implement the Click event handler for the second button like so:

```
Protected Sub btnShowCookie_Click(ByVal sender As Object, ByVal e As EventArgs)
    Handles btnShowCookie.Click
        Dim cookieData As String = ""
        For Each s As String In Request.Cookies
            cookieData &= String.Format("<li><b>Name</b>: {0}, <b>Value</b>: {1}</li>",
                                     s,  Request.Cookies(s).Value)
    Next
            lblCookieData.Text = cookieData
End Sub
```

If you now run the application and click your new button, you will find that the cookie data has indeed been sent by your browser and accessed successfully in your *.aspx code at the server.

■ **Source Code** The CookieStateApp web site is included under the Chapter 34 subdirectory.

The Role of the <sessionState> Element

At this point in the chapter, you have examined numerous ways to remember information about your users. As you have seen, view state and application, cache, session, and cookie data are manipulated programmatically in more or less the same way (via a class indexer). As you have also seen, Global.asax has methods that allow you to intercept and respond to events that occur during your web application's lifetime.

By default, ASP.NET will store session state in-process. The plus side is that access to the information is as fast as possible. However, the downside is that if this AppDomain crashes (for whatever reason) all of the user's state data is destroyed. Furthermore, when you store state data as an in-process *.dll, you cannot interact with a networked web farm. This default mode of storage works just fine if your web application is hosted by a single web server. As you might guess, however, this model is not ideal for a farm of web servers, given that session state is "trapped" within a given AppDomain.

Storing Session Data in the ASP.NET Session State Server

Under ASP.NET, you can instruct the runtime to host the session state *.dll in a surrogate process named the ASP.NET session state server (aspnet_state.exe). When you do so, you are able to offload the *.dll from aspnet_wp.exe into a unique *.exe, which can be located on any machine within the web farm. Even if you intend to run the aspnet_state.exe process on the same machine as the web server, you gain the benefit of partitioning the state data in a unique process (as it is more durable).

To make use of the session state server, the first step is to start the **aspnet_state.exe** Windows service on the target machine by typing the following in a Visual Studio 2010 Command Prompt window (note that you will need admin privileges to do so):

```
net start aspnet_state
```

Alternatively, you can start **aspnet_state.exe** using the Services applet accessed from the Administrative Tools folder of the Control Panel, as shown in Figure 34-9.

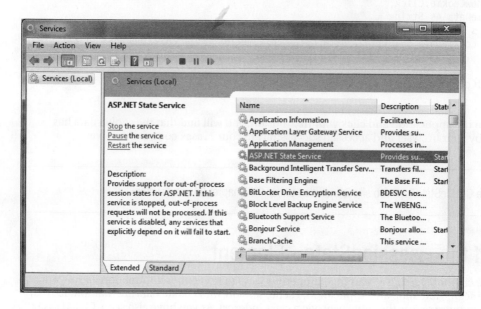

Figure 34-9. *Starting aspnet_state.exe using the Services applet*

The key benefit of this approach is that you can use the Properties window to configure **aspnet_state.exe** to start automatically when the machine boots up. In any case, once the session state server is running, add the following `<sessionState>` element of your **Web.config** file as follows:

```
<system.web>
  <sessionState
    mode="StateServer"
    stateConnectionString="tcpip=127.0.0.1:42626"
    sqlConnectionString="data source=127.0.0.1;Trusted_Connection=yes"
    cookieless="false"
    timeout="20"
  />
...
</system.web>
```

That's it! At this point, the CLR will host session-centric data within **aspnet_state.exe**. In this way, if the AppDomain hosting the web application crashes, the session data is preserved. Moreover, note that the **<sessionState>** element can also support a **stateConnectionString** attribute. The default TCP/IP address value (127.0.0.1) points to the local machine. If you would rather have the .NET runtime use the **aspnet_state.exe** service located on another networked machine (again, think web farms), you are free to update this value.

Storing Session Data in a Dedicated Database

Finally, if you require the highest degree of isolation and durability for your web application, you may choose to have the runtime store all your session state data within Microsoft SQL Server. The appropriate update to the **Web.config** file is simple:

```
<sessionState
  mode="SQLServer"
  stateConnectionString="tcpip=127.0.0.1:42626"
  sqlConnectionString="data source=127.0.0.1;Trusted_Connection=yes"
  cookieless="false"
  timeout="20"
/>
```

However, before you attempt to run the associated web application, you need to ensure that the target machine (specified by the **sqlConnectionString** attribute) has been properly configured. When you install the .NET Framework 4.0 SDK (or Visual Studio 2010), you will be provided with two files named **InstallSqlState.sql** and **UninstallSqlState.sql**, located by default under C:\Windows\Microsoft.NET\Framework*<version>*. On the target machine, you must run the **InstallSqlState.sql** file using a tool such as the Microsoft SQL Server Management Studio (which ships with Microsoft SQL Server).

Once you have run **InstallSqlState.sql**, you will find a new SQL Server database has been created (ASPState), which contains a number of stored procedures called by the ASP.NET runtime, as well as a set of tables used to store the session data itself. (Also, the tempdb database has been updated with a set of tables for swapping purposes.) As you'd guess, configuring your web application to store session data within SQL Server is the slowest of all possible options. The benefit is that user data is as durable as possible (even if the web server is rebooted).

■ **Note** If you make use of the ASP.NET session state server or SQL Server to store your session data, you must make sure that any custom types placed in the **HttpSessionState** object have been marked with the **<Serializable()>** attribute.

Understanding the ASP.NET Profile API

So far you have examined numerous techniques that allow you to remember user-level and application-level bits of data. However, these techniques suffer from one major limitation: they exist only as long as the user is in session and the web application is running! However, many web sites require the ability to persist user information across sessions. For example, perhaps you need to give users the ability to build an account on your site. Maybe you need to persist instances of a ShoppingCart class across sessions (for an online shopping site). Or perhaps you wish to persist basic user preferences (themes, etc.).

While you most certainly could build a custom database (with several stored procedures) to hold such information, you would then need to build a custom code library to interact with these database objects. This is not necessarily a complex task, but the bottom line is that *you* are the individual in charge of building this sort of infrastructure.

To help simplify matters, ASP.NET ships with an out-of-the-box user profile management API and database system for this very purpose. In addition to providing the necessary infrastructure, the Profile API allows you to define the data to be persisted directly within your Web.config file (for purposes of simplification); however, you are also able to persist any <Serializable()> type. Before we get too far ahead of ourselves, let's check out where the Profile API will be storing the specified data.

The ASPNETDB.mdf Database

Every ASP.NET web site built with Visual Studio 2010 can support an App_Data subdirectory. By default, the Profile API (as well as other services, such as the ASP.NET role membership API, which is not examined in this text) is configured to make use of a local SQL Server 2010 database named ASPNETDB.mdf, located within the App_Data folder. This default behavior is due to settings within the machine.config file for the current .NET installation on your machine. In fact, when your code base makes use of any ASP.NET service requiring the App_Data folder, the ASPNETDB.mdf data file will be automatically created on the fly if a copy does not currently exist.

If you'd rather have the ASP.NET runtime communicate with an ASPNETDB.mdf file located on another networked machine, or you'd prefer to install this database on an instance of SQL Server 7.0 (or higher), you will need to manually build ASPNETDB.mdf using the aspnet_regsql.exe command-line utility. Like any good command-line tool, aspnet_regsql.exe provides numerous options; however, if you run the tool with no arguments, like so:

```
aspnet_regsql
```

you will launch a GUI-based wizard that will walk you through the process of creating and installing ASPNETDB.mdf on your machine (and version of SQL Server) of choice.

Now, assuming your site is not using a local copy of the database under the App_Data folder, the final step is to update your Web.config file to point to the unique location of your ASPNETDB.mdf. Assume you have installed ASPNETDB.mdf on a machine named ProductionServer. The following (partial) machine.config file would instruct the Profile API where to find the necessary database items in their default location (you could add a custom Web.config to change these defaults):

```
<configuration>
  <connectionStrings>
    <add name="LocalSqlServer"
         connectionString ="Data Source=ProductionServer;Integrated
         Security=SSPI;Initial Catalog=aspnetdb;"
         providerName="System.Data.SqlClient"/>
  </connectionStrings>
  <system.web>
    <profile>
      <providers>
        <clear/>
        <add name="AspNetSqlProfileProvider"
```

```
            connectionStringName="LocalSqlServer"
            applicationName="/"
            type="System.Web.Profile.SqlProfileProvider, System.Web,
            Version=4.0.0.0,
            Culture=neutral, PublicKeyToken=b03f5f7f11d50a3a" />
      </providers>
    </profile>
  </system.web>
</configuration>
```

Like most *.config files, this looks much worse than it is. Basically we are defining a
<connectionString> element with the necessary data, followed by a named instance of the
SqlProfileProvider (this is the default provider used regardless of physical location of the ASPNETDB.mdf).

■ **Note** For simplicity, I will assume that you'll use the autogenerated ASPNETDB.mdf database located under your web application's App_Data subdirectory.

Defining a User Profile Within Web.config

As mentioned, a user profile is defined within a Web.config file. The really nifty aspect of this approach is
that you can interact with this profile in a strongly typed manner using the inherited Profile property in
your code files. To illustrate this, create a new Empty Web Site named FunWithProfiles, add a new
*.aspx file, and open your Web.config file for editing.

Our goal is to make a profile that models the home address of the users who are in session, as well as
the total number of times they have posted to this site. Not surprisingly, profile data is defined within a
<profile> element using a set of name/data type pairs. Consider the following profile, which is created
within the scope of the <system.web> element:

```
<profile>
  <properties>
    <add name="StreetAddress" type="System.String" />
    <add name="City" type="System.String" />
    <add name="State" type="System.String" />
    <add name="TotalPost" type="System.Int32" />
  </properties>
</profile>
```

Here, we have specified a name and CLR data type for each item in the profile (of course, we could
add additional items for zip code, name, and so forth, but I am sure you get the idea). Strictly speaking,
the type attribute is optional; however, the default is a System.String. As you would guess, there are
many other attributes that can be specified in a profile entry to further qualify how this information
should be persisted in ASPNETDB.mdf. Table 34-4 illustrates some of the core attributes.

Table 34-4. Select Attributes of Profile Data

Attribute	Example Values	Meaning in Life
allowAnonymous	True | False	Restricts or allows anonymous access to this value. If it is set to False, anonymous users won't have access to this profile value.
defaultValue	String	The value to return if the property has not been explicitly set.
Name	String	A unique identifier for this property.
Provider	String	The provider used to manage this value. It overrides the defaultProvider setting in Web.config or machine.config.
readOnly	True | False	Restricts or allows write access (the default is False, i.e. it's not read-only).
serializeAs	String | XML | Binary	The format of a value when persisting in the data store.
type	Primitive | User-defined type	A .NET primitive type or class. Class names must be fully qualified (e.g., MyApp.UserData.ColorPrefs).

We will see some of these attributes in action as we modify the current profile. For now, let's see how to access this data programmatically from within our pages.

Accessing Profile Data Programmatically

Recall that the whole purpose of the ASP.NET Profile API is to automate the process of writing data to (and reading data from) a dedicated database. To test this out for yourself, update the UI of your Default.aspx file with a set of TextBoxes (and descriptive Labels) to gather the street address, city, and state of the user. As well, add a Button (named btnSubmit) and a final Label (named lblUserData) that will be used to display the persisted data, as shown in Figure 34-10.

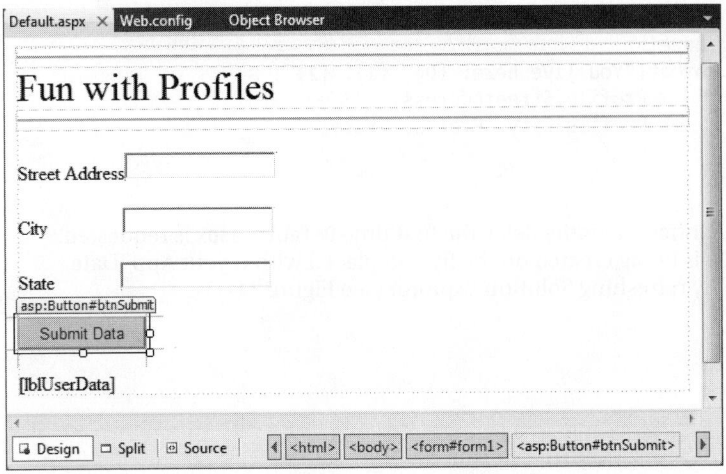

Figure 34-10. The UI of the FunWithProfiles Default.aspx page

Now, within the **Click** event handler of the button, make use of the inherited **Profile** property to persist each point of profile data based on what the user has entered in the related **TextBox**. Once you have persisted each piece of data within **ASPNETDB.mdf**, read each piece of data out of the database and format it into a **string** that is displayed on the **lblUserData** Label type. Finally, handle the page's **Load** event, and display the same information on the **Label** type. In this way, when users come to the page, they can see their current settings. Here is the complete code file:

```
Partial Class _Default
    Inherits System.Web.UI.Page

    Protected Sub Page_Load(ByVal sender As Object, ByVal e As EventArgs)
        Handles Me.Load
    GetUserAddress()
    End Sub

    Protected Sub btnSubmit_Click(ByVal sender As Object, ByVal e As EventArgs)
        Handles btnSubmit.Click
        ' Database writes happening here!
        Profile.StreetAddress = txtStreetAddress.Text
        Profile.City = txtCity.Text
        Profile.State = txtState.Text

        ' Get settings from database.
        GetUserAddress()
    End Sub
```

```
    Private Sub GetUserAddress()
        ' Database reads happening here!
        lblUserData.Text = String.Format("You live here: {0}, {1}, {2}",
                                    Profile.StreetAddress,
                                    Profile.City, Profile.State)
    End Sub
End Class
```

Now if you run this page, you will notice a lengthy delay the first time `Default.aspx` is requested. The reason is that the `ASPNETDB.mdf` file is being created on the fly and placed within your App_Data folder. You can verify this for yourself by refreshing Solution Explorer (see Figure 34-11).

Figure 34-11. Behold ASPNETDB.mdf!

You will also find that the first time you come to this page, the `lblUserData Label` does not display any profile data, as you have not yet entered your data into the correct table of `ASPNETDB.mdf`. Once you enter values in the `TextBox` controls and post back to the server, you will find this `Label` is formatted with the persisted data.

Now, for the really interesting aspect of this technology. If you shut down your browser and rerun your web site, you will find that your previously entered profile data has indeed been persisted, as the `Label` displays the correct information. This begs the obvious question, how were you remembered?

For this example, the Profile API used your Windows network identity, which was obtained via your current machine credentials. However, when you are building public web sites (where the users are not part of a given domain), rest assured that the Profile API integrates with the Forms-based authentication model of ASP.NET and also supports the notion of "anonymous profiles," which allow you to persist profile data for users who do not currently have an active identity on your site.

■ **Note** This edition of the text does not address ASP.NET security topics (such as Forms-based authentication or anonymous profiles). Consult the .NET Framework 4.0 SDK documentation for details.

Grouping Profile Data and Persisting Custom Objects

To wrap up this chapter, allow me to make a few additional comments on how profile data may be defined within a `Web.config` file. The current profile simply defined four pieces of data that were exposed directly from the profile type. When you build more complex profiles, it can be helpful to group related pieces of data under a unique name. Consider the following update:

```
<profile>
  <properties>
    <group name ="Address">
      <add name="StreetAddress" type="String" />
      <add name="City" type="String" />
      <add name="State" type="String" />
    </group>
    <add name="TotalPost" type="Integer" />
  </properties>
</profile>
```

This time we have defined a custom group named `Address` to expose the street address, city, and state of our user. To access this data in our pages would now require us to update our code base by specifying `Profile.Address` to get each subitem. For example, here is the updated `GetUserAddress()` method (the `Click` event handler for the `Button` would need to be updated in a similar manner):

```
Private Sub GetUserAddress()
    ' Database reads happening here!
    lblUserData.Text = String.Format("You live here: {0}, {1}, {2}",
                                Profile.Address.StreetAddress,
                                Profile.Address.City,
                                Profile.Address.State)
End Sub
```

Before you run this example, you need to delete `ASPNETDB.mdf` from your App_Data folder, to ensure the database schema is refreshed. Once you have done so, you should be able to run your web site example without error.

■ **Note** A profile can contain as many groups as you feel are necessary. Simply define multiple `<group>` elements within your `<properties>` scope.

Finally, it is worth pointing out that a profile may also persist (and obtain) custom objects to and from `ASPNETDB.mdf`. To illustrate, assume you wanted to build a custom class (or structure) that will represent the user's address data. The only requirement expected by the Profile API is that the type be marked with the `<Serializable()>` attribute, for example:

```
<Serializable()>
Public Class UserAddress
    Public Street As String = String.Empty
    Public City As String = String.Empty
    Public State As String = String.Empty
End Class
```

With this class in place, our profile definition can now be updated as follows (notice I removed the custom group, although this is not mandatory):

```
<profile>
  <properties>
    <add name="AddressInfo" type="UserAddress" serializeAs ="Binary"/>
    <add name="TotalPost" type="Integer" />
  </properties>
</profile>
```

Note that when you are adding `<Serializable()>` types to a profile, the `type` attribute is the fully qualified named of the type being persisted. As you will see from the Visual Studio 2010 IntelliSense, your core choices are binary, XML, or string data. Now that we are capturing street address information as a custom class type, we (once again) need to update our code base:

```
Private Sub GetUserAddress()
    ' Database reads happening here!
    lblUserData.Text = String.Format("You live here: {0}, {1}, {2}",
                                Profile.AddressInfo.Street,
                                Profile.AddressInfo.City,
                                Profile.AddressInfo.State)
End Sub
```

To be sure, there is much more to the Profile API than I've had space to cover here. For example, the `Profile` property actually encapsulates a type named `ProfileCommon`. Using this type, you are able to programmatically obtain all information for a given user, delete (or add) profiles to `ASPNETDB.mdf`, update aspects of a profile, and so forth.

Moreover, the Profile API has numerous points of extensibility that can allow you to optimize how the profile manager accesses the tables of the `ASPNETDB.mdf` database. As you would expect, there are many ways to decrease the number of "hits" this database takes. Interested readers are encouraged to consult the .NET Framework 4.0 SDK documentation for further details.

■ **Source Code** The FunWithProfiles web site is included under the Chapter 34 subdirectory.

Summary

In this chapter, you rounded out your knowledge of ASP.NET by examining how to leverage the `HttpApplication` type. As you have seen, this type provides a number of default event handlers that allow you to intercept various application- and session-level events. The bulk of this chapter was spent exploring a number of state management techniques. Recall that view state is used to automatically repopulate the values of HTML widgets between postbacks to a specific page. Next, you checked out the distinction of application- and session-level data, cookie management, and the ASP.NET application cache.

Finally, this chapter exposed you to the ASP.NET Profile API. As you have seen, this technology provides an out-of-the-box solution to the issue of persisting user data across sessions. Using your web site's `Web.config` file, you can define any number of profile items (including groups of items and `<Serializable()>` types) that will automatically be persisted into `ASPNETDB.mdf`.

APPENDIX A

■ ■ ■

Programming with Windows Forms

Since the release of the .NET platform (circa 2001), the base class libraries have included a particular API named Windows Forms, represented primarily by the `System.Windows.Forms.dll` assembly. The Windows Forms toolkit provides the types necessary to build desktop graphical user interfaces (GUIs), create custom controls, manage resources (e.g., string tables and icons), and perform other desktop-centric programming tasks. In addition, a separate API named GDI+ (represented by the `System.Drawing.dll` assembly) provides additional types that allow programmers to generate 2D graphics, interact with networked printers, and manipulate image data.

The Windows Forms (and GDI+) APIs remain alive and well within the .NET 4.0 platform, and they will exist within the base class library for quite some time (arguably forever). However, Microsoft has shipped a brand new GUI toolkit called Windows Presentation Foundation (WPF) since the release of .NET 3.0. As you saw in Chapters 27-31, WPF provides a massive amount of horsepower that you can use to build bleeding-edge user interfaces, and it has become the preferred desktop API for today's .NET graphical user interfaces.

The point of this appendix, however, is to provide a tour of the traditional Windows Forms API. One reason it is helpful to understand the original programming model: you can find many existing Windows Forms applications out there that will need to be maintained for some time to come. Also, many desktop GUIs simply might not require the horsepower offered by WPF. When you need to create more traditional business UIs that do not require an assortment of bells and whistles, the Windows Forms API can often fit the bill.

In this appendix, you will learn the Windows Forms programming model, work with the integrated designers of Visual Studio 2010, experiment with numerous Windows Forms controls, and receive an overview of graphics programming using GDI+. You will also pull this information together in a cohesive whole by wrapping things up in a (semi-capable) painting application.

■ **Note** Here's one proof that Windows Forms is not disappearing anytime soon: .NET 4.0 ships with a brand new Windows Forms assembly, `System.Windows.Forms.DataVisualization.dll`. You can use this library to incorporate charting functionality into your programs, complete with annotations; 3D rendering; and hit-testing support. This appendix will not cover this new .NET 4.0 Windows Forms API; however, you can look up the `System.Windows.Forms.DataVisualization.Charting` namespace if you want more information.

The Windows Forms Namespaces

The Windows Forms API consists of hundreds of types (e.g., classes, interfaces, structures, enums, and delegates), most of which are organized within various namespaces of the `System.Windows.Forms.dll` assembly. Figure A-1 shows these namespaces displayed in the Visual Studio 2010 object browser.

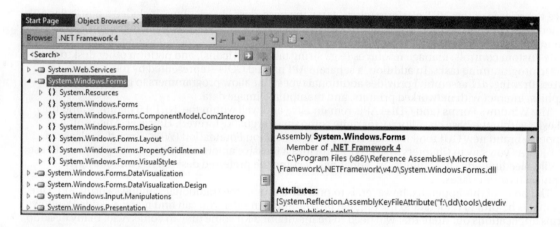

Figure A-1. The namespaces of System.Windows.Forms.dll

Far and away the most important Windows Forms namespace is `System.Windows.Forms`. At a high level, you can group the types within this namespace into the following broad categories:

- *Core infrastructure*: These are types that represent the core operations of a Windows Forms program (e.g., `Form` and `Application`) and various types to facilitate interoperability with legacy ActiveX controls, as well as interoperability with new WPF custom controls.

- *Controls*: These are types used to create graphical UIs (e.g., `Button`, `MenuStrip`, `ProgressBar`, and `DataGridView`), all of which derive from the `Control` base class. Controls are configurable at design time and are visible (by default) at runtime.

- *Components*: These are types that do not derive from the `Control` base class, but still may provide visual features to a Windows Forms program (e.g., `ToolTip` and `ErrorProvider`). Many components (e.g., the `Timer` and `System.ComponentModel.BackgroundWorker`) are not visible at runtime, but can be configured visually at design time.

- *Common dialog boxes*: Windows Forms provides several canned dialog boxes for common operations (e.g., `OpenFileDialog`, `PrintDialog`, and `ColorDialog`). As you would hope, you can certainly build your own custom dialog boxes if the standard dialog boxes do not suit your needs.

Given that the total number of types within `System.Windows.Forms` is well over 100 strong, it would be redundant (not to mention a terrible waste of paper) to list every member of the Windows Forms family. As you work through this appendix, however, you will gain a firm foundation that you can build on. In any case, be sure to check out the .NET Framework 4.0 SDK documentation for additional details.

Building a Simple Windows Forms Application

As you might expect, modern .NET IDEs (e.g., Visual Studio 2010, VB 2010 Express, and SharpDevelop) provide numerous form designers, visual editors, and integrated code-generation tools (wizards) to facilitate the construction of Windows Forms applications. These tools are extremely useful, but they can also hinder the process of learning Windows Forms, because these same tools tend to generate a good deal of boilerplate code that can obscure the core object model. Given this, you will create your first Windows Forms example using a Console Application project as a starting point.

Begin by creating a Console Application named SimpleWinFormsApp. Next, use the Project ➤ Add Reference menu option to set a reference to the `System.Windows.Forms.dll` and `System.Drawing.dll` assemblies through the .NET tab of the resulting dialog box. Next, update your `Module1` file with the following code:

```
' The minimum required windows forms namespaces.
Imports System.Windows.Forms

' This is the application object.
Module Module1
        Sub Main()
         Application.Run(New MainWindow())
         End Sub
End Module

' This is the main window.
Public Class MainWindow
        Inherits Form
End Class
```

■ **Note** When Visual Studio 2010 finds a class that extends System.Windows.Forms.Form, it attempts to open the related GUI designer (provided this class is the first class in the VB 2010 code file). Double-clicking the Module1.vb file from the Solution Explorer opens the designer, but don't do that yet! You will work with the Windows Forms designer in the next example; for now, be sure you right-click on the VB 2010 file containing your code within the Solution Explorer and select the View Code option.

This code represents the absolute simplest Windows Forms application you can build. At a bare minimum, you need a class that extends the Form base class and a Main() method to call the Shared Application.Run() method (you can find more details on Form and Application later in this chapter). Running your application now reveals that you have a resizable, minimizable, maximizable, and closable topmost window (see Figure A-2).

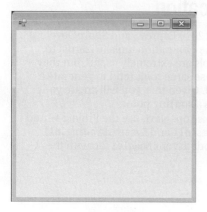

Figure A-2. A simple Windows Forms application

■ **Note** When you run this program, you will notice a command prompt looming in the background of your topmost window. This is because, when you create a Console Application, the /target flag sent to the VB 2010 compiler defaults to /target:exe. You can change this to /target:winexe (preventing the display of the command prompt) by double-clicking the My Project item in the Solution Explorer and changing the Application Type setting to Windows Forms Application using the Application tab.

Granted, the current application is not especially exciting, but it does illustrate how simple a Windows Forms application can be. To spruce things up a bit, you can add a custom constructor to your `MainWindow` class, which allows the caller to set various properties on the window to be displayed:

```vb
' This is the main window.
Public Class MainWindow
    Inherits Form

    Public Sub New()
    End Sub

    Public Sub New(ByVal title As String, ByVal frmHeight As Integer,
                ByVal frmWidth As Integer)
    ' Set various properties from the parent classes.
    Text = title
    Width = frmWidth
    Height = frmHeight
    ' Inherited method to center the form on the screen.
    CenterToScreen()
    End Sub
End Class
```

You can now update the call to `Application.Run()`, as follows:

```vb
Sub Main()
    Application.Run(New MainWindow("My Window", 200, 300))
End Sub
```

This is a step in the right direction, but any window worth its salt requires various user interface elements (e.g., menu systems, status bars, and buttons) to allow for input. To understand how a `Form`-derived type can contain such elements, you must understand the role of the `Controls` property and the underlying controls collection.

Populating the Controls Collection

The `System.Windows.Forms.Control` base class (which is the inheritance chain of the `Form` type) defines a property named `Controls`. This property wraps a custom collection nested in the `Control` class named `ControlsCollection`. This collection (as the name suggests) references each UI element maintained by the derived type. Like other containers, this type supports several methods for inserting, removing, and finding a given UI widget (see Table A-1).

Table A-1. *ControlCollection Members*

Member	Meaning in Life
Add() AddRange()	You use these members to insert a new **Control**-derived type (or array of types) in the collection.
Clear()	This member removes all entries in the collection.
Count	This member returns the number of items in the collection.
Remove() RemoveAt()	You use these members to remove a control from the collection.

When you wish to populate the UI of a **Form**-derived type, you typically follow a predictable series of steps:

- Define a member variable of a given UI element within the **Form**-derived class.

- Configure the look and feel of the UI element.

- Add the UI element to the form's **ControlsCollection** container using a call to **Controls.Add()**.

Assume you wish to update your **MainWindow** class to support a File ➤ Exit menu system. Here are the relevant updates, with code analysis to follow:

```
Public Class MainWindow
    Inherits Form
        ' Members for a simple menu system.
        Private mnuMainMenu As New MenuStrip()
        Private mnuFile As New ToolStripMenuItem()
        Private mnuFileExit As New ToolStripMenuItem()

        Public Sub New(ByVal title As String, ByVal frmHeight As Integer, ByVal frmWidth
As Integer)
            ...
        ' Method to create the menu system.
            BuildMenuSystem()
        End Sub

    Private Sub BuildMenuSystem()
    ' Add the File menu item to the main menu.
    mnuFile.Text = "&File"
    mnuMainMenu.Items.Add(mnuFile)
```

```
' Now add the Exit menu to the File menu.
mnuFileExit.Text = "E&xit"
mnuFile.DropDownItems.Add(mnuFileExit)
AddHandler mnuFileExit.Click, Sub(o, s) Application.Exit()

' Finally, set the menu for this Form.
Controls.Add(Me.mnuMainMenu)
MainMenuStrip = Me.mnuMainMenu
    End Sub
End Class
```

Notice that the MainWindow type now maintains three new member variables. The MenuStrip type represents the entirety of the menu system, while a given ToolStripMenuItem represents any topmost menu item (e.g., File) or submenu item (e.g., Exit) supported by the host.

You configure the menu system within the BuildMenuSystem() helper function. Notice that the text of each ToolStripMenuItem is controlled through the Text property; each menu item has been assigned a string literal that contains an embedded ampersand symbol. As you might already know, this syntax sets the Alt key shortcut. Thus, selecting Alt+F activates the File menu, while selecting Alt+X activates the Exit menu. Also notice that the File ToolStripMenuItem object (mnuFile) adds subitems using the DropDownItems property. The MenuStrip object itself adds a topmost menu item using the Items property.

Once you establish the menu system, you can add it to the controls collection (through the Controls property). Next, you assign your MenuStrip object to the form's MainMenuStrip property. This step might seem redundant, but having a specific property such as MainMenuStrip makes it possible to dynamically establish which menu system to show a user. You might change the menu displayed based on user preferences or security settings.

The only other point of interest is the fact that you handle the Click event of the File ➤ Exit menu; this helps you capture when the user selects this submenu. The Click event works in conjunction with a standard delegate type named System.EventHandler. This event can only call methods that take a System.Object as the first parameter and a System.EventArgs as the second. Here, you use a lambda expression to terminate the entire application with the Application.Exit() method.

Once you recompile and execute this application, you will find your simple window sports a custom menu system (see Figure A-3).

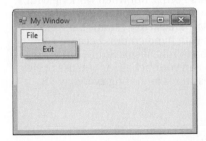

Figure A-3. A simple window, with a simple menu system

The Role of System.EventArgs and System.EventHandler

System.EventHandler is one of many delegate types used within the Windows Forms (and ASP.NET) APIs during the event-handling process. As you have seen, this delegate can only point to methods where the first argument is of type System.Object, which is a reference to the object that sent the event. For example, assume you want to update the implementation of the lambda expression, as follows:

```
AddHandler mnuFileExit.Click,
    Sub(o, s)
        MessageBox.Show(String.Format("{0} sent this event", o.ToString()))
        Application.Exit()
    End Sub
```

You can verify that the mnuFileExit type sent the event because the string is displayed within the message box:

```
"E&xit sent this event"
```

You might be wondering what purpose the second argument, System.EventArgs, serves. In reality, the System.EventArgs type brings little to the table because it simply extends Object and provides practically nothing by way of addition functionality:

```
Public Class EventArgs
        Public Shared ReadOnly Empty As EventArgs
        Shared Sub New()
        Public Sub New()
End Class
```

However, this type is useful in the overall scheme of .NET event handling because it is the parent to many (useful) derived types. For example, the MouseEventArgs type extends EventArgs to provide details regarding the current state of the mouse. KeyEventArgs also extends EventArgs to provide details of the state of the keyboard (such as which key was pressed); PaintEventArgs extends EventArgs to yield graphically relevant data; and so forth. You can also see numerous EventArgs descendents (and the delegates that make use of them) not only when working with Windows Forms, but when working with the WPF and ASP.NET APIs, as well.

While you could continue to build more functionality into your MainWindow (e.g., status bars and dialog boxes) using a simple text editor, you would eventually end up with hand cramps because you have to author all the grungy control configuration logic manually. Thankfully, Visual Studio 2010 provides numerous integrated designers that take care of these details on your behalf. As you use these tools during the remainder of this chapter, always remember that these tools authoring everyday VB 2010 code; there is nothing magical about them whatsoever.

■ **Source Code** You can find the SimpleWinFormsApp project under the Appendix A subdirectory.

The Visual Studio Windows Forms Project Template

When you wish to leverage the Windows Forms designer tools of Visual Studio 2010, your typically begin by selecting the Windows Forms Application project template using the File ➤ New Project menu option. To get comfortable with the core Windows Forms designer tools, create a new application named SimpleVSWinFormsApp (see Figure A-4).

Figure A-4. The Visual Studio Windows Forms Project Template

The Visual Designer Surface

Before you begin to build more interesting Windows applications, you will re-create the previous example leveraging the designer tools. Once you create a new Windows Forms project, you will notice that Visual Studio 2010 presents a designer surface to which you can drag-and-drop any number of controls. You can use this same designer to configure the initial size of the window simply by resizing the form itself using the supplied grab handles (see Figure A-5).

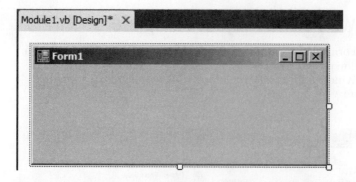

Figure A-5. The visual forms designer

When you wish to configure the look-and-feel of your window (as well as any control placed on a form designer), you do so using the Properties window. Similar to a Windows Presentation Foundation project, this window can be used to assign values to properties, as well as to establish event handlers for the currently selected item on the designer (you select a configuration using the drop-down list box mounted on the top of the Properties window).

Currently, your form is devoid of content, so you see only a listing for the initial Form, which has been given a default name of Form1, as shown in the read-only Name property of Figure A-6.

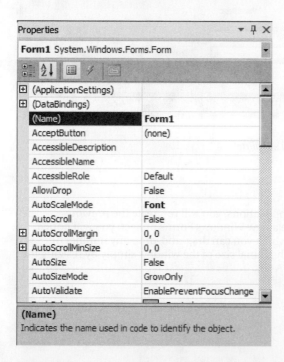

Figure A-6. The Properties window for setting properties and handling events

---

■ **Note** You can configure the Properties window to display its content by category or alphabetically using the first two buttons mounted beneath the drop-down list box. I'd suggest that you sort the items alphabetically to find a given property or event quickly.

The next designer element to be aware of is the Solution Explorer window. All Visual Studio 2010 projects support this window, but it is especially helpful when building Windows Forms applications to be able to (1) change the name of the file and related class for any window quickly, and (2) view the file that contains the designer-maintained code (you'll learn more information on this tidbit in just a moment). For now, right-click the `Form1.vb` icon and select the Rename option. Name this initial window to something more fitting: `MainWindow.vb`. The IDE will ask you if you wish to change the name of your initial class; it's fine to do this.

Dissecting the Initial Form

Each `Form` in a Visual Studio 2010 Windows Application project is composed of two related VB 2010 files, which can be verified using Solution Explorer (note that I renamed this initial class from `Form1` to `MainWindow`). Be aware that the `*.Designer.vb` file is hidden until you click the Show All Files button in Solution Explorer.

Right-click the `MainWindow.vb` icon and select View Code. Here you will see a class type that will contain all of the form's event handlers, custom constructors, member overrides, and any additional member you author yourself. Upon startup, the `Form` type is quite empty:

```
Public Class MainWindow
End Class
```

The first point of interest is it does not appear that the `MainWindow` class is extending the necessary `Form` base class. Rest assured this is the case; however, this detail has been established in the related `*.Designer.vb` file. If you open up the `*.Designer.vb` file, you will find that your `MainWindow` class is further defined via the `Partial` keyword. Recall this keyword allows a single type to be defined across multiple files. Visual Studio 2010 uses this technique to hide the designer-generated code, allowing you to keep focused on the core logic of your `Form`-derived type. Here is the initial definition of this `Partial` class:

```
Partial Class MainWindow
        Private components As System.ComponentModel.IContainer
        Protected Overrides Sub Dispose(ByVal disposing As Boolean)
        Try
            If disposing AndAlso components IsNot Nothing Then
                components.Dispose()
            End If
            Finally
                MyBase.Dispose(disposing)
        End Try
        End Sub
```

```
      Private Sub InitializeComponent()
      components = New System.ComponentModel.Container()
      Me.AutoScaleMode = System.Windows.Forms.AutoScaleMode.Font
      Me.Text = "Form1"
      End Sub
End Class
```

The `IContainer` member variable and `Dispose()` methods are little more than infrastructure used by the Visual Studio designer tools. The `InitializeComponent()` method is invoked by a form's constructor at runtime. Visual Studio also makes use of this same method at design time to render correctly the UI seen on the Forms designer. To see this in action, change the value assigned to the `Text` property of the window to `"My Main Window"`. Once you activate the designer, the form's caption will update accordingly.

When you use the visual design tools (e.g., the Properties window or the form designer), the IDE updates `InitializeComponent()` automatically. To illustrate this aspect of the Windows Forms designer tools, ensure that the Forms designer is the active window within the IDE and find the `Opacity` property listed in the Properties window. Change this value to `0.8` (80%); this gives your window a slightly transparent look-and-feel the next time you compile and run your program. Once you make this change, reexamine the implementation of `InitializeComponent()`:

```
Private Sub InitializeComponent()
        …
        Me.Opacity = 0.8R
End Sub
```

For all practical purposes, you should ignore the `*.Designer.vb` files and allow the IDE to maintain them on your behalf when you build a Windows Forms application using Visual Studio. If you were to author syntactically (or logically) incorrect code within `InitializeComponent()`, you might break the designer. Also, Visual Studio often reformats this method at design time. Thus, if you were to add custom code to `InitializeComponent()`, the IDE might delete it! In any case, remember that each window of a Windows Forms application is composed using Partial classes.

Visually Building a Menu System

To wrap up this look at the Windows Forms visual designer tools and move on to some more illustrative examples, activate the Forms designer window, locate the Toolbox window of Visual Studio 2010, and find the `MenuStrip` control within the Menus & Toolbars node (see Figure A-7).

Figure A-7. Windows Forms controls you can add to your designer surface

Drag a MenuStrip control onto the top of your Forms designer. Notice that Visual Studio responds by activating the menu editor. If you look closely at this editor, you will notice a small triangle on the top-right of the control. Clicking this icon opens a context-sensitive inline editor that allows you to make numerous property settings at once (be aware that many Windows Forms controls have similar inline editors). For example, click the Insert Standard Items option, as shown in Figure A-8.

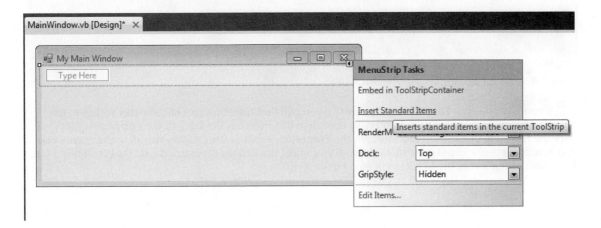

Figure A-8. The inline menu editor

In this example, Visual Studio was kind enough to establish an entire menu system on your behalf. Now open your designer-maintained file (`MainWindow.Designer.vb`) and note the numerous lines of code added to `InitializeComponent()`, as well as several new member variables that represent your menu system (designer tools are good things!). Finally, flip back to the designer and undo the previous operation by clicking the Ctrl+Z keyboard combination. This brings you back to the initial menu editor and removes the generated code. Using the menu designer, type in a topmost File menu item, followed by an Exit submenu (see Figure A-9).

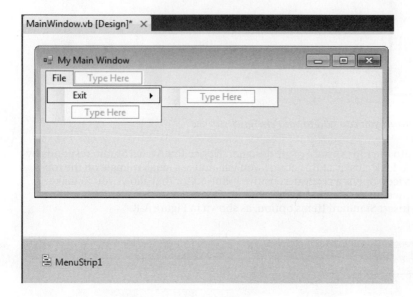

Figure A-9. Manually building our menu system

If you take a look at `InitializeComponent()`, you will find the same sort of code you authored by hand in the first example of this chapter. To complete this exercise, flip back to the Forms designer and click the lightning bolt button mounted on the Properties window. This shows you all of the events you can handle for the selected control. Make sure you select the Exit menu (named `ExitToolStripMenuItem` by default), then locate the `Click` event (see Figure A-10).

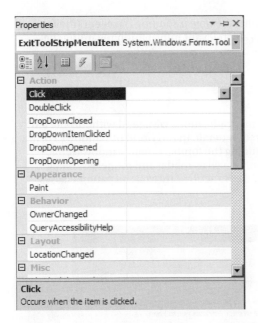

Figure A-10. Establishing Events with the IDE

At this point, you can enter the name of the method to be called when the item is clicked; or, if you feel lazy at this point, you can double-click the event listed in the Properties window. This lets the IDE pick the name of the event handler on your behalf (which follows the pattern, *NameOfControl_NameOfEvent()*). In either case, the IDE will create stub code, and you can fill in the implementation details:

```
Public Class MainWindow
        Private Sub ExitToolStripMenuItem_Click(ByVal sender As Object,
                                        ByVal e As EventArgs)
        Handles ExitToolStripMenuItem.Click
    Application.Exit()
        End Sub
End Class
```

The System.EventHandler Delegate

The ApplicationExit event works in conjunction with the System.EventHandler delegate. This delegate must point to subroutines that conform to the following signature:

```
Sub MyEventHandler(ByVal sender As Object, ByVal args As EventArgs)
```

System.EventHandler is the most primitive delegate used to handle events within Windows Forms, but many variations do exist for other events. As far as EventHandler is concerned, the first parameter of the assigned method is of type System.Object, which represents the object sending the event (the form itself in this case). The second EventArgs parameter contains any relevant information regarding the current event.

The Anatomy of a Form

So far you have examined how to build simple Windows Forms applications with (and without) the aid of Visual Studio; now it's time to examine the Form type in greater detail. In the world of Windows Forms, the Form type represents any window in the application, including the topmost main windows, child windows of a multiple document interface (MDI) application, as well as modal and modeless dialog boxes. As Figure A-11 shows, the Form type gathers a good deal of functionality from its parent classes and the numerous interfaces it implements.

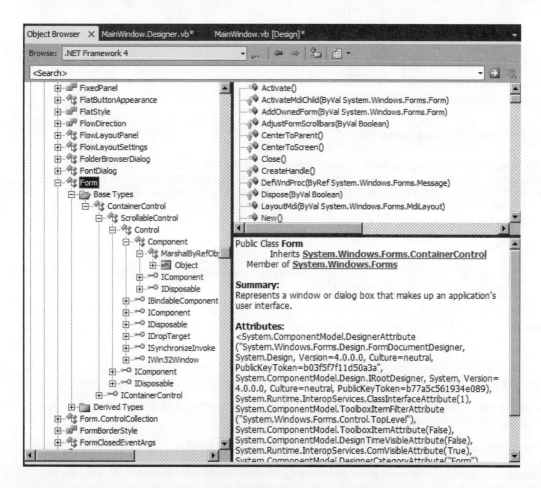

Figure A-11. The inheritance chain of System.Windows.Forms.Form

Table A-2 offers a high-level look at each parent class in the Form's inheritance chain.

Table A-2. Base Classes in the Form Inheritance Chain

Parent Class	Meaning in Life
System.Object	Like any class in .NET, a Form *is-a* object.
System.MarshalByRefObject	Types deriving from this class are accessed remotely through a *reference to* (not a local copy of) the remote type.
System.ComponentModel. Component	This class provides a default implementation of the IComponent interface. In the .NET universe, a component is a type that supports design-time editing, but it is not necessarily visible at runtime.
System.Windows.Forms.Control	This class defines common UI members for all Windows Forms UI controls, including the Form type itself.
System.Windows.Forms. ScrollableControl	This class defines support for horizontal and vertical scrollbars, as well as members, which allow you to manage the viewport shown within the scrollable region.
System.Windows.Forms. ContainerControl	This class provides focus-management functionality for controls that can function as a container for other controls.
System.Windows.Forms.Form	This class represents any custom form, MDI child, or dialog box.

Although the complete derivation of a Form type involves numerous base classes and interfaces, you should keep in mind that you are *not* required to learn the role of each and every member of each and every parent class or implemented interface to be a proficient Windows Forms developer. In fact, you can easily set the majority of the members (specifically, properties and events) you use on a daily basis using the Visual Studio 2010 Properties window. That said, it is important that you understand the functionality provided by the Control and Form parent classes.

The Functionality of the Control Class

The System.Windows.Forms.Control class establishes the common behaviors required by any GUI type. The core members of Control allow you to configure the size and position of a control, capture keyboard and mouse input, get or set the focus/visibility of a member, and so forth. Table A-3 defines some properties of interest, which are grouped by related functionality.

Table A-3. Core Properties of the Control Type

Property	Meaning in Life
BackColor ForeColor BackgroundImage Font Cursor	These properties define the core UI of the control (e.g., colors, font for text, and the mouse cursor to display when the mouse is over the widget).
Anchor Dock AutoSize	These properties control how the control should be positioned within the container.
Top Left Bottom Right Bounds ClientRectangle Height Width	These properties specify the current dimensions of the control.
Enabled Focused Visible	These properties encapsulate a Boolean that specifies the state of the current control.
ModifierKeys	This Shared property checks the current state of the modifier keys (e.g., Shift, Ctrl, and Alt) and returns the state in a Keys type.
MouseButtons	This Shared property checks the current state of the mouse buttons (left, right, and middle mouse buttons) and returns this state in a MouseButtons type.
TabIndex TabStop	You use these properties to configure the tab order of the control.
Opacity	This property determines the opacity of the control (0.0 is completely transparent; 1.0 is completely opaque).
Text	This property indicates the string data associated with this control.
Controls	This property allows you to access a strongly typed collection (e.g., ControlsCollection) that contains any child controls within the current control.

As you might guess, the `Control` class also defines a number of events that allow you to intercept mouse, keyboard, painting, and drag-and-drop activities, among other things. Table A-4 lists some events of interest, grouping them by related functionality.

Table A-4. Events of the Control Type

Event	Meaning in Life
Click DoubleClick MouseEnter MouseLeave MouseDown MouseUp MouseMove MouseHover MouseWheel	These events that let you interact with the mouse.
KeyPress KeyUp KeyDown	These events let you interact with the keyboard.
DragDrop DragEnter DragLeave DragOver	You use these events to monitor drag-and-drop activity.
Paint	This event lets you to interact with the graphical rendering services of GDI+.

Finally, the `Control` base class also defines a several methods that allow you to interact with any `Control`-derived type. As you examine the methods of the `Control` type, notice that a many of them have an `On` prefix, followed by the name of a specific event (e.g., `OnMouseMove`, `OnKeyUp`, and `OnPaint`). Each of these `On`-prefixed Overridable methods is the default event handler for its respective event. If you override any of these Overridable members, you gain the ability to perform any necessary pre- or post-processing of the event before (or after) invoking the parent's default implementation:

```
Public Class MainWindow
        Protected Overrides Sub OnMouseDown(ByVal e As MouseEventArgs)
        ' Add custom code for MouseDown event here.

        ' Call parent implementation when finished.
        MyBase.OnMouseDown(e)
        End Sub
End Class
```

This can be helpful in some circumstances (especially if you want to build a custom control that derives from a standard control), but you will often handle events using the standard VB 2010 event syntax (in fact, this is the default behavior of the Visual Studio designers). When you handle events in this manner, the framework calls your custom event handler once the parent's implementation has completed. For example, this code lets you manually handle the MouseDown event:

```
Public Class MainWindow

        Private Sub MainWindow_MouseDown(ByVal sender As Object,
                                    ByVal e As MouseEventArgs)
            Handles MyBase.MouseDown
         ' Add code for MouseDown event.
        End Sub
End Class
```

You should also be aware of a few other methods, in addition to the just described OnXXX() methods:

- Hide(): Hides the control and sets the Visible property to False.

- Show(): Shows the control and sets the Visible property to True.

- Invalidate(): Forces the control to redraw itself by sending a Paint event (you learn more about graphical rendering using GDI+ later in this chapter).

The Functionality of the Form Class

The Form class is typically (but not necessarily) the direct base class for your custom Form types. In addition to the large set of members inherited from the Control, ScrollableControl, and ContainerControl classes, the Form type adds additional functionality in particular to main windows, MDI child windows, and dialog boxes. Let's start with the core properties in Table A-5.

Table A-5. Properties of the Form Type

Property	Meaning in Life
AcceptButton	Gets or sets the button on the form that is clicked when the user presses the Enter key.
ActiveMdiChild IsMdiChild IsMdiContainer	Used within the context of an MDI application.
CancelButton	Gets or sets the button control that will be clicked when the user presses the Esc key.
ControlBox	Gets or sets a value that indicates whether the form has a control box (e.g., the minimize, maximize, and close icons in the upper right of a window).
FormBorderStyle	Gets or sets the border style of the form. You use this in conjunction with the FormBorderStyle enumeration.

Property	Meaning in Life
Menu	Gets or sets the menu to dock on the form.
MaximizeBox MinimizeBox	Used to determine whether this form will enable the maximize and minimize boxes.
ShowInTaskbar	Determines whether this form will be seen on the Windows taskbar.
StartPosition	Gets or sets the starting position of the form at runtime, as specified by the FormStartPosition enumeration.
WindowState	Configures how the form is to be displayed on startup. You use this in conjunction with the FormWindowState enumeration.

In addition to numerous On-prefixed default event handlers, Table A-6 provides a list of some core methods defined by the Form type.

Table A-6. Key Methods of the Form Type

Method	Meaning in Life
Activate()	Activates a given form and gives it focus.
Close()	Closes the current form.
CenterToScreen()	Places the form in the center of the screen
LayoutMdi()	Arranges each child form (as specified by the MdiLayout enumeration) within the parent form.
Show()	Displays a form as a modeless window.
ShowDialog()	Displays a form as a modal dialog box.

Finally, the Form class defines a number of events, many of which fire during the form's lifetime (see Table A-7).

Table A-7. Select Events of the Form Type

Event	Meaning in Life
Activated	This event occurs whenever the form is *activated*, which means that the form has been given the current focus on the desktop.
FormClosed FormClosing	You use these events to determine when the form is about to close or has closed.
Deactivate	This event occurs whenever the form is *deactivated*, which means the form has lost the current focus on the desktop.
Load	This event occurs after the form has been allocated into memory, but is not yet visible on the screen.
MdiChildActive	This event is sent when a child window is activated.

The Life Cycle of a Form Type

If you have programmed user interfaces using GUI toolkits such as Java Swing, Mac OS X Cocoa, or WPF, you know that *window types* have many events that fire during their lifetime. The same holds true for Windows Forms. Internally, the life of a form begins when the class constructor is called prior to being passed into the `Application.Run()` method.

Once the object has been allocated on the managed heap, the framework fires the `Load` event. Within a `Load` event handler, you are free to configure the look-and-feel of the `Form`, prepare any contained child controls (e.g., `ListBoxes` and `TreeViews`), or allocate resources used during the `Form`'s operation (e.g., database connections and proxies to remote objects).

Once the `Load` event fires, the next event to fire is `Activated`. This event fires when the form receives the focus as the active window on the desktop. The logical counterpart to the `Activated` event is (of course) `Deactivate`, which fires when the form loses the focus as the active window. As you can guess, the `Activated` and `Deactivate` events can fire numerous times over the life of a given `Form` object as the user navigates between active windows and applications.

Two events fire when the user chooses to close a given form: `FormClosing` and `FormClosed`. The `FormClosing` event is fired first and is an ideal place to prompt the end user with the much hated (but useful) message: "Are you *sure* you wish to close this application?" This step gives the user a chance to save any application-centric data before terminating the program.

The `FormClosing` event works in conjunction with the `FormClosingEventHandler` delegate. If you set the `FormClosingEventArgs.Cancel` property to `True`, you prevent the window from being destroyed and instruct it to return to normal operation. If you set `FormClosingEventArgs.Cancel` to `False`, the `FormClosed` event fires, and the Windows Forms application exits, which unloads the AppDomain and terminates the process.

To solidify the sequence of events that take place during a form's lifetime, assume you have a new `MainWindow.vb` file that handles the Load, Activated, Deactivate, FormClosing, and FormClosed events (be sure to add an `Imports` directive for the `System.ComponentModel` namespace to obtain the definition of `CancelEventArgs`).

Within the `Load`, `FormClosed`, `Activated`, and `Deactivate` event handlers, you must update the value of a new `Form`-level `String` member variable (named `lifeTimeInfo`) with a simple message that displays the name of the event that has just been intercepted. Begin by adding this member to your Form derived class:

```
Public Class MainWindow
    Private lifeTimeInfo As String = ""
    ….
End Class
```

The next step is to implement the event handlers. Notice that you display the value of the `lifeTimeInfo` string within a message box in the `FormClosed` event handler:

```
Private Sub MainWindow_Load(ByVal sender As Object, ByVal e As EventArgs)
   Handles MyBase.Load
        lifeTimeInfo &= "Load event" & vbLf
End Sub

Private Sub MainWindow_Activated(ByVal sender As Object, ByVal e AsnEventArgs)
   Handles MyBase.Activated
        lifeTimeInfo = lifeTimeInfo &  "Activate event" & vbLf
End Sub

Private Sub MainWindow_Deactivate(ByVal sender As Object, ByVal e As EventArgs)
   Handles MyBase.Deactivate
        lifeTimeInfo = lifeTimeInfo & "Deactivate event" & vbLf
End Sub

Private Sub MainWindow_FormClosed(ByVal sender As Object, ByVal e As FormClosedEventArgs)
   Handles MyBase.FormClosed
        lifeTimeInfo = lifeTimeInfo & "FormClosed event" & vbLf
        MessageBox.Show(lifeTimeInfo)
End Sub
```

Within the `FormClosing` event handler, you prompt the user to ensure that she wishes to terminate the application using the incoming `FormClosingEventArgs`. In the following code, the `MessageBox.Show()` method returns a `DialogResult` type that contains a value representing which button has been selected by the end user. Here, you craft a message box that displays Yes and No buttons; therefore, you want to discover whether the return value from `Show()` is `DialogResult.No`:

```
Private Sub MainWindow_FormClosing(ByVal sender As Object, ByVal e As FormClosingEventArgs)
   Handles MyBase.FormClosing
            lifeTimeInfo = lifeTimeInfo & "FormClosing event" & vbLf

        ' Show a message box with Yes and No buttons.
        Dim dr As DialogResult = MessageBox.Show("Do you REALLY want to close this app?",
                                        "Closing event!", MessageBoxButtons.YesNo)
```

```
        ' Which button was clicked?
        If dr = DialogResult.No Then
            e.Cancel = True
        Else
            e.Cancel = False
        End If
End Sub
```

Let's make one final adjustment. Currently, the File ➤ Exit menu destroys the entire application, which is a bit aggressive. More often, the File ➤ Exit handler of a top-most window calls the inherited Close() method, which fires the close-centric events and then tears down the application:

```
Private Sub ExitToolStripMenuItem_Click(ByVal sender As Object, ByVal e As EventArgs)
    Handles ExitToolStripMenuItem.Click
        ' Application.Exit()
        Close()
End Sub
```

Now run your application and shift the form into and out of focus a few times (to trigger the Activated and Deactivate events). When you eventually shut down the application, you will see a message box that looks something like the message shown in Figure A-12.

Figure A-12. *The life and times of a Form-derived type*

■ **Source Code** You can find the SimpleVSWinFormsApp project under the Appendix A subdirectory.

Responding to Mouse and Keyboard Activity

You might recall that the Control parent class defines a set of events that allow you to monitor mouse and keyboard activity in a variety of manners. To check this out firsthand, create a new Windows Forms Application project named MouseAndKeyboardEventsApp, rename the initial form to MainWindow.vb (using the Solution Explorer), and handle the MouseMove event using the Properties window. These steps generate the following event handler:

```
Public Class MainWindow
        ' Generated via the Properties window.
        Private Sub MainWindow_MouseMove(ByVal sender As Object, ByVal e As MouseEventArgs)
            Handles MyBase.MouseMove
        End Sub
End Class
```

The MouseMove event works in conjunction with the System.Windows.Forms.MouseEventHandler delegate. This delegate can only call methods where the first parameter is a System.Object, while the second is of type MouseEventArgs. This type contains various members that provide detailed information about the state of the event when mouse-centric events occur:

```
Public Class MouseEventArgs
    Inherits EventArgs

    Public Sub New(ByVal button As MouseButtons, ByVal clicks As Integer,
                ByVal x As Integer,
                ByVal y As Integer, ByVal delta As Integer)
    End Sub

    Public ReadOnly Property Button() As MouseButtons
    Public ReadOnly Property Clicks() As Integer
    Public ReadOnly Property Delta() As Integer
    Public ReadOnly Property Location() As Point
    Public ReadOnly Property X() As Integer
    Public ReadOnly Property Y() As Integer
End Class
```

Most of the Public properties are self-explanatory, but Table A-8 provides more specific details.

Table A-8. Properties of the MouseEventArgs Type

Property	Meaning in Life
Button	Gets which mouse button was pressed, as defined by the MouseButtons enumeration.
Clicks	Gets the number of times the mouse button was pressed and released.

Continued

Property	Meaning in Life
Delta	Gets a signed count of the number of detents (which represents a single notch of the mouse wheel) for the current mouse rotation.
Location	Returns a **Point** that contains the current X and Y location of the mouse.
X	Gets the *x*-coordinate of a mouse click.
Y	Gets the *y*-coordinate of a mouse click.

Now it's time to implement your **MouseMove** handler to display the current X- and Y-position of the mouse on the **Form**'s caption; you do this using the **Location** property:

```
Private Sub MainWindow_MouseMove(ByVal sender As Object, ByVal e As MouseEventArgs)
    Handles MyBase.MouseMove
        Text = String.Format("Mouse Position: {0}", e.Location)
End Sub
```

When you run the application and move the mouse over the window, you find the position displayed on the title area of your **MainWindow** type (see Figure A-13).

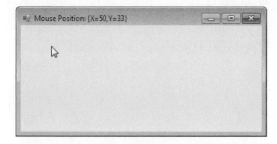

Figure A-13. Intercepting mouse movements

Determining Which Mouse Button Was Clicked

Another common mouse-centric detail to attend to is determining which button has been clicked when a **MouseUp**, **MouseDown**, **MouseClick**, or **MouseDoubleClick** event occurs. When you wish to determine exactly which button was clicked (whether left, right, or middle), you need to examine the **Button** property of the **MouseEventArgs** class. The value of the **Button** property is constrained by the related **MouseButtons** enumeration:

```
Public Enum MouseButtons
      Left
      Middle
      None
      Right
      XButton1
      XButton2
End Enum
```

■ **Note** The XButton1 and XButton2 values allow you to capture forward and backwards navigation buttons that are supported on many mouse-controller devices.

You can see this in action by handling the MouseDown event on your MainWindow type using the Properties window. The following MouseDown event handler displays which mouse button was clicked inside a message box:

```
Private Sub MainWindow_MouseDown(ByVal sender As Object, ByVal e As MouseEventArgs)
    Handles MyBase.MouseDown
      ' Which mouse button was clicked?
      If e.Button = MouseButtons.Left Then
        MessageBox.Show("Left click!")
      End If

      If e.Button = MouseButtons.Right Then
        MessageBox.Show("Right click!")
      End If

      If e.Button = MouseButtons.Middle Then
        MessageBox.Show("Middle click!")
      End If
End Sub
```

Determining Which Key Was Pressed

Windows applications typically define numerous input controls (e.g., the TextBox) where the user can enter information using the keyword. When you capture keyboard input in this manner, you do not need to handle keyboard events explicitly because you can extract the textual data from the control using various properties (e.g., the Text property of the TextBox type).

However, if you need to monitor keyboard input for more exotic purposes (e.g., filtering keystrokes on a control or capturing keypresses on the form itself), the base class libraries provide the KeyUp and KeyDown events. These events work in conjunction with the KeyEventHandler delegate, which can point to any method taking an object as the first parameter and KeyEventArgs as the second. You define this type like this:

```
Public Class KeyEventArgs
        Public Sub New(ByVal keyData As Keys)

        Public Overridable ReadOnly Property Alt() As Boolean
        Public ReadOnly Property Control() As Boolean
        Public Property Handled() As Boolean
        Public ReadOnly Property KeyCode() As Keys
        Public ReadOnly Property KeyData() As Keys
        Public ReadOnly Property KeyValue() As Integer
        Public ReadOnly Property Modifiers() As Keys
        Public Overridable ReadOnly Property Shift() As Boolean
        Public Property SuppressKeyPress() As Boolean
End Class
```

Table A-9 documents some of the more interesting properties supported by **KeyEventArgs**.

Table A-9. Properties of the KeyEventArgs Type

Property	Meaning in Life
Alt	Gets a value that indicates whether the Alt key was pressed.
Control	Gets a value that indicates whether the Ctrl key was pressed.
Handled	Gets or sets a value that indicates whether the event was fully handled in your handler.
KeyCode	Gets the keyboard code for a **KeyDown** or **KeyUp** event.
Modifiers	Indicates which modifier keys (e.g., Ctrl, Shift, and/or Alt) were pressed.
Shift	Gets a value that indicates whether the Shift key was pressed.

You can see this in action by handling the **KeyDown** event as follows:

```
Private Sub MainWindow_KeyDown(ByVal sender As Object, ByVal e As KeyEventArgs)
  Handles MyBase.KeyDown
            Text = String.Format("Key Pressed: {0} Modifiers: {1}",
                            e.KeyCode.ToString(), e.Modifiers.ToString())
End Sub
```

Now compile and run your program. You should be able to determine which mouse button was clicked, as well as which keyboard key was pressed. For example, Figure A-14 shows the result of pressing the Ctrl and Shift keys simultaneously.

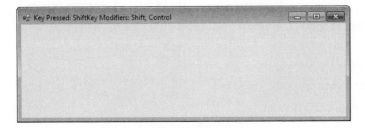

Figure A-14. Intercepting keyboard activity

■ **Source Code** You can find the MouseAndKeyboardEventsApp project under the Appendix A subdirectory.

Designing Dialog Boxes

Within a graphical user interface program, dialog boxes tend to be the primary way to capture user input for use within the application itself. Unlike other GUI APIs you might have used previously, there Windows Forms has no `Dialog` base class. Rather, dialog boxes under Windows Forms are simply types that derive from the `Form` class.

In addition, many dialog boxes are intended to be nonsizable; therefore, you typically want to set the `FormBorderStyle` property to `FormBorderStyle.FixedDialog`. Also, dialog boxes typically set the `MinimizeBox` and `MaximizeBox` properties to `False`. In this way, the dialog box is configured to be a fixed constant. Finally, if you set the `ShowInTaskbar` property to `False`, you will prevent the form from being visible in the Windows taskbar.

Let's look at how to build and manipulate dialog boxes. Begin by creating a new Windows Forms Application project named CarOrderApp and rename the initial `Form1.vb` file to `MainWindow.vb` using Solution Explorer. Next, use the Forms designer to create a simple File ➤ Exit menu, as well as a Tool ➤ Order Automobile... menu item (remember: you create a menu by dragging a MenuStrip from the Toolbox and then configuring the menu items in the designer window). Once you do this, handle the `Click` event for the Exit and Order Automobile submenus using the Properties window.

You implement the File ➤ Exit menu handler so it terminates the application with a call to `Close()`:

```
Private Sub ExitToolStripMenuItem_Click(ByVal sender As Object, ByVal e As EventArgs)
    Handles  ExitToolStripMenuItem.Click
        Close()
End Sub
```

Now use the Project menu of Visual Studio to select the Add Windows Forms menu option and name your new form `OrderAutoDialog.vb` (see Figure A-15).

For this example, design a dialog box that has the expected OK and Cancel buttons (named `btnOK` and `btnCancel`, respectively), as well as three `TextBox` controls named `txtMake`, `txtColor`, and `txtPrice`. Now use the Properties window to finalize the design of your dialog box, as follows:

- Set the `FormBorderStyle` property to `FixedDialog`.

- Set the `MinimizeBox` and `MaximizeBox` properties to `False`.

- Set the `StartPosition` property to `CenterParent`.

- Set the `ShowInTaskbar` property to `False`.

Figure A-15. Inserting new dialog boxes using Visual Studio

The DialogResult Property

Finally, select the OK button and use the Properties window to set the `DialogResult` property to `OK`. Similarly, you can set the `DialogResult` property of the Cancel button to (you guessed it) `Cancel`. As you will see in a moment, the `DialogResult` property is quite useful because it enables the launching form to determine quickly which button the user has clicked; this enables you to take the appropriate action. You can set the `DialogResult` property to any value from the related `DialogResult` enumeration:

```
Public Enum DialogResult
  Abort
  Cancel
  Ignore
  No
  None
  OK
  Retry
  Yes
End Enum
```

Figure A-16 shows one possible design of your dialog box; it even adds in a few descriptive Label controls.

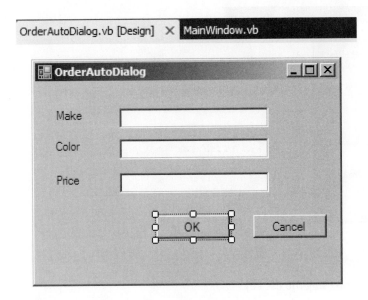

Figure A-16. The OrderAutoDialog type

Configuring the Tab Order

You have created a somewhat interesting dialog box; the next step is to formalize the tab order. As you might know, users expect to be able to shift focus using the Tab key when a form contains multiple GUI widgets. Configuring the tab order for your set of controls requires that you understand two key properties: TabStop and TabIndex.

You can set the TabStop property to True or False, based on whether or not you wish this GUI item to be reachable using the Tab key. Assuming that you set the TabStop property to True for a given control, you can use the TabOrder property to establish the order of activation in the tabbing sequence (which is zero-based), as in this example:

```
' Configure tabbing properties.
txtMake.TabIndex = 0
txtMake.TabStop = True
```

The Tab Order Wizard

You can set the `TabStop` and `TabIndex` manually using the Properties window; however, the Visual Studio 2010 IDE supplies a Tab Order Wizard that you can access by choosing View ➤ Tab Order (be aware that you will not find this menu option unless the Forms designer is active). Once activated, your design-time form displays the current `TabIndex` value for each widget. To change these values, click each item in the order you prefer the controls to tab (see Figure A-17).

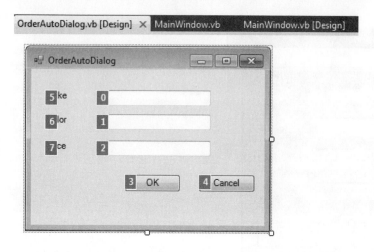

Figure A-17. The Tab Order Wizard

You can exit the Tab Order Wizard by pressing the Esc key.

Setting the Form's Default Input Button

Many user-input forms (especially dialog boxes) have a particular `button` that automatically responds to the user pressing the Enter key. Now assume that you want the `Click` event handler for `btnOK` invoked when the user presses the Enter key. Doing so is as simple as setting the form's `AcceptButton` property in the form's constructor (after the call to the `InitializeComponent()` method) as follows (you can establish this same setting using the Properties window):

```
Public Class OrderAutoDialog
    Public Sub New()
        InitializeComponent()
```

```
            ' When the Enter key is pressed, it is as if
            ' the user clicked the btnOK button.
            Me.AcceptButton = btnOK
         End Sub
End Class
```

■ **Note** Some forms require the ability to simulate clicking the form's Cancel button when the user presses the Esc key. You can accomplish this by assigning the `CancelButton` property of the `Form` to the `Button` object that represents the clicking of the Cancel button.

Displaying Dialog Boxes

When you wish to display a dialog box, you must first decide whether you wish to launch the dialog box in a *modal* or *modeless* fashion. As you might know, modal dialog boxes must be dismissed by the user before he can return to the window that launched the dialog box in the first place; for example, most About boxes are modal in nature. To show a modal dialog box, call `ShowDialog()` off your dialog box object. On the other hand, you can display a modeless dialog box by calling `Show()`, which allows the user to switch focus between the dialog box and the main window (e.g., a Find/Replace dialog box).

For this example, you want to update the Tools ➤ Order Automobile... menu handler of the `MainWindow` type to show the `OrderAutoDialog` object in a modal manner. Consider the following initial code:

```
Private Sub OrderAutomobileToolStripMenuItem_Click(ByVal sender As Object,
                                            ByVal e As EventArgs)
      Handles  OrderAutomobileToolStripMenuItem.Click
          ' Create your dialog object.
          Dim dlg As New OrderAutoDialog()

          ' Show as modal dialog box, and figure out which button
          ' was clicked using the DialogResult return value.
          If dlg.ShowDialog() = DialogResult.OK Then
              ' They clicked OK, so do something...
          End If
End Sub
```

■ **Note** You can optionally call the `ShowDialog()` and `Show()` methods by specifying an object that represents the owner of the dialog box (which for the form loading the dialog box would be represented by `this`). Specifying the owner of a dialog box establishes the z-ordering of the form types and also ensures (in the case of a modeless dialog box) that all owned windows are also disposed of when the main window is destroyed.

Be aware that when you create an instance of a **Form**-derived type (**OrderAutoDialog** in this case), the dialog box is *not* visible on the screen, but simply allocated into memory. It is not until you call **Show()** or **ShowDialog()** that the form becomes visible. Also, notice that **ShowDialog()** returns the **DialogResult** value that has been assigned to the button (the **Show()** method is a **Sub** and therefore has no return value).

Once **ShowDialog()** returns, the form is no longer visible on the screen, but is still in memory. This means you can extract the values in each **TextBox** as follows:

```
Private Sub OrderAutomobileToolStripMenuItem_Click(ByVal sender As Object,
                                                   ByVal e As EventArgs)
    Handles OrderAutomobileToolStripMenuItem.Click
        ' Create your dialog object.
        Dim dlg As New OrderAutoDialog()

        ' Show as modal dialog box, and figure out which button
        ' was clicked using the DialogResult return value.
        If dlg.ShowDialog() = DialogResult.OK Then
            ' Get values in each text box? Compiler errors!
            Dim orderInfo As String = String.Format("Make: {0}, Color: {1}, Cost: {2}",
                        dlg.txtMake.Text.dlg.txtColor.Text, dlg.txtPrice.Text)
            MessageBox.Show(orderInfo, "Information about your order!")
        End If
End Sub
```

The reason you can access the controls is because Visual Studio 2010 declares the controls you add to the Forms designer as *Friend* member variables of the class. You can verify this fact by opening the **OrderAutoDialog.Designer.vb** file.At this point, you can compile and run your application. Once you launch your dialog box, you should be able to see the input data displayed within a message box (provided you click the OK button).

Understanding Form Inheritance

So far, each one of your custom windows/dialog boxes in this chapter has derived directly from **System.Windows.Forms.Form**. However, one intriguing aspect of Windows Forms development is the fact that **Form** types can function as the base class to derived **Forms**. For example, assume you create a .NET code library that contains each of your company's core dialog boxes. Later, you decide that your company's About box is a bit on the bland side, and you wish to add a 3D image of your company logo. Rather than having to re-create the entire About box, you can extend the basic About box, thereby inheriting the core look-and-feel:

```
' ThreeDAboutBox "is-a" AboutBox
Partial Public Class ThreeDAboutBox
    Inherits AboutBox
            ' Add code to render company logo...
End Class
```

To see form inheritance in action, insert a new form into your project using the Project ➤ Add Windows Form menu option. This time, however, pick the Inherited Form icon, and name your new form **ImageOrderAutoDialog.vb** (see Figure A-18).

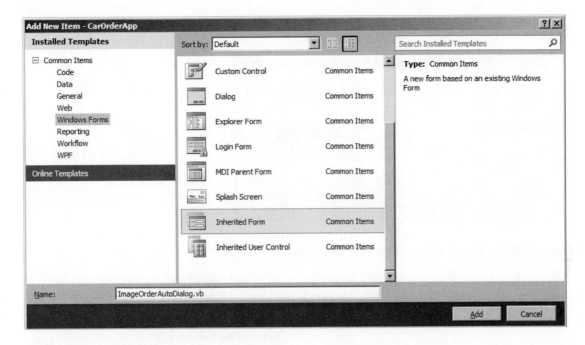

Figure A-18. Adding a derived form to your project

This option brings up the Inheritance Picker dialog box, which shows you each of the forms in your current project. Notice that the Browse button allows you to pick a form in an external .NET assembly. Here, simply pick your OrderAutoDialog class.

■ **Note** You must compile your project at least one time to see the forms of your project in the Inheritance Picker dialog box because this tool reads from the assembly metadata to show you your options.

Once you click the OK button, the visual designer tools show each of the base controls on your parent controls; each control has a small arrow icon mounted on the upper-left of the control (symbolizing inheritance). To complete your derived dialog box, locate the PictureBox control from the Common Controls section of the Toolbox and add one to your derived form. Next, use the Image property to select an image file of your choosing. Figure A-19 shows one possible UI, using a (crude) hand drawing of a junker automobile (a lemon!).

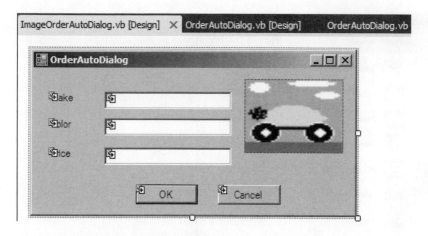

Figure A-19. The UI of the ImageOrderAutoDialog class

With this, you can now update the Tools ➤ Order Automobile... Click event handler to create an instance of your derived type, rather than the OrderAutoDialog base class:

```
Private Sub OrderAutomobileToolStripMenuItem_Click(ByVal sender As Object,
                                                   ByVal e As EventArgs)
    Handles OrderAutomobileToolStripMenuItem.Click
    ' Create the derived dialog object.
    Dim dlg As New ImageOrderAutoDialog()
    ...
End Sub
```

■ **Source Code** You can find the CarOrderApp project under the Appendix A subdirectory.

Rendering Graphical Data Using GDI+

Many GUI applications require the ability to generate graphical data dynamically for display on the surface of a window. For example, perhaps you have selected a set of records from a relational database and wish to render a pie chart (or bar chart) that visually shows items in stock. Or, perhaps you want to re-create some old-school video game using the .NET platform. Regardless of your goal, GDI+ is the API to use when you need to render data graphically within a Windows Forms application. This technology is bundled within the System.Drawing.dll assembly, which defines a number of namespaces (see Figure A-20).

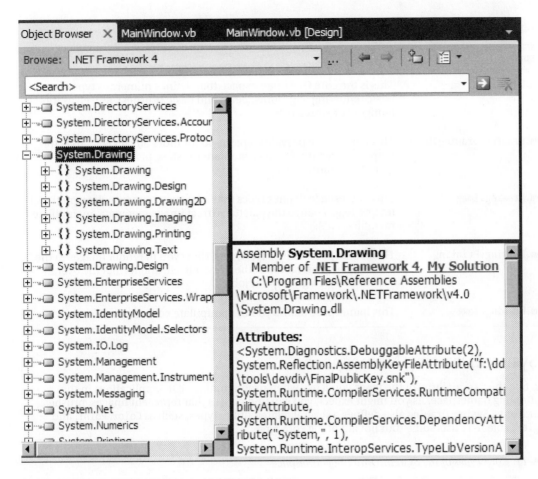

Figure A-20. The namespaces of System.Drawing.dll

■ **Note** A friendly reminder: WPF has its own graphical rendering subsystem and API; you use GDI+ only within a Windows Forms application.

Table A-10 documents the role of the key GDI+ namespaces at a high level.

Table A-10. Core GDI+ Namespaces

Namespace	Meaning in Life
System.Drawing	This is the core GDI+ namespace that defines numerous types for basic rendering (e.g., fonts, pens, and basic brushes), as well as the almighty Graphics type.
System.Drawing.Drawing2D	This namespace provides types used for more advanced 2D/vector graphics functionality (e.g., gradient brushes, pen caps, and geometric transforms).
System.Drawing.Imaging	This namespace defines types that allow you to manipulate graphical images (e.g., change the palette, extract image metadata, manipulate metafiles, etc.).
System.Drawing.Printing	This namespace defines types that allow you to render images to the printed page, interact with the printer itself, and format the overall appearance of a given print job.
System.Drawing.Text	This namespace allows you to manipulate collections of fonts.

The System.Drawing Namespace

You can find the vast majority of the types you'll use when programming GDI+ applications in the System.Drawing namespace. As you might expect, you can find classes that represent images, brushes, pens, and fonts. System.Drawing also defines a several related utility types, such as Color, Point, and Rectangle. Table A-11 lists some (but not all) of the core types.

Table A-11. Core Types of the System.Drawing Namespace

Type	Meaning in Life
Bitmap	This type encapsulates image data (*.bmp or otherwise).
Brush Brushes SolidBrush SystemBrushes TextureBrush	You use brush objects to fill the interiors of graphical shapes, such as rectangles, ellipses, and polygons.
BufferedGraphics	This type provides a graphics buffer for double buffering, which you use to reduce or eliminate flicker caused by redrawing a display surface.

Type	Meaning in Life
Color SystemColors	The Color and SystemColors types define a number of Shared read-only properties you use to obtain specific colors for the construction of various pens/brushes.
Font FontFamily	The Font type encapsulates the characteristics of a given font (e.g., type name, bold, italic, and point size). FontFamily provides an abstraction for a group of fonts that have a similar design, but also certain variations in style.
Graphics	This core class represents a valid drawing surface, as well as several methods to render text, images, and geometric patterns.
Icon SystemIcons	These classes represent custom icons, as well as the set of standard system-supplied icons.
Image ImageAnimator	Image is a MustInherit base class that provides functionality for the Bitmap, Icon, and Cursor types. ImageAnimator provides a way to iterate over a number of Image-derived types at some specified interval.
Pen Pens SystemPens	Pens are objects you use to draw lines and curves. The Pens type defines several Shared properties that return a new Pen of a given color.
Point PointF	These structures represent an (x, y) coordinate mapping to an underlying Integer or Single, respectively.
Rectangle RectangleF	These structures represent a rectangular dimension (again, these map to an underlying Integer or Single).
Size SizeF	These structures represent a given height/width (again, these map to an underlying Integer or Single).
StringFormat	You use this type to encapsulate various features of textual layout (e.g., alignment and line spacing).
Region	This type describes the interior of a geometric image composed of rectangles and paths.

The Role of the Graphics Type

The System.Drawing.Graphics class serves as the gateway to GDI+ rendering functionality. This class not only represents the surface you wish to draw upon (such as a form's surface, a control's surface, or a region of memory), but also defines dozens of members that allow you to render text, images (e.g., icons and bitmaps), and numerous geometric patterns. Table A-12 gives a partial list of members.

Table A-12. Select Members of the Graphics Class

Method	Meaning in Life
FromHdc() FromHwnd() FromImage()	These Shared methods provide a way to obtain a valid Graphics object from a given image (e.g., icon and bitmap) or GUI control.
Clear()	This method fills a Graphics object with a specified color, erasing the current drawing surface in the process.
DrawArc() DrawBeziers() DrawCurve() DrawEllipse() DrawIcon() DrawLine() DrawLines() DrawPie() DrawPath() DrawRectangle() DrawRectangles() DrawString()	You use these methods to render a given image or geometric pattern. All DrawXXX() methods require that you use GDI+ Pen objects.
FillEllipse() FillPie() FillPolygon() FillRectangle() FillPath()	You use these methods to fill the interior of a given geometric shape. All FillXXX() methods require that you use GDI+ Brush objects.

Note that you cannot create the Graphics class directly using the new keyword because there are no publicly defined constructors. So, how do you obtain a valid Graphics object? I'm glad you asked!

Obtaining a Graphics Object with the Paint Event

The most common way to obtain a Graphics object is to use the Visual Studio 2010 Properties window to handle the Paint event on the window you want to render upon. This event is defined in terms of the PaintEventHandler delegate, which can point to any method taking a System.Object as the first parameter and a PaintEventArgs as the second.

The PaintEventArgs parameter contains the Graphics object you need to render onto the Form's surface. For example, create a new Windows Application project named PaintEventApp. Next, use Solution Explorer to rename your initial Form.vb file to MainWindow.vb, and then handle the Paint event using the Properties window. This creates the following stub code:

```
Public Class MainWindow
        Private Sub MainWindow_Paint(ByVal sender As Object, ByVal e As PaintEventArgs)
            Handles MyBase.Paint
        ' Add your painting code here!
        End Sub
End Class
```

Now that you have handled the Paint event, you might wonder when it will fire. The Paint event fires whenever a window becomes *dirty*; a window is considered dirty whenever it is resized, uncovered by another window (partially or completely), or minimized and then restored. In all these cases, the .NET platform ensures that the Paint event handler is called automatically whenever your Form needs to be redrawn. Consider the following implementation of MainWindow_Paint():

```
Private Sub MainWindow_Paint(ByVal sender As Object, ByVal e As PaintEventArgs)
    Handles MyBase.Paint
        ' Get the graphics object for this Form.
        Dim g As Graphics = e.Graphics

        ' Draw a circle.
        g.FillEllipse(Brushes.Blue, 10, 20, 150, 80)
        ' Draw a string in a custom font.
        g.DrawString("Hello GDI+", New Font("Times New Roman", 30), Brushes.Red, 200, 200)

        ' Draw a line with a custom pen.
    Using p As New Pen(Color.YellowGreen, 10)
        g.DrawLine(p, 80, 4, 200, 200)
    End Using
End Sub
```

Once you obtain the Graphics object from the incoming PaintEventArgs parameter, you call FillEllipse(). Notice that this method (as well as any Fill-prefixed method) requires a Brush-derived type as the first parameter. While you could create any number of interesting brush objects from the System.Drawing.Drawing2D namespace (e.g., HatchBrush and LinearGradientBrush), the Brushes utility class provides handy access to a variety of solid-colored brush types.

Next, you make a call to DrawString(), which requires a String to render as its first parameter. Given this, GDI+ provides the Font type, which represents not only the name of the font to use when rendering the textual data, but also related characteristics, such as the point size (30, in this case). Also notice that DrawString() requires a Brush type; as far as GDI+ is concerned, "Hello GDI+" is nothing more than a collection of geometric patterns to fill on the screen. Finally, DrawLine() is called to render a line using a custom Pen type, 10 pixels wide. Figure A-21 shows the output of this rendering logic.

Figure A-21. A simple GDI+ rendering operation

■ **Note** In the preceding code, you explicitly dispose of the Pen object. As a rule, when you directly create a GDI+ type that implements IDisposable, you call the Dispose() method as soon as you are done with the object. Doing this lets you release the underlying resources as soon as possible. If you do not do this, the resources will eventually be freed by the garbage collector in a nondeterministic manner.

Invalidating the Form's Client Area

During the flow of a Windows Forms application, you might need to fire the **Paint** event in your code explicitly, rather than waiting for the window to become *naturally dirty* by the actions of the end user. For example, you might be building a program that allows the user to select from a number of predefined images using a custom dialog box. Once the dialog box is dismissed, you need to draw the newly selected image onto the form's client area. Obviously, if you were to wait for the window to become naturally dirty, the user would not see the change take place until the window was resized or uncovered by another window. To force a window to repaint itself programmatically, you call the inherited **Invalidate()** method:

```
Public Class MainForm
    ...
    Private Sub MainForm_Paint(ByVal sender As Object, ByVal e As PaintEventArgs)
        Handles MyBase.Paint
        Dim g As Graphics = e.Graphics
        ' Render the correct image here.
    End Sub
```

```
      Private Sub GetImageFromDialog()
        ' Show dialog box and get new image.
        ' Repaint the entire client area.
        Invalidate()
      End Sub
End Class
```

The `Invalidate()` method has been overloaded a number of times. This allows you to specify a specific rectangular portion of the form to repaint, rather than having to repaint the entire client area (which is the default). If you wish to update only the extreme upper-left rectangle of the client area, you can write the following code:

```
' Repaint a given rectangular area of the Form.
Private Sub UpdateUpperArea()
        Dim myRect As New Rectangle(0, 0, 75, 150)
        Invalidate(myRect)
End Sub
```

■ **Source Code** You can find the PaintEventApp project under the Appendix A subdirectory.

Building a Complete Windows Forms Application

Let's conclude this introductory look at the Windows Forms and GDI+ APIs by building a complete GUI application that illustrates several of the techniques discussed in this chapter. The program you will create is a rudimentary painting program that allows users to select between two shape types (a circle or rectangle) using the color of their choice to render data to the form. You will also allow end users to save their pictures to a local file on their hard drive for later use with object serialization services.

Building the Main Menu System

Begin by creating a new Windows Forms application named MyPaintProgram and rename your initial `Form1.vb` file to `MainWindow.vb`. Now design a menu system on this initial window that supports a topmost File menu that provides Save…, Load…, and Exit submenus (see Figure A-22).

MainWindow.vb [Design]* ✕

Figure A-22. The File menu system

■ **Note** If you specify a single dash (-) as a menu item, you can define separators within your menu system.

Next, create a second topmost Tools menu that provides options to select a shape and color to use for rendering, as well as an option to clear the form of all graphical data (see Figure A-23).

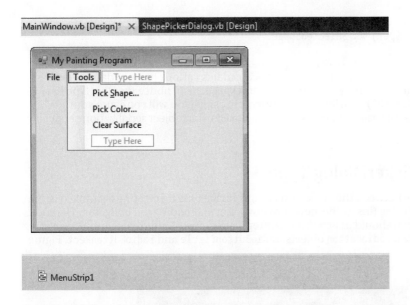

Figure A-23. The Tools Menu System

Finally, handle the `Click` event for each one of these subitems. You will implement each handler as you progress through the example; however, you can finish up the File ➤ Exit menu handler by calling `Close()`:

```
Private Sub ExitToolStripMenuItem_Click(ByVal sender As Object, ByVal e As EventArgs)
    Handles ExitToolStripMenuItem.Click
        Close()
End Sub
```

Defining the ShapeData Type

Recall that this application will allow end users to select from two predefined shapes in a given color. You will provide a way to allow users to save their graphical data to a file, so you want to define a custom class type that encapsulates each of these details; for the sake of simplicity, you do this using VB 2010 automatic properties (see Chapter 5 for more details on how to do this). Begin by adding a new class to your project named **ShapeData.vb** and implementing this type as follows:

```
<Serializable()>
Public Class ShapeData
        ' The upper left of the shape to be drawn.
        Public Property UpperLeftPoint() As Point

        ' The current color of the shape to be drawn.
        Public Property Color() As Color
```

```
        ' The type of shape.
        Public Property ShapeType() As SelectedShape
End Class
```

Here, ShapeData uses three automatic properties that encapsulates various types of data, two of which (Point and Color) are defined in the System.Drawing namespace. Also, notice that this type has been adorned with the <Serializable()> attribute. In an upcoming step, you will configure your MainWindow type to maintain a list of ShapeData types that you persist using object serialization services (see Chapter 20 for more details).

Defining the ShapePickerDialog Type

You can allow the user to choose between the circle or rectangle image type by creating a simple custom dialog box named ShapePickerDialog (insert this new Form now). Beyond adding the obligatory OK and Cancel buttons (each of which you should assign fitting DialogResult values), this dialog box uses of a single GroupBox that maintains two RadioButton objects: radioButtonCircle and radioButtonRect. Figure A-24 shows one possible design.

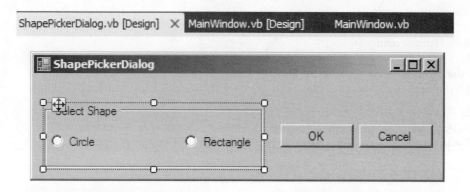

Figure A-24. The ShapePickerDialog type

Now, open the code window for your dialog box by right-clicking the Forms designer and selecting the View Code menu option. At the top of the source code file, define an enumeration (named SelectedShape) that defines names for each possible shape:

```
Public Enum SelectedShape
        Circle
        Rectangle
End Enum
```

Next, update your current `ShapePickerDialog` class type:

- Add an automatic property of type `SelectedShape`. The caller can use this property to determine which shape to render.

- Handle the `Click` event for the OK button using the Properties window.

- Implement this event handler to determine whether the circle radio button has been selected (through the `Checked` property). If so, set your `SelectedShape` property to `SelectedShape.Circle`; otherwise, set this property to `SelectedShape.Rectangle`.

Here is the complete code:

```
Public Class ShapePickerDialog
    Public Property SelectedShape() As SelectedShape

    Private Sub btnOK_Click(ByVal sender As Object, ByVal e As EventArgs)
      Handles btnOK.Click
      If radioButtonCircle.Checked Then
            SelectedShape = SelectedShape.Circle
      Else
            SelectedShape = SelectedShape.Rectangle
      End If
    End Sub
End Class
```

That wraps up the infrastructure of your program. Now all you need to do is implement the `Click` event handlers for the remaining menu items on the main window.

Adding Infrastructure to the MainWindow Type

Returning to the construction of the main window, add three new member variables to this `Form`. These member variables allow you to keep track of the selected shape (through a `SelectedShape` enum member variable), the selected color (represented by a `System.Drawing.Color` member variable), and through each of the rendered images held in a generic `List(Of T)` (where `T` is of type `ShapeData`):

```
Public Class MainWindow

    ' Current shape / color to draw.
    Private currentShape As SelectedShape
    Private currentColor As Color = Color.DarkBlue

    ' This maintains each ShapeData.
    Private shapes As New List(Of ShapeData)()
    ...
End Class
```

Next, you handle the `MouseDown` and `Paint` events for this `Form`-derived type using the Properties window. You will implement them in a later step; for the time being, however, you should find that the IDE has generated the following stub code:

```
Private Sub MainWindow_Paint(ByVal sender As Object, ByVal e As PaintEventArgs)
      Handles MyBase.Paint
End Sub

Private Sub MainWindow_MouseDown(ByVal sender As Object, ByVal e As MouseEventArgs)
      Handles MyBase.MouseDown
End Sub
```

Implementing the Tools Menu Functionality

You can allow a user to set the currentShape member variable by implementing the Click handler for the Tools ➤ Pick Shape... menu option. You use this to launch your custom dialog box; based on a user's selection, you assign this member variable accordingly:

```
Private Sub PickShapeToolStripMenuItem_Click(ByVal sender As Object, ByVal e As EventArgs)
    Handles PickShapeToolStripMenuItem.Click
        ' Load our dialog box and set the correct shape type.
        Dim dlg As New ShapePickerDialog()
        If DialogResult.OK = dlg.ShowDialog() Then
        currentShape = dlg.SelectedShape
        End If
End Sub
```

You can let a user set the currentColor member variable by implementing the Click event handler for the Tools ➤ Pick Color... menu so it uses the System.Windows.Forms.ColorDialog type:

```
Private Sub PickColorToolStripMenuItem_Click(ByVal sender As Object, ByVal e As EventArgs)
      Handles PickColorToolStripMenuItem.Click
          Dim dlg As New ColorDialog()

          If dlg.ShowDialog() = DialogResult.OK Then
          currentColor = dlg.Color
          End If
End Sub
```

If you were to run your program as it now stands and select the Tools ➤ Pick Color menu option, you would get the dialog box shown in Figure A-25.

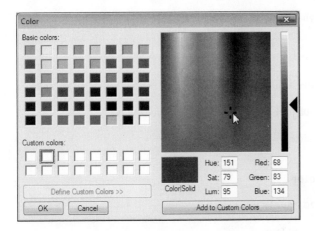

Figure A-25. The stock `ColorDialog` *type*

Finally, you implement the Tools ➤ Clear Surface menu handler so it empties the contents of the `List(Of T)` member variable and programmatically fires the `Paint` event using a call to `Invalidate()`:

```
Private Sub ClearSurfaceToolStripMenuItem_Click(ByVal sender As Object, ByVal e As
EventArgs)
     Handles ClearSurfaceToolStripMenuItem.Click
        shapes.Clear()

        ' This will fire the paint event.
        Invalidate()
End Sub
```

Capturing and Rendering the Graphical Output

Given that a call to `Invalidate()` fires the `Paint` event, you need to author code within the `Paint` event handler. Your goal is to loop through each item in the (currently empty) `List(Of T)` member variable and render a circle or square at the current mouse location. The first step is to implement the `MouseDown` event handler and insert a new `ShapeData` type into the generic `List(Of T)` type, based on the user-selected color, shape type, and current location of the mouse:

```
Private Sub MainWindow_MouseDown(ByVal sender As Object, ByVal e As MouseEventArgs)
   Handles MyBase.MouseDown
            ' Make a ShapeData type based on current user
            ' selections.
            Dim sd As New ShapeData()
            sd.ShapeType = currentShape
            sd.Color = currentColor
            sd.UpperLeftPoint = New Point(e.X, e.Y)
```

```
            ' Add to the List(Of T) and force the form to repaint itself.
            shapes.Add(sd)
            Invalidate()
End Sub
```

At this point, you can implement your **Paint** event handler:

```
Private Sub MainWindow_Paint(ByVal sender As Object, ByVal e As PaintEventArgs)
    Handles MyBase.Paint
        ' Get the Graphics object for this window.
        Dim g As Graphics = e.Graphics

        ' Render each shape in the selected color.
        For Each s As ShapeData In shapes
         ' Render a rectangle or circle 20 x 20 pixels in size
         ' using the correct color.
         If s.ShapeType = SelectedShape.Rectangle Then
                g.FillRectangle(New SolidBrush(s.Color), s.UpperLeftPoint.X,
                s.UpperLeftPoint.Y, 20, 20)
        Else
                g.FillEllipse(New SolidBrush(s.Color), s.UpperLeftPoint.X,
                s.UpperLeftPoint.Y, 20, 20)
        End If
    Next
End Sub
```

If you run your application at this point, you should be able to render any number of shapes in a variety of colors (see Figure A-26).

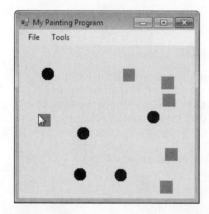

Figure A-26. MyPaintProgram in action

Implementing the Serialization Logic

The final aspect of this project involves implementing Click event handlers for the File ➤ Save... and File ➤ Load... menu items. Given that ShapeData has been marked with the <Serializable()> attribute (and given that List(Of T) itself is serializable), you can quickly save out the current graphical data using the Windows Forms SaveFileDialog type. Begin by updating your Imports directives to specify you are using the System.Runtime.Serialization.Formatters.Binary and System.IO namespaces:

```
' For the binary formatter.
Imports System.Runtime.Serialization.Formatters.Binary
Imports System.IO
```

Now update your File ➤ Save... handler, as follows:

```
Private Sub SaveToolStripMenuItem_Click(ByVal sender As Object, ByVal e As EventArgs)
    Handles SaveToolStripMenuItem.Click
    Using saveDlg As New SaveFileDialog()
        ' Configure the look and feel of the save dialog box.
        saveDlg.InitialDirectory = "."
        saveDlg.Filter = "Shape files (*.shapes)|*.shapes"
        saveDlg.RestoreDirectory = True
        saveDlg.FileName = "MyShapes"

        ' If they click the OK button, open the new
        ' file and serialize the List(Of T).
        If saveDlg.ShowDialog() = DialogResult.OK Then
            Dim myStream As Stream = saveDlg.OpenFile()
            If (myStream IsNot Nothing) Then
                ' Save the shapes!
                Dim myBinaryFormat As New BinaryFormatter()
                myBinaryFormat.Serialize(myStream, shapes)
                myStream.Close()
            End If
        End If
    End Using
End Sub
```

The File ➤ Load event handler opens the selected file and deserializes the data back into the List(Of T) member variable with the help of the Windows Forms OpenFileDialog type:

```
Private Sub LoadToolStripMenuItem_Click(ByVal sender As Object, ByVal e As EventArgs)
    Handles LoadToolStripMenuItem.Click
    Using openDlg As New OpenFileDialog()
        openDlg.InitialDirectory = "."
        openDlg.Filter = "Shape files (*.shapes)|*.shapes"
        openDlg.RestoreDirectory = True
        openDlg.FileName = "MyShapes"
```

```
        If openDlg.ShowDialog() = DialogResult.OK Then
            Dim myStream As Stream = openDlg.OpenFile()
            If (myStream IsNot Nothing) Then
              ' Get the shapes!
              Dim myBinaryFormat As New BinaryFormatter()
              shapes = CType(myBinaryFormat.Deserialize(myStream), List(Of ShapeData))
              myStream.Close()
              Invalidate()
            End If
        End If
    End Using
End Sub
```

After Chapter 20, the overall serialization logic here should look familiar. It is worth pointing out that the SaveFileDialog and OpenFileDialog types both support a Filter property that is assigned a rather cryptic string value. This filter controls a number of settings for the save/open dialog boxes, such as the file extension (*.shapes). You use the FileName property to control what the default name of the file you want to create—MyShapes, in this example.

At this point, your painting application is complete. You should now be able to save and load your current graphical data to any number of *.shapes files. If you want to enhance this Windows Forms program, you might wish to account for additional shapes, or even to allow the user to control the size of the shape to draw or perhaps select the format used to save the data (e.g., binary, XML, or SOAP; see Chapter 20).

Summary

This chapter examined the process of building traditional desktop applications using the Windows Forms and GDI+ APIs, which have been part of the .NET Framework since version 1.0. At minimum, a Windows Forms application consists of a type-extending Form and a Main() method that interacts with the Application type.

When you want to populate your forms with UI elements (e.g., menu systems and GUI input controls), you do so by inserting new objects into the inherited Controls collection. This chapter also showed you how to capture mouse, keyboard, and rendering events. Along the way, you learned about the Graphics type and many ways to generate graphical data at runtime.

As mentioned in this chapter's overview, the Windows Forms API has been (in some ways) superseded by the WPF API introduced with the release of .NET 3.0 (which you learned about in some detail in Part 6 of this book). While it is true that WPF is the choice for supercharged UI front ends, the Windows Forms API remains the simplest (and in many cases, most direct) way to author standard business applications, in-house applications, and simple configuration utilities. For these reasons, Windows Forms will be part of the .NET base class libraries for years to come.

APPENDIX B

■ ■ ■

Platform-Independent .NET Development with Mono

This appendix introduces you to the topic of cross-platform VB and .NET development using an open source implementation of .NET named *Mono* (in case you are wondering about the name, *mono* is a Spanish word for monkey, which is a reference to the various monkey-mascots used by the initial creators of the Mono platform, Ximian Corporation). In this appendix, you will learn about the role of the Common Language Infrastructure (CLI), the overall scope of Mono, and various Mono development tools. At the conclusion of this appendix-and given your work over the course of this book—you will be in a perfect position to dig further into Mono development as you see fit.

■ **Note** If you require a detailed explanation of cross-platform .NET development, I recommend picking up a copy of *Cross-Platform .NET Development: Using Mono, Portable .NET, and Microsoft .NET* by Mark Easton and Jason King (Apress, 2004).

The Platform-Independent Nature of .NET

Historically speaking, when programmers used a Microsoft development language (e.g., VB6) or Microsoft programming framework (e.g., MFC, COM, or ATL), they had to resign themselves to building software that (by-and-large) executed only on the Windows family of operating systems. Many .NET developers, accustomed to previous Microsoft development options, are frequently surprised when they learn that .NET is *platform-independent*. But it's true. You can create, compile, and execute .NET assemblies on operating systems other than Microsoft Windows.

Using open source .NET implementations such as Mono, your .NET applications can find happy homes on numerous operating systems, including Mac OS X, Solaris, AIX, and numerous flavors of Unix/Linux. Mono also provides an installation package for (surprise, surprise) Microsoft Windows. Thus, it is possible to build and run .NET assemblies on the Windows operating system, without ever installing the Microsoft .NET Framework 4.0 SDK or the Visual Studio 2010 IDE.

■ **Note** Be aware that the Microsoft .NET Framework 4.0 SDK and Visual Studio 2010 are your best options for building .NET software for the Windows family of operating systems.

Even after developers learn about .NET code's cross-platform capabilities, they often assume that the scope of platform-independent .NET development is limited to little more than *Hello World* console applications. The reality is that you can build production-ready assemblies that use ADO.NET, Windows Forms (in addition to alternative GUI toolkits such as GTK# and Cocoa#), ASP.NET, LINQ, and XML web services by taking advantage of many of the core namespaces and language features you have seen featured throughout this book.

The Role of the CLI

.NET's cross-platform capabilities are implemented differently than the approach taken by Sun Microsystems and its handling of the Java programming platform. Unlike Java, Microsoft itself does not provide .NET installers for Mac, Linux, and so on. Rather, Microsoft has released a set of formalized specifications that other entities can use as a road map for building .NET distributions for their platform(s) of choice. Collectively, these specifications are termed the *Common Language Infrastructure* (CLI).

As briefly mentioned in Chapter 1, Microsoft submitted two formal specifications to ECMA (European Computer Manufacturers Association) when it released C# and the .NET platform to the world at large. Once approved, Microsoft submitted these same specifications to the International Organization for Standardization (ISO), and these specifications were ratified shortly thereafter.

So, why should you care? These two ECMA specifications provide a road map for other companies, developers, universities, and other organizations to build their own custom distributions of the C# programming language and the .NET platform. The two ECMA specifications in question are:

- *ECMA-334*: Defines the syntax and semantics of the C# programming language.

- *ECMA-335*: Defines many details of the .NET platform, collectively called the *Common Language Infrastructure*.

ECMA-334 tackles the lexical grammar of C# in an extremely rigorous and scientific manner (as you might guess, this level of detail is quite important to those who want to implement a C# compiler). However, ECMA-335 is the meatier of the two specifications, so much so that it has been broken down into six partitions (see Table B-1).

Table B-1. ECMA-335 Specification Partitions

ECMA-335 Partition	Meaning in Life
Partition I: Concepts and Architecture	Describes the overall architecture of the CLI, including the rules of the Common Type System, the Common Language Specification, and the mechanics of the .NET runtime engine.
Partition II: Metadata Definition and Semantics	Describes the details of the .NET metadata format.
Partition III: CIL Instruction Set	Describes the syntax and semantics of the common intermediate language (CIL) programming language.
Partition IV: Profiles and Libraries	Provides a high-level overview of the minimal and complete class libraries that must be supported by a CLI-compatible .NET distribution.
Partition V: Debug Interchange Formats	Provides details of the portable debug interchange format (CILDB). Portable CILDB files provide a standard way to exchange debugging information between CLI producers and consumers.
Partition VI: Annexes	Represents a collection of *odds and ends*; it clarifies topics such as class library design guidelines and the implementation details of a CIL compiler.

The point of this appendix is not to dive into the details of the ECMA-334 and ECMA-335 specifications—nor must you know the ins-and-outs of these documents to understand how to build platform-independent .NET assemblies. However, if you are interested, you can download both of these specifications for free from the ECMA website (`www.ecma-international.org/publications/standards`).

The Mainstream CLI Distributions

To date, you can find two mainstream implementations of the CLI beyond Microsoft's CLR, Microsoft Silverlight, and the Microsoft NET Compact Framework (see Table B-2).

Table B-2. Mainstream .NET CLI Distributions

CLI Distribution	Supporting Website	Meaning in Life
Mono	www.mono-project.com	Mono is an open source and commercially supported distribution of .NET sponsored by Novell Corporation._Mono is targeted to run on many popular flavors of Unix/Linux, Mac OS X, Solaris, and Windows.
Portable .NET	www.gnu.org/software/dotgnu/	Portable .NET is distributed under the GNU General Public License._As the name implies, Portable .NET intends to function on as many operation systems and architectures as possible, including esoteric platforms such as BeOS, Microsoft Xbox, and Sony PlayStation (no, I'm not kidding about the last two!).

Each of the CLI implementations shown in Table B-2 provide a fully function Visual Basic .NET compiler, numerous command-line development tools, a global assembly cache (GAC) implementation, sample code, useful documentation, and dozens of assemblies that constitute the base class libraries.

Beyond implementing the core libraries defined by Partition IV of ECMA-335, Mono and Portable .NET provide Microsoft-compatible implementations of `mscorlib.dll`, `System.Core.dll`, `System.Data.dll`, `System.Web.dll`, `System.Drawing.dll`, and `System.Windows.Forms.dll` (among many others).

The Mono and Portable .NET distributions also ship with a handful of assemblies specifically targeted at Unix/Linux and Mac OS X operating systems. For example, Cocoa# is a .NET wrapper around the preferred Mac OX GUI toolkit, Cocoa. In this appendix, I will not dig into these OS-specific binaries; instead, I'll focus on using the OS-agonistic programming stacks.

■ **Note** This appendix will not examine Portable .NET; however, it is important to know that Mono is not the only platform-independent distribution of the .NET platform available today. I recommend you take some time to play around with Portable .NET in addition to the Mono platform.

The Scope of Mono

Given that Mono is an API built on existing ECMA specifications that originated from Microsoft, you would be correct in assuming that Mono is playing a constant game of catch up as newer versions of Microsoft's .NET platform are released. This means you can build ASP.NET websites, Windows Forms applications, database-centric applications using ADO.NET, and (of course) simple console applications.

Currently, Mono is *not* completely compatible with the new features of VB 2010 or with all aspects of .NET 3.0-4.0. This means that Mono applications are currently unable (again, at the time of this writing) to use the following Microsoft .NET APIs:

- Windows Presentation Foundation (WPF)

- Windows Communication Foundation (WCF)

- Windows Workflow Foundation (WF)

- LINQ to Entities (however, LINQ to Objects and LINQ to XML are supported)

- Any VB 2010 specific language features

Some of these APIs might eventually become part of the standard Mono distribution stacks. For example, according to the Mono website, future versions of the platform (2.8-3.0) will provide support for Visual Basic .NET language features and .NET 3.5-4.0 platform features.

In addition to keeping-step with Microsoft's core .NET APIs and VB .NET language features, Mono also provides an open source distribution of the Silverlight API named *Moonlight*. This enables browsers that run under Linux based operating systems to host and use Silverlight / Moonlight web applications. As you might already know, Microsoft's Silverlight already includes support for Mac OS X; and given the Moonlight API, this technology has truly become cross-platform.

Mono also supports some .NET based technologies that do *not* have a direct Microsoft equivalent. For example, Mono ships with GTK#, a .NET wrapper around a popular Linux-centric GUI framework named GTK. One compelling Mono-centric API is MonoTouch, which allows you to build applications for Apple iPhone and iTouch devices using the VB .NET programming language.

■ **Note** The Mono website includes a page that describes the overall road map of Mono's functionality and the project's plans for future releases (`www.mono-project.com/plans`).

A final point of interest regarding the Mono feature set: Much like Microsoft's .NET Framework 4.0 SDK, the Mono SDK supports several .NET programming languages. While this appendix focuses on VB .NET Mono also provides support for a C# compiler, as well as support for many other .NET-aware programming languages.

Obtaining and Installing Mono

Now that you have a better idea what you can do with the Mono platform, let's turn our attention to obtaining and installing Mono itself. Navigate to the Mono website (`www.mono-project.com`) and locate the Download tab to navigate to the downloads page. Here you can download a variety of installers (see Figure B-1).

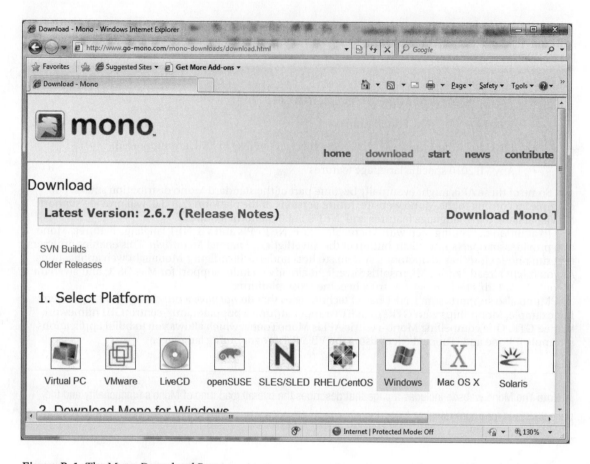

Figure B-1. The Mono Download Page

This appendix assumes that you are installing the Windows distribution of Mono (note that installing Mono will not interfere whatsoever with any existing installation of Microsoft .NET or Visual Studio IDEs). Begin by downloading the current, stable Mono installation package for Microsoft Windows and saving the setup program to your local hard drive.

When you run the setup program, you are given a chance to install a variety of Mono development tools beyond the expected base class libraries and the VB .NET programming tools. Specifically, the installer will ask you whether you wish to include GTK# (the open source .NET GUI API based on the Linux-centric GTK toolkit) and XSP (a stand-alone web server, similar to Microsoft's ASP.NET development web server [`webdev.webserver.exe`]). This appendix also assumes you have opted for a Full Installation, which selects each option in the setup script (see Figure B-2).

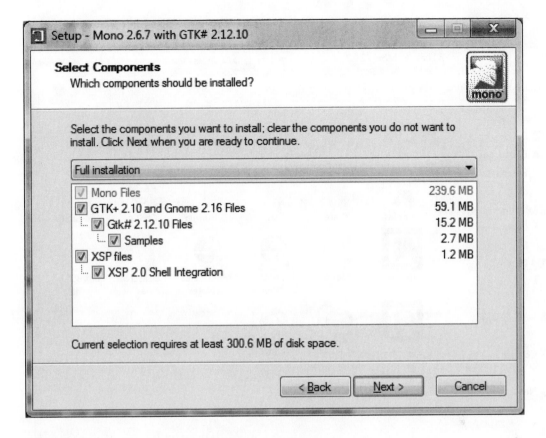

Figure B-2. Select All Options for Your Mono Installation

Examining Mono's Directory Structure

By default, Mono installs under `C:\Program Files\Mono-<version>` (at the time of this writing, the latest version of Mono is 2.6.7; however, your version number will almost certainly be different). Beneath that root, you can find several subdirectories (see Figure B-3).

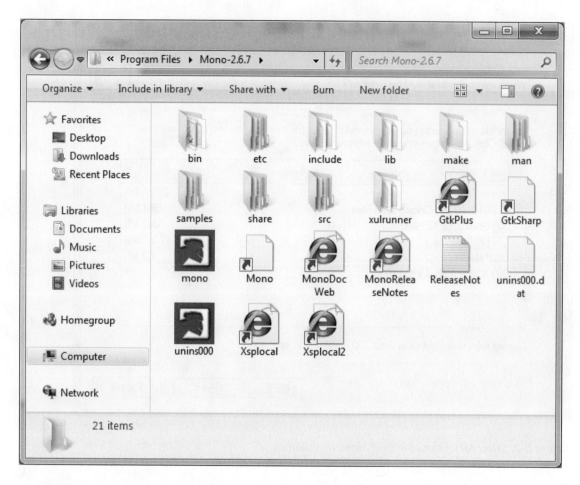

Figure B-3. *The Mono Directory Structure*

For this appendix, you need to concern yourself only with the following subdirectories:

- *bin*: Contains a majority of the Mono development tools, including the VB .NET command-line compilers.

- lib*mono**gac*: Points to the location of Mono's global assembly cache.

Given that you run the vast majority of Mono's development tools from the command line, you will want to use the Mono command prompt, which automatically recognizes each of the command-line development tools. You can activate the command prompt (which is functionally equivalent to the Visual Studio 2010 command prompt) by selecting Start ä All Programs ä Mono <version> For Windows menu option. To test your installation, enter the following command and press the Enter key:

```
mono --version
```

If all is well, you should see various details regarding the Mono runtime environment. Here is the output on my Mono development machine:

```
Mono JIT compiler version 2.6.7 (tarball)
Copyright (C) 2002-2010 Novell, Inc and Contributors. www.mono-project.com
        TLS:            normal
        GC:             Included Boehm (with typed GC and Parallel Mark)

        SIGSEGV:        normal
        Notification:   Thread + polling
        Architecture:   x86

        Disabled:       none
```

The Mono Development Languages

Similar to the Microsoft's CLR distribution, Mono ships with a number of managed compilers:

- **vbnc**: The Mono Visual Basic compiler
- **mcs**: The Mono C# compiler
- **booc**: The Mono Boo language compiler
- **ilasm**: The Mono CIL compilers

The Visual Basic .NET support in Mono is relatively new . Having a native compiler for Visual Basic .NET allows developers to write applications in a Mono-supported platform. It also lets applications that depend on the CodeDOM (ASP.NET, for example) to be developed using Visual Basic .NET, which was not possible before the availability of the VB .NET compiler. The intended goal is to bring the world of human-readable keywords (e.g., **Inherits**, **MustOverride**, and **Implements**) to the world of Unix/Linux and Mac OS X (see **www.mono-project.com/Visual_Basic** for more details).

Boo is an object-oriented, statically typed programming language for the CLI that sports a Python-based syntax. Check out **http://boo.codehaus.org** for more details on the Boo programming language. Finally, as you might have guessed, **ilasm** is the Mono CIL compiler.

Working with the VB 2010 Compiler

The VB .NET compiler for the Mono project was **vbnc**, and it's fully compatible with VB 2010. Like the Microsoft VB 2010 command-line compiler (**vbc.exe**), mono's **vbnc** supports response files, a **/target:** flag (to define the assembly type), an **/out:** flag (to define the name of the compiled assembly), and a **/reference:** flag (to update the manifest of the current assembly with external dependencies). You can view all the options of **vbnc** using the following command:

```
vbnc -?
```

Building Mono Applications using MonoDevelop

When you install Mono, you will not be provided with a graphical IDE. However, this does not mean you must build all of your Mono applications at the command prompt! In addition to the core framework, you can also download the free MonoDevelop IDE. As its name suggests, MonoDevelop was built using the core code base of SharpDevelop (see Chapter 2).

You can download the MonoDevelop IDE from the Mono website, and it supports installation packages for Mac OS X, various Linux distributions, and (surprise!) Microsoft Windows! Once installed, you might be pleased to find an integrated debugger, IntelliSense capabilities, numerous project templates (e.g., ASP.NET and Moonlight). You can get a taste of what the MonoDevelop IDE brings to the table by perusing Figure B-4.

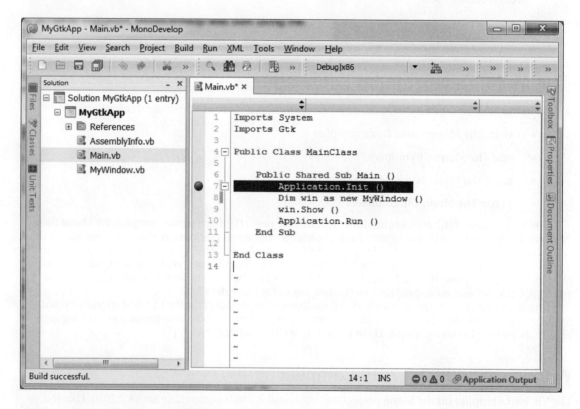

Figure B-4. *The MonoDevelop IDE*

Microsoft-Compatible Mono Development Tools

In addition to the managed compilers, Mono ships with various development tools that are functionally equivalent to tools found in the Microsoft .NET SDK (some of which are identically named). Table B-3 enumerates the mappings between some of the commonly used Mono/Microsoft .NET utilities.

Table B-3. Mono Command-Line Tools and Their Microsoft .NET Counterparts

Mono Utility	Microsoft .NET Utility	Meaning in Life
al	al.exe	Manipulates assembly manifests and builds multifile assemblies (among other things).
gacutil	gacutil.exe	Interacts with the GAC.
mono when run with the -aot option as a startup parameter to the executing assembly	ngen.exe	Performs a precompilation of an assembly's CIL code.
wsdl	wsdl.exe	Generates client-side proxy code for XML web services.
disco	disco.exe	Discovers the URLs of XML web services located on a web server.
xsd	xsd.exe	Generates type definitions from an XSD schema file.
sn	sn.exe	Generates key data for a strongly named assembly.
monodis	ildasm.exe	The CIL disassembler
ilasm	ilasm.exe	The CIL assembler
xsp2	webdev.webserver.exe	A testing and development ASP.NET web server

Mono-Specific Development Tools

Mono also ships with development tools for which no direct Microsoft .NET Framework 3.5 SDK equivalents exist (see Table B-4).

Table B-4. Mono Tools That Have No Direct Microsoft .NET SDK Equivalent

Mono-Specific Development Tool	Meaning in Life
monop	The monop (mono print) utility displays the definition of a specified type using VB .NET syntax (see the next section for a quick example).
SQL#	The Mono Project ships with a graphical front end (SQL#) that allows you to interact with relational databases using a variety of ADO.NET data providers.
Glade 3	This tool is a visual development IDE for building GTK# graphical applications.

■ **Note** You can load SQL# and Glade by using the Windows Start button and navigating to the Applications folder within the Mono installation. Be sure to do this because this illustrates definitively how rich the Mono platform has become.

Using monop

You can use the monop utility (short for mono print) to display the definition of a given type within a specified assembly. As you might suspect, this tool can be quite helpful when you wish to view a method signature quickly, rather than digging through the formal documentation. As a quick test, try entering the following command at a Mono command prompt:

```
monop System.Object
```

You should see the definition of your good friend, System.Object:

```
[Serializable]
public class Object {

        public Object ();

        public static bool Equals (object objA, object objB);
        public static bool ReferenceEquals (object objA, object objB);
        public virtual bool Equals (object obj);
        protected override void Finalize ();
        public virtual int GetHashCode ();
        public Type GetType ();
        protected object MemberwiseClone ();
        public virtual string ToString ();
}
```

■ **Note** The command "monop System.Object" will always show the definition in C# syntax. There is no way to get it displayed in VB .NET format.

Building .NET Applications with Mono

Now let's look at Mono in action. You begin by building a code library named `CoreLibDumper.dll`. This assembly contains a single class type named `CoreLibDumper` that supports a Shared method named `DumpTypeToFile()`. The method takes a String parameter that represents the fully qualified name of any type within `mscorlib.dll` and obtains the related type information through the reflection API (see Chapter 15), dumping the class member signatures to a local file on the hard drive.

Building a Mono Code Library

Create a new folder on your C: drive named `MonoCode`. Within this new folder, create a subfolder named `CorLibDumper` that contains the following VB .NET file (named `CorLibDumper.vb`):

```
' CorLibDumper.vb
Imports System.Reflection
Imports System.IO

' Define assembly version.
<Assembly:AssemblyVersion("1.0.0.0")>

Namespace CorLibDumper
    Public Class TypeDumper
        Public Shared Function DumpTypeToFile(ByVal typeToDisplay As String) As Boolean
            ' Attempt to load type into memory.
            Dim theType As Type = Nothing
            Try
                ' Second parameter to GetType() controls if an
                ' exception should be thrown if the type is not found.
                theType = Type.GetType(typeToDisplay, True)
            Catch
                Return False
            End Try

            ' Create local *.txt file.
            Using sw As StreamWriter = File.CreateText(String.Format("{0}.txt",
theType.FullName))
                ' Now dump type to file.
                sw.WriteLine("Type Name: {0}", theType.FullName)
                sw.WriteLine("Members:")
                For Each mi As MemberInfo In theType.GetMembers()
                    sw.WriteLine(vbTab & "-> {0}", mi.ToString())
                Next
```

```
            End Using
            Return True
         End Function
      End Class
End Namespace
```

Like the Microsoft VB 2010 compiler, Mono's VB .NET compilers support the use of response files (see Chapter 2). While you could compile this file by specifying each required argument manually at the command line, you can instead create a new file named `LibraryBuild.rsp` (in the same location as `CorLibDumper.vb`) that contains the following command set:

```
/target:library
/out:CorLibDumper.dll
CorLibDumper.vb
```

You can now compile your library at the command line, as follows:

```
vbnc @LibraryBuild.rsp
```

This approach is functionally equivalent to the following (more verbose) command set:

```
vbnc /target:library /out:CorLibDumper.dll CorLibDumper.vb
```

Assigning CoreLibDumper.dll a Strong Name

Mono supports the notion of deploying strongly named assemblies (see Chapter 15) to the Mono GAC. To generate the necessary public/private key data, Mono provides the `sn` command-line utility, which functions more or less identically to Microsoft's tool of the same name. For example, the following command generates a new `*.snk` file (specify the `-?` option to view all possible commands):

```
sn -k myTestKeyPair.snk
```

You can tell the VB .NET compiler to use this key data to assign a strong name to `CorLibDumper.dll` by updating your `LibraryBuild.rsp` file with the following additional command:

```
/target:library
/out:CorLibDumper.dll
/keyfile:myTestKeyPair.snk
CorLibDumper.vb
```

Now recompile your assembly:

```
vbnc @LibraryBuild.rsp
```

Viewing the Updated Manifest with monodis

Before you deploy the assembly to the Mono GAC, you should familiarize yourself with the `monodis` command-line tool, which is the functional equivalent of Microsoft's `ildasm.exe` (without the GUI front end). Using `monodis`, you can view the CIL code, manifest, and type metadata for a specified assembly. In this case, you want to view the core details of your (now strongly named) assembly using the `--assembly` flag. Figure B-5 shows the result of the following command set:

```
monodis --assembly CorLibDumper.dll
```

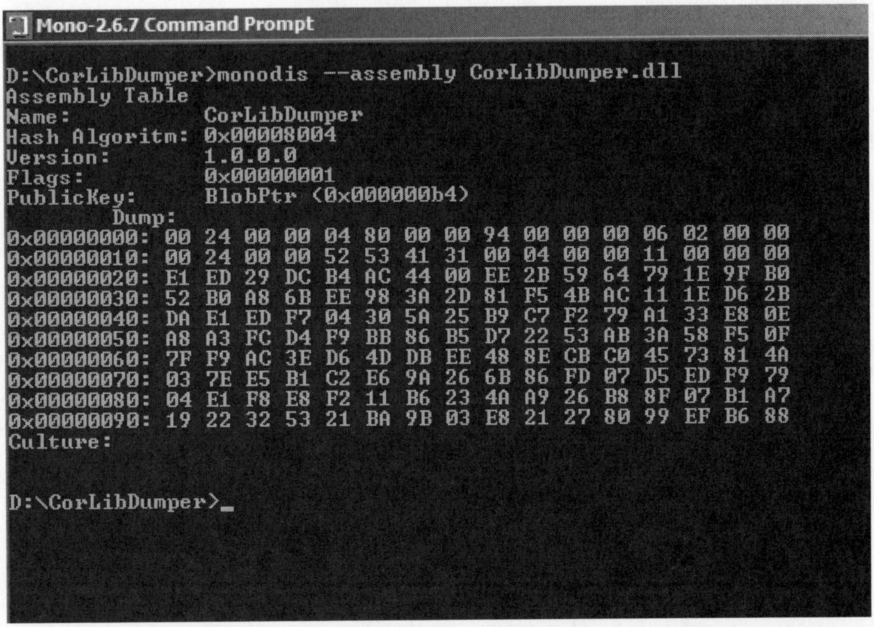

Figure B-5. Viewing the CIL Code, Metadata, and Manifest of an Assembly with monodis

The assembly's manifest now exposes the public key value defined in myTestKeyPair.snk.

Installing Assemblies into the Mono GAC

So far you have provided CorLibDumper.dll with a strong name; you can install it into the Mono GAC using gacutil. Like Microsoft's tool of the same name, Mono's gacutil supports options to install, uninstall, and list the current assemblies installed under C:\Program Files\Mono-<version>\lib\mono\gac. The following command deploys CorLibDumper.dll to the GAC and sets it up as a shared assembly on the machine:

```
gacutil -i CorLibDumper.dll
```

■ **Note** Be sure to use a Mono command prompt to install this binary to the Mono GAC! If you use the Microsoft gacutil.exe program, you'll install CorLibDumper.dll into the Microsoft GAC!

After you run the command, opening the \gac directory should reveal a new folder named CorLibDumper (see Figure B-6). This folder defines a subdirectory that follows the same naming conventions as Microsoft's GAC (versionOfAssembly__publicKeyToken).

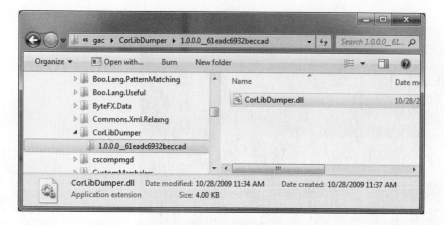

Figure B-6. Deploying Your Code Library to the Mono GAC

■ **Note** Supplying the -1 option to gacutil lists out each assembly in the Mono GAC.

Building a Console Application in Mono

Your first Mono client will be a simple, console-based application named ConsoleClientApp.exe. Create a new file in your C:\MonoCode\CorLibDumper folder, ConsoleClientApp.vb, that contains the following Module1 definition:

```vb
' This client app makes use of the CorLibDumper.dll
' to dump type information to a file.
Imports CorLibDumper

Namespace ConsoleClientApp
    Module Module1
        Sub Main()
            Console.WriteLine("***** The Type Dumper App *****" & vbLf)

            ' Ask user for name of type.
            Dim typeName As String = ""
            Console.Write("Please enter type name: ")
            typeName = Console.ReadLine()
```

```
        ' Now send it to the helper library.
        If TypeDumper.DumpTypeToFile(typeName) Then
                Console.WriteLine("Data saved into {0}.txt", typeName)
        Else
                Console.WriteLine("Error!  Can't find that type...")
        End If
            End Sub
    End Module
End Namespace
```

Notice that the Main() method prompts the user for a fully qualified type name. The TypeDumper.DumpTypeToFile() method uses the user-entered name to dump the type's members to a local file. Next, create a ClientBuild.rsp file for this client application and reference CorLibDumper.dll:

```
/target:exe
/out:ConsoleClientApp.exe
/reference:CorLibDumper.dll
ConsoleClientApp.vb
```

Now, use a Mono command prompt to compile the executable using vbnc, as shown here:

```
vbnc @ClientBuild.rsp
```

Loading Your Client Application in the Mono Runtime

At this point, you can load ConsoleClientApp.exe into the Mono runtime engine by specifying the name of the executable (with the *.exe file extension) as an argument to Mono:

```
mono ConsoleClientApp.exe
```

As a test, enter System.Threading.Thread at the prompt and press the Enter key. You will now find a new file named System.Threading.Thread.txt containing the type's metadata definition (see Figure B-7).

■ **Note** The method signatures are shown in C# syntax. There is no way to get it displayed in VB .NET format.

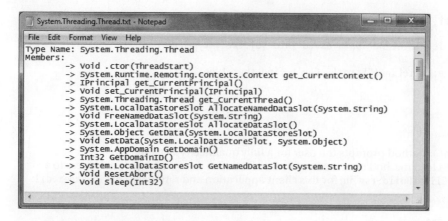

Figure B-7. The Results of Running Your Client Application

Before moving on to a Windows Forms–based client, try the following experiment. Use Windows Explorer to rename the CorLibDumper.dll assembly from the folder containing the client application to DontUseCorLibDumper.dll. You should still be able to run the client application successfully because the only reason you needed access to this assembly when building the client was to update the client manifest. At runtime, the Mono runtime will load the version of CorLibDumper.dll you deployed to the Mono GAC.

However, if you open Windows Explorer and attempt to run your client application by double-clicking ConsoleClientApp.exe, you might be surprised to find a FileNotFoundException is thrown. At first glance, you might assume this is due to the fact that you renamed CorLibDumper.dll from the location of the client application. However, the true reason for the error is that you just loaded ConsoleClientApp.exe into the Microsoft CLR!

To run an application under Mono, you must pass it into the Mono runtime through Mono. If you do not, you will be loading your assembly into the Microsoft CLR, which assumes all shared assemblies are installed into the Microsoft GAC located in the <%windir%>\Assembly directory.

■ **Note** If you double-click your executable using Windows Explorer, you will load your assembly into the Microsoft CLR, not the Mono runtime!

Executing Your Windows Forms Application Under Linux

So far, this appendix has shown you how to create a few assemblies that you could also have compiled using the Microsoft .NET Framework 4.0 SDK. However, the importance of Mono becomes clear when you view Figure B-8, which shows the same exact Windows Forms application running under SuSe Linux. Notice how the Windows Forms application has taken on the correct look and feel of my current desktop theme.

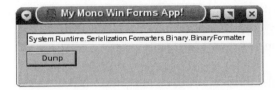

Figure B-8. Executing the Windows Forms Application Under SuSe Linux

---

■ **Source Code** You can find the CorLibDumper project under the Appendix B subdirectory.

The preceding examples shows how you can compile and execute the same exact VB 2010 code shown during this appendix on Linux (or any OS supported by Mono) using the same Mono development tools. In fact, you can deploy or recompile any of the assemblies created in this text that do not use .NET 4.0 programming constructs to a new Mono-aware OS and run them directly using the Mono runtime utility. Because all assemblies contain platform-agonistic CIL code, you do not need to recompile the applications whatsoever.

Who is Using Mono?

In this short appendix, I've tried to capture the promise of the Mono platform in a few simple examples. Granted, if you intend only to build .NET programs for the Windows family of operating systems, you might not have encountered companies or individuals who actively use Mono. Regardless, Mono is alive and well in the programming community for Mac OS X, Linux, and Windows.

For example, navigate to the /Software section of the Mono website:

http://mono-project.com/Software

At this location, you can find a long-running list of commercial products built using Mono, including development tools, server products, video games (including games for the Nintendo Wii and iPhone), and medical point-of-care systems.

If you take a few moments to click the provided links, you will quickly find that Mono is completely equipped to build enterprise-level, real-world .NET software that is truly cross-platform.

Suggestions for Further Study

If you have followed along with the materials presented in this book, you already know a great deal about Mono, given that it is an ECMA-compatible implementation of the CLI. If you want to learn more about Mono's particulars, the best place to begin is with the official Mono website (www.mono-project.com). Specifically, you should examine the page at www.mono-project.com/Use, which serves an entry point to a number of important topics, including database access using ADO.NET, web development using ASP.NET, and so on.

I have also authored some Mono-centric articles for the DevX website (www.devx.com) that you might find interesting:

- "Mono IDEs: Going Beyond the Command Line": This article examines many Mono-aware IDEs.

- "Building Robust UIs in Mono with Gtk#": This article examines building desktop applications using the GTK# toolkit as an alternative to Windows Forms.

Finally, you should familiarize yourself with Mono's documentation website (www.go-mono.com/docs). Here you will find documentation on the Mono base class libraries, development tools, and other topics (see Figure B-9).

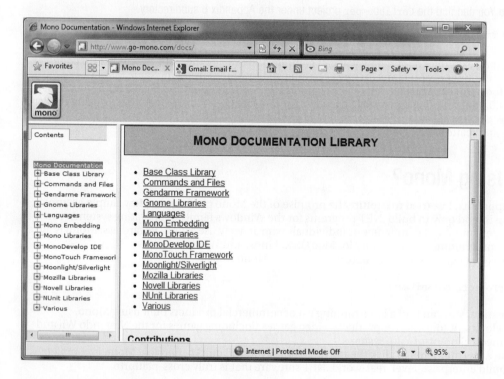

Figure B-9. The Online Mono Documentation

■ **Note** The website with Mono's online documentation is community supported; therefore, don't be too surprised if you find some incomplete documentation links! Given that Mono is an ECMA-compatible distribution of Microsoft .NET, you might prefer to use the feature-rich MSDN online documentation when exploring Mono.

Summary

The point of this appendix was to provide an introduction to the cross-platform nature of the VB .NET programming language and the .NET platform when using the Mono framework. You have seen how Mono ships with a number of command-line tools that allow you to build a wide variety of .NET assemblies, including strongly named assemblies deployed to the GAC, Windows Forms applications, and .NET code libraries.

You've also learned that Mono is not fully compatible with the .NET 3.5 or .NET 4.0 programming APIs (WPF, WCF, WF, or LINQ) or the VB 2010 language features. Efforts are underway (through the Olive project) to bring these aspects of the Microsoft .NET platform to Mono. In any case, if you need to build .NET applications that can execute under a variety of operating systems, the Mono project is a wonderful choice for doing so.

Index

loose resources, WPF

configuring, 1337–1338

including files in project, 1337

LoseFocusStar, 1417

■M

M command, 1308

machine.config file, 1552

magic numbers, 147

main menu system, 1603–1605

Main Window class, 1273

MainControl.xaml file, 1407

MainForm class, 951–952, 1038

MainMenuStrip property, 1567

MainWindow class, 1213–1214

MainWindow type, adding infrastructure to, 1607

MainWindow.g.vb file, 1198, 1214

MainWindow.xaml file, 1199–1200, 1214, 1416

Manage Help Settings tool, 68

ManagedThreadId property, 769

Manager class, 236–238

MANIFEST data, 564

MANIFEST icon, 563, 609

mapping database names to friendly names, 963

Mapping Details window, 1016–1018

mappings, viewing, 1016

markup extensions, XAML, 1211–1213

markup tags, 1488

massive numerical value, 99

master constructor, 180–182, 206

master pages

AdRotator widget, 1496–1497

bread crumbs, establishing with SiteMapPath type, 1496

TreeView control site navigation logic, 1493–1496

Master property, 1499

MasterPageFile attribute, 1498

MasterPage.master file, 1491

MathExtensions class, 495

MathLibrary project, 749

MathLibrary.dll assembly, 749

MathMessage delegate, 457

MAX_IMAGES constant, 1339

MaximumValue property, 1510

.maxstack directive, 718

MaxValue property, 96

MDI (multiple document interface) application, 1576

Me keyword

chaining constructor calls using, 178–181

and constructor flow, 181–183

hidden reference, 720

Me reference, 720

MediaPlayer type, 1322

member parameters, defining in CIL, 714–715

member shadowing, 257–259

members, specifying type parameters for, 389

Menu class, 1245

■T

■ X

You Need the Companion eBook

Your purchase of this book entitles you to buy the companion PDF-version eBook for only $10. Take the weightless companion with you anywhere.

We believe this Apress title will prove so indispensable that you'll want to carry it with you everywhere, which is why we are offering the companion eBook (in PDF format) for $10 to customers who purchase this book now. Convenient and fully searchable, the PDF version of any content-rich, page-heavy Apress book makes a valuable addition to your programming library. You can easily find and copy code—or perform examples by quickly toggling between instructions and the application. Even simultaneously tackling a donut, diet soda, and complex code becomes simplified with hands-free eBooks!

Once you purchase your book, getting the $10 companion eBook is simple:

❶ Visit **www.apress.com/promo/tendollars/**.

❷ Complete a basic registration form to receive a randomly generated question about this title.

❸ Answer the question correctly in 60 seconds, and you will receive a promotional code to redeem for the $10.00 eBook.

Apress®
THE EXPERT'S VOICE™

233 Spring Street, New York, NY 10013

Offer valid through 3/11.